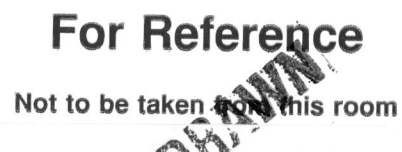
For Reference

Not to be taken from this room

WITHDRAWN

W9-BTF-736

REF
317 3

# STATE RANKINGS
## *2001*

## *A Statistical View of the 50 United States*

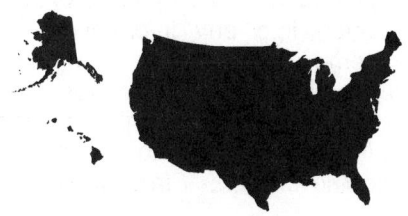

Kathleen O'Leary Morgan and Scott Morgan, Editors

MORGAN
QUITNO

Morgan Quitno Press
© Copyright 2001, All Rights Reserved
512 East 9th Street, P.O. Box 1656
Lawrence, KS 66044-8656
USA
800-457-0742 or 785-841-3534
www.statestats.com

Twelfth Edition

Prospect Heights Public Library
12 N. Elm St.
Prospect Heights, IL 60070-1499

© Copyright 2001 by
Morgan Quitno Corporation
512 East 9th Street, P.O. Box 1656
Lawrence, Kansas 66044-8656
USA
800-457-0742 or 785-841-3534
www.statestats.com

All Rights Reserved

No part of this book may be reproduced in any form, by photostat, microfilm, xerography, or any other means, or incorporated into any information retrieval system, electronic or mechanical, without the written permission of the copyright owner. Copyright is not claimed in any material from U.S. Government sources. However, its arrangement and compilation along with all other material are subject to the copyright. If you are interested in reprinting our material, please call or write. We would be happy to discuss it with you and are usually willing to allow reprinting with the following citation: "*State Rankings 2001*, Morgan Quitno Press, Lawrence, KS."

ISBN: 0-7401-0029-7
ISSN: 1057-3623

*State Rankings 2001* sells for $52.95 ($5.00 shipping) and is only available in paper binding. For those who prefer ranking information tailored to a particular state, we also offer *State Perspectives*, state-specific reports for each of the 50 states. These individual guides provide information on a state's data and rank for each of the categories featured in the national *State Rankings* volume. Perspectives sell for $19.00 or $9.50 if ordered with *State Rankings*. If crime statistics are your interest, please ask about our annual *Crime State Rankings* ($52.95 paper). If you are interested in city and metropolitan crime data, we offer *City Crime Rankings* ($39.95 paper). If you are interested in health statistics for states, please ask about our annual *Health Care State Rankings* ($52.95 paper). All of our data sets are also available in machine readable format. Shipping and handling is $5.00 per order. For information, please visit our website at www.statestats.com.

Twelfth Edition
Printed in the United States of America
April 2001

# PREFACE

Anything and everything you ever wanted to know about the states is found in this twelfth edition of *State Rankings*. Statistics examining state education, transportation, taxes, housing, health, crime, agriculture, energy, environment, finance, social welfare and more are packed into hundreds of easy-to-understand tables. From basic state facts to interesting trivia, *State Rankings* features the most user-friendly, up-to-date collection of state information possible.

**Important Notes About *State Rankings 2001***

This twelfth edition of *State Rankings* is the culmination of our on-going search for interesting state statistics. Our goal is to convert complicated and often convoluted state data into a form that is usable and easy to understand. We have updated the majority of tables in *State Rankings*, added a few new ones and removed others that no longer are pertinent. In all, you'll find 569 tables of state comparisons.

While there are a number of changes in this updated edition of *State Rankings*, its organization and other popular features are the same. These include source information and footnotes clearly shown at the bottom of each page, and national totals, rates and percentages prominently displayed at the top of each table. Every other line is shaded in gray for easier reading. Numerous information-finding tools are provided: a thorough table of contents, table listings at the beginning of each chapter, a detailed index and a chapter thumb index. In addition, a roster of sources, with addresses, phone numbers and internet websites is found in the back of the book.

As in all of our reference books, the numbers shown in *State Rankings* require no additional calculations to convert them from millions, thousands, etc. All states are ranked on a high to low basis, with any ties among the states listed alphabetically for a given ranking. Negative numbers are shown in parentheses "( )." For tables displaying national totals (as opposed to rates, per capita, etc.) a separate column is included that shows what percent of the national total each individual state's total represents. This column is headed by "% of USA." This percentage figure is particularly interesting when compared with a state's share of the nation's population for a particular year.

For those interested in learning basic information about their states, the "State Fast Facts" section is once again featured. Here you'll learn that five states have "Hail!" in their official songs and eight states have chosen pines of some variety as their official tree. You'll also discover that Cardinals, Mockingbirds and Meadowlarks reign as official state birds for 16 states. In addition, find out the lucky winner of our annual "Most Livable State Award."

For those of you needing information for just one state, we once again are offering our *State Perspective* series of publications. These 26-page comb bound reports feature data and ranking information for an individual state, pulled from the national *State Rankings 2001* book. (For example *New York in Perspective* features information about the state of New York only.) They serve as great timesavers for re-searchers who do not want to page through the entire *State Rankings* volume searching for information for their particular state. Purchased individually, *State Perspectives* sell for $19. When purchased with a copy of *State Rankings*, these handy, quick reference guides are just $9.50.

**Other Books From Morgan Quitno Press**

In addition to *State Rankings,* our company offers three other rankings reference books. The first of these, *Health Care State Rankings,* provides an in-depth view of health care by state. Included in this 540-page annual volume are statistics on health care facilities, providers, insurance and finance, incidence of disease, mortality, physical fitness, natality and reproductive health. An annual compilation of state crime data is featured in *Crime State Rankings.* In its eighth edition for 2001, this reference volume contains a huge collection of user-friendly statistics on law enforcement personnel and expenditures, juvenile crime, corrections, arrests and offenses. Our readers' thirst for crime statistics proved to be so popular that we added a companion volume of crime data, *City Crime Rankings,* to our list of titles. This reference book ranks U.S. metropolitan areas and cities of 75,000 or more population in all major crime categories. Numbers of crimes, crime rates and crime trends over one and five years are presented for all major crime categories reported by the FBI.

*City Crime Rankings, 7th Edition* sells for $39.95. *Health Care State Rankings 2001* and *Crime State Rankings 2001* each are available for $52.95. (S/H $5 per order.) All books are paperback. For true data aficionados, we also offer the data in our books on CD-ROM. These electronic editions feature a searchable PDF version of each book as well as the raw data in .dbf, Excel and ASCII formats. CD-ROM and book sets are $152.95 for each of the state books and $139.95 for the *City Crime Rankings* volume.

*State Statistical Trends* is our popular monthly journal that compares changes in life and government for the 50 United States. Each 100-page monthly issue examines a different subject and provides a collection of tables, graphics and commentary showing state multi-year trends. For further information about *Trends* or any of our other publications, check out our website at www.statestats.com or give us a call toll-free at 1-800-457-0742.

Finally, we need to extend a big "thank you" to the many people who help to make this book possible year after year. Our appreciation goes to the government statisticians who provide data and deciphering services. Many thanks also to Joe and Joan Williams, the original editors and creators of *State Rankings*. We appreciate so much the opportunity to continue their legacy of providing a book of interesting and useful state information. Finally, thank you to our readers. We enjoy bringing you this volume and always welcome your suggestions. Please never hesitate to give us a call, send us an e-mail or drop us a note with your ideas.

THE EDITORS

# WHICH STATE IS THE MOST LIVABLE?

When we saw which state had again won our award this year, we thought briefly of completely changing our factors so some other state might possibly come out on top. However, if a state can do what it takes to be #1, it should be amply rewarded. So, winning for a record fifth consecutive year, Minnesota is our year 2001 Most Livable State. Again (how many different ways can we say this?) the same unbeatable performance across-the-board in education, health, low unemployment, funding for the arts and other quality-of-life factors makes it our top state. Even its margin of victory grew. At the bottom, with similar consistency, Mississippi comes in at #50 for the third year in a row.

For 11 years now, Morgan Quitno Press has issued its Most Livable State Award. With the publication of each year's new volume of *State Rankings*, we reexamine our collection of data and select the factors that reflect a state's basic quality of life. The 2001 award is based on 43 factors ranging from median household income to crime rate, sunny days to infant mortality rate.

Unique among the various rankings of states, our Most Livable State Award does not focus on any one category of data. Instead it takes into account a broad range of economic, educational, health-oriented, public safety and environmental statistics.

The Most Livable State Award is one of four such designations announced each year by Morgan Quitno. The Safest City/Metro Area Award is based on statistics from our *City Crime Rankings* volume. The Most Dangerous State designation is announced with our *Crime State Rankings* volume. The Healthiest State Award is based on factors derived from *Health Care State Rankings*. Some view these awards quite seriously, while others look upon them simply as entertainment. Our hope is that the awards foster some meaningful discussion among state leaders and citizens.

While we strive to make our books as objective as possible, these awards give us the opportunity to choose the factors we think tell an interesting story about life in the 50 United States. We note only in passing that number of governors commenting for odd new football leagues was not a factor. Once again in 2001, Minnesota is number one!

Congratulations to the citizens of Minnesota.

THE EDITORS

---

**Negative Factors**
1. Percent Change in Number of Crimes: 1998 to 1999 (Table 26)
2. Crime Rate (Table 27)
3. State Prisoner Incarceration Rate (Table 62)
4. State Cost of Living Index (Table 90)
5. Pupil-Teacher Ratio in Public Elementary and Secondary Schools (Table 123)
6. Unemployment Rate (Table 170)
7. Percent of Nonfarm Employees in Government (Table 181)
8. Electricity Prices (Table 201)
9. Hazardous Waste Sites on the National Priority List per 10,000 Square Miles (Table 213)
10. State & Local Taxes as a Percent of Personal Income (Table 280)
11. Per Capita State and Local Government Debt Outstanding (Table 292)
12. Percent of Population Not Covered by Health Insurance (Table 346)
13. Births of Low Birthweight as a Percent of All Births (Table 361)
14. Teenage Birth Rate (Table 362)
15. Infant Mortality Rate (Table 368)
16. Age-Adjusted Death Rate by Suicide (Table 387)
17. Population per Square Mile (Table 430)
18. Divorce Rate (Table 488)
19. Poverty Rate (Table 500)
20. State and Local Government Spending for Welfare Programs as a Percent of All Spending (Table 507)
21. Percent of Households Receiving Food Stamps (Table 531)
22. Deficient Bridges as a Percent of Total Bridges (Table 550)
23. Highway Fatality Rate (Table 553)
24. Fatalities in Alcohol-Related Crashes as a Percent of All Highway Fatalities (Table 558)

**Positive Factors**
25. Per Capita Gross State Product (Table 94)
26. Percent Change in Per Capita Gross State Product: 1994 to 1998 (Adjusted to Constant 1998 Dollars) (Table 95)
27. Per Capita Personal Income (Table 101)
28. Change in Per Capita Personal Income: 1998 to 1999 (Table 102)
29. Median Household Income (Table 104)
30. Public High School Graduation Rate (Table 128)
31. Percent of Population Graduated from High School (Table 129)
32. Expenditures for Education as a Percent of All State and Local Government Expenditures (Table 135)
33. Percent of Population Graduated from College (Table 149)
34. Books in Public Libraries Per Capita (Table 152)
35. Per Capita State Art Agencies' Legislative Appropriations (Table 154)
36. Annual Average Weekly Earnings of Production Workers on Manufacturing Payrolls (Table 161)
37. Job Growth: 1999 to 2000 (Table 174)
38. Normal Daily Mean Temperature (Table 226)
39. Percent of Days That Are Sunny (Table 227)
40. Homeownership Rate (Table 411)
41. Domestic Migration of Population: 1998 to 1999 (Table 483)
42. Marriage Rate (Table 486)
43. Percent of Eligible Population Reported Voting (Table 498)

# The 2001 Most Livable State Award:

# Minnesota Wins Five Years in a Row

| ALPHA ORDER | | | | | RANK ORDER | | | | |
|---|---|---|---|---|---|---|---|---|---|
| RANK | STATE | LIVABILITY RATING | 00 RANK | CHANGE | RANK | STATE | LIVABILITY RATING | 00 RANK | CHANGE |
| 46 | Alabama | 19.98 | 42 | -4 | 1 | Minnesota | 35.09 | 1 | 0 |
| 37 | Alaska | 22.53 | 41 | 4 | 2 | Colorado | 32.45 | 3 | 1 |
| 36 | Arizona | 22.70 | 39 | 3 | 3 | Iowa | 32.09 | 2 | -1 |
| 44 | Arkansas | 21.00 | 45 | 1 | 4 | Virginia | 31.26 | 8 | 4 |
| 32 | California | 23.50 | 36 | 4 | 5 | Utah | 31.23 | 4 | -1 |
| 2 | Colorado | 32.45 | 3 | 1 | 6 | Connecticut | 29.67 | 13 | 7 |
| 6 | Connecticut | 29.67 | 13 | 7 | 7 | Kansas | 29.56 | 6 | -1 |
| 21 | Delaware | 26.67 | 17 | -4 | 8 | Wisconsin | 29.44 | 6 | -2 |
| 21 | Florida | 22.16 | 40 | 0 | 9 | Massachusetts | 29.33 | 10 | 1 |
| 33 | Georgia | 23.49 | 30 | -3 | 10 | Nebraska | 29.16 | 9 | -1 |
| 34 | Hawaii | 22.98 | 43 | 9 | 11 | New Jersey | 28.98 | 16 | 5 |
| 20 | Idaho | 26.70 | 24 | 4 | 12 | Wyoming | 28.56 | 20 | 8 |
| 31 | Illinois | 23.79 | 29 | -2 | 13 | New Hampshire | 28.51 | 5 | -8 |
| 21 | Indiana | 26.67 | 19 | -2 | 14 | Maryland | 28.49 | 17 | 3 |
| 3 | Iowa | 32.09 | 2 | -1 | 15 | Vermont | 28.28 | 12 | -3 |
| 7 | Kansas | 29.56 | 6 | -1 | 16 | South Dakota | 28.19 | 11 | -5 |
| 43 | Kentucky | 21.77 | 32 | -11 | 17 | Maine | 27.88 | 15 | -2 |
| 49 | Louisiana | 16.76 | 48 | -1 | 18 | Washington | 27.28 | 22 | 4 |
| 17 | Maine | 27.88 | 15 | -2 | 19 | Missouri | 27.12 | 23 | 4 |
| 14 | Maryland | 28.49 | 17 | 3 | 20 | Idaho | 26.70 | 24 | 4 |
| 9 | Massachusetts | 29.33 | 10 | 1 | 21 | Indiana | 26.67 | 19 | -2 |
| 27 | Michigan | 25.12 | 28 | 1 | 21 | Delaware | 26.67 | 17 | -4 |
| 1 | Minnesota | 35.09 | 1 | 0 | 23 | Oregon | 26.37 | 21 | -2 |
| 50 | Mississippi | 16.26 | 50 | 0 | 24 | Ohio | 26.14 | 25 | 1 |
| 19 | Missouri | 27.12 | 23 | 4 | 25 | North Dakota | 25.58 | 14 | -11 |
| 39 | Montana | 22.19 | 33 | -6 | 26 | Nevada | 25.51 | 26 | 0 |
| 10 | Nebraska | 29.16 | 9 | -1 | 27 | Michigan | 25.12 | 28 | 1 |
| 26 | Nevada | 25.51 | 26 | 0 | 28 | Rhode Island | 24.14 | 31 | 3 |
| 13 | New Hampshire | 28.51 | 5 | -8 | 29 | Texas | 23.95 | 27 | -2 |
| 11 | New Jersey | 28.98 | 16 | 5 | 30 | Pennsylvania | 23.81 | 34 | 4 |
| 47 | New Mexico | 19.65 | 47 | 0 | 31 | Illinois | 23.79 | 29 | -2 |
| 35 | New York | 22.74 | 38 | 3 | 32 | California | 23.50 | 36 | 4 |
| 42 | North Carolina | 21.93 | 35 | -7 | 33 | Georgia | 23.49 | 30 | -3 |
| 25 | North Dakota | 25.58 | 14 | -11 | 34 | Hawaii | 22.98 | 43 | 9 |
| 24 | Ohio | 26.14 | 25 | 1 | 35 | New York | 22.74 | 38 | 3 |
| 41 | Oklahoma | 22.02 | 37 | -4 | 36 | Arizona | 22.70 | 39 | 3 |
| 23 | Oregon | 26.37 | 21 | -2 | 37 | Alaska | 22.53 | 41 | 4 |
| 30 | Pennsylvania | 23.81 | 34 | 4 | 38 | South Carolina | 22.35 | 44 | 6 |
| 28 | Rhode Island | 24.14 | 31 | 3 | 39 | Montana | 22.19 | 33 | -6 |
| 38 | South Carolina | 22.35 | 44 | 6 | 40 | Florida | 22.16 | 40 | 0 |
| 16 | South Dakota | 28.19 | 11 | -5 | 41 | Oklahoma | 22.02 | 37 | -4 |
| 45 | Tennessee | 20.40 | 46 | 1 | 42 | North Carolina | 21.93 | 35 | -7 |
| 29 | Texas | 23.95 | 27 | -2 | 43 | Kentucky | 21.77 | 32 | -11 |
| 5 | Utah | 31.23 | 4 | -1 | 44 | Arkansas | 21.00 | 45 | 1 |
| 15 | Vermont | 28.28 | 12 | -3 | 45 | Tennessee | 20.40 | 46 | 1 |
| 4 | Virginia | 31.26 | 8 | 4 | 46 | Alabama | 19.98 | 42 | -4 |
| 18 | Washington | 27.28 | 22 | 4 | 47 | New Mexico | 19.65 | 47 | 0 |
| 48 | West Virginia | 18.62 | 49 | 1 | 48 | West Virginia | 18.62 | 49 | 1 |
| 8 | Wisconsin | 29.44 | 6 | -2 | 49 | Louisiana | 16.76 | 48 | -1 |
| 12 | Wyoming | 28.56 | 20 | 8 | 50 | Mississippi | 16.26 | 50 | 0 |

*METHODOLOGY: To determine a state's "Livability Rating," each state's rankings for 43 categories were averaged. The scale is 1 to 50, the higher the number, the better. Data used are for the most recent year in which comparable numbers are available from most states. All factors were given equal weight. States with no data available for a given category were ranked based only on the remaining factors. In our book, data are listed from highest to lowest. However, for purposes of this award, we inverted rankings for those factors we determined to be "positive." Thus the state with the highest median income in the book (ranking 1st) would be given a number 50 ranking for this award.*

# STATE FAST FACTS

| STATE | NICKNAME | CAPITAL | POPULATION* | AREA** |
|---|---|---|---|---|
| Alabama | Heart of Dixie | Montgomery | 4,447,100 | 52,237 |
| Alaska | The Last Frontier | Juneau | 626,932 | 615,230 |
| Arizona | Grand Canyon State | Phoenix | 5,130,632 | 114,006 |
| Arkansas | The Natural State | Little Rock | 2,673,400 | 53,182 |
| California | Golden State | Sacramento | 33,871,648 | 158,869 |
| Colorado | Centennial State | Denver | 4,301,261 | 104,100 |
| Connecticut | Constitution State | Hartford | 3,405,565 | 5,544 |
| Delaware | First State | Dover | 783,600 | 2,396 |
| Florida | Sunshine State | Tallahassee | 15,982,378 | 59,928 |
| Georgia | Peach State | Atlanta | 8,186,453 | 58,977 |
| Hawaii | Aloha State | Honolulu | 1,211,537 | 6,459 |
| Idaho | Gem State | Boise | 1,293,953 | 83,574 |
| Illinois | Land of Lincoln | Springfield | 12,419,293 | 57,918 |
| Indiana | Hoosier State | Indianapolis | 6,080,485 | 36,420 |
| Iowa | Hawkeye State | Des Moines | 2,926,324 | 56,276 |
| Kansas | Sunflower State | Topeka | 2,688,418 | 82,282 |
| Kentucky | Bluegrass State | Frankfort | 4,041,769 | 40,411 |
| Louisiana | Pelican State | Baton Rouge | 4,468,976 | 49,651 |
| Maine | Pine Tree State | Augusta | 1,274,923 | 33,741 |
| Maryland | Free State | Annapolis | 5,296,486 | 12,297 |
| Massachusetts | Bay State | Boston | 6,349,097 | 9,241 |
| Michigan | Great Lake State | Lansing | 9,938,444 | 96,705 |
| Minnesota | North Star State | St. Paul | 4,919,479 | 86,943 |
| Mississippi | Magnolia State | Jackson | 2,844,658 | 48,286 |
| Missouri | Show Me State | Jefferson City | 5,595,211 | 69,709 |
| Montana | Treasure State | Helena | 902,195 | 147,046 |
| Nebraska | Cornhusker State | Lincoln | 1,711,263 | 77,358 |
| Nevada | Sagebrush State | Carson City | 1,998,257 | 110,567 |
| New Hampshire | Granite State | Concord | 1,235,786 | 9,283 |
| New Jersey | Garden State | Trenton | 8,414,350 | 8,215 |
| New Mexico | Land of Enchantment | Santa Fe | 1,819,046 | 121,598 |
| New York | Empire State | Albany | 18,976,457 | 53,989 |
| North Carolina | Tar Heel State | Raleigh | 8,049,313 | 52,672 |
| North Dakota | Peace Garden State | Bismarck | 642,200 | 70,704 |
| Ohio | Buckeye State | Columbus | 11,353,140 | 44,828 |
| Oklahoma | Sooner State | Oklahoma City | 3,450,654 | 69,903 |
| Oregon | Beaver State | Salem | 3,421,399 | 97,132 |
| Pennsylvania | Keystone State | Harrisburg | 12,281,054 | 46,058 |
| Rhode Island | Ocean State | Providence | 1,048,319 | 1,231 |
| South Carolina | Palmetto State | Columbia | 4,012,012 | 31,189 |
| South Dakota | Mount Rushmore State | Pierre | 754,844 | 77,121 |
| Tennessee | Volunteer State | Nashville | 5,689,283 | 42,146 |
| Texas | Lone Star State | Austin | 20,851,820 | 267,277 |
| Utah | Beehive State | Salt Lake City | 2,233,169 | 84,904 |
| Vermont | Green Mountain State | Montpelier | 608,827 | 9,615 |
| Virginia | Old Dominion | Richmond | 7,078,515 | 42,326 |
| Washington | Evergreen State | Olympia | 5,894,121 | 70,637 |
| West Virginia | Mountain State | Charleston | 1,808,344 | 24,231 |
| Wisconsin | Badger State | Madison | 5,363,675 | 65,499 |
| Wyoming | Equality State | Cheyenne | 493,782 | 97,818 |

*2000 Census resident population counts.
**Total of land and water area in square miles.

| STATE SONG | STATE FLOWER | STATE TREE | STATE BIRD |
|---|---|---|---|
| Alabama | Camellia | Southern Pine | Yellowhammer |
| Alaska's Flag | Forget-Me-Not | Sitka Spruce | Willow Ptarmigan |
| Arizona | Saguaro Cactus Blossom | Palo Verde | Cactus Wren |
| Arkansas | Apple Blossom | Pine | Mockingbird |
| I Love You, California | Golden Poppy | California Redwood | California Valley Quail |
| Where the Columbines Grow | Rocky Mountain Columbine | Colorado Blue Spruce | Lark Bunting |
| Yankee Doodle Dandy | Mountain Laurel | White Oak | American Robin |
| Our Delaware | Peach Blossom | American Holly | Blue Hen Chicken |
| Swanee River | Orange Blossom | Sabal Palmetto Palm | Mockingbird |
| Georgia On My Mind | Cherokee Rose | Live Oak | Brown Thrasher |
| Hawaii Ponoi | Yellow Hibiscus | Candlenut | Nene |
| Here We Have Idaho | Syringa | White Pine | Mountain Bluebird |
| Illinois | Purple Violet | White Oak | Cardinal |
| On the Banks of the Wabash, Far Away | Peony | Tulip Poplar | Cardinal |
| The Song of Iowa | Wild Rose | Oak | Eastern Goldfinch |
| Home on the Range | Sunflower | Cottonwood | Western Meadowlark |
| My Old Kentucky Home | Goldenrod | Tulip Tree | Cardinal |
| Give Me Louisiana | Magnolia | Cypress | Eastern Brown Pelican |
| State of Maine Song | White Pine Cone and Tassel | Eastern White Pine | Chickadee |
| Maryland, My Maryland | Black-eyed Susan | White Oak | Baltimore Oriole |
| All Hail to Massachusetts | Mayflower | American Elm | Chickadee |
| Michigan, My Michigan | Apple Blossom | White Pine | Robin |
| Hail! Minnesota | Pink and White Lady's Slipper | Red Pine | Common Loon |
| Go, Mississippi! | Magnolia | Magnolia | Mockingbird |
| Missouri Waltz | Hawthorn | Dogwood | Bluebird |
| Montana | Bitterroot | Ponderosa Pine | Western Meadowlark |
| Beautiful Nebraska | Goldenrod | Cottonwood | Western Meadowlark |
| Home Means Nevada | Sagebrush | Single-Leaf Pinon | Mountain Bluebird |
| Old New Hampshire | Purple Lilac | White Birch | Purple Finch |
| Ode to New Jersey | Purple Violet | Red Oak | Eastern Goldfinch |
| O Fair New Mexico | Yucca | Pinon | Roadrunner |
| I Love New York | Rose | Sugar Maple | Bluebird |
| The Old North State | Dogwood | Pine | Cardinal |
| North Dakota Hymn | Wild Prairie Rose | American Elm | Western Meadowlark |
| Beautiful Ohio | Scarlet Carnation | Buckeye | Cardinal |
| Oklahoma! | Mistletoe | Redbud | Scissortailed Flycatcher |
| Oregon, My Oregon | Oregon Grape | Douglas Fir | Western Meadowlark |
| Hail! Pennsylvania | Mountain Laurel | Hemlock | Ruffed Grouse |
| Rhode Island | Violet | Red Maple | Rhode Island Red |
| Carolina | Yellow Jessamine | Palmetto | Carolina Wren |
| Hail, South Dakota | Pasque Flower | Black Hills Spruce | Ringnecked Pheasant |
| The Tennessee Waltz | Iris | Tulip Poplar | Mockingbird |
| Texas, Our Texas | Bluebonnet | Pecan | Mockingbird |
| Utah, We Love Thee | Sego Lily | Blue Spruce | Seagull |
| Hail, Vermont | Red Clover | Sugar Maple | Hermit Thrush |
| Carry Me Back to Old Virginia | Dogwood | Dogwood | Cardinal |
| Washington, My Home | Western Rhododendron | Western Hemlock | Willow Goldfinch |
| The West Virginia Hills; This Is My West Virginia; and West Virginia, My Home, Sweet Home | Big Rhododendron | Sugar Maple | Cardinal |
| On Wisconsin! | Wood Violet | Sugar Maple | Robin |
| Wyoming | Indian Paintbrush | Cottonwood | Meadowlark |

# TABLE OF CONTENTS

# TABLE OF CONTENTS (continued)

## III. Defense

## IV. Economy

# TABLE OF CONTENTS (continued)

# TABLE OF CONTENTS (continued)

## VII. Energy and Environment

## VIII. Geography

# TABLE OF CONTENTS (continued)

## IX. Government Finance: Federal

## X. Government Finance: State and Local

# TABLE OF CONTENTS (continued)

# TABLE OF CONTENTS (continued)

## XI. Health

## XII. Housing

# TABLE OF CONTENTS (continued)

## XIII. Population

# TABLE OF CONTENTS (continued)

## XIV. Social Welfare

# TABLE OF CONTENTS (continued)

## XV. Transportation

## XVI. Sources

## XVII. Index

# Date Each State Admitted to Statehood*

| RANK | STATE | DATE OF ADMISSION |
|------|-------|-------------------|
| 22 | Alabama | December 14, 1819 |
| 49 | Alaska | January 3, 1959 |
| 48 | Arizona | February 14, 1912 |
| 25 | Arkansas | June 15, 1836 |
| 31 | California | September 9, 1850 |
| 38 | Colorado | August 1, 1876 |
| 5 | Connecticut | January 9, 1788 |
| 1 | Delaware | December 7, 1787 |
| 27 | Florida | March 3, 1845 |
| 4 | Georgia | January 2, 1788 |
| 50 | Hawaii | August 21, 1959 |
| 43 | Idaho | July 3, 1890 |
| 21 | Illinois | December 3, 1818 |
| 19 | Indiana | December 11, 1816 |
| 29 | Iowa | December 28, 1846 |
| 34 | Kansas | January 29, 1861 |
| 15 | Kentucky | June 1, 1792 |
| 18 | Louisiana | April 30, 1812 |
| 23 | Maine | March 15, 1820 |
| 7 | Maryland | April 28, 1788 |
| 6 | Massachusetts | February 6, 1788 |
| 26 | Michigan | January 26, 1837 |
| 32 | Minnesota | May 11, 1858 |
| 20 | Mississippi | December 10, 1817 |
| 24 | Missouri | August 10, 1821 |
| 41 | Montana | November 8, 1889 |
| 37 | Nebraska | March 1, 1867 |
| 36 | Nevada | October 31, 1864 |
| 9 | New Hampshire | June 21, 1788 |
| 3 | New Jersey | December 18, 1787 |
| 47 | New Mexico | January 6, 1912 |
| 11 | New York | July 26, 1788 |
| 12 | North Carolina | November 21, 1789 |
| 39 | North Dakota | November 2, 1889 |
| 17 | Ohio | March 1, 1803 |
| 46 | Oklahoma | November 16, 1907 |
| 33 | Oregon | February 14, 1859 |
| 2 | Pennsylvania | December 12, 1787 |
| 13 | Rhode Island | May 29, 1790 |
| 8 | South Carolina | May 23, 1788 |
| 39 | South Dakota | November 2, 1889 |
| 16 | Tennessee | June 1, 1796 |
| 28 | Texas | December 29, 1845 |
| 45 | Utah | January 4, 1896 |
| 14 | Vermont | March 4, 1791 |
| 10 | Virginia | June 26, 1788 |
| 42 | Washington | November 11, 1889 |
| 35 | West Virginia | June 20, 1863 |
| 30 | Wisconsin | May 29, 1848 |
| 44 | Wyoming | July 10, 1890 |

| RANK | STATE | DATE OF ADMISSION |
|------|-------|-------------------|
| 1 | Delaware | December 7, 1787 |
| 2 | Pennsylvania | December 12, 1787 |
| 3 | New Jersey | December 18, 1787 |
| 4 | Georgia | January 2, 1788 |
| 5 | Connecticut | January 9, 1788 |
| 6 | Massachusetts | February 6, 1788 |
| 7 | Maryland | April 28, 1788 |
| 8 | South Carolina | May 23, 1788 |
| 9 | New Hampshire | June 21, 1788 |
| 10 | Virginia | June 26, 1788 |
| 11 | New York | July 26, 1788 |
| 12 | North Carolina | November 21, 1789 |
| 13 | Rhode Island | May 29, 1790 |
| 14 | Vermont | March 4, 1791 |
| 15 | Kentucky | June 1, 1792 |
| 16 | Tennessee | June 1, 1796 |
| 17 | Ohio | March 1, 1803 |
| 18 | Louisiana | April 30, 1812 |
| 19 | Indiana | December 11, 1816 |
| 20 | Mississippi | December 10, 1817 |
| 21 | Illinois | December 3, 1818 |
| 22 | Alabama | December 14, 1819 |
| 23 | Maine | March 15, 1820 |
| 24 | Missouri | August 10, 1821 |
| 25 | Arkansas | June 15, 1836 |
| 26 | Michigan | January 26, 1837 |
| 27 | Florida | March 3, 1845 |
| 28 | Texas | December 29, 1845 |
| 29 | Iowa | December 28, 1846 |
| 30 | Wisconsin | May 29, 1848 |
| 31 | California | September 9, 1850 |
| 32 | Minnesota | May 11, 1858 |
| 33 | Oregon | February 14, 1859 |
| 34 | Kansas | January 29, 1861 |
| 35 | West Virginia | June 20, 1863 |
| 36 | Nevada | October 31, 1864 |
| 37 | Nebraska | March 1, 1867 |
| 38 | Colorado | August 1, 1876 |
| 39 | North Dakota | November 2, 1889 |
| 39 | South Dakota | November 2, 1889 |
| 41 | Montana | November 8, 1889 |
| 42 | Washington | November 11, 1889 |
| 43 | Idaho | July 3, 1890 |
| 44 | Wyoming | July 10, 1890 |
| 45 | Utah | January 4, 1896 |
| 46 | Oklahoma | November 16, 1907 |
| 47 | New Mexico | January 6, 1912 |
| 48 | Arizona | February 14, 1912 |
| 49 | Alaska | January 3, 1959 |
| 50 | Hawaii | August 21, 1959 |

Source: U.S. Bureau of the Census
"1980 Census of Population" (vol. 1, part A, PC80-1-A)
*First thirteen states show date of ratification of Constitution.

# I. AGRICULTURE

# Number of Farms in 1999

## National Total = 2,194,070 Farms*

ALPHA ORDER

| RANK | STATE | FARMS | % of USA |
|---|---|---|---|
| 21 | Alabama | 48,000 | 2.2% |
| 50 | Alaska | 570 | 0.0% |
| 40 | Arizona | 7,700 | 0.4% |
| 20 | Arkansas | 48,500 | 2.2% |
| 6 | California | 89,000 | 4.1% |
| 30 | Colorado | 29,000 | 1.3% |
| 45 | Connecticut | 4,000 | 0.2% |
| 48 | Delaware | 2,600 | 0.1% |
| 22 | Florida | 45,000 | 2.1% |
| 18 | Georgia | 50,000 | 2.3% |
| 44 | Hawaii | 5,500 | 0.3% |
| 33 | Idaho | 24,500 | 1.1% |
| 10 | Illinois | 79,000 | 3.6% |
| 12 | Indiana | 65,000 | 3.0% |
| 3 | Iowa | 96,000 | 4.4% |
| 12 | Kansas | 65,000 | 3.0% |
| 4 | Kentucky | 91,000 | 4.1% |
| 29 | Louisiana | 30,000 | 1.4% |
| 41 | Maine | 6,900 | 0.3% |
| 37 | Maryland | 12,400 | 0.6% |
| 43 | Massachusetts | 6,100 | 0.3% |
| 17 | Michigan | 53,000 | 2.4% |
| 8 | Minnesota | 81,000 | 3.7% |
| 23 | Mississippi | 43,000 | 2.0% |
| 2 | Missouri | 110,000 | 5.0% |
| 31 | Montana | 28,000 | 1.3% |
| 16 | Nebraska | 55,000 | 2.5% |
| 47 | Nevada | 3,000 | 0.1% |
| 46 | New Hampshire | 3,100 | 0.1% |
| 38 | New Jersey | 9,600 | 0.4% |
| 35 | New Mexico | 15,500 | 0.7% |
| 26 | New York | 39,000 | 1.8% |
| 15 | North Carolina | 58,000 | 2.6% |
| 28 | North Dakota | 30,500 | 1.4% |
| 9 | Ohio | 80,000 | 3.6% |
| 7 | Oklahoma | 84,000 | 3.8% |
| 24 | Oregon | 40,500 | 1.8% |
| 14 | Pennsylvania | 59,000 | 2.7% |
| 49 | Rhode Island | 700 | 0.0% |
| 32 | South Carolina | 25,000 | 1.1% |
| 27 | South Dakota | 32,500 | 1.5% |
| 4 | Tennessee | 91,000 | 4.1% |
| 1 | Texas | 227,000 | 10.3% |
| 35 | Utah | 15,500 | 0.7% |
| 42 | Vermont | 6,700 | 0.3% |
| 18 | Virginia | 50,000 | 2.3% |
| 25 | Washington | 40,000 | 1.8% |
| 34 | West Virginia | 20,500 | 0.9% |
| 11 | Wisconsin | 78,000 | 3.6% |
| 39 | Wyoming | 9,200 | 0.4% |

RANK ORDER

| RANK | STATE | FARMS | % of USA |
|---|---|---|---|
| 1 | Texas | 227,000 | 10.3% |
| 2 | Missouri | 110,000 | 5.0% |
| 3 | Iowa | 96,000 | 4.4% |
| 4 | Kentucky | 91,000 | 4.1% |
| 4 | Tennessee | 91,000 | 4.1% |
| 6 | California | 89,000 | 4.1% |
| 7 | Oklahoma | 84,000 | 3.8% |
| 8 | Minnesota | 81,000 | 3.7% |
| 9 | Ohio | 80,000 | 3.6% |
| 10 | Illinois | 79,000 | 3.6% |
| 11 | Wisconsin | 78,000 | 3.6% |
| 12 | Indiana | 65,000 | 3.0% |
| 12 | Kansas | 65,000 | 3.0% |
| 14 | Pennsylvania | 59,000 | 2.7% |
| 15 | North Carolina | 58,000 | 2.6% |
| 16 | Nebraska | 55,000 | 2.5% |
| 17 | Michigan | 53,000 | 2.4% |
| 18 | Georgia | 50,000 | 2.3% |
| 18 | Virginia | 50,000 | 2.3% |
| 20 | Arkansas | 48,500 | 2.2% |
| 21 | Alabama | 48,000 | 2.2% |
| 22 | Florida | 45,000 | 2.1% |
| 23 | Mississippi | 43,000 | 2.0% |
| 24 | Oregon | 40,500 | 1.8% |
| 25 | Washington | 40,000 | 1.8% |
| 26 | New York | 39,000 | 1.8% |
| 27 | South Dakota | 32,500 | 1.5% |
| 28 | North Dakota | 30,500 | 1.4% |
| 29 | Louisiana | 30,000 | 1.4% |
| 30 | Colorado | 29,000 | 1.3% |
| 31 | Montana | 28,000 | 1.3% |
| 32 | South Carolina | 25,000 | 1.1% |
| 33 | Idaho | 24,500 | 1.1% |
| 34 | West Virginia | 20,500 | 0.9% |
| 35 | New Mexico | 15,500 | 0.7% |
| 35 | Utah | 15,500 | 0.7% |
| 37 | Maryland | 12,400 | 0.6% |
| 38 | New Jersey | 9,600 | 0.4% |
| 39 | Wyoming | 9,200 | 0.4% |
| 40 | Arizona | 7,700 | 0.4% |
| 41 | Maine | 6,900 | 0.3% |
| 42 | Vermont | 6,700 | 0.3% |
| 43 | Massachusetts | 6,100 | 0.3% |
| 44 | Hawaii | 5,500 | 0.3% |
| 45 | Connecticut | 4,000 | 0.2% |
| 46 | New Hampshire | 3,100 | 0.1% |
| 47 | Nevada | 3,000 | 0.1% |
| 48 | Delaware | 2,600 | 0.1% |
| 49 | Rhode Island | 700 | 0.0% |
| 50 | Alaska | 570 | 0.0% |
|  | District of Columbia | 0 | 0.0% |

Source: U.S. Department of Agriculture, National Agricultural Statistics Service
"Farms and Land in Farms" (http://usda.mannlib.cornell.edu/reports/nassr/other/zfl-bb/fmno0200.txt)
*A farm is any establishment from which $1,000 or more of agricultural products were sold or would normally be sold during the year. This includes places with five or more horses, except horses in boarding stables or racetracks.

# Land in Farms in 1999

## National Total = 947,340,000 Acres*

ALPHA ORDER

| RANK | STATE | ACRES | % of USA |
|---|---|---|---|
| 32 | Alabama | 9,200,000 | 1.0% |
| 44 | Alaska | 910,000 | 0.1% |
| 16 | Arizona | 27,500,000 | 2.9% |
| 22 | Arkansas | 14,650,000 | 1.5% |
| 14 | California | 27,800,000 | 2.9% |
| 11 | Colorado | 31,800,000 | 3.4% |
| 49 | Connecticut | 370,000 | 0.0% |
| 46 | Delaware | 580,000 | 0.1% |
| 29 | Florida | 10,400,000 | 1.1% |
| 28 | Georgia | 11,200,000 | 1.2% |
| 41 | Hawaii | 1,440,000 | 0.2% |
| 24 | Idaho | 11,900,000 | 1.3% |
| 15 | Illinois | 27,700,000 | 2.9% |
| 20 | Indiana | 15,500,000 | 1.6% |
| 10 | Iowa | 33,000,000 | 3.5% |
| 3 | Kansas | 47,500,000 | 5.0% |
| 23 | Kentucky | 13,600,000 | 1.4% |
| 34 | Louisiana | 8,150,000 | 0.9% |
| 43 | Maine | 1,270,000 | 0.1% |
| 40 | Maryland | 2,100,000 | 0.2% |
| 47 | Massachusetts | 570,000 | 0.1% |
| 29 | Michigan | 10,400,000 | 1.1% |
| 13 | Minnesota | 28,800,000 | 3.0% |
| 27 | Mississippi | 11,400,000 | 1.2% |
| 12 | Missouri | 30,100,000 | 3.2% |
| 2 | Montana | 57,000,000 | 6.0% |
| 4 | Nebraska | 46,400,000 | 4.9% |
| 37 | Nevada | 6,800,000 | 0.7% |
| 48 | New Hampshire | 420,000 | 0.0% |
| 45 | New Jersey | 830,000 | 0.1% |
| 5 | New Mexico | 44,700,000 | 4.7% |
| 35 | New York | 7,800,000 | 0.8% |
| 31 | North Carolina | 9,300,000 | 1.0% |
| 7 | North Dakota | 39,400,000 | 4.2% |
| 21 | Ohio | 14,900,000 | 1.6% |
| 9 | Oklahoma | 34,000,000 | 3.6% |
| 17 | Oregon | 17,200,000 | 1.8% |
| 36 | Pennsylvania | 7,700,000 | 0.8% |
| 50 | Rhode Island | 60,000 | 0.0% |
| 38 | South Carolina | 4,850,000 | 0.5% |
| 6 | South Dakota | 44,000,000 | 4.6% |
| 24 | Tennessee | 11,900,000 | 1.3% |
| 1 | Texas | 130,500,000 | 13.8% |
| 26 | Utah | 11,600,000 | 1.2% |
| 42 | Vermont | 1,340,000 | 0.1% |
| 33 | Virginia | 8,600,000 | 0.9% |
| 19 | Washington | 15,700,000 | 1.7% |
| 39 | West Virginia | 3,600,000 | 0.4% |
| 18 | Wisconsin | 16,300,000 | 1.7% |
| 8 | Wyoming | 34,600,000 | 3.7% |

RANK ORDER

| RANK | STATE | ACRES | % of USA |
|---|---|---|---|
| 1 | Texas | 130,500,000 | 13.8% |
| 2 | Montana | 57,000,000 | 6.0% |
| 3 | Kansas | 47,500,000 | 5.0% |
| 4 | Nebraska | 46,400,000 | 4.9% |
| 5 | New Mexico | 44,700,000 | 4.7% |
| 6 | South Dakota | 44,000,000 | 4.6% |
| 7 | North Dakota | 39,400,000 | 4.2% |
| 8 | Wyoming | 34,600,000 | 3.7% |
| 9 | Oklahoma | 34,000,000 | 3.6% |
| 10 | Iowa | 33,000,000 | 3.5% |
| 11 | Colorado | 31,800,000 | 3.4% |
| 12 | Missouri | 30,100,000 | 3.2% |
| 13 | Minnesota | 28,800,000 | 3.0% |
| 14 | California | 27,800,000 | 2.9% |
| 15 | Illinois | 27,700,000 | 2.9% |
| 16 | Arizona | 27,500,000 | 2.9% |
| 17 | Oregon | 17,200,000 | 1.8% |
| 18 | Wisconsin | 16,300,000 | 1.7% |
| 19 | Washington | 15,700,000 | 1.7% |
| 20 | Indiana | 15,500,000 | 1.6% |
| 21 | Ohio | 14,900,000 | 1.6% |
| 22 | Arkansas | 14,650,000 | 1.5% |
| 23 | Kentucky | 13,600,000 | 1.4% |
| 24 | Idaho | 11,900,000 | 1.3% |
| 24 | Tennessee | 11,900,000 | 1.3% |
| 26 | Utah | 11,600,000 | 1.2% |
| 27 | Mississippi | 11,400,000 | 1.2% |
| 28 | Georgia | 11,200,000 | 1.2% |
| 29 | Florida | 10,400,000 | 1.1% |
| 29 | Michigan | 10,400,000 | 1.1% |
| 31 | North Carolina | 9,300,000 | 1.0% |
| 32 | Alabama | 9,200,000 | 1.0% |
| 33 | Virginia | 8,600,000 | 0.9% |
| 34 | Louisiana | 8,150,000 | 0.9% |
| 35 | New York | 7,800,000 | 0.8% |
| 36 | Pennsylvania | 7,700,000 | 0.8% |
| 37 | Nevada | 6,800,000 | 0.7% |
| 38 | South Carolina | 4,850,000 | 0.5% |
| 39 | West Virginia | 3,600,000 | 0.4% |
| 40 | Maryland | 2,100,000 | 0.2% |
| 41 | Hawaii | 1,440,000 | 0.2% |
| 42 | Vermont | 1,340,000 | 0.1% |
| 43 | Maine | 1,270,000 | 0.1% |
| 44 | Alaska | 910,000 | 0.1% |
| 45 | New Jersey | 830,000 | 0.1% |
| 46 | Delaware | 580,000 | 0.1% |
| 47 | Massachusetts | 570,000 | 0.1% |
| 48 | New Hampshire | 420,000 | 0.0% |
| 49 | Connecticut | 370,000 | 0.0% |
| 50 | Rhode Island | 60,000 | 0.0% |
| | District of Columbia | 0 | 0.0% |

Source: U.S. Department of Agriculture, National Agricultural Statistics Service
"Farms and Land in Farms" (http://usda.mannlib.cornell.edu/reports/nassr/other/zfl-bb/fmno0200.txt)
*A farm is any establishment from which $1,000 or more of agricultural products were sold or would normally be sold during the year. This includes places with five or more horses, except horses in boarding stables or racetracks.

3

# Average Number of Acres per Farm in 1999

## National Average = 432 Acres*

ALPHA ORDER

| RANK | STATE | ACRES |
|---|---|---|
| 36 | Alabama | 192 |
| 6 | Alaska | 1,596 |
| 2 | Arizona | 3,571 |
| 22 | Arkansas | 302 |
| 21 | California | 312 |
| 9 | Colorado | 1,097 |
| 47 | Connecticut | 93 |
| 30 | Delaware | 223 |
| 28 | Florida | 231 |
| 29 | Georgia | 224 |
| 26 | Hawaii | 262 |
| 14 | Idaho | 486 |
| 19 | Illinois | 351 |
| 27 | Indiana | 238 |
| 20 | Iowa | 344 |
| 12 | Kansas | 731 |
| 43 | Kentucky | 149 |
| 24 | Louisiana | 272 |
| 38 | Maine | 184 |
| 41 | Maryland | 169 |
| 47 | Massachusetts | 93 |
| 34 | Michigan | 196 |
| 18 | Minnesota | 356 |
| 25 | Mississippi | 265 |
| 23 | Missouri | 274 |
| 5 | Montana | 2,036 |
| 10 | Nebraska | 844 |
| 4 | Nevada | 2,267 |
| 44 | New Hampshire | 135 |
| 49 | New Jersey | 86 |
| 3 | New Mexico | 2,884 |
| 32 | New York | 200 |
| 42 | North Carolina | 160 |
| 8 | North Dakota | 1,292 |
| 37 | Ohio | 186 |
| 16 | Oklahoma | 405 |
| 15 | Oregon | 425 |
| 45 | Pennsylvania | 131 |
| 49 | Rhode Island | 86 |
| 35 | South Carolina | 194 |
| 7 | South Dakota | 1,354 |
| 45 | Tennessee | 131 |
| 13 | Texas | 575 |
| 11 | Utah | 748 |
| 32 | Vermont | 200 |
| 40 | Virginia | 172 |
| 17 | Washington | 393 |
| 39 | West Virginia | 176 |
| 31 | Wisconsin | 209 |
| 1 | Wyoming | 3,761 |

RANK ORDER

| RANK | STATE | ACRES |
|---|---|---|
| 1 | Wyoming | 3,761 |
| 2 | Arizona | 3,571 |
| 3 | New Mexico | 2,884 |
| 4 | Nevada | 2,267 |
| 5 | Montana | 2,036 |
| 6 | Alaska | 1,596 |
| 7 | South Dakota | 1,354 |
| 8 | North Dakota | 1,292 |
| 9 | Colorado | 1,097 |
| 10 | Nebraska | 844 |
| 11 | Utah | 748 |
| 12 | Kansas | 731 |
| 13 | Texas | 575 |
| 14 | Idaho | 486 |
| 15 | Oregon | 425 |
| 16 | Oklahoma | 405 |
| 17 | Washington | 393 |
| 18 | Minnesota | 356 |
| 19 | Illinois | 351 |
| 20 | Iowa | 344 |
| 21 | California | 312 |
| 22 | Arkansas | 302 |
| 23 | Missouri | 274 |
| 24 | Louisiana | 272 |
| 25 | Mississippi | 265 |
| 26 | Hawaii | 262 |
| 27 | Indiana | 238 |
| 28 | Florida | 231 |
| 29 | Georgia | 224 |
| 30 | Delaware | 223 |
| 31 | Wisconsin | 209 |
| 32 | New York | 200 |
| 32 | Vermont | 200 |
| 34 | Michigan | 196 |
| 35 | South Carolina | 194 |
| 36 | Alabama | 192 |
| 37 | Ohio | 186 |
| 38 | Maine | 184 |
| 39 | West Virginia | 176 |
| 40 | Virginia | 172 |
| 41 | Maryland | 169 |
| 42 | North Carolina | 160 |
| 43 | Kentucky | 149 |
| 44 | New Hampshire | 135 |
| 45 | Pennsylvania | 131 |
| 45 | Tennessee | 131 |
| 47 | Connecticut | 93 |
| 47 | Massachusetts | 93 |
| 49 | New Jersey | 86 |
| 49 | Rhode Island | 86 |
|  | District of Columbia** | NA |

Source: U.S. Department of Agriculture, National Agricultural Statistics Service
    "Farms and Land in Farms" (http://usda.mannlib.cornell.edu/reports/nassr/other/zfl-bb/fmno0200.txt)
*A farm is any establishment from which $1,000 or more of agricultural products were sold or would normally be sold during the year.  This includes places with five or more horses, except horses in boarding stables or racetracks.
**Not applicable.

# Percent of Agricultural Land Foreign Owned in 1997

## National Percent = 1.1% of Agricultural Land*

<table>
<tr><td colspan="3">ALPHA ORDER</td><td colspan="3">RANK ORDER</td></tr>
<tr><td>RANK</td><td>STATE</td><td>PERCENT</td><td>RANK</td><td>STATE</td><td>PERCENT</td></tr>
<tr><td>7</td><td>Alabama</td><td>2.1</td><td>1</td><td>Maine</td><td>16.8</td></tr>
<tr><td>NA</td><td>Alaska**</td><td>NA</td><td>2</td><td>Hawaii</td><td>9.0</td></tr>
<tr><td>4</td><td>Arizona</td><td>3.3</td><td>3</td><td>Nevada</td><td>5.3</td></tr>
<tr><td>27</td><td>Arkansas</td><td>0.6</td><td>4</td><td>Arizona</td><td>3.3</td></tr>
<tr><td>7</td><td>California</td><td>2.1</td><td>5</td><td>Florida</td><td>2.8</td></tr>
<tr><td>9</td><td>Colorado</td><td>2.0</td><td>6</td><td>New Mexico</td><td>2.2</td></tr>
<tr><td>42</td><td>Connecticut</td><td>0.1</td><td>7</td><td>Alabama</td><td>2.1</td></tr>
<tr><td>27</td><td>Delaware</td><td>0.6</td><td>7</td><td>California</td><td>2.1</td></tr>
<tr><td>5</td><td>Florida</td><td>2.8</td><td>9</td><td>Colorado</td><td>2.0</td></tr>
<tr><td>10</td><td>Georgia</td><td>1.6</td><td>10</td><td>Georgia</td><td>1.6</td></tr>
<tr><td>2</td><td>Hawaii</td><td>9.0</td><td>10</td><td>Vermont</td><td>1.6</td></tr>
<tr><td>38</td><td>Idaho</td><td>0.2</td><td>12</td><td>Louisiana</td><td>1.4</td></tr>
<tr><td>27</td><td>Illinois</td><td>0.6</td><td>13</td><td>New York</td><td>1.3</td></tr>
<tr><td>32</td><td>Indiana</td><td>0.5</td><td>13</td><td>West Virginia</td><td>1.3</td></tr>
<tr><td>42</td><td>Iowa</td><td>0.1</td><td>15</td><td>Michigan</td><td>1.2</td></tr>
<tr><td>42</td><td>Kansas</td><td>0.1</td><td>16</td><td>Maryland</td><td>1.1</td></tr>
<tr><td>32</td><td>Kentucky</td><td>0.5</td><td>16</td><td>South Carolina</td><td>1.1</td></tr>
<tr><td>12</td><td>Louisiana</td><td>1.4</td><td>18</td><td>New Jersey</td><td>1.0</td></tr>
<tr><td>1</td><td>Maine</td><td>16.8</td><td>18</td><td>Wyoming</td><td>1.0</td></tr>
<tr><td>16</td><td>Maryland</td><td>1.1</td><td>20</td><td>Montana</td><td>0.9</td></tr>
<tr><td>42</td><td>Massachusetts</td><td>0.1</td><td>20</td><td>North Carolina</td><td>0.9</td></tr>
<tr><td>15</td><td>Michigan</td><td>1.2</td><td>20</td><td>Washington</td><td>0.9</td></tr>
<tr><td>27</td><td>Minnesota</td><td>0.6</td><td>23</td><td>Mississippi</td><td>0.8</td></tr>
<tr><td>23</td><td>Mississippi</td><td>0.8</td><td>23</td><td>Ohio</td><td>0.8</td></tr>
<tr><td>38</td><td>Missouri</td><td>0.2</td><td>23</td><td>Oregon</td><td>0.8</td></tr>
<tr><td>20</td><td>Montana</td><td>0.9</td><td>23</td><td>Texas</td><td>0.8</td></tr>
<tr><td>38</td><td>Nebraska</td><td>0.2</td><td>27</td><td>Arkansas</td><td>0.6</td></tr>
<tr><td>3</td><td>Nevada</td><td>5.3</td><td>27</td><td>Delaware</td><td>0.6</td></tr>
<tr><td>36</td><td>New Hampshire</td><td>0.4</td><td>27</td><td>Illinois</td><td>0.6</td></tr>
<tr><td>18</td><td>New Jersey</td><td>1.0</td><td>27</td><td>Minnesota</td><td>0.6</td></tr>
<tr><td>6</td><td>New Mexico</td><td>2.2</td><td>27</td><td>Virginia</td><td>0.6</td></tr>
<tr><td>13</td><td>New York</td><td>1.3</td><td>32</td><td>Indiana</td><td>0.5</td></tr>
<tr><td>20</td><td>North Carolina</td><td>0.9</td><td>32</td><td>Kentucky</td><td>0.5</td></tr>
<tr><td>42</td><td>North Dakota</td><td>0.1</td><td>32</td><td>Pennsylvania</td><td>0.5</td></tr>
<tr><td>23</td><td>Ohio</td><td>0.8</td><td>32</td><td>Utah</td><td>0.5</td></tr>
<tr><td>38</td><td>Oklahoma</td><td>0.2</td><td>36</td><td>New Hampshire</td><td>0.4</td></tr>
<tr><td>23</td><td>Oregon</td><td>0.8</td><td>36</td><td>Tennessee</td><td>0.4</td></tr>
<tr><td>32</td><td>Pennsylvania</td><td>0.5</td><td>38</td><td>Idaho</td><td>0.2</td></tr>
<tr><td>NA</td><td>Rhode Island**</td><td>NA</td><td>38</td><td>Missouri</td><td>0.2</td></tr>
<tr><td>16</td><td>South Carolina</td><td>1.1</td><td>38</td><td>Nebraska</td><td>0.2</td></tr>
<tr><td>42</td><td>South Dakota</td><td>0.1</td><td>38</td><td>Oklahoma</td><td>0.2</td></tr>
<tr><td>36</td><td>Tennessee</td><td>0.4</td><td>42</td><td>Connecticut</td><td>0.1</td></tr>
<tr><td>23</td><td>Texas</td><td>0.8</td><td>42</td><td>Iowa</td><td>0.1</td></tr>
<tr><td>32</td><td>Utah</td><td>0.5</td><td>42</td><td>Kansas</td><td>0.1</td></tr>
<tr><td>10</td><td>Vermont</td><td>1.6</td><td>42</td><td>Massachusetts</td><td>0.1</td></tr>
<tr><td>27</td><td>Virginia</td><td>0.6</td><td>42</td><td>North Dakota</td><td>0.1</td></tr>
<tr><td>20</td><td>Washington</td><td>0.9</td><td>42</td><td>South Dakota</td><td>0.1</td></tr>
<tr><td>13</td><td>West Virginia</td><td>1.3</td><td>42</td><td>Wisconsin</td><td>0.1</td></tr>
<tr><td>42</td><td>Wisconsin</td><td>0.1</td><td>NA</td><td>Alaska**</td><td>NA</td></tr>
<tr><td>18</td><td>Wyoming</td><td>1.0</td><td>NA</td><td>Rhode Island**</td><td>NA</td></tr>
<tr><td></td><td></td><td></td><td></td><td>District of Columbia**</td><td>NA</td></tr>
</table>

Source: U.S. Department of Agriculture, Economic Research Service
   "Foreign Ownership of U.S. Agricultural Land Through December 31, 1997" (September 1998)
*Percent of privately owned agricultural land. Includes both farm, range and forestlands.
**Alaska has 195 acres foreign owned, Rhode Island 17 acres and the District of Columbia has no agricultural land.

# Average per Acre Value of Farmland and Buildings in 2000

## National Average = $1,050 per Acre*

ALPHA ORDER

| RANK | STATE | PER ACRE VALUE |
|------|-------|----------------|
| 20 | Alabama | $1,680 |
| NA | Alaska** | NA |
| 34 | Arizona | 1,140 |
| 27 | Arkansas | 1,250 |
| 6 | California | 2,850 |
| 39 | Colorado | 640 |
| 2 | Connecticut | 6,600 |
| 6 | Delaware | 2,850 |
| 9 | Florida | 2,400 |
| 18 | Georgia | 1,800 |
| NA | Hawaii** | NA |
| 32 | Idaho | 1,170 |
| 13 | Illinois | 2,220 |
| 14 | Indiana | 2,210 |
| 19 | Iowa | 1,750 |
| 42 | Kansas | 590 |
| 23 | Kentucky | 1,590 |
| 27 | Louisiana | 1,250 |
| 29 | Maine | 1,210 |
| 5 | Maryland | 3,500 |
| 4 | Massachusetts | 5,900 |
| 16 | Michigan | 2,100 |
| 26 | Minnesota | 1,270 |
| 31 | Mississippi | 1,180 |
| 30 | Missouri | 1,190 |
| 46 | Montana | 300 |
| 38 | Nebraska | 695 |
| 43 | Nevada | 440 |
| 11 | New Hampshire | 2,300 |
| 1 | New Jersey | 7,100 |
| 48 | New Mexico | 215 |
| 25 | New York | 1,410 |
| 9 | North Carolina | 2,400 |
| 44 | North Dakota | 415 |
| 12 | Ohio | 2,250 |
| 40 | Oklahoma | 634 |
| 36 | Oregon | 1,020 |
| 8 | Pennsylvania | 2,620 |
| 3 | Rhode Island | 6,500 |
| 22 | South Carolina | 1,600 |
| 45 | South Dakota | 380 |
| 16 | Tennessee | 2,100 |
| 41 | Texas | 630 |
| 37 | Utah | 900 |
| 21 | Vermont | 1,640 |
| 15 | Virginia | 2,130 |
| 33 | Washington | 1,150 |
| 35 | West Virginia | 1,060 |
| 24 | Wisconsin | 1,500 |
| 47 | Wyoming | 235 |

RANK ORDER

| RANK | STATE | PER ACRE VALUE |
|------|-------|----------------|
| 1 | New Jersey | $7,100 |
| 2 | Connecticut | 6,600 |
| 3 | Rhode Island | 6,500 |
| 4 | Massachusetts | 5,900 |
| 5 | Maryland | 3,500 |
| 6 | California | 2,850 |
| 6 | Delaware | 2,850 |
| 8 | Pennsylvania | 2,620 |
| 9 | Florida | 2,400 |
| 9 | North Carolina | 2,400 |
| 11 | New Hampshire | 2,300 |
| 12 | Ohio | 2,250 |
| 13 | Illinois | 2,220 |
| 14 | Indiana | 2,210 |
| 15 | Virginia | 2,130 |
| 16 | Michigan | 2,100 |
| 16 | Tennessee | 2,100 |
| 18 | Georgia | 1,800 |
| 19 | Iowa | 1,750 |
| 20 | Alabama | 1,680 |
| 21 | Vermont | 1,640 |
| 22 | South Carolina | 1,600 |
| 23 | Kentucky | 1,590 |
| 24 | Wisconsin | 1,500 |
| 25 | New York | 1,410 |
| 26 | Minnesota | 1,270 |
| 27 | Arkansas | 1,250 |
| 27 | Louisiana | 1,250 |
| 29 | Maine | 1,210 |
| 30 | Missouri | 1,190 |
| 31 | Mississippi | 1,180 |
| 32 | Idaho | 1,170 |
| 33 | Washington | 1,150 |
| 34 | Arizona | 1,140 |
| 35 | West Virginia | 1,060 |
| 36 | Oregon | 1,020 |
| 37 | Utah | 900 |
| 38 | Nebraska | 695 |
| 39 | Colorado | 640 |
| 40 | Oklahoma | 634 |
| 41 | Texas | 630 |
| 42 | Kansas | 590 |
| 43 | Nevada | 440 |
| 44 | North Dakota | 415 |
| 45 | South Dakota | 380 |
| 46 | Montana | 300 |
| 47 | Wyoming | 235 |
| 48 | New Mexico | 215 |
| NA | Alaska** | NA |
| NA | Hawaii** | NA |
| | District of Columbia** | NA |

Source: U.S. Department of Agriculture, Economic Research Service
    "Agricultural Land Values" (http://usda.mannlib.cornell.edu/reports/nassr/other/plr-bb/land0300.txt)
*As of January 1, 2000. Value of farmland and buildings in nominal dollars.
**Not applicable or available.

# Percent Change in Average per Acre Value of Farmland: 1999 to 2000

## National Percent Change = 2.9% Increase*

ALPHA ORDER

| RANK | STATE | PERCENT CHANGE |
|---|---|---|
| 2 | Alabama | 10.5 |
| NA | Alaska** | NA |
| 11 | Arizona | 6.5 |
| 31 | Arkansas | 2.5 |
| 30 | California | 2.9 |
| 36 | Colorado | 1.6 |
| 19 | Connecticut | 4.8 |
| 26 | Delaware | 3.6 |
| 12 | Florida | 6.2 |
| 3 | Georgia | 10.4 |
| NA | Hawaii** | NA |
| 6 | Idaho | 7.3 |
| 47 | Illinois | (1.3) |
| 43 | Indiana | (0.5) |
| 46 | Iowa | (1.1) |
| 35 | Kansas | 1.7 |
| 24 | Kentucky | 3.9 |
| 27 | Louisiana | 3.3 |
| 41 | Maine | 0.8 |
| 13 | Maryland | 6.1 |
| 6 | Massachusetts | 7.3 |
| 1 | Michigan | 13.5 |
| 27 | Minnesota | 3.3 |
| 6 | Mississippi | 7.3 |
| 15 | Missouri | 5.3 |
| 37 | Montana | 1.4 |
| 25 | Nebraska | 3.7 |
| 19 | Nevada | 4.8 |
| 32 | New Hampshire | 2.2 |
| 37 | New Jersey | 1.4 |
| 44 | New Mexico | (0.9) |
| 18 | New York | 5.2 |
| 10 | North Carolina | 6.7 |
| 32 | North Dakota | 2.2 |
| 37 | Ohio | 1.4 |
| 37 | Oklahoma | 1.4 |
| 34 | Oregon | 2.0 |
| 19 | Pennsylvania | 4.8 |
| 42 | Rhode Island | 0.0 |
| 15 | South Carolina | 5.3 |
| 14 | South Dakota | 5.6 |
| 5 | Tennessee | 7.7 |
| 27 | Texas | 3.3 |
| 15 | Utah | 5.3 |
| 22 | Vermont | 4.5 |
| 23 | Virginia | 4.4 |
| 48 | Washington | (3.4) |
| 44 | West Virginia | (0.9) |
| 4 | Wisconsin | 9.5 |
| 9 | Wyoming | 6.8 |

RANK ORDER

| RANK | STATE | PERCENT CHANGE |
|---|---|---|
| 1 | Michigan | 13.5 |
| 2 | Alabama | 10.5 |
| 3 | Georgia | 10.4 |
| 4 | Wisconsin | 9.5 |
| 5 | Tennessee | 7.7 |
| 6 | Idaho | 7.3 |
| 6 | Massachusetts | 7.3 |
| 6 | Mississippi | 7.3 |
| 9 | Wyoming | 6.8 |
| 10 | North Carolina | 6.7 |
| 11 | Arizona | 6.5 |
| 12 | Florida | 6.2 |
| 13 | Maryland | 6.1 |
| 14 | South Dakota | 5.6 |
| 15 | Missouri | 5.3 |
| 15 | South Carolina | 5.3 |
| 15 | Utah | 5.3 |
| 18 | New York | 5.2 |
| 19 | Connecticut | 4.8 |
| 19 | Nevada | 4.8 |
| 19 | Pennsylvania | 4.8 |
| 22 | Vermont | 4.5 |
| 23 | Virginia | 4.4 |
| 24 | Kentucky | 3.9 |
| 25 | Nebraska | 3.7 |
| 26 | Delaware | 3.6 |
| 27 | Louisiana | 3.3 |
| 27 | Minnesota | 3.3 |
| 27 | Texas | 3.3 |
| 30 | California | 2.9 |
| 31 | Arkansas | 2.5 |
| 32 | New Hampshire | 2.2 |
| 32 | North Dakota | 2.2 |
| 34 | Oregon | 2.0 |
| 35 | Kansas | 1.7 |
| 36 | Colorado | 1.6 |
| 37 | Montana | 1.4 |
| 37 | New Jersey | 1.4 |
| 37 | Ohio | 1.4 |
| 37 | Oklahoma | 1.4 |
| 41 | Maine | 0.8 |
| 42 | Rhode Island | 0.0 |
| 43 | Indiana | (0.5) |
| 44 | New Mexico | (0.9) |
| 44 | West Virginia | (0.9) |
| 46 | Iowa | (1.1) |
| 47 | Illinois | (1.3) |
| 48 | Washington | (3.4) |
| NA | Alaska** | NA |
| NA | Hawaii** | NA |
| | District of Columbia** | NA |

Source: U.S. Department of Agriculture, Economic Research Service
    "Agricultural Land Values" (http://usda.mannlib.cornell.edu/reports/nassr/other/plr-bb/land0300.txt)
*As of January 1, 2000. Value of farmland and buildings in nominal dollars.
**Not applicable or available.

# Net Farm Income in 1999

## National Total = $43,397,572,000*

| RANK | STATE | FARM INCOME | % of USA |
|------|-------|-------------|----------|
| 10 | Alabama | $1,449,605,735 | 3.3% |
| 48 | Alaska | 19,587,039 | 0.0% |
| 21 | Arizona | 707,685,953 | 1.6% |
| 6 | Arkansas | 1,830,917,875 | 4.2% |
| 1 | California | 4,986,433,392 | 11.5% |
| 16 | Colorado | 922,905,032 | 2.1% |
| 40 | Connecticut | 139,290,158 | 0.3% |
| 42 | Delaware | 120,678,036 | 0.3% |
| 3 | Florida | 2,815,328,013 | 6.5% |
| 4 | Georgia | 2,099,384,258 | 4.8% |
| 46 | Hawaii | 63,151,139 | 0.1% |
| 18 | Idaho | 873,776,373 | 2.0% |
| 14 | Illinois | 1,007,007,090 | 2.3% |
| 31 | Indiana | 420,822,037 | 1.0% |
| 9 | Iowa | 1,450,175,975 | 3.3% |
| 8 | Kansas | 1,547,850,191 | 3.6% |
| 19 | Kentucky | 846,974,460 | 2.0% |
| 26 | Louisiana | 565,349,759 | 1.3% |
| 43 | Maine | 98,152,418 | 0.2% |
| 34 | Maryland | 337,364,273 | 0.8% |
| 45 | Massachusetts | 64,853,453 | 0.1% |
| 22 | Michigan | 658,574,676 | 1.5% |
| 11 | Minnesota | 1,257,251,889 | 2.9% |
| 15 | Mississippi | 948,997,532 | 2.2% |
| 32 | Missouri | 404,773,069 | 0.9% |
| 28 | Montana | 482,021,568 | 1.1% |
| 7 | Nebraska | 1,650,646,447 | 3.8% |
| 44 | Nevada | 65,039,044 | 0.1% |
| 47 | New Hampshire | 24,691,324 | 0.1% |
| 41 | New Jersey | 127,254,314 | 0.3% |
| 23 | New Mexico | 639,839,435 | 1.5% |
| 25 | New York | 586,536,367 | 1.4% |
| 5 | North Carolina | 1,966,190,161 | 4.5% |
| 29 | North Dakota | 452,136,916 | 1.0% |
| 20 | Ohio | 802,983,390 | 1.9% |
| 13 | Oklahoma | 1,149,787,202 | 2.6% |
| 35 | Oregon | 323,440,998 | 0.7% |
| 24 | Pennsylvania | 627,314,366 | 1.4% |
| 50 | Rhode Island | 11,762,460 | 0.0% |
| 30 | South Carolina | 422,468,747 | 1.0% |
| 12 | South Dakota | 1,189,945,219 | 2.7% |
| 38 | Tennessee | 141,429,814 | 0.3% |
| 2 | Texas | 4,649,677,126 | 10.7% |
| 36 | Utah | 280,457,801 | 0.6% |
| 39 | Vermont | 140,789,572 | 0.3% |
| 33 | Virginia | 395,968,333 | 0.9% |
| 27 | Washington | 519,009,475 | 1.2% |
| 49 | West Virginia | 13,286,706 | 0.0% |
| 17 | Wisconsin | 878,986,151 | 2.0% |
| 37 | Wyoming | 172,842,806 | 0.4% |

| RANK | STATE | FARM INCOME | % of USA |
|------|-------|-------------|----------|
| 1 | California | $4,986,433,392 | 11.5% |
| 2 | Texas | 4,649,677,126 | 10.7% |
| 3 | Florida | 2,815,328,013 | 6.5% |
| 4 | Georgia | 2,099,384,258 | 4.8% |
| 5 | North Carolina | 1,966,190,161 | 4.5% |
| 6 | Arkansas | 1,830,917,875 | 4.2% |
| 7 | Nebraska | 1,650,646,447 | 3.8% |
| 8 | Kansas | 1,547,850,191 | 3.6% |
| 9 | Iowa | 1,450,175,975 | 3.3% |
| 10 | Alabama | 1,449,605,735 | 3.3% |
| 11 | Minnesota | 1,257,251,889 | 2.9% |
| 12 | South Dakota | 1,189,945,219 | 2.7% |
| 13 | Oklahoma | 1,149,787,202 | 2.6% |
| 14 | Illinois | 1,007,007,090 | 2.3% |
| 15 | Mississippi | 948,997,532 | 2.2% |
| 16 | Colorado | 922,905,032 | 2.1% |
| 17 | Wisconsin | 878,986,151 | 2.0% |
| 18 | Idaho | 873,776,373 | 2.0% |
| 19 | Kentucky | 846,974,460 | 2.0% |
| 20 | Ohio | 802,983,390 | 1.9% |
| 21 | Arizona | 707,685,953 | 1.6% |
| 22 | Michigan | 658,574,676 | 1.5% |
| 23 | New Mexico | 639,839,435 | 1.5% |
| 24 | Pennsylvania | 627,314,366 | 1.4% |
| 25 | New York | 586,536,367 | 1.4% |
| 26 | Louisiana | 565,349,759 | 1.3% |
| 27 | Washington | 519,009,475 | 1.2% |
| 28 | Montana | 482,021,568 | 1.1% |
| 29 | North Dakota | 452,136,916 | 1.0% |
| 30 | South Carolina | 422,468,747 | 1.0% |
| 31 | Indiana | 420,822,037 | 1.0% |
| 32 | Missouri | 404,773,069 | 0.9% |
| 33 | Virginia | 395,968,333 | 0.9% |
| 34 | Maryland | 337,364,273 | 0.8% |
| 35 | Oregon | 323,440,998 | 0.7% |
| 36 | Utah | 280,457,801 | 0.6% |
| 37 | Wyoming | 172,842,806 | 0.4% |
| 38 | Tennessee | 141,429,814 | 0.3% |
| 39 | Vermont | 140,789,572 | 0.3% |
| 40 | Connecticut | 139,290,158 | 0.3% |
| 41 | New Jersey | 127,254,314 | 0.3% |
| 42 | Delaware | 120,678,036 | 0.3% |
| 43 | Maine | 98,152,418 | 0.2% |
| 44 | Nevada | 65,039,044 | 0.1% |
| 45 | Massachusetts | 64,853,453 | 0.1% |
| 46 | Hawaii | 63,151,139 | 0.1% |
| 47 | New Hampshire | 24,691,324 | 0.1% |
| 48 | Alaska | 19,587,039 | 0.0% |
| 49 | West Virginia | 13,286,706 | 0.0% |
| 50 | Rhode Island | 11,762,460 | 0.0% |
| | District of Columbia | 0 | 0.0% |

Source: U.S. Department of Agriculture, Economic Research Service
   "State Farm Income Estimates" (http://www.ers.usda.gov/briefing/farmincome/Fist_txt.htm)
*Net farm income is a measure of the net value of production in a given year. It is determined by subtracting total production expenses from gross farm income.

# Farm Income: Cash Receipts from Commodities in 1999

## National Total = $188,609,611,000*

| RANK | STATE | FARM INCOME | % of USA |
|---|---|---|---|
| 23 | Alabama | $3,438,287,000 | 1.8% |
| 50 | Alaska | 47,544,000 | 0.0% |
| 30 | Arizona | 2,178,036,000 | 1.2% |
| 11 | Arkansas | 5,259,413,000 | 2.8% |
| 1 | California | 24,800,670,000 | 13.1% |
| 16 | Colorado | 4,353,604,000 | 2.3% |
| 44 | Connecticut | 482,466,000 | 0.3% |
| 40 | Delaware | 718,258,000 | 0.4% |
| 6 | Florida | 7,065,634,000 | 3.7% |
| 12 | Georgia | 5,240,969,000 | 2.8% |
| 42 | Hawaii | 533,333,000 | 0.3% |
| 24 | Idaho | 3,347,325,000 | 1.8% |
| 8 | Illinois | 6,757,489,000 | 3.6% |
| 15 | Indiana | 4,373,127,000 | 2.3% |
| 3 | Iowa | 9,716,453,000 | 5.2% |
| 5 | Kansas | 7,616,026,000 | 4.0% |
| 22 | Kentucky | 3,456,149,000 | 1.8% |
| 33 | Louisiana | 1,847,599,000 | 1.0% |
| 43 | Maine | 515,207,000 | 0.3% |
| 35 | Maryland | 1,480,998,000 | 0.8% |
| 45 | Massachusetts | 396,130,000 | 0.2% |
| 21 | Michigan | 3,470,098,000 | 1.8% |
| 7 | Minnesota | 7,060,774,000 | 3.7% |
| 25 | Mississippi | 3,173,759,000 | 1.7% |
| 17 | Missouri | 4,255,850,000 | 2.3% |
| 34 | Montana | 1,716,225,000 | 0.9% |
| 4 | Nebraska | 8,555,037,000 | 4.5% |
| 47 | Nevada | 334,272,000 | 0.2% |
| 48 | New Hampshire | 153,135,000 | 0.1% |
| 39 | New Jersey | 740,337,000 | 0.4% |
| 32 | New Mexico | 1,953,423,000 | 1.0% |
| 26 | New York | 3,097,416,000 | 1.6% |
| 9 | North Carolina | 6,687,855,000 | 3.5% |
| 28 | North Dakota | 2,758,886,000 | 1.5% |
| 14 | Ohio | 4,428,837,000 | 2.3% |
| 19 | Oklahoma | 3,990,509,000 | 2.1% |
| 27 | Oregon | 3,052,453,000 | 1.6% |
| 18 | Pennsylvania | 4,070,342,000 | 2.2% |
| 49 | Rhode Island | 47,606,000 | 0.0% |
| 36 | South Carolina | 1,406,077,000 | 0.7% |
| 20 | South Dakota | 3,539,069,000 | 1.9% |
| 31 | Tennessee | 1,974,368,000 | 1.0% |
| 2 | Texas | 13,051,581,000 | 6.9% |
| 37 | Utah | 966,584,000 | 0.5% |
| 41 | Vermont | 540,699,000 | 0.3% |
| 29 | Virginia | 2,283,039,000 | 1.2% |
| 13 | Washington | 4,933,296,000 | 2.6% |
| 46 | West Virginia | 386,598,000 | 0.2% |
| 10 | Wisconsin | 5,596,072,000 | 3.0% |
| 38 | Wyoming | 851,672,000 | 0.5% |

| RANK | STATE | FARM INCOME | % of USA |
|---|---|---|---|
| 1 | California | $24,800,670,000 | 13.1% |
| 2 | Texas | 13,051,581,000 | 6.9% |
| 3 | Iowa | 9,716,453,000 | 5.2% |
| 4 | Nebraska | 8,555,037,000 | 4.5% |
| 5 | Kansas | 7,616,026,000 | 4.0% |
| 6 | Florida | 7,065,634,000 | 3.7% |
| 7 | Minnesota | 7,060,774,000 | 3.7% |
| 8 | Illinois | 6,757,489,000 | 3.6% |
| 9 | North Carolina | 6,687,855,000 | 3.5% |
| 10 | Wisconsin | 5,596,072,000 | 3.0% |
| 11 | Arkansas | 5,259,413,000 | 2.8% |
| 12 | Georgia | 5,240,969,000 | 2.8% |
| 13 | Washington | 4,933,296,000 | 2.6% |
| 14 | Ohio | 4,428,837,000 | 2.3% |
| 15 | Indiana | 4,373,127,000 | 2.3% |
| 16 | Colorado | 4,353,604,000 | 2.3% |
| 17 | Missouri | 4,255,850,000 | 2.3% |
| 18 | Pennsylvania | 4,070,342,000 | 2.2% |
| 19 | Oklahoma | 3,990,509,000 | 2.1% |
| 20 | South Dakota | 3,539,069,000 | 1.9% |
| 21 | Michigan | 3,470,098,000 | 1.8% |
| 22 | Kentucky | 3,456,149,000 | 1.8% |
| 23 | Alabama | 3,438,287,000 | 1.8% |
| 24 | Idaho | 3,347,325,000 | 1.8% |
| 25 | Mississippi | 3,173,759,000 | 1.7% |
| 26 | New York | 3,097,416,000 | 1.6% |
| 27 | Oregon | 3,052,453,000 | 1.6% |
| 28 | North Dakota | 2,758,886,000 | 1.5% |
| 29 | Virginia | 2,283,039,000 | 1.2% |
| 30 | Arizona | 2,178,036,000 | 1.2% |
| 31 | Tennessee | 1,974,368,000 | 1.0% |
| 32 | New Mexico | 1,953,423,000 | 1.0% |
| 33 | Louisiana | 1,847,599,000 | 1.0% |
| 34 | Montana | 1,716,225,000 | 0.9% |
| 35 | Maryland | 1,480,998,000 | 0.8% |
| 36 | South Carolina | 1,406,077,000 | 0.7% |
| 37 | Utah | 966,584,000 | 0.5% |
| 38 | Wyoming | 851,672,000 | 0.5% |
| 39 | New Jersey | 740,337,000 | 0.4% |
| 40 | Delaware | 718,258,000 | 0.4% |
| 41 | Vermont | 540,699,000 | 0.3% |
| 42 | Hawaii | 533,333,000 | 0.3% |
| 43 | Maine | 515,207,000 | 0.3% |
| 44 | Connecticut | 482,466,000 | 0.3% |
| 45 | Massachusetts | 396,130,000 | 0.2% |
| 46 | West Virginia | 386,598,000 | 0.2% |
| 47 | Nevada | 334,272,000 | 0.2% |
| 48 | New Hampshire | 153,135,000 | 0.1% |
| 49 | Rhode Island | 47,606,000 | 0.0% |
| 50 | Alaska | 47,544,000 | 0.0% |
| | District of Columbia | 0 | 0.0% |

*Source: U.S. Department of Agriculture, Economic Research Service*
*"Farm Marketings" (http://www.ers.usda.gov/briefing/farmincome/firkdmu.htm)*
*\*Commodities include crops and livestock.*

# Farm Income: Crops in 1999

## National Total = $93,146,366,000

ALPHA ORDER

| RANK | STATE | FARM INCOME | % of USA |
|---|---|---|---|
| 33 | Alabama | $661,564,000 | 0.7% |
| 50 | Alaska | 18,894,000 | 0.0% |
| 26 | Arizona | 1,190,779,000 | 1.3% |
| 17 | Arkansas | 1,862,815,000 | 2.0% |
| 1 | California | 18,087,032,000 | 19.4% |
| 22 | Colorado | 1,337,821,000 | 1.4% |
| 39 | Connecticut | 302,204,000 | 0.3% |
| 44 | Delaware | 152,609,000 | 0.2% |
| 2 | Florida | 5,702,203,000 | 6.1% |
| 16 | Georgia | 1,906,823,000 | 2.0% |
| 38 | Hawaii | 446,845,000 | 0.5% |
| 19 | Idaho | 1,744,410,000 | 1.9% |
| 3 | Illinois | 5,233,167,000 | 5.6% |
| 10 | Indiana | 2,792,335,000 | 3.0% |
| 4 | Iowa | 5,004,190,000 | 5.4% |
| 12 | Kansas | 2,607,251,000 | 2.8% |
| 23 | Kentucky | 1,297,699,000 | 1.4% |
| 24 | Louisiana | 1,227,563,000 | 1.3% |
| 42 | Maine | 229,331,000 | 0.2% |
| 36 | Maryland | 543,638,000 | 0.6% |
| 40 | Massachusetts | 295,378,000 | 0.3% |
| 14 | Michigan | 2,139,060,000 | 2.3% |
| 6 | Minnesota | 3,513,061,000 | 3.8% |
| 28 | Mississippi | 1,031,013,000 | 1.1% |
| 18 | Missouri | 1,779,318,000 | 1.9% |
| 31 | Montana | 788,508,000 | 0.8% |
| 8 | Nebraska | 3,130,167,000 | 3.4% |
| 45 | Nevada | 117,989,000 | 0.1% |
| 46 | New Hampshire | 90,083,000 | 0.1% |
| 35 | New Jersey | 553,598,000 | 0.6% |
| 37 | New Mexico | 512,634,000 | 0.6% |
| 27 | New York | 1,054,210,000 | 1.1% |
| 9 | North Carolina | 2,837,752,000 | 3.0% |
| 15 | North Dakota | 2,111,684,000 | 2.3% |
| 11 | Ohio | 2,642,582,000 | 2.8% |
| 30 | Oklahoma | 855,084,000 | 0.9% |
| 13 | Oregon | 2,262,383,000 | 2.4% |
| 25 | Pennsylvania | 1,193,081,000 | 1.3% |
| 49 | Rhode Island | 39,147,000 | 0.0% |
| 34 | South Carolina | 632,792,000 | 0.7% |
| 20 | South Dakota | 1,708,809,000 | 1.8% |
| 29 | Tennessee | 963,096,000 | 1.0% |
| 5 | Texas | 4,571,830,000 | 4.9% |
| 41 | Utah | 242,905,000 | 0.3% |
| 47 | Vermont | 66,062,000 | 0.1% |
| 32 | Virginia | 703,535,000 | 0.8% |
| 7 | Washington | 3,274,860,000 | 3.5% |
| 48 | West Virginia | 53,035,000 | 0.1% |
| 21 | Wisconsin | 1,446,753,000 | 1.6% |
| 43 | Wyoming | 172,062,000 | 0.2% |

RANK ORDER

| RANK | STATE | FARM INCOME | % of USA |
|---|---|---|---|
| 1 | California | $18,087,032,000 | 19.4% |
| 2 | Florida | 5,702,203,000 | 6.1% |
| 3 | Illinois | 5,233,167,000 | 5.6% |
| 4 | Iowa | 5,004,190,000 | 5.4% |
| 5 | Texas | 4,571,830,000 | 4.9% |
| 6 | Minnesota | 3,513,061,000 | 3.8% |
| 7 | Washington | 3,274,860,000 | 3.5% |
| 8 | Nebraska | 3,130,167,000 | 3.4% |
| 9 | North Carolina | 2,837,752,000 | 3.0% |
| 10 | Indiana | 2,792,335,000 | 3.0% |
| 11 | Ohio | 2,642,582,000 | 2.8% |
| 12 | Kansas | 2,607,251,000 | 2.8% |
| 13 | Oregon | 2,262,383,000 | 2.4% |
| 14 | Michigan | 2,139,060,000 | 2.3% |
| 15 | North Dakota | 2,111,684,000 | 2.3% |
| 16 | Georgia | 1,906,823,000 | 2.0% |
| 17 | Arkansas | 1,862,815,000 | 2.0% |
| 18 | Missouri | 1,779,318,000 | 1.9% |
| 19 | Idaho | 1,744,410,000 | 1.9% |
| 20 | South Dakota | 1,708,809,000 | 1.8% |
| 21 | Wisconsin | 1,446,753,000 | 1.6% |
| 22 | Colorado | 1,337,821,000 | 1.4% |
| 23 | Kentucky | 1,297,699,000 | 1.4% |
| 24 | Louisiana | 1,227,563,000 | 1.3% |
| 25 | Pennsylvania | 1,193,081,000 | 1.3% |
| 26 | Arizona | 1,190,779,000 | 1.3% |
| 27 | New York | 1,054,210,000 | 1.1% |
| 28 | Mississippi | 1,031,013,000 | 1.1% |
| 29 | Tennessee | 963,096,000 | 1.0% |
| 30 | Oklahoma | 855,084,000 | 0.9% |
| 31 | Montana | 788,508,000 | 0.8% |
| 32 | Virginia | 703,535,000 | 0.8% |
| 33 | Alabama | 661,564,000 | 0.7% |
| 34 | South Carolina | 632,792,000 | 0.7% |
| 35 | New Jersey | 553,598,000 | 0.6% |
| 36 | Maryland | 543,638,000 | 0.6% |
| 37 | New Mexico | 512,634,000 | 0.6% |
| 38 | Hawaii | 446,845,000 | 0.5% |
| 39 | Connecticut | 302,204,000 | 0.3% |
| 40 | Massachusetts | 295,378,000 | 0.3% |
| 41 | Utah | 242,905,000 | 0.3% |
| 42 | Maine | 229,331,000 | 0.2% |
| 43 | Wyoming | 172,062,000 | 0.2% |
| 44 | Delaware | 152,609,000 | 0.2% |
| 45 | Nevada | 117,989,000 | 0.1% |
| 46 | New Hampshire | 90,083,000 | 0.1% |
| 47 | Vermont | 66,062,000 | 0.1% |
| 48 | West Virginia | 53,035,000 | 0.1% |
| 49 | Rhode Island | 39,147,000 | 0.0% |
| 50 | Alaska | 18,894,000 | 0.0% |
| | District of Columbia | 0 | 0.0% |

*Source: U.S. Department of Agriculture, Economic Research Service*
*"Farm Marketings" (http://www.ers.usda.gov/briefing/farmincome/firkdmu.htm)*

# Farm Income: Livestock in 1999

## National Total = $95,463,245,000*

ALPHA ORDER

RANK ORDER

| RANK | STATE | FARM INCOME | % of USA | | RANK | STATE | FARM INCOME | % of USA |
|---|---|---|---|---|---|---|---|---|
| 14 | Alabama | $2,776,723,000 | 2.9% | | 1 | Texas | $8,479,751,000 | 8.9% |
| 49 | Alaska | 28,650,000 | 0.0% | | 2 | California | 6,713,638,000 | 7.0% |
| 30 | Arizona | 987,257,000 | 1.0% | | 3 | Nebraska | 5,424,870,000 | 5.7% |
| 9 | Arkansas | 3,396,598,000 | 3.6% | | 4 | Kansas | 5,008,775,000 | 5.2% |
| 2 | California | 6,713,638,000 | 7.0% | | 5 | Iowa | 4,712,263,000 | 4.9% |
| 12 | Colorado | 3,015,783,000 | 3.2% | | 6 | Wisconsin | 4,149,319,000 | 4.3% |
| 45 | Connecticut | 180,262,000 | 0.2% | | 7 | North Carolina | 3,850,103,000 | 4.0% |
| 39 | Delaware | 565,649,000 | 0.6% | | 8 | Minnesota | 3,547,713,000 | 3.7% |
| 27 | Florida | 1,363,431,000 | 1.4% | | 9 | Arkansas | 3,396,598,000 | 3.6% |
| 10 | Georgia | 3,334,146,000 | 3.5% | | 10 | Georgia | 3,334,146,000 | 3.5% |
| 47 | Hawaii | 86,488,000 | 0.1% | | 11 | Oklahoma | 3,135,425,000 | 3.3% |
| 22 | Idaho | 1,602,915,000 | 1.7% | | 12 | Colorado | 3,015,783,000 | 3.2% |
| 25 | Illinois | 1,524,322,000 | 1.6% | | 13 | Pennsylvania | 2,877,261,000 | 3.0% |
| 23 | Indiana | 1,580,792,000 | 1.7% | | 14 | Alabama | 2,776,723,000 | 2.9% |
| 5 | Iowa | 4,712,263,000 | 4.9% | | 15 | Missouri | 2,476,532,000 | 2.6% |
| 4 | Kansas | 5,008,775,000 | 5.2% | | 16 | Kentucky | 2,158,450,000 | 2.3% |
| 16 | Kentucky | 2,158,450,000 | 2.3% | | 17 | Mississippi | 2,142,746,000 | 2.2% |
| 38 | Louisiana | 620,036,000 | 0.6% | | 18 | New York | 2,043,206,000 | 2.1% |
| 42 | Maine | 285,876,000 | 0.3% | | 19 | South Dakota | 1,830,260,000 | 1.9% |
| 31 | Maryland | 937,360,000 | 1.0% | | 20 | Ohio | 1,786,255,000 | 1.9% |
| 46 | Massachusetts | 100,752,000 | 0.1% | | 21 | Washington | 1,658,436,000 | 1.7% |
| 28 | Michigan | 1,331,038,000 | 1.4% | | 22 | Idaho | 1,602,915,000 | 1.7% |
| 8 | Minnesota | 3,547,713,000 | 3.7% | | 23 | Indiana | 1,580,792,000 | 1.7% |
| 17 | Mississippi | 2,142,746,000 | 2.2% | | 24 | Virginia | 1,579,504,000 | 1.7% |
| 15 | Missouri | 2,476,532,000 | 2.6% | | 25 | Illinois | 1,524,322,000 | 1.6% |
| 32 | Montana | 927,719,000 | 1.0% | | 26 | New Mexico | 1,440,789,000 | 1.5% |
| 3 | Nebraska | 5,424,870,000 | 5.7% | | 27 | Florida | 1,363,431,000 | 1.4% |
| 43 | Nevada | 216,283,000 | 0.2% | | 28 | Michigan | 1,331,038,000 | 1.4% |
| 48 | New Hampshire | 63,052,000 | 0.1% | | 29 | Tennessee | 1,011,272,000 | 1.1% |
| 44 | New Jersey | 186,739,000 | 0.2% | | 30 | Arizona | 987,257,000 | 1.0% |
| 26 | New Mexico | 1,440,789,000 | 1.5% | | 31 | Maryland | 937,360,000 | 1.0% |
| 18 | New York | 2,043,206,000 | 2.1% | | 32 | Montana | 927,719,000 | 1.0% |
| 7 | North Carolina | 3,850,103,000 | 4.0% | | 33 | Oregon | 790,070,000 | 0.8% |
| 37 | North Dakota | 647,202,000 | 0.7% | | 34 | South Carolina | 773,285,000 | 0.8% |
| 20 | Ohio | 1,786,255,000 | 1.9% | | 35 | Utah | 723,679,000 | 0.8% |
| 11 | Oklahoma | 3,135,425,000 | 3.3% | | 36 | Wyoming | 679,610,000 | 0.7% |
| 33 | Oregon | 790,070,000 | 0.8% | | 37 | North Dakota | 647,202,000 | 0.7% |
| 13 | Pennsylvania | 2,877,261,000 | 3.0% | | 38 | Louisiana | 620,036,000 | 0.6% |
| 50 | Rhode Island | 8,459,000 | 0.0% | | 39 | Delaware | 565,649,000 | 0.6% |
| 34 | South Carolina | 773,285,000 | 0.8% | | 40 | Vermont | 472,637,000 | 0.5% |
| 19 | South Dakota | 1,830,260,000 | 1.9% | | 41 | West Virginia | 333,563,000 | 0.3% |
| 29 | Tennessee | 1,011,272,000 | 1.1% | | 42 | Maine | 285,876,000 | 0.3% |
| 1 | Texas | 8,479,751,000 | 8.9% | | 43 | Nevada | 216,283,000 | 0.2% |
| 35 | Utah | 723,679,000 | 0.8% | | 44 | New Jersey | 186,739,000 | 0.2% |
| 40 | Vermont | 472,637,000 | 0.5% | | 45 | Connecticut | 180,262,000 | 0.2% |
| 24 | Virginia | 1,579,504,000 | 1.7% | | 46 | Massachusetts | 100,752,000 | 0.1% |
| 21 | Washington | 1,658,436,000 | 1.7% | | 47 | Hawaii | 86,488,000 | 0.1% |
| 41 | West Virginia | 333,563,000 | 0.3% | | 48 | New Hampshire | 63,052,000 | 0.1% |
| 6 | Wisconsin | 4,149,319,000 | 4.3% | | 49 | Alaska | 28,650,000 | 0.0% |
| 36 | Wyoming | 679,610,000 | 0.7% | | 50 | Rhode Island | 8,459,000 | 0.0% |
| | | | | | | District of Columbia | 0 | 0.0% |

Source: U.S. Department of Agriculture, Economic Research Service
    "Farm Marketings" (http://www.ers.usda.gov/briefing/farmincome/firkdmu.htm)
*Includes livestock products.

# Farm Income: Government Payments in 1999

## National Total = $20,593,972,000*

ALPHA ORDER

| RANK | STATE | PAYMENTS | % of USA |
|---|---|---|---|
| 27 | Alabama | $178,143,950 | 0.9% |
| 48 | Alaska | 1,766,036 | 0.0% |
| 30 | Arizona | 108,030,478 | 0.5% |
| 9 | Arkansas | 768,895,832 | 3.7% |
| 12 | California | 651,294,660 | 3.2% |
| 20 | Colorado | 368,005,258 | 1.8% |
| 45 | Connecticut | 8,708,473 | 0.0% |
| 39 | Delaware | 19,614,675 | 0.1% |
| 35 | Florida | 76,914,465 | 0.4% |
| 21 | Georgia | 360,680,058 | 1.8% |
| 50 | Hawaii | 823,784 | 0.0% |
| 25 | Idaho | 208,845,855 | 1.0% |
| 3 | Illinois | 1,711,033,989 | 8.3% |
| 8 | Indiana | 810,451,448 | 3.9% |
| 2 | Iowa | 1,875,525,227 | 9.1% |
| 4 | Kansas | 1,382,800,169 | 6.7% |
| 24 | Kentucky | 229,102,933 | 1.1% |
| 18 | Louisiana | 411,864,314 | 2.0% |
| 41 | Maine | 11,671,412 | 0.1% |
| 36 | Maryland | 67,357,837 | 0.3% |
| 43 | Massachusetts | 10,162,421 | 0.0% |
| 19 | Michigan | 389,099,218 | 1.9% |
| 6 | Minnesota | 1,256,091,117 | 6.1% |
| 17 | Mississippi | 431,096,055 | 2.1% |
| 11 | Missouri | 688,021,864 | 3.3% |
| 15 | Montana | 487,851,160 | 2.4% |
| 5 | Nebraska | 1,322,090,638 | 6.4% |
| 47 | Nevada | 2,674,423 | 0.0% |
| 46 | New Hampshire | 3,943,565 | 0.0% |
| 44 | New Jersey | 9,955,041 | 0.0% |
| 34 | New Mexico | 92,069,138 | 0.4% |
| 29 | New York | 117,168,479 | 0.6% |
| 22 | North Carolina | 284,725,381 | 1.4% |
| 7 | North Dakota | 951,580,709 | 4.6% |
| 13 | Ohio | 627,714,548 | 3.0% |
| 14 | Oklahoma | 526,401,432 | 2.6% |
| 31 | Oregon | 105,498,722 | 0.5% |
| 33 | Pennsylvania | 94,276,511 | 0.5% |
| 49 | Rhode Island | 877,031 | 0.0% |
| 28 | South Carolina | 127,082,777 | 0.6% |
| 10 | South Dakota | 746,175,543 | 3.6% |
| 26 | Tennessee | 208,224,031 | 1.0% |
| 1 | Texas | 1,914,138,507 | 9.3% |
| 38 | Utah | 30,089,374 | 0.1% |
| 40 | Vermont | 12,242,173 | 0.1% |
| 32 | Virginia | 98,556,006 | 0.5% |
| 23 | Washington | 269,451,605 | 1.3% |
| 16 | West Virginia | 484,133,991 | 2.4% |
| 42 | Wisconsin | 11,101,783 | 0.1% |
| 37 | Wyoming | 39,947,465 | 0.2% |

RANK ORDER

| RANK | STATE | PAYMENTS | % of USA |
|---|---|---|---|
| 1 | Texas | $1,914,138,507 | 9.3% |
| 2 | Iowa | 1,875,525,227 | 9.1% |
| 3 | Illinois | 1,711,033,989 | 8.3% |
| 4 | Kansas | 1,382,800,169 | 6.7% |
| 5 | Nebraska | 1,322,090,638 | 6.4% |
| 6 | Minnesota | 1,256,091,117 | 6.1% |
| 7 | North Dakota | 951,580,709 | 4.6% |
| 8 | Indiana | 810,451,448 | 3.9% |
| 9 | Arkansas | 768,895,832 | 3.7% |
| 10 | South Dakota | 746,175,543 | 3.6% |
| 11 | Missouri | 688,021,864 | 3.3% |
| 12 | California | 651,294,660 | 3.2% |
| 13 | Ohio | 627,714,548 | 3.0% |
| 14 | Oklahoma | 526,401,432 | 2.6% |
| 15 | Montana | 487,851,160 | 2.4% |
| 16 | West Virginia | 484,133,991 | 2.4% |
| 17 | Mississippi | 431,096,055 | 2.1% |
| 18 | Louisiana | 411,864,314 | 2.0% |
| 19 | Michigan | 389,099,218 | 1.9% |
| 20 | Colorado | 368,005,258 | 1.8% |
| 21 | Georgia | 360,680,058 | 1.8% |
| 22 | North Carolina | 284,725,381 | 1.4% |
| 23 | Washington | 269,451,605 | 1.3% |
| 24 | Kentucky | 229,102,933 | 1.1% |
| 25 | Idaho | 208,845,855 | 1.0% |
| 26 | Tennessee | 208,224,031 | 1.0% |
| 27 | Alabama | 178,143,950 | 0.9% |
| 28 | South Carolina | 127,082,777 | 0.6% |
| 29 | New York | 117,168,479 | 0.6% |
| 30 | Arizona | 108,030,478 | 0.5% |
| 31 | Oregon | 105,498,722 | 0.5% |
| 32 | Virginia | 98,556,006 | 0.5% |
| 33 | Pennsylvania | 94,276,511 | 0.5% |
| 34 | New Mexico | 92,069,138 | 0.4% |
| 35 | Florida | 76,914,465 | 0.4% |
| 36 | Maryland | 67,357,837 | 0.3% |
| 37 | Wyoming | 39,947,465 | 0.2% |
| 38 | Utah | 30,089,374 | 0.1% |
| 39 | Delaware | 19,614,675 | 0.1% |
| 40 | Vermont | 12,242,173 | 0.1% |
| 41 | Maine | 11,671,412 | 0.1% |
| 42 | Wisconsin | 11,101,783 | 0.1% |
| 43 | Massachusetts | 10,162,421 | 0.0% |
| 44 | New Jersey | 9,955,041 | 0.0% |
| 45 | Connecticut | 8,708,473 | 0.0% |
| 46 | New Hampshire | 3,943,565 | 0.0% |
| 47 | Nevada | 2,674,423 | 0.0% |
| 48 | Alaska | 1,766,036 | 0.0% |
| 49 | Rhode Island | 877,031 | 0.0% |
| 50 | Hawaii | 823,784 | 0.0% |
| | District of Columbia | 0 | 0.0% |

Source: U.S. Department of Agriculture, Economic Research Service
   "Farm Marketings" (http://www.ers.usda.gov/briefing/farmincome/firkdmu.htm)
*Government payments made directly to farmers in cash.

# Acres Planted in 2000

## National Total = 328,449,000 Acres*

| ALPHA ORDER | | | | | RANK ORDER | | | |
|---|---|---|---|---|---|---|---|---|

| RANK | STATE | ACRES | % of USA | | RANK | STATE | ACRES | % of USA |
|---|---|---|---|---|---|---|---|---|
| 31 | Alabama | 2,085,000 | 0.6% | | 1 | Iowa | 24,990,000 | 7.6% |
| NA | Alaska** | NA | NA | | 2 | Illinois | 23,671,000 | 7.2% |
| 38 | Arizona | 746,000 | 0.2% | | 3 | Texas | 23,309,000 | 7.1% |
| 14 | Arkansas | 8,490,000 | 2.6% | | 4 | Kansas | 22,899,000 | 7.0% |
| 22 | California | 4,738,000 | 1.4% | | 5 | North Dakota | 21,722,000 | 6.6% |
| 17 | Colorado | 6,418,000 | 2.0% | | 6 | Minnesota | 20,293,000 | 6.2% |
| 46 | Connecticut | 103,000 | 0.0% | | 7 | Nebraska | 19,199,000 | 5.8% |
| 41 | Delaware | 500,000 | 0.2% | | 8 | South Dakota | 17,290,000 | 5.3% |
| 36 | Florida | 1,102,000 | 0.3% | | 9 | Missouri | 13,683,000 | 4.2% |
| 26 | Georgia | 3,908,000 | 1.2% | | 10 | Indiana | 12,697,000 | 3.9% |
| 48 | Hawaii | 35,000 | 0.0% | | 11 | Ohio | 10,657,000 | 3.2% |
| 23 | Idaho | 4,502,000 | 1.4% | | 12 | Oklahoma | 10,467,000 | 3.2% |
| 2 | Illinois | 23,671,000 | 7.2% | | 13 | Montana | 8,883,000 | 2.7% |
| 10 | Indiana | 12,697,000 | 3.9% | | 14 | Arkansas | 8,490,000 | 2.6% |
| 1 | Iowa | 24,990,000 | 7.6% | | 15 | Wisconsin | 7,809,000 | 2.4% |
| 4 | Kansas | 22,899,000 | 7.0% | | 16 | Michigan | 6,768,000 | 2.1% |
| 18 | Kentucky | 5,808,000 | 1.8% | | 17 | Colorado | 6,418,000 | 2.0% |
| 27 | Louisiana | 3,775,000 | 1.1% | | 18 | Kentucky | 5,808,000 | 1.8% |
| 44 | Maine | 278,000 | 0.1% | | 19 | Tennessee | 5,062,000 | 1.5% |
| 34 | Maryland | 1,531,000 | 0.5% | | 20 | North Carolina | 4,909,000 | 1.5% |
| 45 | Massachusetts | 124,000 | 0.0% | | 21 | Mississippi | 4,770,000 | 1.5% |
| 16 | Michigan | 6,768,000 | 2.1% | | 22 | California | 4,738,000 | 1.4% |
| 6 | Minnesota | 20,293,000 | 6.2% | | 23 | Idaho | 4,502,000 | 1.4% |
| 21 | Mississippi | 4,770,000 | 1.5% | | 24 | Pennsylvania | 4,237,000 | 1.3% |
| 9 | Missouri | 13,683,000 | 4.2% | | 25 | Washington | 4,185,000 | 1.3% |
| 13 | Montana | 8,883,000 | 2.7% | | 26 | Georgia | 3,908,000 | 1.2% |
| 7 | Nebraska | 19,199,000 | 5.8% | | 27 | Louisiana | 3,775,000 | 1.1% |
| 40 | Nevada | 523,000 | 0.2% | | 28 | New York | 2,924,000 | 0.9% |
| 47 | New Hampshire | 73,000 | 0.0% | | 29 | Virginia | 2,843,000 | 0.9% |
| 42 | New Jersey | 368,000 | 0.1% | | 30 | Oregon | 2,300,000 | 0.7% |
| 35 | New Mexico | 1,294,000 | 0.4% | | 31 | Alabama | 2,085,000 | 0.6% |
| 28 | New York | 2,924,000 | 0.9% | | 32 | Wyoming | 1,703,000 | 0.5% |
| 20 | North Carolina | 4,909,000 | 1.5% | | 33 | South Carolina | 1,675,000 | 0.5% |
| 5 | North Dakota | 21,722,000 | 6.6% | | 34 | Maryland | 1,531,000 | 0.5% |
| 11 | Ohio | 10,657,000 | 3.2% | | 35 | New Mexico | 1,294,000 | 0.4% |
| 12 | Oklahoma | 10,467,000 | 3.2% | | 36 | Florida | 1,102,000 | 0.3% |
| 30 | Oregon | 2,300,000 | 0.7% | | 37 | Utah | 1,089,000 | 0.3% |
| 24 | Pennsylvania | 4,237,000 | 1.3% | | 38 | Arizona | 746,000 | 0.2% |
| 49 | Rhode Island | 12,000 | 0.0% | | 39 | West Virginia | 685,000 | 0.2% |
| 33 | South Carolina | 1,675,000 | 0.5% | | 40 | Nevada | 523,000 | 0.2% |
| 8 | South Dakota | 17,290,000 | 5.3% | | 41 | Delaware | 500,000 | 0.2% |
| 19 | Tennessee | 5,062,000 | 1.5% | | 42 | New Jersey | 368,000 | 0.1% |
| 3 | Texas | 23,309,000 | 7.1% | | 43 | Vermont | 320,000 | 0.1% |
| 37 | Utah | 1,089,000 | 0.3% | | 44 | Maine | 278,000 | 0.1% |
| 43 | Vermont | 320,000 | 0.1% | | 45 | Massachusetts | 124,000 | 0.0% |
| 29 | Virginia | 2,843,000 | 0.9% | | 46 | Connecticut | 103,000 | 0.0% |
| 25 | Washington | 4,185,000 | 1.3% | | 47 | New Hampshire | 73,000 | 0.0% |
| 39 | West Virginia | 685,000 | 0.2% | | 48 | Hawaii | 35,000 | 0.0% |
| 15 | Wisconsin | 7,809,000 | 2.4% | | 49 | Rhode Island | 12,000 | 0.0% |
| 32 | Wyoming | 1,703,000 | 0.5% | | NA | Alaska** | NA | NA |
| | | | | | | District of Columbia** | NA | NA |

Source: U.S. Department of Agriculture, National Agricultural Statistics Service
"Crop Production, 2000 Summary" (Cr Pr 2-1 (01), January 2001)
(http://usda.mannlib.cornell.edu/reports/nassr/field/pcp-bban/cropan01.txt)
*Estimated totals.
**No acreage or not available.

# Acres Harvested in 2000

## National Total = 307,839,000 Acres*

ALPHA ORDER

| RANK | STATE | ACRES | % of USA |
|------|-------|-------|----------|
| 31 | Alabama | 1,895,000 | 0.6% |
| NA | Alaska** | NA | NA |
| 38 | Arizona | 739,000 | 0.2% |
| 12 | Arkansas | 8,234,000 | 2.7% |
| 22 | California | 4,345,000 | 1.4% |
| 17 | Colorado | 5,996,000 | 1.9% |
| 46 | Connecticut | 100,000 | 0.0% |
| 41 | Delaware | 493,000 | 0.2% |
| 35 | Florida | 1,051,000 | 0.3% |
| 27 | Georgia | 3,348,000 | 1.1% |
| 48 | Hawaii | 35,000 | 0.0% |
| 23 | Idaho | 4,323,000 | 1.4% |
| 2 | Illinois | 23,533,000 | 7.6% |
| 10 | Indiana | 12,602,000 | 4.1% |
| 1 | Iowa | 24,828,000 | 8.1% |
| 3 | Kansas | 21,642,000 | 7.0% |
| 18 | Kentucky | 5,531,000 | 1.8% |
| 26 | Louisiana | 3,673,000 | 1.2% |
| 44 | Maine | 273,000 | 0.1% |
| 34 | Maryland | 1,496,000 | 0.5% |
| 45 | Massachusetts | 119,000 | 0.0% |
| 16 | Michigan | 6,653,000 | 2.2% |
| 5 | Minnesota | 19,790,000 | 6.4% |
| 21 | Mississippi | 4,607,000 | 1.5% |
| 9 | Missouri | 13,373,000 | 4.3% |
| 13 | Montana | 8,078,000 | 2.6% |
| 6 | Nebraska | 18,637,000 | 6.1% |
| 40 | Nevada | 518,000 | 0.2% |
| 47 | New Hampshire | 72,000 | 0.0% |
| 42 | New Jersey | 359,000 | 0.1% |
| 37 | New Mexico | 896,000 | 0.3% |
| 28 | New York | 2,888,000 | 0.9% |
| 20 | North Carolina | 4,645,000 | 1.5% |
| 4 | North Dakota | 20,281,000 | 6.6% |
| 11 | Ohio | 10,546,000 | 3.4% |
| 14 | Oklahoma | 7,934,000 | 2.6% |
| 30 | Oregon | 2,236,000 | 0.7% |
| 24 | Pennsylvania | 4,179,000 | 1.4% |
| 49 | Rhode Island | 12,000 | 0.0% |
| 33 | South Carolina | 1,600,000 | 0.5% |
| 7 | South Dakota | 16,870,000 | 5.5% |
| 19 | Tennessee | 4,851,000 | 1.6% |
| 8 | Texas | 16,124,000 | 5.2% |
| 36 | Utah | 1,019,000 | 0.3% |
| 43 | Vermont | 315,000 | 0.1% |
| 29 | Virginia | 2,769,000 | 0.9% |
| 25 | Washington | 4,099,000 | 1.3% |
| 39 | West Virginia | 679,000 | 0.2% |
| 15 | Wisconsin | 7,587,000 | 2.5% |
| 32 | Wyoming | 1,623,000 | 0.5% |

RANK ORDER

| RANK | STATE | ACRES | % of USA |
|------|-------|-------|----------|
| 1 | Iowa | 24,828,000 | 8.1% |
| 2 | Illinois | 23,533,000 | 7.6% |
| 3 | Kansas | 21,642,000 | 7.0% |
| 4 | North Dakota | 20,281,000 | 6.6% |
| 5 | Minnesota | 19,790,000 | 6.4% |
| 6 | Nebraska | 18,637,000 | 6.1% |
| 7 | South Dakota | 16,870,000 | 5.5% |
| 8 | Texas | 16,124,000 | 5.2% |
| 9 | Missouri | 13,373,000 | 4.3% |
| 10 | Indiana | 12,602,000 | 4.1% |
| 11 | Ohio | 10,546,000 | 3.4% |
| 12 | Arkansas | 8,234,000 | 2.7% |
| 13 | Montana | 8,078,000 | 2.6% |
| 14 | Oklahoma | 7,934,000 | 2.6% |
| 15 | Wisconsin | 7,587,000 | 2.5% |
| 16 | Michigan | 6,653,000 | 2.2% |
| 17 | Colorado | 5,996,000 | 1.9% |
| 18 | Kentucky | 5,531,000 | 1.8% |
| 19 | Tennessee | 4,851,000 | 1.6% |
| 20 | North Carolina | 4,645,000 | 1.5% |
| 21 | Mississippi | 4,607,000 | 1.5% |
| 22 | California | 4,345,000 | 1.4% |
| 23 | Idaho | 4,323,000 | 1.4% |
| 24 | Pennsylvania | 4,179,000 | 1.4% |
| 25 | Washington | 4,099,000 | 1.3% |
| 26 | Louisiana | 3,673,000 | 1.2% |
| 27 | Georgia | 3,348,000 | 1.1% |
| 28 | New York | 2,888,000 | 0.9% |
| 29 | Virginia | 2,769,000 | 0.9% |
| 30 | Oregon | 2,236,000 | 0.7% |
| 31 | Alabama | 1,895,000 | 0.6% |
| 32 | Wyoming | 1,623,000 | 0.5% |
| 33 | South Carolina | 1,600,000 | 0.5% |
| 34 | Maryland | 1,496,000 | 0.5% |
| 35 | Florida | 1,051,000 | 0.3% |
| 36 | Utah | 1,019,000 | 0.3% |
| 37 | New Mexico | 896,000 | 0.3% |
| 38 | Arizona | 739,000 | 0.2% |
| 39 | West Virginia | 679,000 | 0.2% |
| 40 | Nevada | 518,000 | 0.2% |
| 41 | Delaware | 493,000 | 0.2% |
| 42 | New Jersey | 359,000 | 0.1% |
| 43 | Vermont | 315,000 | 0.1% |
| 44 | Maine | 273,000 | 0.1% |
| 45 | Massachusetts | 119,000 | 0.0% |
| 46 | Connecticut | 100,000 | 0.0% |
| 47 | New Hampshire | 72,000 | 0.0% |
| 48 | Hawaii | 35,000 | 0.0% |
| 49 | Rhode Island | 12,000 | 0.0% |
| NA | Alaska** | NA | NA |
| | District of Columbia** | NA | NA |

*Source: U.S. Department of Agriculture, National Agricultural Statistics Service*
*"Crop Production, 2000 Summary" (Cr Pr 2-1 (01), January 2001)*
*(http://usda.mannlib.cornell.edu/reports/nassr/field/pcp-bban/cropan01.txt)*
*Estimated totals.
**No acreage or not available.

# Acres Harvested: Corn in 2000

## National Total = 72,732,000 Acres*

ALPHA ORDER

| RANK | STATE | ACRES | % of USA |
|------|-------|-------|----------|
| 29 | Alabama | 165,000 | 0.2% |
| NA | Alaska** | NA | NA |
| 37 | Arizona | 33,000 | 0.0% |
| 28 | Arkansas | 175,000 | 0.2% |
| 27 | California | 235,000 | 0.3% |
| 14 | Colorado | 1,180,000 | 1.6% |
| NA | Connecticut** | NA | NA |
| 30 | Delaware | 156,000 | 0.2% |
| 39 | Florida | 28,000 | 0.0% |
| 24 | Georgia | 300,000 | 0.4% |
| NA | Hawaii** | NA | NA |
| 35 | Idaho | 57,000 | 0.1% |
| 2 | Illinois | 11,050,000 | 15.2% |
| 5 | Indiana | 5,550,000 | 7.6% |
| 1 | Iowa | 12,000,000 | 16.5% |
| 8 | Kansas | 3,200,000 | 4.4% |
| 13 | Kentucky | 1,230,000 | 1.7% |
| 22 | Louisiana | 370,000 | 0.5% |
| NA | Maine** | NA | NA |
| 20 | Maryland | 405,000 | 0.6% |
| NA | Massachusetts** | NA | NA |
| 11 | Michigan | 1,970,000 | 2.7% |
| 4 | Minnesota | 6,600,000 | 9.1% |
| 21 | Mississippi | 385,000 | 0.5% |
| 9 | Missouri | 2,770,000 | 3.8% |
| 41 | Montana | 18,000 | 0.0% |
| 3 | Nebraska | 8,050,000 | 11.1% |
| NA | Nevada** | NA | NA |
| NA | New Hampshire** | NA | NA |
| 32 | New Jersey | 75,000 | 0.1% |
| 33 | New Mexico | 73,000 | 0.1% |
| 19 | New York | 480,000 | 0.7% |
| 17 | North Carolina | 650,000 | 0.9% |
| 16 | North Dakota | 930,000 | 1.3% |
| 7 | Ohio | 3,300,000 | 4.5% |
| 26 | Oklahoma | 270,000 | 0.4% |
| 38 | Oregon | 29,000 | 0.0% |
| 15 | Pennsylvania | 1,080,000 | 1.5% |
| NA | Rhode Island** | NA | NA |
| 25 | South Carolina | 280,000 | 0.4% |
| 6 | South Dakota | 3,850,000 | 5.3% |
| 18 | Tennessee | 590,000 | 0.8% |
| 12 | Texas | 1,900,000 | 2.6% |
| 40 | Utah | 21,000 | 0.0% |
| NA | Vermont** | NA | NA |
| 23 | Virginia | 330,000 | 0.5% |
| 31 | Washington | 100,000 | 0.1% |
| 36 | West Virginia | 35,000 | 0.0% |
| 10 | Wisconsin | 2,750,000 | 3.8% |
| 34 | Wyoming | 62,000 | 0.1% |

RANK ORDER

| RANK | STATE | ACRES | % of USA |
|------|-------|-------|----------|
| 1 | Iowa | 12,000,000 | 16.5% |
| 2 | Illinois | 11,050,000 | 15.2% |
| 3 | Nebraska | 8,050,000 | 11.1% |
| 4 | Minnesota | 6,600,000 | 9.1% |
| 5 | Indiana | 5,550,000 | 7.6% |
| 6 | South Dakota | 3,850,000 | 5.3% |
| 7 | Ohio | 3,300,000 | 4.5% |
| 8 | Kansas | 3,200,000 | 4.4% |
| 9 | Missouri | 2,770,000 | 3.8% |
| 10 | Wisconsin | 2,750,000 | 3.8% |
| 11 | Michigan | 1,970,000 | 2.7% |
| 12 | Texas | 1,900,000 | 2.6% |
| 13 | Kentucky | 1,230,000 | 1.7% |
| 14 | Colorado | 1,180,000 | 1.6% |
| 15 | Pennsylvania | 1,080,000 | 1.5% |
| 16 | North Dakota | 930,000 | 1.3% |
| 17 | North Carolina | 650,000 | 0.9% |
| 18 | Tennessee | 590,000 | 0.8% |
| 19 | New York | 480,000 | 0.7% |
| 20 | Maryland | 405,000 | 0.6% |
| 21 | Mississippi | 385,000 | 0.5% |
| 22 | Louisiana | 370,000 | 0.5% |
| 23 | Virginia | 330,000 | 0.5% |
| 24 | Georgia | 300,000 | 0.4% |
| 25 | South Carolina | 280,000 | 0.4% |
| 26 | Oklahoma | 270,000 | 0.4% |
| 27 | California | 235,000 | 0.3% |
| 28 | Arkansas | 175,000 | 0.2% |
| 29 | Alabama | 165,000 | 0.2% |
| 30 | Delaware | 156,000 | 0.2% |
| 31 | Washington | 100,000 | 0.1% |
| 32 | New Jersey | 75,000 | 0.1% |
| 33 | New Mexico | 73,000 | 0.1% |
| 34 | Wyoming | 62,000 | 0.1% |
| 35 | Idaho | 57,000 | 0.1% |
| 36 | West Virginia | 35,000 | 0.0% |
| 37 | Arizona | 33,000 | 0.0% |
| 38 | Oregon | 29,000 | 0.0% |
| 39 | Florida | 28,000 | 0.0% |
| 40 | Utah | 21,000 | 0.0% |
| 41 | Montana | 18,000 | 0.0% |
| NA | Alaska** | NA | NA |
| NA | Connecticut** | NA | NA |
| NA | Hawaii** | NA | NA |
| NA | Maine** | NA | NA |
| NA | Massachusetts** | NA | NA |
| NA | Nevada** | NA | NA |
| NA | New Hampshire** | NA | NA |
| NA | Rhode Island** | NA | NA |
| NA | Vermont** | NA | NA |
| | District of Columbia** | NA | NA |

Source: U.S. Department of Agriculture, National Agricultural Statistics Service
"Crop Production, 2000 Summary" (Cr Pr 2-1 (01), January 2001)
(http://usda.mannlib.cornell.edu/reports/nassr/field/pcp-bban/cropan01.txt)
*Estimated totals.
**No acreage or not available.

# Acres Harvested: Soybeans in 2000

## National Total = 72,718,000 Acres*

ALPHA ORDER

| RANK | STATE | ACRES | % of USA |
|---|---|---|---|
| 26 | Alabama | 160,000 | 0.2% |
| NA | Alaska** | NA | NA |
| NA | Arizona** | NA | NA |
| 9 | Arkansas | 3,200,000 | 4.4% |
| NA | California** | NA | NA |
| NA | Colorado** | NA | NA |
| NA | Connecticut** | NA | NA |
| 25 | Delaware | 213,000 | 0.3% |
| 30 | Florida | 15,000 | 0.0% |
| 26 | Georgia | 160,000 | 0.2% |
| NA | Hawaii** | NA | NA |
| NA | Idaho** | NA | NA |
| 2 | Illinois | 10,450,000 | 14.4% |
| 4 | Indiana | 5,630,000 | 7.7% |
| 1 | Iowa | 10,680,000 | 14.7% |
| 10 | Kansas | 2,500,000 | 3.4% |
| 16 | Kentucky | 1,180,000 | 1.6% |
| 18 | Louisiana | 870,000 | 1.2% |
| NA | Maine** | NA | NA |
| 19 | Maryland | 515,000 | 0.7% |
| NA | Massachusetts** | NA | NA |
| 11 | Michigan | 2,080,000 | 2.9% |
| 3 | Minnesota | 7,150,000 | 9.8% |
| 13 | Mississippi | 1,580,000 | 2.2% |
| 5 | Missouri | 5,000,000 | 6.9% |
| NA | Montana** | NA | NA |
| 6 | Nebraska | 4,575,000 | 6.3% |
| NA | Nevada** | NA | NA |
| NA | New Hampshire** | NA | NA |
| 29 | New Jersey | 98,000 | 0.1% |
| NA | New Mexico** | NA | NA |
| 28 | New York | 132,000 | 0.2% |
| 15 | North Carolina | 1,360,000 | 1.9% |
| 12 | North Dakota | 1,850,000 | 2.5% |
| 7 | Ohio | 4,440,000 | 6.1% |
| 23 | Oklahoma | 310,000 | 0.4% |
| NA | Oregon** | NA | NA |
| 22 | Pennsylvania | 395,000 | 0.5% |
| NA | Rhode Island** | NA | NA |
| 21 | South Carolina | 440,000 | 0.6% |
| 8 | South Dakota | 4,370,000 | 6.0% |
| 17 | Tennessee | 1,150,000 | 1.6% |
| 24 | Texas | 260,000 | 0.4% |
| NA | Utah** | NA | NA |
| NA | Vermont** | NA | NA |
| 20 | Virginia | 490,000 | 0.7% |
| NA | Washington** | NA | NA |
| 30 | West Virginia | 15,000 | 0.0% |
| 14 | Wisconsin | 1,450,000 | 2.0% |
| NA | Wyoming** | NA | NA |

RANK ORDER

| RANK | STATE | ACRES | % of USA |
|---|---|---|---|
| 1 | Iowa | 10,680,000 | 14.7% |
| 2 | Illinois | 10,450,000 | 14.4% |
| 3 | Minnesota | 7,150,000 | 9.8% |
| 4 | Indiana | 5,630,000 | 7.7% |
| 5 | Missouri | 5,000,000 | 6.9% |
| 6 | Nebraska | 4,575,000 | 6.3% |
| 7 | Ohio | 4,440,000 | 6.1% |
| 8 | South Dakota | 4,370,000 | 6.0% |
| 9 | Arkansas | 3,200,000 | 4.4% |
| 10 | Kansas | 2,500,000 | 3.4% |
| 11 | Michigan | 2,080,000 | 2.9% |
| 12 | North Dakota | 1,850,000 | 2.5% |
| 13 | Mississippi | 1,580,000 | 2.2% |
| 14 | Wisconsin | 1,450,000 | 2.0% |
| 15 | North Carolina | 1,360,000 | 1.9% |
| 16 | Kentucky | 1,180,000 | 1.6% |
| 17 | Tennessee | 1,150,000 | 1.6% |
| 18 | Louisiana | 870,000 | 1.2% |
| 19 | Maryland | 515,000 | 0.7% |
| 20 | Virginia | 490,000 | 0.7% |
| 21 | South Carolina | 440,000 | 0.6% |
| 22 | Pennsylvania | 395,000 | 0.5% |
| 23 | Oklahoma | 310,000 | 0.4% |
| 24 | Texas | 260,000 | 0.4% |
| 25 | Delaware | 213,000 | 0.3% |
| 26 | Alabama | 160,000 | 0.2% |
| 26 | Georgia | 160,000 | 0.2% |
| 28 | New York | 132,000 | 0.2% |
| 29 | New Jersey | 98,000 | 0.1% |
| 30 | Florida | 15,000 | 0.0% |
| 30 | West Virginia | 15,000 | 0.0% |
| NA | Alaska** | NA | NA |
| NA | Arizona** | NA | NA |
| NA | California** | NA | NA |
| NA | Colorado** | NA | NA |
| NA | Connecticut** | NA | NA |
| NA | Hawaii** | NA | NA |
| NA | Idaho** | NA | NA |
| NA | Maine** | NA | NA |
| NA | Massachusetts** | NA | NA |
| NA | Montana** | NA | NA |
| NA | Nevada** | NA | NA |
| NA | New Hampshire** | NA | NA |
| NA | New Mexico** | NA | NA |
| NA | Oregon** | NA | NA |
| NA | Rhode Island** | NA | NA |
| NA | Utah** | NA | NA |
| NA | Vermont** | NA | NA |
| NA | Washington** | NA | NA |
| NA | Wyoming** | NA | NA |
| | District of Columbia** | NA | NA |

*Source: U.S. Department of Agriculture, National Agricultural Statistics Service
"Crop Production, 2000 Summary" (Cr Pr 2-1 (01), January 2001)
(http://usda.mannlib.cornell.edu/reports/nassr/field/pcp-bban/cropan01.txt)*
*Estimated totals.
**No acreage or not available.

# Acres Harvested: Wheat in 2000

## National Total = 53,028,000 Acres*

ALPHA ORDER

RANK ORDER

| RANK | STATE | ACRES | % of USA | | RANK | STATE | ACRES | % of USA |
|------|-------|-------|----------|---|------|-------|-------|----------|
| 36 | Alabama | 90,000 | 0.2% | | 1 | North Dakota | 9,413,000 | 17.8% |
| NA | Alaska** | NA | NA | | 2 | Kansas | 9,400,000 | 17.7% |
| 35 | Arizona | 92,000 | 0.2% | | 3 | Montana | 4,920,000 | 9.3% |
| 13 | Arkansas | 1,100,000 | 2.1% | | 4 | Oklahoma | 4,200,000 | 7.9% |
| 20 | California | 447,000 | 0.8% | | 5 | South Dakota | 2,878,000 | 5.4% |
| 7 | Colorado | 2,396,000 | 4.5% | | 6 | Washington | 2,420,000 | 4.6% |
| NA | Connecticut** | NA | NA | | 7 | Colorado | 2,396,000 | 4.5% |
| 37 | Delaware | 63,000 | 0.1% | | 8 | Texas | 2,200,000 | 4.1% |
| 41 | Florida | 9,000 | 0.0% | | 9 | Minnesota | 1,971,000 | 3.7% |
| 25 | Georgia | 200,000 | 0.4% | | 10 | Nebraska | 1,650,000 | 3.1% |
| NA | Hawaii** | NA | NA | | 11 | Idaho | 1,300,000 | 2.5% |
| 11 | Idaho | 1,300,000 | 2.5% | | 12 | Ohio | 1,110,000 | 2.1% |
| 15 | Illinois | 920,000 | 1.7% | | 13 | Arkansas | 1,100,000 | 2.1% |
| 18 | Indiana | 510,000 | 1.0% | | 14 | Missouri | 950,000 | 1.8% |
| 39 | Iowa | 18,000 | 0.0% | | 15 | Illinois | 920,000 | 1.7% |
| 2 | Kansas | 9,400,000 | 17.7% | | 16 | Oregon | 855,000 | 1.6% |
| 21 | Kentucky | 420,000 | 0.8% | | 17 | North Carolina | 550,000 | 1.0% |
| 28 | Louisiana | 185,000 | 0.3% | | 18 | Indiana | 510,000 | 1.0% |
| NA | Maine** | NA | NA | | 19 | Michigan | 500,000 | 0.9% |
| 25 | Maryland | 200,000 | 0.4% | | 20 | California | 447,000 | 0.8% |
| NA | Massachusetts** | NA | NA | | 21 | Kentucky | 420,000 | 0.8% |
| 19 | Michigan | 500,000 | 0.9% | | 22 | Tennessee | 380,000 | 0.7% |
| 9 | Minnesota | 1,971,000 | 3.7% | | 23 | Mississippi | 235,000 | 0.4% |
| 23 | Mississippi | 235,000 | 0.4% | | 24 | Virginia | 205,000 | 0.4% |
| 14 | Missouri | 950,000 | 1.8% | | 25 | Georgia | 200,000 | 0.4% |
| 3 | Montana | 4,920,000 | 9.3% | | 25 | Maryland | 200,000 | 0.4% |
| 10 | Nebraska | 1,650,000 | 3.1% | | 27 | Pennsylvania | 195,000 | 0.4% |
| 40 | Nevada | 15,000 | 0.0% | | 28 | Louisiana | 185,000 | 0.3% |
| NA | New Hampshire** | NA | NA | | 28 | South Carolina | 185,000 | 0.3% |
| 38 | New Jersey | 35,000 | 0.1% | | 30 | Wyoming | 178,000 | 0.3% |
| 31 | New Mexico | 175,000 | 0.3% | | 31 | New Mexico | 175,000 | 0.3% |
| 34 | New York | 140,000 | 0.3% | | 32 | Utah | 166,000 | 0.3% |
| 17 | North Carolina | 550,000 | 1.0% | | 33 | Wisconsin | 143,000 | 0.3% |
| 1 | North Dakota | 9,413,000 | 17.8% | | 34 | New York | 140,000 | 0.3% |
| 12 | Ohio | 1,110,000 | 2.1% | | 35 | Arizona | 92,000 | 0.2% |
| 4 | Oklahoma | 4,200,000 | 7.9% | | 36 | Alabama | 90,000 | 0.2% |
| 16 | Oregon | 855,000 | 1.6% | | 37 | Delaware | 63,000 | 0.1% |
| 27 | Pennsylvania | 195,000 | 0.4% | | 38 | New Jersey | 35,000 | 0.1% |
| NA | Rhode Island** | NA | NA | | 39 | Iowa | 18,000 | 0.0% |
| 28 | South Carolina | 185,000 | 0.3% | | 40 | Nevada | 15,000 | 0.0% |
| 5 | South Dakota | 2,878,000 | 5.4% | | 41 | Florida | 9,000 | 0.0% |
| 22 | Tennessee | 380,000 | 0.7% | | 41 | West Virginia | 9,000 | 0.0% |
| 8 | Texas | 2,200,000 | 4.1% | | NA | Alaska** | NA | NA |
| 32 | Utah | 166,000 | 0.3% | | NA | Connecticut** | NA | NA |
| NA | Vermont** | NA | NA | | NA | Hawaii** | NA | NA |
| 24 | Virginia | 205,000 | 0.4% | | NA | Maine** | NA | NA |
| 6 | Washington | 2,420,000 | 4.6% | | NA | Massachusetts** | NA | NA |
| 41 | West Virginia | 9,000 | 0.0% | | NA | New Hampshire** | NA | NA |
| 33 | Wisconsin | 143,000 | 0.3% | | NA | Rhode Island** | NA | NA |
| 30 | Wyoming | 178,000 | 0.3% | | NA | Vermont** | NA | NA |
| | | | | | | District of Columbia** | NA | NA |

*Source: U.S. Department of Agriculture, National Agricultural Statistics Service*
   *"Crop Production, 2000 Summary" (Cr Pr 2-1 (01), January 2001)*
      *(http://usda.mannlib.cornell.edu/reports/nassr/field/pcp-bban/cropan01.txt)*
*Estimated totals.*
**No acreage or not available.*

# Cattle on Farms in 2001

## National Total = 97,308,500 Cattle*

ALPHA ORDER

| RANK | STATE | CATTLE | % of USA |
|---|---|---|---|
| 25 | Alabama | 1,360,000 | 1.4% |
| 49 | Alaska | 10,500 | 0.0% |
| 36 | Arizona | 850,000 | 0.9% |
| 17 | Arkansas | 1,810,000 | 1.9% |
| 4 | California | 5,150,000 | 5.3% |
| 10 | Colorado | 3,150,000 | 3.2% |
| 44 | Connecticut | 63,000 | 0.1% |
| 48 | Delaware | 27,000 | 0.0% |
| 18 | Florida | 1,800,000 | 1.8% |
| 27 | Georgia | 1,270,000 | 1.3% |
| 42 | Hawaii | 150,000 | 0.2% |
| 16 | Idaho | 1,970,000 | 2.0% |
| 23 | Illinois | 1,470,000 | 1.5% |
| 34 | Indiana | 880,000 | 0.9% |
| 8 | Iowa | 3,650,000 | 3.8% |
| 2 | Kansas | 6,700,000 | 6.9% |
| 13 | Kentucky | 2,260,000 | 2.3% |
| 35 | Louisiana | 860,000 | 0.9% |
| 43 | Maine | 97,000 | 0.1% |
| 41 | Maryland | 235,000 | 0.2% |
| 45 | Massachusetts | 50,000 | 0.1% |
| 31 | Michigan | 980,000 | 1.0% |
| 11 | Minnesota | 2,550,000 | 2.6% |
| 30 | Mississippi | 1,070,000 | 1.1% |
| 6 | Missouri | 4,250,000 | 4.4% |
| 11 | Montana | 2,550,000 | 2.6% |
| 3 | Nebraska | 6,600,000 | 6.8% |
| 37 | Nevada | 520,000 | 0.5% |
| 47 | New Hampshire | 42,000 | 0.0% |
| 46 | New Jersey | 48,000 | 0.0% |
| 21 | New Mexico | 1,580,000 | 1.6% |
| 24 | New York | 1,380,000 | 1.4% |
| 32 | North Carolina | 950,000 | 1.0% |
| 15 | North Dakota | 1,980,000 | 2.0% |
| 28 | Ohio | 1,240,000 | 1.3% |
| 5 | Oklahoma | 5,050,000 | 5.2% |
| 25 | Oregon | 1,360,000 | 1.4% |
| 20 | Pennsylvania | 1,640,000 | 1.7% |
| 50 | Rhode Island | 6,000 | 0.0% |
| 38 | South Carolina | 445,000 | 0.5% |
| 7 | South Dakota | 4,050,000 | 4.2% |
| 14 | Tennessee | 2,170,000 | 2.2% |
| 1 | Texas | 13,700,000 | 14.1% |
| 33 | Utah | 910,000 | 0.9% |
| 40 | Vermont | 295,000 | 0.3% |
| 19 | Virginia | 1,650,000 | 1.7% |
| 29 | Washington | 1,180,000 | 1.2% |
| 39 | West Virginia | 400,000 | 0.4% |
| 9 | Wisconsin | 3,350,000 | 3.4% |
| 22 | Wyoming | 1,550,000 | 1.6% |

RANK ORDER

| RANK | STATE | CATTLE | % of USA |
|---|---|---|---|
| 1 | Texas | 13,700,000 | 14.1% |
| 2 | Kansas | 6,700,000 | 6.9% |
| 3 | Nebraska | 6,600,000 | 6.8% |
| 4 | California | 5,150,000 | 5.3% |
| 5 | Oklahoma | 5,050,000 | 5.2% |
| 6 | Missouri | 4,250,000 | 4.4% |
| 7 | South Dakota | 4,050,000 | 4.2% |
| 8 | Iowa | 3,650,000 | 3.8% |
| 9 | Wisconsin | 3,350,000 | 3.4% |
| 10 | Colorado | 3,150,000 | 3.2% |
| 11 | Minnesota | 2,550,000 | 2.6% |
| 11 | Montana | 2,550,000 | 2.6% |
| 13 | Kentucky | 2,260,000 | 2.3% |
| 14 | Tennessee | 2,170,000 | 2.2% |
| 15 | North Dakota | 1,980,000 | 2.0% |
| 16 | Idaho | 1,970,000 | 2.0% |
| 17 | Arkansas | 1,810,000 | 1.9% |
| 18 | Florida | 1,800,000 | 1.8% |
| 19 | Virginia | 1,650,000 | 1.7% |
| 20 | Pennsylvania | 1,640,000 | 1.7% |
| 21 | New Mexico | 1,580,000 | 1.6% |
| 22 | Wyoming | 1,550,000 | 1.6% |
| 23 | Illinois | 1,470,000 | 1.5% |
| 24 | New York | 1,380,000 | 1.4% |
| 25 | Alabama | 1,360,000 | 1.4% |
| 25 | Oregon | 1,360,000 | 1.4% |
| 27 | Georgia | 1,270,000 | 1.3% |
| 28 | Ohio | 1,240,000 | 1.3% |
| 29 | Washington | 1,180,000 | 1.2% |
| 30 | Mississippi | 1,070,000 | 1.1% |
| 31 | Michigan | 980,000 | 1.0% |
| 32 | North Carolina | 950,000 | 1.0% |
| 33 | Utah | 910,000 | 0.9% |
| 34 | Indiana | 880,000 | 0.9% |
| 35 | Louisiana | 860,000 | 0.9% |
| 36 | Arizona | 850,000 | 0.9% |
| 37 | Nevada | 520,000 | 0.5% |
| 38 | South Carolina | 445,000 | 0.5% |
| 39 | West Virginia | 400,000 | 0.4% |
| 40 | Vermont | 295,000 | 0.3% |
| 41 | Maryland | 235,000 | 0.2% |
| 42 | Hawaii | 150,000 | 0.2% |
| 43 | Maine | 97,000 | 0.1% |
| 44 | Connecticut | 63,000 | 0.1% |
| 45 | Massachusetts | 50,000 | 0.1% |
| 46 | New Jersey | 48,000 | 0.0% |
| 47 | New Hampshire | 42,000 | 0.0% |
| 48 | Delaware | 27,000 | 0.0% |
| 49 | Alaska | 10,500 | 0.0% |
| 50 | Rhode Island | 6,000 | 0.0% |
| | District of Columbia | 0 | 0.0% |

Source: U.S. Department of Agriculture, National Agricultural Statistics Service
    "Cattle" (http://usda.mannlib.cornell.edu/reports/nassr/livestock/pct-bb/catl0101.txt)
*As of January 1, 2001.

# Milk Cows on Farms in 1999

## National Total = 9,156,000 Milk Cows*

ALPHA ORDER

| RANK | STATE | MILK COWS | % of USA |
|---|---|---|---|
| 38 | Alabama | 27,000 | 0.3% |
| 50 | Alaska | 1,000 | 0.0% |
| 17 | Arizona | 134,000 | 1.5% |
| 34 | Arkansas | 42,000 | 0.5% |
| 1 | California | 1,466,000 | 16.0% |
| 29 | Colorado | 83,000 | 0.9% |
| 37 | Connecticut | 29,000 | 0.3% |
| 46 | Delaware | 11,000 | 0.1% |
| 15 | Florida | 158,000 | 1.7% |
| 25 | Georgia | 89,000 | 1.0% |
| 47 | Hawaii | 8,600 | 0.1% |
| 7 | Idaho | 318,000 | 3.5% |
| 19 | Illinois | 123,000 | 1.3% |
| 16 | Indiana | 136,000 | 1.5% |
| 12 | Iowa | 217,000 | 2.4% |
| 27 | Kansas | 86,000 | 0.9% |
| 18 | Kentucky | 133,000 | 1.5% |
| 32 | Louisiana | 61,000 | 0.7% |
| 34 | Maine | 42,000 | 0.5% |
| 28 | Maryland | 85,000 | 0.9% |
| 39 | Massachusetts | 25,000 | 0.3% |
| 8 | Michigan | 299,000 | 3.3% |
| 5 | Minnesota | 545,000 | 6.0% |
| 36 | Mississippi | 38,000 | 0.4% |
| 14 | Missouri | 159,000 | 1.7% |
| 43 | Montana | 18,000 | 0.2% |
| 30 | Nebraska | 74,000 | 0.8% |
| 39 | Nevada | 25,000 | 0.3% |
| 42 | New Hampshire | 19,000 | 0.2% |
| 45 | New Jersey | 17,000 | 0.2% |
| 11 | New Mexico | 232,000 | 2.5% |
| 3 | New York | 701,000 | 7.7% |
| 31 | North Carolina | 73,000 | 0.8% |
| 33 | North Dakota | 49,000 | 0.5% |
| 9 | Ohio | 260,000 | 2.8% |
| 23 | Oklahoma | 92,000 | 1.0% |
| 25 | Oregon | 89,000 | 1.0% |
| 4 | Pennsylvania | 616,000 | 6.7% |
| 49 | Rhode Island | 2,000 | 0.0% |
| 41 | South Carolina | 24,000 | 0.3% |
| 21 | South Dakota | 102,000 | 1.1% |
| 22 | Tennessee | 97,000 | 1.1% |
| 6 | Texas | 345,000 | 3.8% |
| 23 | Utah | 92,000 | 1.0% |
| 13 | Vermont | 160,000 | 1.7% |
| 20 | Virginia | 121,000 | 1.3% |
| 10 | Washington | 247,000 | 2.7% |
| 43 | West Virginia | 18,000 | 0.2% |
| 2 | Wisconsin | 1,365,000 | 14.9% |
| 48 | Wyoming | 6,000 | 0.1% |

RANK ORDER

| RANK | STATE | MILK COWS | % of USA |
|---|---|---|---|
| 1 | California | 1,466,000 | 16.0% |
| 2 | Wisconsin | 1,365,000 | 14.9% |
| 3 | New York | 701,000 | 7.7% |
| 4 | Pennsylvania | 616,000 | 6.7% |
| 5 | Minnesota | 545,000 | 6.0% |
| 6 | Texas | 345,000 | 3.8% |
| 7 | Idaho | 318,000 | 3.5% |
| 8 | Michigan | 299,000 | 3.3% |
| 9 | Ohio | 260,000 | 2.8% |
| 10 | Washington | 247,000 | 2.7% |
| 11 | New Mexico | 232,000 | 2.5% |
| 12 | Iowa | 217,000 | 2.4% |
| 13 | Vermont | 160,000 | 1.7% |
| 14 | Missouri | 159,000 | 1.7% |
| 15 | Florida | 158,000 | 1.7% |
| 16 | Indiana | 136,000 | 1.5% |
| 17 | Arizona | 134,000 | 1.5% |
| 18 | Kentucky | 133,000 | 1.5% |
| 19 | Illinois | 123,000 | 1.3% |
| 20 | Virginia | 121,000 | 1.3% |
| 21 | South Dakota | 102,000 | 1.1% |
| 22 | Tennessee | 97,000 | 1.1% |
| 23 | Oklahoma | 92,000 | 1.0% |
| 23 | Utah | 92,000 | 1.0% |
| 25 | Georgia | 89,000 | 1.0% |
| 25 | Oregon | 89,000 | 1.0% |
| 27 | Kansas | 86,000 | 0.9% |
| 28 | Maryland | 85,000 | 0.9% |
| 29 | Colorado | 83,000 | 0.9% |
| 30 | Nebraska | 74,000 | 0.8% |
| 31 | North Carolina | 73,000 | 0.8% |
| 32 | Louisiana | 61,000 | 0.7% |
| 33 | North Dakota | 49,000 | 0.5% |
| 34 | Arkansas | 42,000 | 0.5% |
| 34 | Maine | 42,000 | 0.5% |
| 36 | Mississippi | 38,000 | 0.4% |
| 37 | Connecticut | 29,000 | 0.3% |
| 38 | Alabama | 27,000 | 0.3% |
| 39 | Massachusetts | 25,000 | 0.3% |
| 39 | Nevada | 25,000 | 0.3% |
| 41 | South Carolina | 24,000 | 0.3% |
| 42 | New Hampshire | 19,000 | 0.2% |
| 43 | Montana | 18,000 | 0.2% |
| 43 | West Virginia | 18,000 | 0.2% |
| 45 | New Jersey | 17,000 | 0.2% |
| 46 | Delaware | 11,000 | 0.1% |
| 47 | Hawaii | 8,600 | 0.1% |
| 48 | Wyoming | 6,000 | 0.1% |
| 49 | Rhode Island | 2,000 | 0.0% |
| 50 | Alaska | 1,000 | 0.0% |
| | District of Columbia | 0 | 0.0% |

Source: U.S. Department of Agriculture, National Agricultural Statistics Service
"Milk Production, Disposition and Income 1999 Summary" (April 2000)
(http://usda.mannlib.cornell.edu/reports/nassr/dairy/pmp-bbm/milk0400.txt)
*Average number during year. Excludes heifers not yet fresh.

# Milk Production in 1999

## National Total = 162,711,000,000 Pounds of Milk*

ALPHA ORDER

| RANK | STATE | POUNDS | % of USA |
|---|---|---|---|
| 40 | Alabama | 374,000,000 | 0.2% |
| 50 | Alaska | 13,580,000 | 0.0% |
| 13 | Arizona | 2,931,000,000 | 1.8% |
| 36 | Arkansas | 520,000,000 | 0.3% |
| 1 | California | 30,475,000,000 | 18.7% |
| 20 | Colorado | 1,728,000,000 | 1.1% |
| 36 | Connecticut | 520,000,000 | 0.3% |
| 46 | Delaware | 171,000,000 | 0.1% |
| 15 | Florida | 2,398,000,000 | 1.5% |
| 25 | Georgia | 1,449,000,000 | 0.9% |
| 47 | Hawaii | 119,700,000 | 0.1% |
| 6 | Idaho | 6,453,000,000 | 4.0% |
| 18 | Illinois | 2,029,000,000 | 1.2% |
| 17 | Indiana | 2,185,000,000 | 1.3% |
| 12 | Iowa | 3,802,000,000 | 2.3% |
| 27 | Kansas | 1,395,000,000 | 0.9% |
| 22 | Kentucky | 1,645,000,000 | 1.0% |
| 32 | Louisiana | 711,000,000 | 0.4% |
| 33 | Maine | 693,000,000 | 0.4% |
| 28 | Maryland | 1,365,000,000 | 0.8% |
| 39 | Massachusetts | 420,000,000 | 0.3% |
| 9 | Michigan | 5,455,000,000 | 3.4% |
| 5 | Minnesota | 9,478,000,000 | 5.8% |
| 35 | Mississippi | 552,000,000 | 0.3% |
| 16 | Missouri | 2,220,000,000 | 1.4% |
| 43 | Montana | 303,000,000 | 0.2% |
| 31 | Nebraska | 1,139,000,000 | 0.7% |
| 38 | Nevada | 497,000,000 | 0.3% |
| 42 | New Hampshire | 321,000,000 | 0.2% |
| 44 | New Jersey | 280,000,000 | 0.2% |
| 10 | New Mexico | 4,725,000,000 | 2.9% |
| 3 | New York | 12,040,000,000 | 7.4% |
| 30 | North Carolina | 1,216,000,000 | 0.7% |
| 34 | North Dakota | 689,000,000 | 0.4% |
| 11 | Ohio | 4,445,000,000 | 2.7% |
| 29 | Oklahoma | 1,249,000,000 | 0.8% |
| 21 | Oregon | 1,665,000,000 | 1.0% |
| 4 | Pennsylvania | 10,931,000,000 | 6.7% |
| 49 | Rhode Island | 31,000,000 | 0.0% |
| 41 | South Carolina | 369,000,000 | 0.2% |
| 24 | South Dakota | 1,507,000,000 | 0.9% |
| 26 | Tennessee | 1,417,000,000 | 0.9% |
| 7 | Texas | 5,620,000,000 | 3.5% |
| 23 | Utah | 1,613,000,000 | 1.0% |
| 14 | Vermont | 2,712,000,000 | 1.7% |
| 19 | Virginia | 1,879,000,000 | 1.2% |
| 8 | Washington | 5,535,000,000 | 3.4% |
| 45 | West Virginia | 275,000,000 | 0.2% |
| 2 | Wisconsin | 23,071,000,000 | 14.2% |
| 48 | Wyoming | 79,800,000 | 0.0% |

RANK ORDER

| RANK | STATE | POUNDS | % of USA |
|---|---|---|---|
| 1 | California | 30,475,000,000 | 18.7% |
| 2 | Wisconsin | 23,071,000,000 | 14.2% |
| 3 | New York | 12,040,000,000 | 7.4% |
| 4 | Pennsylvania | 10,931,000,000 | 6.7% |
| 5 | Minnesota | 9,478,000,000 | 5.8% |
| 6 | Idaho | 6,453,000,000 | 4.0% |
| 7 | Texas | 5,620,000,000 | 3.5% |
| 8 | Washington | 5,535,000,000 | 3.4% |
| 9 | Michigan | 5,455,000,000 | 3.4% |
| 10 | New Mexico | 4,725,000,000 | 2.9% |
| 11 | Ohio | 4,445,000,000 | 2.7% |
| 12 | Iowa | 3,802,000,000 | 2.3% |
| 13 | Arizona | 2,931,000,000 | 1.8% |
| 14 | Vermont | 2,712,000,000 | 1.7% |
| 15 | Florida | 2,398,000,000 | 1.5% |
| 16 | Missouri | 2,220,000,000 | 1.4% |
| 17 | Indiana | 2,185,000,000 | 1.3% |
| 18 | Illinois | 2,029,000,000 | 1.2% |
| 19 | Virginia | 1,879,000,000 | 1.2% |
| 20 | Colorado | 1,728,000,000 | 1.1% |
| 21 | Oregon | 1,665,000,000 | 1.0% |
| 22 | Kentucky | 1,645,000,000 | 1.0% |
| 23 | Utah | 1,613,000,000 | 1.0% |
| 24 | South Dakota | 1,507,000,000 | 0.9% |
| 25 | Georgia | 1,449,000,000 | 0.9% |
| 26 | Tennessee | 1,417,000,000 | 0.9% |
| 27 | Kansas | 1,395,000,000 | 0.9% |
| 28 | Maryland | 1,365,000,000 | 0.8% |
| 29 | Oklahoma | 1,249,000,000 | 0.8% |
| 30 | North Carolina | 1,216,000,000 | 0.7% |
| 31 | Nebraska | 1,139,000,000 | 0.7% |
| 32 | Louisiana | 711,000,000 | 0.4% |
| 33 | Maine | 693,000,000 | 0.4% |
| 34 | North Dakota | 689,000,000 | 0.4% |
| 35 | Mississippi | 552,000,000 | 0.3% |
| 36 | Arkansas | 520,000,000 | 0.3% |
| 36 | Connecticut | 520,000,000 | 0.3% |
| 38 | Nevada | 497,000,000 | 0.3% |
| 39 | Massachusetts | 420,000,000 | 0.3% |
| 40 | Alabama | 374,000,000 | 0.2% |
| 41 | South Carolina | 369,000,000 | 0.2% |
| 42 | New Hampshire | 321,000,000 | 0.2% |
| 43 | Montana | 303,000,000 | 0.2% |
| 44 | New Jersey | 280,000,000 | 0.2% |
| 45 | West Virginia | 275,000,000 | 0.2% |
| 46 | Delaware | 171,000,000 | 0.1% |
| 47 | Hawaii | 119,700,000 | 0.1% |
| 48 | Wyoming | 79,800,000 | 0.0% |
| 49 | Rhode Island | 31,000,000 | 0.0% |
| 50 | Alaska | 13,580,000 | 0.0% |
| | District of Columbia | 0 | 0.0% |

*Source: U.S. Department of Agriculture, National Agricultural Statistics Service*
*"Milk Production, Disposition and Income 1999 Summary" (April 2000)*
*(http://usda.mannlib.cornell.edu/reports/nassr/dairy/pmp-bbm/milk0400.txt)*
*Excludes milk sucked by calves.*

# Milk Production per Milk Cow in 1999

## National Average = 17,771 Pounds of Milk per Cow*

ALPHA ORDER

| RANK | STATE | POUNDS |
|---|---|---|
| 44 | Alabama | 13,852 |
| 45 | Alaska | 13,580 |
| 2 | Arizona | 21,873 |
| 48 | Arkansas | 12,381 |
| 4 | California | 20,788 |
| 3 | Colorado | 20,819 |
| 10 | Connecticut | 17,931 |
| 31 | Delaware | 15,545 |
| 37 | Florida | 15,177 |
| 27 | Georgia | 16,281 |
| 43 | Hawaii | 13,919 |
| 6 | Idaho | 20,292 |
| 24 | Illinois | 16,496 |
| 29 | Indiana | 16,066 |
| 13 | Iowa | 17,521 |
| 28 | Kansas | 16,221 |
| 49 | Kentucky | 12,368 |
| 50 | Louisiana | 11,656 |
| 23 | Maine | 16,500 |
| 30 | Maryland | 16,059 |
| 21 | Massachusetts | 16,800 |
| 9 | Michigan | 18,244 |
| 14 | Minnesota | 17,391 |
| 40 | Mississippi | 14,526 |
| 42 | Missouri | 13,962 |
| 20 | Montana | 16,833 |
| 34 | Nebraska | 15,392 |
| 7 | Nevada | 19,880 |
| 19 | New Hampshire | 16,895 |
| 25 | New Jersey | 16,471 |
| 5 | New Mexico | 20,366 |
| 15 | New York | 17,175 |
| 22 | North Carolina | 16,658 |
| 41 | North Dakota | 14,061 |
| 16 | Ohio | 17,096 |
| 46 | Oklahoma | 13,576 |
| 8 | Oregon | 18,708 |
| 11 | Pennsylvania | 17,745 |
| 33 | Rhode Island | 15,500 |
| 35 | South Carolina | 15,375 |
| 38 | South Dakota | 14,775 |
| 39 | Tennessee | 14,608 |
| 26 | Texas | 16,290 |
| 12 | Utah | 17,533 |
| 17 | Vermont | 16,950 |
| 32 | Virginia | 15,529 |
| 1 | Washington | 22,409 |
| 36 | West Virginia | 15,278 |
| 18 | Wisconsin | 16,902 |
| 47 | Wyoming | 13,300 |

RANK ORDER

| RANK | STATE | POUNDS |
|---|---|---|
| 1 | Washington | 22,409 |
| 2 | Arizona | 21,873 |
| 3 | Colorado | 20,819 |
| 4 | California | 20,788 |
| 5 | New Mexico | 20,366 |
| 6 | Idaho | 20,292 |
| 7 | Nevada | 19,880 |
| 8 | Oregon | 18,708 |
| 9 | Michigan | 18,244 |
| 10 | Connecticut | 17,931 |
| 11 | Pennsylvania | 17,745 |
| 12 | Utah | 17,533 |
| 13 | Iowa | 17,521 |
| 14 | Minnesota | 17,391 |
| 15 | New York | 17,175 |
| 16 | Ohio | 17,096 |
| 17 | Vermont | 16,950 |
| 18 | Wisconsin | 16,902 |
| 19 | New Hampshire | 16,895 |
| 20 | Montana | 16,833 |
| 21 | Massachusetts | 16,800 |
| 22 | North Carolina | 16,658 |
| 23 | Maine | 16,500 |
| 24 | Illinois | 16,496 |
| 25 | New Jersey | 16,471 |
| 26 | Texas | 16,290 |
| 27 | Georgia | 16,281 |
| 28 | Kansas | 16,221 |
| 29 | Indiana | 16,066 |
| 30 | Maryland | 16,059 |
| 31 | Delaware | 15,545 |
| 32 | Virginia | 15,529 |
| 33 | Rhode Island | 15,500 |
| 34 | Nebraska | 15,392 |
| 35 | South Carolina | 15,375 |
| 36 | West Virginia | 15,278 |
| 37 | Florida | 15,177 |
| 38 | South Dakota | 14,775 |
| 39 | Tennessee | 14,608 |
| 40 | Mississippi | 14,526 |
| 41 | North Dakota | 14,061 |
| 42 | Missouri | 13,962 |
| 43 | Hawaii | 13,919 |
| 44 | Alabama | 13,852 |
| 45 | Alaska | 13,580 |
| 46 | Oklahoma | 13,576 |
| 47 | Wyoming | 13,300 |
| 48 | Arkansas | 12,381 |
| 49 | Kentucky | 12,368 |
| 50 | Louisiana | 11,656 |
| | District of Columbia** | NA |

Source: U.S. Department of Agriculture, National Agricultural Statistics Service
   "Milk Production, Disposition and Income 1999 Summary" (April 2000)
      (http://usda.mannlib.cornell.edu/reports/nassr/dairy/pmp-bbm/milk0400.txt)
*Excludes milk sucked by calves.
**Not applicable.

# Hogs and Pigs on Farms in 2000

## National Total = 59,848,000 Hogs and Pigs*

ALPHA ORDER

| RANK | STATE | HOGS AND PIGS | % of USA |
|---|---|---|---|
| 26 | Alabama | 165,000 | 0.3% |
| 50 | Alaska | 800 | 0.0% |
| 42 | Arizona | 9,000 | 0.0% |
| 16 | Arkansas | 685,000 | 1.1% |
| 28 | California | 150,000 | 0.3% |
| 15 | Colorado | 840,000 | 1.4% |
| 45 | Connecticut | 4,000 | 0.0% |
| 34 | Delaware | 29,000 | 0.0% |
| 32 | Florida | 40,000 | 0.1% |
| 21 | Georgia | 380,000 | 0.6% |
| 37 | Hawaii | 26,000 | 0.0% |
| 38 | Idaho | 24,000 | 0.0% |
| 4 | Illinois | 4,200,000 | 7.0% |
| 5 | Indiana | 3,400,000 | 5.7% |
| 1 | Iowa | 15,400,000 | 25.7% |
| 9 | Kansas | 1,570,000 | 2.6% |
| 19 | Kentucky | 430,000 | 0.7% |
| 34 | Louisiana | 29,000 | 0.0% |
| 44 | Maine | 6,500 | 0.0% |
| 31 | Maryland | 58,000 | 0.1% |
| 39 | Massachusetts | 20,000 | 0.0% |
| 13 | Michigan | 950,000 | 1.6% |
| 3 | Minnesota | 5,800,000 | 9.7% |
| 22 | Mississippi | 315,000 | 0.5% |
| 7 | Missouri | 2,900,000 | 4.8% |
| 27 | Montana | 155,000 | 0.3% |
| 6 | Nebraska | 3,100,000 | 5.2% |
| 43 | Nevada | 7,500 | 0.0% |
| 45 | New Hampshire | 4,000 | 0.0% |
| 40 | New Jersey | 14,000 | 0.0% |
| 47 | New Mexico | 3,000 | 0.0% |
| 30 | New York | 80,000 | 0.1% |
| 2 | North Carolina | 9,400,000 | 15.7% |
| 25 | North Dakota | 185,000 | 0.3% |
| 10 | Ohio | 1,510,000 | 2.5% |
| 8 | Oklahoma | 2,340,000 | 3.9% |
| 33 | Oregon | 32,000 | 0.1% |
| 12 | Pennsylvania | 1,040,000 | 1.7% |
| 47 | Rhode Island | 3,000 | 0.0% |
| 23 | South Carolina | 290,000 | 0.5% |
| 11 | South Dakota | 1,360,000 | 2.3% |
| 24 | Tennessee | 230,000 | 0.4% |
| 14 | Texas | 920,000 | 1.5% |
| 18 | Utah | 550,000 | 0.9% |
| 47 | Vermont | 3,000 | 0.0% |
| 20 | Virginia | 425,000 | 0.7% |
| 36 | Washington | 27,000 | 0.0% |
| 41 | West Virginia | 10,000 | 0.0% |
| 17 | Wisconsin | 620,000 | 1.0% |
| 29 | Wyoming | 108,000 | 0.2% |

RANK ORDER

| RANK | STATE | HOGS AND PIGS | % of USA |
|---|---|---|---|
| 1 | Iowa | 15,400,000 | 25.7% |
| 2 | North Carolina | 9,400,000 | 15.7% |
| 3 | Minnesota | 5,800,000 | 9.7% |
| 4 | Illinois | 4,200,000 | 7.0% |
| 5 | Indiana | 3,400,000 | 5.7% |
| 6 | Nebraska | 3,100,000 | 5.2% |
| 7 | Missouri | 2,900,000 | 4.8% |
| 8 | Oklahoma | 2,340,000 | 3.9% |
| 9 | Kansas | 1,570,000 | 2.6% |
| 10 | Ohio | 1,510,000 | 2.5% |
| 11 | South Dakota | 1,360,000 | 2.3% |
| 12 | Pennsylvania | 1,040,000 | 1.7% |
| 13 | Michigan | 950,000 | 1.6% |
| 14 | Texas | 920,000 | 1.5% |
| 15 | Colorado | 840,000 | 1.4% |
| 16 | Arkansas | 685,000 | 1.1% |
| 17 | Wisconsin | 620,000 | 1.0% |
| 18 | Utah | 550,000 | 0.9% |
| 19 | Kentucky | 430,000 | 0.7% |
| 20 | Virginia | 425,000 | 0.7% |
| 21 | Georgia | 380,000 | 0.6% |
| 22 | Mississippi | 315,000 | 0.5% |
| 23 | South Carolina | 290,000 | 0.5% |
| 24 | Tennessee | 230,000 | 0.4% |
| 25 | North Dakota | 185,000 | 0.3% |
| 26 | Alabama | 165,000 | 0.3% |
| 27 | Montana | 155,000 | 0.3% |
| 28 | California | 150,000 | 0.3% |
| 29 | Wyoming | 108,000 | 0.2% |
| 30 | New York | 80,000 | 0.1% |
| 31 | Maryland | 58,000 | 0.1% |
| 32 | Florida | 40,000 | 0.1% |
| 33 | Oregon | 32,000 | 0.1% |
| 34 | Delaware | 29,000 | 0.0% |
| 34 | Louisiana | 29,000 | 0.0% |
| 36 | Washington | 27,000 | 0.0% |
| 37 | Hawaii | 26,000 | 0.0% |
| 38 | Idaho | 24,000 | 0.0% |
| 39 | Massachusetts | 20,000 | 0.0% |
| 40 | New Jersey | 14,000 | 0.0% |
| 41 | West Virginia | 10,000 | 0.0% |
| 42 | Arizona | 9,000 | 0.0% |
| 43 | Nevada | 7,500 | 0.0% |
| 44 | Maine | 6,500 | 0.0% |
| 45 | Connecticut | 4,000 | 0.0% |
| 45 | New Hampshire | 4,000 | 0.0% |
| 47 | New Mexico | 3,000 | 0.0% |
| 47 | Rhode Island | 3,000 | 0.0% |
| 47 | Vermont | 3,000 | 0.0% |
| 50 | Alaska | 800 | 0.0% |
|  | District of Columbia | 0 | 0.0% |

Source: U.S. Department of Agriculture, National Agricultural Statistics Service
    "Hogs and Pigs" (http://usda.mannlib.cornell.edu/reports/nassr/livestock/php-bb/2000/hgpg1200.txt)
*As of December 1, 2000.

# Chickens in 1999 (Leading States Only)

## National Total = 8,146,010,000 Chickens*

ALPHA ORDER

| RANK | STATE | CHICKENS | % of USA |
|------|-------|----------|----------|
| 3 | Alabama | 971,200,000 | 11.9% |
| NA | Alaska** | NA | NA |
| NA | Arizona** | NA | NA |
| 2 | Arkansas | 1,196,200,000 | 14.7% |
| NA | California** | NA | NA |
| NA | Colorado*** | NA | NA |
| NA | Connecticut*** | NA | NA |
| 9 | Delaware | 251,700,000 | 3.1% |
| 16 | Florida | 122,200,000 | 1.5% |
| 1 | Georgia | 1,239,700,000 | 15.2% |
| 23 | Hawaii | 1,000,000 | 0.0% |
| NA | Idaho*** | NA | NA |
| NA | Illinois*** | NA | NA |
| NA | Indiana** | NA | NA |
| NA | Iowa** | NA | NA |
| NA | Kansas*** | NA | NA |
| 13 | Kentucky | 188,800,000 | 2.3% |
| NA | Louisiana** | NA | NA |
| NA | Maine** | NA | NA |
| 7 | Maryland | 294,400,000 | 3.6% |
| NA | Massachusetts*** | NA | NA |
| 24 | Michigan | 750,000 | 0.0% |
| 19 | Minnesota | 44,200,000 | 0.5% |
| 4 | Mississippi | 735,100,000 | 9.0% |
| 10 | Missouri | 249,700,000 | 3.1% |
| NA | Montana** | NA | NA |
| 21 | Nebraska | 11,500,000 | 0.1% |
| NA | Nevada** | NA | NA |
| NA | New Hampshire*** | NA | NA |
| NA | New Jersey*** | NA | NA |
| NA | New Mexico*** | NA | NA |
| 22 | New York | 2,000,000 | 0.0% |
| 5 | North Carolina | 674,600,000 | 8.3% |
| NA | North Dakota*** | NA | NA |
| 18 | Ohio | 50,500,000 | 0.6% |
| 11 | Oklahoma | 216,400,000 | 2.7% |
| NA | Oregon** | NA | NA |
| 15 | Pennsylvania | 135,300,000 | 1.7% |
| NA | Rhode Island*** | NA | NA |
| 12 | South Carolina | 191,300,000 | 2.3% |
| NA | South Dakota*** | NA | NA |
| 14 | Tennessee | 150,800,000 | 1.9% |
| 6 | Texas | 507,900,000 | 6.2% |
| NA | Utah*** | NA | NA |
| NA | Vermont*** | NA | NA |
| 8 | Virginia | 268,700,000 | 3.3% |
| NA | Washington** | NA | NA |
| 17 | West Virginia | 89,500,000 | 1.1% |
| 20 | Wisconsin | 33,800,000 | 0.4% |
| NA | Wyoming*** | NA | NA |

RANK ORDER

| RANK | STATE | CHICKENS | % of USA |
|------|-------|----------|----------|
| 1 | Georgia | 1,239,700,000 | 15.2% |
| 2 | Arkansas | 1,196,200,000 | 14.7% |
| 3 | Alabama | 971,200,000 | 11.9% |
| 4 | Mississippi | 735,100,000 | 9.0% |
| 5 | North Carolina | 674,600,000 | 8.3% |
| 6 | Texas | 507,900,000 | 6.2% |
| 7 | Maryland | 294,400,000 | 3.6% |
| 8 | Virginia | 268,700,000 | 3.3% |
| 9 | Delaware | 251,700,000 | 3.1% |
| 10 | Missouri | 249,700,000 | 3.1% |
| 11 | Oklahoma | 216,400,000 | 2.7% |
| 12 | South Carolina | 191,300,000 | 2.3% |
| 13 | Kentucky | 188,800,000 | 2.3% |
| 14 | Tennessee | 150,800,000 | 1.9% |
| 15 | Pennsylvania | 135,300,000 | 1.7% |
| 16 | Florida | 122,200,000 | 1.5% |
| 17 | West Virginia | 89,500,000 | 1.1% |
| 18 | Ohio | 50,500,000 | 0.6% |
| 19 | Minnesota | 44,200,000 | 0.5% |
| 20 | Wisconsin | 33,800,000 | 0.4% |
| 21 | Nebraska | 11,500,000 | 0.1% |
| 22 | New York | 2,000,000 | 0.0% |
| 23 | Hawaii | 1,000,000 | 0.0% |
| 24 | Michigan | 750,000 | 0.0% |
| NA | Alaska** | NA | NA |
| NA | Arizona** | NA | NA |
| NA | California** | NA | NA |
| NA | Colorado*** | NA | NA |
| NA | Connecticut*** | NA | NA |
| NA | Idaho*** | NA | NA |
| NA | Illinois*** | NA | NA |
| NA | Indiana** | NA | NA |
| NA | Iowa** | NA | NA |
| NA | Kansas*** | NA | NA |
| NA | Louisiana** | NA | NA |
| NA | Maine** | NA | NA |
| NA | Massachusetts*** | NA | NA |
| NA | Montana** | NA | NA |
| NA | Nevada** | NA | NA |
| NA | New Hampshire*** | NA | NA |
| NA | New Jersey*** | NA | NA |
| NA | New Mexico*** | NA | NA |
| NA | North Dakota*** | NA | NA |
| NA | Oregon** | NA | NA |
| NA | Rhode Island*** | NA | NA |
| NA | South Dakota*** | NA | NA |
| NA | Utah*** | NA | NA |
| NA | Vermont*** | NA | NA |
| NA | Washington** | NA | NA |
| NA | Wyoming*** | NA | NA |
| | District of Columbia*** | NA | NA |

*Source: U.S. Department of Agriculture, National Agricultural Statistics Service
"Poultry - Production and Value 1999 Summary"
(http://usda.mannlib.cornell.edu/reports/nassr/poultry/pbh-bbp/plva0400.txt)*
*Broilers. Total includes numbers for states not shown separately but excludes states producing less than 500,000 birds. **These states produced a combined total of 518,760,000 chickens. They are combined to avoid disclosing individual operations. National total does not include chickens used for egg production. ***Not available.*

# Eggs Produced in 1999

## National Total = 82,711,000,000 Eggs

ALPHA ORDER

| RANK | STATE | EGGS | % of USA |
|---|---|---|---|
| 13 | Alabama | 2,450,000,000 | 3.0% |
| NA | Alaska* | NA | NA |
| NA | Arizona* | NA | NA |
| 8 | Arkansas | 3,458,000,000 | 4.2% |
| 3 | California | 6,606,000,000 | 8.0% |
| 24 | Colorado | 921,000,000 | 1.1% |
| 28 | Connecticut | 828,000,000 | 1.0% |
| 36 | Delaware | 257,000,000 | 0.3% |
| 11 | Florida | 2,772,000,000 | 3.4% |
| 6 | Georgia | 5,172,000,000 | 6.3% |
| 39 | Hawaii | 149,000,000 | 0.2% |
| 37 | Idaho | 255,000,000 | 0.3% |
| 26 | Illinois | 876,000,000 | 1.1% |
| 5 | Indiana | 5,838,000,000 | 7.1% |
| 2 | Iowa | 6,754,000,000 | 8.2% |
| 34 | Kansas | 387,000,000 | 0.5% |
| 23 | Kentucky | 922,000,000 | 1.1% |
| 33 | Louisiana | 481,000,000 | 0.6% |
| 17 | Maine | 1,356,000,000 | 1.6% |
| 25 | Maryland | 894,000,000 | 1.1% |
| 40 | Massachusetts | 109,000,000 | 0.1% |
| 16 | Michigan | 1,533,000,000 | 1.9% |
| 9 | Minnesota | 3,138,000,000 | 3.8% |
| 15 | Mississippi | 1,569,000,000 | 1.9% |
| 14 | Missouri | 1,690,000,000 | 2.0% |
| 41 | Montana | 94,000,000 | 0.1% |
| 10 | Nebraska | 2,837,000,000 | 3.4% |
| NA | Nevada* | NA | NA |
| 43 | New Hampshire | 34,000,000 | 0.0% |
| 31 | New Jersey | 547,000,000 | 0.7% |
| NA | New Mexico* | NA | NA |
| 21 | New York | 1,017,000,000 | 1.2% |
| 12 | North Carolina | 2,587,000,000 | 3.1% |
| NA | North Dakota* | NA | NA |
| 1 | Ohio | 8,193,000,000 | 9.9% |
| 22 | Oklahoma | 945,000,000 | 1.1% |
| 29 | Oregon | 774,000,000 | 0.9% |
| 4 | Pennsylvania | 6,135,000,000 | 7.4% |
| 44 | Rhode Island | 15,000,000 | 0.0% |
| 19 | South Carolina | 1,215,000,000 | 1.5% |
| 30 | South Dakota | 592,000,000 | 0.7% |
| 35 | Tennessee | 274,000,000 | 0.3% |
| 7 | Texas | 4,413,000,000 | 5.3% |
| 32 | Utah | 521,000,000 | 0.6% |
| 42 | Vermont | 65,000,000 | 0.1% |
| 27 | Virginia | 845,000,000 | 1.0% |
| 18 | Washington | 1,312,000,000 | 1.6% |
| 38 | West Virginia | 237,000,000 | 0.3% |
| 20 | Wisconsin | 1,031,000,000 | 1.2% |
| 45 | Wyoming | 3,600,000 | 0.0% |

RANK ORDER

| RANK | STATE | EGGS | % of USA |
|---|---|---|---|
| 1 | Ohio | 8,193,000,000 | 9.9% |
| 2 | Iowa | 6,754,000,000 | 8.2% |
| 3 | California | 6,606,000,000 | 8.0% |
| 4 | Pennsylvania | 6,135,000,000 | 7.4% |
| 5 | Indiana | 5,838,000,000 | 7.1% |
| 6 | Georgia | 5,172,000,000 | 6.3% |
| 7 | Texas | 4,413,000,000 | 5.3% |
| 8 | Arkansas | 3,458,000,000 | 4.2% |
| 9 | Minnesota | 3,138,000,000 | 3.8% |
| 10 | Nebraska | 2,837,000,000 | 3.4% |
| 11 | Florida | 2,772,000,000 | 3.4% |
| 12 | North Carolina | 2,587,000,000 | 3.1% |
| 13 | Alabama | 2,450,000,000 | 3.0% |
| 14 | Missouri | 1,690,000,000 | 2.0% |
| 15 | Mississippi | 1,569,000,000 | 1.9% |
| 16 | Michigan | 1,533,000,000 | 1.9% |
| 17 | Maine | 1,356,000,000 | 1.6% |
| 18 | Washington | 1,312,000,000 | 1.6% |
| 19 | South Carolina | 1,215,000,000 | 1.5% |
| 20 | Wisconsin | 1,031,000,000 | 1.2% |
| 21 | New York | 1,017,000,000 | 1.2% |
| 22 | Oklahoma | 945,000,000 | 1.1% |
| 23 | Kentucky | 922,000,000 | 1.1% |
| 24 | Colorado | 921,000,000 | 1.1% |
| 25 | Maryland | 894,000,000 | 1.1% |
| 26 | Illinois | 876,000,000 | 1.1% |
| 27 | Virginia | 845,000,000 | 1.0% |
| 28 | Connecticut | 828,000,000 | 1.0% |
| 29 | Oregon | 774,000,000 | 0.9% |
| 30 | South Dakota | 592,000,000 | 0.7% |
| 31 | New Jersey | 547,000,000 | 0.7% |
| 32 | Utah | 521,000,000 | 0.6% |
| 33 | Louisiana | 481,000,000 | 0.6% |
| 34 | Kansas | 387,000,000 | 0.5% |
| 35 | Tennessee | 274,000,000 | 0.3% |
| 36 | Delaware | 257,000,000 | 0.3% |
| 37 | Idaho | 255,000,000 | 0.3% |
| 38 | West Virginia | 237,000,000 | 0.3% |
| 39 | Hawaii | 149,000,000 | 0.2% |
| 40 | Massachusetts | 109,000,000 | 0.1% |
| 41 | Montana | 94,000,000 | 0.1% |
| 42 | Vermont | 65,000,000 | 0.1% |
| 43 | New Hampshire | 34,000,000 | 0.0% |
| 44 | Rhode Island | 15,000,000 | 0.0% |
| 45 | Wyoming | 3,600,000 | 0.0% |
| NA | Alaska* | NA | NA |
| NA | Arizona* | NA | NA |
| NA | Nevada* | NA | NA |
| NA | New Mexico* | NA | NA |
| NA | North Dakota* | NA | NA |
| | District of Columbia | 0 | 0.0% |

Source: U.S. Department of Agriculture, National Agricultural Statistics Service
   "Poultry - Production and Value 1999 Summary"
   (http://usda.mannlib.cornell.edu/reports/nassr/poultry/pbh-bbp/plva0400.txt)
*These states produced a combined 604 million eggs. They are combined to avoid disclosing individual operations.

# II. CRIME AND LAW ENFORCEMENT

# Crimes in 1999

## National Total = 11,635,149 Crimes*

ALPHA ORDER

| RANK | STATE | CRIMES | % of USA |
|---|---|---|---|
| 22 | Alabama | 192,819 | 1.7% |
| 46 | Alaska | 27,008 | 0.2% |
| 12 | Arizona | 281,735 | 2.4% |
| 34 | Arkansas | 103,131 | 0.9% |
| 1 | California | 1,261,164 | 10.8% |
| 26 | Colorado | 164,813 | 1.4% |
| 31 | Connecticut | 111,236 | 1.0% |
| 41 | Delaware | 36,456 | 0.3% |
| 3 | Florida | 937,718 | 8.1% |
| 8 | Georgia | 400,968 | 3.4% |
| 38 | Hawaii | 57,324 | 0.5% |
| 40 | Idaho | 39,429 | 0.3% |
| 5 | Illinois | 546,561 | 4.7% |
| 19 | Indiana | 223,808 | 1.9% |
| 35 | Iowa | 92,497 | 0.8% |
| 29 | Kansas | 117,803 | 1.0% |
| 30 | Kentucky | 114,003 | 1.0% |
| 16 | Louisiana | 251,252 | 2.2% |
| 42 | Maine | 36,024 | 0.3% |
| 15 | Maryland | 254,420 | 2.2% |
| 21 | Massachusetts | 201,460 | 1.7% |
| 7 | Michigan | 426,596 | 3.7% |
| 24 | Minnesota | 171,802 | 1.5% |
| 28 | Mississippi | 118,231 | 1.0% |
| 17 | Missouri | 250,363 | 2.2% |
| 43 | Montana | 35,937 | 0.3% |
| 37 | Nebraska | 68,444 | 0.6% |
| 36 | Nevada | 84,185 | 0.7% |
| 45 | New Hampshire | 27,406 | 0.2% |
| 13 | New Jersey | 276,873 | 2.4% |
| 33 | New Mexico | 103,740 | 0.9% |
| 4 | New York | 596,743 | 5.1% |
| 9 | North Carolina | 395,971 | 3.4% |
| 50 | North Dakota | 15,172 | 0.1% |
| 6 | Ohio | 449,880 | 3.9% |
| 27 | Oklahoma | 157,286 | 1.4% |
| 25 | Oregon | 165,866 | 1.4% |
| 10 | Pennsylvania | 373,452 | 3.2% |
| 44 | Rhode Island | 35,497 | 0.3% |
| 20 | South Carolina | 206,907 | 1.8% |
| 47 | South Dakota | 19,386 | 0.2% |
| 14 | Tennessee | 257,413 | 2.2% |
| 2 | Texas | 1,008,567 | 8.7% |
| 32 | Utah | 105,999 | 0.9% |
| 48 | Vermont | 16,735 | 0.1% |
| 18 | Virginia | 231,886 | 2.0% |
| 11 | Washington | 302,509 | 2.6% |
| 39 | West Virginia | 49,161 | 0.4% |
| 23 | Wisconsin | 173,062 | 1.5% |
| 49 | Wyoming | 16,583 | 0.1% |

RANK ORDER

| RANK | STATE | CRIMES | % of USA |
|---|---|---|---|
| 1 | California | 1,261,164 | 10.8% |
| 2 | Texas | 1,008,567 | 8.7% |
| 3 | Florida | 937,718 | 8.1% |
| 4 | New York | 596,743 | 5.1% |
| 5 | Illinois | 546,561 | 4.7% |
| 6 | Ohio | 449,880 | 3.9% |
| 7 | Michigan | 426,596 | 3.7% |
| 8 | Georgia | 400,968 | 3.4% |
| 9 | North Carolina | 395,971 | 3.4% |
| 10 | Pennsylvania | 373,452 | 3.2% |
| 11 | Washington | 302,509 | 2.6% |
| 12 | Arizona | 281,735 | 2.4% |
| 13 | New Jersey | 276,873 | 2.4% |
| 14 | Tennessee | 257,413 | 2.2% |
| 15 | Maryland | 254,420 | 2.2% |
| 16 | Louisiana | 251,252 | 2.2% |
| 17 | Missouri | 250,363 | 2.2% |
| 18 | Virginia | 231,886 | 2.0% |
| 19 | Indiana | 223,808 | 1.9% |
| 20 | South Carolina | 206,907 | 1.8% |
| 21 | Massachusetts | 201,460 | 1.7% |
| 22 | Alabama | 192,819 | 1.7% |
| 23 | Wisconsin | 173,062 | 1.5% |
| 24 | Minnesota | 171,802 | 1.5% |
| 25 | Oregon | 165,866 | 1.4% |
| 26 | Colorado | 164,813 | 1.4% |
| 27 | Oklahoma | 157,286 | 1.4% |
| 28 | Mississippi | 118,231 | 1.0% |
| 29 | Kansas | 117,803 | 1.0% |
| 30 | Kentucky | 114,003 | 1.0% |
| 31 | Connecticut | 111,236 | 1.0% |
| 32 | Utah | 105,999 | 0.9% |
| 33 | New Mexico | 103,740 | 0.9% |
| 34 | Arkansas | 103,131 | 0.9% |
| 35 | Iowa | 92,497 | 0.8% |
| 36 | Nevada | 84,185 | 0.7% |
| 37 | Nebraska | 68,444 | 0.6% |
| 38 | Hawaii | 57,324 | 0.5% |
| 39 | West Virginia | 49,161 | 0.4% |
| 40 | Idaho | 39,429 | 0.3% |
| 41 | Delaware | 36,456 | 0.3% |
| 42 | Maine | 36,024 | 0.3% |
| 43 | Montana | 35,937 | 0.3% |
| 44 | Rhode Island | 35,497 | 0.3% |
| 45 | New Hampshire | 27,406 | 0.2% |
| 46 | Alaska | 27,008 | 0.2% |
| 47 | South Dakota | 19,386 | 0.2% |
| 48 | Vermont | 16,735 | 0.1% |
| 49 | Wyoming | 16,583 | 0.1% |
| 50 | North Dakota | 15,172 | 0.1% |
| | District of Columbia | 41,868 | 0.4% |

Source: Federal Bureau of Investigation
   "Crime in the United States 1999" (Uniform Crime Reports, October 15, 2000)
*Includes murder, rape, robbery, aggravated assault, burglary, larceny-theft and motor vehicle theft.

# Percent Change in Number of Crimes: 1998 to 1999

## National Percent Change = 6.8% Decrease*

| ALPHA ORDER | | | | RANK ORDER | | |
|---|---|---|---|---|---|---|
| RANK | STATE | PERCENT CHANGE | | RANK | STATE | PERCENT CHANGE |
| 6 | Alabama | (3.6) | | 1 | Rhode Island | 2.1 |
| 30 | Alaska | (7.9) | | 2 | South Dakota | 0.1 |
| 32 | Arizona | (8.2) | | 3 | Texas | (0.1) |
| 13 | Arkansas | (5.1) | | 4 | North Carolina | (1.4) |
| 46 | California | (11.1) | | 5 | Mississippi | (2.0) |
| 27 | Colorado | (7.5) | | 6 | Alabama | (3.6) |
| 44 | Connecticut | (10.3) | | 7 | Georgia | (4.0) |
| 35 | Delaware | (8.6) | | 8 | New Hampshire | (4.4) |
| 36 | Florida | (8.7) | | 9 | Massachusetts | (4.6) |
| 7 | Georgia | (4.0) | | 9 | Missouri | (4.6) |
| 42 | Hawaii | (9.9) | | 11 | Maine | (4.8) |
| 49 | Idaho | (13.6) | | 12 | Pennsylvania | (4.9) |
| 19 | Illinois | (6.6) | | 13 | Arkansas | (5.1) |
| 38 | Indiana | (9.0) | | 14 | Louisiana | (5.7) |
| 28 | Iowa | (7.7) | | 15 | Tennessee | (5.9) |
| 31 | Kansas | (8.0) | | 16 | Oklahoma | (6.1) |
| 24 | Kentucky | (7.0) | | 17 | Montana | (6.3) |
| 14 | Louisiana | (5.7) | | 18 | Wisconsin | (6.5) |
| 11 | Maine | (4.8) | | 19 | Illinois | (6.6) |
| 28 | Maryland | (7.7) | | 19 | Nebraska | (6.6) |
| 9 | Massachusetts | (4.6) | | 19 | New Jersey | (6.6) |
| 25 | Michigan | (7.2) | | 19 | South Carolina | (6.6) |
| 43 | Minnesota | (10.1) | | 23 | Virginia | (6.7) |
| 5 | Mississippi | (2.0) | | 24 | Kentucky | (7.0) |
| 9 | Missouri | (4.6) | | 25 | Michigan | (7.2) |
| 17 | Montana | (6.3) | | 26 | Ohio | (7.3) |
| 19 | Nebraska | (6.6) | | 27 | Colorado | (7.5) |
| 36 | Nevada | (8.7) | | 28 | Iowa | (7.7) |
| 8 | New Hampshire | (4.4) | | 28 | Maryland | (7.7) |
| 19 | New Jersey | (6.6) | | 30 | Alaska | (7.9) |
| 46 | New Mexico | (11.1) | | 31 | Kansas | (8.0) |
| 34 | New York | (8.5) | | 32 | Arizona | (8.2) |
| 4 | North Carolina | (1.4) | | 33 | Utah | (8.3) |
| 48 | North Dakota | (11.3) | | 34 | New York | (8.5) |
| 26 | Ohio | (7.3) | | 35 | Delaware | (8.6) |
| 16 | Oklahoma | (6.1) | | 36 | Florida | (8.7) |
| 45 | Oregon | (10.5) | | 36 | Nevada | (8.7) |
| 12 | Pennsylvania | (4.9) | | 38 | Indiana | (9.0) |
| 1 | Rhode Island | 2.1 | | 39 | Washington | (9.4) |
| 19 | South Carolina | (6.6) | | 40 | Wyoming | (9.5) |
| 2 | South Dakota | 0.1 | | 41 | Vermont | (9.8) |
| 15 | Tennessee | (5.9) | | 42 | Hawaii | (9.9) |
| 3 | Texas | (0.1) | | 43 | Minnesota | (10.1) |
| 33 | Utah | (8.3) | | 44 | Connecticut | (10.3) |
| 41 | Vermont | (9.8) | | 45 | Oregon | (10.5) |
| 23 | Virginia | (6.7) | | 46 | California | (11.1) |
| 39 | Washington | (9.4) | | 46 | New Mexico | (11.1) |
| NA | West Virginia** | NA | | 48 | North Dakota | (11.3) |
| 18 | Wisconsin | (6.5) | | 49 | Idaho | (13.6) |
| 40 | Wyoming | (9.5) | | NA | West Virginia** | NA |
| | | | | | District of Columbia | (9.4) |

*Source: Federal Bureau of Investigation*
*"Crime in the United States 1999" (Uniform Crime Reports, October 15, 2000)*
*Includes murder, rape, robbery, aggravated assault, burglary, larceny-theft and motor vehicle theft.*
**Not available.*

# Crime Rate in 1999

## National Rate = 4,266.8 Crimes per 100,000 Population*

ALPHA ORDER

| RANK | STATE | RATE |
|---|---|---|
| 21 | Alabama | 4,412.3 |
| 22 | Alaska | 4,363.2 |
| 3 | Arizona | 5,896.5 |
| 28 | Arkansas | 4,042.8 |
| 30 | California | 3,805.0 |
| 27 | Colorado | 4,063.4 |
| 36 | Connecticut | 3,389.3 |
| 14 | Delaware | 4,835.0 |
| 1 | Florida | 6,205.5 |
| 8 | Georgia | 5,148.5 |
| 13 | Hawaii | 4,837.5 |
| 42 | Idaho | 3,149.3 |
| 19 | Illinois | 4,506.6 |
| 31 | Indiana | 3,765.9 |
| 41 | Iowa | 3,224.0 |
| 20 | Kansas | 4,438.7 |
| 44 | Kentucky | 2,878.1 |
| 4 | Louisiana | 5,746.8 |
| 45 | Maine | 2,875.0 |
| 12 | Maryland | 4,919.2 |
| 40 | Massachusetts | 3,262.5 |
| 23 | Michigan | 4,324.8 |
| 32 | Minnesota | 3,597.2 |
| 24 | Mississippi | 4,269.8 |
| 18 | Missouri | 4,578.7 |
| 26 | Montana | 4,069.9 |
| 25 | Nebraska | 4,108.3 |
| 17 | Nevada | 4,653.7 |
| 50 | New Hampshire | 2,281.9 |
| 35 | New Jersey | 3,400.1 |
| 2 | New Mexico | 5,962.1 |
| 39 | New York | 3,279.3 |
| 7 | North Carolina | 5,175.4 |
| 49 | North Dakota | 2,393.1 |
| 29 | Ohio | 3,996.4 |
| 16 | Oklahoma | 4,683.9 |
| 10 | Oregon | 5,002.0 |
| 43 | Pennsylvania | 3,113.7 |
| 33 | Rhode Island | 3,581.9 |
| 5 | South Carolina | 5,324.4 |
| 48 | South Dakota | 2,644.7 |
| 15 | Tennessee | 4,693.9 |
| 9 | Texas | 5,031.8 |
| 11 | Utah | 4,976.5 |
| 46 | Vermont | 2,817.3 |
| 37 | Virginia | 3,373.9 |
| 6 | Washington | 5,255.5 |
| 47 | West Virginia | 2,720.6 |
| 38 | Wisconsin | 3,296.4 |
| 34 | Wyoming | 3,454.8 |

RANK ORDER

| RANK | STATE | RATE |
|---|---|---|
| 1 | Florida | 6,205.5 |
| 2 | New Mexico | 5,962.1 |
| 3 | Arizona | 5,896.5 |
| 4 | Louisiana | 5,746.8 |
| 5 | South Carolina | 5,324.4 |
| 6 | Washington | 5,255.5 |
| 7 | North Carolina | 5,175.4 |
| 8 | Georgia | 5,148.5 |
| 9 | Texas | 5,031.8 |
| 10 | Oregon | 5,002.0 |
| 11 | Utah | 4,976.5 |
| 12 | Maryland | 4,919.2 |
| 13 | Hawaii | 4,837.5 |
| 14 | Delaware | 4,835.0 |
| 15 | Tennessee | 4,693.9 |
| 16 | Oklahoma | 4,683.9 |
| 17 | Nevada | 4,653.7 |
| 18 | Missouri | 4,578.7 |
| 19 | Illinois | 4,506.6 |
| 20 | Kansas | 4,438.7 |
| 21 | Alabama | 4,412.3 |
| 22 | Alaska | 4,363.2 |
| 23 | Michigan | 4,324.8 |
| 24 | Mississippi | 4,269.8 |
| 25 | Nebraska | 4,108.3 |
| 26 | Montana | 4,069.9 |
| 27 | Colorado | 4,063.4 |
| 28 | Arkansas | 4,042.8 |
| 29 | Ohio | 3,996.4 |
| 30 | California | 3,805.0 |
| 31 | Indiana | 3,765.9 |
| 32 | Minnesota | 3,597.2 |
| 33 | Rhode Island | 3,581.9 |
| 34 | Wyoming | 3,454.8 |
| 35 | New Jersey | 3,400.1 |
| 36 | Connecticut | 3,389.3 |
| 37 | Virginia | 3,373.9 |
| 38 | Wisconsin | 3,296.4 |
| 39 | New York | 3,279.3 |
| 40 | Massachusetts | 3,262.5 |
| 41 | Iowa | 3,224.0 |
| 42 | Idaho | 3,149.3 |
| 43 | Pennsylvania | 3,113.7 |
| 44 | Kentucky | 2,878.1 |
| 45 | Maine | 2,875.0 |
| 46 | Vermont | 2,817.3 |
| 47 | West Virginia | 2,720.6 |
| 48 | South Dakota | 2,644.7 |
| 49 | North Dakota | 2,393.1 |
| 50 | New Hampshire | 2,281.9 |
| | District of Columbia | 8,067.1 |

Source: Federal Bureau of Investigation
    "Crime in the United States 1999" (Uniform Crime Reports, October 15, 2000)
*Includes murder, rape, robbery, aggravated assault, burglary, larceny-theft and motor vehicle theft.

# Percent Change in Crime Rate: 1998 to 1999

## National Percent Change = 7.6% Decrease*

ALPHA ORDER

| RANK | STATE | PERCENT CHANGE |
|------|-------|----------------|
| 6 | Alabama | (4.0) |
| 30 | Alaska | (8.7) |
| 40 | Arizona | (10.3) |
| 11 | Arkansas | (5.6) |
| 48 | California | (12.4) |
| 34 | Colorado | (9.4) |
| 42 | Connecticut | (10.5) |
| 37 | Delaware | (9.8) |
| 38 | Florida | (9.9) |
| 13 | Georgia | (5.8) |
| 32 | Hawaii | (9.3) |
| 49 | Idaho | (15.2) |
| 21 | Illinois | (7.2) |
| 36 | Indiana | (9.7) |
| 27 | Iowa | (7.9) |
| 31 | Kansas | (8.9) |
| 22 | Kentucky | (7.6) |
| 13 | Louisiana | (5.8) |
| 10 | Maine | (5.5) |
| 28 | Maryland | (8.3) |
| 8 | Massachusetts | (5.0) |
| 22 | Michigan | (7.6) |
| 44 | Minnesota | (11.1) |
| 4 | Mississippi | (2.6) |
| 9 | Missouri | (5.1) |
| 16 | Montana | (6.6) |
| 17 | Nebraska | (6.7) |
| 47 | Nevada | (11.9) |
| 12 | New Hampshire | (5.7) |
| 19 | New Jersey | (7.0) |
| 45 | New Mexico | (11.3) |
| 29 | New York | (8.6) |
| 5 | North Carolina | (2.8) |
| 43 | North Dakota | (10.7) |
| 22 | Ohio | (7.6) |
| 15 | Oklahoma | (6.4) |
| 46 | Oregon | (11.4) |
| 7 | Pennsylvania | (4.9) |
| 1 | Rhode Island | 1.8 |
| 25 | South Carolina | (7.8) |
| 2 | South Dakota | 0.8 |
| 18 | Tennessee | (6.8) |
| 3 | Texas | (1.6) |
| 35 | Utah | (9.6) |
| 39 | Vermont | (10.2) |
| 25 | Virginia | (7.8) |
| 41 | Washington | (10.4) |
| NA | West Virginia** | NA |
| 19 | Wisconsin | (7.0) |
| 32 | Wyoming | (9.3) |

RANK ORDER

| RANK | STATE | PERCENT CHANGE |
|------|-------|----------------|
| 1 | Rhode Island | 1.8 |
| 2 | South Dakota | 0.8 |
| 3 | Texas | (1.6) |
| 4 | Mississippi | (2.6) |
| 5 | North Carolina | (2.8) |
| 6 | Alabama | (4.0) |
| 7 | Pennsylvania | (4.9) |
| 8 | Massachusetts | (5.0) |
| 9 | Missouri | (5.1) |
| 10 | Maine | (5.5) |
| 11 | Arkansas | (5.6) |
| 12 | New Hampshire | (5.7) |
| 13 | Georgia | (5.8) |
| 13 | Louisiana | (5.8) |
| 15 | Oklahoma | (6.4) |
| 16 | Montana | (6.6) |
| 17 | Nebraska | (6.7) |
| 18 | Tennessee | (6.8) |
| 19 | New Jersey | (7.0) |
| 19 | Wisconsin | (7.0) |
| 21 | Illinois | (7.2) |
| 22 | Kentucky | (7.6) |
| 22 | Michigan | (7.6) |
| 22 | Ohio | (7.6) |
| 25 | South Carolina | (7.8) |
| 25 | Virginia | (7.8) |
| 27 | Iowa | (7.9) |
| 28 | Maryland | (8.3) |
| 29 | New York | (8.6) |
| 30 | Alaska | (8.7) |
| 31 | Kansas | (8.9) |
| 32 | Hawaii | (9.3) |
| 32 | Wyoming | (9.3) |
| 34 | Colorado | (9.4) |
| 35 | Utah | (9.6) |
| 36 | Indiana | (9.7) |
| 37 | Delaware | (9.8) |
| 38 | Florida | (9.9) |
| 39 | Vermont | (10.2) |
| 40 | Arizona | (10.3) |
| 41 | Washington | (10.4) |
| 42 | Connecticut | (10.5) |
| 43 | North Dakota | (10.7) |
| 44 | Minnesota | (11.1) |
| 45 | New Mexico | (11.3) |
| 46 | Oregon | (11.4) |
| 47 | Nevada | (11.9) |
| 48 | California | (12.4) |
| 49 | Idaho | (15.2) |
| NA | West Virginia** | NA |
| | District of Columbia | (8.7) |

Source: Federal Bureau of Investigation
 "Crime in the United States 1999" (Uniform Crime Reports, October 15, 2000)
*Includes murder, rape, robbery, aggravated assault, burglary, larceny-theft and motor vehicle theft.
**Not available.

# Violent Crimes in 1999

## National Total = 1,430,693 Violent Crimes*

ALPHA ORDER

RANK ORDER

| RANK | STATE | CRIMES | % of USA | | RANK | STATE | CRIMES | % of USA |
|---|---|---|---|---|---|---|---|---|
| 22 | Alabama | 21,421 | 1.5% | | 1 | California | 207,879 | 14.5% |
| 40 | Alaska | 3,909 | 0.3% | | 2 | Florida | 129,044 | 9.0% |
| 18 | Arizona | 26,334 | 1.8% | | 3 | Texas | 112,306 | 7.8% |
| 31 | Arkansas | 10,848 | 0.8% | | 4 | New York | 107,147 | 7.5% |
| 1 | California | 207,879 | 14.5% | | 5 | Illinois | 88,838 | 6.2% |
| 25 | Colorado | 13,811 | 1.0% | | 6 | Michigan | 56,709 | 4.0% |
| 30 | Connecticut | 11,342 | 0.8% | | 7 | Pennsylvania | 50,431 | 3.5% |
| 39 | Delaware | 5,534 | 0.4% | | 8 | Georgia | 41,585 | 2.9% |
| 2 | Florida | 129,044 | 9.0% | | 9 | North Carolina | 41,474 | 2.9% |
| 8 | Georgia | 41,585 | 2.9% | | 10 | Maryland | 38,447 | 2.7% |
| 43 | Hawaii | 2,785 | 0.2% | | 11 | Tennessee | 38,111 | 2.7% |
| 41 | Idaho | 3,066 | 0.2% | | 12 | Ohio | 35,616 | 2.5% |
| 5 | Illinois | 88,838 | 6.2% | | 13 | Massachusetts | 34,023 | 2.4% |
| 19 | Indiana | 22,261 | 1.6% | | 14 | New Jersey | 33,540 | 2.3% |
| 35 | Iowa | 8,034 | 0.6% | | 15 | South Carolina | 32,920 | 2.3% |
| 33 | Kansas | 10,159 | 0.7% | | 16 | Louisiana | 32,033 | 2.2% |
| 29 | Kentucky | 11,908 | 0.8% | | 17 | Missouri | 27,353 | 1.9% |
| 16 | Louisiana | 32,033 | 2.2% | | 18 | Arizona | 26,334 | 1.8% |
| 45 | Maine | 1,406 | 0.1% | | 19 | Indiana | 22,261 | 1.6% |
| 10 | Maryland | 38,447 | 2.7% | | 20 | Washington | 21,716 | 1.5% |
| 13 | Massachusetts | 34,023 | 2.4% | | 21 | Virginia | 21,626 | 1.5% |
| 6 | Michigan | 56,709 | 4.0% | | 22 | Alabama | 21,421 | 1.5% |
| 26 | Minnesota | 13,085 | 0.9% | | 23 | Oklahoma | 17,066 | 1.2% |
| 34 | Mississippi | 9,671 | 0.7% | | 24 | New Mexico | 14,520 | 1.0% |
| 17 | Missouri | 27,353 | 1.9% | | 25 | Colorado | 13,811 | 1.0% |
| 44 | Montana | 1,823 | 0.1% | | 26 | Minnesota | 13,085 | 0.9% |
| 36 | Nebraska | 7,167 | 0.5% | | 27 | Wisconsin | 12,908 | 0.9% |
| 32 | Nevada | 10,311 | 0.7% | | 28 | Oregon | 12,432 | 0.9% |
| 47 | New Hampshire | 1,159 | 0.1% | | 29 | Kentucky | 11,908 | 0.8% |
| 14 | New Jersey | 33,540 | 2.3% | | 30 | Connecticut | 11,342 | 0.8% |
| 24 | New Mexico | 14,520 | 1.0% | | 31 | Arkansas | 10,848 | 0.8% |
| 4 | New York | 107,147 | 7.5% | | 32 | Nevada | 10,311 | 0.7% |
| 9 | North Carolina | 41,474 | 2.9% | | 33 | Kansas | 10,159 | 0.7% |
| 50 | North Dakota | 424 | 0.0% | | 34 | Mississippi | 9,671 | 0.7% |
| 12 | Ohio | 35,616 | 2.5% | | 35 | Iowa | 8,034 | 0.6% |
| 23 | Oklahoma | 17,066 | 1.2% | | 36 | Nebraska | 7,167 | 0.5% |
| 28 | Oregon | 12,432 | 0.9% | | 37 | West Virginia | 6,336 | 0.4% |
| 7 | Pennsylvania | 50,431 | 3.5% | | 38 | Utah | 5,869 | 0.4% |
| 42 | Rhode Island | 2,840 | 0.2% | | 39 | Delaware | 5,534 | 0.4% |
| 15 | South Carolina | 32,920 | 2.3% | | 40 | Alaska | 3,909 | 0.3% |
| 46 | South Dakota | 1,227 | 0.1% | | 41 | Idaho | 3,066 | 0.2% |
| 11 | Tennessee | 38,111 | 2.7% | | 42 | Rhode Island | 2,840 | 0.2% |
| 3 | Texas | 112,306 | 7.8% | | 43 | Hawaii | 2,785 | 0.2% |
| 38 | Utah | 5,869 | 0.4% | | 44 | Montana | 1,823 | 0.1% |
| 49 | Vermont | 676 | 0.0% | | 45 | Maine | 1,406 | 0.1% |
| 21 | Virginia | 21,626 | 1.5% | | 46 | South Dakota | 1,227 | 0.1% |
| 20 | Washington | 21,716 | 1.5% | | 47 | New Hampshire | 1,159 | 0.1% |
| 37 | West Virginia | 6,336 | 0.4% | | 48 | Wyoming | 1,115 | 0.1% |
| 27 | Wisconsin | 12,908 | 0.9% | | 49 | Vermont | 676 | 0.0% |
| 48 | Wyoming | 1,115 | 0.1% | | 50 | North Dakota | 424 | 0.0% |
| | | | | | | District of Columbia | 8,448 | 0.6% |

Source: Federal Bureau of Investigation
 "Crime in the United States 1999" (Uniform Crime Reports, October 15, 2000)
*Violent crimes are offenses of murder, forcible rape, robbery and aggravated assault.

# Percent Change in Number of Violent Crimes: 1998 to 1999

## National Percent Change = 6.7% Decrease*

ALPHA ORDER

RANK ORDER

| RANK | STATE | PERCENT CHANGE | | RANK | STATE | PERCENT CHANGE |
|------|-------|----------------|---|------|-------|----------------|
| 12 | Alabama | (3.9) | | 1 | South Dakota | 7.7 |
| 11 | Alaska | (2.6) | | 2 | Vermont | 7.6 |
| 9 | Arizona | (2.4) | | 3 | Montana | 1.4 |
| 46 | Arkansas | (12.8) | | 4 | Texas | 0.7 |
| 35 | California | (9.6) | | 5 | Pennsylvania | (0.1) |
| 30 | Colorado | (8.0) | | 6 | Wisconsin | (0.8) |
| 17 | Connecticut | (5.4) | | 7 | Tennessee | (1.9) |
| 9 | Delaware | (2.4) | | 8 | Virginia | (2.2) |
| 27 | Florida | (7.8) | | 9 | Arizona | (2.4) |
| 14 | Georgia | (5.0) | | 9 | Delaware | (2.4) |
| 18 | Hawaii | (5.5) | | 11 | Alaska | (2.6) |
| 43 | Idaho | (11.6) | | 12 | Alabama | (3.9) |
| 32 | Illinois | (8.7) | | 13 | Nebraska | (4.5) |
| 45 | Indiana | (12.4) | | 14 | Georgia | (5.0) |
| 37 | Iowa | (9.9) | | 14 | South Carolina | (5.0) |
| 25 | Kansas | (7.4) | | 16 | North Carolina | (5.1) |
| 27 | Kentucky | (7.8) | | 17 | Connecticut | (5.4) |
| 20 | Louisiana | (5.9) | | 18 | Hawaii | (5.5) |
| 38 | Maine | (10.2) | | 18 | Oklahoma | (5.5) |
| 21 | Maryland | (6.0) | | 20 | Louisiana | (5.9) |
| 40 | Massachusetts | (10.9) | | 21 | Maryland | (6.0) |
| 24 | Michigan | (7.0) | | 22 | New Jersey | (6.1) |
| 39 | Minnesota | (10.7) | | 23 | Wyoming | (6.4) |
| 48 | Mississippi | (14.4) | | 24 | Michigan | (7.0) |
| 34 | Missouri | (9.5) | | 25 | Kansas | (7.4) |
| 3 | Montana | 1.4 | | 26 | New York | (7.6) |
| 13 | Nebraska | (4.5) | | 27 | Florida | (7.8) |
| 31 | Nevada | (8.3) | | 27 | Kentucky | (7.8) |
| 32 | New Hampshire | (8.7) | | 29 | Rhode Island | (7.9) |
| 22 | New Jersey | (6.1) | | 30 | Colorado | (8.0) |
| 47 | New Mexico | (13.1) | | 31 | Nevada | (8.3) |
| 26 | New York | (7.6) | | 32 | Illinois | (8.7) |
| 16 | North Carolina | (5.1) | | 32 | New Hampshire | (8.7) |
| 49 | North Dakota | (25.6) | | 34 | Missouri | (9.5) |
| 44 | Ohio | (12.3) | | 35 | California | (9.6) |
| 18 | Oklahoma | (5.5) | | 36 | Oregon | (9.8) |
| 36 | Oregon | (9.8) | | 37 | Iowa | (9.9) |
| 5 | Pennsylvania | (0.1) | | 38 | Maine | (10.2) |
| 29 | Rhode Island | (7.9) | | 39 | Minnesota | (10.7) |
| 14 | South Carolina | (5.0) | | 40 | Massachusetts | (10.9) |
| 1 | South Dakota | 7.7 | | 40 | Washington | (10.9) |
| 7 | Tennessee | (1.9) | | 42 | Utah | (11.1) |
| 4 | Texas | 0.7 | | 43 | Idaho | (11.6) |
| 42 | Utah | (11.1) | | 44 | Ohio | (12.3) |
| 2 | Vermont | 7.6 | | 45 | Indiana | (12.4) |
| 8 | Virginia | (2.2) | | 46 | Arkansas | (12.8) |
| 40 | Washington | (10.9) | | 47 | New Mexico | (13.1) |
| NA | West Virginia** | NA | | 48 | Mississippi | (14.4) |
| 6 | Wisconsin | (0.8) | | 49 | North Dakota | (25.6) |
| 23 | Wyoming | (6.4) | | NA | West Virginia** | NA |
| | | | | | District of Columbia | (6.0) |

Source: Federal Bureau of Investigation
    "Crime in the United States 1999" (Uniform Crime Reports, October 15, 2000)
*Violent crimes are offenses of murder, forcible rape, robbery and aggravated assault.
**Not available.

# Violent Crime Rate in 1999

## National Rate = 524.7 Violent Crimes per 100,000 Population*

ALPHA ORDER

| RANK | STATE | RATE |
|---|---|---|
| 21 | Alabama | 490.2 |
| 9 | Alaska | 631.5 |
| 15 | Arizona | 551.2 |
| 23 | Arkansas | 425.2 |
| 10 | California | 627.2 |
| 33 | Colorado | 340.5 |
| 32 | Connecticut | 345.6 |
| 5 | Delaware | 734.0 |
| 1 | Florida | 854.0 |
| 18 | Georgia | 534.0 |
| 43 | Hawaii | 235.0 |
| 42 | Idaho | 244.9 |
| 7 | Illinois | 732.5 |
| 29 | Indiana | 374.6 |
| 38 | Iowa | 280.0 |
| 26 | Kansas | 382.8 |
| 36 | Kentucky | 300.6 |
| 6 | Louisiana | 732.7 |
| 48 | Maine | 112.2 |
| 4 | Maryland | 743.4 |
| 16 | Massachusetts | 551.0 |
| 12 | Michigan | 574.9 |
| 40 | Minnesota | 274.0 |
| 31 | Mississippi | 349.3 |
| 20 | Missouri | 500.2 |
| 45 | Montana | 206.5 |
| 22 | Nebraska | 430.2 |
| 13 | Nevada | 570.0 |
| 49 | New Hampshire | 96.5 |
| 25 | New Jersey | 411.9 |
| 3 | New Mexico | 834.5 |
| 11 | New York | 588.8 |
| 17 | North Carolina | 542.1 |
| 50 | North Dakota | 66.9 |
| 34 | Ohio | 316.4 |
| 19 | Oklahoma | 508.2 |
| 28 | Oregon | 374.9 |
| 24 | Pennsylvania | 420.5 |
| 37 | Rhode Island | 286.6 |
| 2 | South Carolina | 847.1 |
| 46 | South Dakota | 167.4 |
| 8 | Tennessee | 694.9 |
| 14 | Texas | 560.3 |
| 39 | Utah | 275.5 |
| 47 | Vermont | 113.8 |
| 35 | Virginia | 314.7 |
| 27 | Washington | 377.3 |
| 30 | West Virginia | 350.6 |
| 41 | Wisconsin | 245.9 |
| 44 | Wyoming | 232.3 |

RANK ORDER

| RANK | STATE | RATE |
|---|---|---|
| 1 | Florida | 854.0 |
| 2 | South Carolina | 847.1 |
| 3 | New Mexico | 834.5 |
| 4 | Maryland | 743.4 |
| 5 | Delaware | 734.0 |
| 6 | Louisiana | 732.7 |
| 7 | Illinois | 732.5 |
| 8 | Tennessee | 694.9 |
| 9 | Alaska | 631.5 |
| 10 | California | 627.2 |
| 11 | New York | 588.8 |
| 12 | Michigan | 574.9 |
| 13 | Nevada | 570.0 |
| 14 | Texas | 560.3 |
| 15 | Arizona | 551.2 |
| 16 | Massachusetts | 551.0 |
| 17 | North Carolina | 542.1 |
| 18 | Georgia | 534.0 |
| 19 | Oklahoma | 508.2 |
| 20 | Missouri | 500.2 |
| 21 | Alabama | 490.2 |
| 22 | Nebraska | 430.2 |
| 23 | Arkansas | 425.2 |
| 24 | Pennsylvania | 420.5 |
| 25 | New Jersey | 411.9 |
| 26 | Kansas | 382.8 |
| 27 | Washington | 377.3 |
| 28 | Oregon | 374.9 |
| 29 | Indiana | 374.6 |
| 30 | West Virginia | 350.6 |
| 31 | Mississippi | 349.3 |
| 32 | Connecticut | 345.6 |
| 33 | Colorado | 340.5 |
| 34 | Ohio | 316.4 |
| 35 | Virginia | 314.7 |
| 36 | Kentucky | 300.6 |
| 37 | Rhode Island | 286.6 |
| 38 | Iowa | 280.0 |
| 39 | Utah | 275.5 |
| 40 | Minnesota | 274.0 |
| 41 | Wisconsin | 245.9 |
| 42 | Idaho | 244.9 |
| 43 | Hawaii | 235.0 |
| 44 | Wyoming | 232.3 |
| 45 | Montana | 206.5 |
| 46 | South Dakota | 167.4 |
| 47 | Vermont | 113.8 |
| 48 | Maine | 112.2 |
| 49 | New Hampshire | 96.5 |
| 50 | North Dakota | 66.9 |
| | District of Columbia | 1,627.7 |

Source: Federal Bureau of Investigation
"Crime in the United States 1999" (Uniform Crime Reports, October 15, 2000)
*Violent crimes are offenses of murder, forcible rape, robbery and aggravated assault.
**Not available.

# Percent Change in Violent Crime Rate: 1998 to 1999

## National Percent Change = 7.5% Decrease*

| ALPHA ORDER | | | | RANK ORDER | | |
|---|---|---|---|---|---|---|
| RANK | STATE | PERCENT CHANGE | | RANK | STATE | PERCENT CHANGE |
| 11 | Alabama | (4.3) | | 1 | South Dakota | 8.5 |
| 8 | Alaska | (3.4) | | 2 | Vermont | 7.1 |
| 12 | Arizona | (4.6) | | 3 | Montana | 1.1 |
| 47 | Arkansas | (13.3) | | 4 | Pennsylvania | 0.0 |
| 36 | California | (10.9) | | 5 | Texas | (0.8) |
| 31 | Colorado | (9.9) | | 6 | Wisconsin | (1.3) |
| 15 | Connecticut | (5.7) | | 7 | Tennessee | (2.8) |
| 10 | Delaware | (3.7) | | 8 | Alaska | (3.4) |
| 29 | Florida | (9.0) | | 8 | Virginia | (3.4) |
| 23 | Georgia | (6.8) | | 10 | Delaware | (3.7) |
| 14 | Hawaii | (4.8) | | 11 | Alabama | (4.3) |
| 45 | Idaho | (13.2) | | 12 | Arizona | (4.6) |
| 30 | Illinois | (9.3) | | 13 | Nebraska | (4.7) |
| 44 | Indiana | (13.1) | | 14 | Hawaii | (4.8) |
| 34 | Iowa | (10.1) | | 15 | Connecticut | (5.7) |
| 27 | Kansas | (8.3) | | 16 | Oklahoma | (5.8) |
| 27 | Kentucky | (8.3) | | 17 | Louisiana | (6.0) |
| 17 | Louisiana | (6.0) | | 18 | South Carolina | (6.2) |
| 36 | Maine | (10.9) | | 18 | Wyoming | (6.2) |
| 22 | Maryland | (6.7) | | 20 | New Jersey | (6.4) |
| 38 | Massachusetts | (11.3) | | 20 | North Carolina | (6.4) |
| 24 | Michigan | (7.4) | | 22 | Maryland | (6.7) |
| 40 | Minnesota | (11.7) | | 23 | Georgia | (6.8) |
| 48 | Mississippi | (15.0) | | 24 | Michigan | (7.4) |
| 32 | Missouri | (10.0) | | 25 | New York | (7.7) |
| 3 | Montana | 1.1 | | 26 | Rhode Island | (8.2) |
| 13 | Nebraska | (4.7) | | 27 | Kansas | (8.3) |
| 39 | Nevada | (11.4) | | 27 | Kentucky | (8.3) |
| 32 | New Hampshire | (10.0) | | 29 | Florida | (9.0) |
| 20 | New Jersey | (6.4) | | 30 | Illinois | (9.3) |
| 45 | New Mexico | (13.2) | | 31 | Colorado | (9.9) |
| 25 | New York | (7.7) | | 32 | Missouri | (10.0) |
| 20 | North Carolina | (6.4) | | 32 | New Hampshire | (10.0) |
| 49 | North Dakota | (25.1) | | 34 | Iowa | (10.1) |
| 43 | Ohio | (12.7) | | 35 | Oregon | (10.7) |
| 16 | Oklahoma | (5.8) | | 36 | California | (10.9) |
| 35 | Oregon | (10.7) | | 36 | Maine | (10.9) |
| 4 | Pennsylvania | 0.0 | | 38 | Massachusetts | (11.3) |
| 26 | Rhode Island | (8.2) | | 39 | Nevada | (11.4) |
| 18 | South Carolina | (6.2) | | 40 | Minnesota | (11.7) |
| 1 | South Dakota | 8.5 | | 41 | Washington | (12.0) |
| 7 | Tennessee | (2.8) | | 42 | Utah | (12.3) |
| 5 | Texas | (0.8) | | 43 | Ohio | (12.7) |
| 42 | Utah | (12.3) | | 44 | Indiana | (13.1) |
| 2 | Vermont | 7.1 | | 45 | Idaho | (13.2) |
| 8 | Virginia | (3.4) | | 45 | New Mexico | (13.2) |
| 41 | Washington | (12.0) | | 47 | Arkansas | (13.3) |
| NA | West Virginia** | NA | | 48 | Mississippi | (15.0) |
| 6 | Wisconsin | (1.3) | | 49 | North Dakota | (25.1) |
| 18 | Wyoming | (6.2) | | NA | West Virginia** | NA |
| | | | | | District of Columbia | (5.3) |

Source: Federal Bureau of Investigation
      "Crime in the United States 1999" (Uniform Crime Reports, October 15, 2000)
*Violent crimes are offenses of murder, forcible rape, robbery and aggravated assault.
**Not available.

# Murders in 1999

## National Total = 15,533 Murders*

<table>
<tr><td colspan="4">ALPHA ORDER</td><td colspan="4">RANK ORDER</td></tr>
<tr><td>RANK</td><td>STATE</td><td>MURDERS</td><td>% of USA</td><td>RANK</td><td>STATE</td><td>MURDERS</td><td>% of USA</td></tr>
<tr><td>18</td><td>Alabama</td><td>345</td><td>2.2%</td><td>1</td><td>California</td><td>2,005</td><td>12.9%</td></tr>
<tr><td>37</td><td>Alaska</td><td>53</td><td>0.3%</td><td>2</td><td>Texas</td><td>1,217</td><td>7.8%</td></tr>
<tr><td>16</td><td>Arizona</td><td>384</td><td>2.5%</td><td>3</td><td>Illinois</td><td>937</td><td>6.0%</td></tr>
<tr><td>30</td><td>Arkansas</td><td>143</td><td>0.9%</td><td>4</td><td>New York</td><td>903</td><td>5.8%</td></tr>
<tr><td>1</td><td>California</td><td>2,005</td><td>12.9%</td><td>5</td><td>Florida</td><td>859</td><td>5.5%</td></tr>
<tr><td>24</td><td>Colorado</td><td>185</td><td>1.2%</td><td>6</td><td>Michigan</td><td>695</td><td>4.5%</td></tr>
<tr><td>33</td><td>Connecticut</td><td>107</td><td>0.7%</td><td>7</td><td>Pennsylvania</td><td>592</td><td>3.8%</td></tr>
<tr><td>44</td><td>Delaware</td><td>24</td><td>0.2%</td><td>8</td><td>Georgia</td><td>583</td><td>3.8%</td></tr>
<tr><td>5</td><td>Florida</td><td>859</td><td>5.5%</td><td>9</td><td>North Carolina</td><td>552</td><td>3.6%</td></tr>
<tr><td>8</td><td>Georgia</td><td>583</td><td>3.8%</td><td>10</td><td>Louisiana</td><td>468</td><td>3.0%</td></tr>
<tr><td>38</td><td>Hawaii</td><td>44</td><td>0.3%</td><td>11</td><td>Maryland</td><td>465</td><td>3.0%</td></tr>
<tr><td>43</td><td>Idaho</td><td>25</td><td>0.2%</td><td>12</td><td>Ohio</td><td>397</td><td>2.6%</td></tr>
<tr><td>3</td><td>Illinois</td><td>937</td><td>6.0%</td><td>13</td><td>Virginia</td><td>392</td><td>2.5%</td></tr>
<tr><td>14</td><td>Indiana</td><td>391</td><td>2.5%</td><td>14</td><td>Indiana</td><td>391</td><td>2.5%</td></tr>
<tr><td>40</td><td>Iowa</td><td>43</td><td>0.3%</td><td>14</td><td>Tennessee</td><td>391</td><td>2.5%</td></tr>
<tr><td>29</td><td>Kansas</td><td>160</td><td>1.0%</td><td>16</td><td>Arizona</td><td>384</td><td>2.5%</td></tr>
<tr><td>23</td><td>Kentucky</td><td>212</td><td>1.4%</td><td>17</td><td>Missouri</td><td>359</td><td>2.3%</td></tr>
<tr><td>10</td><td>Louisiana</td><td>468</td><td>3.0%</td><td>18</td><td>Alabama</td><td>345</td><td>2.2%</td></tr>
<tr><td>42</td><td>Maine</td><td>27</td><td>0.2%</td><td>19</td><td>New Jersey</td><td>287</td><td>1.8%</td></tr>
<tr><td>11</td><td>Maryland</td><td>465</td><td>3.0%</td><td>20</td><td>South Carolina</td><td>258</td><td>1.7%</td></tr>
<tr><td>32</td><td>Massachusetts</td><td>122</td><td>0.8%</td><td>21</td><td>Oklahoma</td><td>231</td><td>1.5%</td></tr>
<tr><td>6</td><td>Michigan</td><td>695</td><td>4.5%</td><td>22</td><td>Mississippi</td><td>213</td><td>1.4%</td></tr>
<tr><td>31</td><td>Minnesota</td><td>134</td><td>0.9%</td><td>23</td><td>Kentucky</td><td>212</td><td>1.4%</td></tr>
<tr><td>22</td><td>Mississippi</td><td>213</td><td>1.4%</td><td>24</td><td>Colorado</td><td>185</td><td>1.2%</td></tr>
<tr><td>17</td><td>Missouri</td><td>359</td><td>2.3%</td><td>25</td><td>Wisconsin</td><td>179</td><td>1.2%</td></tr>
<tr><td>45</td><td>Montana</td><td>23</td><td>0.1%</td><td>26</td><td>Washington</td><td>171</td><td>1.1%</td></tr>
<tr><td>36</td><td>Nebraska</td><td>60</td><td>0.4%</td><td>27</td><td>New Mexico</td><td>170</td><td>1.1%</td></tr>
<tr><td>28</td><td>Nevada</td><td>165</td><td>1.1%</td><td>28</td><td>Nevada</td><td>165</td><td>1.1%</td></tr>
<tr><td>46</td><td>New Hampshire</td><td>18</td><td>0.1%</td><td>29</td><td>Kansas</td><td>160</td><td>1.0%</td></tr>
<tr><td>19</td><td>New Jersey</td><td>287</td><td>1.8%</td><td>30</td><td>Arkansas</td><td>143</td><td>0.9%</td></tr>
<tr><td>27</td><td>New Mexico</td><td>170</td><td>1.1%</td><td>31</td><td>Minnesota</td><td>134</td><td>0.9%</td></tr>
<tr><td>4</td><td>New York</td><td>903</td><td>5.8%</td><td>32</td><td>Massachusetts</td><td>122</td><td>0.8%</td></tr>
<tr><td>9</td><td>North Carolina</td><td>552</td><td>3.6%</td><td>33</td><td>Connecticut</td><td>107</td><td>0.7%</td></tr>
<tr><td>50</td><td>North Dakota</td><td>10</td><td>0.1%</td><td>34</td><td>Oregon</td><td>88</td><td>0.6%</td></tr>
<tr><td>12</td><td>Ohio</td><td>397</td><td>2.6%</td><td>35</td><td>West Virginia</td><td>79</td><td>0.5%</td></tr>
<tr><td>21</td><td>Oklahoma</td><td>231</td><td>1.5%</td><td>36</td><td>Nebraska</td><td>60</td><td>0.4%</td></tr>
<tr><td>34</td><td>Oregon</td><td>88</td><td>0.6%</td><td>37</td><td>Alaska</td><td>53</td><td>0.3%</td></tr>
<tr><td>7</td><td>Pennsylvania</td><td>592</td><td>3.8%</td><td>38</td><td>Hawaii</td><td>44</td><td>0.3%</td></tr>
<tr><td>41</td><td>Rhode Island</td><td>36</td><td>0.2%</td><td>38</td><td>Utah</td><td>44</td><td>0.3%</td></tr>
<tr><td>20</td><td>South Carolina</td><td>258</td><td>1.7%</td><td>40</td><td>Iowa</td><td>43</td><td>0.3%</td></tr>
<tr><td>46</td><td>South Dakota</td><td>18</td><td>0.1%</td><td>41</td><td>Rhode Island</td><td>36</td><td>0.2%</td></tr>
<tr><td>14</td><td>Tennessee</td><td>391</td><td>2.5%</td><td>42</td><td>Maine</td><td>27</td><td>0.2%</td></tr>
<tr><td>2</td><td>Texas</td><td>1,217</td><td>7.8%</td><td>43</td><td>Idaho</td><td>25</td><td>0.2%</td></tr>
<tr><td>38</td><td>Utah</td><td>44</td><td>0.3%</td><td>44</td><td>Delaware</td><td>24</td><td>0.2%</td></tr>
<tr><td>48</td><td>Vermont</td><td>17</td><td>0.1%</td><td>45</td><td>Montana</td><td>23</td><td>0.1%</td></tr>
<tr><td>13</td><td>Virginia</td><td>392</td><td>2.5%</td><td>46</td><td>New Hampshire</td><td>18</td><td>0.1%</td></tr>
<tr><td>26</td><td>Washington</td><td>171</td><td>1.1%</td><td>46</td><td>South Dakota</td><td>18</td><td>0.1%</td></tr>
<tr><td>35</td><td>West Virginia</td><td>79</td><td>0.5%</td><td>48</td><td>Vermont</td><td>17</td><td>0.1%</td></tr>
<tr><td>25</td><td>Wisconsin</td><td>179</td><td>1.2%</td><td>49</td><td>Wyoming</td><td>11</td><td>0.1%</td></tr>
<tr><td>49</td><td>Wyoming</td><td>11</td><td>0.1%</td><td>50</td><td>North Dakota</td><td>10</td><td>0.1%</td></tr>
<tr><td></td><td></td><td></td><td></td><td></td><td>District of Columbia</td><td>241</td><td>1.6%</td></tr>
</table>

Source: Federal Bureau of Investigation
    "Crime in the United States 1999" (Uniform Crime Reports, October 15, 2000)
*Includes nonnegligent manslaughter.

# Percent Change in Number of Murders: 1998 to 1999

## National Percent Change = 8.5% Decrease*

ALPHA ORDER

| RANK | STATE | PERCENT CHANGE |
|---|---|---|
| 18 | Alabama | (2.5) |
| 6 | Alaska | 29.3 |
| 13 | Arizona | 2.1 |
| 44 | Arkansas | (28.9) |
| 27 | California | (7.6) |
| 14 | Colorado | 1.1 |
| 42 | Connecticut | (20.7) |
| 9 | Delaware | 14.3 |
| 35 | Florida | (11.2) |
| 21 | Georgia | (5.7) |
| 1 | Hawaii | 83.3 |
| 46 | Idaho | (30.6) |
| 24 | Illinois | (7.0) |
| 37 | Indiana | (13.9) |
| 41 | Iowa | (20.4) |
| 26 | Kansas | (7.5) |
| 33 | Kentucky | (10.5) |
| 40 | Louisiana | (16.4) |
| 12 | Maine | 3.8 |
| 28 | Maryland | (9.4) |
| 16 | Massachusetts | (1.6) |
| 20 | Michigan | (3.6) |
| 11 | Minnesota | 10.7 |
| 48 | Mississippi | (32.4) |
| 31 | Missouri | (10.0) |
| 7 | Montana | 27.8 |
| 8 | Nebraska | 17.6 |
| 19 | Nevada | (2.9) |
| 15 | New Hampshire | 0.0 |
| 36 | New Jersey | (11.7) |
| 33 | New Mexico | (10.5) |
| 17 | New York | (2.3) |
| 30 | North Carolina | (9.8) |
| 4 | North Dakota | 42.9 |
| 32 | Ohio | (10.4) |
| 10 | Oklahoma | 13.2 |
| 45 | Oregon | (30.2) |
| 23 | Pennsylvania | (6.5) |
| 3 | Rhode Island | 50.0 |
| 39 | South Carolina | (15.7) |
| 2 | South Dakota | 80.0 |
| 38 | Tennessee | (15.0) |
| 29 | Texas | (9.6) |
| 47 | Utah | (32.3) |
| 5 | Vermont | 30.8 |
| 25 | Virginia | (7.1) |
| 43 | Washington | (23.7) |
| NA | West Virginia** | NA |
| 22 | Wisconsin | (5.8) |
| 49 | Wyoming | (52.2) |

RANK ORDER

| RANK | STATE | PERCENT CHANGE |
|---|---|---|
| 1 | Hawaii | 83.3 |
| 2 | South Dakota | 80.0 |
| 3 | Rhode Island | 50.0 |
| 4 | North Dakota | 42.9 |
| 5 | Vermont | 30.8 |
| 6 | Alaska | 29.3 |
| 7 | Montana | 27.8 |
| 8 | Nebraska | 17.6 |
| 9 | Delaware | 14.3 |
| 10 | Oklahoma | 13.2 |
| 11 | Minnesota | 10.7 |
| 12 | Maine | 3.8 |
| 13 | Arizona | 2.1 |
| 14 | Colorado | 1.1 |
| 15 | New Hampshire | 0.0 |
| 16 | Massachusetts | (1.6) |
| 17 | New York | (2.3) |
| 18 | Alabama | (2.5) |
| 19 | Nevada | (2.9) |
| 20 | Michigan | (3.6) |
| 21 | Georgia | (5.7) |
| 22 | Wisconsin | (5.8) |
| 23 | Pennsylvania | (6.5) |
| 24 | Illinois | (7.0) |
| 25 | Virginia | (7.1) |
| 26 | Kansas | (7.5) |
| 27 | California | (7.6) |
| 28 | Maryland | (9.4) |
| 29 | Texas | (9.6) |
| 30 | North Carolina | (9.8) |
| 31 | Missouri | (10.0) |
| 32 | Ohio | (10.4) |
| 33 | Kentucky | (10.5) |
| 33 | New Mexico | (10.5) |
| 35 | Florida | (11.2) |
| 36 | New Jersey | (11.7) |
| 37 | Indiana | (13.9) |
| 38 | Tennessee | (15.0) |
| 39 | South Carolina | (15.7) |
| 40 | Louisiana | (16.4) |
| 41 | Iowa | (20.4) |
| 42 | Connecticut | (20.7) |
| 43 | Washington | (23.7) |
| 44 | Arkansas | (28.9) |
| 45 | Oregon | (30.2) |
| 46 | Idaho | (30.6) |
| 47 | Utah | (32.3) |
| 48 | Mississippi | (32.4) |
| 49 | Wyoming | (52.2) |
| NA | West Virginia** | NA |
| | District of Columbia | (7.3) |

Source: Federal Bureau of Investigation
   "Crime in the United States 1999" (Uniform Crime Reports, October 15, 2000)
*Includes nonnegligent manslaughter.
**Not available.

# Murder Rate in 1999

## National Rate = 5.7 Murders per 100,000 Population*

ALPHA ORDER

| RANK | STATE | RATE |
|------|-------|------|
| 7 | Alabama | 7.9 |
| 5 | Alaska | 8.6 |
| 6 | Arizona | 8.0 |
| 23 | Arkansas | 5.6 |
| 19 | California | 6.0 |
| 27 | Colorado | 4.6 |
| 35 | Connecticut | 3.3 |
| 36 | Delaware | 3.2 |
| 21 | Florida | 5.7 |
| 10 | Georgia | 7.5 |
| 29 | Hawaii | 3.7 |
| 46 | Idaho | 2.0 |
| 8 | Illinois | 7.7 |
| 15 | Indiana | 6.6 |
| 49 | Iowa | 1.5 |
| 19 | Kansas | 6.0 |
| 24 | Kentucky | 5.4 |
| 1 | Louisiana | 10.7 |
| 44 | Maine | 2.2 |
| 4 | Maryland | 9.0 |
| 46 | Massachusetts | 2.0 |
| 13 | Michigan | 7.0 |
| 39 | Minnesota | 2.8 |
| 8 | Mississippi | 7.7 |
| 15 | Missouri | 6.6 |
| 41 | Montana | 2.6 |
| 30 | Nebraska | 3.6 |
| 3 | Nevada | 9.1 |
| 49 | New Hampshire | 1.5 |
| 32 | New Jersey | 3.5 |
| 2 | New Mexico | 9.8 |
| 25 | New York | 5.0 |
| 11 | North Carolina | 7.2 |
| 48 | North Dakota | 1.6 |
| 32 | Ohio | 3.5 |
| 14 | Oklahoma | 6.9 |
| 40 | Oregon | 2.7 |
| 26 | Pennsylvania | 4.9 |
| 30 | Rhode Island | 3.6 |
| 15 | South Carolina | 6.6 |
| 42 | South Dakota | 2.5 |
| 12 | Tennessee | 7.1 |
| 18 | Texas | 6.1 |
| 45 | Utah | 2.1 |
| 38 | Vermont | 2.9 |
| 21 | Virginia | 5.7 |
| 37 | Washington | 3.0 |
| 28 | West Virginia | 4.4 |
| 34 | Wisconsin | 3.4 |
| 43 | Wyoming | 2.3 |

RANK ORDER

| RANK | STATE | RATE |
|------|-------|------|
| 1 | Louisiana | 10.7 |
| 2 | New Mexico | 9.8 |
| 3 | Nevada | 9.1 |
| 4 | Maryland | 9.0 |
| 5 | Alaska | 8.6 |
| 6 | Arizona | 8.0 |
| 7 | Alabama | 7.9 |
| 8 | Illinois | 7.7 |
| 8 | Mississippi | 7.7 |
| 10 | Georgia | 7.5 |
| 11 | North Carolina | 7.2 |
| 12 | Tennessee | 7.1 |
| 13 | Michigan | 7.0 |
| 14 | Oklahoma | 6.9 |
| 15 | Indiana | 6.6 |
| 15 | Missouri | 6.6 |
| 15 | South Carolina | 6.6 |
| 18 | Texas | 6.1 |
| 19 | California | 6.0 |
| 19 | Kansas | 6.0 |
| 21 | Florida | 5.7 |
| 21 | Virginia | 5.7 |
| 23 | Arkansas | 5.6 |
| 24 | Kentucky | 5.4 |
| 25 | New York | 5.0 |
| 26 | Pennsylvania | 4.9 |
| 27 | Colorado | 4.6 |
| 28 | West Virginia | 4.4 |
| 29 | Hawaii | 3.7 |
| 30 | Nebraska | 3.6 |
| 30 | Rhode Island | 3.6 |
| 32 | New Jersey | 3.5 |
| 32 | Ohio | 3.5 |
| 34 | Wisconsin | 3.4 |
| 35 | Connecticut | 3.3 |
| 36 | Delaware | 3.2 |
| 37 | Washington | 3.0 |
| 38 | Vermont | 2.9 |
| 39 | Minnesota | 2.8 |
| 40 | Oregon | 2.7 |
| 41 | Montana | 2.6 |
| 42 | South Dakota | 2.5 |
| 43 | Wyoming | 2.3 |
| 44 | Maine | 2.2 |
| 45 | Utah | 2.1 |
| 46 | Idaho | 2.0 |
| 46 | Massachusetts | 2.0 |
| 48 | North Dakota | 1.6 |
| 49 | Iowa | 1.5 |
| 49 | New Hampshire | 1.5 |
| | District of Columbia | 46.4 |

Source: Federal Bureau of Investigation
    "Crime in the United States 1999" (Uniform Crime Reports, October 15, 2000)
*Includes nonnegligent manslaughter.

# Murders with Firearms in 1999

## National Total = 8,256 Murders*

ALPHA ORDER

| RANK | STATE | MURDERS | % of USA |
|------|-------|---------|----------|
| NA | Alabama** | NA | NA |
| 33 | Alaska | 23 | 0.3% |
| 11 | Arizona | 272 | 3.3% |
| 23 | Arkansas | 97 | 1.2% |
| 1 | California | 1,338 | 16.2% |
| 21 | Colorado | 107 | 1.3% |
| 26 | Connecticut | 74 | 0.9% |
| 38 | Delaware | 17 | 0.2% |
| NA | Florida** | NA | NA |
| 8 | Georgia | 360 | 4.4% |
| 34 | Hawaii | 22 | 0.3% |
| 40 | Idaho | 15 | 0.2% |
| 5 | Illinois* | 458 | 5.5% |
| 13 | Indiana | 238 | 2.9% |
| 36 | Iowa | 21 | 0.3% |
| NA | Kansas** | NA | NA |
| 29 | Kentucky | 52 | 0.6% |
| 9 | Louisiana | 315 | 3.8% |
| 38 | Maine | 17 | 0.2% |
| 10 | Maryland | 293 | 3.5% |
| 27 | Massachusetts | 66 | 0.8% |
| 4 | Michigan | 485 | 5.9% |
| 30 | Minnesota | 50 | 0.6% |
| 20 | Mississippi | 112 | 1.4% |
| 15 | Missouri | 213 | 2.6% |
| 43 | Montana | 6 | 0.1% |
| 41 | Nebraska | 7 | 0.1% |
| 22 | Nevada | 103 | 1.2% |
| 45 | New Hampshire | 4 | 0.0% |
| 17 | New Jersey | 151 | 1.8% |
| 25 | New Mexico | 77 | 0.9% |
| 3 | New York | 487 | 5.9% |
| 7 | North Carolina | 362 | 4.4% |
| 45 | North Dakota | 4 | 0.0% |
| 16 | Ohio | 199 | 2.4% |
| 28 | Oklahoma | 56 | 0.7% |
| 31 | Oregon | 46 | 0.6% |
| 6 | Pennsylvania | 407 | 4.9% |
| 37 | Rhode Island | 20 | 0.2% |
| 18 | South Carolina | 146 | 1.8% |
| 44 | South Dakota | 5 | 0.1% |
| 14 | Tennessee | 237 | 2.9% |
| 2 | Texas | 746 | 9.0% |
| 34 | Utah | 22 | 0.3% |
| 41 | Vermont | 7 | 0.1% |
| 12 | Virginia | 243 | 2.9% |
| 24 | Washington | 90 | 1.1% |
| 32 | West Virginia | 44 | 0.5% |
| 19 | Wisconsin | 126 | 1.5% |
| 47 | Wyoming | 3 | 0.0% |

RANK ORDER

| RANK | STATE | MURDERS | % of USA |
|------|-------|---------|----------|
| 1 | California | 1,338 | 16.2% |
| 2 | Texas | 746 | 9.0% |
| 3 | New York | 487 | 5.9% |
| 4 | Michigan | 485 | 5.9% |
| 5 | Illinois* | 458 | 5.5% |
| 6 | Pennsylvania | 407 | 4.9% |
| 7 | North Carolina | 362 | 4.4% |
| 8 | Georgia | 360 | 4.4% |
| 9 | Louisiana | 315 | 3.8% |
| 10 | Maryland | 293 | 3.5% |
| 11 | Arizona | 272 | 3.3% |
| 12 | Virginia | 243 | 2.9% |
| 13 | Indiana | 238 | 2.9% |
| 14 | Tennessee | 237 | 2.9% |
| 15 | Missouri | 213 | 2.6% |
| 16 | Ohio | 199 | 2.4% |
| 17 | New Jersey | 151 | 1.8% |
| 18 | South Carolina | 146 | 1.8% |
| 19 | Wisconsin | 126 | 1.5% |
| 20 | Mississippi | 112 | 1.4% |
| 21 | Colorado | 107 | 1.3% |
| 22 | Nevada | 103 | 1.2% |
| 23 | Arkansas | 97 | 1.2% |
| 24 | Washington | 90 | 1.1% |
| 25 | New Mexico | 77 | 0.9% |
| 26 | Connecticut | 74 | 0.9% |
| 27 | Massachusetts | 66 | 0.8% |
| 28 | Oklahoma | 56 | 0.7% |
| 29 | Kentucky | 52 | 0.6% |
| 30 | Minnesota | 50 | 0.6% |
| 31 | Oregon | 46 | 0.6% |
| 32 | West Virginia | 44 | 0.5% |
| 33 | Alaska | 23 | 0.3% |
| 34 | Hawaii | 22 | 0.3% |
| 34 | Utah | 22 | 0.3% |
| 36 | Iowa | 21 | 0.3% |
| 37 | Rhode Island | 20 | 0.2% |
| 38 | Delaware | 17 | 0.2% |
| 38 | Maine | 17 | 0.2% |
| 40 | Idaho | 15 | 0.2% |
| 41 | Nebraska | 7 | 0.1% |
| 41 | Vermont | 7 | 0.1% |
| 43 | Montana | 6 | 0.1% |
| 44 | South Dakota | 5 | 0.1% |
| 45 | New Hampshire | 4 | 0.0% |
| 45 | North Dakota | 4 | 0.0% |
| 47 | Wyoming | 3 | 0.0% |
| NA | Alabama** | NA | NA |
| NA | Florida** | NA | NA |
| NA | Kansas** | NA | NA |
| | District of Columbia** | NA | NA |

*Source: Federal Bureau of Investigation*
*"Crime in the United States 1999" (Uniform Crime Reports, October 15, 2000)*
*Of the 12,658 murders in 1999 for which supplemental data were received by the F.B.I. There were an additional 2,875 murders for which the type of murder weapon was not reported to the F.B.I. Includes nonnegligent manslaughter. Numbers are for reporting jurisdictions only. Illinois' figure is for Chicago only.*
***Not available.*

# Percent of Murders Involving Firearms in 1999

## National Percent = 65.2% of Murders*

ALPHA ORDER

| RANK | STATE | PERCENT |
|------|-------|---------|
| NA | Alabama** | NA |
| 40 | Alaska | 50.0 |
| 6 | Arizona | 71.2 |
| 16 | Arkansas | 67.8 |
| 18 | California | 66.7 |
| 27 | Colorado | 61.8 |
| 13 | Connecticut | 69.2 |
| 8 | Delaware | 70.8 |
| NA | Florida** | NA |
| 11 | Georgia | 69.8 |
| 38 | Hawaii | 51.2 |
| 25 | Idaho | 62.5 |
| 5 | Illinois* | 71.6 |
| 3 | Indiana | 73.5 |
| 38 | Iowa | 51.2 |
| NA | Kansas** | NA |
| 23 | Kentucky | 64.2 |
| 12 | Louisiana | 69.5 |
| 24 | Maine | 63.0 |
| 2 | Maryland | 74.4 |
| 30 | Massachusetts | 56.4 |
| 15 | Michigan | 67.9 |
| 43 | Minnesota | 38.8 |
| 1 | Mississippi | 78.3 |
| 22 | Missouri | 65.1 |
| 18 | Montana | 66.7 |
| 46 | Nebraska | 26.9 |
| 26 | Nevada | 62.4 |
| 47 | New Hampshire | 22.2 |
| 36 | New Jersey | 52.6 |
| 34 | New Mexico | 54.6 |
| 30 | New York | 56.4 |
| 17 | North Carolina | 67.2 |
| 40 | North Dakota | 50.0 |
| 29 | Ohio | 57.3 |
| 18 | Oklahoma | 66.7 |
| 37 | Oregon | 52.3 |
| 4 | Pennsylvania | 72.7 |
| 32 | Rhode Island | 55.6 |
| 10 | South Carolina | 69.9 |
| 44 | South Dakota | 38.5 |
| 21 | Tennessee | 66.2 |
| 28 | Texas | 61.7 |
| 33 | Utah | 55.0 |
| 42 | Vermont | 41.2 |
| 14 | Virginia | 68.6 |
| 35 | Washington | 54.2 |
| 7 | West Virginia | 71.0 |
| 8 | Wisconsin | 70.8 |
| 45 | Wyoming | 27.3 |

RANK ORDER

| RANK | STATE | PERCENT |
|------|-------|---------|
| 1 | Mississippi | 78.3 |
| 2 | Maryland | 74.4 |
| 3 | Indiana | 73.5 |
| 4 | Pennsylvania | 72.7 |
| 5 | Illinois* | 71.6 |
| 6 | Arizona | 71.2 |
| 7 | West Virginia | 71.0 |
| 8 | Delaware | 70.8 |
| 8 | Wisconsin | 70.8 |
| 10 | South Carolina | 69.9 |
| 11 | Georgia | 69.8 |
| 12 | Louisiana | 69.5 |
| 13 | Connecticut | 69.2 |
| 14 | Virginia | 68.6 |
| 15 | Michigan | 67.9 |
| 16 | Arkansas | 67.8 |
| 17 | North Carolina | 67.2 |
| 18 | California | 66.7 |
| 18 | Montana | 66.7 |
| 18 | Oklahoma | 66.7 |
| 21 | Tennessee | 66.2 |
| 22 | Missouri | 65.1 |
| 23 | Kentucky | 64.2 |
| 24 | Maine | 63.0 |
| 25 | Idaho | 62.5 |
| 26 | Nevada | 62.4 |
| 27 | Colorado | 61.8 |
| 28 | Texas | 61.7 |
| 29 | Ohio | 57.3 |
| 30 | Massachusetts | 56.4 |
| 30 | New York | 56.4 |
| 32 | Rhode Island | 55.6 |
| 33 | Utah | 55.0 |
| 34 | New Mexico | 54.6 |
| 35 | Washington | 54.2 |
| 36 | New Jersey | 52.6 |
| 37 | Oregon | 52.3 |
| 38 | Hawaii | 51.2 |
| 38 | Iowa | 51.2 |
| 40 | Alaska | 50.0 |
| 40 | North Dakota | 50.0 |
| 42 | Vermont | 41.2 |
| 43 | Minnesota | 38.8 |
| 44 | South Dakota | 38.5 |
| 45 | Wyoming | 27.3 |
| 46 | Nebraska | 26.9 |
| 47 | New Hampshire | 22.2 |
| NA | Alabama** | NA |
| NA | Florida** | NA |
| NA | Kansas** | NA |
| | District of Columbia** | NA |

Source: Morgan Quitno Press using data from Federal Bureau of Investigation
  "Crime in the United States 1999" (Uniform Crime Reports, October 15, 2000)
*Of the 12,658 murders in 1999 for which supplemental data were received by the F.B.I. There were an additional 2,875 murders for which the type of murder weapon was not reported to the F.B.I. Murder includes nonnegligent manslaughter. Illinois' percentage is for Chicago only.
**Not available.

37

# Murder Rate with Firearms in 1999

## National Rate = 4.3 Murders per 100,000 Population*

ALPHA ORDER

| RANK | STATE | RATE |
|------|-------|------|
| NA | Alabama** | NA |
| 20 | Alaska | 4.1 |
| 9 | Arizona | 5.9 |
| 20 | Arkansas | 4.1 |
| 22 | California | 4.0 |
| 25 | Colorado | 2.8 |
| 28 | Connecticut | 2.3 |
| 28 | Delaware | 2.3 |
| NA | Florida** | NA |
| 7 | Georgia | 7.6 |
| 31 | Hawaii | 1.9 |
| 41 | Idaho | 1.2 |
| 1 | Illinois* | 16.2 |
| 9 | Indiana | 5.9 |
| 43 | Iowa | 0.9 |
| NA | Kansas** | NA |
| 17 | Kentucky | 4.5 |
| 5 | Louisiana | 8.1 |
| 37 | Maine | 1.4 |
| 2 | Maryland | 9.4 |
| 39 | Massachusetts | 1.3 |
| 12 | Michigan | 5.6 |
| 24 | Minnesota | 3.0 |
| 4 | Mississippi | 8.4 |
| 15 | Missouri | 5.0 |
| 37 | Montana | 1.4 |
| 47 | Nebraska | 0.5 |
| 11 | Nevada | 5.7 |
| 43 | New Hampshire | 0.9 |
| 31 | New Jersey | 1.9 |
| 8 | New Mexico | 6.4 |
| 6 | New York | 7.9 |
| 13 | North Carolina | 5.3 |
| 45 | North Dakota | 0.8 |
| 26 | Ohio | 2.6 |
| 33 | Oklahoma | 1.7 |
| 35 | Oregon | 1.5 |
| 17 | Pennsylvania | 4.5 |
| 30 | Rhode Island | 2.2 |
| 3 | South Carolina | 8.5 |
| 42 | South Dakota | 1.0 |
| 14 | Tennessee | 5.2 |
| 23 | Texas | 3.8 |
| 39 | Utah | 1.3 |
| 35 | Vermont | 1.5 |
| 16 | Virginia | 4.7 |
| 33 | Washington | 1.7 |
| 19 | West Virginia | 4.4 |
| 26 | Wisconsin | 2.6 |
| 46 | Wyoming | 0.7 |

RANK ORDER

| RANK | STATE | RATE |
|------|-------|------|
| 1 | Illinois* | 16.2 |
| 2 | Maryland | 9.4 |
| 3 | South Carolina | 8.5 |
| 4 | Mississippi | 8.4 |
| 5 | Louisiana | 8.1 |
| 6 | New York | 7.9 |
| 7 | Georgia | 7.6 |
| 8 | New Mexico | 6.4 |
| 9 | Arizona | 5.9 |
| 9 | Indiana | 5.9 |
| 11 | Nevada | 5.7 |
| 12 | Michigan | 5.6 |
| 13 | North Carolina | 5.3 |
| 14 | Tennessee | 5.2 |
| 15 | Missouri | 5.0 |
| 16 | Virginia | 4.7 |
| 17 | Kentucky | 4.5 |
| 17 | Pennsylvania | 4.5 |
| 19 | West Virginia | 4.4 |
| 20 | Alaska | 4.1 |
| 20 | Arkansas | 4.1 |
| 22 | California | 4.0 |
| 23 | Texas | 3.8 |
| 24 | Minnesota | 3.0 |
| 25 | Colorado | 2.8 |
| 26 | Ohio | 2.6 |
| 26 | Wisconsin | 2.6 |
| 28 | Connecticut | 2.3 |
| 28 | Delaware | 2.3 |
| 30 | Rhode Island | 2.2 |
| 31 | Hawaii | 1.9 |
| 31 | New Jersey | 1.9 |
| 33 | Oklahoma | 1.7 |
| 33 | Washington | 1.7 |
| 35 | Oregon | 1.5 |
| 35 | Vermont | 1.5 |
| 37 | Maine | 1.4 |
| 37 | Montana | 1.4 |
| 39 | Massachusetts | 1.3 |
| 39 | Utah | 1.3 |
| 41 | Idaho | 1.2 |
| 42 | South Dakota | 1.0 |
| 43 | Iowa | 0.9 |
| 43 | New Hampshire | 0.9 |
| 45 | North Dakota | 0.8 |
| 46 | Wyoming | 0.7 |
| 47 | Nebraska | 0.5 |
| NA | Alabama** | NA |
| NA | Florida** | NA |
| NA | Kansas** | NA |
| | District of Columbia** | NA |

Source: Morgan Quitno Press using data from Federal Bureau of Investigation
    "Crime in the United States 1999" (Uniform Crime Reports, October 15, 2000)
*Of the 12,658 murders in 1999 for which supplemental data were received by the F.B.I. There were an additional 2,875 murders for which the type of murder weapon was not reported to the F.B.I. Includes nonnegligent manslaughter. National and state rates based on population for reporting jurisdictions only. Illinois' rate is for Chicago only. **Not available.

# Rapes in 1999

## National Total = 89,107 Rapes*

ALPHA ORDER

| RANK | STATE | RAPES | % of USA |
|------|-------|-------|----------|
| 20 | Alabama | 1,513 | 1.7% |
| 38 | Alaska | 517 | 0.6% |
| 24 | Arizona | 1,383 | 1.6% |
| 35 | Arkansas | 710 | 0.8% |
| 1 | California | 9,363 | 10.5% |
| 15 | Colorado | 1,679 | 1.9% |
| 36 | Connecticut | 654 | 0.7% |
| 37 | Delaware | 529 | 0.6% |
| 3 | Florida | 6,990 | 7.8% |
| 11 | Georgia | 2,319 | 2.6% |
| 42 | Hawaii | 354 | 0.4% |
| 39 | Idaho | 417 | 0.5% |
| 5 | Illinois | 4,144 | 4.7% |
| 17 | Indiana | 1,607 | 1.8% |
| 34 | Iowa | 780 | 0.9% |
| 28 | Kansas | 1,065 | 1.2% |
| 30 | Kentucky | 1,040 | 1.2% |
| 21 | Louisiana | 1,448 | 1.6% |
| 47 | Maine | 239 | 0.3% |
| 19 | Maryland | 1,551 | 1.7% |
| 16 | Massachusetts | 1,663 | 1.9% |
| 4 | Michigan | 4,849 | 5.4% |
| 13 | Minnesota | 2,038 | 2.3% |
| 27 | Mississippi | 1,156 | 1.3% |
| 22 | Missouri | 1,439 | 1.6% |
| 46 | Montana | 250 | 0.3% |
| 40 | Nebraska | 414 | 0.5% |
| 32 | Nevada | 943 | 1.1% |
| 43 | New Hampshire | 345 | 0.4% |
| 23 | New Jersey | 1,409 | 1.6% |
| 31 | New Mexico | 944 | 1.1% |
| 7 | New York | 3,563 | 4.0% |
| 12 | North Carolina | 2,155 | 2.4% |
| 48 | North Dakota | 142 | 0.2% |
| 6 | Ohio | 4,129 | 4.6% |
| 25 | Oklahoma | 1,375 | 1.5% |
| 26 | Oregon | 1,219 | 1.4% |
| 8 | Pennsylvania | 3,279 | 3.7% |
| 41 | Rhode Island | 391 | 0.4% |
| 18 | South Carolina | 1,587 | 1.8% |
| 45 | South Dakota | 336 | 0.4% |
| 10 | Tennessee | 2,415 | 2.7% |
| 2 | Texas | 7,614 | 8.5% |
| 33 | Utah | 806 | 0.9% |
| 50 | Vermont | 136 | 0.2% |
| 14 | Virginia | 1,720 | 1.9% |
| 9 | Washington | 2,711 | 3.0% |
| 44 | West Virginia | 337 | 0.4% |
| 29 | Wisconsin | 1,055 | 1.2% |
| 49 | Wyoming | 137 | 0.2% |

RANK ORDER

| RANK | STATE | RAPES | % of USA |
|------|-------|-------|----------|
| 1 | California | 9,363 | 10.5% |
| 2 | Texas | 7,614 | 8.5% |
| 3 | Florida | 6,990 | 7.8% |
| 4 | Michigan | 4,849 | 5.4% |
| 5 | Illinois | 4,144 | 4.7% |
| 6 | Ohio | 4,129 | 4.6% |
| 7 | New York | 3,563 | 4.0% |
| 8 | Pennsylvania | 3,279 | 3.7% |
| 9 | Washington | 2,711 | 3.0% |
| 10 | Tennessee | 2,415 | 2.7% |
| 11 | Georgia | 2,319 | 2.6% |
| 12 | North Carolina | 2,155 | 2.4% |
| 13 | Minnesota | 2,038 | 2.3% |
| 14 | Virginia | 1,720 | 1.9% |
| 15 | Colorado | 1,679 | 1.9% |
| 16 | Massachusetts | 1,663 | 1.9% |
| 17 | Indiana | 1,607 | 1.8% |
| 18 | South Carolina | 1,587 | 1.8% |
| 19 | Maryland | 1,551 | 1.7% |
| 20 | Alabama | 1,513 | 1.7% |
| 21 | Louisiana | 1,448 | 1.6% |
| 22 | Missouri | 1,439 | 1.6% |
| 23 | New Jersey | 1,409 | 1.6% |
| 24 | Arizona | 1,383 | 1.6% |
| 25 | Oklahoma | 1,375 | 1.5% |
| 26 | Oregon | 1,219 | 1.4% |
| 27 | Mississippi | 1,156 | 1.3% |
| 28 | Kansas | 1,065 | 1.2% |
| 29 | Wisconsin | 1,055 | 1.2% |
| 30 | Kentucky | 1,040 | 1.2% |
| 31 | New Mexico | 944 | 1.1% |
| 32 | Nevada | 943 | 1.1% |
| 33 | Utah | 806 | 0.9% |
| 34 | Iowa | 780 | 0.9% |
| 35 | Arkansas | 710 | 0.8% |
| 36 | Connecticut | 654 | 0.7% |
| 37 | Delaware | 529 | 0.6% |
| 38 | Alaska | 517 | 0.6% |
| 39 | Idaho | 417 | 0.5% |
| 40 | Nebraska | 414 | 0.5% |
| 41 | Rhode Island | 391 | 0.4% |
| 42 | Hawaii | 354 | 0.4% |
| 43 | New Hampshire | 345 | 0.4% |
| 44 | West Virginia | 337 | 0.4% |
| 45 | South Dakota | 336 | 0.4% |
| 46 | Montana | 250 | 0.3% |
| 47 | Maine | 239 | 0.3% |
| 48 | North Dakota | 142 | 0.2% |
| 49 | Wyoming | 137 | 0.2% |
| 50 | Vermont | 136 | 0.2% |
| | District of Columbia | 248 | 0.3% |

Source: Federal Bureau of Investigation
   "Crime in the United States 1999" (Uniform Crime Reports, October 15, 2000)
*Forcible rape is the carnal knowledge of a female forcibly and against her will. Assaults or attempts to commit rape by force or threat of force are included. However, statutory rape without force and other sex offenses are excluded.

# Percent Change in Number of Rapes: 1998 to 1999

## National Percent Change = 4.3% Decrease*

ALPHA ORDER

| RANK | STATE | PERCENT CHANGE |
|------|-------|----------------|
| 10 | Alabama | 4.9 |
| 2 | Alaska | 22.8 |
| 27 | Arizona | (4.7) |
| 48 | Arkansas | (20.5) |
| 26 | California | (4.3) |
| 42 | Colorado | (10.8) |
| 41 | Connecticut | (10.2) |
| 9 | Delaware | 6.0 |
| 29 | Florida | (5.6) |
| 17 | Georgia | (0.1) |
| 16 | Hawaii | 0.6 |
| 5 | Idaho | 8.0 |
| 15 | Illinois | 1.2 |
| 47 | Indiana | (17.7) |
| 6 | Iowa | 7.1 |
| 29 | Kansas | (5.6) |
| 31 | Kentucky | (6.1) |
| 40 | Louisiana | (10.0) |
| 8 | Maine | 6.2 |
| 38 | Maryland | (9.5) |
| 20 | Massachusetts | (1.4) |
| 23 | Michigan | (2.0) |
| 44 | Minnesota | (13.6) |
| 3 | Mississippi | 12.7 |
| 22 | Missouri | (1.6) |
| 7 | Montana | 6.4 |
| 18 | Nebraska | (0.7) |
| 11 | Nevada | 3.5 |
| 45 | New Hampshire | (13.8) |
| 43 | New Jersey | (13.2) |
| 20 | New Mexico | (1.4) |
| 34 | New York | (7.3) |
| 33 | North Carolina | (6.8) |
| 49 | North Dakota | (33.0) |
| 36 | Ohio | (9.1) |
| 36 | Oklahoma | (9.1) |
| 32 | Oregon | (6.7) |
| 13 | Pennsylvania | 1.7 |
| 4 | Rhode Island | 11.4 |
| 38 | South Carolina | (9.5) |
| 1 | South Dakota | 30.2 |
| 24 | Tennessee | (2.8) |
| 25 | Texas | (3.8) |
| 35 | Utah | (7.9) |
| 46 | Vermont | (16.6) |
| 28 | Virginia | (5.0) |
| 19 | Washington | (1.1) |
| NA | West Virginia** | NA |
| 13 | Wisconsin | 1.7 |
| 12 | Wyoming | 3.0 |

RANK ORDER

| RANK | STATE | PERCENT CHANGE |
|------|-------|----------------|
| 1 | South Dakota | 30.2 |
| 2 | Alaska | 22.8 |
| 3 | Mississippi | 12.7 |
| 4 | Rhode Island | 11.4 |
| 5 | Idaho | 8.0 |
| 6 | Iowa | 7.1 |
| 7 | Montana | 6.4 |
| 8 | Maine | 6.2 |
| 9 | Delaware | 6.0 |
| 10 | Alabama | 4.9 |
| 11 | Nevada | 3.5 |
| 12 | Wyoming | 3.0 |
| 13 | Pennsylvania | 1.7 |
| 13 | Wisconsin | 1.7 |
| 15 | Illinois | 1.2 |
| 16 | Hawaii | 0.6 |
| 17 | Georgia | (0.1) |
| 18 | Nebraska | (0.7) |
| 19 | Washington | (1.1) |
| 20 | Massachusetts | (1.4) |
| 20 | New Mexico | (1.4) |
| 22 | Missouri | (1.6) |
| 23 | Michigan | (2.0) |
| 24 | Tennessee | (2.8) |
| 25 | Texas | (3.8) |
| 26 | California | (4.3) |
| 27 | Arizona | (4.7) |
| 28 | Virginia | (5.0) |
| 29 | Florida | (5.6) |
| 29 | Kansas | (5.6) |
| 31 | Kentucky | (6.1) |
| 32 | Oregon | (6.7) |
| 33 | North Carolina | (6.8) |
| 34 | New York | (7.3) |
| 35 | Utah | (7.9) |
| 36 | Ohio | (9.1) |
| 36 | Oklahoma | (9.1) |
| 38 | Maryland | (9.5) |
| 38 | South Carolina | (9.5) |
| 40 | Louisiana | (10.0) |
| 41 | Connecticut | (10.2) |
| 42 | Colorado | (10.8) |
| 43 | New Jersey | (13.2) |
| 44 | Minnesota | (13.6) |
| 45 | New Hampshire | (13.8) |
| 46 | Vermont | (16.6) |
| 47 | Indiana | (17.7) |
| 48 | Arkansas | (20.5) |
| 49 | North Dakota | (33.0) |
| NA | West Virginia** | NA |
| | District of Columbia | 30.5 |

Source: Federal Bureau of Investigation
"Crime in the United States 1999" (Uniform Crime Reports, October 15, 2000)
*Forcible rape is the carnal knowledge of a female forcibly and against her will. Assaults or attempts to commit rape by force or threat of force are included. However, statutory rape without force and other sex offenses are excluded.
**Not available.

# Rape Rate in 1999

## National Rate = 32.7 Rapes per 100,000 Population*

| RANK | STATE | RATE | | RANK | STATE | RATE |
|------|-------|------|---|------|-------|------|
| 21 | Alabama | 34.6 | | 1 | Alaska | 83.5 |
| 1 | Alaska | 83.5 | | 2 | Delaware | 70.2 |
| 28 | Arizona | 28.9 | | 3 | New Mexico | 54.3 |
| 34 | Arkansas | 27.8 | | 4 | Nevada | 52.1 |
| 32 | California | 28.2 | | 5 | Michigan | 49.2 |
| 12 | Colorado | 41.4 | | 6 | Washington | 47.1 |
| 46 | Connecticut | 19.9 | | 7 | Florida | 46.3 |
| 2 | Delaware | 70.2 | | 8 | South Dakota | 45.8 |
| 7 | Florida | 46.3 | | 9 | Tennessee | 44.0 |
| 27 | Georgia | 29.8 | | 10 | Minnesota | 42.7 |
| 26 | Hawaii | 29.9 | | 11 | Mississippi | 41.7 |
| 23 | Idaho | 33.3 | | 12 | Colorado | 41.4 |
| 22 | Illinois | 34.2 | | 13 | Oklahoma | 40.9 |
| 37 | Indiana | 27.0 | | 14 | South Carolina | 40.8 |
| 36 | Iowa | 27.2 | | 15 | Kansas | 40.1 |
| 15 | Kansas | 40.1 | | 16 | Rhode Island | 39.5 |
| 39 | Kentucky | 26.3 | | 17 | Texas | 38.0 |
| 24 | Louisiana | 33.1 | | 18 | Utah | 37.8 |
| 48 | Maine | 19.1 | | 19 | Oregon | 36.8 |
| 25 | Maryland | 30.0 | | 20 | Ohio | 36.7 |
| 38 | Massachusetts | 26.9 | | 21 | Alabama | 34.6 |
| 5 | Michigan | 49.2 | | 22 | Illinois | 34.2 |
| 10 | Minnesota | 42.7 | | 23 | Idaho | 33.3 |
| 11 | Mississippi | 41.7 | | 24 | Louisiana | 33.1 |
| 39 | Missouri | 26.3 | | 25 | Maryland | 30.0 |
| 31 | Montana | 28.3 | | 26 | Hawaii | 29.9 |
| 42 | Nebraska | 24.8 | | 27 | Georgia | 29.8 |
| 4 | Nevada | 52.1 | | 28 | Arizona | 28.9 |
| 29 | New Hampshire | 28.7 | | 29 | New Hampshire | 28.7 |
| 50 | New Jersey | 17.3 | | 30 | Wyoming | 28.5 |
| 3 | New Mexico | 54.3 | | 31 | Montana | 28.3 |
| 47 | New York | 19.6 | | 32 | California | 28.2 |
| 32 | North Carolina | 28.2 | | 32 | North Carolina | 28.2 |
| 44 | North Dakota | 22.4 | | 34 | Arkansas | 27.8 |
| 20 | Ohio | 36.7 | | 35 | Pennsylvania | 27.3 |
| 13 | Oklahoma | 40.9 | | 36 | Iowa | 27.2 |
| 19 | Oregon | 36.8 | | 37 | Indiana | 27.0 |
| 35 | Pennsylvania | 27.3 | | 38 | Massachusetts | 26.9 |
| 16 | Rhode Island | 39.5 | | 39 | Kentucky | 26.3 |
| 14 | South Carolina | 40.8 | | 39 | Missouri | 26.3 |
| 8 | South Dakota | 45.8 | | 41 | Virginia | 25.0 |
| 9 | Tennessee | 44.0 | | 42 | Nebraska | 24.8 |
| 17 | Texas | 38.0 | | 43 | Vermont | 22.9 |
| 18 | Utah | 37.8 | | 44 | North Dakota | 22.4 |
| 43 | Vermont | 22.9 | | 45 | Wisconsin | 20.1 |
| 41 | Virginia | 25.0 | | 46 | Connecticut | 19.9 |
| 6 | Washington | 47.1 | | 47 | New York | 19.6 |
| 49 | West Virginia | 18.6 | | 48 | Maine | 19.1 |
| 45 | Wisconsin | 20.1 | | 49 | West Virginia | 18.6 |
| 30 | Wyoming | 28.5 | | 50 | New Jersey | 17.3 |
| | | | | | District of Columbia | 47.8 |

ALPHA ORDER

RANK ORDER

Source: Federal Bureau of Investigation
    "Crime in the United States 1999" (Uniform Crime Reports, October 15, 2000)
*Forcible rape is the carnal knowledge of a female forcibly and against her will. Assaults or attempts to commit rape by force or threat of force are included. However, statutory rape without force and other sex offenses are excluded.

# Robberies in 1999

## National Total = 409,670 Robberies*

ALPHA ORDER

| RANK | STATE | ROBBERIES | % of USA |
|---|---|---|---|
| 22 | Alabama | 5,297 | 1.3% |
| 42 | Alaska | 566 | 0.1% |
| 15 | Arizona | 7,288 | 1.8% |
| 34 | Arkansas | 2,024 | 0.5% |
| 1 | California | 60,039 | 14.7% |
| 29 | Colorado | 3,056 | 0.7% |
| 25 | Connecticut | 4,054 | 1.0% |
| 35 | Delaware | 1,492 | 0.4% |
| 3 | Florida | 31,969 | 7.8% |
| 11 | Georgia | 12,962 | 3.2% |
| 39 | Hawaii | 1,044 | 0.3% |
| 46 | Idaho | 223 | 0.1% |
| 5 | Illinois | 26,611 | 6.5% |
| 18 | Indiana | 6,496 | 1.6% |
| 38 | Iowa | 1,051 | 0.3% |
| 33 | Kansas | 2,047 | 0.5% |
| 27 | Kentucky | 3,168 | 0.8% |
| 14 | Louisiana | 7,591 | 1.9% |
| 44 | Maine | 243 | 0.1% |
| 10 | Maryland | 13,636 | 3.3% |
| 19 | Massachusetts | 5,931 | 1.4% |
| 9 | Michigan | 14,103 | 3.4% |
| 26 | Minnesota | 3,917 | 1.0% |
| 28 | Mississippi | 3,091 | 0.8% |
| 16 | Missouri | 7,149 | 1.7% |
| 45 | Montana | 228 | 0.1% |
| 36 | Nebraska | 1,264 | 0.3% |
| 24 | Nevada | 4,209 | 1.0% |
| 43 | New Hampshire | 257 | 0.1% |
| 8 | New Jersey | 14,243 | 3.5% |
| 32 | New Mexico | 2,579 | 0.6% |
| 2 | New York | 43,821 | 10.7% |
| 12 | North Carolina | 12,087 | 3.0% |
| 50 | North Dakota | 56 | 0.0% |
| 7 | Ohio | 14,405 | 3.5% |
| 31 | Oklahoma | 2,785 | 0.7% |
| 30 | Oregon | 2,858 | 0.7% |
| 6 | Pennsylvania | 18,670 | 4.6% |
| 40 | Rhode Island | 788 | 0.2% |
| 21 | South Carolina | 5,760 | 1.4% |
| 47 | South Dakota | 103 | 0.0% |
| 13 | Tennessee | 8,598 | 2.1% |
| 4 | Texas | 29,405 | 7.2% |
| 37 | Utah | 1,158 | 0.3% |
| 49 | Vermont | 65 | 0.0% |
| 17 | Virginia | 6,947 | 1.7% |
| 20 | Washington | 5,808 | 1.4% |
| 41 | West Virginia | 661 | 0.2% |
| 23 | Wisconsin | 4,449 | 1.1% |
| 48 | Wyoming | 74 | 0.0% |

RANK ORDER

| RANK | STATE | ROBBERIES | % of USA |
|---|---|---|---|
| 1 | California | 60,039 | 14.7% |
| 2 | New York | 43,821 | 10.7% |
| 3 | Florida | 31,969 | 7.8% |
| 4 | Texas | 29,405 | 7.2% |
| 5 | Illinois | 26,611 | 6.5% |
| 6 | Pennsylvania | 18,670 | 4.6% |
| 7 | Ohio | 14,405 | 3.5% |
| 8 | New Jersey | 14,243 | 3.5% |
| 9 | Michigan | 14,103 | 3.4% |
| 10 | Maryland | 13,636 | 3.3% |
| 11 | Georgia | 12,962 | 3.2% |
| 12 | North Carolina | 12,087 | 3.0% |
| 13 | Tennessee | 8,598 | 2.1% |
| 14 | Louisiana | 7,591 | 1.9% |
| 15 | Arizona | 7,288 | 1.8% |
| 16 | Missouri | 7,149 | 1.7% |
| 17 | Virginia | 6,947 | 1.7% |
| 18 | Indiana | 6,496 | 1.6% |
| 19 | Massachusetts | 5,931 | 1.4% |
| 20 | Washington | 5,808 | 1.4% |
| 21 | South Carolina | 5,760 | 1.4% |
| 22 | Alabama | 5,297 | 1.3% |
| 23 | Wisconsin | 4,449 | 1.1% |
| 24 | Nevada | 4,209 | 1.0% |
| 25 | Connecticut | 4,054 | 1.0% |
| 26 | Minnesota | 3,917 | 1.0% |
| 27 | Kentucky | 3,168 | 0.8% |
| 28 | Mississippi | 3,091 | 0.8% |
| 29 | Colorado | 3,056 | 0.7% |
| 30 | Oregon | 2,858 | 0.7% |
| 31 | Oklahoma | 2,785 | 0.7% |
| 32 | New Mexico | 2,579 | 0.6% |
| 33 | Kansas | 2,047 | 0.5% |
| 34 | Arkansas | 2,024 | 0.5% |
| 35 | Delaware | 1,492 | 0.4% |
| 36 | Nebraska | 1,264 | 0.3% |
| 37 | Utah | 1,158 | 0.3% |
| 38 | Iowa | 1,051 | 0.3% |
| 39 | Hawaii | 1,044 | 0.3% |
| 40 | Rhode Island | 788 | 0.2% |
| 41 | West Virginia | 661 | 0.2% |
| 42 | Alaska | 566 | 0.1% |
| 43 | New Hampshire | 257 | 0.1% |
| 44 | Maine | 243 | 0.1% |
| 45 | Montana | 228 | 0.1% |
| 46 | Idaho | 223 | 0.1% |
| 47 | South Dakota | 103 | 0.0% |
| 48 | Wyoming | 74 | 0.0% |
| 49 | Vermont | 65 | 0.0% |
| 50 | North Dakota | 56 | 0.0% |
| | District of Columbia | 3,344 | 0.8% |

*Source: Federal Bureau of Investigation*
*"Crime in the United States 1999" (Uniform Crime Reports, October 15, 2000)*
*\*Robbery is the taking or attempting to take anything of value by force or threat of force.*

# Percent Change in Number of Robberies: 1998 to 1999

## National Percent Change = 8.4% Decrease*

ALPHA ORDER

RANK ORDER

| RANK | STATE | PERCENT CHANGE |
|------|-------|----------------|
| 22 | Alabama | (7.0) |
| 3 | Alaska | 6.4 |
| 17 | Arizona | (5.5) |
| 46 | Arkansas | (17.1) |
| 41 | California | (12.7) |
| 19 | Colorado | (5.6) |
| 23 | Connecticut | (7.4) |
| 4 | Delaware | 3.3 |
| 37 | Florida | (11.7) |
| 29 | Georgia | (9.4) |
| 43 | Hawaii | (14.8) |
| 44 | Idaho | (15.5) |
| 34 | Illinois | (11.1) |
| 10 | Indiana | (1.0) |
| 48 | Iowa | (27.8) |
| 32 | Kansas | (10.5) |
| 26 | Kentucky | (8.7) |
| 40 | Louisiana | (12.3) |
| 24 | Maine | (7.6) |
| 34 | Maryland | (11.1) |
| 7 | Massachusetts | (0.1) |
| 25 | Michigan | (7.8) |
| 31 | Minnesota | (10.4) |
| 27 | Mississippi | (8.9) |
| 39 | Missouri | (11.9) |
| 11 | Montana | (1.7) |
| 12 | Nebraska | (2.0) |
| 17 | Nevada | (5.5) |
| 6 | New Hampshire | 0.8 |
| 21 | New Jersey | (5.7) |
| 28 | New Mexico | (9.2) |
| 33 | New York | (10.8) |
| 8 | North Carolina | (0.4) |
| 42 | North Dakota | (13.8) |
| 15 | Ohio | (3.7) |
| 30 | Oklahoma | (9.5) |
| 47 | Oregon | (17.2) |
| 19 | Pennsylvania | (5.6) |
| 1 | Rhode Island | 19.6 |
| 13 | South Carolina | (3.1) |
| 49 | South Dakota | (30.9) |
| 34 | Tennessee | (11.1) |
| 5 | Texas | 2.5 |
| 45 | Utah | (16.4) |
| 2 | Vermont | 16.1 |
| 13 | Virginia | (3.1) |
| 37 | Washington | (11.7) |
| NA | West Virginia** | NA |
| 9 | Wisconsin | (0.6) |
| 16 | Wyoming | (5.1) |

| RANK | STATE | PERCENT CHANGE |
|------|-------|----------------|
| 1 | Rhode Island | 19.6 |
| 2 | Vermont | 16.1 |
| 3 | Alaska | 6.4 |
| 4 | Delaware | 3.3 |
| 5 | Texas | 2.5 |
| 6 | New Hampshire | 0.8 |
| 7 | Massachusetts | (0.1) |
| 8 | North Carolina | (0.4) |
| 9 | Wisconsin | (0.6) |
| 10 | Indiana | (1.0) |
| 11 | Montana | (1.7) |
| 12 | Nebraska | (2.0) |
| 13 | South Carolina | (3.1) |
| 13 | Virginia | (3.1) |
| 15 | Ohio | (3.7) |
| 16 | Wyoming | (5.1) |
| 17 | Arizona | (5.5) |
| 17 | Nevada | (5.5) |
| 19 | Colorado | (5.6) |
| 19 | Pennsylvania | (5.6) |
| 21 | New Jersey | (5.7) |
| 22 | Alabama | (7.0) |
| 23 | Connecticut | (7.4) |
| 24 | Maine | (7.6) |
| 25 | Michigan | (7.8) |
| 26 | Kentucky | (8.7) |
| 27 | Mississippi | (8.9) |
| 28 | New Mexico | (9.2) |
| 29 | Georgia | (9.4) |
| 30 | Oklahoma | (9.5) |
| 31 | Minnesota | (10.4) |
| 32 | Kansas | (10.5) |
| 33 | New York | (10.8) |
| 34 | Illinois | (11.1) |
| 34 | Maryland | (11.1) |
| 34 | Tennessee | (11.1) |
| 37 | Florida | (11.7) |
| 37 | Washington | (11.7) |
| 39 | Missouri | (11.9) |
| 40 | Louisiana | (12.3) |
| 41 | California | (12.7) |
| 42 | North Dakota | (13.8) |
| 43 | Hawaii | (14.8) |
| 44 | Idaho | (15.5) |
| 45 | Utah | (16.4) |
| 46 | Arkansas | (17.1) |
| 47 | Oregon | (17.2) |
| 48 | Iowa | (27.8) |
| 49 | South Dakota | (30.9) |
| NA | West Virginia** | NA |
| | District of Columbia | (7.3) |

Source: Federal Bureau of Investigation
    "Crime in the United States 1999" (Uniform Crime Reports, October 15, 2000)
*Robbery is the taking or attempting to take anything of value by force or threat of force.
**Not available.

# Robbery Rate in 1999

## National Rate = 150.2 Robberies per 100,000 Population*

ALPHA ORDER

| RANK | STATE | RATE |
|------|-------|------|
| 22 | Alabama | 121.2 |
| 28 | Alaska | 91.4 |
| 14 | Arizona | 152.5 |
| 36 | Arkansas | 79.3 |
| 7 | California | 181.1 |
| 39 | Colorado | 75.3 |
| 21 | Connecticut | 123.5 |
| 6 | Delaware | 197.9 |
| 5 | Florida | 211.6 |
| 10 | Georgia | 166.4 |
| 29 | Hawaii | 88.1 |
| 46 | Idaho | 17.8 |
| 4 | Illinois | 219.4 |
| 24 | Indiana | 109.3 |
| 41 | Iowa | 36.6 |
| 37 | Kansas | 77.1 |
| 34 | Kentucky | 80.0 |
| 9 | Louisiana | 173.6 |
| 45 | Maine | 19.4 |
| 1 | Maryland | 263.7 |
| 27 | Massachusetts | 96.0 |
| 18 | Michigan | 143.0 |
| 33 | Minnesota | 82.0 |
| 23 | Mississippi | 111.6 |
| 19 | Missouri | 130.7 |
| 43 | Montana | 25.8 |
| 38 | Nebraska | 75.9 |
| 3 | Nevada | 232.7 |
| 44 | New Hampshire | 21.4 |
| 8 | New Jersey | 174.9 |
| 15 | New Mexico | 148.2 |
| 2 | New York | 240.8 |
| 11 | North Carolina | 158.0 |
| 50 | North Dakota | 8.8 |
| 20 | Ohio | 128.0 |
| 32 | Oklahoma | 82.9 |
| 30 | Oregon | 86.2 |
| 13 | Pennsylvania | 155.7 |
| 35 | Rhode Island | 79.5 |
| 15 | South Carolina | 148.2 |
| 48 | South Dakota | 14.1 |
| 12 | Tennessee | 156.8 |
| 17 | Texas | 146.7 |
| 40 | Utah | 54.4 |
| 49 | Vermont | 10.9 |
| 25 | Virginia | 101.1 |
| 26 | Washington | 100.9 |
| 41 | West Virginia | 36.6 |
| 31 | Wisconsin | 84.7 |
| 47 | Wyoming | 15.4 |

RANK ORDER

| RANK | STATE | RATE |
|------|-------|------|
| 1 | Maryland | 263.7 |
| 2 | New York | 240.8 |
| 3 | Nevada | 232.7 |
| 4 | Illinois | 219.4 |
| 5 | Florida | 211.6 |
| 6 | Delaware | 197.9 |
| 7 | California | 181.1 |
| 8 | New Jersey | 174.9 |
| 9 | Louisiana | 173.6 |
| 10 | Georgia | 166.4 |
| 11 | North Carolina | 158.0 |
| 12 | Tennessee | 156.8 |
| 13 | Pennsylvania | 155.7 |
| 14 | Arizona | 152.5 |
| 15 | New Mexico | 148.2 |
| 15 | South Carolina | 148.2 |
| 17 | Texas | 146.7 |
| 18 | Michigan | 143.0 |
| 19 | Missouri | 130.7 |
| 20 | Ohio | 128.0 |
| 21 | Connecticut | 123.5 |
| 22 | Alabama | 121.2 |
| 23 | Mississippi | 111.6 |
| 24 | Indiana | 109.3 |
| 25 | Virginia | 101.1 |
| 26 | Washington | 100.9 |
| 27 | Massachusetts | 96.0 |
| 28 | Alaska | 91.4 |
| 29 | Hawaii | 88.1 |
| 30 | Oregon | 86.2 |
| 31 | Wisconsin | 84.7 |
| 32 | Oklahoma | 82.9 |
| 33 | Minnesota | 82.0 |
| 34 | Kentucky | 80.0 |
| 35 | Rhode Island | 79.5 |
| 36 | Arkansas | 79.3 |
| 37 | Kansas | 77.1 |
| 38 | Nebraska | 75.9 |
| 39 | Colorado | 75.3 |
| 40 | Utah | 54.4 |
| 41 | Iowa | 36.6 |
| 41 | West Virginia | 36.6 |
| 43 | Montana | 25.8 |
| 44 | New Hampshire | 21.4 |
| 45 | Maine | 19.4 |
| 46 | Idaho | 17.8 |
| 47 | Wyoming | 15.4 |
| 48 | South Dakota | 14.1 |
| 49 | Vermont | 10.9 |
| 50 | North Dakota | 8.8 |

| District of Columbia | 644.3 |
|------|------|

*Source: Federal Bureau of Investigation*
*"Crime in the United States 1999" (Uniform Crime Reports, October 15, 2000)*
*\*Robbery is the taking or attempting to take anything of value by force or threat of force.*

# Aggravated Assaults in 1999

## National Total = 916,383 Aggravated Assaults*

ALPHA ORDER

| RANK | STATE | ASSAULTS | % of USA |
|------|-------|----------|----------|
| 19 | Alabama | 14,266 | 1.6% |
| 40 | Alaska | 2,773 | 0.3% |
| 17 | Arizona | 17,279 | 1.9% |
| 27 | Arkansas | 7,971 | 0.9% |
| 1 | California | 136,472 | 14.9% |
| 25 | Colorado | 8,891 | 1.0% |
| 32 | Connecticut | 6,527 | 0.7% |
| 39 | Delaware | 3,489 | 0.4% |
| 2 | Florida | 89,226 | 9.7% |
| 11 | Georgia | 25,721 | 2.8% |
| 43 | Hawaii | 1,343 | 0.1% |
| 41 | Idaho | 2,401 | 0.3% |
| 5 | Illinois | 57,146 | 6.2% |
| 20 | Indiana | 13,767 | 1.5% |
| 33 | Iowa | 6,160 | 0.7% |
| 31 | Kansas | 6,887 | 0.8% |
| 28 | Kentucky | 7,488 | 0.8% |
| 14 | Louisiana | 22,526 | 2.5% |
| 45 | Maine | 897 | 0.1% |
| 13 | Maryland | 22,795 | 2.5% |
| 10 | Massachusetts | 26,307 | 2.9% |
| 6 | Michigan | 37,062 | 4.0% |
| 30 | Minnesota | 6,996 | 0.8% |
| 36 | Mississippi | 5,211 | 0.6% |
| 15 | Missouri | 18,406 | 2.0% |
| 44 | Montana | 1,322 | 0.1% |
| 34 | Nebraska | 5,429 | 0.6% |
| 37 | Nevada | 4,994 | 0.5% |
| 48 | New Hampshire | 539 | 0.1% |
| 16 | New Jersey | 17,601 | 1.9% |
| 24 | New Mexico | 10,827 | 1.2% |
| 4 | New York | 58,860 | 6.4% |
| 9 | North Carolina | 26,680 | 2.9% |
| 50 | North Dakota | 216 | 0.0% |
| 18 | Ohio | 16,685 | 1.8% |
| 22 | Oklahoma | 12,675 | 1.4% |
| 26 | Oregon | 8,267 | 0.9% |
| 7 | Pennsylvania | 27,890 | 3.0% |
| 42 | Rhode Island | 1,625 | 0.2% |
| 12 | South Carolina | 25,315 | 2.8% |
| 47 | South Dakota | 770 | 0.1% |
| 8 | Tennessee | 26,707 | 2.9% |
| 3 | Texas | 74,070 | 8.1% |
| 38 | Utah | 3,861 | 0.4% |
| 49 | Vermont | 458 | 0.0% |
| 23 | Virginia | 12,567 | 1.4% |
| 21 | Washington | 13,026 | 1.4% |
| 35 | West Virginia | 5,259 | 0.6% |
| 29 | Wisconsin | 7,225 | 0.8% |
| 46 | Wyoming | 893 | 0.1% |

RANK ORDER

| RANK | STATE | ASSAULTS | % of USA |
|------|-------|----------|----------|
| 1 | California | 136,472 | 14.9% |
| 2 | Florida | 89,226 | 9.7% |
| 3 | Texas | 74,070 | 8.1% |
| 4 | New York | 58,860 | 6.4% |
| 5 | Illinois | 57,146 | 6.2% |
| 6 | Michigan | 37,062 | 4.0% |
| 7 | Pennsylvania | 27,890 | 3.0% |
| 8 | Tennessee | 26,707 | 2.9% |
| 9 | North Carolina | 26,680 | 2.9% |
| 10 | Massachusetts | 26,307 | 2.9% |
| 11 | Georgia | 25,721 | 2.8% |
| 12 | South Carolina | 25,315 | 2.8% |
| 13 | Maryland | 22,795 | 2.5% |
| 14 | Louisiana | 22,526 | 2.5% |
| 15 | Missouri | 18,406 | 2.0% |
| 16 | New Jersey | 17,601 | 1.9% |
| 17 | Arizona | 17,279 | 1.9% |
| 18 | Ohio | 16,685 | 1.8% |
| 19 | Alabama | 14,266 | 1.6% |
| 20 | Indiana | 13,767 | 1.5% |
| 21 | Washington | 13,026 | 1.4% |
| 22 | Oklahoma | 12,675 | 1.4% |
| 23 | Virginia | 12,567 | 1.4% |
| 24 | New Mexico | 10,827 | 1.2% |
| 25 | Colorado | 8,891 | 1.0% |
| 26 | Oregon | 8,267 | 0.9% |
| 27 | Arkansas | 7,971 | 0.9% |
| 28 | Kentucky | 7,488 | 0.8% |
| 29 | Wisconsin | 7,225 | 0.8% |
| 30 | Minnesota | 6,996 | 0.8% |
| 31 | Kansas | 6,887 | 0.8% |
| 32 | Connecticut | 6,527 | 0.7% |
| 33 | Iowa | 6,160 | 0.7% |
| 34 | Nebraska | 5,429 | 0.6% |
| 35 | West Virginia | 5,259 | 0.6% |
| 36 | Mississippi | 5,211 | 0.6% |
| 37 | Nevada | 4,994 | 0.5% |
| 38 | Utah | 3,861 | 0.4% |
| 39 | Delaware | 3,489 | 0.4% |
| 40 | Alaska | 2,773 | 0.3% |
| 41 | Idaho | 2,401 | 0.3% |
| 42 | Rhode Island | 1,625 | 0.2% |
| 43 | Hawaii | 1,343 | 0.1% |
| 44 | Montana | 1,322 | 0.1% |
| 45 | Maine | 897 | 0.1% |
| 46 | Wyoming | 893 | 0.1% |
| 47 | South Dakota | 770 | 0.1% |
| 48 | New Hampshire | 539 | 0.1% |
| 49 | Vermont | 458 | 0.0% |
| 50 | North Dakota | 216 | 0.0% |
| | District of Columbia | 4,615 | 0.5% |

Source: Federal Bureau of Investigation
"Crime in the United States 1999" (Uniform Crime Reports, October 15, 2000)
*Aggravated assault is an attack for the purpose of inflicting severe bodily injury.

# Percent Change in Number of Aggravated Assaults: 1998 to 1999

## National Percent Change = 6.2% Decrease*

ALPHA ORDER

| RANK | STATE | PERCENT CHANGE |
|------|-------|----------------|
| 15 | Alabama | (3.5) |
| 30 | Alaska | (8.2) |
| 8 | Arizona | (0.9) |
| 38 | Arkansas | (10.5) |
| 33 | California | (8.5) |
| 32 | Colorado | (8.4) |
| 14 | Connecticut | (3.3) |
| 21 | Delaware | (5.9) |
| 22 | Florida | (6.5) |
| 12 | Georgia | (3.0) |
| 7 | Hawaii | (0.1) |
| 42 | Idaho | (13.7) |
| 30 | Illinois | (8.2) |
| 45 | Indiana | (16.3) |
| 29 | Iowa | (7.8) |
| 23 | Kansas | (6.7) |
| 28 | Kentucky | (7.5) |
| 13 | Louisiana | (3.1) |
| 43 | Maine | (14.7) |
| 11 | Maryland | (2.3) |
| 41 | Massachusetts | (13.6) |
| 27 | Michigan | (7.3) |
| 37 | Minnesota | (10.4) |
| 47 | Mississippi | (20.6) |
| 34 | Missouri | (9.1) |
| 5 | Montana | 0.8 |
| 19 | Nebraska | (5.6) |
| 40 | Nevada | (12.5) |
| 35 | New Hampshire | (9.7) |
| 20 | New Jersey | (5.7) |
| 44 | New Mexico | (14.8) |
| 18 | New York | (5.1) |
| 25 | North Carolina | (6.9) |
| 49 | North Dakota | (24.5) |
| 46 | Ohio | (19.3) |
| 16 | Oklahoma | (4.4) |
| 26 | Oregon | (7.0) |
| 3 | Pennsylvania | 4.0 |
| 48 | Rhode Island | (20.7) |
| 17 | South Carolina | (5.0) |
| 2 | South Dakota | 6.6 |
| 4 | Tennessee | 1.9 |
| 6 | Texas | 0.6 |
| 35 | Utah | (9.7) |
| 1 | Vermont | 15.7 |
| 9 | Virginia | (1.1) |
| 39 | Washington | (12.2) |
| NA | West Virginia** | NA |
| 9 | Wisconsin | (1.1) |
| 23 | Wyoming | (6.7) |

RANK ORDER

| RANK | STATE | PERCENT CHANGE |
|------|-------|----------------|
| 1 | Vermont | 15.7 |
| 2 | South Dakota | 6.6 |
| 3 | Pennsylvania | 4.0 |
| 4 | Tennessee | 1.9 |
| 5 | Montana | 0.8 |
| 6 | Texas | 0.6 |
| 7 | Hawaii | (0.1) |
| 8 | Arizona | (0.9) |
| 9 | Virginia | (1.1) |
| 9 | Wisconsin | (1.1) |
| 11 | Maryland | (2.3) |
| 12 | Georgia | (3.0) |
| 13 | Louisiana | (3.1) |
| 14 | Connecticut | (3.3) |
| 15 | Alabama | (3.5) |
| 16 | Oklahoma | (4.4) |
| 17 | South Carolina | (5.0) |
| 18 | New York | (5.1) |
| 19 | Nebraska | (5.6) |
| 20 | New Jersey | (5.7) |
| 21 | Delaware | (5.9) |
| 22 | Florida | (6.5) |
| 23 | Kansas | (6.7) |
| 23 | Wyoming | (6.7) |
| 25 | North Carolina | (6.9) |
| 26 | Oregon | (7.0) |
| 27 | Michigan | (7.3) |
| 28 | Kentucky | (7.5) |
| 29 | Iowa | (7.8) |
| 30 | Alaska | (8.2) |
| 30 | Illinois | (8.2) |
| 32 | Colorado | (8.4) |
| 33 | California | (8.5) |
| 34 | Missouri | (9.1) |
| 35 | New Hampshire | (9.7) |
| 35 | Utah | (9.7) |
| 37 | Minnesota | (10.4) |
| 38 | Arkansas | (10.5) |
| 39 | Washington | (12.2) |
| 40 | Nevada | (12.5) |
| 41 | Massachusetts | (13.6) |
| 42 | Idaho | (13.7) |
| 43 | Maine | (14.7) |
| 44 | New Mexico | (14.8) |
| 45 | Indiana | (16.3) |
| 46 | Ohio | (19.3) |
| 47 | Mississippi | (20.6) |
| 48 | Rhode Island | (20.7) |
| 49 | North Dakota | (24.5) |
| NA | West Virginia** | NA |
| | District of Columbia | (6.4) |

*Source: Federal Bureau of Investigation*
   *"Crime in the United States 1999" (Uniform Crime Reports, October 15, 2000)*
*Aggravated assault is an attack for the purpose of inflicting severe bodily injury.*
**Not available.*

# Aggravated Assault Rate in 1999

## National Rate = 336.1 Aggravated Assaults per 100,000 Population*

ALPHA ORDER

| RANK | STATE | RATE |
|------|-------|------|
| 19 | Alabama | 326.5 |
| 8 | Alaska | 448.0 |
| 15 | Arizona | 361.6 |
| 22 | Arkansas | 312.5 |
| 11 | California | 411.7 |
| 30 | Colorado | 219.2 |
| 33 | Connecticut | 198.9 |
| 7 | Delaware | 462.7 |
| 3 | Florida | 590.5 |
| 18 | Georgia | 330.3 |
| 45 | Hawaii | 113.3 |
| 34 | Idaho | 191.8 |
| 6 | Illinois | 471.2 |
| 28 | Indiana | 231.7 |
| 32 | Iowa | 214.7 |
| 25 | Kansas | 259.5 |
| 35 | Kentucky | 189.0 |
| 4 | Louisiana | 515.2 |
| 48 | Maine | 71.6 |
| 9 | Maryland | 440.7 |
| 10 | Massachusetts | 426.0 |
| 13 | Michigan | 375.7 |
| 43 | Minnesota | 146.5 |
| 36 | Mississippi | 188.2 |
| 17 | Missouri | 336.6 |
| 41 | Montana | 149.7 |
| 20 | Nebraska | 325.9 |
| 24 | Nevada | 276.1 |
| 49 | New Hampshire | 44.9 |
| 31 | New Jersey | 216.1 |
| 2 | New Mexico | 622.2 |
| 21 | New York | 323.5 |
| 16 | North Carolina | 348.7 |
| 50 | North Dakota | 34.1 |
| 42 | Ohio | 148.2 |
| 12 | Oklahoma | 377.5 |
| 26 | Oregon | 249.3 |
| 27 | Pennsylvania | 232.5 |
| 40 | Rhode Island | 164.0 |
| 1 | South Carolina | 651.4 |
| 46 | South Dakota | 105.0 |
| 5 | Tennessee | 487.0 |
| 14 | Texas | 369.5 |
| 39 | Utah | 181.3 |
| 47 | Vermont | 77.1 |
| 38 | Virginia | 182.8 |
| 29 | Washington | 226.3 |
| 23 | West Virginia | 291.0 |
| 44 | Wisconsin | 137.6 |
| 37 | Wyoming | 186.0 |

RANK ORDER

| RANK | STATE | RATE |
|------|-------|------|
| 1 | South Carolina | 651.4 |
| 2 | New Mexico | 622.2 |
| 3 | Florida | 590.5 |
| 4 | Louisiana | 515.2 |
| 5 | Tennessee | 487.0 |
| 6 | Illinois | 471.2 |
| 7 | Delaware | 462.7 |
| 8 | Alaska | 448.0 |
| 9 | Maryland | 440.7 |
| 10 | Massachusetts | 426.0 |
| 11 | California | 411.7 |
| 12 | Oklahoma | 377.5 |
| 13 | Michigan | 375.7 |
| 14 | Texas | 369.5 |
| 15 | Arizona | 361.6 |
| 16 | North Carolina | 348.7 |
| 17 | Missouri | 336.6 |
| 18 | Georgia | 330.3 |
| 19 | Alabama | 326.5 |
| 20 | Nebraska | 325.9 |
| 21 | New York | 323.5 |
| 22 | Arkansas | 312.5 |
| 23 | West Virginia | 291.0 |
| 24 | Nevada | 276.1 |
| 25 | Kansas | 259.5 |
| 26 | Oregon | 249.3 |
| 27 | Pennsylvania | 232.5 |
| 28 | Indiana | 231.7 |
| 29 | Washington | 226.3 |
| 30 | Colorado | 219.2 |
| 31 | New Jersey | 216.1 |
| 32 | Iowa | 214.7 |
| 33 | Connecticut | 198.9 |
| 34 | Idaho | 191.8 |
| 35 | Kentucky | 189.0 |
| 36 | Mississippi | 188.2 |
| 37 | Wyoming | 186.0 |
| 38 | Virginia | 182.8 |
| 39 | Utah | 181.3 |
| 40 | Rhode Island | 164.0 |
| 41 | Montana | 149.7 |
| 42 | Ohio | 148.2 |
| 43 | Minnesota | 146.5 |
| 44 | Wisconsin | 137.6 |
| 45 | Hawaii | 113.3 |
| 46 | South Dakota | 105.0 |
| 47 | Vermont | 77.1 |
| 48 | Maine | 71.6 |
| 49 | New Hampshire | 44.9 |
| 50 | North Dakota | 34.1 |
| | District of Columbia | 889.2 |

Source: Federal Bureau of Investigation
   "Crime in the United States 1999" (Uniform Crime Reports, October 15, 2000)
*Aggravated assault is an attack for the purpose of inflicting severe bodily injury.

# Property Crimes in 1999

## National Total = 10,204,456 Property Crimes*

ALPHA ORDER

| RANK | STATE | CRIMES | % of USA |
|---|---|---|---|
| 21 | Alabama | 171,398 | 1.7% |
| 46 | Alaska | 23,099 | 0.2% |
| 12 | Arizona | 255,401 | 2.5% |
| 33 | Arkansas | 92,283 | 0.9% |
| 1 | California | 1,053,285 | 10.3% |
| 26 | Colorado | 151,002 | 1.5% |
| 32 | Connecticut | 99,894 | 1.0% |
| 44 | Delaware | 30,922 | 0.3% |
| 3 | Florida | 808,674 | 7.9% |
| 8 | Georgia | 359,383 | 3.5% |
| 38 | Hawaii | 54,539 | 0.5% |
| 40 | Idaho | 36,363 | 0.4% |
| 5 | Illinois | 457,723 | 4.5% |
| 19 | Indiana | 201,547 | 2.0% |
| 35 | Iowa | 84,463 | 0.8% |
| 29 | Kansas | 107,644 | 1.1% |
| 30 | Kentucky | 102,095 | 1.0% |
| 16 | Louisiana | 219,219 | 2.1% |
| 41 | Maine | 34,618 | 0.3% |
| 17 | Maryland | 215,973 | 2.1% |
| 22 | Massachusetts | 167,437 | 1.6% |
| 7 | Michigan | 369,887 | 3.6% |
| 24 | Minnesota | 158,717 | 1.6% |
| 28 | Mississippi | 108,560 | 1.1% |
| 14 | Missouri | 223,010 | 2.2% |
| 42 | Montana | 34,114 | 0.3% |
| 37 | Nebraska | 61,277 | 0.6% |
| 36 | Nevada | 73,874 | 0.7% |
| 45 | New Hampshire | 26,247 | 0.3% |
| 13 | New Jersey | 243,333 | 2.4% |
| 34 | New Mexico | 89,220 | 0.9% |
| 4 | New York | 489,596 | 4.8% |
| 9 | North Carolina | 354,497 | 3.5% |
| 50 | North Dakota | 14,748 | 0.1% |
| 6 | Ohio | 414,264 | 4.1% |
| 27 | Oklahoma | 140,220 | 1.4% |
| 25 | Oregon | 153,434 | 1.5% |
| 10 | Pennsylvania | 323,021 | 3.2% |
| 43 | Rhode Island | 32,657 | 0.3% |
| 20 | South Carolina | 173,987 | 1.7% |
| 47 | South Dakota | 18,159 | 0.2% |
| 15 | Tennessee | 219,302 | 2.1% |
| 2 | Texas | 896,261 | 8.8% |
| 31 | Utah | 100,130 | 1.0% |
| 48 | Vermont | 16,059 | 0.2% |
| 18 | Virginia | 210,260 | 2.1% |
| 11 | Washington | 280,793 | 2.8% |
| 39 | West Virginia | 42,825 | 0.4% |
| 23 | Wisconsin | 160,154 | 1.6% |
| 49 | Wyoming | 15,468 | 0.2% |

RANK ORDER

| RANK | STATE | CRIMES | % of USA |
|---|---|---|---|
| 1 | California | 1,053,285 | 10.3% |
| 2 | Texas | 896,261 | 8.8% |
| 3 | Florida | 808,674 | 7.9% |
| 4 | New York | 489,596 | 4.8% |
| 5 | Illinois | 457,723 | 4.5% |
| 6 | Ohio | 414,264 | 4.1% |
| 7 | Michigan | 369,887 | 3.6% |
| 8 | Georgia | 359,383 | 3.5% |
| 9 | North Carolina | 354,497 | 3.5% |
| 10 | Pennsylvania | 323,021 | 3.2% |
| 11 | Washington | 280,793 | 2.8% |
| 12 | Arizona | 255,401 | 2.5% |
| 13 | New Jersey | 243,333 | 2.4% |
| 14 | Missouri | 223,010 | 2.2% |
| 15 | Tennessee | 219,302 | 2.1% |
| 16 | Louisiana | 219,219 | 2.1% |
| 17 | Maryland | 215,973 | 2.1% |
| 18 | Virginia | 210,260 | 2.1% |
| 19 | Indiana | 201,547 | 2.0% |
| 20 | South Carolina | 173,987 | 1.7% |
| 21 | Alabama | 171,398 | 1.7% |
| 22 | Massachusetts | 167,437 | 1.6% |
| 23 | Wisconsin | 160,154 | 1.6% |
| 24 | Minnesota | 158,717 | 1.6% |
| 25 | Oregon | 153,434 | 1.5% |
| 26 | Colorado | 151,002 | 1.5% |
| 27 | Oklahoma | 140,220 | 1.4% |
| 28 | Mississippi | 108,560 | 1.1% |
| 29 | Kansas | 107,644 | 1.1% |
| 30 | Kentucky | 102,095 | 1.0% |
| 31 | Utah | 100,130 | 1.0% |
| 32 | Connecticut | 99,894 | 1.0% |
| 33 | Arkansas | 92,283 | 0.9% |
| 34 | New Mexico | 89,220 | 0.9% |
| 35 | Iowa | 84,463 | 0.8% |
| 36 | Nevada | 73,874 | 0.7% |
| 37 | Nebraska | 61,277 | 0.6% |
| 38 | Hawaii | 54,539 | 0.5% |
| 39 | West Virginia | 42,825 | 0.4% |
| 40 | Idaho | 36,363 | 0.4% |
| 41 | Maine | 34,618 | 0.3% |
| 42 | Montana | 34,114 | 0.3% |
| 43 | Rhode Island | 32,657 | 0.3% |
| 44 | Delaware | 30,922 | 0.3% |
| 45 | New Hampshire | 26,247 | 0.3% |
| 46 | Alaska | 23,099 | 0.2% |
| 47 | South Dakota | 18,159 | 0.2% |
| 48 | Vermont | 16,059 | 0.2% |
| 49 | Wyoming | 15,468 | 0.2% |
| 50 | North Dakota | 14,748 | 0.1% |
|  | District of Columbia | 33,420 | 0.3% |

Source: Federal Bureau of Investigation
"Crime in the United States 1999" (Uniform Crime Reports, October 15, 2000)
*Property crimes are offenses of burglary, larceny-theft and motor vehicle theft.

# Percent Change in Number of Property Crimes: 1998 to 1999

## National Percent Change = 6.8% Decrease*

ALPHA ORDER

| RANK | STATE | PERCENT CHANGE | RANK | STATE | PERCENT CHANGE |
|------|-------|----------------|------|-------|----------------|
| 7 | Alabama | (3.6) | 1 | Rhode Island | 3.1 |
| 34 | Alaska | (8.8) | 2 | Texas | (0.2) |
| 34 | Arizona | (8.8) | 3 | South Dakota | (0.4) |
| 10 | Arkansas | (4.1) | 4 | Mississippi | (0.7) |
| 48 | California | (11.4) | 5 | North Carolina | (0.9) |
| 27 | Colorado | (7.5) | 6 | Massachusetts | (3.2) |
| 45 | Connecticut | (10.8) | 7 | Alabama | (3.6) |
| 39 | Delaware | (9.7) | 8 | Georgia | (3.8) |
| 34 | Florida | (8.8) | 9 | Missouri | (4.0) |
| 8 | Georgia | (3.8) | 10 | Arkansas | (4.1) |
| 41 | Hawaii | (10.1) | 11 | New Hampshire | (4.2) |
| 49 | Idaho | (13.8) | 12 | Maine | (4.5) |
| 15 | Illinois | (6.2) | 13 | Pennsylvania | (5.6) |
| 32 | Indiana | (8.6) | 14 | Louisiana | (5.7) |
| 27 | Iowa | (7.5) | 15 | Illinois | (6.2) |
| 30 | Kansas | (8.1) | 15 | Oklahoma | (6.2) |
| 24 | Kentucky | (7.0) | 17 | Tennessee | (6.5) |
| 14 | Louisiana | (5.7) | 18 | Montana | (6.7) |
| 12 | Maine | (4.5) | 18 | New Jersey | (6.7) |
| 29 | Maryland | (7.9) | 20 | Nebraska | (6.8) |
| 6 | Massachusetts | (3.2) | 20 | Ohio | (6.8) |
| 25 | Michigan | (7.2) | 22 | South Carolina | (6.9) |
| 41 | Minnesota | (10.1) | 22 | Wisconsin | (6.9) |
| 4 | Mississippi | (0.7) | 24 | Kentucky | (7.0) |
| 9 | Missouri | (4.0) | 25 | Michigan | (7.2) |
| 18 | Montana | (6.7) | 25 | Virginia | (7.2) |
| 20 | Nebraska | (6.8) | 27 | Colorado | (7.5) |
| 34 | Nevada | (8.8) | 27 | Iowa | (7.5) |
| 11 | New Hampshire | (4.2) | 29 | Maryland | (7.9) |
| 18 | New Jersey | (6.7) | 30 | Kansas | (8.1) |
| 45 | New Mexico | (10.8) | 31 | Utah | (8.2) |
| 33 | New York | (8.7) | 32 | Indiana | (8.6) |
| 5 | North Carolina | (0.9) | 33 | New York | (8.7) |
| 45 | North Dakota | (10.8) | 34 | Alaska | (8.8) |
| 20 | Ohio | (6.8) | 34 | Arizona | (8.8) |
| 15 | Oklahoma | (6.2) | 34 | Florida | (8.8) |
| 44 | Oregon | (10.6) | 34 | Nevada | (8.8) |
| 13 | Pennsylvania | (5.6) | 38 | Washington | (9.3) |
| 1 | Rhode Island | 3.1 | 39 | Delaware | (9.7) |
| 22 | South Carolina | (6.9) | 39 | Wyoming | (9.7) |
| 3 | South Dakota | (0.4) | 41 | Hawaii | (10.1) |
| 17 | Tennessee | (6.5) | 41 | Minnesota | (10.1) |
| 2 | Texas | (0.2) | 43 | Vermont | (10.4) |
| 31 | Utah | (8.2) | 44 | Oregon | (10.6) |
| 43 | Vermont | (10.4) | 45 | Connecticut | (10.8) |
| 25 | Virginia | (7.2) | 45 | New Mexico | (10.8) |
| 38 | Washington | (9.3) | 45 | North Dakota | (10.8) |
| NA | West Virginia** | NA | 48 | California | (11.4) |
| 22 | Wisconsin | (6.9) | 49 | Idaho | (13.8) |
| 39 | Wyoming | (9.7) | NA | West Virginia** | NA |
| | | | | District of Columbia | (10.2) |

*Source: Federal Bureau of Investigation*
   *"Crime in the United States 1999" (Uniform Crime Reports, October 15, 2000)*
*\*Property crimes are offenses of burglary, larceny-theft and motor vehicle theft.*
*\*\*Not available.*

# Property Crime Rate in 1999

## National Rate = 3,742.1 Property Crimes per 100,000 Population*

ALPHA ORDER

| RANK | STATE | RATE |
|------|-------|------|
| 20 | Alabama | 3,922.2 |
| 25 | Alaska | 3,731.7 |
| 2 | Arizona | 5,345.4 |
| 29 | Arkansas | 3,617.5 |
| 34 | California | 3,177.8 |
| 26 | Colorado | 3,722.9 |
| 37 | Connecticut | 3,043.7 |
| 15 | Delaware | 4,101.1 |
| 1 | Florida | 5,351.6 |
| 9 | Georgia | 4,614.6 |
| 10 | Hawaii | 4,602.4 |
| 40 | Idaho | 2,904.4 |
| 23 | Illinois | 3,774.1 |
| 30 | Indiana | 3,391.3 |
| 39 | Iowa | 2,944.0 |
| 18 | Kansas | 4,055.9 |
| 46 | Kentucky | 2,577.5 |
| 4 | Louisiana | 5,014.2 |
| 41 | Maine | 2,762.8 |
| 13 | Maryland | 4,175.8 |
| 42 | Massachusetts | 2,711.5 |
| 24 | Michigan | 3,749.9 |
| 31 | Minnesota | 3,323.2 |
| 21 | Mississippi | 3,920.5 |
| 17 | Missouri | 4,078.5 |
| 22 | Montana | 3,863.4 |
| 28 | Nebraska | 3,678.1 |
| 16 | Nevada | 4,083.7 |
| 50 | New Hampshire | 2,185.4 |
| 38 | New Jersey | 2,988.2 |
| 3 | New Mexico | 5,127.6 |
| 45 | New York | 2,690.5 |
| 7 | North Carolina | 4,633.3 |
| 49 | North Dakota | 2,326.2 |
| 27 | Ohio | 3,680.1 |
| 14 | Oklahoma | 4,175.7 |
| 8 | Oregon | 4,627.1 |
| 44 | Pennsylvania | 2,693.2 |
| 32 | Rhode Island | 3,295.4 |
| 11 | South Carolina | 4,477.3 |
| 47 | South Dakota | 2,477.4 |
| 19 | Tennessee | 3,998.9 |
| 12 | Texas | 4,471.5 |
| 6 | Utah | 4,700.9 |
| 43 | Vermont | 2,703.5 |
| 35 | Virginia | 3,059.2 |
| 5 | Washington | 4,878.3 |
| 48 | West Virginia | 2,370.0 |
| 36 | Wisconsin | 3,050.6 |
| 33 | Wyoming | 3,222.5 |

RANK ORDER

| RANK | STATE | RATE |
|------|-------|------|
| 1 | Florida | 5,351.6 |
| 2 | Arizona | 5,345.4 |
| 3 | New Mexico | 5,127.6 |
| 4 | Louisiana | 5,014.2 |
| 5 | Washington | 4,878.3 |
| 6 | Utah | 4,700.9 |
| 7 | North Carolina | 4,633.3 |
| 8 | Oregon | 4,627.1 |
| 9 | Georgia | 4,614.6 |
| 10 | Hawaii | 4,602.4 |
| 11 | South Carolina | 4,477.3 |
| 12 | Texas | 4,471.5 |
| 13 | Maryland | 4,175.8 |
| 14 | Oklahoma | 4,175.7 |
| 15 | Delaware | 4,101.1 |
| 16 | Nevada | 4,083.7 |
| 17 | Missouri | 4,078.5 |
| 18 | Kansas | 4,055.9 |
| 19 | Tennessee | 3,998.9 |
| 20 | Alabama | 3,922.2 |
| 21 | Mississippi | 3,920.5 |
| 22 | Montana | 3,863.4 |
| 23 | Illinois | 3,774.1 |
| 24 | Michigan | 3,749.9 |
| 25 | Alaska | 3,731.7 |
| 26 | Colorado | 3,722.9 |
| 27 | Ohio | 3,680.1 |
| 28 | Nebraska | 3,678.1 |
| 29 | Arkansas | 3,617.5 |
| 30 | Indiana | 3,391.3 |
| 31 | Minnesota | 3,323.2 |
| 32 | Rhode Island | 3,295.4 |
| 33 | Wyoming | 3,222.5 |
| 34 | California | 3,177.8 |
| 35 | Virginia | 3,059.2 |
| 36 | Wisconsin | 3,050.6 |
| 37 | Connecticut | 3,043.7 |
| 38 | New Jersey | 2,988.2 |
| 39 | Iowa | 2,944.0 |
| 40 | Idaho | 2,904.4 |
| 41 | Maine | 2,762.8 |
| 42 | Massachusetts | 2,711.5 |
| 43 | Vermont | 2,703.5 |
| 44 | Pennsylvania | 2,693.2 |
| 45 | New York | 2,690.5 |
| 46 | Kentucky | 2,577.5 |
| 47 | South Dakota | 2,477.4 |
| 48 | West Virginia | 2,370.0 |
| 49 | North Dakota | 2,326.2 |
| 50 | New Hampshire | 2,185.4 |

District of Columbia    6,439.3

Source: Federal Bureau of Investigation
"Crime in the United States 1999" (Uniform Crime Reports, October 15, 2000)
*Property crimes are offenses of burglary, larceny-theft and motor vehicle theft.

# Percent Change in Property Crime Rate: 1998 to 1999

## National Percent Change = 7.6% Decrease*

ALPHA ORDER

| RANK | STATE | PERCENT CHANGE |
|------|-------|----------------|
| 7 | Alabama | (4.0) |
| 33 | Alaska | (9.5) |
| 40 | Arizona | (10.9) |
| 9 | Arkansas | (4.6) |
| 48 | California | (12.7) |
| 32 | Colorado | (9.4) |
| 44 | Connecticut | (11.0) |
| 40 | Delaware | (10.9) |
| 37 | Florida | (10.0) |
| 12 | Georgia | (5.6) |
| 33 | Hawaii | (9.5) |
| 49 | Idaho | (15.4) |
| 16 | Illinois | (6.8) |
| 31 | Indiana | (9.3) |
| 24 | Iowa | (7.7) |
| 30 | Kansas | (9.0) |
| 23 | Kentucky | (7.5) |
| 14 | Louisiana | (5.7) |
| 10 | Maine | (5.2) |
| 28 | Maryland | (8.6) |
| 6 | Massachusetts | (3.7) |
| 24 | Michigan | (7.7) |
| 45 | Minnesota | (11.1) |
| 3 | Mississippi | (1.3) |
| 8 | Missouri | (4.5) |
| 17 | Montana | (7.0) |
| 17 | Nebraska | (7.0) |
| 47 | Nevada | (11.9) |
| 11 | New Hampshire | (5.5) |
| 17 | New Jersey | (7.0) |
| 40 | New Mexico | (10.9) |
| 29 | New York | (8.8) |
| 5 | North Carolina | (2.3) |
| 38 | North Dakota | (10.2) |
| 20 | Ohio | (7.2) |
| 15 | Oklahoma | (6.5) |
| 46 | Oregon | (11.5) |
| 12 | Pennsylvania | (5.6) |
| 1 | Rhode Island | 2.8 |
| 26 | South Carolina | (8.1) |
| 2 | South Dakota | 0.3 |
| 21 | Tennessee | (7.4) |
| 4 | Texas | (1.7) |
| 33 | Utah | (9.5) |
| 40 | Vermont | (10.9) |
| 27 | Virginia | (8.3) |
| 39 | Washington | (10.3) |
| NA | West Virginia** | NA |
| 21 | Wisconsin | (7.4) |
| 33 | Wyoming | (9.5) |

RANK ORDER

| RANK | STATE | PERCENT CHANGE |
|------|-------|----------------|
| 1 | Rhode Island | 2.8 |
| 2 | South Dakota | 0.3 |
| 3 | Mississippi | (1.3) |
| 4 | Texas | (1.7) |
| 5 | North Carolina | (2.3) |
| 6 | Massachusetts | (3.7) |
| 7 | Alabama | (4.0) |
| 8 | Missouri | (4.5) |
| 9 | Arkansas | (4.6) |
| 10 | Maine | (5.2) |
| 11 | New Hampshire | (5.5) |
| 12 | Georgia | (5.6) |
| 12 | Pennsylvania | (5.6) |
| 14 | Louisiana | (5.7) |
| 15 | Oklahoma | (6.5) |
| 16 | Illinois | (6.8) |
| 17 | Montana | (7.0) |
| 17 | Nebraska | (7.0) |
| 17 | New Jersey | (7.0) |
| 20 | Ohio | (7.2) |
| 21 | Tennessee | (7.4) |
| 21 | Wisconsin | (7.4) |
| 23 | Kentucky | (7.5) |
| 24 | Iowa | (7.7) |
| 24 | Michigan | (7.7) |
| 26 | South Carolina | (8.1) |
| 27 | Virginia | (8.3) |
| 28 | Maryland | (8.6) |
| 29 | New York | (8.8) |
| 30 | Kansas | (9.0) |
| 31 | Indiana | (9.3) |
| 32 | Colorado | (9.4) |
| 33 | Alaska | (9.5) |
| 33 | Hawaii | (9.5) |
| 33 | Utah | (9.5) |
| 33 | Wyoming | (9.5) |
| 37 | Florida | (10.0) |
| 38 | North Dakota | (10.2) |
| 39 | Washington | (10.3) |
| 40 | Arizona | (10.9) |
| 40 | Delaware | (10.9) |
| 40 | New Mexico | (10.9) |
| 40 | Vermont | (10.9) |
| 44 | Connecticut | (11.0) |
| 45 | Minnesota | (11.1) |
| 46 | Oregon | (11.5) |
| 47 | Nevada | (11.9) |
| 48 | California | (12.7) |
| 49 | Idaho | (15.4) |
| NA | West Virginia** | NA |

District of Columbia (9.5)

*Source: Federal Bureau of Investigation*
"Crime in the United States 1999" (Uniform Crime Reports, October 15, 2000)
*Property crimes are offenses of burglary, larceny-theft and motor vehicle theft.
**Not available.

# Burglaries in 1999

## National Total = 2,099,739 Burglaries*

ALPHA ORDER

RANK ORDER

| RANK | STATE | BURGLARIES | % of USA |
|---|---|---|---|
| 20 | Alabama | 38,648 | 1.8% |
| 44 | Alaska | 3,787 | 0.2% |
| 13 | Arizona | 49,423 | 2.4% |
| 31 | Arkansas | 21,692 | 1.0% |
| 1 | California | 223,814 | 10.7% |
| 26 | Colorado | 26,979 | 1.3% |
| 33 | Connecticut | 19,298 | 0.9% |
| 43 | Delaware | 5,245 | 0.2% |
| 3 | Florida | 181,378 | 8.6% |
| 9 | Georgia | 71,429 | 3.4% |
| 39 | Hawaii | 9,421 | 0.4% |
| 40 | Idaho | 7,641 | 0.4% |
| 7 | Illinois | 86,390 | 4.1% |
| 18 | Indiana | 42,463 | 2.0% |
| 35 | Iowa | 17,012 | 0.8% |
| 30 | Kansas | 21,874 | 1.0% |
| 29 | Kentucky | 24,199 | 1.2% |
| 14 | Louisiana | 47,775 | 2.3% |
| 41 | Maine | 7,532 | 0.4% |
| 16 | Maryland | 43,230 | 2.1% |
| 22 | Massachusetts | 32,964 | 1.6% |
| 8 | Michigan | 76,736 | 3.7% |
| 25 | Minnesota | 27,706 | 1.3% |
| 24 | Mississippi | 29,109 | 1.4% |
| 17 | Missouri | 42,476 | 2.0% |
| 45 | Montana | 3,784 | 0.2% |
| 38 | Nebraska | 10,158 | 0.5% |
| 34 | Nevada | 17,613 | 0.8% |
| 46 | New Hampshire | 3,698 | 0.2% |
| 15 | New Jersey | 46,998 | 2.2% |
| 32 | New Mexico | 21,481 | 1.0% |
| 5 | New York | 93,217 | 4.4% |
| 4 | North Carolina | 98,457 | 4.7% |
| 50 | North Dakota | 2,337 | 0.1% |
| 6 | Ohio | 87,023 | 4.1% |
| 21 | Oklahoma | 34,472 | 1.6% |
| 27 | Oregon | 26,749 | 1.3% |
| 10 | Pennsylvania | 56,037 | 2.7% |
| 42 | Rhode Island | 6,341 | 0.3% |
| 19 | South Carolina | 39,630 | 1.9% |
| 48 | South Dakota | 3,255 | 0.2% |
| 12 | Tennessee | 51,362 | 2.4% |
| 2 | Texas | 190,362 | 9.1% |
| 36 | Utah | 14,592 | 0.7% |
| 47 | Vermont | 3,537 | 0.2% |
| 23 | Virginia | 32,411 | 1.5% |
| 11 | Washington | 54,652 | 2.6% |
| 37 | West Virginia | 10,303 | 0.5% |
| 28 | Wisconsin | 25,633 | 1.2% |
| 49 | Wyoming | 2,349 | 0.1% |

| RANK | STATE | BURGLARIES | % of USA |
|---|---|---|---|
| 1 | California | 223,814 | 10.7% |
| 2 | Texas | 190,362 | 9.1% |
| 3 | Florida | 181,378 | 8.6% |
| 4 | North Carolina | 98,457 | 4.7% |
| 5 | New York | 93,217 | 4.4% |
| 6 | Ohio | 87,023 | 4.1% |
| 7 | Illinois | 86,390 | 4.1% |
| 8 | Michigan | 76,736 | 3.7% |
| 9 | Georgia | 71,429 | 3.4% |
| 10 | Pennsylvania | 56,037 | 2.7% |
| 11 | Washington | 54,652 | 2.6% |
| 12 | Tennessee | 51,362 | 2.4% |
| 13 | Arizona | 49,423 | 2.4% |
| 14 | Louisiana | 47,775 | 2.3% |
| 15 | New Jersey | 46,998 | 2.2% |
| 16 | Maryland | 43,230 | 2.1% |
| 17 | Missouri | 42,476 | 2.0% |
| 18 | Indiana | 42,463 | 2.0% |
| 19 | South Carolina | 39,630 | 1.9% |
| 20 | Alabama | 38,648 | 1.8% |
| 21 | Oklahoma | 34,472 | 1.6% |
| 22 | Massachusetts | 32,964 | 1.6% |
| 23 | Virginia | 32,411 | 1.5% |
| 24 | Mississippi | 29,109 | 1.4% |
| 25 | Minnesota | 27,706 | 1.3% |
| 26 | Colorado | 26,979 | 1.3% |
| 27 | Oregon | 26,749 | 1.3% |
| 28 | Wisconsin | 25,633 | 1.2% |
| 29 | Kentucky | 24,199 | 1.2% |
| 30 | Kansas | 21,874 | 1.0% |
| 31 | Arkansas | 21,692 | 1.0% |
| 32 | New Mexico | 21,481 | 1.0% |
| 33 | Connecticut | 19,298 | 0.9% |
| 34 | Nevada | 17,613 | 0.8% |
| 35 | Iowa | 17,012 | 0.8% |
| 36 | Utah | 14,592 | 0.7% |
| 37 | West Virginia | 10,303 | 0.5% |
| 38 | Nebraska | 10,158 | 0.5% |
| 39 | Hawaii | 9,421 | 0.4% |
| 40 | Idaho | 7,641 | 0.4% |
| 41 | Maine | 7,532 | 0.4% |
| 42 | Rhode Island | 6,341 | 0.3% |
| 43 | Delaware | 5,245 | 0.2% |
| 44 | Alaska | 3,787 | 0.2% |
| 45 | Montana | 3,784 | 0.2% |
| 46 | New Hampshire | 3,698 | 0.2% |
| 47 | Vermont | 3,537 | 0.2% |
| 48 | South Dakota | 3,255 | 0.2% |
| 49 | Wyoming | 2,349 | 0.1% |
| 50 | North Dakota | 2,337 | 0.1% |
| | District of Columbia | 5,067 | 0.2% |

Source: Federal Bureau of Investigation
   "Crime in the United States 1999" (Uniform Crime Reports, October 15, 2000)
*Burglary is the unlawful entry of a structure to commit a felony or theft. Attempts are included.

# Percent Change in Number of Burglaries: 1998 to 1999

## National Percent Change = 10.0% Decrease*

| RANK | STATE | PERCENT CHANGE |
|---|---|---|
| 14 | Alabama | (7.9) |
| 12 | Alaska | (7.6) |
| 37 | Arizona | (12.5) |
| 14 | Arkansas | (7.9) |
| 47 | California | (16.8) |
| 39 | Colorado | (13.6) |
| 29 | Connecticut | (11.5) |
| 49 | Delaware | (18.0) |
| 23 | Florida | (10.7) |
| 8 | Georgia | (5.7) |
| 46 | Hawaii | (15.7) |
| 21 | Idaho | (10.3) |
| 30 | Illinois | (11.7) |
| 16 | Indiana | (8.8) |
| 32 | Iowa | (11.8) |
| 36 | Kansas | (12.4) |
| 39 | Kentucky | (13.6) |
| 10 | Louisiana | (6.7) |
| 18 | Maine | (9.2) |
| 16 | Maryland | (8.8) |
| 30 | Massachusetts | (11.7) |
| 10 | Michigan | (6.7) |
| 44 | Minnesota | (14.7) |
| 12 | Mississippi | (7.6) |
| 22 | Missouri | (10.5) |
| 48 | Montana | (17.3) |
| 5 | Nebraska | (3.7) |
| 28 | Nevada | (11.4) |
| 6 | New Hampshire | (4.0) |
| 41 | New Jersey | (13.7) |
| 27 | New Mexico | (11.3) |
| 25 | New York | (11.1) |
| 2 | North Carolina | (1.5) |
| 1 | North Dakota | 2.8 |
| 7 | Ohio | (4.2) |
| 20 | Oklahoma | (9.9) |
| 33 | Oregon | (12.1) |
| 33 | Pennsylvania | (12.1) |
| 3 | Rhode Island | (1.7) |
| 25 | South Carolina | (11.1) |
| 9 | South Dakota | (5.9) |
| 33 | Tennessee | (12.1) |
| 4 | Texas | (2.3) |
| 43 | Utah | (14.5) |
| 24 | Vermont | (10.8) |
| 45 | Virginia | (14.9) |
| 19 | Washington | (9.6) |
| NA | West Virginia** | NA |
| 42 | Wisconsin | (13.8) |
| 38 | Wyoming | (12.9) |

| RANK | STATE | PERCENT CHANGE |
|---|---|---|
| 1 | North Dakota | 2.8 |
| 2 | North Carolina | (1.5) |
| 3 | Rhode Island | (1.7) |
| 4 | Texas | (2.3) |
| 5 | Nebraska | (3.7) |
| 6 | New Hampshire | (4.0) |
| 7 | Ohio | (4.2) |
| 8 | Georgia | (5.7) |
| 9 | South Dakota | (5.9) |
| 10 | Louisiana | (6.7) |
| 10 | Michigan | (6.7) |
| 12 | Alaska | (7.6) |
| 12 | Mississippi | (7.6) |
| 14 | Alabama | (7.9) |
| 14 | Arkansas | (7.9) |
| 16 | Indiana | (8.8) |
| 16 | Maryland | (8.8) |
| 18 | Maine | (9.2) |
| 19 | Washington | (9.6) |
| 20 | Oklahoma | (9.9) |
| 21 | Idaho | (10.3) |
| 22 | Missouri | (10.5) |
| 23 | Florida | (10.7) |
| 24 | Vermont | (10.8) |
| 25 | New York | (11.1) |
| 25 | South Carolina | (11.1) |
| 27 | New Mexico | (11.3) |
| 28 | Nevada | (11.4) |
| 29 | Connecticut | (11.5) |
| 30 | Illinois | (11.7) |
| 30 | Massachusetts | (11.7) |
| 32 | Iowa | (11.8) |
| 33 | Oregon | (12.1) |
| 33 | Pennsylvania | (12.1) |
| 33 | Tennessee | (12.1) |
| 36 | Kansas | (12.4) |
| 37 | Arizona | (12.5) |
| 38 | Wyoming | (12.9) |
| 39 | Colorado | (13.6) |
| 39 | Kentucky | (13.6) |
| 41 | New Jersey | (13.7) |
| 42 | Wisconsin | (13.8) |
| 43 | Utah | (14.5) |
| 44 | Minnesota | (14.7) |
| 45 | Virginia | (14.9) |
| 46 | Hawaii | (15.7) |
| 47 | California | (16.8) |
| 48 | Montana | (17.3) |
| 49 | Delaware | (18.0) |
| NA | West Virginia** | NA |
| | District of Columbia | (20.3) |

Source: Federal Bureau of Investigation
"Crime in the United States 1999" (Uniform Crime Reports, October 15, 2000)
*Burglary is the unlawful entry of a structure to commit a felony or theft. Attempts are included.
**Not available.

# Burglary Rate in 1999

## National Rate = 770.0 Burglaries per 100,000 Population*

| RANK | STATE | RATE |
|---|---|---|
| 14 | Alabama | 884.4 |
| 30 | Alaska | 611.8 |
| 6 | Arizona | 1,034.4 |
| 15 | Arkansas | 850.3 |
| 27 | California | 675.3 |
| 28 | Colorado | 665.2 |
| 37 | Connecticut | 588.0 |
| 25 | Delaware | 695.6 |
| 3 | Florida | 1,200.3 |
| 13 | Georgia | 917.2 |
| 19 | Hawaii | 795.0 |
| 32 | Idaho | 610.3 |
| 24 | Illinois | 712.3 |
| 23 | Indiana | 714.5 |
| 36 | Iowa | 593.0 |
| 17 | Kansas | 824.2 |
| 31 | Kentucky | 610.9 |
| 4 | Louisiana | 1,092.7 |
| 34 | Maine | 601.1 |
| 16 | Maryland | 835.8 |
| 41 | Massachusetts | 533.8 |
| 20 | Michigan | 777.9 |
| 38 | Minnesota | 580.1 |
| 5 | Mississippi | 1,051.2 |
| 21 | Missouri | 776.8 |
| 48 | Montana | 428.5 |
| 33 | Nebraska | 609.7 |
| 9 | Nevada | 973.6 |
| 50 | New Hampshire | 307.9 |
| 39 | New Jersey | 577.2 |
| 2 | New Mexico | 1,234.5 |
| 42 | New York | 512.3 |
| 1 | North Carolina | 1,286.9 |
| 49 | North Dakota | 368.6 |
| 22 | Ohio | 773.1 |
| 7 | Oklahoma | 1,026.6 |
| 18 | Oregon | 806.7 |
| 46 | Pennsylvania | 467.2 |
| 29 | Rhode Island | 639.9 |
| 8 | South Carolina | 1,019.8 |
| 47 | South Dakota | 444.1 |
| 12 | Tennessee | 936.6 |
| 10 | Texas | 949.7 |
| 26 | Utah | 685.1 |
| 35 | Vermont | 595.5 |
| 45 | Virginia | 471.6 |
| 11 | Washington | 949.5 |
| 40 | West Virginia | 570.2 |
| 44 | Wisconsin | 488.2 |
| 43 | Wyoming | 489.4 |

| RANK | STATE | RATE |
|---|---|---|
| 1 | North Carolina | 1,286.9 |
| 2 | New Mexico | 1,234.5 |
| 3 | Florida | 1,200.3 |
| 4 | Louisiana | 1,092.7 |
| 5 | Mississippi | 1,051.2 |
| 6 | Arizona | 1,034.4 |
| 7 | Oklahoma | 1,026.6 |
| 8 | South Carolina | 1,019.8 |
| 9 | Nevada | 973.6 |
| 10 | Texas | 949.7 |
| 11 | Washington | 949.5 |
| 12 | Tennessee | 936.6 |
| 13 | Georgia | 917.2 |
| 14 | Alabama | 884.4 |
| 15 | Arkansas | 850.3 |
| 16 | Maryland | 835.8 |
| 17 | Kansas | 824.2 |
| 18 | Oregon | 806.7 |
| 19 | Hawaii | 795.0 |
| 20 | Michigan | 777.9 |
| 21 | Missouri | 776.8 |
| 22 | Ohio | 773.1 |
| 23 | Indiana | 714.5 |
| 24 | Illinois | 712.3 |
| 25 | Delaware | 695.6 |
| 26 | Utah | 685.1 |
| 27 | California | 675.3 |
| 28 | Colorado | 665.2 |
| 29 | Rhode Island | 639.9 |
| 30 | Alaska | 611.8 |
| 31 | Kentucky | 610.9 |
| 32 | Idaho | 610.3 |
| 33 | Nebraska | 609.7 |
| 34 | Maine | 601.1 |
| 35 | Vermont | 595.5 |
| 36 | Iowa | 593.0 |
| 37 | Connecticut | 588.0 |
| 38 | Minnesota | 580.1 |
| 39 | New Jersey | 577.2 |
| 40 | West Virginia | 570.2 |
| 41 | Massachusetts | 533.8 |
| 42 | New York | 512.3 |
| 43 | Wyoming | 489.4 |
| 44 | Wisconsin | 488.2 |
| 45 | Virginia | 471.6 |
| 46 | Pennsylvania | 467.2 |
| 47 | South Dakota | 444.1 |
| 48 | Montana | 428.5 |
| 49 | North Dakota | 368.6 |
| 50 | New Hampshire | 307.9 |
| | District of Columbia | 976.3 |

*Source: Federal Bureau of Investigation*
*"Crime in the United States 1999" (Uniform Crime Reports, October 15, 2000)*
*\*Burglary is the unlawful entry of a structure to commit a felony or theft. Attempts are included.*

# Larcenies and Thefts in 1999

## National Total = 6,957,412 Larcenies and Thefts*

ALPHA ORDER

| RANK | STATE | THEFTS | % of USA |
|---|---|---|---|
| 22 | Alabama | 119,616 | 1.7% |
| 46 | Alaska | 16,654 | 0.2% |
| 12 | Arizona | 167,731 | 2.4% |
| 33 | Arkansas | 63,927 | 0.9% |
| 1 | California | 660,991 | 9.5% |
| 25 | Colorado | 109,228 | 1.6% |
| 30 | Connecticut | 69,299 | 1.0% |
| 43 | Delaware | 22,634 | 0.3% |
| 3 | Florida | 534,105 | 7.7% |
| 7 | Georgia | 247,834 | 3.6% |
| 38 | Hawaii | 40,458 | 0.6% |
| 41 | Idaho | 26,824 | 0.4% |
| 5 | Illinois | 319,219 | 4.6% |
| 19 | Indiana | 138,794 | 2.0% |
| 34 | Iowa | 62,316 | 0.9% |
| 28 | Kansas | 79,722 | 1.1% |
| 31 | Kentucky | 69,265 | 1.0% |
| 16 | Louisiana | 149,749 | 2.2% |
| 42 | Maine | 25,392 | 0.4% |
| 17 | Maryland | 147,296 | 2.1% |
| 26 | Massachusetts | 108,845 | 1.6% |
| 8 | Michigan | 236,351 | 3.4% |
| 23 | Minnesota | 117,736 | 1.7% |
| 32 | Mississippi | 65,919 | 0.9% |
| 15 | Missouri | 157,550 | 2.3% |
| 40 | Montana | 28,434 | 0.4% |
| 36 | Nebraska | 45,679 | 0.7% |
| 37 | Nevada | 43,167 | 0.6% |
| 45 | New Hampshire | 21,195 | 0.3% |
| 13 | New Jersey | 160,978 | 2.3% |
| 35 | New Mexico | 59,613 | 0.9% |
| 4 | New York | 338,118 | 4.9% |
| 9 | North Carolina | 230,463 | 3.3% |
| 50 | North Dakota | 11,375 | 0.2% |
| 6 | Ohio | 288,049 | 4.1% |
| 27 | Oklahoma | 93,616 | 1.3% |
| 24 | Oregon | 113,052 | 1.6% |
| 10 | Pennsylvania | 227,750 | 3.3% |
| 44 | Rhode Island | 22,284 | 0.3% |
| 21 | South Carolina | 119,912 | 1.7% |
| 47 | South Dakota | 14,043 | 0.2% |
| 18 | Tennessee | 142,685 | 2.1% |
| 2 | Texas | 613,862 | 8.8% |
| 29 | Utah | 78,156 | 1.1% |
| 49 | Vermont | 11,610 | 0.2% |
| 14 | Virginia | 159,896 | 2.3% |
| 11 | Washington | 192,334 | 2.8% |
| 39 | West Virginia | 28,760 | 0.4% |
| 20 | Wisconsin | 120,702 | 1.7% |
| 48 | Wyoming | 12,523 | 0.2% |

RANK ORDER

| RANK | STATE | THEFTS | % of USA |
|---|---|---|---|
| 1 | California | 660,991 | 9.5% |
| 2 | Texas | 613,862 | 8.8% |
| 3 | Florida | 534,105 | 7.7% |
| 4 | New York | 338,118 | 4.9% |
| 5 | Illinois | 319,219 | 4.6% |
| 6 | Ohio | 288,049 | 4.1% |
| 7 | Georgia | 247,834 | 3.6% |
| 8 | Michigan | 236,351 | 3.4% |
| 9 | North Carolina | 230,463 | 3.3% |
| 10 | Pennsylvania | 227,750 | 3.3% |
| 11 | Washington | 192,334 | 2.8% |
| 12 | Arizona | 167,731 | 2.4% |
| 13 | New Jersey | 160,978 | 2.3% |
| 14 | Virginia | 159,896 | 2.3% |
| 15 | Missouri | 157,550 | 2.3% |
| 16 | Louisiana | 149,749 | 2.2% |
| 17 | Maryland | 147,296 | 2.1% |
| 18 | Tennessee | 142,685 | 2.1% |
| 19 | Indiana | 138,794 | 2.0% |
| 20 | Wisconsin | 120,702 | 1.7% |
| 21 | South Carolina | 119,912 | 1.7% |
| 22 | Alabama | 119,616 | 1.7% |
| 23 | Minnesota | 117,736 | 1.7% |
| 24 | Oregon | 113,052 | 1.6% |
| 25 | Colorado | 109,228 | 1.6% |
| 26 | Massachusetts | 108,845 | 1.6% |
| 27 | Oklahoma | 93,616 | 1.3% |
| 28 | Kansas | 79,722 | 1.1% |
| 29 | Utah | 78,156 | 1.1% |
| 30 | Connecticut | 69,299 | 1.0% |
| 31 | Kentucky | 69,265 | 1.0% |
| 32 | Mississippi | 65,919 | 0.9% |
| 33 | Arkansas | 63,927 | 0.9% |
| 34 | Iowa | 62,316 | 0.9% |
| 35 | New Mexico | 59,613 | 0.9% |
| 36 | Nebraska | 45,679 | 0.7% |
| 37 | Nevada | 43,167 | 0.6% |
| 38 | Hawaii | 40,458 | 0.6% |
| 39 | West Virginia | 28,760 | 0.4% |
| 40 | Montana | 28,434 | 0.4% |
| 41 | Idaho | 26,824 | 0.4% |
| 42 | Maine | 25,392 | 0.4% |
| 43 | Delaware | 22,634 | 0.3% |
| 44 | Rhode Island | 22,284 | 0.3% |
| 45 | New Hampshire | 21,195 | 0.3% |
| 46 | Alaska | 16,654 | 0.2% |
| 47 | South Dakota | 14,043 | 0.2% |
| 48 | Wyoming | 12,523 | 0.2% |
| 49 | Vermont | 11,610 | 0.2% |
| 50 | North Dakota | 11,375 | 0.2% |
| | District of Columbia | 21,701 | 0.3% |

Source: Federal Bureau of Investigation
   "Crime in the United States 1999" (Uniform Crime Reports, October 15, 2000)
*Larceny and theft is the unlawful taking of property without use of force, violence or fraud. Attempts are included.
Motor vehicle thefts are excluded.

# Percent Change in Number of Larcenies and Thefts: 1998 to 1999

## National Percent Change = 5.7% Decrease*

ALPHA ORDER

| RANK | STATE | PERCENT CHANGE |
|------|-------|----------------|
| 5 | Alabama | (1.1) |
| 45 | Alaska | (10.5) |
| 36 | Arizona | (8.4) |
| 8 | Arkansas | (2.4) |
| 39 | California | (8.7) |
| 22 | Colorado | (5.7) |
| 45 | Connecticut | (10.5) |
| 34 | Delaware | (8.2) |
| 32 | Florida | (7.9) |
| 9 | Georgia | (3.0) |
| 32 | Hawaii | (7.9) |
| 49 | Idaho | (14.5) |
| 20 | Illinois | (5.3) |
| 43 | Indiana | (9.2) |
| 21 | Iowa | (5.6) |
| 26 | Kansas | (6.6) |
| 12 | Kentucky | (3.8) |
| 17 | Louisiana | (4.9) |
| 14 | Maine | (4.0) |
| 30 | Maryland | (7.4) |
| 4 | Massachusetts | (0.4) |
| 37 | Michigan | (8.5) |
| 37 | Minnesota | (8.5) |
| 12 | Mississippi | (3.8) |
| 7 | Missouri | (1.8) |
| 18 | Montana | (5.0) |
| 31 | Nebraska | (7.6) |
| 41 | Nevada | (8.9) |
| 14 | New Hampshire | (4.0) |
| 24 | New Jersey | (6.0) |
| 35 | New Mexico | (8.3) |
| 27 | New York | (6.9) |
| 6 | North Carolina | (1.2) |
| 48 | North Dakota | (13.4) |
| 29 | Ohio | (7.3) |
| 16 | Oklahoma | (4.1) |
| 39 | Oregon | (8.7) |
| 10 | Pennsylvania | (3.4) |
| 1 | Rhode Island | 4.2 |
| 19 | South Carolina | (5.1) |
| 3 | South Dakota | 0.3 |
| 11 | Tennessee | (3.6) |
| 2 | Texas | 1.1 |
| 28 | Utah | (7.2) |
| 47 | Vermont | (11.3) |
| 24 | Virginia | (6.0) |
| 44 | Washington | (10.0) |
| NA | West Virginia** | NA |
| 23 | Wisconsin | (5.8) |
| 42 | Wyoming | (9.0) |

RANK ORDER

| RANK | STATE | PERCENT CHANGE |
|------|-------|----------------|
| 1 | Rhode Island | 4.2 |
| 2 | Texas | 1.1 |
| 3 | South Dakota | 0.3 |
| 4 | Massachusetts | (0.4) |
| 5 | Alabama | (1.1) |
| 6 | North Carolina | (1.2) |
| 7 | Missouri | (1.8) |
| 8 | Arkansas | (2.4) |
| 9 | Georgia | (3.0) |
| 10 | Pennsylvania | (3.4) |
| 11 | Tennessee | (3.6) |
| 12 | Kentucky | (3.8) |
| 12 | Mississippi | (3.8) |
| 14 | Maine | (4.0) |
| 14 | New Hampshire | (4.0) |
| 16 | Oklahoma | (4.1) |
| 17 | Louisiana | (4.9) |
| 18 | Montana | (5.0) |
| 19 | South Carolina | (5.1) |
| 20 | Illinois | (5.3) |
| 21 | Iowa | (5.6) |
| 22 | Colorado | (5.7) |
| 23 | Wisconsin | (5.8) |
| 24 | New Jersey | (6.0) |
| 24 | Virginia | (6.0) |
| 26 | Kansas | (6.6) |
| 27 | New York | (6.9) |
| 28 | Utah | (7.2) |
| 29 | Ohio | (7.3) |
| 30 | Maryland | (7.4) |
| 31 | Nebraska | (7.6) |
| 32 | Florida | (7.9) |
| 32 | Hawaii | (7.9) |
| 34 | Delaware | (8.2) |
| 35 | New Mexico | (8.3) |
| 36 | Arizona | (8.4) |
| 37 | Michigan | (8.5) |
| 37 | Minnesota | (8.5) |
| 39 | California | (8.7) |
| 39 | Oregon | (8.7) |
| 41 | Nevada | (8.9) |
| 42 | Wyoming | (9.0) |
| 43 | Indiana | (9.2) |
| 44 | Washington | (10.0) |
| 45 | Alaska | (10.5) |
| 45 | Connecticut | (10.5) |
| 47 | Vermont | (11.3) |
| 48 | North Dakota | (13.4) |
| 49 | Idaho | (14.5) |
| NA | West Virginia** | NA |
| | District of Columbia | (10.9) |

Source: Federal Bureau of Investigation
     "Crime in the United States 1999" (Uniform Crime Reports, October 15, 2000)
*Larceny and theft is the unlawful taking of property without use of force, violence or fraud.  Attempts are included.
Motor vehicle thefts are excluded.
**Not available.

# Larceny and Theft Rate in 1999

## National Rate = 2,551.4 Larcenies and Thefts per 100,000 Population*

ALPHA ORDER

RANK ORDER

| RANK | STATE | RATE | | RANK | STATE | RATE |
|---|---|---|---|---|---|---|
| 20 | Alabama | 2,737.2 | | 1 | Utah | 3,669.3 |
| 22 | Alaska | 2,690.5 | | 2 | Florida | 3,534.5 |
| 3 | Arizona | 3,510.5 | | 3 | Arizona | 3,510.5 |
| 27 | Arkansas | 2,506.0 | | 4 | New Mexico | 3,426.0 |
| 40 | California | 1,994.2 | | 5 | Louisiana | 3,425.2 |
| 21 | Colorado | 2,693.0 | | 6 | Hawaii | 3,414.2 |
| 38 | Connecticut | 2,111.5 | | 7 | Oregon | 3,409.3 |
| 15 | Delaware | 3,001.9 | | 8 | Washington | 3,341.5 |
| 2 | Florida | 3,534.5 | | 9 | Montana | 3,220.2 |
| 10 | Georgia | 3,182.3 | | 10 | Georgia | 3,182.3 |
| 6 | Hawaii | 3,414.2 | | 11 | South Carolina | 3,085.7 |
| 37 | Idaho | 2,142.5 | | 12 | Texas | 3,062.6 |
| 23 | Illinois | 2,632.1 | | 13 | North Carolina | 3,012.2 |
| 32 | Indiana | 2,335.4 | | 14 | Kansas | 3,003.8 |
| 36 | Iowa | 2,172.0 | | 15 | Delaware | 3,001.9 |
| 14 | Kansas | 3,003.8 | | 16 | Missouri | 2,881.3 |
| 49 | Kentucky | 1,748.7 | | 17 | Maryland | 2,848.0 |
| 5 | Louisiana | 3,425.2 | | 18 | Oklahoma | 2,787.8 |
| 39 | Maine | 2,026.5 | | 19 | Nebraska | 2,741.8 |
| 17 | Maryland | 2,848.0 | | 20 | Alabama | 2,737.2 |
| 48 | Massachusetts | 1,762.7 | | 21 | Colorado | 2,693.0 |
| 29 | Michigan | 2,396.1 | | 22 | Alaska | 2,690.5 |
| 28 | Minnesota | 2,465.2 | | 23 | Illinois | 2,632.1 |
| 31 | Mississippi | 2,380.6 | | 24 | Wyoming | 2,609.0 |
| 16 | Missouri | 2,881.3 | | 25 | Tennessee | 2,601.8 |
| 9 | Montana | 3,220.2 | | 26 | Ohio | 2,558.8 |
| 19 | Nebraska | 2,741.8 | | 27 | Arkansas | 2,506.0 |
| 30 | Nevada | 2,386.2 | | 28 | Minnesota | 2,465.2 |
| 47 | New Hampshire | 1,764.8 | | 29 | Michigan | 2,396.1 |
| 41 | New Jersey | 1,976.9 | | 30 | Nevada | 2,386.2 |
| 4 | New Mexico | 3,426.0 | | 31 | Mississippi | 2,380.6 |
| 45 | New York | 1,858.1 | | 32 | Indiana | 2,335.4 |
| 13 | North Carolina | 3,012.2 | | 33 | Virginia | 2,326.4 |
| 46 | North Dakota | 1,794.2 | | 34 | Wisconsin | 2,299.1 |
| 26 | Ohio | 2,558.8 | | 35 | Rhode Island | 2,248.6 |
| 18 | Oklahoma | 2,787.8 | | 36 | Iowa | 2,172.0 |
| 7 | Oregon | 3,409.3 | | 37 | Idaho | 2,142.5 |
| 44 | Pennsylvania | 1,898.9 | | 38 | Connecticut | 2,111.5 |
| 35 | Rhode Island | 2,248.6 | | 39 | Maine | 2,026.5 |
| 11 | South Carolina | 3,085.7 | | 40 | California | 1,994.2 |
| 43 | South Dakota | 1,915.8 | | 41 | New Jersey | 1,976.9 |
| 25 | Tennessee | 2,601.8 | | 42 | Vermont | 1,954.5 |
| 12 | Texas | 3,062.6 | | 43 | South Dakota | 1,915.8 |
| 1 | Utah | 3,669.3 | | 44 | Pennsylvania | 1,898.9 |
| 42 | Vermont | 1,954.5 | | 45 | New York | 1,858.1 |
| 33 | Virginia | 2,326.4 | | 46 | North Dakota | 1,794.2 |
| 8 | Washington | 3,341.5 | | 47 | New Hampshire | 1,764.8 |
| 50 | West Virginia | 1,591.6 | | 48 | Massachusetts | 1,762.7 |
| 34 | Wisconsin | 2,299.1 | | 49 | Kentucky | 1,748.7 |
| 24 | Wyoming | 2,609.0 | | 50 | West Virginia | 1,591.6 |
| | | | | | District of Columbia | 4,181.3 |

Source: Federal Bureau of Investigation
"Crime in the United States 1999" (Uniform Crime Reports, October 15, 2000)
*Larceny and theft is the unlawful taking of property without use of force, violence or fraud. Attempts are included.
Motor vehicle thefts are excluded.

# Motor Vehicle Thefts in 1999

## National Total = 1,147,305 Motor Vehicle Thefts*

ALPHA ORDER

| RANK | STATE | THEFTS | % of USA |
|------|-------|--------|----------|
| 27 | Alabama | 13,134 | 1.1% |
| 42 | Alaska | 2,658 | 0.2% |
| 10 | Arizona | 38,247 | 3.3% |
| 34 | Arkansas | 6,664 | 0.6% |
| 1 | California | 168,480 | 14.7% |
| 21 | Colorado | 14,795 | 1.3% |
| 30 | Connecticut | 11,297 | 1.0% |
| 41 | Delaware | 3,043 | 0.3% |
| 2 | Florida | 93,191 | 8.1% |
| 7 | Georgia | 40,120 | 3.5% |
| 38 | Hawaii | 4,660 | 0.4% |
| 43 | Idaho | 1,898 | 0.2% |
| 6 | Illinois | 52,114 | 4.5% |
| 19 | Indiana | 20,290 | 1.8% |
| 37 | Iowa | 5,135 | 0.4% |
| 35 | Kansas | 6,048 | 0.5% |
| 31 | Kentucky | 8,631 | 0.8% |
| 18 | Louisiana | 21,695 | 1.9% |
| 45 | Maine | 1,694 | 0.1% |
| 15 | Maryland | 25,447 | 2.2% |
| 13 | Massachusetts | 25,628 | 2.2% |
| 5 | Michigan | 56,800 | 5.0% |
| 26 | Minnesota | 13,275 | 1.2% |
| 25 | Mississippi | 13,532 | 1.2% |
| 17 | Missouri | 22,984 | 2.0% |
| 44 | Montana | 1,896 | 0.2% |
| 36 | Nebraska | 5,440 | 0.5% |
| 28 | Nevada | 13,094 | 1.1% |
| 46 | New Hampshire | 1,354 | 0.1% |
| 11 | New Jersey | 35,357 | 3.1% |
| 32 | New Mexico | 8,126 | 0.7% |
| 4 | New York | 58,261 | 5.1% |
| 14 | North Carolina | 25,577 | 2.2% |
| 47 | North Dakota | 1,036 | 0.1% |
| 9 | Ohio | 39,192 | 3.4% |
| 29 | Oklahoma | 12,132 | 1.1% |
| 24 | Oregon | 13,633 | 1.2% |
| 8 | Pennsylvania | 39,234 | 3.4% |
| 39 | Rhode Island | 4,032 | 0.4% |
| 22 | South Carolina | 14,445 | 1.3% |
| 49 | South Dakota | 861 | 0.1% |
| 16 | Tennessee | 25,255 | 2.2% |
| 3 | Texas | 92,037 | 8.0% |
| 33 | Utah | 7,382 | 0.6% |
| 48 | Vermont | 912 | 0.1% |
| 20 | Virginia | 17,953 | 1.6% |
| 12 | Washington | 33,807 | 2.9% |
| 40 | West Virginia | 3,762 | 0.3% |
| 23 | Wisconsin | 13,819 | 1.2% |
| 50 | Wyoming | 596 | 0.1% |

RANK ORDER

| RANK | STATE | THEFTS | % of USA |
|------|-------|--------|----------|
| 1 | California | 168,480 | 14.7% |
| 2 | Florida | 93,191 | 8.1% |
| 3 | Texas | 92,037 | 8.0% |
| 4 | New York | 58,261 | 5.1% |
| 5 | Michigan | 56,800 | 5.0% |
| 6 | Illinois | 52,114 | 4.5% |
| 7 | Georgia | 40,120 | 3.5% |
| 8 | Pennsylvania | 39,234 | 3.4% |
| 9 | Ohio | 39,192 | 3.4% |
| 10 | Arizona | 38,247 | 3.3% |
| 11 | New Jersey | 35,357 | 3.1% |
| 12 | Washington | 33,807 | 2.9% |
| 13 | Massachusetts | 25,628 | 2.2% |
| 14 | North Carolina | 25,577 | 2.2% |
| 15 | Maryland | 25,447 | 2.2% |
| 16 | Tennessee | 25,255 | 2.2% |
| 17 | Missouri | 22,984 | 2.0% |
| 18 | Louisiana | 21,695 | 1.9% |
| 19 | Indiana | 20,290 | 1.8% |
| 20 | Virginia | 17,953 | 1.6% |
| 21 | Colorado | 14,795 | 1.3% |
| 22 | South Carolina | 14,445 | 1.3% |
| 23 | Wisconsin | 13,819 | 1.2% |
| 24 | Oregon | 13,633 | 1.2% |
| 25 | Mississippi | 13,532 | 1.2% |
| 26 | Minnesota | 13,275 | 1.2% |
| 27 | Alabama | 13,134 | 1.1% |
| 28 | Nevada | 13,094 | 1.1% |
| 29 | Oklahoma | 12,132 | 1.1% |
| 30 | Connecticut | 11,297 | 1.0% |
| 31 | Kentucky | 8,631 | 0.8% |
| 32 | New Mexico | 8,126 | 0.7% |
| 33 | Utah | 7,382 | 0.6% |
| 34 | Arkansas | 6,664 | 0.6% |
| 35 | Kansas | 6,048 | 0.5% |
| 36 | Nebraska | 5,440 | 0.5% |
| 37 | Iowa | 5,135 | 0.4% |
| 38 | Hawaii | 4,660 | 0.4% |
| 39 | Rhode Island | 4,032 | 0.4% |
| 40 | West Virginia | 3,762 | 0.3% |
| 41 | Delaware | 3,043 | 0.3% |
| 42 | Alaska | 2,658 | 0.2% |
| 43 | Idaho | 1,898 | 0.2% |
| 44 | Montana | 1,896 | 0.2% |
| 45 | Maine | 1,694 | 0.1% |
| 46 | New Hampshire | 1,354 | 0.1% |
| 47 | North Dakota | 1,036 | 0.1% |
| 48 | Vermont | 912 | 0.1% |
| 49 | South Dakota | 861 | 0.1% |
| 50 | Wyoming | 596 | 0.1% |
| | District of Columbia | 6,652 | 0.6% |

Source: Federal Bureau of Investigation
"Crime in the United States 1999" (Uniform Crime Reports, October 15, 2000)
*Includes the theft or attempted theft of a self-propelled vehicle. Excludes motorboats, construction equipment, airplanes and farming equipment.

# Percent Change in Number of Motor Vehicle Thefts: 1998 to 1999

## National Percent Change = 7.7% Decrease*

| ALPHA ORDER | | | | RANK ORDER | | |
|---|---|---|---|---|---|---|
| RANK | STATE | PERCENT CHANGE | | RANK | STATE | PERCENT CHANGE |
| 41 | Alabama | (11.7) | | 1 | Mississippi | 45.2 |
| 7 | Alaska | 2.0 | | 2 | South Dakota | 12.8 |
| 20 | Arizona | (5.3) | | 3 | Maine | 12.3 |
| 24 | Arkansas | (7.3) | | 4 | Rhode Island | 5.3 |
| 43 | California | (13.8) | | 5 | Vermont | 4.3 |
| 26 | Colorado | (8.0) | | 6 | North Carolina | 3.9 |
| 38 | Connecticut | (11.1) | | 7 | Alaska | 2.0 |
| 17 | Delaware | (4.5) | | 8 | New Jersey | 0.5 |
| 35 | Florida | (10.6) | | 9 | Illinois | (1.5) |
| 21 | Georgia | (5.7) | | 10 | Virginia | (2.2) |
| 46 | Hawaii | (16.7) | | 11 | Michigan | (2.6) |
| 47 | Idaho | (16.8) | | 12 | Wisconsin | (2.8) |
| 9 | Illinois | (1.5) | | 13 | Massachusetts | (2.9) |
| 16 | Indiana | (4.2) | | 14 | Washington | (4.0) |
| 44 | Iowa | (14.0) | | 15 | Utah | (4.1) |
| 38 | Kansas | (11.1) | | 16 | Indiana | (4.2) |
| 40 | Kentucky | (11.5) | | 17 | Delaware | (4.5) |
| 30 | Louisiana | (8.3) | | 18 | Texas | (4.8) |
| 3 | Maine | 12.3 | | 19 | Nevada | (4.9) |
| 33 | Maryland | (9.8) | | 20 | Arizona | (5.3) |
| 13 | Massachusetts | (2.9) | | 21 | Georgia | (5.7) |
| 11 | Michigan | (2.6) | | 22 | Nebraska | (6.0) |
| 42 | Minnesota | (13.6) | | 23 | Missouri | (6.1) |
| 1 | Mississippi | 45.2 | | 24 | Arkansas | (7.3) |
| 23 | Missouri | (6.1) | | 25 | Montana | (7.5) |
| 25 | Montana | (7.5) | | 26 | Colorado | (8.0) |
| 22 | Nebraska | (6.0) | | 26 | Pennsylvania | (8.0) |
| 19 | Nevada | (4.9) | | 28 | New Hampshire | (8.1) |
| 28 | New Hampshire | (8.1) | | 28 | North Dakota | (8.1) |
| 8 | New Jersey | 0.5 | | 30 | Louisiana | (8.3) |
| 49 | New Mexico | (24.5) | | 31 | Ohio | (8.9) |
| 45 | New York | (14.5) | | 32 | South Carolina | (9.4) |
| 6 | North Carolina | 3.9 | | 33 | Maryland | (9.8) |
| 28 | North Dakota | (8.1) | | 34 | Tennessee | (10.1) |
| 31 | Ohio | (8.9) | | 35 | Florida | (10.6) |
| 35 | Oklahoma | (10.6) | | 35 | Oklahoma | (10.6) |
| 48 | Oregon | (21.0) | | 37 | Wyoming | (10.9) |
| 26 | Pennsylvania | (8.0) | | 38 | Connecticut | (11.1) |
| 4 | Rhode Island | 5.3 | | 38 | Kansas | (11.1) |
| 32 | South Carolina | (9.4) | | 40 | Kentucky | (11.5) |
| 2 | South Dakota | 12.8 | | 41 | Alabama | (11.7) |
| 34 | Tennessee | (10.1) | | 42 | Minnesota | (13.6) |
| 18 | Texas | (4.8) | | 43 | California | (13.8) |
| 15 | Utah | (4.1) | | 44 | Iowa | (14.0) |
| 5 | Vermont | 4.3 | | 45 | New York | (14.5) |
| 10 | Virginia | (2.2) | | 46 | Hawaii | (16.7) |
| 14 | Washington | (4.0) | | 47 | Idaho | (16.8) |
| NA | West Virginia** | NA | | 48 | Oregon | (21.0) |
| 12 | Wisconsin | (2.8) | | 49 | New Mexico | (24.5) |
| 37 | Wyoming | (10.9) | | NA | West Virginia** | NA |
| | | | | | District of Columbia | 2.3 |

Source: Federal Bureau of Investigation
   "Crime in the United States 1999" (Uniform Crime Reports, October 15, 2000)
*Includes the theft or attempted theft of a self-propelled vehicle. Excludes motorboats, construction equipment, airplanes and farming equipment.
**Not available.

# Motor Vehicle Theft Rate in 1999

## National Rate = 420.7 Motor Vehicle Thefts per 100,000 Population*

ALPHA ORDER

| RANK | STATE | RATE |
|---|---|---|
| 34 | Alabama | 300.5 |
| 16 | Alaska | 429.4 |
| 1 | Arizona | 800.5 |
| 37 | Arkansas | 261.2 |
| 7 | California | 508.3 |
| 24 | Colorado | 364.8 |
| 28 | Connecticut | 344.2 |
| 21 | Delaware | 403.6 |
| 3 | Florida | 616.7 |
| 6 | Georgia | 515.2 |
| 22 | Hawaii | 393.2 |
| 46 | Idaho | 151.6 |
| 15 | Illinois | 429.7 |
| 29 | Indiana | 341.4 |
| 43 | Iowa | 179.0 |
| 39 | Kansas | 227.9 |
| 40 | Kentucky | 217.9 |
| 8 | Louisiana | 496.2 |
| 47 | Maine | 135.2 |
| 9 | Maryland | 492.0 |
| 18 | Massachusetts | 415.0 |
| 5 | Michigan | 575.8 |
| 35 | Minnesota | 278.0 |
| 10 | Mississippi | 488.7 |
| 17 | Missouri | 420.3 |
| 41 | Montana | 214.7 |
| 32 | Nebraska | 326.5 |
| 2 | Nevada | 723.8 |
| 50 | New Hampshire | 112.7 |
| 14 | New Jersey | 434.2 |
| 11 | New Mexico | 467.0 |
| 33 | New York | 320.2 |
| 30 | North Carolina | 334.3 |
| 44 | North Dakota | 163.4 |
| 26 | Ohio | 348.2 |
| 25 | Oklahoma | 361.3 |
| 19 | Oregon | 411.1 |
| 31 | Pennsylvania | 327.1 |
| 20 | Rhode Island | 406.9 |
| 23 | South Carolina | 371.7 |
| 49 | South Dakota | 117.5 |
| 12 | Tennessee | 460.5 |
| 13 | Texas | 459.2 |
| 27 | Utah | 346.6 |
| 45 | Vermont | 153.5 |
| 37 | Virginia | 261.2 |
| 4 | Washington | 587.3 |
| 42 | West Virginia | 208.2 |
| 36 | Wisconsin | 263.2 |
| 48 | Wyoming | 124.2 |

RANK ORDER

| RANK | STATE | RATE |
|---|---|---|
| 1 | Arizona | 800.5 |
| 2 | Nevada | 723.8 |
| 3 | Florida | 616.7 |
| 4 | Washington | 587.3 |
| 5 | Michigan | 575.8 |
| 6 | Georgia | 515.2 |
| 7 | California | 508.3 |
| 8 | Louisiana | 496.2 |
| 9 | Maryland | 492.0 |
| 10 | Mississippi | 488.7 |
| 11 | New Mexico | 467.0 |
| 12 | Tennessee | 460.5 |
| 13 | Texas | 459.2 |
| 14 | New Jersey | 434.2 |
| 15 | Illinois | 429.7 |
| 16 | Alaska | 429.4 |
| 17 | Missouri | 420.3 |
| 18 | Massachusetts | 415.0 |
| 19 | Oregon | 411.1 |
| 20 | Rhode Island | 406.9 |
| 21 | Delaware | 403.6 |
| 22 | Hawaii | 393.2 |
| 23 | South Carolina | 371.7 |
| 24 | Colorado | 364.8 |
| 25 | Oklahoma | 361.3 |
| 26 | Ohio | 348.2 |
| 27 | Utah | 346.6 |
| 28 | Connecticut | 344.2 |
| 29 | Indiana | 341.4 |
| 30 | North Carolina | 334.3 |
| 31 | Pennsylvania | 327.1 |
| 32 | Nebraska | 326.5 |
| 33 | New York | 320.2 |
| 34 | Alabama | 300.5 |
| 35 | Minnesota | 278.0 |
| 36 | Wisconsin | 263.2 |
| 37 | Arkansas | 261.2 |
| 37 | Virginia | 261.2 |
| 39 | Kansas | 227.9 |
| 40 | Kentucky | 217.9 |
| 41 | Montana | 214.7 |
| 42 | West Virginia | 208.2 |
| 43 | Iowa | 179.0 |
| 44 | North Dakota | 163.4 |
| 45 | Vermont | 153.5 |
| 46 | Idaho | 151.6 |
| 47 | Maine | 135.2 |
| 48 | Wyoming | 124.2 |
| 49 | South Dakota | 117.5 |
| 50 | New Hampshire | 112.7 |
| | District of Columbia | 1,281.7 |

*Source: Federal Bureau of Investigation*
*"Crime in the United States 1999" (Uniform Crime Reports, October 15, 2000)*
*Includes the theft or attempted theft of a self-propelled vehicle. Excludes motorboats, construction equipment, airplanes and farming equipment.*

# Prisoners in State Correctional Institutions: Year End 1999

## National Total = 1,231,475 State Prisoners*

ALPHA ORDER

| RANK | STATE | PRISONERS | % of USA |
|------|-------|-----------|----------|
| 16 | Alabama | 24,658 | 2.0% |
| 40 | Alaska | 3,949 | 0.3% |
| 15 | Arizona | 25,986 | 2.1% |
| 28 | Arkansas | 11,415 | 0.9% |
| 2 | California | 163,067 | 13.2% |
| 25 | Colorado | 15,670 | 1.3% |
| 23 | Connecticut | 18,639 | 1.5% |
| 34 | Delaware | 6,983 | 0.6% |
| 4 | Florida | 69,596 | 5.7% |
| 8 | Georgia | 42,091 | 3.4% |
| 38 | Hawaii | 4,903 | 0.4% |
| 39 | Idaho | 4,842 | 0.4% |
| 7 | Illinois | 44,660 | 3.6% |
| 22 | Indiana | 19,309 | 1.6% |
| 33 | Iowa | 7,232 | 0.6% |
| 32 | Kansas | 8,567 | 0.7% |
| 26 | Kentucky | 15,317 | 1.2% |
| 10 | Louisiana | 34,066 | 2.8% |
| 47 | Maine | 1,716 | 0.1% |
| 17 | Maryland | 23,095 | 1.9% |
| 29 | Massachusetts | 11,356 | 0.9% |
| 6 | Michigan | 46,617 | 3.8% |
| 35 | Minnesota | 5,969 | 0.5% |
| 24 | Mississippi | 18,247 | 1.5% |
| 14 | Missouri | 26,155 | 2.1% |
| 44 | Montana | 2,954 | 0.2% |
| 41 | Nebraska | 3,688 | 0.3% |
| 31 | Nevada | 9,494 | 0.8% |
| 46 | New Hampshire | 2,257 | 0.2% |
| 12 | New Jersey | 31,493 | 2.6% |
| 37 | New Mexico | 5,124 | 0.4% |
| 3 | New York | 73,233 | 5.9% |
| 13 | North Carolina | 31,086 | 2.5% |
| 50 | North Dakota | 943 | 0.1% |
| 5 | Ohio | 46,842 | 3.8% |
| 19 | Oklahoma | 22,393 | 1.8% |
| 30 | Oregon | 9,810 | 0.8% |
| 9 | Pennsylvania | 36,525 | 3.0% |
| 43 | Rhode Island | 3,003 | 0.2% |
| 20 | South Carolina | 22,008 | 1.8% |
| 45 | South Dakota | 2,506 | 0.2% |
| 18 | Tennessee | 22,502 | 1.8% |
| 1 | Texas | 163,190 | 13.3% |
| 36 | Utah | 5,426 | 0.4% |
| 49 | Vermont | 1,536 | 0.1% |
| 11 | Virginia | 32,453 | 2.6% |
| 27 | Washington | 14,590 | 1.2% |
| 42 | West Virginia | 3,532 | 0.3% |
| 21 | Wisconsin | 20,417 | 1.7% |
| 48 | Wyoming | 1,713 | 0.1% |

RANK ORDER

| RANK | STATE | PRISONERS | % of USA |
|------|-------|-----------|----------|
| 1 | Texas | 163,190 | 13.3% |
| 2 | California | 163,067 | 13.2% |
| 3 | New York | 73,233 | 5.9% |
| 4 | Florida | 69,596 | 5.7% |
| 5 | Ohio | 46,842 | 3.8% |
| 6 | Michigan | 46,617 | 3.8% |
| 7 | Illinois | 44,660 | 3.6% |
| 8 | Georgia | 42,091 | 3.4% |
| 9 | Pennsylvania | 36,525 | 3.0% |
| 10 | Louisiana | 34,066 | 2.8% |
| 11 | Virginia | 32,453 | 2.6% |
| 12 | New Jersey | 31,493 | 2.6% |
| 13 | North Carolina | 31,086 | 2.5% |
| 14 | Missouri | 26,155 | 2.1% |
| 15 | Arizona | 25,986 | 2.1% |
| 16 | Alabama | 24,658 | 2.0% |
| 17 | Maryland | 23,095 | 1.9% |
| 18 | Tennessee | 22,502 | 1.8% |
| 19 | Oklahoma | 22,393 | 1.8% |
| 20 | South Carolina | 22,008 | 1.8% |
| 21 | Wisconsin | 20,417 | 1.7% |
| 22 | Indiana | 19,309 | 1.6% |
| 23 | Connecticut | 18,639 | 1.5% |
| 24 | Mississippi | 18,247 | 1.5% |
| 25 | Colorado | 15,670 | 1.3% |
| 26 | Kentucky | 15,317 | 1.2% |
| 27 | Washington | 14,590 | 1.2% |
| 28 | Arkansas | 11,415 | 0.9% |
| 29 | Massachusetts | 11,356 | 0.9% |
| 30 | Oregon | 9,810 | 0.8% |
| 31 | Nevada | 9,494 | 0.8% |
| 32 | Kansas | 8,567 | 0.7% |
| 33 | Iowa | 7,232 | 0.6% |
| 34 | Delaware | 6,983 | 0.6% |
| 35 | Minnesota | 5,969 | 0.5% |
| 36 | Utah | 5,426 | 0.4% |
| 37 | New Mexico | 5,124 | 0.4% |
| 38 | Hawaii | 4,903 | 0.4% |
| 39 | Idaho | 4,842 | 0.4% |
| 40 | Alaska | 3,949 | 0.3% |
| 41 | Nebraska | 3,688 | 0.3% |
| 42 | West Virginia | 3,532 | 0.3% |
| 43 | Rhode Island | 3,003 | 0.2% |
| 44 | Montana | 2,954 | 0.2% |
| 45 | South Dakota | 2,506 | 0.2% |
| 46 | New Hampshire | 2,257 | 0.2% |
| 47 | Maine | 1,716 | 0.1% |
| 48 | Wyoming | 1,713 | 0.1% |
| 49 | Vermont | 1,536 | 0.1% |
| 50 | North Dakota | 943 | 0.1% |
| | District of Columbia | 8,652 | 0.7% |

*Source: U.S. Department of Justice, Bureau of Justice Statistics
"Prisoners in 1999" (August 2000, NCJ-183476)*
*As of December 31, 1999. Totals reflect all prisoners, including those sentenced to a year or less and those unsentenced. National total does not include 135,246 prisoners under federal jurisdiction. State and federal prisoners combined total 1,366,721.*

# State Prisoner Incarceration Rate in 1999

## National Rate = 434.0 State Prisoners per 100,000 Population*

ALPHA ORDER

| RANK | STATE | RATE |
|---|---|---|
| 5 | Alabama | 548.6 |
| 27 | Alaska | 374.4 |
| 9 | Arizona | 494.8 |
| 16 | Arkansas | 442.6 |
| 11 | California | 481.1 |
| 25 | Colorado | 383.3 |
| 21 | Connecticut | 396.8 |
| 10 | Delaware | 493.4 |
| 14 | Florida | 455.7 |
| 7 | Georgia | 532.1 |
| 35 | Hawaii | 320.5 |
| 23 | Idaho | 384.9 |
| 28 | Illinois | 368.3 |
| 33 | Indiana | 323.7 |
| 40 | Iowa | 251.5 |
| 34 | Kansas | 320.9 |
| 22 | Kentucky | 385.2 |
| 1 | Louisiana | 776.0 |
| 49 | Maine | 133.3 |
| 17 | Maryland | 427.3 |
| 39 | Massachusetts | 266.1 |
| 13 | Michigan | 472.3 |
| 50 | Minnesota | 124.6 |
| 4 | Mississippi | 626.0 |
| 12 | Missouri | 476.7 |
| 32 | Montana | 334.5 |
| 43 | Nebraska | 217.5 |
| 8 | Nevada | 509.4 |
| 47 | New Hampshire | 187.3 |
| 24 | New Jersey | 384.2 |
| 38 | New Mexico | 269.7 |
| 20 | New York | 400.3 |
| 30 | North Carolina | 345.1 |
| 48 | North Dakota | 136.8 |
| 18 | Ohio | 417.0 |
| 3 | Oklahoma | 662.1 |
| 37 | Oregon | 293.3 |
| 36 | Pennsylvania | 304.8 |
| 46 | Rhode Island | 192.7 |
| 6 | South Carolina | 543.3 |
| 31 | South Dakota | 338.9 |
| 19 | Tennessee | 407.7 |
| 2 | Texas | 762.4 |
| 42 | Utah | 244.9 |
| 44 | Vermont | 198.0 |
| 15 | Virginia | 447.4 |
| 41 | Washington | 251.1 |
| 45 | West Virginia | 195.6 |
| 26 | Wisconsin | 374.9 |
| 29 | Wyoming | 355.4 |

RANK ORDER

| RANK | STATE | RATE |
|---|---|---|
| 1 | Louisiana | 776.0 |
| 2 | Texas | 762.4 |
| 3 | Oklahoma | 662.1 |
| 4 | Mississippi | 626.0 |
| 5 | Alabama | 548.6 |
| 6 | South Carolina | 543.3 |
| 7 | Georgia | 532.1 |
| 8 | Nevada | 509.4 |
| 9 | Arizona | 494.8 |
| 10 | Delaware | 493.4 |
| 11 | California | 481.1 |
| 12 | Missouri | 476.7 |
| 13 | Michigan | 472.3 |
| 14 | Florida | 455.7 |
| 15 | Virginia | 447.4 |
| 16 | Arkansas | 442.6 |
| 17 | Maryland | 427.3 |
| 18 | Ohio | 417.0 |
| 19 | Tennessee | 407.7 |
| 20 | New York | 400.3 |
| 21 | Connecticut | 396.8 |
| 22 | Kentucky | 385.2 |
| 23 | Idaho | 384.9 |
| 24 | New Jersey | 384.2 |
| 25 | Colorado | 383.3 |
| 26 | Wisconsin | 374.9 |
| 27 | Alaska | 374.4 |
| 28 | Illinois | 368.3 |
| 29 | Wyoming | 355.4 |
| 30 | North Carolina | 345.1 |
| 31 | South Dakota | 338.9 |
| 32 | Montana | 334.5 |
| 33 | Indiana | 323.7 |
| 34 | Kansas | 320.9 |
| 35 | Hawaii | 320.5 |
| 36 | Pennsylvania | 304.8 |
| 37 | Oregon | 293.3 |
| 38 | New Mexico | 269.7 |
| 39 | Massachusetts | 266.1 |
| 40 | Iowa | 251.5 |
| 41 | Washington | 251.1 |
| 42 | Utah | 244.9 |
| 43 | Nebraska | 217.5 |
| 44 | Vermont | 198.0 |
| 45 | West Virginia | 195.6 |
| 46 | Rhode Island | 192.7 |
| 47 | New Hampshire | 187.3 |
| 48 | North Dakota | 136.8 |
| 49 | Maine | 133.3 |
| 50 | Minnesota | 124.6 |
| | District of Columbia | 1,314.5 |

Source: U.S. Department of Justice, Bureau of Justice Statistics
    "Prisoners in 1999" (August 2000, NCJ-183476)
*As of December 31, 1999. Includes only inmates sentenced to more than one year. Does not include federal
incarceration rate of 42 prisoners per 100,000 population. State and federal combined incarceration rate is 476
prisoners per 100,000 population.

# Percent Change in Number of State Prisoners: 1998 to 1999

## National Percent Change = 2.7% Increase*

ALPHA ORDER

| RANK | STATE | PERCENT CHANGE |
|------|-------|----------------|
| 7 | Alabama | 8.7 |
| 47 | Alaska | (3.6) |
| 31 | Arizona | 1.8 |
| 9 | Arkansas | 7.3 |
| 38 | California | 0.7 |
| 3 | Colorado | 9.5 |
| 14 | Connecticut | 5.9 |
| NA | Delaware** | NA |
| 23 | Florida | 3.5 |
| 10 | Georgia | 7.2 |
| 42 | Hawaii | (0.4) |
| 1 | Idaho | 12.9 |
| 22 | Illinois | 3.7 |
| 39 | Indiana | 0.6 |
| 44 | Iowa | (2.2) |
| 17 | Kansas | 4.7 |
| 29 | Kentucky | 2.2 |
| 15 | Louisiana | 5.7 |
| 34 | Maine | 1.5 |
| 28 | Maryland | 2.3 |
| 48 | Massachusetts | (3.8) |
| 32 | Michigan | 1.6 |
| 13 | Minnesota | 7.1 |
| 4 | Mississippi | 9.4 |
| 16 | Missouri | 4.7 |
| 8 | Montana | 8.0 |
| 41 | Nebraska | 0.3 |
| 43 | Nevada | (1.6) |
| 21 | New Hampshire | 4.1 |
| 35 | New Jersey | 1.2 |
| 37 | New Mexico | 0.9 |
| 27 | New York | 2.6 |
| 45 | North Carolina | (2.7) |
| 25 | North Dakota | 3.1 |
| 46 | Ohio | (3.3) |
| 12 | Oklahoma | 7.2 |
| 5 | Oregon | 9.2 |
| 40 | Pennsylvania | 0.4 |
| 49 | Rhode Island | (12.8) |
| 36 | South Carolina | 1.1 |
| 24 | South Dakota | 3.5 |
| 18 | Tennessee | 4.5 |
| 30 | Texas | 1.9 |
| 20 | Utah | 4.2 |
| 19 | Vermont | 4.3 |
| 11 | Virginia | 7.2 |
| 26 | Washington | 3.0 |
| 33 | West Virginia | 1.6 |
| 2 | Wisconsin | 10.9 |
| 6 | Wyoming | 9.0 |

RANK ORDER

| RANK | STATE | PERCENT CHANGE |
|------|-------|----------------|
| 1 | Idaho | 12.9 |
| 2 | Wisconsin | 10.9 |
| 3 | Colorado | 9.5 |
| 4 | Mississippi | 9.4 |
| 5 | Oregon | 9.2 |
| 6 | Wyoming | 9.0 |
| 7 | Alabama | 8.7 |
| 8 | Montana | 8.0 |
| 9 | Arkansas | 7.3 |
| 10 | Georgia | 7.2 |
| 11 | Virginia | 7.2 |
| 12 | Oklahoma | 7.2 |
| 13 | Minnesota | 7.1 |
| 14 | Connecticut | 5.9 |
| 15 | Louisiana | 5.7 |
| 16 | Missouri | 4.7 |
| 17 | Kansas | 4.7 |
| 18 | Tennessee | 4.5 |
| 19 | Vermont | 4.3 |
| 20 | Utah | 4.2 |
| 21 | New Hampshire | 4.1 |
| 22 | Illinois | 3.7 |
| 23 | Florida | 3.5 |
| 24 | South Dakota | 3.5 |
| 25 | North Dakota | 3.1 |
| 26 | Washington | 3.0 |
| 27 | New York | 2.6 |
| 28 | Maryland | 2.3 |
| 29 | Kentucky | 2.2 |
| 30 | Texas | 1.9 |
| 31 | Arizona | 1.8 |
| 32 | Michigan | 1.6 |
| 33 | West Virginia | 1.6 |
| 34 | Maine | 1.5 |
| 35 | New Jersey | 1.2 |
| 36 | South Carolina | 1.1 |
| 37 | New Mexico | 0.9 |
| 38 | California | 0.7 |
| 39 | Indiana | 0.6 |
| 40 | Pennsylvania | 0.4 |
| 41 | Nebraska | 0.3 |
| 42 | Hawaii | (0.4) |
| 43 | Nevada | (1.6) |
| 44 | Iowa | (2.2) |
| 45 | North Carolina | (2.7) |
| 46 | Ohio | (3.3) |
| 47 | Alaska | (3.6) |
| 48 | Massachusetts | (3.8) |
| 49 | Rhode Island | (12.8) |
| NA | Delaware** | NA |
| | District of Columbia | (12.0) |

*Source: U.S. Department of Justice, Bureau of Justice Statistics*
*"Prisoners in 1999" (August 2000, NCJ-183476)*
*From December 31, 1998 to December 31, 1999. Includes inmates sentenced to more than one year and those sentenced to a year or less or with no sentence. The percent change in number of prisoners under federal jurisdiction during the same period was a 9.9% increase. The combined state and federal increase was 3.4%.*
**Not available.*

# Prisoners Under Sentence of Death in 1999

## National Total = 3,507 State Prisoners*

ALPHA ORDER

| RANK | STATE | PRISONERS | % of USA |
|---|---|---|---|
| 7 | Alabama | 180 | 5.1% |
| NA | Alaska** | NA | NA |
| 10 | Arizona | 116 | 3.3% |
| 19 | Arkansas | 40 | 1.1% |
| 1 | California | 553 | 15.8% |
| 33 | Colorado | 4 | 0.1% |
| 30 | Connecticut | 6 | 0.2% |
| 24 | Delaware | 17 | 0.5% |
| 3 | Florida | 365 | 10.4% |
| 10 | Georgia | 116 | 3.3% |
| NA | Hawaii** | NA | NA |
| 23 | Idaho | 21 | 0.6% |
| 8 | Illinois | 156 | 4.4% |
| 18 | Indiana | 43 | 1.2% |
| NA | Iowa** | NA | NA |
| 35 | Kansas | 3 | 0.1% |
| 20 | Kentucky | 39 | 1.1% |
| 14 | Louisiana | 85 | 2.4% |
| NA | Maine** | NA | NA |
| 24 | Maryland | 17 | 0.5% |
| NA | Massachusetts** | NA | NA |
| NA | Michigan** | NA | NA |
| NA | Minnesota** | NA | NA |
| 17 | Mississippi | 60 | 1.7% |
| 15 | Missouri | 83 | 2.4% |
| 30 | Montana | 6 | 0.2% |
| 29 | Nebraska | 9 | 0.3% |
| 13 | Nevada | 86 | 2.5% |
| 38 | New Hampshire | 0 | 0.0% |
| 26 | New Jersey | 14 | 0.4% |
| 33 | New Mexico | 4 | 0.1% |
| 32 | New York | 5 | 0.1% |
| 5 | North Carolina | 202 | 5.8% |
| NA | North Dakota** | NA | NA |
| 6 | Ohio | 199 | 5.7% |
| 9 | Oklahoma | 139 | 4.0% |
| 22 | Oregon | 25 | 0.7% |
| 4 | Pennsylvania | 230 | 6.6% |
| NA | Rhode Island** | NA | NA |
| 16 | South Carolina | 65 | 1.9% |
| 35 | South Dakota | 3 | 0.1% |
| 12 | Tennessee | 100 | 2.9% |
| 2 | Texas | 460 | 13.1% |
| 28 | Utah | 10 | 0.3% |
| NA | Vermont** | NA | NA |
| 21 | Virginia | 31 | 0.9% |
| 27 | Washington | 13 | 0.4% |
| NA | West Virginia** | NA | NA |
| NA | Wisconsin** | NA | NA |
| 37 | Wyoming | 2 | 0.1% |

RANK ORDER

| RANK | STATE | PRISONERS | % of USA |
|---|---|---|---|
| 1 | California | 553 | 15.8% |
| 2 | Texas | 460 | 13.1% |
| 3 | Florida | 365 | 10.4% |
| 4 | Pennsylvania | 230 | 6.6% |
| 5 | North Carolina | 202 | 5.8% |
| 6 | Ohio | 199 | 5.7% |
| 7 | Alabama | 180 | 5.1% |
| 8 | Illinois | 156 | 4.4% |
| 9 | Oklahoma | 139 | 4.0% |
| 10 | Arizona | 116 | 3.3% |
| 10 | Georgia | 116 | 3.3% |
| 12 | Tennessee | 100 | 2.9% |
| 13 | Nevada | 86 | 2.5% |
| 14 | Louisiana | 85 | 2.4% |
| 15 | Missouri | 83 | 2.4% |
| 16 | South Carolina | 65 | 1.9% |
| 17 | Mississippi | 60 | 1.7% |
| 18 | Indiana | 43 | 1.2% |
| 19 | Arkansas | 40 | 1.1% |
| 20 | Kentucky | 39 | 1.1% |
| 21 | Virginia | 31 | 0.9% |
| 22 | Oregon | 25 | 0.7% |
| 23 | Idaho | 21 | 0.6% |
| 24 | Delaware | 17 | 0.5% |
| 24 | Maryland | 17 | 0.5% |
| 26 | New Jersey | 14 | 0.4% |
| 27 | Washington | 13 | 0.4% |
| 28 | Utah | 10 | 0.3% |
| 29 | Nebraska | 9 | 0.3% |
| 30 | Connecticut | 6 | 0.2% |
| 30 | Montana | 6 | 0.2% |
| 32 | New York | 5 | 0.1% |
| 33 | Colorado | 4 | 0.1% |
| 33 | New Mexico | 4 | 0.1% |
| 35 | Kansas | 3 | 0.1% |
| 35 | South Dakota | 3 | 0.1% |
| 37 | Wyoming | 2 | 0.1% |
| 38 | New Hampshire | 0 | 0.0% |
| NA | Alaska** | NA | NA |
| NA | Hawaii** | NA | NA |
| NA | Iowa** | NA | NA |
| NA | Maine** | NA | NA |
| NA | Massachusetts** | NA | NA |
| NA | Michigan** | NA | NA |
| NA | Minnesota** | NA | NA |
| NA | North Dakota** | NA | NA |
| NA | Rhode Island** | NA | NA |
| NA | Vermont** | NA | NA |
| NA | West Virginia** | NA | NA |
| NA | Wisconsin** | NA | NA |
| | District of Columbia** | NA | NA |

Source: U.S. Department of Justice, Bureau of Justice Statistics
    "Capital Punishment 1999" (Bulletin, December 2000, NCJ-184795)
*As of December 31, 1999.  Does not include 20 federal prisoners under sentence of death.  There were 98
executions in 1999.
**No death penalty as of 12/31/99.

# Adults on State Parole in 1999

## National Total = 641,693 Adults*

ALPHA ORDER

| RANK | STATE | ADULTS | % of USA |
|---|---|---|---|
| 21 | Alabama | 5,005 | 0.8% |
| 45 | Alaska | 493 | 0.1% |
| 28 | Arizona | 3,715 | 0.6% |
| 15 | Arkansas | 7,645 | 1.2% |
| 1 | California | 114,046 | 17.8% |
| 20 | Colorado | 5,263 | 0.8% |
| 35 | Connecticut | 1,526 | 0.2% |
| 42 | Delaware | 634 | 0.1% |
| 17 | Florida | 6,418 | 1.0% |
| 6 | Georgia | 22,003 | 3.4% |
| 32 | Hawaii | 2,252 | 0.4% |
| 38 | Idaho | 1,310 | 0.2% |
| 5 | Illinois | 30,484 | 4.8% |
| 23 | Indiana | 4,539 | 0.7% |
| 31 | Iowa | 2,514 | 0.4% |
| 18 | Kansas | 5,909 | 0.9% |
| 22 | Kentucky | 4,868 | 0.8% |
| 7 | Louisiana | 21,904 | 3.4% |
| 50 | Maine | 31 | 0.0% |
| 11 | Maryland | 15,007 | 2.3% |
| 25 | Massachusetts | 4,304 | 0.7% |
| 10 | Michigan | 15,541 | 2.4% |
| 30 | Minnesota | 3,151 | 0.5% |
| 37 | Mississippi | 1,356 | 0.2% |
| 13 | Missouri | 11,448 | 1.8% |
| 44 | Montana | 549 | 0.1% |
| 43 | Nebraska | 612 | 0.1% |
| 27 | Nevada | 3,893 | 0.6% |
| 40 | New Hampshire | 1,146 | 0.2% |
| 12 | New Jersey | 12,968 | 2.0% |
| 33 | New Mexico | 1,922 | 0.3% |
| 4 | New York | 57,956 | 9.0% |
| 24 | North Carolina | 4,389 | 0.7% |
| 49 | North Dakota | 157 | 0.0% |
| 9 | Ohio | 15,776 | 2.5% |
| 34 | Oklahoma | 1,527 | 0.2% |
| 8 | Oregon | 17,874 | 2.8% |
| 3 | Pennsylvania | 83,702 | 13.0% |
| 47 | Rhode Island | 413 | 0.1% |
| 26 | South Carolina | 3,944 | 0.6% |
| 36 | South Dakota | 1,360 | 0.2% |
| 16 | Tennessee | 7,338 | 1.1% |
| 2 | Texas | 109,310 | 17.0% |
| 29 | Utah | 3,388 | 0.5% |
| 41 | Vermont | 794 | 0.1% |
| 19 | Virginia | 5,860 | 0.9% |
| 48 | Washington | 200 | 0.0% |
| 39 | West Virginia | 1,158 | 0.2% |
| 14 | Wisconsin | 8,530 | 1.3% |
| 46 | Wyoming | 458 | 0.1% |

RANK ORDER

| RANK | STATE | ADULTS | % of USA |
|---|---|---|---|
| 1 | California | 114,046 | 17.8% |
| 2 | Texas | 109,310 | 17.0% |
| 3 | Pennsylvania | 83,702 | 13.0% |
| 4 | New York | 57,956 | 9.0% |
| 5 | Illinois | 30,484 | 4.8% |
| 6 | Georgia | 22,003 | 3.4% |
| 7 | Louisiana | 21,904 | 3.4% |
| 8 | Oregon | 17,874 | 2.8% |
| 9 | Ohio | 15,776 | 2.5% |
| 10 | Michigan | 15,541 | 2.4% |
| 11 | Maryland | 15,007 | 2.3% |
| 12 | New Jersey | 12,968 | 2.0% |
| 13 | Missouri | 11,448 | 1.8% |
| 14 | Wisconsin | 8,530 | 1.3% |
| 15 | Arkansas | 7,645 | 1.2% |
| 16 | Tennessee | 7,338 | 1.1% |
| 17 | Florida | 6,418 | 1.0% |
| 18 | Kansas | 5,909 | 0.9% |
| 19 | Virginia | 5,860 | 0.9% |
| 20 | Colorado | 5,263 | 0.8% |
| 21 | Alabama | 5,005 | 0.8% |
| 22 | Kentucky | 4,868 | 0.8% |
| 23 | Indiana | 4,539 | 0.7% |
| 24 | North Carolina | 4,389 | 0.7% |
| 25 | Massachusetts | 4,304 | 0.7% |
| 26 | South Carolina | 3,944 | 0.6% |
| 27 | Nevada | 3,893 | 0.6% |
| 28 | Arizona | 3,715 | 0.6% |
| 29 | Utah | 3,388 | 0.5% |
| 30 | Minnesota | 3,151 | 0.5% |
| 31 | Iowa | 2,514 | 0.4% |
| 32 | Hawaii | 2,252 | 0.4% |
| 33 | New Mexico | 1,922 | 0.3% |
| 34 | Oklahoma | 1,527 | 0.2% |
| 35 | Connecticut | 1,526 | 0.2% |
| 36 | South Dakota | 1,360 | 0.2% |
| 37 | Mississippi | 1,356 | 0.2% |
| 38 | Idaho | 1,310 | 0.2% |
| 39 | West Virginia | 1,158 | 0.2% |
| 40 | New Hampshire | 1,146 | 0.2% |
| 41 | Vermont | 794 | 0.1% |
| 42 | Delaware | 634 | 0.1% |
| 43 | Nebraska | 612 | 0.1% |
| 44 | Montana | 549 | 0.1% |
| 45 | Alaska | 493 | 0.1% |
| 46 | Wyoming | 458 | 0.1% |
| 47 | Rhode Island | 413 | 0.1% |
| 48 | Washington | 200 | 0.0% |
| 49 | North Dakota | 157 | 0.0% |
| 50 | Maine | 31 | 0.0% |
| | District of Columbia | 5,103 | 0.8% |

Source: U.S. Department of Justice, Bureau of Justice Statistics
     "Probation and Parole in the United States, 1999" (Press Release, July 2000, NCJ-183508)
*As of December 31, 1999.  Does not include 71,020 adults on federal parole.

# Adults on State Probation in 1999

## National Total = 3,740,808 Adults*

| ALPHA ORDER | | | | | RANK ORDER | | | |
|---|---|---|---|---|---|---|---|---|
| RANK | STATE | ADULTS | % of USA | | RANK | STATE | ADULTS | % of USA |
| 24 | Alabama | 41,757 | 1.1% | | 1 | Texas | 447,100 | 12.0% |
| 46 | Alaska | 4,517 | 0.1% | | 2 | California | 332,414 | 8.9% |
| 16 | Arizona | 57,076 | 1.5% | | 3 | Georgia | 307,653 | 8.2% |
| 29 | Arkansas | 30,480 | 0.8% | | 4 | Florida | 292,399 | 7.8% |
| 2 | California | 332,414 | 8.9% | | 5 | Ohio | 184,867 | 4.9% |
| 22 | Colorado | 45,339 | 1.2% | | 6 | New York | 183,686 | 4.9% |
| 17 | Connecticut | 55,070 | 1.5% | | 7 | Michigan | 170,978 | 4.6% |
| 32 | Delaware | 20,976 | 0.6% | | 8 | Washington | 158,213 | 4.2% |
| 4 | Florida | 292,399 | 7.8% | | 9 | Illinois | 134,270 | 3.6% |
| 3 | Georgia | 307,653 | 8.2% | | 10 | New Jersey | 128,634 | 3.4% |
| 37 | Hawaii | 15,707 | 0.4% | | 11 | Pennsylvania | 118,635 | 3.2% |
| 26 | Idaho | 36,705 | 1.0% | | 12 | Indiana | 105,871 | 2.8% |
| 9 | Illinois | 134,270 | 3.6% | | 13 | North Carolina | 105,095 | 2.8% |
| 12 | Indiana | 105,871 | 2.8% | | 14 | Minnesota | 104,615 | 2.8% |
| 34 | Iowa | 19,675 | 0.5% | | 15 | Maryland | 81,286 | 2.2% |
| 36 | Kansas | 17,767 | 0.5% | | 16 | Arizona | 57,076 | 1.5% |
| 35 | Kentucky | 18,988 | 0.5% | | 17 | Connecticut | 55,070 | 1.5% |
| 27 | Louisiana | 35,118 | 0.9% | | 18 | Wisconsin | 54,131 | 1.4% |
| 43 | Maine | 7,524 | 0.2% | | 19 | Missouri | 52,493 | 1.4% |
| 15 | Maryland | 81,286 | 2.2% | | 20 | Massachusetts | 46,267 | 1.2% |
| 20 | Massachusetts | 46,267 | 1.2% | | 21 | Oregon | 45,490 | 1.2% |
| 7 | Michigan | 170,978 | 4.6% | | 22 | Colorado | 45,339 | 1.2% |
| 14 | Minnesota | 104,615 | 2.8% | | 23 | South Carolina | 44,929 | 1.2% |
| 38 | Mississippi | 12,448 | 0.3% | | 24 | Alabama | 41,757 | 1.1% |
| 19 | Missouri | 52,493 | 1.4% | | 25 | Tennessee | 40,060 | 1.1% |
| 45 | Montana | 5,906 | 0.2% | | 26 | Idaho | 36,705 | 1.0% |
| 33 | Nebraska | 20,462 | 0.5% | | 27 | Louisiana | 35,118 | 0.9% |
| 39 | Nevada | 11,787 | 0.3% | | 28 | Virginia | 32,098 | 0.9% |
| 49 | New Hampshire | 3,160 | 0.1% | | 29 | Arkansas | 30,480 | 0.8% |
| 10 | New Jersey | 128,634 | 3.4% | | 30 | Oklahoma | 27,997 | 0.7% |
| 40 | New Mexico | 11,291 | 0.3% | | 31 | Rhode Island | 21,753 | 0.6% |
| 6 | New York | 183,686 | 4.9% | | 32 | Delaware | 20,976 | 0.6% |
| 13 | North Carolina | 105,095 | 2.8% | | 33 | Nebraska | 20,462 | 0.5% |
| 50 | North Dakota | 2,729 | 0.1% | | 34 | Iowa | 19,675 | 0.5% |
| 5 | Ohio | 184,867 | 4.9% | | 35 | Kentucky | 18,988 | 0.5% |
| 30 | Oklahoma | 27,997 | 0.7% | | 36 | Kansas | 17,767 | 0.5% |
| 21 | Oregon | 45,490 | 1.2% | | 37 | Hawaii | 15,707 | 0.4% |
| 11 | Pennsylvania | 118,635 | 3.2% | | 38 | Mississippi | 12,448 | 0.3% |
| 31 | Rhode Island | 21,753 | 0.6% | | 39 | Nevada | 11,787 | 0.3% |
| 23 | South Carolina | 44,929 | 1.2% | | 40 | New Mexico | 11,291 | 0.3% |
| 48 | South Dakota | 3,461 | 0.1% | | 41 | Vermont | 10,541 | 0.3% |
| 25 | Tennessee | 40,060 | 1.1% | | 42 | Utah | 9,426 | 0.3% |
| 1 | Texas | 447,100 | 12.0% | | 43 | Maine | 7,524 | 0.2% |
| 42 | Utah | 9,426 | 0.3% | | 44 | West Virginia | 5,994 | 0.2% |
| 41 | Vermont | 10,541 | 0.3% | | 45 | Montana | 5,906 | 0.2% |
| 28 | Virginia | 32,098 | 0.9% | | 46 | Alaska | 4,517 | 0.1% |
| 8 | Washington | 158,213 | 4.2% | | 47 | Wyoming | 3,841 | 0.1% |
| 44 | West Virginia | 5,994 | 0.2% | | 48 | South Dakota | 3,461 | 0.1% |
| 18 | Wisconsin | 54,131 | 1.4% | | 49 | New Hampshire | 3,160 | 0.1% |
| 47 | Wyoming | 3,841 | 0.1% | | 50 | North Dakota | 2,729 | 0.1% |
| | | | | | | District of Columbia | 12,129 | 0.3% |

*Source: U.S. Department of Justice, Bureau of Justice Statistics*
*"Probation and Parole in the United States, 1999" (Press Release, July 2000, NCJ-183508)*
*As of December 31, 1999. Does not include 32,816 adults on federal probation.*

# Full-Time Sworn Officers in Law Enforcement Agencies in 1996

## National Total = 663,535 Officers*

ALPHA ORDER

RANK ORDER

| RANK | STATE | OFFICERS | % of USA |
|---|---|---|---|
| 22 | Alabama | 9,767 | 1.5% |
| 48 | Alaska | 1,254 | 0.2% |
| 20 | Arizona | 10,088 | 1.5% |
| 31 | Arkansas | 5,819 | 0.9% |
| 2 | California | 69,134 | 10.4% |
| 21 | Colorado | 9,896 | 1.5% |
| 25 | Connecticut | 8,525 | 1.3% |
| 45 | Delaware | 1,660 | 0.3% |
| 5 | Florida | 37,395 | 5.6% |
| 10 | Georgia | 19,115 | 2.9% |
| 38 | Hawaii | 2,989 | 0.5% |
| 40 | Idaho | 2,524 | 0.4% |
| 4 | Illinois | 38,192 | 5.8% |
| 19 | Indiana | 10,931 | 1.6% |
| 33 | Iowa | 5,043 | 0.8% |
| 29 | Kansas | 6,183 | 0.9% |
| 28 | Kentucky | 6,466 | 1.0% |
| 14 | Louisiana | 16,125 | 2.4% |
| 42 | Maine | 2,318 | 0.3% |
| 15 | Maryland | 13,828 | 2.1% |
| 12 | Massachusetts | 17,935 | 2.7% |
| 9 | Michigan | 20,568 | 3.1% |
| 26 | Minnesota | 7,994 | 1.2% |
| 32 | Mississippi | 5,813 | 0.9% |
| 16 | Missouri | 12,998 | 2.0% |
| 44 | Montana | 1,682 | 0.3% |
| 37 | Nebraska | 3,297 | 0.5% |
| 34 | Nevada | 4,363 | 0.7% |
| 43 | New Hampshire | 2,305 | 0.3% |
| 6 | New Jersey | 28,058 | 4.2% |
| 35 | New Mexico | 4,134 | 0.6% |
| 1 | New York | 71,221 | 10.7% |
| 13 | North Carolina | 16,953 | 2.6% |
| 49 | North Dakota | 1,141 | 0.2% |
| 8 | Ohio | 23,811 | 3.6% |
| 27 | Oklahoma | 7,232 | 1.1% |
| 30 | Oregon | 6,064 | 0.9% |
| 7 | Pennsylvania | 24,873 | 3.7% |
| 41 | Rhode Island | 2,422 | 0.4% |
| 24 | South Carolina | 8,675 | 1.3% |
| 46 | South Dakota | 1,464 | 0.2% |
| 18 | Tennessee | 12,152 | 1.8% |
| 3 | Texas | 47,767 | 7.2% |
| 36 | Utah | 3,699 | 0.6% |
| 50 | Vermont | 981 | 0.1% |
| 11 | Virginia | 18,448 | 2.8% |
| 23 | Washington | 9,292 | 1.4% |
| 39 | West Virginia | 2,977 | 0.4% |
| 17 | Wisconsin | 12,678 | 1.9% |
| 47 | Wyoming | 1,377 | 0.2% |

| RANK | STATE | OFFICERS | % of USA |
|---|---|---|---|
| 1 | New York | 71,221 | 10.7% |
| 2 | California | 69,134 | 10.4% |
| 3 | Texas | 47,767 | 7.2% |
| 4 | Illinois | 38,192 | 5.8% |
| 5 | Florida | 37,395 | 5.6% |
| 6 | New Jersey | 28,058 | 4.2% |
| 7 | Pennsylvania | 24,873 | 3.7% |
| 8 | Ohio | 23,811 | 3.6% |
| 9 | Michigan | 20,568 | 3.1% |
| 10 | Georgia | 19,115 | 2.9% |
| 11 | Virginia | 18,448 | 2.8% |
| 12 | Massachusetts | 17,935 | 2.7% |
| 13 | North Carolina | 16,953 | 2.6% |
| 14 | Louisiana | 16,125 | 2.4% |
| 15 | Maryland | 13,828 | 2.1% |
| 16 | Missouri | 12,998 | 2.0% |
| 17 | Wisconsin | 12,678 | 1.9% |
| 18 | Tennessee | 12,152 | 1.8% |
| 19 | Indiana | 10,931 | 1.6% |
| 20 | Arizona | 10,088 | 1.5% |
| 21 | Colorado | 9,896 | 1.5% |
| 22 | Alabama | 9,767 | 1.5% |
| 23 | Washington | 9,292 | 1.4% |
| 24 | South Carolina | 8,675 | 1.3% |
| 25 | Connecticut | 8,525 | 1.3% |
| 26 | Minnesota | 7,994 | 1.2% |
| 27 | Oklahoma | 7,232 | 1.1% |
| 28 | Kentucky | 6,466 | 1.0% |
| 29 | Kansas | 6,183 | 0.9% |
| 30 | Oregon | 6,064 | 0.9% |
| 31 | Arkansas | 5,819 | 0.9% |
| 32 | Mississippi | 5,813 | 0.9% |
| 33 | Iowa | 5,043 | 0.8% |
| 34 | Nevada | 4,363 | 0.7% |
| 35 | New Mexico | 4,134 | 0.6% |
| 36 | Utah | 3,699 | 0.6% |
| 37 | Nebraska | 3,297 | 0.5% |
| 38 | Hawaii | 2,989 | 0.5% |
| 39 | West Virginia | 2,977 | 0.4% |
| 40 | Idaho | 2,524 | 0.4% |
| 41 | Rhode Island | 2,422 | 0.4% |
| 42 | Maine | 2,318 | 0.3% |
| 43 | New Hampshire | 2,305 | 0.3% |
| 44 | Montana | 1,682 | 0.3% |
| 45 | Delaware | 1,660 | 0.3% |
| 46 | South Dakota | 1,464 | 0.2% |
| 47 | Wyoming | 1,377 | 0.2% |
| 48 | Alaska | 1,254 | 0.2% |
| 49 | North Dakota | 1,141 | 0.2% |
| 50 | Vermont | 981 | 0.1% |
| | District of Columbia | 3,909 | 0.6% |

Source: U.S. Department of Justice, Bureau of Justice Statistics
  "Census of State and Local Law Enforcement Agencies, 1996" (Bulletin, June 1998, NCJ-164618)
*Includes state and local police, sheriffs' departments and special police agencies.

# Rate of Full-Time Sworn Officers in Law Enforcement Agencies in 1996

## National Rate = 25 Officers per 10,000 Population*

ALPHA ORDER

| RANK | STATE | RATE |
|------|-------|------|
| 21 | Alabama | 23 |
| 30 | Alaska | 21 |
| 21 | Arizona | 23 |
| 21 | Arkansas | 23 |
| 28 | California | 22 |
| 10 | Colorado | 26 |
| 10 | Connecticut | 26 |
| 21 | Delaware | 23 |
| 10 | Florida | 26 |
| 10 | Georgia | 26 |
| 14 | Hawaii | 25 |
| 30 | Idaho | 21 |
| 4 | Illinois | 32 |
| 39 | Indiana | 19 |
| 43 | Iowa | 18 |
| 17 | Kansas | 24 |
| 46 | Kentucky | 17 |
| 2 | Louisiana | 37 |
| 39 | Maine | 19 |
| 8 | Maryland | 27 |
| 5 | Massachusetts | 29 |
| 30 | Michigan | 21 |
| 46 | Minnesota | 17 |
| 30 | Mississippi | 21 |
| 17 | Missouri | 24 |
| 39 | Montana | 19 |
| 36 | Nebraska | 20 |
| 8 | Nevada | 27 |
| 36 | New Hampshire | 20 |
| 3 | New Jersey | 35 |
| 17 | New Mexico | 24 |
| 1 | New York | 39 |
| 21 | North Carolina | 23 |
| 43 | North Dakota | 18 |
| 30 | Ohio | 21 |
| 28 | Oklahoma | 22 |
| 39 | Oregon | 19 |
| 30 | Pennsylvania | 21 |
| 17 | Rhode Island | 24 |
| 21 | South Carolina | 23 |
| 36 | South Dakota | 20 |
| 21 | Tennessee | 23 |
| 14 | Texas | 25 |
| 43 | Utah | 18 |
| 46 | Vermont | 17 |
| 7 | Virginia | 28 |
| 46 | Washington | 17 |
| 50 | West Virginia | 16 |
| 14 | Wisconsin | 25 |
| 5 | Wyoming | 29 |

RANK ORDER

| RANK | STATE | RATE |
|------|-------|------|
| 1 | New York | 39 |
| 2 | Louisiana | 37 |
| 3 | New Jersey | 35 |
| 4 | Illinois | 32 |
| 5 | Massachusetts | 29 |
| 5 | Wyoming | 29 |
| 7 | Virginia | 28 |
| 8 | Maryland | 27 |
| 8 | Nevada | 27 |
| 10 | Colorado | 26 |
| 10 | Connecticut | 26 |
| 10 | Florida | 26 |
| 10 | Georgia | 26 |
| 14 | Hawaii | 25 |
| 14 | Texas | 25 |
| 14 | Wisconsin | 25 |
| 17 | Kansas | 24 |
| 17 | Missouri | 24 |
| 17 | New Mexico | 24 |
| 17 | Rhode Island | 24 |
| 21 | Alabama | 23 |
| 21 | Arizona | 23 |
| 21 | Arkansas | 23 |
| 21 | Delaware | 23 |
| 21 | North Carolina | 23 |
| 21 | South Carolina | 23 |
| 21 | Tennessee | 23 |
| 28 | California | 22 |
| 28 | Oklahoma | 22 |
| 30 | Alaska | 21 |
| 30 | Idaho | 21 |
| 30 | Michigan | 21 |
| 30 | Mississippi | 21 |
| 30 | Ohio | 21 |
| 30 | Pennsylvania | 21 |
| 36 | Nebraska | 20 |
| 36 | New Hampshire | 20 |
| 36 | South Dakota | 20 |
| 39 | Indiana | 19 |
| 39 | Maine | 19 |
| 39 | Montana | 19 |
| 39 | Oregon | 19 |
| 43 | Iowa | 18 |
| 43 | North Dakota | 18 |
| 43 | Utah | 18 |
| 46 | Kentucky | 17 |
| 46 | Minnesota | 17 |
| 46 | Vermont | 17 |
| 46 | Washington | 17 |
| 50 | West Virginia | 16 |
| | District of Columbia | 72 |

Source: Morgan Quitno Press using data from U.S. Department of Justice, Bureau of Justice Statistics
"Census of State and Local Law Enforcement Agencies, 1996" (Bulletin, June 1998, NCJ-164618)
*Includes state and local police, sheriffs' departments and special police agencies.

# State and Local Government Expenditures for Police Protection in 1997

## National Total = $47,618,740,000*

ALPHA ORDER

| RANK | STATE | EXPENDITURES | % of USA |
|------|-------|--------------|----------|
| 26 | Alabama | $541,374,000 | 1.1% |
| 41 | Alaska | 151,192,000 | 0.3% |
| 16 | Arizona | 869,854,000 | 1.8% |
| 36 | Arkansas | 292,379,000 | 0.6% |
| 1 | California | 7,712,594,000 | 16.2% |
| 22 | Colorado | 649,137,000 | 1.4% |
| 24 | Connecticut | 592,738,000 | 1.2% |
| 45 | Delaware | 131,700,000 | 0.3% |
| 3 | Florida | 3,230,857,000 | 6.8% |
| 11 | Georgia | 1,050,368,000 | 2.2% |
| 38 | Hawaii | 192,287,000 | 0.4% |
| 40 | Idaho | 167,159,000 | 0.4% |
| 5 | Illinois | 2,404,047,000 | 5.0% |
| 23 | Indiana | 644,382,000 | 1.4% |
| 32 | Iowa | 350,462,000 | 0.7% |
| 30 | Kansas | 377,403,000 | 0.8% |
| 29 | Kentucky | 390,992,000 | 0.8% |
| 19 | Louisiana | 759,222,000 | 1.6% |
| 44 | Maine | 137,768,000 | 0.3% |
| 15 | Maryland | 885,188,000 | 1.9% |
| 10 | Massachusetts | 1,114,761,000 | 2.3% |
| 9 | Michigan | 1,563,311,000 | 3.3% |
| 21 | Minnesota | 702,137,000 | 1.5% |
| 33 | Mississippi | 320,027,000 | 0.7% |
| 18 | Missouri | 762,310,000 | 1.6% |
| 46 | Montana | 111,796,000 | 0.2% |
| 37 | Nebraska | 194,494,000 | 0.4% |
| 31 | Nevada | 372,323,000 | 0.8% |
| 42 | New Hampshire | 151,104,000 | 0.3% |
| 8 | New Jersey | 1,763,319,000 | 3.7% |
| 35 | New Mexico | 297,668,000 | 0.6% |
| 2 | New York | 5,132,773,000 | 10.8% |
| 12 | North Carolina | 1,029,038,000 | 2.2% |
| 50 | North Dakota | 56,525,000 | 0.1% |
| 7 | Ohio | 1,809,547,000 | 3.8% |
| 28 | Oklahoma | 401,634,000 | 0.8% |
| 25 | Oregon | 582,016,000 | 1.2% |
| 6 | Pennsylvania | 1,838,949,000 | 3.9% |
| 39 | Rhode Island | 174,864,000 | 0.4% |
| 27 | South Carolina | 494,197,000 | 1.0% |
| 48 | South Dakota | 75,560,000 | 0.2% |
| 20 | Tennessee | 745,792,000 | 1.6% |
| 4 | Texas | 2,760,918,000 | 5.8% |
| 34 | Utah | 305,346,000 | 0.6% |
| 49 | Vermont | 65,119,000 | 0.1% |
| 13 | Virginia | 981,619,000 | 2.1% |
| 17 | Washington | 866,316,000 | 1.8% |
| 43 | West Virginia | 139,666,000 | 0.3% |
| 14 | Wisconsin | 915,904,000 | 1.9% |
| 47 | Wyoming | 78,799,000 | 0.2% |

RANK ORDER

| RANK | STATE | EXPENDITURES | % of USA |
|------|-------|--------------|----------|
| 1 | California | $7,712,594,000 | 16.2% |
| 2 | New York | 5,132,773,000 | 10.8% |
| 3 | Florida | 3,230,857,000 | 6.8% |
| 4 | Texas | 2,760,918,000 | 5.8% |
| 5 | Illinois | 2,404,047,000 | 5.0% |
| 6 | Pennsylvania | 1,838,949,000 | 3.9% |
| 7 | Ohio | 1,809,547,000 | 3.8% |
| 8 | New Jersey | 1,763,319,000 | 3.7% |
| 9 | Michigan | 1,563,311,000 | 3.3% |
| 10 | Massachusetts | 1,114,761,000 | 2.3% |
| 11 | Georgia | 1,050,368,000 | 2.2% |
| 12 | North Carolina | 1,029,038,000 | 2.2% |
| 13 | Virginia | 981,619,000 | 2.1% |
| 14 | Wisconsin | 915,904,000 | 1.9% |
| 15 | Maryland | 885,188,000 | 1.9% |
| 16 | Arizona | 869,854,000 | 1.8% |
| 17 | Washington | 866,316,000 | 1.8% |
| 18 | Missouri | 762,310,000 | 1.6% |
| 19 | Louisiana | 759,222,000 | 1.6% |
| 20 | Tennessee | 745,792,000 | 1.6% |
| 21 | Minnesota | 702,137,000 | 1.5% |
| 22 | Colorado | 649,137,000 | 1.4% |
| 23 | Indiana | 644,382,000 | 1.4% |
| 24 | Connecticut | 592,738,000 | 1.2% |
| 25 | Oregon | 582,016,000 | 1.2% |
| 26 | Alabama | 541,374,000 | 1.1% |
| 27 | South Carolina | 494,197,000 | 1.0% |
| 28 | Oklahoma | 401,634,000 | 0.8% |
| 29 | Kentucky | 390,992,000 | 0.8% |
| 30 | Kansas | 377,403,000 | 0.8% |
| 31 | Nevada | 372,323,000 | 0.8% |
| 32 | Iowa | 350,462,000 | 0.7% |
| 33 | Mississippi | 320,027,000 | 0.7% |
| 34 | Utah | 305,346,000 | 0.6% |
| 35 | New Mexico | 297,668,000 | 0.6% |
| 36 | Arkansas | 292,379,000 | 0.6% |
| 37 | Nebraska | 194,494,000 | 0.4% |
| 38 | Hawaii | 192,287,000 | 0.4% |
| 39 | Rhode Island | 174,864,000 | 0.4% |
| 40 | Idaho | 167,159,000 | 0.4% |
| 41 | Alaska | 151,192,000 | 0.3% |
| 42 | New Hampshire | 151,104,000 | 0.3% |
| 43 | West Virginia | 139,666,000 | 0.3% |
| 44 | Maine | 137,768,000 | 0.3% |
| 45 | Delaware | 131,700,000 | 0.3% |
| 46 | Montana | 111,796,000 | 0.2% |
| 47 | Wyoming | 78,799,000 | 0.2% |
| 48 | South Dakota | 75,560,000 | 0.2% |
| 49 | Vermont | 65,119,000 | 0.1% |
| 50 | North Dakota | 56,525,000 | 0.1% |
| | District of Columbia | 279,805,000 | 0.6% |

Source: Morgan Quitno Press using data from U.S. Bureau of the Census
   "Compendium of Government Finances 1997" (GC97(4)-5, December 2000)
*Direct general expenditures.

# Per Capita State & Local Government Expenditures for Police Protection: 1997

## National Per Capita = $178*

ALPHA ORDER

| RANK | STATE | PER CAPITA |
|---|---|---|
| 38 | Alabama | $125 |
| 2 | Alaska | 248 |
| 8 | Arizona | 191 |
| 43 | Arkansas | 116 |
| 3 | California | 239 |
| 18 | Colorado | 167 |
| 10 | Connecticut | 181 |
| 11 | Delaware | 179 |
| 5 | Florida | 220 |
| 31 | Georgia | 140 |
| 20 | Hawaii | 162 |
| 34 | Idaho | 138 |
| 7 | Illinois | 200 |
| 46 | Indiana | 110 |
| 39 | Iowa | 123 |
| 28 | Kansas | 144 |
| 48 | Kentucky | 100 |
| 15 | Louisiana | 174 |
| 44 | Maine | 111 |
| 15 | Maryland | 174 |
| 9 | Massachusetts | 182 |
| 22 | Michigan | 160 |
| 25 | Minnesota | 150 |
| 41 | Mississippi | 117 |
| 30 | Missouri | 141 |
| 37 | Montana | 127 |
| 41 | Nebraska | 117 |
| 4 | Nevada | 222 |
| 36 | New Hampshire | 129 |
| 6 | New Jersey | 219 |
| 17 | New Mexico | 173 |
| 1 | New York | 283 |
| 32 | North Carolina | 139 |
| 49 | North Dakota | 88 |
| 21 | Ohio | 161 |
| 40 | Oklahoma | 121 |
| 11 | Oregon | 179 |
| 24 | Pennsylvania | 153 |
| 13 | Rhode Island | 177 |
| 35 | South Carolina | 130 |
| 47 | South Dakota | 103 |
| 32 | Tennessee | 139 |
| 29 | Texas | 143 |
| 26 | Utah | 148 |
| 44 | Vermont | 111 |
| 27 | Virginia | 146 |
| 23 | Washington | 155 |
| 50 | West Virginia | 77 |
| 14 | Wisconsin | 176 |
| 19 | Wyoming | 164 |

RANK ORDER

| RANK | STATE | PER CAPITA |
|---|---|---|
| 1 | New York | $283 |
| 2 | Alaska | 248 |
| 3 | California | 239 |
| 4 | Nevada | 222 |
| 5 | Florida | 220 |
| 6 | New Jersey | 219 |
| 7 | Illinois | 200 |
| 8 | Arizona | 191 |
| 9 | Massachusetts | 182 |
| 10 | Connecticut | 181 |
| 11 | Delaware | 179 |
| 11 | Oregon | 179 |
| 13 | Rhode Island | 177 |
| 14 | Wisconsin | 176 |
| 15 | Louisiana | 174 |
| 15 | Maryland | 174 |
| 17 | New Mexico | 173 |
| 18 | Colorado | 167 |
| 19 | Wyoming | 164 |
| 20 | Hawaii | 162 |
| 21 | Ohio | 161 |
| 22 | Michigan | 160 |
| 23 | Washington | 155 |
| 24 | Pennsylvania | 153 |
| 25 | Minnesota | 150 |
| 26 | Utah | 148 |
| 27 | Virginia | 146 |
| 28 | Kansas | 144 |
| 29 | Texas | 143 |
| 30 | Missouri | 141 |
| 31 | Georgia | 140 |
| 32 | North Carolina | 139 |
| 32 | Tennessee | 139 |
| 34 | Idaho | 138 |
| 35 | South Carolina | 130 |
| 36 | New Hampshire | 129 |
| 37 | Montana | 127 |
| 38 | Alabama | 125 |
| 39 | Iowa | 123 |
| 40 | Oklahoma | 121 |
| 41 | Mississippi | 117 |
| 41 | Nebraska | 117 |
| 43 | Arkansas | 116 |
| 44 | Maine | 111 |
| 44 | Vermont | 111 |
| 46 | Indiana | 110 |
| 47 | South Dakota | 103 |
| 48 | Kentucky | 100 |
| 49 | North Dakota | 88 |
| 50 | West Virginia | 77 |
| | District of Columbia | 529 |

Source: Morgan Quitno Press using data from U.S. Bureau of the Census
    "Compendium of Government Finances 1997" (GC97(4)-5, December 2000)
*Direct general expenditures.

# State and Local Government Expenditures for Corrections in 1997

## National Total = $39,946,460,000*

ALPHA ORDER

| RANK | STATE | EXPENDITURES | % of USA |
|---|---|---|---|
| 30 | Alabama | $323,350,000 | 0.8% |
| 38 | Alaska | 149,823,000 | 0.4% |
| 17 | Arizona | 701,806,000 | 1.8% |
| 35 | Arkansas | 240,695,000 | 0.6% |
| 1 | California | 6,209,434,000 | 15.5% |
| 18 | Colorado | 600,124,000 | 1.5% |
| 24 | Connecticut | 493,772,000 | 1.2% |
| 41 | Delaware | 123,147,000 | 0.3% |
| 6 | Florida | 1,526,928,000 | 3.8% |
| 10 | Georgia | 1,199,638,000 | 3.0% |
| 40 | Hawaii | 127,535,000 | 0.3% |
| 39 | Idaho | 132,669,000 | 0.3% |
| 8 | Illinois | 1,310,529,000 | 3.3% |
| 19 | Indiana | 589,048,000 | 1.5% |
| 36 | Iowa | 210,014,000 | 0.5% |
| 32 | Kansas | 246,709,000 | 0.6% |
| 28 | Kentucky | 353,178,000 | 0.9% |
| 26 | Louisiana | 473,284,000 | 1.2% |
| 44 | Maine | 93,664,000 | 0.2% |
| 13 | Maryland | 872,988,000 | 2.2% |
| 14 | Massachusetts | 848,654,000 | 2.1% |
| 5 | Michigan | 1,564,842,000 | 3.9% |
| 25 | Minnesota | 481,101,000 | 1.2% |
| 33 | Mississippi | 245,104,000 | 0.6% |
| 23 | Missouri | 503,566,000 | 1.3% |
| 46 | Montana | 85,844,000 | 0.2% |
| 37 | Nebraska | 151,592,000 | 0.4% |
| 29 | Nevada | 337,816,000 | 0.8% |
| 45 | New Hampshire | 86,026,000 | 0.2% |
| 9 | New Jersey | 1,255,491,000 | 3.1% |
| 31 | New Mexico | 257,714,000 | 0.6% |
| 2 | New York | 3,908,022,000 | 9.8% |
| 11 | North Carolina | 1,088,339,000 | 2.7% |
| 50 | North Dakota | 30,251,000 | 0.1% |
| 7 | Ohio | 1,513,243,000 | 3.8% |
| 27 | Oklahoma | 374,792,000 | 0.9% |
| 21 | Oregon | 579,867,000 | 1.5% |
| 4 | Pennsylvania | 1,740,743,000 | 4.4% |
| 43 | Rhode Island | 119,698,000 | 0.3% |
| 22 | South Carolina | 527,347,000 | 1.3% |
| 47 | South Dakota | 77,435,000 | 0.2% |
| 20 | Tennessee | 587,255,000 | 1.5% |
| 3 | Texas | 3,114,693,000 | 7.8% |
| 34 | Utah | 243,543,000 | 0.6% |
| 49 | Vermont | 43,827,000 | 0.1% |
| 12 | Virginia | 947,965,000 | 2.4% |
| 15 | Washington | 848,304,000 | 2.1% |
| 42 | West Virginia | 121,779,000 | 0.3% |
| 16 | Wisconsin | 702,983,000 | 1.8% |
| 48 | Wyoming | 53,309,000 | 0.1% |

RANK ORDER

| RANK | STATE | EXPENDITURES | % of USA |
|---|---|---|---|
| 1 | California | $6,209,434,000 | 15.5% |
| 2 | New York | 3,908,022,000 | 9.8% |
| 3 | Texas | 3,114,693,000 | 7.8% |
| 4 | Pennsylvania | 1,740,743,000 | 4.4% |
| 5 | Michigan | 1,564,842,000 | 3.9% |
| 6 | Florida | 1,526,928,000 | 3.8% |
| 7 | Ohio | 1,513,243,000 | 3.8% |
| 8 | Illinois | 1,310,529,000 | 3.3% |
| 9 | New Jersey | 1,255,491,000 | 3.1% |
| 10 | Georgia | 1,199,638,000 | 3.0% |
| 11 | North Carolina | 1,088,339,000 | 2.7% |
| 12 | Virginia | 947,965,000 | 2.4% |
| 13 | Maryland | 872,988,000 | 2.2% |
| 14 | Massachusetts | 848,654,000 | 2.1% |
| 15 | Washington | 848,304,000 | 2.1% |
| 16 | Wisconsin | 702,983,000 | 1.8% |
| 17 | Arizona | 701,806,000 | 1.8% |
| 18 | Colorado | 600,124,000 | 1.5% |
| 19 | Indiana | 589,048,000 | 1.5% |
| 20 | Tennessee | 587,255,000 | 1.5% |
| 21 | Oregon | 579,867,000 | 1.5% |
| 22 | South Carolina | 527,347,000 | 1.3% |
| 23 | Missouri | 503,566,000 | 1.3% |
| 24 | Connecticut | 493,772,000 | 1.2% |
| 25 | Minnesota | 481,101,000 | 1.2% |
| 26 | Louisiana | 473,284,000 | 1.2% |
| 27 | Oklahoma | 374,792,000 | 0.9% |
| 28 | Kentucky | 353,178,000 | 0.9% |
| 29 | Nevada | 337,816,000 | 0.8% |
| 30 | Alabama | 323,350,000 | 0.8% |
| 31 | New Mexico | 257,714,000 | 0.6% |
| 32 | Kansas | 246,709,000 | 0.6% |
| 33 | Mississippi | 245,104,000 | 0.6% |
| 34 | Utah | 243,543,000 | 0.6% |
| 35 | Arkansas | 240,695,000 | 0.6% |
| 36 | Iowa | 210,014,000 | 0.5% |
| 37 | Nebraska | 151,592,000 | 0.4% |
| 38 | Alaska | 149,823,000 | 0.4% |
| 39 | Idaho | 132,669,000 | 0.3% |
| 40 | Hawaii | 127,535,000 | 0.3% |
| 41 | Delaware | 123,147,000 | 0.3% |
| 42 | West Virginia | 121,779,000 | 0.3% |
| 43 | Rhode Island | 119,698,000 | 0.3% |
| 44 | Maine | 93,664,000 | 0.2% |
| 45 | New Hampshire | 86,026,000 | 0.2% |
| 46 | Montana | 85,844,000 | 0.2% |
| 47 | South Dakota | 77,435,000 | 0.2% |
| 48 | Wyoming | 53,309,000 | 0.1% |
| 49 | Vermont | 43,827,000 | 0.1% |
| 50 | North Dakota | 30,251,000 | 0.1% |
| | District of Columbia | 300,157,000 | 0.8% |

Source: Morgan Quitno Press using data from U.S. Bureau of the Census
"Compendium of Government Finances 1997" (GC97(4)-5, December 2000)
*Direct general expenditures.

# Per Capita State and Local Government Expenditures for Corrections in 1997

## National Per Capita = $149*

ALPHA ORDER

| RANK | STATE | PER CAPITA |
|---|---|---|
| 44 | Alabama | $75 |
| 1 | Alaska | 246 |
| 12 | Arizona | 154 |
| 38 | Arkansas | 95 |
| 4 | California | 193 |
| 12 | Colorado | 154 |
| 14 | Connecticut | 151 |
| 7 | Delaware | 168 |
| 34 | Florida | 104 |
| 9 | Georgia | 160 |
| 32 | Hawaii | 107 |
| 28 | Idaho | 110 |
| 29 | Illinois | 109 |
| 36 | Indiana | 100 |
| 46 | Iowa | 74 |
| 39 | Kansas | 94 |
| 42 | Kentucky | 90 |
| 29 | Louisiana | 109 |
| 44 | Maine | 75 |
| 6 | Maryland | 171 |
| 20 | Massachusetts | 139 |
| 9 | Michigan | 160 |
| 35 | Minnesota | 103 |
| 42 | Mississippi | 90 |
| 40 | Missouri | 93 |
| 37 | Montana | 98 |
| 41 | Nebraska | 92 |
| 3 | Nevada | 202 |
| 48 | New Hampshire | 73 |
| 11 | New Jersey | 156 |
| 16 | New Mexico | 150 |
| 2 | New York | 215 |
| 17 | North Carolina | 147 |
| 50 | North Dakota | 47 |
| 22 | Ohio | 135 |
| 26 | Oklahoma | 113 |
| 5 | Oregon | 179 |
| 18 | Pennsylvania | 145 |
| 24 | Rhode Island | 121 |
| 20 | South Carolina | 139 |
| 33 | South Dakota | 106 |
| 29 | Tennessee | 109 |
| 8 | Texas | 161 |
| 25 | Utah | 118 |
| 46 | Vermont | 74 |
| 19 | Virginia | 141 |
| 14 | Washington | 151 |
| 49 | West Virginia | 67 |
| 22 | Wisconsin | 135 |
| 27 | Wyoming | 111 |

RANK ORDER

| RANK | STATE | PER CAPITA |
|---|---|---|
| 1 | Alaska | $246 |
| 2 | New York | 215 |
| 3 | Nevada | 202 |
| 4 | California | 193 |
| 5 | Oregon | 179 |
| 6 | Maryland | 171 |
| 7 | Delaware | 168 |
| 8 | Texas | 161 |
| 9 | Georgia | 160 |
| 9 | Michigan | 160 |
| 11 | New Jersey | 156 |
| 12 | Arizona | 154 |
| 12 | Colorado | 154 |
| 14 | Connecticut | 151 |
| 14 | Washington | 151 |
| 16 | New Mexico | 150 |
| 17 | North Carolina | 147 |
| 18 | Pennsylvania | 145 |
| 19 | Virginia | 141 |
| 20 | Massachusetts | 139 |
| 20 | South Carolina | 139 |
| 22 | Ohio | 135 |
| 22 | Wisconsin | 135 |
| 24 | Rhode Island | 121 |
| 25 | Utah | 118 |
| 26 | Oklahoma | 113 |
| 27 | Wyoming | 111 |
| 28 | Idaho | 110 |
| 29 | Illinois | 109 |
| 29 | Louisiana | 109 |
| 29 | Tennessee | 109 |
| 32 | Hawaii | 107 |
| 33 | South Dakota | 106 |
| 34 | Florida | 104 |
| 35 | Minnesota | 103 |
| 36 | Indiana | 100 |
| 37 | Montana | 98 |
| 38 | Arkansas | 95 |
| 39 | Kansas | 94 |
| 40 | Missouri | 93 |
| 41 | Nebraska | 92 |
| 42 | Kentucky | 90 |
| 42 | Mississippi | 90 |
| 44 | Alabama | 75 |
| 44 | Maine | 75 |
| 46 | Iowa | 74 |
| 46 | Vermont | 74 |
| 48 | New Hampshire | 73 |
| 49 | West Virginia | 67 |
| 50 | North Dakota | 47 |

District of Columbia — 568

Source: Morgan Quitno Press using data from U.S. Bureau of the Census
   "Compendium of Government Finances 1997" (GC97(4)-5, December 2000)
*Direct general expenditures.

# III. DEFENSE

# U.S. Department of Defense Domestic Expenditures in 1999

## National Total = $218,861,234,000*

ALPHA ORDER

| RANK | STATE | EXPENDITURES | % of USA |
|------|-------|--------------|----------|
| 14 | Alabama | $5,067,744,000 | 2.3% |
| 33 | Alaska | 1,478,329,000 | 0.7% |
| 9 | Arizona | 6,158,229,000 | 2.8% |
| 37 | Arkansas | 1,033,659,000 | 0.5% |
| 1 | California | 29,072,295,000 | 13.3% |
| 15 | Colorado | 4,833,866,000 | 2.2% |
| 19 | Connecticut | 3,727,230,000 | 1.7% |
| 45 | Delaware | 429,552,000 | 0.2% |
| 4 | Florida | 13,576,583,000 | 6.2% |
| 6 | Georgia | 8,948,953,000 | 4.1% |
| 20 | Hawaii | 3,450,909,000 | 1.6% |
| 43 | Idaho | 562,978,000 | 0.3% |
| 18 | Illinois | 3,799,614,000 | 1.7% |
| 26 | Indiana | 2,571,778,000 | 1.2% |
| 41 | Iowa | 711,812,000 | 0.3% |
| 29 | Kansas | 2,018,086,000 | 0.9% |
| 23 | Kentucky | 3,280,888,000 | 1.5% |
| 25 | Louisiana | 2,830,787,000 | 1.3% |
| 34 | Maine | 1,277,791,000 | 0.6% |
| 5 | Maryland | 9,160,849,000 | 4.2% |
| 11 | Massachusetts | 5,705,545,000 | 2.6% |
| 28 | Michigan | 2,098,941,000 | 1.0% |
| 31 | Minnesota | 1,684,001,000 | 0.8% |
| 24 | Mississippi | 2,952,443,000 | 1.3% |
| 8 | Missouri | 6,216,063,000 | 2.8% |
| 46 | Montana | 407,609,000 | 0.2% |
| 38 | Nebraska | 889,570,000 | 0.4% |
| 36 | Nevada | 1,073,625,000 | 0.5% |
| 42 | New Hampshire | 641,301,000 | 0.3% |
| 17 | New Jersey | 4,415,561,000 | 2.0% |
| 30 | New Mexico | 1,727,688,000 | 0.8% |
| 13 | New York | 5,171,271,000 | 2.4% |
| 12 | North Carolina | 5,610,477,000 | 2.6% |
| 44 | North Dakota | 551,534,000 | 0.3% |
| 16 | Ohio | 4,781,701,000 | 2.2% |
| 21 | Oklahoma | 3,437,738,000 | 1.6% |
| 39 | Oregon | 866,878,000 | 0.4% |
| 10 | Pennsylvania | 6,154,004,000 | 2.8% |
| 40 | Rhode Island | 780,282,000 | 0.4% |
| 22 | South Carolina | 3,325,489,000 | 1.5% |
| 48 | South Dakota | 358,338,000 | 0.2% |
| 27 | Tennessee | 2,204,492,000 | 1.0% |
| 3 | Texas | 17,562,394,000 | 8.0% |
| 32 | Utah | 1,537,838,000 | 0.7% |
| 49 | Vermont | 316,142,000 | 0.1% |
| 2 | Virginia | 23,461,018,000 | 10.7% |
| 7 | Washington | 6,287,031,000 | 2.9% |
| 47 | West Virginia | 404,622,000 | 0.2% |
| 35 | Wisconsin | 1,107,932,000 | 0.5% |
| 50 | Wyoming | 314,432,000 | 0.1% |

RANK ORDER

| RANK | STATE | EXPENDITURES | % of USA |
|------|-------|--------------|----------|
| 1 | California | $29,072,295,000 | 13.3% |
| 2 | Virginia | 23,461,018,000 | 10.7% |
| 3 | Texas | 17,562,394,000 | 8.0% |
| 4 | Florida | 13,576,583,000 | 6.2% |
| 5 | Maryland | 9,160,849,000 | 4.2% |
| 6 | Georgia | 8,948,953,000 | 4.1% |
| 7 | Washington | 6,287,031,000 | 2.9% |
| 8 | Missouri | 6,216,063,000 | 2.8% |
| 9 | Arizona | 6,158,229,000 | 2.8% |
| 10 | Pennsylvania | 6,154,004,000 | 2.8% |
| 11 | Massachusetts | 5,705,545,000 | 2.6% |
| 12 | North Carolina | 5,610,477,000 | 2.6% |
| 13 | New York | 5,171,271,000 | 2.4% |
| 14 | Alabama | 5,067,744,000 | 2.3% |
| 15 | Colorado | 4,833,866,000 | 2.2% |
| 16 | Ohio | 4,781,701,000 | 2.2% |
| 17 | New Jersey | 4,415,561,000 | 2.0% |
| 18 | Illinois | 3,799,614,000 | 1.7% |
| 19 | Connecticut | 3,727,230,000 | 1.7% |
| 20 | Hawaii | 3,450,909,000 | 1.6% |
| 21 | Oklahoma | 3,437,738,000 | 1.6% |
| 22 | South Carolina | 3,325,489,000 | 1.5% |
| 23 | Kentucky | 3,280,888,000 | 1.5% |
| 24 | Mississippi | 2,952,443,000 | 1.3% |
| 25 | Louisiana | 2,830,787,000 | 1.3% |
| 26 | Indiana | 2,571,778,000 | 1.2% |
| 27 | Tennessee | 2,204,492,000 | 1.0% |
| 28 | Michigan | 2,098,941,000 | 1.0% |
| 29 | Kansas | 2,018,086,000 | 0.9% |
| 30 | New Mexico | 1,727,688,000 | 0.8% |
| 31 | Minnesota | 1,684,001,000 | 0.8% |
| 32 | Utah | 1,537,838,000 | 0.7% |
| 33 | Alaska | 1,478,329,000 | 0.7% |
| 34 | Maine | 1,277,791,000 | 0.6% |
| 35 | Wisconsin | 1,107,932,000 | 0.5% |
| 36 | Nevada | 1,073,625,000 | 0.5% |
| 37 | Arkansas | 1,033,659,000 | 0.5% |
| 38 | Nebraska | 889,570,000 | 0.4% |
| 39 | Oregon | 866,878,000 | 0.4% |
| 40 | Rhode Island | 780,282,000 | 0.4% |
| 41 | Iowa | 711,812,000 | 0.3% |
| 42 | New Hampshire | 641,301,000 | 0.3% |
| 43 | Idaho | 562,978,000 | 0.3% |
| 44 | North Dakota | 551,534,000 | 0.3% |
| 45 | Delaware | 429,552,000 | 0.2% |
| 46 | Montana | 407,609,000 | 0.2% |
| 47 | West Virginia | 404,622,000 | 0.2% |
| 48 | South Dakota | 358,338,000 | 0.2% |
| 49 | Vermont | 316,142,000 | 0.1% |
| 50 | Wyoming | 314,432,000 | 0.1% |
| | District of Columbia | 2,823,342,000 | 1.3% |

*Source: U.S. Department of Defense*
     *(http://web1.whs.osd.mil/mmid/l03/fy99/99l03.htm)*
*Expenditures for payroll, grants and prime contracts ($25,000 or more) for civil and military functions. Does not include payroll, contracts or grants to U.S. territories and other countries.*

# Per Capita U.S. Department of Defense Domestic Expenditures in 1999

## National Per Capita = $803*

ALPHA ORDER

| RANK | STATE | PER CAPITA |
|---|---|---|
| 7 | Alabama | $1,160 |
| 3 | Alaska | 2,386 |
| 5 | Arizona | 1,289 |
| 41 | Arkansas | 405 |
| 18 | California | 877 |
| 6 | Colorado | 1,192 |
| 10 | Connecticut | 1,136 |
| 30 | Delaware | 570 |
| 17 | Florida | 898 |
| 8 | Georgia | 1,149 |
| 2 | Hawaii | 2,911 |
| 38 | Idaho | 450 |
| 44 | Illinois | 313 |
| 39 | Indiana | 433 |
| 47 | Iowa | 248 |
| 24 | Kansas | 760 |
| 22 | Kentucky | 828 |
| 28 | Louisiana | 647 |
| 14 | Maine | 1,020 |
| 4 | Maryland | 1,771 |
| 16 | Massachusetts | 924 |
| 49 | Michigan | 213 |
| 43 | Minnesota | 353 |
| 12 | Mississippi | 1,066 |
| 9 | Missouri | 1,137 |
| 37 | Montana | 462 |
| 32 | Nebraska | 534 |
| 29 | Nevada | 593 |
| 32 | New Hampshire | 534 |
| 31 | New Jersey | 542 |
| 15 | New Mexico | 993 |
| 45 | New York | 284 |
| 25 | North Carolina | 733 |
| 20 | North Dakota | 870 |
| 40 | Ohio | 425 |
| 13 | Oklahoma | 1,024 |
| 46 | Oregon | 261 |
| 35 | Pennsylvania | 513 |
| 23 | Rhode Island | 788 |
| 21 | South Carolina | 856 |
| 36 | South Dakota | 489 |
| 42 | Tennessee | 402 |
| 19 | Texas | 876 |
| 26 | Utah | 722 |
| 34 | Vermont | 532 |
| 1 | Virginia | 3,414 |
| 11 | Washington | 1,092 |
| 48 | West Virginia | 224 |
| 50 | Wisconsin | 211 |
| 27 | Wyoming | 656 |

RANK ORDER

| RANK | STATE | PER CAPITA |
|---|---|---|
| 1 | Virginia | $3,414 |
| 2 | Hawaii | 2,911 |
| 3 | Alaska | 2,386 |
| 4 | Maryland | 1,771 |
| 5 | Arizona | 1,289 |
| 6 | Colorado | 1,192 |
| 7 | Alabama | 1,160 |
| 8 | Georgia | 1,149 |
| 9 | Missouri | 1,137 |
| 10 | Connecticut | 1,136 |
| 11 | Washington | 1,092 |
| 12 | Mississippi | 1,066 |
| 13 | Oklahoma | 1,024 |
| 14 | Maine | 1,020 |
| 15 | New Mexico | 993 |
| 16 | Massachusetts | 924 |
| 17 | Florida | 898 |
| 18 | California | 877 |
| 19 | Texas | 876 |
| 20 | North Dakota | 870 |
| 21 | South Carolina | 856 |
| 22 | Kentucky | 828 |
| 23 | Rhode Island | 788 |
| 24 | Kansas | 760 |
| 25 | North Carolina | 733 |
| 26 | Utah | 722 |
| 27 | Wyoming | 656 |
| 28 | Louisiana | 647 |
| 29 | Nevada | 593 |
| 30 | Delaware | 570 |
| 31 | New Jersey | 542 |
| 32 | Nebraska | 534 |
| 32 | New Hampshire | 534 |
| 34 | Vermont | 532 |
| 35 | Pennsylvania | 513 |
| 36 | South Dakota | 489 |
| 37 | Montana | 462 |
| 38 | Idaho | 450 |
| 39 | Indiana | 433 |
| 40 | Ohio | 425 |
| 41 | Arkansas | 405 |
| 42 | Tennessee | 402 |
| 43 | Minnesota | 353 |
| 44 | Illinois | 313 |
| 45 | New York | 284 |
| 46 | Oregon | 261 |
| 47 | Iowa | 248 |
| 48 | West Virginia | 224 |
| 49 | Michigan | 213 |
| 50 | Wisconsin | 211 |

District of Columbia 5,440

Source: Morgan Quitno Press using data from U.S. Department of Defense
(http://web1.whs.osd.mil/mmid/l03/fy99/99l03.htm)
*Expenditures for payroll, grants and prime contracts ($25,000 or more) for civil and military functions. Does not include payroll, contracts or grants to U.S. territories and other countries.

# U.S. Department of Defense Total Contracts in 1999

## National Total = $114,875,139,000*

ALPHA ORDER

| RANK | STATE | CONTRACTS | % of USA |
|---|---|---|---|
| 14 | Alabama | $2,676,744,000 | 2.3% |
| 34 | Alaska | 609,981,000 | 0.5% |
| 8 | Arizona | 4,171,941,000 | 3.6% |
| 41 | Arkansas | 246,056,000 | 0.2% |
| 1 | California | 17,371,558,000 | 15.1% |
| 16 | Colorado | 2,441,790,000 | 2.1% |
| 12 | Connecticut | 3,169,394,000 | 2.8% |
| 49 | Delaware | 91,749,000 | 0.1% |
| 4 | Florida | 6,806,055,000 | 5.9% |
| 9 | Georgia | 4,112,571,000 | 3.6% |
| 28 | Hawaii | 984,849,000 | 0.9% |
| 44 | Idaho | 155,987,000 | 0.1% |
| 22 | Illinois | 1,315,580,000 | 1.1% |
| 18 | Indiana | 1,648,349,000 | 1.4% |
| 36 | Iowa | 419,385,000 | 0.4% |
| 29 | Kansas | 887,380,000 | 0.8% |
| 21 | Kentucky | 1,386,786,000 | 1.2% |
| 20 | Louisiana | 1,441,713,000 | 1.3% |
| 31 | Maine | 686,364,000 | 0.6% |
| 5 | Maryland | 5,466,503,000 | 4.8% |
| 6 | Massachusetts | 4,714,942,000 | 4.1% |
| 24 | Michigan | 1,167,864,000 | 1.0% |
| 23 | Minnesota | 1,212,291,000 | 1.1% |
| 19 | Mississippi | 1,537,891,000 | 1.3% |
| 7 | Missouri | 4,602,627,000 | 4.0% |
| 47 | Montana | 98,006,000 | 0.1% |
| 42 | Nebraska | 225,887,000 | 0.2% |
| 40 | Nevada | 276,131,000 | 0.2% |
| 37 | New Hampshire | 359,907,000 | 0.3% |
| 13 | New Jersey | 2,850,762,000 | 2.5% |
| 33 | New Mexico | 614,173,000 | 0.5% |
| 11 | New York | 3,289,418,000 | 2.9% |
| 27 | North Carolina | 1,039,620,000 | 0.9% |
| 45 | North Dakota | 149,102,000 | 0.1% |
| 15 | Ohio | 2,592,556,000 | 2.3% |
| 25 | Oklahoma | 1,139,932,000 | 1.0% |
| 39 | Oregon | 304,320,000 | 0.3% |
| 10 | Pennsylvania | 3,864,543,000 | 3.4% |
| 38 | Rhode Island | 312,187,000 | 0.3% |
| 30 | South Carolina | 868,545,000 | 0.8% |
| 48 | South Dakota | 93,948,000 | 0.1% |
| 26 | Tennessee | 1,092,565,000 | 1.0% |
| 3 | Texas | 8,666,461,000 | 7.5% |
| 35 | Utah | 532,906,000 | 0.5% |
| 43 | Vermont | 213,552,000 | 0.2% |
| 2 | Virginia | 12,240,573,000 | 10.7% |
| 17 | Washington | 2,296,094,000 | 2.0% |
| 46 | West Virginia | 109,157,000 | 0.1% |
| 32 | Wisconsin | 644,452,000 | 0.6% |
| 50 | Wyoming | 62,038,000 | 0.1% |

RANK ORDER

| RANK | STATE | CONTRACTS | % of USA |
|---|---|---|---|
| 1 | California | $17,371,558,000 | 15.1% |
| 2 | Virginia | 12,240,573,000 | 10.7% |
| 3 | Texas | 8,666,461,000 | 7.5% |
| 4 | Florida | 6,806,055,000 | 5.9% |
| 5 | Maryland | 5,466,503,000 | 4.8% |
| 6 | Massachusetts | 4,714,942,000 | 4.1% |
| 7 | Missouri | 4,602,627,000 | 4.0% |
| 8 | Arizona | 4,171,941,000 | 3.6% |
| 9 | Georgia | 4,112,571,000 | 3.6% |
| 10 | Pennsylvania | 3,864,543,000 | 3.4% |
| 11 | New York | 3,289,418,000 | 2.9% |
| 12 | Connecticut | 3,169,394,000 | 2.8% |
| 13 | New Jersey | 2,850,762,000 | 2.5% |
| 14 | Alabama | 2,676,744,000 | 2.3% |
| 15 | Ohio | 2,592,556,000 | 2.3% |
| 16 | Colorado | 2,441,790,000 | 2.1% |
| 17 | Washington | 2,296,094,000 | 2.0% |
| 18 | Indiana | 1,648,349,000 | 1.4% |
| 19 | Mississippi | 1,537,891,000 | 1.3% |
| 20 | Louisiana | 1,441,713,000 | 1.3% |
| 21 | Kentucky | 1,386,786,000 | 1.2% |
| 22 | Illinois | 1,315,580,000 | 1.1% |
| 23 | Minnesota | 1,212,291,000 | 1.1% |
| 24 | Michigan | 1,167,864,000 | 1.0% |
| 25 | Oklahoma | 1,139,932,000 | 1.0% |
| 26 | Tennessee | 1,092,565,000 | 1.0% |
| 27 | North Carolina | 1,039,620,000 | 0.9% |
| 28 | Hawaii | 984,849,000 | 0.9% |
| 29 | Kansas | 887,380,000 | 0.8% |
| 30 | South Carolina | 868,545,000 | 0.8% |
| 31 | Maine | 686,364,000 | 0.6% |
| 32 | Wisconsin | 644,452,000 | 0.6% |
| 33 | New Mexico | 614,173,000 | 0.5% |
| 34 | Alaska | 609,981,000 | 0.5% |
| 35 | Utah | 532,906,000 | 0.5% |
| 36 | Iowa | 419,385,000 | 0.4% |
| 37 | New Hampshire | 359,907,000 | 0.3% |
| 38 | Rhode Island | 312,187,000 | 0.3% |
| 39 | Oregon | 304,320,000 | 0.3% |
| 40 | Nevada | 276,131,000 | 0.2% |
| 41 | Arkansas | 246,056,000 | 0.2% |
| 42 | Nebraska | 225,887,000 | 0.2% |
| 43 | Vermont | 213,552,000 | 0.2% |
| 44 | Idaho | 155,987,000 | 0.1% |
| 45 | North Dakota | 149,102,000 | 0.1% |
| 46 | West Virginia | 109,157,000 | 0.1% |
| 47 | Montana | 98,006,000 | 0.1% |
| 48 | South Dakota | 93,948,000 | 0.1% |
| 49 | Delaware | 91,749,000 | 0.1% |
| 50 | Wyoming | 62,038,000 | 0.1% |
| | District of Columbia | 1,611,954,000 | 1.4% |

Source: U.S. Department of Defense
  "Estimated Payroll, Contracts & Grants by State/Area" (http://web1.whs.osd.mil/mmid/l03/fy99/99estp.htm)
*Includes prime contracts ($25,000 or more) for civil and military functions. Does not include $10,160,986,000 in contracts to U.S. territories and other countries.

# Per Capita U.S. Department of Defense Contracts in 1999

## National Per Capita = $421*

ALPHA ORDER

| RANK | STATE | PER CAPITA |
|------|-------|------------|
| 9 | Alabama | $613 |
| 3 | Alaska | 985 |
| 5 | Arizona | 873 |
| 48 | Arkansas | 96 |
| 14 | California | 524 |
| 10 | Colorado | 602 |
| 4 | Connecticut | 966 |
| 44 | Delaware | 122 |
| 15 | Florida | 450 |
| 13 | Georgia | 528 |
| 7 | Hawaii | 831 |
| 42 | Idaho | 125 |
| 47 | Illinois | 108 |
| 28 | Indiana | 277 |
| 37 | Iowa | 146 |
| 23 | Kansas | 334 |
| 20 | Kentucky | 350 |
| 24 | Louisiana | 330 |
| 12 | Maine | 548 |
| 2 | Maryland | 1,057 |
| 8 | Massachusetts | 764 |
| 45 | Michigan | 118 |
| 29 | Minnesota | 254 |
| 11 | Mississippi | 555 |
| 6 | Missouri | 842 |
| 46 | Montana | 111 |
| 38 | Nebraska | 136 |
| 36 | Nevada | 153 |
| 27 | New Hampshire | 300 |
| 20 | New Jersey | 350 |
| 19 | New Mexico | 353 |
| 35 | New York | 181 |
| 38 | North Carolina | 136 |
| 31 | North Dakota | 235 |
| 32 | Ohio | 230 |
| 22 | Oklahoma | 339 |
| 49 | Oregon | 92 |
| 25 | Pennsylvania | 322 |
| 26 | Rhode Island | 315 |
| 33 | South Carolina | 224 |
| 41 | South Dakota | 128 |
| 34 | Tennessee | 199 |
| 16 | Texas | 432 |
| 30 | Utah | 250 |
| 18 | Vermont | 360 |
| 1 | Virginia | 1,781 |
| 17 | Washington | 399 |
| 50 | West Virginia | 60 |
| 43 | Wisconsin | 123 |
| 40 | Wyoming | 129 |

RANK ORDER

| RANK | STATE | PER CAPITA |
|------|-------|------------|
| 1 | Virginia | $1,781 |
| 2 | Maryland | 1,057 |
| 3 | Alaska | 985 |
| 4 | Connecticut | 966 |
| 5 | Arizona | 873 |
| 6 | Missouri | 842 |
| 7 | Hawaii | 831 |
| 8 | Massachusetts | 764 |
| 9 | Alabama | 613 |
| 10 | Colorado | 602 |
| 11 | Mississippi | 555 |
| 12 | Maine | 548 |
| 13 | Georgia | 528 |
| 14 | California | 524 |
| 15 | Florida | 450 |
| 16 | Texas | 432 |
| 17 | Washington | 399 |
| 18 | Vermont | 360 |
| 19 | New Mexico | 353 |
| 20 | Kentucky | 350 |
| 20 | New Jersey | 350 |
| 22 | Oklahoma | 339 |
| 23 | Kansas | 334 |
| 24 | Louisiana | 330 |
| 25 | Pennsylvania | 322 |
| 26 | Rhode Island | 315 |
| 27 | New Hampshire | 300 |
| 28 | Indiana | 277 |
| 29 | Minnesota | 254 |
| 30 | Utah | 250 |
| 31 | North Dakota | 235 |
| 32 | Ohio | 230 |
| 33 | South Carolina | 224 |
| 34 | Tennessee | 199 |
| 35 | New York | 181 |
| 36 | Nevada | 153 |
| 37 | Iowa | 146 |
| 38 | Nebraska | 136 |
| 38 | North Carolina | 136 |
| 40 | Wyoming | 129 |
| 41 | South Dakota | 128 |
| 42 | Idaho | 125 |
| 43 | Wisconsin | 123 |
| 44 | Delaware | 122 |
| 45 | Michigan | 118 |
| 46 | Montana | 111 |
| 47 | Illinois | 108 |
| 48 | Arkansas | 96 |
| 49 | Oregon | 92 |
| 50 | West Virginia | 60 |

| | District of Columbia | 3,106 |

*Source: Morgan Quitno Press using data from U.S. Department of Defense
"Estimated Payroll, Contracts & Grants by State/Area" (http://web1.whs.osd.mil/mmid/l03/fy99/99estp.htm)
*Includes prime contracts ($25,000 or more) for civil and military functions.*

# U.S. Department of Defense Contracts for Military Functions in 1999

## National Total = $112,150,705,000*

| RANK | STATE | CONTRACTS | % of USA |
|------|-------|-----------|----------|
| 14 | Alabama | $2,667,870,000 | 2.4% |
| 34 | Alaska | 576,300,000 | 0.5% |
| 8 | Arizona | 4,153,534,000 | 3.7% |
| 43 | Arkansas | 172,064,000 | 0.2% |
| 1 | California | 16,987,383,000 | 15.1% |
| 16 | Colorado | 2,428,668,000 | 2.2% |
| 12 | Connecticut | 3,163,702,000 | 2.8% |
| 48 | Delaware | 87,639,000 | 0.1% |
| 4 | Florida | 6,709,627,000 | 6.0% |
| 9 | Georgia | 4,076,270,000 | 3.6% |
| 28 | Hawaii | 982,357,000 | 0.9% |
| 45 | Idaho | 125,657,000 | 0.1% |
| 21 | Illinois | 1,215,607,000 | 1.1% |
| 18 | Indiana | 1,630,817,000 | 1.5% |
| 36 | Iowa | 392,854,000 | 0.4% |
| 29 | Kansas | 869,923,000 | 0.8% |
| 20 | Kentucky | 1,346,693,000 | 1.2% |
| 22 | Louisiana | 1,169,527,000 | 1.0% |
| 31 | Maine | 680,327,000 | 0.6% |
| 5 | Maryland | 5,422,050,000 | 4.8% |
| 6 | Massachusetts | 4,633,122,000 | 4.1% |
| 24 | Michigan | 1,131,144,000 | 1.0% |
| 23 | Minnesota | 1,161,999,000 | 1.0% |
| 19 | Mississippi | 1,461,672,000 | 1.3% |
| 7 | Missouri | 4,465,894,000 | 4.0% |
| 46 | Montana | 93,307,000 | 0.1% |
| 41 | Nebraska | 220,260,000 | 0.2% |
| 39 | Nevada | 243,318,000 | 0.2% |
| 37 | New Hampshire | 358,119,000 | 0.3% |
| 13 | New Jersey | 2,677,423,000 | 2.4% |
| 33 | New Mexico | 603,883,000 | 0.5% |
| 11 | New York | 3,223,818,000 | 2.9% |
| 27 | North Carolina | 996,498,000 | 0.9% |
| 44 | North Dakota | 132,706,000 | 0.1% |
| 15 | Ohio | 2,554,054,000 | 2.3% |
| 25 | Oklahoma | 1,107,511,000 | 1.0% |
| 40 | Oregon | 234,628,000 | 0.2% |
| 10 | Pennsylvania | 3,785,791,000 | 3.4% |
| 38 | Rhode Island | 310,843,000 | 0.3% |
| 30 | South Carolina | 808,268,000 | 0.7% |
| 47 | South Dakota | 89,222,000 | 0.1% |
| 26 | Tennessee | 1,042,531,000 | 0.9% |
| 3 | Texas | 8,511,126,000 | 7.6% |
| 35 | Utah | 519,461,000 | 0.5% |
| 42 | Vermont | 208,323,000 | 0.2% |
| 2 | Virginia | 12,170,522,000 | 10.9% |
| 17 | Washington | 2,213,743,000 | 2.0% |
| 49 | West Virginia | 67,770,000 | 0.1% |
| 32 | Wisconsin | 614,171,000 | 0.5% |
| 50 | Wyoming | 61,418,000 | 0.1% |

| RANK | STATE | CONTRACTS | % of USA |
|------|-------|-----------|----------|
| 1 | California | $16,987,383,000 | 15.1% |
| 2 | Virginia | 12,170,522,000 | 10.9% |
| 3 | Texas | 8,511,126,000 | 7.6% |
| 4 | Florida | 6,709,627,000 | 6.0% |
| 5 | Maryland | 5,422,050,000 | 4.8% |
| 6 | Massachusetts | 4,633,122,000 | 4.1% |
| 7 | Missouri | 4,465,894,000 | 4.0% |
| 8 | Arizona | 4,153,534,000 | 3.7% |
| 9 | Georgia | 4,076,270,000 | 3.6% |
| 10 | Pennsylvania | 3,785,791,000 | 3.4% |
| 11 | New York | 3,223,818,000 | 2.9% |
| 12 | Connecticut | 3,163,702,000 | 2.8% |
| 13 | New Jersey | 2,677,423,000 | 2.4% |
| 14 | Alabama | 2,667,870,000 | 2.4% |
| 15 | Ohio | 2,554,054,000 | 2.3% |
| 16 | Colorado | 2,428,668,000 | 2.2% |
| 17 | Washington | 2,213,743,000 | 2.0% |
| 18 | Indiana | 1,630,817,000 | 1.5% |
| 19 | Mississippi | 1,461,672,000 | 1.3% |
| 20 | Kentucky | 1,346,693,000 | 1.2% |
| 21 | Illinois | 1,215,607,000 | 1.1% |
| 22 | Louisiana | 1,169,527,000 | 1.0% |
| 23 | Minnesota | 1,161,999,000 | 1.0% |
| 24 | Michigan | 1,131,144,000 | 1.0% |
| 25 | Oklahoma | 1,107,511,000 | 1.0% |
| 26 | Tennessee | 1,042,531,000 | 0.9% |
| 27 | North Carolina | 996,498,000 | 0.9% |
| 28 | Hawaii | 982,357,000 | 0.9% |
| 29 | Kansas | 869,923,000 | 0.8% |
| 30 | South Carolina | 808,268,000 | 0.7% |
| 31 | Maine | 680,327,000 | 0.6% |
| 32 | Wisconsin | 614,171,000 | 0.5% |
| 33 | New Mexico | 603,883,000 | 0.5% |
| 34 | Alaska | 576,300,000 | 0.5% |
| 35 | Utah | 519,461,000 | 0.5% |
| 36 | Iowa | 392,854,000 | 0.4% |
| 37 | New Hampshire | 358,119,000 | 0.3% |
| 38 | Rhode Island | 310,843,000 | 0.3% |
| 39 | Nevada | 243,318,000 | 0.2% |
| 40 | Oregon | 234,628,000 | 0.2% |
| 41 | Nebraska | 220,260,000 | 0.2% |
| 42 | Vermont | 208,323,000 | 0.2% |
| 43 | Arkansas | 172,064,000 | 0.2% |
| 44 | North Dakota | 132,706,000 | 0.1% |
| 45 | Idaho | 125,657,000 | 0.1% |
| 46 | Montana | 93,307,000 | 0.1% |
| 47 | South Dakota | 89,222,000 | 0.1% |
| 48 | Delaware | 87,639,000 | 0.1% |
| 49 | West Virginia | 67,770,000 | 0.1% |
| 50 | Wyoming | 61,418,000 | 0.1% |
| | District of Columbia | 1,589,291,000 | 1.4% |

Source: U.S. Department of Defense
"Estimated Payroll, Contracts & Grants by State/Area" (http://web1.whs.osd.mil/mmid/l03/fy99/99estp.htm)
*Includes prime contracts ($25,000 or more). Does not include $9,919,748,000 in contracts to U.S. territories and other countries.

# U.S. Department of Defense Contracts for Civil Functions in 1999

## National Total = $2,724,434,000*

ALPHA ORDER

| RANK | STATE | CONTRACTS | % of USA |
|------|-------|-----------|----------|
| 39 | Alabama | $8,874,000 | 0.3% |
| 26 | Alaska | 33,681,000 | 1.2% |
| 32 | Arizona | 18,407,000 | 0.7% |
| 12 | Arkansas | 73,992,000 | 2.7% |
| 1 | California | 384,175,000 | 14.1% |
| 37 | Colorado | 13,122,000 | 0.5% |
| 41 | Connecticut | 5,692,000 | 0.2% |
| 46 | Delaware | 4,110,000 | 0.2% |
| 7 | Florida | 96,428,000 | 3.5% |
| 25 | Georgia | 36,301,000 | 1.3% |
| 47 | Hawaii | 2,492,000 | 0.1% |
| 29 | Idaho | 30,330,000 | 1.1% |
| 6 | Illinois | 99,973,000 | 3.7% |
| 33 | Indiana | 17,532,000 | 0.6% |
| 31 | Iowa | 26,531,000 | 1.0% |
| 34 | Kansas | 17,457,000 | 0.6% |
| 22 | Kentucky | 40,093,000 | 1.5% |
| 2 | Louisiana | 272,186,000 | 10.0% |
| 40 | Maine | 6,037,000 | 0.2% |
| 19 | Maryland | 44,453,000 | 1.6% |
| 9 | Massachusetts | 81,820,000 | 3.0% |
| 24 | Michigan | 36,720,000 | 1.3% |
| 17 | Minnesota | 50,292,000 | 1.8% |
| 11 | Mississippi | 76,219,000 | 2.8% |
| 5 | Missouri | 136,733,000 | 5.0% |
| 45 | Montana | 4,699,000 | 0.2% |
| 42 | Nebraska | 5,627,000 | 0.2% |
| 27 | Nevada | 32,813,000 | 1.2% |
| 48 | New Hampshire | 1,788,000 | 0.1% |
| 3 | New Jersey | 173,339,000 | 6.4% |
| 38 | New Mexico | 10,290,000 | 0.4% |
| 15 | New York | 65,600,000 | 2.4% |
| 20 | North Carolina | 43,122,000 | 1.6% |
| 35 | North Dakota | 16,396,000 | 0.6% |
| 23 | Ohio | 38,502,000 | 1.4% |
| 28 | Oklahoma | 32,421,000 | 1.2% |
| 14 | Oregon | 69,692,000 | 2.6% |
| 10 | Pennsylvania | 78,752,000 | 2.9% |
| 49 | Rhode Island | 1,344,000 | 0.0% |
| 16 | South Carolina | 60,277,000 | 2.2% |
| 44 | South Dakota | 4,726,000 | 0.2% |
| 18 | Tennessee | 50,034,000 | 1.8% |
| 4 | Texas | 155,335,000 | 5.7% |
| 36 | Utah | 13,445,000 | 0.5% |
| 43 | Vermont | 5,229,000 | 0.2% |
| 13 | Virginia | 70,051,000 | 2.6% |
| 8 | Washington | 82,351,000 | 3.0% |
| 21 | West Virginia | 41,387,000 | 1.5% |
| 30 | Wisconsin | 30,281,000 | 1.1% |
| 50 | Wyoming | 620,000 | 0.0% |

RANK ORDER

| RANK | STATE | CONTRACTS | % of USA |
|------|-------|-----------|----------|
| 1 | California | $384,175,000 | 14.1% |
| 2 | Louisiana | 272,186,000 | 10.0% |
| 3 | New Jersey | 173,339,000 | 6.4% |
| 4 | Texas | 155,335,000 | 5.7% |
| 5 | Missouri | 136,733,000 | 5.0% |
| 6 | Illinois | 99,973,000 | 3.7% |
| 7 | Florida | 96,428,000 | 3.5% |
| 8 | Washington | 82,351,000 | 3.0% |
| 9 | Massachusetts | 81,820,000 | 3.0% |
| 10 | Pennsylvania | 78,752,000 | 2.9% |
| 11 | Mississippi | 76,219,000 | 2.8% |
| 12 | Arkansas | 73,992,000 | 2.7% |
| 13 | Virginia | 70,051,000 | 2.6% |
| 14 | Oregon | 69,692,000 | 2.6% |
| 15 | New York | 65,600,000 | 2.4% |
| 16 | South Carolina | 60,277,000 | 2.2% |
| 17 | Minnesota | 50,292,000 | 1.8% |
| 18 | Tennessee | 50,034,000 | 1.8% |
| 19 | Maryland | 44,453,000 | 1.6% |
| 20 | North Carolina | 43,122,000 | 1.6% |
| 21 | West Virginia | 41,387,000 | 1.5% |
| 22 | Kentucky | 40,093,000 | 1.5% |
| 23 | Ohio | 38,502,000 | 1.4% |
| 24 | Michigan | 36,720,000 | 1.3% |
| 25 | Georgia | 36,301,000 | 1.3% |
| 26 | Alaska | 33,681,000 | 1.2% |
| 27 | Nevada | 32,813,000 | 1.2% |
| 28 | Oklahoma | 32,421,000 | 1.2% |
| 29 | Idaho | 30,330,000 | 1.1% |
| 30 | Wisconsin | 30,281,000 | 1.1% |
| 31 | Iowa | 26,531,000 | 1.0% |
| 32 | Arizona | 18,407,000 | 0.7% |
| 33 | Indiana | 17,532,000 | 0.6% |
| 34 | Kansas | 17,457,000 | 0.6% |
| 35 | North Dakota | 16,396,000 | 0.6% |
| 36 | Utah | 13,445,000 | 0.5% |
| 37 | Colorado | 13,122,000 | 0.5% |
| 38 | New Mexico | 10,290,000 | 0.4% |
| 39 | Alabama | 8,874,000 | 0.3% |
| 40 | Maine | 6,037,000 | 0.2% |
| 41 | Connecticut | 5,692,000 | 0.2% |
| 42 | Nebraska | 5,627,000 | 0.2% |
| 43 | Vermont | 5,229,000 | 0.2% |
| 44 | South Dakota | 4,726,000 | 0.2% |
| 45 | Montana | 4,699,000 | 0.2% |
| 46 | Delaware | 4,110,000 | 0.2% |
| 47 | Hawaii | 2,492,000 | 0.1% |
| 48 | New Hampshire | 1,788,000 | 0.1% |
| 49 | Rhode Island | 1,344,000 | 0.0% |
| 50 | Wyoming | 620,000 | 0.0% |
| | District of Columbia | 22,663,000 | 0.8% |

*Source: U.S. Department of Defense*
*"Estimated Payroll, Contracts & Grants by State/Area" (http://web1.whs.osd.mil/mmid/l03/fy99/99estp.htm)*
*Includes prime contracts ($25,000 or more).  Does not include $241,238,000 in contracts to U.S. territories and other countries.*

# U.S. Department of Defense Domestic Personnel in 1999

## National Total = 2,863,284 Personnel*

ALPHA ORDER

RANK ORDER

| RANK | STATE | PERSONNEL | % of USA |
|---|---|---|---|
| 15 | Alabama | 65,353 | 2.3% |
| 34 | Alaska | 25,497 | 0.9% |
| 21 | Arizona | 48,094 | 1.7% |
| 33 | Arkansas | 26,109 | 0.9% |
| 1 | California | 272,075 | 9.5% |
| 17 | Colorado | 61,281 | 2.1% |
| 38 | Connecticut | 18,095 | 0.6% |
| 45 | Delaware | 11,372 | 0.4% |
| 6 | Florida | 130,955 | 4.6% |
| 5 | Georgia | 136,305 | 4.8% |
| 19 | Hawaii | 60,715 | 2.1% |
| 44 | Idaho | 13,007 | 0.5% |
| 7 | Illinois | 89,779 | 3.1% |
| 26 | Indiana | 37,716 | 1.3% |
| 37 | Iowa | 18,947 | 0.7% |
| 25 | Kansas | 38,643 | 1.3% |
| 16 | Kentucky | 63,421 | 2.2% |
| 20 | Louisiana | 53,112 | 1.9% |
| 40 | Maine | 15,589 | 0.5% |
| 8 | Maryland | 88,531 | 3.1% |
| 28 | Massachusetts | 34,493 | 1.2% |
| 24 | Michigan | 39,201 | 1.4% |
| 31 | Minnesota | 27,499 | 1.0% |
| 23 | Mississippi | 43,164 | 1.5% |
| 18 | Missouri | 60,750 | 2.1% |
| 46 | Montana | 11,194 | 0.4% |
| 35 | Nebraska | 20,815 | 0.7% |
| 39 | Nevada | 16,303 | 0.6% |
| 49 | New Hampshire | 7,142 | 0.2% |
| 22 | New Jersey | 47,302 | 1.7% |
| 32 | New Mexico | 27,492 | 1.0% |
| 10 | New York | 82,562 | 2.9% |
| 4 | North Carolina | 138,587 | 4.8% |
| 41 | North Dakota | 15,002 | 0.5% |
| 13 | Ohio | 74,177 | 2.6% |
| 14 | Oklahoma | 67,361 | 2.4% |
| 36 | Oregon | 19,282 | 0.7% |
| 11 | Pennsylvania | 81,870 | 2.9% |
| 43 | Rhode Island | 14,065 | 0.5% |
| 12 | South Carolina | 74,498 | 2.6% |
| 47 | South Dakota | 10,773 | 0.4% |
| 27 | Tennessee | 35,571 | 1.2% |
| 2 | Texas | 233,549 | 8.2% |
| 29 | Utah | 30,846 | 1.1% |
| 50 | Vermont | 5,775 | 0.2% |
| 3 | Virginia | 198,854 | 6.9% |
| 9 | Washington | 85,825 | 3.0% |
| 42 | West Virginia | 14,124 | 0.5% |
| 30 | Wisconsin | 28,291 | 1.0% |
| 48 | Wyoming | 8,063 | 0.3% |

| RANK | STATE | PERSONNEL | % of USA |
|---|---|---|---|
| 1 | California | 272,075 | 9.5% |
| 2 | Texas | 233,549 | 8.2% |
| 3 | Virginia | 198,854 | 6.9% |
| 4 | North Carolina | 138,587 | 4.8% |
| 5 | Georgia | 136,305 | 4.8% |
| 6 | Florida | 130,955 | 4.6% |
| 7 | Illinois | 89,779 | 3.1% |
| 8 | Maryland | 88,531 | 3.1% |
| 9 | Washington | 85,825 | 3.0% |
| 10 | New York | 82,562 | 2.9% |
| 11 | Pennsylvania | 81,870 | 2.9% |
| 12 | South Carolina | 74,498 | 2.6% |
| 13 | Ohio | 74,177 | 2.6% |
| 14 | Oklahoma | 67,361 | 2.4% |
| 15 | Alabama | 65,353 | 2.3% |
| 16 | Kentucky | 63,421 | 2.2% |
| 17 | Colorado | 61,281 | 2.1% |
| 18 | Missouri | 60,750 | 2.1% |
| 19 | Hawaii | 60,715 | 2.1% |
| 20 | Louisiana | 53,112 | 1.9% |
| 21 | Arizona | 48,094 | 1.7% |
| 22 | New Jersey | 47,302 | 1.7% |
| 23 | Mississippi | 43,164 | 1.5% |
| 24 | Michigan | 39,201 | 1.4% |
| 25 | Kansas | 38,643 | 1.3% |
| 26 | Indiana | 37,716 | 1.3% |
| 27 | Tennessee | 35,571 | 1.2% |
| 28 | Massachusetts | 34,493 | 1.2% |
| 29 | Utah | 30,846 | 1.1% |
| 30 | Wisconsin | 28,291 | 1.0% |
| 31 | Minnesota | 27,499 | 1.0% |
| 32 | New Mexico | 27,492 | 1.0% |
| 33 | Arkansas | 26,109 | 0.9% |
| 34 | Alaska | 25,497 | 0.9% |
| 35 | Nebraska | 20,815 | 0.7% |
| 36 | Oregon | 19,282 | 0.7% |
| 37 | Iowa | 18,947 | 0.7% |
| 38 | Connecticut | 18,095 | 0.6% |
| 39 | Nevada | 16,303 | 0.6% |
| 40 | Maine | 15,589 | 0.5% |
| 41 | North Dakota | 15,002 | 0.5% |
| 42 | West Virginia | 14,124 | 0.5% |
| 43 | Rhode Island | 14,065 | 0.5% |
| 44 | Idaho | 13,007 | 0.5% |
| 45 | Delaware | 11,372 | 0.4% |
| 46 | Montana | 11,194 | 0.4% |
| 47 | South Dakota | 10,773 | 0.4% |
| 48 | Wyoming | 8,063 | 0.3% |
| 49 | New Hampshire | 7,142 | 0.2% |
| 50 | Vermont | 5,775 | 0.2% |
| | District of Columbia | 34,258 | 1.2% |

*Source: U.S. Department of Defense*
*(http://web1.whs.osd.mil/mmid/l03/fy99/99l03.htm)*
*Includes Active Duty Military, Civilian and Reserve and National Guard personnel. Does not include personnel in U.S. territories or in other countries.*

# U.S. Department of Defense Active Duty Military Personnel in 1999

## National Total = 1,003,093 Personnel*

ALPHA ORDER

| RANK | STATE | PERSONNEL | % of USA |
|---|---|---|---|
| 23 | Alabama | 11,272 | 1.1% |
| 19 | Alaska | 15,684 | 1.6% |
| 15 | Arizona | 21,240 | 2.1% |
| 29 | Arkansas | 4,888 | 0.5% |
| 1 | California | 109,697 | 10.9% |
| 13 | Colorado | 29,247 | 2.9% |
| 31 | Connecticut | 4,412 | 0.4% |
| 33 | Delaware | 3,898 | 0.4% |
| 6 | Florida | 50,731 | 5.1% |
| 5 | Georgia | 62,714 | 6.3% |
| 11 | Hawaii | 32,354 | 3.2% |
| 32 | Idaho | 4,326 | 0.4% |
| 9 | Illinois | 35,674 | 3.6% |
| 43 | Indiana | 991 | 0.1% |
| 48 | Iowa | 443 | 0.0% |
| 18 | Kansas | 16,354 | 1.6% |
| 8 | Kentucky | 36,149 | 3.6% |
| 20 | Louisiana | 15,246 | 1.5% |
| 41 | Maine | 2,136 | 0.2% |
| 12 | Maryland | 29,859 | 3.0% |
| 40 | Massachusetts | 2,535 | 0.3% |
| 42 | Michigan | 1,085 | 0.1% |
| 45 | Minnesota | 862 | 0.1% |
| 21 | Mississippi | 12,069 | 1.2% |
| 17 | Missouri | 17,184 | 1.7% |
| 34 | Montana | 3,663 | 0.4% |
| 24 | Nebraska | 7,988 | 0.8% |
| 25 | Nevada | 7,721 | 0.8% |
| 49 | New Hampshire | 376 | 0.0% |
| 28 | New Jersey | 7,116 | 0.7% |
| 22 | New Mexico | 11,642 | 1.2% |
| 16 | New York | 20,532 | 2.0% |
| 3 | North Carolina | 86,594 | 8.6% |
| 27 | North Dakota | 7,499 | 0.7% |
| 26 | Ohio | 7,668 | 0.8% |
| 14 | Oklahoma | 25,234 | 2.5% |
| 44 | Oregon | 933 | 0.1% |
| 37 | Pennsylvania | 3,261 | 0.3% |
| 36 | Rhode Island | 3,415 | 0.3% |
| 7 | South Carolina | 38,289 | 3.8% |
| 38 | South Dakota | 3,171 | 0.3% |
| 39 | Tennessee | 2,679 | 0.3% |
| 2 | Texas | 108,835 | 10.8% |
| 30 | Utah | 4,844 | 0.5% |
| 50 | Vermont | 125 | 0.0% |
| 4 | Virginia | 80,132 | 8.0% |
| 10 | Washington | 32,398 | 3.2% |
| 46 | West Virginia | 614 | 0.1% |
| 47 | Wisconsin | 578 | 0.1% |
| 35 | Wyoming | 3,496 | 0.3% |

RANK ORDER

| RANK | STATE | PERSONNEL | % of USA |
|---|---|---|---|
| 1 | California | 109,697 | 10.9% |
| 2 | Texas | 108,835 | 10.8% |
| 3 | North Carolina | 86,594 | 8.6% |
| 4 | Virginia | 80,132 | 8.0% |
| 5 | Georgia | 62,714 | 6.3% |
| 6 | Florida | 50,731 | 5.1% |
| 7 | South Carolina | 38,289 | 3.8% |
| 8 | Kentucky | 36,149 | 3.6% |
| 9 | Illinois | 35,674 | 3.6% |
| 10 | Washington | 32,398 | 3.2% |
| 11 | Hawaii | 32,354 | 3.2% |
| 12 | Maryland | 29,859 | 3.0% |
| 13 | Colorado | 29,247 | 2.9% |
| 14 | Oklahoma | 25,234 | 2.5% |
| 15 | Arizona | 21,240 | 2.1% |
| 16 | New York | 20,532 | 2.0% |
| 17 | Missouri | 17,184 | 1.7% |
| 18 | Kansas | 16,354 | 1.6% |
| 19 | Alaska | 15,684 | 1.6% |
| 20 | Louisiana | 15,246 | 1.5% |
| 21 | Mississippi | 12,069 | 1.2% |
| 22 | New Mexico | 11,642 | 1.2% |
| 23 | Alabama | 11,272 | 1.1% |
| 24 | Nebraska | 7,988 | 0.8% |
| 25 | Nevada | 7,721 | 0.8% |
| 26 | Ohio | 7,668 | 0.8% |
| 27 | North Dakota | 7,499 | 0.7% |
| 28 | New Jersey | 7,116 | 0.7% |
| 29 | Arkansas | 4,888 | 0.5% |
| 30 | Utah | 4,844 | 0.5% |
| 31 | Connecticut | 4,412 | 0.4% |
| 32 | Idaho | 4,326 | 0.4% |
| 33 | Delaware | 3,898 | 0.4% |
| 34 | Montana | 3,663 | 0.4% |
| 35 | Wyoming | 3,496 | 0.3% |
| 36 | Rhode Island | 3,415 | 0.3% |
| 37 | Pennsylvania | 3,261 | 0.3% |
| 38 | South Dakota | 3,171 | 0.3% |
| 39 | Tennessee | 2,679 | 0.3% |
| 40 | Massachusetts | 2,535 | 0.3% |
| 41 | Maine | 2,136 | 0.2% |
| 42 | Michigan | 1,085 | 0.1% |
| 43 | Indiana | 991 | 0.1% |
| 44 | Oregon | 933 | 0.1% |
| 45 | Minnesota | 862 | 0.1% |
| 46 | West Virginia | 614 | 0.1% |
| 47 | Wisconsin | 578 | 0.1% |
| 48 | Iowa | 443 | 0.0% |
| 49 | New Hampshire | 376 | 0.0% |
| 50 | Vermont | 125 | 0.0% |
| | District of Columbia | 13,240 | 1.3% |

Source: U.S. Department of Defense
   (http://web1.whs.osd.mil/mmid/l03/fy99/99l03.htm)
*Does not include 6,490 active duty personnel in U.S. territories, 358,255 in other countries or others undistributed. There were 1,367,838 total active duty personnel worldwide in 1999.

# U.S. Department of Defense Domestic Civilian Personnel in 1999

## National Total = 633,600 Personnel*

ALPHA ORDER

| RANK | STATE | PERSONNEL | % of USA |
|------|-------|-----------|----------|
| 10 | Alabama | 20,955 | 3.3% |
| 33 | Alaska | 4,247 | 0.7% |
| 24 | Arizona | 8,117 | 1.3% |
| 34 | Arkansas | 3,570 | 0.6% |
| 2 | California | 64,086 | 10.1% |
| 18 | Colorado | 11,118 | 1.8% |
| 38 | Connecticut | 2,593 | 0.4% |
| 45 | Delaware | 1,370 | 0.2% |
| 6 | Florida | 26,322 | 4.2% |
| 5 | Georgia | 30,678 | 4.8% |
| 12 | Hawaii | 16,318 | 2.6% |
| 44 | Idaho | 1,411 | 0.2% |
| 15 | Illinois | 12,988 | 2.0% |
| 22 | Indiana | 9,266 | 1.5% |
| 43 | Iowa | 1,514 | 0.2% |
| 30 | Kansas | 5,457 | 0.9% |
| 23 | Kentucky | 8,734 | 1.4% |
| 25 | Louisiana | 7,815 | 1.2% |
| 29 | Maine | 5,520 | 0.9% |
| 4 | Maryland | 32,101 | 5.1% |
| 27 | Massachusetts | 6,970 | 1.1% |
| 26 | Michigan | 7,664 | 1.2% |
| 39 | Minnesota | 2,418 | 0.4% |
| 21 | Mississippi | 9,434 | 1.5% |
| 19 | Missouri | 9,516 | 1.5% |
| 47 | Montana | 1,113 | 0.2% |
| 35 | Nebraska | 3,323 | 0.5% |
| 40 | Nevada | 2,068 | 0.3% |
| 48 | New Hampshire | 1,028 | 0.2% |
| 14 | New Jersey | 14,549 | 2.3% |
| 28 | New Mexico | 6,915 | 1.1% |
| 17 | New York | 11,365 | 1.8% |
| 13 | North Carolina | 16,311 | 2.6% |
| 42 | North Dakota | 1,638 | 0.3% |
| 8 | Ohio | 23,544 | 3.7% |
| 11 | Oklahoma | 20,187 | 3.2% |
| 37 | Oregon | 2,908 | 0.5% |
| 7 | Pennsylvania | 25,772 | 4.1% |
| 32 | Rhode Island | 4,352 | 0.7% |
| 20 | South Carolina | 9,495 | 1.5% |
| 46 | South Dakota | 1,264 | 0.2% |
| 31 | Tennessee | 4,939 | 0.8% |
| 3 | Texas | 39,993 | 6.3% |
| 16 | Utah | 12,419 | 2.0% |
| 50 | Vermont | 525 | 0.1% |
| 1 | Virginia | 78,973 | 12.5% |
| 9 | Washington | 22,322 | 3.5% |
| 41 | West Virginia | 1,713 | 0.3% |
| 36 | Wisconsin | 3,119 | 0.5% |
| 49 | Wyoming | 932 | 0.1% |

RANK ORDER

| RANK | STATE | PERSONNEL | % of USA |
|------|-------|-----------|----------|
| 1 | Virginia | 78,973 | 12.5% |
| 2 | California | 64,086 | 10.1% |
| 3 | Texas | 39,993 | 6.3% |
| 4 | Maryland | 32,101 | 5.1% |
| 5 | Georgia | 30,678 | 4.8% |
| 6 | Florida | 26,322 | 4.2% |
| 7 | Pennsylvania | 25,772 | 4.1% |
| 8 | Ohio | 23,544 | 3.7% |
| 9 | Washington | 22,322 | 3.5% |
| 10 | Alabama | 20,955 | 3.3% |
| 11 | Oklahoma | 20,187 | 3.2% |
| 12 | Hawaii | 16,318 | 2.6% |
| 13 | North Carolina | 16,311 | 2.6% |
| 14 | New Jersey | 14,549 | 2.3% |
| 15 | Illinois | 12,988 | 2.0% |
| 16 | Utah | 12,419 | 2.0% |
| 17 | New York | 11,365 | 1.8% |
| 18 | Colorado | 11,118 | 1.8% |
| 19 | Missouri | 9,516 | 1.5% |
| 20 | South Carolina | 9,495 | 1.5% |
| 21 | Mississippi | 9,434 | 1.5% |
| 22 | Indiana | 9,266 | 1.5% |
| 23 | Kentucky | 8,734 | 1.4% |
| 24 | Arizona | 8,117 | 1.3% |
| 25 | Louisiana | 7,815 | 1.2% |
| 26 | Michigan | 7,664 | 1.2% |
| 27 | Massachusetts | 6,970 | 1.1% |
| 28 | New Mexico | 6,915 | 1.1% |
| 29 | Maine | 5,520 | 0.9% |
| 30 | Kansas | 5,457 | 0.9% |
| 31 | Tennessee | 4,939 | 0.8% |
| 32 | Rhode Island | 4,352 | 0.7% |
| 33 | Alaska | 4,247 | 0.7% |
| 34 | Arkansas | 3,570 | 0.6% |
| 35 | Nebraska | 3,323 | 0.5% |
| 36 | Wisconsin | 3,119 | 0.5% |
| 37 | Oregon | 2,908 | 0.5% |
| 38 | Connecticut | 2,593 | 0.4% |
| 39 | Minnesota | 2,418 | 0.4% |
| 40 | Nevada | 2,068 | 0.3% |
| 41 | West Virginia | 1,713 | 0.3% |
| 42 | North Dakota | 1,638 | 0.3% |
| 43 | Iowa | 1,514 | 0.2% |
| 44 | Idaho | 1,411 | 0.2% |
| 45 | Delaware | 1,370 | 0.2% |
| 46 | South Dakota | 1,264 | 0.2% |
| 47 | Montana | 1,113 | 0.2% |
| 48 | New Hampshire | 1,028 | 0.2% |
| 49 | Wyoming | 932 | 0.1% |
| 50 | Vermont | 525 | 0.1% |
| | District of Columbia | 12,651 | 2.0% |

*Source: U.S. Department of Defense*
*(http://web1.whs.osd.mil/mmid/l03/fy99/99l03.htm)*
*Does not include civilian personnel in U.S. territories or civilian personnel in other countries. Includes military and civil functions.*

# U.S. Department of Defense Reserve and National Guard Personnel in 1999

## National Total = 1,226,591 Personnel*

ALPHA ORDER

| RANK | STATE | PERSONNEL | % of USA |
|------|-------|-----------|----------|
| 12 | Alabama | 33,126 | 2.7% |
| 48 | Alaska | 5,566 | 0.5% |
| 27 | Arizona | 18,737 | 1.5% |
| 29 | Arkansas | 17,651 | 1.4% |
| 1 | California | 98,292 | 8.0% |
| 26 | Colorado | 20,916 | 1.7% |
| 36 | Connecticut | 11,090 | 0.9% |
| 45 | Delaware | 6,104 | 0.5% |
| 3 | Florida | 53,902 | 4.4% |
| 7 | Georgia | 42,913 | 3.5% |
| 34 | Hawaii | 12,043 | 1.0% |
| 40 | Idaho | 7,270 | 0.6% |
| 8 | Illinois | 41,117 | 3.4% |
| 17 | Indiana | 27,459 | 2.2% |
| 30 | Iowa | 16,990 | 1.4% |
| 31 | Kansas | 16,832 | 1.4% |
| 28 | Kentucky | 18,538 | 1.5% |
| 15 | Louisiana | 30,051 | 2.4% |
| 39 | Maine | 7,933 | 0.6% |
| 19 | Maryland | 26,571 | 2.2% |
| 21 | Massachusetts | 24,988 | 2.0% |
| 14 | Michigan | 30,452 | 2.5% |
| 23 | Minnesota | 24,219 | 2.0% |
| 25 | Mississippi | 21,661 | 1.8% |
| 11 | Missouri | 34,050 | 2.8% |
| 42 | Montana | 6,418 | 0.5% |
| 37 | Nebraska | 9,504 | 0.8% |
| 41 | Nevada | 6,514 | 0.5% |
| 47 | New Hampshire | 5,738 | 0.5% |
| 20 | New Jersey | 25,637 | 2.1% |
| 38 | New Mexico | 8,935 | 0.7% |
| 5 | New York | 50,665 | 4.1% |
| 10 | North Carolina | 35,682 | 2.9% |
| 46 | North Dakota | 5,865 | 0.5% |
| 6 | Ohio | 42,965 | 3.5% |
| 24 | Oklahoma | 21,940 | 1.8% |
| 32 | Oregon | 15,441 | 1.3% |
| 4 | Pennsylvania | 52,837 | 4.3% |
| 44 | Rhode Island | 6,298 | 0.5% |
| 18 | South Carolina | 26,714 | 2.2% |
| 43 | South Dakota | 6,338 | 0.5% |
| 16 | Tennessee | 27,953 | 2.3% |
| 2 | Texas | 84,721 | 6.9% |
| 33 | Utah | 13,583 | 1.1% |
| 49 | Vermont | 5,125 | 0.4% |
| 9 | Virginia | 39,749 | 3.2% |
| 13 | Washington | 31,105 | 2.5% |
| 35 | West Virginia | 11,797 | 1.0% |
| 22 | Wisconsin | 24,594 | 2.0% |
| 50 | Wyoming | 3,635 | 0.3% |

RANK ORDER

| RANK | STATE | PERSONNEL | % of USA |
|------|-------|-----------|----------|
| 1 | California | 98,292 | 8.0% |
| 2 | Texas | 84,721 | 6.9% |
| 3 | Florida | 53,902 | 4.4% |
| 4 | Pennsylvania | 52,837 | 4.3% |
| 5 | New York | 50,665 | 4.1% |
| 6 | Ohio | 42,965 | 3.5% |
| 7 | Georgia | 42,913 | 3.5% |
| 8 | Illinois | 41,117 | 3.4% |
| 9 | Virginia | 39,749 | 3.2% |
| 10 | North Carolina | 35,682 | 2.9% |
| 11 | Missouri | 34,050 | 2.8% |
| 12 | Alabama | 33,126 | 2.7% |
| 13 | Washington | 31,105 | 2.5% |
| 14 | Michigan | 30,452 | 2.5% |
| 15 | Louisiana | 30,051 | 2.4% |
| 16 | Tennessee | 27,953 | 2.3% |
| 17 | Indiana | 27,459 | 2.2% |
| 18 | South Carolina | 26,714 | 2.2% |
| 19 | Maryland | 26,571 | 2.2% |
| 20 | New Jersey | 25,637 | 2.1% |
| 21 | Massachusetts | 24,988 | 2.0% |
| 22 | Wisconsin | 24,594 | 2.0% |
| 23 | Minnesota | 24,219 | 2.0% |
| 24 | Oklahoma | 21,940 | 1.8% |
| 25 | Mississippi | 21,661 | 1.8% |
| 26 | Colorado | 20,916 | 1.7% |
| 27 | Arizona | 18,737 | 1.5% |
| 28 | Kentucky | 18,538 | 1.5% |
| 29 | Arkansas | 17,651 | 1.4% |
| 30 | Iowa | 16,990 | 1.4% |
| 31 | Kansas | 16,832 | 1.4% |
| 32 | Oregon | 15,441 | 1.3% |
| 33 | Utah | 13,583 | 1.1% |
| 34 | Hawaii | 12,043 | 1.0% |
| 35 | West Virginia | 11,797 | 1.0% |
| 36 | Connecticut | 11,090 | 0.9% |
| 37 | Nebraska | 9,504 | 0.8% |
| 38 | New Mexico | 8,935 | 0.7% |
| 39 | Maine | 7,933 | 0.6% |
| 40 | Idaho | 7,270 | 0.6% |
| 41 | Nevada | 6,514 | 0.5% |
| 42 | Montana | 6,418 | 0.5% |
| 43 | South Dakota | 6,338 | 0.5% |
| 44 | Rhode Island | 6,298 | 0.5% |
| 45 | Delaware | 6,104 | 0.5% |
| 46 | North Dakota | 5,865 | 0.5% |
| 47 | New Hampshire | 5,738 | 0.5% |
| 48 | Alaska | 5,566 | 0.5% |
| 49 | Vermont | 5,125 | 0.4% |
| 50 | Wyoming | 3,635 | 0.3% |
| | District of Columbia | 8,367 | 0.7% |

Source: U.S. Department of Defense
    (http://web1.whs.osd.mil/mmid/l03/fy99/99l03.htm)
*Does not include 18,046 reserve and national guard personnel in U.S. territories.

# U.S. Department of Defense Total Compensation in 1999

## National Total = $101,811,216,000*

| RANK | STATE | TOTAL PAY | % of USA |
|------|-------|-----------|----------|
| 13 | Alabama | $2,352,073,000 | 2.3% |
| 29 | Alaska | 860,085,000 | 0.8% |
| 17 | Arizona | 1,930,868,000 | 1.9% |
| 33 | Arkansas | 759,624,000 | 0.7% |
| 1 | California | 11,394,822,000 | 11.2% |
| 12 | Colorado | 2,359,477,000 | 2.3% |
| 37 | Connecticut | 538,141,000 | 0.5% |
| 43 | Delaware | 325,720,000 | 0.3% |
| 4 | Florida | 6,722,007,000 | 6.6% |
| 5 | Georgia | 4,800,915,000 | 4.7% |
| 11 | Hawaii | 2,422,172,000 | 2.4% |
| 42 | Idaho | 391,225,000 | 0.4% |
| 9 | Illinois | 2,440,230,000 | 2.4% |
| 28 | Indiana | 891,445,000 | 0.9% |
| 45 | Iowa | 264,615,000 | 0.3% |
| 24 | Kansas | 1,117,979,000 | 1.1% |
| 18 | Kentucky | 1,877,023,000 | 1.8% |
| 23 | Louisiana | 1,347,434,000 | 1.3% |
| 35 | Maine | 571,235,000 | 0.6% |
| 8 | Maryland | 3,587,843,000 | 3.5% |
| 31 | Massachusetts | 796,956,000 | 0.8% |
| 30 | Michigan | 848,183,000 | 0.8% |
| 40 | Minnesota | 432,807,000 | 0.4% |
| 22 | Mississippi | 1,394,084,000 | 1.4% |
| 20 | Missouri | 1,590,805,000 | 1.6% |
| 44 | Montana | 299,768,000 | 0.3% |
| 34 | Nebraska | 654,882,000 | 0.6% |
| 32 | Nevada | 791,005,000 | 0.8% |
| 48 | New Hampshire | 254,100,000 | 0.2% |
| 21 | New Jersey | 1,521,093,000 | 1.5% |
| 25 | New Mexico | 1,103,992,000 | 1.1% |
| 19 | New York | 1,787,150,000 | 1.8% |
| 6 | North Carolina | 4,519,786,000 | 4.4% |
| 41 | North Dakota | 391,365,000 | 0.4% |
| 16 | Ohio | 2,136,432,000 | 2.1% |
| 14 | Oklahoma | 2,259,156,000 | 2.2% |
| 36 | Oregon | 544,143,000 | 0.5% |
| 15 | Pennsylvania | 2,175,764,000 | 2.1% |
| 38 | Rhode Island | 458,669,000 | 0.5% |
| 10 | South Carolina | 2,426,677,000 | 2.4% |
| 47 | South Dakota | 258,432,000 | 0.3% |
| 26 | Tennessee | 1,101,582,000 | 1.1% |
| 3 | Texas | 8,811,306,000 | 8.7% |
| 27 | Utah | 976,733,000 | 1.0% |
| 50 | Vermont | 95,849,000 | 0.1% |
| 2 | Virginia | 11,169,951,000 | 11.0% |
| 7 | Washington | 3,951,370,000 | 3.9% |
| 46 | West Virginia | 261,333,000 | 0.3% |
| 39 | Wisconsin | 435,727,000 | 0.4% |
| 49 | Wyoming | 234,371,000 | 0.2% |

| RANK | STATE | TOTAL PAY | % of USA |
|------|-------|-----------|----------|
| 1 | California | $11,394,822,000 | 11.2% |
| 2 | Virginia | 11,169,951,000 | 11.0% |
| 3 | Texas | 8,811,306,000 | 8.7% |
| 4 | Florida | 6,722,007,000 | 6.6% |
| 5 | Georgia | 4,800,915,000 | 4.7% |
| 6 | North Carolina | 4,519,786,000 | 4.4% |
| 7 | Washington | 3,951,370,000 | 3.9% |
| 8 | Maryland | 3,587,843,000 | 3.5% |
| 9 | Illinois | 2,440,230,000 | 2.4% |
| 10 | South Carolina | 2,426,677,000 | 2.4% |
| 11 | Hawaii | 2,422,172,000 | 2.4% |
| 12 | Colorado | 2,359,477,000 | 2.3% |
| 13 | Alabama | 2,352,073,000 | 2.3% |
| 14 | Oklahoma | 2,259,156,000 | 2.2% |
| 15 | Pennsylvania | 2,175,764,000 | 2.1% |
| 16 | Ohio | 2,136,432,000 | 2.1% |
| 17 | Arizona | 1,930,868,000 | 1.9% |
| 18 | Kentucky | 1,877,023,000 | 1.8% |
| 19 | New York | 1,787,150,000 | 1.8% |
| 20 | Missouri | 1,590,805,000 | 1.6% |
| 21 | New Jersey | 1,521,093,000 | 1.5% |
| 22 | Mississippi | 1,394,084,000 | 1.4% |
| 23 | Louisiana | 1,347,434,000 | 1.3% |
| 24 | Kansas | 1,117,979,000 | 1.1% |
| 25 | New Mexico | 1,103,992,000 | 1.1% |
| 26 | Tennessee | 1,101,582,000 | 1.1% |
| 27 | Utah | 976,733,000 | 1.0% |
| 28 | Indiana | 891,445,000 | 0.9% |
| 29 | Alaska | 860,085,000 | 0.8% |
| 30 | Michigan | 848,183,000 | 0.8% |
| 31 | Massachusetts | 796,956,000 | 0.8% |
| 32 | Nevada | 791,005,000 | 0.8% |
| 33 | Arkansas | 759,624,000 | 0.7% |
| 34 | Nebraska | 654,882,000 | 0.6% |
| 35 | Maine | 571,235,000 | 0.6% |
| 36 | Oregon | 544,143,000 | 0.5% |
| 37 | Connecticut | 538,141,000 | 0.5% |
| 38 | Rhode Island | 458,669,000 | 0.5% |
| 39 | Wisconsin | 435,727,000 | 0.4% |
| 40 | Minnesota | 432,807,000 | 0.4% |
| 41 | North Dakota | 391,365,000 | 0.4% |
| 42 | Idaho | 391,225,000 | 0.4% |
| 43 | Delaware | 325,720,000 | 0.3% |
| 44 | Montana | 299,768,000 | 0.3% |
| 45 | Iowa | 264,615,000 | 0.3% |
| 46 | West Virginia | 261,333,000 | 0.3% |
| 47 | South Dakota | 258,432,000 | 0.3% |
| 48 | New Hampshire | 254,100,000 | 0.2% |
| 49 | Wyoming | 234,371,000 | 0.2% |
| 50 | Vermont | 95,849,000 | 0.1% |
|  | District of Columbia | 1,172,812,000 | 1.2% |

Source: U.S. Department of Defense
   "Estimated Payroll, Contracts & Grants by State/Area" (http://web1.whs.osd.mil/mmid/l03/fy99/99estp.htm)
*Includes Civilian Pay, Military Active Duty Pay, Reserve and National Guard Pay and Retired Military Pay. Based on location of recipient. Does not include $9,889,563,000 to recipients in U.S. territories and other countries.

# U.S. Department of Defense Military Active Duty Pay in 1999

## National Total = $37,000,682,000*

ALPHA ORDER

RANK ORDER

| RANK | STATE | PAYROLL | % of USA |
|---|---|---|---|
| 23 | Alabama | $375,660,000 | 1.0% |
| 20 | Alaska | 521,626,000 | 1.4% |
| 15 | Arizona | 668,242,000 | 1.8% |
| 30 | Arkansas | 165,588,000 | 0.4% |
| 2 | California | 4,354,067,000 | 11.8% |
| 13 | Colorado | 965,767,000 | 2.6% |
| 29 | Connecticut | 229,493,000 | 0.6% |
| 33 | Delaware | 132,522,000 | 0.4% |
| 6 | Florida | 2,088,587,000 | 5.6% |
| 5 | Georgia | 2,129,463,000 | 5.8% |
| 8 | Hawaii | 1,295,593,000 | 3.5% |
| 32 | Idaho | 147,021,000 | 0.4% |
| 9 | Illinois | 1,212,454,000 | 3.3% |
| 43 | Indiana | 33,436,000 | 0.1% |
| 49 | Iowa | 14,957,000 | 0.0% |
| 19 | Kansas | 529,002,000 | 1.4% |
| 10 | Kentucky | 1,156,960,000 | 3.1% |
| 21 | Louisiana | 501,812,000 | 1.4% |
| 36 | Maine | 116,154,000 | 0.3% |
| 12 | Maryland | 1,010,247,000 | 2.7% |
| 41 | Massachusetts | 87,025,000 | 0.2% |
| 42 | Michigan | 36,548,000 | 0.1% |
| 45 | Minnesota | 28,845,000 | 0.1% |
| 18 | Mississippi | 533,857,000 | 1.4% |
| 17 | Missouri | 546,657,000 | 1.5% |
| 34 | Montana | 124,566,000 | 0.3% |
| 25 | Nebraska | 271,726,000 | 0.7% |
| 26 | Nevada | 262,816,000 | 0.7% |
| 46 | New Hampshire | 28,416,000 | 0.1% |
| 24 | New Jersey | 311,558,000 | 0.8% |
| 22 | New Mexico | 395,483,000 | 1.1% |
| 16 | New York | 665,113,000 | 1.8% |
| 4 | North Carolina | 2,609,230,000 | 7.1% |
| 28 | North Dakota | 254,988,000 | 0.7% |
| 27 | Ohio | 261,035,000 | 0.7% |
| 14 | Oklahoma | 852,422,000 | 2.3% |
| 44 | Oregon | 31,905,000 | 0.1% |
| 38 | Pennsylvania | 108,964,000 | 0.3% |
| 37 | Rhode Island | 115,978,000 | 0.3% |
| 11 | South Carolina | 1,107,520,000 | 3.0% |
| 39 | South Dakota | 107,726,000 | 0.3% |
| 40 | Tennessee | 90,652,000 | 0.2% |
| 3 | Texas | 3,669,666,000 | 9.9% |
| 31 | Utah | 163,940,000 | 0.4% |
| 50 | Vermont | 5,573,000 | 0.0% |
| 1 | Virginia | 4,469,587,000 | 12.1% |
| 7 | Washington | 1,639,505,000 | 4.4% |
| 47 | West Virginia | 19,954,000 | 0.1% |
| 48 | Wisconsin | 19,614,000 | 0.1% |
| 35 | Wyoming | 118,841,000 | 0.3% |

| RANK | STATE | PAYROLL | % of USA |
|---|---|---|---|
| 1 | Virginia | $4,469,587,000 | 12.1% |
| 2 | California | 4,354,067,000 | 11.8% |
| 3 | Texas | 3,669,666,000 | 9.9% |
| 4 | North Carolina | 2,609,230,000 | 7.1% |
| 5 | Georgia | 2,129,463,000 | 5.8% |
| 6 | Florida | 2,088,587,000 | 5.6% |
| 7 | Washington | 1,639,505,000 | 4.4% |
| 8 | Hawaii | 1,295,593,000 | 3.5% |
| 9 | Illinois | 1,212,454,000 | 3.3% |
| 10 | Kentucky | 1,156,960,000 | 3.1% |
| 11 | South Carolina | 1,107,520,000 | 3.0% |
| 12 | Maryland | 1,010,247,000 | 2.7% |
| 13 | Colorado | 965,767,000 | 2.6% |
| 14 | Oklahoma | 852,422,000 | 2.3% |
| 15 | Arizona | 668,242,000 | 1.8% |
| 16 | New York | 665,113,000 | 1.8% |
| 17 | Missouri | 546,657,000 | 1.5% |
| 18 | Mississippi | 533,857,000 | 1.4% |
| 19 | Kansas | 529,002,000 | 1.4% |
| 20 | Alaska | 521,626,000 | 1.4% |
| 21 | Louisiana | 501,812,000 | 1.4% |
| 22 | New Mexico | 395,483,000 | 1.1% |
| 23 | Alabama | 375,660,000 | 1.0% |
| 24 | New Jersey | 311,558,000 | 0.8% |
| 25 | Nebraska | 271,726,000 | 0.7% |
| 26 | Nevada | 262,816,000 | 0.7% |
| 27 | Ohio | 261,035,000 | 0.7% |
| 28 | North Dakota | 254,988,000 | 0.7% |
| 29 | Connecticut | 229,493,000 | 0.6% |
| 30 | Arkansas | 165,588,000 | 0.4% |
| 31 | Utah | 163,940,000 | 0.4% |
| 32 | Idaho | 147,021,000 | 0.4% |
| 33 | Delaware | 132,522,000 | 0.4% |
| 34 | Montana | 124,566,000 | 0.3% |
| 35 | Wyoming | 118,841,000 | 0.3% |
| 36 | Maine | 116,154,000 | 0.3% |
| 37 | Rhode Island | 115,978,000 | 0.3% |
| 38 | Pennsylvania | 108,964,000 | 0.3% |
| 39 | South Dakota | 107,726,000 | 0.3% |
| 40 | Tennessee | 90,652,000 | 0.2% |
| 41 | Massachusetts | 87,025,000 | 0.2% |
| 42 | Michigan | 36,548,000 | 0.1% |
| 43 | Indiana | 33,436,000 | 0.1% |
| 44 | Oregon | 31,905,000 | 0.1% |
| 45 | Minnesota | 28,845,000 | 0.1% |
| 46 | New Hampshire | 28,416,000 | 0.1% |
| 47 | West Virginia | 19,954,000 | 0.1% |
| 48 | Wisconsin | 19,614,000 | 0.1% |
| 49 | Iowa | 14,957,000 | 0.0% |
| 50 | Vermont | 5,573,000 | 0.0% |
| | District of Columbia | 412,321,000 | 1.1% |

Source: U.S. Department of Defense
   "Estimated Payroll, Contracts & Grants by State/Area" (http://web1.whs.osd.mil/mmid/l03/fy99/99estp.htm)
*Based on location of recipient. Does not include $7,135,374,000 to recipients in U.S. territories and other countries.

# U.S. Department of Defense Civilian Pay in 1999

## National Total = $29,128,436,000*

### ALPHA ORDER

| RANK | STATE | PAYROLL | % of USA |
|---|---|---|---|
| 10 | Alabama | $1,027,104,000 | 3.5% |
| 33 | Alaska | 199,806,000 | 0.7% |
| 24 | Arizona | 343,606,000 | 1.2% |
| 34 | Arkansas | 142,304,000 | 0.5% |
| 2 | California | 3,202,474,000 | 11.0% |
| 18 | Colorado | 450,863,000 | 1.5% |
| 38 | Connecticut | 110,139,000 | 0.4% |
| 44 | Delaware | 52,620,000 | 0.2% |
| 7 | Florida | 1,178,646,000 | 4.0% |
| 5 | Georgia | 1,262,380,000 | 4.3% |
| 11 | Hawaii | 819,825,000 | 2.8% |
| 45 | Idaho | 49,606,000 | 0.2% |
| 15 | Illinois | 611,846,000 | 2.1% |
| 19 | Indiana | 411,755,000 | 1.4% |
| 43 | Iowa | 55,560,000 | 0.2% |
| 32 | Kansas | 210,972,000 | 0.7% |
| 26 | Kentucky | 308,511,000 | 1.1% |
| 28 | Louisiana | 304,372,000 | 1.0% |
| 29 | Maine | 257,630,000 | 0.9% |
| 4 | Maryland | 1,668,397,000 | 5.7% |
| 25 | Massachusetts | 324,316,000 | 1.1% |
| 20 | Michigan | 396,319,000 | 1.4% |
| 39 | Minnesota | 100,331,000 | 0.3% |
| 21 | Mississippi | 391,994,000 | 1.3% |
| 23 | Missouri | 372,256,000 | 1.3% |
| 48 | Montana | 41,722,000 | 0.1% |
| 35 | Nebraska | 135,040,000 | 0.5% |
| 40 | Nevada | 80,289,000 | 0.3% |
| 47 | New Hampshire | 43,818,000 | 0.2% |
| 13 | New Jersey | 797,329,000 | 2.7% |
| 27 | New Mexico | 305,114,000 | 1.0% |
| 17 | New York | 495,738,000 | 1.7% |
| 14 | North Carolina | 640,242,000 | 2.2% |
| 42 | North Dakota | 58,029,000 | 0.2% |
| 8 | Ohio | 1,134,739,000 | 3.9% |
| 12 | Oklahoma | 813,635,000 | 2.8% |
| 36 | Oregon | 128,357,000 | 0.4% |
| 6 | Pennsylvania | 1,208,206,000 | 4.1% |
| 31 | Rhode Island | 221,214,000 | 0.8% |
| 22 | South Carolina | 380,047,000 | 1.3% |
| 46 | South Dakota | 43,867,000 | 0.2% |
| 30 | Tennessee | 226,324,000 | 0.8% |
| 3 | Texas | 1,734,424,000 | 6.0% |
| 16 | Utah | 530,156,000 | 1.8% |
| 50 | Vermont | 20,170,000 | 0.1% |
| 1 | Virginia | 3,926,574,000 | 13.5% |
| 9 | Washington | 1,038,674,000 | 3.6% |
| 41 | West Virginia | 63,950,000 | 0.2% |
| 37 | Wisconsin | 110,421,000 | 0.4% |
| 49 | Wyoming | 33,583,000 | 0.1% |

### RANK ORDER

| RANK | STATE | PAYROLL | % of USA |
|---|---|---|---|
| 1 | Virginia | $3,926,574,000 | 13.5% |
| 2 | California | 3,202,474,000 | 11.0% |
| 3 | Texas | 1,734,424,000 | 6.0% |
| 4 | Maryland | 1,668,397,000 | 5.7% |
| 5 | Georgia | 1,262,380,000 | 4.3% |
| 6 | Pennsylvania | 1,208,206,000 | 4.1% |
| 7 | Florida | 1,178,646,000 | 4.0% |
| 8 | Ohio | 1,134,739,000 | 3.9% |
| 9 | Washington | 1,038,674,000 | 3.6% |
| 10 | Alabama | 1,027,104,000 | 3.5% |
| 11 | Hawaii | 819,825,000 | 2.8% |
| 12 | Oklahoma | 813,635,000 | 2.8% |
| 13 | New Jersey | 797,329,000 | 2.7% |
| 14 | North Carolina | 640,242,000 | 2.2% |
| 15 | Illinois | 611,846,000 | 2.1% |
| 16 | Utah | 530,156,000 | 1.8% |
| 17 | New York | 495,738,000 | 1.7% |
| 18 | Colorado | 450,863,000 | 1.5% |
| 19 | Indiana | 411,755,000 | 1.4% |
| 20 | Michigan | 396,319,000 | 1.4% |
| 21 | Mississippi | 391,994,000 | 1.3% |
| 22 | South Carolina | 380,047,000 | 1.3% |
| 23 | Missouri | 372,256,000 | 1.3% |
| 24 | Arizona | 343,606,000 | 1.2% |
| 25 | Massachusetts | 324,316,000 | 1.1% |
| 26 | Kentucky | 308,511,000 | 1.1% |
| 27 | New Mexico | 305,114,000 | 1.0% |
| 28 | Louisiana | 304,372,000 | 1.0% |
| 29 | Maine | 257,630,000 | 0.9% |
| 30 | Tennessee | 226,324,000 | 0.8% |
| 31 | Rhode Island | 221,214,000 | 0.8% |
| 32 | Kansas | 210,972,000 | 0.7% |
| 33 | Alaska | 199,806,000 | 0.7% |
| 34 | Arkansas | 142,304,000 | 0.5% |
| 35 | Nebraska | 135,040,000 | 0.5% |
| 36 | Oregon | 128,357,000 | 0.4% |
| 37 | Wisconsin | 110,421,000 | 0.4% |
| 38 | Connecticut | 110,139,000 | 0.4% |
| 39 | Minnesota | 100,331,000 | 0.3% |
| 40 | Nevada | 80,289,000 | 0.3% |
| 41 | West Virginia | 63,950,000 | 0.2% |
| 42 | North Dakota | 58,029,000 | 0.2% |
| 43 | Iowa | 55,560,000 | 0.2% |
| 44 | Delaware | 52,620,000 | 0.2% |
| 45 | Idaho | 49,606,000 | 0.2% |
| 46 | South Dakota | 43,867,000 | 0.2% |
| 47 | New Hampshire | 43,818,000 | 0.2% |
| 48 | Montana | 41,722,000 | 0.1% |
| 49 | Wyoming | 33,583,000 | 0.1% |
| 50 | Vermont | 20,170,000 | 0.1% |
| | District of Columbia | 663,142,000 | 2.3% |

Source: U.S. Department of Defense
   "Estimated Payroll, Contracts & Grants by State/Area" (http://web1.whs.osd.mil/mmid/l03/fy99/99estp.htm)
*Based on location of recipient.  Does not include $2,099,624,000 to recipients in U.S. territories and other countries.

# U.S. Department of Defense Reserve and National Guard Pay in 1999

## National Total = $4,721,207,000*

ALPHA ORDER

RANK ORDER

| RANK | STATE | PAYROLL | % of USA |
|---|---|---|---|
| 10 | Alabama | $142,454,000 | 3.0% |
| 46 | Alaska | 25,693,000 | 0.5% |
| 34 | Arizona | 52,899,000 | 1.1% |
| 28 | Arkansas | 76,058,000 | 1.6% |
| 1 | California | 346,745,000 | 7.3% |
| 27 | Colorado | 77,784,000 | 1.6% |
| 37 | Connecticut | 36,716,000 | 0.8% |
| 38 | Delaware | 35,648,000 | 0.8% |
| 6 | Florida | 172,776,000 | 3.7% |
| 7 | Georgia | 162,801,000 | 3.4% |
| 33 | Hawaii | 57,136,000 | 1.2% |
| 43 | Idaho | 27,704,000 | 0.6% |
| 11 | Illinois | 133,487,000 | 2.8% |
| 8 | Indiana | 153,840,000 | 3.3% |
| 31 | Iowa | 65,159,000 | 1.4% |
| 30 | Kansas | 68,114,000 | 1.4% |
| 29 | Kentucky | 69,945,000 | 1.5% |
| 15 | Louisiana | 119,114,000 | 2.5% |
| 39 | Maine | 31,764,000 | 0.7% |
| 14 | Maryland | 119,468,000 | 2.5% |
| 22 | Massachusetts | 96,031,000 | 2.0% |
| 26 | Michigan | 85,405,000 | 1.8% |
| 19 | Minnesota | 102,014,000 | 2.2% |
| 20 | Mississippi | 101,215,000 | 2.1% |
| 5 | Missouri | 175,523,000 | 3.7% |
| 44 | Montana | 26,241,000 | 0.6% |
| 36 | Nebraska | 37,467,000 | 0.8% |
| 49 | Nevada | 18,559,000 | 0.4% |
| 48 | New Hampshire | 21,514,000 | 0.5% |
| 21 | New Jersey | 98,090,000 | 2.1% |
| 40 | New Mexico | 31,415,000 | 0.7% |
| 4 | New York | 186,792,000 | 4.0% |
| 16 | North Carolina | 111,577,000 | 2.4% |
| 42 | North Dakota | 27,814,000 | 0.6% |
| 9 | Ohio | 145,290,000 | 3.1% |
| 24 | Oklahoma | 91,494,000 | 1.9% |
| 32 | Oregon | 64,647,000 | 1.4% |
| 3 | Pennsylvania | 200,822,000 | 4.3% |
| 41 | Rhode Island | 28,662,000 | 0.6% |
| 18 | South Carolina | 108,089,000 | 2.3% |
| 45 | South Dakota | 26,139,000 | 0.6% |
| 17 | Tennessee | 110,411,000 | 2.3% |
| 2 | Texas | 292,601,000 | 6.2% |
| 25 | Utah | 89,480,000 | 1.9% |
| 47 | Vermont | 23,231,000 | 0.5% |
| 12 | Virginia | 121,957,000 | 2.6% |
| 13 | Washington | 121,138,000 | 2.6% |
| 35 | West Virginia | 48,435,000 | 1.0% |
| 23 | Wisconsin | 95,953,000 | 2.0% |
| 50 | Wyoming | 16,801,000 | 0.4% |

| RANK | STATE | PAYROLL | % of USA |
|---|---|---|---|
| 1 | California | $346,745,000 | 7.3% |
| 2 | Texas | 292,601,000 | 6.2% |
| 3 | Pennsylvania | 200,822,000 | 4.3% |
| 4 | New York | 186,792,000 | 4.0% |
| 5 | Missouri | 175,523,000 | 3.7% |
| 6 | Florida | 172,776,000 | 3.7% |
| 7 | Georgia | 162,801,000 | 3.4% |
| 8 | Indiana | 153,840,000 | 3.3% |
| 9 | Ohio | 145,290,000 | 3.1% |
| 10 | Alabama | 142,454,000 | 3.0% |
| 11 | Illinois | 133,487,000 | 2.8% |
| 12 | Virginia | 121,957,000 | 2.6% |
| 13 | Washington | 121,138,000 | 2.6% |
| 14 | Maryland | 119,468,000 | 2.5% |
| 15 | Louisiana | 119,114,000 | 2.5% |
| 16 | North Carolina | 111,577,000 | 2.4% |
| 17 | Tennessee | 110,411,000 | 2.3% |
| 18 | South Carolina | 108,089,000 | 2.3% |
| 19 | Minnesota | 102,014,000 | 2.2% |
| 20 | Mississippi | 101,215,000 | 2.1% |
| 21 | New Jersey | 98,090,000 | 2.1% |
| 22 | Massachusetts | 96,031,000 | 2.0% |
| 23 | Wisconsin | 95,953,000 | 2.0% |
| 24 | Oklahoma | 91,494,000 | 1.9% |
| 25 | Utah | 89,480,000 | 1.9% |
| 26 | Michigan | 85,405,000 | 1.8% |
| 27 | Colorado | 77,784,000 | 1.6% |
| 28 | Arkansas | 76,058,000 | 1.6% |
| 29 | Kentucky | 69,945,000 | 1.5% |
| 30 | Kansas | 68,114,000 | 1.4% |
| 31 | Iowa | 65,159,000 | 1.4% |
| 32 | Oregon | 64,647,000 | 1.4% |
| 33 | Hawaii | 57,136,000 | 1.2% |
| 34 | Arizona | 52,899,000 | 1.1% |
| 35 | West Virginia | 48,435,000 | 1.0% |
| 36 | Nebraska | 37,467,000 | 0.8% |
| 37 | Connecticut | 36,716,000 | 0.8% |
| 38 | Delaware | 35,648,000 | 0.8% |
| 39 | Maine | 31,764,000 | 0.7% |
| 40 | New Mexico | 31,415,000 | 0.7% |
| 41 | Rhode Island | 28,662,000 | 0.6% |
| 42 | North Dakota | 27,814,000 | 0.6% |
| 43 | Idaho | 27,704,000 | 0.6% |
| 44 | Montana | 26,241,000 | 0.6% |
| 45 | South Dakota | 26,139,000 | 0.6% |
| 46 | Alaska | 25,693,000 | 0.5% |
| 47 | Vermont | 23,231,000 | 0.5% |
| 48 | New Hampshire | 21,514,000 | 0.5% |
| 49 | Nevada | 18,559,000 | 0.4% |
| 50 | Wyoming | 16,801,000 | 0.4% |
| | District of Columbia | 41,095,000 | 0.9% |

Source: U.S. Department of Defense

"Estimated Payroll, Contracts & Grants by State/Area" (http://web1.whs.osd.mil/mmid/l03/fy99/99estp.htm)
*Based on location of recipient. Does not include $105,614,000 to recipients in U.S. territories and other countries.

# U.S. Department of Defense Retired Military Pay in 1999

## National Total = $30,960,891,000*

ALPHA ORDER

| RANK | STATE | PAYROLL | % of USA |
|---|---|---|---|
| 11 | Alabama | $806,855,000 | 2.6% |
| 43 | Alaska | 112,960,000 | 0.4% |
| 8 | Arizona | 866,121,000 | 2.8% |
| 22 | Arkansas | 375,674,000 | 1.2% |
| 1 | California | 3,491,536,000 | 11.3% |
| 9 | Colorado | 865,063,000 | 2.8% |
| 39 | Connecticut | 161,793,000 | 0.5% |
| 45 | Delaware | 104,930,000 | 0.3% |
| 2 | Florida | 3,281,998,000 | 10.6% |
| 5 | Georgia | 1,246,271,000 | 4.0% |
| 32 | Hawaii | 249,618,000 | 0.8% |
| 37 | Idaho | 166,894,000 | 0.5% |
| 18 | Illinois | 482,443,000 | 1.6% |
| 30 | Indiana | 292,414,000 | 0.9% |
| 42 | Iowa | 128,939,000 | 0.4% |
| 29 | Kansas | 309,891,000 | 1.0% |
| 25 | Kentucky | 341,607,000 | 1.1% |
| 21 | Louisiana | 422,136,000 | 1.4% |
| 38 | Maine | 165,687,000 | 0.5% |
| 12 | Maryland | 789,731,000 | 2.6% |
| 31 | Massachusetts | 289,584,000 | 0.9% |
| 26 | Michigan | 329,911,000 | 1.1% |
| 35 | Minnesota | 201,617,000 | 0.7% |
| 24 | Mississippi | 367,018,000 | 1.2% |
| 17 | Missouri | 496,369,000 | 1.6% |
| 44 | Montana | 107,239,000 | 0.3% |
| 33 | Nebraska | 210,649,000 | 0.7% |
| 20 | Nevada | 429,341,000 | 1.4% |
| 40 | New Hampshire | 160,352,000 | 0.5% |
| 28 | New Jersey | 314,116,000 | 1.0% |
| 23 | New Mexico | 371,980,000 | 1.2% |
| 19 | New York | 439,507,000 | 1.4% |
| 6 | North Carolina | 1,158,737,000 | 3.7% |
| 49 | North Dakota | 50,534,000 | 0.2% |
| 15 | Ohio | 595,368,000 | 1.9% |
| 16 | Oklahoma | 501,605,000 | 1.6% |
| 27 | Oregon | 319,234,000 | 1.0% |
| 14 | Pennsylvania | 657,772,000 | 2.1% |
| 46 | Rhode Island | 92,815,000 | 0.3% |
| 10 | South Carolina | 831,021,000 | 2.7% |
| 47 | South Dakota | 80,700,000 | 0.3% |
| 13 | Tennessee | 674,195,000 | 2.2% |
| 3 | Texas | 3,114,615,000 | 10.1% |
| 36 | Utah | 193,157,000 | 0.6% |
| 50 | Vermont | 46,875,000 | 0.2% |
| 4 | Virginia | 2,651,833,000 | 8.6% |
| 7 | Washington | 1,152,053,000 | 3.7% |
| 41 | West Virginia | 128,994,000 | 0.4% |
| 34 | Wisconsin | 209,739,000 | 0.7% |
| 48 | Wyoming | 65,146,000 | 0.2% |

RANK ORDER

| RANK | STATE | PAYROLL | % of USA |
|---|---|---|---|
| 1 | California | $3,491,536,000 | 11.3% |
| 2 | Florida | 3,281,998,000 | 10.6% |
| 3 | Texas | 3,114,615,000 | 10.1% |
| 4 | Virginia | 2,651,833,000 | 8.6% |
| 5 | Georgia | 1,246,271,000 | 4.0% |
| 6 | North Carolina | 1,158,737,000 | 3.7% |
| 7 | Washington | 1,152,053,000 | 3.7% |
| 8 | Arizona | 866,121,000 | 2.8% |
| 9 | Colorado | 865,063,000 | 2.8% |
| 10 | South Carolina | 831,021,000 | 2.7% |
| 11 | Alabama | 806,855,000 | 2.6% |
| 12 | Maryland | 789,731,000 | 2.6% |
| 13 | Tennessee | 674,195,000 | 2.2% |
| 14 | Pennsylvania | 657,772,000 | 2.1% |
| 15 | Ohio | 595,368,000 | 1.9% |
| 16 | Oklahoma | 501,605,000 | 1.6% |
| 17 | Missouri | 496,369,000 | 1.6% |
| 18 | Illinois | 482,443,000 | 1.6% |
| 19 | New York | 439,507,000 | 1.4% |
| 20 | Nevada | 429,341,000 | 1.4% |
| 21 | Louisiana | 422,136,000 | 1.4% |
| 22 | Arkansas | 375,674,000 | 1.2% |
| 23 | New Mexico | 371,980,000 | 1.2% |
| 24 | Mississippi | 367,018,000 | 1.2% |
| 25 | Kentucky | 341,607,000 | 1.1% |
| 26 | Michigan | 329,911,000 | 1.1% |
| 27 | Oregon | 319,234,000 | 1.0% |
| 28 | New Jersey | 314,116,000 | 1.0% |
| 29 | Kansas | 309,891,000 | 1.0% |
| 30 | Indiana | 292,414,000 | 0.9% |
| 31 | Massachusetts | 289,584,000 | 0.9% |
| 32 | Hawaii | 249,618,000 | 0.8% |
| 33 | Nebraska | 210,649,000 | 0.7% |
| 34 | Wisconsin | 209,739,000 | 0.7% |
| 35 | Minnesota | 201,617,000 | 0.7% |
| 36 | Utah | 193,157,000 | 0.6% |
| 37 | Idaho | 166,894,000 | 0.5% |
| 38 | Maine | 165,687,000 | 0.5% |
| 39 | Connecticut | 161,793,000 | 0.5% |
| 40 | New Hampshire | 160,352,000 | 0.5% |
| 41 | West Virginia | 128,994,000 | 0.4% |
| 42 | Iowa | 128,939,000 | 0.4% |
| 43 | Alaska | 112,960,000 | 0.4% |
| 44 | Montana | 107,239,000 | 0.3% |
| 45 | Delaware | 104,930,000 | 0.3% |
| 46 | Rhode Island | 92,815,000 | 0.3% |
| 47 | South Dakota | 80,700,000 | 0.3% |
| 48 | Wyoming | 65,146,000 | 0.2% |
| 49 | North Dakota | 50,534,000 | 0.2% |
| 50 | Vermont | 46,875,000 | 0.2% |
| | District of Columbia | 56,254,000 | 0.2% |

*Source: U.S. Department of Defense*
*"Estimated Payroll, Contracts & Grants by State/Area" (http://web1.whs.osd.mil/mmid/l03/fy99/99estp.htm)*
*\*Based on location of recipient. Does not include $548,951,000 to recipients in U.S. territories and other countries.*

# Veterans in 2000

## National Total = 25,497,691 Veterans*

ALPHA ORDER

| RANK | STATE | VETERANS | % of USA |
|------|-------|----------|----------|
| 21 | Alabama | 460,226 | 1.8% |
| 47 | Alaska | 67,781 | 0.3% |
| 18 | Arizona | 509,009 | 2.0% |
| 30 | Arkansas | 281,173 | 1.1% |
| 1 | California | 2,367,685 | 9.3% |
| 24 | Colorado | 409,656 | 1.6% |
| 29 | Connecticut | 283,219 | 1.1% |
| 45 | Delaware | 78,164 | 0.3% |
| 2 | Florida | 1,771,178 | 6.9% |
| 9 | Georgia | 769,351 | 3.0% |
| 43 | Hawaii | 102,566 | 0.4% |
| 41 | Idaho | 124,175 | 0.5% |
| 7 | Illinois | 944,664 | 3.7% |
| 15 | Indiana | 567,045 | 2.2% |
| 31 | Iowa | 267,979 | 1.1% |
| 33 | Kansas | 248,236 | 1.0% |
| 27 | Kentucky | 371,552 | 1.5% |
| 25 | Louisiana | 390,015 | 1.5% |
| 37 | Maine | 164,394 | 0.6% |
| 19 | Maryland | 497,125 | 1.9% |
| 17 | Massachusetts | 543,063 | 2.1% |
| 8 | Michigan | 901,103 | 3.5% |
| 22 | Minnesota | 430,176 | 1.7% |
| 32 | Mississippi | 250,497 | 1.0% |
| 14 | Missouri | 569,046 | 2.2% |
| 42 | Montana | 106,570 | 0.4% |
| 38 | Nebraska | 157,801 | 0.6% |
| 34 | Nevada | 229,422 | 0.9% |
| 39 | New Hampshire | 134,770 | 0.5% |
| 12 | New Jersey | 634,048 | 2.5% |
| 36 | New Mexico | 186,852 | 0.7% |
| 4 | New York | 1,326,086 | 5.2% |
| 10 | North Carolina | 768,084 | 3.0% |
| 49 | North Dakota | 56,986 | 0.2% |
| 6 | Ohio | 1,126,413 | 4.4% |
| 26 | Oklahoma | 373,486 | 1.5% |
| 28 | Oregon | 367,725 | 1.4% |
| 5 | Pennsylvania | 1,235,294 | 4.8% |
| 44 | Rhode Island | 95,334 | 0.4% |
| 23 | South Carolina | 412,104 | 1.6% |
| 46 | South Dakota | 77,333 | 0.3% |
| 16 | Tennessee | 543,205 | 2.1% |
| 3 | Texas | 1,719,676 | 6.7% |
| 40 | Utah | 133,611 | 0.5% |
| 48 | Vermont | 59,317 | 0.2% |
| 11 | Virginia | 713,694 | 2.8% |
| 13 | Washington | 619,208 | 2.4% |
| 35 | West Virginia | 203,226 | 0.8% |
| 20 | Wisconsin | 487,989 | 1.9% |
| 50 | Wyoming | 53,242 | 0.2% |

RANK ORDER

| RANK | STATE | VETERANS | % of USA |
|------|-------|----------|----------|
| 1 | California | 2,367,685 | 9.3% |
| 2 | Florida | 1,771,178 | 6.9% |
| 3 | Texas | 1,719,676 | 6.7% |
| 4 | New York | 1,326,086 | 5.2% |
| 5 | Pennsylvania | 1,235,294 | 4.8% |
| 6 | Ohio | 1,126,413 | 4.4% |
| 7 | Illinois | 944,664 | 3.7% |
| 8 | Michigan | 901,103 | 3.5% |
| 9 | Georgia | 769,351 | 3.0% |
| 10 | North Carolina | 768,084 | 3.0% |
| 11 | Virginia | 713,694 | 2.8% |
| 12 | New Jersey | 634,048 | 2.5% |
| 13 | Washington | 619,208 | 2.4% |
| 14 | Missouri | 569,046 | 2.2% |
| 15 | Indiana | 567,045 | 2.2% |
| 16 | Tennessee | 543,205 | 2.1% |
| 17 | Massachusetts | 543,063 | 2.1% |
| 18 | Arizona | 509,009 | 2.0% |
| 19 | Maryland | 497,125 | 1.9% |
| 20 | Wisconsin | 487,989 | 1.9% |
| 21 | Alabama | 460,226 | 1.8% |
| 22 | Minnesota | 430,176 | 1.7% |
| 23 | South Carolina | 412,104 | 1.6% |
| 24 | Colorado | 409,656 | 1.6% |
| 25 | Louisiana | 390,015 | 1.5% |
| 26 | Oklahoma | 373,486 | 1.5% |
| 27 | Kentucky | 371,552 | 1.5% |
| 28 | Oregon | 367,725 | 1.4% |
| 29 | Connecticut | 283,219 | 1.1% |
| 30 | Arkansas | 281,173 | 1.1% |
| 31 | Iowa | 267,979 | 1.1% |
| 32 | Mississippi | 250,497 | 1.0% |
| 33 | Kansas | 248,236 | 1.0% |
| 34 | Nevada | 229,422 | 0.9% |
| 35 | West Virginia | 203,226 | 0.8% |
| 36 | New Mexico | 186,852 | 0.7% |
| 37 | Maine | 164,394 | 0.6% |
| 38 | Nebraska | 157,801 | 0.6% |
| 39 | New Hampshire | 134,770 | 0.5% |
| 40 | Utah | 133,611 | 0.5% |
| 41 | Idaho | 124,175 | 0.5% |
| 42 | Montana | 106,570 | 0.4% |
| 43 | Hawaii | 102,566 | 0.4% |
| 44 | Rhode Island | 95,334 | 0.4% |
| 45 | Delaware | 78,164 | 0.3% |
| 46 | South Dakota | 77,333 | 0.3% |
| 47 | Alaska | 67,781 | 0.3% |
| 48 | Vermont | 59,317 | 0.2% |
| 49 | North Dakota | 56,986 | 0.2% |
| 50 | Wyoming | 53,242 | 0.2% |
|  | District of Columbia | 48,133 | 0.2% |

Source: U.S. Department of Veterans Affairs, Assistant Secretary for Policy and Planning
"Estimate and Projection of the Veterans Populations 1999-2029"
*As of September 30, 2000. National total includes 268,993 veterans in U.S. territories and overseas.

# Veterans per 1,000 Population 18 and Older in 2000

## National Rate = 125 Veterans*

| ALPHA ORDER | | | RANK ORDER | | |
|---|---|---|---|---|---|
| RANK | STATE | VETERANS | RANK | STATE | VETERANS |
| 18 | Alabama | 139 | 1 | Nevada | 174 |
| 4 | Alaska | 160 | 2 | Maine | 171 |
| 11 | Arizona | 148 | 3 | Montana | 162 |
| 10 | Arkansas | 149 | 4 | Alaska | 160 |
| 48 | California | 98 | 5 | Florida | 153 |
| 21 | Colorado | 137 | 6 | Wyoming | 151 |
| 43 | Connecticut | 115 | 7 | Oklahoma | 151 |
| 22 | Delaware | 137 | 8 | New Hampshire | 150 |
| 5 | Florida | 153 | 9 | New Mexico | 150 |
| 25 | Georgia | 134 | 10 | Arkansas | 149 |
| 45 | Hawaii | 114 | 11 | Arizona | 148 |
| 19 | Idaho | 138 | 12 | Oregon | 148 |
| 46 | Illinois | 106 | 13 | Washington | 145 |
| 31 | Indiana | 128 | 14 | West Virginia | 145 |
| 35 | Iowa | 125 | 15 | South Dakota | 145 |
| 33 | Kansas | 127 | 16 | South Carolina | 141 |
| 37 | Kentucky | 124 | 17 | Missouri | 140 |
| 40 | Louisiana | 123 | 18 | Alabama | 139 |
| 2 | Maine | 171 | 19 | Idaho | 138 |
| 30 | Maryland | 129 | 20 | Virginia | 137 |
| 44 | Massachusetts | 115 | 21 | Colorado | 137 |
| 38 | Michigan | 123 | 22 | Delaware | 137 |
| 39 | Minnesota | 123 | 23 | Pennsylvania | 135 |
| 36 | Mississippi | 124 | 24 | North Carolina | 135 |
| 17 | Missouri | 140 | 25 | Georgia | 134 |
| 3 | Montana | 162 | 26 | Ohio | 134 |
| 29 | Nebraska | 129 | 27 | Tennessee | 131 |
| 1 | Nevada | 174 | 28 | Vermont | 131 |
| 8 | New Hampshire | 150 | 29 | Nebraska | 129 |
| 9 | New Mexico | 150 | 30 | Maryland | 129 |
| 49 | New York | 96 | 31 | Indiana | 128 |
| 24 | North Carolina | 135 | 32 | Rhode Island | 127 |
| 41 | North Dakota | 120 | 33 | Kansas | 127 |
| 26 | Ohio | 134 | 34 | Wisconsin | 125 |
| 7 | Oklahoma | 151 | 35 | Iowa | 125 |
| 12 | Oregon | 148 | 36 | Mississippi | 124 |
| 23 | Pennsylvania | 135 | 37 | Kentucky | 124 |
| 32 | Rhode Island | 127 | 38 | Michigan | 123 |
| 16 | South Carolina | 141 | 39 | Minnesota | 123 |
| 15 | South Dakota | 145 | 40 | Louisiana | 123 |
| 27 | Tennessee | 131 | 41 | North Dakota | 120 |
| 42 | Texas | 120 | 42 | Texas | 120 |
| 50 | Utah | 94 | 43 | Connecticut | 115 |
| 28 | Vermont | 131 | 44 | Massachusetts | 115 |
| 20 | Virginia | 137 | 45 | Hawaii | 114 |
| 13 | Washington | 145 | 46 | Illinois | 106 |
| 14 | West Virginia | 145 | 47 | New Jersey | 103 |
| 34 | Wisconsin | 125 | 48 | California | 98 |
| 6 | Wyoming | 151 | 49 | New York | 96 |
| | | | 50 | Utah | 94 |
| | | | | District of Columbia | 114 |

*Source: Morgan Quitno Press using data from U.S. Department of Veterans Affairs*
   *"Estimate and Projection of the Veterans Populations 1999-2029"*
*As of September 30, 2000. National rate does not include veterans or population in U.S. territories and overseas.*
*Calculated using 1999 population figures for 18 and older.*

# IV. ECONOMY

# State Cost of Living in 1999

## National Average = 1.000*

<u>ALPHA ORDER</u>

| RANK | STATE | COL INDEX |
|---|---|---|
| 39 | Alabama | 0.927 |
| 6 | Alaska | 1.114 |
| 17 | Arizona | 1.004 |
| 47 | Arkansas | 0.910 |
| 14 | California | 1.021 |
| 15 | Colorado | 1.011 |
| 5 | Connecticut | 1.122 |
| 13 | Delaware | 1.030 |
| 32 | Florida | 0.943 |
| 45 | Georgia | 0.917 |
| 1 | Hawaii | 1.217 |
| 29 | Idaho | 0.951 |
| 18 | Illinois | 1.003 |
| 24 | Indiana | 0.963 |
| 34 | Iowa | 0.934 |
| 35 | Kansas | 0.933 |
| 45 | Kentucky | 0.917 |
| 38 | Louisiana | 0.928 |
| 9 | Maine | 1.049 |
| 23 | Maryland | 0.974 |
| 2 | Massachusetts | 1.142 |
| 30 | Michigan | 0.950 |
| 30 | Minnesota | 0.950 |
| 50 | Mississippi | 0.904 |
| 37 | Missouri | 0.929 |
| 26 | Montana | 0.954 |
| 33 | Nebraska | 0.938 |
| 16 | Nevada | 1.008 |
| 8 | New Hampshire | 1.085 |
| 3 | New Jersey | 1.137 |
| 22 | New Mexico | 0.977 |
| 4 | New York | 1.132 |
| 43 | North Carolina | 0.920 |
| 36 | North Dakota | 0.931 |
| 21 | Ohio | 0.980 |
| 42 | Oklahoma | 0.922 |
| 20 | Oregon | 0.989 |
| 10 | Pennsylvania | 1.047 |
| 7 | Rhode Island | 1.107 |
| 41 | South Carolina | 0.923 |
| 43 | South Dakota | 0.920 |
| 39 | Tennessee | 0.927 |
| 48 | Texas | 0.909 |
| 18 | Utah | 1.003 |
| 12 | Vermont | 1.036 |
| 26 | Virginia | 0.954 |
| 11 | Washington | 1.041 |
| 49 | West Virginia | 0.908 |
| 28 | Wisconsin | 0.952 |
| 25 | Wyoming | 0.959 |

<u>RANK ORDER</u>

| RANK | STATE | COL INDEX |
|---|---|---|
| 1 | Hawaii | 1.217 |
| 2 | Massachusetts | 1.142 |
| 3 | New Jersey | 1.137 |
| 4 | New York | 1.132 |
| 5 | Connecticut | 1.122 |
| 6 | Alaska | 1.114 |
| 7 | Rhode Island | 1.107 |
| 8 | New Hampshire | 1.085 |
| 9 | Maine | 1.049 |
| 10 | Pennsylvania | 1.047 |
| 11 | Washington | 1.041 |
| 12 | Vermont | 1.036 |
| 13 | Delaware | 1.030 |
| 14 | California | 1.021 |
| 15 | Colorado | 1.011 |
| 16 | Nevada | 1.008 |
| 17 | Arizona | 1.004 |
| 18 | Illinois | 1.003 |
| 18 | Utah | 1.003 |
| 20 | Oregon | 0.989 |
| 21 | Ohio | 0.980 |
| 22 | New Mexico | 0.977 |
| 23 | Maryland | 0.974 |
| 24 | Indiana | 0.963 |
| 25 | Wyoming | 0.959 |
| 26 | Montana | 0.954 |
| 26 | Virginia | 0.954 |
| 28 | Wisconsin | 0.952 |
| 29 | Idaho | 0.951 |
| 30 | Michigan | 0.950 |
| 30 | Minnesota | 0.950 |
| 32 | Florida | 0.943 |
| 33 | Nebraska | 0.938 |
| 34 | Iowa | 0.934 |
| 35 | Kansas | 0.933 |
| 36 | North Dakota | 0.931 |
| 37 | Missouri | 0.929 |
| 38 | Louisiana | 0.928 |
| 39 | Alabama | 0.927 |
| 39 | Tennessee | 0.927 |
| 41 | South Carolina | 0.923 |
| 42 | Oklahoma | 0.922 |
| 43 | North Carolina | 0.920 |
| 43 | South Dakota | 0.920 |
| 45 | Georgia | 0.917 |
| 45 | Kentucky | 0.917 |
| 47 | Arkansas | 0.910 |
| 48 | Texas | 0.909 |
| 49 | West Virginia | 0.908 |
| 50 | Mississippi | 0.904 |
| | District of Columbia | 1.042 |

Source: Herman B. Leonard and Jay H. Walder

"The Federal Budget and the States, 1999" ( Washington, DC 2001; http://www.ksg.harvard.edu/taubmancenter/)
*A number higher than one reflects a higher cost of living than the average. It measures the relative changes in costs across states and across time for the past 18 years using regional and selected area Consumer Price Indices applied to family budget data.

# Gross State Product in 1998

## National Total = $8,745,219,000,000*

### ALPHA ORDER

| RANK | STATE | G.S.P. | % of USA |
|---|---|---|---|
| 25 | Alabama | $109,833,000,000 | 1.3% |
| 45 | Alaska | 24,236,000,000 | 0.3% |
| 23 | Arizona | 133,801,000,000 | 1.5% |
| 34 | Arkansas | 61,628,000,000 | 0.7% |
| 1 | California | 1,118,945,000,000 | 12.8% |
| 22 | Colorado | 141,791,000,000 | 1.6% |
| 21 | Connecticut | 142,099,000,000 | 1.6% |
| 41 | Delaware | 33,735,000,000 | 0.4% |
| 5 | Florida | 418,851,000,000 | 4.8% |
| 10 | Georgia | 253,769,000,000 | 2.9% |
| 40 | Hawaii | 39,712,000,000 | 0.5% |
| 43 | Idaho | 30,936,000,000 | 0.4% |
| 4 | Illinois | 425,679,000,000 | 4.9% |
| 15 | Indiana | 174,433,000,000 | 2.0% |
| 29 | Iowa | 84,628,000,000 | 1.0% |
| 31 | Kansas | 76,991,000,000 | 0.9% |
| 26 | Kentucky | 107,152,000,000 | 1.2% |
| 24 | Louisiana | 129,251,000,000 | 1.5% |
| 42 | Maine | 32,318,000,000 | 0.4% |
| 16 | Maryland | 164,798,000,000 | 1.9% |
| 11 | Massachusetts | 239,379,000,000 | 2.7% |
| 9 | Michigan | 294,505,000,000 | 3.4% |
| 18 | Minnesota | 161,392,000,000 | 1.8% |
| 33 | Mississippi | 62,216,000,000 | 0.7% |
| 17 | Missouri | 162,772,000,000 | 1.9% |
| 47 | Montana | 19,861,000,000 | 0.2% |
| 36 | Nebraska | 51,737,000,000 | 0.6% |
| 32 | Nevada | 63,044,000,000 | 0.7% |
| 38 | New Hampshire | 41,313,000,000 | 0.5% |
| 8 | New Jersey | 319,201,000,000 | 3.7% |
| 37 | New Mexico | 47,736,000,000 | 0.5% |
| 2 | New York | 706,886,000,000 | 8.1% |
| 12 | North Carolina | 235,752,000,000 | 2.7% |
| 49 | North Dakota | 17,214,000,000 | 0.2% |
| 7 | Ohio | 341,070,000,000 | 3.9% |
| 30 | Oklahoma | 81,655,000,000 | 0.9% |
| 27 | Oregon | 104,771,000,000 | 1.2% |
| 6 | Pennsylvania | 364,039,000,000 | 4.2% |
| 44 | Rhode Island | 30,443,000,000 | 0.3% |
| 28 | South Carolina | 100,350,000,000 | 1.1% |
| 46 | South Dakota | 21,224,000,000 | 0.2% |
| 19 | Tennessee | 159,575,000,000 | 1.8% |
| 3 | Texas | 645,596,000,000 | 7.4% |
| 35 | Utah | 59,624,000,000 | 0.7% |
| 50 | Vermont | 16,257,000,000 | 0.2% |
| 13 | Virginia | 230,825,000,000 | 2.6% |
| 14 | Washington | 192,864,000,000 | 2.2% |
| 39 | West Virginia | 39,938,000,000 | 0.5% |
| 20 | Wisconsin | 157,761,000,000 | 1.8% |
| 48 | Wyoming | 17,530,000,000 | 0.2% |

### RANK ORDER

| RANK | STATE | G.S.P. | % of USA |
|---|---|---|---|
| 1 | California | $1,118,945,000,000 | 12.8% |
| 2 | New York | 706,886,000,000 | 8.1% |
| 3 | Texas | 645,596,000,000 | 7.4% |
| 4 | Illinois | 425,679,000,000 | 4.9% |
| 5 | Florida | 418,851,000,000 | 4.8% |
| 6 | Pennsylvania | 364,039,000,000 | 4.2% |
| 7 | Ohio | 341,070,000,000 | 3.9% |
| 8 | New Jersey | 319,201,000,000 | 3.7% |
| 9 | Michigan | 294,505,000,000 | 3.4% |
| 10 | Georgia | 253,769,000,000 | 2.9% |
| 11 | Massachusetts | 239,379,000,000 | 2.7% |
| 12 | North Carolina | 235,752,000,000 | 2.7% |
| 13 | Virginia | 230,825,000,000 | 2.6% |
| 14 | Washington | 192,864,000,000 | 2.2% |
| 15 | Indiana | 174,433,000,000 | 2.0% |
| 16 | Maryland | 164,798,000,000 | 1.9% |
| 17 | Missouri | 162,772,000,000 | 1.9% |
| 18 | Minnesota | 161,392,000,000 | 1.8% |
| 19 | Tennessee | 159,575,000,000 | 1.8% |
| 20 | Wisconsin | 157,761,000,000 | 1.8% |
| 21 | Connecticut | 142,099,000,000 | 1.6% |
| 22 | Colorado | 141,791,000,000 | 1.6% |
| 23 | Arizona | 133,801,000,000 | 1.5% |
| 24 | Louisiana | 129,251,000,000 | 1.5% |
| 25 | Alabama | 109,833,000,000 | 1.3% |
| 26 | Kentucky | 107,152,000,000 | 1.2% |
| 27 | Oregon | 104,771,000,000 | 1.2% |
| 28 | South Carolina | 100,350,000,000 | 1.1% |
| 29 | Iowa | 84,628,000,000 | 1.0% |
| 30 | Oklahoma | 81,655,000,000 | 0.9% |
| 31 | Kansas | 76,991,000,000 | 0.9% |
| 32 | Nevada | 63,044,000,000 | 0.7% |
| 33 | Mississippi | 62,216,000,000 | 0.7% |
| 34 | Arkansas | 61,628,000,000 | 0.7% |
| 35 | Utah | 59,624,000,000 | 0.7% |
| 36 | Nebraska | 51,737,000,000 | 0.6% |
| 37 | New Mexico | 47,736,000,000 | 0.5% |
| 38 | New Hampshire | 41,313,000,000 | 0.5% |
| 39 | West Virginia | 39,938,000,000 | 0.5% |
| 40 | Hawaii | 39,712,000,000 | 0.5% |
| 41 | Delaware | 33,735,000,000 | 0.4% |
| 42 | Maine | 32,318,000,000 | 0.4% |
| 43 | Idaho | 30,936,000,000 | 0.4% |
| 44 | Rhode Island | 30,443,000,000 | 0.3% |
| 45 | Alaska | 24,236,000,000 | 0.3% |
| 46 | South Dakota | 21,224,000,000 | 0.2% |
| 47 | Montana | 19,861,000,000 | 0.2% |
| 48 | Wyoming | 17,530,000,000 | 0.2% |
| 49 | North Dakota | 17,214,000,000 | 0.2% |
| 50 | Vermont | 16,257,000,000 | 0.2% |
| | District of Columbia | 54,100,000,000 | 0.6% |

Source: U.S. Department of Commerce, Bureau of Economic Analysis
   "Gross State Product Data" (http://www.bea.doc.gov/bea/regional/gsp/)
*G.S.P. is the market value of goods and services produced by the labor and property located in a state.  It is the
state counterpart to the nation's Gross Domestic Product.

# Percent Change in Gross State Product: 1994 to 1998
## (Adjusted to Constant 1998 Dollars)
## National Percent Change = 14.7% Increase*

| RANK | STATE | PERCENT CHANGE |
|---|---|---|
| 34 | Alabama | 11.4 |
| 50 | Alaska | (3.2) |
| 4 | Arizona | 27.0 |
| 41 | Arkansas | 10.3 |
| 15 | California | 15.9 |
| 5 | Colorado | 26.8 |
| 17 | Connecticut | 14.8 |
| 8 | Delaware | 22.7 |
| 13 | Florida | 17.1 |
| 7 | Georgia | 23.3 |
| 49 | Hawaii | (1.8) |
| 20 | Idaho | 13.5 |
| 21 | Illinois | 12.9 |
| 28 | Indiana | 11.8 |
| 38 | Iowa | 10.5 |
| 23 | Kansas | 12.6 |
| 26 | Kentucky | 12.2 |
| 30 | Louisiana | 11.6 |
| 36 | Maine | 10.7 |
| 28 | Maryland | 11.8 |
| 15 | Massachusetts | 15.9 |
| 43 | Michigan | 8.6 |
| 12 | Minnesota | 17.4 |
| 40 | Mississippi | 10.4 |
| 19 | Missouri | 13.8 |
| 46 | Montana | 6.1 |
| 33 | Nebraska | 11.5 |
| 2 | Nevada | 27.8 |
| 2 | New Hampshire | 27.8 |
| 24 | New Jersey | 12.5 |
| 48 | New Mexico | 4.2 |
| 30 | New York | 11.6 |
| 11 | North Carolina | 17.7 |
| 36 | North Dakota | 10.7 |
| 38 | Ohio | 10.5 |
| 30 | Oklahoma | 11.6 |
| 6 | Oregon | 26.5 |
| 42 | Pennsylvania | 10.1 |
| 18 | Rhode Island | 14.1 |
| 25 | South Carolina | 12.3 |
| 35 | South Dakota | 11.2 |
| 27 | Tennessee | 12.0 |
| 9 | Texas | 21.4 |
| 1 | Utah | 28.2 |
| 44 | Vermont | 7.6 |
| 14 | Virginia | 16.8 |
| 10 | Washington | 19.7 |
| 47 | West Virginia | 4.5 |
| 22 | Wisconsin | 12.7 |
| 45 | Wyoming | 7.2 |

| RANK | STATE | PERCENT CHANGE |
|---|---|---|
| 1 | Utah | 28.2 |
| 2 | Nevada | 27.8 |
| 2 | New Hampshire | 27.8 |
| 4 | Arizona | 27.0 |
| 5 | Colorado | 26.8 |
| 6 | Oregon | 26.5 |
| 7 | Georgia | 23.3 |
| 8 | Delaware | 22.7 |
| 9 | Texas | 21.4 |
| 10 | Washington | 19.7 |
| 11 | North Carolina | 17.7 |
| 12 | Minnesota | 17.4 |
| 13 | Florida | 17.1 |
| 14 | Virginia | 16.8 |
| 15 | California | 15.9 |
| 15 | Massachusetts | 15.9 |
| 17 | Connecticut | 14.8 |
| 18 | Rhode Island | 14.1 |
| 19 | Missouri | 13.8 |
| 20 | Idaho | 13.5 |
| 21 | Illinois | 12.9 |
| 22 | Wisconsin | 12.7 |
| 23 | Kansas | 12.6 |
| 24 | New Jersey | 12.5 |
| 25 | South Carolina | 12.3 |
| 26 | Kentucky | 12.2 |
| 27 | Tennessee | 12.0 |
| 28 | Indiana | 11.8 |
| 28 | Maryland | 11.8 |
| 30 | Louisiana | 11.6 |
| 30 | New York | 11.6 |
| 30 | Oklahoma | 11.6 |
| 33 | Nebraska | 11.5 |
| 34 | Alabama | 11.4 |
| 35 | South Dakota | 11.2 |
| 36 | Maine | 10.7 |
| 36 | North Dakota | 10.7 |
| 38 | Iowa | 10.5 |
| 38 | Ohio | 10.5 |
| 40 | Mississippi | 10.4 |
| 41 | Arkansas | 10.3 |
| 42 | Pennsylvania | 10.1 |
| 43 | Michigan | 8.6 |
| 44 | Vermont | 7.6 |
| 45 | Wyoming | 7.2 |
| 46 | Montana | 6.1 |
| 47 | West Virginia | 4.5 |
| 48 | New Mexico | 4.2 |
| 49 | Hawaii | (1.8) |
| 50 | Alaska | (3.2) |

District of Columbia        3.6

*Source: Morgan Quitno Press using data from U.S. Department of Commerce, Bureau of Economic Analysis "Gross State Product Data" (http://www.bea.doc.gov/bea/regional/gsp/)*

*G.S.P. is the market value of goods and services produced by the labor and property located in a state. It is the state counterpart to the nation's Gross Domestic Product. Adjusted for inflation to 1998 dollars using 1982-1984 as the index base period.*

# Average Annual Change in Gross State Product: 1994 to 1998
## (Adjusted to Constant 1998 Dollars)
## National Annual Percent Change = 2.8% Increase*

ALPHA ORDER

| RANK | STATE | PERCENT CHANGE |
|---|---|---|
| 29 | Alabama | 2.2 |
| 50 | Alaska | (0.7) |
| 4 | Arizona | 4.9 |
| 37 | Arkansas | 2.0 |
| 15 | California | 3.0 |
| 4 | Colorado | 4.9 |
| 17 | Connecticut | 2.8 |
| 8 | Delaware | 4.2 |
| 13 | Florida | 3.2 |
| 7 | Georgia | 4.3 |
| 49 | Hawaii | (0.4) |
| 19 | Idaho | 2.6 |
| 21 | Illinois | 2.5 |
| 25 | Indiana | 2.3 |
| 37 | Iowa | 2.0 |
| 22 | Kansas | 2.4 |
| 25 | Kentucky | 2.3 |
| 29 | Louisiana | 2.2 |
| 37 | Maine | 2.0 |
| 29 | Maryland | 2.2 |
| 15 | Massachusetts | 3.0 |
| 43 | Michigan | 1.7 |
| 11 | Minnesota | 3.3 |
| 37 | Mississippi | 2.0 |
| 19 | Missouri | 2.6 |
| 46 | Montana | 1.2 |
| 29 | Nebraska | 2.2 |
| 2 | Nevada | 5.0 |
| 2 | New Hampshire | 5.0 |
| 22 | New Jersey | 2.4 |
| 48 | New Mexico | 0.8 |
| 29 | New York | 2.2 |
| 11 | North Carolina | 3.3 |
| 35 | North Dakota | 2.1 |
| 37 | Ohio | 2.0 |
| 29 | Oklahoma | 2.2 |
| 6 | Oregon | 4.8 |
| 42 | Pennsylvania | 1.9 |
| 18 | Rhode Island | 2.7 |
| 25 | South Carolina | 2.3 |
| 35 | South Dakota | 2.1 |
| 25 | Tennessee | 2.3 |
| 9 | Texas | 4.0 |
| 1 | Utah | 5.1 |
| 44 | Vermont | 1.5 |
| 13 | Virginia | 3.2 |
| 10 | Washington | 3.7 |
| 47 | West Virginia | 0.9 |
| 22 | Wisconsin | 2.4 |
| 45 | Wyoming | 1.4 |

RANK ORDER

| RANK | STATE | PERCENT CHANGE |
|---|---|---|
| 1 | Utah | 5.1 |
| 2 | Nevada | 5.0 |
| 2 | New Hampshire | 5.0 |
| 4 | Arizona | 4.9 |
| 4 | Colorado | 4.9 |
| 6 | Oregon | 4.8 |
| 7 | Georgia | 4.3 |
| 8 | Delaware | 4.2 |
| 9 | Texas | 4.0 |
| 10 | Washington | 3.7 |
| 11 | Minnesota | 3.3 |
| 11 | North Carolina | 3.3 |
| 13 | Florida | 3.2 |
| 13 | Virginia | 3.2 |
| 15 | California | 3.0 |
| 15 | Massachusetts | 3.0 |
| 17 | Connecticut | 2.8 |
| 18 | Rhode Island | 2.7 |
| 19 | Idaho | 2.6 |
| 19 | Missouri | 2.6 |
| 21 | Illinois | 2.5 |
| 22 | Kansas | 2.4 |
| 22 | New Jersey | 2.4 |
| 22 | Wisconsin | 2.4 |
| 25 | Indiana | 2.3 |
| 25 | Kentucky | 2.3 |
| 25 | South Carolina | 2.3 |
| 25 | Tennessee | 2.3 |
| 29 | Alabama | 2.2 |
| 29 | Louisiana | 2.2 |
| 29 | Maryland | 2.2 |
| 29 | Nebraska | 2.2 |
| 29 | New York | 2.2 |
| 29 | Oklahoma | 2.2 |
| 35 | North Dakota | 2.1 |
| 35 | South Dakota | 2.1 |
| 37 | Arkansas | 2.0 |
| 37 | Iowa | 2.0 |
| 37 | Maine | 2.0 |
| 37 | Mississippi | 2.0 |
| 37 | Ohio | 2.0 |
| 42 | Pennsylvania | 1.9 |
| 43 | Michigan | 1.7 |
| 44 | Vermont | 1.5 |
| 45 | Wyoming | 1.4 |
| 46 | Montana | 1.2 |
| 47 | West Virginia | 0.9 |
| 48 | New Mexico | 0.8 |
| 49 | Hawaii | (0.4) |
| 50 | Alaska | (0.7) |
| | District of Columbia | 0.7 |

Source: Morgan Quitno Press using data from U.S. Department of Commerce, Bureau of Economic Analysis
  "Gross State Product Data" (http://www.bea.doc.gov/bea/regional/gsp/)
*G.S.P. is the market value of goods and services produced by the labor and property located in a state. It is the
state counterpart to the nation's Gross Domestic Product. Adjusted for inflation to 1998 dollars using 1982-1984 as
the index base period.

# Per Capita Gross State Product in 1998

## National Per Capita = $32,360*

Source: Morgan Quitno Press using data from U.S. Department of Commerce, Bureau of Economic Analysis "Gross State Product Data" (http://www.bea.doc.gov/bea/regional/gsp/)
*G.S.P. is the market value of goods and services produced by the labor and property located in a state. It is the state counterpart to the nation's Gross Domestic Product.

# Percent Change in Per Capita Gross State Product: 1994 to 1998
## (Adjusted to Constant 1998 Dollars)
## National Percent Change = 10.5% Increase*

ALPHA ORDER

| RANK | STATE | PERCENT CHANGE |
|------|-------|----------------|
| 36 | Alabama | 8.4 |
| 50 | Alaska | (5.5) |
| 11 | Arizona | 12.9 |
| 40 | Arkansas | 6.5 |
| 16 | California | 11.0 |
| 4 | Colorado | 16.8 |
| 7 | Connecticut | 14.6 |
| 4 | Delaware | 16.8 |
| 27 | Florida | 9.7 |
| 9 | Georgia | 13.7 |
| 49 | Hawaii | (3.2) |
| 46 | Idaho | 4.7 |
| 20 | Illinois | 10.4 |
| 33 | Indiana | 8.7 |
| 29 | Iowa | 9.3 |
| 27 | Kansas | 9.7 |
| 31 | Kentucky | 9.0 |
| 21 | Louisiana | 10.2 |
| 26 | Maine | 9.8 |
| 34 | Maryland | 8.6 |
| 8 | Massachusetts | 13.8 |
| 42 | Michigan | 6.0 |
| 10 | Minnesota | 13.4 |
| 38 | Mississippi | 6.8 |
| 18 | Missouri | 10.5 |
| 47 | Montana | 3.1 |
| 32 | Nebraska | 8.9 |
| 38 | Nevada | 6.8 |
| 1 | New Hampshire | 22.1 |
| 23 | New Jersey | 10.0 |
| 48 | New Mexico | (0.6) |
| 15 | New York | 11.6 |
| 22 | North Carolina | 10.1 |
| 16 | North Dakota | 11.0 |
| 29 | Ohio | 9.3 |
| 35 | Oklahoma | 8.5 |
| 2 | Oregon | 18.9 |
| 18 | Pennsylvania | 10.5 |
| 6 | Rhode Island | 14.8 |
| 37 | South Carolina | 7.2 |
| 23 | South Dakota | 10.0 |
| 41 | Tennessee | 6.4 |
| 11 | Texas | 12.9 |
| 3 | Utah | 17.8 |
| 44 | Vermont | 5.4 |
| 13 | Virginia | 12.4 |
| 14 | Washington | 12.2 |
| 45 | West Virginia | 4.9 |
| 23 | Wisconsin | 10.0 |
| 42 | Wyoming | 6.0 |

RANK ORDER

| RANK | STATE | PERCENT CHANGE |
|------|-------|----------------|
| 1 | New Hampshire | 22.1 |
| 2 | Oregon | 18.9 |
| 3 | Utah | 17.8 |
| 4 | Colorado | 16.8 |
| 4 | Delaware | 16.8 |
| 6 | Rhode Island | 14.8 |
| 7 | Connecticut | 14.6 |
| 8 | Massachusetts | 13.8 |
| 9 | Georgia | 13.7 |
| 10 | Minnesota | 13.4 |
| 11 | Arizona | 12.9 |
| 11 | Texas | 12.9 |
| 13 | Virginia | 12.4 |
| 14 | Washington | 12.2 |
| 15 | New York | 11.6 |
| 16 | California | 11.0 |
| 16 | North Dakota | 11.0 |
| 18 | Missouri | 10.5 |
| 18 | Pennsylvania | 10.5 |
| 20 | Illinois | 10.4 |
| 21 | Louisiana | 10.2 |
| 22 | North Carolina | 10.1 |
| 23 | New Jersey | 10.0 |
| 23 | South Dakota | 10.0 |
| 23 | Wisconsin | 10.0 |
| 26 | Maine | 9.8 |
| 27 | Florida | 9.7 |
| 27 | Kansas | 9.7 |
| 29 | Iowa | 9.3 |
| 29 | Ohio | 9.3 |
| 31 | Kentucky | 9.0 |
| 32 | Nebraska | 8.9 |
| 33 | Indiana | 8.7 |
| 34 | Maryland | 8.6 |
| 35 | Oklahoma | 8.5 |
| 36 | Alabama | 8.4 |
| 37 | South Carolina | 7.2 |
| 38 | Mississippi | 6.8 |
| 38 | Nevada | 6.8 |
| 40 | Arkansas | 6.5 |
| 41 | Tennessee | 6.4 |
| 42 | Michigan | 6.0 |
| 42 | Wyoming | 6.0 |
| 44 | Vermont | 5.4 |
| 45 | West Virginia | 4.9 |
| 46 | Idaho | 4.7 |
| 47 | Montana | 3.1 |
| 48 | New Mexico | (0.6) |
| 49 | Hawaii | (3.2) |
| 50 | Alaska | (5.5) |

District of Columbia     12.2

Source: Morgan Quitno Press using data from U.S. Department of Commerce, Bureau of Economic Analysis
    "Gross State Product Data" (http://www.bea.doc.gov/bea/regional/gsp/)
*G.S.P. is the market value of goods and services produced by the labor and property located in a state. It is the
state counterpart to the nation's Gross Domestic Product. Adjusted for inflation to 1998 dollars using 1982-1984 as
the index base period.

# Fortune 500 Companies in 2000

## National Total = 500 Companies*

ALPHA ORDER

| RANK | STATE | COMPANIES | % of USA |
|------|-------|-----------|----------|
| 19 | Alabama | 7 | 1.4% |
| 41 | Alaska | 0 | 0.0% |
| 26 | Arizona | 4 | 0.8% |
| 26 | Arkansas | 4 | 0.8% |
| 2 | California | 53 | 10.6% |
| 23 | Colorado | 5 | 1.0% |
| 9 | Connecticut | 15 | 3.0% |
| 26 | Delaware | 4 | 0.8% |
| 13 | Florida | 14 | 2.8% |
| 9 | Georgia | 15 | 3.0% |
| 41 | Hawaii | 0 | 0.0% |
| 29 | Idaho | 3 | 0.6% |
| 4 | Illinois | 37 | 7.4% |
| 19 | Indiana | 7 | 1.4% |
| 29 | Iowa | 3 | 0.6% |
| 33 | Kansas | 2 | 0.4% |
| 23 | Kentucky | 5 | 1.0% |
| 36 | Louisiana | 1 | 0.2% |
| 33 | Maine | 2 | 0.4% |
| 19 | Maryland | 7 | 1.4% |
| 15 | Massachusetts | 13 | 2.6% |
| 9 | Michigan | 15 | 3.0% |
| 13 | Minnesota | 14 | 2.8% |
| 36 | Mississippi | 1 | 0.2% |
| 9 | Missouri | 15 | 3.0% |
| 41 | Montana | 0 | 0.0% |
| 22 | Nebraska | 6 | 1.2% |
| 36 | Nevada | 1 | 0.2% |
| 41 | New Hampshire | 0 | 0.0% |
| 7 | New Jersey | 24 | 4.8% |
| 41 | New Mexico | 0 | 0.0% |
| 1 | New York | 56 | 11.2% |
| 16 | North Carolina | 12 | 2.4% |
| 41 | North Dakota | 0 | 0.0% |
| 5 | Ohio | 28 | 5.6% |
| 29 | Oklahoma | 3 | 0.6% |
| 33 | Oregon | 2 | 0.4% |
| 5 | Pennsylvania | 28 | 5.6% |
| 29 | Rhode Island | 3 | 0.6% |
| 41 | South Carolina | 0 | 0.0% |
| 36 | South Dakota | 1 | 0.2% |
| 23 | Tennessee | 5 | 1.0% |
| 3 | Texas | 43 | 8.6% |
| 36 | Utah | 1 | 0.2% |
| 41 | Vermont | 0 | 0.0% |
| 8 | Virginia | 20 | 4.0% |
| 17 | Washington | 10 | 2.0% |
| 41 | West Virginia | 0 | 0.0% |
| 18 | Wisconsin | 9 | 1.8% |
| 41 | Wyoming | 0 | 0.0% |

RANK ORDER

| RANK | STATE | COMPANIES | % of USA |
|------|-------|-----------|----------|
| 1 | New York | 56 | 11.2% |
| 2 | California | 53 | 10.6% |
| 3 | Texas | 43 | 8.6% |
| 4 | Illinois | 37 | 7.4% |
| 5 | Ohio | 28 | 5.6% |
| 5 | Pennsylvania | 28 | 5.6% |
| 7 | New Jersey | 24 | 4.8% |
| 8 | Virginia | 20 | 4.0% |
| 9 | Connecticut | 15 | 3.0% |
| 9 | Georgia | 15 | 3.0% |
| 9 | Michigan | 15 | 3.0% |
| 9 | Missouri | 15 | 3.0% |
| 13 | Florida | 14 | 2.8% |
| 13 | Minnesota | 14 | 2.8% |
| 15 | Massachusetts | 13 | 2.6% |
| 16 | North Carolina | 12 | 2.4% |
| 17 | Washington | 10 | 2.0% |
| 18 | Wisconsin | 9 | 1.8% |
| 19 | Alabama | 7 | 1.4% |
| 19 | Indiana | 7 | 1.4% |
| 19 | Maryland | 7 | 1.4% |
| 22 | Nebraska | 6 | 1.2% |
| 23 | Colorado | 5 | 1.0% |
| 23 | Kentucky | 5 | 1.0% |
| 23 | Tennessee | 5 | 1.0% |
| 26 | Arizona | 4 | 0.8% |
| 26 | Arkansas | 4 | 0.8% |
| 26 | Delaware | 4 | 0.8% |
| 29 | Idaho | 3 | 0.6% |
| 29 | Iowa | 3 | 0.6% |
| 29 | Oklahoma | 3 | 0.6% |
| 29 | Rhode Island | 3 | 0.6% |
| 33 | Kansas | 2 | 0.4% |
| 33 | Maine | 2 | 0.4% |
| 33 | Oregon | 2 | 0.4% |
| 36 | Louisiana | 1 | 0.2% |
| 36 | Mississippi | 1 | 0.2% |
| 36 | Nevada | 1 | 0.2% |
| 36 | South Dakota | 1 | 0.2% |
| 36 | Utah | 1 | 0.2% |
| 41 | Alaska | 0 | 0.0% |
| 41 | Hawaii | 0 | 0.0% |
| 41 | Montana | 0 | 0.0% |
| 41 | New Hampshire | 0 | 0.0% |
| 41 | New Mexico | 0 | 0.0% |
| 41 | North Dakota | 0 | 0.0% |
| 41 | South Carolina | 0 | 0.0% |
| 41 | Vermont | 0 | 0.0% |
| 41 | West Virginia | 0 | 0.0% |
| 41 | Wyoming | 0 | 0.0% |
| | District of Columbia | 2 | 0.4% |

Source: Fortune Magazine
*"Fortune 5 Hundred Ranked Within States" (April 17, 2000)*
*By state where each company's headquarters is located.

# New Business Incorporations in 1998

## National Total = 760,925 New Incorporations*

ALPHA ORDER

| RANK | STATE | NEW CORPS | % of USA |
|------|-------|-----------|----------|
| 26 | Alabama | 7,559 | 1.0% |
| 49 | Alaska | 995 | 0.1% |
| 21 | Arizona | 11,499 | 1.5% |
| 32 | Arkansas | 6,029 | 0.8% |
| 4 | California | 46,935 | 6.2% |
| 16 | Colorado | 14,392 | 1.9% |
| 41 | Connecticut | 2,617 | 0.3% |
| 3 | Delaware | 48,074 | 6.3% |
| 1 | Florida | 109,355 | 14.4% |
| 9 | Georgia | 28,916 | 3.8% |
| 36 | Hawaii | 3,792 | 0.5% |
| 44 | Idaho | 2,322 | 0.3% |
| 6 | Illinois | 35,319 | 4.6% |
| 19 | Indiana | 11,996 | 1.6% |
| 35 | Iowa | 4,173 | 0.5% |
| 34 | Kansas | 4,780 | 0.6% |
| 25 | Kentucky | 7,867 | 1.0% |
| 23 | Louisiana | 9,196 | 1.2% |
| 40 | Maine | 2,669 | 0.4% |
| 15 | Maryland | 16,714 | 2.2% |
| 20 | Massachusetts | 11,798 | 1.6% |
| 8 | Michigan | 28,983 | 3.8% |
| 17 | Minnesota | 12,481 | 1.6% |
| 33 | Mississippi | 5,003 | 0.7% |
| 22 | Missouri | 9,579 | 1.3% |
| 38 | Montana | 2,812 | 0.4% |
| 37 | Nebraska | 3,348 | 0.4% |
| 10 | Nevada | 27,571 | 3.6% |
| 42 | New Hampshire | 2,346 | 0.3% |
| 7 | New Jersey | 29,282 | 3.8% |
| 39 | New Mexico | 2,763 | 0.4% |
| 2 | New York | 72,568 | 9.5% |
| 13 | North Carolina | 17,762 | 2.3% |
| 50 | North Dakota | 762 | 0.1% |
| 14 | Ohio | 17,134 | 2.3% |
| 28 | Oklahoma | 7,349 | 1.0% |
| 24 | Oregon | 8,393 | 1.1% |
| 11 | Pennsylvania | 18,852 | 2.5% |
| 43 | Rhode Island | 2,334 | 0.3% |
| 27 | South Carolina | 7,524 | 1.0% |
| 47 | South Dakota | 1,515 | 0.2% |
| 31 | Tennessee | 6,463 | 0.8% |
| 5 | Texas | 38,829 | 5.1% |
| 30 | Utah | 6,864 | 0.9% |
| 48 | Vermont | 1,217 | 0.2% |
| 12 | Virginia | 17,808 | 2.3% |
| 18 | Washington | 12,179 | 1.6% |
| 45 | West Virginia | 1,908 | 0.3% |
| 29 | Wisconsin | 7,049 | 0.9% |
| 46 | Wyoming | 1,897 | 0.2% |

RANK ORDER

| RANK | STATE | NEW CORPS | % of USA |
|------|-------|-----------|----------|
| 1 | Florida | 109,355 | 14.4% |
| 2 | New York | 72,568 | 9.5% |
| 3 | Delaware | 48,074 | 6.3% |
| 4 | California | 46,935 | 6.2% |
| 5 | Texas | 38,829 | 5.1% |
| 6 | Illinois | 35,319 | 4.6% |
| 7 | New Jersey | 29,282 | 3.8% |
| 8 | Michigan | 28,983 | 3.8% |
| 9 | Georgia | 28,916 | 3.8% |
| 10 | Nevada | 27,571 | 3.6% |
| 11 | Pennsylvania | 18,852 | 2.5% |
| 12 | Virginia | 17,808 | 2.3% |
| 13 | North Carolina | 17,762 | 2.3% |
| 14 | Ohio | 17,134 | 2.3% |
| 15 | Maryland | 16,714 | 2.2% |
| 16 | Colorado | 14,392 | 1.9% |
| 17 | Minnesota | 12,481 | 1.6% |
| 18 | Washington | 12,179 | 1.6% |
| 19 | Indiana | 11,996 | 1.6% |
| 20 | Massachusetts | 11,798 | 1.6% |
| 21 | Arizona | 11,499 | 1.5% |
| 22 | Missouri | 9,579 | 1.3% |
| 23 | Louisiana | 9,196 | 1.2% |
| 24 | Oregon | 8,393 | 1.1% |
| 25 | Kentucky | 7,867 | 1.0% |
| 26 | Alabama | 7,559 | 1.0% |
| 27 | South Carolina | 7,524 | 1.0% |
| 28 | Oklahoma | 7,349 | 1.0% |
| 29 | Wisconsin | 7,049 | 0.9% |
| 30 | Utah | 6,864 | 0.9% |
| 31 | Tennessee | 6,463 | 0.8% |
| 32 | Arkansas | 6,029 | 0.8% |
| 33 | Mississippi | 5,003 | 0.7% |
| 34 | Kansas | 4,780 | 0.6% |
| 35 | Iowa | 4,173 | 0.5% |
| 36 | Hawaii | 3,792 | 0.5% |
| 37 | Nebraska | 3,348 | 0.4% |
| 38 | Montana | 2,812 | 0.4% |
| 39 | New Mexico | 2,763 | 0.4% |
| 40 | Maine | 2,669 | 0.4% |
| 41 | Connecticut | 2,617 | 0.3% |
| 42 | New Hampshire | 2,346 | 0.3% |
| 43 | Rhode Island | 2,334 | 0.3% |
| 44 | Idaho | 2,322 | 0.3% |
| 45 | West Virginia | 1,908 | 0.3% |
| 46 | Wyoming | 1,897 | 0.2% |
| 47 | South Dakota | 1,515 | 0.2% |
| 48 | Vermont | 1,217 | 0.2% |
| 49 | Alaska | 995 | 0.1% |
| 50 | North Dakota | 762 | 0.1% |
| | District of Columbia | 1,353 | 0.2% |

*Source: Economic Analysis Department, The Dun & Bradstreet Corporation*
*"New Business Incorporations" (http://www.dnb.com/newsview/nbi98.htm)*
*\*Estimated. Not seasonally adjusted.*

# Percent Change in New Business Incorporations: 1997 to 1998

## National Percent Change = 4.7% Decrease*

ALPHA ORDER

RANK ORDER

| RANK | STATE | PERCENT CHANGE | RANK | STATE | PERCENT CHANGE |
|------|-------|----------------|------|-------|----------------|
| 13 | Alabama | (2.4) | 1 | South Dakota | 5.2 |
| 24 | Alaska | (6.4) | 2 | Arizona | 2.1 |
| 2 | Arizona | 2.1 | 2 | Nevada | 2.1 |
| 40 | Arkansas | (12.1) | 4 | Mississippi | 1.9 |
| 7 | California | (0.3) | 5 | Florida | 1.0 |
| 33 | Colorado | (8.2) | 6 | Hawaii | 0.0 |
| 50 | Connecticut | (22.5) | 7 | California | (0.3) |
| 32 | Delaware | (7.9) | 8 | Texas | (1.2) |
| 5 | Florida | 1.0 | 9 | Georgia | (1.4) |
| 9 | Georgia | (1.4) | 9 | Kansas | (1.4) |
| 6 | Hawaii | 0.0 | 9 | Minnesota | (1.4) |
| 25 | Idaho | (6.7) | 12 | Illinois | (2.1) |
| 12 | Illinois | (2.1) | 13 | Alabama | (2.4) |
| 21 | Indiana | (5.8) | 14 | New York | (2.5) |
| 37 | Iowa | (11.1) | 14 | Washington | (2.5) |
| 9 | Kansas | (1.4) | 16 | Virginia | (4.8) |
| 23 | Kentucky | (6.3) | 17 | Nebraska | (5.0) |
| 48 | Louisiana | (17.5) | 18 | Massachusetts | (5.1) |
| 20 | Maine | (5.5) | 19 | New Mexico | (5.3) |
| 29 | Maryland | (7.5) | 20 | Maine | (5.5) |
| 18 | Massachusetts | (5.1) | 21 | Indiana | (5.8) |
| 28 | Michigan | (7.3) | 22 | Utah | (6.0) |
| 9 | Minnesota | (1.4) | 23 | Kentucky | (6.3) |
| 4 | Mississippi | 1.9 | 24 | Alaska | (6.4) |
| 26 | Missouri | (6.8) | 25 | Idaho | (6.7) |
| 41 | Montana | (12.6) | 26 | Missouri | (6.8) |
| 17 | Nebraska | (5.0) | 27 | North Carolina | (6.9) |
| 2 | Nevada | 2.1 | 28 | Michigan | (7.3) |
| 46 | New Hampshire | (15.9) | 29 | Maryland | (7.5) |
| 44 | New Jersey | (14.8) | 30 | South Carolina | (7.7) |
| 19 | New Mexico | (5.3) | 31 | West Virginia | (7.8) |
| 14 | New York | (2.5) | 32 | Delaware | (7.9) |
| 27 | North Carolina | (6.9) | 33 | Colorado | (8.2) |
| 49 | North Dakota | (18.3) | 34 | Oregon | (9.6) |
| 44 | Ohio | (14.8) | 35 | Pennsylvania | (9.8) |
| 36 | Oklahoma | (10.0) | 36 | Oklahoma | (10.0) |
| 34 | Oregon | (9.6) | 37 | Iowa | (11.1) |
| 35 | Pennsylvania | (9.8) | 38 | Wisconsin | (11.5) |
| 39 | Rhode Island | (11.9) | 39 | Rhode Island | (11.9) |
| 30 | South Carolina | (7.7) | 40 | Arkansas | (12.1) |
| 1 | South Dakota | 5.2 | 41 | Montana | (12.6) |
| 42 | Tennessee | (13.8) | 42 | Tennessee | (13.8) |
| 8 | Texas | (1.2) | 43 | Vermont | (14.1) |
| 22 | Utah | (6.0) | 44 | New Jersey | (14.8) |
| 43 | Vermont | (14.1) | 44 | Ohio | (14.8) |
| 16 | Virginia | (4.8) | 46 | New Hampshire | (15.9) |
| 14 | Washington | (2.5) | 47 | Wyoming | (16.3) |
| 31 | West Virginia | (7.8) | 48 | Louisiana | (17.5) |
| 38 | Wisconsin | (11.5) | 49 | North Dakota | (18.3) |
| 47 | Wyoming | (16.3) | 50 | Connecticut | (22.5) |
| | | | | District of Columbia | (7.5) |

Source: Economic Analysis Department, The Dun & Bradstreet Corporation
"New Business Incorporations" (http://www.dnb.com/newsview/nbi98.htm)
*Estimated. Not seasonally adjusted.

# Personal Income in 1999

## National Total = $7,783,152,000,000*

### ALPHA ORDER

| RANK | STATE | INCOME | % of USA |
|------|-------|--------|----------|
| 24 | Alabama | $100,452,000,000 | 1.3% |
| 47 | Alaska | 17,704,000,000 | 0.2% |
| 23 | Arizona | 120,360,000,000 | 1.5% |
| 33 | Arkansas | 56,752,000,000 | 0.7% |
| 1 | California | 991,382,000,000 | 12.7% |
| 22 | Colorado | 127,955,000,000 | 1.6% |
| 21 | Connecticut | 128,983,000,000 | 1.7% |
| 44 | Delaware | 23,192,000,000 | 0.3% |
| 4 | Florida | 419,792,000,000 | 5.4% |
| 11 | Georgia | 212,929,000,000 | 2.7% |
| 40 | Hawaii | 32,653,000,000 | 0.4% |
| 43 | Idaho | 28,582,000,000 | 0.4% |
| 5 | Illinois | 377,744,000,000 | 4.9% |
| 16 | Indiana | 155,365,000,000 | 2.0% |
| 30 | Iowa | 73,499,000,000 | 0.9% |
| 31 | Kansas | 71,194,000,000 | 0.9% |
| 26 | Kentucky | 92,036,000,000 | 1.2% |
| 25 | Louisiana | 99,887,000,000 | 1.3% |
| 41 | Maine | 30,828,000,000 | 0.4% |
| 15 | Maryland | 167,895,000,000 | 2.2% |
| 10 | Massachusetts | 219,533,000,000 | 2.8% |
| 9 | Michigan | 277,296,000,000 | 3.6% |
| 17 | Minnesota | 147,050,000,000 | 1.9% |
| 32 | Mississippi | 57,278,000,000 | 0.7% |
| 18 | Missouri | 144,235,000,000 | 1.9% |
| 45 | Montana | 19,438,000,000 | 0.2% |
| 36 | Nebraska | 45,065,000,000 | 0.6% |
| 34 | Nevada | 56,127,000,000 | 0.7% |
| 39 | New Hampshire | 37,372,000,000 | 0.5% |
| 8 | New Jersey | 289,503,000,000 | 3.7% |
| 37 | New Mexico | 38,020,000,000 | 0.5% |
| 2 | New York | 616,678,000,000 | 7.9% |
| 13 | North Carolina | 198,943,000,000 | 2.6% |
| 49 | North Dakota | 14,773,000,000 | 0.2% |
| 7 | Ohio | 305,643,000,000 | 3.9% |
| 29 | Oklahoma | 77,077,000,000 | 1.0% |
| 28 | Oregon | 89,614,000,000 | 1.2% |
| 6 | Pennsylvania | 343,088,000,000 | 4.4% |
| 42 | Rhode Island | 29,107,000,000 | 0.4% |
| 27 | South Carolina | 91,490,000,000 | 1.2% |
| 46 | South Dakota | 18,361,000,000 | 0.2% |
| 20 | Tennessee | 140,234,000,000 | 1.8% |
| 3 | Texas | 538,345,000,000 | 6.9% |
| 35 | Utah | 49,600,000,000 | 0.6% |
| 48 | Vermont | 15,371,000,000 | 0.2% |
| 12 | Virginia | 204,736,000,000 | 2.6% |
| 14 | Washington | 174,948,000,000 | 2.2% |
| 38 | West Virginia | 37,884,000,000 | 0.5% |
| 19 | Wisconsin | 143,811,000,000 | 1.8% |
| 50 | Wyoming | 12,660,000,000 | 0.2% |

### RANK ORDER

| RANK | STATE | INCOME | % of USA |
|------|-------|--------|----------|
| 1 | California | $991,382,000,000 | 12.7% |
| 2 | New York | 616,678,000,000 | 7.9% |
| 3 | Texas | 538,345,000,000 | 6.9% |
| 4 | Florida | 419,792,000,000 | 5.4% |
| 5 | Illinois | 377,744,000,000 | 4.9% |
| 6 | Pennsylvania | 343,088,000,000 | 4.4% |
| 7 | Ohio | 305,643,000,000 | 3.9% |
| 8 | New Jersey | 289,503,000,000 | 3.7% |
| 9 | Michigan | 277,296,000,000 | 3.6% |
| 10 | Massachusetts | 219,533,000,000 | 2.8% |
| 11 | Georgia | 212,929,000,000 | 2.7% |
| 12 | Virginia | 204,736,000,000 | 2.6% |
| 13 | North Carolina | 198,943,000,000 | 2.6% |
| 14 | Washington | 174,948,000,000 | 2.2% |
| 15 | Maryland | 167,895,000,000 | 2.2% |
| 16 | Indiana | 155,365,000,000 | 2.0% |
| 17 | Minnesota | 147,050,000,000 | 1.9% |
| 18 | Missouri | 144,235,000,000 | 1.9% |
| 19 | Wisconsin | 143,811,000,000 | 1.8% |
| 20 | Tennessee | 140,234,000,000 | 1.8% |
| 21 | Connecticut | 128,983,000,000 | 1.7% |
| 22 | Colorado | 127,955,000,000 | 1.6% |
| 23 | Arizona | 120,360,000,000 | 1.5% |
| 24 | Alabama | 100,452,000,000 | 1.3% |
| 25 | Louisiana | 99,887,000,000 | 1.3% |
| 26 | Kentucky | 92,036,000,000 | 1.2% |
| 27 | South Carolina | 91,490,000,000 | 1.2% |
| 28 | Oregon | 89,614,000,000 | 1.2% |
| 29 | Oklahoma | 77,077,000,000 | 1.0% |
| 30 | Iowa | 73,499,000,000 | 0.9% |
| 31 | Kansas | 71,194,000,000 | 0.9% |
| 32 | Mississippi | 57,278,000,000 | 0.7% |
| 33 | Arkansas | 56,752,000,000 | 0.7% |
| 34 | Nevada | 56,127,000,000 | 0.7% |
| 35 | Utah | 49,600,000,000 | 0.6% |
| 36 | Nebraska | 45,065,000,000 | 0.6% |
| 37 | New Mexico | 38,020,000,000 | 0.5% |
| 38 | West Virginia | 37,884,000,000 | 0.5% |
| 39 | New Hampshire | 37,372,000,000 | 0.5% |
| 40 | Hawaii | 32,653,000,000 | 0.4% |
| 41 | Maine | 30,828,000,000 | 0.4% |
| 42 | Rhode Island | 29,107,000,000 | 0.4% |
| 43 | Idaho | 28,582,000,000 | 0.4% |
| 44 | Delaware | 23,192,000,000 | 0.3% |
| 45 | Montana | 19,438,000,000 | 0.2% |
| 46 | South Dakota | 18,361,000,000 | 0.2% |
| 47 | Alaska | 17,704,000,000 | 0.2% |
| 48 | Vermont | 15,371,000,000 | 0.2% |
| 49 | North Dakota | 14,773,000,000 | 0.2% |
| 50 | Wyoming | 12,660,000,000 | 0.2% |
| | District of Columbia | 20,686,000,000 | 0.3% |

Source: U.S. Department of Commerce, Bureau of Economic Analysis
"1999 State Per Capita Personal Income" (http://www.bea.doc.gov/bea/newsrel/spi0900.htm)
*Revised estimates. The national total shown here is the sum of the state estimates. It differs from the national income and product accounts (NIPA) estimate of personal income because it omits the earnings of federal civilian and military personnel stationed abroad and of U.S. residents employed abroad temporarily by private U.S. firms.

# Change in Personal Income: 1998 to 1999

## National Percent Change = 5.4% Increase*

ALPHA ORDER

RANK ORDER

| RANK | STATE | PERCENT CHANGE |
|---|---|---|
| 34 | Alabama | 4.4 |
| 47 | Alaska | 3.1 |
| 6 | Arizona | 6.9 |
| 21 | Arkansas | 5.2 |
| 4 | California | 7.3 |
| 1 | Colorado | 8.0 |
| 21 | Connecticut | 5.2 |
| 18 | Delaware | 5.4 |
| 32 | Florida | 4.6 |
| 7 | Georgia | 6.7 |
| 48 | Hawaii | 2.6 |
| 11 | Idaho | 5.9 |
| 34 | Illinois | 4.4 |
| 34 | Indiana | 4.4 |
| 45 | Iowa | 3.4 |
| 25 | Kansas | 5.0 |
| 31 | Kentucky | 4.7 |
| 49 | Louisiana | 2.4 |
| 25 | Maine | 5.0 |
| 10 | Maryland | 6.1 |
| 5 | Massachusetts | 7.0 |
| 19 | Michigan | 5.3 |
| 17 | Minnesota | 5.5 |
| 39 | Mississippi | 4.0 |
| 34 | Missouri | 4.4 |
| 42 | Montana | 3.6 |
| 28 | Nebraska | 4.9 |
| 1 | Nevada | 8.0 |
| 9 | New Hampshire | 6.2 |
| 38 | New Jersey | 4.2 |
| 42 | New Mexico | 3.6 |
| 19 | New York | 5.3 |
| 42 | North Carolina | 3.6 |
| 50 | North Dakota | 1.7 |
| 39 | Ohio | 4.0 |
| 39 | Oklahoma | 4.0 |
| 21 | Oregon | 5.2 |
| 33 | Pennsylvania | 4.5 |
| 21 | Rhode Island | 5.2 |
| 15 | South Carolina | 5.7 |
| 16 | South Dakota | 5.6 |
| 25 | Tennessee | 5.0 |
| 13 | Texas | 5.8 |
| 11 | Utah | 5.9 |
| 28 | Vermont | 4.9 |
| 8 | Virginia | 6.4 |
| 3 | Washington | 7.4 |
| 46 | West Virginia | 3.3 |
| 28 | Wisconsin | 4.9 |
| 13 | Wyoming | 5.8 |

| RANK | STATE | PERCENT CHANGE |
|---|---|---|
| 1 | Colorado | 8.0 |
| 1 | Nevada | 8.0 |
| 3 | Washington | 7.4 |
| 4 | California | 7.3 |
| 5 | Massachusetts | 7.0 |
| 6 | Arizona | 6.9 |
| 7 | Georgia | 6.7 |
| 8 | Virginia | 6.4 |
| 9 | New Hampshire | 6.2 |
| 10 | Maryland | 6.1 |
| 11 | Idaho | 5.9 |
| 11 | Utah | 5.9 |
| 13 | Texas | 5.8 |
| 13 | Wyoming | 5.8 |
| 15 | South Carolina | 5.7 |
| 16 | South Dakota | 5.6 |
| 17 | Minnesota | 5.5 |
| 18 | Delaware | 5.4 |
| 19 | Michigan | 5.3 |
| 19 | New York | 5.3 |
| 21 | Arkansas | 5.2 |
| 21 | Connecticut | 5.2 |
| 21 | Oregon | 5.2 |
| 21 | Rhode Island | 5.2 |
| 25 | Kansas | 5.0 |
| 25 | Maine | 5.0 |
| 25 | Tennessee | 5.0 |
| 28 | Nebraska | 4.9 |
| 28 | Vermont | 4.9 |
| 28 | Wisconsin | 4.9 |
| 31 | Kentucky | 4.7 |
| 32 | Florida | 4.6 |
| 33 | Pennsylvania | 4.5 |
| 34 | Alabama | 4.4 |
| 34 | Illinois | 4.4 |
| 34 | Indiana | 4.4 |
| 34 | Missouri | 4.4 |
| 38 | New Jersey | 4.2 |
| 39 | Mississippi | 4.0 |
| 39 | Ohio | 4.0 |
| 39 | Oklahoma | 4.0 |
| 42 | Montana | 3.6 |
| 42 | New Mexico | 3.6 |
| 42 | North Carolina | 3.6 |
| 45 | Iowa | 3.4 |
| 46 | West Virginia | 3.3 |
| 47 | Alaska | 3.1 |
| 48 | Hawaii | 2.6 |
| 49 | Louisiana | 2.4 |
| 50 | North Dakota | 1.7 |
| | District of Columbia | 5.2 |

Source: U.S. Department of Commerce, Bureau of Economic Analysis
"1999 State Per Capita Personal Income" (http://www.bea.doc.gov/bea/newsrel/spi0900.htm)
*Based on revised estimates.

# Per Capita Personal Income in 1999

## National Per Capita = $28,542*

ALPHA ORDER

RANK ORDER

| RANK | STATE | PER CAPITA | | RANK | STATE | PER CAPITA |
|------|-------|-----------|---|------|-------|-----------|
| 42 | Alabama | $22,987 | | 1 | Connecticut | $39,300 |
| 17 | Alaska | 28,577 | | 2 | Massachusetts | 35,551 |
| 35 | Arizona | 25,189 | | 2 | New Jersey | 35,551 |
| 46 | Arkansas | 22,244 | | 4 | New York | 33,890 |
| 13 | California | 29,910 | | 5 | Maryland | 32,465 |
| 6 | Colorado | 31,546 | | 6 | Colorado | 31,546 |
| 1 | Connecticut | 39,300 | | 7 | Illinois | 31,145 |
| 11 | Delaware | 30,778 | | 8 | New Hampshire | 31,114 |
| 19 | Florida | 27,780 | | 9 | Nevada | 31,022 |
| 22 | Georgia | 27,340 | | 10 | Minnesota | 30,793 |
| 20 | Hawaii | 27,544 | | 11 | Delaware | 30,778 |
| 45 | Idaho | 22,835 | | 12 | Washington | 30,392 |
| 7 | Illinois | 31,145 | | 13 | California | 29,910 |
| 30 | Indiana | 26,143 | | 14 | Virginia | 29,789 |
| 33 | Iowa | 25,615 | | 15 | Rhode Island | 29,377 |
| 27 | Kansas | 26,824 | | 16 | Pennsylvania | 28,605 |
| 41 | Kentucky | 23,237 | | 17 | Alaska | 28,577 |
| 44 | Louisiana | 22,847 | | 18 | Michigan | 28,113 |
| 37 | Maine | 24,603 | | 19 | Florida | 27,780 |
| 5 | Maryland | 32,465 | | 20 | Hawaii | 27,544 |
| 2 | Massachusetts | 35,551 | | 21 | Wisconsin | 27,390 |
| 18 | Michigan | 28,113 | | 22 | Georgia | 27,340 |
| 10 | Minnesota | 30,793 | | 23 | Ohio | 27,152 |
| 50 | Mississippi | 20,688 | | 24 | Nebraska | 27,049 |
| 29 | Missouri | 26,376 | | 25 | Oregon | 27,023 |
| 47 | Montana | 22,019 | | 26 | Texas | 26,858 |
| 24 | Nebraska | 27,049 | | 27 | Kansas | 26,824 |
| 9 | Nevada | 31,022 | | 28 | Wyoming | 26,396 |
| 8 | New Hampshire | 31,114 | | 29 | Missouri | 26,376 |
| 2 | New Jersey | 35,551 | | 30 | Indiana | 26,143 |
| 48 | New Mexico | 21,853 | | 31 | North Carolina | 26,003 |
| 4 | New York | 33,890 | | 32 | Vermont | 25,889 |
| 31 | North Carolina | 26,003 | | 33 | Iowa | 25,615 |
| 39 | North Dakota | 23,313 | | 34 | Tennessee | 25,574 |
| 23 | Ohio | 27,152 | | 35 | Arizona | 25,189 |
| 43 | Oklahoma | 22,953 | | 36 | South Dakota | 25,045 |
| 25 | Oregon | 27,023 | | 37 | Maine | 24,603 |
| 16 | Pennsylvania | 28,605 | | 38 | South Carolina | 23,545 |
| 15 | Rhode Island | 29,377 | | 39 | North Dakota | 23,313 |
| 38 | South Carolina | 23,545 | | 40 | Utah | 23,288 |
| 36 | South Dakota | 25,045 | | 41 | Kentucky | 23,237 |
| 34 | Tennessee | 25,574 | | 42 | Alabama | 22,987 |
| 26 | Texas | 26,858 | | 43 | Oklahoma | 22,953 |
| 40 | Utah | 23,288 | | 44 | Louisiana | 22,847 |
| 32 | Vermont | 25,889 | | 45 | Idaho | 22,835 |
| 14 | Virginia | 29,789 | | 46 | Arkansas | 22,244 |
| 12 | Washington | 30,392 | | 47 | Montana | 22,019 |
| 49 | West Virginia | 20,966 | | 48 | New Mexico | 21,853 |
| 21 | Wisconsin | 27,390 | | 49 | West Virginia | 20,966 |
| 28 | Wyoming | 26,396 | | 50 | Mississippi | 20,688 |
| | | | | | District of Columbia | 39,858 |

*Source: U.S. Department of Commerce, Bureau of Economic Analysis*
  *"1999 State Per Capita Personal Income" (http://www.bea.doc.gov/bea/newsrel/spi0900.htm)*
*\*Revised estimates. The national figure is based on the sum of the state estimates. It differs from the national income and product accounts (NIPA) estimate of personal income because it omits the earnings of federal civilian and military personnel stationed abroad and of U.S. residents employed abroad temporarily by private U.S. firms.*

# Change in Per Capita Personal Income: 1998 to 1999

## National Percent Change = 4.5% Increase*

ALPHA ORDER

| RANK | STATE | PERCENT CHANGE |
|---|---|---|
| 33 | Alabama | 3.9 |
| 47 | Alaska | 2.4 |
| 20 | Arizona | 4.4 |
| 14 | Arkansas | 4.6 |
| 4 | California | 5.8 |
| 5 | Colorado | 5.6 |
| 10 | Connecticut | 4.9 |
| 27 | Delaware | 4.1 |
| 43 | Florida | 3.2 |
| 14 | Georgia | 4.6 |
| 45 | Hawaii | 3.1 |
| 26 | Idaho | 4.2 |
| 33 | Illinois | 3.9 |
| 35 | Indiana | 3.8 |
| 45 | Iowa | 3.1 |
| 20 | Kansas | 4.4 |
| 32 | Kentucky | 4.0 |
| 49 | Louisiana | 2.2 |
| 14 | Maine | 4.6 |
| 6 | Maryland | 5.2 |
| 1 | Massachusetts | 6.5 |
| 10 | Michigan | 4.9 |
| 20 | Minnesota | 4.4 |
| 40 | Mississippi | 3.4 |
| 35 | Missouri | 3.8 |
| 42 | Montana | 3.3 |
| 14 | Nebraska | 4.6 |
| 27 | Nevada | 4.1 |
| 13 | New Hampshire | 4.8 |
| 38 | New Jersey | 3.6 |
| 43 | New Mexico | 3.2 |
| 8 | New York | 5.1 |
| 49 | North Carolina | 2.2 |
| 47 | North Dakota | 2.4 |
| 35 | Ohio | 3.8 |
| 40 | Oklahoma | 3.4 |
| 27 | Oregon | 4.1 |
| 14 | Pennsylvania | 4.6 |
| 10 | Rhode Island | 4.9 |
| 20 | South Carolina | 4.4 |
| 6 | South Dakota | 5.2 |
| 27 | Tennessee | 4.1 |
| 27 | Texas | 4.1 |
| 19 | Utah | 4.5 |
| 20 | Vermont | 4.4 |
| 8 | Virginia | 5.1 |
| 2 | Washington | 6.1 |
| 38 | West Virginia | 3.6 |
| 20 | Wisconsin | 4.4 |
| 3 | Wyoming | 5.9 |

RANK ORDER

| RANK | STATE | PERCENT CHANGE |
|---|---|---|
| 1 | Massachusetts | 6.5 |
| 2 | Washington | 6.1 |
| 3 | Wyoming | 5.9 |
| 4 | California | 5.8 |
| 5 | Colorado | 5.6 |
| 6 | Maryland | 5.2 |
| 6 | South Dakota | 5.2 |
| 8 | New York | 5.1 |
| 8 | Virginia | 5.1 |
| 10 | Connecticut | 4.9 |
| 10 | Michigan | 4.9 |
| 10 | Rhode Island | 4.9 |
| 13 | New Hampshire | 4.8 |
| 14 | Arkansas | 4.6 |
| 14 | Georgia | 4.6 |
| 14 | Maine | 4.6 |
| 14 | Nebraska | 4.6 |
| 14 | Pennsylvania | 4.6 |
| 19 | Utah | 4.5 |
| 20 | Arizona | 4.4 |
| 20 | Kansas | 4.4 |
| 20 | Minnesota | 4.4 |
| 20 | South Carolina | 4.4 |
| 20 | Vermont | 4.4 |
| 20 | Wisconsin | 4.4 |
| 26 | Idaho | 4.2 |
| 27 | Delaware | 4.1 |
| 27 | Nevada | 4.1 |
| 27 | Oregon | 4.1 |
| 27 | Tennessee | 4.1 |
| 27 | Texas | 4.1 |
| 32 | Kentucky | 4.0 |
| 33 | Alabama | 3.9 |
| 33 | Illinois | 3.9 |
| 35 | Indiana | 3.8 |
| 35 | Missouri | 3.8 |
| 35 | Ohio | 3.8 |
| 38 | New Jersey | 3.6 |
| 38 | West Virginia | 3.6 |
| 40 | Mississippi | 3.4 |
| 40 | Oklahoma | 3.4 |
| 42 | Montana | 3.3 |
| 43 | Florida | 3.2 |
| 43 | New Mexico | 3.2 |
| 45 | Hawaii | 3.1 |
| 45 | Iowa | 3.1 |
| 47 | Alaska | 2.4 |
| 47 | North Dakota | 2.4 |
| 49 | Louisiana | 2.2 |
| 49 | North Carolina | 2.2 |
| | District of Columbia | 5.7 |

Source: U.S. Department of Commerce, Bureau of Economic Analysis
    "1999 State Per Capita Personal Income" (http://www.bea.doc.gov/bea/newsrel/spi0900.htm)
*Based on revised estimates.

# Per Capita Disposable Personal Income in 1999

## National Per Capita = $24,322*

| ALPHA ORDER | | | RANK ORDER | | |
|---|---|---|---|---|---|
| RANK | STATE | PER CAPITA | RANK | STATE | PER CAPITA |
| 42 | Alabama | $20,170 | 1 | Connecticut | $31,697 |
| 16 | Alaska | 25,022 | 2 | New Jersey | 29,683 |
| 36 | Arizona | 21,721 | 3 | Massachusetts | 29,294 |
| 46 | Arkansas | 19,532 | 4 | New York | 28,020 |
| 14 | California | 25,195 | 5 | Maryland | 27,116 |
| 8 | Colorado | 26,674 | 6 | New Hampshire | 26,973 |
| 1 | Connecticut | 31,697 | 7 | Nevada | 26,685 |
| 12 | Delaware | 26,021 | 8 | Colorado | 26,674 |
| 19 | Florida | 23,981 | 9 | Illinois | 26,384 |
| 22 | Georgia | 23,378 | 10 | Minnesota | 26,113 |
| 18 | Hawaii | 24,075 | 11 | Washington | 26,041 |
| 45 | Idaho | 19,883 | 12 | Delaware | 26,021 |
| 9 | Illinois | 26,384 | 13 | Rhode Island | 25,342 |
| 34 | Indiana | 22,279 | 14 | California | 25,195 |
| 33 | Iowa | 22,296 | 15 | Virginia | 25,139 |
| 26 | Kansas | 23,146 | 16 | Alaska | 25,022 |
| 43 | Kentucky | 20,033 | 17 | Pennsylvania | 24,456 |
| 41 | Louisiana | 20,171 | 18 | Hawaii | 24,075 |
| 37 | Maine | 21,165 | 19 | Florida | 23,981 |
| 5 | Maryland | 27,116 | 20 | Michigan | 23,836 |
| 3 | Massachusetts | 29,294 | 21 | Texas | 23,544 |
| 20 | Michigan | 23,836 | 22 | Georgia | 23,378 |
| 10 | Minnesota | 26,113 | 23 | Nebraska | 23,370 |
| 50 | Mississippi | 18,467 | 24 | Wisconsin | 23,163 |
| 28 | Missouri | 22,745 | 25 | Ohio | 23,150 |
| 47 | Montana | 19,303 | 26 | Kansas | 23,146 |
| 23 | Nebraska | 23,370 | 27 | Oregon | 23,003 |
| 7 | Nevada | 26,685 | 28 | Missouri | 22,745 |
| 6 | New Hampshire | 26,973 | 29 | Tennessee | 22,674 |
| 2 | New Jersey | 29,683 | 30 | Wyoming | 22,654 |
| 48 | New Mexico | 19,229 | 31 | South Dakota | 22,463 |
| 4 | New York | 28,020 | 32 | Vermont | 22,318 |
| 35 | North Carolina | 22,227 | 33 | Iowa | 22,296 |
| 38 | North Dakota | 20,692 | 34 | Indiana | 22,279 |
| 25 | Ohio | 23,150 | 35 | North Carolina | 22,227 |
| 44 | Oklahoma | 20,023 | 36 | Arizona | 21,721 |
| 27 | Oregon | 23,003 | 37 | Maine | 21,165 |
| 17 | Pennsylvania | 24,456 | 38 | North Dakota | 20,692 |
| 13 | Rhode Island | 25,342 | 39 | South Carolina | 20,555 |
| 39 | South Carolina | 20,555 | 40 | Utah | 20,222 |
| 31 | South Dakota | 22,463 | 41 | Louisiana | 20,171 |
| 29 | Tennessee | 22,674 | 42 | Alabama | 20,170 |
| 21 | Texas | 23,544 | 43 | Kentucky | 20,033 |
| 40 | Utah | 20,222 | 44 | Oklahoma | 20,023 |
| 32 | Vermont | 22,318 | 45 | Idaho | 19,883 |
| 15 | Virginia | 25,139 | 46 | Arkansas | 19,532 |
| 11 | Washington | 26,041 | 47 | Montana | 19,303 |
| 49 | West Virginia | 18,498 | 48 | New Mexico | 19,229 |
| 24 | Wisconsin | 23,163 | 49 | West Virginia | 18,498 |
| 30 | Wyoming | 22,654 | 50 | Mississippi | 18,467 |
| | | | | District of Columbia | 32,905 |

Source: U.S. Department of Commerce, Bureau of Economic Analysis
    "Survey of Current Business" (October 2000)

*Revised estimates. Disposable personal income is personal income less personal tax and nontax payments. It is the income available to persons for spending or saving.

# Median Household Income in 1999

## National Median = $39,657*

ALPHA ORDER

| RANK | STATE | INCOME |
|---|---|---|
| 37 | Alabama | $35,478 |
| 1 | Alaska | 51,046 |
| 34 | Arizona | 36,337 |
| 50 | Arkansas | 28,398 |
| 17 | California | 42,262 |
| 5 | Colorado | 46,950 |
| 4 | Connecticut | 47,997 |
| 11 | Delaware | 44,627 |
| 40 | Florida | 35,081 |
| 24 | Georgia | 39,003 |
| 16 | Hawaii | 42,864 |
| 36 | Idaho | 36,023 |
| 12 | Illinois | 44,459 |
| 19 | Indiana | 40,635 |
| 28 | Iowa | 38,047 |
| 29 | Kansas | 37,618 |
| 39 | Kentucky | 35,226 |
| 44 | Louisiana | 33,218 |
| 33 | Maine | 36,459 |
| 2 | Maryland | 50,630 |
| 13 | Massachusetts | 43,697 |
| 14 | Michigan | 43,066 |
| 6 | Minnesota | 46,802 |
| 48 | Mississippi | 30,628 |
| 21 | Missouri | 40,166 |
| 47 | Montana | 31,280 |
| 30 | Nebraska | 37,338 |
| 18 | Nevada | 40,882 |
| 9 | New Hampshire | 44,891 |
| 3 | New Jersey | 50,234 |
| 46 | New Mexico | 31,981 |
| 27 | New York | 38,479 |
| 32 | North Carolina | 37,057 |
| 45 | North Dakota | 32,238 |
| 25 | Ohio | 38,970 |
| 43 | Oklahoma | 33,311 |
| 22 | Oregon | 39,768 |
| 26 | Pennsylvania | 38,938 |
| 20 | Rhode Island | 40,213 |
| 38 | South Carolina | 35,376 |
| 42 | South Dakota | 33,438 |
| 41 | Tennessee | 34,393 |
| 31 | Texas | 37,320 |
| 8 | Utah | 45,257 |
| 23 | Vermont | 39,419 |
| 10 | Virginia | 44,884 |
| 7 | Washington | 46,788 |
| 49 | West Virginia | 28,420 |
| 15 | Wisconsin | 43,055 |
| 35 | Wyoming | 36,039 |

RANK ORDER

| RANK | STATE | INCOME |
|---|---|---|
| 1 | Alaska | $51,046 |
| 2 | Maryland | 50,630 |
| 3 | New Jersey | 50,234 |
| 4 | Connecticut | 47,997 |
| 5 | Colorado | 46,950 |
| 6 | Minnesota | 46,802 |
| 7 | Washington | 46,788 |
| 8 | Utah | 45,257 |
| 9 | New Hampshire | 44,891 |
| 10 | Virginia | 44,884 |
| 11 | Delaware | 44,627 |
| 12 | Illinois | 44,459 |
| 13 | Massachusetts | 43,697 |
| 14 | Michigan | 43,066 |
| 15 | Wisconsin | 43,055 |
| 16 | Hawaii | 42,864 |
| 17 | California | 42,262 |
| 18 | Nevada | 40,882 |
| 19 | Indiana | 40,635 |
| 20 | Rhode Island | 40,213 |
| 21 | Missouri | 40,166 |
| 22 | Oregon | 39,768 |
| 23 | Vermont | 39,419 |
| 24 | Georgia | 39,003 |
| 25 | Ohio | 38,970 |
| 26 | Pennsylvania | 38,938 |
| 27 | New York | 38,479 |
| 28 | Iowa | 38,047 |
| 29 | Kansas | 37,618 |
| 30 | Nebraska | 37,338 |
| 31 | Texas | 37,320 |
| 32 | North Carolina | 37,057 |
| 33 | Maine | 36,459 |
| 34 | Arizona | 36,337 |
| 35 | Wyoming | 36,039 |
| 36 | Idaho | 36,023 |
| 37 | Alabama | 35,478 |
| 38 | South Carolina | 35,376 |
| 39 | Kentucky | 35,226 |
| 40 | Florida | 35,081 |
| 41 | Tennessee | 34,393 |
| 42 | South Dakota | 33,438 |
| 43 | Oklahoma | 33,311 |
| 44 | Louisiana | 33,218 |
| 45 | North Dakota | 32,238 |
| 46 | New Mexico | 31,981 |
| 47 | Montana | 31,280 |
| 48 | Mississippi | 30,628 |
| 49 | West Virginia | 28,420 |
| 50 | Arkansas | 28,398 |
| | District of Columbia | 35,309 |

Source: U.S. Bureau of the Census
   "Median Income of Households by State" (http://www.census.gov/hhes/income/income99/99tabled.html)
*Three-year average: 1997-1999.

# Per Capita Total Taxes in 1999

## National Per Capita = $10,298*

| ALPHA ORDER | | | RANK ORDER | | |
|---|---|---|---|---|---|
| RANK | STATE | TAXES | RANK | STATE | TAXES |
| 43 | Alabama | $7,621 | 1 | Connecticut | $16,139 |
| 35 | Alaska | 8,608 | 2 | New Jersey | 13,785 |
| 31 | Arizona | 9,041 | 3 | New York | 13,420 |
| 47 | Arkansas | 7,222 | 4 | Massachusetts | 13,016 |
| 10 | California | 10,879 | 5 | Illinois | 11,638 |
| 14 | Colorado | 10,414 | 6 | Minnesota | 11,560 |
| 1 | Connecticut | 16,139 | 7 | Maryland | 11,410 |
| 11 | Delaware | 10,802 | 8 | Washington | 11,359 |
| 16 | Florida | 10,337 | 9 | Nevada | 10,997 |
| 23 | Georgia | 9,512 | 10 | California | 10,879 |
| 22 | Hawaii | 9,613 | 11 | Delaware | 10,802 |
| 42 | Idaho | 7,656 | 12 | Michigan | 10,514 |
| 5 | Illinois | 11,638 | 13 | Rhode Island | 10,479 |
| 29 | Indiana | 9,062 | 14 | Colorado | 10,414 |
| 28 | Iowa | 9,101 | 15 | New Hampshire | 10,400 |
| 25 | Kansas | 9,481 | 16 | Florida | 10,337 |
| 39 | Kentucky | 7,985 | 17 | Wisconsin | 10,312 |
| 40 | Louisiana | 7,912 | 18 | Pennsylvania | 10,189 |
| 30 | Maine | 9,052 | 19 | Virginia | 10,133 |
| 7 | Maryland | 11,410 | 20 | Ohio | 9,713 |
| 4 | Massachusetts | 13,016 | 21 | Oregon | 9,648 |
| 12 | Michigan | 10,514 | 22 | Hawaii | 9,613 |
| 6 | Minnesota | 11,560 | 23 | Georgia | 9,512 |
| 49 | Mississippi | 6,925 | 24 | Nebraska | 9,500 |
| 27 | Missouri | 9,189 | 25 | Kansas | 9,481 |
| 48 | Montana | 7,199 | 26 | Texas | 9,338 |
| 24 | Nebraska | 9,500 | 27 | Missouri | 9,189 |
| 9 | Nevada | 10,997 | 28 | Iowa | 9,101 |
| 15 | New Hampshire | 10,400 | 29 | Indiana | 9,062 |
| 2 | New Jersey | 13,785 | 30 | Maine | 9,052 |
| 46 | New Mexico | 7,400 | 31 | Arizona | 9,041 |
| 3 | New York | 13,420 | 32 | Vermont | 8,946 |
| 33 | North Carolina | 8,941 | 33 | North Carolina | 8,941 |
| 45 | North Dakota | 7,483 | 34 | Wyoming | 8,651 |
| 20 | Ohio | 9,713 | 35 | Alaska | 8,608 |
| 44 | Oklahoma | 7,609 | 36 | Tennessee | 8,484 |
| 21 | Oregon | 9,648 | 37 | South Carolina | 8,117 |
| 18 | Pennsylvania | 10,189 | 38 | Utah | 8,031 |
| 13 | Rhode Island | 10,479 | 39 | Kentucky | 7,985 |
| 37 | South Carolina | 8,117 | 40 | Louisiana | 7,912 |
| 41 | South Dakota | 7,831 | 41 | South Dakota | 7,831 |
| 36 | Tennessee | 8,484 | 42 | Idaho | 7,656 |
| 26 | Texas | 9,338 | 43 | Alabama | 7,621 |
| 38 | Utah | 8,031 | 44 | Oklahoma | 7,609 |
| 32 | Vermont | 8,946 | 45 | North Dakota | 7,483 |
| 19 | Virginia | 10,133 | 46 | New Mexico | 7,400 |
| 8 | Washington | 11,359 | 47 | Arkansas | 7,222 |
| 50 | West Virginia | 6,801 | 48 | Montana | 7,199 |
| 17 | Wisconsin | 10,312 | 49 | Mississippi | 6,925 |
| 34 | Wyoming | 8,651 | 50 | West Virginia | 6,801 |
| | | | | District of Columbia | 15,150 |

Source: The Tax Foundation
   "The Price of Civilized Society" (http://www.taxfoundation.org)
*Includes federal, state and local taxes.

# Per Capita Total Taxes as a Percent of
# Per Capita Personal Income in 1999
# National Percent = 36.1% of Per Capita Personal Income*

ALPHA ORDER

| RANK | STATE | PERCENT |
|---|---|---|
| 40 | Alabama | 33.2 |
| 50 | Alaska | 30.1 |
| 13 | Arizona | 35.9 |
| 46 | Arkansas | 32.5 |
| 12 | California | 36.4 |
| 43 | Colorado | 33.0 |
| 1 | Connecticut | 41.1 |
| 21 | Delaware | 35.1 |
| 9 | Florida | 37.2 |
| 25 | Georgia | 34.8 |
| 24 | Hawaii | 34.9 |
| 37 | Idaho | 33.5 |
| 6 | Illinois | 37.4 |
| 28 | Indiana | 34.7 |
| 18 | Iowa | 35.5 |
| 20 | Kansas | 35.3 |
| 33 | Kentucky | 34.4 |
| 29 | Louisiana | 34.6 |
| 10 | Maine | 36.8 |
| 21 | Maryland | 35.1 |
| 11 | Massachusetts | 36.6 |
| 6 | Michigan | 37.4 |
| 5 | Minnesota | 37.5 |
| 37 | Mississippi | 33.5 |
| 25 | Missouri | 34.8 |
| 45 | Montana | 32.7 |
| 21 | Nebraska | 35.1 |
| 19 | Nevada | 35.4 |
| 39 | New Hampshire | 33.4 |
| 3 | New Jersey | 38.8 |
| 36 | New Mexico | 33.9 |
| 2 | New York | 39.6 |
| 33 | North Carolina | 34.4 |
| 48 | North Dakota | 32.1 |
| 14 | Ohio | 35.8 |
| 40 | Oklahoma | 33.2 |
| 15 | Oregon | 35.7 |
| 17 | Pennsylvania | 35.6 |
| 15 | Rhode Island | 35.7 |
| 31 | South Carolina | 34.5 |
| 49 | South Dakota | 31.3 |
| 40 | Tennessee | 33.2 |
| 25 | Texas | 34.8 |
| 31 | Utah | 34.5 |
| 29 | Vermont | 34.6 |
| 35 | Virginia | 34.0 |
| 6 | Washington | 37.4 |
| 47 | West Virginia | 32.4 |
| 4 | Wisconsin | 37.6 |
| 44 | Wyoming | 32.8 |

RANK ORDER

| RANK | STATE | PERCENT |
|---|---|---|
| 1 | Connecticut | 41.1 |
| 2 | New York | 39.6 |
| 3 | New Jersey | 38.8 |
| 4 | Wisconsin | 37.6 |
| 5 | Minnesota | 37.5 |
| 6 | Illinois | 37.4 |
| 6 | Michigan | 37.4 |
| 6 | Washington | 37.4 |
| 9 | Florida | 37.2 |
| 10 | Maine | 36.8 |
| 11 | Massachusetts | 36.6 |
| 12 | California | 36.4 |
| 13 | Arizona | 35.9 |
| 14 | Ohio | 35.8 |
| 15 | Oregon | 35.7 |
| 15 | Rhode Island | 35.7 |
| 17 | Pennsylvania | 35.6 |
| 18 | Iowa | 35.5 |
| 19 | Nevada | 35.4 |
| 20 | Kansas | 35.3 |
| 21 | Delaware | 35.1 |
| 21 | Maryland | 35.1 |
| 21 | Nebraska | 35.1 |
| 24 | Hawaii | 34.9 |
| 25 | Georgia | 34.8 |
| 25 | Missouri | 34.8 |
| 25 | Texas | 34.8 |
| 28 | Indiana | 34.7 |
| 29 | Louisiana | 34.6 |
| 29 | Vermont | 34.6 |
| 31 | South Carolina | 34.5 |
| 31 | Utah | 34.5 |
| 33 | Kentucky | 34.4 |
| 33 | North Carolina | 34.4 |
| 35 | Virginia | 34.0 |
| 36 | New Mexico | 33.9 |
| 37 | Idaho | 33.5 |
| 37 | Mississippi | 33.5 |
| 39 | New Hampshire | 33.4 |
| 40 | Alabama | 33.2 |
| 40 | Oklahoma | 33.2 |
| 40 | Tennessee | 33.2 |
| 43 | Colorado | 33.0 |
| 44 | Wyoming | 32.8 |
| 45 | Montana | 32.7 |
| 46 | Arkansas | 32.5 |
| 47 | West Virginia | 32.4 |
| 48 | North Dakota | 32.1 |
| 49 | South Dakota | 31.3 |
| 50 | Alaska | 30.1 |
| | District of Columbia | 38.0 |

*Source: Morgan Quitno Press using data from The Tax Foundation*
*"The Price of Civilized Society" (http://www.taxfoundation.org) and*
*U.S. Department of Commerce, Bureau of Economic Analysis*
*"1999 State Per Capita Personal Income" (http://www.bea.doc.gov/bea/newsrel/spi0900.htm)*
*Includes federal, state and local taxes.*

# Retail Sales in 1997

## National Total = $2,545,881,473,000*

### ALPHA ORDER

| RANK | STATE | RETAIL SALES | % of USA |
|------|-------|-------------|----------|
| 21 | Alabama | $37,614,376,000 | 1.5% |
| 45 | Alaska | 6,598,019,000 | 0.3% |
| 19 | Arizona | 44,916,454,000 | 1.8% |
| 30 | Arkansas | 21,903,527,000 | 0.9% |
| NA | California** | NA | NA |
| 20 | Colorado | 42,188,444,000 | 1.7% |
| 23 | Connecticut | 35,832,852,000 | 1.4% |
| 42 | Delaware | 8,555,393,000 | 0.3% |
| 2 | Florida | 158,693,907,000 | 6.2% |
| 10 | Georgia | 74,096,020,000 | 2.9% |
| 39 | Hawaii | 12,837,212,000 | 0.5% |
| 40 | Idaho | 11,510,569,000 | 0.5% |
| 5 | Illinois | 111,805,925,000 | 4.4% |
| 13 | Indiana | 59,181,921,000 | 2.3% |
| 28 | Iowa | 26,283,470,000 | 1.0% |
| 29 | Kansas | 23,080,403,000 | 0.9% |
| 25 | Kentucky | 34,364,705,000 | 1.3% |
| 22 | Louisiana | 37,222,865,000 | 1.5% |
| 38 | Maine | 13,275,829,000 | 0.5% |
| 18 | Maryland | 48,297,830,000 | 1.9% |
| 12 | Massachusetts | 62,533,487,000 | 2.5% |
| 7 | Michigan | 96,836,422,000 | 3.8% |
| 17 | Minnesota | 48,814,277,000 | 1.9% |
| 31 | Mississippi | 20,923,871,000 | 0.8% |
| 15 | Missouri | 52,001,235,000 | 2.0% |
| 44 | Montana | 8,014,759,000 | 0.3% |
| 34 | Nebraska | 16,350,932,000 | 0.6% |
| 33 | Nevada | 19,019,702,000 | 0.7% |
| 35 | New Hampshire | 16,264,348,000 | 0.6% |
| 8 | New Jersey | 81,672,814,000 | 3.2% |
| 36 | New Mexico | 15,585,757,000 | 0.6% |
| 3 | New York | 148,865,467,000 | 5.8% |
| 9 | North Carolina | 74,507,525,000 | 2.9% |
| 46 | North Dakota | 6,382,015,000 | 0.3% |
| 6 | Ohio | 107,417,375,000 | 4.2% |
| 27 | Oklahoma | 28,306,597,000 | 1.1% |
| 26 | Oregon | 34,066,578,000 | 1.3% |
| 4 | Pennsylvania | 113,092,636,000 | 4.4% |
| 43 | Rhode Island | 8,207,824,000 | 0.3% |
| 24 | South Carolina | 34,912,588,000 | 1.4% |
| 41 | South Dakota | 9,872,544,000 | 0.4% |
| 14 | Tennessee | 52,750,245,000 | 2.1% |
| 1 | Texas | 183,274,112,000 | 7.2% |
| 32 | Utah | 20,110,336,000 | 0.8% |
| 47 | Vermont | 6,018,347,000 | 0.2% |
| 11 | Virginia | 64,575,911,000 | 2.5% |
| NA | Washington** | NA | NA |
| 37 | West Virginia | 14,639,608,000 | 0.6% |
| 16 | Wisconsin | 51,066,574,000 | 2.0% |
| NA | Wyoming** | NA | NA |

### RANK ORDER

| RANK | STATE | RETAIL SALES | % of USA |
|------|-------|-------------|----------|
| 1 | Texas | $183,274,112,000 | 7.2% |
| 2 | Florida | 158,693,907,000 | 6.2% |
| 3 | New York | 148,865,467,000 | 5.8% |
| 4 | Pennsylvania | 113,092,636,000 | 4.4% |
| 5 | Illinois | 111,805,925,000 | 4.4% |
| 6 | Ohio | 107,417,375,000 | 4.2% |
| 7 | Michigan | 96,836,422,000 | 3.8% |
| 8 | New Jersey | 81,672,814,000 | 3.2% |
| 9 | North Carolina | 74,507,525,000 | 2.9% |
| 10 | Georgia | 74,096,020,000 | 2.9% |
| 11 | Virginia | 64,575,911,000 | 2.5% |
| 12 | Massachusetts | 62,533,487,000 | 2.5% |
| 13 | Indiana | 59,181,921,000 | 2.3% |
| 14 | Tennessee | 52,750,245,000 | 2.1% |
| 15 | Missouri | 52,001,235,000 | 2.0% |
| 16 | Wisconsin | 51,066,574,000 | 2.0% |
| 17 | Minnesota | 48,814,277,000 | 1.9% |
| 18 | Maryland | 48,297,830,000 | 1.9% |
| 19 | Arizona | 44,916,454,000 | 1.8% |
| 20 | Colorado | 42,188,444,000 | 1.7% |
| 21 | Alabama | 37,614,376,000 | 1.5% |
| 22 | Louisiana | 37,222,865,000 | 1.5% |
| 23 | Connecticut | 35,832,852,000 | 1.4% |
| 24 | South Carolina | 34,912,588,000 | 1.4% |
| 25 | Kentucky | 34,364,705,000 | 1.3% |
| 26 | Oregon | 34,066,578,000 | 1.3% |
| 27 | Oklahoma | 28,306,597,000 | 1.1% |
| 28 | Iowa | 26,283,470,000 | 1.0% |
| 29 | Kansas | 23,080,403,000 | 0.9% |
| 30 | Arkansas | 21,903,527,000 | 0.9% |
| 31 | Mississippi | 20,923,871,000 | 0.8% |
| 32 | Utah | 20,110,336,000 | 0.8% |
| 33 | Nevada | 19,019,702,000 | 0.7% |
| 34 | Nebraska | 16,350,932,000 | 0.6% |
| 35 | New Hampshire | 16,264,348,000 | 0.6% |
| 36 | New Mexico | 15,585,757,000 | 0.6% |
| 37 | West Virginia | 14,639,608,000 | 0.6% |
| 38 | Maine | 13,275,829,000 | 0.5% |
| 39 | Hawaii | 12,837,212,000 | 0.5% |
| 40 | Idaho | 11,510,569,000 | 0.5% |
| 41 | South Dakota | 9,872,544,000 | 0.4% |
| 42 | Delaware | 8,555,393,000 | 0.3% |
| 43 | Rhode Island | 8,207,824,000 | 0.3% |
| 44 | Montana | 8,014,759,000 | 0.3% |
| 45 | Alaska | 6,598,019,000 | 0.3% |
| 46 | North Dakota | 6,382,015,000 | 0.3% |
| 47 | Vermont | 6,018,347,000 | 0.2% |
| NA | California** | NA | NA |
| NA | Washington** | NA | NA |
| NA | Wyoming** | NA | NA |
| | District of Columbia** | NA | NA |

Source: U.S. Bureau of the Census
     "1997 Economic Census, Comparative Statistics"
*National total includes states not shown separately.  Sales are net after deductions for returns and refunds.  Sales do not include credit charges or taxes collected on sales.
**Not available.

# Per Capita Retail Sales in 1997

## National Per Capita = $9,628 in Sales*

ALPHA ORDER

| RANK | STATE | PER CAPITA |
|------|-------|------------|
| 40 | Alabama | $8,706 |
| 7 | Alaska | 10,837 |
| 22 | Arizona | 9,867 |
| 41 | Arkansas | 8,678 |
| NA | California** | NA |
| 6 | Colorado | 10,842 |
| 5 | Connecticut | 10,963 |
| 3 | Delaware | 11,640 |
| 8 | Florida | 10,808 |
| 19 | Georgia | 9,898 |
| 9 | Hawaii | 10,794 |
| 29 | Idaho | 9,508 |
| 33 | Illinois | 9,308 |
| 16 | Indiana | 10,078 |
| 35 | Iowa | 9,208 |
| 38 | Kansas | 8,822 |
| 39 | Kentucky | 8,794 |
| 42 | Louisiana | 8,554 |
| 10 | Maine | 10,661 |
| 30 | Maryland | 9,483 |
| 13 | Massachusetts | 10,225 |
| 20 | Michigan | 9,896 |
| 12 | Minnesota | 10,413 |
| 47 | Mississippi | 7,659 |
| 26 | Missouri | 9,617 |
| 36 | Montana | 9,121 |
| 21 | Nebraska | 9,874 |
| 4 | Nevada | 11,351 |
| 1 | New Hampshire | 13,863 |
| 15 | New Jersey | 10,140 |
| 37 | New Mexico | 9,046 |
| 45 | New York | 8,205 |
| 17 | North Carolina | 10,030 |
| 18 | North Dakota | 9,957 |
| 28 | Ohio | 9,580 |
| 43 | Oklahoma | 8,541 |
| 11 | Oregon | 10,504 |
| 32 | Pennsylvania | 9,412 |
| 44 | Rhode Island | 8,316 |
| 34 | South Carolina | 9,212 |
| 2 | South Dakota | 13,508 |
| 24 | Tennessee | 9,808 |
| 31 | Texas | 9,469 |
| 25 | Utah | 9,737 |
| 14 | Vermont | 10,224 |
| 27 | Virginia | 9,591 |
| NA | Washington** | NA |
| 46 | West Virginia | 8,063 |
| 23 | Wisconsin | 9,820 |
| NA | Wyoming** | NA |

RANK ORDER

| RANK | STATE | PER CAPITA |
|------|-------|------------|
| 1 | New Hampshire | $13,863 |
| 2 | South Dakota | 13,508 |
| 3 | Delaware | 11,640 |
| 4 | Nevada | 11,351 |
| 5 | Connecticut | 10,963 |
| 6 | Colorado | 10,842 |
| 7 | Alaska | 10,837 |
| 8 | Florida | 10,808 |
| 9 | Hawaii | 10,794 |
| 10 | Maine | 10,661 |
| 11 | Oregon | 10,504 |
| 12 | Minnesota | 10,413 |
| 13 | Massachusetts | 10,225 |
| 14 | Vermont | 10,224 |
| 15 | New Jersey | 10,140 |
| 16 | Indiana | 10,078 |
| 17 | North Carolina | 10,030 |
| 18 | North Dakota | 9,957 |
| 19 | Georgia | 9,898 |
| 20 | Michigan | 9,896 |
| 21 | Nebraska | 9,874 |
| 22 | Arizona | 9,867 |
| 23 | Wisconsin | 9,820 |
| 24 | Tennessee | 9,808 |
| 25 | Utah | 9,737 |
| 26 | Missouri | 9,617 |
| 27 | Virginia | 9,591 |
| 28 | Ohio | 9,580 |
| 29 | Idaho | 9,508 |
| 30 | Maryland | 9,483 |
| 31 | Texas | 9,469 |
| 32 | Pennsylvania | 9,412 |
| 33 | Illinois | 9,308 |
| 34 | South Carolina | 9,212 |
| 35 | Iowa | 9,208 |
| 36 | Montana | 9,121 |
| 37 | New Mexico | 9,046 |
| 38 | Kansas | 8,822 |
| 39 | Kentucky | 8,794 |
| 40 | Alabama | 8,706 |
| 41 | Arkansas | 8,678 |
| 42 | Louisiana | 8,554 |
| 43 | Oklahoma | 8,541 |
| 44 | Rhode Island | 8,316 |
| 45 | New York | 8,205 |
| 46 | West Virginia | 8,063 |
| 47 | Mississippi | 7,659 |
| NA | California** | NA |
| NA | Washington** | NA |
| NA | Wyoming** | NA |
| | District of Columbia** | NA |

Source: Morgan Quitno Press using data from U.S. Bureau of the Census
    "1997 Economic Census, Comparative Statistics"
*National rate based only on sales and population of reporting states. Sales are net after deductions for returns and refunds. Sales do not include credit charges or taxes collected on sales.
**Not available.

# Bankruptcy Filings in 2000

## National Total = 1,262,102 Bankruptcies*

ALPHA ORDER

| RANK | STATE | BANKRUPTCIES | % of USA |
|------|-------|--------------|----------|
| 14 | Alabama | 32,345 | 2.6% |
| 50 | Alaska | 1,412 | 0.1% |
| 20 | Arizona | 21,205 | 1.7% |
| 26 | Arkansas | 16,683 | 1.3% |
| 1 | California | 150,870 | 12.0% |
| 28 | Colorado | 15,458 | 1.2% |
| 34 | Connecticut | 10,968 | 0.9% |
| 40 | Delaware | 4,849 | 0.4% |
| 2 | Florida | 73,438 | 5.8% |
| 6 | Georgia | 58,574 | 4.6% |
| 42 | Hawaii | 4,667 | 0.4% |
| 37 | Idaho | 7,155 | 0.6% |
| 3 | Illinois | 61,953 | 4.9% |
| 11 | Indiana | 37,587 | 3.0% |
| 36 | Iowa | 8,245 | 0.7% |
| 33 | Kansas | 11,509 | 0.9% |
| 21 | Kentucky | 20,895 | 1.7% |
| 19 | Louisiana | 22,832 | 1.8% |
| 43 | Maine | 4,036 | 0.3% |
| 16 | Maryland | 30,833 | 2.4% |
| 27 | Massachusetts | 16,125 | 1.3% |
| 12 | Michigan | 36,575 | 2.9% |
| 29 | Minnesota | 15,320 | 1.2% |
| 23 | Mississippi | 18,220 | 1.4% |
| 18 | Missouri | 25,978 | 2.1% |
| 45 | Montana | 3,358 | 0.3% |
| 39 | Nebraska | 5,552 | 0.4% |
| 31 | Nevada | 14,182 | 1.1% |
| 44 | New Hampshire | 3,784 | 0.3% |
| 10 | New Jersey | 37,956 | 3.0% |
| 38 | New Mexico | 7,039 | 0.6% |
| 5 | New York | 60,002 | 4.8% |
| 17 | North Carolina | 26,315 | 2.1% |
| 48 | North Dakota | 1,988 | 0.2% |
| 7 | Ohio | 53,592 | 4.2% |
| 22 | Oklahoma | 19,082 | 1.5% |
| 24 | Oregon | 18,040 | 1.4% |
| 9 | Pennsylvania | 44,096 | 3.5% |
| 41 | Rhode Island | 4,702 | 0.4% |
| 32 | South Carolina | 11,725 | 0.9% |
| 46 | South Dakota | 2,099 | 0.2% |
| 8 | Tennessee | 48,138 | 3.8% |
| 4 | Texas | 61,809 | 4.9% |
| 30 | Utah | 14,738 | 1.2% |
| 49 | Vermont | 1,497 | 0.1% |
| 13 | Virginia | 36,509 | 2.9% |
| 15 | Washington | 31,325 | 2.5% |
| 35 | West Virginia | 8,447 | 0.7% |
| 25 | Wisconsin | 17,901 | 1.4% |
| 47 | Wyoming | 2,010 | 0.2% |

RANK ORDER

| RANK | STATE | BANKRUPTCIES | % of USA |
|------|-------|--------------|----------|
| 1 | California | 150,870 | 12.0% |
| 2 | Florida | 73,438 | 5.8% |
| 3 | Illinois | 61,953 | 4.9% |
| 4 | Texas | 61,809 | 4.9% |
| 5 | New York | 60,002 | 4.8% |
| 6 | Georgia | 58,574 | 4.6% |
| 7 | Ohio | 53,592 | 4.2% |
| 8 | Tennessee | 48,138 | 3.8% |
| 9 | Pennsylvania | 44,096 | 3.5% |
| 10 | New Jersey | 37,956 | 3.0% |
| 11 | Indiana | 37,587 | 3.0% |
| 12 | Michigan | 36,575 | 2.9% |
| 13 | Virginia | 36,509 | 2.9% |
| 14 | Alabama | 32,345 | 2.6% |
| 15 | Washington | 31,325 | 2.5% |
| 16 | Maryland | 30,833 | 2.4% |
| 17 | North Carolina | 26,315 | 2.1% |
| 18 | Missouri | 25,978 | 2.1% |
| 19 | Louisiana | 22,832 | 1.8% |
| 20 | Arizona | 21,205 | 1.7% |
| 21 | Kentucky | 20,895 | 1.7% |
| 22 | Oklahoma | 19,082 | 1.5% |
| 23 | Mississippi | 18,220 | 1.4% |
| 24 | Oregon | 18,040 | 1.4% |
| 25 | Wisconsin | 17,901 | 1.4% |
| 26 | Arkansas | 16,683 | 1.3% |
| 27 | Massachusetts | 16,125 | 1.3% |
| 28 | Colorado | 15,458 | 1.2% |
| 29 | Minnesota | 15,320 | 1.2% |
| 30 | Utah | 14,738 | 1.2% |
| 31 | Nevada | 14,182 | 1.1% |
| 32 | South Carolina | 11,725 | 0.9% |
| 33 | Kansas | 11,509 | 0.9% |
| 34 | Connecticut | 10,968 | 0.9% |
| 35 | West Virginia | 8,447 | 0.7% |
| 36 | Iowa | 8,245 | 0.7% |
| 37 | Idaho | 7,155 | 0.6% |
| 38 | New Mexico | 7,039 | 0.6% |
| 39 | Nebraska | 5,552 | 0.4% |
| 40 | Delaware | 4,849 | 0.4% |
| 41 | Rhode Island | 4,702 | 0.4% |
| 42 | Hawaii | 4,667 | 0.4% |
| 43 | Maine | 4,036 | 0.3% |
| 44 | New Hampshire | 3,784 | 0.3% |
| 45 | Montana | 3,358 | 0.3% |
| 46 | South Dakota | 2,099 | 0.2% |
| 47 | Wyoming | 2,010 | 0.2% |
| 48 | North Dakota | 1,988 | 0.2% |
| 49 | Vermont | 1,497 | 0.1% |
| 50 | Alaska | 1,412 | 0.1% |
| | District of Columbia | 2,501 | 0.2% |

Source: Morgan Quitno Press using data from Administrative Office of the U.S. Courts
 "Table F, U.S. Bankruptcy Courts"
*For 12 months through September 2000. Includes business (36,065) and Non-Business (1,226,037) filings.
Includes all chapters of bankruptcy. National total includes 15,983 bankruptcies in U.S. territories.

# Personal Bankruptcy Rate in 2000

## National Rate = 430 Personal Bankruptcies per 100,000 Population*

ALPHA ORDER

| RANK | STATE | RATE |
|------|-------|------|
| 2 | Alabama | 717 |
| 50 | Alaska | 208 |
| 26 | Arizona | 398 |
| 7 | Arkansas | 614 |
| 24 | California | 432 |
| 32 | Colorado | 351 |
| 36 | Connecticut | 319 |
| 40 | Delaware | 296 |
| 21 | Florida | 450 |
| 3 | Georgia | 704 |
| 28 | Hawaii | 380 |
| 10 | Idaho | 531 |
| 16 | Illinois | 489 |
| 8 | Indiana | 611 |
| 46 | Iowa | 274 |
| 25 | Kansas | 422 |
| 13 | Kentucky | 509 |
| 15 | Louisiana | 497 |
| 39 | Maine | 303 |
| 9 | Maryland | 569 |
| 48 | Massachusetts | 247 |
| 29 | Michigan | 362 |
| 44 | Minnesota | 281 |
| 6 | Mississippi | 634 |
| 19 | Missouri | 458 |
| 31 | Montana | 355 |
| 37 | Nebraska | 317 |
| 4 | Nevada | 694 |
| 45 | New Hampshire | 280 |
| 22 | New Jersey | 443 |
| 30 | New Mexico | 359 |
| 38 | New York | 306 |
| 34 | North Carolina | 321 |
| 40 | North Dakota | 296 |
| 18 | Ohio | 460 |
| 11 | Oklahoma | 529 |
| 17 | Oregon | 471 |
| 33 | Pennsylvania | 347 |
| 23 | Rhode Island | 440 |
| 42 | South Carolina | 288 |
| 47 | South Dakota | 262 |
| 1 | Tennessee | 835 |
| 43 | Texas | 284 |
| 5 | Utah | 639 |
| 49 | Vermont | 235 |
| 14 | Virginia | 504 |
| 12 | Washington | 520 |
| 20 | West Virginia | 452 |
| 34 | Wisconsin | 321 |
| 27 | Wyoming | 397 |

RANK ORDER

| RANK | STATE | RATE |
|------|-------|------|
| 1 | Tennessee | 835 |
| 2 | Alabama | 717 |
| 3 | Georgia | 704 |
| 4 | Nevada | 694 |
| 5 | Utah | 639 |
| 6 | Mississippi | 634 |
| 7 | Arkansas | 614 |
| 8 | Indiana | 611 |
| 9 | Maryland | 569 |
| 10 | Idaho | 531 |
| 11 | Oklahoma | 529 |
| 12 | Washington | 520 |
| 13 | Kentucky | 509 |
| 14 | Virginia | 504 |
| 15 | Louisiana | 497 |
| 16 | Illinois | 489 |
| 17 | Oregon | 471 |
| 18 | Ohio | 460 |
| 19 | Missouri | 458 |
| 20 | West Virginia | 452 |
| 21 | Florida | 450 |
| 22 | New Jersey | 443 |
| 23 | Rhode Island | 440 |
| 24 | California | 432 |
| 25 | Kansas | 422 |
| 26 | Arizona | 398 |
| 27 | Wyoming | 397 |
| 28 | Hawaii | 380 |
| 29 | Michigan | 362 |
| 30 | New Mexico | 359 |
| 31 | Montana | 355 |
| 32 | Colorado | 351 |
| 33 | Pennsylvania | 347 |
| 34 | North Carolina | 321 |
| 34 | Wisconsin | 321 |
| 36 | Connecticut | 319 |
| 37 | Nebraska | 317 |
| 38 | New York | 306 |
| 39 | Maine | 303 |
| 40 | Delaware | 296 |
| 40 | North Dakota | 296 |
| 42 | South Carolina | 288 |
| 43 | Texas | 284 |
| 44 | Minnesota | 281 |
| 45 | New Hampshire | 280 |
| 46 | Iowa | 274 |
| 47 | South Dakota | 262 |
| 48 | Massachusetts | 247 |
| 49 | Vermont | 235 |
| 50 | Alaska | 208 |
| | District of Columbia | 425 |

Source: Morgan Quitno Press using data from Administrative Office of the U.S. Courts
    "Table F-2 U.S. Bankruptcy Courts"
*For 12 months through September 2000. National rate does not include bankruptcies or population in U.S. territories. Includes all nonbusiness bankruptcies.

# Percent Change in Personal Bankruptcy Rate: 1999 to 2000

## National Percent Change = 9.7% Decrease*

ALPHA ORDER

| RANK | STATE | PERCENT CHANGE |
|------|-------|----------------|
| 1 | Alabama | 3.8 |
| 28 | Alaska | (7.6) |
| 44 | Arizona | (15.3) |
| 15 | Arkansas | (4.1) |
| 50 | California | (22.3) |
| 40 | Colorado | (13.5) |
| 42 | Connecticut | (14.5) |
| 32 | Delaware | (9.5) |
| 34 | Florida | (10.4) |
| 19 | Georgia | (4.7) |
| 47 | Hawaii | (20.0) |
| 17 | Idaho | (4.3) |
| 26 | Illinois | (7.2) |
| 16 | Indiana | (4.2) |
| 24 | Iowa | (6.8) |
| 13 | Kansas | (3.9) |
| 9 | Kentucky | (2.7) |
| 8 | Louisiana | (2.4) |
| 25 | Maine | (7.1) |
| 31 | Maryland | (8.4) |
| 48 | Massachusetts | (20.3) |
| 10 | Michigan | (3.2) |
| 35 | Minnesota | (10.5) |
| 7 | Mississippi | (0.8) |
| 30 | Missouri | (8.2) |
| 23 | Montana | (6.6) |
| 18 | Nebraska | (4.5) |
| 43 | Nevada | (14.7) |
| 45 | New Hampshire | (15.7) |
| 39 | New Jersey | (13.1) |
| 33 | New Mexico | (10.0) |
| 46 | New York | (19.5) |
| 19 | North Carolina | (4.7) |
| 27 | North Dakota | (7.5) |
| 10 | Ohio | (3.2) |
| 38 | Oklahoma | (11.7) |
| 3 | Oregon | 1.1 |
| 12 | Pennsylvania | (3.6) |
| 41 | Rhode Island | (13.9) |
| 6 | South Carolina | (0.7) |
| 29 | South Dakota | (8.1) |
| 5 | Tennessee | (0.5) |
| 37 | Texas | (11.5) |
| 4 | Utah | 0.8 |
| 48 | Vermont | (20.3) |
| 36 | Virginia | (10.6) |
| 13 | Washington | (3.9) |
| 2 | West Virginia | 3.0 |
| 19 | Wisconsin | (4.7) |
| 22 | Wyoming | (5.5) |

RANK ORDER

| RANK | STATE | PERCENT CHANGE |
|------|-------|----------------|
| 1 | Alabama | 3.8 |
| 2 | West Virginia | 3.0 |
| 3 | Oregon | 1.1 |
| 4 | Utah | 0.8 |
| 5 | Tennessee | (0.5) |
| 6 | South Carolina | (0.7) |
| 7 | Mississippi | (0.8) |
| 8 | Louisiana | (2.4) |
| 9 | Kentucky | (2.7) |
| 10 | Michigan | (3.2) |
| 10 | Ohio | (3.2) |
| 12 | Pennsylvania | (3.6) |
| 13 | Kansas | (3.9) |
| 13 | Washington | (3.9) |
| 15 | Arkansas | (4.1) |
| 16 | Indiana | (4.2) |
| 17 | Idaho | (4.3) |
| 18 | Nebraska | (4.5) |
| 19 | Georgia | (4.7) |
| 19 | North Carolina | (4.7) |
| 19 | Wisconsin | (4.7) |
| 22 | Wyoming | (5.5) |
| 23 | Montana | (6.6) |
| 24 | Iowa | (6.8) |
| 25 | Maine | (7.1) |
| 26 | Illinois | (7.2) |
| 27 | North Dakota | (7.5) |
| 28 | Alaska | (7.6) |
| 29 | South Dakota | (8.1) |
| 30 | Missouri | (8.2) |
| 31 | Maryland | (8.4) |
| 32 | Delaware | (9.5) |
| 33 | New Mexico | (10.0) |
| 34 | Florida | (10.4) |
| 35 | Minnesota | (10.5) |
| 36 | Virginia | (10.6) |
| 37 | Texas | (11.5) |
| 38 | Oklahoma | (11.7) |
| 39 | New Jersey | (13.1) |
| 40 | Colorado | (13.5) |
| 41 | Rhode Island | (13.9) |
| 42 | Connecticut | (14.5) |
| 43 | Nevada | (14.7) |
| 44 | Arizona | (15.3) |
| 45 | New Hampshire | (15.7) |
| 46 | New York | (19.5) |
| 47 | Hawaii | (20.0) |
| 48 | Massachusetts | (20.3) |
| 48 | Vermont | (20.3) |
| 50 | California | (22.3) |
| | District of Columbia | (15.8) |

Source: Morgan Quitno Press using data from Administrative Office of the U.S. Courts
    "Table F-2 U.S. Bankruptcy Courts"
*For 12 months through September 1999 and 2000.  National rate does not include bankruptcies or population in
U.S. territories. Includes all nonbusiness bankruptcies.

# Insured Commercial Banks in 2000

## National Total = 8,375 Banks*

ALPHA ORDER

| RANK | STATE | BANKS | % of USA |
|---|---|---|---|
| 20 | Alabama | 158 | 1.9% |
| 50 | Alaska | 6 | 0.1% |
| 40 | Arizona | 42 | 0.5% |
| 17 | Arkansas | 188 | 2.2% |
| 9 | California | 310 | 3.7% |
| 18 | Colorado | 185 | 2.2% |
| 43 | Connecticut | 23 | 0.3% |
| 41 | Delaware | 32 | 0.4% |
| 12 | Florida | 267 | 3.2% |
| 7 | Georgia | 338 | 4.0% |
| 48 | Hawaii | 8 | 0.1% |
| 45 | Idaho | 17 | 0.2% |
| 2 | Illinois | 711 | 8.5% |
| 21 | Indiana | 153 | 1.8% |
| 4 | Iowa | 434 | 5.2% |
| 5 | Kansas | 376 | 4.5% |
| 13 | Kentucky | 245 | 2.9% |
| 22 | Louisiana | 150 | 1.8% |
| 46 | Maine | 16 | 0.2% |
| 33 | Maryland | 75 | 0.9% |
| 38 | Massachusetts | 44 | 0.5% |
| 19 | Michigan | 168 | 2.0% |
| 3 | Minnesota | 492 | 5.9% |
| 27 | Mississippi | 97 | 1.2% |
| 6 | Missouri | 361 | 4.3% |
| 28 | Montana | 85 | 1.0% |
| 11 | Nebraska | 279 | 3.3% |
| 42 | Nevada | 30 | 0.4% |
| 46 | New Hampshire | 16 | 0.2% |
| 32 | New Jersey | 77 | 0.9% |
| 36 | New Mexico | 51 | 0.6% |
| 22 | New York | 150 | 1.8% |
| 34 | North Carolina | 72 | 0.9% |
| 25 | North Dakota | 111 | 1.3% |
| 14 | Ohio | 215 | 2.6% |
| 10 | Oklahoma | 292 | 3.5% |
| 39 | Oregon | 43 | 0.5% |
| 16 | Pennsylvania | 190 | 2.3% |
| 49 | Rhode Island | 7 | 0.1% |
| 30 | South Carolina | 78 | 0.9% |
| 26 | South Dakota | 98 | 1.2% |
| 15 | Tennessee | 193 | 2.3% |
| 1 | Texas | 725 | 8.7% |
| 35 | Utah | 54 | 0.6% |
| 44 | Vermont | 18 | 0.2% |
| 24 | Virginia | 148 | 1.8% |
| 29 | Washington | 81 | 1.0% |
| 30 | West Virginia | 78 | 0.9% |
| 8 | Wisconsin | 316 | 3.8% |
| 37 | Wyoming | 48 | 0.6% |

RANK ORDER

| RANK | STATE | BANKS | % of USA |
|---|---|---|---|
| 1 | Texas | 725 | 8.7% |
| 2 | Illinois | 711 | 8.5% |
| 3 | Minnesota | 492 | 5.9% |
| 4 | Iowa | 434 | 5.2% |
| 5 | Kansas | 376 | 4.5% |
| 6 | Missouri | 361 | 4.3% |
| 7 | Georgia | 338 | 4.0% |
| 8 | Wisconsin | 316 | 3.8% |
| 9 | California | 310 | 3.7% |
| 10 | Oklahoma | 292 | 3.5% |
| 11 | Nebraska | 279 | 3.3% |
| 12 | Florida | 267 | 3.2% |
| 13 | Kentucky | 245 | 2.9% |
| 14 | Ohio | 215 | 2.6% |
| 15 | Tennessee | 193 | 2.3% |
| 16 | Pennsylvania | 190 | 2.3% |
| 17 | Arkansas | 188 | 2.2% |
| 18 | Colorado | 185 | 2.2% |
| 19 | Michigan | 168 | 2.0% |
| 20 | Alabama | 158 | 1.9% |
| 21 | Indiana | 153 | 1.8% |
| 22 | Louisiana | 150 | 1.8% |
| 22 | New York | 150 | 1.8% |
| 24 | Virginia | 148 | 1.8% |
| 25 | North Dakota | 111 | 1.3% |
| 26 | South Dakota | 98 | 1.2% |
| 27 | Mississippi | 97 | 1.2% |
| 28 | Montana | 85 | 1.0% |
| 29 | Washington | 81 | 1.0% |
| 30 | South Carolina | 78 | 0.9% |
| 30 | West Virginia | 78 | 0.9% |
| 32 | New Jersey | 77 | 0.9% |
| 33 | Maryland | 75 | 0.9% |
| 34 | North Carolina | 72 | 0.9% |
| 35 | Utah | 54 | 0.6% |
| 36 | New Mexico | 51 | 0.6% |
| 37 | Wyoming | 48 | 0.6% |
| 38 | Massachusetts | 44 | 0.5% |
| 39 | Oregon | 43 | 0.5% |
| 40 | Arizona | 42 | 0.5% |
| 41 | Delaware | 32 | 0.4% |
| 42 | Nevada | 30 | 0.4% |
| 43 | Connecticut | 23 | 0.3% |
| 44 | Vermont | 18 | 0.2% |
| 45 | Idaho | 17 | 0.2% |
| 46 | Maine | 16 | 0.2% |
| 46 | New Hampshire | 16 | 0.2% |
| 48 | Hawaii | 8 | 0.1% |
| 49 | Rhode Island | 7 | 0.1% |
| 50 | Alaska | 6 | 0.1% |
| | District of Columbia | 6 | 0.1% |

Source: Federal Deposit Insurance Corporation
    "FDIC Insured Commercial Banks by State"
    (Third Quarter, 2000, http://www.fdic.gov/bank/statistical/statistics/sectiond.html)
*FDIC-Insured institutions.  Total includes 18 banks in U.S. territories.

# Assets of Insured Commercial Banks in 2000

## National Total = $6,064,084,000,000*

### ALPHA ORDER

| RANK | STATE | ASSETS | % of USA |
|---|---|---|---|
| 8 | Alabama | $179,415,000,000 | 3.0% |
| 48 | Alaska | 5,983,000,000 | 0.1% |
| 23 | Arizona | 56,190,000,000 | 0.9% |
| 35 | Arkansas | 25,006,000,000 | 0.4% |
| 5 | California | 305,119,000,000 | 5.0% |
| 27 | Colorado | 46,084,000,000 | 0.8% |
| 49 | Connecticut | 3,124,000,000 | 0.1% |
| 12 | Delaware | 138,308,000,000 | 2.3% |
| 21 | Florida | 57,521,000,000 | 0.9% |
| 10 | Georgia | 162,940,000,000 | 2.7% |
| 36 | Hawaii | 23,987,000,000 | 0.4% |
| 50 | Idaho | 2,403,000,000 | 0.0% |
| 3 | Illinois | 350,445,000,000 | 5.8% |
| 18 | Indiana | 80,926,000,000 | 1.3% |
| 28 | Iowa | 43,354,000,000 | 0.7% |
| 32 | Kansas | 36,569,000,000 | 0.6% |
| 25 | Kentucky | 50,275,000,000 | 0.8% |
| 24 | Louisiana | 50,345,000,000 | 0.8% |
| 45 | Maine | 9,304,000,000 | 0.2% |
| 26 | Maryland | 46,572,000,000 | 0.8% |
| 14 | Massachusetts | 104,572,000,000 | 1.7% |
| 13 | Michigan | 133,670,000,000 | 2.2% |
| 7 | Minnesota | 181,132,000,000 | 3.0% |
| 33 | Mississippi | 33,933,000,000 | 0.6% |
| 20 | Missouri | 61,739,000,000 | 1.0% |
| 44 | Montana | 10,567,000,000 | 0.2% |
| 34 | Nebraska | 29,042,000,000 | 0.5% |
| 30 | Nevada | 38,741,000,000 | 0.6% |
| 37 | New Hampshire | 22,607,000,000 | 0.4% |
| 15 | New Jersey | 95,102,000,000 | 1.6% |
| 42 | New Mexico | 15,100,000,000 | 0.2% |
| 1 | New York | 1,240,134,000,000 | 20.5% |
| 2 | North Carolina | 988,237,000,000 | 16.3% |
| 40 | North Dakota | 17,823,000,000 | 0.3% |
| 4 | Ohio | 349,226,000,000 | 5.8% |
| 29 | Oklahoma | 41,604,000,000 | 0.7% |
| 41 | Oregon | 17,682,000,000 | 0.3% |
| 6 | Pennsylvania | 196,371,000,000 | 3.2% |
| 9 | Rhode Island | 177,282,000,000 | 2.9% |
| 38 | South Carolina | 22,513,000,000 | 0.4% |
| 31 | South Dakota | 36,867,000,000 | 0.6% |
| 17 | Tennessee | 86,855,000,000 | 1.4% |
| 11 | Texas | 162,051,000,000 | 2.7% |
| 16 | Utah | 88,525,000,000 | 1.5% |
| 46 | Vermont | 7,596,000,000 | 0.1% |
| 22 | Virginia | 57,319,000,000 | 0.9% |
| 43 | Washington | 14,631,000,000 | 0.2% |
| 39 | West Virginia | 22,409,000,000 | 0.4% |
| 19 | Wisconsin | 77,321,000,000 | 1.3% |
| 47 | Wyoming | 7,258,000,000 | 0.1% |

### RANK ORDER

| RANK | STATE | ASSETS | % of USA |
|---|---|---|---|
| 1 | New York | $1,240,134,000,000 | 20.5% |
| 2 | North Carolina | 988,237,000,000 | 16.3% |
| 3 | Illinois | 350,445,000,000 | 5.8% |
| 4 | Ohio | 349,226,000,000 | 5.8% |
| 5 | California | 305,119,000,000 | 5.0% |
| 6 | Pennsylvania | 196,371,000,000 | 3.2% |
| 7 | Minnesota | 181,132,000,000 | 3.0% |
| 8 | Alabama | 179,415,000,000 | 3.0% |
| 9 | Rhode Island | 177,282,000,000 | 2.9% |
| 10 | Georgia | 162,940,000,000 | 2.7% |
| 11 | Texas | 162,051,000,000 | 2.7% |
| 12 | Delaware | 138,308,000,000 | 2.3% |
| 13 | Michigan | 133,670,000,000 | 2.2% |
| 14 | Massachusetts | 104,572,000,000 | 1.7% |
| 15 | New Jersey | 95,102,000,000 | 1.6% |
| 16 | Utah | 88,525,000,000 | 1.5% |
| 17 | Tennessee | 86,855,000,000 | 1.4% |
| 18 | Indiana | 80,926,000,000 | 1.3% |
| 19 | Wisconsin | 77,321,000,000 | 1.3% |
| 20 | Missouri | 61,739,000,000 | 1.0% |
| 21 | Florida | 57,521,000,000 | 0.9% |
| 22 | Virginia | 57,319,000,000 | 0.9% |
| 23 | Arizona | 56,190,000,000 | 0.9% |
| 24 | Louisiana | 50,345,000,000 | 0.8% |
| 25 | Kentucky | 50,275,000,000 | 0.8% |
| 26 | Maryland | 46,572,000,000 | 0.8% |
| 27 | Colorado | 46,084,000,000 | 0.8% |
| 28 | Iowa | 43,354,000,000 | 0.7% |
| 29 | Oklahoma | 41,604,000,000 | 0.7% |
| 30 | Nevada | 38,741,000,000 | 0.6% |
| 31 | South Dakota | 36,867,000,000 | 0.6% |
| 32 | Kansas | 36,569,000,000 | 0.6% |
| 33 | Mississippi | 33,933,000,000 | 0.6% |
| 34 | Nebraska | 29,042,000,000 | 0.5% |
| 35 | Arkansas | 25,006,000,000 | 0.4% |
| 36 | Hawaii | 23,987,000,000 | 0.4% |
| 37 | New Hampshire | 22,607,000,000 | 0.4% |
| 38 | South Carolina | 22,513,000,000 | 0.4% |
| 39 | West Virginia | 22,409,000,000 | 0.4% |
| 40 | North Dakota | 17,823,000,000 | 0.3% |
| 41 | Oregon | 17,682,000,000 | 0.3% |
| 42 | New Mexico | 15,100,000,000 | 0.2% |
| 43 | Washington | 14,631,000,000 | 0.2% |
| 44 | Montana | 10,567,000,000 | 0.2% |
| 45 | Maine | 9,304,000,000 | 0.2% |
| 46 | Vermont | 7,596,000,000 | 0.1% |
| 47 | Wyoming | 7,258,000,000 | 0.1% |
| 48 | Alaska | 5,983,000,000 | 0.1% |
| 49 | Connecticut | 3,124,000,000 | 0.1% |
| 50 | Idaho | 2,403,000,000 | 0.0% |
| | District of Columbia | 759,000,000 | 0.0% |

Source: Federal Deposit Insurance Corporation
   "FDIC Insured Commercial Banks by State"
   (Third Quarter, 2000, http://www.fdic.gov/bank/statistical/statistics/sectiond.html)
*FDIC-Insured institutions.  Total includes assets in banks in U.S. territories.

# Savings Institutions in 2000

## National Total = 1,613 Savings Institutions*

| RANK | STATE | INSTITUTIONS | % of USA |
|---|---|---|---|
| 30 | Alabama | 12 | 0.7% |
| 47 | Alaska | 2 | 0.1% |
| 43 | Arizona | 4 | 0.2% |
| 31 | Arkansas | 10 | 0.6% |
| 10 | California | 48 | 3.0% |
| 31 | Colorado | 10 | 0.6% |
| 10 | Connecticut | 48 | 3.0% |
| 37 | Delaware | 6 | 0.4% |
| 12 | Florida | 45 | 2.8% |
| 22 | Georgia | 24 | 1.5% |
| 47 | Hawaii | 2 | 0.1% |
| 47 | Idaho | 2 | 0.1% |
| 4 | Illinois | 117 | 7.3% |
| 7 | Indiana | 68 | 4.2% |
| 20 | Iowa | 25 | 1.5% |
| 28 | Kansas | 17 | 1.1% |
| 16 | Kentucky | 34 | 2.1% |
| 17 | Louisiana | 33 | 2.0% |
| 19 | Maine | 26 | 1.6% |
| 8 | Maryland | 64 | 4.0% |
| 1 | Massachusetts | 186 | 11.5% |
| 22 | Michigan | 24 | 1.5% |
| 25 | Minnesota | 21 | 1.3% |
| 35 | Mississippi | 8 | 0.5% |
| 14 | Missouri | 40 | 2.5% |
| 39 | Montana | 5 | 0.3% |
| 29 | Nebraska | 15 | 0.9% |
| 47 | Nevada | 2 | 0.1% |
| 26 | New Hampshire | 19 | 1.2% |
| 6 | New Jersey | 71 | 4.4% |
| 31 | New Mexico | 10 | 0.6% |
| 5 | New York | 84 | 5.2% |
| 13 | North Carolina | 44 | 2.7% |
| 43 | North Dakota | 4 | 0.2% |
| 2 | Ohio | 131 | 8.1% |
| 34 | Oklahoma | 9 | 0.6% |
| 39 | Oregon | 5 | 0.3% |
| 3 | Pennsylvania | 119 | 7.4% |
| 37 | Rhode Island | 6 | 0.4% |
| 18 | South Carolina | 30 | 1.9% |
| 43 | South Dakota | 4 | 0.2% |
| 20 | Tennessee | 25 | 1.5% |
| 9 | Texas | 49 | 3.0% |
| 39 | Utah | 5 | 0.3% |
| 39 | Vermont | 5 | 0.3% |
| 26 | Virginia | 19 | 1.2% |
| 24 | Washington | 23 | 1.4% |
| 36 | West Virginia | 7 | 0.4% |
| 15 | Wisconsin | 39 | 2.4% |
| 43 | Wyoming | 4 | 0.2% |

| RANK | STATE | INSTITUTIONS | % of USA |
|---|---|---|---|
| 1 | Massachusetts | 186 | 11.5% |
| 2 | Ohio | 131 | 8.1% |
| 3 | Pennsylvania | 119 | 7.4% |
| 4 | Illinois | 117 | 7.3% |
| 5 | New York | 84 | 5.2% |
| 6 | New Jersey | 71 | 4.4% |
| 7 | Indiana | 68 | 4.2% |
| 8 | Maryland | 64 | 4.0% |
| 9 | Texas | 49 | 3.0% |
| 10 | California | 48 | 3.0% |
| 10 | Connecticut | 48 | 3.0% |
| 12 | Florida | 45 | 2.8% |
| 13 | North Carolina | 44 | 2.7% |
| 14 | Missouri | 40 | 2.5% |
| 15 | Wisconsin | 39 | 2.4% |
| 16 | Kentucky | 34 | 2.1% |
| 17 | Louisiana | 33 | 2.0% |
| 18 | South Carolina | 30 | 1.9% |
| 19 | Maine | 26 | 1.6% |
| 20 | Iowa | 25 | 1.5% |
| 20 | Tennessee | 25 | 1.5% |
| 22 | Georgia | 24 | 1.5% |
| 22 | Michigan | 24 | 1.5% |
| 24 | Washington | 23 | 1.4% |
| 25 | Minnesota | 21 | 1.3% |
| 26 | New Hampshire | 19 | 1.2% |
| 26 | Virginia | 19 | 1.2% |
| 28 | Kansas | 17 | 1.1% |
| 29 | Nebraska | 15 | 0.9% |
| 30 | Alabama | 12 | 0.7% |
| 31 | Arkansas | 10 | 0.6% |
| 31 | Colorado | 10 | 0.6% |
| 31 | New Mexico | 10 | 0.6% |
| 34 | Oklahoma | 9 | 0.6% |
| 35 | Mississippi | 8 | 0.5% |
| 36 | West Virginia | 7 | 0.4% |
| 37 | Delaware | 6 | 0.4% |
| 37 | Rhode Island | 6 | 0.4% |
| 39 | Montana | 5 | 0.3% |
| 39 | Oregon | 5 | 0.3% |
| 39 | Utah | 5 | 0.3% |
| 39 | Vermont | 5 | 0.3% |
| 43 | Arizona | 4 | 0.2% |
| 43 | North Dakota | 4 | 0.2% |
| 43 | South Dakota | 4 | 0.2% |
| 43 | Wyoming | 4 | 0.2% |
| 47 | Alaska | 2 | 0.1% |
| 47 | Hawaii | 2 | 0.1% |
| 47 | Idaho | 2 | 0.1% |
| 47 | Nevada | 2 | 0.1% |
| | District of Columbia | 1 | 0.1% |

*Source: Federal Deposit Insurance Corporation*
*"FDIC Insured Savings Institutions By State"*
*(Third Quarter, 2000, http://www.fdic.gov/bank/statistical/statistics/sectionf.html)*
*FDIC-Insured institutions. Total includes two institutions in U.S. territories.

# Assets of Savings Institutions in 2000

## National Total = 1,204,277,000,000*

ALPHA ORDER

| RANK | STATE | ASSETS | % of USA |
|---|---|---|---|
| 35 | Alabama | $2,224,000,000 | 0.2% |
| 50 | Alaska | 296,000,000 | 0.0% |
| 47 | Arizona | 785,000,000 | 0.1% |
| 31 | Arkansas | 3,466,000,000 | 0.3% |
| 1 | California | 343,452,000,000 | 28.5% |
| 46 | Colorado | 826,000,000 | 0.1% |
| 8 | Connecticut | 45,300,000,000 | 3.8% |
| 17 | Delaware | 11,800,000,000 | 1.0% |
| 13 | Florida | 22,901,000,000 | 1.9% |
| 24 | Georgia | 6,698,000,000 | 0.6% |
| 26 | Hawaii | 6,482,000,000 | 0.5% |
| 48 | Idaho | 567,000,000 | 0.0% |
| 10 | Illinois | 39,486,000,000 | 3.3% |
| 15 | Indiana | 16,788,000,000 | 1.4% |
| 30 | Iowa | 4,045,000,000 | 0.3% |
| 18 | Kansas | 11,371,000,000 | 0.9% |
| 32 | Kentucky | 3,225,000,000 | 0.3% |
| 29 | Louisiana | 4,443,000,000 | 0.4% |
| 23 | Maine | 7,240,000,000 | 0.6% |
| 20 | Maryland | 8,376,000,000 | 0.7% |
| 6 | Massachusetts | 60,991,000,000 | 5.1% |
| 11 | Michigan | 34,793,000,000 | 2.9% |
| 34 | Minnesota | 2,852,000,000 | 0.2% |
| 42 | Mississippi | 976,000,000 | 0.1% |
| 22 | Missouri | 7,303,000,000 | 0.6% |
| 38 | Montana | 1,541,000,000 | 0.1% |
| 16 | Nebraska | 16,463,000,000 | 1.4% |
| 44 | Nevada | 910,000,000 | 0.1% |
| 19 | New Hampshire | 9,098,000,000 | 0.8% |
| 9 | New Jersey | 42,387,000,000 | 3.5% |
| 33 | New Mexico | 3,116,000,000 | 0.3% |
| 2 | New York | 130,535,000,000 | 10.8% |
| 27 | North Carolina | 6,430,000,000 | 0.5% |
| 43 | North Dakota | 972,000,000 | 0.1% |
| 4 | Ohio | 71,248,000,000 | 5.9% |
| 25 | Oklahoma | 6,601,000,000 | 0.5% |
| 36 | Oregon | 2,213,000,000 | 0.2% |
| 3 | Pennsylvania | 78,084,000,000 | 6.5% |
| 37 | Rhode Island | 1,945,000,000 | 0.2% |
| 21 | South Carolina | 8,310,000,000 | 0.7% |
| 41 | South Dakota | 1,019,000,000 | 0.1% |
| 28 | Tennessee | 5,150,000,000 | 0.4% |
| 5 | Texas | 63,700,000,000 | 5.3% |
| 39 | Utah | 1,494,000,000 | 0.1% |
| 40 | Vermont | 1,025,000,000 | 0.1% |
| 12 | Virginia | 28,189,000,000 | 2.3% |
| 7 | Washington | 56,495,000,000 | 4.7% |
| 45 | West Virginia | 857,000,000 | 0.1% |
| 14 | Wisconsin | 18,887,000,000 | 1.6% |
| 49 | Wyoming | 388,000,000 | 0.0% |

RANK ORDER

| RANK | STATE | ASSETS | % of USA |
|---|---|---|---|
| 1 | California | $343,452,000,000 | 28.5% |
| 2 | New York | 130,535,000,000 | 10.8% |
| 3 | Pennsylvania | 78,084,000,000 | 6.5% |
| 4 | Ohio | 71,248,000,000 | 5.9% |
| 5 | Texas | 63,700,000,000 | 5.3% |
| 6 | Massachusetts | 60,991,000,000 | 5.1% |
| 7 | Washington | 56,495,000,000 | 4.7% |
| 8 | Connecticut | 45,300,000,000 | 3.8% |
| 9 | New Jersey | 42,387,000,000 | 3.5% |
| 10 | Illinois | 39,486,000,000 | 3.3% |
| 11 | Michigan | 34,793,000,000 | 2.9% |
| 12 | Virginia | 28,189,000,000 | 2.3% |
| 13 | Florida | 22,901,000,000 | 1.9% |
| 14 | Wisconsin | 18,887,000,000 | 1.6% |
| 15 | Indiana | 16,788,000,000 | 1.4% |
| 16 | Nebraska | 16,463,000,000 | 1.4% |
| 17 | Delaware | 11,800,000,000 | 1.0% |
| 18 | Kansas | 11,371,000,000 | 0.9% |
| 19 | New Hampshire | 9,098,000,000 | 0.8% |
| 20 | Maryland | 8,376,000,000 | 0.7% |
| 21 | South Carolina | 8,310,000,000 | 0.7% |
| 22 | Missouri | 7,303,000,000 | 0.6% |
| 23 | Maine | 7,240,000,000 | 0.6% |
| 24 | Georgia | 6,698,000,000 | 0.6% |
| 25 | Oklahoma | 6,601,000,000 | 0.5% |
| 26 | Hawaii | 6,482,000,000 | 0.5% |
| 27 | North Carolina | 6,430,000,000 | 0.5% |
| 28 | Tennessee | 5,150,000,000 | 0.4% |
| 29 | Louisiana | 4,443,000,000 | 0.4% |
| 30 | Iowa | 4,045,000,000 | 0.3% |
| 31 | Arkansas | 3,466,000,000 | 0.3% |
| 32 | Kentucky | 3,225,000,000 | 0.3% |
| 33 | New Mexico | 3,116,000,000 | 0.3% |
| 34 | Minnesota | 2,852,000,000 | 0.2% |
| 35 | Alabama | 2,224,000,000 | 0.2% |
| 36 | Oregon | 2,213,000,000 | 0.2% |
| 37 | Rhode Island | 1,945,000,000 | 0.2% |
| 38 | Montana | 1,541,000,000 | 0.1% |
| 39 | Utah | 1,494,000,000 | 0.1% |
| 40 | Vermont | 1,025,000,000 | 0.1% |
| 41 | South Dakota | 1,019,000,000 | 0.1% |
| 42 | Mississippi | 976,000,000 | 0.1% |
| 43 | North Dakota | 972,000,000 | 0.1% |
| 44 | Nevada | 910,000,000 | 0.1% |
| 45 | West Virginia | 857,000,000 | 0.1% |
| 46 | Colorado | 826,000,000 | 0.1% |
| 47 | Arizona | 785,000,000 | 0.1% |
| 48 | Idaho | 567,000,000 | 0.0% |
| 49 | Wyoming | 388,000,000 | 0.0% |
| 50 | Alaska | 296,000,000 | 0.0% |
| | District of Columbia | 253,000,000 | 0.0% |

Source: Federal Deposit Insurance Corporation
   "FDIC Insured Savings Institutions By State"
   (Third Quarter, 2000, http://www.fdic.gov/bank/statistical/statistics/sectionf.html)
*FDIC-Insured institutions.  Total includes assets in two institutions in U.S. territories.

# V. EDUCATION

# School-Age Population as a Percent of Total Population in 1999

## National Percent = 18.8% of Population is School-Age*

ALPHA ORDER

| RANK | STATE | PERCENT |
|---|---|---|
| 43 | Alabama | 17.7 |
| 1 | Alaska | 23.7 |
| 9 | Arizona | 19.9 |
| 27 | Arkansas | 18.9 |
| 13 | California | 19.4 |
| 20 | Colorado | 19.2 |
| 31 | Connecticut | 18.6 |
| 46 | Delaware | 17.6 |
| 49 | Florida | 17.3 |
| 23 | Georgia | 19.0 |
| 46 | Hawaii | 17.6 |
| 4 | Idaho | 20.6 |
| 23 | Illinois | 19.0 |
| 28 | Indiana | 18.8 |
| 29 | Iowa | 18.7 |
| 13 | Kansas | 19.4 |
| 39 | Kentucky | 17.8 |
| 8 | Louisiana | 20.0 |
| 39 | Maine | 17.8 |
| 31 | Maryland | 18.6 |
| 48 | Massachusetts | 17.4 |
| 16 | Michigan | 19.3 |
| 9 | Minnesota | 19.9 |
| 9 | Mississippi | 19.9 |
| 23 | Missouri | 19.0 |
| 16 | Montana | 19.3 |
| 12 | Nebraska | 19.7 |
| 16 | Nevada | 19.3 |
| 20 | New Hampshire | 19.2 |
| 38 | New Jersey | 17.9 |
| 3 | New Mexico | 20.9 |
| 43 | New York | 17.7 |
| 33 | North Carolina | 18.4 |
| 22 | North Dakota | 19.1 |
| 29 | Ohio | 18.7 |
| 16 | Oklahoma | 19.3 |
| 34 | Oregon | 18.3 |
| 39 | Pennsylvania | 17.8 |
| 35 | Rhode Island | 18.1 |
| 35 | South Carolina | 18.1 |
| 6 | South Dakota | 20.2 |
| 39 | Tennessee | 17.8 |
| 5 | Texas | 20.4 |
| 2 | Utah | 23.3 |
| 35 | Vermont | 18.1 |
| 43 | Virginia | 17.7 |
| 23 | Washington | 19.0 |
| 50 | West Virginia | 16.8 |
| 13 | Wisconsin | 19.4 |
| 7 | Wyoming | 20.1 |

RANK ORDER

| RANK | STATE | PERCENT |
|---|---|---|
| 1 | Alaska | 23.7 |
| 2 | Utah | 23.3 |
| 3 | New Mexico | 20.9 |
| 4 | Idaho | 20.6 |
| 5 | Texas | 20.4 |
| 6 | South Dakota | 20.2 |
| 7 | Wyoming | 20.1 |
| 8 | Louisiana | 20.0 |
| 9 | Arizona | 19.9 |
| 9 | Minnesota | 19.9 |
| 9 | Mississippi | 19.9 |
| 12 | Nebraska | 19.7 |
| 13 | California | 19.4 |
| 13 | Kansas | 19.4 |
| 13 | Wisconsin | 19.4 |
| 16 | Michigan | 19.3 |
| 16 | Montana | 19.3 |
| 16 | Nevada | 19.3 |
| 16 | Oklahoma | 19.3 |
| 20 | Colorado | 19.2 |
| 20 | New Hampshire | 19.2 |
| 22 | North Dakota | 19.1 |
| 23 | Georgia | 19.0 |
| 23 | Illinois | 19.0 |
| 23 | Missouri | 19.0 |
| 23 | Washington | 19.0 |
| 27 | Arkansas | 18.9 |
| 28 | Indiana | 18.8 |
| 29 | Iowa | 18.7 |
| 29 | Ohio | 18.7 |
| 31 | Connecticut | 18.6 |
| 31 | Maryland | 18.6 |
| 33 | North Carolina | 18.4 |
| 34 | Oregon | 18.3 |
| 35 | Rhode Island | 18.1 |
| 35 | South Carolina | 18.1 |
| 35 | Vermont | 18.1 |
| 38 | New Jersey | 17.9 |
| 39 | Kentucky | 17.8 |
| 39 | Maine | 17.8 |
| 39 | Pennsylvania | 17.8 |
| 39 | Tennessee | 17.8 |
| 43 | Alabama | 17.7 |
| 43 | New York | 17.7 |
| 43 | Virginia | 17.7 |
| 46 | Delaware | 17.6 |
| 46 | Hawaii | 17.6 |
| 48 | Massachusetts | 17.4 |
| 49 | Florida | 17.3 |
| 50 | West Virginia | 16.8 |
| | District of Columbia | 13.1 |

Source: Morgan Quitno Press using data from U.S. Bureau of the Census
"Population Estimates for the U.S., Regions, and States by Selected Age Groups and Sex" (ST-99-9, March 9, 2000)
(http://www.census.gov/population/estimates/state/st-99-09.txt)
*Five- to 17-year-olds as of July 1, 1999.

# Public Elementary and Secondary School Districts in 1999

## National Total = 14,498 School Districts*

ALPHA ORDER

| RANK | STATE | DISTRICTS | % of USA |
|---|---|---|---|
| 35 | Alabama | 128 | 0.9% |
| 43 | Alaska | 53 | 0.4% |
| 16 | Arizona | 353 | 2.4% |
| 17 | Arkansas | 310 | 2.1% |
| 2 | California | 988 | 6.8% |
| 27 | Colorado | 176 | 1.2% |
| 30 | Connecticut | 166 | 1.1% |
| 48 | Delaware | 19 | 0.1% |
| 41 | Florida | 67 | 0.5% |
| 26 | Georgia | 180 | 1.2% |
| 50 | Hawaii | 1 | 0.0% |
| 37 | Idaho | 112 | 0.8% |
| 3 | Illinois | 936 | 6.5% |
| 20 | Indiana | 292 | 2.0% |
| 15 | Iowa | 375 | 2.6% |
| 18 | Kansas | 304 | 2.1% |
| 27 | Kentucky | 176 | 1.2% |
| 40 | Louisiana | 70 | 0.5% |
| 24 | Maine | 224 | 1.5% |
| 47 | Maryland | 24 | 0.2% |
| 22 | Massachusetts | 244 | 1.7% |
| 5 | Michigan | 687 | 4.7% |
| 14 | Minnesota | 387 | 2.7% |
| 32 | Mississippi | 152 | 1.0% |
| 10 | Missouri | 523 | 3.6% |
| 12 | Montana | 456 | 3.1% |
| 7 | Nebraska | 596 | 4.1% |
| 49 | Nevada | 17 | 0.1% |
| 31 | New Hampshire | 165 | 1.1% |
| 8 | New Jersey | 581 | 4.0% |
| 39 | New Mexico | 89 | 0.6% |
| 4 | New York | 705 | 4.9% |
| 36 | North Carolina | 120 | 0.8% |
| 23 | North Dakota | 229 | 1.6% |
| 6 | Ohio | 625 | 4.3% |
| 9 | Oklahoma | 547 | 3.8% |
| 25 | Oregon | 197 | 1.4% |
| 11 | Pennsylvania | 500 | 3.4% |
| 46 | Rhode Island | 36 | 0.2% |
| 38 | South Carolina | 90 | 0.6% |
| 29 | South Dakota | 173 | 1.2% |
| 33 | Tennessee | 137 | 0.9% |
| 1 | Texas | 1,042 | 7.2% |
| 45 | Utah | 40 | 0.3% |
| 21 | Vermont | 248 | 1.7% |
| 34 | Virginia | 132 | 0.9% |
| 19 | Washington | 296 | 2.0% |
| 42 | West Virginia | 55 | 0.4% |
| 13 | Wisconsin | 426 | 2.9% |
| 44 | Wyoming | 48 | 0.3% |

RANK ORDER

| RANK | STATE | DISTRICTS | % of USA |
|---|---|---|---|
| 1 | Texas | 1,042 | 7.2% |
| 2 | California | 988 | 6.8% |
| 3 | Illinois | 936 | 6.5% |
| 4 | New York | 705 | 4.9% |
| 5 | Michigan | 687 | 4.7% |
| 6 | Ohio | 625 | 4.3% |
| 7 | Nebraska | 596 | 4.1% |
| 8 | New Jersey | 581 | 4.0% |
| 9 | Oklahoma | 547 | 3.8% |
| 10 | Missouri | 523 | 3.6% |
| 11 | Pennsylvania | 500 | 3.4% |
| 12 | Montana | 456 | 3.1% |
| 13 | Wisconsin | 426 | 2.9% |
| 14 | Minnesota | 387 | 2.7% |
| 15 | Iowa | 375 | 2.6% |
| 16 | Arizona | 353 | 2.4% |
| 17 | Arkansas | 310 | 2.1% |
| 18 | Kansas | 304 | 2.1% |
| 19 | Washington | 296 | 2.0% |
| 20 | Indiana | 292 | 2.0% |
| 21 | Vermont | 248 | 1.7% |
| 22 | Massachusetts | 244 | 1.7% |
| 23 | North Dakota | 229 | 1.6% |
| 24 | Maine | 224 | 1.5% |
| 25 | Oregon | 197 | 1.4% |
| 26 | Georgia | 180 | 1.2% |
| 27 | Colorado | 176 | 1.2% |
| 27 | Kentucky | 176 | 1.2% |
| 29 | South Dakota | 173 | 1.2% |
| 30 | Connecticut | 166 | 1.1% |
| 31 | New Hampshire | 165 | 1.1% |
| 32 | Mississippi | 152 | 1.0% |
| 33 | Tennessee | 137 | 0.9% |
| 34 | Virginia | 132 | 0.9% |
| 35 | Alabama | 128 | 0.9% |
| 36 | North Carolina | 120 | 0.8% |
| 37 | Idaho | 112 | 0.8% |
| 38 | South Carolina | 90 | 0.6% |
| 39 | New Mexico | 89 | 0.6% |
| 40 | Louisiana | 70 | 0.5% |
| 41 | Florida | 67 | 0.5% |
| 42 | West Virginia | 55 | 0.4% |
| 43 | Alaska | 53 | 0.4% |
| 44 | Wyoming | 48 | 0.3% |
| 45 | Utah | 40 | 0.3% |
| 46 | Rhode Island | 36 | 0.2% |
| 47 | Maryland | 24 | 0.2% |
| 48 | Delaware | 19 | 0.1% |
| 49 | Nevada | 17 | 0.1% |
| 50 | Hawaii | 1 | 0.0% |
|  | District of Columbia | 1 | 0.0% |

Source: U.S. Department of Education, Office of Educational Research and Improvement
    "Overview of Public Elementary and Secondary Schools and Districts: School Year 1998-1999"
*Estimates for 1998-99.  Regular school districts, including supervisory union components.

# Public Elementary and Secondary Schools in 1999

## National Total = 88,548 Schools*

ALPHA ORDER

RANK ORDER

| RANK | STATE | SCHOOLS | % of USA |
|------|-------|---------|----------|
| 26 | Alabama | 1,364 | 1.5% |
| 44 | Alaska | 497 | 0.6% |
| 23 | Arizona | 1,511 | 1.7% |
| 31 | Arkansas | 1,106 | 1.2% |
| 1 | California | 8,334 | 9.4% |
| 21 | Colorado | 1,539 | 1.7% |
| 32 | Connecticut | 1,069 | 1.2% |
| 50 | Delaware | 185 | 0.2% |
| 8 | Florida | 3,044 | 3.4% |
| 17 | Georgia | 1,843 | 2.1% |
| 49 | Hawaii | 253 | 0.3% |
| 41 | Idaho | 649 | 0.7% |
| 3 | Illinois | 4,251 | 4.8% |
| 15 | Indiana | 1,886 | 2.1% |
| 22 | Iowa | 1,538 | 1.7% |
| 25 | Kansas | 1,437 | 1.6% |
| 27 | Kentucky | 1,346 | 1.5% |
| 24 | Louisiana | 1,500 | 1.7% |
| 40 | Maine | 690 | 0.8% |
| 29 | Maryland | 1,326 | 1.5% |
| 16 | Massachusetts | 1,874 | 2.1% |
| 6 | Michigan | 3,656 | 4.1% |
| 14 | Minnesota | 2,054 | 2.3% |
| 35 | Mississippi | 874 | 1.0% |
| 10 | Missouri | 2,221 | 2.5% |
| 34 | Montana | 886 | 1.0% |
| 28 | Nebraska | 1,333 | 1.5% |
| 45 | Nevada | 461 | 0.5% |
| 43 | New Hampshire | 516 | 0.6% |
| 9 | New Jersey | 2,317 | 2.6% |
| 39 | New Mexico | 745 | 0.8% |
| 4 | New York | 4,224 | 4.8% |
| 12 | North Carolina | 2,095 | 2.4% |
| 42 | North Dakota | 555 | 0.6% |
| 5 | Ohio | 3,732 | 4.2% |
| 18 | Oklahoma | 1,818 | 2.1% |
| 30 | Oregon | 1,271 | 1.4% |
| 7 | Pennsylvania | 3,139 | 3.5% |
| 48 | Rhode Island | 318 | 0.4% |
| 33 | South Carolina | 1,058 | 1.2% |
| 37 | South Dakota | 770 | 0.9% |
| 20 | Tennessee | 1,554 | 1.8% |
| 2 | Texas | 7,228 | 8.2% |
| 38 | Utah | 769 | 0.9% |
| 47 | Vermont | 358 | 0.4% |
| 19 | Virginia | 1,815 | 2.0% |
| 13 | Washington | 2,066 | 2.3% |
| 36 | West Virginia | 816 | 0.9% |
| 11 | Wisconsin | 2,109 | 2.4% |
| 46 | Wyoming | 384 | 0.4% |

| RANK | STATE | SCHOOLS | % of USA |
|------|-------|---------|----------|
| 1 | California | 8,334 | 9.4% |
| 2 | Texas | 7,228 | 8.2% |
| 3 | Illinois | 4,251 | 4.8% |
| 4 | New York | 4,224 | 4.8% |
| 5 | Ohio | 3,732 | 4.2% |
| 6 | Michigan | 3,656 | 4.1% |
| 7 | Pennsylvania | 3,139 | 3.5% |
| 8 | Florida | 3,044 | 3.4% |
| 9 | New Jersey | 2,317 | 2.6% |
| 10 | Missouri | 2,221 | 2.5% |
| 11 | Wisconsin | 2,109 | 2.4% |
| 12 | North Carolina | 2,095 | 2.4% |
| 13 | Washington | 2,066 | 2.3% |
| 14 | Minnesota | 2,054 | 2.3% |
| 15 | Indiana | 1,886 | 2.1% |
| 16 | Massachusetts | 1,874 | 2.1% |
| 17 | Georgia | 1,843 | 2.1% |
| 18 | Oklahoma | 1,818 | 2.1% |
| 19 | Virginia | 1,815 | 2.0% |
| 20 | Tennessee | 1,554 | 1.8% |
| 21 | Colorado | 1,539 | 1.7% |
| 22 | Iowa | 1,538 | 1.7% |
| 23 | Arizona | 1,511 | 1.7% |
| 24 | Louisiana | 1,500 | 1.7% |
| 25 | Kansas | 1,437 | 1.6% |
| 26 | Alabama | 1,364 | 1.5% |
| 27 | Kentucky | 1,346 | 1.5% |
| 28 | Nebraska | 1,333 | 1.5% |
| 29 | Maryland | 1,326 | 1.5% |
| 30 | Oregon | 1,271 | 1.4% |
| 31 | Arkansas | 1,106 | 1.2% |
| 32 | Connecticut | 1,069 | 1.2% |
| 33 | South Carolina | 1,058 | 1.2% |
| 34 | Montana | 886 | 1.0% |
| 35 | Mississippi | 874 | 1.0% |
| 36 | West Virginia | 816 | 0.9% |
| 37 | South Dakota | 770 | 0.9% |
| 38 | Utah | 769 | 0.9% |
| 39 | New Mexico | 745 | 0.8% |
| 40 | Maine | 690 | 0.8% |
| 41 | Idaho | 649 | 0.7% |
| 42 | North Dakota | 555 | 0.6% |
| 43 | New Hampshire | 516 | 0.6% |
| 44 | Alaska | 497 | 0.6% |
| 45 | Nevada | 461 | 0.5% |
| 46 | Wyoming | 384 | 0.4% |
| 47 | Vermont | 358 | 0.4% |
| 48 | Rhode Island | 318 | 0.4% |
| 49 | Hawaii | 253 | 0.3% |
| 50 | Delaware | 185 | 0.2% |
|  | District of Columbia | 164 | 0.2% |

*Source: U.S. Department of Education, Office of Educational Research and Improvement*
*"Overview of Public Elementary and Secondary Schools and Districts: School Year 1998-1999"*
*\*Estimates for 1998-99. Includes special education, alternative and other schools not classified by grade span.*

# Private Elementary and Secondary Schools in 1998

## National Total = 27,402 Private Schools*

ALPHA ORDER

| RANK | STATE | SCHOOLS | % of USA |
|---|---|---|---|
| 25 | Alabama | 333 | 1.2% |
| 48 | Alaska | 70 | 0.3% |
| 28 | Arizona | 283 | 1.0% |
| 33 | Arkansas | 196 | 0.7% |
| 1 | California | 3,332 | 12.2% |
| 23 | Colorado | 353 | 1.3% |
| 24 | Connecticut | 339 | 1.2% |
| 41 | Delaware | 103 | 0.4% |
| 4 | Florida | 1,481 | 5.4% |
| 16 | Georgia | 588 | 2.1% |
| 40 | Hawaii | 126 | 0.5% |
| 46 | Idaho | 82 | 0.3% |
| 5 | Illinois | 1,408 | 5.1% |
| 11 | Indiana | 768 | 2.8% |
| 29 | Iowa | 277 | 1.0% |
| 30 | Kansas | 241 | 0.9% |
| 22 | Kentucky | 370 | 1.4% |
| 21 | Louisiana | 452 | 1.6% |
| 38 | Maine | 135 | 0.5% |
| 13 | Maryland | 655 | 2.4% |
| 12 | Massachusetts | 657 | 2.4% |
| 7 | Michigan | 1,096 | 4.0% |
| 17 | Minnesota | 580 | 2.1% |
| 32 | Mississippi | 212 | 0.8% |
| 14 | Missouri | 602 | 2.2% |
| 43 | Montana | 94 | 0.3% |
| 31 | Nebraska | 236 | 0.9% |
| 47 | Nevada | 71 | 0.3% |
| 37 | New Hampshire | 148 | 0.5% |
| 10 | New Jersey | 901 | 3.3% |
| 34 | New Mexico | 182 | 0.7% |
| 3 | New York | 1,924 | 7.0% |
| 18 | North Carolina | 550 | 2.0% |
| 49 | North Dakota | 60 | 0.2% |
| 9 | Ohio | 991 | 3.6% |
| 35 | Oklahoma | 177 | 0.6% |
| 26 | Oregon | 327 | 1.2% |
| 2 | Pennsylvania | 1,989 | 7.3% |
| 39 | Rhode Island | 130 | 0.5% |
| 27 | South Carolina | 316 | 1.2% |
| 44 | South Dakota | 91 | 0.3% |
| 19 | Tennessee | 513 | 1.9% |
| 6 | Texas | 1,329 | 4.9% |
| 45 | Utah | 83 | 0.3% |
| 42 | Vermont | 101 | 0.4% |
| 15 | Virginia | 591 | 2.2% |
| 20 | Washington | 496 | 1.8% |
| 36 | West Virginia | 159 | 0.6% |
| 8 | Wisconsin | 1,073 | 3.9% |
| 50 | Wyoming | 43 | 0.2% |

RANK ORDER

| RANK | STATE | SCHOOLS | % of USA |
|---|---|---|---|
| 1 | California | 3,332 | 12.2% |
| 2 | Pennsylvania | 1,989 | 7.3% |
| 3 | New York | 1,924 | 7.0% |
| 4 | Florida | 1,481 | 5.4% |
| 5 | Illinois | 1,408 | 5.1% |
| 6 | Texas | 1,329 | 4.9% |
| 7 | Michigan | 1,096 | 4.0% |
| 8 | Wisconsin | 1,073 | 3.9% |
| 9 | Ohio | 991 | 3.6% |
| 10 | New Jersey | 901 | 3.3% |
| 11 | Indiana | 768 | 2.8% |
| 12 | Massachusetts | 657 | 2.4% |
| 13 | Maryland | 655 | 2.4% |
| 14 | Missouri | 602 | 2.2% |
| 15 | Virginia | 591 | 2.2% |
| 16 | Georgia | 588 | 2.1% |
| 17 | Minnesota | 580 | 2.1% |
| 18 | North Carolina | 550 | 2.0% |
| 19 | Tennessee | 513 | 1.9% |
| 20 | Washington | 496 | 1.8% |
| 21 | Louisiana | 452 | 1.6% |
| 22 | Kentucky | 370 | 1.4% |
| 23 | Colorado | 353 | 1.3% |
| 24 | Connecticut | 339 | 1.2% |
| 25 | Alabama | 333 | 1.2% |
| 26 | Oregon | 327 | 1.2% |
| 27 | South Carolina | 316 | 1.2% |
| 28 | Arizona | 283 | 1.0% |
| 29 | Iowa | 277 | 1.0% |
| 30 | Kansas | 241 | 0.9% |
| 31 | Nebraska | 236 | 0.9% |
| 32 | Mississippi | 212 | 0.8% |
| 33 | Arkansas | 196 | 0.7% |
| 34 | New Mexico | 182 | 0.7% |
| 35 | Oklahoma | 177 | 0.6% |
| 36 | West Virginia | 159 | 0.6% |
| 37 | New Hampshire | 148 | 0.5% |
| 38 | Maine | 135 | 0.5% |
| 39 | Rhode Island | 130 | 0.5% |
| 40 | Hawaii | 126 | 0.5% |
| 41 | Delaware | 103 | 0.4% |
| 42 | Vermont | 101 | 0.4% |
| 43 | Montana | 94 | 0.3% |
| 44 | South Dakota | 91 | 0.3% |
| 45 | Utah | 83 | 0.3% |
| 46 | Idaho | 82 | 0.3% |
| 47 | Nevada | 71 | 0.3% |
| 48 | Alaska | 70 | 0.3% |
| 49 | North Dakota | 60 | 0.2% |
| 50 | Wyoming | 43 | 0.2% |
| | District of Columbia | 87 | 0.3% |

Source: U.S. Department of Education, Office of Educational Research and Improvement
    "Private School Universe Survey, 1997-98" (NCES 1999-319, August 1999)
*Estimate for 1997-98.

# Percent of Elementary/Secondary School Students in Private Schools in 1998

## National Percent = 10.1% of Students*

| ALPHA ORDER | | | | RANK ORDER | | |
|---|---|---|---|---|---|---|
| **RANK** | **STATE** | **PERCENT** | | **RANK** | **STATE** | **PERCENT** |
| 26 | Alabama | 9.2 | | 1 | Delaware | 18.8 |
| 45 | Alaska | 4.5 | | 2 | Pennsylvania | 16.1 |
| 42 | Arizona | 5.1 | | 3 | Louisiana | 15.9 |
| 40 | Arkansas | 5.5 | | 4 | Hawaii | 15.5 |
| 21 | California | 9.7 | | 5 | Rhode Island | 14.7 |
| 35 | Colorado | 7.1 | | 6 | New York | 14.4 |
| 12 | Connecticut | 12.1 | | 7 | New Jersey | 14.3 |
| 1 | Delaware | 18.8 | | 8 | Wisconsin | 14.1 |
| 16 | Florida | 10.9 | | 9 | Maryland | 13.9 |
| 32 | Georgia | 7.5 | | 10 | Illinois | 13.1 |
| 4 | Hawaii | 15.5 | | 11 | Nebraska | 12.4 |
| 48 | Idaho | 3.7 | | 12 | Connecticut | 12.1 |
| 10 | Illinois | 13.1 | | 12 | Massachusetts | 12.1 |
| 23 | Indiana | 9.6 | | 14 | Ohio | 12.0 |
| 25 | Iowa | 9.3 | | 15 | Missouri | 11.5 |
| 30 | Kansas | 7.9 | | 16 | Florida | 10.9 |
| 19 | Kentucky | 9.8 | | 17 | Michigan | 10.0 |
| 3 | Louisiana | 15.9 | | 18 | Vermont | 9.9 |
| 31 | Maine | 7.6 | | 19 | Kentucky | 9.8 |
| 9 | Maryland | 13.9 | | 19 | Mississippi | 9.8 |
| 12 | Massachusetts | 12.1 | | 21 | California | 9.7 |
| 17 | Michigan | 10.0 | | 21 | Minnesota | 9.7 |
| 21 | Minnesota | 9.7 | | 23 | Indiana | 9.6 |
| 19 | Mississippi | 9.8 | | 24 | New Hampshire | 9.5 |
| 15 | Missouri | 11.5 | | 25 | Iowa | 9.3 |
| 43 | Montana | 4.8 | | 26 | Alabama | 9.2 |
| 11 | Nebraska | 12.4 | | 27 | Tennessee | 8.8 |
| 47 | Nevada | 4.1 | | 28 | Virginia | 8.3 |
| 24 | New Hampshire | 9.5 | | 29 | South Carolina | 8.0 |
| 7 | New Jersey | 14.3 | | 30 | Kansas | 7.9 |
| 41 | New Mexico | 5.2 | | 31 | Maine | 7.6 |
| 6 | New York | 14.4 | | 32 | Georgia | 7.5 |
| 36 | North Carolina | 6.5 | | 33 | Oregon | 7.4 |
| 38 | North Dakota | 5.9 | | 34 | Washington | 7.2 |
| 14 | Ohio | 12.0 | | 35 | Colorado | 7.1 |
| 46 | Oklahoma | 4.2 | | 36 | North Carolina | 6.5 |
| 33 | Oregon | 7.4 | | 36 | South Dakota | 6.5 |
| 2 | Pennsylvania | 16.1 | | 38 | North Dakota | 5.9 |
| 5 | Rhode Island | 14.7 | | 39 | Texas | 5.6 |
| 29 | South Carolina | 8.0 | | 40 | Arkansas | 5.5 |
| 36 | South Dakota | 6.5 | | 41 | New Mexico | 5.2 |
| 27 | Tennessee | 8.8 | | 42 | Arizona | 5.1 |
| '39 | Texas | 5.6 | | 43 | Montana | 4.8 |
| 50 | Utah | 2.5 | | 44 | West Virginia | 4.7 |
| 18 | Vermont | 9.9 | | 45 | Alaska | 4.5 |
| 28 | Virginia | 8.3 | | 46 | Oklahoma | 4.2 |
| 34 | Washington | 7.2 | | 47 | Nevada | 4.1 |
| 44 | West Virginia | 4.7 | | 48 | Idaho | 3.7 |
| 8 | Wisconsin | 14.1 | | 49 | Wyoming | 2.6 |
| 49 | Wyoming | 2.6 | | 50 | Utah | 2.5 |
| | | | | | District of Columbia | 22.6 |

Source: Morgan Quitno Press using data from U.S. Dept. of Education, Office of Educational Research and Improvement
"Private School Universe Survey, 1997-98" (NCES 1999-319, August 1999)
*Estimate for 1997-98.

# Percent of Public Elementary and Secondary Students with Individualized Education Plans (IEP's) in 1999
## National Percent = 12.3% of Students*

<table>
<tr><td colspan="3">ALPHA ORDER</td><td colspan="3">RANK ORDER</td></tr>
<tr><th>RANK</th><th>STATE</th><th>PERCENT</th><th>RANK</th><th>STATE</th><th>PERCENT</th></tr>
<tr><td>16</td><td>Alabama</td><td>13.4</td><td>1</td><td>New Mexico</td><td>18.2</td></tr>
<tr><td>21</td><td>Alaska</td><td>13.1</td><td>2</td><td>Rhode Island</td><td>17.9</td></tr>
<tr><td>48</td><td>Arizona</td><td>10.1</td><td>3</td><td>Massachusetts</td><td>17.6</td></tr>
<tr><td>37</td><td>Arkansas</td><td>11.3</td><td>4</td><td>West Virginia</td><td>16.8</td></tr>
<tr><td>40</td><td>California</td><td>11.1</td><td>5</td><td>Nebraska</td><td>14.9</td></tr>
<tr><td>47</td><td>Colorado</td><td>10.2</td><td>6</td><td>Indiana</td><td>14.7</td></tr>
<tr><td>12</td><td>Connecticut</td><td>14.1</td><td>6</td><td>Maine</td><td>14.7</td></tr>
<tr><td>24</td><td>Delaware</td><td>12.9</td><td>8</td><td>Florida</td><td>14.6</td></tr>
<tr><td>8</td><td>Florida</td><td>14.6</td><td>9</td><td>New York</td><td>14.5</td></tr>
<tr><td>43</td><td>Georgia</td><td>10.9</td><td>10</td><td>Missouri</td><td>14.4</td></tr>
<tr><td>46</td><td>Hawaii</td><td>10.3</td><td>11</td><td>Tennessee</td><td>14.2</td></tr>
<tr><td>39</td><td>Idaho</td><td>11.2</td><td>12</td><td>Connecticut</td><td>14.1</td></tr>
<tr><td>13</td><td>Illinois</td><td>13.6</td><td>13</td><td>Illinois</td><td>13.6</td></tr>
<tr><td>6</td><td>Indiana</td><td>14.7</td><td>13</td><td>Iowa</td><td>13.6</td></tr>
<tr><td>13</td><td>Iowa</td><td>13.6</td><td>13</td><td>Virginia</td><td>13.6</td></tr>
<tr><td>28</td><td>Kansas</td><td>12.3</td><td>16</td><td>Alabama</td><td>13.4</td></tr>
<tr><td>16</td><td>Kentucky</td><td>13.4</td><td>16</td><td>Kentucky</td><td>13.4</td></tr>
<tr><td>31</td><td>Louisiana</td><td>12.2</td><td>16</td><td>New Hampshire</td><td>13.4</td></tr>
<tr><td>6</td><td>Maine</td><td>14.7</td><td>19</td><td>South Carolina</td><td>13.3</td></tr>
<tr><td>21</td><td>Maryland</td><td>13.1</td><td>20</td><td>Wisconsin</td><td>13.2</td></tr>
<tr><td>3</td><td>Massachusetts</td><td>17.6</td><td>21</td><td>Alaska</td><td>13.1</td></tr>
<tr><td>50</td><td>Michigan</td><td>4.9</td><td>21</td><td>Maryland</td><td>13.1</td></tr>
<tr><td>26</td><td>Minnesota</td><td>12.7</td><td>23</td><td>North Carolina</td><td>13.0</td></tr>
<tr><td>28</td><td>Mississippi</td><td>12.3</td><td>24</td><td>Delaware</td><td>12.9</td></tr>
<tr><td>10</td><td>Missouri</td><td>14.4</td><td>25</td><td>Wyoming</td><td>12.8</td></tr>
<tr><td>33</td><td>Montana</td><td>11.6</td><td>26</td><td>Minnesota</td><td>12.7</td></tr>
<tr><td>5</td><td>Nebraska</td><td>14.9</td><td>26</td><td>Oklahoma</td><td>12.7</td></tr>
<tr><td>44</td><td>Nevada</td><td>10.7</td><td>28</td><td>Kansas</td><td>12.3</td></tr>
<tr><td>16</td><td>New Hampshire</td><td>13.4</td><td>28</td><td>Mississippi</td><td>12.3</td></tr>
<tr><td>49</td><td>New Jersey</td><td>6.7</td><td>28</td><td>Texas</td><td>12.3</td></tr>
<tr><td>1</td><td>New Mexico</td><td>18.2</td><td>31</td><td>Louisiana</td><td>12.2</td></tr>
<tr><td>9</td><td>New York</td><td>14.5</td><td>32</td><td>Ohio</td><td>12.0</td></tr>
<tr><td>23</td><td>North Carolina</td><td>13.0</td><td>33</td><td>Montana</td><td>11.6</td></tr>
<tr><td>37</td><td>North Dakota</td><td>11.3</td><td>33</td><td>South Dakota</td><td>11.6</td></tr>
<tr><td>32</td><td>Ohio</td><td>12.0</td><td>35</td><td>Utah</td><td>11.5</td></tr>
<tr><td>26</td><td>Oklahoma</td><td>12.7</td><td>36</td><td>Vermont</td><td>11.4</td></tr>
<tr><td>41</td><td>Oregon</td><td>11.0</td><td>37</td><td>Arkansas</td><td>11.3</td></tr>
<tr><td>41</td><td>Pennsylvania</td><td>11.0</td><td>37</td><td>North Dakota</td><td>11.3</td></tr>
<tr><td>2</td><td>Rhode Island</td><td>17.9</td><td>39</td><td>Idaho</td><td>11.2</td></tr>
<tr><td>19</td><td>South Carolina</td><td>13.3</td><td>40</td><td>California</td><td>11.1</td></tr>
<tr><td>33</td><td>South Dakota</td><td>11.6</td><td>41</td><td>Oregon</td><td>11.0</td></tr>
<tr><td>11</td><td>Tennessee</td><td>14.2</td><td>41</td><td>Pennsylvania</td><td>11.0</td></tr>
<tr><td>28</td><td>Texas</td><td>12.3</td><td>43</td><td>Georgia</td><td>10.9</td></tr>
<tr><td>35</td><td>Utah</td><td>11.5</td><td>44</td><td>Nevada</td><td>10.7</td></tr>
<tr><td>36</td><td>Vermont</td><td>11.4</td><td>44</td><td>Washington</td><td>10.7</td></tr>
<tr><td>13</td><td>Virginia</td><td>13.6</td><td>46</td><td>Hawaii</td><td>10.3</td></tr>
<tr><td>44</td><td>Washington</td><td>10.7</td><td>47</td><td>Colorado</td><td>10.2</td></tr>
<tr><td>4</td><td>West Virginia</td><td>16.8</td><td>48</td><td>Arizona</td><td>10.1</td></tr>
<tr><td>20</td><td>Wisconsin</td><td>13.2</td><td>49</td><td>New Jersey</td><td>6.7</td></tr>
<tr><td>25</td><td>Wyoming</td><td>12.8</td><td>50</td><td>Michigan</td><td>4.9</td></tr>
<tr><td></td><td></td><td></td><td></td><td>District of Columbia</td><td>11.4</td></tr>
</table>

Source: U.S. Department of Education, National Center for Education Statistics
"Overview of Public Elementary and Secondary Schools and Districts" (June 2000)
*These plans are for students participating in various special education services. For school year 1998-99.

# Enrollment in Public Elementary and Secondary Schools in 1999

## National Total = 46,772,445 Students*

ALPHA ORDER

| RANK | STATE | STUDENTS | % of USA |
|---|---|---|---|
| 22 | Alabama | 730,342 | 1.6% |
| 45 | Alaska | 136,658 | 0.3% |
| 19 | Arizona | 872,428 | 1.9% |
| 34 | Arkansas | 426,984 | 0.9% |
| 1 | California | 6,050,609 | 12.9% |
| 24 | Colorado | 708,109 | 1.5% |
| 28 | Connecticut | 554,087 | 1.2% |
| 47 | Delaware | 113,622 | 0.2% |
| 4 | Florida | 2,380,232 | 5.1% |
| 9 | Georgia | 1,422,762 | 3.0% |
| 42 | Hawaii | 185,036 | 0.4% |
| 39 | Idaho | 245,100 | 0.5% |
| 5 | Illinois | 2,035,450 | 4.4% |
| 14 | Indiana | 993,985 | 2.1% |
| 31 | Iowa | 498,836 | 1.1% |
| 33 | Kansas | 469,376 | 1.0% |
| 26 | Kentucky | 637,007 | 1.4% |
| 23 | Louisiana | 710,159 | 1.5% |
| 40 | Maine | 219,000 | 0.5% |
| 21 | Maryland | 846,709 | 1.8% |
| 15 | Massachusetts | 975,815 | 2.1% |
| 8 | Michigan | 1,712,300 | 3.7% |
| 20 | Minnesota | 857,023 | 1.8% |
| 30 | Mississippi | 499,359 | 1.1% |
| 17 | Missouri | 893,052 | 1.9% |
| 43 | Montana | 157,236 | 0.3% |
| 38 | Nebraska | 287,752 | 0.6% |
| 35 | Nevada | 326,616 | 0.7% |
| 41 | New Hampshire | 208,812 | 0.4% |
| 10 | New Jersey | 1,287,996 | 2.8% |
| 36 | New Mexico | 324,222 | 0.7% |
| 3 | New York | 2,884,000 | 6.2% |
| 11 | North Carolina | 1,256,063 | 2.7% |
| 48 | North Dakota | 111,705 | 0.2% |
| 6 | Ohio | 1,837,000 | 3.9% |
| 27 | Oklahoma | 633,361 | 1.4% |
| 29 | Oregon | 545,059 | 1.2% |
| 7 | Pennsylvania | 1,817,530 | 3.9% |
| 44 | Rhode Island | 156,458 | 0.3% |
| 25 | South Carolina | 646,850 | 1.4% |
| 46 | South Dakota | 130,863 | 0.3% |
| 16 | Tennessee | 908,722 | 1.9% |
| 2 | Texas | 4,025,923 | 8.6% |
| 32 | Utah | 477,775 | 1.0% |
| 49 | Vermont | 106,069 | 0.2% |
| 12 | Virginia | 1,133,994 | 2.4% |
| 13 | Washington | 1,002,044 | 2.1% |
| 37 | West Virginia | 290,936 | 0.6% |
| 18 | Wisconsin | 878,900 | 1.9% |
| 50 | Wyoming | 91,757 | 0.2% |

RANK ORDER

| RANK | STATE | STUDENTS | % of USA |
|---|---|---|---|
| 1 | California | 6,050,609 | 12.9% |
| 2 | Texas | 4,025,923 | 8.6% |
| 3 | New York | 2,884,000 | 6.2% |
| 4 | Florida | 2,380,232 | 5.1% |
| 5 | Illinois | 2,035,450 | 4.4% |
| 6 | Ohio | 1,837,000 | 3.9% |
| 7 | Pennsylvania | 1,817,530 | 3.9% |
| 8 | Michigan | 1,712,300 | 3.7% |
| 9 | Georgia | 1,422,762 | 3.0% |
| 10 | New Jersey | 1,287,996 | 2.8% |
| 11 | North Carolina | 1,256,063 | 2.7% |
| 12 | Virginia | 1,133,994 | 2.4% |
| 13 | Washington | 1,002,044 | 2.1% |
| 14 | Indiana | 993,985 | 2.1% |
| 15 | Massachusetts | 975,815 | 2.1% |
| 16 | Tennessee | 908,722 | 1.9% |
| 17 | Missouri | 893,052 | 1.9% |
| 18 | Wisconsin | 878,900 | 1.9% |
| 19 | Arizona | 872,428 | 1.9% |
| 20 | Minnesota | 857,023 | 1.8% |
| 21 | Maryland | 846,709 | 1.8% |
| 22 | Alabama | 730,342 | 1.6% |
| 23 | Louisiana | 710,159 | 1.5% |
| 24 | Colorado | 708,109 | 1.5% |
| 25 | South Carolina | 646,850 | 1.4% |
| 26 | Kentucky | 637,007 | 1.4% |
| 27 | Oklahoma | 633,361 | 1.4% |
| 28 | Connecticut | 554,087 | 1.2% |
| 29 | Oregon | 545,059 | 1.2% |
| 30 | Mississippi | 499,359 | 1.1% |
| 31 | Iowa | 498,836 | 1.1% |
| 32 | Utah | 477,775 | 1.0% |
| 33 | Kansas | 469,376 | 1.0% |
| 34 | Arkansas | 426,984 | 0.9% |
| 35 | Nevada | 326,616 | 0.7% |
| 36 | New Mexico | 324,222 | 0.7% |
| 37 | West Virginia | 290,936 | 0.6% |
| 38 | Nebraska | 287,752 | 0.6% |
| 39 | Idaho | 245,100 | 0.5% |
| 40 | Maine | 219,000 | 0.5% |
| 41 | New Hampshire | 208,812 | 0.4% |
| 42 | Hawaii | 185,036 | 0.4% |
| 43 | Montana | 157,236 | 0.3% |
| 44 | Rhode Island | 156,458 | 0.3% |
| 45 | Alaska | 136,658 | 0.3% |
| 46 | South Dakota | 130,863 | 0.3% |
| 47 | Delaware | 113,622 | 0.2% |
| 48 | North Dakota | 111,705 | 0.2% |
| 49 | Vermont | 106,069 | 0.2% |
| 50 | Wyoming | 91,757 | 0.2% |
| | District of Columbia | 70,762 | 0.2% |

*Source: U.S. Department of Education, Office of Educational Research and Improvement*
*"Early Estimates of Public Elementary and Secondary Education Statistics: 1999-2000" (May 2000)*
*Fall 1999.

# Pupil-Teacher Ratio in Public Elementary and Secondary Schools in 2000

## National Ratio = 16.2 Pupils per Teacher*

ALPHA ORDER

| RANK | STATE | RATIO |
|------|-------|-------|
| 30 | Alabama | 15.1 |
| 11 | Alaska | 17.1 |
| 4 | Arizona | 19.2 |
| 21 | Arkansas | 15.9 |
| 2 | California | 20.7 |
| 10 | Colorado | 17.2 |
| 43 | Connecticut | 13.9 |
| 25 | Delaware | 15.5 |
| 7 | Florida | 18.1 |
| 23 | Georgia | 15.8 |
| 9 | Hawaii | 17.6 |
| 13 | Idaho | 16.8 |
| 18 | Illinois | 16.0 |
| 12 | Indiana | 16.9 |
| 34 | Iowa | 14.8 |
| 36 | Kansas | 14.6 |
| 18 | Kentucky | 16.0 |
| 32 | Louisiana | 15.0 |
| 49 | Maine | 12.8 |
| 14 | Maryland | 16.7 |
| 47 | Massachusetts | 13.6 |
| 6 | Michigan | 18.4 |
| 21 | Minnesota | 15.9 |
| 17 | Mississippi | 16.2 |
| 38 | Missouri | 14.1 |
| 26 | Montana | 15.4 |
| 41 | Nebraska | 14.0 |
| 5 | Nevada | 18.7 |
| 26 | New Hampshire | 15.4 |
| 48 | New Jersey | 13.5 |
| 15 | New Mexico | 16.4 |
| 41 | New York | 14.0 |
| 23 | North Carolina | 15.8 |
| 38 | North Dakota | 14.1 |
| 18 | Ohio | 16.0 |
| 28 | Oklahoma | 15.2 |
| 7 | Oregon | 18.1 |
| 16 | Pennsylvania | 16.3 |
| 43 | Rhode Island | 13.9 |
| 35 | South Carolina | 14.7 |
| 38 | South Dakota | 14.1 |
| 32 | Tennessee | 15.0 |
| 30 | Texas | 15.1 |
| 1 | Utah | 22.3 |
| 50 | Vermont | 12.4 |
| 43 | Virginia | 13.9 |
| 3 | Washington | 20.0 |
| 37 | West Virginia | 14.3 |
| 28 | Wisconsin | 15.2 |
| 43 | Wyoming | 13.9 |

RANK ORDER

| RANK | STATE | RATIO |
|------|-------|-------|
| 1 | Utah | 22.3 |
| 2 | California | 20.7 |
| 3 | Washington | 20.0 |
| 4 | Arizona | 19.2 |
| 5 | Nevada | 18.7 |
| 6 | Michigan | 18.4 |
| 7 | Florida | 18.1 |
| 7 | Oregon | 18.1 |
| 9 | Hawaii | 17.6 |
| 10 | Colorado | 17.2 |
| 11 | Alaska | 17.1 |
| 12 | Indiana | 16.9 |
| 13 | Idaho | 16.8 |
| 14 | Maryland | 16.7 |
| 15 | New Mexico | 16.4 |
| 16 | Pennsylvania | 16.3 |
| 17 | Mississippi | 16.2 |
| 18 | Illinois | 16.0 |
| 18 | Kentucky | 16.0 |
| 18 | Ohio | 16.0 |
| 21 | Arkansas | 15.9 |
| 21 | Minnesota | 15.9 |
| 23 | Georgia | 15.8 |
| 23 | North Carolina | 15.8 |
| 25 | Delaware | 15.5 |
| 26 | Montana | 15.4 |
| 26 | New Hampshire | 15.4 |
| 28 | Oklahoma | 15.2 |
| 28 | Wisconsin | 15.2 |
| 30 | Alabama | 15.1 |
| 30 | Texas | 15.1 |
| 32 | Louisiana | 15.0 |
| 32 | Tennessee | 15.0 |
| 34 | Iowa | 14.8 |
| 35 | South Carolina | 14.7 |
| 36 | Kansas | 14.6 |
| 37 | West Virginia | 14.3 |
| 38 | Missouri | 14.1 |
| 38 | North Dakota | 14.1 |
| 38 | South Dakota | 14.1 |
| 41 | Nebraska | 14.0 |
| 41 | New York | 14.0 |
| 43 | Connecticut | 13.9 |
| 43 | Rhode Island | 13.9 |
| 43 | Virginia | 13.9 |
| 43 | Wyoming | 13.9 |
| 47 | Massachusetts | 13.6 |
| 48 | New Jersey | 13.5 |
| 49 | Maine | 12.8 |
| 50 | Vermont | 12.4 |
| | District of Columbia | 13.6 |

*Source: U.S. Department of Education, Office of Educational Research and Improvement*
*"Early Estimates of Public Elementary and Secondary Education Statistics: 1999-2000" (May 2000)*
*School year 1999-2000.

# Teachers in Public Elementary and Secondary Schools in 2000

## National Total = 2,887,233 Teachers*

ALPHA ORDER

| RANK | STATE | TEACHERS | % of USA |
|---|---|---|---|
| 21 | Alabama | 48,269 | 1.7% |
| 47 | Alaska | 7,992 | 0.3% |
| 23 | Arizona | 45,540 | 1.6% |
| 33 | Arkansas | 26,836 | 0.9% |
| 1 | California | 292,455 | 10.1% |
| 26 | Colorado | 41,104 | 1.4% |
| 27 | Connecticut | 39,918 | 1.4% |
| 49 | Delaware | 7,311 | 0.3% |
| 4 | Florida | 131,249 | 4.5% |
| 10 | Georgia | 90,286 | 3.1% |
| 43 | Hawaii | 10,510 | 0.4% |
| 40 | Idaho | 14,600 | 0.5% |
| 5 | Illinois | 127,216 | 4.4% |
| 16 | Indiana | 58,843 | 2.0% |
| 29 | Iowa | 33,744 | 1.2% |
| 30 | Kansas | 32,240 | 1.1% |
| 28 | Kentucky | 39,813 | 1.4% |
| 22 | Louisiana | 47,363 | 1.6% |
| 39 | Maine | 17,170 | 0.6% |
| 19 | Maryland | 50,801 | 1.8% |
| 13 | Massachusetts | 71,922 | 2.5% |
| 9 | Michigan | 93,100 | 3.2% |
| 18 | Minnesota | 53,747 | 1.9% |
| 31 | Mississippi | 30,736 | 1.1% |
| 14 | Missouri | 63,500 | 2.2% |
| 44 | Montana | 10,200 | 0.4% |
| 35 | Nebraska | 20,609 | 0.7% |
| 38 | Nevada | 17,486 | 0.6% |
| 41 | New Hampshire | 13,559 | 0.5% |
| 8 | New Jersey | 95,223 | 3.3% |
| 37 | New Mexico | 19,802 | 0.7% |
| 3 | New York | 206,000 | 7.1% |
| 12 | North Carolina | 79,498 | 2.8% |
| 48 | North Dakota | 7,904 | 0.3% |
| 6 | Ohio | 114,600 | 4.0% |
| 25 | Oklahoma | 41,557 | 1.4% |
| 32 | Oregon | 30,086 | 1.0% |
| 7 | Pennsylvania | 111,250 | 3.9% |
| 42 | Rhode Island | 11,235 | 0.4% |
| 24 | South Carolina | 43,870 | 1.5% |
| 45 | South Dakota | 9,250 | 0.3% |
| 15 | Tennessee | 60,474 | 2.1% |
| 2 | Texas | 266,878 | 9.2% |
| 34 | Utah | 21,400 | 0.7% |
| 46 | Vermont | 8,549 | 0.3% |
| 11 | Virginia | 81,751 | 2.8% |
| 20 | Washington | 50,009 | 1.7% |
| 36 | West Virginia | 20,316 | 0.7% |
| 17 | Wisconsin | 57,670 | 2.0% |
| 50 | Wyoming | 6,600 | 0.2% |

RANK ORDER

| RANK | STATE | TEACHERS | % of USA |
|---|---|---|---|
| 1 | California | 292,455 | 10.1% |
| 2 | Texas | 266,878 | 9.2% |
| 3 | New York | 206,000 | 7.1% |
| 4 | Florida | 131,249 | 4.5% |
| 5 | Illinois | 127,216 | 4.4% |
| 6 | Ohio | 114,600 | 4.0% |
| 7 | Pennsylvania | 111,250 | 3.9% |
| 8 | New Jersey | 95,223 | 3.3% |
| 9 | Michigan | 93,100 | 3.2% |
| 10 | Georgia | 90,286 | 3.1% |
| 11 | Virginia | 81,751 | 2.8% |
| 12 | North Carolina | 79,498 | 2.8% |
| 13 | Massachusetts | 71,922 | 2.5% |
| 14 | Missouri | 63,500 | 2.2% |
| 15 | Tennessee | 60,474 | 2.1% |
| 16 | Indiana | 58,843 | 2.0% |
| 17 | Wisconsin | 57,670 | 2.0% |
| 18 | Minnesota | 53,747 | 1.9% |
| 19 | Maryland | 50,801 | 1.8% |
| 20 | Washington | 50,009 | 1.7% |
| 21 | Alabama | 48,269 | 1.7% |
| 22 | Louisiana | 47,363 | 1.6% |
| 23 | Arizona | 45,540 | 1.6% |
| 24 | South Carolina | 43,870 | 1.5% |
| 25 | Oklahoma | 41,557 | 1.4% |
| 26 | Colorado | 41,104 | 1.4% |
| 27 | Connecticut | 39,918 | 1.4% |
| 28 | Kentucky | 39,813 | 1.4% |
| 29 | Iowa | 33,744 | 1.2% |
| 30 | Kansas | 32,240 | 1.1% |
| 31 | Mississippi | 30,736 | 1.1% |
| 32 | Oregon | 30,086 | 1.0% |
| 33 | Arkansas | 26,836 | 0.9% |
| 34 | Utah | 21,400 | 0.7% |
| 35 | Nebraska | 20,609 | 0.7% |
| 36 | West Virginia | 20,316 | 0.7% |
| 37 | New Mexico | 19,802 | 0.7% |
| 38 | Nevada | 17,486 | 0.6% |
| 39 | Maine | 17,170 | 0.6% |
| 40 | Idaho | 14,600 | 0.5% |
| 41 | New Hampshire | 13,559 | 0.5% |
| 42 | Rhode Island | 11,235 | 0.4% |
| 43 | Hawaii | 10,510 | 0.4% |
| 44 | Montana | 10,200 | 0.4% |
| 45 | South Dakota | 9,250 | 0.3% |
| 46 | Vermont | 8,549 | 0.3% |
| 47 | Alaska | 7,992 | 0.3% |
| 48 | North Dakota | 7,904 | 0.3% |
| 49 | Delaware | 7,311 | 0.3% |
| 50 | Wyoming | 6,600 | 0.2% |
| | District of Columbia | 5,192 | 0.2% |

*Source: U.S. Department of Education, Office of Educational Research and Improvement*
*"Early Estimates of Public Elementary and Secondary Education Statistics: 1999-2000" (May 2000)*
*School year 1999-2000.

# Average Salary of Teachers in 1999

## National Average = $40,582*

| ALPHA ORDER | | | | RANK ORDER | | |
|---|---|---|---|---|---|---|
| **RANK** | **STATE** | **SALARY** | | **RANK** | **STATE** | **SALARY** |
| 30 | Alabama | $35,820 | | 1 | Connecticut | $51,584 |
| 6 | Alaska | 46,845 | | 2 | New Jersey | 51,193 |
| 33 | Arizona | 35,025 | | 3 | New York | 49,437 |
| 45 | Arkansas | 32,350 | | 4 | Pennsylvania | 48,457 |
| 9 | California | 45,400 | | 5 | Michigan | 48,207 |
| 22 | Colorado | 38,025 | | 6 | Alaska | 46,845 |
| 1 | Connecticut | 51,584 | | 7 | Rhode Island | 45,650 |
| 11 | Delaware | 43,164 | | 8 | Illinois | 45,569 |
| 29 | Florida | 35,916 | | 9 | California | 45,400 |
| 18 | Georgia | 39,675 | | 10 | Massachusetts | 45,075 |
| 17 | Hawaii | 40,377 | | 11 | Delaware | 43,164 |
| 39 | Idaho | 34,063 | | 12 | Oregon | 42,833 |
| 8 | Illinois | 45,569 | | 13 | Maryland | 42,526 |
| 14 | Indiana | 41,163 | | 14 | Indiana | 41,163 |
| 34 | Iowa | 34,927 | | 15 | Wisconsin | 40,657 |
| 24 | Kansas | 37,405 | | 16 | Ohio | 40,566 |
| 31 | Kentucky | 35,526 | | 17 | Hawaii | 40,377 |
| 43 | Louisiana | 32,510 | | 18 | Georgia | 39,675 |
| 35 | Maine | 34,906 | | 19 | Minnesota | 39,458 |
| 13 | Maryland | 42,526 | | 20 | Nevada | 38,883 |
| 10 | Massachusetts | 45,075 | | 21 | Washington | 38,692 |
| 5 | Michigan | 48,207 | | 22 | Colorado | 38,025 |
| 19 | Minnesota | 39,458 | | 23 | Virginia | 37,475 |
| 48 | Mississippi | 29,530 | | 24 | Kansas | 37,405 |
| 36 | Missouri | 34,746 | | 24 | New Hampshire | 37,405 |
| 46 | Montana | 31,356 | | 26 | Vermont | 36,800 |
| 42 | Nebraska | 32,880 | | 27 | Tennessee | 36,500 |
| 20 | Nevada | 38,883 | | 28 | North Carolina | 36,098 |
| 24 | New Hampshire | 37,405 | | 29 | Florida | 35,916 |
| 2 | New Jersey | 51,193 | | 30 | Alabama | 35,820 |
| 44 | New Mexico | 32,398 | | 31 | Kentucky | 35,526 |
| 3 | New York | 49,437 | | 32 | Texas | 35,041 |
| 28 | North Carolina | 36,098 | | 33 | Arizona | 35,025 |
| 49 | North Dakota | 28,976 | | 34 | Iowa | 34,927 |
| 16 | Ohio | 40,566 | | 35 | Maine | 34,906 |
| 47 | Oklahoma | 31,149 | | 36 | Missouri | 34,746 |
| 12 | Oregon | 42,833 | | 37 | South Carolina | 34,506 |
| 4 | Pennsylvania | 48,457 | | 38 | West Virginia | 34,244 |
| 7 | Rhode Island | 45,650 | | 39 | Idaho | 34,063 |
| 37 | South Carolina | 34,506 | | 40 | Wyoming | 33,500 |
| 50 | South Dakota | 28,552 | | 41 | Utah | 32,950 |
| 27 | Tennessee | 36,500 | | 42 | Nebraska | 32,880 |
| 32 | Texas | 35,041 | | 43 | Louisiana | 32,510 |
| 41 | Utah | 32,950 | | 44 | New Mexico | 32,398 |
| 26 | Vermont | 36,800 | | 45 | Arkansas | 32,350 |
| 23 | Virginia | 37,475 | | 46 | Montana | 31,356 |
| 21 | Washington | 38,692 | | 47 | Oklahoma | 31,149 |
| 38 | West Virginia | 34,244 | | 48 | Mississippi | 29,530 |
| 15 | Wisconsin | 40,657 | | 49 | North Dakota | 28,976 |
| 40 | Wyoming | 33,500 | | 50 | South Dakota | 28,552 |
| | | | | | District of Columbia | 47,150 |

Source: National Education Association, Washington, D.C.
   "Rankings & Estimates" (Copyright © 1999, NEA, used with permission)
*For 1998-99.

# Public High School Graduates in 2000

## National Total = 2,545,317 Graduates*

ALPHA ORDER

RANK ORDER

| RANK | STATE | GRADUATES | % of USA | | RANK | STATE | GRADUATES | % of USA |
|---|---|---|---|---|---|---|---|---|
| 23 | Alabama | 37,893 | 1.5% | | 1 | California | 303,169 | 11.9% |
| 47 | Alaska | 6,975 | 0.3% | | 2 | Texas | 212,966 | 8.4% |
| 20 | Arizona | 42,369 | 1.7% | | 3 | New York | 141,800 | 5.6% |
| 33 | Arkansas | 26,622 | 1.0% | | 4 | Ohio | 115,000 | 4.5% |
| 1 | California | 303,169 | 11.9% | | 5 | Pennsylvania | 114,160 | 4.5% |
| 22 | Colorado | 38,078 | 1.5% | | 6 | Illinois | 111,230 | 4.4% |
| 30 | Connecticut | 29,858 | 1.2% | | 7 | Michigan | 100,600 | 4.0% |
| 49 | Delaware | 6,356 | 0.2% | | 8 | Florida | 99,930 | 3.9% |
| 8 | Florida | 99,930 | 3.9% | | 9 | New Jersey | 68,946 | 2.7% |
| 11 | Georgia | 66,635 | 2.6% | | 10 | Virginia | 66,868 | 2.6% |
| 43 | Hawaii | 10,152 | 0.4% | | 11 | Georgia | 66,635 | 2.6% |
| 38 | Idaho | 15,700 | 0.6% | | 12 | North Carolina | 61,463 | 2.4% |
| 6 | Illinois | 111,230 | 4.4% | | 13 | Wisconsin | 59,438 | 2.3% |
| 14 | Indiana | 58,364 | 2.3% | | 14 | Indiana | 58,364 | 2.3% |
| 28 | Iowa | 34,149 | 1.3% | | 15 | Minnesota | 57,603 | 2.3% |
| 31 | Kansas | 28,964 | 1.1% | | 16 | Washington | 57,246 | 2.2% |
| 24 | Kentucky | 36,956 | 1.5% | | 17 | Missouri | 53,500 | 2.1% |
| 26 | Louisiana | 35,184 | 1.4% | | 18 | Massachusetts | 50,537 | 2.0% |
| 40 | Maine | 12,871 | 0.5% | | 19 | Maryland | 48,106 | 1.9% |
| 19 | Maryland | 48,106 | 1.9% | | 20 | Arizona | 42,369 | 1.7% |
| 18 | Massachusetts | 50,537 | 2.0% | | 21 | Tennessee | 41,719 | 1.6% |
| 7 | Michigan | 100,600 | 4.0% | | 22 | Colorado | 38,078 | 1.5% |
| 15 | Minnesota | 57,603 | 2.3% | | 23 | Alabama | 37,893 | 1.5% |
| 34 | Mississippi | 26,375 | 1.0% | | 24 | Kentucky | 36,956 | 1.5% |
| 17 | Missouri | 53,500 | 2.1% | | 25 | Oklahoma | 36,759 | 1.4% |
| 41 | Montana | 10,893 | 0.4% | | 26 | Louisiana | 35,184 | 1.4% |
| 35 | Nebraska | 22,093 | 0.9% | | 27 | South Carolina | 34,500 | 1.4% |
| 39 | Nevada | 13,922 | 0.5% | | 28 | Iowa | 34,149 | 1.3% |
| 42 | New Hampshire | 10,383 | 0.4% | | 29 | Utah | 32,303 | 1.3% |
| 9 | New Jersey | 68,946 | 2.7% | | 30 | Connecticut | 29,858 | 1.2% |
| 37 | New Mexico | 17,254 | 0.7% | | 31 | Kansas | 28,964 | 1.1% |
| 3 | New York | 141,800 | 5.6% | | 32 | Oregon | 28,700 | 1.1% |
| 12 | North Carolina | 61,463 | 2.4% | | 33 | Arkansas | 26,622 | 1.0% |
| 45 | North Dakota | 8,635 | 0.3% | | 34 | Mississippi | 26,375 | 1.0% |
| 4 | Ohio | 115,000 | 4.5% | | 35 | Nebraska | 22,093 | 0.9% |
| 25 | Oklahoma | 36,759 | 1.4% | | 36 | West Virginia | 19,582 | 0.8% |
| 32 | Oregon | 28,700 | 1.1% | | 37 | New Mexico | 17,254 | 0.7% |
| 5 | Pennsylvania | 114,160 | 4.5% | | 38 | Idaho | 15,700 | 0.6% |
| 46 | Rhode Island | 7,498 | 0.3% | | 39 | Nevada | 13,922 | 0.5% |
| 27 | South Carolina | 34,500 | 1.4% | | 40 | Maine | 12,871 | 0.5% |
| 44 | South Dakota | 9,420 | 0.4% | | 41 | Montana | 10,893 | 0.4% |
| 21 | Tennessee | 41,719 | 1.6% | | 42 | New Hampshire | 10,383 | 0.4% |
| 2 | Texas | 212,966 | 8.4% | | 43 | Hawaii | 10,152 | 0.4% |
| 29 | Utah | 32,303 | 1.3% | | 44 | South Dakota | 9,420 | 0.4% |
| 48 | Vermont | 6,763 | 0.3% | | 45 | North Dakota | 8,635 | 0.3% |
| 10 | Virginia | 66,868 | 2.6% | | 46 | Rhode Island | 7,498 | 0.3% |
| 16 | Washington | 57,246 | 2.2% | | 47 | Alaska | 6,975 | 0.3% |
| 36 | West Virginia | 19,582 | 0.8% | | 48 | Vermont | 6,763 | 0.3% |
| 13 | Wisconsin | 59,438 | 2.3% | | 49 | Delaware | 6,356 | 0.2% |
| 50 | Wyoming | 6,300 | 0.2% | | 50 | Wyoming | 6,300 | 0.2% |
| | | | | | | District of Columbia | 2,530 | 0.1% |

Source: U.S. Department of Education, National Center for Education Statistics
   "Digest of Education Statistics 2000 (NCES 2001-34, January 2001)
*Estimate for 1999-2000. Excludes persons receiving high school equivalency certificates and graduates of federal schools for American Indians.

# Percent Change in Public High School Graduates: 1996 to 2000

## National Percent Change = 12.0% Increase*

ALPHA ORDER

RANK ORDER

| RANK | STATE | PERCENT CHANGE | RANK | STATE | PERCENT CHANGE |
|---|---|---|---|---|---|
| 29 | Alabama | 8.1 | 1 | Arizona | 41.2 |
| 8 | Alaska | 17.3 | 2 | Nevada | 34.2 |
| 1 | Arizona | 41.2 | 3 | Texas | 23.9 |
| 40 | Arkansas | 6.1 | 4 | Utah | 22.9 |
| 9 | California | 17.0 | 5 | Nebraska | 22.6 |
| 10 | Colorado | 16.8 | 6 | Georgia | 18.4 |
| 18 | Connecticut | 13.4 | 7 | Michigan | 17.6 |
| 19 | Delaware | 13.3 | 8 | Alaska | 17.3 |
| 23 | Florida | 12.0 | 9 | California | 17.0 |
| 6 | Georgia | 18.4 | 10 | Colorado | 16.8 |
| 29 | Hawaii | 8.1 | 11 | Vermont | 15.3 |
| 37 | Idaho | 7.0 | 12 | Maryland | 15.1 |
| 39 | Illinois | 6.3 | 13 | Virginia | 15.0 |
| 43 | Indiana | 3.6 | 14 | Washington | 14.8 |
| 32 | Iowa | 7.8 | 15 | Mississippi | 14.5 |
| 22 | Kansas | 12.3 | 16 | South Carolina | 14.3 |
| 46 | Kentucky | 0.9 | 17 | Minnesota | 14.1 |
| 48 | Louisiana | (3.5) | 18 | Connecticut | 13.4 |
| 28 | Maine | 9.1 | 19 | Delaware | 13.3 |
| 12 | Maryland | 15.1 | 20 | Wisconsin | 12.9 |
| 42 | Massachusetts | 5.3 | 21 | Ohio | 12.6 |
| 7 | Michigan | 17.6 | 22 | Kansas | 12.3 |
| 17 | Minnesota | 14.1 | 23 | Florida | 12.0 |
| 15 | Mississippi | 14.5 | 23 | New Mexico | 12.0 |
| 27 | Missouri | 9.2 | 25 | Oklahoma | 11.2 |
| 36 | Montana | 7.4 | 26 | South Dakota | 10.4 |
| 5 | Nebraska | 22.6 | 27 | Missouri | 9.2 |
| 2 | Nevada | 34.2 | 28 | Maine | 9.1 |
| 44 | New Hampshire | 2.9 | 29 | Alabama | 8.1 |
| 45 | New Jersey | 1.8 | 29 | Hawaii | 8.1 |
| 23 | New Mexico | 12.0 | 31 | Oregon | 8.0 |
| 41 | New York | 5.5 | 32 | Iowa | 7.8 |
| 32 | North Carolina | 7.8 | 32 | North Carolina | 7.8 |
| 35 | North Dakota | 7.6 | 34 | Pennsylvania | 7.7 |
| 21 | Ohio | 12.6 | 35 | North Dakota | 7.6 |
| 25 | Oklahoma | 11.2 | 36 | Montana | 7.4 |
| 31 | Oregon | 8.0 | 37 | Idaho | 7.0 |
| 34 | Pennsylvania | 7.7 | 38 | Wyoming | 6.9 |
| 47 | Rhode Island | (2.5) | 39 | Illinois | 6.3 |
| 16 | South Carolina | 14.3 | 40 | Arkansas | 6.1 |
| 26 | South Dakota | 10.4 | 41 | New York | 5.5 |
| 50 | Tennessee | (4.7) | 42 | Massachusetts | 5.3 |
| 3 | Texas | 23.9 | 43 | Indiana | 3.6 |
| 4 | Utah | 22.9 | 44 | New Hampshire | 2.9 |
| 11 | Vermont | 15.3 | 45 | New Jersey | 1.8 |
| 13 | Virginia | 15.0 | 46 | Kentucky | 0.9 |
| 14 | Washington | 14.8 | 47 | Rhode Island | (2.5) |
| 49 | West Virginia | (3.7) | 48 | Louisiana | (3.5) |
| 20 | Wisconsin | 12.9 | 49 | West Virginia | (3.7) |
| 38 | Wyoming | 6.9 | 50 | Tennessee | (4.7) |
| | | | | District of Columbia | (6.2) |

Source: Morgan Quitno Press using data from U.S. Dept of Education, National Center for Education Statistics
    "Digest of Education Statistics 2000 (NCES 2001-34, January 2001)
*Estimate for 1999-2000. Excludes persons receiving high school equivalency certificates and graduates of federal
schools for American Indians.

# Public High School Graduation Rate in 2000

## National Rate = 67.0% Graduated*

ALPHA ORDER

| RANK | STATE | PERCENT |
|------|-------|---------|
| 42 | Alabama | 59.0 |
| 33 | Alaska | 65.7 |
| 34 | Arizona | 65.6 |
| 23 | Arkansas | 71.6 |
| 30 | California | 67.2 |
| 29 | Colorado | 69.0 |
| 20 | Connecticut | 72.8 |
| 37 | Delaware | 63.2 |
| 49 | Florida | 51.7 |
| 46 | Georgia | 55.7 |
| 38 | Hawaii | 62.4 |
| 15 | Idaho | 74.7 |
| 26 | Illinois | 70.7 |
| 28 | Indiana | 69.8 |
| 4 | Iowa | 83.5 |
| 16 | Kansas | 74.1 |
| 31 | Kentucky | 66.0 |
| 50 | Louisiana | 51.5 |
| 6 | Maine | 81.2 |
| 18 | Maryland | 73.7 |
| 24 | Massachusetts | 71.4 |
| 21 | Michigan | 72.5 |
| 3 | Minnesota | 84.0 |
| 41 | Mississippi | 60.9 |
| 17 | Missouri | 74.0 |
| 10 | Montana | 78.0 |
| 1 | Nebraska | 91.9 |
| 32 | Nevada | 65.8 |
| 35 | New Hampshire | 64.9 |
| 8 | New Jersey | 79.2 |
| 45 | New Mexico | 57.7 |
| 43 | New York | 58.6 |
| 44 | North Carolina | 58.1 |
| 2 | North Dakota | 84.4 |
| 22 | Ohio | 71.7 |
| 25 | Oklahoma | 71.1 |
| 36 | Oregon | 64.2 |
| 14 | Pennsylvania | 75.1 |
| 40 | Rhode Island | 61.5 |
| 46 | South Carolina | 55.7 |
| 11 | South Dakota | 75.4 |
| 48 | Tennessee | 55.0 |
| 39 | Texas | 61.9 |
| 5 | Utah | 83.4 |
| 7 | Vermont | 79.7 |
| 11 | Virginia | 75.4 |
| 27 | Washington | 70.4 |
| 13 | West Virginia | 75.3 |
| 9 | Wisconsin | 79.1 |
| 19 | Wyoming | 73.2 |

RANK ORDER

| RANK | STATE | PERCENT |
|------|-------|---------|
| 1 | Nebraska | 91.9 |
| 2 | North Dakota | 84.4 |
| 3 | Minnesota | 84.0 |
| 4 | Iowa | 83.5 |
| 5 | Utah | 83.4 |
| 6 | Maine | 81.2 |
| 7 | Vermont | 79.7 |
| 8 | New Jersey | 79.2 |
| 9 | Wisconsin | 79.1 |
| 10 | Montana | 78.0 |
| 11 | South Dakota | 75.4 |
| 11 | Virginia | 75.4 |
| 13 | West Virginia | 75.3 |
| 14 | Pennsylvania | 75.1 |
| 15 | Idaho | 74.7 |
| 16 | Kansas | 74.1 |
| 17 | Missouri | 74.0 |
| 18 | Maryland | 73.7 |
| 19 | Wyoming | 73.2 |
| 20 | Connecticut | 72.8 |
| 21 | Michigan | 72.5 |
| 22 | Ohio | 71.7 |
| 23 | Arkansas | 71.6 |
| 24 | Massachusetts | 71.4 |
| 25 | Oklahoma | 71.1 |
| 26 | Illinois | 70.7 |
| 27 | Washington | 70.4 |
| 28 | Indiana | 69.8 |
| 29 | Colorado | 69.0 |
| 30 | California | 67.2 |
| 31 | Kentucky | 66.0 |
| 32 | Nevada | 65.8 |
| 33 | Alaska | 65.7 |
| 34 | Arizona | 65.6 |
| 35 | New Hampshire | 64.9 |
| 36 | Oregon | 64.2 |
| 37 | Delaware | 63.2 |
| 38 | Hawaii | 62.4 |
| 39 | Texas | 61.9 |
| 40 | Rhode Island | 61.5 |
| 41 | Mississippi | 60.9 |
| 42 | Alabama | 59.0 |
| 43 | New York | 58.6 |
| 44 | North Carolina | 58.1 |
| 45 | New Mexico | 57.7 |
| 46 | Georgia | 55.7 |
| 46 | South Carolina | 55.7 |
| 48 | Tennessee | 55.0 |
| 49 | Florida | 51.7 |
| 50 | Louisiana | 51.5 |

District of Columbia   51.1

Source: Morgan Quitno Press using data from U.S. Dept of Education, National Center for Education Statistics
    "Digest of Education Statistics 2000 (NCES 2001-34, January 2001)
*Calculated by comparing estimated number of public high school graduates in 2000 with 9th grade enrollment in Fall 1996.  Data exclude ungraded pupils and have not been adjusted for interstate migration or switching to private schools.

# Percent of Population Graduated from High School in 2000

## National Percent = 84.1% of Population*

ALPHA ORDER

| RANK | STATE | PERCENT |
|------|-------|---------|
| 49 | Alabama | 77.5 |
| 5 | Alaska | 90.4 |
| 31 | Arizona | 85.1 |
| 40 | Arkansas | 81.7 |
| 42 | California | 81.2 |
| 9 | Colorado | 89.7 |
| 13 | Connecticut | 88.2 |
| 25 | Delaware | 86.1 |
| 34 | Florida | 84.0 |
| 37 | Georgia | 82.6 |
| 17 | Hawaii | 87.4 |
| 23 | Idaho | 86.2 |
| 29 | Illinois | 85.5 |
| 33 | Indiana | 84.6 |
| 9 | Iowa | 89.7 |
| 14 | Kansas | 88.1 |
| 48 | Kentucky | 78.7 |
| 43 | Louisiana | 80.8 |
| 12 | Maine | 89.3 |
| 27 | Maryland | 85.7 |
| 31 | Massachusetts | 85.1 |
| 23 | Michigan | 86.2 |
| 3 | Minnesota | 90.8 |
| 44 | Mississippi | 80.3 |
| 21 | Missouri | 86.6 |
| 11 | Montana | 89.6 |
| 5 | Nebraska | 90.4 |
| 36 | Nevada | 82.8 |
| 14 | New Hampshire | 88.1 |
| 18 | New Jersey | 87.3 |
| 39 | New Mexico | 82.2 |
| 38 | New York | 82.5 |
| 46 | North Carolina | 79.2 |
| 29 | North Dakota | 85.5 |
| 19 | Ohio | 87.0 |
| 25 | Oklahoma | 86.1 |
| 14 | Oregon | 88.1 |
| 27 | Pennsylvania | 85.7 |
| 41 | Rhode Island | 81.3 |
| 35 | South Carolina | 83.0 |
| 1 | South Dakota | 91.8 |
| 45 | Tennessee | 79.9 |
| 46 | Texas | 79.2 |
| 4 | Utah | 90.7 |
| 7 | Vermont | 90.0 |
| 21 | Virginia | 86.6 |
| 1 | Washington | 91.8 |
| 50 | West Virginia | 77.1 |
| 20 | Wisconsin | 86.7 |
| 7 | Wyoming | 90.0 |

RANK ORDER

| RANK | STATE | PERCENT |
|------|-------|---------|
| 1 | South Dakota | 91.8 |
| 1 | Washington | 91.8 |
| 3 | Minnesota | 90.8 |
| 4 | Utah | 90.7 |
| 5 | Alaska | 90.4 |
| 5 | Nebraska | 90.4 |
| 7 | Vermont | 90.0 |
| 7 | Wyoming | 90.0 |
| 9 | Colorado | 89.7 |
| 9 | Iowa | 89.7 |
| 11 | Montana | 89.6 |
| 12 | Maine | 89.3 |
| 13 | Connecticut | 88.2 |
| 14 | Kansas | 88.1 |
| 14 | New Hampshire | 88.1 |
| 14 | Oregon | 88.1 |
| 17 | Hawaii | 87.4 |
| 18 | New Jersey | 87.3 |
| 19 | Ohio | 87.0 |
| 20 | Wisconsin | 86.7 |
| 21 | Missouri | 86.6 |
| 21 | Virginia | 86.6 |
| 23 | Idaho | 86.2 |
| 23 | Michigan | 86.2 |
| 25 | Delaware | 86.1 |
| 25 | Oklahoma | 86.1 |
| 27 | Maryland | 85.7 |
| 27 | Pennsylvania | 85.7 |
| 29 | Illinois | 85.5 |
| 29 | North Dakota | 85.5 |
| 31 | Arizona | 85.1 |
| 31 | Massachusetts | 85.1 |
| 33 | Indiana | 84.6 |
| 34 | Florida | 84.0 |
| 35 | South Carolina | 83.0 |
| 36 | Nevada | 82.8 |
| 37 | Georgia | 82.6 |
| 38 | New York | 82.5 |
| 39 | New Mexico | 82.2 |
| 40 | Arkansas | 81.7 |
| 41 | Rhode Island | 81.3 |
| 42 | California | 81.2 |
| 43 | Louisiana | 80.8 |
| 44 | Mississippi | 80.3 |
| 45 | Tennessee | 79.9 |
| 46 | North Carolina | 79.2 |
| 46 | Texas | 79.2 |
| 48 | Kentucky | 78.7 |
| 49 | Alabama | 77.5 |
| 50 | West Virginia | 77.1 |
| | District of Columbia | 83.2 |

Source: U.S. Bureau of the Census
    "Educational Attainment in the United States: March 2000"
    (http://www.census.gov/population/www/socdemo/educ-attn.html)
*Persons age 25 and older.

# High School Dropout Rate in 1998

## National Rate = 4.8%*

ALPHA ORDER

| RANK | STATE | RATE |
|---|---|---|
| 20 | Alabama | 4.8 |
| 23 | Alaska | 4.6 |
| 3 | Arizona | 9.4 |
| 11 | Arkansas | 5.4 |
| NA | California** | NA |
| 9 | Colorado | 5.8 |
| 30 | Connecticut | 3.5 |
| 22 | Delaware | 4.7 |
| NA | Florida** | NA |
| 4 | Georgia | 7.3 |
| NA | Hawaii** | NA |
| 7 | Idaho | 6.7 |
| 6 | Illinois | 6.9 |
| NA | Indiana** | NA |
| 35 | Iowa | 2.9 |
| 27 | Kansas | 4.2 |
| 12 | Kentucky | 5.2 |
| 1 | Louisiana | 11.4 |
| 32 | Maine | 3.2 |
| 26 | Maryland | 4.3 |
| 32 | Massachusetts | 3.2 |
| NA | Michigan** | NA |
| 18 | Minnesota | 4.9 |
| 9 | Mississippi | 5.8 |
| 12 | Missouri | 5.2 |
| 24 | Montana | 4.4 |
| 24 | Nebraska | 4.4 |
| 2 | Nevada | 10.1 |
| NA | New Hampshire** | NA |
| 30 | New Jersey | 3.5 |
| 5 | New Mexico | 7.1 |
| NA | New York** | NA |
| NA | North Carolina** | NA |
| 36 | North Dakota | 2.8 |
| 16 | Ohio | 5.1 |
| NA | Oklahoma** | NA |
| NA | Oregon** | NA |
| 29 | Pennsylvania | 3.9 |
| 18 | Rhode Island | 4.9 |
| NA | South Carolina** | NA |
| 34 | South Dakota | 3.1 |
| 17 | Tennessee | 5.0 |
| NA | Texas** | NA |
| 12 | Utah | 5.2 |
| 12 | Vermont | 5.2 |
| 20 | Virginia | 4.8 |
| NA | Washington** | NA |
| 28 | West Virginia | 4.1 |
| 36 | Wisconsin | 2.8 |
| 8 | Wyoming | 6.4 |

RANK ORDER

| RANK | STATE | RATE |
|---|---|---|
| 1 | Louisiana | 11.4 |
| 2 | Nevada | 10.1 |
| 3 | Arizona | 9.4 |
| 4 | Georgia | 7.3 |
| 5 | New Mexico | 7.1 |
| 6 | Illinois | 6.9 |
| 7 | Idaho | 6.7 |
| 8 | Wyoming | 6.4 |
| 9 | Colorado | 5.8 |
| 9 | Mississippi | 5.8 |
| 11 | Arkansas | 5.4 |
| 12 | Kentucky | 5.2 |
| 12 | Missouri | 5.2 |
| 12 | Utah | 5.2 |
| 12 | Vermont | 5.2 |
| 16 | Ohio | 5.1 |
| 17 | Tennessee | 5.0 |
| 18 | Minnesota | 4.9 |
| 18 | Rhode Island | 4.9 |
| 20 | Alabama | 4.8 |
| 20 | Virginia | 4.8 |
| 22 | Delaware | 4.7 |
| 23 | Alaska | 4.6 |
| 24 | Montana | 4.4 |
| 24 | Nebraska | 4.4 |
| 26 | Maryland | 4.3 |
| 27 | Kansas | 4.2 |
| 28 | West Virginia | 4.1 |
| 29 | Pennsylvania | 3.9 |
| 30 | Connecticut | 3.5 |
| 30 | New Jersey | 3.5 |
| 32 | Maine | 3.2 |
| 32 | Massachusetts | 3.2 |
| 34 | South Dakota | 3.1 |
| 35 | Iowa | 2.9 |
| 36 | North Dakota | 2.8 |
| 36 | Wisconsin | 2.8 |
| NA | California** | NA |
| NA | Florida** | NA |
| NA | Hawaii** | NA |
| NA | Indiana** | NA |
| NA | Michigan** | NA |
| NA | New Hampshire** | NA |
| NA | New York** | NA |
| NA | North Carolina** | NA |
| NA | Oklahoma** | NA |
| NA | Oregon** | NA |
| NA | South Carolina** | NA |
| NA | Texas** | NA |
| NA | Washington** | NA |
| | District of Columbia | 12.8 |

Source: U.S. Department of Education, National Center for Educational Statistics
   "Dropout Rates in the United States: 1999" (NCES 2001-022, November 2000)
*"Event" dropout rates showing the proportion of youth, ages 15-24 who dropped out of grades 10-12 in the 12 months preceding October 1998.
**Not available.

# ACT Average Composite Scores in 2000

## National Average = 21.0*

| RANK | STATE | SCORE | | RANK | STATE | SCORE |
|------|-------|-------|--|------|-------|-------|
| **ALPHA ORDER** | | | | **RANK ORDER** | | |
| 41 | Alabama | 20.2 | | 1 | Oregon | 22.7 |
| 29 | Alaska | 21.3 | | 2 | New Hampshire | 22.5 |
| 17 | Arizona | 21.5 | | 3 | Washington | 22.4 |
| 39 | Arkansas | 20.3 | | 4 | New York | 22.2 |
| 23 | California | 21.4 | | 4 | Vermont | 22.2 |
| 17 | Colorado | 21.5 | | 4 | Wisconsin | 22.2 |
| 29 | Connecticut | 21.3 | | 7 | Iowa | 22.0 |
| 36 | Delaware | 20.6 | | 7 | Minnesota | 22.0 |
| 36 | Florida | 20.6 | | 9 | Maine | 21.9 |
| 46 | Georgia | 19.9 | | 9 | Massachusetts | 21.9 |
| 13 | Hawaii | 21.6 | | 11 | Montana | 21.8 |
| 23 | Idaho | 21.4 | | 12 | Nebraska | 21.7 |
| 17 | Illinois | 21.5 | | 13 | Hawaii | 21.6 |
| 23 | Indiana | 21.4 | | 13 | Kansas | 21.6 |
| 7 | Iowa | 22.0 | | 13 | Missouri | 21.6 |
| 13 | Kansas | 21.6 | | 13 | Wyoming | 21.6 |
| 43 | Kentucky | 20.1 | | 17 | Arizona | 21.5 |
| 47 | Louisiana | 19.6 | | 17 | Colorado | 21.5 |
| 9 | Maine | 21.9 | | 17 | Illinois | 21.5 |
| 34 | Maryland | 20.7 | | 17 | Nevada | 21.5 |
| 9 | Massachusetts | 21.9 | | 17 | South Dakota | 21.5 |
| 29 | Michigan | 21.3 | | 17 | Utah | 21.5 |
| 7 | Minnesota | 22.0 | | 23 | California | 21.4 |
| 50 | Mississippi | 18.7 | | 23 | Idaho | 21.4 |
| 13 | Missouri | 21.6 | | 23 | Indiana | 21.4 |
| 11 | Montana | 21.8 | | 23 | North Dakota | 21.4 |
| 12 | Nebraska | 21.7 | | 23 | Ohio | 21.4 |
| 17 | Nevada | 21.5 | | 23 | Pennsylvania | 21.4 |
| 2 | New Hampshire | 22.5 | | 29 | Alaska | 21.3 |
| 34 | New Jersey | 20.7 | | 29 | Connecticut | 21.3 |
| 43 | New Mexico | 20.1 | | 29 | Michigan | 21.3 |
| 4 | New York | 22.2 | | 32 | Rhode Island | 21.1 |
| 48 | North Carolina | 19.5 | | 33 | Oklahoma | 20.8 |
| 23 | North Dakota | 21.4 | | 34 | Maryland | 20.7 |
| 23 | Ohio | 21.4 | | 34 | New Jersey | 20.7 |
| 33 | Oklahoma | 20.8 | | 36 | Delaware | 20.6 |
| 1 | Oregon | 22.7 | | 36 | Florida | 20.6 |
| 23 | Pennsylvania | 21.4 | | 38 | Virginia | 20.5 |
| 32 | Rhode Island | 21.1 | | 39 | Arkansas | 20.3 |
| 49 | South Carolina | 19.3 | | 39 | Texas | 20.3 |
| 17 | South Dakota | 21.5 | | 41 | Alabama | 20.2 |
| 45 | Tennessee | 20.0 | | 41 | West Virginia | 20.2 |
| 39 | Texas | 20.3 | | 43 | Kentucky | 20.1 |
| 17 | Utah | 21.5 | | 43 | New Mexico | 20.1 |
| 4 | Vermont | 22.2 | | 45 | Tennessee | 20.0 |
| 38 | Virginia | 20.5 | | 46 | Georgia | 19.9 |
| 3 | Washington | 22.4 | | 47 | Louisiana | 19.6 |
| 41 | West Virginia | 20.2 | | 48 | North Carolina | 19.5 |
| 4 | Wisconsin | 22.2 | | 49 | South Carolina | 19.3 |
| 13 | Wyoming | 21.6 | | 50 | Mississippi | 18.7 |
| | | | | | District of Columbia | 17.8 |

Source: The American College Testing Program (copyright 1999)

"ACT Average Composite Scores by State" (press release: http://www.act.org/news/data/00/00states.html)
*The ACT score range is 1 to 36. More than one million 2000 U.S. high school graduates took the test. Caution should be used in using ACT scores to compare states. The percentage of high school students taking the test varies greatly from one state to another.

# Scholastic Assessment Test (SAT) Scores in 2000

## National Average = 1,019 Composite Score*

ALPHA ORDER

| RANK | STATE | AVERAGE SCORE |
|---|---|---|
| 16 | Alabama | 1,114 |
| 30 | Alaska | 1,034 |
| 27 | Arizona | 1,044 |
| 14 | Arkansas | 1,117 |
| 36 | California | 1,015 |
| 24 | Colorado | 1,071 |
| 34 | Connecticut | 1,017 |
| 44 | Delaware | 998 |
| 44 | Florida | 998 |
| 49 | Georgia | 974 |
| 39 | Hawaii | 1,007 |
| 22 | Idaho | 1,081 |
| 6 | Illinois | 1,154 |
| 43 | Indiana | 999 |
| 2 | Iowa | 1,189 |
| 6 | Kansas | 1,154 |
| 18 | Kentucky | 1,098 |
| 13 | Louisiana | 1,120 |
| 41 | Maine | 1,004 |
| 35 | Maryland | 1,016 |
| 32 | Massachusetts | 1,024 |
| 11 | Michigan | 1,126 |
| 4 | Minnesota | 1,175 |
| 17 | Mississippi | 1,111 |
| 8 | Missouri | 1,149 |
| 21 | Montana | 1,089 |
| 10 | Nebraska | 1,131 |
| 31 | Nevada | 1,027 |
| 28 | New Hampshire | 1,039 |
| 37 | New Jersey | 1,011 |
| 19 | New Mexico | 1,092 |
| 42 | New York | 1,000 |
| 48 | North Carolina | 988 |
| 1 | North Dakota | 1,197 |
| 23 | Ohio | 1,072 |
| 12 | Oklahoma | 1,123 |
| 25 | Oregon | 1,054 |
| 46 | Pennsylvania | 995 |
| 40 | Rhode Island | 1,005 |
| 50 | South Carolina | 966 |
| 4 | South Dakota | 1,175 |
| 15 | Tennessee | 1,116 |
| 47 | Texas | 993 |
| 9 | Utah | 1,139 |
| 33 | Vermont | 1,021 |
| 38 | Virginia | 1,009 |
| 25 | Washington | 1,054 |
| 29 | West Virginia | 1,037 |
| 3 | Wisconsin | 1,181 |
| 20 | Wyoming | 1,090 |

RANK ORDER

| RANK | STATE | AVERAGE SCORE |
|---|---|---|
| 1 | North Dakota | 1,197 |
| 2 | Iowa | 1,189 |
| 3 | Wisconsin | 1,181 |
| 4 | Minnesota | 1,175 |
| 4 | South Dakota | 1,175 |
| 6 | Illinois | 1,154 |
| 6 | Kansas | 1,154 |
| 8 | Missouri | 1,149 |
| 9 | Utah | 1,139 |
| 10 | Nebraska | 1,131 |
| 11 | Michigan | 1,126 |
| 12 | Oklahoma | 1,123 |
| 13 | Louisiana | 1,120 |
| 14 | Arkansas | 1,117 |
| 15 | Tennessee | 1,116 |
| 16 | Alabama | 1,114 |
| 17 | Mississippi | 1,111 |
| 18 | Kentucky | 1,098 |
| 19 | New Mexico | 1,092 |
| 20 | Wyoming | 1,090 |
| 21 | Montana | 1,089 |
| 22 | Idaho | 1,081 |
| 23 | Ohio | 1,072 |
| 24 | Colorado | 1,071 |
| 25 | Oregon | 1,054 |
| 25 | Washington | 1,054 |
| 27 | Arizona | 1,044 |
| 28 | New Hampshire | 1,039 |
| 29 | West Virginia | 1,037 |
| 30 | Alaska | 1,034 |
| 31 | Nevada | 1,027 |
| 32 | Massachusetts | 1,024 |
| 33 | Vermont | 1,021 |
| 34 | Connecticut | 1,017 |
| 35 | Maryland | 1,016 |
| 36 | California | 1,015 |
| 37 | New Jersey | 1,011 |
| 38 | Virginia | 1,009 |
| 39 | Hawaii | 1,007 |
| 40 | Rhode Island | 1,005 |
| 41 | Maine | 1,004 |
| 42 | New York | 1,000 |
| 43 | Indiana | 999 |
| 44 | Delaware | 998 |
| 44 | Florida | 998 |
| 46 | Pennsylvania | 995 |
| 47 | Texas | 993 |
| 48 | North Carolina | 988 |
| 49 | Georgia | 974 |
| 50 | South Carolina | 966 |
| | District of Columbia | 980 |

Source: The College Board, New York, NY
"SAT averages by state for 1990 and 1997-2000" (http://www.collegeboard.org/press/senior00/html/table3.html)
*National cumulative score based on an average of 505 verbal score and 514 math score. The College Board strongly cautions against comparing states based on SAT scores alone. The percentage of high school students taking the test varies greatly from one state to another. The SAT was formerly known as the Scholastic Aptitude Test.

# Education Expenditures by State and Local Governments in 1997

## National Total = $419,053,165,000*

ALPHA ORDER

| RANK | STATE | EXPENDITURES | % of USA |
|------|-------|--------------|----------|
| 22 | Alabama | $6,270,431,000 | 1.5% |
| 42 | Alaska | 1,586,116,000 | 0.4% |
| 23 | Arizona | 6,176,156,000 | 1.5% |
| 34 | Arkansas | 3,457,869,000 | 0.8% |
| 1 | California | 46,730,864,000 | 11.2% |
| 21 | Colorado | 6,455,568,000 | 1.5% |
| 27 | Connecticut | 5,400,879,000 | 1.3% |
| 45 | Delaware | 1,476,201,000 | 0.4% |
| 4 | Florida | 18,735,050,000 | 4.5% |
| 10 | Georgia | 11,625,235,000 | 2.8% |
| 44 | Hawaii | 1,557,280,000 | 0.4% |
| 40 | Idaho | 1,846,215,000 | 0.4% |
| 7 | Illinois | 17,437,988,000 | 4.2% |
| 15 | Indiana | 9,585,056,000 | 2.3% |
| 29 | Iowa | 4,902,901,000 | 1.2% |
| 31 | Kansas | 4,145,336,000 | 1.0% |
| 28 | Kentucky | 5,355,366,000 | 1.3% |
| 24 | Louisiana | 5,930,806,000 | 1.4% |
| 39 | Maine | 1,927,285,000 | 0.5% |
| 18 | Maryland | 8,296,630,000 | 2.0% |
| 16 | Massachusetts | 8,842,486,000 | 2.1% |
| 6 | Michigan | 18,217,057,000 | 4.3% |
| 17 | Minnesota | 8,617,647,000 | 2.1% |
| 32 | Mississippi | 3,711,573,000 | 0.9% |
| 19 | Missouri | 7,513,907,000 | 1.8% |
| 46 | Montana | 1,450,956,000 | 0.3% |
| 36 | Nebraska | 2,855,342,000 | 0.7% |
| 38 | Nevada | 2,394,176,000 | 0.6% |
| 41 | New Hampshire | 1,769,410,000 | 0.4% |
| 9 | New Jersey | 15,013,065,000 | 3.6% |
| 35 | New Mexico | 2,968,963,000 | 0.7% |
| 2 | New York | 34,009,092,000 | 8.1% |
| 11 | North Carolina | 11,017,475,000 | 2.6% |
| 48 | North Dakota | 1,055,407,000 | 0.3% |
| 8 | Ohio | 17,337,102,000 | 4.1% |
| 30 | Oklahoma | 4,776,044,000 | 1.1% |
| 26 | Oregon | 5,539,625,000 | 1.3% |
| 5 | Pennsylvania | 18,577,751,000 | 4.4% |
| 43 | Rhode Island | 1,576,724,000 | 0.4% |
| 25 | South Carolina | 5,613,239,000 | 1.3% |
| 50 | South Dakota | 976,909,000 | 0.2% |
| 20 | Tennessee | 6,863,653,000 | 1.6% |
| 3 | Texas | 30,367,466,000 | 7.2% |
| 33 | Utah | 3,581,996,000 | 0.9% |
| 47 | Vermont | 1,120,188,000 | 0.3% |
| 12 | Virginia | 10,418,976,000 | 2.5% |
| 13 | Washington | 9,811,547,000 | 2.3% |
| 37 | West Virginia | 2,772,941,000 | 0.7% |
| 14 | Wisconsin | 9,715,508,000 | 2.3% |
| 49 | Wyoming | 994,619,000 | 0.2% |

RANK ORDER

| RANK | STATE | EXPENDITURES | % of USA |
|------|-------|--------------|----------|
| 1 | California | $46,730,864,000 | 11.2% |
| 2 | New York | 34,009,092,000 | 8.1% |
| 3 | Texas | 30,367,466,000 | 7.2% |
| 4 | Florida | 18,735,050,000 | 4.5% |
| 5 | Pennsylvania | 18,577,751,000 | 4.4% |
| 6 | Michigan | 18,217,057,000 | 4.3% |
| 7 | Illinois | 17,437,988,000 | 4.2% |
| 8 | Ohio | 17,337,102,000 | 4.1% |
| 9 | New Jersey | 15,013,065,000 | 3.6% |
| 10 | Georgia | 11,625,235,000 | 2.8% |
| 11 | North Carolina | 11,017,475,000 | 2.6% |
| 12 | Virginia | 10,418,976,000 | 2.5% |
| 13 | Washington | 9,811,547,000 | 2.3% |
| 14 | Wisconsin | 9,715,508,000 | 2.3% |
| 15 | Indiana | 9,585,056,000 | 2.3% |
| 16 | Massachusetts | 8,842,486,000 | 2.1% |
| 17 | Minnesota | 8,617,647,000 | 2.1% |
| 18 | Maryland | 8,296,630,000 | 2.0% |
| 19 | Missouri | 7,513,907,000 | 1.8% |
| 20 | Tennessee | 6,863,653,000 | 1.6% |
| 21 | Colorado | 6,455,568,000 | 1.5% |
| 22 | Alabama | 6,270,431,000 | 1.5% |
| 23 | Arizona | 6,176,156,000 | 1.5% |
| 24 | Louisiana | 5,930,806,000 | 1.4% |
| 25 | South Carolina | 5,613,239,000 | 1.3% |
| 26 | Oregon | 5,539,625,000 | 1.3% |
| 27 | Connecticut | 5,400,879,000 | 1.3% |
| 28 | Kentucky | 5,355,366,000 | 1.3% |
| 29 | Iowa | 4,902,901,000 | 1.2% |
| 30 | Oklahoma | 4,776,044,000 | 1.1% |
| 31 | Kansas | 4,145,336,000 | 1.0% |
| 32 | Mississippi | 3,711,573,000 | 0.9% |
| 33 | Utah | 3,581,996,000 | 0.9% |
| 34 | Arkansas | 3,457,869,000 | 0.8% |
| 35 | New Mexico | 2,968,963,000 | 0.7% |
| 36 | Nebraska | 2,855,342,000 | 0.7% |
| 37 | West Virginia | 2,772,941,000 | 0.7% |
| 38 | Nevada | 2,394,176,000 | 0.6% |
| 39 | Maine | 1,927,285,000 | 0.5% |
| 40 | Idaho | 1,846,215,000 | 0.4% |
| 41 | New Hampshire | 1,769,410,000 | 0.4% |
| 42 | Alaska | 1,586,116,000 | 0.4% |
| 43 | Rhode Island | 1,576,724,000 | 0.4% |
| 44 | Hawaii | 1,557,280,000 | 0.4% |
| 45 | Delaware | 1,476,201,000 | 0.4% |
| 46 | Montana | 1,450,956,000 | 0.3% |
| 47 | Vermont | 1,120,188,000 | 0.3% |
| 48 | North Dakota | 1,055,407,000 | 0.3% |
| 49 | Wyoming | 994,619,000 | 0.2% |
| 50 | South Dakota | 976,909,000 | 0.2% |
| | District of Columbia | 673,089,000 | 0.2% |

Source: U.S. Bureau of the Census, Governments Division
"Compendium of Government Finances: 1997" (2000) (http://www.census.gov/govs/www/cog.html)
*Direct general expenditures for higher, secondary, elementary and "other" education. Includes capital outlays.

# Per Capita State and Local Government Expenditures for Education in 1997

## National Per Capita = $1,565*

ALPHA ORDER

RANK ORDER

| RANK | STATE | PER CAPITA |
|---|---|---|
| 36 | Alabama | $1,451 |
| 1 | Alaska | 2,605 |
| 46 | Arizona | 1,357 |
| 42 | Arkansas | 1,370 |
| 37 | California | 1,450 |
| 16 | Colorado | 1,659 |
| 17 | Connecticut | 1,652 |
| 3 | Delaware | 2,008 |
| 49 | Florida | 1,276 |
| 25 | Georgia | 1,553 |
| 48 | Hawaii | 1,309 |
| 31 | Idaho | 1,525 |
| 35 | Illinois | 1,452 |
| 20 | Indiana | 1,632 |
| 14 | Iowa | 1,718 |
| 23 | Kansas | 1,584 |
| 42 | Kentucky | 1,370 |
| 44 | Louisiana | 1,363 |
| 26 | Maine | 1,548 |
| 21 | Maryland | 1,629 |
| 38 | Massachusetts | 1,446 |
| 8 | Michigan | 1,862 |
| 9 | Minnesota | 1,838 |
| 45 | Mississippi | 1,359 |
| 41 | Missouri | 1,390 |
| 18 | Montana | 1,651 |
| 12 | Nebraska | 1,724 |
| 40 | Nevada | 1,429 |
| 32 | New Hampshire | 1,508 |
| 7 | New Jersey | 1,864 |
| 13 | New Mexico | 1,723 |
| 5 | New York | 1,874 |
| 33 | North Carolina | 1,483 |
| 19 | North Dakota | 1,647 |
| 28 | Ohio | 1,546 |
| 39 | Oklahoma | 1,441 |
| 15 | Oregon | 1,708 |
| 28 | Pennsylvania | 1,546 |
| 22 | Rhode Island | 1,598 |
| 34 | South Carolina | 1,481 |
| 47 | South Dakota | 1,337 |
| 49 | Tennessee | 1,276 |
| 24 | Texas | 1,569 |
| 11 | Utah | 1,734 |
| 4 | Vermont | 1,903 |
| 27 | Virginia | 1,547 |
| 10 | Washington | 1,751 |
| 30 | West Virginia | 1,527 |
| 6 | Wisconsin | 1,868 |
| 2 | Wyoming | 2,072 |

| RANK | STATE | PER CAPITA |
|---|---|---|
| 1 | Alaska | $2,605 |
| 2 | Wyoming | 2,072 |
| 3 | Delaware | 2,008 |
| 4 | Vermont | 1,903 |
| 5 | New York | 1,874 |
| 6 | Wisconsin | 1,868 |
| 7 | New Jersey | 1,864 |
| 8 | Michigan | 1,862 |
| 9 | Minnesota | 1,838 |
| 10 | Washington | 1,751 |
| 11 | Utah | 1,734 |
| 12 | Nebraska | 1,724 |
| 13 | New Mexico | 1,723 |
| 14 | Iowa | 1,718 |
| 15 | Oregon | 1,708 |
| 16 | Colorado | 1,659 |
| 17 | Connecticut | 1,652 |
| 18 | Montana | 1,651 |
| 19 | North Dakota | 1,647 |
| 20 | Indiana | 1,632 |
| 21 | Maryland | 1,629 |
| 22 | Rhode Island | 1,598 |
| 23 | Kansas | 1,584 |
| 24 | Texas | 1,569 |
| 25 | Georgia | 1,553 |
| 26 | Maine | 1,548 |
| 27 | Virginia | 1,547 |
| 28 | Ohio | 1,546 |
| 28 | Pennsylvania | 1,546 |
| 30 | West Virginia | 1,527 |
| 31 | Idaho | 1,525 |
| 32 | New Hampshire | 1,508 |
| 33 | North Carolina | 1,483 |
| 34 | South Carolina | 1,481 |
| 35 | Illinois | 1,452 |
| 36 | Alabama | 1,451 |
| 37 | California | 1,450 |
| 38 | Massachusetts | 1,446 |
| 39 | Oklahoma | 1,441 |
| 40 | Nevada | 1,429 |
| 41 | Missouri | 1,390 |
| 42 | Arkansas | 1,370 |
| 42 | Kentucky | 1,370 |
| 44 | Louisiana | 1,363 |
| 45 | Mississippi | 1,359 |
| 46 | Arizona | 1,357 |
| 47 | South Dakota | 1,337 |
| 48 | Hawaii | 1,309 |
| 49 | Florida | 1,276 |
| 49 | Tennessee | 1,276 |
| | District of Columbia | 1,273 |

Source: Morgan Quitno Press using data from U.S. Bureau of the Census, Governments Division
"Compendium of Government Finances: 1997" (2000) (http://www.census.gov/govs/www/cog.html)
*Direct general expenditures for higher, secondary, elementary and "other" education.  Includes capital outlays.

# Expenditures for Education as a Percent of
# All State and Local Government Expenditures in 1997
## National Percent = 33.5%*

ALPHA ORDER

| RANK | STATE | PERCENT |
|------|-------|---------|
| 19 | Alabama | 36.4 |
| 49 | Alaska | 23.7 |
| 31 | Arizona | 34.8 |
| 15 | Arkansas | 36.7 |
| 46 | California | 29.1 |
| 14 | Colorado | 36.9 |
| 43 | Connecticut | 30.4 |
| 12 | Delaware | 37.4 |
| 45 | Florida | 29.5 |
| 24 | Georgia | 35.6 |
| 50 | Hawaii | 23.2 |
| 10 | Idaho | 37.9 |
| 39 | Illinois | 32.8 |
| 1 | Indiana | 41.0 |
| 9 | Iowa | 38.1 |
| 11 | Kansas | 37.6 |
| 32 | Kentucky | 34.4 |
| 42 | Louisiana | 31.5 |
| 38 | Maine | 33.3 |
| 20 | Maryland | 36.3 |
| 47 | Massachusetts | 27.8 |
| 4 | Michigan | 39.7 |
| 33 | Minnesota | 34.3 |
| 37 | Mississippi | 33.4 |
| 15 | Missouri | 36.7 |
| 13 | Montana | 37.1 |
| 7 | Nebraska | 38.4 |
| 44 | Nevada | 30.2 |
| 22 | New Hampshire | 35.9 |
| 15 | New Jersey | 36.7 |
| 26 | New Mexico | 35.4 |
| 48 | New York | 26.9 |
| 27 | North Carolina | 35.3 |
| 28 | North Dakota | 35.2 |
| 21 | Ohio | 36.0 |
| 6 | Oklahoma | 39.1 |
| 35 | Oregon | 33.5 |
| 30 | Pennsylvania | 35.0 |
| 40 | Rhode Island | 32.3 |
| 28 | South Carolina | 35.2 |
| 35 | South Dakota | 33.5 |
| 40 | Tennessee | 32.3 |
| 4 | Texas | 39.7 |
| 3 | Utah | 39.8 |
| 2 | Vermont | 40.3 |
| 18 | Virginia | 36.5 |
| 34 | Washington | 34.0 |
| 23 | West Virginia | 35.8 |
| 7 | Wisconsin | 38.4 |
| 25 | Wyoming | 35.5 |

RANK ORDER

| RANK | STATE | PERCENT |
|------|-------|---------|
| 1 | Indiana | 41.0 |
| 2 | Vermont | 40.3 |
| 3 | Utah | 39.8 |
| 4 | Michigan | 39.7 |
| 4 | Texas | 39.7 |
| 6 | Oklahoma | 39.1 |
| 7 | Nebraska | 38.4 |
| 7 | Wisconsin | 38.4 |
| 9 | Iowa | 38.1 |
| 10 | Idaho | 37.9 |
| 11 | Kansas | 37.6 |
| 12 | Delaware | 37.4 |
| 13 | Montana | 37.1 |
| 14 | Colorado | 36.9 |
| 15 | Arkansas | 36.7 |
| 15 | Missouri | 36.7 |
| 15 | New Jersey | 36.7 |
| 18 | Virginia | 36.5 |
| 19 | Alabama | 36.4 |
| 20 | Maryland | 36.3 |
| 21 | Ohio | 36.0 |
| 22 | New Hampshire | 35.9 |
| 23 | West Virginia | 35.8 |
| 24 | Georgia | 35.6 |
| 25 | Wyoming | 35.5 |
| 26 | New Mexico | 35.4 |
| 27 | North Carolina | 35.3 |
| 28 | North Dakota | 35.2 |
| 28 | South Carolina | 35.2 |
| 30 | Pennsylvania | 35.0 |
| 31 | Arizona | 34.8 |
| 32 | Kentucky | 34.4 |
| 33 | Minnesota | 34.3 |
| 34 | Washington | 34.0 |
| 35 | Oregon | 33.5 |
| 35 | South Dakota | 33.5 |
| 37 | Mississippi | 33.4 |
| 38 | Maine | 33.3 |
| 39 | Illinois | 32.8 |
| 40 | Rhode Island | 32.3 |
| 40 | Tennessee | 32.3 |
| 42 | Louisiana | 31.5 |
| 43 | Connecticut | 30.4 |
| 44 | Nevada | 30.2 |
| 45 | Florida | 29.5 |
| 46 | California | 29.1 |
| 47 | Massachusetts | 27.8 |
| 48 | New York | 26.9 |
| 49 | Alaska | 23.7 |
| 50 | Hawaii | 23.2 |
|  | District of Columbia | 15.5 |

Source: Morgan Quitno Press using data from U.S. Bureau of the Census, Governments Division
"Compendium of Government Finances: 1997" (2000) (http://www.census.gov/govs/www/cog.html)
*Direct general expenditures for higher, secondary, elementary and "other" education as a percent of all direct
general expenditures. Includes capital outlays.

# Elementary and Secondary Education Expenditures by State and Local Governments in 1997
## National Total = $294,598,418,000*

ALPHA ORDER

| RANK | STATE | EXPENDITURES | % of USA |
|---|---|---|---|
| 25 | Alabama | $3,923,428,000 | 1.3% |
| 42 | Alaska | 1,221,896,000 | 0.4% |
| 22 | Arizona | 4,185,545,000 | 1.4% |
| 33 | Arkansas | 2,266,975,000 | 0.8% |
| 1 | California | 32,310,299,000 | 11.0% |
| 23 | Colorado | 4,144,654,000 | 1.4% |
| 21 | Connecticut | 4,272,902,000 | 1.5% |
| 46 | Delaware | 862,181,000 | 0.3% |
| 4 | Florida | 14,247,654,000 | 4.8% |
| 10 | Georgia | 8,160,239,000 | 2.8% |
| 45 | Hawaii | 946,995,000 | 0.3% |
| 41 | Idaho | 1,263,821,000 | 0.4% |
| 7 | Illinois | 12,457,238,000 | 4.2% |
| 16 | Indiana | 6,244,092,000 | 2.1% |
| 30 | Iowa | 2,963,673,000 | 1.0% |
| 31 | Kansas | 2,735,758,000 | 0.9% |
| 28 | Kentucky | 3,410,018,000 | 1.2% |
| 24 | Louisiana | 3,973,770,000 | 1.3% |
| 39 | Maine | 1,428,364,000 | 0.5% |
| 18 | Maryland | 5,687,075,000 | 1.9% |
| 14 | Massachusetts | 6,659,802,000 | 2.3% |
| 6 | Michigan | 12,493,457,000 | 4.2% |
| 17 | Minnesota | 6,225,875,000 | 2.1% |
| 32 | Mississippi | 2,284,073,000 | 0.8% |
| 19 | Missouri | 5,337,208,000 | 1.8% |
| 44 | Montana | 954,144,000 | 0.3% |
| 36 | Nebraska | 1,879,526,000 | 0.6% |
| 37 | Nevada | 1,811,101,000 | 0.6% |
| 40 | New Hampshire | 1,331,472,000 | 0.5% |
| 8 | New Jersey | 11,891,635,000 | 4.0% |
| 38 | New Mexico | 1,787,559,000 | 0.6% |
| 2 | New York | 27,107,927,000 | 9.2% |
| 12 | North Carolina | 6,942,293,000 | 2.4% |
| 50 | North Dakota | 606,314,000 | 0.2% |
| 9 | Ohio | 11,841,308,000 | 4.0% |
| 29 | Oklahoma | 3,234,155,000 | 1.1% |
| 27 | Oregon | 3,658,712,000 | 1.2% |
| 5 | Pennsylvania | 13,108,015,000 | 4.4% |
| 43 | Rhode Island | 1,127,279,000 | 0.4% |
| 26 | South Carolina | 3,789,744,000 | 1.3% |
| 48 | South Dakota | 693,632,000 | 0.2% |
| 20 | Tennessee | 4,627,207,000 | 1.6% |
| 3 | Texas | 21,901,900,000 | 7.4% |
| 34 | Utah | 2,125,185,000 | 0.7% |
| 47 | Vermont | 727,998,000 | 0.2% |
| 11 | Virginia | 7,171,432,000 | 2.4% |
| 15 | Washington | 6,640,379,000 | 2.3% |
| 35 | West Virginia | 1,917,890,000 | 0.7% |
| 13 | Wisconsin | 6,739,841,000 | 2.3% |
| 49 | Wyoming | 676,778,000 | 0.2% |

RANK ORDER

| RANK | STATE | EXPENDITURES | % of USA |
|---|---|---|---|
| 1 | California | $32,310,299,000 | 11.0% |
| 2 | New York | 27,107,927,000 | 9.2% |
| 3 | Texas | 21,901,900,000 | 7.4% |
| 4 | Florida | 14,247,654,000 | 4.8% |
| 5 | Pennsylvania | 13,108,015,000 | 4.4% |
| 6 | Michigan | 12,493,457,000 | 4.2% |
| 7 | Illinois | 12,457,238,000 | 4.2% |
| 8 | New Jersey | 11,891,635,000 | 4.0% |
| 9 | Ohio | 11,841,308,000 | 4.0% |
| 10 | Georgia | 8,160,239,000 | 2.8% |
| 11 | Virginia | 7,171,432,000 | 2.4% |
| 12 | North Carolina | 6,942,293,000 | 2.4% |
| 13 | Wisconsin | 6,739,841,000 | 2.3% |
| 14 | Massachusetts | 6,659,802,000 | 2.3% |
| 15 | Washington | 6,640,379,000 | 2.3% |
| 16 | Indiana | 6,244,092,000 | 2.1% |
| 17 | Minnesota | 6,225,875,000 | 2.1% |
| 18 | Maryland | 5,687,075,000 | 1.9% |
| 19 | Missouri | 5,337,208,000 | 1.8% |
| 20 | Tennessee | 4,627,207,000 | 1.6% |
| 21 | Connecticut | 4,272,902,000 | 1.5% |
| 22 | Arizona | 4,185,545,000 | 1.4% |
| 23 | Colorado | 4,144,654,000 | 1.4% |
| 24 | Louisiana | 3,973,770,000 | 1.3% |
| 25 | Alabama | 3,923,428,000 | 1.3% |
| 26 | South Carolina | 3,789,744,000 | 1.3% |
| 27 | Oregon | 3,658,712,000 | 1.2% |
| 28 | Kentucky | 3,410,018,000 | 1.2% |
| 29 | Oklahoma | 3,234,155,000 | 1.1% |
| 30 | Iowa | 2,963,673,000 | 1.0% |
| 31 | Kansas | 2,735,758,000 | 0.9% |
| 32 | Mississippi | 2,284,073,000 | 0.8% |
| 33 | Arkansas | 2,266,975,000 | 0.8% |
| 34 | Utah | 2,125,185,000 | 0.7% |
| 35 | West Virginia | 1,917,890,000 | 0.7% |
| 36 | Nebraska | 1,879,526,000 | 0.6% |
| 37 | Nevada | 1,811,101,000 | 0.6% |
| 38 | New Mexico | 1,787,559,000 | 0.6% |
| 39 | Maine | 1,428,364,000 | 0.5% |
| 40 | New Hampshire | 1,331,472,000 | 0.5% |
| 41 | Idaho | 1,263,821,000 | 0.4% |
| 42 | Alaska | 1,221,896,000 | 0.4% |
| 43 | Rhode Island | 1,127,279,000 | 0.4% |
| 44 | Montana | 954,144,000 | 0.3% |
| 45 | Hawaii | 946,995,000 | 0.3% |
| 46 | Delaware | 862,181,000 | 0.3% |
| 47 | Vermont | 727,998,000 | 0.2% |
| 48 | South Dakota | 693,632,000 | 0.2% |
| 49 | Wyoming | 676,778,000 | 0.2% |
| 50 | North Dakota | 606,314,000 | 0.2% |
|  | District of Columbia | 598,000,000 | 0.2% |

Source: U.S. Bureau of the Census, Governments Division
   "Compendium of Government Finances: 1997" (2000) (http://www.census.gov/govs/www/cog.html)
*Direct general expenditures.  Includes capital outlays.

# Per Capita State and Local Government Expenditures
## For Elementary and Secondary Education in 1997
## National Per Capita = $1,100*

ALPHA ORDER

| RANK | STATE | PER CAPITA |
|------|-------|-----------|
| 45 | Alabama | $908 |
| 1 | Alaska | 2,007 |
| 43 | Arizona | 919 |
| 46 | Arkansas | 898 |
| 35 | California | 1,003 |
| 24 | Colorado | 1,065 |
| 6 | Connecticut | 1,307 |
| 11 | Delaware | 1,173 |
| 39 | Florida | 970 |
| 20 | Georgia | 1,090 |
| 50 | Hawaii | 796 |
| 30 | Idaho | 1,044 |
| 33 | Illinois | 1,037 |
| 26 | Indiana | 1,063 |
| 31 | Iowa | 1,038 |
| 29 | Kansas | 1,046 |
| 47 | Kentucky | 873 |
| 44 | Louisiana | 913 |
| 12 | Maine | 1,147 |
| 18 | Maryland | 1,117 |
| 21 | Massachusetts | 1,089 |
| 8 | Michigan | 1,277 |
| 5 | Minnesota | 1,328 |
| 49 | Mississippi | 836 |
| 37 | Missouri | 987 |
| 22 | Montana | 1,086 |
| 14 | Nebraska | 1,135 |
| 23 | Nevada | 1,081 |
| 14 | New Hampshire | 1,135 |
| 3 | New Jersey | 1,476 |
| 31 | New Mexico | 1,038 |
| 2 | New York | 1,494 |
| 42 | North Carolina | 935 |
| 41 | North Dakota | 946 |
| 27 | Ohio | 1,056 |
| 38 | Oklahoma | 976 |
| 17 | Oregon | 1,128 |
| 19 | Pennsylvania | 1,091 |
| 13 | Rhode Island | 1,142 |
| 36 | South Carolina | 1,000 |
| 40 | South Dakota | 949 |
| 48 | Tennessee | 860 |
| 16 | Texas | 1,132 |
| 34 | Utah | 1,029 |
| 9 | Vermont | 1,237 |
| 24 | Virginia | 1,065 |
| 10 | Washington | 1,185 |
| 27 | West Virginia | 1,056 |
| 7 | Wisconsin | 1,296 |
| 4 | Wyoming | 1,410 |

RANK ORDER

| RANK | STATE | PER CAPITA |
|------|-------|-----------|
| 1 | Alaska | $2,007 |
| 2 | New York | 1,494 |
| 3 | New Jersey | 1,476 |
| 4 | Wyoming | 1,410 |
| 5 | Minnesota | 1,328 |
| 6 | Connecticut | 1,307 |
| 7 | Wisconsin | 1,296 |
| 8 | Michigan | 1,277 |
| 9 | Vermont | 1,237 |
| 10 | Washington | 1,185 |
| 11 | Delaware | 1,173 |
| 12 | Maine | 1,147 |
| 13 | Rhode Island | 1,142 |
| 14 | Nebraska | 1,135 |
| 14 | New Hampshire | 1,135 |
| 16 | Texas | 1,132 |
| 17 | Oregon | 1,128 |
| 18 | Maryland | 1,117 |
| 19 | Pennsylvania | 1,091 |
| 20 | Georgia | 1,090 |
| 21 | Massachusetts | 1,089 |
| 22 | Montana | 1,086 |
| 23 | Nevada | 1,081 |
| 24 | Colorado | 1,065 |
| 24 | Virginia | 1,065 |
| 26 | Indiana | 1,063 |
| 27 | Ohio | 1,056 |
| 27 | West Virginia | 1,056 |
| 29 | Kansas | 1,046 |
| 30 | Idaho | 1,044 |
| 31 | Iowa | 1,038 |
| 31 | New Mexico | 1,038 |
| 33 | Illinois | 1,037 |
| 34 | Utah | 1,029 |
| 35 | California | 1,003 |
| 36 | South Carolina | 1,000 |
| 37 | Missouri | 987 |
| 38 | Oklahoma | 976 |
| 39 | Florida | 970 |
| 40 | South Dakota | 949 |
| 41 | North Dakota | 946 |
| 42 | North Carolina | 935 |
| 43 | Arizona | 919 |
| 44 | Louisiana | 913 |
| 45 | Alabama | 908 |
| 46 | Arkansas | 898 |
| 47 | Kentucky | 873 |
| 48 | Tennessee | 860 |
| 49 | Mississippi | 836 |
| 50 | Hawaii | 796 |
| | District of Columbia | 1,131 |

Source: Morgan Quitno Press using data from U.S. Bureau of the Census, Governments Division
"Compendium of Government Finances: 1997" (2000) (http://www.census.gov/govs/www/cog.html)
*Direct general expenditures. Includes capital outlays.

# Expenditures for Elementary and Secondary Education
## As a Percent of All State and Local Government Expenditures in 1997
### National Percent = 23.5%*

ALPHA ORDER

| RANK | STATE | PERCENT |
|------|-------|---------|
| 35 | Alabama | 22.8 |
| 49 | Alaska | 18.2 |
| 28 | Arizona | 23.6 |
| 23 | Arkansas | 24.1 |
| 48 | California | 20.1 |
| 27 | Colorado | 23.7 |
| 24 | Connecticut | 24.0 |
| 39 | Delaware | 21.9 |
| 36 | Florida | 22.5 |
| 13 | Georgia | 25.0 |
| 50 | Hawaii | 14.1 |
| 10 | Idaho | 25.9 |
| 30 | Illinois | 23.5 |
| 5 | Indiana | 26.7 |
| 32 | Iowa | 23.0 |
| 15 | Kansas | 24.8 |
| 39 | Kentucky | 21.9 |
| 44 | Louisiana | 21.1 |
| 18 | Maine | 24.7 |
| 14 | Maryland | 24.9 |
| 45 | Massachusetts | 21.0 |
| 3 | Michigan | 27.2 |
| 15 | Minnesota | 24.8 |
| 46 | Mississippi | 20.6 |
| 9 | Missouri | 26.1 |
| 21 | Montana | 24.4 |
| 11 | Nebraska | 25.3 |
| 34 | Nevada | 22.9 |
| 4 | New Hampshire | 27.0 |
| 1 | New Jersey | 29.1 |
| 43 | New Mexico | 21.3 |
| 42 | New York | 21.5 |
| 37 | North Carolina | 22.2 |
| 47 | North Dakota | 20.2 |
| 20 | Ohio | 24.6 |
| 7 | Oklahoma | 26.5 |
| 38 | Oregon | 22.1 |
| 18 | Pennsylvania | 24.7 |
| 31 | Rhode Island | 23.1 |
| 25 | South Carolina | 23.8 |
| 25 | South Dakota | 23.8 |
| 41 | Tennessee | 21.8 |
| 2 | Texas | 28.7 |
| 28 | Utah | 23.6 |
| 8 | Vermont | 26.2 |
| 12 | Virginia | 25.1 |
| 32 | Washington | 23.0 |
| 15 | West Virginia | 24.8 |
| 6 | Wisconsin | 26.6 |
| 22 | Wyoming | 24.2 |

RANK ORDER

| RANK | STATE | PERCENT |
|------|-------|---------|
| 1 | New Jersey | 29.1 |
| 2 | Texas | 28.7 |
| 3 | Michigan | 27.2 |
| 4 | New Hampshire | 27.0 |
| 5 | Indiana | 26.7 |
| 6 | Wisconsin | 26.6 |
| 7 | Oklahoma | 26.5 |
| 8 | Vermont | 26.2 |
| 9 | Missouri | 26.1 |
| 10 | Idaho | 25.9 |
| 11 | Nebraska | 25.3 |
| 12 | Virginia | 25.1 |
| 13 | Georgia | 25.0 |
| 14 | Maryland | 24.9 |
| 15 | Kansas | 24.8 |
| 15 | Minnesota | 24.8 |
| 15 | West Virginia | 24.8 |
| 18 | Maine | 24.7 |
| 18 | Pennsylvania | 24.7 |
| 20 | Ohio | 24.6 |
| 21 | Montana | 24.4 |
| 22 | Wyoming | 24.2 |
| 23 | Arkansas | 24.1 |
| 24 | Connecticut | 24.0 |
| 25 | South Carolina | 23.8 |
| 25 | South Dakota | 23.8 |
| 27 | Colorado | 23.7 |
| 28 | Arizona | 23.6 |
| 28 | Utah | 23.6 |
| 30 | Illinois | 23.5 |
| 31 | Rhode Island | 23.1 |
| 32 | Iowa | 23.0 |
| 32 | Washington | 23.0 |
| 34 | Nevada | 22.9 |
| 35 | Alabama | 22.8 |
| 36 | Florida | 22.5 |
| 37 | North Carolina | 22.2 |
| 38 | Oregon | 22.1 |
| 39 | Delaware | 21.9 |
| 39 | Kentucky | 21.9 |
| 41 | Tennessee | 21.8 |
| 42 | New York | 21.5 |
| 43 | New Mexico | 21.3 |
| 44 | Louisiana | 21.1 |
| 45 | Massachusetts | 21.0 |
| 46 | Mississippi | 20.6 |
| 47 | North Dakota | 20.2 |
| 48 | California | 20.1 |
| 49 | Alaska | 18.2 |
| 50 | Hawaii | 14.1 |
| | District of Columbia | 13.8 |

Source: Morgan Quitno Press using data from U.S. Bureau of the Census, Governments Division
"Compendium of Government Finances: 1997" (2000) (http://www.census.gov/govs/www/cog.html)
*Direct general expenditures for elementary and secondary education as a percent of all direct general expenditures. Includes capital outlays.

# Expenditures per Pupil in Elementary and Secondary Schools in 2000

## National Average = $6,585 per Pupil*

| ALPHA ORDER | | | | RANK ORDER | | |
|---|---|---|---|---|---|---|
| RANK | STATE | PER PUPIL | | RANK | STATE | PER PUPIL |
| 45 | Alabama | $5,010 | | 1 | New Jersey | $9,963 |
| 4 | Alaska | 8,717 | | 2 | Connecticut | 9,872 |
| 49 | Arizona | 4,754 | | 3 | New York | 9,146 |
| 47 | Arkansas | 4,864 | | 4 | Alaska | 8,717 |
| 36 | California | 5,832 | | 5 | Rhode Island | 8,315 |
| 37 | Colorado | 5,823 | | 6 | Massachusetts | 8,284 |
| 2 | Connecticut | 9,872 | | 7 | West Virginia | 8,114 |
| 10 | Delaware | 7,666 | | 8 | Pennsylvania | 8,045 |
| 38 | Florida | 5,737 | | 9 | Wisconsin | 7,894 |
| 35 | Georgia | 5,835 | | 10 | Delaware | 7,666 |
| 26 | Hawaii | 6,193 | | 11 | Minnesota | 7,585 |
| 46 | Idaho | 4,878 | | 12 | Wyoming | 7,356 |
| 31 | Illinois | 6,075 | | 13 | Vermont | 7,309 |
| 17 | Indiana | 7,048 | | 14 | Maryland | 7,297 |
| 24 | Iowa | 6,485 | | 15 | Michigan | 7,269 |
| 27 | Kansas | 6,185 | | 16 | Oregon | 7,069 |
| 22 | Kentucky | 6,539 | | 17 | Indiana | 7,048 |
| 30 | Louisiana | 6,088 | | 18 | Maine | 6,937 |
| 18 | Maine | 6,937 | | 19 | New Hampshire | 6,932 |
| 14 | Maryland | 7,297 | | 20 | Virginia | 6,913 |
| 6 | Massachusetts | 8,284 | | 21 | Ohio | 6,554 |
| 15 | Michigan | 7,269 | | 22 | Kentucky | 6,539 |
| 11 | Minnesota | 7,585 | | 23 | Washington | 6,514 |
| 48 | Mississippi | 4,827 | | 24 | Iowa | 6,485 |
| 39 | Missouri | 5,655 | | 25 | Montana | 6,209 |
| 25 | Montana | 6,209 | | 26 | Hawaii | 6,193 |
| 28 | Nebraska | 6,156 | | 27 | Kansas | 6,185 |
| 40 | Nevada | 5,597 | | 28 | Nebraska | 6,156 |
| 19 | New Hampshire | 6,932 | | 29 | South Carolina | 6,092 |
| 1 | New Jersey | 9,963 | | 30 | Louisiana | 6,088 |
| 33 | New Mexico | 5,895 | | 31 | Illinois | 6,075 |
| 3 | New York | 9,146 | | 32 | North Dakota | 5,949 |
| 42 | North Carolina | 5,431 | | 33 | New Mexico | 5,895 |
| 32 | North Dakota | 5,949 | | 34 | Texas | 5,870 |
| 21 | Ohio | 6,554 | | 35 | Georgia | 5,835 |
| 41 | Oklahoma | 5,533 | | 36 | California | 5,832 |
| 16 | Oregon | 7,069 | | 37 | Colorado | 5,823 |
| 8 | Pennsylvania | 8,045 | | 38 | Florida | 5,737 |
| 5 | Rhode Island | 8,315 | | 39 | Missouri | 5,655 |
| 29 | South Carolina | 6,092 | | 40 | Nevada | 5,597 |
| 43 | South Dakota | 5,417 | | 41 | Oklahoma | 5,533 |
| 44 | Tennessee | 5,282 | | 42 | North Carolina | 5,431 |
| 34 | Texas | 5,870 | | 43 | South Dakota | 5,417 |
| 50 | Utah | 3,991 | | 44 | Tennessee | 5,282 |
| 13 | Vermont | 7,309 | | 45 | Alabama | 5,010 |
| 20 | Virginia | 6,913 | | 46 | Idaho | 4,878 |
| 23 | Washington | 6,514 | | 47 | Arkansas | 4,864 |
| 7 | West Virginia | 8,114 | | 48 | Mississippi | 4,827 |
| 9 | Wisconsin | 7,894 | | 49 | Arizona | 4,754 |
| 12 | Wyoming | 7,356 | | 50 | Utah | 3,991 |
| | | | | | District of Columbia | 8,672 |

Source: U.S. Department of Education, Office of Educational Research and Improvement
"Early Estimates of Public Elementary and Secondary Education Statistics: 1999-2000" (May 2000)
*School year 1999-2000.

# Higher Education Expenditures by State and Local Governments in 1997

## National Total = $106,061,001,000*

ALPHA ORDER

| RANK | STATE | EXPENDITURES | % of USA |
|------|-------|-------------:|---------:|
| 20 | Alabama | $1,979,473,000 | 1.9% |
| 48 | Alaska | 304,638,000 | 0.3% |
| 22 | Arizona | 1,696,816,000 | 1.6% |
| 34 | Arkansas | 914,356,000 | 0.9% |
| 1 | California | 12,347,422,000 | 11.6% |
| 17 | Colorado | 2,131,596,000 | 2.0% |
| 35 | Connecticut | 909,575,000 | 0.9% |
| 41 | Delaware | 498,589,000 | 0.5% |
| 8 | Florida | 3,797,248,000 | 3.6% |
| 15 | Georgia | 2,539,760,000 | 2.4% |
| 38 | Hawaii | 589,625,000 | 0.6% |
| 40 | Idaho | 514,735,000 | 0.5% |
| 7 | Illinois | 3,995,320,000 | 3.8% |
| 10 | Indiana | 2,954,836,000 | 2.8% |
| 23 | Iowa | 1,687,355,000 | 1.6% |
| 31 | Kansas | 1,265,286,000 | 1.2% |
| 27 | Kentucky | 1,560,128,000 | 1.5% |
| 26 | Louisiana | 1,642,488,000 | 1.5% |
| 43 | Maine | 404,826,000 | 0.4% |
| 16 | Maryland | 2,239,627,000 | 2.1% |
| 24 | Massachusetts | 1,680,292,000 | 1.6% |
| 4 | Michigan | 5,215,377,000 | 4.9% |
| 18 | Minnesota | 2,022,356,000 | 1.9% |
| 32 | Mississippi | 1,224,667,000 | 1.2% |
| 21 | Missouri | 1,863,197,000 | 1.8% |
| 42 | Montana | 412,572,000 | 0.4% |
| 36 | Nebraska | 887,491,000 | 0.8% |
| 39 | Nevada | 534,567,000 | 0.5% |
| 45 | New Hampshire | 383,712,000 | 0.4% |
| 13 | New Jersey | 2,689,557,000 | 2.5% |
| 33 | New Mexico | 1,069,769,000 | 1.0% |
| 3 | New York | 5,587,746,000 | 5.3% |
| 9 | North Carolina | 3,636,142,000 | 3.4% |
| 44 | North Dakota | 393,583,000 | 0.4% |
| 5 | Ohio | 4,550,747,000 | 4.3% |
| 29 | Oklahoma | 1,367,707,000 | 1.3% |
| 25 | Oregon | 1,666,057,000 | 1.6% |
| 6 | Pennsylvania | 4,124,801,000 | 3.9% |
| 46 | Rhode Island | 339,838,000 | 0.3% |
| 28 | South Carolina | 1,558,546,000 | 1.5% |
| 50 | South Dakota | 242,398,000 | 0.2% |
| 19 | Tennessee | 1,990,089,000 | 1.9% |
| 2 | Texas | 7,765,484,000 | 7.3% |
| 30 | Utah | 1,314,161,000 | 1.2% |
| 47 | Vermont | 319,672,000 | 0.3% |
| 11 | Virginia | 2,841,785,000 | 2.7% |
| 12 | Washington | 2,723,308,000 | 2.6% |
| 37 | West Virginia | 690,299,000 | 0.7% |
| 14 | Wisconsin | 2,641,317,000 | 2.5% |
| 49 | Wyoming | 274,976,000 | 0.3% |

RANK ORDER

| RANK | STATE | EXPENDITURES | % of USA |
|------|-------|-------------:|---------:|
| 1 | California | $12,347,422,000 | 11.6% |
| 2 | Texas | 7,765,484,000 | 7.3% |
| 3 | New York | 5,587,746,000 | 5.3% |
| 4 | Michigan | 5,215,377,000 | 4.9% |
| 5 | Ohio | 4,550,747,000 | 4.3% |
| 6 | Pennsylvania | 4,124,801,000 | 3.9% |
| 7 | Illinois | 3,995,320,000 | 3.8% |
| 8 | Florida | 3,797,248,000 | 3.6% |
| 9 | North Carolina | 3,636,142,000 | 3.4% |
| 10 | Indiana | 2,954,836,000 | 2.8% |
| 11 | Virginia | 2,841,785,000 | 2.7% |
| 12 | Washington | 2,723,308,000 | 2.6% |
| 13 | New Jersey | 2,689,557,000 | 2.5% |
| 14 | Wisconsin | 2,641,317,000 | 2.5% |
| 15 | Georgia | 2,539,760,000 | 2.4% |
| 16 | Maryland | 2,239,627,000 | 2.1% |
| 17 | Colorado | 2,131,596,000 | 2.0% |
| 18 | Minnesota | 2,022,356,000 | 1.9% |
| 19 | Tennessee | 1,990,089,000 | 1.9% |
| 20 | Alabama | 1,979,473,000 | 1.9% |
| 21 | Missouri | 1,863,197,000 | 1.8% |
| 22 | Arizona | 1,696,816,000 | 1.6% |
| 23 | Iowa | 1,687,355,000 | 1.6% |
| 24 | Massachusetts | 1,680,292,000 | 1.6% |
| 25 | Oregon | 1,666,057,000 | 1.6% |
| 26 | Louisiana | 1,642,488,000 | 1.5% |
| 27 | Kentucky | 1,560,128,000 | 1.5% |
| 28 | South Carolina | 1,558,546,000 | 1.5% |
| 29 | Oklahoma | 1,367,707,000 | 1.3% |
| 30 | Utah | 1,314,161,000 | 1.2% |
| 31 | Kansas | 1,265,286,000 | 1.2% |
| 32 | Mississippi | 1,224,667,000 | 1.2% |
| 33 | New Mexico | 1,069,769,000 | 1.0% |
| 34 | Arkansas | 914,356,000 | 0.9% |
| 35 | Connecticut | 909,575,000 | 0.9% |
| 36 | Nebraska | 887,491,000 | 0.8% |
| 37 | West Virginia | 690,299,000 | 0.7% |
| 38 | Hawaii | 589,625,000 | 0.6% |
| 39 | Nevada | 534,567,000 | 0.5% |
| 40 | Idaho | 514,735,000 | 0.5% |
| 41 | Delaware | 498,589,000 | 0.5% |
| 42 | Montana | 412,572,000 | 0.4% |
| 43 | Maine | 404,826,000 | 0.4% |
| 44 | North Dakota | 393,583,000 | 0.4% |
| 45 | New Hampshire | 383,712,000 | 0.4% |
| 46 | Rhode Island | 339,838,000 | 0.3% |
| 47 | Vermont | 319,672,000 | 0.3% |
| 48 | Alaska | 304,638,000 | 0.3% |
| 49 | Wyoming | 274,976,000 | 0.3% |
| 50 | South Dakota | 242,398,000 | 0.2% |
| | District of Columbia | 75,089,000 | 0.1% |

*Source: U.S. Bureau of the Census, Governments Division*
*"Compendium of Government Finances: 1997" (2000) (http://www.census.gov/govs/www/cog.html)*
*Direct general expenditures. Includes capital outlays.*

# Per Capita State and Local Government Expenditures
## For Higher Education in 1997
## National Per Capita = $396*

| ALPHA ORDER | | | | RANK ORDER | | |
|---|---|---|---|---|---|---|
| RANK | STATE | PER CAPITA | | RANK | STATE | PER CAPITA |
| 20 | Alabama | $458 | | 1 | Delaware | $678 |
| 14 | Alaska | 500 | | 2 | Utah | 636 |
| 34 | Arizona | 373 | | 3 | New Mexico | 621 |
| 36 | Arkansas | 362 | | 4 | North Dakota | 614 |
| 31 | California | 383 | | 5 | Iowa | 591 |
| 7 | Colorado | 548 | | 6 | Wyoming | 573 |
| 48 | Connecticut | 278 | | 7 | Colorado | 548 |
| 1 | Delaware | 678 | | 8 | Vermont | 543 |
| 50 | Florida | 259 | | 9 | Nebraska | 536 |
| 40 | Georgia | 339 | | 10 | Michigan | 533 |
| 15 | Hawaii | 496 | | 11 | Oregon | 514 |
| 24 | Idaho | 425 | | 12 | Wisconsin | 508 |
| 42 | Illinois | 333 | | 13 | Indiana | 503 |
| 13 | Indiana | 503 | | 14 | Alaska | 500 |
| 5 | Iowa | 591 | | 15 | Hawaii | 496 |
| 18 | Kansas | 484 | | 16 | North Carolina | 489 |
| 30 | Kentucky | 399 | | 17 | Washington | 486 |
| 33 | Louisiana | 377 | | 18 | Kansas | 484 |
| 45 | Maine | 325 | | 19 | Montana | 470 |
| 22 | Maryland | 440 | | 20 | Alabama | 458 |
| 49 | Massachusetts | 275 | | 21 | Mississippi | 448 |
| 10 | Michigan | 533 | | 22 | Maryland | 440 |
| 23 | Minnesota | 431 | | 23 | Minnesota | 431 |
| 21 | Mississippi | 448 | | 24 | Idaho | 425 |
| 37 | Missouri | 345 | | 25 | Virginia | 422 |
| 19 | Montana | 470 | | 26 | Oklahoma | 413 |
| 9 | Nebraska | 536 | | 27 | South Carolina | 411 |
| 46 | Nevada | 319 | | 28 | Ohio | 406 |
| 44 | New Hampshire | 327 | | 29 | Texas | 401 |
| 41 | New Jersey | 334 | | 30 | Kentucky | 399 |
| 3 | New Mexico | 621 | | 31 | California | 383 |
| 47 | New York | 308 | | 32 | West Virginia | 380 |
| 16 | North Carolina | 489 | | 33 | Louisiana | 377 |
| 4 | North Dakota | 614 | | 34 | Arizona | 373 |
| 28 | Ohio | 406 | | 35 | Tennessee | 370 |
| 26 | Oklahoma | 413 | | 36 | Arkansas | 362 |
| 11 | Oregon | 514 | | 37 | Missouri | 345 |
| 39 | Pennsylvania | 343 | | 38 | Rhode Island | 344 |
| 38 | Rhode Island | 344 | | 39 | Pennsylvania | 343 |
| 27 | South Carolina | 411 | | 40 | Georgia | 339 |
| 43 | South Dakota | 332 | | 41 | New Jersey | 334 |
| 35 | Tennessee | 370 | | 42 | Illinois | 333 |
| 29 | Texas | 401 | | 43 | South Dakota | 332 |
| 2 | Utah | 636 | | 44 | New Hampshire | 327 |
| 8 | Vermont | 543 | | 45 | Maine | 325 |
| 25 | Virginia | 422 | | 46 | Nevada | 319 |
| 17 | Washington | 486 | | 47 | New York | 308 |
| 32 | West Virginia | 380 | | 48 | Connecticut | 278 |
| 12 | Wisconsin | 508 | | 49 | Massachusetts | 275 |
| 6 | Wyoming | 573 | | 50 | Florida | 259 |
| | | | | | District of Columbia | 142 |

Source: Morgan Quitno Press using data from U.S. Bureau of the Census, Governments Division
"Compendium of Government Finances: 1997" (2000) (http://www.census.gov/govs/www/cog.html)
*Direct general expenditures. Includes capital outlays.

# Expenditures for Higher Education as a Percent
## Of All State and Local Government Expenditures in 1997
## National Percent = 8.5%*

ALPHA ORDER

| RANK | STATE | PERCENT |
|---|---|---|
| 10 | Alabama | 11.5 |
| 49 | Alaska | 4.5 |
| 27 | Arizona | 9.5 |
| 26 | Arkansas | 9.7 |
| 40 | California | 7.7 |
| 7 | Colorado | 12.2 |
| 48 | Connecticut | 5.1 |
| 5 | Delaware | 12.6 |
| 46 | Florida | 6.0 |
| 37 | Georgia | 7.8 |
| 33 | Hawaii | 8.8 |
| 16 | Idaho | 10.6 |
| 41 | Illinois | 7.5 |
| 5 | Indiana | 12.6 |
| 2 | Iowa | 13.1 |
| 10 | Kansas | 11.5 |
| 21 | Kentucky | 10.0 |
| 34 | Louisiana | 8.7 |
| 42 | Maine | 7.0 |
| 23 | Maryland | 9.8 |
| 47 | Massachusetts | 5.3 |
| 13 | Michigan | 11.4 |
| 36 | Minnesota | 8.1 |
| 15 | Mississippi | 11.0 |
| 31 | Missouri | 9.1 |
| 16 | Montana | 10.6 |
| 8 | Nebraska | 11.9 |
| 44 | Nevada | 6.8 |
| 37 | New Hampshire | 7.8 |
| 45 | New Jersey | 6.6 |
| 4 | New Mexico | 12.8 |
| 50 | New York | 4.4 |
| 9 | North Carolina | 11.6 |
| 2 | North Dakota | 13.1 |
| 27 | Ohio | 9.5 |
| 14 | Oklahoma | 11.2 |
| 20 | Oregon | 10.1 |
| 37 | Pennsylvania | 7.8 |
| 42 | Rhode Island | 7.0 |
| 23 | South Carolina | 9.8 |
| 35 | South Dakota | 8.3 |
| 29 | Tennessee | 9.4 |
| 19 | Texas | 10.2 |
| 1 | Utah | 14.6 |
| 10 | Vermont | 11.5 |
| 21 | Virginia | 10.0 |
| 29 | Washington | 9.4 |
| 32 | West Virginia | 8.9 |
| 18 | Wisconsin | 10.4 |
| 23 | Wyoming | 9.8 |

RANK ORDER

| RANK | STATE | PERCENT |
|---|---|---|
| 1 | Utah | 14.6 |
| 2 | Iowa | 13.1 |
| 2 | North Dakota | 13.1 |
| 4 | New Mexico | 12.8 |
| 5 | Delaware | 12.6 |
| 5 | Indiana | 12.6 |
| 7 | Colorado | 12.2 |
| 8 | Nebraska | 11.9 |
| 9 | North Carolina | 11.6 |
| 10 | Alabama | 11.5 |
| 10 | Kansas | 11.5 |
| 10 | Vermont | 11.5 |
| 13 | Michigan | 11.4 |
| 14 | Oklahoma | 11.2 |
| 15 | Mississippi | 11.0 |
| 16 | Idaho | 10.6 |
| 16 | Montana | 10.6 |
| 18 | Wisconsin | 10.4 |
| 19 | Texas | 10.2 |
| 20 | Oregon | 10.1 |
| 21 | Kentucky | 10.0 |
| 21 | Virginia | 10.0 |
| 23 | Maryland | 9.8 |
| 23 | South Carolina | 9.8 |
| 23 | Wyoming | 9.8 |
| 26 | Arkansas | 9.7 |
| 27 | Arizona | 9.5 |
| 27 | Ohio | 9.5 |
| 29 | Tennessee | 9.4 |
| 29 | Washington | 9.4 |
| 31 | Missouri | 9.1 |
| 32 | West Virginia | 8.9 |
| 33 | Hawaii | 8.8 |
| 34 | Louisiana | 8.7 |
| 35 | South Dakota | 8.3 |
| 36 | Minnesota | 8.1 |
| 37 | Georgia | 7.8 |
| 37 | New Hampshire | 7.8 |
| 37 | Pennsylvania | 7.8 |
| 40 | California | 7.7 |
| 41 | Illinois | 7.5 |
| 42 | Maine | 7.0 |
| 42 | Rhode Island | 7.0 |
| 44 | Nevada | 6.8 |
| 45 | New Jersey | 6.6 |
| 46 | Florida | 6.0 |
| 47 | Massachusetts | 5.3 |
| 48 | Connecticut | 5.1 |
| 49 | Alaska | 4.5 |
| 50 | New York | 4.4 |

| District of Columbia | 1.7 |
|---|---|

Source: Morgan Quitno Press using data from U.S. Bureau of the Census, Governments Division
   "Compendium of Government Finances: 1997" (2000) (http://www.census.gov/govs/www/cog.html)
*Direct general expenditures for higher education as a percent of all direct general expenditures. Includes capital outlays.

# Average Student Costs at Public Institutions of Higher Education in 2000

## National Average = $8,265*

ALPHA ORDER

| RANK | STATE | AVERAGE COSTS |
|---|---|---|
| 38 | Alabama | $6,742 |
| 19 | Alaska | 8,333 |
| 30 | Arizona | 7,362 |
| 45 | Arkansas | 6,416 |
| 13 | California | 9,183 |
| 23 | Colorado | 7,994 |
| 7 | Connecticut | 10,136 |
| 10 | Delaware | 9,876 |
| 28 | Florida | 7,474 |
| 31 | Georgia | 7,295 |
| 22 | Hawaii | 8,056 |
| 47 | Idaho | 6,323 |
| 16 | Illinois | 9,002 |
| 17 | Indiana | 8,845 |
| 34 | Iowa | 7,210 |
| 46 | Kansas | 6,324 |
| 43 | Kentucky | 6,481 |
| 49 | Louisiana | 5,910 |
| 14 | Maine | 9,089 |
| 6 | Maryland | 10,345 |
| 12 | Massachusetts | 9,212 |
| 11 | Michigan | 9,513 |
| 26 | Minnesota | 7,665 |
| 44 | Mississippi | 6,456 |
| 21 | Missouri | 8,185 |
| 29 | Montana | 7,463 |
| 33 | Nebraska | 7,258 |
| 24 | Nevada | 7,812 |
| 3 | New Hampshire | 11,052 |
| 2 | New Jersey | 11,450 |
| 39 | New Mexico | 6,600 |
| 8 | New York | 9,998 |
| 42 | North Carolina | 6,483 |
| 37 | North Dakota | 6,994 |
| 9 | Ohio | 9,900 |
| 50 | Oklahoma | 5,735 |
| 15 | Oregon | 9,065 |
| 5 | Pennsylvania | 10,534 |
| 4 | Rhode Island | 10,595 |
| 25 | South Carolina | 7,703 |
| 41 | South Dakota | 6,520 |
| 40 | Tennessee | 6,555 |
| 27 | Texas | 7,497 |
| 48 | Utah | 6,299 |
| 1 | Vermont | 12,478 |
| 18 | Virginia | 8,619 |
| 20 | Washington | 8,314 |
| 35 | West Virginia | 7,105 |
| 32 | Wisconsin | 7,268 |
| 36 | Wyoming | 7,091 |

RANK ORDER

| RANK | STATE | AVERAGE COSTS |
|---|---|---|
| 1 | Vermont | $12,478 |
| 2 | New Jersey | 11,450 |
| 3 | New Hampshire | 11,052 |
| 4 | Rhode Island | 10,595 |
| 5 | Pennsylvania | 10,534 |
| 6 | Maryland | 10,345 |
| 7 | Connecticut | 10,136 |
| 8 | New York | 9,998 |
| 9 | Ohio | 9,900 |
| 10 | Delaware | 9,876 |
| 11 | Michigan | 9,513 |
| 12 | Massachusetts | 9,212 |
| 13 | California | 9,183 |
| 14 | Maine | 9,089 |
| 15 | Oregon | 9,065 |
| 16 | Illinois | 9,002 |
| 17 | Indiana | 8,845 |
| 18 | Virginia | 8,619 |
| 19 | Alaska | 8,333 |
| 20 | Washington | 8,314 |
| 21 | Missouri | 8,185 |
| 22 | Hawaii | 8,056 |
| 23 | Colorado | 7,994 |
| 24 | Nevada | 7,812 |
| 25 | South Carolina | 7,703 |
| 26 | Minnesota | 7,665 |
| 27 | Texas | 7,497 |
| 28 | Florida | 7,474 |
| 29 | Montana | 7,463 |
| 30 | Arizona | 7,362 |
| 31 | Georgia | 7,295 |
| 32 | Wisconsin | 7,268 |
| 33 | Nebraska | 7,258 |
| 34 | Iowa | 7,210 |
| 35 | West Virginia | 7,105 |
| 36 | Wyoming | 7,091 |
| 37 | North Dakota | 6,994 |
| 38 | Alabama | 6,742 |
| 39 | New Mexico | 6,600 |
| 40 | Tennessee | 6,555 |
| 41 | South Dakota | 6,520 |
| 42 | North Carolina | 6,483 |
| 43 | Kentucky | 6,481 |
| 44 | Mississippi | 6,456 |
| 45 | Arkansas | 6,416 |
| 46 | Kansas | 6,324 |
| 47 | Idaho | 6,323 |
| 48 | Utah | 6,299 |
| 49 | Louisiana | 5,910 |
| 50 | Oklahoma | 5,735 |
| | District of Columbia** | NA |

Source: U.S. Department of Education, National Center for Educational Statistics
   "Digest of Education Statistics 2000" (NCES 2001-034)
*Preliminary data for 1999-00 school year. Based on average in-state tuition, room and board and fees for full-time students in public four-year institutions for an entire academic year.
**Not available.

# Average Student Costs at Private Institutions of Higher Education in 2000

## National Average = $20,805*

ALPHA ORDER

| RANK | STATE | AVERAGE COSTS |
|---|---|---|
| 43 | Alabama | $13,548 |
| 41 | Alaska | 13,728 |
| 40 | Arizona | 13,964 |
| 47 | Arkansas | 12,040 |
| 11 | California | 22,751 |
| 19 | Colorado | 20,013 |
| 2 | Connecticut | 27,212 |
| 42 | Delaware | 13,726 |
| 24 | Florida | 18,405 |
| 23 | Georgia | 18,620 |
| 34 | Hawaii | 15,171 |
| 28 | Idaho | 16,885 |
| 13 | Illinois | 20,881 |
| 14 | Indiana | 20,825 |
| 21 | Iowa | 18,691 |
| 36 | Kansas | 14,998 |
| 39 | Kentucky | 13,990 |
| 16 | Louisiana | 20,623 |
| 3 | Maine | 26,785 |
| 5 | Maryland | 24,795 |
| 1 | Massachusetts | 27,860 |
| 33 | Michigan | 15,354 |
| 17 | Minnesota | 20,475 |
| 46 | Mississippi | 12,569 |
| 29 | Missouri | 16,839 |
| 44 | Montana | 13,335 |
| 32 | Nebraska | 15,613 |
| 45 | Nevada | 12,881 |
| 9 | New Hampshire | 23,213 |
| 10 | New Jersey | 23,154 |
| 37 | New Mexico | 14,771 |
| 7 | New York | 24,047 |
| 22 | North Carolina | 18,678 |
| 48 | North Dakota | 10,932 |
| 15 | Ohio | 20,748 |
| 38 | Oklahoma | 14,409 |
| 12 | Oregon | 22,023 |
| 8 | Pennsylvania | 23,651 |
| 4 | Rhode Island | 25,124 |
| 30 | South Carolina | 16,501 |
| 35 | South Dakota | 15,008 |
| 27 | Tennessee | 17,020 |
| 31 | Texas | 16,032 |
| 49 | Utah | 7,893 |
| 6 | Vermont | 24,629 |
| 25 | Virginia | 17,853 |
| 18 | Washington | 20,313 |
| 26 | West Virginia | 17,047 |
| 20 | Wisconsin | 19,385 |
| NA | Wyoming** | NA |

RANK ORDER

| RANK | STATE | AVERAGE COSTS |
|---|---|---|
| 1 | Massachusetts | $27,860 |
| 2 | Connecticut | 27,212 |
| 3 | Maine | 26,785 |
| 4 | Rhode Island | 25,124 |
| 5 | Maryland | 24,795 |
| 6 | Vermont | 24,629 |
| 7 | New York | 24,047 |
| 8 | Pennsylvania | 23,651 |
| 9 | New Hampshire | 23,213 |
| 10 | New Jersey | 23,154 |
| 11 | California | 22,751 |
| 12 | Oregon | 22,023 |
| 13 | Illinois | 20,881 |
| 14 | Indiana | 20,825 |
| 15 | Ohio | 20,748 |
| 16 | Louisiana | 20,623 |
| 17 | Minnesota | 20,475 |
| 18 | Washington | 20,313 |
| 19 | Colorado | 20,013 |
| 20 | Wisconsin | 19,385 |
| 21 | Iowa | 18,691 |
| 22 | North Carolina | 18,678 |
| 23 | Georgia | 18,620 |
| 24 | Florida | 18,405 |
| 25 | Virginia | 17,853 |
| 26 | West Virginia | 17,047 |
| 27 | Tennessee | 17,020 |
| 28 | Idaho | 16,885 |
| 29 | Missouri | 16,839 |
| 30 | South Carolina | 16,501 |
| 31 | Texas | 16,032 |
| 32 | Nebraska | 15,613 |
| 33 | Michigan | 15,354 |
| 34 | Hawaii | 15,171 |
| 35 | South Dakota | 15,008 |
| 36 | Kansas | 14,998 |
| 37 | New Mexico | 14,771 |
| 38 | Oklahoma | 14,409 |
| 39 | Kentucky | 13,990 |
| 40 | Arizona | 13,964 |
| 41 | Alaska | 13,728 |
| 42 | Delaware | 13,726 |
| 43 | Alabama | 13,548 |
| 44 | Montana | 13,335 |
| 45 | Nevada | 12,881 |
| 46 | Mississippi | 12,569 |
| 47 | Arkansas | 12,040 |
| 48 | North Dakota | 10,932 |
| 49 | Utah | 7,893 |
| NA | Wyoming** | NA |
| | District of Columbia | 25,381 |

Source: U.S. Department of Education, National Center for Educational Statistics
    "Digest of Education Statistics 2000" (NCES 2001-034)
*Preliminary data for 1999-00 school year. Based on average in-state tuition, room and board and fees for full-time students in private four-year institutions for an entire academic year.
**Not available or not applicable.

# Institutions of Higher Education in 1999

## National Total = 4,070 Institutions*

ALPHA ORDER

| RANK | STATE | INSTITUTIONS | % of USA |
|------|-------|--------------|----------|
| 18 | Alabama | 78 | 1.9% |
| 50 | Alaska | 8 | 0.2% |
| 23 | Arizona | 65 | 1.6% |
| 32 | Arkansas | 45 | 1.1% |
| 1 | California | 403 | 9.9% |
| 19 | Colorado | 71 | 1.7% |
| 34 | Connecticut | 41 | 1.0% |
| 48 | Delaware | 10 | 0.2% |
| 7 | Florida | 147 | 3.6% |
| 13 | Georgia | 103 | 2.5% |
| 44 | Hawaii | 20 | 0.5% |
| 45 | Idaho | 15 | 0.4% |
| 5 | Illinois | 175 | 4.3% |
| 14 | Indiana | 94 | 2.3% |
| 25 | Iowa | 59 | 1.4% |
| 25 | Kansas | 59 | 1.4% |
| 21 | Kentucky | 67 | 1.6% |
| 16 | Louisiana | 85 | 2.1% |
| 36 | Maine | 34 | 0.8% |
| 25 | Maryland | 59 | 1.4% |
| 8 | Massachusetts | 129 | 3.2% |
| 12 | Michigan | 112 | 2.8% |
| 10 | Minnesota | 116 | 2.9% |
| 31 | Mississippi | 46 | 1.1% |
| 11 | Missouri | 113 | 2.8% |
| 38 | Montana | 28 | 0.7% |
| 35 | Nebraska | 37 | 0.9% |
| 45 | Nevada | 15 | 0.4% |
| 39 | New Hampshire | 27 | 0.7% |
| 28 | New Jersey | 58 | 1.4% |
| 33 | New Mexico | 44 | 1.1% |
| 2 | New York | 320 | 7.9% |
| 9 | North Carolina | 120 | 2.9% |
| 42 | North Dakota | 21 | 0.5% |
| 6 | Ohio | 173 | 4.3% |
| 30 | Oklahoma | 48 | 1.2% |
| 29 | Oregon | 54 | 1.3% |
| 3 | Pennsylvania | 250 | 6.1% |
| 47 | Rhode Island | 12 | 0.3% |
| 24 | South Carolina | 62 | 1.5% |
| 40 | South Dakota | 25 | 0.6% |
| 17 | Tennessee | 84 | 2.1% |
| 4 | Texas | 199 | 4.9% |
| 42 | Utah | 21 | 0.5% |
| 40 | Vermont | 25 | 0.6% |
| 15 | Virginia | 92 | 2.3% |
| 19 | Washington | 71 | 1.7% |
| 37 | West Virginia | 33 | 0.8% |
| 22 | Wisconsin | 66 | 1.6% |
| 49 | Wyoming | 9 | 0.2% |

RANK ORDER

| RANK | STATE | INSTITUTIONS | % of USA |
|------|-------|--------------|----------|
| 1 | California | 403 | 9.9% |
| 2 | New York | 320 | 7.9% |
| 3 | Pennsylvania | 250 | 6.1% |
| 4 | Texas | 199 | 4.9% |
| 5 | Illinois | 175 | 4.3% |
| 6 | Ohio | 173 | 4.3% |
| 7 | Florida | 147 | 3.6% |
| 8 | Massachusetts | 129 | 3.2% |
| 9 | North Carolina | 120 | 2.9% |
| 10 | Minnesota | 116 | 2.9% |
| 11 | Missouri | 113 | 2.8% |
| 12 | Michigan | 112 | 2.8% |
| 13 | Georgia | 103 | 2.5% |
| 14 | Indiana | 94 | 2.3% |
| 15 | Virginia | 92 | 2.3% |
| 16 | Louisiana | 85 | 2.1% |
| 17 | Tennessee | 84 | 2.1% |
| 18 | Alabama | 78 | 1.9% |
| 19 | Colorado | 71 | 1.7% |
| 19 | Washington | 71 | 1.7% |
| 21 | Kentucky | 67 | 1.6% |
| 22 | Wisconsin | 66 | 1.6% |
| 23 | Arizona | 65 | 1.6% |
| 24 | South Carolina | 62 | 1.5% |
| 25 | Iowa | 59 | 1.4% |
| 25 | Kansas | 59 | 1.4% |
| 25 | Maryland | 59 | 1.4% |
| 28 | New Jersey | 58 | 1.4% |
| 29 | Oregon | 54 | 1.3% |
| 30 | Oklahoma | 48 | 1.2% |
| 31 | Mississippi | 46 | 1.1% |
| 32 | Arkansas | 45 | 1.1% |
| 33 | New Mexico | 44 | 1.1% |
| 34 | Connecticut | 41 | 1.0% |
| 35 | Nebraska | 37 | 0.9% |
| 36 | Maine | 34 | 0.8% |
| 37 | West Virginia | 33 | 0.8% |
| 38 | Montana | 28 | 0.7% |
| 39 | New Hampshire | 27 | 0.7% |
| 40 | South Dakota | 25 | 0.6% |
| 40 | Vermont | 25 | 0.6% |
| 42 | North Dakota | 21 | 0.5% |
| 42 | Utah | 21 | 0.5% |
| 44 | Hawaii | 20 | 0.5% |
| 45 | Idaho | 15 | 0.4% |
| 45 | Nevada | 15 | 0.4% |
| 47 | Rhode Island | 12 | 0.3% |
| 48 | Delaware | 10 | 0.2% |
| 49 | Wyoming | 9 | 0.2% |
| 50 | Alaska | 8 | 0.2% |
|  | District of Columbia | 17 | 0.4% |

Source: U.S. Department of Education, National Center for Education Statistics
   "Digest of Education Statistics 2000" (NCES 2001-034, January 2001)
*For 1998-99 school year.  Includes 5 U.S. Service Schools not shown by state.  Consists of 2,343 four-year and
1,727 two-year public and private degree-granting institutions.

# Enrollment in Institutions of High Education in 1998

## National Total = 14,549,189 Students*

ALPHA ORDER

| RANK | STATE | STUDENTS | % of USA |
|---|---|---|---|
| 24 | Alabama | 216,268 | 1.5% |
| 50 | Alaska | 27,652 | 0.2% |
| 16 | Arizona | 302,123 | 2.1% |
| 34 | Arkansas | 113,751 | 0.8% |
| 1 | California | 1,970,592 | 13.5% |
| 21 | Colorado | 257,247 | 1.8% |
| 31 | Connecticut | 153,336 | 1.1% |
| 44 | Delaware | 46,260 | 0.3% |
| 5 | Florida | 661,312 | 4.5% |
| 15 | Georgia | 303,685 | 2.1% |
| 41 | Hawaii | 61,681 | 0.4% |
| 40 | Idaho | 63,085 | 0.4% |
| 4 | Illinois | 729,234 | 5.0% |
| 17 | Indiana | 299,604 | 2.1% |
| 25 | Iowa | 181,944 | 1.3% |
| 29 | Kansas | 177,639 | 1.2% |
| 27 | Kentucky | 180,576 | 1.2% |
| 23 | Louisiana | 221,110 | 1.5% |
| 43 | Maine | 56,986 | 0.4% |
| 20 | Maryland | 265,173 | 1.8% |
| 9 | Massachusetts | 415,616 | 2.9% |
| 7 | Michigan | 557,011 | 3.8% |
| 19 | Minnesota | 278,997 | 1.9% |
| 33 | Mississippi | 132,438 | 0.9% |
| 13 | Missouri | 311,383 | 2.1% |
| 45 | Montana | 44,150 | 0.3% |
| 35 | Nebraska | 111,123 | 0.8% |
| 38 | Nevada | 83,155 | 0.6% |
| 42 | New Hampshire | 60,784 | 0.4% |
| 12 | New Jersey | 325,898 | 2.2% |
| 36 | New Mexico | 109,002 | 0.7% |
| 2 | New York | 1,014,271 | 7.0% |
| 10 | North Carolina | 387,407 | 2.7% |
| 47 | North Dakota | 39,441 | 0.3% |
| 8 | Ohio | 542,201 | 3.7% |
| 28 | Oklahoma | 178,642 | 1.2% |
| 30 | Oregon | 171,153 | 1.2% |
| 6 | Pennsylvania | 595,805 | 4.1% |
| 39 | Rhode Island | 73,970 | 0.5% |
| 26 | South Carolina | 181,353 | 1.2% |
| 46 | South Dakota | 41,545 | 0.3% |
| 22 | Tennessee | 251,410 | 1.7% |
| 3 | Texas | 982,227 | 6.8% |
| 32 | Utah | 151,232 | 1.0% |
| 48 | Vermont | 37,054 | 0.3% |
| 11 | Virginia | 370,142 | 2.5% |
| 18 | Washington | 298,974 | 2.1% |
| 37 | West Virginia | 88,107 | 0.6% |
| 14 | Wisconsin | 309,354 | 2.1% |
| 49 | Wyoming | 29,707 | 0.2% |

RANK ORDER

| RANK | STATE | STUDENTS | % of USA |
|---|---|---|---|
| 1 | California | 1,970,592 | 13.5% |
| 2 | New York | 1,014,271 | 7.0% |
| 3 | Texas | 982,227 | 6.8% |
| 4 | Illinois | 729,234 | 5.0% |
| 5 | Florida | 661,312 | 4.5% |
| 6 | Pennsylvania | 595,805 | 4.1% |
| 7 | Michigan | 557,011 | 3.8% |
| 8 | Ohio | 542,201 | 3.7% |
| 9 | Massachusetts | 415,616 | 2.9% |
| 10 | North Carolina | 387,407 | 2.7% |
| 11 | Virginia | 370,142 | 2.5% |
| 12 | New Jersey | 325,898 | 2.2% |
| 13 | Missouri | 311,383 | 2.1% |
| 14 | Wisconsin | 309,354 | 2.1% |
| 15 | Georgia | 303,685 | 2.1% |
| 16 | Arizona | 302,123 | 2.1% |
| 17 | Indiana | 299,604 | 2.1% |
| 18 | Washington | 298,974 | 2.1% |
| 19 | Minnesota | 278,997 | 1.9% |
| 20 | Maryland | 265,173 | 1.8% |
| 21 | Colorado | 257,247 | 1.8% |
| 22 | Tennessee | 251,410 | 1.7% |
| 23 | Louisiana | 221,110 | 1.5% |
| 24 | Alabama | 216,268 | 1.5% |
| 25 | Iowa | 181,944 | 1.3% |
| 26 | South Carolina | 181,353 | 1.2% |
| 27 | Kentucky | 180,576 | 1.2% |
| 28 | Oklahoma | 178,642 | 1.2% |
| 29 | Kansas | 177,639 | 1.2% |
| 30 | Oregon | 171,153 | 1.2% |
| 31 | Connecticut | 153,336 | 1.1% |
| 32 | Utah | 151,232 | 1.0% |
| 33 | Mississippi | 132,438 | 0.9% |
| 34 | Arkansas | 113,751 | 0.8% |
| 35 | Nebraska | 111,123 | 0.8% |
| 36 | New Mexico | 109,002 | 0.7% |
| 37 | West Virginia | 88,107 | 0.6% |
| 38 | Nevada | 83,155 | 0.6% |
| 39 | Rhode Island | 73,970 | 0.5% |
| 40 | Idaho | 63,085 | 0.4% |
| 41 | Hawaii | 61,681 | 0.4% |
| 42 | New Hampshire | 60,784 | 0.4% |
| 43 | Maine | 56,986 | 0.4% |
| 44 | Delaware | 46,260 | 0.3% |
| 45 | Montana | 44,150 | 0.3% |
| 46 | South Dakota | 41,545 | 0.3% |
| 47 | North Dakota | 39,441 | 0.3% |
| 48 | Vermont | 37,054 | 0.3% |
| 49 | Wyoming | 29,707 | 0.2% |
| 50 | Alaska | 27,652 | 0.2% |
| | District of Columbia | 72,388 | 0.5% |

Source: U.S. Department of Education, National Center for Education Statistics
    "Digest of Education Statistics 2000" (NCES 2001-034, January 2001)
*Fall 1998 enrollment. Includes full-time and part-time students at Title IV eligible, degree-granting four-year and two-year institutions.

# Enrollment in Public Institutions of Higher Education in 1998

## National Total = 11,176,184 Students*

ALPHA ORDER

| RANK | STATE | STUDENTS | % of USA |
|---|---|---|---|
| 22 | Alabama | 190,685 | 1.7% |
| 49 | Alaska | 26,296 | 0.2% |
| 11 | Arizona | 268,102 | 2.4% |
| 33 | Arkansas | 102,264 | 0.9% |
| 1 | California | 1,666,330 | 14.9% |
| 18 | Colorado | 216,351 | 1.9% |
| 35 | Connecticut | 94,299 | 0.8% |
| 44 | Delaware | 37,362 | 0.3% |
| 5 | Florida | 531,921 | 4.8% |
| 15 | Georgia | 229,928 | 2.1% |
| 40 | Hawaii | 45,270 | 0.4% |
| 39 | Idaho | 51,330 | 0.5% |
| 4 | Illinois | 533,294 | 4.8% |
| 16 | Indiana | 228,450 | 2.0% |
| 30 | Iowa | 129,302 | 1.2% |
| 25 | Kansas | 158,672 | 1.4% |
| 28 | Kentucky | 146,344 | 1.3% |
| 23 | Louisiana | 189,896 | 1.7% |
| 42 | Maine | 38,636 | 0.3% |
| 17 | Maryland | 219,055 | 2.0% |
| 24 | Massachusetts | 178,376 | 1.6% |
| 6 | Michigan | 462,580 | 4.1% |
| 19 | Minnesota | 207,807 | 1.9% |
| 31 | Mississippi | 120,831 | 1.1% |
| 20 | Missouri | 194,462 | 1.7% |
| 41 | Montana | 38,768 | 0.3% |
| 36 | Nebraska | 89,040 | 0.8% |
| 37 | Nevada | 79,147 | 0.7% |
| 47 | New Hampshire | 32,187 | 0.3% |
| 12 | New Jersey | 260,092 | 2.3% |
| 34 | New Mexico | 101,170 | 0.9% |
| 3 | New York | 567,202 | 5.1% |
| 9 | North Carolina | 314,110 | 2.8% |
| 45 | North Dakota | 35,264 | 0.3% |
| 7 | Ohio | 408,487 | 3.7% |
| 26 | Oklahoma | 155,796 | 1.4% |
| 29 | Oregon | 144,423 | 1.3% |
| 8 | Pennsylvania | 338,047 | 3.0% |
| 43 | Rhode Island | 38,368 | 0.3% |
| 27 | South Carolina | 152,542 | 1.4% |
| 46 | South Dakota | 34,088 | 0.3% |
| 21 | Tennessee | 193,393 | 1.7% |
| 2 | Texas | 852,736 | 7.6% |
| 32 | Utah | 111,315 | 1.0% |
| 50 | Vermont | 20,549 | 0.2% |
| 10 | Virginia | 305,455 | 2.7% |
| 13 | Washington | 257,047 | 2.3% |
| 38 | West Virginia | 76,322 | 0.7% |
| 14 | Wisconsin | 254,635 | 2.3% |
| 48 | Wyoming | 28,757 | 0.3% |

RANK ORDER

| RANK | STATE | STUDENTS | % of USA |
|---|---|---|---|
| 1 | California | 1,666,330 | 14.9% |
| 2 | Texas | 852,736 | 7.6% |
| 3 | New York | 567,202 | 5.1% |
| 4 | Illinois | 533,294 | 4.8% |
| 5 | Florida | 531,921 | 4.8% |
| 6 | Michigan | 462,580 | 4.1% |
| 7 | Ohio | 408,487 | 3.7% |
| 8 | Pennsylvania | 338,047 | 3.0% |
| 9 | North Carolina | 314,110 | 2.8% |
| 10 | Virginia | 305,455 | 2.7% |
| 11 | Arizona | 268,102 | 2.4% |
| 12 | New Jersey | 260,092 | 2.3% |
| 13 | Washington | 257,047 | 2.3% |
| 14 | Wisconsin | 254,635 | 2.3% |
| 15 | Georgia | 229,928 | 2.1% |
| 16 | Indiana | 228,450 | 2.0% |
| 17 | Maryland | 219,055 | 2.0% |
| 18 | Colorado | 216,351 | 1.9% |
| 19 | Minnesota | 207,807 | 1.9% |
| 20 | Missouri | 194,462 | 1.7% |
| 21 | Tennessee | 193,393 | 1.7% |
| 22 | Alabama | 190,685 | 1.7% |
| 23 | Louisiana | 189,896 | 1.7% |
| 24 | Massachusetts | 178,376 | 1.6% |
| 25 | Kansas | 158,672 | 1.4% |
| 26 | Oklahoma | 155,796 | 1.4% |
| 27 | South Carolina | 152,542 | 1.4% |
| 28 | Kentucky | 146,344 | 1.3% |
| 29 | Oregon | 144,423 | 1.3% |
| 30 | Iowa | 129,302 | 1.2% |
| 31 | Mississippi | 120,831 | 1.1% |
| 32 | Utah | 111,315 | 1.0% |
| 33 | Arkansas | 102,264 | 0.9% |
| 34 | New Mexico | 101,170 | 0.9% |
| 35 | Connecticut | 94,299 | 0.8% |
| 36 | Nebraska | 89,040 | 0.8% |
| 37 | Nevada | 79,147 | 0.7% |
| 38 | West Virginia | 76,322 | 0.7% |
| 39 | Idaho | 51,330 | 0.5% |
| 40 | Hawaii | 45,270 | 0.4% |
| 41 | Montana | 38,768 | 0.3% |
| 42 | Maine | 38,636 | 0.3% |
| 43 | Rhode Island | 38,368 | 0.3% |
| 44 | Delaware | 37,362 | 0.3% |
| 45 | North Dakota | 35,264 | 0.3% |
| 46 | South Dakota | 34,088 | 0.3% |
| 47 | New Hampshire | 32,187 | 0.3% |
| 48 | Wyoming | 28,757 | 0.3% |
| 49 | Alaska | 26,296 | 0.2% |
| 50 | Vermont | 20,549 | 0.2% |
| | District of Columbia | 5,410 | 0.0% |

Source: U.S. Department of Education, National Center for Education Statistics
    "Digest of Education Statistics 2000" (NCES 2001-034, January 2001)
*Fall 1998 enrollment.  Includes full-time and part-time students at Title IV eligible, degree-granting four-year and two-year institutions.

# Enrollment in Private Institutions of Higher Education in 1998

## National Total = 3,373,005 Students*

ALPHA ORDER

| RANK | STATE | STUDENTS | % of USA |
|---|---|---|---|
| 32 | Alabama | 25,583 | 0.8% |
| 49 | Alaska | 1,356 | 0.0% |
| 27 | Arizona | 34,021 | 1.0% |
| 42 | Arkansas | 11,487 | 0.3% |
| 2 | California | 304,262 | 9.0% |
| 23 | Colorado | 40,896 | 1.2% |
| 17 | Connecticut | 59,037 | 1.8% |
| 43 | Delaware | 8,898 | 0.3% |
| 8 | Florida | 129,391 | 3.8% |
| 11 | Georgia | 73,757 | 2.2% |
| 38 | Hawaii | 16,411 | 0.5% |
| 40 | Idaho | 11,755 | 0.3% |
| 5 | Illinois | 195,940 | 5.8% |
| 14 | Indiana | 71,154 | 2.1% |
| 20 | Iowa | 52,642 | 1.6% |
| 35 | Kansas | 18,967 | 0.6% |
| 26 | Kentucky | 34,232 | 1.0% |
| 28 | Louisiana | 31,214 | 0.9% |
| 36 | Maine | 18,350 | 0.5% |
| 21 | Maryland | 46,118 | 1.4% |
| 4 | Massachusetts | 237,240 | 7.0% |
| 10 | Michigan | 94,431 | 2.8% |
| 13 | Minnesota | 71,190 | 2.1% |
| 41 | Mississippi | 11,607 | 0.3% |
| 9 | Missouri | 116,921 | 3.5% |
| 46 | Montana | 5,382 | 0.2% |
| 34 | Nebraska | 22,083 | 0.7% |
| 48 | Nevada | 4,008 | 0.1% |
| 30 | New Hampshire | 28,597 | 0.8% |
| 15 | New Jersey | 65,806 | 2.0% |
| 44 | New Mexico | 7,832 | 0.2% |
| 1 | New York | 447,069 | 13.3% |
| 12 | North Carolina | 73,297 | 2.2% |
| 47 | North Dakota | 4,177 | 0.1% |
| 6 | Ohio | 133,714 | 4.0% |
| 33 | Oklahoma | 22,846 | 0.7% |
| 31 | Oregon | 26,730 | 0.8% |
| 3 | Pennsylvania | 257,758 | 7.6% |
| 25 | Rhode Island | 35,602 | 1.1% |
| 29 | South Carolina | 28,811 | 0.9% |
| 45 | South Dakota | 7,457 | 0.2% |
| 18 | Tennessee | 58,017 | 1.7% |
| 7 | Texas | 129,491 | 3.8% |
| 24 | Utah | 39,917 | 1.2% |
| 37 | Vermont | 16,505 | 0.5% |
| 16 | Virginia | 64,687 | 1.9% |
| 22 | Washington | 41,927 | 1.2% |
| 39 | West Virginia | 11,785 | 0.3% |
| 19 | Wisconsin | 54,719 | 1.6% |
| 50 | Wyoming | 950 | 0.0% |

RANK ORDER

| RANK | STATE | STUDENTS | % of USA |
|---|---|---|---|
| 1 | New York | 447,069 | 13.3% |
| 2 | California | 304,262 | 9.0% |
| 3 | Pennsylvania | 257,758 | 7.6% |
| 4 | Massachusetts | 237,240 | 7.0% |
| 5 | Illinois | 195,940 | 5.8% |
| 6 | Ohio | 133,714 | 4.0% |
| 7 | Texas | 129,491 | 3.8% |
| 8 | Florida | 129,391 | 3.8% |
| 9 | Missouri | 116,921 | 3.5% |
| 10 | Michigan | 94,431 | 2.8% |
| 11 | Georgia | 73,757 | 2.2% |
| 12 | North Carolina | 73,297 | 2.2% |
| 13 | Minnesota | 71,190 | 2.1% |
| 14 | Indiana | 71,154 | 2.1% |
| 15 | New Jersey | 65,806 | 2.0% |
| 16 | Virginia | 64,687 | 1.9% |
| 17 | Connecticut | 59,037 | 1.8% |
| 18 | Tennessee | 58,017 | 1.7% |
| 19 | Wisconsin | 54,719 | 1.6% |
| 20 | Iowa | 52,642 | 1.6% |
| 21 | Maryland | 46,118 | 1.4% |
| 22 | Washington | 41,927 | 1.2% |
| 23 | Colorado | 40,896 | 1.2% |
| 24 | Utah | 39,917 | 1.2% |
| 25 | Rhode Island | 35,602 | 1.1% |
| 26 | Kentucky | 34,232 | 1.0% |
| 27 | Arizona | 34,021 | 1.0% |
| 28 | Louisiana | 31,214 | 0.9% |
| 29 | South Carolina | 28,811 | 0.9% |
| 30 | New Hampshire | 28,597 | 0.8% |
| 31 | Oregon | 26,730 | 0.8% |
| 32 | Alabama | 25,583 | 0.8% |
| 33 | Oklahoma | 22,846 | 0.7% |
| 34 | Nebraska | 22,083 | 0.7% |
| 35 | Kansas | 18,967 | 0.6% |
| 36 | Maine | 18,350 | 0.5% |
| 37 | Vermont | 16,505 | 0.5% |
| 38 | Hawaii | 16,411 | 0.5% |
| 39 | West Virginia | 11,785 | 0.3% |
| 40 | Idaho | 11,755 | 0.3% |
| 41 | Mississippi | 11,607 | 0.3% |
| 42 | Arkansas | 11,487 | 0.3% |
| 43 | Delaware | 8,898 | 0.3% |
| 44 | New Mexico | 7,832 | 0.2% |
| 45 | South Dakota | 7,457 | 0.2% |
| 46 | Montana | 5,382 | 0.2% |
| 47 | North Dakota | 4,177 | 0.1% |
| 48 | Nevada | 4,008 | 0.1% |
| 49 | Alaska | 1,356 | 0.0% |
| 50 | Wyoming | 950 | 0.0% |
| | District of Columbia | 66,978 | 2.0% |

*Source: U.S. Department of Education, National Center for Education Statistics*
*"Digest of Education Statistics 2000" (NCES 2001-034, January 2001)*
*Fall 1998 enrollment. Includes full-time and part-time students at Title IV eligible, degree-granting four-year and two-year institutions.*

# Percent of Population Graduated from College as of 2000

## National Percent = 25.6% of Population*

ALPHA ORDER

RANK ORDER

| RANK | STATE | PERCENT | | RANK | STATE | PERCENT |
|---|---|---|---|---|---|---|
| 43 | Alabama | 20.4 | | 1 | Colorado | 34.6 |
| 12 | Alaska | 28.1 | | 2 | Massachusetts | 32.7 |
| 23 | Arizona | 24.6 | | 3 | Maryland | 32.3 |
| 48 | Arkansas | 18.4 | | 4 | Virginia | 31.9 |
| 13 | California | 27.5 | | 5 | Connecticut | 31.6 |
| 1 | Colorado | 34.6 | | 6 | Minnesota | 31.2 |
| 5 | Connecticut | 31.6 | | 7 | New Hampshire | 30.1 |
| 28 | Delaware | 24.0 | | 7 | New Jersey | 30.1 |
| 36 | Florida | 22.8 | | 9 | Vermont | 28.8 |
| 34 | Georgia | 23.1 | | 10 | New York | 28.7 |
| 19 | Hawaii | 26.3 | | 11 | Washington | 28.6 |
| 44 | Idaho | 20.0 | | 12 | Alaska | 28.1 |
| 16 | Illinois | 27.1 | | 13 | California | 27.5 |
| 49 | Indiana | 17.1 | | 14 | Kansas | 27.3 |
| 22 | Iowa | 25.5 | | 15 | Oregon | 27.2 |
| 14 | Kansas | 27.3 | | 16 | Illinois | 27.1 |
| 42 | Kentucky | 20.5 | | 17 | Rhode Island | 26.4 |
| 38 | Louisiana | 22.5 | | 17 | Utah | 26.4 |
| 27 | Maine | 24.1 | | 19 | Hawaii | 26.3 |
| 3 | Maryland | 32.3 | | 20 | Missouri | 26.2 |
| 2 | Massachusetts | 32.7 | | 21 | South Dakota | 25.7 |
| 35 | Michigan | 23.0 | | 22 | Iowa | 25.5 |
| 6 | Minnesota | 31.2 | | 23 | Arizona | 24.6 |
| 47 | Mississippi | 18.7 | | 23 | Nebraska | 24.6 |
| 20 | Missouri | 26.2 | | 23 | Ohio | 24.6 |
| 30 | Montana | 23.8 | | 26 | Pennsylvania | 24.3 |
| 23 | Nebraska | 24.6 | | 27 | Maine | 24.1 |
| 45 | Nevada | 19.3 | | 28 | Delaware | 24.0 |
| 7 | New Hampshire | 30.1 | | 29 | Texas | 23.9 |
| 7 | New Jersey | 30.1 | | 30 | Montana | 23.8 |
| 32 | New Mexico | 23.6 | | 30 | Wisconsin | 23.8 |
| 10 | New York | 28.7 | | 32 | New Mexico | 23.6 |
| 33 | North Carolina | 23.2 | | 33 | North Carolina | 23.2 |
| 37 | North Dakota | 22.6 | | 34 | Georgia | 23.1 |
| 23 | Ohio | 24.6 | | 35 | Michigan | 23.0 |
| 38 | Oklahoma | 22.5 | | 36 | Florida | 22.8 |
| 15 | Oregon | 27.2 | | 37 | North Dakota | 22.6 |
| 26 | Pennsylvania | 24.3 | | 38 | Louisiana | 22.5 |
| 17 | Rhode Island | 26.4 | | 38 | Oklahoma | 22.5 |
| 46 | South Carolina | 19.0 | | 40 | Tennessee | 22.0 |
| 21 | South Dakota | 25.7 | | 41 | Wyoming | 20.6 |
| 40 | Tennessee | 22.0 | | 42 | Kentucky | 20.5 |
| 29 | Texas | 23.9 | | 43 | Alabama | 20.4 |
| 17 | Utah | 26.4 | | 44 | Idaho | 20.0 |
| 9 | Vermont | 28.8 | | 45 | Nevada | 19.3 |
| 4 | Virginia | 31.9 | | 46 | South Carolina | 19.0 |
| 11 | Washington | 28.6 | | 47 | Mississippi | 18.7 |
| 50 | West Virginia | 15.3 | | 48 | Arkansas | 18.4 |
| 30 | Wisconsin | 23.8 | | 49 | Indiana | 17.1 |
| 41 | Wyoming | 20.6 | | 50 | West Virginia | 15.3 |
| | | | | | District of Columbia | 38.3 |

Source: U.S. Bureau of the Census
 "Educational Attainment in the United States: March 2000"
 (http://www.census.gov/population/www/socdemo/educ-attn.html)
*Persons age 25 and older having completed a Bachelor's degree or more.

# Public Libraries and Branches in 1997

## National Total = 16,090 Libraries and Branches*

ALPHA ORDER

| RANK | STATE | LIBRARIES | % of USA |
|---|---|---|---|
| 24 | Alabama | 274 | 1.7% |
| 42 | Alaska | 103 | 0.6% |
| 38 | Arizona | 164 | 1.0% |
| 31 | Arkansas | 203 | 1.3% |
| 2 | California | 1,039 | 6.5% |
| 25 | Colorado | 249 | 1.5% |
| 26 | Connecticut | 245 | 1.5% |
| 50 | Delaware | 30 | 0.2% |
| 12 | Florida | 438 | 2.7% |
| 15 | Georgia | 368 | 2.3% |
| 49 | Hawaii | 49 | 0.3% |
| 39 | Idaho | 143 | 0.9% |
| 3 | Illinois | 779 | 4.8% |
| 13 | Indiana | 427 | 2.7% |
| 8 | Iowa | 556 | 3.5% |
| 14 | Kansas | 374 | 2.3% |
| 35 | Kentucky | 187 | 1.2% |
| 19 | Louisiana | 317 | 2.0% |
| 23 | Maine | 276 | 1.7% |
| 34 | Maryland | 189 | 1.2% |
| 9 | Massachusetts | 489 | 3.0% |
| 6 | Michigan | 652 | 4.1% |
| 17 | Minnesota | 362 | 2.2% |
| 28 | Mississippi | 242 | 1.5% |
| 18 | Missouri | 354 | 2.2% |
| 41 | Montana | 106 | 0.7% |
| 26 | Nebraska | 245 | 1.5% |
| 46 | Nevada | 83 | 0.5% |
| 29 | New Hampshire | 239 | 1.5% |
| 11 | New Jersey | 452 | 2.8% |
| 44 | New Mexico | 92 | 0.6% |
| 1 | New York | 1,077 | 6.7% |
| 16 | North Carolina | 364 | 2.3% |
| 45 | North Dakota | 88 | 0.5% |
| 5 | Ohio | 690 | 4.3% |
| 30 | Oklahoma | 208 | 1.3% |
| 32 | Oregon | 200 | 1.2% |
| 7 | Pennsylvania | 644 | 4.0% |
| 48 | Rhode Island | 72 | 0.4% |
| 36 | South Carolina | 181 | 1.1% |
| 40 | South Dakota | 129 | 0.8% |
| 22 | Tennessee | 286 | 1.8% |
| 4 | Texas | 776 | 4.8% |
| 43 | Utah | 100 | 0.6% |
| 33 | Vermont | 198 | 1.2% |
| 20 | Virginia | 311 | 1.9% |
| 20 | Washington | 311 | 1.9% |
| 37 | West Virginia | 173 | 1.1% |
| 10 | Wisconsin | 455 | 2.8% |
| 47 | Wyoming | 74 | 0.5% |

RANK ORDER

| RANK | STATE | LIBRARIES | % of USA |
|---|---|---|---|
| 1 | New York | 1,077 | 6.7% |
| 2 | California | 1,039 | 6.5% |
| 3 | Illinois | 779 | 4.8% |
| 4 | Texas | 776 | 4.8% |
| 5 | Ohio | 690 | 4.3% |
| 6 | Michigan | 652 | 4.1% |
| 7 | Pennsylvania | 644 | 4.0% |
| 8 | Iowa | 556 | 3.5% |
| 9 | Massachusetts | 489 | 3.0% |
| 10 | Wisconsin | 455 | 2.8% |
| 11 | New Jersey | 452 | 2.8% |
| 12 | Florida | 438 | 2.7% |
| 13 | Indiana | 427 | 2.7% |
| 14 | Kansas | 374 | 2.3% |
| 15 | Georgia | 368 | 2.3% |
| 16 | North Carolina | 364 | 2.3% |
| 17 | Minnesota | 362 | 2.2% |
| 18 | Missouri | 354 | 2.2% |
| 19 | Louisiana | 317 | 2.0% |
| 20 | Virginia | 311 | 1.9% |
| 20 | Washington | 311 | 1.9% |
| 22 | Tennessee | 286 | 1.8% |
| 23 | Maine | 276 | 1.7% |
| 24 | Alabama | 274 | 1.7% |
| 25 | Colorado | 249 | 1.5% |
| 26 | Connecticut | 245 | 1.5% |
| 26 | Nebraska | 245 | 1.5% |
| 28 | Mississippi | 242 | 1.5% |
| 29 | New Hampshire | 239 | 1.5% |
| 30 | Oklahoma | 208 | 1.3% |
| 31 | Arkansas | 203 | 1.3% |
| 32 | Oregon | 200 | 1.2% |
| 33 | Vermont | 198 | 1.2% |
| 34 | Maryland | 189 | 1.2% |
| 35 | Kentucky | 187 | 1.2% |
| 36 | South Carolina | 181 | 1.1% |
| 37 | West Virginia | 173 | 1.1% |
| 38 | Arizona | 164 | 1.0% |
| 39 | Idaho | 143 | 0.9% |
| 40 | South Dakota | 129 | 0.8% |
| 41 | Montana | 106 | 0.7% |
| 42 | Alaska | 103 | 0.6% |
| 43 | Utah | 100 | 0.6% |
| 44 | New Mexico | 92 | 0.6% |
| 45 | North Dakota | 88 | 0.5% |
| 46 | Nevada | 83 | 0.5% |
| 47 | Wyoming | 74 | 0.5% |
| 48 | Rhode Island | 72 | 0.4% |
| 49 | Hawaii | 49 | 0.3% |
| 50 | Delaware | 30 | 0.2% |
| | District of Columbia | 27 | 0.2% |

*Source: U.S. Dept. of Education, Office of Educational Research & Improvement
"Public Libraries in the United States: FY 1997" (NCES 2000-316, June 2000)
*For fiscal year 1997. Does not include bookmobiles.*

# Rate of Public Libraries and Branches in 1997

## National Rate = 0.60 Libraries per 10,000 Population*

ALPHA ORDER

RANK ORDER

| RANK | STATE | RATE | | RANK | STATE | RATE |
|------|-------|------|---|------|-------|------|
| 27 | Alabama | 0.63 | | 1 | Vermont | 3.36 |
| 6 | Alaska | 1.69 | | 2 | Maine | 2.22 |
| 48 | Arizona | 0.36 | | 3 | New Hampshire | 2.04 |
| 16 | Arkansas | 0.80 | | 4 | Iowa | 1.95 |
| 49 | California | 0.32 | | 5 | South Dakota | 1.77 |
| 26 | Colorado | 0.64 | | 6 | Alaska | 1.69 |
| 19 | Connecticut | 0.75 | | 7 | Wyoming | 1.54 |
| 44 | Delaware | 0.41 | | 8 | Nebraska | 1.48 |
| 50 | Florida | 0.30 | | 9 | Kansas | 1.43 |
| 38 | Georgia | 0.49 | | 10 | North Dakota | 1.37 |
| 44 | Hawaii | 0.41 | | 11 | Montana | 1.21 |
| 12 | Idaho | 1.18 | | 12 | Idaho | 1.18 |
| 24 | Illinois | 0.65 | | 13 | West Virginia | 0.95 |
| 20 | Indiana | 0.73 | | 14 | Mississippi | 0.89 |
| 4 | Iowa | 1.95 | | 15 | Wisconsin | 0.87 |
| 9 | Kansas | 1.43 | | 16 | Arkansas | 0.80 |
| 40 | Kentucky | 0.48 | | 16 | Massachusetts | 0.80 |
| 20 | Louisiana | 0.73 | | 18 | Minnesota | 0.77 |
| 2 | Maine | 2.22 | | 19 | Connecticut | 0.75 |
| 47 | Maryland | 0.37 | | 20 | Indiana | 0.73 |
| 16 | Massachusetts | 0.80 | | 20 | Louisiana | 0.73 |
| 23 | Michigan | 0.67 | | 20 | Rhode Island | 0.73 |
| 18 | Minnesota | 0.77 | | 23 | Michigan | 0.67 |
| 14 | Mississippi | 0.89 | | 24 | Illinois | 0.65 |
| 24 | Missouri | 0.65 | | 24 | Missouri | 0.65 |
| 11 | Montana | 1.21 | | 26 | Colorado | 0.64 |
| 8 | Nebraska | 1.48 | | 27 | Alabama | 0.63 |
| 37 | Nevada | 0.50 | | 27 | Oklahoma | 0.63 |
| 3 | New Hampshire | 2.04 | | 29 | Ohio | 0.62 |
| 32 | New Jersey | 0.56 | | 29 | Oregon | 0.62 |
| 35 | New Mexico | 0.53 | | 31 | New York | 0.59 |
| 31 | New York | 0.59 | | 32 | New Jersey | 0.56 |
| 38 | North Carolina | 0.49 | | 33 | Washington | 0.55 |
| 10 | North Dakota | 1.37 | | 34 | Pennsylvania | 0.54 |
| 29 | Ohio | 0.62 | | 35 | New Mexico | 0.53 |
| 27 | Oklahoma | 0.63 | | 35 | Tennessee | 0.53 |
| 29 | Oregon | 0.62 | | 37 | Nevada | 0.50 |
| 34 | Pennsylvania | 0.54 | | 38 | Georgia | 0.49 |
| 20 | Rhode Island | 0.73 | | 38 | North Carolina | 0.49 |
| 40 | South Carolina | 0.48 | | 40 | Kentucky | 0.48 |
| 5 | South Dakota | 1.77 | | 40 | South Carolina | 0.48 |
| 35 | Tennessee | 0.53 | | 40 | Utah | 0.48 |
| 46 | Texas | 0.40 | | 43 | Virginia | 0.46 |
| 40 | Utah | 0.48 | | 44 | Delaware | 0.41 |
| 1 | Vermont | 3.36 | | 44 | Hawaii | 0.41 |
| 43 | Virginia | 0.46 | | 46 | Texas | 0.40 |
| 33 | Washington | 0.55 | | 47 | Maryland | 0.37 |
| 13 | West Virginia | 0.95 | | 48 | Arizona | 0.36 |
| 15 | Wisconsin | 0.87 | | 49 | California | 0.32 |
| 7 | Wyoming | 1.54 | | 50 | Florida | 0.30 |
| | | | | | District of Columbia | 0.51 |

Source: Morgan Quitno Press using data from U.S. Dept. of Education, Office of Educational Research & Improvement
   "Public Libraries in the United States: FY 1997" (NCES 2000-316, June 2000)
*For fiscal year 1997. Does not include bookmobiles.

# Books in Public Libraries Per Capita in 1997

## National Per Capita = 2.8 Books*

ALPHA ORDER

| RANK | STATE | BOOKS PER CAPITA |
|---|---|---|
| 39 | Alabama | 2.1 |
| 20 | Alaska | 3.3 |
| 48 | Arizona | 1.8 |
| 35 | Arkansas | 2.2 |
| 45 | California | 1.9 |
| 29 | Colorado | 2.6 |
| 9 | Connecticut | 4.4 |
| 35 | Delaware | 2.2 |
| 48 | Florida | 1.8 |
| 45 | Georgia | 1.9 |
| 29 | Hawaii | 2.6 |
| 21 | Idaho | 3.2 |
| 15 | Illinois | 3.8 |
| 10 | Indiana | 4.3 |
| 13 | Iowa | 4.0 |
| 6 | Kansas | 4.6 |
| 39 | Kentucky | 2.1 |
| 34 | Louisiana | 2.3 |
| 2 | Maine | 5.3 |
| 27 | Maryland | 2.7 |
| 4 | Massachusetts | 4.8 |
| 26 | Michigan | 2.8 |
| 23 | Minnesota | 2.9 |
| 42 | Mississippi | 2.0 |
| 12 | Missouri | 4.1 |
| 22 | Montana | 3.0 |
| 18 | Nebraska | 3.7 |
| 35 | Nevada | 2.2 |
| 7 | New Hampshire | 4.5 |
| 15 | New Jersey | 3.8 |
| 23 | New Mexico | 2.9 |
| 7 | New York | 4.5 |
| 42 | North Carolina | 2.0 |
| 15 | North Dakota | 3.8 |
| 13 | Ohio | 4.0 |
| 39 | Oklahoma | 2.1 |
| 32 | Oregon | 2.5 |
| 35 | Pennsylvania | 2.2 |
| 11 | Rhode Island | 4.2 |
| 45 | South Carolina | 1.9 |
| 3 | South Dakota | 4.9 |
| 50 | Tennessee | 1.6 |
| 42 | Texas | 2.0 |
| 29 | Utah | 2.6 |
| 1 | Vermont | 5.4 |
| 32 | Virginia | 2.5 |
| 23 | Washington | 2.9 |
| 27 | West Virginia | 2.7 |
| 19 | Wisconsin | 3.4 |
| 5 | Wyoming | 4.7 |

RANK ORDER

| RANK | STATE | BOOKS PER CAPITA |
|---|---|---|
| 1 | Vermont | 5.4 |
| 2 | Maine | 5.3 |
| 3 | South Dakota | 4.9 |
| 4 | Massachusetts | 4.8 |
| 5 | Wyoming | 4.7 |
| 6 | Kansas | 4.6 |
| 7 | New Hampshire | 4.5 |
| 7 | New York | 4.5 |
| 9 | Connecticut | 4.4 |
| 10 | Indiana | 4.3 |
| 11 | Rhode Island | 4.2 |
| 12 | Missouri | 4.1 |
| 13 | Iowa | 4.0 |
| 13 | Ohio | 4.0 |
| 15 | Illinois | 3.8 |
| 15 | New Jersey | 3.8 |
| 15 | North Dakota | 3.8 |
| 18 | Nebraska | 3.7 |
| 19 | Wisconsin | 3.4 |
| 20 | Alaska | 3.3 |
| 21 | Idaho | 3.2 |
| 22 | Montana | 3.0 |
| 23 | Minnesota | 2.9 |
| 23 | New Mexico | 2.9 |
| 23 | Washington | 2.9 |
| 26 | Michigan | 2.8 |
| 27 | Maryland | 2.7 |
| 27 | West Virginia | 2.7 |
| 29 | Colorado | 2.6 |
| 29 | Hawaii | 2.6 |
| 29 | Utah | 2.6 |
| 32 | Oregon | 2.5 |
| 32 | Virginia | 2.5 |
| 34 | Louisiana | 2.3 |
| 35 | Arkansas | 2.2 |
| 35 | Delaware | 2.2 |
| 35 | Nevada | 2.2 |
| 35 | Pennsylvania | 2.2 |
| 39 | Alabama | 2.1 |
| 39 | Kentucky | 2.1 |
| 39 | Oklahoma | 2.1 |
| 42 | Mississippi | 2.0 |
| 42 | North Carolina | 2.0 |
| 42 | Texas | 2.0 |
| 45 | California | 1.9 |
| 45 | Georgia | 1.9 |
| 45 | South Carolina | 1.9 |
| 48 | Arizona | 1.8 |
| 48 | Florida | 1.8 |
| 50 | Tennessee | 1.6 |
| | District of Columbia | 5.3 |

Source: U.S. Dept. of Education, Office of Educational Research & Improvement
"Public Libraries in the United States: FY 1997" (NCES 2000-316, June 2000)
*For fiscal year 1997. Includes serial volumes but not serial subscriptions.

# State Art Agencies' Legislative Appropriations in 2000

## National Total = $327,430,755*

ALPHA ORDER

RANK ORDER

| RANK | STATE | FUNDING | % of USA | | RANK | STATE | FUNDING | % of USA |
|------|-------|---------|----------|---|------|-------|---------|----------|
| 21 | Alabama | $4,200,875 | 1.3% | | 1 | New York | $50,169,000 | 15.3% |
| 47 | Alaska | 455,800 | 0.1% | | 2 | Florida | 27,896,619 | 8.5% |
| 25 | Arizona | 3,730,700 | 1.1% | | 3 | Michigan | 21,704,100 | 6.6% |
| 38 | Arkansas | 1,348,916 | 0.4% | | 4 | New Jersey | 19,359,000 | 5.9% |
| 5 | California | 19,355,000 | 5.9% | | 5 | California | 19,355,000 | 5.9% |
| 32 | Colorado | 1,863,183 | 0.6% | | 6 | Massachusetts | 17,366,146 | 5.3% |
| 12 | Connecticut | 9,608,560 | 2.9% | | 7 | Ohio | 16,456,606 | 5.0% |
| 35 | Delaware | 1,560,300 | 0.5% | | 8 | Minnesota | 13,064,000 | 4.0% |
| 2 | Florida | 27,896,619 | 8.5% | | 9 | Illinois | 12,197,900 | 3.7% |
| 19 | Georgia | 4,403,816 | 1.3% | | 10 | Pennsylvania | 12,000,000 | 3.7% |
| 14 | Hawaii | 5,977,405 | 1.8% | | 11 | Maryland | 10,342,393 | 3.2% |
| 42 | Idaho | 912,800 | 0.3% | | 12 | Connecticut | 9,608,560 | 2.9% |
| 9 | Illinois | 12,197,900 | 3.7% | | 13 | North Carolina | 7,520,757 | 2.3% |
| 23 | Indiana | 3,842,783 | 1.2% | | 14 | Hawaii | 5,977,405 | 1.8% |
| 33 | Iowa | 1,817,807 | 0.6% | | 15 | Missouri | 5,559,354 | 1.7% |
| 34 | Kansas | 1,629,755 | 0.5% | | 16 | Texas | 5,284,429 | 1.6% |
| 24 | Kentucky | 3,820,600 | 1.2% | | 17 | Louisiana | 5,041,770 | 1.5% |
| 17 | Louisiana | 5,041,770 | 1.5% | | 18 | South Carolina | 4,894,467 | 1.5% |
| 40 | Maine | 1,239,557 | 0.4% | | 19 | Georgia | 4,403,816 | 1.3% |
| 11 | Maryland | 10,342,393 | 3.2% | | 20 | Virginia | 4,322,183 | 1.3% |
| 6 | Massachusetts | 17,366,146 | 5.3% | | 21 | Alabama | 4,200,875 | 1.3% |
| 3 | Michigan | 21,704,100 | 6.6% | | 22 | Oklahoma | 4,083,091 | 1.2% |
| 8 | Minnesota | 13,064,000 | 4.0% | | 23 | Indiana | 3,842,783 | 1.2% |
| 29 | Mississippi | 2,230,193 | 0.7% | | 24 | Kentucky | 3,820,600 | 1.2% |
| 15 | Missouri | 5,559,354 | 1.7% | | 25 | Arizona | 3,730,700 | 1.1% |
| 50 | Montana | 273,221 | 0.1% | | 26 | Utah | 2,646,000 | 0.8% |
| 39 | Nebraska | 1,337,446 | 0.4% | | 27 | Wisconsin | 2,537,300 | 0.8% |
| 36 | Nevada | 1,410,429 | 0.4% | | 28 | Washington | 2,339,982 | 0.7% |
| 44 | New Hampshire | 590,779 | 0.2% | | 29 | Mississippi | 2,230,193 | 0.7% |
| 4 | New Jersey | 19,359,000 | 5.9% | | 30 | New Mexico | 2,212,600 | 0.7% |
| 30 | New Mexico | 2,212,600 | 0.7% | | 31 | Tennessee | 1,863,200 | 0.6% |
| 1 | New York | 50,169,000 | 15.3% | | 32 | Colorado | 1,863,183 | 0.6% |
| 13 | North Carolina | 7,520,757 | 2.3% | | 33 | Iowa | 1,817,807 | 0.6% |
| 48 | North Dakota | 390,123 | 0.1% | | 34 | Kansas | 1,629,755 | 0.5% |
| 7 | Ohio | 16,456,606 | 5.0% | | 35 | Delaware | 1,560,300 | 0.5% |
| 22 | Oklahoma | 4,083,091 | 1.2% | | 36 | Nevada | 1,410,429 | 0.4% |
| 37 | Oregon | 1,386,671 | 0.4% | | 37 | Oregon | 1,386,671 | 0.4% |
| 10 | Pennsylvania | 12,000,000 | 3.7% | | 38 | Arkansas | 1,348,916 | 0.4% |
| 43 | Rhode Island | 856,185 | 0.3% | | 39 | Nebraska | 1,337,446 | 0.4% |
| 18 | South Carolina | 4,894,467 | 1.5% | | 40 | Maine | 1,239,557 | 0.4% |
| 46 | South Dakota | 481,003 | 0.1% | | 41 | West Virginia | 1,224,097 | 0.4% |
| 31 | Tennessee | 1,863,200 | 0.6% | | 42 | Idaho | 912,800 | 0.3% |
| 16 | Texas | 5,284,429 | 1.6% | | 43 | Rhode Island | 856,185 | 0.3% |
| 26 | Utah | 2,646,000 | 0.8% | | 44 | New Hampshire | 590,779 | 0.2% |
| 45 | Vermont | 547,739 | 0.2% | | 45 | Vermont | 547,739 | 0.2% |
| 20 | Virginia | 4,322,183 | 1.3% | | 46 | South Dakota | 481,003 | 0.1% |
| 28 | Washington | 2,339,982 | 0.7% | | 47 | Alaska | 455,800 | 0.1% |
| 41 | West Virginia | 1,224,097 | 0.4% | | 48 | North Dakota | 390,123 | 0.1% |
| 27 | Wisconsin | 2,537,300 | 0.8% | | 49 | Wyoming | 342,115 | 0.1% |
| 49 | Wyoming | 342,115 | 0.1% | | 50 | Montana | 273,221 | 0.1% |
| | | | | | | District of Columbia | 1,732,000 | 0.5% |

*Source: National Assembly of State Arts Agencies*
*"Legislative Appropriations Annual Survey" (March 2000)*
*Fiscal year 2000. Does not include line item appropriations. Line items are legislative appropriations that are not controlled by the state art agencies but are passed through their budgets directly to another entity. National total does not include $15,619,566 in appropriations in U.S. territories.*

# Per Capita State Art Agencies' Legislative Appropriations in 2000

## National Per Capita = $1.25*

| ALPHA ORDER | | | RANK ORDER | | |
|---|---|---|---|---|---|
| RANK | STATE | PER CAPITA | RANK | STATE | PER CAPITA |
| 22 | Alabama | $0.97 | 1 | Hawaii | $5.01 |
| 30 | Alaska | 0.74 | 2 | Connecticut | 2.93 |
| 28 | Arizona | 0.80 | 3 | Massachusetts | 2.83 |
| 42 | Arkansas | 0.53 | 4 | Minnesota | 2.76 |
| 40 | California | 0.59 | 4 | New York | 2.76 |
| 45 | Colorado | 0.47 | 6 | New Jersey | 2.39 |
| 2 | Connecticut | 2.93 | 7 | Michigan | 2.21 |
| 8 | Delaware | 2.10 | 8 | Delaware | 2.10 |
| 10 | Florida | 1.87 | 9 | Maryland | 2.01 |
| 41 | Georgia | 0.58 | 10 | Florida | 1.87 |
| 1 | Hawaii | 5.01 | 11 | Ohio | 1.47 |
| 30 | Idaho | 0.74 | 12 | South Carolina | 1.28 |
| 18 | Illinois | 1.01 | 13 | New Mexico | 1.27 |
| 34 | Indiana | 0.65 | 14 | Utah | 1.26 |
| 36 | Iowa | 0.64 | 15 | Oklahoma | 1.22 |
| 38 | Kansas | 0.62 | 16 | Louisiana | 1.15 |
| 22 | Kentucky | 0.97 | 17 | Missouri | 1.02 |
| 16 | Louisiana | 1.15 | 18 | Illinois | 1.01 |
| 19 | Maine | 1.00 | 19 | Maine | 1.00 |
| 9 | Maryland | 2.01 | 19 | North Carolina | 1.00 |
| 3 | Massachusetts | 2.83 | 19 | Pennsylvania | 1.00 |
| 7 | Michigan | 2.21 | 22 | Alabama | 0.97 |
| 4 | Minnesota | 2.76 | 22 | Kentucky | 0.97 |
| 26 | Mississippi | 0.81 | 24 | Vermont | 0.93 |
| 17 | Missouri | 1.02 | 25 | Rhode Island | 0.87 |
| 49 | Montana | 0.31 | 26 | Mississippi | 0.81 |
| 28 | Nebraska | 0.80 | 26 | Nevada | 0.81 |
| 26 | Nevada | 0.81 | 28 | Arizona | 0.80 |
| 43 | New Hampshire | 0.50 | 28 | Nebraska | 0.80 |
| 6 | New Jersey | 2.39 | 30 | Alaska | 0.74 |
| 13 | New Mexico | 1.27 | 30 | Idaho | 0.74 |
| 4 | New York | 2.76 | 32 | Wyoming | 0.71 |
| 19 | North Carolina | 1.00 | 33 | West Virginia | 0.68 |
| 39 | North Dakota | 0.61 | 34 | Indiana | 0.65 |
| 11 | Ohio | 1.47 | 34 | South Dakota | 0.65 |
| 15 | Oklahoma | 1.22 | 36 | Iowa | 0.64 |
| 46 | Oregon | 0.42 | 36 | Virginia | 0.64 |
| 19 | Pennsylvania | 1.00 | 38 | Kansas | 0.62 |
| 25 | Rhode Island | 0.87 | 39 | North Dakota | 0.61 |
| 12 | South Carolina | 1.28 | 40 | California | 0.59 |
| 34 | South Dakota | 0.65 | 41 | Georgia | 0.58 |
| 48 | Tennessee | 0.34 | 42 | Arkansas | 0.53 |
| 50 | Texas | 0.27 | 43 | New Hampshire | 0.50 |
| 14 | Utah | 1.26 | 44 | Wisconsin | 0.49 |
| 24 | Vermont | 0.93 | 45 | Colorado | 0.47 |
| 36 | Virginia | 0.64 | 46 | Oregon | 0.42 |
| 47 | Washington | 0.41 | 47 | Washington | 0.41 |
| 33 | West Virginia | 0.68 | 48 | Tennessee | 0.34 |
| 44 | Wisconsin | 0.49 | 49 | Montana | 0.31 |
| 32 | Wyoming | 0.71 | 50 | Texas | 0.27 |
| | | | District of Columbia | | 3.31 |

Source: National Assembly of State Arts Agencies
"Legislative Appropriations Annual Survey" (March 2000)
*Fiscal year 2000. Does not include line item appropriations. Line items are legislative appropriations that are not controlled by the state art agencies but are passed through their budgets directly to another entity.

# Federal Allocations for Head Start Program in 1999

## National Total = $4,502,423,000*

### ALPHA ORDER

| RANK | STATE | ALLOCATIONS | % of USA |
|---|---|---|---|
| 18 | Alabama | $71,983,000 | 1.6% |
| 49 | Alaska | 8,786,000 | 0.2% |
| 23 | Arizona | 62,444,000 | 1.4% |
| 29 | Arkansas | 43,449,000 | 1.0% |
| 1 | California | 554,366,000 | 12.3% |
| 28 | Colorado | 46,602,000 | 1.0% |
| 31 | Connecticut | 37,906,000 | 0.8% |
| 48 | Delaware | 8,873,000 | 0.2% |
| 7 | Florida | 169,996,000 | 3.8% |
| 10 | Georgia | 112,040,000 | 2.5% |
| 39 | Hawaii | 15,786,000 | 0.4% |
| 41 | Idaho | 14,121,000 | 0.3% |
| 4 | Illinois | 192,580,000 | 4.3% |
| 22 | Indiana | 65,226,000 | 1.4% |
| 33 | Iowa | 36,038,000 | 0.8% |
| 35 | Kansas | 32,958,000 | 0.7% |
| 17 | Kentucky | 76,409,000 | 1.7% |
| 11 | Louisiana | 100,196,000 | 2.2% |
| 38 | Maine | 18,695,000 | 0.4% |
| 25 | Maryland | 54,966,000 | 1.2% |
| 16 | Massachusetts | 78,544,000 | 1.7% |
| 6 | Michigan | 171,121,000 | 3.8% |
| 27 | Minnesota | 51,740,000 | 1.1% |
| 9 | Mississippi | 117,375,000 | 2.6% |
| 15 | Missouri | 78,622,000 | 1.7% |
| 42 | Montana | 13,839,000 | 0.3% |
| 36 | Nebraska | 23,890,000 | 0.5% |
| 44 | Nevada | 11,484,000 | 0.3% |
| 47 | New Hampshire | 9,114,000 | 0.2% |
| 12 | New Jersey | 94,945,000 | 2.1% |
| 34 | New Mexico | 35,363,000 | 0.8% |
| 2 | New York | 304,283,000 | 6.8% |
| 13 | North Carolina | 93,979,000 | 2.1% |
| 45 | North Dakota | 10,561,000 | 0.2% |
| 5 | Ohio | 178,271,000 | 4.0% |
| 26 | Oklahoma | 54,422,000 | 1.2% |
| 30 | Oregon | 40,118,000 | 0.9% |
| 8 | Pennsylvania | 165,674,000 | 3.7% |
| 40 | Rhode Island | 15,330,000 | 0.3% |
| 24 | South Carolina | 56,280,000 | 1.2% |
| 43 | South Dakota | 12,708,000 | 0.3% |
| 14 | Tennessee | 81,387,000 | 1.8% |
| 3 | Texas | 299,891,000 | 6.7% |
| 37 | Utah | 23,185,000 | 0.5% |
| 46 | Vermont | 9,691,000 | 0.2% |
| 21 | Virginia | 66,246,000 | 1.5% |
| 19 | Washington | 69,601,000 | 1.5% |
| 32 | West Virginia | 36,062,000 | 0.8% |
| 20 | Wisconsin | 67,582,000 | 1.5% |
| 50 | Wyoming | 7,546,000 | 0.2% |

### RANK ORDER

| RANK | STATE | ALLOCATIONS | % of USA |
|---|---|---|---|
| 1 | California | $554,366,000 | 12.3% |
| 2 | New York | 304,283,000 | 6.8% |
| 3 | Texas | 299,891,000 | 6.7% |
| 4 | Illinois | 192,580,000 | 4.3% |
| 5 | Ohio | 178,271,000 | 4.0% |
| 6 | Michigan | 171,121,000 | 3.8% |
| 7 | Florida | 169,996,000 | 3.8% |
| 8 | Pennsylvania | 165,674,000 | 3.7% |
| 9 | Mississippi | 117,375,000 | 2.6% |
| 10 | Georgia | 112,040,000 | 2.5% |
| 11 | Louisiana | 100,196,000 | 2.2% |
| 12 | New Jersey | 94,945,000 | 2.1% |
| 13 | North Carolina | 93,979,000 | 2.1% |
| 14 | Tennessee | 81,387,000 | 1.8% |
| 15 | Missouri | 78,622,000 | 1.7% |
| 16 | Massachusetts | 78,544,000 | 1.7% |
| 17 | Kentucky | 76,409,000 | 1.7% |
| 18 | Alabama | 71,983,000 | 1.6% |
| 19 | Washington | 69,601,000 | 1.5% |
| 20 | Wisconsin | 67,582,000 | 1.5% |
| 21 | Virginia | 66,246,000 | 1.5% |
| 22 | Indiana | 65,226,000 | 1.4% |
| 23 | Arizona | 62,444,000 | 1.4% |
| 24 | South Carolina | 56,280,000 | 1.2% |
| 25 | Maryland | 54,966,000 | 1.2% |
| 26 | Oklahoma | 54,422,000 | 1.2% |
| 27 | Minnesota | 51,740,000 | 1.1% |
| 28 | Colorado | 46,602,000 | 1.0% |
| 29 | Arkansas | 43,449,000 | 1.0% |
| 30 | Oregon | 40,118,000 | 0.9% |
| 31 | Connecticut | 37,906,000 | 0.8% |
| 32 | West Virginia | 36,062,000 | 0.8% |
| 33 | Iowa | 36,038,000 | 0.8% |
| 34 | New Mexico | 35,363,000 | 0.8% |
| 35 | Kansas | 32,958,000 | 0.7% |
| 36 | Nebraska | 23,890,000 | 0.5% |
| 37 | Utah | 23,185,000 | 0.5% |
| 38 | Maine | 18,695,000 | 0.4% |
| 39 | Hawaii | 15,786,000 | 0.4% |
| 40 | Rhode Island | 15,330,000 | 0.3% |
| 41 | Idaho | 14,121,000 | 0.3% |
| 42 | Montana | 13,839,000 | 0.3% |
| 43 | South Dakota | 12,708,000 | 0.3% |
| 44 | Nevada | 11,484,000 | 0.3% |
| 45 | North Dakota | 10,561,000 | 0.2% |
| 46 | Vermont | 9,691,000 | 0.2% |
| 47 | New Hampshire | 9,114,000 | 0.2% |
| 48 | Delaware | 8,873,000 | 0.2% |
| 49 | Alaska | 8,786,000 | 0.2% |
| 50 | Wyoming | 7,546,000 | 0.2% |
| | District of Columbia | 19,201,000 | 0.4% |

Source: U.S. Department of Education, National Center for Educational Statistics
    "Digest of Education Statistics 2000" (January 2001)
*For fiscal year 1999. National total includes $308,313,000 to Migrant and Native American programs and
$172,634,000 to U.S. territories.

# Enrollment in Head Start in 1999

## National Total = 829,958 Enrollees*

| ALPHA ORDER | | | | | RANK ORDER | | | |
|---|---|---|---|---|---|---|---|---|
| RANK | STATE | | ENROLLEES | % of USA | RANK | STATE | ENROLLEES | % of USA |
| 15 | Alabama | | 15,263 | 1.8% | 1 | California | 86,459 | 10.4% |
| 50 | Alaska | | 1,281 | 0.2% | 2 | Texas | 58,173 | 7.0% |
| 24 | Arizona | | 11,127 | 1.3% | 3 | New York | 45,040 | 5.4% |
| 25 | Arkansas | | 10,097 | 1.2% | 4 | Ohio | 36,454 | 4.4% |
| 1 | California | | 86,459 | 10.4% | 5 | Illinois | 35,211 | 4.2% |
| 29 | Colorado | | 9,135 | 1.1% | 6 | Michigan | 33,422 | 4.0% |
| 34 | Connecticut | | 6,825 | 0.8% | 7 | Florida | 30,792 | 3.7% |
| 44 | Delaware | | 2,126 | 0.3% | 8 | Pennsylvania | 29,124 | 3.5% |
| 7 | Florida | | 30,792 | 3.7% | 9 | Mississippi | 25,091 | 3.0% |
| 10 | Georgia | | 21,121 | 2.5% | 10 | Georgia | 21,121 | 2.5% |
| 40 | Hawaii | | 2,799 | 0.3% | 11 | Louisiana | 20,703 | 2.5% |
| 43 | Idaho | | 2,266 | 0.3% | 12 | North Carolina | 17,394 | 2.1% |
| 5 | Illinois | | 35,211 | 4.2% | 13 | Missouri | 16,191 | 2.0% |
| 19 | Indiana | | 13,057 | 1.6% | 14 | Kentucky | 15,281 | 1.8% |
| 32 | Iowa | | 7,003 | 0.8% | 15 | Alabama | 15,263 | 1.8% |
| 33 | Kansas | | 7,000 | 0.8% | 16 | Tennessee | 14,753 | 1.8% |
| 14 | Kentucky | | 15,281 | 1.8% | 17 | New Jersey | 14,443 | 1.7% |
| 11 | Louisiana | | 20,703 | 2.5% | 18 | Wisconsin | 13,113 | 1.6% |
| 38 | Maine | | 3,618 | 0.4% | 19 | Indiana | 13,057 | 1.6% |
| 28 | Maryland | | 9,626 | 1.2% | 20 | Virginia | 12,243 | 1.5% |
| 22 | Massachusetts | | 12,094 | 1.5% | 21 | Oklahoma | 12,217 | 1.5% |
| 6 | Michigan | | 33,422 | 4.0% | 22 | Massachusetts | 12,094 | 1.5% |
| 27 | Minnesota | | 9,630 | 1.2% | 23 | South Carolina | 11,207 | 1.4% |
| 9 | Mississippi | | 25,091 | 3.0% | 24 | Arizona | 11,127 | 1.3% |
| 13 | Missouri | | 16,191 | 2.0% | 25 | Arkansas | 10,097 | 1.2% |
| 41 | Montana | | 2,678 | 0.3% | 26 | Washington | 9,831 | 1.2% |
| 37 | Nebraska | | 4,518 | 0.5% | 27 | Minnesota | 9,630 | 1.2% |
| 45 | Nevada | | 2,035 | 0.2% | 28 | Maryland | 9,626 | 1.2% |
| 49 | New Hampshire | | 1,425 | 0.2% | 29 | Colorado | 9,135 | 1.1% |
| 17 | New Jersey | | 14,443 | 1.7% | 30 | New Mexico | 7,108 | 0.9% |
| 30 | New Mexico | | 7,108 | 0.9% | 31 | West Virginia | 7,043 | 0.8% |
| 3 | New York | | 45,040 | 5.4% | 32 | Iowa | 7,003 | 0.8% |
| 12 | North Carolina | | 17,394 | 2.1% | 33 | Kansas | 7,000 | 0.8% |
| 46 | North Dakota | | 2,002 | 0.2% | 34 | Connecticut | 6,825 | 0.8% |
| 4 | Ohio | | 36,454 | 4.4% | 35 | Oregon | 5,480 | 0.7% |
| 21 | Oklahoma | | 12,217 | 1.5% | 36 | Utah | 4,679 | 0.6% |
| 35 | Oregon | | 5,480 | 0.7% | 37 | Nebraska | 4,518 | 0.5% |
| 8 | Pennsylvania | | 29,124 | 3.5% | 38 | Maine | 3,618 | 0.4% |
| 39 | Rhode Island | | 2,817 | 0.3% | 39 | Rhode Island | 2,817 | 0.3% |
| 23 | South Carolina | | 11,207 | 1.4% | 40 | Hawaii | 2,799 | 0.3% |
| 42 | South Dakota | | 2,485 | 0.3% | 41 | Montana | 2,678 | 0.3% |
| 16 | Tennessee | | 14,753 | 1.8% | 42 | South Dakota | 2,485 | 0.3% |
| 2 | Texas | | 58,173 | 7.0% | 43 | Idaho | 2,266 | 0.3% |
| 36 | Utah | | 4,679 | 0.6% | 44 | Delaware | 2,126 | 0.3% |
| 48 | Vermont | | 1,438 | 0.2% | 45 | Nevada | 2,035 | 0.2% |
| 20 | Virginia | | 12,243 | 1.5% | 46 | North Dakota | 2,002 | 0.2% |
| 26 | Washington | | 9,831 | 1.2% | 47 | Wyoming | 1,500 | 0.2% |
| 31 | West Virginia | | 7,043 | 0.8% | 48 | Vermont | 1,438 | 0.2% |
| 18 | Wisconsin | | 13,113 | 1.6% | 49 | New Hampshire | 1,425 | 0.2% |
| 47 | Wyoming | | 1,500 | 0.2% | 50 | Alaska | 1,281 | 0.2% |
| | | | | | | District of Columbia | 3,279 | 0.4% |

*Source: U.S. Department of Education, National Center for Educational Statistics*
*"Digest of Education Statistics 2000" (January 2001)*
*For fiscal year 1999. National total includes 59,369 enrollees in Migrant and Native American programs and 40,889 enrollees in U.S. territories.

# VI. EMPLOYMENT AND LABOR

# Average Annual Pay in 1999

## National Average = $33,313*

<table>
<tr><td colspan="3"><u>ALPHA ORDER</u></td><td colspan="3"><u>RANK ORDER</u></td></tr>
<tr><td>RANK</td><td>STATE</td><td>ANNUAL PAY</td><td>RANK</td><td>STATE</td><td>ANNUAL PAY</td></tr>
<tr><td>31</td><td>Alabama</td><td>$28,069</td><td>1</td><td>Connecticut</td><td>$42,653</td></tr>
<tr><td>12</td><td>Alaska</td><td>34,034</td><td>2</td><td>New York</td><td>42,133</td></tr>
<tr><td>23</td><td>Arizona</td><td>30,523</td><td>3</td><td>Massachusetts</td><td>40,331</td></tr>
<tr><td>46</td><td>Arkansas</td><td>25,371</td><td>4</td><td>New Jersey**</td><td>39,516</td></tr>
<tr><td>5</td><td>California</td><td>37,564</td><td>5</td><td>California</td><td>37,564</td></tr>
<tr><td>11</td><td>Colorado</td><td>34,192</td><td>6</td><td>Illinois</td><td>36,279</td></tr>
<tr><td>1</td><td>Connecticut</td><td>42,653</td><td>7</td><td>Washington</td><td>35,736</td></tr>
<tr><td>9</td><td>Delaware</td><td>35,102</td><td>8</td><td>Michigan</td><td>35,734</td></tr>
<tr><td>30</td><td>Florida</td><td>28,911</td><td>9</td><td>Delaware</td><td>35,102</td></tr>
<tr><td>17</td><td>Georgia</td><td>32,339</td><td>10</td><td>Maryland</td><td>34,472</td></tr>
<tr><td>26</td><td>Hawaii</td><td>29,771</td><td>11</td><td>Colorado</td><td>34,192</td></tr>
<tr><td>42</td><td>Idaho</td><td>26,042</td><td>12</td><td>Alaska</td><td>34,034</td></tr>
<tr><td>6</td><td>Illinois</td><td>36,279</td><td>13</td><td>Minnesota</td><td>33,487</td></tr>
<tr><td>24</td><td>Indiana</td><td>30,027</td><td>14</td><td>Virginia</td><td>33,015</td></tr>
<tr><td>38</td><td>Iowa</td><td>26,939</td><td>15</td><td>Texas</td><td>32,895</td></tr>
<tr><td>32</td><td>Kansas</td><td>28,029</td><td>16</td><td>Pennsylvania</td><td>32,694</td></tr>
<tr><td>34</td><td>Kentucky</td><td>27,748</td><td>17</td><td>Georgia</td><td>32,339</td></tr>
<tr><td>36</td><td>Louisiana</td><td>27,221</td><td>18</td><td>New Hampshire</td><td>32,139</td></tr>
<tr><td>39</td><td>Maine</td><td>26,887</td><td>19</td><td>Ohio</td><td>31,396</td></tr>
<tr><td>10</td><td>Maryland</td><td>34,472</td><td>20</td><td>Nevada</td><td>31,213</td></tr>
<tr><td>3</td><td>Massachusetts</td><td>40,331</td><td>21</td><td>Rhode Island</td><td>31,177</td></tr>
<tr><td>8</td><td>Michigan</td><td>35,734</td><td>22</td><td>Oregon</td><td>30,867</td></tr>
<tr><td>13</td><td>Minnesota</td><td>33,487</td><td>23</td><td>Arizona</td><td>30,523</td></tr>
<tr><td>47</td><td>Mississippi</td><td>24,392</td><td>24</td><td>Indiana</td><td>30,027</td></tr>
<tr><td>25</td><td>Missouri</td><td>29,958</td><td>25</td><td>Missouri</td><td>29,958</td></tr>
<tr><td>50</td><td>Montana</td><td>23,253</td><td>26</td><td>Hawaii</td><td>29,771</td></tr>
<tr><td>40</td><td>Nebraska</td><td>26,633</td><td>27</td><td>Wisconsin</td><td>29,597</td></tr>
<tr><td>20</td><td>Nevada</td><td>31,213</td><td>28</td><td>Tennessee</td><td>29,518</td></tr>
<tr><td>18</td><td>New Hampshire</td><td>32,139</td><td>29</td><td>North Carolina</td><td>29,453</td></tr>
<tr><td>4</td><td>New Jersey**</td><td>39,516</td><td>30</td><td>Florida</td><td>28,911</td></tr>
<tr><td>41</td><td>New Mexico</td><td>26,270</td><td>31</td><td>Alabama</td><td>28,069</td></tr>
<tr><td>2</td><td>New York</td><td>42,133</td><td>32</td><td>Kansas</td><td>28,029</td></tr>
<tr><td>29</td><td>North Carolina</td><td>29,453</td><td>33</td><td>Utah</td><td>27,884</td></tr>
<tr><td>49</td><td>North Dakota</td><td>23,753</td><td>34</td><td>Kentucky</td><td>27,748</td></tr>
<tr><td>19</td><td>Ohio</td><td>31,396</td><td>35</td><td>Vermont</td><td>27,595</td></tr>
<tr><td>44</td><td>Oklahoma</td><td>25,748</td><td>36</td><td>Louisiana</td><td>27,221</td></tr>
<tr><td>22</td><td>Oregon</td><td>30,867</td><td>37</td><td>South Carolina</td><td>27,124</td></tr>
<tr><td>16</td><td>Pennsylvania</td><td>32,694</td><td>38</td><td>Iowa</td><td>26,939</td></tr>
<tr><td>21</td><td>Rhode Island</td><td>31,177</td><td>39</td><td>Maine</td><td>26,887</td></tr>
<tr><td>37</td><td>South Carolina</td><td>27,124</td><td>40</td><td>Nebraska</td><td>26,633</td></tr>
<tr><td>48</td><td>South Dakota</td><td>23,765</td><td>41</td><td>New Mexico</td><td>26,270</td></tr>
<tr><td>28</td><td>Tennessee</td><td>29,518</td><td>42</td><td>Idaho</td><td>26,042</td></tr>
<tr><td>15</td><td>Texas</td><td>32,895</td><td>43</td><td>West Virginia</td><td>26,008</td></tr>
<tr><td>33</td><td>Utah</td><td>27,884</td><td>44</td><td>Oklahoma</td><td>25,748</td></tr>
<tr><td>35</td><td>Vermont</td><td>27,595</td><td>45</td><td>Wyoming</td><td>25,639</td></tr>
<tr><td>14</td><td>Virginia</td><td>33,015</td><td>46</td><td>Arkansas</td><td>25,371</td></tr>
<tr><td>7</td><td>Washington</td><td>35,736</td><td>47</td><td>Mississippi</td><td>24,392</td></tr>
<tr><td>43</td><td>West Virginia</td><td>26,008</td><td>48</td><td>South Dakota</td><td>23,765</td></tr>
<tr><td>27</td><td>Wisconsin</td><td>29,597</td><td>49</td><td>North Dakota</td><td>23,753</td></tr>
<tr><td>45</td><td>Wyoming</td><td>25,639</td><td>50</td><td>Montana</td><td>23,253</td></tr>
<tr><td></td><td></td><td></td><td></td><td>District of Columbia</td><td>50,742</td></tr>
</table>

*Source: U.S. Department of Labor, Bureau of Labor Statistics*
   *"Average Annual Pay by State and Industry, 1999" (News Release USDL 00-339, November 17, 2000)*
*\*Computed by dividing total annual pay of employees covered by unemployment insurance programs by the average monthly number of these employees. Includes bonuses, cash value of meals and lodging, tips and, in many states, employer contributions to certain deferred compensation plans such as 401(k) plans. Preliminary data.*
*\*\*New Jersey's figure is for 1998.*

# Percent Change in Average Annual Pay: 1998 to 1999

## National Percent Change = 4.3% Increase*

ALPHA ORDER

| RANK | STATE | PERCENT CHANGE |
|---|---|---|
| 22 | Alabama | 3.8 |
| 49 | Alaska | 0.6 |
| 17 | Arizona | 4.1 |
| 18 | Arkansas | 3.9 |
| 3 | California | 6.3 |
| 4 | Colorado | 6.0 |
| 15 | Connecticut | 4.3 |
| 36 | Delaware | 3.3 |
| 43 | Florida | 2.6 |
| 6 | Georgia | 4.8 |
| 44 | Hawaii | 2.5 |
| 7 | Idaho | 4.7 |
| 8 | Illinois | 4.5 |
| 40 | Indiana | 3.2 |
| 31 | Iowa | 3.5 |
| 12 | Kansas | 4.4 |
| 18 | Kentucky | 3.9 |
| 48 | Louisiana | 1.2 |
| 18 | Maine | 3.9 |
| 31 | Maryland | 3.5 |
| 2 | Massachusetts | 6.8 |
| 31 | Michigan | 3.5 |
| 12 | Minnesota | 4.4 |
| 46 | Mississippi | 2.4 |
| 29 | Missouri | 3.6 |
| 42 | Montana | 2.7 |
| 15 | Nebraska | 4.3 |
| 36 | Nevada | 3.3 |
| 18 | New Hampshire | 3.9 |
| NA | New Jersey** | NA |
| 47 | New Mexico | 2.2 |
| 29 | New York | 3.6 |
| 8 | North Carolina | 4.5 |
| 36 | North Dakota | 3.3 |
| 36 | Ohio | 3.3 |
| 44 | Oklahoma | 2.5 |
| 8 | Oregon | 4.5 |
| 31 | Pennsylvania | 3.5 |
| 35 | Rhode Island | 3.4 |
| 24 | South Carolina | 3.7 |
| 8 | South Dakota | 4.5 |
| 24 | Tennessee | 3.7 |
| 12 | Texas | 4.4 |
| 22 | Utah | 3.8 |
| 24 | Vermont | 3.7 |
| 5 | Virginia | 5.2 |
| 1 | Washington | 8.0 |
| 41 | West Virginia | 2.9 |
| 24 | Wisconsin | 3.7 |
| 24 | Wyoming | 3.7 |

RANK ORDER

| RANK | STATE | PERCENT CHANGE |
|---|---|---|
| 1 | Washington | 8.0 |
| 2 | Massachusetts | 6.8 |
| 3 | California | 6.3 |
| 4 | Colorado | 6.0 |
| 5 | Virginia | 5.2 |
| 6 | Georgia | 4.8 |
| 7 | Idaho | 4.7 |
| 8 | Illinois | 4.5 |
| 8 | North Carolina | 4.5 |
| 8 | Oregon | 4.5 |
| 8 | South Dakota | 4.5 |
| 12 | Kansas | 4.4 |
| 12 | Minnesota | 4.4 |
| 12 | Texas | 4.4 |
| 15 | Connecticut | 4.3 |
| 15 | Nebraska | 4.3 |
| 17 | Arizona | 4.1 |
| 18 | Arkansas | 3.9 |
| 18 | Kentucky | 3.9 |
| 18 | Maine | 3.9 |
| 18 | New Hampshire | 3.9 |
| 22 | Alabama | 3.8 |
| 22 | Utah | 3.8 |
| 24 | South Carolina | 3.7 |
| 24 | Tennessee | 3.7 |
| 24 | Vermont | 3.7 |
| 24 | Wisconsin | 3.7 |
| 24 | Wyoming | 3.7 |
| 29 | Missouri | 3.6 |
| 29 | New York | 3.6 |
| 31 | Iowa | 3.5 |
| 31 | Maryland | 3.5 |
| 31 | Michigan | 3.5 |
| 31 | Pennsylvania | 3.5 |
| 35 | Rhode Island | 3.4 |
| 36 | Delaware | 3.3 |
| 36 | Nevada | 3.3 |
| 36 | North Dakota | 3.3 |
| 36 | Ohio | 3.3 |
| 40 | Indiana | 3.2 |
| 41 | West Virginia | 2.9 |
| 42 | Montana | 2.7 |
| 43 | Florida | 2.6 |
| 44 | Hawaii | 2.5 |
| 44 | Oklahoma | 2.5 |
| 46 | Mississippi | 2.4 |
| 47 | New Mexico | 2.2 |
| 48 | Louisiana | 1.2 |
| 49 | Alaska | 0.6 |
| NA | New Jersey** | NA |
|  | District of Columbia | 4.7 |

Source: U.S. Department of Labor, Bureau of Labor Statistics
   "Average Annual Pay by State and Industry, 1999" (News Release USDL 00-339, November 17, 2000)
*Computed by dividing total annual pay of employees covered by unemployment insurance programs by the average monthly number of these employees. Includes bonuses, cash value of meals and lodging, tips and, in many states, employer contributions to certain deferred compensation plans such as 401(k) plans. Preliminary data.
**Not available.

# State Minimum Wage Rates in 2001

## National Rate = $5.15 per Hour*

### ALPHA ORDER

| RANK | STATE | MINIMUM WAGE |
|---|---|---|
| NA | Alabama** | NA |
| 9 | Alaska | 5.65 |
| NA | Arizona** | NA |
| 11 | Arkansas | 5.15 |
| 5 | California | 6.25 |
| 11 | Colorado | 5.15 |
| 4 | Connecticut | 6.40 |
| 6 | Delaware | 6.15 |
| NA | Florida** | NA |
| 41 | Georgia | 3.25 |
| 10 | Hawaii | 5.25 |
| 11 | Idaho | 5.15 |
| 11 | Illinois | 5.15 |
| 11 | Indiana | 5.15 |
| 11 | Iowa | 5.15 |
| 42 | Kansas | 2.65 |
| 11 | Kentucky | 5.15 |
| NA | Louisiana** | NA |
| 11 | Maine | 5.15 |
| 11 | Maryland | 5.15 |
| 1 | Massachusetts | 6.75 |
| 11 | Michigan | 5.15 |
| 11 | Minnesota | 5.15 |
| NA | Mississippi** | NA |
| 11 | Missouri | 5.15 |
| 11 | Montana | 5.15 |
| 11 | Nebraska | 5.15 |
| 11 | Nevada | 5.15 |
| 11 | New Hampshire | 5.15 |
| 11 | New Jersey | 5.15 |
| 38 | New Mexico | 4.25 |
| 11 | New York | 5.15 |
| 11 | North Carolina | 5.15 |
| 11 | North Dakota | 5.15 |
| 38 | Ohio | 4.25 |
| 11 | Oklahoma | 5.15 |
| 3 | Oregon | 6.50 |
| 11 | Pennsylvania | 5.15 |
| 6 | Rhode Island | 6.15 |
| NA | South Carolina** | NA |
| 11 | South Dakota | 5.15 |
| NA | Tennessee** | NA |
| 40 | Texas | 3.35 |
| 11 | Utah | 5.15 |
| 8 | Vermont | 5.75 |
| 11 | Virginia | 5.15 |
| 2 | Washington | 6.72 |
| 11 | West Virginia | 5.15 |
| 11 | Wisconsin | 5.15 |
| 43 | Wyoming | 1.60 |

### RANK ORDER

| RANK | STATE | MINIMUM WAGE |
|---|---|---|
| 1 | Massachusetts | $6.75 |
| 2 | Washington | 6.72 |
| 3 | Oregon | 6.50 |
| 4 | Connecticut | 6.40 |
| 5 | California | 6.25 |
| 6 | Delaware | 6.15 |
| 6 | Rhode Island | 6.15 |
| 8 | Vermont | 5.75 |
| 9 | Alaska | 5.65 |
| 10 | Hawaii | 5.25 |
| 11 | Arkansas | 5.15 |
| 11 | Colorado | 5.15 |
| 11 | Idaho | 5.15 |
| 11 | Illinois | 5.15 |
| 11 | Indiana | 5.15 |
| 11 | Iowa | 5.15 |
| 11 | Kentucky | 5.15 |
| 11 | Maine | 5.15 |
| 11 | Maryland | 5.15 |
| 11 | Michigan | 5.15 |
| 11 | Minnesota | 5.15 |
| 11 | Missouri | 5.15 |
| 11 | Montana | 5.15 |
| 11 | Nebraska | 5.15 |
| 11 | Nevada | 5.15 |
| 11 | New Hampshire | 5.15 |
| 11 | New Jersey | 5.15 |
| 11 | New York | 5.15 |
| 11 | North Carolina | 5.15 |
| 11 | North Dakota | 5.15 |
| 11 | Oklahoma | 5.15 |
| 11 | Pennsylvania | 5.15 |
| 11 | South Dakota | 5.15 |
| 11 | Utah | 5.15 |
| 11 | Virginia | 5.15 |
| 11 | West Virginia | 5.15 |
| 11 | Wisconsin | 5.15 |
| 38 | New Mexico | 4.25 |
| 38 | Ohio | 4.25 |
| 40 | Texas | 3.35 |
| 41 | Georgia | 3.25 |
| 42 | Kansas | 2.65 |
| 43 | Wyoming | 1.60 |
| NA | Alabama** | NA |
| NA | Arizona** | NA |
| NA | Florida** | NA |
| NA | Louisiana** | NA |
| NA | Mississippi** | NA |
| NA | South Carolina** | NA |
| NA | Tennessee** | NA |
| | District of Columbia | 6.15 |

*Source: U.S. Department of Labor, Employment Standards Administration*
*"Minimum Wage Laws in the States" (http://www.dol.gov/dol/esa/public/minwage/america.htm)*
*\*As of January 1, 2001. State minimum wage rates are for those employers and jobs not covered by the federal program.*
*\*\*No separate state program.*

# Average Hourly Earnings of Production Workers
## On Manufacturing Payrolls in 2000
## National Average = $14.69*

ALPHA ORDER

| RANK | STATE | HOURLY EARNINGS |
|------|-------|-----------------|
| 40 | Alabama | $13.10 |
| 7 | Alaska | 15.96 |
| 42 | Arizona | 12.89 |
| 46 | Arkansas | 12.29 |
| 26 | California | 14.47 |
| 12 | Colorado | 15.42 |
| 5 | Connecticut | 16.01 |
| 4 | Delaware | 16.71 |
| 45 | Florida | 12.45 |
| 39 | Georgia | 13.13 |
| 35 | Hawaii | 13.67 |
| 24 | Idaho | 14.59 |
| 25 | Illinois | 14.52 |
| 6 | Indiana | 15.98 |
| 19 | Iowa | 14.87 |
| 13 | Kansas | 15.23 |
| 16 | Kentucky | 15.12 |
| 9 | Louisiana | 15.61 |
| 21 | Maine | 14.76 |
| 17 | Maryland | 15.11 |
| 18 | Massachusetts | 15.00 |
| 1 | Michigan | 19.82 |
| 11 | Minnesota | 15.46 |
| 48 | Mississippi | 11.94 |
| 19 | Missouri | 14.87 |
| 27 | Montana | 14.44 |
| 37 | Nebraska | 13.35 |
| 30 | Nevada | 14.22 |
| 33 | New Hampshire | 13.86 |
| 8 | New Jersey | 15.72 |
| 36 | New Mexico | 13.61 |
| 27 | New York | 14.44 |
| 41 | North Carolina | 12.95 |
| 43 | North Dakota | 12.68 |
| 3 | Ohio | 16.96 |
| 34 | Oklahoma | 13.69 |
| 14 | Oregon | 15.22 |
| 22 | Pennsylvania | 14.68 |
| 47 | Rhode Island | 12.25 |
| 49 | South Carolina | 11.03 |
| 50 | South Dakota | 10.81 |
| 38 | Tennessee | 13.18 |
| 44 | Texas | 12.48 |
| 32 | Utah | 13.93 |
| 29 | Vermont | 14.29 |
| 31 | Virginia | 14.16 |
| 2 | Washington | 17.34 |
| 23 | West Virginia | 14.65 |
| 15 | Wisconsin | 15.21 |
| 10 | Wyoming | 15.54 |

RANK ORDER

| RANK | STATE | HOURLY EARNINGS |
|------|-------|-----------------|
| 1 | Michigan | $19.82 |
| 2 | Washington | 17.34 |
| 3 | Ohio | 16.96 |
| 4 | Delaware | 16.71 |
| 5 | Connecticut | 16.01 |
| 6 | Indiana | 15.98 |
| 7 | Alaska | 15.96 |
| 8 | New Jersey | 15.72 |
| 9 | Louisiana | 15.61 |
| 10 | Wyoming | 15.54 |
| 11 | Minnesota | 15.46 |
| 12 | Colorado | 15.42 |
| 13 | Kansas | 15.23 |
| 14 | Oregon | 15.22 |
| 15 | Wisconsin | 15.21 |
| 16 | Kentucky | 15.12 |
| 17 | Maryland | 15.11 |
| 18 | Massachusetts | 15.00 |
| 19 | Iowa | 14.87 |
| 19 | Missouri | 14.87 |
| 21 | Maine | 14.76 |
| 22 | Pennsylvania | 14.68 |
| 23 | West Virginia | 14.65 |
| 24 | Idaho | 14.59 |
| 25 | Illinois | 14.52 |
| 26 | California | 14.47 |
| 27 | Montana | 14.44 |
| 27 | New York | 14.44 |
| 29 | Vermont | 14.29 |
| 30 | Nevada | 14.22 |
| 31 | Virginia | 14.16 |
| 32 | Utah | 13.93 |
| 33 | New Hampshire | 13.86 |
| 34 | Oklahoma | 13.69 |
| 35 | Hawaii | 13.67 |
| 36 | New Mexico | 13.61 |
| 37 | Nebraska | 13.35 |
| 38 | Tennessee | 13.18 |
| 39 | Georgia | 13.13 |
| 40 | Alabama | 13.10 |
| 41 | North Carolina | 12.95 |
| 42 | Arizona | 12.89 |
| 43 | North Dakota | 12.68 |
| 44 | Texas | 12.48 |
| 45 | Florida | 12.45 |
| 46 | Arkansas | 12.29 |
| 47 | Rhode Island | 12.25 |
| 48 | Mississippi | 11.94 |
| 49 | South Carolina | 11.03 |
| 50 | South Dakota | 10.81 |

District of Columbia**          NA

*Source: U.S. Department of Labor, Bureau of Labor Statistics*
*unpublished data for December 2000*
*\*Preliminary.  Not seasonally adjusted.*
*\*\*Not available*

# Average Weekly Earnings of Production Workers
## On Manufacturing Payrolls in 2000
### National Average = $605.23*

ALPHA ORDER

| RANK | STATE | WEEKLY EARNINGS |
|------|-------|-----------------|
| 37 | Alabama | $543.65 |
| 25 | Alaska | 590.52 |
| 43 | Arizona | 519.47 |
| 48 | Arkansas | 473.17 |
| 21 | California | 610.63 |
| 9 | Colorado | 652.27 |
| 5 | Connecticut | 690.03 |
| 2 | Delaware | 728.56 |
| 41 | Florida | 530.37 |
| 35 | Georgia | 547.52 |
| 36 | Hawaii | 545.43 |
| 30 | Idaho | 573.39 |
| 26 | Illinois | 586.61 |
| 8 | Indiana | 656.78 |
| 17 | Iowa | 614.13 |
| 20 | Kansas | 610.72 |
| 10 | Kentucky | 642.60 |
| 6 | Louisiana | 685.28 |
| 18 | Maine | 612.54 |
| 19 | Maryland | 611.96 |
| 12 | Massachusetts | 631.50 |
| 1 | Michigan | 822.53 |
| 11 | Minnesota | 636.95 |
| 47 | Mississippi | 479.99 |
| 28 | Missouri | 575.47 |
| 33 | Montana | 551.61 |
| 34 | Nebraska | 548.69 |
| 15 | Nevada | 618.57 |
| 29 | New Hampshire | 575.19 |
| 7 | New Jersey | 663.38 |
| 44 | New Mexico | 502.21 |
| 24 | New York | 593.48 |
| 40 | North Carolina | 533.54 |
| 45 | North Dakota | 499.59 |
| 3 | Ohio | 720.80 |
| 39 | Oklahoma | 533.91 |
| 22 | Oregon | 607.28 |
| 16 | Pennsylvania | 615.09 |
| 46 | Rhode Island | 490.00 |
| 49 | South Carolina | 464.36 |
| 50 | South Dakota | 463.75 |
| 42 | Tennessee | 527.20 |
| 38 | Texas | 537.89 |
| 32 | Utah | 562.77 |
| 31 | Vermont | 570.17 |
| 23 | Virginia | 597.55 |
| 4 | Washington | 697.07 |
| 27 | West Virginia | 584.54 |
| 13 | Wisconsin | 625.13 |
| 14 | Wyoming | 623.15 |

RANK ORDER

| RANK | STATE | WEEKLY EARNINGS |
|------|-------|-----------------|
| 1 | Michigan | $822.53 |
| 2 | Delaware | 728.56 |
| 3 | Ohio | 720.80 |
| 4 | Washington | 697.07 |
| 5 | Connecticut | 690.03 |
| 6 | Louisiana | 685.28 |
| 7 | New Jersey | 663.38 |
| 8 | Indiana | 656.78 |
| 9 | Colorado | 652.27 |
| 10 | Kentucky | 642.60 |
| 11 | Minnesota | 636.95 |
| 12 | Massachusetts | 631.50 |
| 13 | Wisconsin | 625.13 |
| 14 | Wyoming | 623.15 |
| 15 | Nevada | 618.57 |
| 16 | Pennsylvania | 615.09 |
| 17 | Iowa | 614.13 |
| 18 | Maine | 612.54 |
| 19 | Maryland | 611.96 |
| 20 | Kansas | 610.72 |
| 21 | California | 610.63 |
| 22 | Oregon | 607.28 |
| 23 | Virginia | 597.55 |
| 24 | New York | 593.48 |
| 25 | Alaska | 590.52 |
| 26 | Illinois | 586.61 |
| 27 | West Virginia | 584.54 |
| 28 | Missouri | 575.47 |
| 29 | New Hampshire | 575.19 |
| 30 | Idaho | 573.39 |
| 31 | Vermont | 570.17 |
| 32 | Utah | 562.77 |
| 33 | Montana | 551.61 |
| 34 | Nebraska | 548.69 |
| 35 | Georgia | 547.52 |
| 36 | Hawaii | 545.43 |
| 37 | Alabama | 543.65 |
| 38 | Texas | 537.89 |
| 39 | Oklahoma | 533.91 |
| 40 | North Carolina | 533.54 |
| 41 | Florida | 530.37 |
| 42 | Tennessee | 527.20 |
| 43 | Arizona | 519.47 |
| 44 | New Mexico | 502.21 |
| 45 | North Dakota | 499.59 |
| 46 | Rhode Island | 490.00 |
| 47 | Mississippi | 479.99 |
| 48 | Arkansas | 473.17 |
| 49 | South Carolina | 464.36 |
| 50 | South Dakota | 463.75 |
| | District of Columbia** | NA |

Source: U.S. Department of Labor, Bureau of Labor Statistics
unpublished data for December 2000
*Preliminary. Not seasonally adjusted.
**Not available

# Average Work Week of Production Workers On Manufacturing Payrolls in 2000
## National Average = 41.2 Hours per Week*

ALPHA ORDER

| RANK | STATE | WEEKLY HOURS |
|------|-------|--------------|
| 18 | Alabama | 41.5 |
| 49 | Alaska | 37.0 |
| 32 | Arizona | 40.3 |
| 47 | Arkansas | 38.5 |
| 11 | California | 42.2 |
| 10 | Colorado | 42.3 |
| 4 | Connecticut | 43.1 |
| 2 | Delaware | 43.6 |
| 7 | Florida | 42.6 |
| 17 | Georgia | 41.7 |
| 39 | Hawaii | 39.9 |
| 44 | Idaho | 39.3 |
| 30 | Illinois | 40.4 |
| 25 | Indiana | 41.1 |
| 22 | Iowa | 41.3 |
| 35 | Kansas | 40.1 |
| 8 | Kentucky | 42.5 |
| 1 | Louisiana | 43.9 |
| 18 | Maine | 41.5 |
| 29 | Maryland | 40.5 |
| 14 | Massachusetts | 42.1 |
| 18 | Michigan | 41.5 |
| 23 | Minnesota | 41.2 |
| 33 | Mississippi | 40.2 |
| 46 | Missouri | 38.7 |
| 48 | Montana | 38.2 |
| 25 | Nebraska | 41.1 |
| 3 | Nevada | 43.5 |
| 18 | New Hampshire | 41.5 |
| 11 | New Jersey | 42.2 |
| 50 | New Mexico | 36.9 |
| 25 | New York | 41.1 |
| 23 | North Carolina | 41.2 |
| 43 | North Dakota | 39.4 |
| 8 | Ohio | 42.5 |
| 45 | Oklahoma | 39.0 |
| 39 | Oregon | 39.9 |
| 16 | Pennsylvania | 41.9 |
| 37 | Rhode Island | 40.0 |
| 14 | South Carolina | 42.1 |
| 6 | South Dakota | 42.9 |
| 37 | Tennessee | 40.0 |
| 4 | Texas | 43.1 |
| 30 | Utah | 40.4 |
| 39 | Vermont | 39.9 |
| 11 | Virginia | 42.2 |
| 33 | Washington | 40.2 |
| 39 | West Virginia | 39.9 |
| 25 | Wisconsin | 41.1 |
| 35 | Wyoming | 40.1 |

RANK ORDER

| RANK | STATE | WEEKLY HOURS |
|------|-------|--------------|
| 1 | Louisiana | 43.9 |
| 2 | Delaware | 43.6 |
| 3 | Nevada | 43.5 |
| 4 | Connecticut | 43.1 |
| 4 | Texas | 43.1 |
| 6 | South Dakota | 42.9 |
| 7 | Florida | 42.6 |
| 8 | Kentucky | 42.5 |
| 8 | Ohio | 42.5 |
| 10 | Colorado | 42.3 |
| 11 | California | 42.2 |
| 11 | New Jersey | 42.2 |
| 11 | Virginia | 42.2 |
| 14 | Massachusetts | 42.1 |
| 14 | South Carolina | 42.1 |
| 16 | Pennsylvania | 41.9 |
| 17 | Georgia | 41.7 |
| 18 | Alabama | 41.5 |
| 18 | Maine | 41.5 |
| 18 | Michigan | 41.5 |
| 18 | New Hampshire | 41.5 |
| 22 | Iowa | 41.3 |
| 23 | Minnesota | 41.2 |
| 23 | North Carolina | 41.2 |
| 25 | Indiana | 41.1 |
| 25 | Nebraska | 41.1 |
| 25 | New York | 41.1 |
| 25 | Wisconsin | 41.1 |
| 29 | Maryland | 40.5 |
| 30 | Illinois | 40.4 |
| 30 | Utah | 40.4 |
| 32 | Arizona | 40.3 |
| 33 | Mississippi | 40.2 |
| 33 | Washington | 40.2 |
| 35 | Kansas | 40.1 |
| 35 | Wyoming | 40.1 |
| 37 | Rhode Island | 40.0 |
| 37 | Tennessee | 40.0 |
| 39 | Hawaii | 39.9 |
| 39 | Oregon | 39.9 |
| 39 | Vermont | 39.9 |
| 39 | West Virginia | 39.9 |
| 43 | North Dakota | 39.4 |
| 44 | Idaho | 39.3 |
| 45 | Oklahoma | 39.0 |
| 46 | Missouri | 38.7 |
| 47 | Arkansas | 38.5 |
| 48 | Montana | 38.2 |
| 49 | Alaska | 37.0 |
| 50 | New Mexico | 36.9 |

District of Columbia**          NA

*Source: U.S. Department of Labor, Bureau of Labor Statistics*
*unpublished data for December 2000*
*Preliminary. Not seasonally adjusted.*
**Not available*

# Average Weekly Unemployment Benefit in 2000

## National Average = $220.64 a Week*

ALPHA ORDER

| RANK | STATE | BENEFIT |
|---|---|---|
| 49 | Alabama | $159.41 |
| 39 | Alaska | 189.86 |
| 47 | Arizona | 162.51 |
| 31 | Arkansas | 210.08 |
| 48 | California | 160.00 |
| 7 | Colorado | 255.86 |
| 15 | Connecticut | 235.06 |
| 26 | Delaware | 214.85 |
| 23 | Florida | 220.21 |
| 30 | Georgia | 211.89 |
| 4 | Hawaii | 283.67 |
| 33 | Idaho | 209.46 |
| 9 | Illinois | 251.58 |
| 22 | Indiana | 222.19 |
| 13 | Iowa | 238.42 |
| 11 | Kansas | 247.09 |
| 20 | Kentucky | 224.78 |
| 44 | Louisiana | 182.06 |
| 36 | Maine | 202.29 |
| 29 | Maryland | 212.51 |
| 1 | Massachusetts | 293.45 |
| 12 | Michigan | 244.12 |
| 2 | Minnesota | 290.51 |
| 50 | Mississippi | 156.62 |
| 43 | Missouri | 186.22 |
| 42 | Montana | 187.92 |
| 41 | Nebraska | 188.00 |
| 21 | Nevada | 222.43 |
| 24 | New Hampshire | 217.21 |
| 3 | New Jersey | 289.61 |
| 46 | New Mexico | 180.43 |
| 10 | New York | 247.48 |
| 18 | North Carolina | 231.18 |
| 32 | North Dakota | 210.01 |
| 14 | Ohio | 236.40 |
| 27 | Oklahoma | 214.40 |
| 17 | Oregon | 232.62 |
| 6 | Pennsylvania | 264.76 |
| 8 | Rhode Island | 253.48 |
| 38 | South Carolina | 190.18 |
| 45 | South Dakota | 180.86 |
| 40 | Tennessee | 188.74 |
| 19 | Texas | 227.11 |
| 28 | Utah | 213.89 |
| 25 | Vermont | 215.55 |
| 35 | Virginia | 203.88 |
| 5 | Washington | 280.94 |
| 37 | West Virginia | 197.53 |
| 16 | Wisconsin | 233.11 |
| 34 | Wyoming | 207.10 |

RANK ORDER

| RANK | STATE | BENEFIT |
|---|---|---|
| 1 | Massachusetts | $293.45 |
| 2 | Minnesota | 290.51 |
| 3 | New Jersey | 289.61 |
| 4 | Hawaii | 283.67 |
| 5 | Washington | 280.94 |
| 6 | Pennsylvania | 264.76 |
| 7 | Colorado | 255.86 |
| 8 | Rhode Island | 253.48 |
| 9 | Illinois | 251.58 |
| 10 | New York | 247.48 |
| 11 | Kansas | 247.09 |
| 12 | Michigan | 244.12 |
| 13 | Iowa | 238.42 |
| 14 | Ohio | 236.40 |
| 15 | Connecticut | 235.06 |
| 16 | Wisconsin | 233.11 |
| 17 | Oregon | 232.62 |
| 18 | North Carolina | 231.18 |
| 19 | Texas | 227.11 |
| 20 | Kentucky | 224.78 |
| 21 | Nevada | 222.43 |
| 22 | Indiana | 222.19 |
| 23 | Florida | 220.21 |
| 24 | New Hampshire | 217.21 |
| 25 | Vermont | 215.55 |
| 26 | Delaware | 214.85 |
| 27 | Oklahoma | 214.40 |
| 28 | Utah | 213.89 |
| 29 | Maryland | 212.51 |
| 30 | Georgia | 211.89 |
| 31 | Arkansas | 210.08 |
| 32 | North Dakota | 210.01 |
| 33 | Idaho | 209.46 |
| 34 | Wyoming | 207.10 |
| 35 | Virginia | 203.88 |
| 36 | Maine | 202.29 |
| 37 | West Virginia | 197.53 |
| 38 | South Carolina | 190.18 |
| 39 | Alaska | 189.86 |
| 40 | Tennessee | 188.74 |
| 41 | Nebraska | 188.00 |
| 42 | Montana | 187.92 |
| 43 | Missouri | 186.22 |
| 44 | Louisiana | 182.06 |
| 45 | South Dakota | 180.86 |
| 46 | New Mexico | 180.43 |
| 47 | Arizona | 162.51 |
| 48 | California | 160.00 |
| 49 | Alabama | 159.41 |
| 50 | Mississippi | 156.62 |
| | District of Columbia | 241.03 |

*Source: U.S. Department of Labor, Bureau of Labor Statistics unpublished data*

# Workers' Compensation Benefit Payments in 1998

## National Total = $44,696,415,000*

ALPHA ORDER

RANK ORDER

| RANK | STATE | PAYMENTS | % of USA | | RANK | STATE | PAYMENTS | % of USA |
|---|---|---|---|---|---|---|---|---|
| 18 | Alabama | $615,316,000 | 1.4% | | 1 | California | $7,374,486,000 | 16.5% |
| 45 | Alaska | 110,866,000 | 0.2% | | 2 | New York | 2,556,658,000 | 5.7% |
| 29 | Arizona | 417,673,000 | 0.9% | | 3 | Pennsylvania | 2,447,908,000 | 5.5% |
| 41 | Arkansas | 161,146,000 | 0.4% | | 4 | Ohio | 2,335,022,000 | 5.2% |
| 1 | California | 7,374,486,000 | 16.5% | | 5 | Florida | 2,207,984,000 | 4.9% |
| 15 | Colorado | 656,894,000 | 1.5% | | 6 | Illinois | 1,687,070,000 | 3.8% |
| 14 | Connecticut | 711,130,000 | 1.6% | | 7 | Washington | 1,481,587,000 | 3.3% |
| 43 | Delaware | 118,511,000 | 0.3% | | 8 | Texas | 1,465,009,000 | 3.3% |
| 5 | Florida | 2,207,984,000 | 4.9% | | 9 | Michigan | 1,366,963,000 | 3.1% |
| 11 | Georgia | 807,582,000 | 1.8% | | 10 | New Jersey | 954,696,000 | 2.1% |
| 36 | Hawaii | 194,680,000 | 0.4% | | 11 | Georgia | 807,582,000 | 1.8% |
| 38 | Idaho | 165,764,000 | 0.4% | | 12 | North Carolina | 765,817,000 | 1.7% |
| 6 | Illinois | 1,687,070,000 | 3.8% | | 13 | Minnesota | 732,300,000 | 1.6% |
| 28 | Indiana | 439,268,000 | 1.0% | | 14 | Connecticut | 711,130,000 | 1.6% |
| 32 | Iowa | 292,002,000 | 0.7% | | 15 | Colorado | 656,894,000 | 1.5% |
| 31 | Kansas | 318,352,000 | 0.7% | | 16 | Massachusetts | 641,409,000 | 1.4% |
| 23 | Kentucky | 510,938,000 | 1.1% | | 17 | Wisconsin | 621,973,000 | 1.4% |
| 30 | Louisiana | 364,656,000 | 0.8% | | 18 | Alabama | 615,316,000 | 1.4% |
| 33 | Maine | 288,146,000 | 0.6% | | 19 | Virginia | 591,068,000 | 1.3% |
| 24 | Maryland | 510,577,000 | 1.1% | | 20 | Missouri | 527,587,000 | 1.2% |
| 16 | Massachusetts | 641,409,000 | 1.4% | | 21 | Oklahoma | 520,181,000 | 1.2% |
| 9 | Michigan | 1,366,963,000 | 3.1% | | 22 | Tennessee | 517,846,000 | 1.2% |
| 13 | Minnesota | 732,300,000 | 1.6% | | 23 | Kentucky | 510,938,000 | 1.1% |
| 35 | Mississippi | 234,700,000 | 0.5% | | 24 | Maryland | 510,577,000 | 1.1% |
| 20 | Missouri | 527,587,000 | 1.2% | | 25 | Oregon | 492,854,000 | 1.1% |
| 42 | Montana | 155,019,000 | 0.3% | | 26 | South Carolina | 483,606,000 | 1.1% |
| 39 | Nebraska | 164,382,000 | 0.4% | | 27 | West Virginia | 463,555,000 | 1.0% |
| 34 | Nevada | 288,095,000 | 0.6% | | 28 | Indiana | 439,268,000 | 1.0% |
| 40 | New Hampshire | 163,883,000 | 0.4% | | 29 | Arizona | 417,673,000 | 0.9% |
| 10 | New Jersey | 954,696,000 | 2.1% | | 30 | Louisiana | 364,656,000 | 0.8% |
| 44 | New Mexico | 116,799,000 | 0.3% | | 31 | Kansas | 318,352,000 | 0.7% |
| 2 | New York | 2,556,658,000 | 5.7% | | 32 | Iowa | 292,002,000 | 0.7% |
| 12 | North Carolina | 765,817,000 | 1.7% | | 33 | Maine | 288,146,000 | 0.6% |
| 48 | North Dakota | 81,403,000 | 0.2% | | 34 | Nevada | 288,095,000 | 0.6% |
| 4 | Ohio | 2,335,022,000 | 5.2% | | 35 | Mississippi | 234,700,000 | 0.5% |
| 21 | Oklahoma | 520,181,000 | 1.2% | | 36 | Hawaii | 194,680,000 | 0.4% |
| 25 | Oregon | 492,854,000 | 1.1% | | 37 | Utah | 168,643,000 | 0.4% |
| 3 | Pennsylvania | 2,447,908,000 | 5.5% | | 38 | Idaho | 165,764,000 | 0.4% |
| 46 | Rhode Island | 104,199,000 | 0.2% | | 39 | Nebraska | 164,382,000 | 0.4% |
| 26 | South Carolina | 483,606,000 | 1.1% | | 40 | New Hampshire | 163,883,000 | 0.4% |
| 50 | South Dakota | 72,722,000 | 0.2% | | 41 | Arkansas | 161,146,000 | 0.4% |
| 22 | Tennessee | 517,846,000 | 1.2% | | 42 | Montana | 155,019,000 | 0.3% |
| 8 | Texas | 1,465,009,000 | 3.3% | | 43 | Delaware | 118,511,000 | 0.3% |
| 37 | Utah | 168,643,000 | 0.4% | | 44 | New Mexico | 116,799,000 | 0.3% |
| 47 | Vermont | 87,925,000 | 0.2% | | 45 | Alaska | 110,866,000 | 0.2% |
| 19 | Virginia | 591,068,000 | 1.3% | | 46 | Rhode Island | 104,199,000 | 0.2% |
| 7 | Washington | 1,481,587,000 | 3.3% | | 47 | Vermont | 87,925,000 | 0.2% |
| 27 | West Virginia | 463,555,000 | 1.0% | | 48 | North Dakota | 81,403,000 | 0.2% |
| 17 | Wisconsin | 621,973,000 | 1.4% | | 49 | Wyoming | 74,469,000 | 0.2% |
| 49 | Wyoming | 74,469,000 | 0.2% | | 50 | South Dakota | 72,722,000 | 0.2% |
| | | | | | | District of Columbia | 70,608,000 | 0.2% |

Source: Morgan Quitno Press using data from National Academy of Social Insurance (Washington, DC)
   unpublished data
*Estimated payments from private insurance, state and federal funds and self insurance.  National total includes
payments for federal civilian employee program, Black Lung Program and other federal programs.

# Workers' Compensation Benefit Payment per Employee in 1998

## National Average = $352 per Employee*

ALPHA ORDER

| RANK | STATE | AVERAGE |
|------|-------|---------|
| 14 | Alabama | $325 |
| 9 | Alaska | 405 |
| 40 | Arizona | 198 |
| 50 | Arkansas | 143 |
| 3 | California | 537 |
| 15 | Colorado | 317 |
| 6 | Connecticut | 428 |
| 22 | Delaware | 290 |
| 13 | Florida | 326 |
| 34 | Georgia | 213 |
| 10 | Hawaii | 373 |
| 16 | Idaho | 316 |
| 25 | Illinois | 285 |
| 49 | Indiana | 152 |
| 37 | Iowa | 201 |
| 30 | Kansas | 241 |
| 22 | Kentucky | 290 |
| 43 | Louisiana | 193 |
| 4 | Maine | 504 |
| 33 | Maryland | 220 |
| 39 | Massachusetts | 199 |
| 21 | Michigan | 300 |
| 25 | Minnesota | 285 |
| 35 | Mississippi | 209 |
| 41 | Missouri | 196 |
| 8 | Montana | 414 |
| 44 | Nebraska | 186 |
| 20 | Nevada | 303 |
| 24 | New Hampshire | 286 |
| 29 | New Jersey | 249 |
| 48 | New Mexico | 161 |
| 18 | New York | 310 |
| 36 | North Carolina | 203 |
| 28 | North Dakota | 256 |
| 7 | Ohio | 426 |
| 11 | Oklahoma | 360 |
| 17 | Oregon | 311 |
| 5 | Pennsylvania | 446 |
| 31 | Rhode Island | 228 |
| 27 | South Carolina | 266 |
| 37 | South Dakota | 201 |
| 41 | Tennessee | 196 |
| 46 | Texas | 163 |
| 46 | Utah | 163 |
| 19 | Vermont | 308 |
| 45 | Virginia | 176 |
| 2 | Washington | 565 |
| 1 | West Virginia | 636 |
| 31 | Wisconsin | 228 |
| 12 | Wyoming | 327 |

RANK ORDER

| RANK | STATE | AVERAGE |
|------|-------|---------|
| 1 | West Virginia | $636 |
| 2 | Washington | 565 |
| 3 | California | 537 |
| 4 | Maine | 504 |
| 5 | Pennsylvania | 446 |
| 6 | Connecticut | 428 |
| 7 | Ohio | 426 |
| 8 | Montana | 414 |
| 9 | Alaska | 405 |
| 10 | Hawaii | 373 |
| 11 | Oklahoma | 360 |
| 12 | Wyoming | 327 |
| 13 | Florida | 326 |
| 14 | Alabama | 325 |
| 15 | Colorado | 317 |
| 16 | Idaho | 316 |
| 17 | Oregon | 311 |
| 18 | New York | 310 |
| 19 | Vermont | 308 |
| 20 | Nevada | 303 |
| 21 | Michigan | 300 |
| 22 | Delaware | 290 |
| 22 | Kentucky | 290 |
| 24 | New Hampshire | 286 |
| 25 | Illinois | 285 |
| 25 | Minnesota | 285 |
| 27 | South Carolina | 266 |
| 28 | North Dakota | 256 |
| 29 | New Jersey | 249 |
| 30 | Kansas | 241 |
| 31 | Rhode Island | 228 |
| 31 | Wisconsin | 228 |
| 33 | Maryland | 220 |
| 34 | Georgia | 213 |
| 35 | Mississippi | 209 |
| 36 | North Carolina | 203 |
| 37 | Iowa | 201 |
| 37 | South Dakota | 201 |
| 39 | Massachusetts | 199 |
| 40 | Arizona | 198 |
| 41 | Missouri | 196 |
| 41 | Tennessee | 196 |
| 43 | Louisiana | 193 |
| 44 | Nebraska | 186 |
| 45 | Virginia | 176 |
| 46 | Texas | 163 |
| 46 | Utah | 163 |
| 48 | New Mexico | 161 |
| 49 | Indiana | 152 |
| 50 | Arkansas | 143 |
| | District of Columbia | 116 |

Source: Morgan Quitno Press using data from National Academy of Social Insurance (Washington, DC) unpublished data

*Estimated payments from private insurance, state and federal funds and self insurance. National rate includes payments for federal civilian employee program, Black Lung Program and other federal programs. Total divided by number of employees on nonfarm payrolls in 1998.

# Percent Change in Workers' Compensation Benefit Payments: 1996 to 1998

## National Percent Change = 5.5% Increase*

ALPHA ORDER

| RANK | STATE | PERCENT CHANGE |
|------|-------|----------------|
| 9 | Alabama | 17.2 |
| 35 | Alaska | (9.1) |
| 34 | Arizona | (9.0) |
| 22 | Arkansas | 0.7 |
| 12 | California | 8.0 |
| 28 | Colorado | (3.3) |
| 14 | Connecticut | 5.8 |
| 18 | Delaware | 3.1 |
| 44 | Florida | (18.4) |
| 26 | Georgia | (1.8) |
| 49 | Hawaii | (32.4) |
| 3 | Idaho | 29.5 |
| 19 | Illinois | 2.7 |
| 13 | Indiana | 7.1 |
| 10 | Iowa | 11.9 |
| 8 | Kansas | 17.9 |
| 21 | Kentucky | 0.8 |
| 50 | Louisiana | (34.5) |
| 32 | Maine | (8.2) |
| 40 | Maryland | (14.5) |
| 33 | Massachusetts | (8.4) |
| 38 | Michigan | (12.3) |
| 25 | Minnesota | (1.0) |
| 16 | Mississippi | 4.8 |
| 42 | Missouri | (14.8) |
| 17 | Montana | 3.3 |
| 43 | Nebraska | (17.4) |
| 48 | Nevada | (24.8) |
| 39 | New Hampshire | (12.8) |
| 20 | New Jersey | 2.5 |
| 47 | New Mexico | (22.6) |
| 24 | New York | (0.1) |
| 1 | North Carolina | 52.9 |
| 5 | North Dakota | 21.5 |
| 30 | Ohio | (4.0) |
| 45 | Oklahoma | (19.4) |
| 27 | Oregon | (2.6) |
| 29 | Pennsylvania | (3.4) |
| 41 | Rhode Island | (14.6) |
| 2 | South Carolina | 30.0 |
| 36 | South Dakota | (11.3) |
| 6 | Tennessee | 19.9 |
| 46 | Texas | (19.5) |
| 11 | Utah | 8.8 |
| 7 | Vermont | 18.8 |
| 15 | Virginia | 5.5 |
| 4 | Washington | 24.2 |
| 37 | West Virginia | (11.5) |
| 30 | Wisconsin | (4.0) |
| 23 | Wyoming | 0.6 |

RANK ORDER

| RANK | STATE | PERCENT CHANGE |
|------|-------|----------------|
| 1 | North Carolina | 52.9 |
| 2 | South Carolina | 30.0 |
| 3 | Idaho | 29.5 |
| 4 | Washington | 24.2 |
| 5 | North Dakota | 21.5 |
| 6 | Tennessee | 19.9 |
| 7 | Vermont | 18.8 |
| 8 | Kansas | 17.9 |
| 9 | Alabama | 17.2 |
| 10 | Iowa | 11.9 |
| 11 | Utah | 8.8 |
| 12 | California | 8.0 |
| 13 | Indiana | 7.1 |
| 14 | Connecticut | 5.8 |
| 15 | Virginia | 5.5 |
| 16 | Mississippi | 4.8 |
| 17 | Montana | 3.3 |
| 18 | Delaware | 3.1 |
| 19 | Illinois | 2.7 |
| 20 | New Jersey | 2.5 |
| 21 | Kentucky | 0.8 |
| 22 | Arkansas | 0.7 |
| 23 | Wyoming | 0.6 |
| 24 | New York | (0.1) |
| 25 | Minnesota | (1.0) |
| 26 | Georgia | (1.8) |
| 27 | Oregon | (2.6) |
| 28 | Colorado | (3.3) |
| 29 | Pennsylvania | (3.4) |
| 30 | Ohio | (4.0) |
| 30 | Wisconsin | (4.0) |
| 32 | Maine | (8.2) |
| 33 | Massachusetts | (8.4) |
| 34 | Arizona | (9.0) |
| 35 | Alaska | (9.1) |
| 36 | South Dakota | (11.3) |
| 37 | West Virginia | (11.5) |
| 38 | Michigan | (12.3) |
| 39 | New Hampshire | (12.8) |
| 40 | Maryland | (14.5) |
| 41 | Rhode Island | (14.6) |
| 42 | Missouri | (14.8) |
| 43 | Nebraska | (17.4) |
| 44 | Florida | (18.4) |
| 45 | Oklahoma | (19.4) |
| 46 | Texas | (19.5) |
| 47 | New Mexico | (22.6) |
| 48 | Nevada | (24.8) |
| 49 | Hawaii | (32.4) |
| 50 | Louisiana | (34.5) |

District of Columbia (21.5)

*Source: Morgan Quitno Press using data from National Academy of Social Insurance (Washington, DC) unpublished data*
*\*Estimated payments from private insurance, state and federal funds and self insurance. National total includes payments for federal civilian employee program, Black Lung Program and other federal programs.*

# Civilian Labor Force in 2000

## National Total = 140,863,000 Workers*

ALPHA ORDER

| RANK | STATE | WORKERS | % of USA |
|---|---|---|---|
| 23 | Alabama | 2,154,000 | 1.5% |
| 49 | Alaska | 322,000 | 0.2% |
| 21 | Arizona | 2,347,000 | 1.7% |
| 33 | Arkansas | 1,238,000 | 0.9% |
| 1 | California | 17,091,000 | 12.1% |
| 22 | Colorado | 2,276,000 | 1.6% |
| 28 | Connecticut | 1,746,000 | 1.2% |
| 45 | Delaware | 409,000 | 0.3% |
| 4 | Florida | 7,490,000 | 5.3% |
| 10 | Georgia | 4,173,000 | 3.0% |
| 42 | Hawaii | 595,000 | 0.4% |
| 41 | Idaho | 658,000 | 0.5% |
| 5 | Illinois | 6,419,000 | 4.6% |
| 14 | Indiana | 3,084,000 | 2.2% |
| 30 | Iowa | 1,563,000 | 1.1% |
| 31 | Kansas | 1,411,000 | 1.0% |
| 26 | Kentucky | 1,982,000 | 1.4% |
| 24 | Louisiana | 2,030,000 | 1.4% |
| 39 | Maine | 689,000 | 0.5% |
| 18 | Maryland | 2,805,000 | 2.0% |
| 13 | Massachusetts | 3,237,000 | 2.3% |
| 8 | Michigan | 5,201,000 | 3.7% |
| 20 | Minnesota | 2,739,000 | 1.9% |
| 32 | Mississippi | 1,326,000 | 0.9% |
| 17 | Missouri | 2,930,000 | 2.1% |
| 44 | Montana | 479,000 | 0.3% |
| 36 | Nebraska | 924,000 | 0.7% |
| 35 | Nevada | 986,000 | 0.7% |
| 40 | New Hampshire | 686,000 | 0.5% |
| 9 | New Jersey | 4,188,000 | 3.0% |
| 37 | New Mexico | 833,000 | 0.6% |
| 3 | New York | 8,941,000 | 6.3% |
| 11 | North Carolina | 3,958,000 | 2.8% |
| 47 | North Dakota | 339,000 | 0.2% |
| 7 | Ohio | 5,783,000 | 4.1% |
| 29 | Oklahoma | 1,648,000 | 1.2% |
| 27 | Oregon | 1,803,000 | 1.3% |
| 6 | Pennsylvania | 5,972,000 | 4.2% |
| 43 | Rhode Island | 505,000 | 0.4% |
| 25 | South Carolina | 1,985,000 | 1.4% |
| 46 | South Dakota | 401,000 | 0.3% |
| 19 | Tennessee | 2,798,000 | 2.0% |
| 2 | Texas | 10,325,000 | 7.3% |
| 34 | Utah | 1,104,000 | 0.8% |
| 48 | Vermont | 332,000 | 0.2% |
| 12 | Virginia | 3,610,000 | 2.6% |
| 15 | Washington | 3,045,000 | 2.2% |
| 38 | West Virginia | 825,000 | 0.6% |
| 16 | Wisconsin | 2,935,000 | 2.1% |
| 50 | Wyoming | 267,000 | 0.2% |

RANK ORDER

| RANK | STATE | WORKERS | % of USA |
|---|---|---|---|
| 1 | California | 17,091,000 | 12.1% |
| 2 | Texas | 10,325,000 | 7.3% |
| 3 | New York | 8,941,000 | 6.3% |
| 4 | Florida | 7,490,000 | 5.3% |
| 5 | Illinois | 6,419,000 | 4.6% |
| 6 | Pennsylvania | 5,972,000 | 4.2% |
| 7 | Ohio | 5,783,000 | 4.1% |
| 8 | Michigan | 5,201,000 | 3.7% |
| 9 | New Jersey | 4,188,000 | 3.0% |
| 10 | Georgia | 4,173,000 | 3.0% |
| 11 | North Carolina | 3,958,000 | 2.8% |
| 12 | Virginia | 3,610,000 | 2.6% |
| 13 | Massachusetts | 3,237,000 | 2.3% |
| 14 | Indiana | 3,084,000 | 2.2% |
| 15 | Washington | 3,045,000 | 2.2% |
| 16 | Wisconsin | 2,935,000 | 2.1% |
| 17 | Missouri | 2,930,000 | 2.1% |
| 18 | Maryland | 2,805,000 | 2.0% |
| 19 | Tennessee | 2,798,000 | 2.0% |
| 20 | Minnesota | 2,739,000 | 1.9% |
| 21 | Arizona | 2,347,000 | 1.7% |
| 22 | Colorado | 2,276,000 | 1.6% |
| 23 | Alabama | 2,154,000 | 1.5% |
| 24 | Louisiana | 2,030,000 | 1.4% |
| 25 | South Carolina | 1,985,000 | 1.4% |
| 26 | Kentucky | 1,982,000 | 1.4% |
| 27 | Oregon | 1,803,000 | 1.3% |
| 28 | Connecticut | 1,746,000 | 1.2% |
| 29 | Oklahoma | 1,648,000 | 1.2% |
| 30 | Iowa | 1,563,000 | 1.1% |
| 31 | Kansas | 1,411,000 | 1.0% |
| 32 | Mississippi | 1,326,000 | 0.9% |
| 33 | Arkansas | 1,238,000 | 0.9% |
| 34 | Utah | 1,104,000 | 0.8% |
| 35 | Nevada | 986,000 | 0.7% |
| 36 | Nebraska | 924,000 | 0.7% |
| 37 | New Mexico | 833,000 | 0.6% |
| 38 | West Virginia | 825,000 | 0.6% |
| 39 | Maine | 689,000 | 0.5% |
| 40 | New Hampshire | 686,000 | 0.5% |
| 41 | Idaho | 658,000 | 0.5% |
| 42 | Hawaii | 595,000 | 0.4% |
| 43 | Rhode Island | 505,000 | 0.4% |
| 44 | Montana | 479,000 | 0.3% |
| 45 | Delaware | 409,000 | 0.3% |
| 46 | South Dakota | 401,000 | 0.3% |
| 47 | North Dakota | 339,000 | 0.2% |
| 48 | Vermont | 332,000 | 0.2% |
| 49 | Alaska | 322,000 | 0.2% |
| 50 | Wyoming | 267,000 | 0.2% |
| | District of Columbia | 279,000 | 0.2% |

Source: U.S. Department of Labor, Bureau of Labor Statistics
    "State and Regional Unemployment, 2000 Annual Averages" (press release, February 23, 2001)
*Annual averages for 2000.  National total calculated through a different formula.

# Employed Civilian Labor Force in 2000

## National Total = 135,208,000 Employed Workers*

ALPHA ORDER

| RANK | STATE | EMPLOYED | % of USA |
|---|---|---|---|
| 23 | Alabama | 2,055,000 | 1.5% |
| 49 | Alaska | 301,000 | 0.2% |
| 21 | Arizona | 2,256,000 | 1.7% |
| 33 | Arkansas | 1,183,000 | 0.9% |
| 1 | California | 16,246,000 | 12.0% |
| 22 | Colorado | 2,213,000 | 1.6% |
| 28 | Connecticut | 1,707,000 | 1.3% |
| 45 | Delaware | 393,000 | 0.3% |
| 4 | Florida | 7,221,000 | 5.3% |
| 10 | Georgia | 4,019,000 | 3.0% |
| 42 | Hawaii | 570,000 | 0.4% |
| 41 | Idaho | 626,000 | 0.5% |
| 5 | Illinois | 6,140,000 | 4.5% |
| 14 | Indiana | 2,984,000 | 2.2% |
| 30 | Iowa | 1,522,000 | 1.1% |
| 31 | Kansas | 1,359,000 | 1.0% |
| 26 | Kentucky | 1,900,000 | 1.4% |
| 24 | Louisiana | 1,917,000 | 1.4% |
| 40 | Maine | 665,000 | 0.5% |
| 18 | Maryland | 2,697,000 | 2.0% |
| 13 | Massachusetts | 3,151,000 | 2.3% |
| 8 | Michigan | 5,016,000 | 3.7% |
| 20 | Minnesota | 2,649,000 | 2.0% |
| 32 | Mississippi | 1,251,000 | 0.9% |
| 17 | Missouri | 2,828,000 | 2.1% |
| 44 | Montana | 456,000 | 0.3% |
| 36 | Nebraska | 897,000 | 0.7% |
| 35 | Nevada | 946,000 | 0.7% |
| 39 | New Hampshire | 666,000 | 0.5% |
| 9 | New Jersey | 4,030,000 | 3.0% |
| 37 | New Mexico | 792,000 | 0.6% |
| 3 | New York | 8,533,000 | 6.3% |
| 11 | North Carolina | 3,814,000 | 2.8% |
| 47 | North Dakota | 329,000 | 0.2% |
| 7 | Ohio | 5,546,000 | 4.1% |
| 29 | Oklahoma | 1,598,000 | 1.2% |
| 27 | Oregon | 1,715,000 | 1.3% |
| 6 | Pennsylvania | 5,722,000 | 4.2% |
| 43 | Rhode Island | 484,000 | 0.4% |
| 25 | South Carolina | 1,909,000 | 1.4% |
| 46 | South Dakota | 392,000 | 0.3% |
| 19 | Tennessee | 2,688,000 | 2.0% |
| 2 | Texas | 9,887,000 | 7.3% |
| 34 | Utah | 1,068,000 | 0.8% |
| 48 | Vermont | 322,000 | 0.2% |
| 12 | Virginia | 3,530,000 | 2.6% |
| 15 | Washington | 2,888,000 | 2.1% |
| 38 | West Virginia | 779,000 | 0.6% |
| 16 | Wisconsin | 2,831,000 | 2.1% |
| 50 | Wyoming | 257,000 | 0.2% |

RANK ORDER

| RANK | STATE | EMPLOYED | % of USA |
|---|---|---|---|
| 1 | California | 16,246,000 | 12.0% |
| 2 | Texas | 9,887,000 | 7.3% |
| 3 | New York | 8,533,000 | 6.3% |
| 4 | Florida | 7,221,000 | 5.3% |
| 5 | Illinois | 6,140,000 | 4.5% |
| 6 | Pennsylvania | 5,722,000 | 4.2% |
| 7 | Ohio | 5,546,000 | 4.1% |
| 8 | Michigan | 5,016,000 | 3.7% |
| 9 | New Jersey | 4,030,000 | 3.0% |
| 10 | Georgia | 4,019,000 | 3.0% |
| 11 | North Carolina | 3,814,000 | 2.8% |
| 12 | Virginia | 3,530,000 | 2.6% |
| 13 | Massachusetts | 3,151,000 | 2.3% |
| 14 | Indiana | 2,984,000 | 2.2% |
| 15 | Washington | 2,888,000 | 2.1% |
| 16 | Wisconsin | 2,831,000 | 2.1% |
| 17 | Missouri | 2,828,000 | 2.1% |
| 18 | Maryland | 2,697,000 | 2.0% |
| 19 | Tennessee | 2,688,000 | 2.0% |
| 20 | Minnesota | 2,649,000 | 2.0% |
| 21 | Arizona | 2,256,000 | 1.7% |
| 22 | Colorado | 2,213,000 | 1.6% |
| 23 | Alabama | 2,055,000 | 1.5% |
| 24 | Louisiana | 1,917,000 | 1.4% |
| 25 | South Carolina | 1,909,000 | 1.4% |
| 26 | Kentucky | 1,900,000 | 1.4% |
| 27 | Oregon | 1,715,000 | 1.3% |
| 28 | Connecticut | 1,707,000 | 1.3% |
| 29 | Oklahoma | 1,598,000 | 1.2% |
| 30 | Iowa | 1,522,000 | 1.1% |
| 31 | Kansas | 1,359,000 | 1.0% |
| 32 | Mississippi | 1,251,000 | 0.9% |
| 33 | Arkansas | 1,183,000 | 0.9% |
| 34 | Utah | 1,068,000 | 0.8% |
| 35 | Nevada | 946,000 | 0.7% |
| 36 | Nebraska | 897,000 | 0.7% |
| 37 | New Mexico | 792,000 | 0.6% |
| 38 | West Virginia | 779,000 | 0.6% |
| 39 | New Hampshire | 666,000 | 0.5% |
| 40 | Maine | 665,000 | 0.5% |
| 41 | Idaho | 626,000 | 0.5% |
| 42 | Hawaii | 570,000 | 0.4% |
| 43 | Rhode Island | 484,000 | 0.4% |
| 44 | Montana | 456,000 | 0.3% |
| 45 | Delaware | 393,000 | 0.3% |
| 46 | South Dakota | 392,000 | 0.3% |
| 47 | North Dakota | 329,000 | 0.2% |
| 48 | Vermont | 322,000 | 0.2% |
| 49 | Alaska | 301,000 | 0.2% |
| 50 | Wyoming | 257,000 | 0.2% |
| | District of Columbia | 263,000 | 0.2% |

Source: U.S. Department of Labor, Bureau of Labor Statistics
  "State and Regional Unemployment, 2000 Annual Averages" (press release, February 23, 2001)
*Annual averages for 2000. National total calculated through a different formula.

# Unemployed Civilian Labor Force in 2000

## National Total = 5,655,000 Unemployed Workers*

ALPHA ORDER

| RANK | STATE | UNEMPLOYED | % of USA |
|------|-------|-----------:|---------:|
| 19 | Alabama | 99,000 | 1.8% |
| 43 | Alaska | 21,000 | 0.4% |
| 20 | Arizona | 91,000 | 1.6% |
| 29 | Arkansas | 55,000 | 1.0% |
| 1 | California | 845,000 | 14.9% |
| 28 | Colorado | 63,000 | 1.1% |
| 36 | Connecticut | 39,000 | 0.7% |
| 46 | Delaware | 16,000 | 0.3% |
| 5 | Florida | 269,000 | 4.8% |
| 11 | Georgia | 154,000 | 2.7% |
| 40 | Hawaii | 26,000 | 0.5% |
| 38 | Idaho | 32,000 | 0.6% |
| 4 | Illinois | 279,000 | 4.9% |
| 18 | Indiana | 100,000 | 1.8% |
| 33 | Iowa | 41,000 | 0.7% |
| 30 | Kansas | 52,000 | 0.9% |
| 24 | Kentucky | 82,000 | 1.5% |
| 13 | Louisiana | 112,000 | 2.0% |
| 41 | Maine | 24,000 | 0.4% |
| 15 | Maryland | 108,000 | 1.9% |
| 23 | Massachusetts | 86,000 | 1.5% |
| 8 | Michigan | 185,000 | 3.3% |
| 21 | Minnesota | 90,000 | 1.6% |
| 27 | Mississippi | 75,000 | 1.3% |
| 17 | Missouri | 101,000 | 1.8% |
| 41 | Montana | 24,000 | 0.4% |
| 39 | Nebraska | 28,000 | 0.5% |
| 34 | Nevada | 40,000 | 0.7% |
| 45 | New Hampshire | 19,000 | 0.3% |
| 10 | New Jersey | 157,000 | 2.8% |
| 34 | New Mexico | 40,000 | 0.7% |
| 3 | New York | 408,000 | 7.2% |
| 12 | North Carolina | 144,000 | 2.5% |
| 47 | North Dakota | 10,000 | 0.2% |
| 7 | Ohio | 237,000 | 4.2% |
| 31 | Oklahoma | 50,000 | 0.9% |
| 22 | Oregon | 87,000 | 1.5% |
| 6 | Pennsylvania | 250,000 | 4.4% |
| 43 | Rhode Island | 21,000 | 0.4% |
| 26 | South Carolina | 77,000 | 1.4% |
| 50 | South Dakota | 9,000 | 0.2% |
| 14 | Tennessee | 110,000 | 1.9% |
| 2 | Texas | 437,000 | 7.7% |
| 37 | Utah | 36,000 | 0.6% |
| 47 | Vermont | 10,000 | 0.2% |
| 25 | Virginia | 80,000 | 1.4% |
| 9 | Washington | 158,000 | 2.8% |
| 32 | West Virginia | 46,000 | 0.8% |
| 16 | Wisconsin | 104,000 | 1.8% |
| 47 | Wyoming | 10,000 | 0.2% |

RANK ORDER

| RANK | STATE | UNEMPLOYED | % of USA |
|------|-------|-----------:|---------:|
| 1 | California | 845,000 | 14.9% |
| 2 | Texas | 437,000 | 7.7% |
| 3 | New York | 408,000 | 7.2% |
| 4 | Illinois | 279,000 | 4.9% |
| 5 | Florida | 269,000 | 4.8% |
| 6 | Pennsylvania | 250,000 | 4.4% |
| 7 | Ohio | 237,000 | 4.2% |
| 8 | Michigan | 185,000 | 3.3% |
| 9 | Washington | 158,000 | 2.8% |
| 10 | New Jersey | 157,000 | 2.8% |
| 11 | Georgia | 154,000 | 2.7% |
| 12 | North Carolina | 144,000 | 2.5% |
| 13 | Louisiana | 112,000 | 2.0% |
| 14 | Tennessee | 110,000 | 1.9% |
| 15 | Maryland | 108,000 | 1.9% |
| 16 | Wisconsin | 104,000 | 1.8% |
| 17 | Missouri | 101,000 | 1.8% |
| 18 | Indiana | 100,000 | 1.8% |
| 19 | Alabama | 99,000 | 1.8% |
| 20 | Arizona | 91,000 | 1.6% |
| 21 | Minnesota | 90,000 | 1.6% |
| 22 | Oregon | 87,000 | 1.5% |
| 23 | Massachusetts | 86,000 | 1.5% |
| 24 | Kentucky | 82,000 | 1.5% |
| 25 | Virginia | 80,000 | 1.4% |
| 26 | South Carolina | 77,000 | 1.4% |
| 27 | Mississippi | 75,000 | 1.3% |
| 28 | Colorado | 63,000 | 1.1% |
| 29 | Arkansas | 55,000 | 1.0% |
| 30 | Kansas | 52,000 | 0.9% |
| 31 | Oklahoma | 50,000 | 0.9% |
| 32 | West Virginia | 46,000 | 0.8% |
| 33 | Iowa | 41,000 | 0.7% |
| 34 | Nevada | 40,000 | 0.7% |
| 34 | New Mexico | 40,000 | 0.7% |
| 36 | Connecticut | 39,000 | 0.7% |
| 37 | Utah | 36,000 | 0.6% |
| 38 | Idaho | 32,000 | 0.6% |
| 39 | Nebraska | 28,000 | 0.5% |
| 40 | Hawaii | 26,000 | 0.5% |
| 41 | Maine | 24,000 | 0.4% |
| 41 | Montana | 24,000 | 0.4% |
| 43 | Alaska | 21,000 | 0.4% |
| 43 | Rhode Island | 21,000 | 0.4% |
| 45 | New Hampshire | 19,000 | 0.3% |
| 46 | Delaware | 16,000 | 0.3% |
| 47 | North Dakota | 10,000 | 0.2% |
| 47 | Vermont | 10,000 | 0.2% |
| 47 | Wyoming | 10,000 | 0.2% |
| 50 | South Dakota | 9,000 | 0.2% |
| | District of Columbia | 16,000 | 0.3% |

Source: U.S. Department of Labor, Bureau of Labor Statistics
"State and Regional Unemployment, 2000 Annual Averages" (press release, February 23, 2001)
*Annual averages for 2000. National total calculated through a different formula.

# Unemployment Rate in 2000

## National Rate = 4.0% of Labor Force Unemployed*

ALPHA ORDER

| RANK | STATE | PERCENT |
|------|-------|---------|
| 11 | Alabama | 4.6 |
| 1 | Alaska | 6.6 |
| 23 | Arizona | 3.9 |
| 13 | Arkansas | 4.4 |
| 6 | California | 4.9 |
| 45 | Colorado | 2.7 |
| 48 | Connecticut | 2.3 |
| 22 | Delaware | 4.0 |
| 31 | Florida | 3.6 |
| 29 | Georgia | 3.7 |
| 15 | Hawaii | 4.3 |
| 6 | Idaho | 4.9 |
| 13 | Illinois | 4.4 |
| 38 | Indiana | 3.2 |
| 46 | Iowa | 2.6 |
| 29 | Kansas | 3.7 |
| 18 | Kentucky | 4.1 |
| 3 | Louisiana | 5.5 |
| 34 | Maine | 3.5 |
| 23 | Maryland | 3.9 |
| 46 | Massachusetts | 2.6 |
| 31 | Michigan | 3.6 |
| 37 | Minnesota | 3.3 |
| 2 | Mississippi | 5.7 |
| 34 | Missouri | 3.5 |
| 6 | Montana | 4.9 |
| 40 | Nebraska | 3.0 |
| 18 | Nevada | 4.1 |
| 44 | New Hampshire | 2.8 |
| 28 | New Jersey | 3.8 |
| 6 | New Mexico | 4.9 |
| 11 | New York | 4.6 |
| 31 | North Carolina | 3.6 |
| 40 | North Dakota | 3.0 |
| 18 | Ohio | 4.1 |
| 40 | Oklahoma | 3.0 |
| 6 | Oregon | 4.9 |
| 16 | Pennsylvania | 4.2 |
| 18 | Rhode Island | 4.1 |
| 23 | South Carolina | 3.9 |
| 48 | South Dakota | 2.3 |
| 23 | Tennessee | 3.9 |
| 16 | Texas | 4.2 |
| 38 | Utah | 3.2 |
| 43 | Vermont | 2.9 |
| 50 | Virginia | 2.2 |
| 5 | Washington | 5.2 |
| 3 | West Virginia | 5.5 |
| 34 | Wisconsin | 3.5 |
| 23 | Wyoming | 3.9 |

RANK ORDER

| RANK | STATE | PERCENT |
|------|-------|---------|
| 1 | Alaska | 6.6 |
| 2 | Mississippi | 5.7 |
| 3 | Louisiana | 5.5 |
| 3 | West Virginia | 5.5 |
| 5 | Washington | 5.2 |
| 6 | California | 4.9 |
| 6 | Idaho | 4.9 |
| 6 | Montana | 4.9 |
| 6 | New Mexico | 4.9 |
| 6 | Oregon | 4.9 |
| 11 | Alabama | 4.6 |
| 11 | New York | 4.6 |
| 13 | Arkansas | 4.4 |
| 13 | Illinois | 4.4 |
| 15 | Hawaii | 4.3 |
| 16 | Pennsylvania | 4.2 |
| 16 | Texas | 4.2 |
| 18 | Kentucky | 4.1 |
| 18 | Nevada | 4.1 |
| 18 | Ohio | 4.1 |
| 18 | Rhode Island | 4.1 |
| 22 | Delaware | 4.0 |
| 23 | Arizona | 3.9 |
| 23 | Maryland | 3.9 |
| 23 | South Carolina | 3.9 |
| 23 | Tennessee | 3.9 |
| 23 | Wyoming | 3.9 |
| 28 | New Jersey | 3.8 |
| 29 | Georgia | 3.7 |
| 29 | Kansas | 3.7 |
| 31 | Florida | 3.6 |
| 31 | Michigan | 3.6 |
| 31 | North Carolina | 3.6 |
| 34 | Maine | 3.5 |
| 34 | Missouri | 3.5 |
| 34 | Wisconsin | 3.5 |
| 37 | Minnesota | 3.3 |
| 38 | Indiana | 3.2 |
| 38 | Utah | 3.2 |
| 40 | Nebraska | 3.0 |
| 40 | North Dakota | 3.0 |
| 40 | Oklahoma | 3.0 |
| 43 | Vermont | 2.9 |
| 44 | New Hampshire | 2.8 |
| 45 | Colorado | 2.7 |
| 46 | Iowa | 2.6 |
| 46 | Massachusetts | 2.6 |
| 48 | Connecticut | 2.3 |
| 48 | South Dakota | 2.3 |
| 50 | Virginia | 2.2 |

District of Columbia — 5.8

*Source: U.S. Department of Labor, Bureau of Labor Statistics*
    *"State and Regional Unemployment, 2000 Annual Averages" (press release, February 23, 2001)*
*Annual averages for 2000. National rate calculated through a different formula.*

# Women in Civilian Labor Force in 1999

## National Total = 64,855,000 Women*

ALPHA ORDER

| RANK | STATE | WOMEN | % of USA |
|------|-------|-------|----------|
| 23 | Alabama | 1,007,000 | 1.6% |
| 49 | Alaska | 145,000 | 0.2% |
| 21 | Arizona | 1,093,000 | 1.7% |
| 33 | Arkansas | 570,000 | 0.9% |
| 1 | California | 7,471,000 | 11.5% |
| 22 | Colorado | 1,032,000 | 1.6% |
| 27 | Connecticut | 810,000 | 1.2% |
| 46 | Delaware | 185,000 | 0.3% |
| 4 | Florida | 3,425,000 | 5.3% |
| 9 | Georgia | 1,956,000 | 3.0% |
| 41 | Hawaii | 298,000 | 0.5% |
| 42 | Idaho | 292,000 | 0.5% |
| 5 | Illinois | 3,005,000 | 4.6% |
| 15 | Indiana | 1,428,000 | 2.2% |
| 30 | Iowa | 733,000 | 1.1% |
| 31 | Kansas | 678,000 | 1.0% |
| 26 | Kentucky | 897,000 | 1.4% |
| 24 | Louisiana | 991,000 | 1.5% |
| 39 | Maine | 321,000 | 0.5% |
| 17 | Maryland | 1,338,000 | 2.1% |
| 13 | Massachusetts | 1,552,000 | 2.4% |
| 8 | Michigan | 2,344,000 | 3.6% |
| 20 | Minnesota | 1,275,000 | 2.0% |
| 32 | Mississippi | 604,000 | 0.9% |
| 19 | Missouri | 1,303,000 | 2.0% |
| 44 | Montana | 221,000 | 0.3% |
| 35 | Nebraska | 430,000 | 0.7% |
| 36 | Nevada | 425,000 | 0.7% |
| 40 | New Hampshire | 311,000 | 0.5% |
| 10 | New Jersey | 1,950,000 | 3.0% |
| 38 | New Mexico | 379,000 | 0.6% |
| 3 | New York | 4,171,000 | 6.4% |
| 11 | North Carolina | 1,814,000 | 2.8% |
| 47 | North Dakota | 160,000 | 0.2% |
| 7 | Ohio | 2,717,000 | 4.2% |
| 29 | Oklahoma | 774,000 | 1.2% |
| 28 | Oregon | 806,000 | 1.2% |
| 6 | Pennsylvania | 2,812,000 | 4.3% |
| 43 | Rhode Island | 240,000 | 0.4% |
| 25 | South Carolina | 936,000 | 1.4% |
| 45 | South Dakota | 190,000 | 0.3% |
| 18 | Tennessee | 1,336,000 | 2.1% |
| 2 | Texas | 4,622,000 | 7.1% |
| 34 | Utah | 490,000 | 0.8% |
| 47 | Vermont | 160,000 | 0.2% |
| 12 | Virginia | 1,651,000 | 2.5% |
| 14 | Washington | 1,434,000 | 2.2% |
| 37 | West Virginia | 382,000 | 0.6% |
| 16 | Wisconsin | 1,359,000 | 2.1% |
| 50 | Wyoming | 122,000 | 0.2% |

RANK ORDER

| RANK | STATE | WOMEN | % of USA |
|------|-------|-------|----------|
| 1 | California | 7,471,000 | 11.5% |
| 2 | Texas | 4,622,000 | 7.1% |
| 3 | New York | 4,171,000 | 6.4% |
| 4 | Florida | 3,425,000 | 5.3% |
| 5 | Illinois | 3,005,000 | 4.6% |
| 6 | Pennsylvania | 2,812,000 | 4.3% |
| 7 | Ohio | 2,717,000 | 4.2% |
| 8 | Michigan | 2,344,000 | 3.6% |
| 9 | Georgia | 1,956,000 | 3.0% |
| 10 | New Jersey | 1,950,000 | 3.0% |
| 11 | North Carolina | 1,814,000 | 2.8% |
| 12 | Virginia | 1,651,000 | 2.5% |
| 13 | Massachusetts | 1,552,000 | 2.4% |
| 14 | Washington | 1,434,000 | 2.2% |
| 15 | Indiana | 1,428,000 | 2.2% |
| 16 | Wisconsin | 1,359,000 | 2.1% |
| 17 | Maryland | 1,338,000 | 2.1% |
| 18 | Tennessee | 1,336,000 | 2.1% |
| 19 | Missouri | 1,303,000 | 2.0% |
| 20 | Minnesota | 1,275,000 | 2.0% |
| 21 | Arizona | 1,093,000 | 1.7% |
| 22 | Colorado | 1,032,000 | 1.6% |
| 23 | Alabama | 1,007,000 | 1.6% |
| 24 | Louisiana | 991,000 | 1.5% |
| 25 | South Carolina | 936,000 | 1.4% |
| 26 | Kentucky | 897,000 | 1.4% |
| 27 | Connecticut | 810,000 | 1.2% |
| 28 | Oregon | 806,000 | 1.2% |
| 29 | Oklahoma | 774,000 | 1.2% |
| 30 | Iowa | 733,000 | 1.1% |
| 31 | Kansas | 678,000 | 1.0% |
| 32 | Mississippi | 604,000 | 0.9% |
| 33 | Arkansas | 570,000 | 0.9% |
| 34 | Utah | 490,000 | 0.8% |
| 35 | Nebraska | 430,000 | 0.7% |
| 36 | Nevada | 425,000 | 0.7% |
| 37 | West Virginia | 382,000 | 0.6% |
| 38 | New Mexico | 379,000 | 0.6% |
| 39 | Maine | 321,000 | 0.5% |
| 40 | New Hampshire | 311,000 | 0.5% |
| 41 | Hawaii | 298,000 | 0.5% |
| 42 | Idaho | 292,000 | 0.5% |
| 43 | Rhode Island | 240,000 | 0.4% |
| 44 | Montana | 221,000 | 0.3% |
| 45 | South Dakota | 190,000 | 0.3% |
| 46 | Delaware | 185,000 | 0.3% |
| 47 | North Dakota | 160,000 | 0.2% |
| 47 | Vermont | 160,000 | 0.2% |
| 49 | Alaska | 145,000 | 0.2% |
| 50 | Wyoming | 122,000 | 0.2% |
| | District of Columbia | 145,000 | 0.2% |

Source: U.S. Department of Labor, Bureau of Labor Statistics
   "Geographic Profiles of Employment and Unemployment, 1999"
*Annual averages.

# Percent of Women in the Civilian Labor Force in 1999

## National Percent = 60.0% of Women*

| ALPHA ORDER | | | | RANK ORDER | | |
|---|---|---|---|---|---|---|
| RANK | STATE | PERCENT | | RANK | STATE | PERCENT |
| 42 | Alabama | 56.7 | | 1 | Minnesota | 69.9 |
| 5 | Alaska | 66.6 | | 2 | South Dakota | 68.2 |
| 38 | Arizona | 58.4 | | 3 | Wisconsin | 67.2 |
| 44 | Arkansas | 56.4 | | 4 | Colorado | 66.9 |
| 40 | California | 58.1 | | 5 | Alaska | 66.6 |
| 4 | Colorado | 66.9 | | 5 | Nebraska | 66.6 |
| 23 | Connecticut | 61.7 | | 7 | Vermont | 66.5 |
| 25 | Delaware | 61.5 | | 8 | Kansas | 66.3 |
| 47 | Florida | 55.4 | | 9 | New Hampshire | 66.2 |
| 18 | Georgia | 63.1 | | 10 | Iowa | 66.1 |
| 14 | Hawaii | 63.6 | | 11 | North Dakota | 65.2 |
| 22 | Idaho | 62.0 | | 12 | Maryland | 64.9 |
| 19 | Illinois | 63.0 | | 13 | Wyoming | 64.3 |
| 28 | Indiana | 61.1 | | 14 | Hawaii | 63.6 |
| 10 | Iowa | 66.1 | | 14 | Montana | 63.6 |
| 8 | Kansas | 66.3 | | 16 | Utah | 63.3 |
| 42 | Kentucky | 56.7 | | 16 | Washington | 63.3 |
| 45 | Louisiana | 56.0 | | 18 | Georgia | 63.1 |
| 21 | Maine | 62.4 | | 19 | Illinois | 63.0 |
| 12 | Maryland | 64.9 | | 19 | Massachusetts | 63.0 |
| 19 | Massachusetts | 63.0 | | 21 | Maine | 62.4 |
| 27 | Michigan | 61.2 | | 22 | Idaho | 62.0 |
| 1 | Minnesota | 69.9 | | 23 | Connecticut | 61.7 |
| 49 | Mississippi | 53.9 | | 23 | Nevada | 61.7 |
| 26 | Missouri | 61.4 | | 25 | Delaware | 61.5 |
| 14 | Montana | 63.6 | | 26 | Missouri | 61.4 |
| 5 | Nebraska | 66.6 | | 27 | Michigan | 61.2 |
| 23 | Nevada | 61.7 | | 28 | Indiana | 61.1 |
| 9 | New Hampshire | 66.2 | | 29 | Rhode Island | 60.8 |
| 36 | New Jersey | 59.5 | | 30 | Oregon | 60.6 |
| 48 | New Mexico | 55.3 | | 30 | Virginia | 60.6 |
| 46 | New York | 55.8 | | 32 | North Carolina | 60.3 |
| 32 | North Carolina | 60.3 | | 32 | Ohio | 60.3 |
| 11 | North Dakota | 65.2 | | 32 | Texas | 60.3 |
| 32 | Ohio | 60.3 | | 35 | Tennessee | 59.7 |
| 38 | Oklahoma | 58.4 | | 36 | New Jersey | 59.5 |
| 30 | Oregon | 60.6 | | 37 | South Carolina | 59.2 |
| 41 | Pennsylvania | 57.5 | | 38 | Arizona | 58.4 |
| 29 | Rhode Island | 60.8 | | 38 | Oklahoma | 58.4 |
| 37 | South Carolina | 59.2 | | 40 | California | 58.1 |
| 2 | South Dakota | 68.2 | | 41 | Pennsylvania | 57.5 |
| 35 | Tennessee | 59.7 | | 42 | Alabama | 56.7 |
| 32 | Texas | 60.3 | | 42 | Kentucky | 56.7 |
| 16 | Utah | 63.3 | | 44 | Arkansas | 56.4 |
| 7 | Vermont | 66.5 | | 45 | Louisiana | 56.0 |
| 30 | Virginia | 60.6 | | 46 | New York | 55.8 |
| 16 | Washington | 63.3 | | 47 | Florida | 55.4 |
| 50 | West Virginia | 49.9 | | 48 | New Mexico | 55.3 |
| 3 | Wisconsin | 67.2 | | 49 | Mississippi | 53.9 |
| 13 | Wyoming | 64.3 | | 50 | West Virginia | 49.9 |
| | | | | | District of Columbia | 64.3 |

Source: U.S. Department of Labor, Bureau of Labor Statistics
    "Geographic Profiles of Employment and Unemployment, 1999"
*Annual averages.

# Percent of Civilian Labor Force Comprised of Women in 1999

## National Percent = 46.5% of Civilian Labor Force*

ALPHA ORDER

| RANK | STATE | PERCENT |
|------|-------|---------|
| 25 | Alabama | 46.9 |
| 40 | Alaska | 46.0 |
| 39 | Arizona | 46.2 |
| 31 | Arkansas | 46.6 |
| 49 | California | 45.0 |
| 43 | Colorado | 45.6 |
| 4 | Connecticut | 47.9 |
| 8 | Delaware | 47.6 |
| 36 | Florida | 46.5 |
| 5 | Georgia | 47.8 |
| 1 | Hawaii | 50.1 |
| 50 | Idaho | 44.6 |
| 20 | Illinois | 47.1 |
| 37 | Indiana | 46.4 |
| 31 | Iowa | 46.6 |
| 15 | Kansas | 47.3 |
| 45 | Kentucky | 45.5 |
| 3 | Louisiana | 48.3 |
| 5 | Maine | 47.8 |
| 2 | Maryland | 48.4 |
| 15 | Massachusetts | 47.3 |
| 43 | Michigan | 45.6 |
| 18 | Minnesota | 47.2 |
| 8 | Mississippi | 47.6 |
| 41 | Missouri | 45.8 |
| 31 | Montana | 46.6 |
| 18 | Nebraska | 47.2 |
| 48 | Nevada | 45.1 |
| 30 | New Hampshire | 46.7 |
| 37 | New Jersey | 46.4 |
| 27 | New Mexico | 46.8 |
| 22 | New York | 47.0 |
| 27 | North Carolina | 46.8 |
| 12 | North Dakota | 47.5 |
| 15 | Ohio | 47.3 |
| 22 | Oklahoma | 47.0 |
| 41 | Oregon | 45.8 |
| 20 | Pennsylvania | 47.1 |
| 8 | Rhode Island | 47.6 |
| 7 | South Carolina | 47.7 |
| 12 | South Dakota | 47.5 |
| 14 | Tennessee | 47.4 |
| 46 | Texas | 45.3 |
| 47 | Utah | 45.2 |
| 8 | Vermont | 47.6 |
| 25 | Virginia | 46.9 |
| 31 | Washington | 46.6 |
| 27 | West Virginia | 46.8 |
| 22 | Wisconsin | 47.0 |
| 31 | Wyoming | 46.6 |

RANK ORDER

| RANK | STATE | PERCENT |
|------|-------|---------|
| 1 | Hawaii | 50.1 |
| 2 | Maryland | 48.4 |
| 3 | Louisiana | 48.3 |
| 4 | Connecticut | 47.9 |
| 5 | Georgia | 47.8 |
| 5 | Maine | 47.8 |
| 7 | South Carolina | 47.7 |
| 8 | Delaware | 47.6 |
| 8 | Mississippi | 47.6 |
| 8 | Rhode Island | 47.6 |
| 8 | Vermont | 47.6 |
| 12 | North Dakota | 47.5 |
| 12 | South Dakota | 47.5 |
| 14 | Tennessee | 47.4 |
| 15 | Kansas | 47.3 |
| 15 | Massachusetts | 47.3 |
| 15 | Ohio | 47.3 |
| 18 | Minnesota | 47.2 |
| 18 | Nebraska | 47.2 |
| 20 | Illinois | 47.1 |
| 20 | Pennsylvania | 47.1 |
| 22 | New York | 47.0 |
| 22 | Oklahoma | 47.0 |
| 22 | Wisconsin | 47.0 |
| 25 | Alabama | 46.9 |
| 25 | Virginia | 46.9 |
| 27 | New Mexico | 46.8 |
| 27 | North Carolina | 46.8 |
| 27 | West Virginia | 46.8 |
| 30 | New Hampshire | 46.7 |
| 31 | Arkansas | 46.6 |
| 31 | Iowa | 46.6 |
| 31 | Montana | 46.6 |
| 31 | Washington | 46.6 |
| 31 | Wyoming | 46.6 |
| 36 | Florida | 46.5 |
| 37 | Indiana | 46.4 |
| 37 | New Jersey | 46.4 |
| 39 | Arizona | 46.2 |
| 40 | Alaska | 46.0 |
| 41 | Missouri | 45.8 |
| 41 | Oregon | 45.8 |
| 43 | Colorado | 45.6 |
| 43 | Michigan | 45.6 |
| 45 | Kentucky | 45.5 |
| 46 | Texas | 45.3 |
| 47 | Utah | 45.2 |
| 48 | Nevada | 45.1 |
| 49 | California | 45.0 |
| 50 | Idaho | 44.6 |

District of Columbia — 51.4

Source: Morgan Quitno Press using data from U.S. Department of Labor, Bureau of Labor Statistics
"Geographic Profiles of Employment and Unemployment, 1999"
*Annual averages.

# Job Growth: 1999 to 2000

## National Percent Change = 1.4% Increase*

ALPHA ORDER

| RANK | STATE | PERCENT CHANGE |
|------|-------|----------------|
| 47 | Alabama | 0.0 |
| 29 | Alaska | 1.3 |
| 2 | Arizona | 3.7 |
| 11 | Arkansas | 2.1 |
| 5 | California | 3.1 |
| 9 | Colorado | 2.3 |
| 34 | Connecticut | 1.0 |
| 23 | Delaware | 1.6 |
| 2 | Florida | 3.7 |
| 32 | Georgia | 1.2 |
| 10 | Hawaii | 2.2 |
| 4 | Idaho | 3.5 |
| 38 | Illinois | 0.7 |
| 46 | Indiana | 0.1 |
| 16 | Iowa | 1.9 |
| 16 | Kansas | 1.9 |
| 23 | Kentucky | 1.6 |
| 35 | Louisiana | 0.9 |
| 19 | Maine | 1.8 |
| 11 | Maryland | 2.1 |
| 21 | Massachusetts | 1.7 |
| 43 | Michigan | 0.4 |
| 26 | Minnesota | 1.5 |
| 49 | Mississippi | (0.8) |
| 33 | Missouri | 1.1 |
| 21 | Montana | 1.7 |
| 50 | Nebraska | (0.9) |
| 1 | Nevada | 4.9 |
| 44 | New Hampshire | 0.3 |
| 29 | New Jersey | 1.3 |
| 13 | New Mexico | 2.0 |
| 19 | New York | 1.8 |
| 40 | North Carolina | 0.6 |
| 48 | North Dakota | (0.1) |
| 42 | Ohio | 0.5 |
| 29 | Oklahoma | 1.3 |
| 40 | Oregon | 0.6 |
| 44 | Pennsylvania | 0.3 |
| 26 | Rhode Island | 1.5 |
| 23 | South Carolina | 1.6 |
| 38 | South Dakota | 0.7 |
| 36 | Tennessee | 0.8 |
| 6 | Texas | 2.8 |
| 7 | Utah | 2.4 |
| 16 | Vermont | 1.9 |
| 13 | Virginia | 2.0 |
| 13 | Washington | 2.0 |
| 36 | West Virginia | 0.8 |
| 28 | Wisconsin | 1.4 |
| 7 | Wyoming | 2.4 |

RANK ORDER

| RANK | STATE | PERCENT CHANGE |
|------|-------|----------------|
| 1 | Nevada | 4.9 |
| 2 | Arizona | 3.7 |
| 2 | Florida | 3.7 |
| 4 | Idaho | 3.5 |
| 5 | California | 3.1 |
| 6 | Texas | 2.8 |
| 7 | Utah | 2.4 |
| 7 | Wyoming | 2.4 |
| 9 | Colorado | 2.3 |
| 10 | Hawaii | 2.2 |
| 11 | Arkansas | 2.1 |
| 11 | Maryland | 2.1 |
| 13 | New Mexico | 2.0 |
| 13 | Virginia | 2.0 |
| 13 | Washington | 2.0 |
| 16 | Iowa | 1.9 |
| 16 | Kansas | 1.9 |
| 16 | Vermont | 1.9 |
| 19 | Maine | 1.8 |
| 19 | New York | 1.8 |
| 21 | Massachusetts | 1.7 |
| 21 | Montana | 1.7 |
| 23 | Delaware | 1.6 |
| 23 | Kentucky | 1.6 |
| 23 | South Carolina | 1.6 |
| 26 | Minnesota | 1.5 |
| 26 | Rhode Island | 1.5 |
| 28 | Wisconsin | 1.4 |
| 29 | Alaska | 1.3 |
| 29 | New Jersey | 1.3 |
| 29 | Oklahoma | 1.3 |
| 32 | Georgia | 1.2 |
| 33 | Missouri | 1.1 |
| 34 | Connecticut | 1.0 |
| 35 | Louisiana | 0.9 |
| 36 | Tennessee | 0.8 |
| 36 | West Virginia | 0.8 |
| 38 | Illinois | 0.7 |
| 38 | South Dakota | 0.7 |
| 40 | North Carolina | 0.6 |
| 40 | Oregon | 0.6 |
| 42 | Ohio | 0.5 |
| 43 | Michigan | 0.4 |
| 44 | New Hampshire | 0.3 |
| 44 | Pennsylvania | 0.3 |
| 46 | Indiana | 0.1 |
| 47 | Alabama | 0.0 |
| 48 | North Dakota | (0.1) |
| 49 | Mississippi | (0.8) |
| 50 | Nebraska | (0.9) |

| District of Columbia | 1.0 |
|---|---|

*Source: Morgan Quitno Press using data from U.S. Department of Labor, Bureau of Labor Statistics*
    *"Regional and State Employment and Unemployment" (press release, January 19, 2001)*
*Nonfarm jobs. December 1999 to December 2000, seasonally adjusted. National figure based on nonfarm*
*employment from a different survey.*

# Employees on Nonfarm Payrolls in 2000

## National Total = 131,861,000 Employees*

ALPHA ORDER

| RANK | STATE | EMPLOYEES | % of USA |
|---|---|---|---|
| 23 | Alabama | 1,941,300 | 1.5% |
| 49 | Alaska | 284,000 | 0.2% |
| 21 | Arizona | 2,285,600 | 1.7% |
| 32 | Arkansas | 1,177,500 | 0.9% |
| 1 | California | 14,614,400 | 11.1% |
| 22 | Colorado | 2,216,900 | 1.7% |
| 27 | Connecticut | 1,697,300 | 1.3% |
| 44 | Delaware | 424,100 | 0.3% |
| 4 | Florida | 7,278,900 | 5.5% |
| 9 | Georgia | 3,993,600 | 3.0% |
| 42 | Hawaii | 548,500 | 0.4% |
| 41 | Idaho | 568,200 | 0.4% |
| 5 | Illinois | 6,026,000 | 4.6% |
| 14 | Indiana | 2,989,700 | 2.3% |
| 29 | Iowa | 1,501,600 | 1.1% |
| 31 | Kansas | 1,365,100 | 1.0% |
| 26 | Kentucky | 1,843,500 | 1.4% |
| 24 | Louisiana | 1,923,800 | 1.5% |
| 40 | Maine | 603,700 | 0.5% |
| 20 | Maryland | 2,460,100 | 1.9% |
| 13 | Massachusetts | 3,320,500 | 2.5% |
| 8 | Michigan | 4,600,300 | 3.5% |
| 19 | Minnesota | 2,673,500 | 2.0% |
| 33 | Mississippi | 1,147,800 | 0.9% |
| 16 | Missouri | 2,770,300 | 2.1% |
| 45 | Montana | 393,200 | 0.3% |
| 36 | Nebraska | 886,400 | 0.7% |
| 35 | Nevada | 1,056,500 | 0.8% |
| 39 | New Hampshire | 612,600 | 0.5% |
| 10 | New Jersey | 3,949,100 | 3.0% |
| 37 | New Mexico | 750,500 | 0.6% |
| 3 | New York | 8,683,200 | 6.6% |
| 11 | North Carolina | 3,910,300 | 3.0% |
| 47 | North Dakota | 325,800 | 0.2% |
| 6 | Ohio | 5,605,800 | 4.3% |
| 30 | Oklahoma | 1,495,200 | 1.1% |
| 28 | Oregon | 1,598,000 | 1.2% |
| 7 | Pennsylvania | 5,597,300 | 4.2% |
| 43 | Rhode Island | 474,600 | 0.4% |
| 25 | South Carolina | 1,885,200 | 1.4% |
| 46 | South Dakota | 381,300 | 0.3% |
| 18 | Tennessee | 2,714,500 | 2.1% |
| 2 | Texas | 9,521,000 | 7.2% |
| 34 | Utah | 1,087,200 | 0.8% |
| 48 | Vermont | 297,800 | 0.2% |
| 12 | Virginia | 3,511,100 | 2.7% |
| 17 | Washington | 2,718,900 | 2.1% |
| 38 | West Virginia | 734,100 | 0.6% |
| 15 | Wisconsin | 2,833,300 | 2.1% |
| 50 | Wyoming | 240,700 | 0.2% |

RANK ORDER

| RANK | STATE | EMPLOYEES | % of USA |
|---|---|---|---|
| 1 | California | 14,614,400 | 11.1% |
| 2 | Texas | 9,521,000 | 7.2% |
| 3 | New York | 8,683,200 | 6.6% |
| 4 | Florida | 7,278,900 | 5.5% |
| 5 | Illinois | 6,026,000 | 4.6% |
| 6 | Ohio | 5,605,800 | 4.3% |
| 7 | Pennsylvania | 5,597,300 | 4.2% |
| 8 | Michigan | 4,600,300 | 3.5% |
| 9 | Georgia | 3,993,600 | 3.0% |
| 10 | New Jersey | 3,949,100 | 3.0% |
| 11 | North Carolina | 3,910,300 | 3.0% |
| 12 | Virginia | 3,511,100 | 2.7% |
| 13 | Massachusetts | 3,320,500 | 2.5% |
| 14 | Indiana | 2,989,700 | 2.3% |
| 15 | Wisconsin | 2,833,300 | 2.1% |
| 16 | Missouri | 2,770,300 | 2.1% |
| 17 | Washington | 2,718,900 | 2.1% |
| 18 | Tennessee | 2,714,500 | 2.1% |
| 19 | Minnesota | 2,673,500 | 2.0% |
| 20 | Maryland | 2,460,100 | 1.9% |
| 21 | Arizona | 2,285,600 | 1.7% |
| 22 | Colorado | 2,216,900 | 1.7% |
| 23 | Alabama | 1,941,300 | 1.5% |
| 24 | Louisiana | 1,923,800 | 1.5% |
| 25 | South Carolina | 1,885,200 | 1.4% |
| 26 | Kentucky | 1,843,500 | 1.4% |
| 27 | Connecticut | 1,697,300 | 1.3% |
| 28 | Oregon | 1,598,000 | 1.2% |
| 29 | Iowa | 1,501,600 | 1.1% |
| 30 | Oklahoma | 1,495,200 | 1.1% |
| 31 | Kansas | 1,365,100 | 1.0% |
| 32 | Arkansas | 1,177,500 | 0.9% |
| 33 | Mississippi | 1,147,800 | 0.9% |
| 34 | Utah | 1,087,200 | 0.8% |
| 35 | Nevada | 1,056,500 | 0.8% |
| 36 | Nebraska | 886,400 | 0.7% |
| 37 | New Mexico | 750,500 | 0.6% |
| 38 | West Virginia | 734,100 | 0.6% |
| 39 | New Hampshire | 612,600 | 0.5% |
| 40 | Maine | 603,700 | 0.5% |
| 41 | Idaho | 568,200 | 0.4% |
| 42 | Hawaii | 548,500 | 0.4% |
| 43 | Rhode Island | 474,600 | 0.4% |
| 44 | Delaware | 424,100 | 0.3% |
| 45 | Montana | 393,200 | 0.3% |
| 46 | South Dakota | 381,300 | 0.3% |
| 47 | North Dakota | 325,800 | 0.2% |
| 48 | Vermont | 297,800 | 0.2% |
| 49 | Alaska | 284,000 | 0.2% |
| 50 | Wyoming | 240,700 | 0.2% |
| | District of Columbia | 627,100 | 0.5% |

*Source: U.S. Department of Labor, Bureau of Labor Statistics*
*"Regional and State Employment and Unemployment" (press release, January 19, 2001)*
*\*Seasonally adjusted preliminary data as of December 2000. National total calculated through a different formula.*

# Employees in Construction in 2000

## National Total = 6,716,000 Employees*

ALPHA ORDER

| RANK | STATE | EMPLOYEES | % of USA |
|------|-------|-----------|----------|
| 25 | Alabama | 106,800 | 1.6% |
| 50 | Alaska | 14,100 | 0.2% |
| 14 | Arizona | 160,100 | 2.4% |
| 34 | Arkansas | 55,500 | 0.8% |
| 1 | California | 762,600 | 11.4% |
| 13 | Colorado | 162,100 | 2.4% |
| 32 | Connecticut | 64,600 | 1.0% |
| 42 | Delaware | 24,200 | 0.4% |
| 3 | Florida | 380,500 | 5.7% |
| 10 | Georgia | 200,500 | 3.0% |
| 43 | Hawaii** | 23,300 | 0.3% |
| 38 | Idaho | 39,400 | 0.6% |
| 5 | Illinois | 256,600 | 3.8% |
| 17 | Indiana | 145,700 | 2.2% |
| 30 | Iowa | 69,800 | 1.0% |
| 31 | Kansas | 69,400 | 1.0% |
| 28 | Kentucky | 87,800 | 1.3% |
| 18 | Louisiana | 132,700 | 2.0% |
| 40 | Maine | 31,600 | 0.5% |
| 15 | Maryland | 157,800 | 2.3% |
| 21 | Massachusetts | 131,400 | 2.0% |
| 11 | Michigan | 197,400 | 2.9% |
| 24 | Minnesota | 119,700 | 1.8% |
| 35 | Mississippi | 52,300 | 0.8% |
| 19 | Missouri | 132,600 | 2.0% |
| 44 | Montana | 20,300 | 0.3% |
| 37 | Nebraska | 41,300 | 0.6% |
| 26 | Nevada | 93,900 | 1.4% |
| 41 | New Hampshire | 26,200 | 0.4% |
| 16 | New Jersey | 147,500 | 2.2% |
| 36 | New Mexico | 45,600 | 0.7% |
| 4 | New York | 334,800 | 5.0% |
| 8 | North Carolina | 232,900 | 3.5% |
| 48 | North Dakota | 16,200 | 0.2% |
| 6 | Ohio | 240,500 | 3.6% |
| 33 | Oklahoma | 60,700 | 0.9% |
| 27 | Oregon | 88,300 | 1.3% |
| 7 | Pennsylvania | 238,800 | 3.6% |
| 45 | Rhode Island | 19,300 | 0.3% |
| 23 | South Carolina | 122,500 | 1.8% |
| 46 | South Dakota | 17,800 | 0.3% |
| 20 | Tennessee | 131,600 | 2.0% |
| 2 | Texas | 563,200 | 8.4% |
| 29 | Utah | 74,800 | 1.1% |
| 49 | Vermont | 14,400 | 0.2% |
| 9 | Virginia | 209,800 | 3.1% |
| 12 | Washington | 167,700 | 2.5% |
| 39 | West Virginia | 34,500 | 0.5% |
| 22 | Wisconsin | 123,500 | 1.8% |
| 47 | Wyoming | 17,600 | 0.3% |

RANK ORDER

| RANK | STATE | EMPLOYEES | % of USA |
|------|-------|-----------|----------|
| 1 | California | 762,600 | 11.4% |
| 2 | Texas | 563,200 | 8.4% |
| 3 | Florida | 380,500 | 5.7% |
| 4 | New York | 334,800 | 5.0% |
| 5 | Illinois | 256,600 | 3.8% |
| 6 | Ohio | 240,500 | 3.6% |
| 7 | Pennsylvania | 238,800 | 3.6% |
| 8 | North Carolina | 232,900 | 3.5% |
| 9 | Virginia | 209,800 | 3.1% |
| 10 | Georgia | 200,500 | 3.0% |
| 11 | Michigan | 197,400 | 2.9% |
| 12 | Washington | 167,700 | 2.5% |
| 13 | Colorado | 162,100 | 2.4% |
| 14 | Arizona | 160,100 | 2.4% |
| 15 | Maryland | 157,800 | 2.3% |
| 16 | New Jersey | 147,500 | 2.2% |
| 17 | Indiana | 145,700 | 2.2% |
| 18 | Louisiana | 132,700 | 2.0% |
| 19 | Missouri | 132,600 | 2.0% |
| 20 | Tennessee | 131,600 | 2.0% |
| 21 | Massachusetts | 131,400 | 2.0% |
| 22 | Wisconsin | 123,500 | 1.8% |
| 23 | South Carolina | 122,500 | 1.8% |
| 24 | Minnesota | 119,700 | 1.8% |
| 25 | Alabama | 106,800 | 1.6% |
| 26 | Nevada | 93,900 | 1.4% |
| 27 | Oregon | 88,300 | 1.3% |
| 28 | Kentucky | 87,800 | 1.3% |
| 29 | Utah | 74,800 | 1.1% |
| 30 | Iowa | 69,800 | 1.0% |
| 31 | Kansas | 69,400 | 1.0% |
| 32 | Connecticut | 64,600 | 1.0% |
| 33 | Oklahoma | 60,700 | 0.9% |
| 34 | Arkansas | 55,500 | 0.8% |
| 35 | Mississippi | 52,300 | 0.8% |
| 36 | New Mexico | 45,600 | 0.7% |
| 37 | Nebraska | 41,300 | 0.6% |
| 38 | Idaho | 39,400 | 0.6% |
| 39 | West Virginia | 34,500 | 0.5% |
| 40 | Maine | 31,600 | 0.5% |
| 41 | New Hampshire | 26,200 | 0.4% |
| 42 | Delaware | 24,200 | 0.4% |
| 43 | Hawaii** | 23,300 | 0.3% |
| 44 | Montana | 20,300 | 0.3% |
| 45 | Rhode Island | 19,300 | 0.3% |
| 46 | South Dakota | 17,800 | 0.3% |
| 47 | Wyoming | 17,600 | 0.3% |
| 48 | North Dakota | 16,200 | 0.2% |
| 49 | Vermont | 14,400 | 0.2% |
| 50 | Alaska | 14,100 | 0.2% |
| | District of Columbia | 10,200 | 0.2% |

Source: U.S. Department of Labor, Bureau of Labor Statistics
"Regional and State Employment and Unemployment" (press release, January 19, 2001)
*Seasonally adjusted preliminary data as of December 2000.  National total calculated through a different formula.
**Hawaii's figure includes employees in mining.

# Percent of Nonfarm Employees in Construction in 2000

## National Percent = 5.1% of Employees*

ALPHA ORDER

| RANK | STATE | PERCENT |
|------|-------|---------|
| 16 | Alabama | 5.5 |
| 23 | Alaska | 5.0 |
| 4 | Arizona | 7.0 |
| 31 | Arkansas | 4.7 |
| 18 | California | 5.2 |
| 2 | Colorado | 7.3 |
| 49 | Connecticut | 3.8 |
| 15 | Delaware | 5.7 |
| 18 | Florida | 5.2 |
| 23 | Georgia | 5.0 |
| 44 | Hawaii** | 4.2 |
| 5 | Idaho | 6.9 |
| 39 | Illinois | 4.3 |
| 26 | Indiana | 4.9 |
| 35 | Iowa | 4.6 |
| 22 | Kansas | 5.1 |
| 27 | Kentucky | 4.8 |
| 5 | Louisiana | 6.9 |
| 18 | Maine | 5.2 |
| 9 | Maryland | 6.4 |
| 47 | Massachusetts | 4.0 |
| 39 | Michigan | 4.3 |
| 37 | Minnesota | 4.5 |
| 35 | Mississippi | 4.6 |
| 27 | Missouri | 4.8 |
| 18 | Montana | 5.2 |
| 31 | Nebraska | 4.7 |
| 1 | Nevada | 8.9 |
| 39 | New Hampshire | 4.3 |
| 50 | New Jersey | 3.7 |
| 11 | New Mexico | 6.1 |
| 48 | New York | 3.9 |
| 12 | North Carolina | 6.0 |
| 23 | North Dakota | 5.0 |
| 39 | Ohio | 4.3 |
| 45 | Oklahoma | 4.1 |
| 16 | Oregon | 5.5 |
| 39 | Pennsylvania | 4.3 |
| 45 | Rhode Island | 4.1 |
| 8 | South Carolina | 6.5 |
| 31 | South Dakota | 4.7 |
| 27 | Tennessee | 4.8 |
| 14 | Texas | 5.9 |
| 5 | Utah | 6.9 |
| 27 | Vermont | 4.8 |
| 12 | Virginia | 6.0 |
| 10 | Washington | 6.2 |
| 31 | West Virginia | 4.7 |
| 38 | Wisconsin | 4.4 |
| 2 | Wyoming | 7.3 |

RANK ORDER

| RANK | STATE | PERCENT |
|------|-------|---------|
| 1 | Nevada | 8.9 |
| 2 | Colorado | 7.3 |
| 2 | Wyoming | 7.3 |
| 4 | Arizona | 7.0 |
| 5 | Idaho | 6.9 |
| 5 | Louisiana | 6.9 |
| 5 | Utah | 6.9 |
| 8 | South Carolina | 6.5 |
| 9 | Maryland | 6.4 |
| 10 | Washington | 6.2 |
| 11 | New Mexico | 6.1 |
| 12 | North Carolina | 6.0 |
| 12 | Virginia | 6.0 |
| 14 | Texas | 5.9 |
| 15 | Delaware | 5.7 |
| 16 | Alabama | 5.5 |
| 16 | Oregon | 5.5 |
| 18 | California | 5.2 |
| 18 | Florida | 5.2 |
| 18 | Maine | 5.2 |
| 18 | Montana | 5.2 |
| 22 | Kansas | 5.1 |
| 23 | Alaska | 5.0 |
| 23 | Georgia | 5.0 |
| 23 | North Dakota | 5.0 |
| 26 | Indiana | 4.9 |
| 27 | Kentucky | 4.8 |
| 27 | Missouri | 4.8 |
| 27 | Tennessee | 4.8 |
| 27 | Vermont | 4.8 |
| 31 | Arkansas | 4.7 |
| 31 | Nebraska | 4.7 |
| 31 | South Dakota | 4.7 |
| 31 | West Virginia | 4.7 |
| 35 | Iowa | 4.6 |
| 35 | Mississippi | 4.6 |
| 37 | Minnesota | 4.5 |
| 38 | Wisconsin | 4.4 |
| 39 | Illinois | 4.3 |
| 39 | Michigan | 4.3 |
| 39 | New Hampshire | 4.3 |
| 39 | Ohio | 4.3 |
| 39 | Pennsylvania | 4.3 |
| 44 | Hawaii** | 4.2 |
| 45 | Oklahoma | 4.1 |
| 45 | Rhode Island | 4.1 |
| 47 | Massachusetts | 4.0 |
| 48 | New York | 3.9 |
| 49 | Connecticut | 3.8 |
| 50 | New Jersey | 3.7 |
| | District of Columbia | 1.6 |

Source: Morgan Quitno Press using data from U.S. Department of Labor, Bureau of Labor Statistics
    "Regional and State Employment and Unemployment" (press release, January 19, 2001)
*Seasonally adjusted preliminary data as of December 2000. National percent calculated through a different formula.
**Hawaii's figure includes employees in mining.

# Employees in Finance, Insurance and Real Estate in 2000

## National Total = 7,660,000 Employees*

ALPHA ORDER

| RANK | STATE | EMPLOYEES | % of USA |
|---|---|---|---|
| 25 | Alabama | 92,600 | 1.2% |
| 48 | Alaska | 12,800 | 0.2% |
| 17 | Arizona | 148,300 | 1.9% |
| 35 | Arkansas | 47,900 | 0.6% |
| 1 | California | 840,700 | 11.0% |
| 22 | Colorado | 140,900 | 1.8% |
| 19 | Connecticut | 142,300 | 1.9% |
| 34 | Delaware | 51,600 | 0.7% |
| 4 | Florida | 469,600 | 6.1% |
| 11 | Georgia | 205,500 | 2.7% |
| 38 | Hawaii | 34,500 | 0.5% |
| 45 | Idaho | 23,800 | 0.3% |
| 5 | Illinois | 409,200 | 5.3% |
| 18 | Indiana | 145,100 | 1.9% |
| 26 | Iowa | 86,800 | 1.1% |
| 31 | Kansas | 64,600 | 0.8% |
| 30 | Kentucky | 72,100 | 0.9% |
| 27 | Louisiana | 85,500 | 1.1% |
| 41 | Maine | 31,100 | 0.4% |
| 21 | Maryland | 141,000 | 1.8% |
| 9 | Massachusetts | 232,000 | 3.0% |
| 10 | Michigan | 208,300 | 2.7% |
| 15 | Minnesota | 160,200 | 2.1% |
| 37 | Mississippi | 42,400 | 0.6% |
| 14 | Missouri | 170,100 | 2.2% |
| 46 | Montana | 18,400 | 0.2% |
| 32 | Nebraska | 60,600 | 0.8% |
| 36 | Nevada | 45,500 | 0.6% |
| 39 | New Hampshire | 33,400 | 0.4% |
| 8 | New Jersey | 262,300 | 3.4% |
| 40 | New Mexico | 33,000 | 0.4% |
| 2 | New York | 754,000 | 9.8% |
| 12 | North Carolina | 192,600 | 2.5% |
| 47 | North Dakota | 16,400 | 0.2% |
| 7 | Ohio | 315,000 | 4.1% |
| 29 | Oklahoma | 75,300 | 1.0% |
| 24 | Oregon | 96,100 | 1.3% |
| 6 | Pennsylvania | 325,000 | 4.2% |
| 43 | Rhode Island | 29,800 | 0.4% |
| 28 | South Carolina | 84,200 | 1.1% |
| 44 | South Dakota | 25,900 | 0.3% |
| 23 | Tennessee | 131,000 | 1.7% |
| 3 | Texas | 541,100 | 7.1% |
| 33 | Utah | 58,100 | 0.8% |
| 49 | Vermont | 12,600 | 0.2% |
| 13 | Virginia | 190,500 | 2.5% |
| 20 | Washington | 141,100 | 1.8% |
| 42 | West Virginia | 29,900 | 0.4% |
| 16 | Wisconsin | 152,500 | 2.0% |
| 50 | Wyoming | 8,500 | 0.1% |

RANK ORDER

| RANK | STATE | EMPLOYEES | % of USA |
|---|---|---|---|
| 1 | California | 840,700 | 11.0% |
| 2 | New York | 754,000 | 9.8% |
| 3 | Texas | 541,100 | 7.1% |
| 4 | Florida | 469,600 | 6.1% |
| 5 | Illinois | 409,200 | 5.3% |
| 6 | Pennsylvania | 325,000 | 4.2% |
| 7 | Ohio | 315,000 | 4.1% |
| 8 | New Jersey | 262,300 | 3.4% |
| 9 | Massachusetts | 232,000 | 3.0% |
| 10 | Michigan | 208,300 | 2.7% |
| 11 | Georgia | 205,500 | 2.7% |
| 12 | North Carolina | 192,600 | 2.5% |
| 13 | Virginia | 190,500 | 2.5% |
| 14 | Missouri | 170,100 | 2.2% |
| 15 | Minnesota | 160,200 | 2.1% |
| 16 | Wisconsin | 152,500 | 2.0% |
| 17 | Arizona | 148,300 | 1.9% |
| 18 | Indiana | 145,100 | 1.9% |
| 19 | Connecticut | 142,300 | 1.9% |
| 20 | Washington | 141,100 | 1.8% |
| 21 | Maryland | 141,000 | 1.8% |
| 22 | Colorado | 140,900 | 1.8% |
| 23 | Tennessee | 131,000 | 1.7% |
| 24 | Oregon | 96,100 | 1.3% |
| 25 | Alabama | 92,600 | 1.2% |
| 26 | Iowa | 86,800 | 1.1% |
| 27 | Louisiana | 85,500 | 1.1% |
| 28 | South Carolina | 84,200 | 1.1% |
| 29 | Oklahoma | 75,300 | 1.0% |
| 30 | Kentucky | 72,100 | 0.9% |
| 31 | Kansas | 64,600 | 0.8% |
| 32 | Nebraska | 60,600 | 0.8% |
| 33 | Utah | 58,100 | 0.8% |
| 34 | Delaware | 51,600 | 0.7% |
| 35 | Arkansas | 47,900 | 0.6% |
| 36 | Nevada | 45,500 | 0.6% |
| 37 | Mississippi | 42,400 | 0.6% |
| 38 | Hawaii | 34,500 | 0.5% |
| 39 | New Hampshire | 33,400 | 0.4% |
| 40 | New Mexico | 33,000 | 0.4% |
| 41 | Maine | 31,100 | 0.4% |
| 42 | West Virginia | 29,900 | 0.4% |
| 43 | Rhode Island | 29,800 | 0.4% |
| 44 | South Dakota | 25,900 | 0.3% |
| 45 | Idaho | 23,800 | 0.3% |
| 46 | Montana | 18,400 | 0.2% |
| 47 | North Dakota | 16,400 | 0.2% |
| 48 | Alaska | 12,800 | 0.2% |
| 49 | Vermont | 12,600 | 0.2% |
| 50 | Wyoming | 8,500 | 0.1% |
| | District of Columbia | 32,300 | 0.4% |

Source: U.S. Department of Labor, Bureau of Labor Statistics
  "Regional and State Employment and Unemployment" (press release, January 19, 2001)
*Seasonally adjusted preliminary data as of December 2000.  National total calculated through a different formula.

# Percent of Nonfarm Employees in Finance, Insurance and Real Estate in 2000

## National Percent = 5.8% of Employees*

ALPHA ORDER

| RANK | STATE | PERCENT |
|------|-------|---------|
| 34 | Alabama | 4.8 |
| 38 | Alaska | 4.5 |
| 9 | Arizona | 6.5 |
| 46 | Arkansas | 4.1 |
| 17 | California | 5.8 |
| 11 | Colorado | 6.4 |
| 3 | Connecticut | 8.4 |
| 1 | Delaware | 12.2 |
| 9 | Florida | 6.5 |
| 29 | Georgia | 5.1 |
| 12 | Hawaii | 6.3 |
| 44 | Idaho | 4.2 |
| 5 | Illinois | 6.8 |
| 32 | Indiana | 4.9 |
| 17 | Iowa | 5.8 |
| 36 | Kansas | 4.7 |
| 48 | Kentucky | 3.9 |
| 41 | Louisiana | 4.4 |
| 27 | Maine | 5.2 |
| 20 | Maryland | 5.7 |
| 4 | Massachusetts | 7.0 |
| 38 | Michigan | 4.5 |
| 15 | Minnesota | 6.0 |
| 49 | Mississippi | 3.7 |
| 14 | Missouri | 6.1 |
| 36 | Montana | 4.7 |
| 5 | Nebraska | 6.8 |
| 43 | Nevada | 4.3 |
| 23 | New Hampshire | 5.5 |
| 8 | New Jersey | 6.6 |
| 41 | New Mexico | 4.4 |
| 2 | New York | 8.7 |
| 32 | North Carolina | 4.9 |
| 30 | North Dakota | 5.0 |
| 22 | Ohio | 5.6 |
| 30 | Oklahoma | 5.0 |
| 15 | Oregon | 6.0 |
| 17 | Pennsylvania | 5.8 |
| 12 | Rhode Island | 6.3 |
| 38 | South Carolina | 4.5 |
| 5 | South Dakota | 6.8 |
| 34 | Tennessee | 4.8 |
| 20 | Texas | 5.7 |
| 26 | Utah | 5.3 |
| 44 | Vermont | 4.2 |
| 24 | Virginia | 5.4 |
| 27 | Washington | 5.2 |
| 46 | West Virginia | 4.1 |
| 24 | Wisconsin | 5.4 |
| 50 | Wyoming | 3.5 |

RANK ORDER

| RANK | STATE | PERCENT |
|------|-------|---------|
| 1 | Delaware | 12.2 |
| 2 | New York | 8.7 |
| 3 | Connecticut | 8.4 |
| 4 | Massachusetts | 7.0 |
| 5 | Illinois | 6.8 |
| 5 | Nebraska | 6.8 |
| 5 | South Dakota | 6.8 |
| 8 | New Jersey | 6.6 |
| 9 | Arizona | 6.5 |
| 9 | Florida | 6.5 |
| 11 | Colorado | 6.4 |
| 12 | Hawaii | 6.3 |
| 12 | Rhode Island | 6.3 |
| 14 | Missouri | 6.1 |
| 15 | Minnesota | 6.0 |
| 15 | Oregon | 6.0 |
| 17 | California | 5.8 |
| 17 | Iowa | 5.8 |
| 17 | Pennsylvania | 5.8 |
| 20 | Maryland | 5.7 |
| 20 | Texas | 5.7 |
| 22 | Ohio | 5.6 |
| 23 | New Hampshire | 5.5 |
| 24 | Virginia | 5.4 |
| 24 | Wisconsin | 5.4 |
| 26 | Utah | 5.3 |
| 27 | Maine | 5.2 |
| 27 | Washington | 5.2 |
| 29 | Georgia | 5.1 |
| 30 | North Dakota | 5.0 |
| 30 | Oklahoma | 5.0 |
| 32 | Indiana | 4.9 |
| 32 | North Carolina | 4.9 |
| 34 | Alabama | 4.8 |
| 34 | Tennessee | 4.8 |
| 36 | Kansas | 4.7 |
| 36 | Montana | 4.7 |
| 38 | Alaska | 4.5 |
| 38 | Michigan | 4.5 |
| 38 | South Carolina | 4.5 |
| 41 | Louisiana | 4.4 |
| 41 | New Mexico | 4.4 |
| 43 | Nevada | 4.3 |
| 44 | Idaho | 4.2 |
| 44 | Vermont | 4.2 |
| 46 | Arkansas | 4.1 |
| 46 | West Virginia | 4.1 |
| 48 | Kentucky | 3.9 |
| 49 | Mississippi | 3.7 |
| 50 | Wyoming | 3.5 |

District of Columbia 5.2

Source: Morgan Quitno Press using data from U.S. Department of Labor, Bureau of Labor Statistics
"Regional and State Employment and Unemployment" (press release, January 19, 2001)
*Seasonally adjusted preliminary data as of December 2000. National percent calculated through a different formula.

# Employees in Government in 2000

## National Total = 20,414,000 Employees*

ALPHA ORDER

| RANK | STATE | EMPLOYEES | % of USA |
|---|---|---|---|
| 23 | Alabama | 356,600 | 1.7% |
| 44 | Alaska | 74,100 | 0.4% |
| 22 | Arizona | 367,100 | 1.8% |
| 33 | Arkansas | 192,100 | 0.9% |
| 1 | California | 2,335,400 | 11.4% |
| 24 | Colorado | 350,400 | 1.7% |
| 30 | Connecticut | 243,200 | 1.2% |
| 49 | Delaware | 57,700 | 0.3% |
| 4 | Florida | 999,200 | 4.9% |
| 11 | Georgia | 595,800 | 2.9% |
| 39 | Hawaii | 114,600 | 0.6% |
| 40 | Idaho | 109,400 | 0.5% |
| 5 | Illinois | 834,200 | 4.1% |
| 18 | Indiana | 408,000 | 2.0% |
| 31 | Iowa | 242,800 | 1.2% |
| 29 | Kansas | 246,200 | 1.2% |
| 26 | Kentucky | 311,500 | 1.5% |
| 21 | Louisiana | 369,000 | 1.8% |
| 41 | Maine | 99,000 | 0.5% |
| 14 | Maryland | 450,500 | 2.2% |
| 16 | Massachusetts | 423,900 | 2.1% |
| 8 | Michigan | 682,100 | 3.3% |
| 20 | Minnesota | 394,000 | 1.9% |
| 32 | Mississippi | 232,100 | 1.1% |
| 15 | Missouri | 432,200 | 2.1% |
| 43 | Montana | 80,600 | 0.4% |
| 36 | Nebraska | 153,600 | 0.8% |
| 38 | Nevada | 125,600 | 0.6% |
| 42 | New Hampshire | 82,700 | 0.4% |
| 12 | New Jersey | 585,900 | 2.9% |
| 35 | New Mexico | 184,300 | 0.9% |
| 3 | New York | 1,447,600 | 7.1% |
| 10 | North Carolina | 623,500 | 3.1% |
| 45 | North Dakota | 73,500 | 0.4% |
| 6 | Ohio | 789,800 | 3.9% |
| 27 | Oklahoma | 288,300 | 1.4% |
| 28 | Oregon | 261,500 | 1.3% |
| 7 | Pennsylvania | 714,900 | 3.5% |
| 47 | Rhode Island | 63,100 | 0.3% |
| 25 | South Carolina | 313,200 | 1.5% |
| 46 | South Dakota | 72,500 | 0.4% |
| 19 | Tennessee | 398,000 | 1.9% |
| 2 | Texas | 1,592,700 | 7.8% |
| 34 | Utah | 185,600 | 0.9% |
| 50 | Vermont | 48,900 | 0.2% |
| 9 | Virginia | 629,800 | 3.1% |
| 13 | Washington | 482,500 | 2.4% |
| 37 | West Virginia | 140,400 | 0.7% |
| 17 | Wisconsin | 414,000 | 2.0% |
| 48 | Wyoming | 60,100 | 0.3% |

RANK ORDER

| RANK | STATE | EMPLOYEES | % of USA |
|---|---|---|---|
| 1 | California | 2,335,400 | 11.4% |
| 2 | Texas | 1,592,700 | 7.8% |
| 3 | New York | 1,447,600 | 7.1% |
| 4 | Florida | 999,200 | 4.9% |
| 5 | Illinois | 834,200 | 4.1% |
| 6 | Ohio | 789,800 | 3.9% |
| 7 | Pennsylvania | 714,900 | 3.5% |
| 8 | Michigan | 682,100 | 3.3% |
| 9 | Virginia | 629,800 | 3.1% |
| 10 | North Carolina | 623,500 | 3.1% |
| 11 | Georgia | 595,800 | 2.9% |
| 12 | New Jersey | 585,900 | 2.9% |
| 13 | Washington | 482,500 | 2.4% |
| 14 | Maryland | 450,500 | 2.2% |
| 15 | Missouri | 432,200 | 2.1% |
| 16 | Massachusetts | 423,900 | 2.1% |
| 17 | Wisconsin | 414,000 | 2.0% |
| 18 | Indiana | 408,000 | 2.0% |
| 19 | Tennessee | 398,000 | 1.9% |
| 20 | Minnesota | 394,000 | 1.9% |
| 21 | Louisiana | 369,000 | 1.8% |
| 22 | Arizona | 367,100 | 1.8% |
| 23 | Alabama | 356,600 | 1.7% |
| 24 | Colorado | 350,400 | 1.7% |
| 25 | South Carolina | 313,200 | 1.5% |
| 26 | Kentucky | 311,500 | 1.5% |
| 27 | Oklahoma | 288,300 | 1.4% |
| 28 | Oregon | 261,500 | 1.3% |
| 29 | Kansas | 246,200 | 1.2% |
| 30 | Connecticut | 243,200 | 1.2% |
| 31 | Iowa | 242,800 | 1.2% |
| 32 | Mississippi | 232,100 | 1.1% |
| 33 | Arkansas | 192,100 | 0.9% |
| 34 | Utah | 185,600 | 0.9% |
| 35 | New Mexico | 184,300 | 0.9% |
| 36 | Nebraska | 153,600 | 0.8% |
| 37 | West Virginia | 140,400 | 0.7% |
| 38 | Nevada | 125,600 | 0.6% |
| 39 | Hawaii | 114,600 | 0.6% |
| 40 | Idaho | 109,400 | 0.5% |
| 41 | Maine | 99,000 | 0.5% |
| 42 | New Hampshire | 82,700 | 0.4% |
| 43 | Montana | 80,600 | 0.4% |
| 44 | Alaska | 74,100 | 0.4% |
| 45 | North Dakota | 73,500 | 0.4% |
| 46 | South Dakota | 72,500 | 0.4% |
| 47 | Rhode Island | 63,100 | 0.3% |
| 48 | Wyoming | 60,100 | 0.3% |
| 49 | Delaware | 57,700 | 0.3% |
| 50 | Vermont | 48,900 | 0.2% |
| | District of Columbia | 223,500 | 1.1% |

*Source: U.S. Department of Labor, Bureau of Labor Statistics*
   *"Regional and State Employment and Unemployment" (press release, January 19, 2001)*
*Seasonally adjusted preliminary data as of December 2000. National total calculated through a different formula.*

# Percent of Nonfarm Employees in Government in 2000

## National Percent = 15.5% of Employees*

ALPHA ORDER

| RANK | STATE | PERCENT |
|------|-------|---------|
| 13 | Alabama | 18.4 |
| 1 | Alaska | 26.1 |
| 29 | Arizona | 16.1 |
| 27 | Arkansas | 16.3 |
| 30 | California | 16.0 |
| 32 | Colorado | 15.8 |
| 40 | Connecticut | 14.3 |
| 44 | Delaware | 13.6 |
| 43 | Florida | 13.7 |
| 34 | Georgia | 14.9 |
| 5 | Hawaii | 20.9 |
| 8 | Idaho | 19.3 |
| 42 | Illinois | 13.8 |
| 44 | Indiana | 13.6 |
| 28 | Iowa | 16.2 |
| 15 | Kansas | 18.0 |
| 20 | Kentucky | 16.9 |
| 10 | Louisiana | 19.2 |
| 24 | Maine | 16.4 |
| 14 | Maryland | 18.3 |
| 48 | Massachusetts | 12.8 |
| 35 | Michigan | 14.8 |
| 37 | Minnesota | 14.7 |
| 7 | Mississippi | 20.2 |
| 33 | Missouri | 15.6 |
| 6 | Montana | 20.5 |
| 18 | Nebraska | 17.3 |
| 50 | Nevada | 11.9 |
| 46 | New Hampshire | 13.5 |
| 35 | New Jersey | 14.8 |
| 3 | New Mexico | 24.6 |
| 21 | New York | 16.7 |
| 31 | North Carolina | 15.9 |
| 4 | North Dakota | 22.6 |
| 41 | Ohio | 14.1 |
| 8 | Oklahoma | 19.3 |
| 24 | Oregon | 16.4 |
| 48 | Pennsylvania | 12.8 |
| 47 | Rhode Island | 13.3 |
| 23 | South Carolina | 16.6 |
| 12 | South Dakota | 19.0 |
| 37 | Tennessee | 14.7 |
| 21 | Texas | 16.7 |
| 19 | Utah | 17.1 |
| 24 | Vermont | 16.4 |
| 16 | Virginia | 17.9 |
| 17 | Washington | 17.7 |
| 11 | West Virginia | 19.1 |
| 39 | Wisconsin | 14.6 |
| 2 | Wyoming | 25.0 |

RANK ORDER

| RANK | STATE | PERCENT |
|------|-------|---------|
| 1 | Alaska | 26.1 |
| 2 | Wyoming | 25.0 |
| 3 | New Mexico | 24.6 |
| 4 | North Dakota | 22.6 |
| 5 | Hawaii | 20.9 |
| 6 | Montana | 20.5 |
| 7 | Mississippi | 20.2 |
| 8 | Idaho | 19.3 |
| 8 | Oklahoma | 19.3 |
| 10 | Louisiana | 19.2 |
| 11 | West Virginia | 19.1 |
| 12 | South Dakota | 19.0 |
| 13 | Alabama | 18.4 |
| 14 | Maryland | 18.3 |
| 15 | Kansas | 18.0 |
| 16 | Virginia | 17.9 |
| 17 | Washington | 17.7 |
| 18 | Nebraska | 17.3 |
| 19 | Utah | 17.1 |
| 20 | Kentucky | 16.9 |
| 21 | New York | 16.7 |
| 21 | Texas | 16.7 |
| 23 | South Carolina | 16.6 |
| 24 | Maine | 16.4 |
| 24 | Oregon | 16.4 |
| 24 | Vermont | 16.4 |
| 27 | Arkansas | 16.3 |
| 28 | Iowa | 16.2 |
| 29 | Arizona | 16.1 |
| 30 | California | 16.0 |
| 31 | North Carolina | 15.9 |
| 32 | Colorado | 15.8 |
| 33 | Missouri | 15.6 |
| 34 | Georgia | 14.9 |
| 35 | Michigan | 14.8 |
| 35 | New Jersey | 14.8 |
| 37 | Minnesota | 14.7 |
| 37 | Tennessee | 14.7 |
| 39 | Wisconsin | 14.6 |
| 40 | Connecticut | 14.3 |
| 41 | Ohio | 14.1 |
| 42 | Illinois | 13.8 |
| 43 | Florida | 13.7 |
| 44 | Delaware | 13.6 |
| 44 | Indiana | 13.6 |
| 46 | New Hampshire | 13.5 |
| 47 | Rhode Island | 13.3 |
| 48 | Massachusetts | 12.8 |
| 48 | Pennsylvania | 12.8 |
| 50 | Nevada | 11.9 |

| | District of Columbia | 35.6 |

Source: Morgan Quitno Press using data from U.S. Department of Labor, Bureau of Labor Statistics
    "Regional and State Employment and Unemployment" (press release, January 19, 2001)
*Seasonally adjusted preliminary data as of December 2000. National percent calculated through a different formula.

# Employees in Manufacturing in 2000

## National Total = 18,304,000 Employees*

ALPHA ORDER

| RANK | STATE | EMPLOYEES | % of USA |
|---|---|---|---|
| 19 | Alabama | 356,700 | 1.9% |
| 49 | Alaska | 13,900 | 0.1% |
| 28 | Arizona | 216,800 | 1.2% |
| 25 | Arkansas | 253,000 | 1.4% |
| 1 | California | 1,924,800 | 10.5% |
| 30 | Colorado | 205,400 | 1.1% |
| 23 | Connecticut | 263,400 | 1.4% |
| 41 | Delaware | 58,400 | 0.3% |
| 13 | Florida | 488,400 | 2.7% |
| 11 | Georgia | 598,000 | 3.3% |
| 48 | Hawaii | 16,900 | 0.1% |
| 39 | Idaho | 75,600 | 0.4% |
| 5 | Illinois | 946,700 | 5.2% |
| 9 | Indiana | 681,200 | 3.7% |
| 24 | Iowa | 261,700 | 1.4% |
| 29 | Kansas | 212,700 | 1.2% |
| 22 | Kentucky | 314,400 | 1.7% |
| 31 | Louisiana | 186,100 | 1.0% |
| 37 | Maine | 84,200 | 0.5% |
| 33 | Maryland | 175,100 | 1.0% |
| 16 | Massachusetts | 431,600 | 2.4% |
| 4 | Michigan | 952,000 | 5.2% |
| 15 | Minnesota | 439,400 | 2.4% |
| 27 | Mississippi | 236,600 | 1.3% |
| 17 | Missouri | 399,100 | 2.2% |
| 46 | Montana | 24,600 | 0.1% |
| 35 | Nebraska | 116,200 | 0.6% |
| 44 | Nevada | 45,000 | 0.2% |
| 36 | New Hampshire | 106,100 | 0.6% |
| 14 | New Jersey | 455,400 | 2.5% |
| 45 | New Mexico | 42,600 | 0.2% |
| 7 | New York | 873,500 | 4.8% |
| 8 | North Carolina | 764,400 | 4.2% |
| 47 | North Dakota | 24,200 | 0.1% |
| 3 | Ohio | 1,070,300 | 5.8% |
| 32 | Oklahoma | 182,800 | 1.0% |
| 26 | Oregon | 242,300 | 1.3% |
| 6 | Pennsylvania | 921,900 | 5.0% |
| 40 | Rhode Island | 73,800 | 0.4% |
| 21 | South Carolina | 338,800 | 1.9% |
| 42 | South Dakota | 49,100 | 0.3% |
| 12 | Tennessee | 496,600 | 2.7% |
| 2 | Texas | 1,086,900 | 5.9% |
| 34 | Utah | 131,800 | 0.7% |
| 43 | Vermont | 48,400 | 0.3% |
| 18 | Virginia | 391,300 | 2.1% |
| 20 | Washington | 347,500 | 1.9% |
| 38 | West Virginia | 81,000 | 0.4% |
| 10 | Wisconsin | 610,800 | 3.3% |
| 50 | Wyoming | 11,500 | 0.1% |

RANK ORDER

| RANK | STATE | EMPLOYEES | % of USA |
|---|---|---|---|
| 1 | California | 1,924,800 | 10.5% |
| 2 | Texas | 1,086,900 | 5.9% |
| 3 | Ohio | 1,070,300 | 5.8% |
| 4 | Michigan | 952,000 | 5.2% |
| 5 | Illinois | 946,700 | 5.2% |
| 6 | Pennsylvania | 921,900 | 5.0% |
| 7 | New York | 873,500 | 4.8% |
| 8 | North Carolina | 764,400 | 4.2% |
| 9 | Indiana | 681,200 | 3.7% |
| 10 | Wisconsin | 610,800 | 3.3% |
| 11 | Georgia | 598,000 | 3.3% |
| 12 | Tennessee | 496,600 | 2.7% |
| 13 | Florida | 488,400 | 2.7% |
| 14 | New Jersey | 455,400 | 2.5% |
| 15 | Minnesota | 439,400 | 2.4% |
| 16 | Massachusetts | 431,600 | 2.4% |
| 17 | Missouri | 399,100 | 2.2% |
| 18 | Virginia | 391,300 | 2.1% |
| 19 | Alabama | 356,700 | 1.9% |
| 20 | Washington | 347,500 | 1.9% |
| 21 | South Carolina | 338,800 | 1.9% |
| 22 | Kentucky | 314,400 | 1.7% |
| 23 | Connecticut | 263,400 | 1.4% |
| 24 | Iowa | 261,700 | 1.4% |
| 25 | Arkansas | 253,000 | 1.4% |
| 26 | Oregon | 242,300 | 1.3% |
| 27 | Mississippi | 236,600 | 1.3% |
| 28 | Arizona | 216,800 | 1.2% |
| 29 | Kansas | 212,700 | 1.2% |
| 30 | Colorado | 205,400 | 1.1% |
| 31 | Louisiana | 186,100 | 1.0% |
| 32 | Oklahoma | 182,800 | 1.0% |
| 33 | Maryland | 175,100 | 1.0% |
| 34 | Utah | 131,800 | 0.7% |
| 35 | Nebraska | 116,200 | 0.6% |
| 36 | New Hampshire | 106,100 | 0.6% |
| 37 | Maine | 84,200 | 0.5% |
| 38 | West Virginia | 81,000 | 0.4% |
| 39 | Idaho | 75,600 | 0.4% |
| 40 | Rhode Island | 73,800 | 0.4% |
| 41 | Delaware | 58,400 | 0.3% |
| 42 | South Dakota | 49,100 | 0.3% |
| 43 | Vermont | 48,400 | 0.3% |
| 44 | Nevada | 45,000 | 0.2% |
| 45 | New Mexico | 42,600 | 0.2% |
| 46 | Montana | 24,600 | 0.1% |
| 47 | North Dakota | 24,200 | 0.1% |
| 48 | Hawaii | 16,900 | 0.1% |
| 49 | Alaska | 13,900 | 0.1% |
| 50 | Wyoming | 11,500 | 0.1% |
| | District of Columbia | 12,200 | 0.1% |

Source: U.S. Department of Labor, Bureau of Labor Statistics
    "Regional and State Employment and Unemployment" (press release, January 19, 2001)
*Seasonally adjusted preliminary data as of December 2000. National total calculated through a different formula.

# Percent of Nonfarm Employees in Manufacturing in 2000

## National Percent = 13.9% of Employees*

ALPHA ORDER

| RANK | STATE | PERCENT |
|------|-------|---------|
| 8 | Alabama | 18.4 |
| 47 | Alaska | 4.9 |
| 40 | Arizona | 9.5 |
| 3 | Arkansas | 21.5 |
| 27 | California | 13.2 |
| 41 | Colorado | 9.3 |
| 19 | Connecticut | 15.5 |
| 25 | Delaware | 13.8 |
| 44 | Florida | 6.7 |
| 22 | Georgia | 15.0 |
| 50 | Hawaii | 3.1 |
| 26 | Idaho | 13.3 |
| 17 | Illinois | 15.7 |
| 1 | Indiana | 22.8 |
| 11 | Iowa | 17.4 |
| 18 | Kansas | 15.6 |
| 13 | Kentucky | 17.1 |
| 39 | Louisiana | 9.7 |
| 24 | Maine | 13.9 |
| 43 | Maryland | 7.1 |
| 29 | Massachusetts | 13.0 |
| 4 | Michigan | 20.7 |
| 15 | Minnesota | 16.4 |
| 5 | Mississippi | 20.6 |
| 23 | Missouri | 14.4 |
| 45 | Montana | 6.3 |
| 28 | Nebraska | 13.1 |
| 49 | Nevada | 4.3 |
| 12 | New Hampshire | 17.3 |
| 34 | New Jersey | 11.5 |
| 46 | New Mexico | 5.7 |
| 38 | New York | 10.1 |
| 6 | North Carolina | 19.5 |
| 42 | North Dakota | 7.4 |
| 7 | Ohio | 19.1 |
| 32 | Oklahoma | 12.2 |
| 21 | Oregon | 15.2 |
| 14 | Pennsylvania | 16.5 |
| 19 | Rhode Island | 15.5 |
| 10 | South Carolina | 18.0 |
| 30 | South Dakota | 12.9 |
| 9 | Tennessee | 18.3 |
| 35 | Texas | 11.4 |
| 33 | Utah | 12.1 |
| 16 | Vermont | 16.3 |
| 36 | Virginia | 11.1 |
| 31 | Washington | 12.8 |
| 37 | West Virginia | 11.0 |
| 2 | Wisconsin | 21.6 |
| 48 | Wyoming | 4.8 |

RANK ORDER

| RANK | STATE | PERCENT |
|------|-------|---------|
| 1 | Indiana | 22.8 |
| 2 | Wisconsin | 21.6 |
| 3 | Arkansas | 21.5 |
| 4 | Michigan | 20.7 |
| 5 | Mississippi | 20.6 |
| 6 | North Carolina | 19.5 |
| 7 | Ohio | 19.1 |
| 8 | Alabama | 18.4 |
| 9 | Tennessee | 18.3 |
| 10 | South Carolina | 18.0 |
| 11 | Iowa | 17.4 |
| 12 | New Hampshire | 17.3 |
| 13 | Kentucky | 17.1 |
| 14 | Pennsylvania | 16.5 |
| 15 | Minnesota | 16.4 |
| 16 | Vermont | 16.3 |
| 17 | Illinois | 15.7 |
| 18 | Kansas | 15.6 |
| 19 | Connecticut | 15.5 |
| 19 | Rhode Island | 15.5 |
| 21 | Oregon | 15.2 |
| 22 | Georgia | 15.0 |
| 23 | Missouri | 14.4 |
| 24 | Maine | 13.9 |
| 25 | Delaware | 13.8 |
| 26 | Idaho | 13.3 |
| 27 | California | 13.2 |
| 28 | Nebraska | 13.1 |
| 29 | Massachusetts | 13.0 |
| 30 | South Dakota | 12.9 |
| 31 | Washington | 12.8 |
| 32 | Oklahoma | 12.2 |
| 33 | Utah | 12.1 |
| 34 | New Jersey | 11.5 |
| 35 | Texas | 11.4 |
| 36 | Virginia | 11.1 |
| 37 | West Virginia | 11.0 |
| 38 | New York | 10.1 |
| 39 | Louisiana | 9.7 |
| 40 | Arizona | 9.5 |
| 41 | Colorado | 9.3 |
| 42 | North Dakota | 7.4 |
| 43 | Maryland | 7.1 |
| 44 | Florida | 6.7 |
| 45 | Montana | 6.3 |
| 46 | New Mexico | 5.7 |
| 47 | Alaska | 4.9 |
| 48 | Wyoming | 4.8 |
| 49 | Nevada | 4.3 |
| 50 | Hawaii | 3.1 |
| | District of Columbia | 1.9 |

Source: Morgan Quitno Press using data from U.S. Department of Labor, Bureau of Labor Statistics
   "Regional and State Employment and Unemployment" (press release, January 19, 2001)
*Seasonally adjusted preliminary data as of December 2000. National percent calculated through a different formula.

# Employees in Mining in 2000

## National Total = 540,000 Employees*

ALPHA ORDER

| RANK | STATE | EMPLOYEES | % of USA |
|------|-------|-----------|----------|
| NA | Alabama** | NA | NA |
| 14 | Alaska | 9,900 | 1.8% |
| 15 | Arizona | 9,800 | 1.8% |
| 29 | Arkansas | 3,100 | 0.6% |
| 4 | California | 22,900 | 4.2% |
| 10 | Colorado | 12,800 | 2.4% |
| 39 | Connecticut | 800 | 0.1% |
| NA | Delaware** | NA | NA |
| NA | Florida** | NA | NA |
| NA | Georgia** | NA | NA |
| NA | Hawaii** | NA | NA |
| 30 | Idaho | 2,400 | 0.4% |
| 13 | Illinois | 10,500 | 1.9% |
| 21 | Indiana | 6,000 | 1.1% |
| 32 | Iowa | 2,200 | 0.4% |
| 20 | Kansas | 6,600 | 1.2% |
| 6 | Kentucky | 20,500 | 3.8% |
| 2 | Louisiana | 47,700 | 8.8% |
| NA | Maine** | NA | NA |
| 35 | Maryland | 1,500 | 0.3% |
| 36 | Massachusetts | 1,400 | 0.3% |
| 19 | Michigan | 6,900 | 1.3% |
| 18 | Minnesota | 7,200 | 1.3% |
| NA | Mississippi** | NA | NA |
| 22 | Missouri | 5,100 | 0.9% |
| 25 | Montana | 4,000 | 0.7% |
| 37 | Nebraska | 1,200 | 0.2% |
| 12 | Nevada | 11,000 | 2.0% |
| NA | New Hampshire** | NA | NA |
| 32 | New Jersey | 2,200 | 0.4% |
| 9 | New Mexico | 14,600 | 2.7% |
| 23 | New York | 4,400 | 0.8% |
| 25 | North Carolina | 4,000 | 0.7% |
| 27 | North Dakota | 3,300 | 0.6% |
| 11 | Ohio | 12,100 | 2.2% |
| 3 | Oklahoma | 27,600 | 5.1% |
| 34 | Oregon | 1,700 | 0.3% |
| 7 | Pennsylvania | 19,000 | 3.5% |
| NA | Rhode Island** | NA | NA |
| NA | South Carolina** | NA | NA |
| 38 | South Dakota | 1,100 | 0.2% |
| 24 | Tennessee | 4,200 | 0.8% |
| 1 | Texas | 144,600 | 26.8% |
| 17 | Utah | 7,600 | 1.4% |
| 40 | Vermont | 600 | 0.1% |
| 15 | Virginia | 9,800 | 1.8% |
| 27 | Washington | 3,300 | 0.6% |
| 5 | West Virginia | 20,600 | 3.8% |
| 30 | Wisconsin | 2,400 | 0.4% |
| 8 | Wyoming | 17,100 | 3.2% |

RANK ORDER

| RANK | STATE | EMPLOYEES | % of USA |
|------|-------|-----------|----------|
| 1 | Texas | 144,600 | 26.8% |
| 2 | Louisiana | 47,700 | 8.8% |
| 3 | Oklahoma | 27,600 | 5.1% |
| 4 | California | 22,900 | 4.2% |
| 5 | West Virginia | 20,600 | 3.8% |
| 6 | Kentucky | 20,500 | 3.8% |
| 7 | Pennsylvania | 19,000 | 3.5% |
| 8 | Wyoming | 17,100 | 3.2% |
| 9 | New Mexico | 14,600 | 2.7% |
| 10 | Colorado | 12,800 | 2.4% |
| 11 | Ohio | 12,100 | 2.2% |
| 12 | Nevada | 11,000 | 2.0% |
| 13 | Illinois | 10,500 | 1.9% |
| 14 | Alaska | 9,900 | 1.8% |
| 15 | Arizona | 9,800 | 1.8% |
| 15 | Virginia | 9,800 | 1.8% |
| 17 | Utah | 7,600 | 1.4% |
| 18 | Minnesota | 7,200 | 1.3% |
| 19 | Michigan | 6,900 | 1.3% |
| 20 | Kansas | 6,600 | 1.2% |
| 21 | Indiana | 6,000 | 1.1% |
| 22 | Missouri | 5,100 | 0.9% |
| 23 | New York | 4,400 | 0.8% |
| 24 | Tennessee | 4,200 | 0.8% |
| 25 | Montana | 4,000 | 0.7% |
| 25 | North Carolina | 4,000 | 0.7% |
| 27 | North Dakota | 3,300 | 0.6% |
| 27 | Washington | 3,300 | 0.6% |
| 29 | Arkansas | 3,100 | 0.6% |
| 30 | Idaho | 2,400 | 0.4% |
| 30 | Wisconsin | 2,400 | 0.4% |
| 32 | Iowa | 2,200 | 0.4% |
| 32 | New Jersey | 2,200 | 0.4% |
| 34 | Oregon | 1,700 | 0.3% |
| 35 | Maryland | 1,500 | 0.3% |
| 36 | Massachusetts | 1,400 | 0.3% |
| 37 | Nebraska | 1,200 | 0.2% |
| 38 | South Dakota | 1,100 | 0.2% |
| 39 | Connecticut | 800 | 0.1% |
| 40 | Vermont | 600 | 0.1% |
| NA | Alabama** | NA | NA |
| NA | Delaware** | NA | NA |
| NA | Florida** | NA | NA |
| NA | Georgia** | NA | NA |
| NA | Hawaii** | NA | NA |
| NA | Maine** | NA | NA |
| NA | Mississippi** | NA | NA |
| NA | New Hampshire** | NA | NA |
| NA | Rhode Island** | NA | NA |
| NA | South Carolina** | NA | NA |
| | District of Columbia** | NA | NA |

Source: U.S. Department of Labor, Bureau of Labor Statistics
"Regional and State Employment and Unemployment" (press release, January 19, 2001)
*Seasonally adjusted preliminary data as of December 1999. National total calculated through a different formula.
**None or not available.

# Percent of Nonfarm Employees in Mining in 2000

## National Percent = 0.41% of Employees*

<table>
<tr><td colspan="3">ALPHA ORDER</td><td colspan="3">RANK ORDER</td></tr>
<tr><td>RANK</td><td>STATE</td><td>PERCENT</td><td>RANK</td><td>STATE</td><td>PERCENT</td></tr>
<tr><td>NA</td><td>Alabama**</td><td>NA</td><td>1</td><td>Wyoming</td><td>7.10</td></tr>
<tr><td>2</td><td>Alaska</td><td>3.49</td><td>2</td><td>Alaska</td><td>3.49</td></tr>
<tr><td>15</td><td>Arizona</td><td>0.43</td><td>3</td><td>West Virginia</td><td>2.81</td></tr>
<tr><td>21</td><td>Arkansas</td><td>0.26</td><td>4</td><td>Louisiana</td><td>2.48</td></tr>
<tr><td>27</td><td>California</td><td>0.16</td><td>5</td><td>New Mexico</td><td>1.95</td></tr>
<tr><td>13</td><td>Colorado</td><td>0.58</td><td>6</td><td>Oklahoma</td><td>1.85</td></tr>
<tr><td>38</td><td>Connecticut</td><td>0.05</td><td>7</td><td>Texas</td><td>1.52</td></tr>
<tr><td>NA</td><td>Delaware**</td><td>NA</td><td>8</td><td>Kentucky</td><td>1.11</td></tr>
<tr><td>NA</td><td>Florida**</td><td>NA</td><td>9</td><td>Nevada</td><td>1.04</td></tr>
<tr><td>NA</td><td>Georgia**</td><td>NA</td><td>10</td><td>Montana</td><td>1.02</td></tr>
<tr><td>NA</td><td>Hawaii**</td><td>NA</td><td>11</td><td>North Dakota</td><td>1.01</td></tr>
<tr><td>16</td><td>Idaho</td><td>0.42</td><td>12</td><td>Utah</td><td>0.70</td></tr>
<tr><td>26</td><td>Illinois</td><td>0.17</td><td>13</td><td>Colorado</td><td>0.58</td></tr>
<tr><td>23</td><td>Indiana</td><td>0.20</td><td>14</td><td>Kansas</td><td>0.48</td></tr>
<tr><td>28</td><td>Iowa</td><td>0.15</td><td>15</td><td>Arizona</td><td>0.43</td></tr>
<tr><td>14</td><td>Kansas</td><td>0.48</td><td>16</td><td>Idaho</td><td>0.42</td></tr>
<tr><td>8</td><td>Kentucky</td><td>1.11</td><td>17</td><td>Pennsylvania</td><td>0.34</td></tr>
<tr><td>4</td><td>Louisiana</td><td>2.48</td><td>18</td><td>South Dakota</td><td>0.29</td></tr>
<tr><td>NA</td><td>Maine**</td><td>NA</td><td>19</td><td>Virginia</td><td>0.28</td></tr>
<tr><td>36</td><td>Maryland</td><td>0.06</td><td>20</td><td>Minnesota</td><td>0.27</td></tr>
<tr><td>40</td><td>Massachusetts</td><td>0.04</td><td>21</td><td>Arkansas</td><td>0.26</td></tr>
<tr><td>28</td><td>Michigan</td><td>0.15</td><td>22</td><td>Ohio</td><td>0.22</td></tr>
<tr><td>20</td><td>Minnesota</td><td>0.27</td><td>23</td><td>Indiana</td><td>0.20</td></tr>
<tr><td>NA</td><td>Mississippi**</td><td>NA</td><td>23</td><td>Vermont</td><td>0.20</td></tr>
<tr><td>25</td><td>Missouri</td><td>0.18</td><td>25</td><td>Missouri</td><td>0.18</td></tr>
<tr><td>10</td><td>Montana</td><td>1.02</td><td>26</td><td>Illinois</td><td>0.17</td></tr>
<tr><td>31</td><td>Nebraska</td><td>0.14</td><td>27</td><td>California</td><td>0.16</td></tr>
<tr><td>9</td><td>Nevada</td><td>1.04</td><td>28</td><td>Iowa</td><td>0.15</td></tr>
<tr><td>NA</td><td>New Hampshire**</td><td>NA</td><td>28</td><td>Michigan</td><td>0.15</td></tr>
<tr><td>36</td><td>New Jersey</td><td>0.06</td><td>28</td><td>Tennessee</td><td>0.15</td></tr>
<tr><td>5</td><td>New Mexico</td><td>1.95</td><td>31</td><td>Nebraska</td><td>0.14</td></tr>
<tr><td>38</td><td>New York</td><td>0.05</td><td>32</td><td>Washington</td><td>0.12</td></tr>
<tr><td>34</td><td>North Carolina</td><td>0.10</td><td>33</td><td>Oregon</td><td>0.11</td></tr>
<tr><td>11</td><td>North Dakota</td><td>1.01</td><td>34</td><td>North Carolina</td><td>0.10</td></tr>
<tr><td>22</td><td>Ohio</td><td>0.22</td><td>35</td><td>Wisconsin</td><td>0.08</td></tr>
<tr><td>6</td><td>Oklahoma</td><td>1.85</td><td>36</td><td>Maryland</td><td>0.06</td></tr>
<tr><td>33</td><td>Oregon</td><td>0.11</td><td>36</td><td>New Jersey</td><td>0.06</td></tr>
<tr><td>17</td><td>Pennsylvania</td><td>0.34</td><td>38</td><td>Connecticut</td><td>0.05</td></tr>
<tr><td>NA</td><td>Rhode Island**</td><td>NA</td><td>38</td><td>New York</td><td>0.05</td></tr>
<tr><td>NA</td><td>South Carolina**</td><td>NA</td><td>40</td><td>Massachusetts</td><td>0.04</td></tr>
<tr><td>18</td><td>South Dakota</td><td>0.29</td><td>NA</td><td>Alabama**</td><td>NA</td></tr>
<tr><td>28</td><td>Tennessee</td><td>0.15</td><td>NA</td><td>Delaware**</td><td>NA</td></tr>
<tr><td>7</td><td>Texas</td><td>1.52</td><td>NA</td><td>Florida**</td><td>NA</td></tr>
<tr><td>12</td><td>Utah</td><td>0.70</td><td>NA</td><td>Georgia**</td><td>NA</td></tr>
<tr><td>23</td><td>Vermont</td><td>0.20</td><td>NA</td><td>Hawaii**</td><td>NA</td></tr>
<tr><td>19</td><td>Virginia</td><td>0.28</td><td>NA</td><td>Maine**</td><td>NA</td></tr>
<tr><td>32</td><td>Washington</td><td>0.12</td><td>NA</td><td>Mississippi**</td><td>NA</td></tr>
<tr><td>3</td><td>West Virginia</td><td>2.81</td><td>NA</td><td>New Hampshire**</td><td>NA</td></tr>
<tr><td>35</td><td>Wisconsin</td><td>0.08</td><td>NA</td><td>Rhode Island**</td><td>NA</td></tr>
<tr><td>1</td><td>Wyoming</td><td>7.10</td><td>NA</td><td>South Carolina**</td><td>NA</td></tr>
<tr><td></td><td></td><td></td><td></td><td>District of Columbia**</td><td>NA</td></tr>
</table>

*Source: Morgan Quitno Press using data from U.S. Department of Labor, Bureau of Labor Statistics*
   *"Regional and State Employment and Unemployment" (press release, January 19, 2001)*
*Seasonally adjusted preliminary data as of December 2000. National percent calculated through a different formula.*
**None or not available.*

# Employees in Service Industries in 2000

## National Total = 40,800,000 Employees*

ALPHA ORDER

| RANK | STATE | EMPLOYEES | % of USA |
|------|-------|-----------|----------|
| 27 | Alabama | 469,400 | 1.2% |
| 49 | Alaska | 73,900 | 0.2% |
| 21 | Arizona | 735,100 | 1.8% |
| 34 | Arkansas | 280,700 | 0.7% |
| 1 | California | 4,661,400 | 11.4% |
| 22 | Colorado | 676,100 | 1.7% |
| 24 | Connecticut | 541,100 | 1.3% |
| 44 | Delaware | 121,800 | 0.3% |
| 3 | Florida | 2,784,800 | 6.8% |
| 12 | Georgia | 1,102,000 | 2.7% |
| 40 | Hawaii | 180,300 | 0.4% |
| 43 | Idaho | 145,600 | 0.4% |
| 5 | Illinois | 1,860,200 | 4.6% |
| 19 | Indiana | 744,600 | 1.8% |
| 31 | Iowa | 400,300 | 1.0% |
| 32 | Kansas | 359,100 | 0.9% |
| 25 | Kentucky | 490,200 | 1.2% |
| 23 | Louisiana | 544,000 | 1.3% |
| 39 | Maine | 181,500 | 0.4% |
| 14 | Maryland | 855,900 | 2.1% |
| 10 | Massachusetts | 1,208,300 | 3.0% |
| 9 | Michigan | 1,283,700 | 3.1% |
| 16 | Minnesota | 782,900 | 1.9% |
| 35 | Mississippi | 269,700 | 0.7% |
| 15 | Missouri | 802,800 | 2.0% |
| 45 | Montana | 119,100 | 0.3% |
| 36 | Nebraska | 244,000 | 0.6% |
| 28 | Nevada | 456,900 | 1.1% |
| 41 | New Hampshire | 180,000 | 0.4% |
| 8 | New Jersey | 1,303,000 | 3.2% |
| 38 | New Mexico | 218,400 | 0.5% |
| 2 | New York | 3,079,300 | 7.5% |
| 13 | North Carolina | 1,042,000 | 2.6% |
| 47 | North Dakota | 92,300 | 0.2% |
| 7 | Ohio | 1,585,200 | 3.9% |
| 30 | Oklahoma | 433,300 | 1.1% |
| 29 | Oregon | 439,000 | 1.1% |
| 6 | Pennsylvania | 1,823,600 | 4.5% |
| 42 | Rhode Island | 162,900 | 0.4% |
| 26 | South Carolina | 476,100 | 1.2% |
| 46 | South Dakota | 104,700 | 0.3% |
| 20 | Tennessee | 737,500 | 1.8% |
| 4 | Texas | 2,712,900 | 6.6% |
| 33 | Utah | 312,900 | 0.8% |
| 48 | Vermont | 91,400 | 0.2% |
| 11 | Virginia | 1,138,100 | 2.8% |
| 17 | Washington | 778,100 | 1.9% |
| 37 | West Virginia | 225,800 | 0.6% |
| 18 | Wisconsin | 748,400 | 1.8% |
| 50 | Wyoming | 56,800 | 0.1% |

RANK ORDER

| RANK | STATE | EMPLOYEES | % of USA |
|------|-------|-----------|----------|
| 1 | California | 4,661,400 | 11.4% |
| 2 | New York | 3,079,300 | 7.5% |
| 3 | Florida | 2,784,800 | 6.8% |
| 4 | Texas | 2,712,900 | 6.6% |
| 5 | Illinois | 1,860,200 | 4.6% |
| 6 | Pennsylvania | 1,823,600 | 4.5% |
| 7 | Ohio | 1,585,200 | 3.9% |
| 8 | New Jersey | 1,303,000 | 3.2% |
| 9 | Michigan | 1,283,700 | 3.1% |
| 10 | Massachusetts | 1,208,300 | 3.0% |
| 11 | Virginia | 1,138,100 | 2.8% |
| 12 | Georgia | 1,102,000 | 2.7% |
| 13 | North Carolina | 1,042,000 | 2.6% |
| 14 | Maryland | 855,900 | 2.1% |
| 15 | Missouri | 802,800 | 2.0% |
| 16 | Minnesota | 782,900 | 1.9% |
| 17 | Washington | 778,100 | 1.9% |
| 18 | Wisconsin | 748,400 | 1.8% |
| 19 | Indiana | 744,600 | 1.8% |
| 20 | Tennessee | 737,500 | 1.8% |
| 21 | Arizona | 735,100 | 1.8% |
| 22 | Colorado | 676,100 | 1.7% |
| 23 | Louisiana | 544,000 | 1.3% |
| 24 | Connecticut | 541,100 | 1.3% |
| 25 | Kentucky | 490,200 | 1.2% |
| 26 | South Carolina | 476,100 | 1.2% |
| 27 | Alabama | 469,400 | 1.2% |
| 28 | Nevada | 456,900 | 1.1% |
| 29 | Oregon | 439,000 | 1.1% |
| 30 | Oklahoma | 433,300 | 1.1% |
| 31 | Iowa | 400,300 | 1.0% |
| 32 | Kansas | 359,100 | 0.9% |
| 33 | Utah | 312,900 | 0.8% |
| 34 | Arkansas | 280,700 | 0.7% |
| 35 | Mississippi | 269,700 | 0.7% |
| 36 | Nebraska | 244,000 | 0.6% |
| 37 | West Virginia | 225,800 | 0.6% |
| 38 | New Mexico | 218,400 | 0.5% |
| 39 | Maine | 181,500 | 0.4% |
| 40 | Hawaii | 180,300 | 0.4% |
| 41 | New Hampshire | 180,000 | 0.4% |
| 42 | Rhode Island | 162,900 | 0.4% |
| 43 | Idaho | 145,600 | 0.4% |
| 44 | Delaware | 121,800 | 0.3% |
| 45 | Montana | 119,100 | 0.3% |
| 46 | South Dakota | 104,700 | 0.3% |
| 47 | North Dakota | 92,300 | 0.2% |
| 48 | Vermont | 91,400 | 0.2% |
| 49 | Alaska | 73,900 | 0.2% |
| 50 | Wyoming | 56,800 | 0.1% |
| | District of Columbia | 282,900 | 0.7% |

Source: U.S. Department of Labor, Bureau of Labor Statistics
"Regional and State Employment and Unemployment" (press release, January 19, 2001)
*Seasonally adjusted preliminary data as of December 2000. National total calculated through a different formula.

# Percent of Nonfarm Employees in Service Industries in 2000

## National Percent = 30.9% of Employees*

RANK ORDER

| RANK | STATE | PERCENT | RANK | STATE | PERCENT |
|------|-------|---------|------|-------|---------|
| 47 | Alabama | 24.2 | 1 | Nevada | 43.2 |
| 43 | Alaska | 26.0 | 2 | Florida | 38.3 |
| 11 | Arizona | 32.2 | 3 | Massachusetts | 36.4 |
| 48 | Arkansas | 23.8 | 4 | New York | 35.5 |
| 12 | California | 31.9 | 5 | Maryland | 34.8 |
| 17 | Colorado | 30.5 | 6 | Rhode Island | 34.3 |
| 12 | Connecticut | 31.9 | 7 | New Jersey | 33.0 |
| 26 | Delaware | 28.7 | 8 | Hawaii | 32.9 |
| 2 | Florida | 38.3 | 9 | Pennsylvania | 32.6 |
| 33 | Georgia | 27.6 | 10 | Virginia | 32.4 |
| 8 | Hawaii | 32.9 | 11 | Arizona | 32.2 |
| 44 | Idaho | 25.6 | 12 | California | 31.9 |
| 14 | Illinois | 30.9 | 12 | Connecticut | 31.9 |
| 46 | Indiana | 24.9 | 14 | Illinois | 30.9 |
| 38 | Iowa | 26.7 | 15 | West Virginia | 30.8 |
| 42 | Kansas | 26.3 | 16 | Vermont | 30.7 |
| 39 | Kentucky | 26.6 | 17 | Colorado | 30.5 |
| 29 | Louisiana | 28.3 | 18 | Montana | 30.3 |
| 19 | Maine | 30.1 | 19 | Maine | 30.1 |
| 5 | Maryland | 34.8 | 20 | New Hampshire | 29.4 |
| 3 | Massachusetts | 36.4 | 21 | Minnesota | 29.3 |
| 32 | Michigan | 27.9 | 22 | New Mexico | 29.1 |
| 21 | Minnesota | 29.3 | 23 | Missouri | 29.0 |
| 50 | Mississippi | 23.5 | 23 | Oklahoma | 29.0 |
| 23 | Missouri | 29.0 | 25 | Utah | 28.8 |
| 18 | Montana | 30.3 | 26 | Delaware | 28.7 |
| 34 | Nebraska | 27.5 | 27 | Washington | 28.6 |
| 1 | Nevada | 43.2 | 28 | Texas | 28.5 |
| 20 | New Hampshire | 29.4 | 29 | Louisiana | 28.3 |
| 7 | New Jersey | 33.0 | 29 | North Dakota | 28.3 |
| 22 | New Mexico | 29.1 | 29 | Ohio | 28.3 |
| 4 | New York | 35.5 | 32 | Michigan | 27.9 |
| 39 | North Carolina | 26.6 | 33 | Georgia | 27.6 |
| 29 | North Dakota | 28.3 | 34 | Nebraska | 27.5 |
| 29 | Ohio | 28.3 | 34 | Oregon | 27.5 |
| 23 | Oklahoma | 29.0 | 34 | South Dakota | 27.5 |
| 34 | Oregon | 27.5 | 37 | Tennessee | 27.2 |
| 9 | Pennsylvania | 32.6 | 38 | Iowa | 26.7 |
| 6 | Rhode Island | 34.3 | 39 | Kentucky | 26.6 |
| 45 | South Carolina | 25.3 | 39 | North Carolina | 26.6 |
| 34 | South Dakota | 27.5 | 41 | Wisconsin | 26.4 |
| 37 | Tennessee | 27.2 | 42 | Kansas | 26.3 |
| 28 | Texas | 28.5 | 43 | Alaska | 26.0 |
| 25 | Utah | 28.8 | 44 | Idaho | 25.6 |
| 16 | Vermont | 30.7 | 45 | South Carolina | 25.3 |
| 10 | Virginia | 32.4 | 46 | Indiana | 24.9 |
| 27 | Washington | 28.6 | 47 | Alabama | 24.2 |
| 15 | West Virginia | 30.8 | 48 | Arkansas | 23.8 |
| 41 | Wisconsin | 26.4 | 49 | Wyoming | 23.6 |
| 49 | Wyoming | 23.6 | 50 | Mississippi | 23.5 |

| | | | | District of Columbia | 45.1 |

Source: Morgan Quitno Press using data from U.S. Department of Labor, Bureau of Labor Statistics
    "Regional and State Employment and Unemployment" (press release, January 19, 2001)
*Seasonally adjusted preliminary data as of December 2000.  National percent calculated through a different formula.

# Employees in Transportation and Public Utilities in 2000

## National Total = 7,086,000*

ALPHA ORDER

| RANK | STATE | EMPLOYEES | % of USA |
|---|---|---|---|
| 25 | Alabama | 96,500 | 1.4% |
| 41 | Alaska | 26,900 | 0.4% |
| 23 | Arizona | 111,500 | 1.6% |
| 32 | Arkansas | 72,300 | 1.0% |
| 1 | California | 759,100 | 10.7% |
| 17 | Colorado | 142,000 | 2.0% |
| 30 | Connecticut | 79,000 | 1.1% |
| 46 | Delaware | 18,200 | 0.3% |
| 4 | Florida | 368,900 | 5.2% |
| 7 | Georgia | 269,400 | 3.8% |
| 37 | Hawaii** | 42,200 | 0.6% |
| 40 | Idaho | 27,600 | 0.4% |
| 5 | Illinois | 351,900 | 5.0% |
| 15 | Indiana | 146,800 | 2.1% |
| 31 | Iowa | 74,200 | 1.0% |
| 28 | Kansas | 81,000 | 1.1% |
| 24 | Kentucky | 108,800 | 1.5% |
| 22 | Louisiana | 115,000 | 1.6% |
| 42 | Maine | 24,400 | 0.3% |
| 21 | Maryland | 117,300 | 1.7% |
| 18 | Massachusetts | 141,900 | 2.0% |
| 12 | Michigan | 177,200 | 2.5% |
| 19 | Minnesota | 134,700 | 1.9% |
| 34 | Mississippi | 57,800 | 0.8% |
| 14 | Missouri | 173,800 | 2.5% |
| 43 | Montana | 22,400 | 0.3% |
| 35 | Nebraska | 57,200 | 0.8% |
| 36 | Nevada | 57,100 | 0.8% |
| 44 | New Hampshire | 21,300 | 0.3% |
| 8 | New Jersey | 263,200 | 3.7% |
| 39 | New Mexico | 36,900 | 0.5% |
| 3 | New York | 429,500 | 6.1% |
| 11 | North Carolina | 180,500 | 2.5% |
| 45 | North Dakota | 18,700 | 0.3% |
| 9 | Ohio | 249,300 | 3.5% |
| 27 | Oklahoma | 82,000 | 1.2% |
| 29 | Oregon | 80,300 | 1.1% |
| 6 | Pennsylvania | 298,700 | 4.2% |
| 48 | Rhode Island | 16,500 | 0.2% |
| 26 | South Carolina | 90,700 | 1.3% |
| 47 | South Dakota | 16,700 | 0.2% |
| 13 | Tennessee | 174,200 | 2.5% |
| 2 | Texas | 595,100 | 8.4% |
| 33 | Utah | 60,800 | 0.9% |
| 50 | Vermont | 12,900 | 0.2% |
| 10 | Virginia | 187,800 | 2.7% |
| 16 | Washington | 144,000 | 2.0% |
| 38 | West Virginia | 37,700 | 0.5% |
| 20 | Wisconsin | 134,300 | 1.9% |
| 49 | Wyoming | 14,300 | 0.2% |

RANK ORDER

| RANK | STATE | EMPLOYEES | % of USA |
|---|---|---|---|
| 1 | California | 759,100 | 10.7% |
| 2 | Texas | 595,100 | 8.4% |
| 3 | New York | 429,500 | 6.1% |
| 4 | Florida | 368,900 | 5.2% |
| 5 | Illinois | 351,900 | 5.0% |
| 6 | Pennsylvania | 298,700 | 4.2% |
| 7 | Georgia | 269,400 | 3.8% |
| 8 | New Jersey | 263,200 | 3.7% |
| 9 | Ohio | 249,300 | 3.5% |
| 10 | Virginia | 187,800 | 2.7% |
| 11 | North Carolina | 180,500 | 2.5% |
| 12 | Michigan | 177,200 | 2.5% |
| 13 | Tennessee | 174,200 | 2.5% |
| 14 | Missouri | 173,800 | 2.5% |
| 15 | Indiana | 146,800 | 2.1% |
| 16 | Washington | 144,000 | 2.0% |
| 17 | Colorado | 142,000 | 2.0% |
| 18 | Massachusetts | 141,900 | 2.0% |
| 19 | Minnesota | 134,700 | 1.9% |
| 20 | Wisconsin | 134,300 | 1.9% |
| 21 | Maryland | 117,300 | 1.7% |
| 22 | Louisiana | 115,000 | 1.6% |
| 23 | Arizona | 111,500 | 1.6% |
| 24 | Kentucky | 108,800 | 1.5% |
| 25 | Alabama | 96,500 | 1.4% |
| 26 | South Carolina | 90,700 | 1.3% |
| 27 | Oklahoma | 82,000 | 1.2% |
| 28 | Kansas | 81,000 | 1.1% |
| 29 | Oregon | 80,300 | 1.1% |
| 30 | Connecticut | 79,000 | 1.1% |
| 31 | Iowa | 74,200 | 1.0% |
| 32 | Arkansas | 72,300 | 1.0% |
| 33 | Utah | 60,800 | 0.9% |
| 34 | Mississippi | 57,800 | 0.8% |
| 35 | Nebraska | 57,200 | 0.8% |
| 36 | Nevada | 57,100 | 0.8% |
| 37 | Hawaii** | 42,200 | 0.6% |
| 38 | West Virginia | 37,700 | 0.5% |
| 39 | New Mexico | 36,900 | 0.5% |
| 40 | Idaho | 27,600 | 0.4% |
| 41 | Alaska | 26,900 | 0.4% |
| 42 | Maine | 24,400 | 0.3% |
| 43 | Montana | 22,400 | 0.3% |
| 44 | New Hampshire | 21,300 | 0.3% |
| 45 | North Dakota | 18,700 | 0.3% |
| 46 | Delaware | 18,200 | 0.3% |
| 47 | South Dakota | 16,700 | 0.2% |
| 48 | Rhode Island | 16,500 | 0.2% |
| 49 | Wyoming | 14,300 | 0.2% |
| 50 | Vermont | 12,900 | 0.2% |
| | District of Columbia | 17,500 | 0.2% |

*Source: U.S. Department of Labor, Bureau of Labor Statistics*
   *"Regional and State Employment and Unemployment" (press release, January 19, 2001)*
*Seasonally adjusted preliminary data as of December 2000. National total calculated through a different formula.*
**Hawaii's figure is not seasonally adjusted.*

# Percent of Nonfarm Employees in Transportation and Public Utilities in 2000

## National Percent = 5.4% of Employees*

ALPHA ORDER

RANK ORDER

| RANK | STATE | PERCENT | | RANK | STATE | PERCENT |
|---|---|---|---|---|---|---|
| 27 | Alabama | 5.0 | | 1 | Alaska | 9.5 |
| 1 | Alaska | 9.5 | | 2 | Hawaii** | 7.7 |
| 31 | Arizona | 4.9 | | 3 | Georgia | 6.7 |
| 10 | Arkansas | 6.1 | | 3 | New Jersey | 6.7 |
| 24 | California | 5.2 | | 5 | Nebraska | 6.5 |
| 6 | Colorado | 6.4 | | 6 | Colorado | 6.4 |
| 39 | Connecticut | 4.7 | | 6 | Tennessee | 6.4 |
| 44 | Delaware | 4.3 | | 8 | Missouri | 6.3 |
| 25 | Florida | 5.1 | | 8 | Texas | 6.3 |
| 3 | Georgia | 6.7 | | 10 | Arkansas | 6.1 |
| 2 | Hawaii** | 7.7 | | 11 | Louisiana | 6.0 |
| 31 | Idaho | 4.9 | | 12 | Kansas | 5.9 |
| 15 | Illinois | 5.8 | | 12 | Kentucky | 5.9 |
| 31 | Indiana | 4.9 | | 12 | Wyoming | 5.9 |
| 31 | Iowa | 4.9 | | 15 | Illinois | 5.8 |
| 12 | Kansas | 5.9 | | 16 | Montana | 5.7 |
| 12 | Kentucky | 5.9 | | 16 | North Dakota | 5.7 |
| 11 | Louisiana | 6.0 | | 18 | Utah | 5.6 |
| 47 | Maine | 4.0 | | 19 | Oklahoma | 5.5 |
| 37 | Maryland | 4.8 | | 20 | Nevada | 5.4 |
| 44 | Massachusetts | 4.3 | | 21 | Pennsylvania | 5.3 |
| 48 | Michigan | 3.9 | | 21 | Virginia | 5.3 |
| 27 | Minnesota | 5.0 | | 21 | Washington | 5.3 |
| 27 | Mississippi | 5.0 | | 24 | California | 5.2 |
| 8 | Missouri | 6.3 | | 25 | Florida | 5.1 |
| 16 | Montana | 5.7 | | 25 | West Virginia | 5.1 |
| 5 | Nebraska | 6.5 | | 27 | Alabama | 5.0 |
| 20 | Nevada | 5.4 | | 27 | Minnesota | 5.0 |
| 49 | New Hampshire | 3.5 | | 27 | Mississippi | 5.0 |
| 3 | New Jersey | 6.7 | | 27 | Oregon | 5.0 |
| 31 | New Mexico | 4.9 | | 31 | Arizona | 4.9 |
| 31 | New York | 4.9 | | 31 | Idaho | 4.9 |
| 41 | North Carolina | 4.6 | | 31 | Indiana | 4.9 |
| 16 | North Dakota | 5.7 | | 31 | Iowa | 4.9 |
| 42 | Ohio | 4.4 | | 31 | New Mexico | 4.9 |
| 19 | Oklahoma | 5.5 | | 31 | New York | 4.9 |
| 27 | Oregon | 5.0 | | 37 | Maryland | 4.8 |
| 21 | Pennsylvania | 5.3 | | 37 | South Carolina | 4.8 |
| 49 | Rhode Island | 3.5 | | 39 | Connecticut | 4.7 |
| 37 | South Carolina | 4.8 | | 39 | Wisconsin | 4.7 |
| 42 | South Dakota | 4.4 | | 41 | North Carolina | 4.6 |
| 6 | Tennessee | 6.4 | | 42 | Ohio | 4.4 |
| 8 | Texas | 6.3 | | 42 | South Dakota | 4.4 |
| 18 | Utah | 5.6 | | 44 | Delaware | 4.3 |
| 44 | Vermont | 4.3 | | 44 | Massachusetts | 4.3 |
| 21 | Virginia | 5.3 | | 44 | Vermont | 4.3 |
| 21 | Washington | 5.3 | | 47 | Maine | 4.0 |
| 25 | West Virginia | 5.1 | | 48 | Michigan | 3.9 |
| 39 | Wisconsin | 4.7 | | 49 | New Hampshire | 3.5 |
| 12 | Wyoming | 5.9 | | 49 | Rhode Island | 3.5 |
| | | | | | District of Columbia | 2.8 |

Source: Morgan Quitno Press using data from U.S. Department of Labor, Bureau of Labor Statistics
   "Regional and State Employment and Unemployment" (press release, January 19, 2001)
*Seasonally adjusted preliminary data as of December 2000. National percent calculated through a different formula.
**Hawaii's figure is not seasonally adjusted.

# Employees in Wholesale and Retail Trade in 2000

## National Total = 30,341,000 Employees*

ALPHA ORDER

| RANK | STATE | EMPLOYEES | % of USA |
|---|---|---|---|
| 24 | Alabama | 453,700 | 1.5% |
| 49 | Alaska | 58,400 | 0.2% |
| 21 | Arizona | 536,900 | 1.8% |
| 32 | Arkansas | 272,900 | 0.9% |
| 1 | California | 3,307,500 | 10.9% |
| 22 | Colorado | 527,200 | 1.7% |
| 29 | Connecticut | 362,900 | 1.2% |
| 46 | Delaware | 92,100 | 0.3% |
| 3 | Florida | 1,781,200 | 5.9% |
| 9 | Georgia | 1,014,700 | 3.3% |
| 42 | Hawaii | 136,700 | 0.5% |
| 41 | Idaho | 144,400 | 0.5% |
| 5 | Illinois | 1,356,700 | 4.5% |
| 14 | Indiana | 712,300 | 2.3% |
| 28 | Iowa | 363,800 | 1.2% |
| 31 | Kansas | 325,500 | 1.1% |
| 26 | Kentucky | 438,200 | 1.4% |
| 25 | Louisiana | 443,800 | 1.5% |
| 40 | Maine | 151,800 | 0.5% |
| 20 | Maryland | 561,000 | 1.8% |
| 13 | Massachusetts | 750,000 | 2.5% |
| 8 | Michigan | 1,092,700 | 3.6% |
| 19 | Minnesota | 635,400 | 2.1% |
| 34 | Mississippi | 250,700 | 0.8% |
| 16 | Missouri | 654,600 | 2.2% |
| 44 | Montana | 103,800 | 0.3% |
| 36 | Nebraska | 212,300 | 0.7% |
| 35 | Nevada | 221,500 | 0.7% |
| 39 | New Hampshire | 162,500 | 0.5% |
| 10 | New Jersey | 929,600 | 3.1% |
| 37 | New Mexico | 175,100 | 0.6% |
| 4 | New York | 1,760,100 | 5.8% |
| 11 | North Carolina | 870,400 | 2.9% |
| 47 | North Dakota | 81,200 | 0.3% |
| 6 | Ohio | 1,343,600 | 4.4% |
| 30 | Oklahoma | 345,200 | 1.1% |
| 27 | Oregon | 388,800 | 1.3% |
| 7 | Pennsylvania | 1,255,400 | 4.1% |
| 43 | Rhode Island | 109,000 | 0.4% |
| 23 | South Carolina | 458,000 | 1.5% |
| 45 | South Dakota | 93,500 | 0.3% |
| 18 | Tennessee | 641,400 | 2.1% |
| 2 | Texas | 2,284,500 | 7.5% |
| 33 | Utah | 255,600 | 0.8% |
| 48 | Vermont | 68,600 | 0.2% |
| 12 | Virginia | 754,000 | 2.5% |
| 15 | Washington | 654,700 | 2.2% |
| 38 | West Virginia | 164,200 | 0.5% |
| 17 | Wisconsin | 647,400 | 2.1% |
| 50 | Wyoming | 54,800 | 0.2% |

RANK ORDER

| RANK | STATE | EMPLOYEES | % of USA |
|---|---|---|---|
| 1 | California | 3,307,500 | 10.9% |
| 2 | Texas | 2,284,500 | 7.5% |
| 3 | Florida | 1,781,200 | 5.9% |
| 4 | New York | 1,760,100 | 5.8% |
| 5 | Illinois | 1,356,700 | 4.5% |
| 6 | Ohio | 1,343,600 | 4.4% |
| 7 | Pennsylvania | 1,255,400 | 4.1% |
| 8 | Michigan | 1,092,700 | 3.6% |
| 9 | Georgia | 1,014,700 | 3.3% |
| 10 | New Jersey | 929,600 | 3.1% |
| 11 | North Carolina | 870,400 | 2.9% |
| 12 | Virginia | 754,000 | 2.5% |
| 13 | Massachusetts | 750,000 | 2.5% |
| 14 | Indiana | 712,300 | 2.3% |
| 15 | Washington | 654,700 | 2.2% |
| 16 | Missouri | 654,600 | 2.2% |
| 17 | Wisconsin | 647,400 | 2.1% |
| 18 | Tennessee | 641,400 | 2.1% |
| 19 | Minnesota | 635,400 | 2.1% |
| 20 | Maryland | 561,000 | 1.8% |
| 21 | Arizona | 536,900 | 1.8% |
| 22 | Colorado | 527,200 | 1.7% |
| 23 | South Carolina | 458,000 | 1.5% |
| 24 | Alabama | 453,700 | 1.5% |
| 25 | Louisiana | 443,800 | 1.5% |
| 26 | Kentucky | 438,200 | 1.4% |
| 27 | Oregon | 388,800 | 1.3% |
| 28 | Iowa | 363,800 | 1.2% |
| 29 | Connecticut | 362,900 | 1.2% |
| 30 | Oklahoma | 345,200 | 1.1% |
| 31 | Kansas | 325,500 | 1.1% |
| 32 | Arkansas | 272,900 | 0.9% |
| 33 | Utah | 255,600 | 0.8% |
| 34 | Mississippi | 250,700 | 0.8% |
| 35 | Nevada | 221,500 | 0.7% |
| 36 | Nebraska | 212,300 | 0.7% |
| 37 | New Mexico | 175,100 | 0.6% |
| 38 | West Virginia | 164,200 | 0.5% |
| 39 | New Hampshire | 162,500 | 0.5% |
| 40 | Maine | 151,800 | 0.5% |
| 41 | Idaho | 144,400 | 0.5% |
| 42 | Hawaii | 136,700 | 0.5% |
| 43 | Rhode Island | 109,000 | 0.4% |
| 44 | Montana | 103,800 | 0.3% |
| 45 | South Dakota | 93,500 | 0.3% |
| 46 | Delaware | 92,100 | 0.3% |
| 47 | North Dakota | 81,200 | 0.3% |
| 48 | Vermont | 68,600 | 0.2% |
| 49 | Alaska | 58,400 | 0.2% |
| 50 | Wyoming | 54,800 | 0.2% |
| | District of Columbia | 48,400 | 0.2% |

*Source: U.S. Department of Labor, Bureau of Labor Statistics*
*"Regional and State Employment and Unemployment" (press release, January 19, 2001)*
*\*Seasonally adjusted preliminary data as of December 2000. National total calculated through a different formula.*

# Percent of Nonfarm Employees in Wholesale and Retail Trade in 2000

## National Percent = 23.0% of Employees*

<table>
<tr><td colspan="3">ALPHA ORDER</td><td colspan="3">RANK ORDER</td></tr>
<tr><td>RANK</td><td>STATE</td><td>PERCENT</td><td>RANK</td><td>STATE</td><td>PERCENT</td></tr>
<tr><td>28</td><td>Alabama</td><td>23.4</td><td>1</td><td>New Hampshire</td><td>26.5</td></tr>
<tr><td>49</td><td>Alaska</td><td>20.6</td><td>2</td><td>Montana</td><td>26.4</td></tr>
<tr><td>25</td><td>Arizona</td><td>23.5</td><td>3</td><td>Georgia</td><td>25.4</td></tr>
<tr><td>30</td><td>Arkansas</td><td>23.2</td><td>3</td><td>Idaho</td><td>25.4</td></tr>
<tr><td>38</td><td>California</td><td>22.6</td><td>5</td><td>Maine</td><td>25.1</td></tr>
<tr><td>17</td><td>Colorado</td><td>23.8</td><td>6</td><td>Hawaii</td><td>24.9</td></tr>
<tr><td>47</td><td>Connecticut</td><td>21.4</td><td>6</td><td>North Dakota</td><td>24.9</td></tr>
<tr><td>45</td><td>Delaware</td><td>21.7</td><td>8</td><td>Florida</td><td>24.5</td></tr>
<tr><td>8</td><td>Florida</td><td>24.5</td><td>8</td><td>South Dakota</td><td>24.5</td></tr>
<tr><td>3</td><td>Georgia</td><td>25.4</td><td>10</td><td>Oregon</td><td>24.3</td></tr>
<tr><td>6</td><td>Hawaii</td><td>24.9</td><td>10</td><td>South Carolina</td><td>24.3</td></tr>
<tr><td>3</td><td>Idaho</td><td>25.4</td><td>12</td><td>Iowa</td><td>24.2</td></tr>
<tr><td>40</td><td>Illinois</td><td>22.5</td><td>13</td><td>Washington</td><td>24.1</td></tr>
<tr><td>17</td><td>Indiana</td><td>23.8</td><td>14</td><td>Nebraska</td><td>24.0</td></tr>
<tr><td>12</td><td>Iowa</td><td>24.2</td><td>14</td><td>Ohio</td><td>24.0</td></tr>
<tr><td>17</td><td>Kansas</td><td>23.8</td><td>14</td><td>Texas</td><td>24.0</td></tr>
<tr><td>17</td><td>Kentucky</td><td>23.8</td><td>17</td><td>Colorado</td><td>23.8</td></tr>
<tr><td>31</td><td>Louisiana</td><td>23.1</td><td>17</td><td>Indiana</td><td>23.8</td></tr>
<tr><td>5</td><td>Maine</td><td>25.1</td><td>17</td><td>Kansas</td><td>23.8</td></tr>
<tr><td>35</td><td>Maryland</td><td>22.8</td><td>17</td><td>Kentucky</td><td>23.8</td></tr>
<tr><td>38</td><td>Massachusetts</td><td>22.6</td><td>17</td><td>Michigan</td><td>23.8</td></tr>
<tr><td>17</td><td>Michigan</td><td>23.8</td><td>17</td><td>Minnesota</td><td>23.8</td></tr>
<tr><td>17</td><td>Minnesota</td><td>23.8</td><td>23</td><td>Missouri</td><td>23.6</td></tr>
<tr><td>44</td><td>Mississippi</td><td>21.8</td><td>23</td><td>Tennessee</td><td>23.6</td></tr>
<tr><td>23</td><td>Missouri</td><td>23.6</td><td>25</td><td>Arizona</td><td>23.5</td></tr>
<tr><td>2</td><td>Montana</td><td>26.4</td><td>25</td><td>New Jersey</td><td>23.5</td></tr>
<tr><td>14</td><td>Nebraska</td><td>24.0</td><td>25</td><td>Utah</td><td>23.5</td></tr>
<tr><td>48</td><td>Nevada</td><td>21.0</td><td>28</td><td>Alabama</td><td>23.4</td></tr>
<tr><td>1</td><td>New Hampshire</td><td>26.5</td><td>29</td><td>New Mexico</td><td>23.3</td></tr>
<tr><td>25</td><td>New Jersey</td><td>23.5</td><td>30</td><td>Arkansas</td><td>23.2</td></tr>
<tr><td>29</td><td>New Mexico</td><td>23.3</td><td>31</td><td>Louisiana</td><td>23.1</td></tr>
<tr><td>50</td><td>New York</td><td>20.3</td><td>31</td><td>Oklahoma</td><td>23.1</td></tr>
<tr><td>43</td><td>North Carolina</td><td>22.3</td><td>33</td><td>Rhode Island</td><td>23.0</td></tr>
<tr><td>6</td><td>North Dakota</td><td>24.9</td><td>33</td><td>Vermont</td><td>23.0</td></tr>
<tr><td>14</td><td>Ohio</td><td>24.0</td><td>35</td><td>Maryland</td><td>22.8</td></tr>
<tr><td>31</td><td>Oklahoma</td><td>23.1</td><td>35</td><td>Wisconsin</td><td>22.8</td></tr>
<tr><td>10</td><td>Oregon</td><td>24.3</td><td>35</td><td>Wyoming</td><td>22.8</td></tr>
<tr><td>41</td><td>Pennsylvania</td><td>22.4</td><td>38</td><td>California</td><td>22.6</td></tr>
<tr><td>33</td><td>Rhode Island</td><td>23.0</td><td>38</td><td>Massachusetts</td><td>22.6</td></tr>
<tr><td>10</td><td>South Carolina</td><td>24.3</td><td>40</td><td>Illinois</td><td>22.5</td></tr>
<tr><td>8</td><td>South Dakota</td><td>24.5</td><td>41</td><td>Pennsylvania</td><td>22.4</td></tr>
<tr><td>23</td><td>Tennessee</td><td>23.6</td><td>41</td><td>West Virginia</td><td>22.4</td></tr>
<tr><td>14</td><td>Texas</td><td>24.0</td><td>43</td><td>North Carolina</td><td>22.3</td></tr>
<tr><td>25</td><td>Utah</td><td>23.5</td><td>44</td><td>Mississippi</td><td>21.8</td></tr>
<tr><td>33</td><td>Vermont</td><td>23.0</td><td>45</td><td>Delaware</td><td>21.7</td></tr>
<tr><td>46</td><td>Virginia</td><td>21.5</td><td>46</td><td>Virginia</td><td>21.5</td></tr>
<tr><td>13</td><td>Washington</td><td>24.1</td><td>47</td><td>Connecticut</td><td>21.4</td></tr>
<tr><td>41</td><td>West Virginia</td><td>22.4</td><td>48</td><td>Nevada</td><td>21.0</td></tr>
<tr><td>35</td><td>Wisconsin</td><td>22.8</td><td>49</td><td>Alaska</td><td>20.6</td></tr>
<tr><td>35</td><td>Wyoming</td><td>22.8</td><td>50</td><td>New York</td><td>20.3</td></tr>
<tr><td></td><td></td><td></td><td></td><td>District of Columbia</td><td>7.7</td></tr>
</table>

Source: Morgan Quitno Press using data from U.S. Department of Labor, Bureau of Labor Statistics
"Regional and State Employment and Unemployment" (press release, January 19, 2001)
*Seasonally adjusted preliminary data as of December 2000. National percent calculated through a different formula.

# VII. ENERGY AND ENVIRONMENT

# Energy Consumption in 1997

## National Total = 94,063,600,000,000,000 Btu's*

ALPHA ORDER

| RANK | STATE | BTU'S | % of USA |
|------|-------|-------|----------|
| 17 | Alabama | 1,977,500,000,000,000 | 2.1% |
| 35 | Alaska | 697,300,000,000,000 | 0.7% |
| 26 | Arizona | 1,152,400,000,000,000 | 1.2% |
| 32 | Arkansas | 1,030,200,000,000,000 | 1.1% |
| 2 | California | 7,727,500,000,000,000 | 8.2% |
| 28 | Colorado | 1,133,400,000,000,000 | 1.2% |
| 34 | Connecticut | 795,800,000,000,000 | 0.8% |
| 46 | Delaware | 267,200,000,000,000 | 0.3% |
| 8 | Florida | 3,614,700,000,000,000 | 3.8% |
| 11 | Georgia | 2,588,400,000,000,000 | 2.8% |
| 48 | Hawaii | 239,500,000,000,000 | 0.3% |
| 41 | Idaho | 497,700,000,000,000 | 0.5% |
| 7 | Illinois | 3,900,200,000,000,000 | 4.1% |
| 10 | Indiana | 2,683,600,000,000,000 | 2.9% |
| 27 | Iowa | 1,136,400,000,000,000 | 1.2% |
| 31 | Kansas | 1,033,100,000,000,000 | 1.1% |
| 19 | Kentucky | 1,809,600,000,000,000 | 1.9% |
| 5 | Louisiana | 4,093,000,000,000,000 | 4.4% |
| 40 | Maine | 553,400,000,000,000 | 0.6% |
| 25 | Maryland | 1,360,000,000,000,000 | 1.4% |
| 22 | Massachusetts | 1,534,100,000,000,000 | 1.6% |
| 9 | Michigan | 3,259,100,000,000,000 | 3.5% |
| 21 | Minnesota | 1,685,800,000,000,000 | 1.8% |
| 30 | Mississippi | 1,123,700,000,000,000 | 1.2% |
| 20 | Missouri | 1,748,900,000,000,000 | 1.9% |
| 43 | Montana | 377,500,000,000,000 | 0.4% |
| 38 | Nebraska | 617,100,000,000,000 | 0.7% |
| 39 | Nevada | 584,400,000,000,000 | 0.6% |
| 45 | New Hampshir | 303,900,000,000,000 | 0.3% |
| 12 | New Jersey | 2,585,400,000,000,000 | 2.7% |
| 37 | New Mexico | 647,100,000,000,000 | 0.7% |
| 4 | New York | 4,093,200,000,000,000 | 4.4% |
| 13 | North Carolina | 2,425,200,000,000,000 | 2.6% |
| 44 | North Dakota | 355,800,000,000,000 | 0.4% |
| 3 | Ohio | 4,144,300,000,000,000 | 4.4% |
| 24 | Oklahoma | 1,405,200,000,000,000 | 1.5% |
| 29 | Oregon | 1,132,900,000,000,000 | 1.2% |
| 6 | Pennsylvania | 3,900,700,000,000,000 | 4.1% |
| 49 | Rhode Island | 235,100,000,000,000 | 0.2% |
| 23 | South Carolina | 1,474,200,000,000,000 | 1.6% |
| 47 | South Dakota | 241,900,000,000,000 | 0.3% |
| 16 | Tennessee | 2,084,200,000,000,000 | 2.2% |
| 1 | Texas | 11,396,100,000,000,000 | 12.1% |
| 36 | Utah | 691,200,000,000,000 | 0.7% |
| 50 | Vermont | 167,100,000,000,000 | 0.2% |
| 15 | Virginia | 2,126,400,000,000,000 | 2.3% |
| 14 | Washington | 2,164,200,000,000,000 | 2.3% |
| 33 | West Virginia | 809,200,000,000,000 | 0.9% |
| 18 | Wisconsin | 1,835,400,000,000,000 | 2.0% |
| 42 | Wyoming | 428,300,000,000,000 | 0.5% |

RANK ORDER

| RANK | STATE | BTU'S | % of USA |
|------|-------|-------|----------|
| 1 | Texas | 11,396,100,000,000,000 | 12.1% |
| 2 | California | 7,727,500,000,000,000 | 8.2% |
| 3 | Ohio | 4,144,300,000,000,000 | 4.4% |
| 4 | New York | 4,093,200,000,000,000 | 4.4% |
| 5 | Louisiana | 4,093,000,000,000,000 | 4.4% |
| 6 | Pennsylvania | 3,900,700,000,000,000 | 4.1% |
| 7 | Illinois | 3,900,200,000,000,000 | 4.1% |
| 8 | Florida | 3,614,700,000,000,000 | 3.8% |
| 9 | Michigan | 3,259,100,000,000,000 | 3.5% |
| 10 | Indiana | 2,683,600,000,000,000 | 2.9% |
| 11 | Georgia | 2,588,400,000,000,000 | 2.8% |
| 12 | New Jersey | 2,585,400,000,000,000 | 2.7% |
| 13 | North Carolina | 2,425,200,000,000,000 | 2.6% |
| 14 | Washington | 2,164,200,000,000,000 | 2.3% |
| 15 | Virginia | 2,126,400,000,000,000 | 2.3% |
| 16 | Tennessee | 2,084,200,000,000,000 | 2.2% |
| 17 | Alabama | 1,977,500,000,000,000 | 2.1% |
| 18 | Wisconsin | 1,835,400,000,000,000 | 2.0% |
| 19 | Kentucky | 1,809,600,000,000,000 | 1.9% |
| 20 | Missouri | 1,748,900,000,000,000 | 1.9% |
| 21 | Minnesota | 1,685,800,000,000,000 | 1.8% |
| 22 | Massachusetts | 1,534,100,000,000,000 | 1.6% |
| 23 | South Carolina | 1,474,200,000,000,000 | 1.6% |
| 24 | Oklahoma | 1,405,200,000,000,000 | 1.5% |
| 25 | Maryland | 1,360,000,000,000,000 | 1.4% |
| 26 | Arizona | 1,152,400,000,000,000 | 1.2% |
| 27 | Iowa | 1,136,400,000,000,000 | 1.2% |
| 28 | Colorado | 1,133,400,000,000,000 | 1.2% |
| 29 | Oregon | 1,132,900,000,000,000 | 1.2% |
| 30 | Mississippi | 1,123,700,000,000,000 | 1.2% |
| 31 | Kansas | 1,033,100,000,000,000 | 1.1% |
| 32 | Arkansas | 1,030,200,000,000,000 | 1.1% |
| 33 | West Virginia | 809,200,000,000,000 | 0.9% |
| 34 | Connecticut | 795,800,000,000,000 | 0.8% |
| 35 | Alaska | 697,300,000,000,000 | 0.7% |
| 36 | Utah | 691,200,000,000,000 | 0.7% |
| 37 | New Mexico | 647,100,000,000,000 | 0.7% |
| 38 | Nebraska | 617,100,000,000,000 | 0.7% |
| 39 | Nevada | 584,400,000,000,000 | 0.6% |
| 40 | Maine | 553,400,000,000,000 | 0.6% |
| 41 | Idaho | 497,700,000,000,000 | 0.5% |
| 42 | Wyoming | 428,300,000,000,000 | 0.5% |
| 43 | Montana | 377,500,000,000,000 | 0.4% |
| 44 | North Dakota | 355,800,000,000,000 | 0.4% |
| 45 | New Hampshir | 303,900,000,000,000 | 0.3% |
| 46 | Delaware | 267,200,000,000,000 | 0.3% |
| 47 | South Dakota | 241,900,000,000,000 | 0.3% |
| 48 | Hawaii | 239,500,000,000,000 | 0.3% |
| 49 | Rhode Island | 235,100,000,000,000 | 0.2% |
| 50 | Vermont | 167,100,000,000,000 | 0.2% |
| | District of Columbia | 176,600,000,000,000 | 0.2% |

Source: U.S. Department of Energy, Energy Information Administration
     "State Energy Data Report 1997" (DOE/EIA-0214(97), September 1999)
*British Thermal Units: The amount of heat required to raise the temperature of one pound of water one degree.

# Per Capita Energy Consumption in 1997

## National Per Capita = 351,267,208 Btu's*

<table>
<tr><td colspan="3">ALPHA ORDER</td><td colspan="3">RANK ORDER</td></tr>
<tr><td>RANK</td><td>STATE</td><td>BTU'S PER CAPITA</td><td>RANK</td><td>STATE</td><td>BTU'S PER CAPITA</td></tr>
<tr><td>7</td><td>Alabama</td><td>457,724,856</td><td>1</td><td>Alaska</td><td>1,145,281,401</td></tr>
<tr><td>1</td><td>Alaska</td><td>1,145,281,401</td><td>2</td><td>Louisiana</td><td>940,618,975</td></tr>
<tr><td>43</td><td>Arizona</td><td>253,151,933</td><td>3</td><td>Wyoming</td><td>892,234,043</td></tr>
<tr><td>15</td><td>Arkansas</td><td>408,160,516</td><td>4</td><td>Texas</td><td>588,780,604</td></tr>
<tr><td>47</td><td>California</td><td>239,852,568</td><td>5</td><td>North Dakota</td><td>555,117,834</td></tr>
<tr><td>39</td><td>Colorado</td><td>291,265,654</td><td>6</td><td>Kentucky</td><td>463,071,956</td></tr>
<tr><td>46</td><td>Connecticut</td><td>243,474,558</td><td>7</td><td>Alabama</td><td>457,724,856</td></tr>
<tr><td>24</td><td>Delaware</td><td>363,525,545</td><td>8</td><td>Indiana</td><td>456,987,554</td></tr>
<tr><td>45</td><td>Florida</td><td>246,176,792</td><td>9</td><td>West Virginia</td><td>445,695,830</td></tr>
<tr><td>29</td><td>Georgia</td><td>345,761,087</td><td>10</td><td>Maine</td><td>444,421,245</td></tr>
<tr><td>50</td><td>Hawaii</td><td>201,375,237</td><td>11</td><td>Montana</td><td>429,608,993</td></tr>
<tr><td>14</td><td>Idaho</td><td>411,105,549</td><td>12</td><td>Oklahoma</td><td>423,986,176</td></tr>
<tr><td>34</td><td>Illinois</td><td>324,705,247</td><td>13</td><td>Mississippi</td><td>411,336,593</td></tr>
<tr><td>8</td><td>Indiana</td><td>456,987,554</td><td>14</td><td>Idaho</td><td>411,105,549</td></tr>
<tr><td>16</td><td>Iowa</td><td>398,122,755</td><td>15</td><td>Arkansas</td><td>408,160,516</td></tr>
<tr><td>17</td><td>Kansas</td><td>394,864,733</td><td>16</td><td>Iowa</td><td>398,122,755</td></tr>
<tr><td>6</td><td>Kentucky</td><td>463,071,956</td><td>17</td><td>Kansas</td><td>394,864,733</td></tr>
<tr><td>2</td><td>Louisiana</td><td>940,618,975</td><td>18</td><td>South Carolina</td><td>388,964,203</td></tr>
<tr><td>10</td><td>Maine</td><td>444,421,245</td><td>19</td><td>Tennessee</td><td>387,510,637</td></tr>
<tr><td>41</td><td>Maryland</td><td>267,037,692</td><td>20</td><td>Washington</td><td>386,181,201</td></tr>
<tr><td>44</td><td>Massachusetts</td><td>250,855,371</td><td>21</td><td>New Mexico</td><td>375,579,170</td></tr>
<tr><td>31</td><td>Michigan</td><td>333,055,710</td><td>22</td><td>Nebraska</td><td>372,635,477</td></tr>
<tr><td>25</td><td>Minnesota</td><td>359,619,995</td><td>23</td><td>Ohio</td><td>369,614,336</td></tr>
<tr><td>13</td><td>Mississippi</td><td>411,336,593</td><td>24</td><td>Delaware</td><td>363,525,545</td></tr>
<tr><td>36</td><td>Missouri</td><td>323,444,322</td><td>25</td><td>Minnesota</td><td>359,619,995</td></tr>
<tr><td>11</td><td>Montana</td><td>429,608,993</td><td>26</td><td>Wisconsin</td><td>352,945,588</td></tr>
<tr><td>22</td><td>Nebraska</td><td>372,635,477</td><td>27</td><td>Oregon</td><td>349,309,675</td></tr>
<tr><td>28</td><td>Nevada</td><td>348,774,544</td><td>28</td><td>Nevada</td><td>348,774,544</td></tr>
<tr><td>42</td><td>New Hampshire</td><td>259,026,507</td><td>29</td><td>Georgia</td><td>345,761,087</td></tr>
<tr><td>37</td><td>New Jersey</td><td>321,001,100</td><td>30</td><td>Utah</td><td>334,657,211</td></tr>
<tr><td>21</td><td>New Mexico</td><td>375,579,170</td><td>31</td><td>Michigan</td><td>333,055,710</td></tr>
<tr><td>49</td><td>New York</td><td>225,605,384</td><td>32</td><td>South Dakota</td><td>330,982,206</td></tr>
<tr><td>33</td><td>North Carolina</td><td>326,464,811</td><td>33</td><td>North Carolina</td><td>326,464,811</td></tr>
<tr><td>5</td><td>North Dakota</td><td>555,117,834</td><td>34</td><td>Illinois</td><td>324,705,247</td></tr>
<tr><td>23</td><td>Ohio</td><td>369,614,336</td><td>35</td><td>Pennsylvania</td><td>324,628,525</td></tr>
<tr><td>12</td><td>Oklahoma</td><td>423,986,176</td><td>36</td><td>Missouri</td><td>323,444,322</td></tr>
<tr><td>27</td><td>Oregon</td><td>349,309,675</td><td>37</td><td>New Jersey</td><td>321,001,100</td></tr>
<tr><td>35</td><td>Pennsylvania</td><td>324,628,525</td><td>38</td><td>Virginia</td><td>315,823,337</td></tr>
<tr><td>48</td><td>Rhode Island</td><td>238,204,761</td><td>39</td><td>Colorado</td><td>291,265,654</td></tr>
<tr><td>18</td><td>South Carolina</td><td>388,964,203</td><td>40</td><td>Vermont</td><td>283,862,638</td></tr>
<tr><td>32</td><td>South Dakota</td><td>330,982,206</td><td>41</td><td>Maryland</td><td>267,037,692</td></tr>
<tr><td>19</td><td>Tennessee</td><td>387,510,637</td><td>42</td><td>New Hampshire</td><td>259,026,507</td></tr>
<tr><td>4</td><td>Texas</td><td>588,780,604</td><td>43</td><td>Arizona</td><td>253,151,933</td></tr>
<tr><td>30</td><td>Utah</td><td>334,657,211</td><td>44</td><td>Massachusetts</td><td>250,855,371</td></tr>
<tr><td>40</td><td>Vermont</td><td>283,862,638</td><td>45</td><td>Florida</td><td>246,176,792</td></tr>
<tr><td>38</td><td>Virginia</td><td>315,823,337</td><td>46</td><td>Connecticut</td><td>243,474,558</td></tr>
<tr><td>20</td><td>Washington</td><td>386,181,201</td><td>47</td><td>California</td><td>239,852,568</td></tr>
<tr><td>9</td><td>West Virginia</td><td>445,695,830</td><td>48</td><td>Rhode Island</td><td>238,204,761</td></tr>
<tr><td>26</td><td>Wisconsin</td><td>352,945,588</td><td>49</td><td>New York</td><td>225,605,384</td></tr>
<tr><td>3</td><td>Wyoming</td><td>892,234,043</td><td>50</td><td>Hawaii</td><td>201,375,237</td></tr>
<tr><td></td><td></td><td></td><td></td><td>District of Columbia</td><td>333,994,009</td></tr>
</table>

Source: Morgan Quitno Press using data from U.S. Department of Energy, Energy Information Administration
    "State Energy Data Report 1997" (DOE/EIA-0214(97), September 1999)
*British Thermal Units: The amount of heat required to raise the temperature of one pound of water one degree.

# Average Annual Percent Change in Per Capita Energy Use: 1995 to 1997

## National Percent Change = 1.0% Increase Annually*

ALPHA ORDER

| RANK | STATE | PERCENT CHANGE |
|------|-------|----------------|
| 33 | Alabama | 0.5 |
| 38 | Alaska | 0.2 |
| 18 | Arizona | 1.5 |
| 29 | Arkansas | 0.7 |
| 41 | California | (0.1) |
| 29 | Colorado | 0.7 |
| 32 | Connecticut | 0.6 |
| 46 | Delaware | (0.7) |
| 43 | Florida | (0.4) |
| 45 | Georgia | (0.5) |
| 50 | Hawaii | (3.5) |
| 7 | Idaho | 2.5 |
| 36 | Illinois | 0.3 |
| 23 | Indiana | 1.0 |
| 5 | Iowa | 2.9 |
| 48 | Kansas | (1.3) |
| 34 | Kentucky | 0.4 |
| 4 | Louisiana | 3.3 |
| 3 | Maine | 3.4 |
| 20 | Maryland | 1.2 |
| 25 | Massachusetts | 0.9 |
| 25 | Michigan | 0.9 |
| 21 | Minnesota | 1.1 |
| 12 | Mississippi | 2.2 |
| 14 | Missouri | 1.8 |
| 47 | Montana | (0.8) |
| 7 | Nebraska | 2.5 |
| 42 | Nevada | (0.3) |
| 12 | New Hampshire | 2.2 |
| 38 | New Jersey | 0.2 |
| 2 | New Mexico | 5.0 |
| 10 | New York | 2.3 |
| 34 | North Carolina | 0.4 |
| 28 | North Dakota | 0.8 |
| 25 | Ohio | 0.9 |
| 23 | Oklahoma | 1.0 |
| 10 | Oregon | 2.3 |
| 36 | Pennsylvania | 0.3 |
| 40 | Rhode Island | 0.1 |
| 21 | South Carolina | 1.1 |
| 16 | South Dakota | 1.6 |
| 19 | Tennessee | 1.3 |
| 9 | Texas | 2.4 |
| 15 | Utah | 1.7 |
| 1 | Vermont | 5.1 |
| 29 | Virginia | 0.7 |
| 49 | Washington | (1.4) |
| 43 | West Virginia | (0.4) |
| 16 | Wisconsin | 1.6 |
| 6 | Wyoming | 2.7 |

RANK ORDER

| RANK | STATE | PERCENT CHANGE |
|------|-------|----------------|
| 1 | Vermont | 5.1 |
| 2 | New Mexico | 5.0 |
| 3 | Maine | 3.4 |
| 4 | Louisiana | 3.3 |
| 5 | Iowa | 2.9 |
| 6 | Wyoming | 2.7 |
| 7 | Idaho | 2.5 |
| 7 | Nebraska | 2.5 |
| 9 | Texas | 2.4 |
| 10 | New York | 2.3 |
| 10 | Oregon | 2.3 |
| 12 | Mississippi | 2.2 |
| 12 | New Hampshire | 2.2 |
| 14 | Missouri | 1.8 |
| 15 | Utah | 1.7 |
| 16 | South Dakota | 1.6 |
| 16 | Wisconsin | 1.6 |
| 18 | Arizona | 1.5 |
| 19 | Tennessee | 1.3 |
| 20 | Maryland | 1.2 |
| 21 | Minnesota | 1.1 |
| 21 | South Carolina | 1.1 |
| 23 | Indiana | 1.0 |
| 23 | Oklahoma | 1.0 |
| 25 | Massachusetts | 0.9 |
| 25 | Michigan | 0.9 |
| 25 | Ohio | 0.9 |
| 28 | North Dakota | 0.8 |
| 29 | Arkansas | 0.7 |
| 29 | Colorado | 0.7 |
| 29 | Virginia | 0.7 |
| 32 | Connecticut | 0.6 |
| 33 | Alabama | 0.5 |
| 34 | Kentucky | 0.4 |
| 34 | North Carolina | 0.4 |
| 36 | Illinois | 0.3 |
| 36 | Pennsylvania | 0.3 |
| 38 | Alaska | 0.2 |
| 38 | New Jersey | 0.2 |
| 40 | Rhode Island | 0.1 |
| 41 | California | (0.1) |
| 42 | Nevada | (0.3) |
| 43 | Florida | (0.4) |
| 43 | West Virginia | (0.4) |
| 45 | Georgia | (0.5) |
| 46 | Delaware | (0.7) |
| 47 | Montana | (0.8) |
| 48 | Kansas | (1.3) |
| 49 | Washington | (1.4) |
| 50 | Hawaii | (3.5) |

District of Columbia 1.9

*Source: Morgan Quitno Press using data from U.S. Department of Energy, Energy Information Administration
"State Energy Data Report 1997" (DOE/EIA-0214(97), September 1999)*
*British Thermal Units: The amount of heat required to raise the temperature of one pound of water one degree.
Table shows annual average change in Btu's per capita for two year period from 1995 to 1997.*

# Energy Prices in 1997

## National Rate = $8.82 per Million Btu's*

ALPHA ORDER

RANK ORDER

| RANK | STATE | RATE |
|---|---|---|
| 40 | Alabama | $7.81 |
| 47 | Alaska | 6.69 |
| 3 | Arizona | 11.75 |
| 28 | Arkansas | 8.65 |
| 10 | California | 10.27 |
| 27 | Colorado | 8.68 |
| 2 | Connecticut | 12.56 |
| 13 | Delaware | 9.98 |
| 9 | Florida | 10.99 |
| 23 | Georgia | 8.86 |
| 1 | Hawaii | 13.34 |
| 39 | Idaho | 8.01 |
| 20 | Illinois | 9.03 |
| 45 | Indiana | 7.31 |
| 37 | Iowa | 8.10 |
| 25 | Kansas | 8.77 |
| 41 | Kentucky | 7.72 |
| 50 | Louisiana | 5.81 |
| 24 | Maine | 8.82 |
| 10 | Maryland | 10.27 |
| 6 | Massachusetts | 11.35 |
| 36 | Michigan | 8.18 |
| 32 | Minnesota | 8.46 |
| 30 | Mississippi | 8.59 |
| 19 | Missouri | 9.15 |
| 33 | Montana | 8.41 |
| 31 | Nebraska | 8.47 |
| 14 | Nevada | 9.81 |
| 4 | New Hampshire | 11.58 |
| 15 | New Jersey | 9.46 |
| 16 | New Mexico | 9.45 |
| 7 | New York | 11.18 |
| 12 | North Carolina | 10.11 |
| 49 | North Dakota | 6.25 |
| 21 | Ohio | 9.01 |
| 38 | Oklahoma | 8.07 |
| 34 | Oregon | 8.40 |
| 17 | Pennsylvania | 9.32 |
| 8 | Rhode Island | 11.04 |
| 25 | South Carolina | 8.77 |
| 22 | South Dakota | 8.98 |
| 29 | Tennessee | 8.60 |
| 46 | Texas | 6.94 |
| 43 | Utah | 7.58 |
| 5 | Vermont | 11.36 |
| 17 | Virginia | 9.32 |
| 42 | Washington | 7.64 |
| 44 | West Virginia | 7.33 |
| 35 | Wisconsin | 8.25 |
| 48 | Wyoming | 6.51 |

| RANK | STATE | RATE |
|---|---|---|
| 1 | Hawaii | $13.34 |
| 2 | Connecticut | 12.56 |
| 3 | Arizona | 11.75 |
| 4 | New Hampshire | 11.58 |
| 5 | Vermont | 11.36 |
| 6 | Massachusetts | 11.35 |
| 7 | New York | 11.18 |
| 8 | Rhode Island | 11.04 |
| 9 | Florida | 10.99 |
| 10 | California | 10.27 |
| 10 | Maryland | 10.27 |
| 12 | North Carolina | 10.11 |
| 13 | Delaware | 9.98 |
| 14 | Nevada | 9.81 |
| 15 | New Jersey | 9.46 |
| 16 | New Mexico | 9.45 |
| 17 | Pennsylvania | 9.32 |
| 17 | Virginia | 9.32 |
| 19 | Missouri | 9.15 |
| 20 | Illinois | 9.03 |
| 21 | Ohio | 9.01 |
| 22 | South Dakota | 8.98 |
| 23 | Georgia | 8.86 |
| 24 | Maine | 8.82 |
| 25 | Kansas | 8.77 |
| 25 | South Carolina | 8.77 |
| 27 | Colorado | 8.68 |
| 28 | Arkansas | 8.65 |
| 29 | Tennessee | 8.60 |
| 30 | Mississippi | 8.59 |
| 31 | Nebraska | 8.47 |
| 32 | Minnesota | 8.46 |
| 33 | Montana | 8.41 |
| 34 | Oregon | 8.40 |
| 35 | Wisconsin | 8.25 |
| 36 | Michigan | 8.18 |
| 37 | Iowa | 8.10 |
| 38 | Oklahoma | 8.07 |
| 39 | Idaho | 8.01 |
| 40 | Alabama | 7.81 |
| 41 | Kentucky | 7.72 |
| 42 | Washington | 7.64 |
| 43 | Utah | 7.58 |
| 44 | West Virginia | 7.33 |
| 45 | Indiana | 7.31 |
| 46 | Texas | 6.94 |
| 47 | Alaska | 6.69 |
| 48 | Wyoming | 6.51 |
| 49 | North Dakota | 6.25 |
| 50 | Louisiana | 5.81 |
| | District of Columbia | 12.84 |

Source: U.S. Department of Energy, Energy Information Administration
    "State Energy Price and Expenditure Report 1997" (July 2000)
*British Thermal Units: The amount of heat required to raise the temperature of one pound of water one degree.

# Energy Expenditures in 1997

## National Total = $567,318,000,000

ALPHA ORDER

| RANK | STATE | EXPENDITURES | % of USA |
|------|-------|-------------:|---------:|
| 21 | Alabama | $9,816,000,000 | 1.7% |
| 43 | Alaska | 2,180,000,000 | 0.4% |
| 24 | Arizona | 8,574,000,000 | 1.5% |
| 33 | Arkansas | 5,812,000,000 | 1.0% |
| 1 | California | 55,187,000,000 | 9.7% |
| 28 | Colorado | 6,881,000,000 | 1.2% |
| 27 | Connecticut | 7,248,000,000 | 1.3% |
| 48 | Delaware | 1,692,000,000 | 0.3% |
| 6 | Florida | 25,117,000,000 | 4.4% |
| 11 | Georgia | 15,642,000,000 | 2.8% |
| 42 | Hawaii | 2,288,000,000 | 0.4% |
| 40 | Idaho | 2,550,000,000 | 0.4% |
| 7 | Illinois | 25,089,000,000 | 4.4% |
| 13 | Indiana | 14,106,000,000 | 2.5% |
| 29 | Iowa | 6,649,000,000 | 1.2% |
| 32 | Kansas | 5,850,000,000 | 1.0% |
| 23 | Kentucky | 9,045,000,000 | 1.6% |
| 12 | Louisiana | 15,120,000,000 | 2.7% |
| 39 | Maine | 3,158,000,000 | 0.6% |
| 22 | Maryland | 9,583,000,000 | 1.7% |
| 15 | Massachusetts | 13,087,000,000 | 2.3% |
| 8 | Michigan | 19,758,000,000 | 3.5% |
| 20 | Minnesota | 9,869,000,000 | 1.7% |
| 31 | Mississippi | 5,963,000,000 | 1.1% |
| 17 | Missouri | 11,532,000,000 | 2.0% |
| 44 | Montana | 2,171,000,000 | 0.4% |
| 35 | Nebraska | 3,814,000,000 | 0.7% |
| 37 | Nevada | 3,637,000,000 | 0.6% |
| 41 | New Hampshire | 2,525,000,000 | 0.4% |
| 9 | New Jersey | 18,764,000,000 | 3.3% |
| 38 | New Mexico | 3,427,000,000 | 0.6% |
| 3 | New York | 34,089,000,000 | 6.0% |
| 10 | North Carolina | 15,823,000,000 | 2.8% |
| 47 | North Dakota | 1,699,000,000 | 0.3% |
| 5 | Ohio | 25,556,000,000 | 4.5% |
| 26 | Oklahoma | 7,333,000,000 | 1.3% |
| 30 | Oregon | 6,058,000,000 | 1.1% |
| 4 | Pennsylvania | 25,810,000,000 | 4.5% |
| 45 | Rhode Island | 2,044,000,000 | 0.4% |
| 25 | South Carolina | 8,177,000,000 | 1.4% |
| 49 | South Dakota | 1,629,000,000 | 0.3% |
| 16 | Tennessee | 11,604,000,000 | 2.0% |
| 2 | Texas | 55,070,000,000 | 9.7% |
| 36 | Utah | 3,708,000,000 | 0.7% |
| 50 | Vermont | 1,368,000,000 | 0.2% |
| 14 | Virginia | 13,451,000,000 | 2.4% |
| 18 | Washington | 10,330,000,000 | 1.8% |
| 34 | West Virginia | 4,002,000,000 | 0.7% |
| 19 | Wisconsin | 10,156,000,000 | 1.8% |
| 46 | Wyoming | 1,873,000,000 | 0.3% |

RANK ORDER

| RANK | STATE | EXPENDITURES | % of USA |
|------|-------|-------------:|---------:|
| 1 | California | $55,187,000,000 | 9.7% |
| 2 | Texas | 55,070,000,000 | 9.7% |
| 3 | New York | 34,089,000,000 | 6.0% |
| 4 | Pennsylvania | 25,810,000,000 | 4.5% |
| 5 | Ohio | 25,556,000,000 | 4.5% |
| 6 | Florida | 25,117,000,000 | 4.4% |
| 7 | Illinois | 25,089,000,000 | 4.4% |
| 8 | Michigan | 19,758,000,000 | 3.5% |
| 9 | New Jersey | 18,764,000,000 | 3.3% |
| 10 | North Carolina | 15,823,000,000 | 2.8% |
| 11 | Georgia | 15,642,000,000 | 2.8% |
| 12 | Louisiana | 15,120,000,000 | 2.7% |
| 13 | Indiana | 14,106,000,000 | 2.5% |
| 14 | Virginia | 13,451,000,000 | 2.4% |
| 15 | Massachusetts | 13,087,000,000 | 2.3% |
| 16 | Tennessee | 11,604,000,000 | 2.0% |
| 17 | Missouri | 11,532,000,000 | 2.0% |
| 18 | Washington | 10,330,000,000 | 1.8% |
| 19 | Wisconsin | 10,156,000,000 | 1.8% |
| 20 | Minnesota | 9,869,000,000 | 1.7% |
| 21 | Alabama | 9,816,000,000 | 1.7% |
| 22 | Maryland | 9,583,000,000 | 1.7% |
| 23 | Kentucky | 9,045,000,000 | 1.6% |
| 24 | Arizona | 8,574,000,000 | 1.5% |
| 25 | South Carolina | 8,177,000,000 | 1.4% |
| 26 | Oklahoma | 7,333,000,000 | 1.3% |
| 27 | Connecticut | 7,248,000,000 | 1.3% |
| 28 | Colorado | 6,881,000,000 | 1.2% |
| 29 | Iowa | 6,649,000,000 | 1.2% |
| 30 | Oregon | 6,058,000,000 | 1.1% |
| 31 | Mississippi | 5,963,000,000 | 1.1% |
| 32 | Kansas | 5,850,000,000 | 1.0% |
| 33 | Arkansas | 5,812,000,000 | 1.0% |
| 34 | West Virginia | 4,002,000,000 | 0.7% |
| 35 | Nebraska | 3,814,000,000 | 0.7% |
| 36 | Utah | 3,708,000,000 | 0.7% |
| 37 | Nevada | 3,637,000,000 | 0.6% |
| 38 | New Mexico | 3,427,000,000 | 0.6% |
| 39 | Maine | 3,158,000,000 | 0.6% |
| 40 | Idaho | 2,550,000,000 | 0.4% |
| 41 | New Hampshire | 2,525,000,000 | 0.4% |
| 42 | Hawaii | 2,288,000,000 | 0.4% |
| 43 | Alaska | 2,180,000,000 | 0.4% |
| 44 | Montana | 2,171,000,000 | 0.4% |
| 45 | Rhode Island | 2,044,000,000 | 0.4% |
| 46 | Wyoming | 1,873,000,000 | 0.3% |
| 47 | North Dakota | 1,699,000,000 | 0.3% |
| 48 | Delaware | 1,692,000,000 | 0.3% |
| 49 | South Dakota | 1,629,000,000 | 0.3% |
| 50 | Vermont | 1,368,000,000 | 0.2% |
| | District of Columbia | 1,334,000,000 | 0.2% |

*Source: U.S. Department of Energy, Energy Information Administration*
*"State Energy Price and Expenditure Report 1997" (July 2000)*

# Per Capita Energy Expenditures in 1997

## National Per Capita = $2,119

<table>
<tr><td colspan="3"><u>ALPHA ORDER</u></td><td colspan="3"><u>RANK ORDER</u></td></tr>
<tr><td>RANK</td><td>STATE</td><td>PER CAPITA</td><td>RANK</td><td>STATE</td><td>PER CAPITA</td></tr>
<tr><td>17</td><td>Alabama</td><td>$2,271</td><td>1</td><td>Wyoming</td><td>$3,902</td></tr>
<tr><td>2</td><td>Alaska</td><td>3,575</td><td>2</td><td>Alaska</td><td>3,575</td></tr>
<tr><td>42</td><td>Arizona</td><td>1,883</td><td>3</td><td>Louisiana</td><td>3,473</td></tr>
<tr><td>13</td><td>Arkansas</td><td>2,304</td><td>4</td><td>Texas</td><td>2,841</td></tr>
<tr><td>49</td><td>California</td><td>1,715</td><td>5</td><td>North Dakota</td><td>2,651</td></tr>
<tr><td>48</td><td>Colorado</td><td>1,768</td><td>6</td><td>Maine</td><td>2,543</td></tr>
<tr><td>19</td><td>Connecticut</td><td>2,218</td><td>7</td><td>Montana</td><td>2,471</td></tr>
<tr><td>15</td><td>Delaware</td><td>2,301</td><td>8</td><td>Indiana</td><td>2,405</td></tr>
<tr><td>50</td><td>Florida</td><td>1,711</td><td>9</td><td>Iowa</td><td>2,330</td></tr>
<tr><td>35</td><td>Georgia</td><td>2,088</td><td>10</td><td>New Jersey</td><td>2,328</td></tr>
<tr><td>41</td><td>Hawaii</td><td>1,920</td><td>11</td><td>Vermont</td><td>2,324</td></tr>
<tr><td>32</td><td>Idaho</td><td>2,109</td><td>12</td><td>Kentucky</td><td>2,313</td></tr>
<tr><td>34</td><td>Illinois</td><td>2,093</td><td>13</td><td>Arkansas</td><td>2,304</td></tr>
<tr><td>8</td><td>Indiana</td><td>2,405</td><td>14</td><td>Nebraska</td><td>2,302</td></tr>
<tr><td>9</td><td>Iowa</td><td>2,330</td><td>15</td><td>Delaware</td><td>2,301</td></tr>
<tr><td>18</td><td>Kansas</td><td>2,249</td><td>16</td><td>Ohio</td><td>2,283</td></tr>
<tr><td>12</td><td>Kentucky</td><td>2,313</td><td>17</td><td>Alabama</td><td>2,271</td></tr>
<tr><td>3</td><td>Louisiana</td><td>3,473</td><td>18</td><td>Kansas</td><td>2,249</td></tr>
<tr><td>6</td><td>Maine</td><td>2,543</td><td>19</td><td>Connecticut</td><td>2,218</td></tr>
<tr><td>43</td><td>Maryland</td><td>1,881</td><td>20</td><td>Oklahoma</td><td>2,208</td></tr>
<tr><td>29</td><td>Massachusetts</td><td>2,140</td><td>20</td><td>South Dakota</td><td>2,208</td></tr>
<tr><td>37</td><td>Michigan</td><td>2,020</td><td>22</td><td>West Virginia</td><td>2,204</td></tr>
<tr><td>33</td><td>Minnesota</td><td>2,105</td><td>23</td><td>Mississippi</td><td>2,183</td></tr>
<tr><td>23</td><td>Mississippi</td><td>2,183</td><td>24</td><td>Nevada</td><td>2,166</td></tr>
<tr><td>30</td><td>Missouri</td><td>2,132</td><td>25</td><td>Tennessee</td><td>2,160</td></tr>
<tr><td>7</td><td>Montana</td><td>2,471</td><td>26</td><td>South Carolina</td><td>2,159</td></tr>
<tr><td>14</td><td>Nebraska</td><td>2,302</td><td>27</td><td>New Hampshire</td><td>2,154</td></tr>
<tr><td>24</td><td>Nevada</td><td>2,166</td><td>28</td><td>Pennsylvania</td><td>2,149</td></tr>
<tr><td>27</td><td>New Hampshire</td><td>2,154</td><td>29</td><td>Massachusetts</td><td>2,140</td></tr>
<tr><td>10</td><td>New Jersey</td><td>2,328</td><td>30</td><td>Missouri</td><td>2,132</td></tr>
<tr><td>39</td><td>New Mexico</td><td>1,988</td><td>31</td><td>North Carolina</td><td>2,129</td></tr>
<tr><td>44</td><td>New York</td><td>1,879</td><td>32</td><td>Idaho</td><td>2,109</td></tr>
<tr><td>31</td><td>North Carolina</td><td>2,129</td><td>33</td><td>Minnesota</td><td>2,105</td></tr>
<tr><td>5</td><td>North Dakota</td><td>2,651</td><td>34</td><td>Illinois</td><td>2,093</td></tr>
<tr><td>16</td><td>Ohio</td><td>2,283</td><td>35</td><td>Georgia</td><td>2,088</td></tr>
<tr><td>20</td><td>Oklahoma</td><td>2,208</td><td>36</td><td>Rhode Island</td><td>2,070</td></tr>
<tr><td>45</td><td>Oregon</td><td>1,868</td><td>37</td><td>Michigan</td><td>2,020</td></tr>
<tr><td>28</td><td>Pennsylvania</td><td>2,149</td><td>38</td><td>Virginia</td><td>1,996</td></tr>
<tr><td>36</td><td>Rhode Island</td><td>2,070</td><td>39</td><td>New Mexico</td><td>1,988</td></tr>
<tr><td>26</td><td>South Carolina</td><td>2,159</td><td>40</td><td>Wisconsin</td><td>1,953</td></tr>
<tr><td>20</td><td>South Dakota</td><td>2,208</td><td>41</td><td>Hawaii</td><td>1,920</td></tr>
<tr><td>25</td><td>Tennessee</td><td>2,160</td><td>42</td><td>Arizona</td><td>1,883</td></tr>
<tr><td>4</td><td>Texas</td><td>2,841</td><td>43</td><td>Maryland</td><td>1,881</td></tr>
<tr><td>47</td><td>Utah</td><td>1,795</td><td>44</td><td>New York</td><td>1,879</td></tr>
<tr><td>11</td><td>Vermont</td><td>2,324</td><td>45</td><td>Oregon</td><td>1,868</td></tr>
<tr><td>38</td><td>Virginia</td><td>1,996</td><td>46</td><td>Washington</td><td>1,840</td></tr>
<tr><td>46</td><td>Washington</td><td>1,840</td><td>47</td><td>Utah</td><td>1,795</td></tr>
<tr><td>22</td><td>West Virginia</td><td>2,204</td><td>48</td><td>Colorado</td><td>1,768</td></tr>
<tr><td>40</td><td>Wisconsin</td><td>1,953</td><td>49</td><td>California</td><td>1,715</td></tr>
<tr><td>1</td><td>Wyoming</td><td>3,902</td><td>50</td><td>Florida</td><td>1,711</td></tr>
<tr><td></td><td></td><td></td><td></td><td>District of Columbia</td><td>2,518</td></tr>
</table>

*Source: U.S. Department of Energy, Energy Information Administration
"State Energy Price and Expenditure Report 1997" (July 2000)*

# Expenditures on Coal in 1997

## National Total = $27,522,000,000

ALPHA ORDER

| RANK | STATE | EXPENDITURES | % of USA |
|------|-------|--------------|----------|
| 6 | Alabama | $1,345,000,000 | 4.9% |
| 44 | Alaska | 26,000,000 | 0.1% |
| 17 | Arizona | 534,000,000 | 1.9% |
| 22 | Arkansas | 406,000,000 | 1.5% |
| 39 | California | 87,000,000 | 0.3% |
| 28 | Colorado | 362,000,000 | 1.3% |
| 42 | Connecticut | 54,000,000 | 0.2% |
| 40 | Delaware | 75,000,000 | 0.3% |
| 8 | Florida | 1,205,000,000 | 4.4% |
| 7 | Georgia | 1,234,000,000 | 4.5% |
| 48 | Hawaii | 6,000,000 | 0.0% |
| 46 | Idaho | 13,000,000 | 0.0% |
| 5 | Illinois | 1,492,000,000 | 5.4% |
| 4 | Indiana | 1,782,000,000 | 6.5% |
| 23 | Iowa | 402,000,000 | 1.5% |
| 31 | Kansas | 318,000,000 | 1.2% |
| 10 | Kentucky | 1,107,000,000 | 4.0% |
| 30 | Louisiana | 333,000,000 | 1.2% |
| 47 | Maine | 12,000,000 | 0.0% |
| 20 | Maryland | 432,000,000 | 1.6% |
| 33 | Massachusetts | 211,000,000 | 0.8% |
| 11 | Michigan | 1,102,000,000 | 4.0% |
| 24 | Minnesota | 391,000,000 | 1.4% |
| 34 | Mississippi | 205,000,000 | 0.7% |
| 14 | Missouri | 635,000,000 | 2.3% |
| 38 | Montana | 113,000,000 | 0.4% |
| 37 | Nebraska | 120,000,000 | 0.4% |
| 32 | Nevada | 232,000,000 | 0.8% |
| 41 | New Hampshire | 73,000,000 | 0.3% |
| 36 | New Jersey | 132,000,000 | 0.5% |
| 26 | New Mexico | 385,000,000 | 1.4% |
| 19 | New York | 463,000,000 | 1.7% |
| 12 | North Carolina | 1,067,000,000 | 3.9% |
| 21 | North Dakota | 411,000,000 | 1.5% |
| 3 | Ohio | 1,898,000,000 | 6.9% |
| 29 | Oklahoma | 349,000,000 | 1.3% |
| 45 | Oregon | 21,000,000 | 0.1% |
| 1 | Pennsylvania | 2,113,000,000 | 7.7% |
| 49 | Rhode Island* | 0 | 0.0% |
| 16 | South Carolina | 539,000,000 | 2.0% |
| 43 | South Dakota | 42,000,000 | 0.2% |
| 13 | Tennessee | 789,000,000 | 2.9% |
| 2 | Texas | 1,900,000,000 | 6.9% |
| 27 | Utah | 374,000,000 | 1.4% |
| 49 | Vermont* | 0 | 0.0% |
| 18 | Virginia | 525,000,000 | 1.9% |
| 35 | Washington | 136,000,000 | 0.5% |
| 9 | West Virginia | 1,119,000,000 | 4.1% |
| 15 | Wisconsin | 562,000,000 | 2.0% |
| 25 | Wyoming | 389,000,000 | 1.4% |

RANK ORDER

| RANK | STATE | EXPENDITURES | % of USA |
|------|-------|--------------|----------|
| 1 | Pennsylvania | $2,113,000,000 | 7.7% |
| 2 | Texas | 1,900,000,000 | 6.9% |
| 3 | Ohio | 1,898,000,000 | 6.9% |
| 4 | Indiana | 1,782,000,000 | 6.5% |
| 5 | Illinois | 1,492,000,000 | 5.4% |
| 6 | Alabama | 1,345,000,000 | 4.9% |
| 7 | Georgia | 1,234,000,000 | 4.5% |
| 8 | Florida | 1,205,000,000 | 4.4% |
| 9 | West Virginia | 1,119,000,000 | 4.1% |
| 10 | Kentucky | 1,107,000,000 | 4.0% |
| 11 | Michigan | 1,102,000,000 | 4.0% |
| 12 | North Carolina | 1,067,000,000 | 3.9% |
| 13 | Tennessee | 789,000,000 | 2.9% |
| 14 | Missouri | 635,000,000 | 2.3% |
| 15 | Wisconsin | 562,000,000 | 2.0% |
| 16 | South Carolina | 539,000,000 | 2.0% |
| 17 | Arizona | 534,000,000 | 1.9% |
| 18 | Virginia | 525,000,000 | 1.9% |
| 19 | New York | 463,000,000 | 1.7% |
| 20 | Maryland | 432,000,000 | 1.6% |
| 21 | North Dakota | 411,000,000 | 1.5% |
| 22 | Arkansas | 406,000,000 | 1.5% |
| 23 | Iowa | 402,000,000 | 1.5% |
| 24 | Minnesota | 391,000,000 | 1.4% |
| 25 | Wyoming | 389,000,000 | 1.4% |
| 26 | New Mexico | 385,000,000 | 1.4% |
| 27 | Utah | 374,000,000 | 1.4% |
| 28 | Colorado | 362,000,000 | 1.3% |
| 29 | Oklahoma | 349,000,000 | 1.3% |
| 30 | Louisiana | 333,000,000 | 1.2% |
| 31 | Kansas | 318,000,000 | 1.2% |
| 32 | Nevada | 232,000,000 | 0.8% |
| 33 | Massachusetts | 211,000,000 | 0.8% |
| 34 | Mississippi | 205,000,000 | 0.7% |
| 35 | Washington | 136,000,000 | 0.5% |
| 36 | New Jersey | 132,000,000 | 0.5% |
| 37 | Nebraska | 120,000,000 | 0.4% |
| 38 | Montana | 113,000,000 | 0.4% |
| 39 | California | 87,000,000 | 0.3% |
| 40 | Delaware | 75,000,000 | 0.3% |
| 41 | New Hampshire | 73,000,000 | 0.3% |
| 42 | Connecticut | 54,000,000 | 0.2% |
| 43 | South Dakota | 42,000,000 | 0.2% |
| 44 | Alaska | 26,000,000 | 0.1% |
| 45 | Oregon | 21,000,000 | 0.1% |
| 46 | Idaho | 13,000,000 | 0.0% |
| 47 | Maine | 12,000,000 | 0.0% |
| 48 | Hawaii | 6,000,000 | 0.0% |
| 49 | Rhode Island* | 0 | 0.0% |
| 49 | Vermont* | 0 | 0.0% |
| | District of Columbia | 2,000,000 | 0.0% |

*Source: U.S. Department of Energy, Energy Information Administration*
*"State Energy Price and Expenditure Report 1997" (July 2000)*
*Value less than 0.5 million dollars.

# Coal Prices in 1997

## National Rate = $1.31 per Million Btu's*

ALPHA ORDER

| RANK | STATE | RATE |
|---|---|---|
| 16 | Alabama | $1.57 |
| 4 | Alaska | 2.18 |
| 24 | Arizona | 1.45 |
| 13 | Arkansas | 1.64 |
| 7 | California | 1.78 |
| 42 | Colorado | 1.02 |
| 6 | Connecticut | 1.92 |
| 17 | Delaware | 1.55 |
| 10 | Florida | 1.73 |
| 15 | Georgia | 1.60 |
| 7 | Hawaii | 1.78 |
| 5 | Idaho | 1.97 |
| 17 | Illinois | 1.55 |
| 34 | Indiana | 1.25 |
| 41 | Iowa | 1.03 |
| 42 | Kansas | 1.02 |
| 39 | Kentucky | 1.12 |
| 23 | Louisiana | 1.48 |
| 3 | Maine | 2.56 |
| 21 | Maryland | 1.49 |
| 11 | Massachusetts | 1.71 |
| 27 | Michigan | 1.42 |
| 37 | Minnesota | 1.15 |
| 17 | Mississippi | 1.55 |
| 46 | Missouri | 0.95 |
| 49 | Montana | 0.70 |
| 50 | Nebraska | 0.62 |
| 28 | Nevada | 1.39 |
| 13 | New Hampshire | 1.64 |
| 9 | New Jersey | 1.76 |
| 31 | New Mexico | 1.34 |
| 20 | New York | 1.51 |
| 24 | North Carolina | 1.45 |
| 40 | North Dakota | 1.06 |
| 30 | Ohio | 1.35 |
| 46 | Oklahoma | 0.95 |
| 32 | Oregon | 1.27 |
| 24 | Pennsylvania | 1.45 |
| 2 | Rhode Island | 3.50 |
| 21 | South Carolina | 1.49 |
| 45 | South Dakota | 1.00 |
| 36 | Tennessee | 1.17 |
| 33 | Texas | 1.26 |
| 42 | Utah | 1.02 |
| 1 | Vermont | 3.74 |
| 29 | Virginia | 1.37 |
| 12 | Washington | 1.69 |
| 35 | West Virginia | 1.21 |
| 37 | Wisconsin | 1.15 |
| 48 | Wyoming | 0.83 |

RANK ORDER

| RANK | STATE | RATE |
|---|---|---|
| 1 | Vermont | $3.74 |
| 2 | Rhode Island | 3.50 |
| 3 | Maine | 2.56 |
| 4 | Alaska | 2.18 |
| 5 | Idaho | 1.97 |
| 6 | Connecticut | 1.92 |
| 7 | California | 1.78 |
| 7 | Hawaii | 1.78 |
| 9 | New Jersey | 1.76 |
| 10 | Florida | 1.73 |
| 11 | Massachusetts | 1.71 |
| 12 | Washington | 1.69 |
| 13 | Arkansas | 1.64 |
| 13 | New Hampshire | 1.64 |
| 15 | Georgia | 1.60 |
| 16 | Alabama | 1.57 |
| 17 | Delaware | 1.55 |
| 17 | Illinois | 1.55 |
| 17 | Mississippi | 1.55 |
| 20 | New York | 1.51 |
| 21 | Maryland | 1.49 |
| 21 | South Carolina | 1.49 |
| 23 | Louisiana | 1.48 |
| 24 | Arizona | 1.45 |
| 24 | North Carolina | 1.45 |
| 24 | Pennsylvania | 1.45 |
| 27 | Michigan | 1.42 |
| 28 | Nevada | 1.39 |
| 29 | Virginia | 1.37 |
| 30 | Ohio | 1.35 |
| 31 | New Mexico | 1.34 |
| 32 | Oregon | 1.27 |
| 33 | Texas | 1.26 |
| 34 | Indiana | 1.25 |
| 35 | West Virginia | 1.21 |
| 36 | Tennessee | 1.17 |
| 37 | Minnesota | 1.15 |
| 37 | Wisconsin | 1.15 |
| 39 | Kentucky | 1.12 |
| 40 | North Dakota | 1.06 |
| 41 | Iowa | 1.03 |
| 42 | Colorado | 1.02 |
| 42 | Kansas | 1.02 |
| 42 | Utah | 1.02 |
| 45 | South Dakota | 1.00 |
| 46 | Missouri | 0.95 |
| 46 | Oklahoma | 0.95 |
| 48 | Wyoming | 0.83 |
| 49 | Montana | 0.70 |
| 50 | Nebraska | 0.62 |
| | District of Columbia | 1.97 |

Source: U.S. Department of Energy, Energy Information Administration
   "State Energy Price and Expenditure Report 1997" (July 2000)
*British Thermal Units: The amount of heat required to raise the temperature of one pound of water one degree.

# Expenditures on Electricity in 1997

## National Total = $213,645,000,000

| RANK | STATE | EXPENDITURES | % of USA |
|---|---|---|---|
| 20 | Alabama | $3,884,000,000 | 1.8% |
| 48 | Alaska | 485,000,000 | 0.2% |
| 17 | Arizona | 4,019,000,000 | 1.9% |
| 30 | Arkansas | 2,216,000,000 | 1.0% |
| 1 | California | 21,568,000,000 | 10.1% |
| 29 | Colorado | 2,244,000,000 | 1.1% |
| 26 | Connecticut | 2,991,000,000 | 1.4% |
| 44 | Delaware | 704,000,000 | 0.3% |
| 4 | Florida | 12,588,000,000 | 5.9% |
| 11 | Georgia | 6,484,000,000 | 3.0% |
| 38 | Hawaii | 1,152,000,000 | 0.5% |
| 42 | Idaho | 821,000,000 | 0.4% |
| 7 | Illinois | 9,688,000,000 | 4.5% |
| 14 | Indiana | 4,668,000,000 | 2.2% |
| 32 | Iowa | 2,157,000,000 | 1.0% |
| 33 | Kansas | 2,025,000,000 | 0.9% |
| 25 | Kentucky | 3,067,000,000 | 1.4% |
| 16 | Louisiana | 4,442,000,000 | 2.1% |
| 39 | Maine | 1,137,000,000 | 0.5% |
| 19 | Maryland | 3,928,000,000 | 1.8% |
| 13 | Massachusetts | 4,993,000,000 | 2.3% |
| 10 | Michigan | 6,806,000,000 | 3.2% |
| 24 | Minnesota | 3,090,000,000 | 1.4% |
| 28 | Mississippi | 2,326,000,000 | 1.1% |
| 18 | Missouri | 4,002,000,000 | 1.9% |
| 45 | Montana | 611,000,000 | 0.3% |
| 36 | Nebraska | 1,196,000,000 | 0.6% |
| 34 | Nevada | 1,338,000,000 | 0.6% |
| 40 | New Hampshire | 1,059,000,000 | 0.5% |
| 9 | New Jersey | 6,925,000,000 | 3.2% |
| 37 | New Mexico | 1,172,000,000 | 0.5% |
| 3 | New York | 14,682,000,000 | 6.9% |
| 8 | North Carolina | 7,068,000,000 | 3.3% |
| 50 | North Dakota | 466,000,000 | 0.2% |
| 6 | Ohio | 9,831,000,000 | 4.6% |
| 27 | Oklahoma | 2,398,000,000 | 1.1% |
| 31 | Oregon | 2,197,000,000 | 1.0% |
| 5 | Pennsylvania | 10,157,000,000 | 4.8% |
| 43 | Rhode Island | 716,000,000 | 0.3% |
| 21 | South Carolina | 3,771,000,000 | 1.8% |
| 49 | South Dakota | 483,000,000 | 0.2% |
| 15 | Tennessee | 4,587,000,000 | 2.1% |
| 2 | Texas | 17,386,000,000 | 8.1% |
| 41 | Utah | 1,042,000,000 | 0.5% |
| 46 | Vermont | 525,000,000 | 0.2% |
| 12 | Virginia | 5,349,000,000 | 2.5% |
| 22 | Washington | 3,531,000,000 | 1.7% |
| 35 | West Virginia | 1,308,000,000 | 0.6% |
| 23 | Wisconsin | 3,113,000,000 | 1.5% |
| 47 | Wyoming | 499,000,000 | 0.2% |

| RANK | STATE | EXPENDITURES | % of USA |
|---|---|---|---|
| 1 | California | $21,568,000,000 | 10.1% |
| 2 | Texas | 17,386,000,000 | 8.1% |
| 3 | New York | 14,682,000,000 | 6.9% |
| 4 | Florida | 12,588,000,000 | 5.9% |
| 5 | Pennsylvania | 10,157,000,000 | 4.8% |
| 6 | Ohio | 9,831,000,000 | 4.6% |
| 7 | Illinois | 9,688,000,000 | 4.5% |
| 8 | North Carolina | 7,068,000,000 | 3.3% |
| 9 | New Jersey | 6,925,000,000 | 3.2% |
| 10 | Michigan | 6,806,000,000 | 3.2% |
| 11 | Georgia | 6,484,000,000 | 3.0% |
| 12 | Virginia | 5,349,000,000 | 2.5% |
| 13 | Massachusetts | 4,993,000,000 | 2.3% |
| 14 | Indiana | 4,668,000,000 | 2.2% |
| 15 | Tennessee | 4,587,000,000 | 2.1% |
| 16 | Louisiana | 4,442,000,000 | 2.1% |
| 17 | Arizona | 4,019,000,000 | 1.9% |
| 18 | Missouri | 4,002,000,000 | 1.9% |
| 19 | Maryland | 3,928,000,000 | 1.8% |
| 20 | Alabama | 3,884,000,000 | 1.8% |
| 21 | South Carolina | 3,771,000,000 | 1.8% |
| 22 | Washington | 3,531,000,000 | 1.7% |
| 23 | Wisconsin | 3,113,000,000 | 1.5% |
| 24 | Minnesota | 3,090,000,000 | 1.4% |
| 25 | Kentucky | 3,067,000,000 | 1.4% |
| 26 | Connecticut | 2,991,000,000 | 1.4% |
| 27 | Oklahoma | 2,398,000,000 | 1.1% |
| 28 | Mississippi | 2,326,000,000 | 1.1% |
| 29 | Colorado | 2,244,000,000 | 1.1% |
| 30 | Arkansas | 2,216,000,000 | 1.0% |
| 31 | Oregon | 2,197,000,000 | 1.0% |
| 32 | Iowa | 2,157,000,000 | 1.0% |
| 33 | Kansas | 2,025,000,000 | 0.9% |
| 34 | Nevada | 1,338,000,000 | 0.6% |
| 35 | West Virginia | 1,308,000,000 | 0.6% |
| 36 | Nebraska | 1,196,000,000 | 0.6% |
| 37 | New Mexico | 1,172,000,000 | 0.5% |
| 38 | Hawaii | 1,152,000,000 | 0.5% |
| 39 | Maine | 1,137,000,000 | 0.5% |
| 40 | New Hampshire | 1,059,000,000 | 0.5% |
| 41 | Utah | 1,042,000,000 | 0.5% |
| 42 | Idaho | 821,000,000 | 0.4% |
| 43 | Rhode Island | 716,000,000 | 0.3% |
| 44 | Delaware | 704,000,000 | 0.3% |
| 45 | Montana | 611,000,000 | 0.3% |
| 46 | Vermont | 525,000,000 | 0.2% |
| 47 | Wyoming | 499,000,000 | 0.2% |
| 48 | Alaska | 485,000,000 | 0.2% |
| 49 | South Dakota | 483,000,000 | 0.2% |
| 50 | North Dakota | 466,000,000 | 0.2% |
| | District of Columbia | 747,000,000 | 0.3% |

*Source: U.S. Department of Energy, Energy Information Administration*
*"State Energy Price and Expenditure Report 1997" (July 2000)*

# Electricity Prices in 1997

## National Rate = $20.15 per Million Btu's*

ALPHA ORDER

| RANK | STATE | RATE |
|------|-------|------|
| 38 | Alabama | $15.76 |
| 8 | Alaska | 29.57 |
| 14 | Arizona | 21.63 |
| 26 | Arkansas | 18.17 |
| 10 | California | 28.06 |
| 30 | Colorado | 17.50 |
| 6 | Connecticut | 30.83 |
| 17 | Delaware | 20.56 |
| 15 | Florida | 21.08 |
| 21 | Georgia | 18.72 |
| 1 | Hawaii | 36.71 |
| 50 | Idaho | 11.33 |
| 13 | Illinois | 22.65 |
| 40 | Indiana | 15.55 |
| 31 | Iowa | 17.49 |
| 22 | Kansas | 18.53 |
| 49 | Kentucky | 11.86 |
| 29 | Louisiana | 17.70 |
| 11 | Maine | 27.86 |
| 18 | Maryland | 20.46 |
| 7 | Massachusetts | 30.70 |
| 16 | Michigan | 20.68 |
| 35 | Minnesota | 16.48 |
| 32 | Mississippi | 17.46 |
| 28 | Missouri | 17.86 |
| 43 | Montana | 15.31 |
| 41 | Nebraska | 15.53 |
| 34 | Nevada | 16.49 |
| 2 | New Hampshire | 34.17 |
| 5 | New Jersey | 30.93 |
| 19 | New Mexico | 20.11 |
| 3 | New York | 32.61 |
| 20 | North Carolina | 19.00 |
| 33 | North Dakota | 16.59 |
| 23 | Ohio | 18.40 |
| 37 | Oklahoma | 15.93 |
| 46 | Oregon | 13.52 |
| 12 | Pennsylvania | 23.48 |
| 4 | Rhode Island | 31.37 |
| 36 | South Carolina | 16.13 |
| 24 | South Dakota | 18.23 |
| 39 | Tennessee | 15.60 |
| 24 | Texas | 18.23 |
| 44 | Utah | 15.25 |
| 9 | Vermont | 28.99 |
| 27 | Virginia | 18.02 |
| 48 | Washington | 11.90 |
| 45 | West Virginia | 14.75 |
| 42 | Wisconsin | 15.35 |
| 47 | Wyoming | 12.78 |

RANK ORDER

| RANK | STATE | RATE |
|------|-------|------|
| 1 | Hawaii | $36.71 |
| 2 | New Hampshire | 34.17 |
| 3 | New York | 32.61 |
| 4 | Rhode Island | 31.37 |
| 5 | New Jersey | 30.93 |
| 6 | Connecticut | 30.83 |
| 7 | Massachusetts | 30.70 |
| 8 | Alaska | 29.57 |
| 9 | Vermont | 28.99 |
| 10 | California | 28.06 |
| 11 | Maine | 27.86 |
| 12 | Pennsylvania | 23.48 |
| 13 | Illinois | 22.65 |
| 14 | Arizona | 21.63 |
| 15 | Florida | 21.08 |
| 16 | Michigan | 20.68 |
| 17 | Delaware | 20.56 |
| 18 | Maryland | 20.46 |
| 19 | New Mexico | 20.11 |
| 20 | North Carolina | 19.00 |
| 21 | Georgia | 18.72 |
| 22 | Kansas | 18.53 |
| 23 | Ohio | 18.40 |
| 24 | South Dakota | 18.23 |
| 24 | Texas | 18.23 |
| 26 | Arkansas | 18.17 |
| 27 | Virginia | 18.02 |
| 28 | Missouri | 17.86 |
| 29 | Louisiana | 17.70 |
| 30 | Colorado | 17.50 |
| 31 | Iowa | 17.49 |
| 32 | Mississippi | 17.46 |
| 33 | North Dakota | 16.59 |
| 34 | Nevada | 16.49 |
| 35 | Minnesota | 16.48 |
| 36 | South Carolina | 16.13 |
| 37 | Oklahoma | 15.93 |
| 38 | Alabama | 15.76 |
| 39 | Tennessee | 15.60 |
| 40 | Indiana | 15.55 |
| 41 | Nebraska | 15.53 |
| 42 | Wisconsin | 15.35 |
| 43 | Montana | 15.31 |
| 44 | Utah | 15.25 |
| 45 | West Virginia | 14.75 |
| 46 | Oregon | 13.52 |
| 47 | Wyoming | 12.78 |
| 48 | Washington | 11.90 |
| 49 | Kentucky | 11.86 |
| 50 | Idaho | 11.33 |
|  | District of Columbia | 21.65 |

Source: U.S. Department of Energy, Energy Information Administration
    "State Energy Price and Expenditure Report 1997" (July 2000)
*British Thermal Units: The amount of heat required to raise the temperature of one pound of water one degree.

# Electricity Costs for Industrial Users in 1997

## National Rate = $13.29 per Million Btu's*

| RANK | STATE | RATE |
| --- | --- | --- |
| 41 | Alabama | $10.86 |
| 7 | Alaska | 21.93 |
| 14 | Arizona | 14.80 |
| 22 | Arkansas | 13.03 |
| 9 | California | 20.38 |
| 28 | Colorado | 12.55 |
| 6 | Connecticut | 22.74 |
| 17 | Delaware | 14.13 |
| 15 | Florida | 14.76 |
| 31 | Georgia | 12.10 |
| 1 | Hawaii | 30.25 |
| 49 | Idaho | 7.61 |
| 12 | Illinois | 15.51 |
| 36 | Indiana | 11.45 |
| 35 | Iowa | 11.59 |
| 19 | Kansas | 13.23 |
| 48 | Kentucky | 8.22 |
| 25 | Louisiana | 12.87 |
| 10 | Maine | 18.63 |
| 29 | Maryland | 12.33 |
| 3 | Massachusetts | 25.73 |
| 16 | Michigan | 14.56 |
| 27 | Minnesota | 12.70 |
| 32 | Mississippi | 12.08 |
| 21 | Missouri | 13.07 |
| 42 | Montana | 10.72 |
| 44 | Nebraska | 10.59 |
| 20 | Nevada | 13.13 |
| 2 | New Hampshire | 26.55 |
| 5 | New Jersey | 23.77 |
| 24 | New Mexico | 12.94 |
| 13 | New York | 15.23 |
| 18 | North Carolina | 13.82 |
| 26 | North Dakota | 12.83 |
| 30 | Ohio | 12.20 |
| 43 | Oklahoma | 10.65 |
| 47 | Oregon | 9.46 |
| 11 | Pennsylvania | 17.25 |
| 4 | Rhode Island | 24.98 |
| 39 | South Carolina | 10.87 |
| 23 | South Dakota | 12.96 |
| 37 | Tennessee | 11.17 |
| 33 | Texas | 11.88 |
| 45 | Utah | 10.22 |
| 8 | Vermont | 21.82 |
| 34 | Virginia | 11.73 |
| 50 | Washington | 7.58 |
| 39 | West Virginia | 10.87 |
| 38 | Wisconsin | 10.89 |
| 46 | Wyoming | 10.14 |

| RANK | STATE | RATE |
| --- | --- | --- |
| 1 | Hawaii | $30.25 |
| 2 | New Hampshire | 26.55 |
| 3 | Massachusetts | 25.73 |
| 4 | Rhode Island | 24.98 |
| 5 | New Jersey | 23.77 |
| 6 | Connecticut | 22.74 |
| 7 | Alaska | 21.93 |
| 8 | Vermont | 21.82 |
| 9 | California | 20.38 |
| 10 | Maine | 18.63 |
| 11 | Pennsylvania | 17.25 |
| 12 | Illinois | 15.51 |
| 13 | New York | 15.23 |
| 14 | Arizona | 14.80 |
| 15 | Florida | 14.76 |
| 16 | Michigan | 14.56 |
| 17 | Delaware | 14.13 |
| 18 | North Carolina | 13.82 |
| 19 | Kansas | 13.23 |
| 20 | Nevada | 13.13 |
| 21 | Missouri | 13.07 |
| 22 | Arkansas | 13.03 |
| 23 | South Dakota | 12.96 |
| 24 | New Mexico | 12.94 |
| 25 | Louisiana | 12.87 |
| 26 | North Dakota | 12.83 |
| 27 | Minnesota | 12.70 |
| 28 | Colorado | 12.55 |
| 29 | Maryland | 12.33 |
| 30 | Ohio | 12.20 |
| 31 | Georgia | 12.10 |
| 32 | Mississippi | 12.08 |
| 33 | Texas | 11.88 |
| 34 | Virginia | 11.73 |
| 35 | Iowa | 11.59 |
| 36 | Indiana | 11.45 |
| 37 | Tennessee | 11.17 |
| 38 | Wisconsin | 10.89 |
| 39 | South Carolina | 10.87 |
| 39 | West Virginia | 10.87 |
| 41 | Alabama | 10.86 |
| 42 | Montana | 10.72 |
| 43 | Oklahoma | 10.65 |
| 44 | Nebraska | 10.59 |
| 45 | Utah | 10.22 |
| 46 | Wyoming | 10.14 |
| 47 | Oregon | 9.46 |
| 48 | Kentucky | 8.22 |
| 49 | Idaho | 7.61 |
| 50 | Washington | 7.58 |
| | District of Columbia | 12.97 |

Source: U.S. Department of Energy, Energy Information Administration
   "State Energy Price and Expenditure Report 1997" (July 2000)
*British Thermal Units: The amount of heat required to raise the temperature of one pound of water one degree.
Industrial users include manufacturing, mining, construction, agriculture, fisheries and forestry.

# Expenditures on Natural Gas in 1997

## National Total = $91,769,000,000

ALPHA ORDER

| RANK | STATE | EXPENDITURES | % of USA |
|---|---|---|---|
| 20 | Alabama | $1,298,000,000 | 1.4% |
| 41 | Alaska | 252,000,000 | 0.3% |
| 35 | Arizona | 574,000,000 | 0.6% |
| 27 | Arkansas | 981,000,000 | 1.1% |
| 2 | California | 8,879,000,000 | 9.7% |
| 24 | Colorado | 1,097,000,000 | 1.2% |
| 28 | Connecticut | 932,000,000 | 1.0% |
| 43 | Delaware | 232,000,000 | 0.3% |
| 14 | Florida | 1,928,000,000 | 2.1% |
| 13 | Georgia | 1,995,000,000 | 2.2% |
| 49 | Hawaii | 42,000,000 | 0.0% |
| 44 | Idaho | 226,000,000 | 0.2% |
| 4 | Illinois | 5,382,000,000 | 5.9% |
| 10 | Indiana | 2,743,000,000 | 3.0% |
| 22 | Iowa | 1,220,000,000 | 1.3% |
| 25 | Kansas | 1,083,000,000 | 1.2% |
| 26 | Kentucky | 1,036,000,000 | 1.1% |
| 8 | Louisiana | 3,751,000,000 | 4.1% |
| 48 | Maine | 43,000,000 | 0.0% |
| 22 | Maryland | 1,220,000,000 | 1.3% |
| 11 | Massachusetts | 2,622,000,000 | 2.9% |
| 7 | Michigan | 4,264,000,000 | 4.6% |
| 17 | Minnesota | 1,537,000,000 | 1.7% |
| 30 | Mississippi | 749,000,000 | 0.8% |
| 16 | Missouri | 1,615,000,000 | 1.8% |
| 40 | Montana | 258,000,000 | 0.3% |
| 32 | Nebraska | 612,000,000 | 0.7% |
| 34 | Nevada | 590,000,000 | 0.6% |
| 47 | New Hampshire | 146,000,000 | 0.2% |
| 9 | New Jersey | 3,532,000,000 | 3.8% |
| 38 | New Mexico | 512,000,000 | 0.6% |
| 3 | New York | 7,913,000,000 | 8.6% |
| 21 | North Carolina | 1,275,000,000 | 1.4% |
| 45 | North Dakota | 163,000,000 | 0.2% |
| 5 | Ohio | 5,139,000,000 | 5.6% |
| 15 | Oklahoma | 1,884,000,000 | 2.1% |
| 33 | Oregon | 610,000,000 | 0.7% |
| 6 | Pennsylvania | 4,314,000,000 | 4.7% |
| 39 | Rhode Island | 473,000,000 | 0.5% |
| 31 | South Carolina | 741,000,000 | 0.8% |
| 46 | South Dakota | 158,000,000 | 0.2% |
| 19 | Tennessee | 1,340,000,000 | 1.5% |
| 1 | Texas | 10,365,000,000 | 11.3% |
| 37 | Utah | 529,000,000 | 0.6% |
| 50 | Vermont | 40,000,000 | 0.0% |
| 18 | Virginia | 1,448,000,000 | 1.6% |
| 29 | Washington | 909,000,000 | 1.0% |
| 36 | West Virginia | 568,000,000 | 0.6% |
| 12 | Wisconsin | 2,014,000,000 | 2.2% |
| 42 | Wyoming | 250,000,000 | 0.3% |

RANK ORDER

| RANK | STATE | EXPENDITURES | % of USA |
|---|---|---|---|
| 1 | Texas | $10,365,000,000 | 11.3% |
| 2 | California | 8,879,000,000 | 9.7% |
| 3 | New York | 7,913,000,000 | 8.6% |
| 4 | Illinois | 5,382,000,000 | 5.9% |
| 5 | Ohio | 5,139,000,000 | 5.6% |
| 6 | Pennsylvania | 4,314,000,000 | 4.7% |
| 7 | Michigan | 4,264,000,000 | 4.6% |
| 8 | Louisiana | 3,751,000,000 | 4.1% |
| 9 | New Jersey | 3,532,000,000 | 3.8% |
| 10 | Indiana | 2,743,000,000 | 3.0% |
| 11 | Massachusetts | 2,622,000,000 | 2.9% |
| 12 | Wisconsin | 2,014,000,000 | 2.2% |
| 13 | Georgia | 1,995,000,000 | 2.2% |
| 14 | Florida | 1,928,000,000 | 2.1% |
| 15 | Oklahoma | 1,884,000,000 | 2.1% |
| 16 | Missouri | 1,615,000,000 | 1.8% |
| 17 | Minnesota | 1,537,000,000 | 1.7% |
| 18 | Virginia | 1,448,000,000 | 1.6% |
| 19 | Tennessee | 1,340,000,000 | 1.5% |
| 20 | Alabama | 1,298,000,000 | 1.4% |
| 21 | North Carolina | 1,275,000,000 | 1.4% |
| 22 | Iowa | 1,220,000,000 | 1.3% |
| 22 | Maryland | 1,220,000,000 | 1.3% |
| 24 | Colorado | 1,097,000,000 | 1.2% |
| 25 | Kansas | 1,083,000,000 | 1.2% |
| 26 | Kentucky | 1,036,000,000 | 1.1% |
| 27 | Arkansas | 981,000,000 | 1.1% |
| 28 | Connecticut | 932,000,000 | 1.0% |
| 29 | Washington | 909,000,000 | 1.0% |
| 30 | Mississippi | 749,000,000 | 0.8% |
| 31 | South Carolina | 741,000,000 | 0.8% |
| 32 | Nebraska | 612,000,000 | 0.7% |
| 33 | Oregon | 610,000,000 | 0.7% |
| 34 | Nevada | 590,000,000 | 0.6% |
| 35 | Arizona | 574,000,000 | 0.6% |
| 36 | West Virginia | 568,000,000 | 0.6% |
| 37 | Utah | 529,000,000 | 0.6% |
| 38 | New Mexico | 512,000,000 | 0.6% |
| 39 | Rhode Island | 473,000,000 | 0.5% |
| 40 | Montana | 258,000,000 | 0.3% |
| 41 | Alaska | 252,000,000 | 0.3% |
| 42 | Wyoming | 250,000,000 | 0.3% |
| 43 | Delaware | 232,000,000 | 0.3% |
| 44 | Idaho | 226,000,000 | 0.2% |
| 45 | North Dakota | 163,000,000 | 0.2% |
| 46 | South Dakota | 158,000,000 | 0.2% |
| 47 | New Hampshire | 146,000,000 | 0.2% |
| 48 | Maine | 43,000,000 | 0.0% |
| 49 | Hawaii | 42,000,000 | 0.0% |
| 50 | Vermont | 40,000,000 | 0.0% |
| | District of Columbia | 281,000,000 | 0.3% |

*Source: U.S. Department of Energy, Energy Information Administration*
    *"State Energy Price and Expenditure Report 1997" (July 2000)*

# Natural Gas Prices in 1997

## National Rate = $4.62 per Million Btu's*

| ALPHA ORDER | | | | RANK ORDER | | |
|:---|:---|---:|---|:---|:---|---:|
| **RANK** | **STATE** | **RATE** | | **RANK** | **STATE** | **RATE** |
| 30 | Alabama | $4.69 | | 1 | Hawaii** | $15.88 |
| 50 | Alaska | 2.07 | | 2 | New Hampshire | 6.94 |
| 20 | Arizona | 5.00 | | 3 | Maine | 6.86 |
| 36 | Arkansas | 4.29 | | 4 | Massachusetts | 6.79 |
| 25 | California | 4.88 | | 5 | Connecticut | 6.75 |
| 37 | Colorado | 4.22 | | 6 | Pennsylvania | 6.50 |
| 5 | Connecticut | 6.75 | | 7 | New York | 6.32 |
| 23 | Delaware | 4.90 | | 8 | Virginia | 6.07 |
| 41 | Florida | 3.85 | | 9 | North Carolina | 5.95 |
| 13 | Georgia | 5.62 | | 10 | Missouri | 5.79 |
| 1 | Hawaii** | 15.88 | | 11 | Maryland | 5.78 |
| 46 | Idaho | 3.55 | | 12 | Ohio | 5.69 |
| 19 | Illinois | 5.03 | | 13 | Georgia | 5.62 |
| 18 | Indiana | 5.08 | | 13 | Rhode Island | 5.62 |
| 21 | Iowa | 4.97 | | 15 | New Jersey | 5.61 |
| 35 | Kansas | 4.48 | | 16 | Tennessee | 5.12 |
| 21 | Kentucky | 4.97 | | 17 | Wisconsin | 5.11 |
| 49 | Louisiana | 2.80 | | 18 | Indiana | 5.08 |
| 3 | Maine | 6.86 | | 19 | Illinois | 5.03 |
| 11 | Maryland | 5.78 | | 20 | Arizona | 5.00 |
| 4 | Massachusetts | 6.79 | | 21 | Iowa | 4.97 |
| 34 | Michigan | 4.52 | | 21 | Kentucky | 4.97 |
| 31 | Minnesota | 4.58 | | 23 | Delaware | 4.90 |
| 44 | Mississippi | 3.70 | | 23 | Vermont | 4.90 |
| 10 | Missouri | 5.79 | | 25 | California | 4.88 |
| 28 | Montana | 4.76 | | 26 | Nebraska | 4.79 |
| 26 | Nebraska | 4.79 | | 26 | South Dakota | 4.79 |
| 32 | Nevada | 4.57 | | 28 | Montana | 4.76 |
| 2 | New Hampshire | 6.94 | | 28 | South Carolina | 4.76 |
| 15 | New Jersey | 5.61 | | 30 | Alabama | 4.69 |
| 40 | New Mexico | 3.88 | | 31 | Minnesota | 4.58 |
| 7 | New York | 6.32 | | 32 | Nevada | 4.57 |
| 9 | North Carolina | 5.95 | | 32 | West Virginia | 4.57 |
| 43 | North Dakota | 3.73 | | 34 | Michigan | 4.52 |
| 12 | Ohio | 5.69 | | 35 | Kansas | 4.48 |
| 37 | Oklahoma | 4.22 | | 36 | Arkansas | 4.29 |
| 45 | Oregon | 3.67 | | 37 | Colorado | 4.22 |
| 6 | Pennsylvania | 6.50 | | 37 | Oklahoma | 4.22 |
| 13 | Rhode Island | 5.62 | | 39 | Washington | 4.07 |
| 28 | South Carolina | 4.76 | | 40 | New Mexico | 3.88 |
| 26 | South Dakota | 4.79 | | 41 | Florida | 3.85 |
| 16 | Tennessee | 5.12 | | 42 | Utah | 3.83 |
| 48 | Texas | 3.08 | | 43 | North Dakota | 3.73 |
| 42 | Utah | 3.83 | | 44 | Mississippi | 3.70 |
| 23 | Vermont | 4.90 | | 45 | Oregon | 3.67 |
| 8 | Virginia | 6.07 | | 46 | Idaho | 3.55 |
| 39 | Washington | 4.07 | | 47 | Wyoming | 3.54 |
| 32 | West Virginia | 4.57 | | 48 | Texas | 3.08 |
| 17 | Wisconsin | 5.11 | | 49 | Louisiana | 2.80 |
| 47 | Wyoming | 3.54 | | 50 | Alaska | 2.07 |
| | | | | | District of Columbia | 8.15 |

Source: U.S. Department of Energy, Energy Information Administration
"State Energy Price and Expenditure Report 1997" (July 2000)
*British Thermal Units: The amount of heat required to raise the temperature of one pound of water one degree.
**Hawaii's rate is based on small quantities of liquefied natural gas.

# Natural Gas Costs for Industrial Users in 1997

## National Rate = $3.58 per Million Btu's*

ALPHA ORDER

RANK ORDER

| RANK | STATE | RATE | | RANK | STATE | RATE |
|------|-------|------|---|------|-------|------|
| 34 | Alabama | $3.51 | | 1 | Hawaii | $10.48 |
| 50 | Alaska | 1.54 | | 2 | Nevada | 7.58 |
| 33 | Arizona | 3.52 | | 3 | Massachusetts | 5.67 |
| 29 | Arkansas | 3.66 | | 4 | Maine | 5.47 |
| 20 | California | 4.11 | | 5 | New York | 4.92 |
| 31 | Colorado | 3.62 | | 6 | New Hampshire | 4.85 |
| 10 | Connecticut | 4.60 | | 7 | Missouri | 4.73 |
| 16 | Delaware | 4.25 | | 8 | Ohio | 4.72 |
| 18 | Florida | 4.18 | | 9 | Montana | 4.65 |
| 14 | Georgia | 4.44 | | 10 | Connecticut | 4.60 |
| 1 | Hawaii | 10.48 | | 11 | North Carolina | 4.50 |
| 47 | Idaho | 2.68 | | 12 | Virginia | 4.48 |
| 26 | Illinois | 3.89 | | 13 | Pennsylvania | 4.45 |
| 15 | Indiana | 4.28 | | 14 | Georgia | 4.44 |
| 22 | Iowa | 4.07 | | 15 | Indiana | 4.28 |
| 36 | Kansas | 3.31 | | 16 | Delaware | 4.25 |
| 24 | Kentucky | 3.99 | | 17 | Rhode Island | 4.23 |
| 48 | Louisiana | 2.53 | | 18 | Florida | 4.18 |
| 4 | Maine | 5.47 | | 19 | Oklahoma | 4.15 |
| 39 | Maryland | 3.14 | | 20 | California | 4.11 |
| 3 | Massachusetts | 5.67 | | 21 | Wisconsin | 4.08 |
| 27 | Michigan | 3.86 | | 22 | Iowa | 4.07 |
| 38 | Minnesota | 3.22 | | 23 | Tennessee | 4.05 |
| 35 | Mississippi | 3.44 | | 24 | Kentucky | 3.99 |
| 7 | Missouri | 4.73 | | 25 | South Dakota | 3.95 |
| 9 | Montana | 4.65 | | 26 | Illinois | 3.89 |
| 27 | Nebraska | 3.86 | | 27 | Michigan | 3.86 |
| 2 | Nevada | 7.58 | | 27 | Nebraska | 3.86 |
| 6 | New Hampshire | 4.85 | | 29 | Arkansas | 3.66 |
| 30 | New Jersey | 3.65 | | 30 | New Jersey | 3.65 |
| 42 | New Mexico | 2.93 | | 31 | Colorado | 3.62 |
| 5 | New York | 4.92 | | 32 | South Carolina | 3.61 |
| 11 | North Carolina | 4.50 | | 33 | Arizona | 3.52 |
| 43 | North Dakota | 2.90 | | 34 | Alabama | 3.51 |
| 8 | Ohio | 4.72 | | 35 | Mississippi | 3.44 |
| 19 | Oklahoma | 4.15 | | 36 | Kansas | 3.31 |
| 44 | Oregon | 2.89 | | 37 | Wyoming | 3.26 |
| 13 | Pennsylvania | 4.45 | | 38 | Minnesota | 3.22 |
| 17 | Rhode Island | 4.23 | | 39 | Maryland | 3.14 |
| 32 | South Carolina | 3.61 | | 40 | Vermont | 3.03 |
| 25 | South Dakota | 3.95 | | 41 | Washington | 3.02 |
| 23 | Tennessee | 4.05 | | 42 | New Mexico | 2.93 |
| 45 | Texas | 2.74 | | 43 | North Dakota | 2.90 |
| 49 | Utah | 2.45 | | 44 | Oregon | 2.89 |
| 40 | Vermont | 3.03 | | 45 | Texas | 2.74 |
| 12 | Virginia | 4.48 | | 46 | West Virginia | 2.72 |
| 41 | Washington | 3.02 | | 47 | Idaho | 2.68 |
| 46 | West Virginia | 2.72 | | 48 | Louisiana | 2.53 |
| 21 | Wisconsin | 4.08 | | 49 | Utah | 2.45 |
| 37 | Wyoming | 3.26 | | 50 | Alaska | 1.54 |
| | | | | | District of Columbia** | NA |

Source: U.S. Department of Energy, Energy Information Administration
    "State Energy Price and Expenditure Report 1997" (July 2000)
*British Thermal Units: The amount of heat required to raise the temperature of one pound of water one degree.
Industrial users include manufacturing, mining, construction, agriculture, fisheries and forestry.
**Not available.

# Average Price of Natural Gas Delivered to Residential Customers in 1999

## National Average = $6.69 per Thousand Cubic Feet*

ALPHA ORDER

| RANK | STATE | RATE |
|------|-------|------|
| 12 | Alabama | $8.34 |
| 49 | Alaska | 3.64 |
| 6 | Arizona | 9.13 |
| 19 | Arkansas | 7.22 |
| 24 | California | 6.62 |
| 41 | Colorado | 5.38 |
| 3 | Connecticut | 10.54 |
| 8 | Delaware | 8.63 |
| 2 | Florida | 11.59 |
| NA | Georgia** | NA |
| 1 | Hawaii | 18.97 |
| 40 | Idaho | 5.42 |
| 39 | Illinois | 5.50 |
| 31 | Indiana | 6.03 |
| 29 | Iowa | 6.10 |
| 33 | Kansas | 5.98 |
| 37 | Kentucky | 5.72 |
| 23 | Louisiana | 6.83 |
| 16 | Maine | 7.47 |
| 11 | Maryland | 8.41 |
| 5 | Massachusetts | 9.25 |
| 45 | Michigan | 5.13 |
| 38 | Minnesota | 5.56 |
| 32 | Mississippi | 5.99 |
| 26 | Missouri | 6.36 |
| 44 | Montana | 5.16 |
| 47 | Nebraska | 5.06 |
| 21 | Nevada | 7.14 |
| 15 | New Hampshire | 7.67 |
| 17 | New Jersey | 7.46 |
| 48 | New Mexico | 5.03 |
| 7 | New York | 9.12 |
| 13 | North Carolina | 8.33 |
| 43 | North Dakota | 5.32 |
| 27 | Ohio | 6.24 |
| 34 | Oklahoma | 5.97 |
| 22 | Oregon | 7.13 |
| 14 | Pennsylvania | 8.30 |
| 4 | Rhode Island | 9.53 |
| 10 | South Carolina | 8.46 |
| 36 | South Dakota | 5.83 |
| 25 | Tennessee | 6.55 |
| 30 | Texas | 6.09 |
| 42 | Utah | 5.37 |
| 20 | Vermont | 7.18 |
| 9 | Virginia | 8.61 |
| 35 | Washington | 5.88 |
| 18 | West Virginia | 7.42 |
| 28 | Wisconsin | 6.17 |
| 46 | Wyoming | 5.11 |

RANK ORDER

| RANK | STATE | RATE |
|------|-------|------|
| 1 | Hawaii | $18.97 |
| 2 | Florida | 11.59 |
| 3 | Connecticut | 10.54 |
| 4 | Rhode Island | 9.53 |
| 5 | Massachusetts | 9.25 |
| 6 | Arizona | 9.13 |
| 7 | New York | 9.12 |
| 8 | Delaware | 8.63 |
| 9 | Virginia | 8.61 |
| 10 | South Carolina | 8.46 |
| 11 | Maryland | 8.41 |
| 12 | Alabama | 8.34 |
| 13 | North Carolina | 8.33 |
| 14 | Pennsylvania | 8.30 |
| 15 | New Hampshire | 7.67 |
| 16 | Maine | 7.47 |
| 17 | New Jersey | 7.46 |
| 18 | West Virginia | 7.42 |
| 19 | Arkansas | 7.22 |
| 20 | Vermont | 7.18 |
| 21 | Nevada | 7.14 |
| 22 | Oregon | 7.13 |
| 23 | Louisiana | 6.83 |
| 24 | California | 6.62 |
| 25 | Tennessee | 6.55 |
| 26 | Missouri | 6.36 |
| 27 | Ohio | 6.24 |
| 28 | Wisconsin | 6.17 |
| 29 | Iowa | 6.10 |
| 30 | Texas | 6.09 |
| 31 | Indiana | 6.03 |
| 32 | Mississippi | 5.99 |
| 33 | Kansas | 5.98 |
| 34 | Oklahoma | 5.97 |
| 35 | Washington | 5.88 |
| 36 | South Dakota | 5.83 |
| 37 | Kentucky | 5.72 |
| 38 | Minnesota | 5.56 |
| 39 | Illinois | 5.50 |
| 40 | Idaho | 5.42 |
| 41 | Colorado | 5.38 |
| 42 | Utah | 5.37 |
| 43 | North Dakota | 5.32 |
| 44 | Montana | 5.16 |
| 45 | Michigan | 5.13 |
| 46 | Wyoming | 5.11 |
| 47 | Nebraska | 5.06 |
| 48 | New Mexico | 5.03 |
| 49 | Alaska | 3.64 |
| NA | Georgia** | NA |
| | District of Columbia | 8.70 |

Source: U.S. Department of Energy, Energy Information Administration
    "Average Price of Natural Gas" (http://www.eia.doe.gov/neic/rankings/gasresprice.htm)
*Preliminary.
**Not available.

# Expenditures on Motor Gasoline in 1997

## National Total = $149,549,000,000

ALPHA ORDER

| RANK | STATE | EXPENDITURES | % of USA |
|---|---|---|---|
| 21 | Alabama | $2,730,000,000 | 1.8% |
| 49 | Alaska | 395,000,000 | 0.3% |
| 22 | Arizona | 2,698,000,000 | 1.8% |
| 32 | Arkansas | 1,612,000,000 | 1.1% |
| 1 | California | 17,266,000,000 | 11.5% |
| 24 | Colorado | 2,402,000,000 | 1.6% |
| 27 | Connecticut | 2,049,000,000 | 1.4% |
| 46 | Delaware | 466,000,000 | 0.3% |
| 3 | Florida | 7,712,000,000 | 5.2% |
| 11 | Georgia | 4,314,000,000 | 2.9% |
| 43 | Hawaii | 598,000,000 | 0.4% |
| 40 | Idaho | 795,000,000 | 0.5% |
| 7 | Illinois | 5,880,000,000 | 3.9% |
| 15 | Indiana | 3,341,000,000 | 2.2% |
| 30 | Iowa | 1,761,000,000 | 1.2% |
| 33 | Kansas | 1,495,000,000 | 1.0% |
| 23 | Kentucky | 2,540,000,000 | 1.7% |
| 25 | Louisiana | 2,363,000,000 | 1.6% |
| 39 | Maine | 870,000,000 | 0.6% |
| 20 | Maryland | 2,888,000,000 | 1.9% |
| 14 | Massachusetts | 3,406,000,000 | 2.3% |
| 8 | Michigan | 5,329,000,000 | 3.6% |
| 18 | Minnesota | 3,038,000,000 | 2.0% |
| 31 | Mississippi | 1,722,000,000 | 1.2% |
| 13 | Missouri | 3,422,000,000 | 2.3% |
| 42 | Montana | 654,000,000 | 0.4% |
| 38 | Nebraska | 995,000,000 | 0.7% |
| 36 | Nevada | 1,100,000,000 | 0.7% |
| 41 | New Hampshire | 777,000,000 | 0.5% |
| 10 | New Jersey | 4,404,000,000 | 2.9% |
| 35 | New Mexico | 1,142,000,000 | 0.8% |
| 4 | New York | 6,853,000,000 | 4.6% |
| 9 | North Carolina | 4,538,000,000 | 3.0% |
| 47 | North Dakota | 436,000,000 | 0.3% |
| 6 | Ohio | 6,035,000,000 | 4.0% |
| 28 | Oklahoma | 2,000,000,000 | 1.3% |
| 29 | Oregon | 1,950,000,000 | 1.3% |
| 5 | Pennsylvania | 6,124,000,000 | 4.1% |
| 45 | Rhode Island | 521,000,000 | 0.3% |
| 26 | South Carolina | 2,271,000,000 | 1.5% |
| 44 | South Dakota | 536,000,000 | 0.4% |
| 17 | Tennessee | 3,329,000,000 | 2.2% |
| 2 | Texas | 11,163,000,000 | 7.5% |
| 34 | Utah | 1,203,000,000 | 0.8% |
| 48 | Vermont | 410,000,000 | 0.3% |
| 12 | Virginia | 4,095,000,000 | 2.7% |
| 16 | Washington | 3,340,000,000 | 2.2% |
| 37 | West Virginia | 1,061,000,000 | 0.7% |
| 19 | Wisconsin | 2,926,000,000 | 2.0% |
| 50 | Wyoming | 375,000,000 | 0.3% |

RANK ORDER

| RANK | STATE | EXPENDITURES | % of USA |
|---|---|---|---|
| 1 | California | $17,266,000,000 | 11.5% |
| 2 | Texas | 11,163,000,000 | 7.5% |
| 3 | Florida | 7,712,000,000 | 5.2% |
| 4 | New York | 6,853,000,000 | 4.6% |
| 5 | Pennsylvania | 6,124,000,000 | 4.1% |
| 6 | Ohio | 6,035,000,000 | 4.0% |
| 7 | Illinois | 5,880,000,000 | 3.9% |
| 8 | Michigan | 5,329,000,000 | 3.6% |
| 9 | North Carolina | 4,538,000,000 | 3.0% |
| 10 | New Jersey | 4,404,000,000 | 2.9% |
| 11 | Georgia | 4,314,000,000 | 2.9% |
| 12 | Virginia | 4,095,000,000 | 2.7% |
| 13 | Missouri | 3,422,000,000 | 2.3% |
| 14 | Massachusetts | 3,406,000,000 | 2.3% |
| 15 | Indiana | 3,341,000,000 | 2.2% |
| 16 | Washington | 3,340,000,000 | 2.2% |
| 17 | Tennessee | 3,329,000,000 | 2.2% |
| 18 | Minnesota | 3,038,000,000 | 2.0% |
| 19 | Wisconsin | 2,926,000,000 | 2.0% |
| 20 | Maryland | 2,888,000,000 | 1.9% |
| 21 | Alabama | 2,730,000,000 | 1.8% |
| 22 | Arizona | 2,698,000,000 | 1.8% |
| 23 | Kentucky | 2,540,000,000 | 1.7% |
| 24 | Colorado | 2,402,000,000 | 1.6% |
| 25 | Louisiana | 2,363,000,000 | 1.6% |
| 26 | South Carolina | 2,271,000,000 | 1.5% |
| 27 | Connecticut | 2,049,000,000 | 1.4% |
| 28 | Oklahoma | 2,000,000,000 | 1.3% |
| 29 | Oregon | 1,950,000,000 | 1.3% |
| 30 | Iowa | 1,761,000,000 | 1.2% |
| 31 | Mississippi | 1,722,000,000 | 1.2% |
| 32 | Arkansas | 1,612,000,000 | 1.1% |
| 33 | Kansas | 1,495,000,000 | 1.0% |
| 34 | Utah | 1,203,000,000 | 0.8% |
| 35 | New Mexico | 1,142,000,000 | 0.8% |
| 36 | Nevada | 1,100,000,000 | 0.7% |
| 37 | West Virginia | 1,061,000,000 | 0.7% |
| 38 | Nebraska | 995,000,000 | 0.7% |
| 39 | Maine | 870,000,000 | 0.6% |
| 40 | Idaho | 795,000,000 | 0.5% |
| 41 | New Hampshire | 777,000,000 | 0.5% |
| 42 | Montana | 654,000,000 | 0.4% |
| 43 | Hawaii | 598,000,000 | 0.4% |
| 44 | South Dakota | 536,000,000 | 0.4% |
| 45 | Rhode Island | 521,000,000 | 0.3% |
| 46 | Delaware | 466,000,000 | 0.3% |
| 47 | North Dakota | 436,000,000 | 0.3% |
| 48 | Vermont | 410,000,000 | 0.3% |
| 49 | Alaska | 395,000,000 | 0.3% |
| 50 | Wyoming | 375,000,000 | 0.3% |
|  | District of Columbia | 220,000,000 | 0.1% |

Source: U.S. Department of Energy, Energy Information Administration
"State Energy Price and Expenditure Report 1997" (July 2000)

# Gasoline Used in 1999

## National Total = 131,781,369,000 Gallons*

<table>
<tr><td colspan="4">ALPHA ORDER</td><td colspan="4">RANK ORDER</td></tr>
<tr><td>RANK</td><td>STATE</td><td>GALLONS</td><td>% of USA</td><td>RANK</td><td>STATE</td><td>GALLONS</td><td>% of USA</td></tr>
<tr><td>20</td><td>Alabama</td><td>2,465,157,000</td><td>1.9%</td><td>1</td><td>California</td><td>14,448,971,000</td><td>11.0%</td></tr>
<tr><td>50</td><td>Alaska</td><td>296,187,000</td><td>0.2%</td><td>2</td><td>Texas</td><td>10,402,329,000</td><td>7.9%</td></tr>
<tr><td>22</td><td>Arizona</td><td>2,347,337,000</td><td>1.8%</td><td>3</td><td>Florida</td><td>7,430,234,000</td><td>5.6%</td></tr>
<tr><td>32</td><td>Arkansas</td><td>1,442,892,000</td><td>1.1%</td><td>4</td><td>New York</td><td>5,705,550,000</td><td>4.3%</td></tr>
<tr><td>1</td><td>California</td><td>14,448,971,000</td><td>11.0%</td><td>5</td><td>Michigan</td><td>5,176,493,000</td><td>3.9%</td></tr>
<tr><td>26</td><td>Colorado</td><td>2,016,686,000</td><td>1.5%</td><td>6</td><td>Ohio</td><td>5,169,428,000</td><td>3.9%</td></tr>
<tr><td>31</td><td>Connecticut</td><td>1,549,645,000</td><td>1.2%</td><td>7</td><td>Illinois</td><td>5,077,156,000</td><td>3.9%</td></tr>
<tr><td>45</td><td>Delaware</td><td>395,743,000</td><td>0.3%</td><td>8</td><td>Pennsylvania</td><td>5,019,247,000</td><td>3.8%</td></tr>
<tr><td>3</td><td>Florida</td><td>7,430,234,000</td><td>5.6%</td><td>9</td><td>Georgia</td><td>4,696,857,000</td><td>3.6%</td></tr>
<tr><td>9</td><td>Georgia</td><td>4,696,857,000</td><td>3.6%</td><td>10</td><td>North Carolina</td><td>4,165,057,000</td><td>3.2%</td></tr>
<tr><td>46</td><td>Hawaii</td><td>384,469,000</td><td>0.3%</td><td>11</td><td>New Jersey</td><td>3,921,103,000</td><td>3.0%</td></tr>
<tr><td>40</td><td>Idaho</td><td>680,667,000</td><td>0.5%</td><td>12</td><td>Virginia</td><td>3,623,739,000</td><td>2.7%</td></tr>
<tr><td>7</td><td>Illinois</td><td>5,077,156,000</td><td>3.9%</td><td>13</td><td>Indiana</td><td>3,100,989,000</td><td>2.4%</td></tr>
<tr><td>13</td><td>Indiana</td><td>3,100,989,000</td><td>2.4%</td><td>14</td><td>Missouri</td><td>3,041,007,000</td><td>2.3%</td></tr>
<tr><td>29</td><td>Iowa</td><td>1,581,953,000</td><td>1.2%</td><td>15</td><td>Tennessee</td><td>2,981,829,000</td><td>2.3%</td></tr>
<tr><td>33</td><td>Kansas</td><td>1,441,672,000</td><td>1.1%</td><td>16</td><td>Massachusetts</td><td>2,710,909,000</td><td>2.1%</td></tr>
<tr><td>25</td><td>Kentucky</td><td>2,175,614,000</td><td>1.7%</td><td>17</td><td>Washington</td><td>2,710,388,000</td><td>2.1%</td></tr>
<tr><td>23</td><td>Louisiana</td><td>2,267,899,000</td><td>1.7%</td><td>18</td><td>Minnesota</td><td>2,561,743,000</td><td>1.9%</td></tr>
<tr><td>39</td><td>Maine</td><td>690,950,000</td><td>0.5%</td><td>19</td><td>Wisconsin</td><td>2,522,246,000</td><td>1.9%</td></tr>
<tr><td>21</td><td>Maryland</td><td>2,429,149,000</td><td>1.8%</td><td>20</td><td>Alabama</td><td>2,465,157,000</td><td>1.9%</td></tr>
<tr><td>16</td><td>Massachusetts</td><td>2,710,909,000</td><td>2.1%</td><td>21</td><td>Maryland</td><td>2,429,149,000</td><td>1.8%</td></tr>
<tr><td>5</td><td>Michigan</td><td>5,176,493,000</td><td>3.9%</td><td>22</td><td>Arizona</td><td>2,347,337,000</td><td>1.8%</td></tr>
<tr><td>18</td><td>Minnesota</td><td>2,561,743,000</td><td>1.9%</td><td>23</td><td>Louisiana</td><td>2,267,899,000</td><td>1.7%</td></tr>
<tr><td>28</td><td>Mississippi</td><td>1,642,919,000</td><td>1.2%</td><td>24</td><td>South Carolina</td><td>2,256,199,000</td><td>1.7%</td></tr>
<tr><td>14</td><td>Missouri</td><td>3,041,007,000</td><td>2.3%</td><td>25</td><td>Kentucky</td><td>2,175,614,000</td><td>1.7%</td></tr>
<tr><td>42</td><td>Montana</td><td>507,240,000</td><td>0.4%</td><td>26</td><td>Colorado</td><td>2,016,686,000</td><td>1.5%</td></tr>
<tr><td>37</td><td>Nebraska</td><td>877,212,000</td><td>0.7%</td><td>27</td><td>Oklahoma</td><td>1,863,554,000</td><td>1.4%</td></tr>
<tr><td>36</td><td>Nevada</td><td>924,288,000</td><td>0.7%</td><td>28</td><td>Mississippi</td><td>1,642,919,000</td><td>1.2%</td></tr>
<tr><td>41</td><td>New Hampshire</td><td>669,363,000</td><td>0.5%</td><td>29</td><td>Iowa</td><td>1,581,953,000</td><td>1.2%</td></tr>
<tr><td>11</td><td>New Jersey</td><td>3,921,103,000</td><td>3.0%</td><td>30</td><td>Oregon</td><td>1,564,739,000</td><td>1.2%</td></tr>
<tr><td>35</td><td>New Mexico</td><td>949,739,000</td><td>0.7%</td><td>31</td><td>Connecticut</td><td>1,549,645,000</td><td>1.2%</td></tr>
<tr><td>4</td><td>New York</td><td>5,705,550,000</td><td>4.3%</td><td>32</td><td>Arkansas</td><td>1,442,892,000</td><td>1.1%</td></tr>
<tr><td>10</td><td>North Carolina</td><td>4,165,057,000</td><td>3.2%</td><td>33</td><td>Kansas</td><td>1,441,672,000</td><td>1.1%</td></tr>
<tr><td>47</td><td>North Dakota</td><td>373,370,000</td><td>0.3%</td><td>34</td><td>Utah</td><td>990,530,000</td><td>0.8%</td></tr>
<tr><td>6</td><td>Ohio</td><td>5,169,428,000</td><td>3.9%</td><td>35</td><td>New Mexico</td><td>949,739,000</td><td>0.7%</td></tr>
<tr><td>27</td><td>Oklahoma</td><td>1,863,554,000</td><td>1.4%</td><td>36</td><td>Nevada</td><td>924,288,000</td><td>0.7%</td></tr>
<tr><td>30</td><td>Oregon</td><td>1,564,739,000</td><td>1.2%</td><td>37</td><td>Nebraska</td><td>877,212,000</td><td>0.7%</td></tr>
<tr><td>8</td><td>Pennsylvania</td><td>5,019,247,000</td><td>3.8%</td><td>38</td><td>West Virginia</td><td>832,670,000</td><td>0.6%</td></tr>
<tr><td>44</td><td>Rhode Island</td><td>409,826,000</td><td>0.3%</td><td>39</td><td>Maine</td><td>690,950,000</td><td>0.5%</td></tr>
<tr><td>24</td><td>South Carolina</td><td>2,256,199,000</td><td>1.7%</td><td>40</td><td>Idaho</td><td>680,667,000</td><td>0.5%</td></tr>
<tr><td>43</td><td>South Dakota</td><td>443,560,000</td><td>0.3%</td><td>41</td><td>New Hampshire</td><td>669,363,000</td><td>0.5%</td></tr>
<tr><td>15</td><td>Tennessee</td><td>2,981,829,000</td><td>2.3%</td><td>42</td><td>Montana</td><td>507,240,000</td><td>0.4%</td></tr>
<tr><td>2</td><td>Texas</td><td>10,402,329,000</td><td>7.9%</td><td>43</td><td>South Dakota</td><td>443,560,000</td><td>0.3%</td></tr>
<tr><td>34</td><td>Utah</td><td>990,530,000</td><td>0.8%</td><td>44</td><td>Rhode Island</td><td>409,826,000</td><td>0.3%</td></tr>
<tr><td>49</td><td>Vermont</td><td>329,047,000</td><td>0.2%</td><td>45</td><td>Delaware</td><td>395,743,000</td><td>0.3%</td></tr>
<tr><td>12</td><td>Virginia</td><td>3,623,739,000</td><td>2.7%</td><td>46</td><td>Hawaii</td><td>384,469,000</td><td>0.3%</td></tr>
<tr><td>17</td><td>Washington</td><td>2,710,388,000</td><td>2.1%</td><td>47</td><td>North Dakota</td><td>373,370,000</td><td>0.3%</td></tr>
<tr><td>38</td><td>West Virginia</td><td>832,670,000</td><td>0.6%</td><td>48</td><td>Wyoming</td><td>345,910,000</td><td>0.3%</td></tr>
<tr><td>19</td><td>Wisconsin</td><td>2,522,246,000</td><td>1.9%</td><td>49</td><td>Vermont</td><td>329,047,000</td><td>0.2%</td></tr>
<tr><td>48</td><td>Wyoming</td><td>345,910,000</td><td>0.3%</td><td>50</td><td>Alaska</td><td>296,187,000</td><td>0.2%</td></tr>
<tr><td></td><td></td><td></td><td></td><td></td><td>District of Columbia</td><td>169,908,000</td><td>0.1%</td></tr>
</table>

Source: U.S. Department of Transportation, Federal Highway Administration
"Highway Statistics 1999" (Table MF-21)
*Includes gasoline for highway and nonhighway uses. "Gasoline" includes gasohol but excludes "special fuels" such as diesel.

# Per Capita Gasoline Used in 1999

## National Per Capita = 483 Gallons*

| ALPHA ORDER | | | | RANK ORDER | | |
|---|---|---|---|---|---|---|
| RANK | STATE | GALLONS | | RANK | STATE | GALLONS |
| 9 | Alabama | 564 | | 1 | Wyoming | 721 |
| 36 | Alaska | 478 | | 2 | South Dakota | 605 |
| 33 | Arizona | 491 | | 3 | Georgia | 603 |
| 8 | Arkansas | 566 | | 4 | Mississippi | 593 |
| 45 | California | 436 | | 5 | North Dakota | 589 |
| 31 | Colorado | 497 | | 6 | South Carolina | 581 |
| 37 | Connecticut | 472 | | 7 | Montana | 575 |
| 25 | Delaware | 525 | | 8 | Arkansas | 566 |
| 32 | Florida | 492 | | 9 | Alabama | 564 |
| 3 | Georgia | 603 | | 10 | New Hampshire | 557 |
| 49 | Hawaii | 324 | | 11 | Missouri | 556 |
| 18 | Idaho | 544 | | 12 | Oklahoma | 555 |
| 46 | Illinois | 419 | | 13 | Vermont | 554 |
| 27 | Indiana | 522 | | 14 | Iowa | 551 |
| 14 | Iowa | 551 | | 14 | Maine | 551 |
| 21 | Kansas | 543 | | 16 | Kentucky | 549 |
| 16 | Kentucky | 549 | | 17 | New Mexico | 546 |
| 28 | Louisiana | 519 | | 18 | Idaho | 544 |
| 14 | Maine | 551 | | 18 | North Carolina | 544 |
| 40 | Maryland | 470 | | 18 | Tennessee | 544 |
| 44 | Massachusetts | 439 | | 21 | Kansas | 543 |
| 25 | Michigan | 525 | | 22 | Minnesota | 536 |
| 22 | Minnesota | 536 | | 23 | Nebraska | 527 |
| 4 | Mississippi | 593 | | 23 | Virginia | 527 |
| 11 | Missouri | 556 | | 25 | Delaware | 525 |
| 7 | Montana | 575 | | 25 | Michigan | 525 |
| 23 | Nebraska | 527 | | 27 | Indiana | 522 |
| 30 | Nevada | 511 | | 28 | Louisiana | 519 |
| 10 | New Hampshire | 557 | | 28 | Texas | 519 |
| 34 | New Jersey | 482 | | 30 | Nevada | 511 |
| 17 | New Mexico | 546 | | 31 | Colorado | 497 |
| 50 | New York | 314 | | 32 | Florida | 492 |
| 18 | North Carolina | 544 | | 33 | Arizona | 491 |
| 5 | North Dakota | 589 | | 34 | New Jersey | 482 |
| 43 | Ohio | 459 | | 35 | Wisconsin | 480 |
| 12 | Oklahoma | 555 | | 36 | Alaska | 478 |
| 37 | Oregon | 472 | | 37 | Connecticut | 472 |
| 47 | Pennsylvania | 418 | | 37 | Oregon | 472 |
| 48 | Rhode Island | 414 | | 39 | Washington | 471 |
| 6 | South Carolina | 581 | | 40 | Maryland | 470 |
| 2 | South Dakota | 605 | | 41 | Utah | 465 |
| 18 | Tennessee | 544 | | 42 | West Virginia | 461 |
| 28 | Texas | 519 | | 43 | Ohio | 459 |
| 41 | Utah | 465 | | 44 | Massachusetts | 439 |
| 13 | Vermont | 554 | | 45 | California | 436 |
| 23 | Virginia | 527 | | 46 | Illinois | 419 |
| 39 | Washington | 471 | | 47 | Pennsylvania | 418 |
| 42 | West Virginia | 461 | | 48 | Rhode Island | 414 |
| 35 | Wisconsin | 480 | | 49 | Hawaii | 324 |
| 1 | Wyoming | 721 | | 50 | New York | 314 |
| | | | | | District of Columbia | 327 |

Source: Morgan Quitno Press using data from U.S. Department of Transportation, Federal Highway Administration "Highway Statistics 1999" (Table MF-21)

*Includes gasoline for highway and nonhighway uses. "Gasoline" includes gasohol but excludes "special fuels" such as diesel.

# Daily Production of Crude Oil in 1999

## National Total = 5,881,458 Barrels a Day*

ALPHA ORDER

| RANK | STATE | BARRELS | % of USA |
|------|-------|---------|----------|
| 15 | Alabama | 30,479 | 0.5% |
| 2 | Alaska | 1,049,858 | 17.9% |
| 30 | Arizona | 181 | 0.0% |
| 17 | Arkansas | 19,600 | 0.3% |
| 3 | California | 747,997 | 12.7% |
| 10 | Colorado | 50,597 | 0.9% |
| NA | Connecticut** | NA | NA |
| NA | Delaware** | NA | NA |
| 19 | Florida | 13,411 | 0.2% |
| NA | Georgia** | NA | NA |
| NA | Hawaii** | NA | NA |
| NA | Idaho** | NA | NA |
| 14 | Illinois | 33,055 | 0.6% |
| 22 | Indiana | 5,381 | 0.1% |
| NA | Iowa** | NA | NA |
| 9 | Kansas | 79,578 | 1.4% |
| 20 | Kentucky | 7,608 | 0.1% |
| 4 | Louisiana | 328,789 | 5.6% |
| NA | Maine** | NA | NA |
| NA | Maryland** | NA | NA |
| NA | Massachusetts** | NA | NA |
| 16 | Michigan | 21,466 | 0.4% |
| NA | Minnesota** | NA | NA |
| 11 | Mississippi | 49,175 | 0.8% |
| 29 | Missouri | 252 | 0.0% |
| 13 | Montana | 40,929 | 0.7% |
| 21 | Nebraska | 7,290 | 0.1% |
| 26 | Nevada | 1,934 | 0.0% |
| NA | New Hampshire** | NA | NA |
| NA | New Jersey** | NA | NA |
| 6 | New Mexico | 176,375 | 3.0% |
| 28 | New York | 562 | 0.0% |
| NA | North Carolina** | NA | NA |
| 8 | North Dakota | 90,090 | 1.5% |
| 18 | Ohio | 16,351 | 0.3% |
| 5 | Oklahoma | 193,307 | 3.3% |
| NA | Oregon** | NA | NA |
| 23 | Pennsylvania | 4,027 | 0.1% |
| NA | Rhode Island** | NA | NA |
| NA | South Carolina** | NA | NA |
| 25 | South Dakota | 3,014 | 0.1% |
| 27 | Tennessee | 945 | 0.0% |
| 1 | Texas | 1,230,775 | 20.9% |
| 12 | Utah | 44,529 | 0.8% |
| NA | Vermont** | NA | NA |
| 31 | Virginia | 22 | 0.0% |
| NA | Washington** | NA | NA |
| 23 | West Virginia | 4,027 | 0.1% |
| NA | Wisconsin** | NA | NA |
| 7 | Wyoming | 167,471 | 2.8% |

RANK ORDER

| RANK | STATE | BARRELS | % of USA |
|------|-------|---------|----------|
| 1 | Texas | 1,230,775 | 20.9% |
| 2 | Alaska | 1,049,858 | 17.9% |
| 3 | California | 747,997 | 12.7% |
| 4 | Louisiana | 328,789 | 5.6% |
| 5 | Oklahoma | 193,307 | 3.3% |
| 6 | New Mexico | 176,375 | 3.0% |
| 7 | Wyoming | 167,471 | 2.8% |
| 8 | North Dakota | 90,090 | 1.5% |
| 9 | Kansas | 79,578 | 1.4% |
| 10 | Colorado | 50,597 | 0.9% |
| 11 | Mississippi | 49,175 | 0.8% |
| 12 | Utah | 44,529 | 0.8% |
| 13 | Montana | 40,929 | 0.7% |
| 14 | Illinois | 33,055 | 0.6% |
| 15 | Alabama | 30,479 | 0.5% |
| 16 | Michigan | 21,466 | 0.4% |
| 17 | Arkansas | 19,600 | 0.3% |
| 18 | Ohio | 16,351 | 0.3% |
| 19 | Florida | 13,411 | 0.2% |
| 20 | Kentucky | 7,608 | 0.1% |
| 21 | Nebraska | 7,290 | 0.1% |
| 22 | Indiana | 5,381 | 0.1% |
| 23 | Pennsylvania | 4,027 | 0.1% |
| 23 | West Virginia | 4,027 | 0.1% |
| 25 | South Dakota | 3,014 | 0.1% |
| 26 | Nevada | 1,934 | 0.0% |
| 27 | Tennessee | 945 | 0.0% |
| 28 | New York | 562 | 0.0% |
| 29 | Missouri | 252 | 0.0% |
| 30 | Arizona | 181 | 0.0% |
| 31 | Virginia | 22 | 0.0% |
| NA | Connecticut** | NA | NA |
| NA | Delaware** | NA | NA |
| NA | Georgia** | NA | NA |
| NA | Hawaii** | NA | NA |
| NA | Idaho** | NA | NA |
| NA | Iowa** | NA | NA |
| NA | Maine** | NA | NA |
| NA | Maryland** | NA | NA |
| NA | Massachusetts** | NA | NA |
| NA | Minnesota** | NA | NA |
| NA | New Hampshire** | NA | NA |
| NA | New Jersey** | NA | NA |
| NA | North Carolina** | NA | NA |
| NA | Oregon** | NA | NA |
| NA | Rhode Island** | NA | NA |
| NA | South Carolina** | NA | NA |
| NA | Vermont** | NA | NA |
| NA | Washington** | NA | NA |
| NA | Wisconsin** | NA | NA |
| | District of Columbia** | NA | NA |

*Source: U.S. Department of Energy, Energy Information Administration*
    *"Production of Crude Oil by PAD District and State, 1999" (http://www.eia.doe.gov/neic/rankings/crudebystate.htm)*
*\*National total includes 1,462,381 barrels in federal offshore production. Figures for Alaska, California, Louisiana and Texas include state offshore production.*
*\*\*No reported production.*

# Power Plants in 1999

## National Total = 3,043 Power Plants*

ALPHA ORDER

| RANK | STATE | POWER PLANTS | % of USA |
|------|-------|--------------|----------|
| 32 | Alabama | 35 | 1.2% |
| 3 | Alaska | 166 | 5.5% |
| 33 | Arizona | 33 | 1.1% |
| 33 | Arkansas | 33 | 1.1% |
| 1 | California | 295 | 9.7% |
| 16 | Colorado | 67 | 2.2% |
| 36 | Connecticut | 30 | 1.0% |
| 49 | Delaware | 11 | 0.4% |
| 14 | Florida | 69 | 2.3% |
| 23 | Georgia | 53 | 1.7% |
| 46 | Hawaii | 17 | 0.6% |
| 25 | Idaho | 47 | 1.5% |
| 14 | Illinois | 69 | 2.3% |
| 27 | Indiana | 41 | 1.3% |
| 7 | Iowa | 118 | 3.9% |
| 9 | Kansas | 95 | 3.1% |
| 37 | Kentucky | 29 | 1.0% |
| 31 | Louisiana | 36 | 1.2% |
| 21 | Maine | 58 | 1.9% |
| 40 | Maryland | 22 | 0.7% |
| 29 | Massachusetts | 37 | 1.2% |
| 5 | Michigan | 136 | 4.5% |
| 8 | Minnesota | 108 | 3.5% |
| 42 | Mississippi | 21 | 0.7% |
| 10 | Missouri | 86 | 2.8% |
| 38 | Montana | 27 | 0.9% |
| 11 | Nebraska | 81 | 2.7% |
| 40 | Nevada | 22 | 0.7% |
| 48 | New Hampshire | 15 | 0.5% |
| 35 | New Jersey | 31 | 1.0% |
| 45 | New Mexico | 18 | 0.6% |
| 2 | New York | 169 | 5.6% |
| 22 | North Carolina | 54 | 1.8% |
| 47 | North Dakota | 16 | 0.5% |
| 18 | Ohio | 64 | 2.1% |
| 28 | Oklahoma | 40 | 1.3% |
| 19 | Oregon | 60 | 2.0% |
| 17 | Pennsylvania | 65 | 2.1% |
| 50 | Rhode Island | 2 | 0.1% |
| 24 | South Carolina | 50 | 1.6% |
| 44 | South Dakota | 20 | 0.7% |
| 29 | Tennessee | 37 | 1.2% |
| 4 | Texas | 137 | 4.5% |
| 12 | Utah | 79 | 2.6% |
| 20 | Vermont | 59 | 1.9% |
| 25 | Virginia | 47 | 1.5% |
| 13 | Washington | 72 | 2.4% |
| 42 | West Virginia | 21 | 0.7% |
| 6 | Wisconsin | 119 | 3.9% |
| 39 | Wyoming | 24 | 0.8% |

RANK ORDER

| RANK | STATE | POWER PLANTS | % of USA |
|------|-------|--------------|----------|
| 1 | California | 295 | 9.7% |
| 2 | New York | 169 | 5.6% |
| 3 | Alaska | 166 | 5.5% |
| 4 | Texas | 137 | 4.5% |
| 5 | Michigan | 136 | 4.5% |
| 6 | Wisconsin | 119 | 3.9% |
| 7 | Iowa | 118 | 3.9% |
| 8 | Minnesota | 108 | 3.5% |
| 9 | Kansas | 95 | 3.1% |
| 10 | Missouri | 86 | 2.8% |
| 11 | Nebraska | 81 | 2.7% |
| 12 | Utah | 79 | 2.6% |
| 13 | Washington | 72 | 2.4% |
| 14 | Florida | 69 | 2.3% |
| 14 | Illinois | 69 | 2.3% |
| 16 | Colorado | 67 | 2.2% |
| 17 | Pennsylvania | 65 | 2.1% |
| 18 | Ohio | 64 | 2.1% |
| 19 | Oregon | 60 | 2.0% |
| 20 | Vermont | 59 | 1.9% |
| 21 | Maine | 58 | 1.9% |
| 22 | North Carolina | 54 | 1.8% |
| 23 | Georgia | 53 | 1.7% |
| 24 | South Carolina | 50 | 1.6% |
| 25 | Idaho | 47 | 1.5% |
| 25 | Virginia | 47 | 1.5% |
| 27 | Indiana | 41 | 1.3% |
| 28 | Oklahoma | 40 | 1.3% |
| 29 | Massachusetts | 37 | 1.2% |
| 29 | Tennessee | 37 | 1.2% |
| 31 | Louisiana | 36 | 1.2% |
| 32 | Alabama | 35 | 1.2% |
| 33 | Arizona | 33 | 1.1% |
| 33 | Arkansas | 33 | 1.1% |
| 35 | New Jersey | 31 | 1.0% |
| 36 | Connecticut | 30 | 1.0% |
| 37 | Kentucky | 29 | 1.0% |
| 38 | Montana | 27 | 0.9% |
| 39 | Wyoming | 24 | 0.8% |
| 40 | Maryland | 22 | 0.7% |
| 40 | Nevada | 22 | 0.7% |
| 42 | Mississippi | 21 | 0.7% |
| 42 | West Virginia | 21 | 0.7% |
| 44 | South Dakota | 20 | 0.7% |
| 45 | New Mexico | 18 | 0.6% |
| 46 | Hawaii | 17 | 0.6% |
| 47 | North Dakota | 16 | 0.5% |
| 48 | New Hampshire | 15 | 0.5% |
| 49 | Delaware | 11 | 0.4% |
| 50 | Rhode Island | 2 | 0.1% |
| | District of Columbia | 2 | 0.1% |

*Source: U.S. Department of Energy, Energy Information Agency*
   *"Inventory of Electric Utility Power Plants in the United States 1999"*
*As of January 1, 1999. Each unique site reported by electric utilities, regardless of the number of generators at that site, is counted as a single plant.*

# Hazardous Waste Sites on the National Priority List in 2001

## National Total = 1,293 Sites*

ALPHA ORDER

| RANK | STATE | SITES | % of USA |
|---|---|---|---|
| 26 | Alabama | 15 | 1.2% |
| 44 | Alaska | 7 | 0.5% |
| 39 | Arizona | 10 | 0.8% |
| 33 | Arkansas | 12 | 0.9% |
| 2 | California | 99 | 7.7% |
| 22 | Colorado | 17 | 1.3% |
| 24 | Connecticut | 16 | 1.2% |
| 22 | Delaware | 17 | 1.3% |
| 6 | Florida | 53 | 4.1% |
| 26 | Georgia | 15 | 1.2% |
| 45 | Hawaii | 3 | 0.2% |
| 41 | Idaho | 9 | 0.7% |
| 8 | Illinois | 43 | 3.3% |
| 14 | Indiana | 29 | 2.2% |
| 26 | Iowa | 15 | 1.2% |
| 33 | Kansas | 12 | 0.9% |
| 26 | Kentucky | 15 | 1.2% |
| 24 | Louisiana | 16 | 1.2% |
| 33 | Maine | 12 | 0.9% |
| 21 | Maryland | 18 | 1.4% |
| 12 | Massachusetts | 33 | 2.6% |
| 5 | Michigan | 69 | 5.3% |
| 18 | Minnesota | 24 | 1.9% |
| 45 | Mississippi | 3 | 0.2% |
| 16 | Missouri | 25 | 1.9% |
| 30 | Montana | 14 | 1.1% |
| 39 | Nebraska | 10 | 0.8% |
| 49 | Nevada | 1 | 0.1% |
| 20 | New Hampshire | 19 | 1.5% |
| 1 | New Jersey | 114 | 8.8% |
| 32 | New Mexico | 13 | 1.0% |
| 4 | New York | 89 | 6.9% |
| 15 | North Carolina | 26 | 2.0% |
| 50 | North Dakota | 0 | 0.0% |
| 11 | Ohio | 35 | 2.7% |
| 33 | Oklahoma | 12 | 0.9% |
| 33 | Oregon | 12 | 0.9% |
| 3 | Pennsylvania | 97 | 7.5% |
| 33 | Rhode Island | 12 | 0.9% |
| 16 | South Carolina | 25 | 1.9% |
| 47 | South Dakota | 2 | 0.2% |
| 30 | Tennessee | 14 | 1.1% |
| 10 | Texas | 38 | 2.9% |
| 19 | Utah | 20 | 1.5% |
| 43 | Vermont | 8 | 0.6% |
| 13 | Virginia | 31 | 2.4% |
| 7 | Washington | 48 | 3.7% |
| 41 | West Virginia | 9 | 0.7% |
| 9 | Wisconsin | 41 | 3.2% |
| 47 | Wyoming | 2 | 0.2% |

RANK ORDER

| RANK | STATE | SITES | % of USA |
|---|---|---|---|
| 1 | New Jersey | 114 | 8.8% |
| 2 | California | 99 | 7.7% |
| 3 | Pennsylvania | 97 | 7.5% |
| 4 | New York | 89 | 6.9% |
| 5 | Michigan | 69 | 5.3% |
| 6 | Florida | 53 | 4.1% |
| 7 | Washington | 48 | 3.7% |
| 8 | Illinois | 43 | 3.3% |
| 9 | Wisconsin | 41 | 3.2% |
| 10 | Texas | 38 | 2.9% |
| 11 | Ohio | 35 | 2.7% |
| 12 | Massachusetts | 33 | 2.6% |
| 13 | Virginia | 31 | 2.4% |
| 14 | Indiana | 29 | 2.2% |
| 15 | North Carolina | 26 | 2.0% |
| 16 | Missouri | 25 | 1.9% |
| 16 | South Carolina | 25 | 1.9% |
| 18 | Minnesota | 24 | 1.9% |
| 19 | Utah | 20 | 1.5% |
| 20 | New Hampshire | 19 | 1.5% |
| 21 | Maryland | 18 | 1.4% |
| 22 | Colorado | 17 | 1.3% |
| 22 | Delaware | 17 | 1.3% |
| 24 | Connecticut | 16 | 1.2% |
| 24 | Louisiana | 16 | 1.2% |
| 26 | Alabama | 15 | 1.2% |
| 26 | Georgia | 15 | 1.2% |
| 26 | Iowa | 15 | 1.2% |
| 26 | Kentucky | 15 | 1.2% |
| 30 | Montana | 14 | 1.1% |
| 30 | Tennessee | 14 | 1.1% |
| 32 | New Mexico | 13 | 1.0% |
| 33 | Arkansas | 12 | 0.9% |
| 33 | Kansas | 12 | 0.9% |
| 33 | Maine | 12 | 0.9% |
| 33 | Oklahoma | 12 | 0.9% |
| 33 | Oregon | 12 | 0.9% |
| 33 | Rhode Island | 12 | 0.9% |
| 39 | Arizona | 10 | 0.8% |
| 39 | Nebraska | 10 | 0.8% |
| 41 | Idaho | 9 | 0.7% |
| 41 | West Virginia | 9 | 0.7% |
| 43 | Vermont | 8 | 0.6% |
| 44 | Alaska | 7 | 0.5% |
| 45 | Hawaii | 3 | 0.2% |
| 45 | Mississippi | 3 | 0.2% |
| 47 | South Dakota | 2 | 0.2% |
| 47 | Wyoming | 2 | 0.2% |
| 49 | Nevada | 1 | 0.1% |
| 50 | North Dakota | 0 | 0.0% |
| | District of Columbia | 1 | 0.1% |

Source: U.S. Environmental Protection Agency, Office of Emergency and Remedial Response
    "Proposed National Priorities List (NPL) Sites-by State" (February 7, 2001)
*Includes final and proposed General Superfund and Federal Facilities Sites. National total includes nine sites in Puerto Rico, two in Guam and two in the Virgin Islands.

# Hazardous Waste Sites on the National Priority List
## Per 10,000 Square Miles in 2001
## National Rate = 3.4 Sites per 10,000 Square Miles*

ALPHA ORDER

RANK ORDER

| RANK | STATE | RATE | | RANK | STATE | RATE |
|------|-------|------|---|------|-------|------|
| 29 | Alabama | 2.9 | | 1 | New Jersey | 138.8 |
| 48 | Alaska | 0.1 | | 2 | Rhode Island | 97.5 |
| 44 | Arizona | 0.9 | | 3 | Delaware | 71.0 |
| 34 | Arkansas | 2.3 | | 4 | Massachusetts | 35.7 |
| 20 | California | 6.2 | | 5 | Connecticut | 28.9 |
| 36 | Colorado | 1.6 | | 6 | Pennsylvania | 21.1 |
| 5 | Connecticut | 28.9 | | 7 | New Hampshire | 20.5 |
| 3 | Delaware | 71.0 | | 8 | New York | 16.5 |
| 10 | Florida | 8.8 | | 9 | Maryland | 14.6 |
| 32 | Georgia | 2.5 | | 10 | Florida | 8.8 |
| 22 | Hawaii | 4.6 | | 11 | Vermont | 8.3 |
| 41 | Idaho | 1.1 | | 12 | Indiana | 8.0 |
| 15 | Illinois | 7.4 | | 12 | South Carolina | 8.0 |
| 12 | Indiana | 8.0 | | 14 | Ohio | 7.8 |
| 31 | Iowa | 2.7 | | 15 | Illinois | 7.4 |
| 37 | Kansas | 1.5 | | 16 | Virginia | 7.3 |
| 23 | Kentucky | 3.7 | | 17 | Michigan | 7.1 |
| 28 | Louisiana | 3.2 | | 18 | Washington | 6.8 |
| 25 | Maine | 3.6 | | 19 | Wisconsin | 6.3 |
| 9 | Maryland | 14.6 | | 20 | California | 6.2 |
| 4 | Massachusetts | 35.7 | | 21 | North Carolina | 4.9 |
| 17 | Michigan | 7.1 | | 22 | Hawaii | 4.6 |
| 30 | Minnesota | 2.8 | | 23 | Kentucky | 3.7 |
| 45 | Mississippi | 0.6 | | 23 | West Virginia | 3.7 |
| 25 | Missouri | 3.6 | | 25 | Maine | 3.6 |
| 43 | Montana | 1.0 | | 25 | Missouri | 3.6 |
| 39 | Nebraska | 1.3 | | 27 | Tennessee | 3.3 |
| 48 | Nevada | 0.1 | | 28 | Louisiana | 3.2 |
| 7 | New Hampshire | 20.5 | | 29 | Alabama | 2.9 |
| 1 | New Jersey | 138.8 | | 30 | Minnesota | 2.8 |
| 41 | New Mexico | 1.1 | | 31 | Iowa | 2.7 |
| 8 | New York | 16.5 | | 32 | Georgia | 2.5 |
| 21 | North Carolina | 4.9 | | 33 | Utah | 2.4 |
| 50 | North Dakota | 0.0 | | 34 | Arkansas | 2.3 |
| 14 | Ohio | 7.8 | | 35 | Oklahoma | 1.7 |
| 35 | Oklahoma | 1.7 | | 36 | Colorado | 1.6 |
| 40 | Oregon | 1.2 | | 37 | Kansas | 1.5 |
| 6 | Pennsylvania | 21.1 | | 38 | Texas | 1.4 |
| 2 | Rhode Island | 97.5 | | 39 | Nebraska | 1.3 |
| 12 | South Carolina | 8.0 | | 40 | Oregon | 1.2 |
| 46 | South Dakota | 0.3 | | 41 | Idaho | 1.1 |
| 27 | Tennessee | 3.3 | | 41 | New Mexico | 1.1 |
| 38 | Texas | 1.4 | | 43 | Montana | 1.0 |
| 33 | Utah | 2.4 | | 44 | Arizona | 0.9 |
| 11 | Vermont | 8.3 | | 45 | Mississippi | 0.6 |
| 16 | Virginia | 7.3 | | 46 | South Dakota | 0.3 |
| 18 | Washington | 6.8 | | 47 | Wyoming | 0.2 |
| 23 | West Virginia | 3.7 | | 48 | Alaska | 0.1 |
| 19 | Wisconsin | 6.3 | | 48 | Nevada | 0.1 |
| 47 | Wyoming | 0.2 | | 50 | North Dakota | 0.0 |

District of Columbia**      NA

Source: Morgan Quitno Press using data from U.S. EPA, Office of Emergency and Remedial Response
    "Proposed National Priorities List (NPL) Sites-by State" (February 7, 2001)
*Includes final and proposed General Superfund and Federal Facilities Sites. National rate excludes sites and
square miles in Puerto Rico, Guam and the Virgin Islands. Based on land and water area of states.
**The District of Columbia has one site in its 68 square miles.

# Pollution Released in 1998

## National Total = 7,288,214,893 Pounds of Toxins*

ALPHA ORDER

| RANK | STATE | POUNDS | % of USA |
|------|-------|--------|----------|
| 12 | Alabama | 147,971,814 | 2.0% |
| 6 | Alaska | 307,019,139 | 4.2% |
| 2 | Arizona | 1,069,459,422 | 14.7% |
| 33 | Arkansas | 39,015,235 | 0.5% |
| 26 | California | 70,690,378 | 1.0% |
| 38 | Colorado | 30,257,725 | 0.4% |
| 45 | Connecticut | 9,964,122 | 0.1% |
| 44 | Delaware | 13,167,440 | 0.2% |
| 13 | Florida | 146,950,228 | 2.0% |
| 19 | Georgia | 116,050,668 | 1.6% |
| 48 | Hawaii | 3,612,853 | 0.0% |
| 23 | Idaho | 99,581,448 | 1.4% |
| 11 | Illinois | 169,297,551 | 2.3% |
| 9 | Indiana | 189,475,570 | 2.6% |
| 30 | Iowa | 49,019,069 | 0.7% |
| 32 | Kansas | 40,063,944 | 0.5% |
| 22 | Kentucky | 101,459,789 | 1.4% |
| 10 | Louisiana | 188,608,079 | 2.6% |
| 46 | Maine | 9,746,764 | 0.1% |
| 34 | Maryland | 38,916,981 | 0.5% |
| 43 | Massachusetts | 14,947,545 | 0.2% |
| 14 | Michigan | 140,944,017 | 1.9% |
| 36 | Minnesota | 32,376,326 | 0.4% |
| 25 | Mississippi | 71,751,244 | 1.0% |
| 16 | Missouri | 136,845,034 | 1.9% |
| 18 | Montana | 123,520,951 | 1.7% |
| 42 | Nebraska | 21,281,764 | 0.3% |
| 1 | Nevada | 1,271,722,674 | 17.4% |
| 47 | New Hampshire | 7,061,002 | 0.1% |
| 37 | New Jersey | 30,763,455 | 0.4% |
| 7 | New Mexico | 260,119,315 | 3.6% |
| 27 | New York | 70,444,506 | 1.0% |
| 17 | North Carolina | 133,397,919 | 1.8% |
| 39 | North Dakota | 23,382,206 | 0.3% |
| 4 | Ohio | 336,268,276 | 4.6% |
| 31 | Oklahoma | 41,831,334 | 0.6% |
| 29 | Oregon | 55,140,807 | 0.8% |
| 8 | Pennsylvania | 216,164,765 | 3.0% |
| 49 | Rhode Island | 2,273,531 | 0.0% |
| 20 | South Carolina | 107,300,428 | 1.5% |
| 41 | South Dakota | 22,310,732 | 0.3% |
| 15 | Tennessee | 139,312,649 | 1.9% |
| 5 | Texas | 312,239,546 | 4.3% |
| 3 | Utah | 574,225,505 | 7.9% |
| 50 | Vermont | 412,965 | 0.0% |
| 24 | Virginia | 79,924,886 | 1.1% |
| 35 | Washington | 34,491,128 | 0.5% |
| 21 | West Virginia | 103,840,324 | 1.4% |
| 28 | Wisconsin | 60,732,242 | 0.8% |
| 40 | Wyoming | 22,781,837 | 0.3% |

RANK ORDER

| RANK | STATE | POUNDS | % of USA |
|------|-------|--------|----------|
| 1 | Nevada | 1,271,722,674 | 17.4% |
| 2 | Arizona | 1,069,459,422 | 14.7% |
| 3 | Utah | 574,225,505 | 7.9% |
| 4 | Ohio | 336,268,276 | 4.6% |
| 5 | Texas | 312,239,546 | 4.3% |
| 6 | Alaska | 307,019,139 | 4.2% |
| 7 | New Mexico | 260,119,315 | 3.6% |
| 8 | Pennsylvania | 216,164,765 | 3.0% |
| 9 | Indiana | 189,475,570 | 2.6% |
| 10 | Louisiana | 188,608,079 | 2.6% |
| 11 | Illinois | 169,297,551 | 2.3% |
| 12 | Alabama | 147,971,814 | 2.0% |
| 13 | Florida | 146,950,228 | 2.0% |
| 14 | Michigan | 140,944,017 | 1.9% |
| 15 | Tennessee | 139,312,649 | 1.9% |
| 16 | Missouri | 136,845,034 | 1.9% |
| 17 | North Carolina | 133,397,919 | 1.8% |
| 18 | Montana | 123,520,951 | 1.7% |
| 19 | Georgia | 116,050,668 | 1.6% |
| 20 | South Carolina | 107,300,428 | 1.5% |
| 21 | West Virginia | 103,840,324 | 1.4% |
| 22 | Kentucky | 101,459,789 | 1.4% |
| 23 | Idaho | 99,581,448 | 1.4% |
| 24 | Virginia | 79,924,886 | 1.1% |
| 25 | Mississippi | 71,751,244 | 1.0% |
| 26 | California | 70,690,378 | 1.0% |
| 27 | New York | 70,444,506 | 1.0% |
| 28 | Wisconsin | 60,732,242 | 0.8% |
| 29 | Oregon | 55,140,807 | 0.8% |
| 30 | Iowa | 49,019,069 | 0.7% |
| 31 | Oklahoma | 41,831,334 | 0.6% |
| 32 | Kansas | 40,063,944 | 0.5% |
| 33 | Arkansas | 39,015,235 | 0.5% |
| 34 | Maryland | 38,916,981 | 0.5% |
| 35 | Washington | 34,491,128 | 0.5% |
| 36 | Minnesota | 32,376,326 | 0.4% |
| 37 | New Jersey | 30,763,455 | 0.4% |
| 38 | Colorado | 30,257,725 | 0.4% |
| 39 | North Dakota | 23,382,206 | 0.3% |
| 40 | Wyoming | 22,781,837 | 0.3% |
| 41 | South Dakota | 22,310,732 | 0.3% |
| 42 | Nebraska | 21,281,764 | 0.3% |
| 43 | Massachusetts | 14,947,545 | 0.2% |
| 44 | Delaware | 13,167,440 | 0.2% |
| 45 | Connecticut | 9,964,122 | 0.1% |
| 46 | Maine | 9,746,764 | 0.1% |
| 47 | New Hampshire | 7,061,002 | 0.1% |
| 48 | Hawaii | 3,612,853 | 0.0% |
| 49 | Rhode Island | 2,273,531 | 0.0% |
| 50 | Vermont | 412,965 | 0.0% |
| | District of Columbia | 77,761 | 0.0% |

*Source: U.S. Environmental Protection Agency, Office of Pollution Prevention and Toxics Information Management "1998 Toxics Release Inventory"*

*National total does not include 19,059,770 pounds of toxins in U.S. territories. Includes discharges to air, surface water, underground injection and surface land. Includes both original (or manufacturing) industries and those added by EPA since it began tracking releases. Because industries have been added it is not possible to show trends except for the original industries. Those figures are shown in tables 215 and 216.*

# Pollution Released by Manufacturing Plants in 1998

## National Total = 2,488,406,889 Pounds of Toxins*

ALPHA ORDER

| RANK | STATE | POUNDS | % of USA |
|---|---|---|---|
| 9 | Alabama | 89,519,922 | 3.6% |
| 47 | Alaska | 1,948,559 | 0.1% |
| 18 | Arizona | 54,346,031 | 2.2% |
| 20 | Arkansas | 50,743,995 | 2.0% |
| 22 | California | 43,688,750 | 1.8% |
| 42 | Colorado | 5,473,006 | 0.2% |
| 39 | Connecticut | 7,604,324 | 0.3% |
| 41 | Delaware | 5,503,568 | 0.2% |
| 11 | Florida | 78,499,582 | 3.2% |
| 13 | Georgia | 64,867,232 | 2.6% |
| 49 | Hawaii | 435,831 | 0.0% |
| 32 | Idaho | 22,750,923 | 0.9% |
| 6 | Illinois | 116,483,095 | 4.7% |
| 5 | Indiana | 120,941,009 | 4.9% |
| 24 | Iowa | 40,100,994 | 1.6% |
| 28 | Kansas | 29,137,835 | 1.2% |
| 23 | Kentucky | 41,033,286 | 1.6% |
| 2 | Louisiana | 175,603,883 | 7.1% |
| 37 | Maine | 9,636,269 | 0.4% |
| 36 | Maryland | 13,251,453 | 0.5% |
| 40 | Massachusetts | 7,278,796 | 0.3% |
| 10 | Michigan | 83,648,982 | 3.4% |
| 34 | Minnesota | 19,870,654 | 0.8% |
| 14 | Mississippi | 60,520,702 | 2.4% |
| 16 | Missouri | 57,045,614 | 2.3% |
| 19 | Montana | 51,377,382 | 2.1% |
| 35 | Nebraska | 16,186,981 | 0.7% |
| 43 | Nevada | 4,204,845 | 0.2% |
| 45 | New Hampshire | 2,970,927 | 0.1% |
| 33 | New Jersey | 19,959,412 | 0.8% |
| 30 | New Mexico | 24,827,806 | 1.0% |
| 25 | New York | 35,489,850 | 1.4% |
| 12 | North Carolina | 76,800,683 | 3.1% |
| 46 | North Dakota | 2,449,976 | 0.1% |
| 3 | Ohio | 153,558,752 | 6.2% |
| 31 | Oklahoma | 24,397,829 | 1.0% |
| 26 | Oregon | 33,180,800 | 1.3% |
| 4 | Pennsylvania | 145,737,350 | 5.9% |
| 48 | Rhode Island | 1,751,380 | 0.1% |
| 15 | South Carolina | 59,695,616 | 2.4% |
| 44 | South Dakota | 3,251,231 | 0.1% |
| 8 | Tennessee | 94,907,549 | 3.8% |
| 1 | Texas | 262,681,842 | 10.6% |
| 7 | Utah | 106,252,499 | 4.3% |
| 50 | Vermont | 417,357 | 0.0% |
| 17 | Virginia | 56,848,332 | 2.3% |
| 27 | Washington | 32,108,843 | 1.3% |
| 29 | West Virginia | 26,185,485 | 1.1% |
| 21 | Wisconsin | 43,780,692 | 1.8% |
| 38 | Wyoming | 9,437,664 | 0.4% |

RANK ORDER

| RANK | STATE | POUNDS | % of USA |
|---|---|---|---|
| 1 | Texas | 262,681,842 | 10.6% |
| 2 | Louisiana | 175,603,883 | 7.1% |
| 3 | Ohio | 153,558,752 | 6.2% |
| 4 | Pennsylvania | 145,737,350 | 5.9% |
| 5 | Indiana | 120,941,009 | 4.9% |
| 6 | Illinois | 116,483,095 | 4.7% |
| 7 | Utah | 106,252,499 | 4.3% |
| 8 | Tennessee | 94,907,549 | 3.8% |
| 9 | Alabama | 89,519,922 | 3.6% |
| 10 | Michigan | 83,648,982 | 3.4% |
| 11 | Florida | 78,499,582 | 3.2% |
| 12 | North Carolina | 76,800,683 | 3.1% |
| 13 | Georgia | 64,867,232 | 2.6% |
| 14 | Mississippi | 60,520,702 | 2.4% |
| 15 | South Carolina | 59,695,616 | 2.4% |
| 16 | Missouri | 57,045,614 | 2.3% |
| 17 | Virginia | 56,848,332 | 2.3% |
| 18 | Arizona | 54,346,031 | 2.2% |
| 19 | Montana | 51,377,382 | 2.1% |
| 20 | Arkansas | 50,743,995 | 2.0% |
| 21 | Wisconsin | 43,780,692 | 1.8% |
| 22 | California | 43,688,750 | 1.8% |
| 23 | Kentucky | 41,033,286 | 1.6% |
| 24 | Iowa | 40,100,994 | 1.6% |
| 25 | New York | 35,489,850 | 1.4% |
| 26 | Oregon | 33,180,800 | 1.3% |
| 27 | Washington | 32,108,843 | 1.3% |
| 28 | Kansas | 29,137,835 | 1.2% |
| 29 | West Virginia | 26,185,485 | 1.1% |
| 30 | New Mexico | 24,827,806 | 1.0% |
| 31 | Oklahoma | 24,397,829 | 1.0% |
| 32 | Idaho | 22,750,923 | 0.9% |
| 33 | New Jersey | 19,959,412 | 0.8% |
| 34 | Minnesota | 19,870,654 | 0.8% |
| 35 | Nebraska | 16,186,981 | 0.7% |
| 36 | Maryland | 13,251,453 | 0.5% |
| 37 | Maine | 9,636,269 | 0.4% |
| 38 | Wyoming | 9,437,664 | 0.4% |
| 39 | Connecticut | 7,604,324 | 0.3% |
| 40 | Massachusetts | 7,278,796 | 0.3% |
| 41 | Delaware | 5,503,568 | 0.2% |
| 42 | Colorado | 5,473,006 | 0.2% |
| 43 | Nevada | 4,204,845 | 0.2% |
| 44 | South Dakota | 3,251,231 | 0.1% |
| 45 | New Hampshire | 2,970,927 | 0.1% |
| 46 | North Dakota | 2,449,976 | 0.1% |
| 47 | Alaska | 1,948,559 | 0.1% |
| 48 | Rhode Island | 1,751,380 | 0.1% |
| 49 | Hawaii | 435,831 | 0.0% |
| 50 | Vermont | 417,357 | 0.0% |
| | District of Columbia | 11,511 | 0.0% |

*Source: U.S. Environmental Protection Agency, Office of Pollution Prevention and Toxics Information Management "1998 Toxics Release Inventory"*

*National total does not include 8,352,976 pounds of toxins in U.S. territories. Includes discharges to air, surface water, underground injection and surface land by what are labeled by the EPA as "original industries" for which data have been collected since 1988. An additional 4,799,808,004 pounds (excluding territories) of toxins were released by industries that have been added by EPA (see table 214).*

# Percent Change in Pollution Released by Manufacturing Plants: 1995 to 1998

## National Percent Change = 5.2% Decrease*

ALPHA ORDER

| RANK | STATE | PERCENT CHANGE |
|------|-------|----------------|
| 40 | Alabama | (22.2) |
| 50 | Alaska | (71.5) |
| 2 | Arizona | 34.2 |
| 4 | Arkansas | 31.0 |
| 42 | California | (22.4) |
| 14 | Colorado | 3.1 |
| 46 | Connecticut | (35.9) |
| 19 | Delaware | (0.3) |
| 23 | Florida | (3.7) |
| 11 | Georgia | 6.3 |
| 45 | Hawaii | (33.6) |
| 1 | Idaho | 41.1 |
| 23 | Illinois | (3.7) |
| 12 | Indiana | 5.2 |
| 15 | Iowa | 3.0 |
| 18 | Kansas | (0.1) |
| 30 | Kentucky | (15.5) |
| 22 | Louisiana | (2.6) |
| 31 | Maine | (16.2) |
| 43 | Maryland | (27.5) |
| 44 | Massachusetts | (27.9) |
| 35 | Michigan | (18.7) |
| 36 | Minnesota | (18.8) |
| 20 | Mississippi | (1.5) |
| 26 | Missouri | (6.7) |
| 5 | Montana | 17.0 |
| 10 | Nebraska | 6.7 |
| 8 | Nevada | 7.2 |
| 16 | New Hampshire | 1.6 |
| 13 | New Jersey | 3.8 |
| 48 | New Mexico | (44.9) |
| 34 | New York | (18.4) |
| 39 | North Carolina | (20.5) |
| 32 | North Dakota | (16.5) |
| 21 | Ohio | (2.4) |
| 36 | Oklahoma | (18.8) |
| 6 | Oregon | 16.2 |
| 7 | Pennsylvania | 12.4 |
| 49 | Rhode Island | (48.6) |
| 17 | South Carolina | 0.5 |
| 41 | South Dakota | (22.3) |
| 29 | Tennessee | (14.5) |
| 28 | Texas | (14.1) |
| 3 | Utah | 33.1 |
| 47 | Vermont | (39.8) |
| 25 | Virginia | (5.2) |
| 9 | Washington | 7.1 |
| 38 | West Virginia | (19.6) |
| 27 | Wisconsin | (7.0) |
| 33 | Wyoming | (16.9) |

RANK ORDER

| RANK | STATE | PERCENT CHANGE |
|------|-------|----------------|
| 1 | Idaho | 41.1 |
| 2 | Arizona | 34.2 |
| 3 | Utah | 33.1 |
| 4 | Arkansas | 31.0 |
| 5 | Montana | 17.0 |
| 6 | Oregon | 16.2 |
| 7 | Pennsylvania | 12.4 |
| 8 | Nevada | 7.2 |
| 9 | Washington | 7.1 |
| 10 | Nebraska | 6.7 |
| 11 | Georgia | 6.3 |
| 12 | Indiana | 5.2 |
| 13 | New Jersey | 3.8 |
| 14 | Colorado | 3.1 |
| 15 | Iowa | 3.0 |
| 16 | New Hampshire | 1.6 |
| 17 | South Carolina | 0.5 |
| 18 | Kansas | (0.1) |
| 19 | Delaware | (0.3) |
| 20 | Mississippi | (1.5) |
| 21 | Ohio | (2.4) |
| 22 | Louisiana | (2.6) |
| 23 | Florida | (3.7) |
| 23 | Illinois | (3.7) |
| 25 | Virginia | (5.2) |
| 26 | Missouri | (6.7) |
| 27 | Wisconsin | (7.0) |
| 28 | Texas | (14.1) |
| 29 | Tennessee | (14.5) |
| 30 | Kentucky | (15.5) |
| 31 | Maine | (16.2) |
| 32 | North Dakota | (16.5) |
| 33 | Wyoming | (16.9) |
| 34 | New York | (18.4) |
| 35 | Michigan | (18.7) |
| 36 | Minnesota | (18.8) |
| 36 | Oklahoma | (18.8) |
| 38 | West Virginia | (19.6) |
| 39 | North Carolina | (20.5) |
| 40 | Alabama | (22.2) |
| 41 | South Dakota | (22.3) |
| 42 | California | (22.4) |
| 43 | Maryland | (27.5) |
| 44 | Massachusetts | (27.9) |
| 45 | Hawaii | (33.6) |
| 46 | Connecticut | (35.9) |
| 47 | Vermont | (39.8) |
| 48 | New Mexico | (44.9) |
| 49 | Rhode Island | (48.6) |
| 50 | Alaska | (71.5) |
| | District of Columbia | (79.8) |

*Source: U.S. Environmental Protection Agency, Office of Pollution Prevention and Toxics Information Management "1998 Toxics Release Inventory"*

*\*National rate does not include toxins in U.S. territories. Includes discharges to air, surface water, underground injection and surface land by what are labeled by the EPA as "original industries" for which data have been collected since 1988. Additional toxins were released by industries that have been added by EPA (see table 214).*

# Toxic Waste Sent Out of State in 1998

## National Total = 1,657,203,350 Pounds of Toxins*

| ALPHA ORDER | | | | | RANK ORDER | | | |
|---|---|---|---|---|---|---|---|---|
| RANK | STATE | POUNDS | % of USA | | RANK | STATE | POUNDS | % of USA |
| 19 | Alabama | 40,778,206 | 2.5% | | 1 | Ohio | 140,233,311 | 8.5% |
| 50 | Alaska | 32,302 | 0.0% | | 2 | Indiana | 115,890,037 | 7.0% |
| 24 | Arizona | 21,949,772 | 1.3% | | 3 | Texas | 101,541,111 | 6.1% |
| 18 | Arkansas | 41,470,668 | 2.5% | | 4 | Michigan | 100,786,776 | 6.1% |
| 21 | California | 23,936,355 | 1.4% | | 5 | Illinois | 80,085,860 | 4.8% |
| 28 | Colorado | 19,415,737 | 1.2% | | 6 | North Carolina | 78,152,170 | 4.7% |
| 30 | Connecticut | 18,032,956 | 1.1% | | 7 | New York | 75,148,237 | 4.5% |
| 34 | Delaware | 14,048,745 | 0.8% | | 8 | Pennsylvania | 66,304,282 | 4.0% |
| 31 | Florida | 17,336,484 | 1.0% | | 9 | Georgia | 59,754,421 | 3.6% |
| 9 | Georgia | 59,754,421 | 3.6% | | 10 | Kansas | 57,938,070 | 3.5% |
| 48 | Hawaii | 103,637 | 0.0% | | 11 | Tennessee | 55,337,655 | 3.3% |
| 41 | Idaho | 1,988,639 | 0.1% | | 12 | Kentucky | 52,604,432 | 3.2% |
| 5 | Illinois | 80,085,860 | 4.8% | | 13 | New Jersey | 49,710,382 | 3.0% |
| 2 | Indiana | 115,890,037 | 7.0% | | 14 | South Carolina | 48,980,456 | 3.0% |
| 15 | Iowa | 47,130,636 | 2.8% | | 15 | Iowa | 47,130,636 | 2.8% |
| 10 | Kansas | 57,938,070 | 3.5% | | 16 | Wisconsin | 45,841,966 | 2.8% |
| 12 | Kentucky | 52,604,432 | 3.2% | | 17 | Missouri | 41,984,172 | 2.5% |
| 20 | Louisiana | 39,324,481 | 2.4% | | 18 | Arkansas | 41,470,668 | 2.5% |
| 40 | Maine | 2,041,256 | 0.1% | | 19 | Alabama | 40,778,206 | 2.5% |
| 37 | Maryland | 9,056,766 | 0.5% | | 20 | Louisiana | 39,324,481 | 2.4% |
| 23 | Massachusetts | 22,958,253 | 1.4% | | 21 | California | 23,936,355 | 1.4% |
| 4 | Michigan | 100,786,776 | 6.1% | | 22 | Virginia | 23,405,452 | 1.4% |
| 33 | Minnesota | 14,234,087 | 0.9% | | 23 | Massachusetts | 22,958,253 | 1.4% |
| 27 | Mississippi | 20,000,640 | 1.2% | | 24 | Arizona | 21,949,772 | 1.3% |
| 17 | Missouri | 41,984,172 | 2.5% | | 25 | Nebraska | 21,702,168 | 1.3% |
| 49 | Montana | 71,799 | 0.0% | | 26 | Oklahoma | 21,516,257 | 1.3% |
| 25 | Nebraska | 21,702,168 | 1.3% | | 27 | Mississippi | 20,000,640 | 1.2% |
| 42 | Nevada | 1,549,725 | 0.1% | | 28 | Colorado | 19,415,737 | 1.2% |
| 32 | New Hampshire | 14,427,339 | 0.9% | | 29 | West Virginia | 18,126,598 | 1.1% |
| 13 | New Jersey | 49,710,382 | 3.0% | | 30 | Connecticut | 18,032,956 | 1.1% |
| 44 | New Mexico | 1,037,661 | 0.1% | | 31 | Florida | 17,336,484 | 1.0% |
| 7 | New York | 75,148,237 | 4.5% | | 32 | New Hampshire | 14,427,339 | 0.9% |
| 6 | North Carolina | 78,152,170 | 4.7% | | 33 | Minnesota | 14,234,087 | 0.9% |
| 47 | North Dakota | 112,632 | 0.0% | | 34 | Delaware | 14,048,745 | 0.8% |
| 1 | Ohio | 140,233,311 | 8.5% | | 35 | Rhode Island | 11,581,223 | 0.7% |
| 26 | Oklahoma | 21,516,257 | 1.3% | | 36 | Oregon | 10,345,130 | 0.6% |
| 36 | Oregon | 10,345,130 | 0.6% | | 37 | Maryland | 9,056,766 | 0.5% |
| 8 | Pennsylvania | 66,304,282 | 4.0% | | 38 | Washington | 4,798,657 | 0.3% |
| 35 | Rhode Island | 11,581,223 | 0.7% | | 39 | Utah | 2,312,828 | 0.1% |
| 14 | South Carolina | 48,980,456 | 3.0% | | 40 | Maine | 2,041,256 | 0.1% |
| 43 | South Dakota | 1,087,109 | 0.1% | | 41 | Idaho | 1,988,639 | 0.1% |
| 11 | Tennessee | 55,337,655 | 3.3% | | 42 | Nevada | 1,549,725 | 0.1% |
| 3 | Texas | 101,541,111 | 6.1% | | 43 | South Dakota | 1,087,109 | 0.1% |
| 39 | Utah | 2,312,828 | 0.1% | | 44 | New Mexico | 1,037,661 | 0.1% |
| 45 | Vermont | 873,135 | 0.1% | | 45 | Vermont | 873,135 | 0.1% |
| 22 | Virginia | 23,405,452 | 1.4% | | 46 | Wyoming | 115,379 | 0.0% |
| 38 | Washington | 4,798,657 | 0.3% | | 47 | North Dakota | 112,632 | 0.0% |
| 29 | West Virginia | 18,126,598 | 1.1% | | 48 | Hawaii | 103,637 | 0.0% |
| 16 | Wisconsin | 45,841,966 | 2.8% | | 49 | Montana | 71,799 | 0.0% |
| 46 | Wyoming | 115,379 | 0.0% | | 50 | Alaska | 32,302 | 0.0% |
| | | | | | | District of Columbia | 7,300 | 0.0% |

Source: U.S. Environmental Protection Agency, Office of Pollution Prevention and Toxics Information Management
"1998 Toxics Release Inventory"
*Off-site transfers for further waste management. This includes disposal, recycling and treatment. National total
does not include 12,024,016 pounds of toxins shipped from U.S. territories or labeled as "other."

# Toxic Waste Received In State in 1998

## National Total = 1,544,678,462 Pounds of Toxins*

| RANK | STATE | POUNDS | % of USA |
|------|-------|--------|----------|
| 11 | Alabama | 53,729,752 | 3.5% |
| 44 | Alaska | 68,884 | 0.0% |
| 23 | Arizona | 15,267,726 | 1.0% |
| 14 | Arkansas | 36,758,670 | 2.4% |
| 13 | California | 39,672,275 | 2.6% |
| 39 | Colorado | 779,131 | 0.1% |
| 8 | Connecticut | 66,061,499 | 4.3% |
| 37 | Delaware | 1,246,830 | 0.1% |
| 29 | Florida | 4,672,396 | 0.3% |
| 27 | Georgia | 6,687,358 | 0.4% |
| 47 | Hawaii | 6,300 | 0.0% |
| 42 | Idaho | 271,974 | 0.0% |
| 1 | Illinois | 166,029,409 | 10.7% |
| 2 | Indiana | 165,406,010 | 10.7% |
| 17 | Iowa | 26,188,559 | 1.7% |
| 26 | Kansas | 7,171,940 | 0.5% |
| 25 | Kentucky | 12,875,512 | 0.8% |
| 16 | Louisiana | 29,838,571 | 1.9% |
| 48 | Maine | 2,386 | 0.0% |
| 24 | Maryland | 14,831,506 | 1.0% |
| 31 | Massachusetts | 3,140,813 | 0.2% |
| 6 | Michigan | 92,541,974 | 6.0% |
| 19 | Minnesota | 19,661,370 | 1.3% |
| 32 | Mississippi | 3,112,097 | 0.2% |
| 5 | Missouri | 107,364,122 | 7.0% |
| 30 | Montana | 3,764,496 | 0.2% |
| 28 | Nebraska | 6,393,743 | 0.4% |
| 40 | Nevada | 778,213 | 0.1% |
| 45 | New Hampshire | 47,667 | 0.0% |
| 9 | New Jersey | 59,807,562 | 3.9% |
| 41 | New Mexico | 376,377 | 0.0% |
| 10 | New York | 55,697,575 | 3.6% |
| 21 | North Carolina | 16,684,948 | 1.1% |
| 49 | North Dakota | 301 | 0.0% |
| 3 | Ohio | 146,549,648 | 9.5% |
| 36 | Oklahoma | 2,104,359 | 0.1% |
| 38 | Oregon | 1,025,840 | 0.1% |
| 4 | Pennsylvania | 140,721,580 | 9.1% |
| 35 | Rhode Island | 2,436,889 | 0.2% |
| 12 | South Carolina | 46,280,817 | 3.0% |
| 50 | South Dakota | 0 | 0.0% |
| 15 | Tennessee | 36,391,552 | 2.4% |
| 7 | Texas | 92,083,753 | 6.0% |
| 33 | Utah | 2,856,569 | 0.2% |
| 46 | Vermont | 17,742 | 0.0% |
| 22 | Virginia | 15,730,969 | 1.0% |
| 34 | Washington | 2,822,972 | 0.2% |
| 20 | West Virginia | 18,246,460 | 1.2% |
| 18 | Wisconsin | 20,293,026 | 1.3% |
| 43 | Wyoming | 177,040 | 0.0% |

| RANK | STATE | POUNDS | % of USA |
|------|-------|--------|----------|
| 1 | Illinois | 166,029,409 | 10.7% |
| 2 | Indiana | 165,406,010 | 10.7% |
| 3 | Ohio | 146,549,648 | 9.5% |
| 4 | Pennsylvania | 140,721,580 | 9.1% |
| 5 | Missouri | 107,364,122 | 7.0% |
| 6 | Michigan | 92,541,974 | 6.0% |
| 7 | Texas | 92,083,753 | 6.0% |
| 8 | Connecticut | 66,061,499 | 4.3% |
| 9 | New Jersey | 59,807,562 | 3.9% |
| 10 | New York | 55,697,575 | 3.6% |
| 11 | Alabama | 53,729,752 | 3.5% |
| 12 | South Carolina | 46,280,817 | 3.0% |
| 13 | California | 39,672,275 | 2.6% |
| 14 | Arkansas | 36,758,670 | 2.4% |
| 15 | Tennessee | 36,391,552 | 2.4% |
| 16 | Louisiana | 29,838,571 | 1.9% |
| 17 | Iowa | 26,188,559 | 1.7% |
| 18 | Wisconsin | 20,293,026 | 1.3% |
| 19 | Minnesota | 19,661,370 | 1.3% |
| 20 | West Virginia | 18,246,460 | 1.2% |
| 21 | North Carolina | 16,684,948 | 1.1% |
| 22 | Virginia | 15,730,969 | 1.0% |
| 23 | Arizona | 15,267,726 | 1.0% |
| 24 | Maryland | 14,831,506 | 1.0% |
| 25 | Kentucky | 12,875,512 | 0.8% |
| 26 | Kansas | 7,171,940 | 0.5% |
| 27 | Georgia | 6,687,358 | 0.4% |
| 28 | Nebraska | 6,393,743 | 0.4% |
| 29 | Florida | 4,672,396 | 0.3% |
| 30 | Montana | 3,764,496 | 0.2% |
| 31 | Massachusetts | 3,140,813 | 0.2% |
| 32 | Mississippi | 3,112,097 | 0.2% |
| 33 | Utah | 2,856,569 | 0.2% |
| 34 | Washington | 2,822,972 | 0.2% |
| 35 | Rhode Island | 2,436,889 | 0.2% |
| 36 | Oklahoma | 2,104,359 | 0.1% |
| 37 | Delaware | 1,246,830 | 0.1% |
| 38 | Oregon | 1,025,840 | 0.1% |
| 39 | Colorado | 779,131 | 0.1% |
| 40 | Nevada | 778,213 | 0.1% |
| 41 | New Mexico | 376,377 | 0.0% |
| 42 | Idaho | 271,974 | 0.0% |
| 43 | Wyoming | 177,040 | 0.0% |
| 44 | Alaska | 68,884 | 0.0% |
| 45 | New Hampshire | 47,667 | 0.0% |
| 46 | Vermont | 17,742 | 0.0% |
| 47 | Hawaii | 6,300 | 0.0% |
| 48 | Maine | 2,386 | 0.0% |
| 49 | North Dakota | 301 | 0.0% |
| 50 | South Dakota | 0 | 0.0% |
| | District of Columbia | 1,300 | 0.0% |

Source: U.S. Environmental Protection Agency, Office of Pollution Prevention and Toxics Information Management
"1998 Toxics Release Inventory"
*Transfers into state for further waste management. This includes disposal, recycling and treatment. National total
does not include 123,805,601 pounds of toxins in U.S. territories or labeled as "other." These were shipped either
out of the country or to sites not identified by state by the reporting facility.

# Per Capita Daily Fresh Water Withdrawn in 1995

## National Per Capita = 1,516 Gallons per Day*

ALPHA ORDER

| RANK | STATE | GALLONS |
|------|-------|---------|
| 18 | Alabama | 1,666 |
| 48 | Alaska | 547 |
| 21 | Arizona | 1,586 |
| 6 | Arkansas | 3,548 |
| 26 | California | 1,457 |
| 5 | Colorado | 3,692 |
| 28 | Connecticut | 1,363 |
| 11 | Delaware | 2,088 |
| 31 | Florida | 1,283 |
| 42 | Georgia | 810 |
| 19 | Hawaii | 1,635 |
| 2 | Idaho | 12,961 |
| 17 | Illinois | 1,674 |
| 23 | Indiana | 1,578 |
| 37 | Iowa | 1,067 |
| 13 | Kansas | 2,026 |
| 36 | Kentucky | 1,146 |
| 9 | Louisiana | 2,276 |
| 50 | Maine | 263 |
| 24 | Maryland | 1,539 |
| 41 | Massachusetts | 909 |
| 32 | Michigan | 1,253 |
| 45 | Minnesota | 736 |
| 34 | Mississippi | 1,189 |
| 29 | Missouri | 1,320 |
| 3 | Montana | 10,201 |
| 4 | Nebraska | 6,421 |
| 25 | Nevada | 1,507 |
| 35 | New Hampshire | 1,152 |
| 44 | New Jersey | 767 |
| 12 | New Mexico | 2,086 |
| 40 | New York | 926 |
| 30 | North Carolina | 1,293 |
| 15 | North Dakota | 1,746 |
| 39 | Ohio | 941 |
| 47 | Oklahoma | 625 |
| 8 | Oregon | 2,518 |
| 43 | Pennsylvania | 804 |
| 49 | Rhode Island | 415 |
| 16 | South Carolina | 1,676 |
| 46 | South Dakota | 632 |
| 14 | Tennessee | 1,927 |
| 22 | Texas | 1,585 |
| 10 | Utah | 2,256 |
| 38 | Vermont | 969 |
| 33 | Virginia | 1,251 |
| 20 | Washington | 1,631 |
| 7 | West Virginia | 2,538 |
| 27 | Wisconsin | 1,411 |
| 1 | Wyoming | 14,756 |

RANK ORDER

| RANK | STATE | GALLONS |
|------|-------|---------|
| 1 | Wyoming | 14,756 |
| 2 | Idaho | 12,961 |
| 3 | Montana | 10,201 |
| 4 | Nebraska | 6,421 |
| 5 | Colorado | 3,692 |
| 6 | Arkansas | 3,548 |
| 7 | West Virginia | 2,538 |
| 8 | Oregon | 2,518 |
| 9 | Louisiana | 2,276 |
| 10 | Utah | 2,256 |
| 11 | Delaware | 2,088 |
| 12 | New Mexico | 2,086 |
| 13 | Kansas | 2,026 |
| 14 | Tennessee | 1,927 |
| 15 | North Dakota | 1,746 |
| 16 | South Carolina | 1,676 |
| 17 | Illinois | 1,674 |
| 18 | Alabama | 1,666 |
| 19 | Hawaii | 1,635 |
| 20 | Washington | 1,631 |
| 21 | Arizona | 1,586 |
| 22 | Texas | 1,585 |
| 23 | Indiana | 1,578 |
| 24 | Maryland | 1,539 |
| 25 | Nevada | 1,507 |
| 26 | California | 1,457 |
| 27 | Wisconsin | 1,411 |
| 28 | Connecticut | 1,363 |
| 29 | Missouri | 1,320 |
| 30 | North Carolina | 1,293 |
| 31 | Florida | 1,283 |
| 32 | Michigan | 1,253 |
| 33 | Virginia | 1,251 |
| 34 | Mississippi | 1,189 |
| 35 | New Hampshire | 1,152 |
| 36 | Kentucky | 1,146 |
| 37 | Iowa | 1,067 |
| 38 | Vermont | 969 |
| 39 | Ohio | 941 |
| 40 | New York | 926 |
| 41 | Massachusetts | 909 |
| 42 | Georgia | 810 |
| 43 | Pennsylvania | 804 |
| 44 | New Jersey | 767 |
| 45 | Minnesota | 736 |
| 46 | South Dakota | 632 |
| 47 | Oklahoma | 625 |
| 48 | Alaska | 547 |
| 49 | Rhode Island | 415 |
| 50 | Maine | 263 |

District of Columbia — 18

Source: Morgan Quitno Press using data from U.S. Department of Interior, U.S. Geological Survey
"Estimated Water Use in the United States in 1995" (circular 1200)
*National per capita does not include water or population for Puerto Rico or the Virgin Islands. Includes water used for irrigation, public supply, industrial and thermo-electric power.

# VIII. GEOGRAPHY

# Total Area of States in Square Miles in 2000

## National Total = 3,717,796 Square Miles*

ALPHA ORDER

RANK ORDER

| RANK | STATE | MILES | % of USA |
|------|-------|-------|----------|
| 30 | Alabama | 52,237 | 1.4% |
| 1 | Alaska | 615,230 | 16.6% |
| 6 | Arizona | 114,006 | 3.1% |
| 28 | Arkansas | 53,182 | 1.4% |
| 3 | California | 158,869 | 4.3% |
| 8 | Colorado | 104,100 | 2.8% |
| 48 | Connecticut | 5,544 | 0.2% |
| 49 | Delaware | 2,396 | 0.1% |
| 23 | Florida | 59,928 | 1.6% |
| 24 | Georgia | 58,977 | 1.6% |
| 47 | Hawaii | 6,459 | 0.2% |
| 14 | Idaho | 83,574 | 2.3% |
| 25 | Illinois | 57,918 | 1.6% |
| 38 | Indiana | 36,420 | 1.0% |
| 26 | Iowa | 56,276 | 1.5% |
| 15 | Kansas | 82,282 | 2.2% |
| 37 | Kentucky | 40,411 | 1.1% |
| 31 | Louisiana | 49,651 | 1.3% |
| 39 | Maine | 33,741 | 0.9% |
| 42 | Maryland | 12,297 | 0.3% |
| 45 | Massachusetts | 9,241 | 0.3% |
| 11 | Michigan | 96,705 | 2.6% |
| 12 | Minnesota | 86,943 | 2.3% |
| 32 | Mississippi | 48,286 | 1.3% |
| 21 | Missouri | 69,709 | 1.9% |
| 4 | Montana | 147,046 | 4.0% |
| 16 | Nebraska | 77,358 | 2.1% |
| 7 | Nevada | 110,567 | 3.0% |
| 44 | New Hampshire | 9,283 | 0.3% |
| 46 | New Jersey | 8,215 | 0.2% |
| 5 | New Mexico | 121,598 | 3.3% |
| 27 | New York | 53,989 | 1.5% |
| 29 | North Carolina | 52,672 | 1.4% |
| 18 | North Dakota | 70,704 | 1.9% |
| 34 | Ohio | 44,828 | 1.2% |
| 20 | Oklahoma | 69,903 | 1.9% |
| 10 | Oregon | 97,132 | 2.6% |
| 33 | Pennsylvania | 46,058 | 1.2% |
| 50 | Rhode Island | 1,231 | 0.0% |
| 40 | South Carolina | 31,189 | 0.8% |
| 17 | South Dakota | 77,121 | 2.1% |
| 36 | Tennessee | 42,146 | 1.1% |
| 2 | Texas | 267,277 | 7.2% |
| 13 | Utah | 84,904 | 2.3% |
| 43 | Vermont | 9,615 | 0.3% |
| 35 | Virginia | 42,326 | 1.1% |
| 19 | Washington | 70,637 | 1.9% |
| 41 | West Virginia | 24,231 | 0.7% |
| 22 | Wisconsin | 65,499 | 1.8% |
| 9 | Wyoming | 97,818 | 2.6% |

| RANK | STATE | MILES | % of USA |
|------|-------|-------|----------|
| 1 | Alaska | 615,230 | 16.6% |
| 2 | Texas | 267,277 | 7.2% |
| 3 | California | 158,869 | 4.3% |
| 4 | Montana | 147,046 | 4.0% |
| 5 | New Mexico | 121,598 | 3.3% |
| 6 | Arizona | 114,006 | 3.1% |
| 7 | Nevada | 110,567 | 3.0% |
| 8 | Colorado | 104,100 | 2.8% |
| 9 | Wyoming | 97,818 | 2.6% |
| 10 | Oregon | 97,132 | 2.6% |
| 11 | Michigan | 96,705 | 2.6% |
| 12 | Minnesota | 86,943 | 2.3% |
| 13 | Utah | 84,904 | 2.3% |
| 14 | Idaho | 83,574 | 2.3% |
| 15 | Kansas | 82,282 | 2.2% |
| 16 | Nebraska | 77,358 | 2.1% |
| 17 | South Dakota | 77,121 | 2.1% |
| 18 | North Dakota | 70,704 | 1.9% |
| 19 | Washington | 70,637 | 1.9% |
| 20 | Oklahoma | 69,903 | 1.9% |
| 21 | Missouri | 69,709 | 1.9% |
| 22 | Wisconsin | 65,499 | 1.8% |
| 23 | Florida | 59,928 | 1.6% |
| 24 | Georgia | 58,977 | 1.6% |
| 25 | Illinois | 57,918 | 1.6% |
| 26 | Iowa | 56,276 | 1.5% |
| 27 | New York | 53,989 | 1.5% |
| 28 | Arkansas | 53,182 | 1.4% |
| 29 | North Carolina | 52,672 | 1.4% |
| 30 | Alabama | 52,237 | 1.4% |
| 31 | Louisiana | 49,651 | 1.3% |
| 32 | Mississippi | 48,286 | 1.3% |
| 33 | Pennsylvania | 46,058 | 1.2% |
| 34 | Ohio | 44,828 | 1.2% |
| 35 | Virginia | 42,326 | 1.1% |
| 36 | Tennessee | 42,146 | 1.1% |
| 37 | Kentucky | 40,411 | 1.1% |
| 38 | Indiana | 36,420 | 1.0% |
| 39 | Maine | 33,741 | 0.9% |
| 40 | South Carolina | 31,189 | 0.8% |
| 41 | West Virginia | 24,231 | 0.7% |
| 42 | Maryland | 12,297 | 0.3% |
| 43 | Vermont | 9,615 | 0.3% |
| 44 | New Hampshire | 9,283 | 0.3% |
| 45 | Massachusetts | 9,241 | 0.3% |
| 46 | New Jersey | 8,215 | 0.2% |
| 47 | Hawaii | 6,459 | 0.2% |
| 48 | Connecticut | 5,544 | 0.2% |
| 49 | Delaware | 2,396 | 0.1% |
| 50 | Rhode Island | 1,231 | 0.0% |
| | District of Columbia | 68 | 0.0% |

Source: U.S. Bureau of the Census
"1990 Census of Population and Housing" (Series CPH-1)
*Total of land and water area. These totals are revised. Excludes territorial water which was included in previous reports.

# Land Area of States in Square Miles in 2000

## National Total = 3,536,278 Square Miles of Land Area*

ALPHA ORDER

| RANK | STATE | MILES | % of USA |
|---|---|---|---|
| 28 | Alabama | 50,750 | 1.4% |
| 1 | Alaska | 570,374 | 16.1% |
| 6 | Arizona | 113,642 | 3.2% |
| 27 | Arkansas | 52,075 | 1.5% |
| 3 | California | 155,973 | 4.4% |
| 8 | Colorado | 103,729 | 2.9% |
| 48 | Connecticut | 4,845 | 0.1% |
| 49 | Delaware | 1,955 | 0.1% |
| 26 | Florida | 53,937 | 1.5% |
| 21 | Georgia | 57,919 | 1.6% |
| 47 | Hawaii | 6,423 | 0.2% |
| 11 | Idaho | 82,751 | 2.3% |
| 24 | Illinois | 55,593 | 1.6% |
| 38 | Indiana | 35,870 | 1.0% |
| 23 | Iowa | 55,875 | 1.6% |
| 13 | Kansas | 81,823 | 2.3% |
| 36 | Kentucky | 39,732 | 1.1% |
| 33 | Louisiana | 43,566 | 1.2% |
| 39 | Maine | 30,865 | 0.9% |
| 42 | Maryland | 9,775 | 0.3% |
| 45 | Massachusetts | 7,838 | 0.2% |
| 22 | Michigan | 56,809 | 1.6% |
| 14 | Minnesota | 79,617 | 2.3% |
| 31 | Mississippi | 46,914 | 1.3% |
| 18 | Missouri | 68,898 | 2.0% |
| 4 | Montana | 145,556 | 4.1% |
| 15 | Nebraska | 76,878 | 2.2% |
| 7 | Nevada | 109,806 | 3.1% |
| 44 | New Hampshire | 8,969 | 0.3% |
| 46 | New Jersey | 7,419 | 0.2% |
| 5 | New Mexico | 121,364 | 3.4% |
| 30 | New York | 47,224 | 1.3% |
| 29 | North Carolina | 48,718 | 1.4% |
| 17 | North Dakota | 68,994 | 2.0% |
| 35 | Ohio | 40,953 | 1.2% |
| 19 | Oklahoma | 68,679 | 1.9% |
| 10 | Oregon | 96,002 | 2.7% |
| 32 | Pennsylvania | 44,820 | 1.3% |
| 50 | Rhode Island | 1,045 | 0.0% |
| 40 | South Carolina | 30,111 | 0.9% |
| 16 | South Dakota | 75,896 | 2.2% |
| 34 | Tennessee | 41,219 | 1.2% |
| 2 | Texas | 261,914 | 7.4% |
| 12 | Utah | 82,168 | 2.3% |
| 43 | Vermont | 9,249 | 0.3% |
| 37 | Virginia | 39,598 | 1.1% |
| 20 | Washington | 66,581 | 1.9% |
| 41 | West Virginia | 24,087 | 0.7% |
| 25 | Wisconsin | 54,314 | 1.5% |
| 9 | Wyoming | 97,105 | 2.8% |

RANK ORDER

| RANK | STATE | MILES | % of USA |
|---|---|---|---|
| 1 | Alaska | 570,374 | 16.1% |
| 2 | Texas | 261,914 | 7.4% |
| 3 | California | 155,973 | 4.4% |
| 4 | Montana | 145,556 | 4.1% |
| 5 | New Mexico | 121,364 | 3.4% |
| 6 | Arizona | 113,642 | 3.2% |
| 7 | Nevada | 109,806 | 3.1% |
| 8 | Colorado | 103,729 | 2.9% |
| 9 | Wyoming | 97,105 | 2.8% |
| 10 | Oregon | 96,002 | 2.7% |
| 11 | Idaho | 82,751 | 2.3% |
| 12 | Utah | 82,168 | 2.3% |
| 13 | Kansas | 81,823 | 2.3% |
| 14 | Minnesota | 79,617 | 2.3% |
| 15 | Nebraska | 76,878 | 2.2% |
| 16 | South Dakota | 75,896 | 2.2% |
| 17 | North Dakota | 68,994 | 2.0% |
| 18 | Missouri | 68,898 | 2.0% |
| 19 | Oklahoma | 68,679 | 1.9% |
| 20 | Washington | 66,581 | 1.9% |
| 21 | Georgia | 57,919 | 1.6% |
| 22 | Michigan | 56,809 | 1.6% |
| 23 | Iowa | 55,875 | 1.6% |
| 24 | Illinois | 55,593 | 1.6% |
| 25 | Wisconsin | 54,314 | 1.5% |
| 26 | Florida | 53,937 | 1.5% |
| 27 | Arkansas | 52,075 | 1.5% |
| 28 | Alabama | 50,750 | 1.4% |
| 29 | North Carolina | 48,718 | 1.4% |
| 30 | New York | 47,224 | 1.3% |
| 31 | Mississippi | 46,914 | 1.3% |
| 32 | Pennsylvania | 44,820 | 1.3% |
| 33 | Louisiana | 43,566 | 1.2% |
| 34 | Tennessee | 41,219 | 1.2% |
| 35 | Ohio | 40,953 | 1.2% |
| 36 | Kentucky | 39,732 | 1.1% |
| 37 | Virginia | 39,598 | 1.1% |
| 38 | Indiana | 35,870 | 1.0% |
| 39 | Maine | 30,865 | 0.9% |
| 40 | South Carolina | 30,111 | 0.9% |
| 41 | West Virginia | 24,087 | 0.7% |
| 42 | Maryland | 9,775 | 0.3% |
| 43 | Vermont | 9,249 | 0.3% |
| 44 | New Hampshire | 8,969 | 0.3% |
| 45 | Massachusetts | 7,838 | 0.2% |
| 46 | New Jersey | 7,419 | 0.2% |
| 47 | Hawaii | 6,423 | 0.2% |
| 48 | Connecticut | 4,845 | 0.1% |
| 49 | Delaware | 1,955 | 0.1% |
| 50 | Rhode Island | 1,045 | 0.0% |
| | District of Columbia | 61 | 0.0% |

*Source: U.S. Bureau of the Census*
*"1990 Census of Population and Housing" (Series CPH-1)*
*Revised totals. Includes dry land temporarily or partially covered by water, such as marshland, swamps, etc.;*
*streams and canals under one-eighth mile wide; and lakes, reservoirs and ponds under 40 acres.*

# Water Area of States in Square Miles in 2000

## National Total = 181,518 Square Miles of Water*

ALPHA ORDER

| RANK | STATE | MILES | % of USA |
|---|---|---|---|
| 20 | Alabama | 1,486 | 0.8% |
| 1 | Alaska | 44,856 | 24.7% |
| 45 | Arizona | 364 | 0.2% |
| 27 | Arkansas | 1,107 | 0.6% |
| 12 | California | 2,895 | 1.6% |
| 43 | Colorado | 371 | 0.2% |
| 36 | Connecticut | 698 | 0.4% |
| 41 | Delaware | 442 | 0.2% |
| 7 | Florida | 5,991 | 3.3% |
| 29 | Georgia | 1,058 | 0.6% |
| 50 | Hawaii | 36 | 0.0% |
| 31 | Idaho | 823 | 0.5% |
| 17 | Illinois | 2,325 | 1.3% |
| 38 | Indiana | 550 | 0.3% |
| 42 | Iowa | 401 | 0.2% |
| 40 | Kansas | 459 | 0.3% |
| 37 | Kentucky | 679 | 0.4% |
| 6 | Louisiana | 6,085 | 3.4% |
| 13 | Maine | 2,876 | 1.6% |
| 16 | Maryland | 2,522 | 1.4% |
| 21 | Massachusetts | 1,403 | 0.8% |
| 2 | Michigan | 39,895 | 22.0% |
| 4 | Minnesota | 7,326 | 4.0% |
| 22 | Mississippi | 1,372 | 0.8% |
| 32 | Missouri | 811 | 0.5% |
| 19 | Montana | 1,490 | 0.8% |
| 39 | Nebraska | 481 | 0.3% |
| 34 | Nevada | 761 | 0.4% |
| 46 | New Hampshire | 314 | 0.2% |
| 33 | New Jersey | 796 | 0.4% |
| 47 | New Mexico | 234 | 0.1% |
| 5 | New York | 6,766 | 3.7% |
| 10 | North Carolina | 3,954 | 2.2% |
| 18 | North Dakota | 1,710 | 0.9% |
| 11 | Ohio | 3,875 | 2.1% |
| 25 | Oklahoma | 1,224 | 0.7% |
| 26 | Oregon | 1,129 | 0.6% |
| 23 | Pennsylvania | 1,239 | 0.7% |
| 48 | Rhode Island | 186 | 0.1% |
| 28 | South Carolina | 1,078 | 0.6% |
| 24 | South Dakota | 1,225 | 0.7% |
| 30 | Tennessee | 926 | 0.5% |
| 8 | Texas | 5,363 | 3.0% |
| 14 | Utah | 2,736 | 1.5% |
| 44 | Vermont | 366 | 0.2% |
| 15 | Virginia | 2,729 | 1.5% |
| 9 | Washington | 4,055 | 2.2% |
| 49 | West Virginia | 145 | 0.1% |
| 3 | Wisconsin | 11,186 | 6.2% |
| 35 | Wyoming | 714 | 0.4% |

RANK ORDER

| RANK | STATE | MILES | % of USA |
|---|---|---|---|
| 1 | Alaska | 44,856 | 24.7% |
| 2 | Michigan | 39,895 | 22.0% |
| 3 | Wisconsin | 11,186 | 6.2% |
| 4 | Minnesota | 7,326 | 4.0% |
| 5 | New York | 6,766 | 3.7% |
| 6 | Louisiana | 6,085 | 3.4% |
| 7 | Florida | 5,991 | 3.3% |
| 8 | Texas | 5,363 | 3.0% |
| 9 | Washington | 4,055 | 2.2% |
| 10 | North Carolina | 3,954 | 2.2% |
| 11 | Ohio | 3,875 | 2.1% |
| 12 | California | 2,895 | 1.6% |
| 13 | Maine | 2,876 | 1.6% |
| 14 | Utah | 2,736 | 1.5% |
| 15 | Virginia | 2,729 | 1.5% |
| 16 | Maryland | 2,522 | 1.4% |
| 17 | Illinois | 2,325 | 1.3% |
| 18 | North Dakota | 1,710 | 0.9% |
| 19 | Montana | 1,490 | 0.8% |
| 20 | Alabama | 1,486 | 0.8% |
| 21 | Massachusetts | 1,403 | 0.8% |
| 22 | Mississippi | 1,372 | 0.8% |
| 23 | Pennsylvania | 1,239 | 0.7% |
| 24 | South Dakota | 1,225 | 0.7% |
| 25 | Oklahoma | 1,224 | 0.7% |
| 26 | Oregon | 1,129 | 0.6% |
| 27 | Arkansas | 1,107 | 0.6% |
| 28 | South Carolina | 1,078 | 0.6% |
| 29 | Georgia | 1,058 | 0.6% |
| 30 | Tennessee | 926 | 0.5% |
| 31 | Idaho | 823 | 0.5% |
| 32 | Missouri | 811 | 0.5% |
| 33 | New Jersey | 796 | 0.4% |
| 34 | Nevada | 761 | 0.4% |
| 35 | Wyoming | 714 | 0.4% |
| 36 | Connecticut | 698 | 0.4% |
| 37 | Kentucky | 679 | 0.4% |
| 38 | Indiana | 550 | 0.3% |
| 39 | Nebraska | 481 | 0.3% |
| 40 | Kansas | 459 | 0.3% |
| 41 | Delaware | 442 | 0.2% |
| 42 | Iowa | 401 | 0.2% |
| 43 | Colorado | 371 | 0.2% |
| 44 | Vermont | 366 | 0.2% |
| 45 | Arizona | 364 | 0.2% |
| 46 | New Hampshire | 314 | 0.2% |
| 47 | New Mexico | 234 | 0.1% |
| 48 | Rhode Island | 186 | 0.1% |
| 49 | West Virginia | 145 | 0.1% |
| 50 | Hawaii | 36 | 0.0% |
| | District of Columbia | 7 | 0.0% |

Source: U.S. Bureau of the Census
     "1990 Census of Population and Housing" (Series CPH-1)
*Revised totals. Includes permanent inland water surface, such as lakes, reservoirs, and ponds having an area of 40 acres or more, canals one-eighth mile or more in width; coastal waters behind or sheltered by headlands or islands separated by less than 1 nautical mile of water, and islands sunder 40 acres in area. Excludes areas of oceans, bays, etc., lying within U.S. jurisdiction but not defined as inland water.

# Highest Point of Elevation in Feet

## National High Point = 20,320 Feet Above Sea Level (Mt. McKinley, Alaska)

ALPHA ORDER

| RANK | STATE | HIGHEST POINT |
|---|---|---|
| 35 | Alabama | 2,405 |
| 1 | Alaska | 20,320 |
| 12 | Arizona | 12,633 |
| 34 | Arkansas | 2,753 |
| 2 | California | 14,494 |
| 3 | Colorado | 14,433 |
| 36 | Connecticut | 2,380 |
| 49 | Delaware | 448 |
| 50 | Florida | 345 |
| 25 | Georgia | 4,784 |
| 6 | Hawaii | 13,796 |
| 11 | Idaho | 12,662 |
| 45 | Illinois | 1,235 |
| 44 | Indiana | 1,257 |
| 42 | Iowa | 1,670 |
| 28 | Kansas | 4,039 |
| 27 | Kentucky | 4,139 |
| 48 | Louisiana | 535 |
| 22 | Maine | 5,267 |
| 32 | Maryland | 3,360 |
| 31 | Massachusetts | 3,487 |
| 38 | Michigan | 1,979 |
| 37 | Minnesota | 2,301 |
| 47 | Mississippi | 806 |
| 41 | Missouri | 1,772 |
| 10 | Montana | 12,799 |
| 20 | Nebraska | 5,424 |
| 9 | Nevada | 13,140 |
| 18 | New Hampshire | 6,288 |
| 40 | New Jersey | 1,803 |
| 8 | New Mexico | 13,161 |
| 21 | New York | 5,344 |
| 16 | North Carolina | 6,684 |
| 30 | North Dakota | 3,506 |
| 43 | Ohio | 1,549 |
| 23 | Oklahoma | 4,973 |
| 13 | Oregon | 11,239 |
| 33 | Pennsylvania | 3,213 |
| 46 | Rhode Island | 812 |
| 29 | South Carolina | 3,560 |
| 15 | South Dakota | 7,242 |
| 17 | Tennessee | 6,643 |
| 14 | Texas | 8,749 |
| 7 | Utah | 13,528 |
| 26 | Vermont | 4,393 |
| 19 | Virginia | 5,729 |
| 4 | Washington | 14,410 |
| 24 | West Virginia | 4,861 |
| 39 | Wisconsin | 1,951 |
| 5 | Wyoming | 13,804 |

RANK ORDER

| RANK | STATE | HIGHEST POINT |
|---|---|---|
| 1 | Alaska | 20,320 |
| 2 | California | 14,494 |
| 3 | Colorado | 14,433 |
| 4 | Washington | 14,410 |
| 5 | Wyoming | 13,804 |
| 6 | Hawaii | 13,796 |
| 7 | Utah | 13,528 |
| 8 | New Mexico | 13,161 |
| 9 | Nevada | 13,140 |
| 10 | Montana | 12,799 |
| 11 | Idaho | 12,662 |
| 12 | Arizona | 12,633 |
| 13 | Oregon | 11,239 |
| 14 | Texas | 8,749 |
| 15 | South Dakota | 7,242 |
| 16 | North Carolina | 6,684 |
| 17 | Tennessee | 6,643 |
| 18 | New Hampshire | 6,288 |
| 19 | Virginia | 5,729 |
| 20 | Nebraska | 5,424 |
| 21 | New York | 5,344 |
| 22 | Maine | 5,267 |
| 23 | Oklahoma | 4,973 |
| 24 | West Virginia | 4,861 |
| 25 | Georgia | 4,784 |
| 26 | Vermont | 4,393 |
| 27 | Kentucky | 4,139 |
| 28 | Kansas | 4,039 |
| 29 | South Carolina | 3,560 |
| 30 | North Dakota | 3,506 |
| 31 | Massachusetts | 3,487 |
| 32 | Maryland | 3,360 |
| 33 | Pennsylvania | 3,213 |
| 34 | Arkansas | 2,753 |
| 35 | Alabama | 2,405 |
| 36 | Connecticut | 2,380 |
| 37 | Minnesota | 2,301 |
| 38 | Michigan | 1,979 |
| 39 | Wisconsin | 1,951 |
| 40 | New Jersey | 1,803 |
| 41 | Missouri | 1,772 |
| 42 | Iowa | 1,670 |
| 43 | Ohio | 1,549 |
| 44 | Indiana | 1,257 |
| 45 | Illinois | 1,235 |
| 46 | Rhode Island | 812 |
| 47 | Mississippi | 806 |
| 48 | Louisiana | 535 |
| 49 | Delaware | 448 |
| 50 | Florida | 345 |
| | District of Columbia | 410 |

*Source: U.S. Department of Interior, U.S. Geological Survey
"Elevations and Distances in the United States, 1990"*

# Lowest Point of Elevation in Feet

## National Low Point = 282 Feet Below Sea Level (Death Valley, California)*

ALPHA ORDER

| RANK | STATE | LOWEST POINT |
|---|---|---|
| 3 | Alabama | 0 |
| 3 | Alaska | 0 |
| 26 | Arizona | 70 |
| 25 | Arkansas | 55 |
| 1 | California | (282) |
| 50 | Colorado | 3,350 |
| 3 | Connecticut | 0 |
| 3 | Delaware | 0 |
| 3 | Florida | 0 |
| 3 | Georgia | 0 |
| 3 | Hawaii | 0 |
| 42 | Idaho | 710 |
| 32 | Illinois | 279 |
| 34 | Indiana | 320 |
| 37 | Iowa | 480 |
| 41 | Kansas | 679 |
| 31 | Kentucky | 257 |
| 2 | Louisiana | (8) |
| 3 | Maine | 0 |
| 3 | Maryland | 0 |
| 3 | Massachusetts | 0 |
| 38 | Michigan | 571 |
| 40 | Minnesota | 600 |
| 3 | Mississippi | 0 |
| 29 | Missouri | 230 |
| 46 | Montana | 1,800 |
| 44 | Nebraska | 840 |
| 36 | Nevada | 479 |
| 3 | New Hampshire | 0 |
| 3 | New Jersey | 0 |
| 48 | New Mexico | 2,842 |
| 3 | New York | 0 |
| 3 | North Carolina | 0 |
| 43 | North Dakota | 750 |
| 35 | Ohio | 455 |
| 33 | Oklahoma | 289 |
| 3 | Oregon | 0 |
| 3 | Pennsylvania | 0 |
| 3 | Rhode Island | 0 |
| 3 | South Carolina | 0 |
| 45 | South Dakota | 966 |
| 28 | Tennessee | 178 |
| 3 | Texas | 0 |
| 47 | Utah | 2,000 |
| 27 | Vermont | 95 |
| 3 | Virginia | 0 |
| 3 | Washington | 0 |
| 30 | West Virginia | 240 |
| 39 | Wisconsin | 579 |
| 49 | Wyoming | 3,099 |

RANK ORDER

| RANK | STATE | LOWEST POINT |
|---|---|---|
| 1 | California | (282) |
| 2 | Louisiana | (8) |
| 3 | Alabama* | 0 |
| 3 | Alaska | 0 |
| 3 | Connecticut | 0 |
| 3 | Delaware | 0 |
| 3 | Florida | 0 |
| 3 | Georgia | 0 |
| 3 | Hawaii | 0 |
| 3 | Maine | 0 |
| 3 | Maryland | 0 |
| 3 | Massachusetts | 0 |
| 3 | Mississippi | 0 |
| 3 | New Hampshire | 0 |
| 3 | New Jersey | 0 |
| 3 | New York | 0 |
| 3 | North Carolina | 0 |
| 3 | Oregon | 0 |
| 3 | Pennsylvania | 0 |
| 3 | Rhode Island | 0 |
| 3 | South Carolina | 0 |
| 3 | Texas | 0 |
| 3 | Virginia | 0 |
| 3 | Washington | 0 |
| 25 | Arkansas | 55 |
| 26 | Arizona | 70 |
| 27 | Vermont | 95 |
| 28 | Tennessee | 178 |
| 29 | Missouri | 230 |
| 30 | West Virginia | 240 |
| 31 | Kentucky | 257 |
| 32 | Illinois | 279 |
| 33 | Oklahoma | 289 |
| 34 | Indiana | 320 |
| 35 | Ohio | 455 |
| 36 | Nevada | 479 |
| 37 | Iowa | 480 |
| 38 | Michigan | 571 |
| 39 | Wisconsin | 579 |
| 40 | Minnesota | 600 |
| 41 | Kansas | 679 |
| 42 | Idaho | 710 |
| 43 | North Dakota | 750 |
| 44 | Nebraska | 840 |
| 45 | South Dakota | 966 |
| 46 | Montana | 1,800 |
| 47 | Utah | 2,000 |
| 48 | New Mexico | 2,842 |
| 49 | Wyoming | 3,099 |
| 50 | Colorado | 3,350 |
| | District of Columbia | 1 |

*Source: U.S. Department of Interior, U.S. Geological Survey*
*"Elevations and Distances in the United States, 1990"*
*States with "0" have sea level as lowest point.*

# Approximate Mean Elevation in Feet

## Approximate National Mean Elevation = 2,500 Feet Above Sea Level

ALPHA ORDER

| RANK | STATE | MEAN ELEVATION |
|------|-------|----------------|
| 40 | Alabama | 500 |
| 15 | Alaska | 1,900 |
| 7 | Arizona | 4,100 |
| 36 | Arkansas | 650 |
| 11 | California | 2,900 |
| 1 | Colorado | 6,800 |
| 40 | Connecticut | 500 |
| 50 | Delaware | 60 |
| 48 | Florida | 100 |
| 37 | Georgia | 600 |
| 10 | Hawaii | 3,030 |
| 6 | Idaho | 5,000 |
| 37 | Illinois | 600 |
| 34 | Indiana | 700 |
| 22 | Iowa | 1,100 |
| 14 | Kansas | 2,000 |
| 33 | Kentucky | 750 |
| 48 | Louisiana | 100 |
| 37 | Maine | 600 |
| 43 | Maryland | 350 |
| 40 | Massachusetts | 500 |
| 29 | Michigan | 900 |
| 21 | Minnesota | 1,200 |
| 45 | Mississippi | 300 |
| 32 | Missouri | 800 |
| 8 | Montana | 3,400 |
| 12 | Nebraska | 2,600 |
| 5 | Nevada | 5,500 |
| 25 | New Hampshire | 1,000 |
| 46 | New Jersey | 250 |
| 4 | New Mexico | 5,700 |
| 25 | New York | 1,000 |
| 34 | North Carolina | 700 |
| 15 | North Dakota | 1,900 |
| 31 | Ohio | 850 |
| 20 | Oklahoma | 1,300 |
| 9 | Oregon | 3,300 |
| 22 | Pennsylvania | 1,100 |
| 47 | Rhode Island | 200 |
| 43 | South Carolina | 350 |
| 13 | South Dakota | 2,200 |
| 29 | Tennessee | 900 |
| 17 | Texas | 1,700 |
| 3 | Utah | 6,100 |
| 25 | Vermont | 1,000 |
| 28 | Virginia | 950 |
| 17 | Washington | 1,700 |
| 19 | West Virginia | 1,500 |
| 24 | Wisconsin | 1,050 |
| 2 | Wyoming | 6,700 |

RANK ORDER

| RANK | STATE | MEAN ELEVATION |
|------|-------|----------------|
| 1 | Colorado | 6,800 |
| 2 | Wyoming | 6,700 |
| 3 | Utah | 6,100 |
| 4 | New Mexico | 5,700 |
| 5 | Nevada | 5,500 |
| 6 | Idaho | 5,000 |
| 7 | Arizona | 4,100 |
| 8 | Montana | 3,400 |
| 9 | Oregon | 3,300 |
| 10 | Hawaii | 3,030 |
| 11 | California | 2,900 |
| 12 | Nebraska | 2,600 |
| 13 | South Dakota | 2,200 |
| 14 | Kansas | 2,000 |
| 15 | Alaska | 1,900 |
| 15 | North Dakota | 1,900 |
| 17 | Texas | 1,700 |
| 17 | Washington | 1,700 |
| 19 | West Virginia | 1,500 |
| 20 | Oklahoma | 1,300 |
| 21 | Minnesota | 1,200 |
| 22 | Iowa | 1,100 |
| 22 | Pennsylvania | 1,100 |
| 24 | Wisconsin | 1,050 |
| 25 | New Hampshire | 1,000 |
| 25 | New York | 1,000 |
| 25 | Vermont | 1,000 |
| 28 | Virginia | 950 |
| 29 | Michigan | 900 |
| 29 | Tennessee | 900 |
| 31 | Ohio | 850 |
| 32 | Missouri | 800 |
| 33 | Kentucky | 750 |
| 34 | Indiana | 700 |
| 34 | North Carolina | 700 |
| 36 | Arkansas | 650 |
| 37 | Georgia | 600 |
| 37 | Illinois | 600 |
| 37 | Maine | 600 |
| 40 | Alabama | 500 |
| 40 | Connecticut | 500 |
| 40 | Massachusetts | 500 |
| 43 | Maryland | 350 |
| 43 | South Carolina | 350 |
| 45 | Mississippi | 300 |
| 46 | New Jersey | 250 |
| 47 | Rhode Island | 200 |
| 48 | Florida | 100 |
| 48 | Louisiana | 100 |
| 50 | Delaware | 60 |

District of Columbia — 150

*Source: U.S. Department of Interior, U.S. Geological Survey*
*"Elevations and Distances in the United States, 1983"*

# Normal Daily Mean Temperature*

## ALPHA ORDER

| RANK | STATE | MEAN TEMPERATURE |
|---|---|---|
| 5 | Alabama | 67.5 |
| 50 | Alaska | 40.6 |
| 2 | Arizona | 72.6 |
| 9 | Arkansas | 61.8 |
| 10 | California** | 61.3 |
| 34 | Colorado | 50.3 |
| 35 | Connecticut | 49.9 |
| 22 | Delaware | 54.2 |
| 3 | Florida** | 72.0 |
| 10 | Georgia | 61.3 |
| 1 | Hawaii | 77.2 |
| 30 | Idaho | 50.9 |
| 35 | Illinois** | 49.9 |
| 25 | Indiana | 52.3 |
| 35 | Iowa | 49.9 |
| 16 | Kansas | 56.2 |
| 18 | Kentucky | 56.1 |
| 4 | Louisiana | 68.1 |
| 43 | Maine | 45.4 |
| 19 | Maryland | 55.1 |
| 29 | Massachusetts | 51.3 |
| 47 | Michigan** | 44.2 |
| 48 | Minnesota** | 41.7 |
| 7 | Mississippi | 64.2 |
| 21 | Missouri** | 54.9 |
| 45 | Montana | 44.8 |
| 32 | Nebraska | 50.6 |
| 31 | Nevada | 50.8 |
| 44 | New Hampshire | 45.1 |
| 24 | New Jersey | 53.0 |
| 16 | New Mexico | 56.2 |
| 35 | New York** | 49.9 |
| 14 | North Carolina** | 59.7 |
| 49 | North Dakota | 41.6 |
| 28 | Ohio** | 51.4 |
| 13 | Oklahoma | 60.0 |
| 23 | Oregon | 53.6 |
| 25 | Pennsylvania** | 52.3 |
| 33 | Rhode Island | 50.4 |
| 8 | South Carolina | 63.1 |
| 42 | South Dakota | 45.5 |
| 12 | Tennessee** | 60.7 |
| 6 | Texas** | 65.5 |
| 27 | Utah | 52.0 |
| 46 | Vermont | 44.6 |
| 15 | Virginia** | 58.5 |
| 39 | Washington** | 49.7 |
| 20 | West Virginia | 55.0 |
| 40 | Wisconsin | 46.1 |
| 41 | Wyoming | 45.6 |

## RANK ORDER

| RANK | STATE | MEAN TEMPERATURE |
|---|---|---|
| 1 | Hawaii | 77.2 |
| 2 | Arizona | 72.6 |
| 3 | Florida** | 72.0 |
| 4 | Louisiana | 68.1 |
| 5 | Alabama | 67.5 |
| 6 | Texas** | 65.5 |
| 7 | Mississippi | 64.2 |
| 8 | South Carolina | 63.1 |
| 9 | Arkansas | 61.8 |
| 10 | California** | 61.3 |
| 10 | Georgia | 61.3 |
| 12 | Tennessee** | 60.7 |
| 13 | Oklahoma | 60.0 |
| 14 | North Carolina** | 59.7 |
| 15 | Virginia** | 58.5 |
| 16 | Kansas | 56.2 |
| 16 | New Mexico | 56.2 |
| 18 | Kentucky | 56.1 |
| 19 | Maryland | 55.1 |
| 20 | West Virginia | 55.0 |
| 21 | Missouri** | 54.9 |
| 22 | Delaware | 54.2 |
| 23 | Oregon | 53.6 |
| 24 | New Jersey | 53.0 |
| 25 | Indiana | 52.3 |
| 25 | Pennsylvania** | 52.3 |
| 27 | Utah | 52.0 |
| 28 | Ohio** | 51.4 |
| 29 | Massachusetts | 51.3 |
| 30 | Idaho | 50.9 |
| 31 | Nevada | 50.8 |
| 32 | Nebraska | 50.6 |
| 33 | Rhode Island | 50.4 |
| 34 | Colorado | 50.3 |
| 35 | Connecticut | 49.9 |
| 35 | Illinois** | 49.9 |
| 35 | Iowa | 49.9 |
| 35 | New York** | 49.9 |
| 39 | Washington** | 49.7 |
| 40 | Wisconsin | 46.1 |
| 41 | Wyoming | 45.6 |
| 42 | South Dakota | 45.5 |
| 43 | Maine | 45.4 |
| 44 | New Hampshire | 45.1 |
| 45 | Montana | 44.8 |
| 46 | Vermont | 44.6 |
| 47 | Michigan** | 44.2 |
| 48 | Minnesota** | 41.7 |
| 49 | North Dakota | 41.6 |
| 50 | Alaska | 40.6 |
|  | District of Columbia | 58.0 |

Source: U.S. Department of Commerce, National Oceanic and Atmospheric Administration
   "Climatography of the United States" (No. 81)
*Based on standard 30 year period, 1961-1990.
**Temperatures from multiple reporting cities within one state were averaged to determine a state's mean temperature.

# Percent of Days That Are Sunny*

ALPHA ORDER

ALPHA ORDER

| RANK | STATE | PERCENT OF DAYS SUNNY |
|------|-------|------------------------|
| 13 | Alabama | 60 |
| 50 | Alaska | 23 |
| 1 | Arizona | 81 |
| 13 | Arkansas | 60 |
| 4 | California** | 72 |
| 6 | Colorado | 67 |
| 37 | Connecticut | 52 |
| 29 | Delaware | 55 |
| 8 | Florida** | 65 |
| 17 | Georgia | 59 |
| 3 | Hawaii | 74 |
| 21 | Idaho | 58 |
| 35 | Illinois** | 53 |
| 41 | Indiana | 51 |
| 29 | Iowa | 55 |
| 11 | Kansas | 62 |
| 35 | Kentucky | 53 |
| 13 | Louisiana | 60 |
| 29 | Maine | 55 |
| 21 | Maryland | 58 |
| 29 | Massachusetts | 55 |
| 46 | Michigan** | 46 |
| 37 | Minnesota** | 52 |
| 17 | Mississippi | 59 |
| 25 | Missouri** | 57 |
| 41 | Montana | 51 |
| 17 | Nebraska | 59 |
| 5 | Nevada | 69 |
| 29 | New Hampshire | 55 |
| 28 | New Jersey | 56 |
| 2 | New Mexico | 76 |
| 37 | New York** | 52 |
| 17 | North Carolina** | 59 |
| 29 | North Dakota | 55 |
| 45 | Ohio** | 47 |
| 9 | Oklahoma | 64 |
| 49 | Oregon | 39 |
| 43 | Pennsylvania** | 50 |
| 21 | Rhode Island | 58 |
| 13 | South Carolina | 60 |
| 25 | South Dakota | 57 |
| 21 | Tennessee** | 58 |
| 6 | Texas** | 67 |
| 11 | Utah | 62 |
| 47 | Vermont | 44 |
| 25 | Virginia** | 57 |
| 48 | Washington** | 43 |
| 44 | West Virginia | 48 |
| 37 | Wisconsin | 52 |
| 9 | Wyoming | 64 |

RANK ORDER

| RANK | STATE | PERCENT OF DAYS SUNNY |
|------|-------|------------------------|
| 1 | Arizona | 81 |
| 2 | New Mexico | 76 |
| 3 | Hawaii | 74 |
| 4 | California** | 72 |
| 5 | Nevada | 69 |
| 6 | Colorado | 67 |
| 6 | Texas** | 67 |
| 8 | Florida** | 65 |
| 9 | Oklahoma | 64 |
| 9 | Wyoming | 64 |
| 11 | Kansas | 62 |
| 11 | Utah | 62 |
| 13 | Alabama | 60 |
| 13 | Arkansas | 60 |
| 13 | Louisiana | 60 |
| 13 | South Carolina | 60 |
| 17 | Georgia | 59 |
| 17 | Mississippi | 59 |
| 17 | Nebraska | 59 |
| 17 | North Carolina** | 59 |
| 21 | Idaho | 58 |
| 21 | Maryland | 58 |
| 21 | Rhode Island | 58 |
| 21 | Tennessee** | 58 |
| 25 | Missouri** | 57 |
| 25 | South Dakota | 57 |
| 25 | Virginia** | 57 |
| 28 | New Jersey | 56 |
| 29 | Delaware | 55 |
| 29 | Iowa | 55 |
| 29 | Maine | 55 |
| 29 | Massachusetts | 55 |
| 29 | New Hampshire | 55 |
| 29 | North Dakota | 55 |
| 35 | Illinois** | 53 |
| 35 | Kentucky | 53 |
| 37 | Connecticut | 52 |
| 37 | Minnesota** | 52 |
| 37 | New York** | 52 |
| 37 | Wisconsin | 52 |
| 41 | Indiana | 51 |
| 41 | Montana | 51 |
| 43 | Pennsylvania** | 50 |
| 44 | West Virginia | 48 |
| 45 | Ohio** | 47 |
| 46 | Michigan** | 46 |
| 47 | Vermont | 44 |
| 48 | Washington** | 43 |
| 49 | Oregon | 39 |
| 50 | Alaska | 23 |
| | District of Columbia | 55 |

Source: U.S. Department of Commerce, National Oceanic and Atmospheric Administration
   "Comparative Climatic Data" (annual)
*Averages over various years.
**Percentages from multiple reporting cities within one state were averaged to determine a state's average percentage of sunny days.

# Average Wind Speed (M.P.H.)*

ALPHA ORDER

ALPHA ORDER

| RANK | STATE | MILES PER HOUR |
|------|-------|----------------|
| 30 | Alabama | 8.8 |
| 38 | Alaska | 8.3 |
| 49 | Arizona | 6.2 |
| 43 | Arkansas | 7.8 |
| 38 | California** | 8.3 |
| 34 | Colorado | 8.6 |
| 36 | Connecticut | 8.4 |
| 25 | Delaware | 9.0 |
| 34 | Florida** | 8.6 |
| 23 | Georgia | 9.1 |
| 7 | Hawaii | 11.3 |
| 32 | Idaho | 8.7 |
| 13 | Illinois** | 10.2 |
| 19 | Indiana | 9.6 |
| 10 | Iowa | 10.7 |
| 5 | Kansas | 12.2 |
| 38 | Kentucky | 8.3 |
| 41 | Louisiana | 8.2 |
| 32 | Maine | 8.7 |
| 27 | Maryland | 8.9 |
| 3 | Massachusetts | 12.4 |
| 18 | Michigan** | 9.8 |
| 9 | Minnesota** | 10.8 |
| 45 | Mississippi | 7.1 |
| 13 | Missouri** | 10.2 |
| 2 | Montana | 12.6 |
| 11 | Nebraska | 10.5 |
| 48 | Nevada | 6.6 |
| 47 | New Hampshire | 6.7 |
| 17 | New Jersey | 9.9 |
| 27 | New Mexico | 8.9 |
| 16 | New York** | 10.0 |
| 44 | North Carolina** | 7.5 |
| 13 | North Dakota | 10.2 |
| 20 | Ohio** | 9.3 |
| 4 | Oklahoma | 12.3 |
| 42 | Oregon | 7.9 |
| 20 | Pennsylvania** | 9.3 |
| 12 | Rhode Island | 10.4 |
| 46 | South Carolina | 6.8 |
| 8 | South Dakota | 11.1 |
| 36 | Tennessee** | 8.4 |
| 23 | Texas** | 9.1 |
| 30 | Utah | 8.8 |
| 25 | Vermont | 9.0 |
| 22 | Virginia** | 9.2 |
| 27 | Washington** | 8.9 |
| 50 | West Virginia | 5.9 |
| 6 | Wisconsin | 11.5 |
| 1 | Wyoming | 12.9 |

RANK ORDER

| RANK | STATE | MILES PER HOUR |
|------|-------|----------------|
| 1 | Wyoming | 12.9 |
| 2 | Montana | 12.6 |
| 3 | Massachusetts | 12.4 |
| 4 | Oklahoma | 12.3 |
| 5 | Kansas | 12.2 |
| 6 | Wisconsin | 11.5 |
| 7 | Hawaii | 11.3 |
| 8 | South Dakota | 11.1 |
| 9 | Minnesota** | 10.8 |
| 10 | Iowa | 10.7 |
| 11 | Nebraska | 10.5 |
| 12 | Rhode Island | 10.4 |
| 13 | Illinois** | 10.2 |
| 13 | Missouri** | 10.2 |
| 13 | North Dakota | 10.2 |
| 16 | New York** | 10.0 |
| 17 | New Jersey | 9.9 |
| 18 | Michigan** | 9.8 |
| 19 | Indiana | 9.6 |
| 20 | Ohio** | 9.3 |
| 20 | Pennsylvania** | 9.3 |
| 22 | Virginia** | 9.2 |
| 23 | Georgia | 9.1 |
| 23 | Texas** | 9.1 |
| 25 | Delaware | 9.0 |
| 25 | Vermont | 9.0 |
| 27 | Maryland | 8.9 |
| 27 | New Mexico | 8.9 |
| 27 | Washington** | 8.9 |
| 30 | Alabama | 8.8 |
| 30 | Utah | 8.8 |
| 32 | Idaho | 8.7 |
| 32 | Maine | 8.7 |
| 34 | Colorado | 8.6 |
| 34 | Florida** | 8.6 |
| 36 | Connecticut | 8.4 |
| 36 | Tennessee** | 8.4 |
| 38 | Alaska | 8.3 |
| 38 | California** | 8.3 |
| 38 | Kentucky | 8.3 |
| 41 | Louisiana | 8.2 |
| 42 | Oregon | 7.9 |
| 43 | Arkansas | 7.8 |
| 44 | North Carolina** | 7.5 |
| 45 | Mississippi | 7.1 |
| 46 | South Carolina | 6.8 |
| 47 | New Hampshire | 6.7 |
| 48 | Nevada | 6.6 |
| 49 | Arizona | 6.2 |
| 50 | West Virginia | 5.9 |
| | District of Columbia | 9.4 |

Source: U.S. Department of Commerce, National Oceanic and Atmospheric Administration
  "Comparative Climatic Data" (annual)
*Averages over various years.
**Wind speeds from multiple reporting cities within one state were averaged to determine a state's average wind speed.

# Tornadoes in 1999

## National Total = 1,351 Tornadoes

| RANK | STATE | TORNADOES | % of USA |
|------|-------|-----------|----------|
| 17 | Alabama | 23 | 1.7% |
| NA | Alaska* | NA | NA |
| 31 | Arizona | 5 | 0.4% |
| 3 | Arkansas | 107 | 7.9% |
| 32 | California | 3 | 0.2% |
| 12 | Colorado | 41 | 3.0% |
| 44 | Connecticut | 0 | 0.0% |
| 44 | Delaware | 0 | 0.0% |
| 8 | Florida | 60 | 4.4% |
| 23 | Georgia | 12 | 0.9% |
| NA | Hawaii* | NA | NA |
| 38 | Idaho | 1 | 0.1% |
| 5 | Illinois | 65 | 4.8% |
| 25 | Indiana | 10 | 0.7% |
| 8 | Iowa | 60 | 4.4% |
| 6 | Kansas | 64 | 4.7% |
| 30 | Kentucky | 6 | 0.4% |
| 7 | Louisiana | 63 | 4.7% |
| 38 | Maine | 1 | 0.1% |
| 32 | Maryland | 3 | 0.2% |
| 44 | Massachusetts | 0 | 0.0% |
| 25 | Michigan | 10 | 0.7% |
| 16 | Minnesota | 36 | 2.7% |
| 11 | Mississippi | 44 | 3.3% |
| 12 | Missouri | 41 | 3.0% |
| 19 | Montana | 22 | 1.6% |
| 4 | Nebraska | 102 | 7.5% |
| 38 | Nevada | 1 | 0.1% |
| 35 | New Hampshire | 2 | 0.1% |
| 35 | New Jersey | 2 | 0.1% |
| 29 | New Mexico | 8 | 0.6% |
| 38 | New York | 1 | 0.1% |
| 15 | North Carolina | 37 | 2.7% |
| 10 | North Dakota | 58 | 4.3% |
| 21 | Ohio | 19 | 1.4% |
| 2 | Oklahoma | 142 | 10.5% |
| 38 | Oregon | 1 | 0.1% |
| 27 | Pennsylvania | 9 | 0.7% |
| 44 | Rhode Island | 0 | 0.0% |
| 22 | South Carolina | 17 | 1.3% |
| 12 | South Dakota | 41 | 3.0% |
| 17 | Tennessee | 23 | 1.7% |
| 1 | Texas | 165 | 12.2% |
| 32 | Utah | 3 | 0.2% |
| 44 | Vermont | 0 | 0.0% |
| 27 | Virginia | 9 | 0.7% |
| 35 | Washington | 2 | 0.1% |
| 38 | West Virginia | 1 | 0.1% |
| 24 | Wisconsin | 11 | 0.8% |
| 20 | Wyoming | 20 | 1.5% |

| RANK | STATE | TORNADOES | % of USA |
|------|-------|-----------|----------|
| 1 | Texas | 165 | 12.2% |
| 2 | Oklahoma | 142 | 10.5% |
| 3 | Arkansas | 107 | 7.9% |
| 4 | Nebraska | 102 | 7.5% |
| 5 | Illinois | 65 | 4.8% |
| 6 | Kansas | 64 | 4.7% |
| 7 | Louisiana | 63 | 4.7% |
| 8 | Florida | 60 | 4.4% |
| 8 | Iowa | 60 | 4.4% |
| 10 | North Dakota | 58 | 4.3% |
| 11 | Mississippi | 44 | 3.3% |
| 12 | Colorado | 41 | 3.0% |
| 12 | Missouri | 41 | 3.0% |
| 12 | South Dakota | 41 | 3.0% |
| 15 | North Carolina | 37 | 2.7% |
| 16 | Minnesota | 36 | 2.7% |
| 17 | Alabama | 23 | 1.7% |
| 17 | Tennessee | 23 | 1.7% |
| 19 | Montana | 22 | 1.6% |
| 20 | Wyoming | 20 | 1.5% |
| 21 | Ohio | 19 | 1.4% |
| 22 | South Carolina | 17 | 1.3% |
| 23 | Georgia | 12 | 0.9% |
| 24 | Wisconsin | 11 | 0.8% |
| 25 | Indiana | 10 | 0.7% |
| 25 | Michigan | 10 | 0.7% |
| 27 | Pennsylvania | 9 | 0.7% |
| 27 | Virginia | 9 | 0.7% |
| 29 | New Mexico | 8 | 0.6% |
| 30 | Kentucky | 6 | 0.4% |
| 31 | Arizona | 5 | 0.4% |
| 32 | California | 3 | 0.2% |
| 32 | Maryland | 3 | 0.2% |
| 32 | Utah | 3 | 0.2% |
| 35 | New Hampshire | 2 | 0.1% |
| 35 | New Jersey | 2 | 0.1% |
| 35 | Washington | 2 | 0.1% |
| 38 | Idaho | 1 | 0.1% |
| 38 | Maine | 1 | 0.1% |
| 38 | Nevada | 1 | 0.1% |
| 38 | New York | 1 | 0.1% |
| 38 | Oregon | 1 | 0.1% |
| 38 | West Virginia | 1 | 0.1% |
| 44 | Connecticut | 0 | 0.0% |
| 44 | Delaware | 0 | 0.0% |
| 44 | Massachusetts | 0 | 0.0% |
| 44 | Rhode Island | 0 | 0.0% |
| 44 | Vermont | 0 | 0.0% |
| NA | Alaska* | NA | NA |
| NA | Hawaii* | NA | NA |
| | District of Columbia | 0 | 0.0% |

*Source: National Weather Service, Storm Prediction Center
    unpublished data*
*Not available.

# Tornadoes: 1950 to 1999

## National Total = 40,516 Tornadoes*

ALPHA ORDER

| RANK | STATE | TORNADOES | % of USA |
|------|-------|-----------|----------|
| 14 | Alabama | 1,059 | 2.6% |
| 50 | Alaska | 1 | 0.0% |
| 34 | Arizona | 180 | 0.4% |
| 13 | Arkansas | 1,094 | 2.7% |
| 31 | California | 288 | 0.7% |
| 8 | Colorado | 1,385 | 3.4% |
| 44 | Connecticut | 69 | 0.2% |
| 46 | Delaware | 55 | 0.1% |
| 3 | Florida | 2,454 | 6.1% |
| 16 | Georgia | 1,000 | 2.5% |
| 48 | Hawaii | 28 | 0.1% |
| 36 | Idaho | 141 | 0.3% |
| 7 | Illinois | 1,470 | 3.6% |
| 17 | Indiana | 985 | 2.4% |
| 6 | Iowa | 1,595 | 3.9% |
| 4 | Kansas | 2,449 | 6.0% |
| 27 | Kentucky | 486 | 1.2% |
| 11 | Louisiana | 1,263 | 3.1% |
| 40 | Maine | 88 | 0.2% |
| 33 | Maryland | 206 | 0.5% |
| 35 | Massachusetts | 143 | 0.4% |
| 21 | Michigan | 783 | 1.9% |
| 15 | Minnesota | 1,041 | 2.6% |
| 12 | Mississippi | 1,203 | 3.0% |
| 9 | Missouri | 1,306 | 3.2% |
| 30 | Montana | 303 | 0.7% |
| 5 | Nebraska | 1,957 | 4.8% |
| 45 | Nevada | 61 | 0.2% |
| 41 | New Hampshire | 78 | 0.2% |
| 37 | New Jersey | 126 | 0.3% |
| 28 | New Mexico | 441 | 1.1% |
| 31 | New York | 288 | 0.7% |
| 20 | North Carolina | 784 | 1.9% |
| 18 | North Dakota | 954 | 2.4% |
| 22 | Ohio | 724 | 1.8% |
| 2 | Oklahoma | 2,710 | 6.7% |
| 43 | Oregon | 70 | 0.2% |
| 25 | Pennsylvania | 562 | 1.4% |
| 49 | Rhode Island | 8 | 0.0% |
| 24 | South Carolina | 577 | 1.4% |
| 10 | South Dakota | 1,294 | 3.2% |
| 23 | Tennessee | 648 | 1.6% |
| 1 | Texas | 6,336 | 15.6% |
| 39 | Utah | 92 | 0.2% |
| 47 | Vermont | 32 | 0.1% |
| 29 | Virginia | 346 | 0.9% |
| 42 | Washington | 72 | 0.2% |
| 38 | West Virginia | 101 | 0.2% |
| 19 | Wisconsin | 921 | 2.3% |
| 26 | Wyoming | 511 | 1.3% |

RANK ORDER

| RANK | STATE | TORNADOES | % of USA |
|------|-------|-----------|----------|
| 1 | Texas | 6,336 | 15.6% |
| 2 | Oklahoma | 2,710 | 6.7% |
| 3 | Florida | 2,454 | 6.1% |
| 4 | Kansas | 2,449 | 6.0% |
| 5 | Nebraska | 1,957 | 4.8% |
| 6 | Iowa | 1,595 | 3.9% |
| 7 | Illinois | 1,470 | 3.6% |
| 8 | Colorado | 1,385 | 3.4% |
| 9 | Missouri | 1,306 | 3.2% |
| 10 | South Dakota | 1,294 | 3.2% |
| 11 | Louisiana | 1,263 | 3.1% |
| 12 | Mississippi | 1,203 | 3.0% |
| 13 | Arkansas | 1,094 | 2.7% |
| 14 | Alabama | 1,059 | 2.6% |
| 15 | Minnesota | 1,041 | 2.6% |
| 16 | Georgia | 1,000 | 2.5% |
| 17 | Indiana | 985 | 2.4% |
| 18 | North Dakota | 954 | 2.4% |
| 19 | Wisconsin | 921 | 2.3% |
| 20 | North Carolina | 784 | 1.9% |
| 21 | Michigan | 783 | 1.9% |
| 22 | Ohio | 724 | 1.8% |
| 23 | Tennessee | 648 | 1.6% |
| 24 | South Carolina | 577 | 1.4% |
| 25 | Pennsylvania | 562 | 1.4% |
| 26 | Wyoming | 511 | 1.3% |
| 27 | Kentucky | 486 | 1.2% |
| 28 | New Mexico | 441 | 1.1% |
| 29 | Virginia | 346 | 0.9% |
| 30 | Montana | 303 | 0.7% |
| 31 | California | 288 | 0.7% |
| 31 | New York | 288 | 0.7% |
| 33 | Maryland | 206 | 0.5% |
| 34 | Arizona | 180 | 0.4% |
| 35 | Massachusetts | 143 | 0.4% |
| 36 | Idaho | 141 | 0.3% |
| 37 | New Jersey | 126 | 0.3% |
| 38 | West Virginia | 101 | 0.2% |
| 39 | Utah | 92 | 0.2% |
| 40 | Maine | 88 | 0.2% |
| 41 | New Hampshire | 78 | 0.2% |
| 42 | Washington | 72 | 0.2% |
| 43 | Oregon | 70 | 0.2% |
| 44 | Connecticut | 69 | 0.2% |
| 45 | Nevada | 61 | 0.2% |
| 46 | Delaware | 55 | 0.1% |
| 47 | Vermont | 32 | 0.1% |
| 48 | Hawaii | 28 | 0.1% |
| 49 | Rhode Island | 8 | 0.0% |
| 50 | Alaska | 1 | 0.0% |
| | District of Columbia | 1 | 0.0% |

*Source: Morgan Quitno Press using data from the National Weather Service, Storm Prediction Center unpublished data*

*State totals include tornadoes that crossed state borders and were counted for each state they entered.*

# Fatalities Caused by Tornadoes: 1950 to 2000

## National Total = 4,501 Fatalities

ALPHA ORDER

RANK ORDER

| RANK | STATE | FATALITIES | % of USA | | RANK | STATE | FATALITIES | % of USA |
|------|-------|-----------|----------|---|------|-------|-----------|----------|
| 3 | Alabama | 337 | 7.5% | | 1 | Texas | 518 | 11.5% |
| 41 | Alaska | 0 | 0.0% | | 2 | Mississippi | 389 | 8.6% |
| 31 | Arizona | 3 | 0.1% | | 3 | Alabama | 337 | 7.5% |
| 4 | Arkansas | 328 | 7.3% | | 4 | Arkansas | 328 | 7.3% |
| 41 | California | 0 | 0.0% | | 5 | Oklahoma | 264 | 5.9% |
| 33 | Colorado | 2 | 0.0% | | 6 | Michigan | 239 | 5.3% |
| 30 | Connecticut | 4 | 0.1% | | 7 | Indiana | 221 | 4.9% |
| 33 | Delaware | 2 | 0.0% | | 8 | Kansas | 205 | 4.6% |
| 15 | Florida | 130 | 2.9% | | 9 | Tennessee | 204 | 4.5% |
| 13 | Georgia | 151 | 3.4% | | 10 | Illinois | 186 | 4.1% |
| 41 | Hawaii | 0 | 0.0% | | 11 | Ohio | 179 | 4.0% |
| 41 | Idaho | 0 | 0.0% | | 12 | Missouri | 155 | 3.4% |
| 10 | Illinois | 186 | 4.1% | | 13 | Georgia | 151 | 3.4% |
| 7 | Indiana | 221 | 4.9% | | 14 | Louisiana | 143 | 3.2% |
| 22 | Iowa | 64 | 1.4% | | 15 | Florida | 130 | 2.9% |
| 8 | Kansas | 205 | 4.6% | | 16 | Kentucky | 111 | 2.5% |
| 16 | Kentucky | 111 | 2.5% | | 17 | Massachusetts | 102 | 2.3% |
| 14 | Louisiana | 143 | 3.2% | | 18 | Wisconsin | 95 | 2.1% |
| 39 | Maine | 1 | 0.0% | | 19 | Minnesota | 92 | 2.0% |
| 33 | Maryland | 2 | 0.0% | | 20 | North Carolina | 85 | 1.9% |
| 17 | Massachusetts | 102 | 2.3% | | 21 | Pennsylvania | 81 | 1.8% |
| 6 | Michigan | 239 | 5.3% | | 22 | Iowa | 64 | 1.4% |
| 19 | Minnesota | 92 | 2.0% | | 23 | South Carolina | 52 | 1.2% |
| 2 | Mississippi | 389 | 8.6% | | 24 | Nebraska | 51 | 1.1% |
| 12 | Missouri | 155 | 3.4% | | 25 | Virginia | 27 | 0.6% |
| 33 | Montana | 2 | 0.0% | | 26 | North Dakota | 23 | 0.5% |
| 24 | Nebraska | 51 | 1.1% | | 27 | New York | 21 | 0.5% |
| 41 | Nevada | 0 | 0.0% | | 28 | South Dakota | 18 | 0.4% |
| 41 | New Hampshire | 0 | 0.0% | | 29 | Washington | 6 | 0.1% |
| 41 | New Jersey | 0 | 0.0% | | 30 | Connecticut | 4 | 0.1% |
| 31 | New Mexico | 3 | 0.1% | | 31 | Arizona | 3 | 0.1% |
| 27 | New York | 21 | 0.5% | | 31 | New Mexico | 3 | 0.1% |
| 20 | North Carolina | 85 | 1.9% | | 33 | Colorado | 2 | 0.0% |
| 26 | North Dakota | 23 | 0.5% | | 33 | Delaware | 2 | 0.0% |
| 11 | Ohio | 179 | 4.0% | | 33 | Maryland | 2 | 0.0% |
| 5 | Oklahoma | 264 | 5.9% | | 33 | Montana | 2 | 0.0% |
| 41 | Oregon | 0 | 0.0% | | 33 | West Virginia | 2 | 0.0% |
| 21 | Pennsylvania | 81 | 1.8% | | 33 | Wyoming | 2 | 0.0% |
| 41 | Rhode Island | 0 | 0.0% | | 39 | Maine | 1 | 0.0% |
| 23 | South Carolina | 52 | 1.2% | | 39 | Utah | 1 | 0.0% |
| 28 | South Dakota | 18 | 0.4% | | 41 | Alaska | 0 | 0.0% |
| 9 | Tennessee | 204 | 4.5% | | 41 | California | 0 | 0.0% |
| 1 | Texas | 518 | 11.5% | | 41 | Hawaii | 0 | 0.0% |
| 39 | Utah | 1 | 0.0% | | 41 | Idaho | 0 | 0.0% |
| 41 | Vermont | 0 | 0.0% | | 41 | Nevada | 0 | 0.0% |
| 25 | Virginia | 27 | 0.6% | | 41 | New Hampshire | 0 | 0.0% |
| 29 | Washington | 6 | 0.1% | | 41 | New Jersey | 0 | 0.0% |
| 33 | West Virginia | 2 | 0.0% | | 41 | Oregon | 0 | 0.0% |
| 18 | Wisconsin | 95 | 2.1% | | 41 | Rhode Island | 0 | 0.0% |
| 33 | Wyoming | 2 | 0.0% | | 41 | Vermont | 0 | 0.0% |
| | | | | | | District of Columbia | 0 | 0.0% |

*Source: Morgan Quitno Press using data from National Weather Service, Storm Prediction Center*
  *unpublished data*

# Land in Metropolitan Areas in 2000

## National Total = 705,940.1 Square Miles*

ALPHA ORDER

| RANK | STATE | MILES | % of USA |
|------|-------|-------|----------|
| 14 | Alabama | 16,797.5 | 2.4% |
| 44 | Alaska | 1,697.6 | 0.2% |
| 2 | Arizona | 61,207.0 | 8.7% |
| 27 | Arkansas | 8,664.2 | 1.2% |
| 1 | California | 92,546.6 | 13.1% |
| 9 | Colorado | 18,940.9 | 2.7% |
| 41 | Connecticut | 3,836.0 | 0.5% |
| 47 | Delaware | 1,017.0 | 0.1% |
| 5 | Florida | 31,332.4 | 4.4% |
| 20 | Georgia | 12,881.6 | 1.8% |
| 49 | Hawaii | 600.2 | 0.1% |
| 42 | Idaho | 3,009.5 | 0.4% |
| 13 | Illinois | 16,907.9 | 2.4% |
| 19 | Indiana | 13,689.5 | 1.9% |
| 34 | Iowa | 6,520.2 | 0.9% |
| 36 | Kansas | 5,642.9 | 0.8% |
| 33 | Kentucky | 6,533.7 | 0.9% |
| 16 | Louisiana | 15,241.1 | 2.2% |
| 45 | Maine | 1,490.1 | 0.2% |
| 35 | Maryland | 6,161.2 | 0.9% |
| 38 | Massachusetts | 5,488.6 | 0.8% |
| 15 | Michigan | 15,965.8 | 2.3% |
| 12 | Minnesota | 16,971.8 | 2.4% |
| 37 | Mississippi | 5,589.9 | 0.8% |
| 23 | Missouri | 12,138.9 | 1.7% |
| 29 | Montana | 7,951.6 | 1.1% |
| 43 | Nebraska | 2,624.3 | 0.4% |
| 4 | Nevada | 32,400.4 | 4.6% |
| 46 | New Hampshire | 1,398.5 | 0.2% |
| 31 | New Jersey | 7,418.8 | 1.1% |
| 26 | New Mexico | 11,769.6 | 1.7% |
| 6 | New York | 22,288.0 | 3.2% |
| 11 | North Carolina | 17,799.5 | 2.5% |
| 32 | North Dakota | 6,763.2 | 1.0% |
| 10 | Ohio | 18,298.8 | 2.6% |
| 25 | Oklahoma | 12,064.2 | 1.7% |
| 18 | Oregon | 14,341.8 | 2.0% |
| 7 | Pennsylvania | 21,481.7 | 3.0% |
| 48 | Rhode Island | 991.1 | 0.1% |
| 24 | South Carolina | 12,115.8 | 1.7% |
| 39 | South Dakota | 4,163.7 | 0.6% |
| 22 | Tennessee | 12,332.8 | 1.7% |
| 3 | Texas | 52,523.3 | 7.4% |
| 30 | Utah | 7,608.1 | 1.1% |
| 50 | Vermont | 561.9 | 0.1% |
| 17 | Virginia | 14,575.1 | 2.1% |
| 8 | Washington | 18,976.7 | 2.7% |
| 40 | West Virginia | 3,847.8 | 0.5% |
| 21 | Wisconsin | 12,683.6 | 1.8% |
| 28 | Wyoming | 8,026.3 | 1.1% |

RANK ORDER

| RANK | STATE | MILES | % of USA |
|------|-------|-------|----------|
| 1 | California | 92,546.6 | 13.1% |
| 2 | Arizona | 61,207.0 | 8.7% |
| 3 | Texas | 52,523.3 | 7.4% |
| 4 | Nevada | 32,400.4 | 4.6% |
| 5 | Florida | 31,332.4 | 4.4% |
| 6 | New York | 22,288.0 | 3.2% |
| 7 | Pennsylvania | 21,481.7 | 3.0% |
| 8 | Washington | 18,976.7 | 2.7% |
| 9 | Colorado | 18,940.9 | 2.7% |
| 10 | Ohio | 18,298.8 | 2.6% |
| 11 | North Carolina | 17,799.5 | 2.5% |
| 12 | Minnesota | 16,971.8 | 2.4% |
| 13 | Illinois | 16,907.9 | 2.4% |
| 14 | Alabama | 16,797.5 | 2.4% |
| 15 | Michigan | 15,965.8 | 2.3% |
| 16 | Louisiana | 15,241.1 | 2.2% |
| 17 | Virginia | 14,575.1 | 2.1% |
| 18 | Oregon | 14,341.8 | 2.0% |
| 19 | Indiana | 13,689.5 | 1.9% |
| 20 | Georgia | 12,881.6 | 1.8% |
| 21 | Wisconsin | 12,683.6 | 1.8% |
| 22 | Tennessee | 12,332.8 | 1.7% |
| 23 | Missouri | 12,138.9 | 1.7% |
| 24 | South Carolina | 12,115.8 | 1.7% |
| 25 | Oklahoma | 12,064.2 | 1.7% |
| 26 | New Mexico | 11,769.6 | 1.7% |
| 27 | Arkansas | 8,664.2 | 1.2% |
| 28 | Wyoming | 8,026.3 | 1.1% |
| 29 | Montana | 7,951.6 | 1.1% |
| 30 | Utah | 7,608.1 | 1.1% |
| 31 | New Jersey | 7,418.8 | 1.1% |
| 32 | North Dakota | 6,763.2 | 1.0% |
| 33 | Kentucky | 6,533.7 | 0.9% |
| 34 | Iowa | 6,520.2 | 0.9% |
| 35 | Maryland | 6,161.2 | 0.9% |
| 36 | Kansas | 5,642.9 | 0.8% |
| 37 | Mississippi | 5,589.9 | 0.8% |
| 38 | Massachusetts | 5,488.6 | 0.8% |
| 39 | South Dakota | 4,163.7 | 0.6% |
| 40 | West Virginia | 3,847.8 | 0.5% |
| 41 | Connecticut | 3,836.0 | 0.5% |
| 42 | Idaho | 3,009.5 | 0.4% |
| 43 | Nebraska | 2,624.3 | 0.4% |
| 44 | Alaska | 1,697.6 | 0.2% |
| 45 | Maine | 1,490.1 | 0.2% |
| 46 | New Hampshire | 1,398.5 | 0.2% |
| 47 | Delaware | 1,017.0 | 0.1% |
| 48 | Rhode Island | 991.1 | 0.1% |
| 49 | Hawaii | 600.2 | 0.1% |
| 50 | Vermont | 561.9 | 0.1% |
| | District of Columbia | 61.4 | 0.0% |

*Source: Morgan Quitno Press using data from U.S. Bureau of the Census
unpublished data*

*"Metropolitan" refers to metropolitan statistical areas and consolidated metropolitan statistical areas as defined by
the U.S. Office of Management and Budget, July 1, 1999.*

# Percent of Land in Metropolitan Areas in 2000

## National Percent = 20.0% of Land*

ALPHA ORDER

| RANK | STATE | PERCENT |
|------|-------|---------|
| 18 | Alabama | 33.1 |
| 50 | Alaska | 0.3 |
| 8 | Arizona | 53.9 |
| 31 | Arkansas | 16.6 |
| 6 | California | 59.3 |
| 28 | Colorado | 18.3 |
| 3 | Connecticut | 79.2 |
| 9 | Delaware | 52.0 |
| 7 | Florida | 58.0 |
| 25 | Georgia | 22.2 |
| 40 | Hawaii | 9.3 |
| 48 | Idaho | 3.6 |
| 19 | Illinois | 30.4 |
| 14 | Indiana | 38.2 |
| 37 | Iowa | 11.7 |
| 43 | Kansas | 6.9 |
| 32 | Kentucky | 16.4 |
| 17 | Louisiana | 35.0 |
| 47 | Maine | 4.8 |
| 5 | Maryland | 63.0 |
| 4 | Massachusetts | 70.0 |
| 23 | Michigan | 28.1 |
| 26 | Minnesota | 21.3 |
| 36 | Mississippi | 11.9 |
| 29 | Missouri | 17.6 |
| 45 | Montana | 5.5 |
| 49 | Nebraska | 3.4 |
| 21 | Nevada | 29.5 |
| 34 | New Hampshire | 15.6 |
| 1 | New Jersey | 100.0 |
| 39 | New Mexico | 9.7 |
| 11 | New York | 47.2 |
| 16 | North Carolina | 36.5 |
| 38 | North Dakota | 9.8 |
| 12 | Ohio | 44.7 |
| 29 | Oklahoma | 17.6 |
| 35 | Oregon | 14.9 |
| 10 | Pennsylvania | 47.9 |
| 2 | Rhode Island | 94.8 |
| 13 | South Carolina | 40.2 |
| 45 | South Dakota | 5.5 |
| 20 | Tennessee | 29.9 |
| 27 | Texas | 20.1 |
| 40 | Utah | 9.3 |
| 44 | Vermont | 6.1 |
| 15 | Virginia | 36.8 |
| 22 | Washington | 28.5 |
| 33 | West Virginia | 16.0 |
| 24 | Wisconsin | 23.4 |
| 42 | Wyoming | 8.3 |

RANK ORDER

| RANK | STATE | PERCENT |
|------|-------|---------|
| 1 | New Jersey | 100.0 |
| 2 | Rhode Island | 94.8 |
| 3 | Connecticut | 79.2 |
| 4 | Massachusetts | 70.0 |
| 5 | Maryland | 63.0 |
| 6 | California | 59.3 |
| 7 | Florida | 58.0 |
| 8 | Arizona | 53.9 |
| 9 | Delaware | 52.0 |
| 10 | Pennsylvania | 47.9 |
| 11 | New York | 47.2 |
| 12 | Ohio | 44.7 |
| 13 | South Carolina | 40.2 |
| 14 | Indiana | 38.2 |
| 15 | Virginia | 36.8 |
| 16 | North Carolina | 36.5 |
| 17 | Louisiana | 35.0 |
| 18 | Alabama | 33.1 |
| 19 | Illinois | 30.4 |
| 20 | Tennessee | 29.9 |
| 21 | Nevada | 29.5 |
| 22 | Washington | 28.5 |
| 23 | Michigan | 28.1 |
| 24 | Wisconsin | 23.4 |
| 25 | Georgia | 22.2 |
| 26 | Minnesota | 21.3 |
| 27 | Texas | 20.1 |
| 28 | Colorado | 18.3 |
| 29 | Missouri | 17.6 |
| 29 | Oklahoma | 17.6 |
| 31 | Arkansas | 16.6 |
| 32 | Kentucky | 16.4 |
| 33 | West Virginia | 16.0 |
| 34 | New Hampshire | 15.6 |
| 35 | Oregon | 14.9 |
| 36 | Mississippi | 11.9 |
| 37 | Iowa | 11.7 |
| 38 | North Dakota | 9.8 |
| 39 | New Mexico | 9.7 |
| 40 | Hawaii | 9.3 |
| 40 | Utah | 9.3 |
| 42 | Wyoming | 8.3 |
| 43 | Kansas | 6.9 |
| 44 | Vermont | 6.1 |
| 45 | Montana | 5.5 |
| 45 | South Dakota | 5.5 |
| 47 | Maine | 4.8 |
| 48 | Idaho | 3.6 |
| 49 | Nebraska | 3.4 |
| 50 | Alaska | 0.3 |
| | District of Columbia | 100.0 |

Source: Morgan Quitno Press using data from U.S. Bureau of the Census
    unpublished data
*"Metropolitan" refers to metropolitan statistical areas and consolidated metropolitan statistical areas as defined by
the U.S. Office of Management and Budget, July 1, 1999.

# Land in Nonmetropolitan Areas in 2000

## National Total = 2,830,398.3 Square Miles*

| ALPHA ORDER | | | | | RANK ORDER | | | |
|---|---|---|---|---|---|---|---|---|

| RANK | STATE | MILES | % of USA |
|---|---|---|---|
| 28 | Alabama | 33,952.7 | 1.2% |
| 1 | Alaska | 568,675.9 | 20.1% |
| 19 | Arizona | 52,435.2 | 1.9% |
| 23 | Arkansas | 43,411.1 | 1.5% |
| 14 | California | 63,426.7 | 2.2% |
| 6 | Colorado | 84,787.9 | 3.0% |
| 47 | Connecticut | 1,009.4 | 0.0% |
| 48 | Delaware | 937.7 | 0.0% |
| 37 | Florida | 22,664.9 | 0.8% |
| 22 | Georgia | 45,037.2 | 1.6% |
| 44 | Hawaii | 5,823.2 | 0.2% |
| 8 | Idaho | 79,741.4 | 2.8% |
| 27 | Illinois | 38,685.4 | 1.4% |
| 39 | Indiana | 22,180.7 | 0.8% |
| 20 | Iowa | 49,354.7 | 1.7% |
| 10 | Kansas | 76,180.1 | 2.7% |
| 29 | Kentucky | 33,198.7 | 1.2% |
| 33 | Louisiana | 28,325.0 | 1.0% |
| 31 | Maine | 29,374.4 | 1.0% |
| 45 | Maryland | 3,613.5 | 0.1% |
| 46 | Massachusetts | 2,349.3 | 0.1% |
| 26 | Michigan | 40,843.4 | 1.4% |
| 15 | Minnesota | 62,644.7 | 2.2% |
| 25 | Mississippi | 41,323.8 | 1.5% |
| 17 | Missouri | 56,759.2 | 2.0% |
| 3 | Montana | 137,604.7 | 4.9% |
| 12 | Nebraska | 74,253.3 | 2.6% |
| 9 | Nevada | 77,405.1 | 2.7% |
| 43 | New Hampshire | 7,570.8 | 0.3% |
| 50 | New Jersey | 0.0 | 0.0% |
| 4 | New Mexico | 109,594.9 | 3.9% |
| 35 | New York | 24,935.8 | 0.9% |
| 30 | North Carolina | 30,918.6 | 1.1% |
| 16 | North Dakota | 62,231.0 | 2.2% |
| 38 | Ohio | 22,653.8 | 0.8% |
| 18 | Oklahoma | 56,614.4 | 2.0% |
| 7 | Oregon | 81,660.6 | 2.9% |
| 36 | Pennsylvania | 23,337.9 | 0.8% |
| 49 | Rhode Island | 53.9 | 0.0% |
| 41 | South Carolina | 17,995.3 | 0.6% |
| 13 | South Dakota | 71,732.3 | 2.5% |
| 32 | Tennessee | 28,886.7 | 1.0% |
| 2 | Texas | 209,391.0 | 7.4% |
| 11 | Utah | 74,560.0 | 2.6% |
| 42 | Vermont | 8,687.5 | 0.3% |
| 34 | Virginia | 25,022.7 | 0.9% |
| 21 | Washington | 47,604.6 | 1.7% |
| 40 | West Virginia | 20,238.8 | 0.7% |
| 24 | Wisconsin | 41,630.1 | 1.5% |
| 5 | Wyoming | 89,078.3 | 3.1% |

| RANK | STATE | MILES | % of USA |
|---|---|---|---|
| 1 | Alaska | 568,675.9 | 20.1% |
| 2 | Texas | 209,391.0 | 7.4% |
| 3 | Montana | 137,604.7 | 4.9% |
| 4 | New Mexico | 109,594.9 | 3.9% |
| 5 | Wyoming | 89,078.3 | 3.1% |
| 6 | Colorado | 84,787.9 | 3.0% |
| 7 | Oregon | 81,660.6 | 2.9% |
| 8 | Idaho | 79,741.4 | 2.8% |
| 9 | Nevada | 77,405.1 | 2.7% |
| 10 | Kansas | 76,180.1 | 2.7% |
| 11 | Utah | 74,560.0 | 2.6% |
| 12 | Nebraska | 74,253.3 | 2.6% |
| 13 | South Dakota | 71,732.3 | 2.5% |
| 14 | California | 63,426.7 | 2.2% |
| 15 | Minnesota | 62,644.7 | 2.2% |
| 16 | North Dakota | 62,231.0 | 2.2% |
| 17 | Missouri | 56,759.2 | 2.0% |
| 18 | Oklahoma | 56,614.4 | 2.0% |
| 19 | Arizona | 52,435.2 | 1.9% |
| 20 | Iowa | 49,354.7 | 1.7% |
| 21 | Washington | 47,604.6 | 1.7% |
| 22 | Georgia | 45,037.2 | 1.6% |
| 23 | Arkansas | 43,411.1 | 1.5% |
| 24 | Wisconsin | 41,630.1 | 1.5% |
| 25 | Mississippi | 41,323.8 | 1.5% |
| 26 | Michigan | 40,843.4 | 1.4% |
| 27 | Illinois | 38,685.4 | 1.4% |
| 28 | Alabama | 33,952.7 | 1.2% |
| 29 | Kentucky | 33,198.7 | 1.2% |
| 30 | North Carolina | 30,918.6 | 1.1% |
| 31 | Maine | 29,374.4 | 1.0% |
| 32 | Tennessee | 28,886.7 | 1.0% |
| 33 | Louisiana | 28,325.0 | 1.0% |
| 34 | Virginia | 25,022.7 | 0.9% |
| 35 | New York | 24,935.8 | 0.9% |
| 36 | Pennsylvania | 23,337.9 | 0.8% |
| 37 | Florida | 22,664.9 | 0.8% |
| 38 | Ohio | 22,653.8 | 0.8% |
| 39 | Indiana | 22,180.7 | 0.8% |
| 40 | West Virginia | 20,238.8 | 0.7% |
| 41 | South Carolina | 17,995.3 | 0.6% |
| 42 | Vermont | 8,687.5 | 0.3% |
| 43 | New Hampshire | 7,570.8 | 0.3% |
| 44 | Hawaii | 5,823.2 | 0.2% |
| 45 | Maryland | 3,613.5 | 0.1% |
| 46 | Massachusetts | 2,349.3 | 0.1% |
| 47 | Connecticut | 1,009.4 | 0.0% |
| 48 | Delaware | 937.7 | 0.0% |
| 49 | Rhode Island | 53.9 | 0.0% |
| 50 | New Jersey | 0.0 | 0.0% |
| | District of Columbia | 0.0 | 0.0% |

Source: Morgan Quitno Press using data from U.S. Bureau of the Census
    unpublished data

*"Nonmetropolitan" refers to areas outside of metropolitan statistical areas and consolidated metropolitan statistical areas as defined by the U.S. Office of Management and Budget, July 1, 1999.

# Percent of Land in Nonmetropolitan Areas in 2000

## National Percent = 80.0% of Land*

| ALPHA ORDER | | | RANK ORDER | | |
|---|---|---|---|---|---|
| RANK | STATE | PERCENT | RANK | STATE | PERCENT |
| 33 | Alabama | 66.9 | 1 | Alaska | 99.7 |
| 1 | Alaska | 99.7 | 2 | Nebraska | 96.6 |
| 43 | Arizona | 46.1 | 3 | Idaho | 96.4 |
| 20 | Arkansas | 83.4 | 4 | Maine | 95.2 |
| 45 | California | 40.7 | 5 | Montana | 94.5 |
| 23 | Colorado | 81.7 | 5 | South Dakota | 94.5 |
| 48 | Connecticut | 20.8 | 7 | Vermont | 93.9 |
| 42 | Delaware | 48.0 | 8 | Kansas | 93.1 |
| 44 | Florida | 42.0 | 9 | Wyoming | 91.7 |
| 26 | Georgia | 77.8 | 10 | Hawaii | 90.7 |
| 10 | Hawaii | 90.7 | 10 | Utah | 90.7 |
| 3 | Idaho | 96.4 | 12 | New Mexico | 90.3 |
| 32 | Illinois | 69.6 | 13 | North Dakota | 90.2 |
| 37 | Indiana | 61.8 | 14 | Iowa | 88.3 |
| 14 | Iowa | 88.3 | 15 | Mississippi | 88.1 |
| 8 | Kansas | 93.1 | 16 | Oregon | 85.1 |
| 19 | Kentucky | 83.6 | 17 | New Hampshire | 84.4 |
| 34 | Louisiana | 65.0 | 18 | West Virginia | 84.0 |
| 4 | Maine | 95.2 | 19 | Kentucky | 83.6 |
| 46 | Maryland | 37.0 | 20 | Arkansas | 83.4 |
| 47 | Massachusetts | 30.0 | 21 | Missouri | 82.4 |
| 28 | Michigan | 71.9 | 21 | Oklahoma | 82.4 |
| 25 | Minnesota | 78.7 | 23 | Colorado | 81.7 |
| 15 | Mississippi | 88.1 | 24 | Texas | 79.9 |
| 21 | Missouri | 82.4 | 25 | Minnesota | 78.7 |
| 5 | Montana | 94.5 | 26 | Georgia | 77.8 |
| 2 | Nebraska | 96.6 | 27 | Wisconsin | 76.6 |
| 30 | Nevada | 70.5 | 28 | Michigan | 71.9 |
| 17 | New Hampshire | 84.4 | 29 | Washington | 71.5 |
| 50 | New Jersey | 0.0 | 30 | Nevada | 70.5 |
| 12 | New Mexico | 90.3 | 31 | Tennessee | 70.1 |
| 40 | New York | 52.8 | 32 | Illinois | 69.6 |
| 35 | North Carolina | 63.5 | 33 | Alabama | 66.9 |
| 13 | North Dakota | 90.2 | 34 | Louisiana | 65.0 |
| 39 | Ohio | 55.3 | 35 | North Carolina | 63.5 |
| 21 | Oklahoma | 82.4 | 36 | Virginia | 63.2 |
| 16 | Oregon | 85.1 | 37 | Indiana | 61.8 |
| 41 | Pennsylvania | 52.1 | 38 | South Carolina | 59.8 |
| 49 | Rhode Island | 5.2 | 39 | Ohio | 55.3 |
| 38 | South Carolina | 59.8 | 40 | New York | 52.8 |
| 5 | South Dakota | 94.5 | 41 | Pennsylvania | 52.1 |
| 31 | Tennessee | 70.1 | 42 | Delaware | 48.0 |
| 24 | Texas | 79.9 | 43 | Arizona | 46.1 |
| 10 | Utah | 90.7 | 44 | Florida | 42.0 |
| 7 | Vermont | 93.9 | 45 | California | 40.7 |
| 36 | Virginia | 63.2 | 46 | Maryland | 37.0 |
| 29 | Washington | 71.5 | 47 | Massachusetts | 30.0 |
| 18 | West Virginia | 84.0 | 48 | Connecticut | 20.8 |
| 27 | Wisconsin | 76.6 | 49 | Rhode Island | 5.2 |
| 9 | Wyoming | 91.7 | 50 | New Jersey | 0.0 |
| | | | | District of Columbia | 0.0 |

Source: Morgan Quitno Press using data from U.S. Bureau of the Census
    unpublished data
*"Nonmetropolitan" refers to areas outside of metropolitan statistical areas and consolidated metropolitan statistical areas as defined by the U.S. Office of Management and Budget, July 1, 1999.

# Acres of Land Owned by the Federal Government in 1999

## National Total = 630,265,626 Acres*

ALPHA ORDER

| RANK | STATE | ACRES | % of USA |
|---|---|---|---|
| 28 | Alabama | 1,234,298 | 0.2% |
| 1 | Alaska | 227,995,892 | 36.2% |
| 6 | Arizona | 32,388,815 | 5.1% |
| 15 | Arkansas | 3,238,351 | 0.5% |
| 3 | California | 43,713,267 | 6.9% |
| 11 | Colorado | 24,239,407 | 3.8% |
| 48 | Connecticut | 14,412 | 0.0% |
| 49 | Delaware | 7,967 | 0.0% |
| 16 | Florida | 3,066,386 | 0.5% |
| 23 | Georgia | 1,864,308 | 0.3% |
| 37 | Hawaii | 618,327 | 0.1% |
| 5 | Idaho | 33,078,708 | 5.2% |
| 38 | Illinois | 574,025 | 0.1% |
| 39 | Indiana | 501,159 | 0.1% |
| 42 | Iowa | 195,397 | 0.0% |
| 34 | Kansas | 673,370 | 0.1% |
| 29 | Kentucky | 1,233,910 | 0.2% |
| 31 | Louisiana | 1,158,942 | 0.2% |
| 43 | Maine | 168,471 | 0.0% |
| 44 | Maryland | 166,899 | 0.0% |
| 47 | Massachusetts | 71,584 | 0.0% |
| 14 | Michigan | 4,078,885 | 0.6% |
| 13 | Minnesota | 4,206,078 | 0.7% |
| 26 | Mississippi | 1,647,295 | 0.3% |
| 21 | Missouri | 2,094,689 | 0.3% |
| 10 | Montana | 25,782,664 | 4.1% |
| 36 | Nebraska | 646,677 | 0.1% |
| 2 | Nevada | 58,226,016 | 9.2% |
| 33 | New Hampshire | 758,844 | 0.1% |
| 45 | New Jersey | 118,829 | 0.0% |
| 9 | New Mexico | 26,625,968 | 4.2% |
| 46 | New York | 105,545 | 0.0% |
| 19 | North Carolina | 2,355,724 | 0.4% |
| 24 | North Dakota | 1,771,115 | 0.3% |
| 40 | Ohio | 392,226 | 0.1% |
| 27 | Oklahoma | 1,323,205 | 0.2% |
| 7 | Oregon | 32,314,759 | 5.1% |
| 35 | Pennsylvania | 669,526 | 0.1% |
| 50 | Rhode Island | 3,957 | 0.0% |
| 32 | South Carolina | 1,107,347 | 0.2% |
| 17 | South Dakota | 2,661,645 | 0.4% |
| 25 | Tennessee | 1,657,952 | 0.3% |
| 18 | Texas | 2,568,392 | 0.4% |
| 4 | Utah | 34,005,401 | 5.4% |
| 41 | Vermont | 371,995 | 0.1% |
| 20 | Virginia | 2,283,993 | 0.4% |
| 12 | Washington | 12,152,494 | 1.9% |
| 30 | West Virginia | 1,178,474 | 0.2% |
| 22 | Wisconsin | 1,872,007 | 0.3% |
| 8 | Wyoming | 31,071,152 | 4.9% |

RANK ORDER

| RANK | STATE | ACRES | % of USA |
|---|---|---|---|
| 1 | Alaska | 227,995,892 | 36.2% |
| 2 | Nevada | 58,226,016 | 9.2% |
| 3 | California | 43,713,267 | 6.9% |
| 4 | Utah | 34,005,401 | 5.4% |
| 5 | Idaho | 33,078,708 | 5.2% |
| 6 | Arizona | 32,388,815 | 5.1% |
| 7 | Oregon | 32,314,759 | 5.1% |
| 8 | Wyoming | 31,071,152 | 4.9% |
| 9 | New Mexico | 26,625,968 | 4.2% |
| 10 | Montana | 25,782,664 | 4.1% |
| 11 | Colorado | 24,239,407 | 3.8% |
| 12 | Washington | 12,152,494 | 1.9% |
| 13 | Minnesota | 4,206,078 | 0.7% |
| 14 | Michigan | 4,078,885 | 0.6% |
| 15 | Arkansas | 3,238,351 | 0.5% |
| 16 | Florida | 3,066,386 | 0.5% |
| 17 | South Dakota | 2,661,645 | 0.4% |
| 18 | Texas | 2,568,392 | 0.4% |
| 19 | North Carolina | 2,355,724 | 0.4% |
| 20 | Virginia | 2,283,993 | 0.4% |
| 21 | Missouri | 2,094,689 | 0.3% |
| 22 | Wisconsin | 1,872,007 | 0.3% |
| 23 | Georgia | 1,864,308 | 0.3% |
| 24 | North Dakota | 1,771,115 | 0.3% |
| 25 | Tennessee | 1,657,952 | 0.3% |
| 26 | Mississippi | 1,647,295 | 0.3% |
| 27 | Oklahoma | 1,323,205 | 0.2% |
| 28 | Alabama | 1,234,298 | 0.2% |
| 29 | Kentucky | 1,233,910 | 0.2% |
| 30 | West Virginia | 1,178,474 | 0.2% |
| 31 | Louisiana | 1,158,942 | 0.2% |
| 32 | South Carolina | 1,107,347 | 0.2% |
| 33 | New Hampshire | 758,844 | 0.1% |
| 34 | Kansas | 673,370 | 0.1% |
| 35 | Pennsylvania | 669,526 | 0.1% |
| 36 | Nebraska | 646,677 | 0.1% |
| 37 | Hawaii | 618,327 | 0.1% |
| 38 | Illinois | 574,025 | 0.1% |
| 39 | Indiana | 501,159 | 0.1% |
| 40 | Ohio | 392,226 | 0.1% |
| 41 | Vermont | 371,995 | 0.1% |
| 42 | Iowa | 195,397 | 0.0% |
| 43 | Maine | 168,471 | 0.0% |
| 44 | Maryland | 166,899 | 0.0% |
| 45 | New Jersey | 118,829 | 0.0% |
| 46 | New York | 105,545 | 0.0% |
| 47 | Massachusetts | 71,584 | 0.0% |
| 48 | Connecticut | 14,412 | 0.0% |
| 49 | Delaware | 7,967 | 0.0% |
| 50 | Rhode Island | 3,957 | 0.0% |
| | District of Columbia | 8,880 | 0.0% |

*Source: Government Services Administration, Office of Governmentwide Real Property Policy*
*"Summary Report of Real Property Owned by the United States Throughout the World" (June 2000)*
*(http://www.gsa.gov/attachments/GSA_PUBLICATIONS/extpub/owned-99pos.pdf)*
*\*As of September 30, 1999.  Does not include 382,338 acres owned by the federal government in U.S. territories or in foreign countries.*

# Percent of Land Owned by the Federal Government in 1999

## National Percent = 27.7%*

ALPHA ORDER

| RANK | STATE | PERCENT |
|------|-------|---------|
| 33 | Alabama | 3.8 |
| 4 | Alaska | 62.4 |
| 7 | Arizona | 44.6 |
| 16 | Arkansas | 9.6 |
| 8 | California | 43.6 |
| 9 | Colorado | 36.5 |
| 48 | Connecticut | 0.5 |
| 46 | Delaware | 0.6 |
| 18 | Florida | 8.8 |
| 28 | Georgia | 5.0 |
| 13 | Hawaii | 15.1 |
| 3 | Idaho | 62.5 |
| 39 | Illinois | 1.6 |
| 38 | Indiana | 2.2 |
| 48 | Iowa | 0.5 |
| 43 | Kansas | 1.3 |
| 29 | Kentucky | 4.8 |
| 31 | Louisiana | 4.0 |
| 45 | Maine | 0.8 |
| 35 | Maryland | 2.6 |
| 42 | Massachusetts | 1.4 |
| 15 | Michigan | 11.2 |
| 19 | Minnesota | 8.2 |
| 25 | Mississippi | 5.5 |
| 30 | Missouri | 4.7 |
| 12 | Montana | 27.6 |
| 43 | Nebraska | 1.3 |
| 1 | Nevada | 82.9 |
| 14 | New Hampshire | 13.2 |
| 36 | New Jersey | 2.5 |
| 10 | New Mexico | 34.2 |
| 50 | New York | 0.3 |
| 21 | North Carolina | 7.5 |
| 31 | North Dakota | 4.0 |
| 40 | Ohio | 1.5 |
| 34 | Oklahoma | 3.0 |
| 5 | Oregon | 52.5 |
| 37 | Pennsylvania | 2.3 |
| 46 | Rhode Island | 0.6 |
| 24 | South Carolina | 5.7 |
| 26 | South Dakota | 5.4 |
| 23 | Tennessee | 6.2 |
| 40 | Texas | 1.5 |
| 2 | Utah | 64.5 |
| 22 | Vermont | 6.3 |
| 17 | Virginia | 9.0 |
| 11 | Washington | 28.5 |
| 20 | West Virginia | 7.6 |
| 27 | Wisconsin | 5.3 |
| 6 | Wyoming | 49.8 |

RANK ORDER

| RANK | STATE | PERCENT |
|------|-------|---------|
| 1 | Nevada | 82.9 |
| 2 | Utah | 64.5 |
| 3 | Idaho | 62.5 |
| 4 | Alaska | 62.4 |
| 5 | Oregon | 52.5 |
| 6 | Wyoming | 49.8 |
| 7 | Arizona | 44.6 |
| 8 | California | 43.6 |
| 9 | Colorado | 36.5 |
| 10 | New Mexico | 34.2 |
| 11 | Washington | 28.5 |
| 12 | Montana | 27.6 |
| 13 | Hawaii | 15.1 |
| 14 | New Hampshire | 13.2 |
| 15 | Michigan | 11.2 |
| 16 | Arkansas | 9.6 |
| 17 | Virginia | 9.0 |
| 18 | Florida | 8.8 |
| 19 | Minnesota | 8.2 |
| 20 | West Virginia | 7.6 |
| 21 | North Carolina | 7.5 |
| 22 | Vermont | 6.3 |
| 23 | Tennessee | 6.2 |
| 24 | South Carolina | 5.7 |
| 25 | Mississippi | 5.5 |
| 26 | South Dakota | 5.4 |
| 27 | Wisconsin | 5.3 |
| 28 | Georgia | 5.0 |
| 29 | Kentucky | 4.8 |
| 30 | Missouri | 4.7 |
| 31 | Louisiana | 4.0 |
| 31 | North Dakota | 4.0 |
| 33 | Alabama | 3.8 |
| 34 | Oklahoma | 3.0 |
| 35 | Maryland | 2.6 |
| 36 | New Jersey | 2.5 |
| 37 | Pennsylvania | 2.3 |
| 38 | Indiana | 2.2 |
| 39 | Illinois | 1.6 |
| 40 | Ohio | 1.5 |
| 40 | Texas | 1.5 |
| 42 | Massachusetts | 1.4 |
| 43 | Kansas | 1.3 |
| 43 | Nebraska | 1.3 |
| 45 | Maine | 0.8 |
| 46 | Delaware | 0.6 |
| 46 | Rhode Island | 0.6 |
| 48 | Connecticut | 0.5 |
| 48 | Iowa | 0.5 |
| 50 | New York | 0.3 |

| District of Columbia | 22.7 |
|----------------------|------|

Source: Government Services Administration, Office of Governmentwide Real Property Policy
"Summary Report of Real Property Owned by the United States Throughout the World" (June 2000)
(http://www.gsa.gov/attachments/GSA_PUBLICATIONS/extpub/owned-99pos.pdf)
*As of September 30, 1999. National rate does not include acres owned by the federal government in U.S. territories or in foreign countries.

# Percent of Nonfederal Land That is Developed: 1997

## National Percent = 6.6% of Nonfederal Land*

ALPHA ORDER

| RANK | STATE | PERCENT |
|------|-------|---------|
| 22 | Alabama | 7.2 |
| NA | Alaska** | NA |
| 43 | Arizona | 3.5 |
| 33 | Arkansas | 4.7 |
| 17 | California | 10.3 |
| 37 | Colorado | 3.9 |
| 4 | Connecticut | 28.6 |
| 6 | Delaware | 18.6 |
| 7 | Florida | 16.9 |
| 14 | Georgia | 11.4 |
| 31 | Hawaii | 4.8 |
| 37 | Idaho | 3.9 |
| 20 | Illinois | 9.1 |
| 18 | Indiana | 10.1 |
| 31 | Iowa | 4.8 |
| 39 | Kansas | 3.8 |
| 22 | Kentucky | 7.2 |
| 25 | Louisiana | 6.2 |
| 40 | Maine | 3.7 |
| 5 | Maryland | 20.4 |
| 3 | Massachusetts | 30.4 |
| 15 | Michigan | 10.8 |
| 34 | Minnesota | 4.6 |
| 29 | Mississippi | 5.3 |
| 27 | Missouri | 6.0 |
| 49 | Montana | 1.6 |
| 44 | Nebraska | 2.5 |
| 41 | Nevada | 3.6 |
| 11 | New Hampshire | 11.9 |
| 1 | New Jersey | 39.1 |
| 45 | New Mexico | 2.3 |
| 16 | New York | 10.7 |
| 10 | North Carolina | 13.6 |
| 45 | North Dakota | 2.3 |
| 9 | Ohio | 14.1 |
| 35 | Oklahoma | 4.5 |
| 36 | Oregon | 4.1 |
| 8 | Pennsylvania | 14.3 |
| 2 | Rhode Island | 30.5 |
| 13 | South Carolina | 11.6 |
| 47 | South Dakota | 2.1 |
| 19 | Tennessee | 9.5 |
| 30 | Texas | 5.2 |
| 41 | Utah | 3.6 |
| 28 | Vermont | 5.8 |
| 12 | Virginia | 11.7 |
| 24 | Washington | 6.8 |
| 25 | West Virginia | 6.2 |
| 21 | Wisconsin | 7.4 |
| 48 | Wyoming | 1.9 |

RANK ORDER

| RANK | STATE | PERCENT |
|------|-------|---------|
| 1 | New Jersey | 39.1 |
| 2 | Rhode Island | 30.5 |
| 3 | Massachusetts | 30.4 |
| 4 | Connecticut | 28.6 |
| 5 | Maryland | 20.4 |
| 6 | Delaware | 18.6 |
| 7 | Florida | 16.9 |
| 8 | Pennsylvania | 14.3 |
| 9 | Ohio | 14.1 |
| 10 | North Carolina | 13.6 |
| 11 | New Hampshire | 11.9 |
| 12 | Virginia | 11.7 |
| 13 | South Carolina | 11.6 |
| 14 | Georgia | 11.4 |
| 15 | Michigan | 10.8 |
| 16 | New York | 10.7 |
| 17 | California | 10.3 |
| 18 | Indiana | 10.1 |
| 19 | Tennessee | 9.5 |
| 20 | Illinois | 9.1 |
| 21 | Wisconsin | 7.4 |
| 22 | Alabama | 7.2 |
| 22 | Kentucky | 7.2 |
| 24 | Washington | 6.8 |
| 25 | Louisiana | 6.2 |
| 25 | West Virginia | 6.2 |
| 27 | Missouri | 6.0 |
| 28 | Vermont | 5.8 |
| 29 | Mississippi | 5.3 |
| 30 | Texas | 5.2 |
| 31 | Hawaii | 4.8 |
| 31 | Iowa | 4.8 |
| 33 | Arkansas | 4.7 |
| 34 | Minnesota | 4.6 |
| 35 | Oklahoma | 4.5 |
| 36 | Oregon | 4.1 |
| 37 | Colorado | 3.9 |
| 37 | Idaho | 3.9 |
| 39 | Kansas | 3.8 |
| 40 | Maine | 3.7 |
| 41 | Nevada | 3.6 |
| 41 | Utah | 3.6 |
| 43 | Arizona | 3.5 |
| 44 | Nebraska | 2.5 |
| 45 | New Mexico | 2.3 |
| 45 | North Dakota | 2.3 |
| 47 | South Dakota | 2.1 |
| 48 | Wyoming | 1.9 |
| 49 | Montana | 1.6 |
| NA | Alaska** | NA |
| | District of Columbia** | NA |

*Source: Morgan Quitno Press using data from U.S. Department of Agriculture, Natural Resources Conservation Service "National Resources Inventory" (http://www.nhq.nrcs.usda.gov/NRI/1997/) (December 2000)*
*Revised figures. Excludes Alaska and the District of Columbia. "Developed" is defined as urban or built-up areas of a quarter acre or more and rural transportation land such as highways, railroads and associated rights-of-way.*
***Not available.*

# Percent Change in Number of Acres Developed: 1992 to 1997

## National Percent Change = 12.8% Increase*

ALPHA ORDER

| RANK | STATE | PERCENT CHANGE |
|------|-------|----------------|
| 10 | Alabama | 16.3 |
| NA | Alaska** | NA |
| 36 | Arizona | 8.3 |
| 19 | Arkansas | 13.6 |
| 26 | California | 11.3 |
| 39 | Colorado | 7.3 |
| 44 | Connecticut | 4.7 |
| 24 | Delaware | 11.4 |
| 6 | Florida | 18.9 |
| 1 | Georgia | 27.4 |
| 46 | Hawaii | 3.9 |
| 17 | Idaho | 13.9 |
| 34 | Illinois | 8.4 |
| 31 | Indiana | 9.5 |
| 45 | Iowa | 4.2 |
| 42 | Kansas | 5.2 |
| 13 | Kentucky | 15.8 |
| 33 | Louisiana | 9.0 |
| 7 | Maine | 18.5 |
| 8 | Maryland | 16.8 |
| 9 | Massachusetts | 16.7 |
| 24 | Michigan | 11.4 |
| 21 | Minnesota | 11.9 |
| 10 | Mississippi | 16.3 |
| 30 | Missouri | 9.8 |
| 37 | Montana | 8.0 |
| 43 | Nebraska | 4.8 |
| 38 | Nevada | 7.5 |
| 21 | New Hampshire | 11.9 |
| 18 | New Jersey | 13.7 |
| 3 | New Mexico | 23.2 |
| 28 | New York | 11.1 |
| 14 | North Carolina | 15.1 |
| 48 | North Dakota | 3.4 |
| 27 | Ohio | 11.2 |
| 29 | Oklahoma | 10.1 |
| 32 | Oregon | 9.3 |
| 12 | Pennsylvania | 15.9 |
| 48 | Rhode Island | 3.4 |
| 4 | South Carolina | 20.9 |
| 40 | South Dakota | 6.4 |
| 5 | Tennessee | 20.4 |
| 23 | Texas | 11.6 |
| 16 | Utah | 14.0 |
| 47 | Vermont | 3.8 |
| 14 | Virginia | 15.1 |
| 20 | Washington | 13.2 |
| 2 | West Virginia | 25.4 |
| 34 | Wisconsin | 8.4 |
| 41 | Wyoming | 5.6 |

RANK ORDER

| RANK | STATE | PERCENT CHANGE |
|------|-------|----------------|
| 1 | Georgia | 27.4 |
| 2 | West Virginia | 25.4 |
| 3 | New Mexico | 23.2 |
| 4 | South Carolina | 20.9 |
| 5 | Tennessee | 20.4 |
| 6 | Florida | 18.9 |
| 7 | Maine | 18.5 |
| 8 | Maryland | 16.8 |
| 9 | Massachusetts | 16.7 |
| 10 | Alabama | 16.3 |
| 10 | Mississippi | 16.3 |
| 12 | Pennsylvania | 15.9 |
| 13 | Kentucky | 15.8 |
| 14 | North Carolina | 15.1 |
| 14 | Virginia | 15.1 |
| 16 | Utah | 14.0 |
| 17 | Idaho | 13.9 |
| 18 | New Jersey | 13.7 |
| 19 | Arkansas | 13.6 |
| 20 | Washington | 13.2 |
| 21 | Minnesota | 11.9 |
| 21 | New Hampshire | 11.9 |
| 23 | Texas | 11.6 |
| 24 | Delaware | 11.4 |
| 24 | Michigan | 11.4 |
| 26 | California | 11.3 |
| 27 | Ohio | 11.2 |
| 28 | New York | 11.1 |
| 29 | Oklahoma | 10.1 |
| 30 | Missouri | 9.8 |
| 31 | Indiana | 9.5 |
| 32 | Oregon | 9.3 |
| 33 | Louisiana | 9.0 |
| 34 | Illinois | 8.4 |
| 34 | Wisconsin | 8.4 |
| 36 | Arizona | 8.3 |
| 37 | Montana | 8.0 |
| 38 | Nevada | 7.5 |
| 39 | Colorado | 7.3 |
| 40 | South Dakota | 6.4 |
| 41 | Wyoming | 5.6 |
| 42 | Kansas | 5.2 |
| 43 | Nebraska | 4.8 |
| 44 | Connecticut | 4.7 |
| 45 | Iowa | 4.2 |
| 46 | Hawaii | 3.9 |
| 47 | Vermont | 3.8 |
| 48 | North Dakota | 3.4 |
| 48 | Rhode Island | 3.4 |
| NA | Alaska** | NA |
| | District of Columbia** | NA |

Source: Morgan Quitno Press using data from U.S. Department of Agriculture, Natural Resources Conservation Service
"National Resources Inventory" (http://www.nhq.nrcs.usda.gov/NRI/1997/) (December 2000)
*Revised figures.  Excludes Alaska and the District of Columbia.  "Developed" is defined as urban or built-up areas
of a quarter acre or more and rural transportation land such as highways, railroads and associated rights-of-way.
**Not available.

# State Parks, Recreation Areas and Natural Areas in 2000

## National Total = 5,660 Areas*

ALPHA ORDER

| RANK | STATE | AREAS | % of USA |
|------|-------|-------|----------|
| 50 | Alabama | 23 | 0.4% |
| 12 | Alaska | 138 | 2.4% |
| 45 | Arizona | 28 | 0.5% |
| 28 | Arkansas | 66 | 1.2% |
| 4 | California | 263 | 4.6% |
| 6 | Colorado | 236 | 4.2% |
| 13 | Connecticut | 130 | 2.3% |
| 47 | Delaware | 25 | 0.4% |
| 11 | Florida | 145 | 2.6% |
| 31 | Georgia | 64 | 1.1% |
| 27 | Hawaii | 67 | 1.2% |
| 46 | Idaho | 27 | 0.5% |
| 2 | Illinois | 384 | 6.8% |
| 41 | Indiana | 33 | 0.6% |
| 9 | Iowa | 174 | 3.1% |
| 48 | Kansas | 24 | 0.4% |
| 38 | Kentucky | 49 | 0.9% |
| 35 | Louisiana | 56 | 1.0% |
| 10 | Maine | 168 | 3.0% |
| 18 | Maryland | 98 | 1.7% |
| 6 | Massachusetts | 236 | 4.2% |
| 19 | Michigan | 95 | 1.7% |
| 24 | Minnesota | 79 | 1.4% |
| 44 | Mississippi | 29 | 0.5% |
| 21 | Missouri | 85 | 1.5% |
| 3 | Montana | 355 | 6.3% |
| 21 | Nebraska | 85 | 1.5% |
| 48 | Nevada | 24 | 0.4% |
| 23 | New Hampshire | 84 | 1.5% |
| 16 | New Jersey | 115 | 2.0% |
| 42 | New Mexico | 31 | 0.5% |
| 1 | New York | 651 | 11.5% |
| 34 | North Carolina | 57 | 1.0% |
| 42 | North Dakota | 31 | 0.5% |
| 26 | Ohio | 73 | 1.3% |
| 37 | Oklahoma | 51 | 0.9% |
| 8 | Oregon | 224 | 4.0% |
| 15 | Pennsylvania | 117 | 2.1% |
| 25 | Rhode Island | 74 | 1.3% |
| 33 | South Carolina | 58 | 1.0% |
| 20 | South Dakota | 86 | 1.5% |
| 17 | Tennessee | 108 | 1.9% |
| 14 | Texas | 122 | 2.2% |
| 36 | Utah | 54 | 1.0% |
| 28 | Vermont | 66 | 1.2% |
| 32 | Virginia | 61 | 1.1% |
| 4 | Washington | 263 | 4.6% |
| 39 | West Virginia | 47 | 0.8% |
| 30 | Wisconsin | 65 | 1.1% |
| 40 | Wyoming | 36 | 0.6% |

RANK ORDER

| RANK | STATE | AREAS | % of USA |
|------|-------|-------|----------|
| 1 | New York | 651 | 11.5% |
| 2 | Illinois | 384 | 6.8% |
| 3 | Montana | 355 | 6.3% |
| 4 | California | 263 | 4.6% |
| 4 | Washington | 263 | 4.6% |
| 6 | Colorado | 236 | 4.2% |
| 6 | Massachusetts | 236 | 4.2% |
| 8 | Oregon | 224 | 4.0% |
| 9 | Iowa | 174 | 3.1% |
| 10 | Maine | 168 | 3.0% |
| 11 | Florida | 145 | 2.6% |
| 12 | Alaska | 138 | 2.4% |
| 13 | Connecticut | 130 | 2.3% |
| 14 | Texas | 122 | 2.2% |
| 15 | Pennsylvania | 117 | 2.1% |
| 16 | New Jersey | 115 | 2.0% |
| 17 | Tennessee | 108 | 1.9% |
| 18 | Maryland | 98 | 1.7% |
| 19 | Michigan | 95 | 1.7% |
| 20 | South Dakota | 86 | 1.5% |
| 21 | Missouri | 85 | 1.5% |
| 21 | Nebraska | 85 | 1.5% |
| 23 | New Hampshire | 84 | 1.5% |
| 24 | Minnesota | 79 | 1.4% |
| 25 | Rhode Island | 74 | 1.3% |
| 26 | Ohio | 73 | 1.3% |
| 27 | Hawaii | 67 | 1.2% |
| 28 | Arkansas | 66 | 1.2% |
| 28 | Vermont | 66 | 1.2% |
| 30 | Wisconsin | 65 | 1.1% |
| 31 | Georgia | 64 | 1.1% |
| 32 | Virginia | 61 | 1.1% |
| 33 | South Carolina | 58 | 1.0% |
| 34 | North Carolina | 57 | 1.0% |
| 35 | Louisiana | 56 | 1.0% |
| 36 | Utah | 54 | 1.0% |
| 37 | Oklahoma | 51 | 0.9% |
| 38 | Kentucky | 49 | 0.9% |
| 39 | West Virginia | 47 | 0.8% |
| 40 | Wyoming | 36 | 0.6% |
| 41 | Indiana | 33 | 0.6% |
| 42 | New Mexico | 31 | 0.5% |
| 42 | North Dakota | 31 | 0.5% |
| 44 | Mississippi | 29 | 0.5% |
| 45 | Arizona | 28 | 0.5% |
| 46 | Idaho | 27 | 0.5% |
| 47 | Delaware | 25 | 0.4% |
| 48 | Kansas | 24 | 0.4% |
| 48 | Nevada | 24 | 0.4% |
| 50 | Alabama | 23 | 0.4% |
| | District of Columbia** | NA | NA |

Source: The National Association of State Parks Directors
    "2000 Annual Information Exchange"
*Includes state parks, recreation areas, natural areas and other areas.
**Not available.

# Visitors to State Parks and Recreational Areas in 2000

## National Total = 766,842,123 Visitors*

<table>
<tr><td colspan="4">ALPHA ORDER</td><td colspan="4">RANK ORDER</td></tr>
<tr><td>RANK</td><td>STATE</td><td>VISITORS</td><td>% of USA</td><td>RANK</td><td>STATE</td><td>VISITORS</td><td>% of USA</td></tr>
<tr><td>35</td><td>Alabama</td><td>5,922,501</td><td>0.8%</td><td>1</td><td>California</td><td>76,735,500</td><td>10.0%</td></tr>
<tr><td>41</td><td>Alaska</td><td>3,855,292</td><td>0.5%</td><td>2</td><td>New York</td><td>61,960,119</td><td>8.1%</td></tr>
<tr><td>45</td><td>Arizona</td><td>2,180,136</td><td>0.3%</td><td>3</td><td>Ohio</td><td>60,220,437</td><td>7.9%</td></tr>
<tr><td>33</td><td>Arkansas</td><td>6,460,116</td><td>0.8%</td><td>4</td><td>Washington</td><td>48,137,786</td><td>6.3%</td></tr>
<tr><td>1</td><td>California</td><td>76,735,500</td><td>10.0%</td><td>5</td><td>Illinois</td><td>41,891,391</td><td>5.5%</td></tr>
<tr><td>24</td><td>Colorado</td><td>9,508,291</td><td>1.2%</td><td>6</td><td>Oregon</td><td>38,752,416</td><td>5.1%</td></tr>
<tr><td>28</td><td>Connecticut</td><td>7,958,945</td><td>1.0%</td><td>7</td><td>Pennsylvania</td><td>36,019,224</td><td>4.7%</td></tr>
<tr><td>40</td><td>Delaware</td><td>3,976,706</td><td>0.5%</td><td>8</td><td>Tennessee</td><td>31,833,942</td><td>4.2%</td></tr>
<tr><td>18</td><td>Florida</td><td>14,645,202</td><td>1.9%</td><td>9</td><td>Michigan</td><td>27,745,450</td><td>3.6%</td></tr>
<tr><td>14</td><td>Georgia</td><td>15,344,111</td><td>2.0%</td><td>10</td><td>Texas</td><td>21,445,680</td><td>2.8%</td></tr>
<tr><td>15</td><td>Hawaii</td><td>15,071,000</td><td>2.0%</td><td>11</td><td>Indiana</td><td>18,651,721</td><td>2.4%</td></tr>
<tr><td>44</td><td>Idaho</td><td>2,354,402</td><td>0.3%</td><td>12</td><td>Missouri</td><td>17,708,509</td><td>2.3%</td></tr>
<tr><td>5</td><td>Illinois</td><td>41,891,391</td><td>5.5%</td><td>13</td><td>Oklahoma</td><td>15,546,393</td><td>2.0%</td></tr>
<tr><td>11</td><td>Indiana</td><td>18,651,721</td><td>2.4%</td><td>14</td><td>Georgia</td><td>15,344,111</td><td>2.0%</td></tr>
<tr><td>17</td><td>Iowa</td><td>14,736,022</td><td>1.9%</td><td>15</td><td>Hawaii</td><td>15,071,000</td><td>2.0%</td></tr>
<tr><td>30</td><td>Kansas</td><td>7,100,000</td><td>0.9%</td><td>16</td><td>New Jersey</td><td>15,018,648</td><td>2.0%</td></tr>
<tr><td>29</td><td>Kentucky</td><td>7,575,000</td><td>1.0%</td><td>17</td><td>Iowa</td><td>14,736,022</td><td>1.9%</td></tr>
<tr><td>48</td><td>Louisiana</td><td>1,468,802</td><td>0.2%</td><td>18</td><td>Florida</td><td>14,645,202</td><td>1.9%</td></tr>
<tr><td>43</td><td>Maine</td><td>2,453,959</td><td>0.3%</td><td>19</td><td>Wisconsin</td><td>14,181,383</td><td>1.8%</td></tr>
<tr><td>22</td><td>Maryland</td><td>10,779,544</td><td>1.4%</td><td>20</td><td>Massachusetts</td><td>13,496,687</td><td>1.8%</td></tr>
<tr><td>20</td><td>Massachusetts</td><td>13,496,687</td><td>1.8%</td><td>21</td><td>North Carolina</td><td>13,268,971</td><td>1.7%</td></tr>
<tr><td>9</td><td>Michigan</td><td>27,745,450</td><td>3.6%</td><td>22</td><td>Maryland</td><td>10,779,544</td><td>1.4%</td></tr>
<tr><td>26</td><td>Minnesota</td><td>8,406,793</td><td>1.1%</td><td>23</td><td>South Carolina</td><td>9,563,510</td><td>1.2%</td></tr>
<tr><td>39</td><td>Mississippi</td><td>4,277,307</td><td>0.6%</td><td>24</td><td>Colorado</td><td>9,508,291</td><td>1.2%</td></tr>
<tr><td>12</td><td>Missouri</td><td>17,708,509</td><td>2.3%</td><td>25</td><td>Nebraska</td><td>9,368,428</td><td>1.2%</td></tr>
<tr><td>47</td><td>Montana</td><td>1,506,835</td><td>0.2%</td><td>26</td><td>Minnesota</td><td>8,406,793</td><td>1.1%</td></tr>
<tr><td>25</td><td>Nebraska</td><td>9,368,428</td><td>1.2%</td><td>27</td><td>West Virginia</td><td>8,249,096</td><td>1.1%</td></tr>
<tr><td>42</td><td>Nevada</td><td>2,666,079</td><td>0.3%</td><td>28</td><td>Connecticut</td><td>7,958,945</td><td>1.0%</td></tr>
<tr><td>38</td><td>New Hampshire</td><td>4,361,478</td><td>0.6%</td><td>29</td><td>Kentucky</td><td>7,575,000</td><td>1.0%</td></tr>
<tr><td>16</td><td>New Jersey</td><td>15,018,648</td><td>2.0%</td><td>30</td><td>Kansas</td><td>7,100,000</td><td>0.9%</td></tr>
<tr><td>37</td><td>New Mexico</td><td>4,725,298</td><td>0.6%</td><td>31</td><td>Utah</td><td>6,957,511</td><td>0.9%</td></tr>
<tr><td>2</td><td>New York</td><td>61,960,119</td><td>8.1%</td><td>32</td><td>South Dakota</td><td>6,843,188</td><td>0.9%</td></tr>
<tr><td>21</td><td>North Carolina</td><td>13,268,971</td><td>1.7%</td><td>33</td><td>Arkansas</td><td>6,460,116</td><td>0.8%</td></tr>
<tr><td>49</td><td>North Dakota</td><td>1,068,424</td><td>0.1%</td><td>34</td><td>Rhode Island</td><td>6,332,073</td><td>0.8%</td></tr>
<tr><td>3</td><td>Ohio</td><td>60,220,437</td><td>7.9%</td><td>35</td><td>Alabama</td><td>5,922,501</td><td>0.8%</td></tr>
<tr><td>13</td><td>Oklahoma</td><td>15,546,393</td><td>2.0%</td><td>36</td><td>Virginia</td><td>5,519,760</td><td>0.7%</td></tr>
<tr><td>6</td><td>Oregon</td><td>38,752,416</td><td>5.1%</td><td>37</td><td>New Mexico</td><td>4,725,298</td><td>0.6%</td></tr>
<tr><td>7</td><td>Pennsylvania</td><td>36,019,224</td><td>4.7%</td><td>38</td><td>New Hampshire</td><td>4,361,478</td><td>0.6%</td></tr>
<tr><td>34</td><td>Rhode Island</td><td>6,332,073</td><td>0.8%</td><td>39</td><td>Mississippi</td><td>4,277,307</td><td>0.6%</td></tr>
<tr><td>23</td><td>South Carolina</td><td>9,563,510</td><td>1.2%</td><td>40</td><td>Delaware</td><td>3,976,706</td><td>0.5%</td></tr>
<tr><td>32</td><td>South Dakota</td><td>6,843,188</td><td>0.9%</td><td>41</td><td>Alaska</td><td>3,855,292</td><td>0.5%</td></tr>
<tr><td>8</td><td>Tennessee</td><td>31,833,942</td><td>4.2%</td><td>42</td><td>Nevada</td><td>2,666,079</td><td>0.3%</td></tr>
<tr><td>10</td><td>Texas</td><td>21,445,680</td><td>2.8%</td><td>43</td><td>Maine</td><td>2,453,959</td><td>0.3%</td></tr>
<tr><td>31</td><td>Utah</td><td>6,957,511</td><td>0.9%</td><td>44</td><td>Idaho</td><td>2,354,402</td><td>0.3%</td></tr>
<tr><td>50</td><td>Vermont</td><td>834,350</td><td>0.1%</td><td>45</td><td>Arizona</td><td>2,180,136</td><td>0.3%</td></tr>
<tr><td>36</td><td>Virginia</td><td>5,519,760</td><td>0.7%</td><td>46</td><td>Wyoming</td><td>2,157,707</td><td>0.3%</td></tr>
<tr><td>4</td><td>Washington</td><td>48,137,786</td><td>6.3%</td><td>47</td><td>Montana</td><td>1,506,835</td><td>0.2%</td></tr>
<tr><td>27</td><td>West Virginia</td><td>8,249,096</td><td>1.1%</td><td>48</td><td>Louisiana</td><td>1,468,802</td><td>0.2%</td></tr>
<tr><td>19</td><td>Wisconsin</td><td>14,181,383</td><td>1.8%</td><td>49</td><td>North Dakota</td><td>1,068,424</td><td>0.1%</td></tr>
<tr><td>46</td><td>Wyoming</td><td>2,157,707</td><td>0.3%</td><td>50</td><td>Vermont</td><td>834,350</td><td>0.1%</td></tr>
<tr><td></td><td></td><td></td><td></td><td></td><td>District of Columbia**</td><td>NA</td><td>NA</td></tr>
</table>

Source: The National Association of State Parks Directors
   "2000 Annual Information Exchange"
*Includes state parks, recreation areas and natural areas.  Includes day and overnight visitors.
**Not available.

# IX. GOVERNMENT FINANCE: FEDERAL

# Internal Revenue Service Gross Collections in 1998

## National Total = $1,769,408,739,000*

ALPHA ORDER

| RANK | STATE | COLLECTIONS | % of USA |
|------|-------|-------------|----------|
| 26 | Alabama | $17,152,680,000 | 1.0% |
| 47 | Alaska | 2,684,859,000 | 0.2% |
| 23 | Arizona | 20,766,004,000 | 1.2% |
| 31 | Arkansas | 14,758,616,000 | 0.8% |
| 1 | California | 199,106,248,000 | 11.3% |
| 22 | Colorado | 29,722,488,000 | 1.7% |
| 18 | Connecticut | 34,954,399,000 | 2.0% |
| 36 | Delaware | 8,518,240,000 | 0.5% |
| 5 | Florida | 80,937,975,000 | 4.6% |
| 11 | Georgia | 50,774,604,000 | 2.9% |
| 43 | Hawaii | 4,690,970,000 | 0.3% |
| 41 | Idaho | 5,346,069,000 | 0.3% |
| 4 | Illinois | 104,534,765,000 | 5.9% |
| 21 | Indiana | 31,622,947,000 | 1.8% |
| 32 | Iowa | 13,422,663,000 | 0.8% |
| 30 | Kansas | 15,320,021,000 | 0.9% |
| 28 | Kentucky | 16,537,667,000 | 0.9% |
| 24 | Louisiana | 18,557,393,000 | 1.0% |
| 44 | Maine | 4,624,951,000 | 0.3% |
| 13 | Maryland** | 45,983,274,000 | 2.6% |
| 10 | Massachusetts | 52,617,476,000 | 3.0% |
| 9 | Michigan | 67,368,949,000 | 3.8% |
| 12 | Minnesota | 46,902,395,000 | 2.7% |
| 37 | Mississippi | 8,385,437,000 | 0.5% |
| 15 | Missouri | 39,701,056,000 | 2.2% |
| 46 | Montana | 2,723,967,000 | 0.2% |
| 33 | Nebraska | 12,103,297,000 | 0.7% |
| 34 | Nevada | 9,506,900,000 | 0.5% |
| 39 | New Hampshire | 6,289,975,000 | 0.4% |
| 7 | New Jersey | 78,929,409,000 | 4.5% |
| 40 | New Mexico | 5,602,113,000 | 0.3% |
| 2 | New York | 165,747,347,000 | 9.4% |
| 16 | North Carolina | 38,320,349,000 | 2.2% |
| 49 | North Dakota | 2,517,333,000 | 0.1% |
| 8 | Ohio | 77,527,507,000 | 4.4% |
| 25 | Oklahoma | 17,549,708,000 | 1.0% |
| 27 | Oregon | 16,818,174,000 | 1.0% |
| 6 | Pennsylvania | 80,341,881,000 | 4.5% |
| 38 | Rhode Island | 6,669,034,000 | 0.4% |
| 29 | South Carolina | 15,743,615,000 | 0.9% |
| 45 | South Dakota | 3,071,404,000 | 0.2% |
| 20 | Tennessee | 31,955,521,000 | 1.8% |
| 3 | Texas | 122,356,312,000 | 6.9% |
| 35 | Utah | 9,209,126,000 | 0.5% |
| 48 | Vermont | 2,614,490,000 | 0.1% |
| 14 | Virginia | 39,897,986,000 | 2.3% |
| 17 | Washington | 36,981,487,000 | 2.1% |
| 42 | West Virginia | 4,808,922,000 | 0.3% |
| 19 | Wisconsin | 32,371,429,000 | 1.8% |
| 50 | Wyoming | 2,307,868,000 | 0.1% |

RANK ORDER

| RANK | STATE | COLLECTIONS | % of USA |
|------|-------|-------------|----------|
| 1 | California | $199,106,248,000 | 11.3% |
| 2 | New York | 165,747,347,000 | 9.4% |
| 3 | Texas | 122,356,312,000 | 6.9% |
| 4 | Illinois | 104,534,765,000 | 5.9% |
| 5 | Florida | 80,937,975,000 | 4.6% |
| 6 | Pennsylvania | 80,341,881,000 | 4.5% |
| 7 | New Jersey | 78,929,409,000 | 4.5% |
| 8 | Ohio | 77,527,507,000 | 4.4% |
| 9 | Michigan | 67,368,949,000 | 3.8% |
| 10 | Massachusetts | 52,617,476,000 | 3.0% |
| 11 | Georgia | 50,774,604,000 | 2.9% |
| 12 | Minnesota | 46,902,395,000 | 2.7% |
| 13 | Maryland** | 45,983,274,000 | 2.6% |
| 14 | Virginia | 39,897,986,000 | 2.3% |
| 15 | Missouri | 39,701,056,000 | 2.2% |
| 16 | North Carolina | 38,320,349,000 | 2.2% |
| 17 | Washington | 36,981,487,000 | 2.1% |
| 18 | Connecticut | 34,954,399,000 | 2.0% |
| 19 | Wisconsin | 32,371,429,000 | 1.8% |
| 20 | Tennessee | 31,955,521,000 | 1.8% |
| 21 | Indiana | 31,622,947,000 | 1.8% |
| 22 | Colorado | 29,722,488,000 | 1.7% |
| 23 | Arizona | 20,766,004,000 | 1.2% |
| 24 | Louisiana | 18,557,393,000 | 1.0% |
| 25 | Oklahoma | 17,549,708,000 | 1.0% |
| 26 | Alabama | 17,152,680,000 | 1.0% |
| 27 | Oregon | 16,818,174,000 | 1.0% |
| 28 | Kentucky | 16,537,667,000 | 0.9% |
| 29 | South Carolina | 15,743,615,000 | 0.9% |
| 30 | Kansas | 15,320,021,000 | 0.9% |
| 31 | Arkansas | 14,758,616,000 | 0.8% |
| 32 | Iowa | 13,422,663,000 | 0.8% |
| 33 | Nebraska | 12,103,297,000 | 0.7% |
| 34 | Nevada | 9,506,900,000 | 0.5% |
| 35 | Utah | 9,209,126,000 | 0.5% |
| 36 | Delaware | 8,518,240,000 | 0.5% |
| 37 | Mississippi | 8,385,437,000 | 0.5% |
| 38 | Rhode Island | 6,669,034,000 | 0.4% |
| 39 | New Hampshire | 6,289,975,000 | 0.4% |
| 40 | New Mexico | 5,602,113,000 | 0.3% |
| 41 | Idaho | 5,346,069,000 | 0.3% |
| 42 | West Virginia | 4,808,922,000 | 0.3% |
| 43 | Hawaii | 4,690,970,000 | 0.3% |
| 44 | Maine | 4,624,951,000 | 0.3% |
| 45 | South Dakota | 3,071,404,000 | 0.2% |
| 46 | Montana | 2,723,967,000 | 0.2% |
| 47 | Alaska | 2,684,859,000 | 0.2% |
| 48 | Vermont | 2,614,490,000 | 0.1% |
| 49 | North Dakota | 2,517,333,000 | 0.1% |
| 50 | Wyoming | 2,307,868,000 | 0.1% |
| | District of Columbia** | NA | NA |

Source: U.S. Department of the Treasury, Internal Revenue Service
"Internal Revenue Gross Collections" (http://www.irs.gov/tax_stats/soi/other_tc.html)
*Total includes $12,451,437,000 from U.S. citizens abroad and other miscellaneous returns not shown separately.
**Maryland's figure includes the District of Columbia.

# Federal Individual Income Tax Collections in 1998

## National Total = $1,485,865,050,000*

ALPHA ORDER

| RANK | STATE | COLLECTIONS | % of USA |
|---|---|---|---|
| 25 | Alabama | $14,898,138,061 | 1.0% |
| 46 | Alaska | 2,522,057,676 | 0.2% |
| 23 | Arizona | 17,587,099,741 | 1.2% |
| 32 | Arkansas | 11,045,493,441 | 0.7% |
| 1 | California | 169,353,210,750 | 11.4% |
| 22 | Colorado | 27,102,523,526 | 1.8% |
| 18 | Connecticut | 28,314,191,741 | 1.9% |
| 38 | Delaware | 5,677,666,371 | 0.4% |
| 5 | Florida | 73,300,997,713 | 4.9% |
| 12 | Georgia | 39,852,204,592 | 2.7% |
| 44 | Hawaii | 4,123,307,425 | 0.3% |
| 41 | Idaho | 4,762,145,596 | 0.3% |
| 4 | Illinois | 85,249,823,205 | 5.7% |
| 19 | Indiana | 28,191,255,489 | 1.9% |
| 31 | Iowa | 11,353,145,881 | 0.8% |
| 29 | Kansas | 12,798,575,225 | 0.9% |
| 27 | Kentucky | 14,330,974,331 | 1.0% |
| 24 | Louisiana | 16,458,101,387 | 1.1% |
| 43 | Maine | 4,165,905,764 | 0.3% |
| 11 | Maryland** | 40,729,497,394 | 2.7% |
| 10 | Massachusetts | 46,116,571,516 | 3.1% |
| 9 | Michigan | 59,353,357,158 | 4.0% |
| 13 | Minnesota | 39,471,901,629 | 2.7% |
| 36 | Mississippi | 7,457,021,510 | 0.5% |
| 17 | Missouri | 32,494,007,368 | 2.2% |
| 47 | Montana | 2,475,872,831 | 0.2% |
| 33 | Nebraska | 9,190,664,643 | 0.6% |
| 34 | Nevada | 8,519,764,467 | 0.6% |
| 37 | New Hampshire | 5,786,474,295 | 0.4% |
| 7 | New Jersey | 65,451,052,585 | 4.4% |
| 40 | New Mexico | 5,185,688,063 | 0.3% |
| 2 | New York | 138,114,076,551 | 9.3% |
| 16 | North Carolina | 32,543,196,105 | 2.2% |
| 49 | North Dakota | 2,297,613,820 | 0.2% |
| 8 | Ohio | 63,543,579,911 | 4.3% |
| 30 | Oklahoma | 12,646,290,898 | 0.9% |
| 26 | Oregon | 14,896,813,919 | 1.0% |
| 6 | Pennsylvania | 67,407,133,794 | 4.5% |
| 39 | Rhode Island | 5,319,782,790 | 0.4% |
| 28 | South Carolina | 14,294,942,893 | 1.0% |
| 45 | South Dakota | 2,720,382,959 | 0.2% |
| 20 | Tennessee | 27,941,591,512 | 1.9% |
| 3 | Texas | 94,404,751,394 | 6.4% |
| 35 | Utah | 8,227,165,366 | 0.6% |
| 48 | Vermont | 2,322,624,014 | 0.2% |
| 15 | Virginia | 33,164,427,129 | 2.2% |
| 14 | Washington | 33,165,428,836 | 2.2% |
| 42 | West Virginia | 4,338,353,104 | 0.3% |
| 21 | Wisconsin | 27,568,466,176 | 1.9% |
| 50 | Wyoming | 1,906,714,945 | 0.1% |

RANK ORDER

| RANK | STATE | COLLECTIONS | % of USA |
|---|---|---|---|
| 1 | California | $169,353,210,750 | 11.4% |
| 2 | New York | 138,114,076,551 | 9.3% |
| 3 | Texas | 94,404,751,394 | 6.4% |
| 4 | Illinois | 85,249,823,205 | 5.7% |
| 5 | Florida | 73,300,997,713 | 4.9% |
| 6 | Pennsylvania | 67,407,133,794 | 4.5% |
| 7 | New Jersey | 65,451,052,585 | 4.4% |
| 8 | Ohio | 63,543,579,911 | 4.3% |
| 9 | Michigan | 59,353,357,158 | 4.0% |
| 10 | Massachusetts | 46,116,571,516 | 3.1% |
| 11 | Maryland** | 40,729,497,394 | 2.7% |
| 12 | Georgia | 39,852,204,592 | 2.7% |
| 13 | Minnesota | 39,471,901,629 | 2.7% |
| 14 | Washington | 33,165,428,836 | 2.2% |
| 15 | Virginia | 33,164,427,129 | 2.2% |
| 16 | North Carolina | 32,543,196,105 | 2.2% |
| 17 | Missouri | 32,494,007,368 | 2.2% |
| 18 | Connecticut | 28,314,191,741 | 1.9% |
| 19 | Indiana | 28,191,255,489 | 1.9% |
| 20 | Tennessee | 27,941,591,512 | 1.9% |
| 21 | Wisconsin | 27,568,466,176 | 1.9% |
| 22 | Colorado | 27,102,523,526 | 1.8% |
| 23 | Arizona | 17,587,099,741 | 1.2% |
| 24 | Louisiana | 16,458,101,387 | 1.1% |
| 25 | Alabama | 14,898,138,061 | 1.0% |
| 26 | Oregon | 14,896,813,919 | 1.0% |
| 27 | Kentucky | 14,330,974,331 | 1.0% |
| 28 | South Carolina | 14,294,942,893 | 1.0% |
| 29 | Kansas | 12,798,575,225 | 0.9% |
| 30 | Oklahoma | 12,646,290,898 | 0.9% |
| 31 | Iowa | 11,353,145,881 | 0.8% |
| 32 | Arkansas | 11,045,493,441 | 0.7% |
| 33 | Nebraska | 9,190,664,643 | 0.6% |
| 34 | Nevada | 8,519,764,467 | 0.6% |
| 35 | Utah | 8,227,165,366 | 0.6% |
| 36 | Mississippi | 7,457,021,510 | 0.5% |
| 37 | New Hampshire | 5,786,474,295 | 0.4% |
| 38 | Delaware | 5,677,666,371 | 0.4% |
| 39 | Rhode Island | 5,319,782,790 | 0.4% |
| 40 | New Mexico | 5,185,688,063 | 0.3% |
| 41 | Idaho | 4,762,145,596 | 0.3% |
| 42 | West Virginia | 4,338,353,104 | 0.3% |
| 43 | Maine | 4,165,905,764 | 0.3% |
| 44 | Hawaii | 4,123,307,425 | 0.3% |
| 45 | South Dakota | 2,720,382,959 | 0.2% |
| 46 | Alaska | 2,522,057,676 | 0.2% |
| 47 | Montana | 2,475,872,831 | 0.2% |
| 48 | Vermont | 2,322,624,014 | 0.2% |
| 49 | North Dakota | 2,297,613,820 | 0.2% |
| 50 | Wyoming | 1,906,714,945 | 0.1% |
| | District of Columbia** | NA | NA |

Source: U.S. Department of the Treasury, Internal Revenue Service
"Internal Revenue Gross Collections" (http://www.irs.gov/tax_stats/soi/other_tc.html)
*Total includes $5,723,022,321 from U.S. citizens abroad and other miscellaneous returns not shown separately.
**Maryland's figure includes the District of Columbia.

# Average Revenue Collection per Federal Individual Income Tax Return in 1998

## National Average = $12,080 per Return*

ALPHA ORDER

| RANK | STATE | AVERAGE |
|------|-------|---------|
| 42 | Alabama | $7,992 |
| 45 | Alaska | 7,350 |
| 35 | Arizona | 8,938 |
| 26 | Arkansas | 10,218 |
| 13 | California | 12,241 |
| 9 | Colorado | 14,274 |
| 1 | Connecticut | 17,681 |
| 5 | Delaware | 15,924 |
| 24 | Florida | 10,631 |
| 15 | Georgia | 11,815 |
| 44 | Hawaii | 7,477 |
| 32 | Idaho | 9,139 |
| 7 | Illinois | 15,338 |
| 25 | Indiana | 10,355 |
| 36 | Iowa | 8,624 |
| 23 | Kansas | 10,884 |
| 37 | Kentucky | 8,609 |
| 33 | Louisiana | 9,017 |
| 46 | Maine | 7,255 |
| 8 | Maryland** | 14,575 |
| 6 | Massachusetts | 15,591 |
| 10 | Michigan | 13,413 |
| 2 | Minnesota | 17,633 |
| 48 | Mississippi | 6,547 |
| 11 | Missouri | 13,241 |
| 49 | Montana | 6,122 |
| 17 | Nebraska | 11,703 |
| 27 | Nevada | 10,169 |
| 29 | New Hampshire | 9,874 |
| 4 | New Jersey | 16,957 |
| 47 | New Mexico | 6,858 |
| 3 | New York | 17,024 |
| 30 | North Carolina | 9,405 |
| 43 | North Dakota | 7,647 |
| 16 | Ohio | 11,712 |
| 34 | Oklahoma | 8,954 |
| 28 | Oregon | 9,911 |
| 14 | Pennsylvania | 12,067 |
| 18 | Rhode Island | 11,471 |
| 39 | South Carolina | 8,327 |
| 41 | South Dakota | 7,997 |
| 19 | Tennessee | 11,371 |
| 20 | Texas | 11,176 |
| 31 | Utah | 9,394 |
| 40 | Vermont | 8,231 |
| 22 | Virginia | 10,968 |
| 12 | Washington | 12,711 |
| 50 | West Virginia | 5,949 |
| 21 | Wisconsin | 11,127 |
| 38 | Wyoming | 8,414 |

RANK ORDER

| RANK | STATE | AVERAGE |
|------|-------|---------|
| 1 | Connecticut | $17,681 |
| 2 | Minnesota | 17,633 |
| 3 | New York | 17,024 |
| 4 | New Jersey | 16,957 |
| 5 | Delaware | 15,924 |
| 6 | Massachusetts | 15,591 |
| 7 | Illinois | 15,338 |
| 8 | Maryland** | 14,575 |
| 9 | Colorado | 14,274 |
| 10 | Michigan | 13,413 |
| 11 | Missouri | 13,241 |
| 12 | Washington | 12,711 |
| 13 | California | 12,241 |
| 14 | Pennsylvania | 12,067 |
| 15 | Georgia | 11,815 |
| 16 | Ohio | 11,712 |
| 17 | Nebraska | 11,703 |
| 18 | Rhode Island | 11,471 |
| 19 | Tennessee | 11,371 |
| 20 | Texas | 11,176 |
| 21 | Wisconsin | 11,127 |
| 22 | Virginia | 10,968 |
| 23 | Kansas | 10,884 |
| 24 | Florida | 10,631 |
| 25 | Indiana | 10,355 |
| 26 | Arkansas | 10,218 |
| 27 | Nevada | 10,169 |
| 28 | Oregon | 9,911 |
| 29 | New Hampshire | 9,874 |
| 30 | North Carolina | 9,405 |
| 31 | Utah | 9,394 |
| 32 | Idaho | 9,139 |
| 33 | Louisiana | 9,017 |
| 34 | Oklahoma | 8,954 |
| 35 | Arizona | 8,938 |
| 36 | Iowa | 8,624 |
| 37 | Kentucky | 8,609 |
| 38 | Wyoming | 8,414 |
| 39 | South Carolina | 8,327 |
| 40 | Vermont | 8,231 |
| 41 | South Dakota | 7,997 |
| 42 | Alabama | 7,992 |
| 43 | North Dakota | 7,647 |
| 44 | Hawaii | 7,477 |
| 45 | Alaska | 7,350 |
| 46 | Maine | 7,255 |
| 47 | New Mexico | 6,858 |
| 48 | Mississippi | 6,547 |
| 49 | Montana | 6,122 |
| 50 | West Virginia | 5,949 |

District of Columbia**      NA

Source: Morgan Quitno Press using data from U.S. Department of the Treasury, Internal Revenue Service
"Internal Revenue Gross Collections" (http://www.irs.gov/tax_stats/soi/other_tc.html) and
"Number of Returns Filed" (http://www.irs.gov/tax_stats/soi/other_nr.html)
*Total includes collections and returns from U.S. citizens abroad and other miscellaneous returns not shown separately.
**Maryland's figure includes the District of Columbia.

# Adjusted Gross Income in 1998

## National Total = $5,381,508,195,000*

ALPHA ORDER

ALPHA ORDER

| RANK | STATE | A.G.I. | % of USA |
|------|-------|--------|----------|
| 24 | Alabama | $66,477,023,000 | 1.2% |
| 46 | Alaska | 12,585,446,000 | 0.2% |
| 23 | Arizona | 84,085,281,000 | 1.6% |
| 34 | Arkansas | 35,790,307,000 | 0.7% |
| 1 | California | 662,213,474,000 | 12.3% |
| 22 | Colorado | 89,914,628,000 | 1.7% |
| 19 | Connecticut | 99,009,753,000 | 1.8% |
| 44 | Delaware | 16,251,783,000 | 0.3% |
| 4 | Florida | 298,975,854,000 | 5.6% |
| 12 | Georgia | 144,775,467,000 | 2.7% |
| 40 | Hawaii | 20,874,106,000 | 0.4% |
| 43 | Idaho | 18,761,513,000 | 0.3% |
| 5 | Illinois | 265,944,914,000 | 4.9% |
| 16 | Indiana | 109,635,954,000 | 2.0% |
| 29 | Iowa | 49,309,047,000 | 0.9% |
| 31 | Kansas | 48,374,124,000 | 0.9% |
| 28 | Kentucky | 60,044,619,000 | 1.1% |
| 25 | Louisiana | 64,331,671,000 | 1.2% |
| 41 | Maine | 20,600,117,000 | 0.4% |
| 15 | Maryland | 118,590,440,000 | 2.2% |
| 10 | Massachusetts | 156,029,895,000 | 2.9% |
| 9 | Michigan | 196,297,150,000 | 3.6% |
| 18 | Minnesota | 103,136,590,000 | 1.9% |
| 33 | Mississippi | 35,837,358,000 | 0.7% |
| 20 | Missouri | 96,350,012,000 | 1.8% |
| 45 | Montana | 12,696,338,000 | 0.2% |
| 36 | Nebraska | 30,330,132,000 | 0.6% |
| 32 | Nevada | 40,372,767,000 | 0.8% |
| 37 | New Hampshire | 27,685,270,000 | 0.5% |
| 7 | New Jersey | 212,726,616,000 | 4.0% |
| 38 | New Mexico | 25,134,158,000 | 0.5% |
| 2 | New York | 406,380,576,000 | 7.6% |
| 13 | North Carolina | 136,960,436,000 | 2.5% |
| 49 | North Dakota | 9,663,534,000 | 0.2% |
| 8 | Ohio | 211,365,125,000 | 3.9% |
| 30 | Oklahoma | 48,921,751,000 | 0.9% |
| 27 | Oregon | 60,751,301,000 | 1.1% |
| 6 | Pennsylvania | 233,941,334,000 | 4.3% |
| 42 | Rhode Island | 19,581,453,000 | 0.4% |
| 26 | South Carolina | 62,046,607,000 | 1.2% |
| 47 | South Dakota | 11,489,256,000 | 0.2% |
| 21 | Tennessee | 93,660,048,000 | 1.7% |
| 3 | Texas | 356,996,730,000 | 6.6% |
| 35 | Utah | 34,954,436,000 | 0.6% |
| 48 | Vermont | 10,797,468,000 | 0.2% |
| 11 | Virginia | 145,882,225,000 | 2.7% |
| 14 | Washington | 126,664,857,000 | 2.4% |
| 39 | West Virginia | 23,574,268,000 | 0.4% |
| 17 | Wisconsin | 103,178,696,000 | 1.9% |
| 50 | Wyoming | 9,382,037,000 | 0.2% |

RANK ORDER

| RANK | STATE | A.G.I. | % of USA |
|------|-------|--------|----------|
| 1 | California | $662,213,474,000 | 12.3% |
| 2 | New York | 406,380,576,000 | 7.6% |
| 3 | Texas | 356,996,730,000 | 6.6% |
| 4 | Florida | 298,975,854,000 | 5.6% |
| 5 | Illinois | 265,944,914,000 | 4.9% |
| 6 | Pennsylvania | 233,941,334,000 | 4.3% |
| 7 | New Jersey | 212,726,616,000 | 4.0% |
| 8 | Ohio | 211,365,125,000 | 3.9% |
| 9 | Michigan | 196,297,150,000 | 3.6% |
| 10 | Massachusetts | 156,029,895,000 | 2.9% |
| 11 | Virginia | 145,882,225,000 | 2.7% |
| 12 | Georgia | 144,775,467,000 | 2.7% |
| 13 | North Carolina | 136,960,436,000 | 2.5% |
| 14 | Washington | 126,664,857,000 | 2.4% |
| 15 | Maryland | 118,590,440,000 | 2.2% |
| 16 | Indiana | 109,635,954,000 | 2.0% |
| 17 | Wisconsin | 103,178,696,000 | 1.9% |
| 18 | Minnesota | 103,136,590,000 | 1.9% |
| 19 | Connecticut | 99,009,753,000 | 1.8% |
| 20 | Missouri | 96,350,012,000 | 1.8% |
| 21 | Tennessee | 93,660,048,000 | 1.7% |
| 22 | Colorado | 89,914,628,000 | 1.7% |
| 23 | Arizona | 84,085,281,000 | 1.6% |
| 24 | Alabama | 66,477,023,000 | 1.2% |
| 25 | Louisiana | 64,331,671,000 | 1.2% |
| 26 | South Carolina | 62,046,607,000 | 1.2% |
| 27 | Oregon | 60,751,301,000 | 1.1% |
| 28 | Kentucky | 60,044,619,000 | 1.1% |
| 29 | Iowa | 49,309,047,000 | 0.9% |
| 30 | Oklahoma | 48,921,751,000 | 0.9% |
| 31 | Kansas | 48,374,124,000 | 0.9% |
| 32 | Nevada | 40,372,767,000 | 0.8% |
| 33 | Mississippi | 35,837,358,000 | 0.7% |
| 34 | Arkansas | 35,790,307,000 | 0.7% |
| 35 | Utah | 34,954,436,000 | 0.6% |
| 36 | Nebraska | 30,330,132,000 | 0.6% |
| 37 | New Hampshire | 27,685,270,000 | 0.5% |
| 38 | New Mexico | 25,134,158,000 | 0.5% |
| 39 | West Virginia | 23,574,268,000 | 0.4% |
| 40 | Hawaii | 20,874,106,000 | 0.4% |
| 41 | Maine | 20,600,117,000 | 0.4% |
| 42 | Rhode Island | 19,581,453,000 | 0.4% |
| 43 | Idaho | 18,761,513,000 | 0.3% |
| 44 | Delaware | 16,251,783,000 | 0.3% |
| 45 | Montana | 12,696,338,000 | 0.2% |
| 46 | Alaska | 12,585,446,000 | 0.2% |
| 47 | South Dakota | 11,489,256,000 | 0.2% |
| 48 | Vermont | 10,797,468,000 | 0.2% |
| 49 | North Dakota | 9,663,534,000 | 0.2% |
| 50 | Wyoming | 9,382,037,000 | 0.2% |
| | District of Columbia | 13,461,355,000 | 0.3% |

*Source: U.S. Department of the Treasury, Internal Revenue Service*
*"Individual Tax Statistics" (http://www.irs.gov/tax_stats/soi/ind_st.html)*
*Total includes $38,712,895,000 from U.S. citizens abroad and other miscellaneous returns not shown separately.*

# Per Capita Adjusted Gross Income in 1998

## National Per Capita = $19,770*

ALPHA ORDER

| RANK | STATE | PER CAPITA | | RANK | STATE | PER CAPITA |
|---|---|---|---|---|---|---|
| 40 | Alabama | $15,278 | | 1 | Connecticut | $30,254 |
| 14 | Alaska | 20,457 | | 2 | New Jersey | 26,277 |
| 31 | Arizona | 18,016 | | 3 | Massachusetts | 25,394 |
| 48 | Arkansas | 14,101 | | 4 | New Hampshire | 23,347 |
| 15 | California | 20,262 | | 5 | Nevada | 23,153 |
| 7 | Colorado | 22,654 | | 6 | Maryland | 23,117 |
| 1 | Connecticut | 30,254 | | 7 | Colorado | 22,654 |
| 11 | Delaware | 21,842 | | 8 | New York | 22,379 |
| 16 | Florida | 20,054 | | 9 | Washington | 22,269 |
| 22 | Georgia | 18,958 | | 10 | Illinois | 22,034 |
| 33 | Hawaii | 17,534 | | 11 | Delaware | 21,842 |
| 42 | Idaho | 15,242 | | 12 | Minnesota | 21,821 |
| 10 | Illinois | 22,034 | | 13 | Virginia | 21,487 |
| 24 | Indiana | 18,558 | | 14 | Alaska | 20,457 |
| 35 | Iowa | 17,235 | | 15 | California | 20,262 |
| 26 | Kansas | 18,333 | | 16 | Florida | 20,054 |
| 41 | Kentucky | 15,262 | | 17 | Michigan | 19,989 |
| 44 | Louisiana | 14,746 | | 18 | Rhode Island | 19,825 |
| 37 | Maine | 16,512 | | 19 | Wisconsin | 19,758 |
| 6 | Maryland | 23,117 | | 20 | Wyoming | 19,544 |
| 3 | Massachusetts | 25,394 | | 21 | Pennsylvania | 19,491 |
| 17 | Michigan | 19,989 | | 22 | Georgia | 18,958 |
| 12 | Minnesota | 21,821 | | 23 | Ohio | 18,808 |
| 49 | Mississippi | 13,025 | | 24 | Indiana | 18,558 |
| 32 | Missouri | 17,719 | | 25 | Oregon | 18,510 |
| 47 | Montana | 14,435 | | 26 | Kansas | 18,333 |
| 28 | Nebraska | 18,263 | | 27 | Vermont | 18,283 |
| 5 | Nevada | 23,153 | | 28 | Nebraska | 18,263 |
| 4 | New Hampshire | 23,347 | | 29 | North Carolina | 18,150 |
| 2 | New Jersey | 26,277 | | 30 | Texas | 18,110 |
| 46 | New Mexico | 14,499 | | 31 | Arizona | 18,016 |
| 8 | New York | 22,379 | | 32 | Missouri | 17,719 |
| 29 | North Carolina | 18,150 | | 33 | Hawaii | 17,534 |
| 43 | North Dakota | 15,151 | | 34 | Tennessee | 17,240 |
| 23 | Ohio | 18,808 | | 35 | Iowa | 17,235 |
| 45 | Oklahoma | 14,650 | | 36 | Utah | 16,641 |
| 25 | Oregon | 18,510 | | 37 | Maine | 16,512 |
| 21 | Pennsylvania | 19,491 | | 38 | South Carolina | 16,160 |
| 18 | Rhode Island | 19,825 | | 39 | South Dakota | 15,722 |
| 38 | South Carolina | 16,160 | | 40 | Alabama | 15,278 |
| 39 | South Dakota | 15,722 | | 41 | Kentucky | 15,262 |
| 34 | Tennessee | 17,240 | | 42 | Idaho | 15,242 |
| 30 | Texas | 18,110 | | 43 | North Dakota | 15,151 |
| 36 | Utah | 16,641 | | 44 | Louisiana | 14,746 |
| 27 | Vermont | 18,283 | | 45 | Oklahoma | 14,650 |
| 13 | Virginia | 21,487 | | 46 | New Mexico | 14,499 |
| 9 | Washington | 22,269 | | 47 | Montana | 14,435 |
| 50 | West Virginia | 13,012 | | 48 | Arkansas | 14,101 |
| 19 | Wisconsin | 19,758 | | 49 | Mississippi | 13,025 |
| 20 | Wyoming | 19,544 | | 50 | West Virginia | 13,012 |
| | | | | | District of Columbia | 25,816 |

RANK ORDER

Source: Morgan Quitno Press using data from U.S. Department of the Treasury, Internal Revenue Service
"Individual Tax Statistics" (http://www.irs.gov/tax_stats/soi/ind_st.html)
*National per capita does not include income from U.S. citizens abroad and other miscellaneous returns not shown separately.

# Federal Corporate Income Tax Collections in 1998

## National Total = $213,270,011,000*

ALPHA ORDER

| RANK | STATE | COLLECTIONS | % of USA |
|---|---|---|---|
| 25 | Alabama | $1,867,009,031 | 0.9% |
| 49 | Alaska | 116,307,522 | 0.1% |
| 27 | Arizona | 1,677,560,763 | 0.8% |
| 19 | Arkansas | 3,197,093,968 | 1.5% |
| 2 | California | 22,318,124,363 | 10.5% |
| 29 | Colorado | 1,653,622,818 | 0.8% |
| 11 | Connecticut | 5,538,491,083 | 2.6% |
| 22 | Delaware | 2,728,998,937 | 1.3% |
| 13 | Florida | 5,181,627,179 | 2.4% |
| 8 | Georgia | 8,301,288,405 | 3.9% |
| 40 | Hawaii | 390,821,259 | 0.2% |
| 39 | Idaho | 529,050,417 | 0.2% |
| 3 | Illinois | 14,925,281,591 | 7.0% |
| 24 | Indiana | 2,686,637,114 | 1.3% |
| 26 | Iowa | 1,819,549,890 | 0.9% |
| 32 | Kansas | 1,498,865,225 | 0.7% |
| 30 | Kentucky | 1,636,095,326 | 0.8% |
| 28 | Louisiana | 1,673,507,431 | 0.8% |
| 44 | Maine | 281,013,605 | 0.1% |
| 17 | Maryland** | 4,288,856,280 | 2.0% |
| 12 | Massachusetts | 5,320,841,824 | 2.5% |
| 9 | Michigan | 7,148,835,883 | 3.4% |
| 10 | Minnesota | 6,029,892,991 | 2.8% |
| 38 | Mississippi | 616,071,950 | 0.3% |
| 15 | Missouri | 5,024,164,813 | 2.4% |
| 48 | Montana | 173,790,078 | 0.1% |
| 23 | Nebraska | 2,722,068,315 | 1.3% |
| 36 | Nevada | 765,792,614 | 0.4% |
| 41 | New Hampshire | 343,259,381 | 0.2% |
| 5 | New Jersey | 10,965,126,637 | 5.1% |
| 46 | New Mexico | 225,196,839 | 0.1% |
| 1 | New York | 23,516,463,410 | 11.0% |
| 14 | North Carolina | 5,088,077,005 | 2.4% |
| 47 | North Dakota | 181,056,723 | 0.1% |
| 6 | Ohio | 10,276,095,808 | 4.8% |
| 33 | Oklahoma | 1,231,651,621 | 0.6% |
| 31 | Oregon | 1,524,647,804 | 0.7% |
| 7 | Pennsylvania | 10,186,205,641 | 4.8% |
| 34 | Rhode Island | 1,179,306,767 | 0.6% |
| 35 | South Carolina | 1,099,466,531 | 0.5% |
| 42 | South Dakota | 309,792,691 | 0.1% |
| 20 | Tennessee | 3,192,618,220 | 1.5% |
| 4 | Texas | 14,526,238,486 | 6.8% |
| 37 | Utah | 758,817,132 | 0.4% |
| 45 | Vermont | 227,313,215 | 0.1% |
| 16 | Virginia | 4,799,631,598 | 2.3% |
| 21 | Washington | 2,889,509,811 | 1.4% |
| 43 | West Virginia | 291,563,989 | 0.1% |
| 18 | Wisconsin | 4,201,754,946 | 2.0% |
| 50 | Wyoming | 78,819,274 | 0.0% |

RANK ORDER

| RANK | STATE | COLLECTIONS | % of USA |
|---|---|---|---|
| 1 | New York | $23,516,463,410 | 11.0% |
| 2 | California | 22,318,124,363 | 10.5% |
| 3 | Illinois | 14,925,281,591 | 7.0% |
| 4 | Texas | 14,526,238,486 | 6.8% |
| 5 | New Jersey | 10,965,126,637 | 5.1% |
| 6 | Ohio | 10,276,095,808 | 4.8% |
| 7 | Pennsylvania | 10,186,205,641 | 4.8% |
| 8 | Georgia | 8,301,288,405 | 3.9% |
| 9 | Michigan | 7,148,835,883 | 3.4% |
| 10 | Minnesota | 6,029,892,991 | 2.8% |
| 11 | Connecticut | 5,538,491,083 | 2.6% |
| 12 | Massachusetts | 5,320,841,824 | 2.5% |
| 13 | Florida | 5,181,627,179 | 2.4% |
| 14 | North Carolina | 5,088,077,005 | 2.4% |
| 15 | Missouri | 5,024,164,813 | 2.4% |
| 16 | Virginia | 4,799,631,598 | 2.3% |
| 17 | Maryland** | 4,288,856,280 | 2.0% |
| 18 | Wisconsin | 4,201,754,946 | 2.0% |
| 19 | Arkansas | 3,197,093,968 | 1.5% |
| 20 | Tennessee | 3,192,618,220 | 1.5% |
| 21 | Washington | 2,889,509,811 | 1.4% |
| 22 | Delaware | 2,728,998,937 | 1.3% |
| 23 | Nebraska | 2,722,068,315 | 1.3% |
| 24 | Indiana | 2,686,637,114 | 1.3% |
| 25 | Alabama | 1,867,009,031 | 0.9% |
| 26 | Iowa | 1,819,549,890 | 0.9% |
| 27 | Arizona | 1,677,560,763 | 0.8% |
| 28 | Louisiana | 1,673,507,431 | 0.8% |
| 29 | Colorado | 1,653,622,818 | 0.8% |
| 30 | Kentucky | 1,636,095,326 | 0.8% |
| 31 | Oregon | 1,524,647,804 | 0.7% |
| 32 | Kansas | 1,498,865,225 | 0.7% |
| 33 | Oklahoma | 1,231,651,621 | 0.6% |
| 34 | Rhode Island | 1,179,306,767 | 0.6% |
| 35 | South Carolina | 1,099,466,531 | 0.5% |
| 36 | Nevada | 765,792,614 | 0.4% |
| 37 | Utah | 758,817,132 | 0.4% |
| 38 | Mississippi | 616,071,950 | 0.3% |
| 39 | Idaho | 529,050,417 | 0.2% |
| 40 | Hawaii | 390,821,259 | 0.2% |
| 41 | New Hampshire | 343,259,381 | 0.2% |
| 42 | South Dakota | 309,792,691 | 0.1% |
| 43 | West Virginia | 291,563,989 | 0.1% |
| 44 | Maine | 281,013,605 | 0.1% |
| 45 | Vermont | 227,313,215 | 0.1% |
| 46 | New Mexico | 225,196,839 | 0.1% |
| 47 | North Dakota | 181,056,723 | 0.1% |
| 48 | Montana | 173,790,078 | 0.1% |
| 49 | Alaska | 116,307,522 | 0.1% |
| 50 | Wyoming | 78,819,274 | 0.0% |
| | District of Columbia** | NA | NA |

Source: U.S. Department of the Treasury, Internal Revenue Service
    "Internal Revenue Gross Collections" (http://www.irs.gov/tax_stats/soi/other_tc.html)
*Total includes $6,066,136,479 from international sources and others not distributed by state.
**Maryland's figure includes the District of Columbia.

# Average Revenue Collection per Federal Corporate Income Tax Return in 1998

## National Average = $40,153 per Return*

| ALPHA ORDER | | | | RANK ORDER | | |
|---|---|---|---|---|---|---|
| RANK | STATE | AVERAGE | | RANK | STATE | AVERAGE |
| 25 | Alabama | $31,019 | | 1 | Delaware | $124,243 |
| 45 | Alaska | 11,580 | | 2 | Connecticut | 78,078 |
| 32 | Arizona | 20,711 | | 3 | Nebraska | 77,389 |
| 4 | Arkansas | 73,542 | | 4 | Arkansas | 73,542 |
| 11 | California | 51,197 | | 5 | Minnesota | 61,927 |
| 40 | Colorado | 15,459 | | 6 | Illinois | 59,950 |
| 2 | Connecticut | 78,078 | | 7 | Georgia | 55,507 |
| 1 | Delaware | 124,243 | | 8 | Ohio | 54,410 |
| 46 | Florida | 10,712 | | 9 | Pennsylvania | 54,367 |
| 7 | Georgia | 55,507 | | 10 | Missouri | 54,236 |
| 41 | Hawaii | 14,712 | | 11 | California | 51,197 |
| 31 | Idaho | 22,868 | | 12 | Tennessee | 48,582 |
| 6 | Illinois | 59,950 | | 13 | Wisconsin | 47,355 |
| 27 | Indiana | 26,330 | | 14 | New York | 46,397 |
| 22 | Iowa | 35,394 | | 15 | Rhode Island | 46,171 |
| 24 | Kansas | 33,042 | | 16 | New Jersey | 45,153 |
| 28 | Kentucky | 26,015 | | 17 | Texas | 44,546 |
| 34 | Louisiana | 19,251 | | 18 | Massachusetts | 39,086 |
| 47 | Maine | 10,495 | | 19 | North Carolina | 38,586 |
| 23 | Maryland** | 33,164 | | 20 | Michigan | 37,288 |
| 18 | Massachusetts | 39,086 | | 21 | Virginia | 36,856 |
| 20 | Michigan | 37,288 | | 22 | Iowa | 35,394 |
| 5 | Minnesota | 61,927 | | 23 | Maryland** | 33,164 |
| 38 | Mississippi | 16,927 | | 24 | Kansas | 33,042 |
| 10 | Missouri | 54,236 | | 25 | Alabama | 31,019 |
| 49 | Montana | 7,951 | | 26 | Washington | 27,307 |
| 3 | Nebraska | 77,389 | | 27 | Indiana | 26,330 |
| 36 | Nevada | 18,109 | | 28 | Kentucky | 26,015 |
| 43 | New Hampshire | 13,028 | | 29 | South Dakota | 23,031 |
| 16 | New Jersey | 45,153 | | 30 | Oregon | 22,941 |
| 48 | New Mexico | 8,548 | | 31 | Idaho | 22,868 |
| 14 | New York | 46,397 | | 32 | Arizona | 20,711 |
| 19 | North Carolina | 38,586 | | 33 | Oklahoma | 19,624 |
| 39 | North Dakota | 16,064 | | 34 | Louisiana | 19,251 |
| 8 | Ohio | 54,410 | | 35 | Utah | 19,236 |
| 33 | Oklahoma | 19,624 | | 36 | Nevada | 18,109 |
| 30 | Oregon | 22,941 | | 37 | South Carolina | 17,003 |
| 9 | Pennsylvania | 54,367 | | 38 | Mississippi | 16,927 |
| 15 | Rhode Island | 46,171 | | 39 | North Dakota | 16,064 |
| 37 | South Carolina | 17,003 | | 40 | Colorado | 15,459 |
| 29 | South Dakota | 23,031 | | 41 | Hawaii | 14,712 |
| 12 | Tennessee | 48,582 | | 42 | Vermont | 13,797 |
| 17 | Texas | 44,546 | | 43 | New Hampshire | 13,028 |
| 35 | Utah | 19,236 | | 44 | West Virginia | 12,982 |
| 42 | Vermont | 13,797 | | 45 | Alaska | 11,580 |
| 21 | Virginia | 36,856 | | 46 | Florida | 10,712 |
| 26 | Washington | 27,307 | | 47 | Maine | 10,495 |
| 44 | West Virginia | 12,982 | | 48 | New Mexico | 8,548 |
| 13 | Wisconsin | 47,355 | | 49 | Montana | 7,951 |
| 50 | Wyoming | 6,780 | | 50 | Wyoming | 6,780 |

District of Columbia**    NA

Source: Morgan Quitno Press using data from U.S. Department of the Treasury, Internal Revenue Service
"Internal Revenue Gross Collections" (http://www.irs.gov/tax_stats/soi/other_tc.html) and
"Number of Returns Filed" (http://www.irs.gov/tax_stats/soi/other_nr.html)
*Total includes collections and returns from international sources and other miscellaneous returns not shown separately.
**Maryland's figure includes the District of Columbia.

# Federal Tax Returns Filed in 1998

## National Total = 224,453,283 Returns*

ALPHA ORDER

ALPHA ORDER

| RANK | STATE | RETURNS | % of USA |
|------|-------|---------|----------|
| 25 | Alabama | 3,069,356 | 1.4% |
| 48 | Alaska | 588,172 | 0.3% |
| 22 | Arizona | 3,632,482 | 1.6% |
| 32 | Arkansas | 1,919,571 | 0.9% |
| 1 | California | 25,847,472 | 11.5% |
| 21 | Colorado | 3,740,750 | 1.7% |
| 24 | Connecticut | 3,113,923 | 1.4% |
| 45 | Delaware | 669,766 | 0.3% |
| 4 | Florida | 13,559,368 | 6.0% |
| 11 | Georgia | 5,708,080 | 2.5% |
| 41 | Hawaii | 1,028,339 | 0.5% |
| 42 | Idaho | 981,156 | 0.4% |
| 5 | Illinois | 10,100,188 | 4.5% |
| 16 | Indiana | 4,666,736 | 2.1% |
| 30 | Iowa | 2,496,111 | 1.1% |
| 31 | Kansas | 2,267,089 | 1.0% |
| 27 | Kentucky | 2,856,712 | 1.3% |
| 23 | Louisiana | 3,137,668 | 1.4% |
| 40 | Maine | 1,086,275 | 0.5% |
| 14 | Maryland** | 5,306,496 | 2.4% |
| 12 | Massachusetts | 5,689,109 | 2.5% |
| 8 | Michigan | 7,645,377 | 3.4% |
| 19 | Minnesota | 4,146,521 | 1.8% |
| 33 | Mississippi | 1,839,787 | 0.8% |
| 17 | Missouri | 4,529,271 | 2.0% |
| 44 | Montana | 841,360 | 0.4% |
| 35 | Nebraska | 1,482,509 | 0.7% |
| 36 | Nevada | 1,479,511 | 0.7% |
| 39 | New Hampshire | 1,096,168 | 0.5% |
| 9 | New Jersey | 7,453,981 | 3.3% |
| 37 | New Mexico | 1,335,486 | 0.6% |
| 2 | New York | 15,278,385 | 6.8% |
| 10 | North Carolina | 5,987,600 | 2.7% |
| 47 | North Dakota | 600,470 | 0.3% |
| 7 | Ohio | 9,338,728 | 4.2% |
| 29 | Oklahoma | 2,663,768 | 1.2% |
| 26 | Oregon | 2,971,976 | 1.3% |
| 6 | Pennsylvania | 9,953,898 | 4.4% |
| 43 | Rhode Island | 880,460 | 0.4% |
| 28 | South Carolina | 2,833,096 | 1.3% |
| 46 | South Dakota | 667,407 | 0.3% |
| 20 | Tennessee | 4,100,821 | 1.8% |
| 3 | Texas | 15,038,042 | 6.7% |
| 34 | Utah | 1,544,067 | 0.7% |
| 49 | Vermont | 580,479 | 0.3% |
| 13 | Virginia | 5,342,266 | 2.4% |
| 15 | Washington | 5,052,152 | 2.3% |
| 38 | West Virginia | 1,237,196 | 0.6% |
| 18 | Wisconsin | 4,511,094 | 2.0% |
| 50 | Wyoming | 460,500 | 0.2% |

RANK ORDER

| RANK | STATE | RETURNS | % of USA |
|------|-------|---------|----------|
| 1 | California | 25,847,472 | 11.5% |
| 2 | New York | 15,278,385 | 6.8% |
| 3 | Texas | 15,038,042 | 6.7% |
| 4 | Florida | 13,559,368 | 6.0% |
| 5 | Illinois | 10,100,188 | 4.5% |
| 6 | Pennsylvania | 9,953,898 | 4.4% |
| 7 | Ohio | 9,338,728 | 4.2% |
| 8 | Michigan | 7,645,377 | 3.4% |
| 9 | New Jersey | 7,453,981 | 3.3% |
| 10 | North Carolina | 5,987,600 | 2.7% |
| 11 | Georgia | 5,708,080 | 2.5% |
| 12 | Massachusetts | 5,689,109 | 2.5% |
| 13 | Virginia | 5,342,266 | 2.4% |
| 14 | Maryland** | 5,306,496 | 2.4% |
| 15 | Washington | 5,052,152 | 2.3% |
| 16 | Indiana | 4,666,736 | 2.1% |
| 17 | Missouri | 4,529,271 | 2.0% |
| 18 | Wisconsin | 4,511,094 | 2.0% |
| 19 | Minnesota | 4,146,521 | 1.8% |
| 20 | Tennessee | 4,100,821 | 1.8% |
| 21 | Colorado | 3,740,750 | 1.7% |
| 22 | Arizona | 3,632,482 | 1.6% |
| 23 | Louisiana | 3,137,668 | 1.4% |
| 24 | Connecticut | 3,113,923 | 1.4% |
| 25 | Alabama | 3,069,356 | 1.4% |
| 26 | Oregon | 2,971,976 | 1.3% |
| 27 | Kentucky | 2,856,712 | 1.3% |
| 28 | South Carolina | 2,833,096 | 1.3% |
| 29 | Oklahoma | 2,663,768 | 1.2% |
| 30 | Iowa | 2,496,111 | 1.1% |
| 31 | Kansas | 2,267,089 | 1.0% |
| 32 | Arkansas | 1,919,571 | 0.9% |
| 33 | Mississippi | 1,839,787 | 0.8% |
| 34 | Utah | 1,544,067 | 0.7% |
| 35 | Nebraska | 1,482,509 | 0.7% |
| 36 | Nevada | 1,479,511 | 0.7% |
| 37 | New Mexico | 1,335,486 | 0.6% |
| 38 | West Virginia | 1,237,196 | 0.6% |
| 39 | New Hampshire | 1,096,168 | 0.5% |
| 40 | Maine | 1,086,275 | 0.5% |
| 41 | Hawaii | 1,028,339 | 0.5% |
| 42 | Idaho | 981,156 | 0.4% |
| 43 | Rhode Island | 880,460 | 0.4% |
| 44 | Montana | 841,360 | 0.4% |
| 45 | Delaware | 669,766 | 0.3% |
| 46 | South Dakota | 667,407 | 0.3% |
| 47 | North Dakota | 600,470 | 0.3% |
| 48 | Alaska | 588,172 | 0.3% |
| 49 | Vermont | 580,479 | 0.3% |
| 50 | Wyoming | 460,500 | 0.2% |
|  | District of Columbia** | NA | NA |

Source: U.S. Department of the Treasury, Internal Revenue Service
   "Number of Returns Filed" (http://www.irs.gov/tax_stats/soi/other_nr.html)
*Total includes returns from international sources and other miscellaneous returns not shown separately.
**Maryland's figure includes the District of Columbia.

# Federal Individual Income Tax Returns Filed in 1998

## National Total = 122,999,969 Returns*

ALPHA ORDER

| RANK | STATE | RETURNS | % of USA |
|------|-------|---------|----------|
| 23 | Alabama | 1,864,166 | 1.5% |
| 46 | Alaska | 343,157 | 0.3% |
| 21 | Arizona | 1,967,756 | 1.6% |
| 33 | Arkansas | 1,080,969 | 0.9% |
| 1 | California | 13,834,364 | 11.2% |
| 22 | Colorado | 1,898,751 | 1.5% |
| 27 | Connecticut | 1,601,374 | 1.3% |
| 45 | Delaware | 356,547 | 0.3% |
| 4 | Florida | 6,895,229 | 5.6% |
| 11 | Georgia | 3,373,071 | 2.7% |
| 41 | Hawaii | 551,494 | 0.4% |
| 42 | Idaho | 521,079 | 0.4% |
| 6 | Illinois | 5,557,968 | 4.5% |
| 15 | Indiana | 2,722,416 | 2.2% |
| 30 | Iowa | 1,316,521 | 1.1% |
| 31 | Kansas | 1,175,954 | 1.0% |
| 26 | Kentucky | 1,664,629 | 1.4% |
| 24 | Louisiana | 1,825,171 | 1.5% |
| 40 | Maine | 574,177 | 0.5% |
| 14 | Maryland** | 2,794,535 | 2.3% |
| 13 | Massachusetts | 2,957,958 | 2.4% |
| 8 | Michigan | 4,424,929 | 3.6% |
| 20 | Minnesota | 2,238,539 | 1.8% |
| 32 | Mississippi | 1,139,085 | 0.9% |
| 19 | Missouri | 2,454,082 | 2.0% |
| 44 | Montana | 404,445 | 0.3% |
| 36 | Nebraska | 785,294 | 0.6% |
| 35 | Nevada | 837,849 | 0.7% |
| 39 | New Hampshire | 586,042 | 0.5% |
| 9 | New Jersey | 3,859,863 | 3.1% |
| 37 | New Mexico | 756,124 | 0.6% |
| 3 | New York | 8,112,815 | 6.6% |
| 10 | North Carolina | 3,460,182 | 2.8% |
| 48 | North Dakota | 300,450 | 0.2% |
| 7 | Ohio | 5,425,406 | 4.4% |
| 29 | Oklahoma | 1,412,435 | 1.1% |
| 28 | Oregon | 1,503,062 | 1.2% |
| 5 | Pennsylvania | 5,585,879 | 4.5% |
| 43 | Rhode Island | 463,753 | 0.4% |
| 25 | South Carolina | 1,716,702 | 1.4% |
| 47 | South Dakota | 340,172 | 0.3% |
| 18 | Tennessee | 2,457,252 | 2.0% |
| 2 | Texas | 8,447,225 | 6.9% |
| 34 | Utah | 875,834 | 0.7% |
| 49 | Vermont | 282,171 | 0.2% |
| 12 | Virginia | 3,023,809 | 2.5% |
| 16 | Washington | 2,609,291 | 2.1% |
| 38 | West Virginia | 729,243 | 0.6% |
| 17 | Wisconsin | 2,477,620 | 2.0% |
| 50 | Wyoming | 226,606 | 0.2% |

RANK ORDER

| RANK | STATE | RETURNS | % of USA |
|------|-------|---------|----------|
| 1 | California | 13,834,364 | 11.2% |
| 2 | Texas | 8,447,225 | 6.9% |
| 3 | New York | 8,112,815 | 6.6% |
| 4 | Florida | 6,895,229 | 5.6% |
| 5 | Pennsylvania | 5,585,879 | 4.5% |
| 6 | Illinois | 5,557,968 | 4.5% |
| 7 | Ohio | 5,425,406 | 4.4% |
| 8 | Michigan | 4,424,929 | 3.6% |
| 9 | New Jersey | 3,859,863 | 3.1% |
| 10 | North Carolina | 3,460,182 | 2.8% |
| 11 | Georgia | 3,373,071 | 2.7% |
| 12 | Virginia | 3,023,809 | 2.5% |
| 13 | Massachusetts | 2,957,958 | 2.4% |
| 14 | Maryland** | 2,794,535 | 2.3% |
| 15 | Indiana | 2,722,416 | 2.2% |
| 16 | Washington | 2,609,291 | 2.1% |
| 17 | Wisconsin | 2,477,620 | 2.0% |
| 18 | Tennessee | 2,457,252 | 2.0% |
| 19 | Missouri | 2,454,082 | 2.0% |
| 20 | Minnesota | 2,238,539 | 1.8% |
| 21 | Arizona | 1,967,756 | 1.6% |
| 22 | Colorado | 1,898,751 | 1.5% |
| 23 | Alabama | 1,864,166 | 1.5% |
| 24 | Louisiana | 1,825,171 | 1.5% |
| 25 | South Carolina | 1,716,702 | 1.4% |
| 26 | Kentucky | 1,664,629 | 1.4% |
| 27 | Connecticut | 1,601,374 | 1.3% |
| 28 | Oregon | 1,503,062 | 1.2% |
| 29 | Oklahoma | 1,412,435 | 1.1% |
| 30 | Iowa | 1,316,521 | 1.1% |
| 31 | Kansas | 1,175,954 | 1.0% |
| 32 | Mississippi | 1,139,085 | 0.9% |
| 33 | Arkansas | 1,080,969 | 0.9% |
| 34 | Utah | 875,834 | 0.7% |
| 35 | Nevada | 837,849 | 0.7% |
| 36 | Nebraska | 785,294 | 0.6% |
| 37 | New Mexico | 756,124 | 0.6% |
| 38 | West Virginia | 729,243 | 0.6% |
| 39 | New Hampshire | 586,042 | 0.5% |
| 40 | Maine | 574,177 | 0.5% |
| 41 | Hawaii | 551,494 | 0.4% |
| 42 | Idaho | 521,079 | 0.4% |
| 43 | Rhode Island | 463,753 | 0.4% |
| 44 | Montana | 404,445 | 0.3% |
| 45 | Delaware | 356,547 | 0.3% |
| 46 | Alaska | 343,157 | 0.3% |
| 47 | South Dakota | 340,172 | 0.3% |
| 48 | North Dakota | 300,450 | 0.2% |
| 49 | Vermont | 282,171 | 0.2% |
| 50 | Wyoming | 226,606 | 0.2% |
| | District of Columbia** | NA | NA |

Source: U.S. Department of the Treasury, Internal Revenue Service
    "Number of Returns Filed" (http://www.irs.gov/tax_stats/soi/other_nr.html)
*Total includes returns from international sources and other miscellaneous returns not shown separately.
**Maryland's figure includes the District of Columbia.

# Federal Corporate Income Tax Returns Filed in 1998

## National Total = 5,311,411 Returns*

ALPHA ORDER

| RANK | STATE | RETURNS | % of USA |
|---|---|---|---|
| 29 | Alabama | 60,190 | 1.1% |
| 50 | Alaska | 10,044 | 0.2% |
| 22 | Arizona | 80,997 | 1.5% |
| 32 | Arkansas | 43,473 | 0.8% |
| 3 | California | 435,923 | 8.2% |
| 15 | Colorado | 106,965 | 2.0% |
| 23 | Connecticut | 70,935 | 1.3% |
| 44 | Delaware | 21,965 | 0.4% |
| 2 | Florida | 483,741 | 9.1% |
| 10 | Georgia | 149,554 | 2.8% |
| 38 | Hawaii | 26,565 | 0.5% |
| 42 | Idaho | 23,135 | 0.4% |
| 5 | Illinois | 248,964 | 4.7% |
| 17 | Indiana | 102,039 | 1.9% |
| 30 | Iowa | 51,409 | 1.0% |
| 31 | Kansas | 45,362 | 0.9% |
| 27 | Kentucky | 62,890 | 1.2% |
| 21 | Louisiana | 86,929 | 1.6% |
| 37 | Maine | 26,775 | 0.5% |
| 14 | Maryland** | 129,321 | 2.4% |
| 11 | Massachusetts | 136,132 | 2.6% |
| 7 | Michigan | 191,720 | 3.6% |
| 18 | Minnesota | 97,371 | 1.8% |
| 35 | Mississippi | 36,395 | 0.7% |
| 19 | Missouri | 92,635 | 1.7% |
| 45 | Montana | 21,859 | 0.4% |
| 36 | Nebraska | 35,174 | 0.7% |
| 33 | Nevada | 42,287 | 0.8% |
| 39 | New Hampshire | 26,347 | 0.5% |
| 6 | New Jersey | 242,843 | 4.6% |
| 40 | New Mexico | 26,344 | 0.5% |
| 1 | New York | 506,854 | 9.5% |
| 12 | North Carolina | 131,863 | 2.5% |
| 49 | North Dakota | 11,271 | 0.2% |
| 8 | Ohio | 188,863 | 3.6% |
| 28 | Oklahoma | 62,761 | 1.2% |
| 24 | Oregon | 66,459 | 1.3% |
| 9 | Pennsylvania | 187,361 | 3.5% |
| 41 | Rhode Island | 25,542 | 0.5% |
| 26 | South Carolina | 64,663 | 1.2% |
| 47 | South Dakota | 13,451 | 0.3% |
| 25 | Tennessee | 65,716 | 1.2% |
| 4 | Texas | 326,094 | 6.1% |
| 34 | Utah | 39,447 | 0.7% |
| 46 | Vermont | 16,476 | 0.3% |
| 13 | Virginia | 130,227 | 2.5% |
| 16 | Washington | 105,815 | 2.0% |
| 43 | West Virginia | 22,459 | 0.4% |
| 20 | Wisconsin | 88,728 | 1.7% |
| 48 | Wyoming | 11,626 | 0.2% |

RANK ORDER

| RANK | STATE | RETURNS | % of USA |
|---|---|---|---|
| 1 | New York | 506,854 | 9.5% |
| 2 | Florida | 483,741 | 9.1% |
| 3 | California | 435,923 | 8.2% |
| 4 | Texas | 326,094 | 6.1% |
| 5 | Illinois | 248,964 | 4.7% |
| 6 | New Jersey | 242,843 | 4.6% |
| 7 | Michigan | 191,720 | 3.6% |
| 8 | Ohio | 188,863 | 3.6% |
| 9 | Pennsylvania | 187,361 | 3.5% |
| 10 | Georgia | 149,554 | 2.8% |
| 11 | Massachusetts | 136,132 | 2.6% |
| 12 | North Carolina | 131,863 | 2.5% |
| 13 | Virginia | 130,227 | 2.5% |
| 14 | Maryland** | 129,321 | 2.4% |
| 15 | Colorado | 106,965 | 2.0% |
| 16 | Washington | 105,815 | 2.0% |
| 17 | Indiana | 102,039 | 1.9% |
| 18 | Minnesota | 97,371 | 1.8% |
| 19 | Missouri | 92,635 | 1.7% |
| 20 | Wisconsin | 88,728 | 1.7% |
| 21 | Louisiana | 86,929 | 1.6% |
| 22 | Arizona | 80,997 | 1.5% |
| 23 | Connecticut | 70,935 | 1.3% |
| 24 | Oregon | 66,459 | 1.3% |
| 25 | Tennessee | 65,716 | 1.2% |
| 26 | South Carolina | 64,663 | 1.2% |
| 27 | Kentucky | 62,890 | 1.2% |
| 28 | Oklahoma | 62,761 | 1.2% |
| 29 | Alabama | 60,190 | 1.1% |
| 30 | Iowa | 51,409 | 1.0% |
| 31 | Kansas | 45,362 | 0.9% |
| 32 | Arkansas | 43,473 | 0.8% |
| 33 | Nevada | 42,287 | 0.8% |
| 34 | Utah | 39,447 | 0.7% |
| 35 | Mississippi | 36,395 | 0.7% |
| 36 | Nebraska | 35,174 | 0.7% |
| 37 | Maine | 26,775 | 0.5% |
| 38 | Hawaii | 26,565 | 0.5% |
| 39 | New Hampshire | 26,347 | 0.5% |
| 40 | New Mexico | 26,344 | 0.5% |
| 41 | Rhode Island | 25,542 | 0.5% |
| 42 | Idaho | 23,135 | 0.4% |
| 43 | West Virginia | 22,459 | 0.4% |
| 44 | Delaware | 21,965 | 0.4% |
| 45 | Montana | 21,859 | 0.4% |
| 46 | Vermont | 16,476 | 0.3% |
| 47 | South Dakota | 13,451 | 0.3% |
| 48 | Wyoming | 11,626 | 0.2% |
| 49 | North Dakota | 11,271 | 0.2% |
| 50 | Alaska | 10,044 | 0.2% |
| | District of Columbia** | NA | NA |

Source: U.S. Department of the Treasury, Internal Revenue Service
   "Number of Returns Filed" (http://www.irs.gov/tax_stats/soi/other_nr.html)
*Total includes returns from international sources and other miscellaneous returns not shown separately.
**Maryland's figure includes the District of Columbia.

# Federal Tax Refunds in 1998

## National Total = 90,426,491 Refunds*

ALPHA ORDER

| RANK | STATE | REFUNDS | % of USA |
|------|-------|---------|----------|
| 26 | Alabama | 1,042,776 | 1.2% |
| 49 | Alaska | 150,879 | 0.2% |
| 22 | Arizona | 1,188,872 | 1.3% |
| 33 | Arkansas | 563,673 | 0.6% |
| 2 | California | 8,318,195 | 9.2% |
| 24 | Colorado | 1,153,643 | 1.3% |
| 25 | Connecticut | 1,087,291 | 1.2% |
| 45 | Delaware | 191,565 | 0.2% |
| 7 | Florida | 3,648,628 | 4.0% |
| 16 | Georgia | 1,678,641 | 1.9% |
| 41 | Hawaii | 306,586 | 0.3% |
| 42 | Idaho | 301,137 | 0.3% |
| 10 | Illinois | 3,052,328 | 3.4% |
| 17 | Indiana | 1,635,623 | 1.8% |
| 31 | Iowa | 620,471 | 0.7% |
| 30 | Kansas | 632,947 | 0.7% |
| 27 | Kentucky | 963,865 | 1.1% |
| 5 | Louisiana | 4,569,060 | 5.1% |
| 39 | Maine | 338,009 | 0.4% |
| 15 | Maryland** | 1,759,727 | 1.9% |
| 14 | Massachusetts | 1,863,320 | 2.1% |
| 4 | Michigan | 7,681,151 | 8.5% |
| 23 | Minnesota | 1,186,716 | 1.3% |
| 32 | Mississippi | 577,937 | 0.6% |
| 21 | Missouri | 1,309,853 | 1.4% |
| 44 | Montana | 224,556 | 0.2% |
| 38 | Nebraska | 430,639 | 0.5% |
| 35 | Nevada | 473,307 | 0.5% |
| 40 | New Hampshire | 329,099 | 0.4% |
| 11 | New Jersey | 2,298,130 | 2.5% |
| 37 | New Mexico | 435,190 | 0.5% |
| 3 | New York | 7,919,130 | 8.8% |
| 12 | North Carolina | 1,947,216 | 2.2% |
| 48 | North Dakota | 167,598 | 0.2% |
| 8 | Ohio | 3,602,202 | 4.0% |
| 28 | Oklahoma | 808,621 | 0.9% |
| 6 | Oregon | 4,558,356 | 5.0% |
| 9 | Pennsylvania | 3,206,892 | 3.5% |
| 43 | Rhode Island | 293,674 | 0.3% |
| 29 | South Carolina | 761,406 | 0.8% |
| 46 | South Dakota | 184,430 | 0.2% |
| 19 | Tennessee | 1,474,114 | 1.6% |
| 1 | Texas | 8,603,667 | 9.5% |
| 34 | Utah | 542,803 | 0.6% |
| 47 | Vermont | 169,525 | 0.2% |
| 18 | Virginia | 1,619,941 | 1.8% |
| 13 | Washington | 1,902,759 | 2.1% |
| 36 | West Virginia | 443,587 | 0.5% |
| 20 | Wisconsin | 1,379,140 | 1.5% |
| 50 | Wyoming | 124,385 | 0.1% |

RANK ORDER

| RANK | STATE | REFUNDS | % of USA |
|------|-------|---------|----------|
| 1 | Texas | 8,603,667 | 9.5% |
| 2 | California | 8,318,195 | 9.2% |
| 3 | New York | 7,919,130 | 8.8% |
| 4 | Michigan | 7,681,151 | 8.5% |
| 5 | Louisiana | 4,569,060 | 5.1% |
| 6 | Oregon | 4,558,356 | 5.0% |
| 7 | Florida | 3,648,628 | 4.0% |
| 8 | Ohio | 3,602,202 | 4.0% |
| 9 | Pennsylvania | 3,206,892 | 3.5% |
| 10 | Illinois | 3,052,328 | 3.4% |
| 11 | New Jersey | 2,298,130 | 2.5% |
| 12 | North Carolina | 1,947,216 | 2.2% |
| 13 | Washington | 1,902,759 | 2.1% |
| 14 | Massachusetts | 1,863,320 | 2.1% |
| 15 | Maryland** | 1,759,727 | 1.9% |
| 16 | Georgia | 1,678,641 | 1.9% |
| 17 | Indiana | 1,635,623 | 1.8% |
| 18 | Virginia | 1,619,941 | 1.8% |
| 19 | Tennessee | 1,474,114 | 1.6% |
| 20 | Wisconsin | 1,379,140 | 1.5% |
| 21 | Missouri | 1,309,853 | 1.4% |
| 22 | Arizona | 1,188,872 | 1.3% |
| 23 | Minnesota | 1,186,716 | 1.3% |
| 24 | Colorado | 1,153,643 | 1.3% |
| 25 | Connecticut | 1,087,291 | 1.2% |
| 26 | Alabama | 1,042,776 | 1.2% |
| 27 | Kentucky | 963,865 | 1.1% |
| 28 | Oklahoma | 808,621 | 0.9% |
| 29 | South Carolina | 761,406 | 0.8% |
| 30 | Kansas | 632,947 | 0.7% |
| 31 | Iowa | 620,471 | 0.7% |
| 32 | Mississippi | 577,937 | 0.6% |
| 33 | Arkansas | 563,673 | 0.6% |
| 34 | Utah | 542,803 | 0.6% |
| 35 | Nevada | 473,307 | 0.5% |
| 36 | West Virginia | 443,587 | 0.5% |
| 37 | New Mexico | 435,190 | 0.5% |
| 38 | Nebraska | 430,639 | 0.5% |
| 39 | Maine | 338,009 | 0.4% |
| 40 | New Hampshire | 329,099 | 0.4% |
| 41 | Hawaii | 306,586 | 0.3% |
| 42 | Idaho | 301,137 | 0.3% |
| 43 | Rhode Island | 293,674 | 0.3% |
| 44 | Montana | 224,556 | 0.2% |
| 45 | Delaware | 191,565 | 0.2% |
| 46 | South Dakota | 184,430 | 0.2% |
| 47 | Vermont | 169,525 | 0.2% |
| 48 | North Dakota | 167,598 | 0.2% |
| 49 | Alaska | 150,879 | 0.2% |
| 50 | Wyoming | 124,385 | 0.1% |
| | District of Columbia** | NA | NA |

Source: U.S. Department of the Treasury, Internal Revenue Service
 "Number of Internal Revenue Refunds Issued" (http://www.irs.gov/tax_stats/soi/other_tr.html)
*Total includes refunds to international sources and other miscellaneous refunds not shown separately.
**Maryland's figure includes the District of Columbia.

# Value of Federal Tax Refunds in 1998

## National Total = $155,133,259,000*

ALPHA ORDER

| RANK | STATE | REFUNDS | % of USA |
|---|---|---|---|
| 26 | Alabama | $1,349,154,000 | 0.9% |
| 46 | Alaska | 198,467,000 | 0.1% |
| 25 | Arizona | 1,689,519,000 | 1.1% |
| 32 | Arkansas | 651,615,000 | 0.4% |
| 2 | California | 15,343,049,000 | 9.9% |
| 21 | Colorado | 1,946,142,000 | 1.3% |
| 17 | Connecticut | 2,456,403,000 | 1.6% |
| 45 | Delaware | 215,736,000 | 0.1% |
| 6 | Florida | 5,881,743,000 | 3.8% |
| 15 | Georgia | 2,570,854,000 | 1.7% |
| 40 | Hawaii | 394,335,000 | 0.3% |
| 43 | Idaho | 343,353,000 | 0.2% |
| 8 | Illinois | 5,429,462,000 | 3.5% |
| 18 | Indiana | 2,215,266,000 | 1.4% |
| 35 | Iowa | 615,528,000 | 0.4% |
| 30 | Kansas | 820,227,000 | 0.5% |
| 28 | Kentucky | 1,099,795,000 | 0.7% |
| 5 | Louisiana | 5,981,379,000 | 3.9% |
| 42 | Maine | 376,025,000 | 0.2% |
| 12 | Maryland** | 4,491,588,000 | 2.9% |
| 13 | Massachusetts | 3,445,275,000 | 2.2% |
| 4 | Michigan | 6,200,589,000 | 4.0% |
| 24 | Minnesota | 1,787,248,000 | 1.2% |
| 31 | Mississippi | 685,584,000 | 0.4% |
| 22 | Missouri | 1,910,027,000 | 1.2% |
| 44 | Montana | 241,138,000 | 0.2% |
| 37 | Nebraska | 480,503,000 | 0.3% |
| 33 | Nevada | 651,174,000 | 0.4% |
| 39 | New Hampshire | 425,248,000 | 0.3% |
| 10 | New Jersey | 5,165,594,000 | 3.3% |
| 36 | New Mexico | 523,639,000 | 0.3% |
| 3 | New York | 13,101,866,000 | 8.4% |
| 16 | North Carolina | 2,490,559,000 | 1.6% |
| 49 | North Dakota | 171,798,000 | 0.1% |
| 9 | Ohio | 5,414,788,000 | 3.5% |
| 27 | Oklahoma | 1,162,367,000 | 0.7% |
| 7 | Oregon | 5,783,355,000 | 3.7% |
| 11 | Pennsylvania | 4,521,212,000 | 2.9% |
| 41 | Rhode Island | 380,971,000 | 0.2% |
| 29 | South Carolina | 866,336,000 | 0.6% |
| 48 | South Dakota | 183,460,000 | 0.1% |
| 20 | Tennessee | 2,184,649,000 | 1.4% |
| 1 | Texas | 15,880,679,000 | 10.2% |
| 34 | Utah | 633,777,000 | 0.4% |
| 47 | Vermont | 191,165,000 | 0.1% |
| 19 | Virginia | 2,192,412,000 | 1.4% |
| 14 | Washington | 3,419,110,000 | 2.2% |
| 38 | West Virginia | 472,791,000 | 0.3% |
| 23 | Wisconsin | 1,874,838,000 | 1.2% |
| 50 | Wyoming | 144,999,000 | 0.1% |

RANK ORDER

| RANK | STATE | REFUNDS | % of USA |
|---|---|---|---|
| 1 | Texas | $15,880,679,000 | 10.2% |
| 2 | California | 15,343,049,000 | 9.9% |
| 3 | New York | 13,101,866,000 | 8.4% |
| 4 | Michigan | 6,200,589,000 | 4.0% |
| 5 | Louisiana | 5,981,379,000 | 3.9% |
| 6 | Florida | 5,881,743,000 | 3.8% |
| 7 | Oregon | 5,783,355,000 | 3.7% |
| 8 | Illinois | 5,429,462,000 | 3.5% |
| 9 | Ohio | 5,414,788,000 | 3.5% |
| 10 | New Jersey | 5,165,594,000 | 3.3% |
| 11 | Pennsylvania | 4,521,212,000 | 2.9% |
| 12 | Maryland** | 4,491,588,000 | 2.9% |
| 13 | Massachusetts | 3,445,275,000 | 2.2% |
| 14 | Washington | 3,419,110,000 | 2.2% |
| 15 | Georgia | 2,570,854,000 | 1.7% |
| 16 | North Carolina | 2,490,559,000 | 1.6% |
| 17 | Connecticut | 2,456,403,000 | 1.6% |
| 18 | Indiana | 2,215,266,000 | 1.4% |
| 19 | Virginia | 2,192,412,000 | 1.4% |
| 20 | Tennessee | 2,184,649,000 | 1.4% |
| 21 | Colorado | 1,946,142,000 | 1.3% |
| 22 | Missouri | 1,910,027,000 | 1.2% |
| 23 | Wisconsin | 1,874,838,000 | 1.2% |
| 24 | Minnesota | 1,787,248,000 | 1.2% |
| 25 | Arizona | 1,689,519,000 | 1.1% |
| 26 | Alabama | 1,349,154,000 | 0.9% |
| 27 | Oklahoma | 1,162,367,000 | 0.7% |
| 28 | Kentucky | 1,099,795,000 | 0.7% |
| 29 | South Carolina | 866,336,000 | 0.6% |
| 30 | Kansas | 820,227,000 | 0.5% |
| 31 | Mississippi | 685,584,000 | 0.4% |
| 32 | Arkansas | 651,615,000 | 0.4% |
| 33 | Nevada | 651,174,000 | 0.4% |
| 34 | Utah | 633,777,000 | 0.4% |
| 35 | Iowa | 615,528,000 | 0.4% |
| 36 | New Mexico | 523,639,000 | 0.3% |
| 37 | Nebraska | 480,503,000 | 0.3% |
| 38 | West Virginia | 472,791,000 | 0.3% |
| 39 | New Hampshire | 425,248,000 | 0.3% |
| 40 | Hawaii | 394,335,000 | 0.3% |
| 41 | Rhode Island | 380,971,000 | 0.2% |
| 42 | Maine | 376,025,000 | 0.2% |
| 43 | Idaho | 343,353,000 | 0.2% |
| 44 | Montana | 241,138,000 | 0.2% |
| 45 | Delaware | 215,736,000 | 0.1% |
| 46 | Alaska | 198,467,000 | 0.1% |
| 47 | Vermont | 191,165,000 | 0.1% |
| 48 | South Dakota | 183,460,000 | 0.1% |
| 49 | North Dakota | 171,798,000 | 0.1% |
| 50 | Wyoming | 144,999,000 | 0.1% |
| | District of Columbia** | NA | NA |

Source: U.S. Department of the Treasury, Internal Revenue Service
"Amount Internal Revenue Refunds, Including Interest" (http://www.irs.gov/tax_stats/soi/other_tr.html)
*Total includes refunds to international sources and other miscellaneous refunds not shown separately.
**Maryland's figure includes the District of Columbia.

# Average Federal Tax Refund in 1998

## National Average = $1,716*

ALPHA ORDER

| RANK | STATE | REFUND |
|------|-------|--------|
| 28 | Alabama | $1,294 |
| 24 | Alaska | 1,315 |
| 18 | Arizona | 1,421 |
| 37 | Arkansas | 1,156 |
| 6 | California | 1,845 |
| 9 | Colorado | 1,687 |
| 2 | Connecticut | 2,259 |
| 42 | Delaware | 1,126 |
| 11 | Florida | 1,612 |
| 12 | Georgia | 1,532 |
| 30 | Hawaii | 1,286 |
| 39 | Idaho | 1,140 |
| 8 | Illinois | 1,779 |
| 22 | Indiana | 1,354 |
| 49 | Iowa | 992 |
| 27 | Kansas | 1,296 |
| 38 | Kentucky | 1,141 |
| 25 | Louisiana | 1,309 |
| 44 | Maine | 1,112 |
| 1 | Maryland** | 2,552 |
| 4 | Massachusetts | 1,849 |
| 50 | Michigan | 807 |
| 13 | Minnesota | 1,506 |
| 34 | Mississippi | 1,186 |
| 16 | Missouri | 1,458 |
| 45 | Montana | 1,074 |
| 43 | Nebraska | 1,116 |
| 20 | Nevada | 1,376 |
| 29 | New Hampshire | 1,292 |
| 3 | New Jersey | 2,248 |
| 33 | New Mexico | 1,203 |
| 10 | New York | 1,654 |
| 31 | North Carolina | 1,279 |
| 47 | North Dakota | 1,025 |
| 14 | Ohio | 1,503 |
| 17 | Oklahoma | 1,437 |
| 32 | Oregon | 1,269 |
| 19 | Pennsylvania | 1,410 |
| 26 | Rhode Island | 1,297 |
| 40 | South Carolina | 1,138 |
| 48 | South Dakota | 995 |
| 15 | Tennessee | 1,482 |
| 5 | Texas | 1,846 |
| 35 | Utah | 1,168 |
| 41 | Vermont | 1,128 |
| 23 | Virginia | 1,353 |
| 7 | Washington | 1,797 |
| 46 | West Virginia | 1,066 |
| 21 | Wisconsin | 1,359 |
| 36 | Wyoming | 1,166 |

RANK ORDER

| RANK | STATE | REFUND |
|------|-------|--------|
| 1 | Maryland** | $2,552 |
| 2 | Connecticut | 2,259 |
| 3 | New Jersey | 2,248 |
| 4 | Massachusetts | 1,849 |
| 5 | Texas | 1,846 |
| 6 | California | 1,845 |
| 7 | Washington | 1,797 |
| 8 | Illinois | 1,779 |
| 9 | Colorado | 1,687 |
| 10 | New York | 1,654 |
| 11 | Florida | 1,612 |
| 12 | Georgia | 1,532 |
| 13 | Minnesota | 1,506 |
| 14 | Ohio | 1,503 |
| 15 | Tennessee | 1,482 |
| 16 | Missouri | 1,458 |
| 17 | Oklahoma | 1,437 |
| 18 | Arizona | 1,421 |
| 19 | Pennsylvania | 1,410 |
| 20 | Nevada | 1,376 |
| 21 | Wisconsin | 1,359 |
| 22 | Indiana | 1,354 |
| 23 | Virginia | 1,353 |
| 24 | Alaska | 1,315 |
| 25 | Louisiana | 1,309 |
| 26 | Rhode Island | 1,297 |
| 27 | Kansas | 1,296 |
| 28 | Alabama | 1,294 |
| 29 | New Hampshire | 1,292 |
| 30 | Hawaii | 1,286 |
| 31 | North Carolina | 1,279 |
| 32 | Oregon | 1,269 |
| 33 | New Mexico | 1,203 |
| 34 | Mississippi | 1,186 |
| 35 | Utah | 1,168 |
| 36 | Wyoming | 1,166 |
| 37 | Arkansas | 1,156 |
| 38 | Kentucky | 1,141 |
| 39 | Idaho | 1,140 |
| 40 | South Carolina | 1,138 |
| 41 | Vermont | 1,128 |
| 42 | Delaware | 1,126 |
| 43 | Nebraska | 1,116 |
| 44 | Maine | 1,112 |
| 45 | Montana | 1,074 |
| 46 | West Virginia | 1,066 |
| 47 | North Dakota | 1,025 |
| 48 | South Dakota | 995 |
| 49 | Iowa | 992 |
| 50 | Michigan | 807 |

District of Columbia**                    NA

*Source: Morgan Quitno Press using data from U.S. Department of the Treasury, Internal Revenue Service*
*"Amount Internal Revenue Refunds, Including Interest" (http://www.irs.gov/tax_stats/soi/other_tr.html) and*
*"Number of Internal Revenue Refunds Issued" (http://www.irs.gov/tax_stats/soi/other_tr.html)*
*\*Total includes refunds to international sources and other miscellaneous refunds not shown separately.*
*\*\*Maryland's figure includes the District of Columbia.*

# Value of Federal Individual Income Tax Refunds in 1998

## National Total = $120,803,308,000*

ALPHA ORDER

| RANK | STATE | REFUNDS | % of USA |
|------|-------|---------|----------|
| 25 | Alabama | $1,223,613,000 | 1.0% |
| 46 | Alaska | 182,900,000 | 0.2% |
| 21 | Arizona | 1,398,803,000 | 1.2% |
| 32 | Arkansas | 604,179,000 | 0.5% |
| 2 | California | 11,853,576,000 | 9.8% |
| 24 | Colorado | 1,360,425,000 | 1.1% |
| 19 | Connecticut | 1,660,974,000 | 1.4% |
| 45 | Delaware | 212,472,000 | 0.2% |
| 7 | Florida | 4,564,619,000 | 3.8% |
| 16 | Georgia | 2,002,309,000 | 1.7% |
| 41 | Hawaii | 359,750,000 | 0.3% |
| 43 | Idaho | 317,489,000 | 0.3% |
| 8 | Illinois | 3,876,237,000 | 3.2% |
| 18 | Indiana | 1,783,419,000 | 1.5% |
| 35 | Iowa | 563,375,000 | 0.5% |
| 30 | Kansas | 701,595,000 | 0.6% |
| 27 | Kentucky | 1,033,855,000 | 0.9% |
| 4 | Louisiana | 5,724,189,000 | 4.7% |
| 42 | Maine | 357,823,000 | 0.3% |
| 14 | Maryland** | 2,206,766,000 | 1.8% |
| 12 | Massachusetts | 2,623,306,000 | 2.2% |
| 6 | Michigan | 4,896,048,000 | 4.1% |
| 26 | Minnesota | 1,182,008,000 | 1.0% |
| 31 | Mississippi | 633,412,000 | 0.5% |
| 23 | Missouri | 1,369,602,000 | 1.1% |
| 44 | Montana | 223,868,000 | 0.2% |
| 38 | Nebraska | 446,606,000 | 0.4% |
| 33 | Nevada | 599,811,000 | 0.5% |
| 39 | New Hampshire | 402,005,000 | 0.3% |
| 11 | New Jersey | 3,395,022,000 | 2.8% |
| 36 | New Mexico | 491,418,000 | 0.4% |
| 3 | New York | 9,826,589,000 | 8.1% |
| 15 | North Carolina | 2,100,525,000 | 1.7% |
| 49 | North Dakota | 157,706,000 | 0.1% |
| 9 | Ohio | 3,674,294,000 | 3.0% |
| 28 | Oklahoma | 855,286,000 | 0.7% |
| 5 | Oregon | 5,680,590,000 | 4.7% |
| 10 | Pennsylvania | 3,533,466,000 | 2.9% |
| 40 | Rhode Island | 372,023,000 | 0.3% |
| 29 | South Carolina | 814,036,000 | 0.7% |
| 48 | South Dakota | 171,249,000 | 0.1% |
| 20 | Tennessee | 1,654,137,000 | 1.4% |
| 1 | Texas | 12,685,430,000 | 10.5% |
| 34 | Utah | 592,274,000 | 0.5% |
| 47 | Vermont | 181,759,000 | 0.2% |
| 17 | Virginia | 1,783,964,000 | 1.5% |
| 13 | Washington | 2,224,567,000 | 1.8% |
| 37 | West Virginia | 451,090,000 | 0.4% |
| 22 | Wisconsin | 1,395,255,000 | 1.2% |
| 50 | Wyoming | 134,231,000 | 0.1% |

RANK ORDER

| RANK | STATE | REFUNDS | % of USA |
|------|-------|---------|----------|
| 1 | Texas | $12,685,430,000 | 10.5% |
| 2 | California | 11,853,576,000 | 9.8% |
| 3 | New York | 9,826,589,000 | 8.1% |
| 4 | Louisiana | 5,724,189,000 | 4.7% |
| 5 | Oregon | 5,680,590,000 | 4.7% |
| 6 | Michigan | 4,896,048,000 | 4.1% |
| 7 | Florida | 4,564,619,000 | 3.8% |
| 8 | Illinois | 3,876,237,000 | 3.2% |
| 9 | Ohio | 3,674,294,000 | 3.0% |
| 10 | Pennsylvania | 3,533,466,000 | 2.9% |
| 11 | New Jersey | 3,395,022,000 | 2.8% |
| 12 | Massachusetts | 2,623,306,000 | 2.2% |
| 13 | Washington | 2,224,567,000 | 1.8% |
| 14 | Maryland** | 2,206,766,000 | 1.8% |
| 15 | North Carolina | 2,100,525,000 | 1.7% |
| 16 | Georgia | 2,002,309,000 | 1.7% |
| 17 | Virginia | 1,783,964,000 | 1.5% |
| 18 | Indiana | 1,783,419,000 | 1.5% |
| 19 | Connecticut | 1,660,974,000 | 1.4% |
| 20 | Tennessee | 1,654,137,000 | 1.4% |
| 21 | Arizona | 1,398,803,000 | 1.2% |
| 22 | Wisconsin | 1,395,255,000 | 1.2% |
| 23 | Missouri | 1,369,602,000 | 1.1% |
| 24 | Colorado | 1,360,425,000 | 1.1% |
| 25 | Alabama | 1,223,613,000 | 1.0% |
| 26 | Minnesota | 1,182,008,000 | 1.0% |
| 27 | Kentucky | 1,033,855,000 | 0.9% |
| 28 | Oklahoma | 855,286,000 | 0.7% |
| 29 | South Carolina | 814,036,000 | 0.7% |
| 30 | Kansas | 701,595,000 | 0.6% |
| 31 | Mississippi | 633,412,000 | 0.5% |
| 32 | Arkansas | 604,179,000 | 0.5% |
| 33 | Nevada | 599,811,000 | 0.5% |
| 34 | Utah | 592,274,000 | 0.5% |
| 35 | Iowa | 563,375,000 | 0.5% |
| 36 | New Mexico | 491,418,000 | 0.4% |
| 37 | West Virginia | 451,090,000 | 0.4% |
| 38 | Nebraska | 446,606,000 | 0.4% |
| 39 | New Hampshire | 402,005,000 | 0.3% |
| 40 | Rhode Island | 372,023,000 | 0.3% |
| 41 | Hawaii | 359,750,000 | 0.3% |
| 42 | Maine | 357,823,000 | 0.3% |
| 43 | Idaho | 317,489,000 | 0.3% |
| 44 | Montana | 223,868,000 | 0.2% |
| 45 | Delaware | 212,472,000 | 0.2% |
| 46 | Alaska | 182,900,000 | 0.2% |
| 47 | Vermont | 181,759,000 | 0.2% |
| 48 | South Dakota | 171,249,000 | 0.1% |
| 49 | North Dakota | 157,706,000 | 0.1% |
| 50 | Wyoming | 134,231,000 | 0.1% |
| | District of Columbia** | NA | NA |

Source: U.S. Department of the Treasury, Internal Revenue Service
   "Amount Internal Revenue Refunds, Including Interest" (http://www.irs.gov/tax_stats/soi/other_tr.html)
*Total includes refunds to international sources and other miscellaneous refunds not shown separately.
**Maryland's figure includes the District of Columbia.

# Average Value of Federal Individual Income Tax Refunds in 1998

## National Average = $1,377*

ALPHA ORDER

| RANK | STATE | REFUNDS |
|------|-------|---------|
| 21 | Alabama | $1,214 |
| 11 | Alaska | 1,275 |
| 19 | Arizona | 1,218 |
| 32 | Arkansas | 1,119 |
| 4 | California | 1,481 |
| 17 | Colorado | 1,228 |
| 1 | Connecticut | 1,579 |
| 25 | Delaware | 1,151 |
| 8 | Florida | 1,309 |
| 16 | Georgia | 1,245 |
| 20 | Hawaii | 1,216 |
| 37 | Idaho | 1,105 |
| 6 | Illinois | 1,316 |
| 31 | Indiana | 1,122 |
| 49 | Iowa | 947 |
| 24 | Kansas | 1,152 |
| 36 | Kentucky | 1,107 |
| 12 | Louisiana | 1,274 |
| 39 | Maine | 1,092 |
| 10 | Maryland** | 1,295 |
| 5 | Massachusetts | 1,446 |
| 50 | Michigan | 645 |
| 46 | Minnesota | 1,031 |
| 27 | Mississippi | 1,140 |
| 40 | Missouri | 1,088 |
| 43 | Montana | 1,056 |
| 42 | Nebraska | 1,082 |
| 7 | Nevada | 1,314 |
| 13 | New Hampshire | 1,268 |
| 2 | New Jersey | 1,545 |
| 22 | New Mexico | 1,171 |
| 14 | New York | 1,264 |
| 32 | North Carolina | 1,119 |
| 47 | North Dakota | 987 |
| 41 | Ohio | 1,085 |
| 38 | Oklahoma | 1,101 |
| 15 | Oregon | 1,255 |
| 29 | Pennsylvania | 1,132 |
| 9 | Rhode Island | 1,296 |
| 35 | South Carolina | 1,113 |
| 48 | South Dakota | 973 |
| 23 | Tennessee | 1,167 |
| 3 | Texas | 1,509 |
| 30 | Utah | 1,131 |
| 34 | Vermont | 1,118 |
| 26 | Virginia | 1,142 |
| 18 | Washington | 1,227 |
| 44 | West Virginia | 1,050 |
| 44 | Wisconsin | 1,050 |
| 27 | Wyoming | 1,140 |

RANK ORDER

| RANK | STATE | REFUNDS |
|------|-------|---------|
| 1 | Connecticut | $1,579 |
| 2 | New Jersey | 1,545 |
| 3 | Texas | 1,509 |
| 4 | California | 1,481 |
| 5 | Massachusetts | 1,446 |
| 6 | Illinois | 1,316 |
| 7 | Nevada | 1,314 |
| 8 | Florida | 1,309 |
| 9 | Rhode Island | 1,296 |
| 10 | Maryland** | 1,295 |
| 11 | Alaska | 1,275 |
| 12 | Louisiana | 1,274 |
| 13 | New Hampshire | 1,268 |
| 14 | New York | 1,264 |
| 15 | Oregon | 1,255 |
| 16 | Georgia | 1,245 |
| 17 | Colorado | 1,228 |
| 18 | Washington | 1,227 |
| 19 | Arizona | 1,218 |
| 20 | Hawaii | 1,216 |
| 21 | Alabama | 1,214 |
| 22 | New Mexico | 1,171 |
| 23 | Tennessee | 1,167 |
| 24 | Kansas | 1,152 |
| 25 | Delaware | 1,151 |
| 26 | Virginia | 1,142 |
| 27 | Mississippi | 1,140 |
| 27 | Wyoming | 1,140 |
| 29 | Pennsylvania | 1,132 |
| 30 | Utah | 1,131 |
| 31 | Indiana | 1,122 |
| 32 | Arkansas | 1,119 |
| 32 | North Carolina | 1,119 |
| 34 | Vermont | 1,118 |
| 35 | South Carolina | 1,113 |
| 36 | Kentucky | 1,107 |
| 37 | Idaho | 1,105 |
| 38 | Oklahoma | 1,101 |
| 39 | Maine | 1,092 |
| 40 | Missouri | 1,088 |
| 41 | Ohio | 1,085 |
| 42 | Nebraska | 1,082 |
| 43 | Montana | 1,056 |
| 44 | West Virginia | 1,050 |
| 44 | Wisconsin | 1,050 |
| 46 | Minnesota | 1,031 |
| 47 | North Dakota | 987 |
| 48 | South Dakota | 973 |
| 49 | Iowa | 947 |
| 50 | Michigan | 645 |

District of Columbia**     NA

Source: Morgan Quitno Press using data from U.S. Department of the Treasury, Internal Revenue Service
"Amount Internal Revenue Refunds, Including Interest" (http://www.irs.gov/tax_stats/soi/other_tr.html) and
"Number of Internal Revenue Refunds Issued" (http://www.irs.gov/tax_stats/soi/other_tr.html)
*Total includes refunds to international sources and other miscellaneous refunds not shown separately.
**Maryland's figure includes the District of Columbia.

# Value of Federal Corporate Income Tax Refunds in 1998

## National Total = $27,560,085,000*

ALPHA ORDER

| RANK | STATE | REFUNDS | % of USA |
|------|-------|---------|----------|
| 27 | Alabama | $96,844,000 | 0.4% |
| 44 | Alaska | 11,181,000 | 0.0% |
| 24 | Arizona | 257,168,000 | 0.9% |
| 33 | Arkansas | 31,315,000 | 0.1% |
| 3 | California | 2,887,675,000 | 10.5% |
| 15 | Colorado | 513,633,000 | 1.9% |
| 13 | Connecticut | 731,396,000 | 2.7% |
| 50 | Delaware | (2,262,000) | 0.0% |
| 9 | Florida | 1,124,333,000 | 4.1% |
| 16 | Georgia | 504,881,000 | 1.8% |
| 36 | Hawaii | 26,564,000 | 0.1% |
| 39 | Idaho | 17,063,000 | 0.1% |
| 7 | Illinois | 1,349,892,000 | 4.9% |
| 20 | Indiana | 398,750,000 | 1.4% |
| 30 | Iowa | 38,862,000 | 0.1% |
| 26 | Kansas | 104,898,000 | 0.4% |
| 29 | Kentucky | 39,404,000 | 0.1% |
| 25 | Louisiana | 154,301,000 | 0.6% |
| 41 | Maine | 14,042,000 | 0.1% |
| 4 | Maryland** | 2,159,618,000 | 7.8% |
| 12 | Massachusetts | 770,774,000 | 2.8% |
| 8 | Michigan | 1,127,974,000 | 4.1% |
| 14 | Minnesota | 570,951,000 | 2.1% |
| 31 | Mississippi | 38,328,000 | 0.1% |
| 17 | Missouri | 477,010,000 | 1.7% |
| 43 | Montana | 12,478,000 | 0.0% |
| 37 | Nebraska | 24,910,000 | 0.1% |
| 32 | Nevada | 37,208,000 | 0.1% |
| 40 | New Hampshire | 15,026,000 | 0.1% |
| 5 | New Jersey | 1,591,531,000 | 5.8% |
| 38 | New Mexico | 20,108,000 | 0.1% |
| 1 | New York | 3,068,925,000 | 11.1% |
| 22 | North Carolina | 334,802,000 | 1.2% |
| 45 | North Dakota | 10,717,000 | 0.0% |
| 6 | Ohio | 1,446,373,000 | 5.2% |
| 23 | Oklahoma | 281,190,000 | 1.0% |
| 28 | Oregon | 85,932,000 | 0.3% |
| 11 | Pennsylvania | 904,107,000 | 3.3% |
| 49 | Rhode Island | 4,193,000 | 0.0% |
| 34 | South Carolina | 30,530,000 | 0.1% |
| 46 | South Dakota | 9,140,000 | 0.0% |
| 18 | Tennessee | 452,475,000 | 1.6% |
| 2 | Texas | 2,947,300,000 | 10.7% |
| 35 | Utah | 28,808,000 | 0.1% |
| 48 | Vermont | 6,759,000 | 0.0% |
| 21 | Virginia | 358,632,000 | 1.3% |
| 10 | Washington | 1,083,958,000 | 3.9% |
| 42 | West Virginia | 13,876,000 | 0.1% |
| 19 | Wisconsin | 434,212,000 | 1.6% |
| 47 | Wyoming | 7,958,000 | 0.0% |

RANK ORDER

| RANK | STATE | REFUNDS | % of USA |
|------|-------|---------|----------|
| 1 | New York | $3,068,925,000 | 11.1% |
| 2 | Texas | 2,947,300,000 | 10.7% |
| 3 | California | 2,887,675,000 | 10.5% |
| 4 | Maryland** | 2,159,618,000 | 7.8% |
| 5 | New Jersey | 1,591,531,000 | 5.8% |
| 6 | Ohio | 1,446,373,000 | 5.2% |
| 7 | Illinois | 1,349,892,000 | 4.9% |
| 8 | Michigan | 1,127,974,000 | 4.1% |
| 9 | Florida | 1,124,333,000 | 4.1% |
| 10 | Washington | 1,083,958,000 | 3.9% |
| 11 | Pennsylvania | 904,107,000 | 3.3% |
| 12 | Massachusetts | 770,774,000 | 2.8% |
| 13 | Connecticut | 731,396,000 | 2.7% |
| 14 | Minnesota | 570,951,000 | 2.1% |
| 15 | Colorado | 513,633,000 | 1.9% |
| 16 | Georgia | 504,881,000 | 1.8% |
| 17 | Missouri | 477,010,000 | 1.7% |
| 18 | Tennessee | 452,475,000 | 1.6% |
| 19 | Wisconsin | 434,212,000 | 1.6% |
| 20 | Indiana | 398,750,000 | 1.4% |
| 21 | Virginia | 358,632,000 | 1.3% |
| 22 | North Carolina | 334,802,000 | 1.2% |
| 23 | Oklahoma | 281,190,000 | 1.0% |
| 24 | Arizona | 257,168,000 | 0.9% |
| 25 | Louisiana | 154,301,000 | 0.6% |
| 26 | Kansas | 104,898,000 | 0.4% |
| 27 | Alabama | 96,844,000 | 0.4% |
| 28 | Oregon | 85,932,000 | 0.3% |
| 29 | Kentucky | 39,404,000 | 0.1% |
| 30 | Iowa | 38,862,000 | 0.1% |
| 31 | Mississippi | 38,328,000 | 0.1% |
| 32 | Nevada | 37,208,000 | 0.1% |
| 33 | Arkansas | 31,315,000 | 0.1% |
| 34 | South Carolina | 30,530,000 | 0.1% |
| 35 | Utah | 28,808,000 | 0.1% |
| 36 | Hawaii | 26,564,000 | 0.1% |
| 37 | Nebraska | 24,910,000 | 0.1% |
| 38 | New Mexico | 20,108,000 | 0.1% |
| 39 | Idaho | 17,063,000 | 0.1% |
| 40 | New Hampshire | 15,026,000 | 0.1% |
| 41 | Maine | 14,042,000 | 0.1% |
| 42 | West Virginia | 13,876,000 | 0.1% |
| 43 | Montana | 12,478,000 | 0.0% |
| 44 | Alaska | 11,181,000 | 0.0% |
| 45 | North Dakota | 10,717,000 | 0.0% |
| 46 | South Dakota | 9,140,000 | 0.0% |
| 47 | Wyoming | 7,958,000 | 0.0% |
| 48 | Vermont | 6,759,000 | 0.0% |
| 49 | Rhode Island | 4,193,000 | 0.0% |
| 50 | Delaware | (2,262,000) | 0.0% |
| | District of Columbia** | NA | NA |

Source: U.S. Department of the Treasury, Internal Revenue Service
"Amount Internal Revenue Refunds, Including Interest" (http://www.irs.gov/tax_stats/soi/other_tr.html)
*Total includes refunds to international sources and other miscellaneous refunds not shown separately.
**Maryland's figure includes the District of Columbia.

# Average Value of Federal Corporate Income Tax Refunds in 1998

## National Average = $49,384*

ALPHA ORDER

| RANK | STATE | REFUNDS |
|------|-------|---------|
| 26 | Alabama | $18,422 |
| 30 | Alaska | 10,119 |
| 20 | Arizona | 35,942 |
| 35 | Arkansas | 8,716 |
| 11 | California | 56,882 |
| 10 | Colorado | 58,560 |
| 2 | Connecticut | 122,573 |
| 50 | Delaware | (1,568) |
| 13 | Florida | 50,575 |
| 19 | Georgia | 40,772 |
| 34 | Hawaii | 8,741 |
| 38 | Idaho | 7,007 |
| 8 | Illinois | 64,790 |
| 17 | Indiana | 48,753 |
| 46 | Iowa | 5,393 |
| 24 | Kansas | 19,860 |
| 33 | Kentucky | 9,096 |
| 25 | Louisiana | 19,701 |
| 42 | Maine | 6,063 |
| 1 | Maryland** | 197,713 |
| 7 | Massachusetts | 67,975 |
| 14 | Michigan | 50,426 |
| 9 | Minnesota | 62,584 |
| 31 | Mississippi | 9,601 |
| 18 | Missouri | 43,670 |
| 48 | Montana | 3,247 |
| 44 | Nebraska | 5,830 |
| 28 | Nevada | 11,613 |
| 41 | New Hampshire | 6,362 |
| 4 | New Jersey | 117,612 |
| 36 | New Mexico | 8,177 |
| 3 | New York | 122,039 |
| 23 | North Carolina | 26,629 |
| 40 | North Dakota | 6,567 |
| 27 | Ohio | 13,725 |
| 15 | Oklahoma | 50,078 |
| 29 | Oregon | 10,887 |
| 6 | Pennsylvania | 71,857 |
| 49 | Rhode Island | 3,063 |
| 37 | South Carolina | 7,123 |
| 47 | South Dakota | 4,973 |
| 12 | Tennessee | 52,068 |
| 5 | Texas | 88,021 |
| 32 | Utah | 9,216 |
| 43 | Vermont | 6,040 |
| 22 | Virginia | 32,671 |
| 16 | Washington | 49,582 |
| 39 | West Virginia | 6,720 |
| 21 | Wisconsin | 33,896 |
| 45 | Wyoming | 5,469 |

RANK ORDER

| RANK | STATE | REFUNDS |
|------|-------|---------|
| 1 | Maryland** | $197,713 |
| 2 | Connecticut | 122,573 |
| 3 | New York | 122,039 |
| 4 | New Jersey | 117,612 |
| 5 | Texas | 88,021 |
| 6 | Pennsylvania | 71,857 |
| 7 | Massachusetts | 67,975 |
| 8 | Illinois | 64,790 |
| 9 | Minnesota | 62,584 |
| 10 | Colorado | 58,560 |
| 11 | California | 56,882 |
| 12 | Tennessee | 52,068 |
| 13 | Florida | 50,575 |
| 14 | Michigan | 50,426 |
| 15 | Oklahoma | 50,078 |
| 16 | Washington | 49,582 |
| 17 | Indiana | 48,753 |
| 18 | Missouri | 43,670 |
| 19 | Georgia | 40,772 |
| 20 | Arizona | 35,942 |
| 21 | Wisconsin | 33,896 |
| 22 | Virginia | 32,671 |
| 23 | North Carolina | 26,629 |
| 24 | Kansas | 19,860 |
| 25 | Louisiana | 19,701 |
| 26 | Alabama | 18,422 |
| 27 | Ohio | 13,725 |
| 28 | Nevada | 11,613 |
| 29 | Oregon | 10,887 |
| 30 | Alaska | 10,119 |
| 31 | Mississippi | 9,601 |
| 32 | Utah | 9,216 |
| 33 | Kentucky | 9,096 |
| 34 | Hawaii | 8,741 |
| 35 | Arkansas | 8,716 |
| 36 | New Mexico | 8,177 |
| 37 | South Carolina | 7,123 |
| 38 | Idaho | 7,007 |
| 39 | West Virginia | 6,720 |
| 40 | North Dakota | 6,567 |
| 41 | New Hampshire | 6,362 |
| 42 | Maine | 6,063 |
| 43 | Vermont | 6,040 |
| 44 | Nebraska | 5,830 |
| 45 | Wyoming | 5,469 |
| 46 | Iowa | 5,393 |
| 47 | South Dakota | 4,973 |
| 48 | Montana | 3,247 |
| 49 | Rhode Island | 3,063 |
| 50 | Delaware | (1,568) |

District of Columbia**    NA

*Source: Morgan Quitno Press using data from U.S. Department of the Treasury, Internal Revenue Service*
*"Amount Internal Revenue Refunds, Including Interest" (http://www.irs.gov/tax_stats/soi/other_tr.html) and*
*"Number of Internal Revenue Refunds Issued" (http://www.irs.gov/tax_stats/soi/other_tr.html)*
*Total includes refunds to international sources and other miscellaneous refunds not shown separately.*
**Maryland's figure includes the District of Columbia.*

# Federal Government Expenditures in 1999

## National Total = $1,531,627,134,000*

ALPHA ORDER

| RANK | STATE | EXPENDITURES | % of USA |
|------|-------|--------------|----------|
| 20 | Alabama | $26,775,609,000 | 1.7% |
| 45 | Alaska | 5,278,716,000 | 0.3% |
| 18 | Arizona | 26,959,312,000 | 1.8% |
| 33 | Arkansas | 13,630,841,000 | 0.9% |
| 1 | California | 166,049,702,000 | 10.8% |
| 24 | Colorado | 21,755,429,000 | 1.4% |
| 27 | Connecticut | 19,240,532,000 | 1.3% |
| 48 | Delaware | 3,765,734,000 | 0.2% |
| 4 | Florida | 87,214,874,000 | 5.7% |
| 12 | Georgia | 39,214,972,000 | 2.6% |
| 38 | Hawaii | 8,568,210,000 | 0.6% |
| 42 | Idaho | 6,164,663,000 | 0.4% |
| 7 | Illinois | 55,835,956,000 | 3.6% |
| 19 | Indiana | 26,828,143,000 | 1.8% |
| 30 | Iowa | 15,601,525,000 | 1.0% |
| 32 | Kansas | 14,447,019,000 | 0.9% |
| 23 | Kentucky | 22,198,101,000 | 1.4% |
| 21 | Louisiana | 24,384,278,000 | 1.6% |
| 40 | Maine | 7,281,484,000 | 0.5% |
| 10 | Maryland | 41,990,244,000 | 2.7% |
| 13 | Massachusetts | 37,803,042,000 | 2.5% |
| 9 | Michigan | 43,871,642,000 | 2.9% |
| 25 | Minnesota | 21,665,794,000 | 1.4% |
| 29 | Mississippi | 16,487,905,000 | 1.1% |
| 15 | Missouri | 33,231,031,000 | 2.2% |
| 41 | Montana | 6,225,014,000 | 0.4% |
| 37 | Nebraska | 8,793,324,000 | 0.6% |
| 39 | Nevada | 7,941,909,000 | 0.5% |
| 44 | New Hampshire | 5,301,370,000 | 0.3% |
| 11 | New Jersey | 40,397,603,000 | 2.6% |
| 34 | New Mexico | 13,580,214,000 | 0.9% |
| 2 | New York | 101,808,595,000 | 6.6% |
| 14 | North Carolina | 37,227,647,000 | 2.4% |
| 47 | North Dakota | 4,535,216,000 | 0.3% |
| 8 | Ohio | 53,262,163,000 | 3.5% |
| 28 | Oklahoma | 19,188,707,000 | 1.3% |
| 31 | Oregon | 15,592,249,000 | 1.0% |
| 5 | Pennsylvania | 69,448,043,000 | 4.5% |
| 43 | Rhode Island | 6,036,064,000 | 0.4% |
| 26 | South Carolina | 20,833,188,000 | 1.4% |
| 46 | South Dakota | 4,909,015,000 | 0.3% |
| 17 | Tennessee | 30,866,835,000 | 2.0% |
| 3 | Texas | 97,987,610,000 | 6.4% |
| 36 | Utah | 9,238,662,000 | 0.6% |
| 49 | Vermont | 3,114,291,000 | 0.2% |
| 6 | Virginia | 57,842,231,000 | 3.8% |
| 16 | Washington | 31,993,052,000 | 2.1% |
| 35 | West Virginia | 11,028,116,000 | 0.7% |
| 22 | Wisconsin | 22,603,768,000 | 1.5% |
| 50 | Wyoming | 2,916,241,000 | 0.2% |

RANK ORDER

| RANK | STATE | EXPENDITURES | % of USA |
|------|-------|--------------|----------|
| 1 | California | $166,049,702,000 | 10.8% |
| 2 | New York | 101,808,595,000 | 6.6% |
| 3 | Texas | 97,987,610,000 | 6.4% |
| 4 | Florida | 87,214,874,000 | 5.7% |
| 5 | Pennsylvania | 69,448,043,000 | 4.5% |
| 6 | Virginia | 57,842,231,000 | 3.8% |
| 7 | Illinois | 55,835,956,000 | 3.6% |
| 8 | Ohio | 53,262,163,000 | 3.5% |
| 9 | Michigan | 43,871,642,000 | 2.9% |
| 10 | Maryland | 41,990,244,000 | 2.7% |
| 11 | New Jersey | 40,397,603,000 | 2.6% |
| 12 | Georgia | 39,214,972,000 | 2.6% |
| 13 | Massachusetts | 37,803,042,000 | 2.5% |
| 14 | North Carolina | 37,227,647,000 | 2.4% |
| 15 | Missouri | 33,231,031,000 | 2.2% |
| 16 | Washington | 31,993,052,000 | 2.1% |
| 17 | Tennessee | 30,866,835,000 | 2.0% |
| 18 | Arizona | 26,959,312,000 | 1.8% |
| 19 | Indiana | 26,828,143,000 | 1.8% |
| 20 | Alabama | 26,775,609,000 | 1.7% |
| 21 | Louisiana | 24,384,278,000 | 1.6% |
| 22 | Wisconsin | 22,603,768,000 | 1.5% |
| 23 | Kentucky | 22,198,101,000 | 1.4% |
| 24 | Colorado | 21,755,429,000 | 1.4% |
| 25 | Minnesota | 21,665,794,000 | 1.4% |
| 26 | South Carolina | 20,833,188,000 | 1.4% |
| 27 | Connecticut | 19,240,532,000 | 1.3% |
| 28 | Oklahoma | 19,188,707,000 | 1.3% |
| 29 | Mississippi | 16,487,905,000 | 1.1% |
| 30 | Iowa | 15,601,525,000 | 1.0% |
| 31 | Oregon | 15,592,249,000 | 1.0% |
| 32 | Kansas | 14,447,019,000 | 0.9% |
| 33 | Arkansas | 13,630,841,000 | 0.9% |
| 34 | New Mexico | 13,580,214,000 | 0.9% |
| 35 | West Virginia | 11,028,116,000 | 0.7% |
| 36 | Utah | 9,238,662,000 | 0.6% |
| 37 | Nebraska | 8,793,324,000 | 0.6% |
| 38 | Hawaii | 8,568,210,000 | 0.6% |
| 39 | Nevada | 7,941,909,000 | 0.5% |
| 40 | Maine | 7,281,484,000 | 0.5% |
| 41 | Montana | 6,225,014,000 | 0.4% |
| 42 | Idaho | 6,164,663,000 | 0.4% |
| 43 | Rhode Island | 6,036,064,000 | 0.4% |
| 44 | New Hampshire | 5,301,370,000 | 0.3% |
| 45 | Alaska | 5,278,716,000 | 0.3% |
| 46 | South Dakota | 4,909,015,000 | 0.3% |
| 47 | North Dakota | 4,535,216,000 | 0.3% |
| 48 | Delaware | 3,765,734,000 | 0.2% |
| 49 | Vermont | 3,114,291,000 | 0.2% |
| 50 | Wyoming | 2,916,241,000 | 0.2% |
|  | District of Columbia | 27,033,665,000 | 1.8% |

*Source: U.S. Bureau of the Census*
   *"Consolidated Federal Funds Report: 1999" (CFFR/99, Revised August 2000)*
*Total includes $14,853,000,000 in U.S. territories ($12,982,000,000 in Puerto Rico) and $20,825,000,000 in expenditures not distributed by state.*

# Per Capita Federal Government Expenditures in 1999

## National Per Capita = $5,486*

ALPHA ORDER

RANK ORDER

| RANK | STATE | PER CAPITA | | RANK | STATE | PER CAPITA |
|---|---|---|---|---|---|---|
| 9 | Alabama | $6,127 | | 1 | Alaska | $8,521 |
| 1 | Alaska | 8,521 | | 2 | Virginia | 8,416 |
| 21 | Arizona | 5,642 | | 3 | Maryland | 8,119 |
| 31 | Arkansas | 5,343 | | 4 | New Mexico | 7,805 |
| 35 | California | 5,010 | | 5 | Hawaii | 7,228 |
| 29 | Colorado | 5,364 | | 6 | North Dakota | 7,157 |
| 16 | Connecticut | 5,862 | | 7 | Montana | 7,052 |
| 36 | Delaware | 4,997 | | 8 | South Dakota | 6,696 |
| 19 | Florida | 5,772 | | 9 | Alabama | 6,127 |
| 34 | Georgia | 5,035 | | 10 | Massachusetts | 6,122 |
| 5 | Hawaii | 7,228 | | 11 | West Virginia | 6,103 |
| 38 | Idaho | 4,925 | | 12 | Rhode Island | 6,092 |
| 43 | Illinois | 4,604 | | 13 | Wyoming | 6,081 |
| 45 | Indiana | 4,514 | | 14 | Missouri | 6,077 |
| 28 | Iowa | 5,437 | | 15 | Mississippi | 5,955 |
| 27 | Kansas | 5,443 | | 16 | Connecticut | 5,862 |
| 23 | Kentucky | 5,604 | | 17 | Maine | 5,811 |
| 25 | Louisiana | 5,577 | | 18 | Pennsylvania | 5,790 |
| 17 | Maine | 5,811 | | 19 | Florida | 5,772 |
| 3 | Maryland | 8,119 | | 20 | Oklahoma | 5,714 |
| 10 | Massachusetts | 6,122 | | 21 | Arizona | 5,642 |
| 46 | Michigan | 4,448 | | 22 | Tennessee | 5,629 |
| 44 | Minnesota | 4,537 | | 23 | Kentucky | 5,604 |
| 15 | Mississippi | 5,955 | | 24 | New York | 5,595 |
| 14 | Missouri | 6,077 | | 25 | Louisiana | 5,577 |
| 7 | Montana | 7,052 | | 26 | Washington | 5,558 |
| 32 | Nebraska | 5,278 | | 27 | Kansas | 5,443 |
| 48 | Nevada | 4,390 | | 28 | Iowa | 5,437 |
| 47 | New Hampshire | 4,414 | | 29 | Colorado | 5,364 |
| 37 | New Jersey | 4,961 | | 30 | South Carolina | 5,361 |
| 4 | New Mexico | 7,805 | | 31 | Arkansas | 5,343 |
| 24 | New York | 5,595 | | 32 | Nebraska | 5,278 |
| 40 | North Carolina | 4,866 | | 33 | Vermont | 5,245 |
| 6 | North Dakota | 7,157 | | 34 | Georgia | 5,035 |
| 41 | Ohio | 4,732 | | 35 | California | 5,010 |
| 20 | Oklahoma | 5,714 | | 36 | Delaware | 4,997 |
| 42 | Oregon | 4,702 | | 37 | New Jersey | 4,961 |
| 18 | Pennsylvania | 5,790 | | 38 | Idaho | 4,925 |
| 12 | Rhode Island | 6,092 | | 39 | Texas | 4,889 |
| 30 | South Carolina | 5,361 | | 40 | North Carolina | 4,866 |
| 8 | South Dakota | 6,696 | | 41 | Ohio | 4,732 |
| 22 | Tennessee | 5,629 | | 42 | Oregon | 4,702 |
| 39 | Texas | 4,889 | | 43 | Illinois | 4,604 |
| 49 | Utah | 4,338 | | 44 | Minnesota | 4,537 |
| 33 | Vermont | 5,245 | | 45 | Indiana | 4,514 |
| 2 | Virginia | 8,416 | | 46 | Michigan | 4,448 |
| 26 | Washington | 5,558 | | 47 | New Hampshire | 4,414 |
| 11 | West Virginia | 6,103 | | 48 | Nevada | 4,390 |
| 50 | Wisconsin | 4,305 | | 49 | Utah | 4,338 |
| 13 | Wyoming | 6,081 | | 50 | Wisconsin | 4,305 |
| | | | | | District of Columbia | 52,088 |

Source: Morgan Quitno Press using data from U.S. Bureau of the Census
  "Consolidated Federal Funds Report: 1999" (CFFR/99, Revised August 2000)
*National per capita excludes expenditures and population for territories and undistributed amounts.

# Federal Government Grants in 1999

## National Total = $294,468,691,000*

ALPHA ORDER

| RANK | STATE | GRANTS | % of USA |
|---|---|---|---|
| 21 | Alabama | $4,631,811,000 | 1.6% |
| 37 | Alaska | 1,929,338,000 | 0.7% |
| 22 | Arizona | 4,537,187,000 | 1.5% |
| 32 | Arkansas | 2,614,236,000 | 0.9% |
| 1 | California | 36,369,740,000 | 12.4% |
| 28 | Colorado | 3,445,685,000 | 1.2% |
| 26 | Connecticut | 3,845,740,000 | 1.3% |
| 50 | Delaware | 825,078,000 | 0.3% |
| 5 | Florida | 11,190,873,000 | 3.8% |
| 12 | Georgia | 6,751,504,000 | 2.3% |
| 42 | Hawaii | 1,334,569,000 | 0.5% |
| 44 | Idaho | 1,176,832,000 | 0.4% |
| 6 | Illinois | 10,586,241,000 | 3.6% |
| 20 | Indiana | 4,705,833,000 | 1.6% |
| 33 | Iowa | 2,595,290,000 | 0.9% |
| 35 | Kansas | 2,182,764,000 | 0.7% |
| 24 | Kentucky | 4,395,096,000 | 1.5% |
| 17 | Louisiana | 5,227,879,000 | 1.8% |
| 38 | Maine | 1,664,301,000 | 0.6% |
| 14 | Maryland | 5,743,960,000 | 2.0% |
| 9 | Massachusetts | 8,838,202,000 | 3.0% |
| 8 | Michigan | 9,764,029,000 | 3.3% |
| 23 | Minnesota | 4,498,501,000 | 1.5% |
| 29 | Mississippi | 3,387,313,000 | 1.2% |
| 16 | Missouri | 5,478,456,000 | 1.9% |
| 41 | Montana | 1,399,432,000 | 0.5% |
| 39 | Nebraska | 1,651,241,000 | 0.6% |
| 43 | Nevada | 1,249,010,000 | 0.4% |
| 45 | New Hampshire | 1,120,006,000 | 0.4% |
| 11 | New Jersey | 7,261,564,000 | 2.5% |
| 31 | New Mexico | 2,749,967,000 | 0.9% |
| 2 | New York | 28,869,892,000 | 9.8% |
| 10 | North Carolina | 7,608,000,000 | 2.6% |
| 47 | North Dakota | 1,009,480,000 | 0.3% |
| 7 | Ohio | 10,254,389,000 | 3.5% |
| 30 | Oklahoma | 3,230,741,000 | 1.1% |
| 27 | Oregon | 3,518,292,000 | 1.2% |
| 4 | Pennsylvania | 13,140,671,000 | 4.5% |
| 40 | Rhode Island | 1,410,994,000 | 0.5% |
| 25 | South Carolina | 3,878,727,000 | 1.3% |
| 46 | South Dakota | 1,055,805,000 | 0.4% |
| 13 | Tennessee | 5,900,009,000 | 2.0% |
| 3 | Texas | 18,369,834,000 | 6.2% |
| 36 | Utah | 1,993,680,000 | 0.7% |
| 49 | Vermont | 883,237,000 | 0.3% |
| 19 | Virginia | 4,748,850,000 | 1.6% |
| 15 | Washington | 5,720,345,000 | 1.9% |
| 34 | West Virginia | 2,489,854,000 | 0.8% |
| 18 | Wisconsin | 4,841,740,000 | 1.6% |
| 48 | Wyoming | 933,361,000 | 0.3% |

RANK ORDER

| RANK | STATE | GRANTS | % of USA |
|---|---|---|---|
| 1 | California | $36,369,740,000 | 12.4% |
| 2 | New York | 28,869,892,000 | 9.8% |
| 3 | Texas | 18,369,834,000 | 6.2% |
| 4 | Pennsylvania | 13,140,671,000 | 4.5% |
| 5 | Florida | 11,190,873,000 | 3.8% |
| 6 | Illinois | 10,586,241,000 | 3.6% |
| 7 | Ohio | 10,254,389,000 | 3.5% |
| 8 | Michigan | 9,764,029,000 | 3.3% |
| 9 | Massachusetts | 8,838,202,000 | 3.0% |
| 10 | North Carolina | 7,608,000,000 | 2.6% |
| 11 | New Jersey | 7,261,564,000 | 2.5% |
| 12 | Georgia | 6,751,504,000 | 2.3% |
| 13 | Tennessee | 5,900,009,000 | 2.0% |
| 14 | Maryland | 5,743,960,000 | 2.0% |
| 15 | Washington | 5,720,345,000 | 1.9% |
| 16 | Missouri | 5,478,456,000 | 1.9% |
| 17 | Louisiana | 5,227,879,000 | 1.8% |
| 18 | Wisconsin | 4,841,740,000 | 1.6% |
| 19 | Virginia | 4,748,850,000 | 1.6% |
| 20 | Indiana | 4,705,833,000 | 1.6% |
| 21 | Alabama | 4,631,811,000 | 1.6% |
| 22 | Arizona | 4,537,187,000 | 1.5% |
| 23 | Minnesota | 4,498,501,000 | 1.5% |
| 24 | Kentucky | 4,395,096,000 | 1.5% |
| 25 | South Carolina | 3,878,727,000 | 1.3% |
| 26 | Connecticut | 3,845,740,000 | 1.3% |
| 27 | Oregon | 3,518,292,000 | 1.2% |
| 28 | Colorado | 3,445,685,000 | 1.2% |
| 29 | Mississippi | 3,387,313,000 | 1.2% |
| 30 | Oklahoma | 3,230,741,000 | 1.1% |
| 31 | New Mexico | 2,749,967,000 | 0.9% |
| 32 | Arkansas | 2,614,236,000 | 0.9% |
| 33 | Iowa | 2,595,290,000 | 0.9% |
| 34 | West Virginia | 2,489,854,000 | 0.8% |
| 35 | Kansas | 2,182,764,000 | 0.7% |
| 36 | Utah | 1,993,680,000 | 0.7% |
| 37 | Alaska | 1,929,338,000 | 0.7% |
| 38 | Maine | 1,664,301,000 | 0.6% |
| 39 | Nebraska | 1,651,241,000 | 0.6% |
| 40 | Rhode Island | 1,410,994,000 | 0.5% |
| 41 | Montana | 1,399,432,000 | 0.5% |
| 42 | Hawaii | 1,334,569,000 | 0.5% |
| 43 | Nevada | 1,249,010,000 | 0.4% |
| 44 | Idaho | 1,176,832,000 | 0.4% |
| 45 | New Hampshire | 1,120,006,000 | 0.4% |
| 46 | South Dakota | 1,055,805,000 | 0.4% |
| 47 | North Dakota | 1,009,480,000 | 0.3% |
| 48 | Wyoming | 933,361,000 | 0.3% |
| 49 | Vermont | 883,237,000 | 0.3% |
| 50 | Delaware | 825,078,000 | 0.3% |
| | District of Columbia | 5,292,757,000 | 1.8% |

Source: U.S. Bureau of the Census
   "Consolidated Federal Funds Report: 1999" (CFFR/99, Revised August 2000)
*Total includes $5,918,000,000 in U.S. territories ($5,284,000,000 in Puerto Rico) and $248,000,000 in expenditures not distributed by state.

# Per Capita Expenditures for Federal Government Grants in 1999

## National Per Capita = $1,057*

ALPHA ORDER

| RANK | STATE | PER CAPITA |
|------|-------|-----------|
| 24 | Alabama | $1,060 |
| 1 | Alaska | 3,114 |
| 33 | Arizona | 950 |
| 25 | Arkansas | 1,025 |
| 19 | California | 1,097 |
| 45 | Colorado | 850 |
| 15 | Connecticut | 1,172 |
| 21 | Delaware | 1,095 |
| 48 | Florida | 741 |
| 44 | Georgia | 867 |
| 16 | Hawaii | 1,126 |
| 35 | Idaho | 940 |
| 43 | Illinois | 873 |
| 47 | Indiana | 792 |
| 41 | Iowa | 904 |
| 46 | Kansas | 822 |
| 18 | Kentucky | 1,110 |
| 14 | Louisiana | 1,196 |
| 12 | Maine | 1,328 |
| 17 | Maryland | 1,111 |
| 9 | Massachusetts | 1,431 |
| 31 | Michigan | 990 |
| 34 | Minnesota | 942 |
| 13 | Mississippi | 1,223 |
| 26 | Missouri | 1,002 |
| 5 | Montana | 1,585 |
| 30 | Nebraska | 991 |
| 50 | Nevada | 690 |
| 37 | New Hampshire | 932 |
| 42 | New Jersey | 892 |
| 6 | New Mexico | 1,581 |
| 4 | New York | 1,587 |
| 28 | North Carolina | 994 |
| 3 | North Dakota | 1,593 |
| 40 | Ohio | 911 |
| 32 | Oklahoma | 962 |
| 23 | Oregon | 1,061 |
| 20 | Pennsylvania | 1,096 |
| 10 | Rhode Island | 1,424 |
| 27 | South Carolina | 998 |
| 8 | South Dakota | 1,440 |
| 22 | Tennessee | 1,076 |
| 39 | Texas | 916 |
| 36 | Utah | 936 |
| 7 | Vermont | 1,488 |
| 49 | Virginia | 691 |
| 28 | Washington | 994 |
| 11 | West Virginia | 1,378 |
| 38 | Wisconsin | 922 |
| 2 | Wyoming | 1,946 |

RANK ORDER

| RANK | STATE | PER CAPITA |
|------|-------|-----------|
| 1 | Alaska | $3,114 |
| 2 | Wyoming | 1,946 |
| 3 | North Dakota | 1,593 |
| 4 | New York | 1,587 |
| 5 | Montana | 1,585 |
| 6 | New Mexico | 1,581 |
| 7 | Vermont | 1,488 |
| 8 | South Dakota | 1,440 |
| 9 | Massachusetts | 1,431 |
| 10 | Rhode Island | 1,424 |
| 11 | West Virginia | 1,378 |
| 12 | Maine | 1,328 |
| 13 | Mississippi | 1,223 |
| 14 | Louisiana | 1,196 |
| 15 | Connecticut | 1,172 |
| 16 | Hawaii | 1,126 |
| 17 | Maryland | 1,111 |
| 18 | Kentucky | 1,110 |
| 19 | California | 1,097 |
| 20 | Pennsylvania | 1,096 |
| 21 | Delaware | 1,095 |
| 22 | Tennessee | 1,076 |
| 23 | Oregon | 1,061 |
| 24 | Alabama | 1,060 |
| 25 | Arkansas | 1,025 |
| 26 | Missouri | 1,002 |
| 27 | South Carolina | 998 |
| 28 | North Carolina | 994 |
| 28 | Washington | 994 |
| 30 | Nebraska | 991 |
| 31 | Michigan | 990 |
| 32 | Oklahoma | 962 |
| 33 | Arizona | 950 |
| 34 | Minnesota | 942 |
| 35 | Idaho | 940 |
| 36 | Utah | 936 |
| 37 | New Hampshire | 932 |
| 38 | Wisconsin | 922 |
| 39 | Texas | 916 |
| 40 | Ohio | 911 |
| 41 | Iowa | 904 |
| 42 | New Jersey | 892 |
| 43 | Illinois | 873 |
| 44 | Georgia | 867 |
| 45 | Colorado | 850 |
| 46 | Kansas | 822 |
| 47 | Indiana | 792 |
| 48 | Florida | 741 |
| 49 | Virginia | 691 |
| 50 | Nevada | 690 |
| | District of Columbia | 10,198 |

Source: Morgan Quitno Press using data from U.S. Bureau of the Census
"Consolidated Federal Funds Report: 1999" (CFFR/99, Revised August 2000)
*National per capita excludes expenditures and population for territories and undistributed amounts.

# Federal Government Procurement Contract Awards in 1999

## National Total = $208,093,944,000*

### ALPHA ORDER

| RANK | STATE | CONTRACTS | % of USA |
|------|-------|-----------|----------|
| 18 | Alabama | $3,696,424,000 | 1.8% |
| 36 | Alaska | 845,475,000 | 0.4% |
| 11 | Arizona | 4,781,631,000 | 2.3% |
| 45 | Arkansas | 466,826,000 | 0.2% |
| 1 | California | 25,795,110,000 | 12.4% |
| 15 | Colorado | 4,442,531,000 | 2.1% |
| 19 | Connecticut | 3,636,348,000 | 1.7% |
| 49 | Delaware | 221,241,000 | 0.1% |
| 5 | Florida | 8,639,271,000 | 4.2% |
| 10 | Georgia | 5,150,040,000 | 2.5% |
| 33 | Hawaii | 1,141,351,000 | 0.5% |
| 35 | Idaho | 870,063,000 | 0.4% |
| 20 | Illinois | 3,480,314,000 | 1.7% |
| 24 | Indiana | 2,221,836,000 | 1.1% |
| 34 | Iowa | 897,901,000 | 0.4% |
| 32 | Kansas | 1,263,169,000 | 0.6% |
| 23 | Kentucky | 2,274,856,000 | 1.1% |
| 21 | Louisiana | 2,666,608,000 | 1.3% |
| 37 | Maine | 802,591,000 | 0.4% |
| 4 | Maryland | 10,583,522,000 | 5.1% |
| 8 | Massachusetts | 5,753,282,000 | 2.8% |
| 25 | Michigan | 2,064,872,000 | 1.0% |
| 28 | Minnesota | 1,807,300,000 | 0.9% |
| 27 | Mississippi | 1,939,318,000 | 0.9% |
| 9 | Missouri | 5,705,264,000 | 2.7% |
| 42 | Montana | 519,983,000 | 0.2% |
| 44 | Nebraska | 470,313,000 | 0.2% |
| 38 | Nevada | 801,551,000 | 0.4% |
| 43 | New Hampshire | 481,685,000 | 0.2% |
| 16 | New Jersey | 4,206,178,000 | 2.0% |
| 17 | New Mexico | 3,931,018,000 | 1.9% |
| 6 | New York | 6,772,795,000 | 3.3% |
| 26 | North Carolina | 2,049,792,000 | 1.0% |
| 48 | North Dakota | 254,593,000 | 0.1% |
| 14 | Ohio | 4,507,562,000 | 2.2% |
| 29 | Oklahoma | 1,669,541,000 | 0.8% |
| 39 | Oregon | 765,495,000 | 0.4% |
| 7 | Pennsylvania | 5,933,771,000 | 2.9% |
| 46 | Rhode Island | 421,046,000 | 0.2% |
| 22 | South Carolina | 2,540,236,000 | 1.2% |
| 41 | South Dakota | 523,765,000 | 0.3% |
| 13 | Tennessee | 4,520,355,000 | 2.2% |
| 3 | Texas | 14,502,452,000 | 7.0% |
| 31 | Utah | 1,268,269,000 | 0.6% |
| 47 | Vermont | 276,143,000 | 0.1% |
| 2 | Virginia | 19,044,421,000 | 9.2% |
| 12 | Washington | 4,614,416,000 | 2.2% |
| 40 | West Virginia | 625,242,000 | 0.3% |
| 30 | Wisconsin | 1,433,390,000 | 0.7% |
| 50 | Wyoming | 199,210,000 | 0.1% |

### RANK ORDER

| RANK | STATE | CONTRACTS | % of USA |
|------|-------|-----------|----------|
| 1 | California | $25,795,110,000 | 12.4% |
| 2 | Virginia | 19,044,421,000 | 9.2% |
| 3 | Texas | 14,502,452,000 | 7.0% |
| 4 | Maryland | 10,583,522,000 | 5.1% |
| 5 | Florida | 8,639,271,000 | 4.2% |
| 6 | New York | 6,772,795,000 | 3.3% |
| 7 | Pennsylvania | 5,933,771,000 | 2.9% |
| 8 | Massachusetts | 5,753,282,000 | 2.8% |
| 9 | Missouri | 5,705,264,000 | 2.7% |
| 10 | Georgia | 5,150,040,000 | 2.5% |
| 11 | Arizona | 4,781,631,000 | 2.3% |
| 12 | Washington | 4,614,416,000 | 2.2% |
| 13 | Tennessee | 4,520,355,000 | 2.2% |
| 14 | Ohio | 4,507,562,000 | 2.2% |
| 15 | Colorado | 4,442,531,000 | 2.1% |
| 16 | New Jersey | 4,206,178,000 | 2.0% |
| 17 | New Mexico | 3,931,018,000 | 1.9% |
| 18 | Alabama | 3,696,424,000 | 1.8% |
| 19 | Connecticut | 3,636,348,000 | 1.7% |
| 20 | Illinois | 3,480,314,000 | 1.7% |
| 21 | Louisiana | 2,666,608,000 | 1.3% |
| 22 | South Carolina | 2,540,236,000 | 1.2% |
| 23 | Kentucky | 2,274,856,000 | 1.1% |
| 24 | Indiana | 2,221,836,000 | 1.1% |
| 25 | Michigan | 2,064,872,000 | 1.0% |
| 26 | North Carolina | 2,049,792,000 | 1.0% |
| 27 | Mississippi | 1,939,318,000 | 0.9% |
| 28 | Minnesota | 1,807,300,000 | 0.9% |
| 29 | Oklahoma | 1,669,541,000 | 0.8% |
| 30 | Wisconsin | 1,433,390,000 | 0.7% |
| 31 | Utah | 1,268,269,000 | 0.6% |
| 32 | Kansas | 1,263,169,000 | 0.6% |
| 33 | Hawaii | 1,141,351,000 | 0.5% |
| 34 | Iowa | 897,901,000 | 0.4% |
| 35 | Idaho | 870,063,000 | 0.4% |
| 36 | Alaska | 845,475,000 | 0.4% |
| 37 | Maine | 802,591,000 | 0.4% |
| 38 | Nevada | 801,551,000 | 0.4% |
| 39 | Oregon | 765,495,000 | 0.4% |
| 40 | West Virginia | 625,242,000 | 0.3% |
| 41 | South Dakota | 523,765,000 | 0.3% |
| 42 | Montana | 519,983,000 | 0.2% |
| 43 | New Hampshire | 481,685,000 | 0.2% |
| 44 | Nebraska | 470,313,000 | 0.2% |
| 45 | Arkansas | 466,826,000 | 0.2% |
| 46 | Rhode Island | 421,046,000 | 0.2% |
| 47 | Vermont | 276,143,000 | 0.1% |
| 48 | North Dakota | 254,593,000 | 0.1% |
| 49 | Delaware | 221,241,000 | 0.1% |
| 50 | Wyoming | 199,210,000 | 0.1% |
| | District of Columbia | 6,403,378,000 | 3.1% |

Source: U.S. Bureau of the Census
   "Consolidated Federal Funds Report: 1999" (CFFR/99, Revised August 2000)
*Total includes $933,000,000 in U.S. territories ($525,000,000 in Puerto Rico) and $17,276,894,000 in expenditures not distributed by state.

# Per Capita Expenditures for Federal Government Procurement Contract Awards in 1999
## National Per Capita = $696*

ALPHA ORDER

| RANK | STATE | PER CAPITA |
|------|-------|------------|
| 11 | Alabama | $846 |
| 4 | Alaska | 1,365 |
| 8 | Arizona | 1,001 |
| 50 | Arkansas | 183 |
| 14 | California | 778 |
| 6 | Colorado | 1,095 |
| 5 | Connecticut | 1,108 |
| 43 | Delaware | 294 |
| 26 | Florida | 572 |
| 19 | Georgia | 661 |
| 9 | Hawaii | 963 |
| 18 | Idaho | 695 |
| 44 | Illinois | 287 |
| 39 | Indiana | 374 |
| 42 | Iowa | 313 |
| 30 | Kansas | 476 |
| 25 | Kentucky | 574 |
| 22 | Louisiana | 610 |
| 21 | Maine | 641 |
| 3 | Maryland | 2,046 |
| 10 | Massachusetts | 932 |
| 49 | Michigan | 209 |
| 38 | Minnesota | 378 |
| 17 | Mississippi | 700 |
| 7 | Missouri | 1,043 |
| 24 | Montana | 589 |
| 45 | Nebraska | 282 |
| 32 | Nevada | 443 |
| 36 | New Hampshire | 401 |
| 27 | New Jersey | 517 |
| 2 | New Mexico | 2,259 |
| 40 | New York | 372 |
| 47 | North Carolina | 268 |
| 35 | North Dakota | 402 |
| 37 | Ohio | 400 |
| 28 | Oklahoma | 497 |
| 48 | Oregon | 231 |
| 29 | Pennsylvania | 495 |
| 33 | Rhode Island | 425 |
| 20 | South Carolina | 654 |
| 16 | South Dakota | 714 |
| 12 | Tennessee | 824 |
| 15 | Texas | 724 |
| 23 | Utah | 595 |
| 31 | Vermont | 465 |
| 1 | Virginia | 2,771 |
| 13 | Washington | 802 |
| 41 | West Virginia | 346 |
| 46 | Wisconsin | 273 |
| 34 | Wyoming | 415 |

RANK ORDER

| RANK | STATE | PER CAPITA |
|------|-------|------------|
| 1 | Virginia | $2,771 |
| 2 | New Mexico | 2,259 |
| 3 | Maryland | 2,046 |
| 4 | Alaska | 1,365 |
| 5 | Connecticut | 1,108 |
| 6 | Colorado | 1,095 |
| 7 | Missouri | 1,043 |
| 8 | Arizona | 1,001 |
| 9 | Hawaii | 963 |
| 10 | Massachusetts | 932 |
| 11 | Alabama | 846 |
| 12 | Tennessee | 824 |
| 13 | Washington | 802 |
| 14 | California | 778 |
| 15 | Texas | 724 |
| 16 | South Dakota | 714 |
| 17 | Mississippi | 700 |
| 18 | Idaho | 695 |
| 19 | Georgia | 661 |
| 20 | South Carolina | 654 |
| 21 | Maine | 641 |
| 22 | Louisiana | 610 |
| 23 | Utah | 595 |
| 24 | Montana | 589 |
| 25 | Kentucky | 574 |
| 26 | Florida | 572 |
| 27 | New Jersey | 517 |
| 28 | Oklahoma | 497 |
| 29 | Pennsylvania | 495 |
| 30 | Kansas | 476 |
| 31 | Vermont | 465 |
| 32 | Nevada | 443 |
| 33 | Rhode Island | 425 |
| 34 | Wyoming | 415 |
| 35 | North Dakota | 402 |
| 36 | New Hampshire | 401 |
| 37 | Ohio | 400 |
| 38 | Minnesota | 378 |
| 39 | Indiana | 374 |
| 40 | New York | 372 |
| 41 | West Virginia | 346 |
| 42 | Iowa | 313 |
| 43 | Delaware | 294 |
| 44 | Illinois | 287 |
| 45 | Nebraska | 282 |
| 46 | Wisconsin | 273 |
| 47 | North Carolina | 268 |
| 48 | Oregon | 231 |
| 49 | Michigan | 209 |
| 50 | Arkansas | 183 |

District of Columbia — 12,338

*Source: Morgan Quitno Press using data from U.S. Bureau of the Census "Consolidated Federal Funds Report: 1999" (CFFR/99, Revised August 2000)*
*National per capita excludes expenditures and population for territories and undistributed amounts.*

# Federal Government Direct Payments for Individuals in 1999

## National Total = $851,785,998,000*

ALPHA ORDER

| RANK | STATE | PAYMENTS | % of USA |
|---|---|---|---|
| 19 | Alabama | $15,649,550,000 | 1.8% |
| 50 | Alaska | 1,232,115,000 | 0.1% |
| 20 | Arizona | 14,979,220,000 | 1.8% |
| 32 | Arkansas | 9,434,143,000 | 1.1% |
| 1 | California | 86,151,640,000 | 10.1% |
| 29 | Colorado | 10,368,070,000 | 1.2% |
| 28 | Connecticut | 10,408,821,000 | 1.2% |
| 47 | Delaware | 2,313,517,000 | 0.3% |
| 2 | Florida | 59,549,810,000 | 7.0% |
| 12 | Georgia | 21,021,758,000 | 2.5% |
| 40 | Hawaii | 3,656,186,000 | 0.4% |
| 43 | Idaho | 3,424,923,000 | 0.4% |
| 6 | Illinois | 35,769,431,000 | 4.2% |
| 15 | Indiana | 17,928,759,000 | 2.1% |
| 27 | Iowa | 11,138,349,000 | 1.3% |
| 33 | Kansas | 9,248,716,000 | 1.1% |
| 24 | Kentucky | 12,912,886,000 | 1.5% |
| 22 | Louisiana | 14,324,844,000 | 1.7% |
| 39 | Maine | 4,019,540,000 | 0.5% |
| 17 | Maryland | 17,317,245,000 | 2.0% |
| 13 | Massachusetts | 20,292,708,000 | 2.4% |
| 8 | Michigan | 29,110,341,000 | 3.4% |
| 23 | Minnesota | 13,581,733,000 | 1.6% |
| 31 | Mississippi | 9,462,728,000 | 1.1% |
| 14 | Missouri | 18,733,911,000 | 2.2% |
| 41 | Montana | 3,638,832,000 | 0.4% |
| 35 | Nebraska | 5,679,569,000 | 0.7% |
| 37 | Nevada | 4,988,740,000 | 0.6% |
| 44 | New Hampshire | 3,246,368,000 | 0.4% |
| 9 | New Jersey | 25,331,094,000 | 3.0% |
| 36 | New Mexico | 5,252,842,000 | 0.6% |
| 3 | New York | 58,644,692,000 | 6.9% |
| 10 | North Carolina | 22,294,735,000 | 2.6% |
| 46 | North Dakota | 2,653,059,000 | 0.3% |
| 7 | Ohio | 34,159,295,000 | 4.0% |
| 26 | Oklahoma | 11,527,813,000 | 1.4% |
| 30 | Oregon | 9,802,593,000 | 1.2% |
| 5 | Pennsylvania | 44,950,028,000 | 5.3% |
| 42 | Rhode Island | 3,481,476,000 | 0.4% |
| 25 | South Carolina | 11,972,988,000 | 1.4% |
| 45 | South Dakota | 2,770,481,000 | 0.3% |
| 16 | Tennessee | 17,728,593,000 | 2.1% |
| 4 | Texas | 53,317,475,000 | 6.3% |
| 38 | Utah | 4,507,662,000 | 0.5% |
| 48 | Vermont | 1,653,518,000 | 0.2% |
| 11 | Virginia | 21,998,904,000 | 2.6% |
| 18 | Washington | 16,789,608,000 | 2.0% |
| 34 | West Virginia | 7,001,619,000 | 0.8% |
| 21 | Wisconsin | 14,815,001,000 | 1.7% |
| 49 | Wyoming | 1,373,936,000 | 0.2% |

RANK ORDER

| RANK | STATE | PAYMENTS | % of USA |
|---|---|---|---|
| 1 | California | $86,151,640,000 | 10.1% |
| 2 | Florida | 59,549,810,000 | 7.0% |
| 3 | New York | 58,644,692,000 | 6.9% |
| 4 | Texas | 53,317,475,000 | 6.3% |
| 5 | Pennsylvania | 44,950,028,000 | 5.3% |
| 6 | Illinois | 35,769,431,000 | 4.2% |
| 7 | Ohio | 34,159,295,000 | 4.0% |
| 8 | Michigan | 29,110,341,000 | 3.4% |
| 9 | New Jersey | 25,331,094,000 | 3.0% |
| 10 | North Carolina | 22,294,735,000 | 2.6% |
| 11 | Virginia | 21,998,904,000 | 2.6% |
| 12 | Georgia | 21,021,758,000 | 2.5% |
| 13 | Massachusetts | 20,292,708,000 | 2.4% |
| 14 | Missouri | 18,733,911,000 | 2.2% |
| 15 | Indiana | 17,928,759,000 | 2.1% |
| 16 | Tennessee | 17,728,593,000 | 2.1% |
| 17 | Maryland | 17,317,245,000 | 2.0% |
| 18 | Washington | 16,789,608,000 | 2.0% |
| 19 | Alabama | 15,649,550,000 | 1.8% |
| 20 | Arizona | 14,979,220,000 | 1.8% |
| 21 | Wisconsin | 14,815,001,000 | 1.7% |
| 22 | Louisiana | 14,324,844,000 | 1.7% |
| 23 | Minnesota | 13,581,733,000 | 1.6% |
| 24 | Kentucky | 12,912,886,000 | 1.5% |
| 25 | South Carolina | 11,972,988,000 | 1.4% |
| 26 | Oklahoma | 11,527,813,000 | 1.4% |
| 27 | Iowa | 11,138,349,000 | 1.3% |
| 28 | Connecticut | 10,408,821,000 | 1.2% |
| 29 | Colorado | 10,368,070,000 | 1.2% |
| 30 | Oregon | 9,802,593,000 | 1.2% |
| 31 | Mississippi | 9,462,728,000 | 1.1% |
| 32 | Arkansas | 9,434,143,000 | 1.1% |
| 33 | Kansas | 9,248,716,000 | 1.1% |
| 34 | West Virginia | 7,001,619,000 | 0.8% |
| 35 | Nebraska | 5,679,569,000 | 0.7% |
| 36 | New Mexico | 5,252,842,000 | 0.6% |
| 37 | Nevada | 4,988,740,000 | 0.6% |
| 38 | Utah | 4,507,662,000 | 0.5% |
| 39 | Maine | 4,019,540,000 | 0.5% |
| 40 | Hawaii | 3,656,186,000 | 0.4% |
| 41 | Montana | 3,638,832,000 | 0.4% |
| 42 | Rhode Island | 3,481,476,000 | 0.4% |
| 43 | Idaho | 3,424,923,000 | 0.4% |
| 44 | New Hampshire | 3,246,368,000 | 0.4% |
| 45 | South Dakota | 2,770,481,000 | 0.3% |
| 46 | North Dakota | 2,653,059,000 | 0.3% |
| 47 | Delaware | 2,313,517,000 | 0.3% |
| 48 | Vermont | 1,653,518,000 | 0.2% |
| 49 | Wyoming | 1,373,936,000 | 0.2% |
| 50 | Alaska | 1,232,115,000 | 0.1% |
| | District of Columbia | 3,362,364,000 | 0.4% |

Source: U.S. Bureau of the Census
"Consolidated Federal Funds Report: 1999" (CFFR/99, Revised August 2000)
*Total includes $6,808,000,000 in U.S. territories ($6,334,000,000 in Puerto Rico) and $4,000,000 in expenditures not distributed by state. "Direct Payments" include Social Security, Medicare, federal retirement, disability payments, veterans benefits, food stamps, student loans and other programs.

# Per Capita Expenditures for Federal Government
## Direct Payments for Individuals in 1999
### National Per Capita = $3,099*

ALPHA ORDER

| RANK | STATE | PER CAPITA |
|------|-------|-----------|
| 9 | Alabama | $3,581 |
| 50 | Alaska | 1,989 |
| 25 | Arizona | 3,135 |
| 8 | Arkansas | 3,698 |
| 47 | California | 2,599 |
| 48 | Colorado | 2,556 |
| 24 | Connecticut | 3,171 |
| 29 | Delaware | 3,070 |
| 3 | Florida | 3,941 |
| 45 | Georgia | 2,699 |
| 27 | Hawaii | 3,084 |
| 43 | Idaho | 2,736 |
| 35 | Illinois | 2,949 |
| 32 | Indiana | 3,017 |
| 4 | Iowa | 3,882 |
| 11 | Kansas | 3,485 |
| 19 | Kentucky | 3,260 |
| 18 | Louisiana | 3,276 |
| 22 | Maine | 3,208 |
| 16 | Maryland | 3,349 |
| 17 | Massachusetts | 3,286 |
| 34 | Michigan | 2,951 |
| 39 | Minnesota | 2,844 |
| 14 | Mississippi | 3,418 |
| 13 | Missouri | 3,426 |
| 2 | Montana | 4,122 |
| 15 | Nebraska | 3,409 |
| 42 | Nevada | 2,757 |
| 44 | New Hampshire | 2,703 |
| 26 | New Jersey | 3,111 |
| 31 | New Mexico | 3,019 |
| 21 | New York | 3,223 |
| 37 | North Carolina | 2,914 |
| 1 | North Dakota | 4,187 |
| 30 | Ohio | 3,035 |
| 12 | Oklahoma | 3,433 |
| 33 | Oregon | 2,956 |
| 7 | Pennsylvania | 3,748 |
| 10 | Rhode Island | 3,514 |
| 28 | South Carolina | 3,081 |
| 6 | South Dakota | 3,779 |
| 20 | Tennessee | 3,233 |
| 46 | Texas | 2,660 |
| 49 | Utah | 2,116 |
| 41 | Vermont | 2,785 |
| 23 | Virginia | 3,201 |
| 36 | Washington | 2,917 |
| 5 | West Virginia | 3,875 |
| 40 | Wisconsin | 2,822 |
| 38 | Wyoming | 2,865 |

RANK ORDER

| RANK | STATE | PER CAPITA |
|------|-------|-----------|
| 1 | North Dakota | $4,187 |
| 2 | Montana | 4,122 |
| 3 | Florida | 3,941 |
| 4 | Iowa | 3,882 |
| 5 | West Virginia | 3,875 |
| 6 | South Dakota | 3,779 |
| 7 | Pennsylvania | 3,748 |
| 8 | Arkansas | 3,698 |
| 9 | Alabama | 3,581 |
| 10 | Rhode Island | 3,514 |
| 11 | Kansas | 3,485 |
| 12 | Oklahoma | 3,433 |
| 13 | Missouri | 3,426 |
| 14 | Mississippi | 3,418 |
| 15 | Nebraska | 3,409 |
| 16 | Maryland | 3,349 |
| 17 | Massachusetts | 3,286 |
| 18 | Louisiana | 3,276 |
| 19 | Kentucky | 3,260 |
| 20 | Tennessee | 3,233 |
| 21 | New York | 3,223 |
| 22 | Maine | 3,208 |
| 23 | Virginia | 3,201 |
| 24 | Connecticut | 3,171 |
| 25 | Arizona | 3,135 |
| 26 | New Jersey | 3,111 |
| 27 | Hawaii | 3,084 |
| 28 | South Carolina | 3,081 |
| 29 | Delaware | 3,070 |
| 30 | Ohio | 3,035 |
| 31 | New Mexico | 3,019 |
| 32 | Indiana | 3,017 |
| 33 | Oregon | 2,956 |
| 34 | Michigan | 2,951 |
| 35 | Illinois | 2,949 |
| 36 | Washington | 2,917 |
| 37 | North Carolina | 2,914 |
| 38 | Wyoming | 2,865 |
| 39 | Minnesota | 2,844 |
| 40 | Wisconsin | 2,822 |
| 41 | Vermont | 2,785 |
| 42 | Nevada | 2,757 |
| 43 | Idaho | 2,736 |
| 44 | New Hampshire | 2,703 |
| 45 | Georgia | 2,699 |
| 46 | Texas | 2,660 |
| 47 | California | 2,599 |
| 48 | Colorado | 2,556 |
| 49 | Utah | 2,116 |
| 50 | Alaska | 1,989 |

District of Columbia 6,479

*Source: Morgan Quitno Press using data from U.S. Bureau of the Census
"Consolidated Federal Funds Report: 1999" (CFFR/99, Revised August 2000)*
*National per capita excludes expenditures and population for territories not shown separately. "Direct Payments" include Social Security, Medicare, federal retirement, disability payments, veterans benefits, food stamps, student loans and other programs.*

# Federal Government Salaries and Wages in 1999

## National Total = $177,278,501,000*

ALPHA ORDER

| RANK | STATE | SALARIES | % of USA |
|------|-------|----------|----------|
| 18 | Alabama | $2,797,824,000 | 1.6% |
| 35 | Alaska | 1,271,788,000 | 0.7% |
| 21 | Arizona | 2,661,274,000 | 1.5% |
| 36 | Arkansas | 1,115,636,000 | 0.6% |
| 1 | California | 17,733,212,000 | 10.0% |
| 14 | Colorado | 3,499,143,000 | 2.0% |
| 34 | Connecticut | 1,349,623,000 | 0.8% |
| 49 | Delaware | 405,898,000 | 0.2% |
| 5 | Florida | 7,834,920,000 | 4.4% |
| 7 | Georgia | 6,291,670,000 | 3.5% |
| 24 | Hawaii | 2,436,104,000 | 1.4% |
| 43 | Idaho | 692,845,000 | 0.4% |
| 8 | Illinois | 5,999,970,000 | 3.4% |
| 26 | Indiana | 1,971,715,000 | 1.1% |
| 38 | Iowa | 969,985,000 | 0.5% |
| 28 | Kansas | 1,752,370,000 | 1.0% |
| 22 | Kentucky | 2,615,263,000 | 1.5% |
| 25 | Louisiana | 2,164,947,000 | 1.2% |
| 41 | Maine | 795,052,000 | 0.4% |
| 4 | Maryland | 8,345,517,000 | 4.7% |
| 17 | Massachusetts | 2,918,850,000 | 1.6% |
| 16 | Michigan | 2,932,400,000 | 1.7% |
| 27 | Minnesota | 1,778,260,000 | 1.0% |
| 29 | Mississippi | 1,698,546,000 | 1.0% |
| 15 | Missouri | 3,313,400,000 | 1.9% |
| 44 | Montana | 666,767,000 | 0.4% |
| 37 | Nebraska | 992,201,000 | 0.6% |
| 40 | Nevada | 902,608,000 | 0.5% |
| 47 | New Hampshire | 453,311,000 | 0.3% |
| 13 | New Jersey | 3,598,767,000 | 2.0% |
| 30 | New Mexico | 1,646,387,000 | 0.9% |
| 6 | New York | 7,521,216,000 | 4.2% |
| 10 | North Carolina | 5,275,120,000 | 3.0% |
| 45 | North Dakota | 618,084,000 | 0.3% |
| 12 | Ohio | 4,340,917,000 | 2.4% |
| 19 | Oklahoma | 2,760,612,000 | 1.6% |
| 32 | Oregon | 1,505,869,000 | 0.8% |
| 9 | Pennsylvania | 5,423,573,000 | 3.1% |
| 42 | Rhode Island | 722,548,000 | 0.4% |
| 23 | South Carolina | 2,441,237,000 | 1.4% |
| 46 | South Dakota | 558,964,000 | 0.3% |
| 20 | Tennessee | 2,717,878,000 | 1.5% |
| 3 | Texas | 11,797,849,000 | 6.7% |
| 33 | Utah | 1,469,051,000 | 0.8% |
| 50 | Vermont | 301,393,000 | 0.2% |
| 2 | Virginia | 12,050,056,000 | 6.8% |
| 11 | Washington | 4,868,683,000 | 2.7% |
| 39 | West Virginia | 911,401,000 | 0.5% |
| 31 | Wisconsin | 1,513,637,000 | 0.9% |
| 48 | Wyoming | 409,734,000 | 0.2% |

RANK ORDER

| RANK | STATE | SALARIES | % of USA |
|------|-------|----------|----------|
| 1 | California | $17,733,212,000 | 10.0% |
| 2 | Virginia | 12,050,056,000 | 6.8% |
| 3 | Texas | 11,797,849,000 | 6.7% |
| 4 | Maryland | 8,345,517,000 | 4.7% |
| 5 | Florida | 7,834,920,000 | 4.4% |
| 6 | New York | 7,521,216,000 | 4.2% |
| 7 | Georgia | 6,291,670,000 | 3.5% |
| 8 | Illinois | 5,999,970,000 | 3.4% |
| 9 | Pennsylvania | 5,423,573,000 | 3.1% |
| 10 | North Carolina | 5,275,120,000 | 3.0% |
| 11 | Washington | 4,868,683,000 | 2.7% |
| 12 | Ohio | 4,340,917,000 | 2.4% |
| 13 | New Jersey | 3,598,767,000 | 2.0% |
| 14 | Colorado | 3,499,143,000 | 2.0% |
| 15 | Missouri | 3,313,400,000 | 1.9% |
| 16 | Michigan | 2,932,400,000 | 1.7% |
| 17 | Massachusetts | 2,918,850,000 | 1.6% |
| 18 | Alabama | 2,797,824,000 | 1.6% |
| 19 | Oklahoma | 2,760,612,000 | 1.6% |
| 20 | Tennessee | 2,717,878,000 | 1.5% |
| 21 | Arizona | 2,661,274,000 | 1.5% |
| 22 | Kentucky | 2,615,263,000 | 1.5% |
| 23 | South Carolina | 2,441,237,000 | 1.4% |
| 24 | Hawaii | 2,436,104,000 | 1.4% |
| 25 | Louisiana | 2,164,947,000 | 1.2% |
| 26 | Indiana | 1,971,715,000 | 1.1% |
| 27 | Minnesota | 1,778,260,000 | 1.0% |
| 28 | Kansas | 1,752,370,000 | 1.0% |
| 29 | Mississippi | 1,698,546,000 | 1.0% |
| 30 | New Mexico | 1,646,387,000 | 0.9% |
| 31 | Wisconsin | 1,513,637,000 | 0.9% |
| 32 | Oregon | 1,505,869,000 | 0.8% |
| 33 | Utah | 1,469,051,000 | 0.8% |
| 34 | Connecticut | 1,349,623,000 | 0.8% |
| 35 | Alaska | 1,271,788,000 | 0.7% |
| 36 | Arkansas | 1,115,636,000 | 0.6% |
| 37 | Nebraska | 992,201,000 | 0.6% |
| 38 | Iowa | 969,985,000 | 0.5% |
| 39 | West Virginia | 911,401,000 | 0.5% |
| 40 | Nevada | 902,608,000 | 0.5% |
| 41 | Maine | 795,052,000 | 0.4% |
| 42 | Rhode Island | 722,548,000 | 0.4% |
| 43 | Idaho | 692,845,000 | 0.4% |
| 44 | Montana | 666,767,000 | 0.4% |
| 45 | North Dakota | 618,084,000 | 0.3% |
| 46 | South Dakota | 558,964,000 | 0.3% |
| 47 | New Hampshire | 453,311,000 | 0.3% |
| 48 | Wyoming | 409,734,000 | 0.2% |
| 49 | Delaware | 405,898,000 | 0.2% |
| 50 | Vermont | 301,393,000 | 0.2% |
| | District of Columbia | 11,975,166,000 | 6.8% |

*Source: U.S. Bureau of the Census*
*"Consolidated Federal Funds Report: 1999" (CFFR/99, Revised August 2000)*
*\*Total includes $1,193,000,000 in U.S. territories ($839,000,000 in Puerto Rico) and $3,296,000,000 in expenditures not distributed by state.*

# Per Capita Expenditures for Federal Government Salaries and Wages in 1999

## National Per Capita = $634*

ALPHA ORDER

| RANK | STATE | PER CAPITA |
|---|---|---|
| 19 | Alabama | $640 |
| 2 | Alaska | 2,053 |
| 26 | Arizona | 557 |
| 41 | Arkansas | 437 |
| 29 | California | 535 |
| 7 | Colorado | 863 |
| 43 | Connecticut | 411 |
| 28 | Delaware | 539 |
| 30 | Florida | 518 |
| 11 | Georgia | 808 |
| 1 | Hawaii | 2,055 |
| 27 | Idaho | 554 |
| 35 | Illinois | 495 |
| 48 | Indiana | 332 |
| 47 | Iowa | 338 |
| 17 | Kansas | 660 |
| 17 | Kentucky | 660 |
| 35 | Louisiana | 495 |
| 20 | Maine | 634 |
| 4 | Maryland | 1,614 |
| 37 | Massachusetts | 473 |
| 49 | Michigan | 297 |
| 46 | Minnesota | 372 |
| 22 | Mississippi | 613 |
| 23 | Missouri | 606 |
| 13 | Montana | 755 |
| 24 | Nebraska | 596 |
| 33 | Nevada | 499 |
| 45 | New Hampshire | 377 |
| 40 | New Jersey | 442 |
| 6 | New Mexico | 946 |
| 42 | New York | 413 |
| 16 | North Carolina | 689 |
| 5 | North Dakota | 975 |
| 44 | Ohio | 386 |
| 10 | Oklahoma | 822 |
| 38 | Oregon | 454 |
| 39 | Pennsylvania | 452 |
| 14 | Rhode Island | 729 |
| 21 | South Carolina | 628 |
| 12 | South Dakota | 762 |
| 34 | Tennessee | 496 |
| 25 | Texas | 589 |
| 15 | Utah | 690 |
| 31 | Vermont | 508 |
| 3 | Virginia | 1,753 |
| 9 | Washington | 846 |
| 32 | West Virginia | 504 |
| 50 | Wisconsin | 288 |
| 8 | Wyoming | 854 |

RANK ORDER

| RANK | STATE | PER CAPITA |
|---|---|---|
| 1 | Hawaii | $2,055 |
| 2 | Alaska | 2,053 |
| 3 | Virginia | 1,753 |
| 4 | Maryland | 1,614 |
| 5 | North Dakota | 975 |
| 6 | New Mexico | 946 |
| 7 | Colorado | 863 |
| 8 | Wyoming | 854 |
| 9 | Washington | 846 |
| 10 | Oklahoma | 822 |
| 11 | Georgia | 808 |
| 12 | South Dakota | 762 |
| 13 | Montana | 755 |
| 14 | Rhode Island | 729 |
| 15 | Utah | 690 |
| 16 | North Carolina | 689 |
| 17 | Kansas | 660 |
| 17 | Kentucky | 660 |
| 19 | Alabama | 640 |
| 20 | Maine | 634 |
| 21 | South Carolina | 628 |
| 22 | Mississippi | 613 |
| 23 | Missouri | 606 |
| 24 | Nebraska | 596 |
| 25 | Texas | 589 |
| 26 | Arizona | 557 |
| 27 | Idaho | 554 |
| 28 | Delaware | 539 |
| 29 | California | 535 |
| 30 | Florida | 518 |
| 31 | Vermont | 508 |
| 32 | West Virginia | 504 |
| 33 | Nevada | 499 |
| 34 | Tennessee | 496 |
| 35 | Illinois | 495 |
| 35 | Louisiana | 495 |
| 37 | Massachusetts | 473 |
| 38 | Oregon | 454 |
| 39 | Pennsylvania | 452 |
| 40 | New Jersey | 442 |
| 41 | Arkansas | 437 |
| 42 | New York | 413 |
| 43 | Connecticut | 411 |
| 44 | Ohio | 386 |
| 45 | New Hampshire | 377 |
| 46 | Minnesota | 372 |
| 47 | Iowa | 338 |
| 48 | Indiana | 332 |
| 49 | Michigan | 297 |
| 50 | Wisconsin | 288 |
|  | District of Columbia | 23,074 |

Source: Morgan Quitno Press using data from U.S. Bureau of the Census
"Consolidated Federal Funds Report: 1999" (CFFR/99, Revised August 2000)
*National per capita excludes expenditures and population for territories and undistributed amounts.

# Federal Civilian Employees in 1998

## National Total = 2,706,420 Employees*

ALPHA ORDER

RANK ORDER

| RANK | STATE | EMPLOYEES | % of USA | | RANK | STATE | EMPLOYEES | % of USA |
|------|-------|-----------|----------|---|------|-------|-----------|----------|
| 19 | Alabama | 51,936 | 1.9% | | 1 | California | 265,472 | 9.8% |
| 39 | Alaska | 14,354 | 0.5% | | 2 | Texas | 174,561 | 6.4% |
| 20 | Arizona | 43,229 | 1.6% | | 3 | Virginia | 146,551 | 5.4% |
| 35 | Arkansas | 20,579 | 0.8% | | 4 | New York | 139,425 | 5.2% |
| 1 | California | 265,472 | 9.8% | | 5 | Maryland | 130,889 | 4.8% |
| 17 | Colorado | 53,730 | 2.0% | | 6 | Florida | 115,605 | 4.3% |
| 34 | Connecticut | 22,986 | 0.8% | | 7 | Pennsylvania | 112,680 | 4.2% |
| 50 | Delaware | 5,481 | 0.2% | | 8 | Illinois | 98,341 | 3.6% |
| 6 | Florida | 115,605 | 4.3% | | 9 | Georgia | 87,752 | 3.2% |
| 9 | Georgia | 87,752 | 3.2% | | 10 | Ohio | 86,502 | 3.2% |
| 33 | Hawaii | 23,784 | 0.9% | | 11 | New Jersey | 64,519 | 2.4% |
| 44 | Idaho | 10,730 | 0.4% | | 12 | Washington | 62,892 | 2.3% |
| 8 | Illinois | 98,341 | 3.6% | | 13 | Michigan | 59,054 | 2.2% |
| 22 | Indiana | 38,319 | 1.4% | | 14 | Missouri | 56,837 | 2.1% |
| 36 | Iowa | 19,921 | 0.7% | | 15 | North Carolina | 56,758 | 2.1% |
| 31 | Kansas | 25,479 | 0.9% | | 16 | Massachusetts | 55,552 | 2.1% |
| 25 | Kentucky | 31,090 | 1.1% | | 17 | Colorado | 53,730 | 2.0% |
| 24 | Louisiana | 34,805 | 1.3% | | 18 | Tennessee | 52,402 | 1.9% |
| 40 | Maine | 13,369 | 0.5% | | 19 | Alabama | 51,936 | 1.9% |
| 5 | Maryland | 130,889 | 4.8% | | 20 | Arizona | 43,229 | 1.6% |
| 16 | Massachusetts | 55,552 | 2.1% | | 21 | Oklahoma | 42,529 | 1.6% |
| 13 | Michigan | 59,054 | 2.2% | | 22 | Indiana | 38,319 | 1.4% |
| 23 | Minnesota | 34,806 | 1.3% | | 23 | Minnesota | 34,806 | 1.3% |
| 32 | Mississippi | 24,652 | 0.9% | | 24 | Louisiana | 34,805 | 1.3% |
| 14 | Missouri | 56,837 | 2.1% | | 25 | Kentucky | 31,090 | 1.1% |
| 42 | Montana | 11,296 | 0.4% | | 26 | Wisconsin | 30,557 | 1.1% |
| 38 | Nebraska | 15,487 | 0.6% | | 27 | Oregon | 29,541 | 1.1% |
| 41 | Nevada | 12,909 | 0.5% | | 28 | Utah | 28,028 | 1.0% |
| 46 | New Hampshire | 8,326 | 0.3% | | 29 | South Carolina | 27,052 | 1.0% |
| 11 | New Jersey | 64,519 | 2.4% | | 30 | New Mexico | 25,895 | 1.0% |
| 30 | New Mexico | 25,895 | 1.0% | | 31 | Kansas | 25,479 | 0.9% |
| 4 | New York | 139,425 | 5.2% | | 32 | Mississippi | 24,652 | 0.9% |
| 15 | North Carolina | 56,758 | 2.1% | | 33 | Hawaii | 23,784 | 0.9% |
| 47 | North Dakota | 7,664 | 0.3% | | 34 | Connecticut | 22,986 | 0.8% |
| 10 | Ohio | 86,502 | 3.2% | | 35 | Arkansas | 20,579 | 0.8% |
| 21 | Oklahoma | 42,529 | 1.6% | | 36 | Iowa | 19,921 | 0.7% |
| 27 | Oregon | 29,541 | 1.1% | | 37 | West Virginia | 18,299 | 0.7% |
| 7 | Pennsylvania | 112,680 | 4.2% | | 38 | Nebraska | 15,487 | 0.6% |
| 43 | Rhode Island | 11,178 | 0.4% | | 39 | Alaska | 14,354 | 0.5% |
| 29 | South Carolina | 27,052 | 1.0% | | 40 | Maine | 13,369 | 0.5% |
| 45 | South Dakota | 9,593 | 0.4% | | 41 | Nevada | 12,909 | 0.5% |
| 18 | Tennessee | 52,402 | 1.9% | | 42 | Montana | 11,296 | 0.4% |
| 2 | Texas | 174,561 | 6.4% | | 43 | Rhode Island | 11,178 | 0.4% |
| 28 | Utah | 28,028 | 1.0% | | 44 | Idaho | 10,730 | 0.4% |
| 49 | Vermont | 5,757 | 0.2% | | 45 | South Dakota | 9,593 | 0.4% |
| 3 | Virginia | 146,551 | 5.4% | | 46 | New Hampshire | 8,326 | 0.3% |
| 12 | Washington | 62,892 | 2.3% | | 47 | North Dakota | 7,664 | 0.3% |
| 37 | West Virginia | 18,299 | 0.7% | | 48 | Wyoming | 6,190 | 0.2% |
| 26 | Wisconsin | 30,557 | 1.1% | | 49 | Vermont | 5,757 | 0.2% |
| 48 | Wyoming | 6,190 | 0.2% | | 50 | Delaware | 5,481 | 0.2% |
| | | | | | | District of Columbia | 181,077 | 6.7% |

Source: U.S. Bureau of the Census
    "Federal Government Civilian Employment by State" (http://www.census.gov/govs/apes/96fedst.txt)
*Includes full-time and part-time employees. Figures do not include employees based outside the U.S., seasonal employees and employees of Public Health Service, Central Intelligence Agency, National Security Agency and the Defense Intelligence Agency. As of December 31, 1998.

# Rate of Federal Civilian Employees in 1998

## National Rate = 100 Federal Employees per 10,000 Population*

ALPHA ORDER

RANK ORDER

| RANK | STATE | RATE | | RANK | STATE | RATE |
|---|---|---|---|---|---|---|
| 13 | Alabama | 119 | | 1 | Maryland | 255 |
| 2 | Alaska | 233 | | 2 | Alaska | 233 |
| 24 | Arizona | 93 | | 3 | Virginia | 216 |
| 31 | Arkansas | 81 | | 4 | Hawaii | 200 |
| 31 | California | 81 | | 5 | New Mexico | 149 |
| 6 | Colorado | 135 | | 6 | Colorado | 135 |
| 44 | Connecticut | 70 | | 7 | Utah | 133 |
| 41 | Delaware | 74 | | 8 | South Dakota | 131 |
| 37 | Florida | 78 | | 9 | Wyoming | 129 |
| 14 | Georgia | 115 | | 10 | Montana | 128 |
| 4 | Hawaii | 200 | | 11 | Oklahoma | 127 |
| 30 | Idaho | 87 | | 12 | North Dakota | 120 |
| 31 | Illinois | 81 | | 13 | Alabama | 119 |
| 48 | Indiana | 65 | | 14 | Georgia | 115 |
| 44 | Iowa | 70 | | 15 | Rhode Island | 113 |
| 20 | Kansas | 97 | | 16 | Washington | 111 |
| 36 | Kentucky | 79 | | 17 | Maine | 107 |
| 34 | Louisiana | 80 | | 18 | Missouri | 105 |
| 17 | Maine | 107 | | 19 | West Virginia | 101 |
| 1 | Maryland | 255 | | 20 | Kansas | 97 |
| 26 | Massachusetts | 90 | | 20 | Vermont | 97 |
| 49 | Michigan | 60 | | 22 | Tennessee | 96 |
| 41 | Minnesota | 74 | | 23 | Pennsylvania | 94 |
| 26 | Mississippi | 90 | | 24 | Arizona | 93 |
| 18 | Missouri | 105 | | 24 | Nebraska | 93 |
| 10 | Montana | 128 | | 26 | Massachusetts | 90 |
| 24 | Nebraska | 93 | | 26 | Mississippi | 90 |
| 41 | Nevada | 74 | | 26 | Oregon | 90 |
| 44 | New Hampshire | 70 | | 29 | Texas | 89 |
| 34 | New Jersey | 80 | | 30 | Idaho | 87 |
| 5 | New Mexico | 149 | | 31 | Arkansas | 81 |
| 38 | New York | 77 | | 31 | California | 81 |
| 40 | North Carolina | 75 | | 31 | Illinois | 81 |
| 12 | North Dakota | 120 | | 34 | Louisiana | 80 |
| 38 | Ohio | 77 | | 34 | New Jersey | 80 |
| 11 | Oklahoma | 127 | | 36 | Kentucky | 79 |
| 26 | Oregon | 90 | | 37 | Florida | 78 |
| 23 | Pennsylvania | 94 | | 38 | New York | 77 |
| 15 | Rhode Island | 113 | | 38 | Ohio | 77 |
| 44 | South Carolina | 70 | | 40 | North Carolina | 75 |
| 8 | South Dakota | 131 | | 41 | Delaware | 74 |
| 22 | Tennessee | 96 | | 41 | Minnesota | 74 |
| 29 | Texas | 89 | | 41 | Nevada | 74 |
| 7 | Utah | 133 | | 44 | Connecticut | 70 |
| 20 | Vermont | 97 | | 44 | Iowa | 70 |
| 3 | Virginia | 216 | | 44 | New Hampshire | 70 |
| 16 | Washington | 111 | | 44 | South Carolina | 70 |
| 19 | West Virginia | 101 | | 48 | Indiana | 65 |
| 50 | Wisconsin | 59 | | 49 | Michigan | 60 |
| 9 | Wyoming | 129 | | 50 | Wisconsin | 59 |
| | | | | | District of Columbia | 3,473 |

Source: Morgan Quitno Press using data from U.S. Bureau of the Census
"Federal Government Civilian Employment by State" (http://www.census.gov/govs/apes/96fedst.txt)
*Includes full-time and part-time employees. Figures do not include employees based outside the U.S., seasonal employees and employees of Public Health Service, Central Intelligence Agency, National Security Agency and the Defense Intelligence Agency. As of December 31, 1998.

# X. GOVERNMENT FINANCE: STATE AND LOCAL

# X. GOVERNMENT FINANCE: STATE AND LOCAL

# State and Local Government Total Revenue in 1997

## National Total = $1,614,771,342,000*

| ALPHA ORDER | | | | RANK ORDER | | | |
|---|---|---|---|---|---|---|---|
| RANK | STATE | REVENUE | % of USA | RANK | STATE | REVENUE | % of USA |
| 26 | Alabama | $21,171,584,000 | 1.3% | 1 | California | $209,645,735,000 | 13.0% |
| 35 | Alaska | 11,304,564,000 | 0.7% | 2 | New York | 160,058,820,000 | 9.9% |
| 23 | Arizona | 22,290,022,000 | 1.4% | 3 | Texas | 103,919,811,000 | 6.4% |
| 33 | Arkansas | 11,916,510,000 | 0.7% | 4 | Florida | 76,174,148,000 | 4.7% |
| 1 | California | 209,645,735,000 | 13.0% | 5 | Pennsylvania | 72,272,643,000 | 4.5% |
| 22 | Colorado | 22,540,188,000 | 1.4% | 6 | Illinois | 66,654,128,000 | 4.1% |
| 25 | Connecticut | 22,045,152,000 | 1.4% | 7 | Ohio | 66,018,054,000 | 4.1% |
| 45 | Delaware | 5,132,212,000 | 0.3% | 8 | Michigan | 61,749,190,000 | 3.8% |
| 4 | Florida | 76,174,148,000 | 4.7% | 9 | New Jersey | 53,524,622,000 | 3.3% |
| 11 | Georgia | 40,024,721,000 | 2.5% | 10 | Washington | 40,032,443,000 | 2.5% |
| 40 | Hawaii | 8,144,623,000 | 0.5% | 11 | Georgia | 40,024,721,000 | 2.5% |
| 42 | Idaho | 5,965,502,000 | 0.4% | 12 | North Carolina | 39,047,955,000 | 2.4% |
| 6 | Illinois | 66,654,128,000 | 4.1% | 13 | Massachusetts | 38,228,578,000 | 2.4% |
| 19 | Indiana | 28,240,641,000 | 1.7% | 14 | Virginia | 36,657,548,000 | 2.3% |
| 30 | Iowa | 14,643,600,000 | 0.9% | 15 | Wisconsin | 33,573,416,000 | 2.1% |
| 32 | Kansas | 13,098,247,000 | 0.8% | 16 | Minnesota | 33,271,712,000 | 2.1% |
| 27 | Kentucky | 20,281,268,000 | 1.3% | 17 | Maryland | 30,877,020,000 | 1.9% |
| 21 | Louisiana | 23,394,570,000 | 1.4% | 18 | Tennessee | 28,683,824,000 | 1.8% |
| 41 | Maine | 7,303,112,000 | 0.5% | 19 | Indiana | 28,240,641,000 | 1.7% |
| 17 | Maryland | 30,877,020,000 | 1.9% | 20 | Missouri | 25,823,519,000 | 1.6% |
| 13 | Massachusetts | 38,228,578,000 | 2.4% | 21 | Louisiana | 23,394,570,000 | 1.4% |
| 8 | Michigan | 61,749,190,000 | 3.8% | 22 | Colorado | 22,540,188,000 | 1.4% |
| 16 | Minnesota | 33,271,712,000 | 2.1% | 23 | Arizona | 22,290,022,000 | 1.4% |
| 31 | Mississippi | 13,235,439,000 | 0.8% | 24 | Oregon | 22,112,711,000 | 1.4% |
| 20 | Missouri | 25,823,519,000 | 1.6% | 25 | Connecticut | 22,045,152,000 | 1.4% |
| 46 | Montana | 4,770,140,000 | 0.3% | 26 | Alabama | 21,171,584,000 | 1.3% |
| 36 | Nebraska | 10,707,656,000 | 0.7% | 27 | Kentucky | 20,281,268,000 | 1.3% |
| 38 | Nevada | 10,105,496,000 | 0.6% | 28 | South Carolina | 19,880,543,000 | 1.2% |
| 44 | New Hampshire | 5,686,127,000 | 0.4% | 29 | Oklahoma | 16,106,732,000 | 1.0% |
| 9 | New Jersey | 53,524,622,000 | 3.3% | 30 | Iowa | 14,643,600,000 | 0.9% |
| 37 | New Mexico | 10,338,783,000 | 0.6% | 31 | Mississippi | 13,235,439,000 | 0.8% |
| 2 | New York | 160,058,820,000 | 9.9% | 32 | Kansas | 13,098,247,000 | 0.8% |
| 12 | North Carolina | 39,047,955,000 | 2.4% | 33 | Arkansas | 11,916,510,000 | 0.7% |
| 47 | North Dakota | 3,789,522,000 | 0.2% | 34 | Utah | 11,859,981,000 | 0.7% |
| 7 | Ohio | 66,018,054,000 | 4.1% | 35 | Alaska | 11,304,564,000 | 0.7% |
| 29 | Oklahoma | 16,106,732,000 | 1.0% | 36 | Nebraska | 10,707,656,000 | 0.7% |
| 24 | Oregon | 22,112,711,000 | 1.4% | 37 | New Mexico | 10,338,783,000 | 0.6% |
| 5 | Pennsylvania | 72,272,643,000 | 4.5% | 38 | Nevada | 10,105,496,000 | 0.6% |
| 43 | Rhode Island | 5,912,057,000 | 0.4% | 39 | West Virginia | 9,563,140,000 | 0.6% |
| 28 | South Carolina | 19,880,543,000 | 1.2% | 40 | Hawaii | 8,144,623,000 | 0.5% |
| 49 | South Dakota | 3,495,569,000 | 0.2% | 41 | Maine | 7,303,112,000 | 0.5% |
| 18 | Tennessee | 28,683,824,000 | 1.8% | 42 | Idaho | 5,965,502,000 | 0.4% |
| 3 | Texas | 103,919,811,000 | 6.4% | 43 | Rhode Island | 5,912,057,000 | 0.4% |
| 34 | Utah | 11,859,981,000 | 0.7% | 44 | New Hampshire | 5,686,127,000 | 0.4% |
| 50 | Vermont | 3,379,648,000 | 0.2% | 45 | Delaware | 5,132,212,000 | 0.3% |
| 14 | Virginia | 36,657,548,000 | 2.3% | 46 | Montana | 4,770,140,000 | 0.3% |
| 10 | Washington | 40,032,443,000 | 2.5% | 47 | North Dakota | 3,789,522,000 | 0.2% |
| 39 | West Virginia | 9,563,140,000 | 0.6% | 48 | Wyoming | 3,729,258,000 | 0.2% |
| 15 | Wisconsin | 33,573,416,000 | 2.1% | 49 | South Dakota | 3,495,569,000 | 0.2% |
| 48 | Wyoming | 3,729,258,000 | 0.2% | 50 | Vermont | 3,379,648,000 | 0.2% |
| | | | | | District of Columbia | 6,388,858,000 | 0.4% |

Source: U.S. Bureau of the Census, Governments Division
   "Compendium of Government Finances: 1997" (2000) (http://www.census.gov/govs/www/cog.html)
*Total revenue includes all money received from external sources.  This includes taxes, intergovernmental transfers and insurance trust revenue and revenue from government owned utilities and other commercial or auxiliary enterprise.

# Per Capita State and Local Government Total Revenue in 1997

## National Per Capita = $6,030*

ALPHA ORDER

| RANK | STATE | PER CAPITA |
|------|-------|-----------|
| 42 | Alabama | $4,901 |
| 1 | Alaska | 18,567 |
| 43 | Arizona | 4,897 |
| 50 | Arkansas | 4,721 |
| 11 | California | 6,507 |
| 24 | Colorado | 5,792 |
| 9 | Connecticut | 6,745 |
| 6 | Delaware | 6,982 |
| 38 | Florida | 5,188 |
| 32 | Georgia | 5,347 |
| 7 | Hawaii | 6,848 |
| 41 | Idaho | 4,928 |
| 27 | Illinois | 5,549 |
| 47 | Indiana | 4,809 |
| 39 | Iowa | 5,130 |
| 40 | Kansas | 5,006 |
| 37 | Kentucky | 5,190 |
| 30 | Louisiana | 5,376 |
| 23 | Maine | 5,865 |
| 16 | Maryland | 6,063 |
| 15 | Massachusetts | 6,251 |
| 14 | Michigan | 6,310 |
| 5 | Minnesota | 7,098 |
| 46 | Mississippi | 4,845 |
| 49 | Missouri | 4,776 |
| 29 | Montana | 5,429 |
| 12 | Nebraska | 6,466 |
| 17 | Nevada | 6,031 |
| 45 | New Hampshire | 4,847 |
| 10 | New Jersey | 6,646 |
| 19 | New Mexico | 6,001 |
| 2 | New York | 8,822 |
| 35 | North Carolina | 5,256 |
| 21 | North Dakota | 5,912 |
| 22 | Ohio | 5,888 |
| 44 | Oklahoma | 4,860 |
| 8 | Oregon | 6,818 |
| 18 | Pennsylvania | 6,015 |
| 20 | Rhode Island | 5,990 |
| 36 | South Carolina | 5,245 |
| 48 | South Dakota | 4,783 |
| 33 | Tennessee | 5,333 |
| 31 | Texas | 5,369 |
| 25 | Utah | 5,742 |
| 26 | Vermont | 5,741 |
| 28 | Virginia | 5,445 |
| 4 | Washington | 7,143 |
| 34 | West Virginia | 5,267 |
| 13 | Wisconsin | 6,456 |
| 3 | Wyoming | 7,769 |

RANK ORDER

| RANK | STATE | PER CAPITA |
|------|-------|-----------|
| 1 | Alaska | $18,567 |
| 2 | New York | 8,822 |
| 3 | Wyoming | 7,769 |
| 4 | Washington | 7,143 |
| 5 | Minnesota | 7,098 |
| 6 | Delaware | 6,982 |
| 7 | Hawaii | 6,848 |
| 8 | Oregon | 6,818 |
| 9 | Connecticut | 6,745 |
| 10 | New Jersey | 6,646 |
| 11 | California | 6,507 |
| 12 | Nebraska | 6,466 |
| 13 | Wisconsin | 6,456 |
| 14 | Michigan | 6,310 |
| 15 | Massachusetts | 6,251 |
| 16 | Maryland | 6,063 |
| 17 | Nevada | 6,031 |
| 18 | Pennsylvania | 6,015 |
| 19 | New Mexico | 6,001 |
| 20 | Rhode Island | 5,990 |
| 21 | North Dakota | 5,912 |
| 22 | Ohio | 5,888 |
| 23 | Maine | 5,865 |
| 24 | Colorado | 5,792 |
| 25 | Utah | 5,742 |
| 26 | Vermont | 5,741 |
| 27 | Illinois | 5,549 |
| 28 | Virginia | 5,445 |
| 29 | Montana | 5,429 |
| 30 | Louisiana | 5,376 |
| 31 | Texas | 5,369 |
| 32 | Georgia | 5,347 |
| 33 | Tennessee | 5,333 |
| 34 | West Virginia | 5,267 |
| 35 | North Carolina | 5,256 |
| 36 | South Carolina | 5,245 |
| 37 | Kentucky | 5,190 |
| 38 | Florida | 5,188 |
| 39 | Iowa | 5,130 |
| 40 | Kansas | 5,006 |
| 41 | Idaho | 4,928 |
| 42 | Alabama | 4,901 |
| 43 | Arizona | 4,897 |
| 44 | Oklahoma | 4,860 |
| 45 | New Hampshire | 4,847 |
| 46 | Mississippi | 4,845 |
| 47 | Indiana | 4,809 |
| 48 | South Dakota | 4,783 |
| 49 | Missouri | 4,776 |
| 50 | Arkansas | 4,721 |

District of Columbia** 12,083

*Source: Morgan Quitno Press using data from U.S. Bureau of the Census, Governments Division
"Compendium of Government Finances: 1997" (2000) (http://www.census.gov/govs/www/cog.html)*
*Total revenue includes all money received from external sources. This includes taxes, intergovernmental transfers and insurance trust revenue and revenue from government owned utilities and other commercial or auxiliary enterprise.*

# State and Local Government Revenue from the Federal Government in 1997

## National Total = $244,606,988,000

ALPHA ORDER

| RANK | STATE | REVENUE | % of USA |
|---|---|---|---|
| 22 | Alabama | $3,830,775,000 | 1.6% |
| 40 | Alaska | 1,209,919,000 | 0.5% |
| 25 | Arizona | 3,414,793,000 | 1.4% |
| 30 | Arkansas | 2,385,708,000 | 1.0% |
| 1 | California | 31,398,763,000 | 12.8% |
| 29 | Colorado | 2,932,770,000 | 1.2% |
| 27 | Connecticut | 3,231,624,000 | 1.3% |
| 49 | Delaware | 698,675,000 | 0.3% |
| 7 | Florida | 9,248,463,000 | 3.8% |
| 9 | Georgia | 6,564,766,000 | 2.7% |
| 37 | Hawaii | 1,423,902,000 | 0.6% |
| 44 | Idaho | 907,129,000 | 0.4% |
| 5 | Illinois | 9,674,700,000 | 4.0% |
| 20 | Indiana | 3,975,251,000 | 1.6% |
| 32 | Iowa | 2,192,500,000 | 0.9% |
| 35 | Kansas | 1,947,440,000 | 0.8% |
| 24 | Kentucky | 3,679,065,000 | 1.5% |
| 14 | Louisiana | 4,589,578,000 | 1.9% |
| 38 | Maine | 1,373,420,000 | 0.6% |
| 19 | Maryland | 4,024,976,000 | 1.6% |
| 12 | Massachusetts | 6,092,947,000 | 2.5% |
| 8 | Michigan | 8,660,245,000 | 3.5% |
| 23 | Minnesota | 3,820,721,000 | 1.6% |
| 28 | Mississippi | 2,978,331,000 | 1.2% |
| 18 | Missouri | 4,106,291,000 | 1.7% |
| 42 | Montana | 1,033,729,000 | 0.4% |
| 39 | Nebraska | 1,306,815,000 | 0.5% |
| 43 | Nevada | 966,375,000 | 0.4% |
| 45 | New Hampshire | 891,484,000 | 0.4% |
| 11 | New Jersey | 6,398,466,000 | 2.6% |
| 34 | New Mexico | 2,139,020,000 | 0.9% |
| 2 | New York | 27,544,065,000 | 11.3% |
| 10 | North Carolina | 6,521,352,000 | 2.7% |
| 47 | North Dakota | 851,476,000 | 0.3% |
| 6 | Ohio | 9,636,850,000 | 3.9% |
| 31 | Oklahoma | 2,262,848,000 | 0.9% |
| 17 | Oregon | 4,165,219,000 | 1.7% |
| 4 | Pennsylvania | 11,065,489,000 | 4.5% |
| 41 | Rhode Island | 1,153,850,000 | 0.5% |
| 26 | South Carolina | 3,308,768,000 | 1.4% |
| 48 | South Dakota | 734,371,000 | 0.3% |
| 13 | Tennessee | 5,303,498,000 | 2.2% |
| 3 | Texas | 14,841,159,000 | 6.1% |
| 36 | Utah | 1,818,348,000 | 0.7% |
| 50 | Vermont | 681,927,000 | 0.3% |
| 21 | Virginia | 3,872,648,000 | 1.6% |
| 15 | Washington | 4,565,138,000 | 1.9% |
| 33 | West Virginia | 2,145,195,000 | 0.9% |
| 16 | Wisconsin | 4,172,977,000 | 1.7% |
| 46 | Wyoming | 868,710,000 | 0.4% |

RANK ORDER

| RANK | STATE | REVENUE | % of USA |
|---|---|---|---|
| 1 | California | $31,398,763,000 | 12.8% |
| 2 | New York | 27,544,065,000 | 11.3% |
| 3 | Texas | 14,841,159,000 | 6.1% |
| 4 | Pennsylvania | 11,065,489,000 | 4.5% |
| 5 | Illinois | 9,674,700,000 | 4.0% |
| 6 | Ohio | 9,636,850,000 | 3.9% |
| 7 | Florida | 9,248,463,000 | 3.8% |
| 8 | Michigan | 8,660,245,000 | 3.5% |
| 9 | Georgia | 6,564,766,000 | 2.7% |
| 10 | North Carolina | 6,521,352,000 | 2.7% |
| 11 | New Jersey | 6,398,466,000 | 2.6% |
| 12 | Massachusetts | 6,092,947,000 | 2.5% |
| 13 | Tennessee | 5,303,498,000 | 2.2% |
| 14 | Louisiana | 4,589,578,000 | 1.9% |
| 15 | Washington | 4,565,138,000 | 1.9% |
| 16 | Wisconsin | 4,172,977,000 | 1.7% |
| 17 | Oregon | 4,165,219,000 | 1.7% |
| 18 | Missouri | 4,106,291,000 | 1.7% |
| 19 | Maryland | 4,024,976,000 | 1.6% |
| 20 | Indiana | 3,975,251,000 | 1.6% |
| 21 | Virginia | 3,872,648,000 | 1.6% |
| 22 | Alabama | 3,830,775,000 | 1.6% |
| 23 | Minnesota | 3,820,721,000 | 1.6% |
| 24 | Kentucky | 3,679,065,000 | 1.5% |
| 25 | Arizona | 3,414,793,000 | 1.4% |
| 26 | South Carolina | 3,308,768,000 | 1.4% |
| 27 | Connecticut | 3,231,624,000 | 1.3% |
| 28 | Mississippi | 2,978,331,000 | 1.2% |
| 29 | Colorado | 2,932,770,000 | 1.2% |
| 30 | Arkansas | 2,385,708,000 | 1.0% |
| 31 | Oklahoma | 2,262,848,000 | 0.9% |
| 32 | Iowa | 2,192,500,000 | 0.9% |
| 33 | West Virginia | 2,145,195,000 | 0.9% |
| 34 | New Mexico | 2,139,020,000 | 0.9% |
| 35 | Kansas | 1,947,440,000 | 0.8% |
| 36 | Utah | 1,818,348,000 | 0.7% |
| 37 | Hawaii | 1,423,902,000 | 0.6% |
| 38 | Maine | 1,373,420,000 | 0.6% |
| 39 | Nebraska | 1,306,815,000 | 0.5% |
| 40 | Alaska | 1,209,919,000 | 0.5% |
| 41 | Rhode Island | 1,153,850,000 | 0.5% |
| 42 | Montana | 1,033,729,000 | 0.4% |
| 43 | Nevada | 966,375,000 | 0.4% |
| 44 | Idaho | 907,129,000 | 0.4% |
| 45 | New Hampshire | 891,484,000 | 0.4% |
| 46 | Wyoming | 868,710,000 | 0.4% |
| 47 | North Dakota | 851,476,000 | 0.3% |
| 48 | South Dakota | 734,371,000 | 0.3% |
| 49 | Delaware | 698,675,000 | 0.3% |
| 50 | Vermont | 681,927,000 | 0.3% |
| | District of Columbia | 1,994,459,000 | 0.8% |

Source: U.S. Bureau of the Census, Governments Division
"Compendium of Government Finances: 1997" (2000) (http://www.census.gov/govs/www/cog.html)

# Per Capita State and Local Government Revenue
## From the Federal Government in 1997
## National Per Capita = $913

| RANK | STATE | PER CAPITA |
|------|-------|------------|
| 24 | Alabama | $887 |
| 1 | Alaska | 1,987 |
| 43 | Arizona | 750 |
| 21 | Arkansas | 945 |
| 19 | California | 975 |
| 42 | Colorado | 754 |
| 17 | Connecticut | 989 |
| 20 | Delaware | 951 |
| 48 | Florida | 630 |
| 28 | Georgia | 877 |
| 7 | Hawaii | 1,197 |
| 44 | Idaho | 749 |
| 33 | Illinois | 805 |
| 47 | Indiana | 677 |
| 38 | Iowa | 768 |
| 45 | Kansas | 744 |
| 22 | Kentucky | 941 |
| 14 | Louisiana | 1,055 |
| 12 | Maine | 1,103 |
| 36 | Maryland | 790 |
| 16 | Massachusetts | 996 |
| 25 | Michigan | 885 |
| 31 | Minnesota | 815 |
| 13 | Mississippi | 1,090 |
| 41 | Missouri | 759 |
| 9 | Montana | 1,176 |
| 37 | Nebraska | 789 |
| 49 | Nevada | 577 |
| 40 | New Hampshire | 760 |
| 35 | New Jersey | 794 |
| 6 | New Mexico | 1,241 |
| 3 | New York | 1,518 |
| 27 | North Carolina | 878 |
| 4 | North Dakota | 1,328 |
| 30 | Ohio | 859 |
| 46 | Oklahoma | 683 |
| 5 | Oregon | 1,284 |
| 23 | Pennsylvania | 921 |
| 10 | Rhode Island | 1,169 |
| 29 | South Carolina | 873 |
| 15 | South Dakota | 1,005 |
| 18 | Tennessee | 986 |
| 39 | Texas | 767 |
| 26 | Utah | 880 |
| 11 | Vermont | 1,158 |
| 50 | Virginia | 575 |
| 31 | Washington | 815 |
| 8 | West Virginia | 1,182 |
| 34 | Wisconsin | 802 |
| 2 | Wyoming | 1,810 |

| RANK | STATE | PER CAPITA |
|------|-------|------------|
| 1 | Alaska | $1,987 |
| 2 | Wyoming | 1,810 |
| 3 | New York | 1,518 |
| 4 | North Dakota | 1,328 |
| 5 | Oregon | 1,284 |
| 6 | New Mexico | 1,241 |
| 7 | Hawaii | 1,197 |
| 8 | West Virginia | 1,182 |
| 9 | Montana | 1,176 |
| 10 | Rhode Island | 1,169 |
| 11 | Vermont | 1,158 |
| 12 | Maine | 1,103 |
| 13 | Mississippi | 1,090 |
| 14 | Louisiana | 1,055 |
| 15 | South Dakota | 1,005 |
| 16 | Massachusetts | 996 |
| 17 | Connecticut | 989 |
| 18 | Tennessee | 986 |
| 19 | California | 975 |
| 20 | Delaware | 951 |
| 21 | Arkansas | 945 |
| 22 | Kentucky | 941 |
| 23 | Pennsylvania | 921 |
| 24 | Alabama | 887 |
| 25 | Michigan | 885 |
| 26 | Utah | 880 |
| 27 | North Carolina | 878 |
| 28 | Georgia | 877 |
| 29 | South Carolina | 873 |
| 30 | Ohio | 859 |
| 31 | Minnesota | 815 |
| 31 | Washington | 815 |
| 33 | Illinois | 805 |
| 34 | Wisconsin | 802 |
| 35 | New Jersey | 794 |
| 36 | Maryland | 790 |
| 37 | Nebraska | 789 |
| 38 | Iowa | 768 |
| 39 | Texas | 767 |
| 40 | New Hampshire | 760 |
| 41 | Missouri | 759 |
| 42 | Colorado | 754 |
| 43 | Arizona | 750 |
| 44 | Idaho | 749 |
| 45 | Kansas | 744 |
| 46 | Oklahoma | 683 |
| 47 | Indiana | 677 |
| 48 | Florida | 630 |
| 49 | Nevada | 577 |
| 50 | Virginia | 575 |
| | District of Columbia | 3,772 |

*Source: Morgan Quitno Press using data from U.S. Bureau of the Census, Governments Division*
*"Compendium of Government Finances: 1997" (2000) (http://www.census.gov/govs/www/cog.html)*

# Percent of State and Local Government Revenue
# From the Federal Government in 1997
## National Percent = 15.1%*

ALPHA ORDER

| RANK | STATE | PERCENT |
|---|---|---|
| 15 | Alabama | 18.1 |
| 48 | Alaska | 10.7 |
| 25 | Arizona | 15.3 |
| 9 | Arkansas | 20.0 |
| 29 | California | 15.0 |
| 40 | Colorado | 13.0 |
| 32 | Connecticut | 14.7 |
| 39 | Delaware | 13.6 |
| 44 | Florida | 12.1 |
| 21 | Georgia | 16.4 |
| 17 | Hawaii | 17.5 |
| 28 | Idaho | 15.2 |
| 34 | Illinois | 14.5 |
| 36 | Indiana | 14.1 |
| 29 | Iowa | 15.0 |
| 31 | Kansas | 14.9 |
| 15 | Kentucky | 18.1 |
| 10 | Louisiana | 19.6 |
| 12 | Maine | 18.8 |
| 40 | Maryland | 13.0 |
| 22 | Massachusetts | 15.9 |
| 37 | Michigan | 14.0 |
| 46 | Minnesota | 11.5 |
| 2 | Mississippi | 22.5 |
| 22 | Missouri | 15.9 |
| 5 | Montana | 21.7 |
| 43 | Nebraska | 12.2 |
| 50 | Nevada | 9.6 |
| 24 | New Hampshire | 15.7 |
| 45 | New Jersey | 12.0 |
| 7 | New Mexico | 20.7 |
| 18 | New York | 17.2 |
| 19 | North Carolina | 16.7 |
| 2 | North Dakota | 22.5 |
| 33 | Ohio | 14.6 |
| 37 | Oklahoma | 14.0 |
| 12 | Oregon | 18.8 |
| 25 | Pennsylvania | 15.3 |
| 11 | Rhode Island | 19.5 |
| 20 | South Carolina | 16.6 |
| 6 | South Dakota | 21.0 |
| 14 | Tennessee | 18.5 |
| 35 | Texas | 14.3 |
| 25 | Utah | 15.3 |
| 8 | Vermont | 20.2 |
| 49 | Virginia | 10.6 |
| 47 | Washington | 11.4 |
| 4 | West Virginia | 22.4 |
| 42 | Wisconsin | 12.4 |
| 1 | Wyoming | 23.3 |

RANK ORDER

| RANK | STATE | PERCENT |
|---|---|---|
| 1 | Wyoming | 23.3 |
| 2 | Mississippi | 22.5 |
| 2 | North Dakota | 22.5 |
| 4 | West Virginia | 22.4 |
| 5 | Montana | 21.7 |
| 6 | South Dakota | 21.0 |
| 7 | New Mexico | 20.7 |
| 8 | Vermont | 20.2 |
| 9 | Arkansas | 20.0 |
| 10 | Louisiana | 19.6 |
| 11 | Rhode Island | 19.5 |
| 12 | Maine | 18.8 |
| 12 | Oregon | 18.8 |
| 14 | Tennessee | 18.5 |
| 15 | Alabama | 18.1 |
| 15 | Kentucky | 18.1 |
| 17 | Hawaii | 17.5 |
| 18 | New York | 17.2 |
| 19 | North Carolina | 16.7 |
| 20 | South Carolina | 16.6 |
| 21 | Georgia | 16.4 |
| 22 | Massachusetts | 15.9 |
| 22 | Missouri | 15.9 |
| 24 | New Hampshire | 15.7 |
| 25 | Arizona | 15.3 |
| 25 | Pennsylvania | 15.3 |
| 25 | Utah | 15.3 |
| 28 | Idaho | 15.2 |
| 29 | California | 15.0 |
| 29 | Iowa | 15.0 |
| 31 | Kansas | 14.9 |
| 32 | Connecticut | 14.7 |
| 33 | Ohio | 14.6 |
| 34 | Illinois | 14.5 |
| 35 | Texas | 14.3 |
| 36 | Indiana | 14.1 |
| 37 | Michigan | 14.0 |
| 37 | Oklahoma | 14.0 |
| 39 | Delaware | 13.6 |
| 40 | Colorado | 13.0 |
| 40 | Maryland | 13.0 |
| 42 | Wisconsin | 12.4 |
| 43 | Nebraska | 12.2 |
| 44 | Florida | 12.1 |
| 45 | New Jersey | 12.0 |
| 46 | Minnesota | 11.5 |
| 47 | Washington | 11.4 |
| 48 | Alaska | 10.7 |
| 49 | Virginia | 10.6 |
| 50 | Nevada | 9.6 |
| | District of Columbia | 31.2 |

Source: Morgan Quitno Press using data from U.S. Bureau of the Census, Governments Division
"Compendium of Government Finances: 1997" (2000) (http://www.census.gov/govs/www/cog.html)
*As a percent of total revenue.

# State and Local Government Own Source Revenue in 1997

## National Total = $1,044,610,195,000*

ALPHA ORDER

RANK ORDER

| RANK | STATE | REVENUE | % of USA | RANK | STATE | REVENUE | % of USA |
|---|---|---|---|---|---|---|---|
| 26 | Alabama | $13,134,763,000 | 1.3% | 1 | California | $130,280,957,000 | 12.5% |
| 33 | Alaska | 7,832,826,000 | 0.7% | 2 | New York | 102,387,554,000 | 9.8% |
| 24 | Arizona | 14,277,597,000 | 1.4% | 3 | Texas | 63,814,080,000 | 6.1% |
| 34 | Arkansas | 7,486,866,000 | 0.7% | 4 | Florida | 54,509,045,000 | 5.2% |
| 1 | California | 130,280,957,000 | 12.5% | 5 | Illinois | 45,394,856,000 | 4.3% |
| 23 | Colorado | 15,379,408,000 | 1.5% | 6 | Pennsylvania | 44,249,012,000 | 4.2% |
| 20 | Connecticut | 16,602,978,000 | 1.6% | 7 | Ohio | 40,232,861,000 | 3.9% |
| 45 | Delaware | 3,529,731,000 | 0.3% | 8 | Michigan | 38,339,364,000 | 3.7% |
| 4 | Florida | 54,509,045,000 | 5.2% | 9 | New Jersey | 37,402,749,000 | 3.6% |
| 11 | Georgia | 26,392,933,000 | 2.5% | 10 | Massachusetts | 26,751,720,000 | 2.6% |
| 40 | Hawaii | 5,375,877,000 | 0.5% | 11 | Georgia | 26,392,933,000 | 2.5% |
| 42 | Idaho | 4,040,267,000 | 0.4% | 12 | North Carolina | 26,048,492,000 | 2.5% |
| 5 | Illinois | 45,394,856,000 | 4.3% | 13 | Virginia | 24,697,747,000 | 2.4% |
| 16 | Indiana | 21,465,138,000 | 2.1% | 14 | Washington | 23,613,896,000 | 2.3% |
| 29 | Iowa | 10,807,955,000 | 1.0% | 15 | Minnesota | 22,284,891,000 | 2.1% |
| 31 | Kansas | 9,690,133,000 | 0.9% | 16 | Indiana | 21,465,138,000 | 2.1% |
| 27 | Kentucky | 12,855,674,000 | 1.2% | 17 | Wisconsin | 21,207,549,000 | 2.0% |
| 22 | Louisiana | 15,570,357,000 | 1.5% | 18 | Maryland | 19,851,755,000 | 1.9% |
| 41 | Maine | 4,677,327,000 | 0.4% | 19 | Missouri | 17,445,270,000 | 1.7% |
| 18 | Maryland | 19,851,755,000 | 1.9% | 20 | Connecticut | 16,602,978,000 | 1.6% |
| 10 | Massachusetts | 26,751,720,000 | 2.6% | 21 | Tennessee | 15,853,524,000 | 1.5% |
| 8 | Michigan | 38,339,364,000 | 3.7% | 22 | Louisiana | 15,570,357,000 | 1.5% |
| 15 | Minnesota | 22,284,891,000 | 2.1% | 23 | Colorado | 15,379,408,000 | 1.5% |
| 32 | Mississippi | 8,256,258,000 | 0.8% | 24 | Arizona | 14,277,597,000 | 1.4% |
| 19 | Missouri | 17,445,270,000 | 1.7% | 25 | Oregon | 13,411,483,000 | 1.3% |
| 46 | Montana | 3,017,338,000 | 0.3% | 26 | Alabama | 13,134,763,000 | 1.3% |
| 38 | Nebraska | 6,610,352,000 | 0.6% | 27 | Kentucky | 12,855,674,000 | 1.2% |
| 37 | Nevada | 6,692,541,000 | 0.6% | 28 | South Carolina | 12,563,863,000 | 1.2% |
| 43 | New Hampshire | 3,963,659,000 | 0.4% | 29 | Iowa | 10,807,955,000 | 1.0% |
| 9 | New Jersey | 37,402,749,000 | 3.6% | 30 | Oklahoma | 10,577,525,000 | 1.0% |
| 36 | New Mexico | 6,708,269,000 | 0.6% | 31 | Kansas | 9,690,133,000 | 0.9% |
| 2 | New York | 102,387,554,000 | 9.8% | 32 | Mississippi | 8,256,258,000 | 0.8% |
| 12 | North Carolina | 26,048,492,000 | 2.5% | 33 | Alaska | 7,832,826,000 | 0.7% |
| 47 | North Dakota | 2,462,238,000 | 0.2% | 34 | Arkansas | 7,486,866,000 | 0.7% |
| 7 | Ohio | 40,232,861,000 | 3.9% | 35 | Utah | 7,092,652,000 | 0.7% |
| 30 | Oklahoma | 10,577,525,000 | 1.0% | 36 | New Mexico | 6,708,269,000 | 0.6% |
| 25 | Oregon | 13,411,483,000 | 1.3% | 37 | Nevada | 6,692,541,000 | 0.6% |
| 6 | Pennsylvania | 44,249,012,000 | 4.2% | 38 | Nebraska | 6,610,352,000 | 0.6% |
| 44 | Rhode Island | 3,874,929,000 | 0.4% | 39 | West Virginia | 5,843,825,000 | 0.6% |
| 28 | South Carolina | 12,563,863,000 | 1.2% | 40 | Hawaii | 5,375,877,000 | 0.5% |
| 50 | South Dakota | 2,215,325,000 | 0.2% | 41 | Maine | 4,677,327,000 | 0.4% |
| 21 | Tennessee | 15,853,524,000 | 1.5% | 42 | Idaho | 4,040,267,000 | 0.4% |
| 3 | Texas | 63,814,080,000 | 6.1% | 43 | New Hampshire | 3,963,659,000 | 0.4% |
| 35 | Utah | 7,092,652,000 | 0.7% | 44 | Rhode Island | 3,874,929,000 | 0.4% |
| 49 | Vermont | 2,243,086,000 | 0.2% | 45 | Delaware | 3,529,731,000 | 0.3% |
| 13 | Virginia | 24,697,747,000 | 2.4% | 46 | Montana | 3,017,338,000 | 0.3% |
| 14 | Washington | 23,613,896,000 | 2.3% | 47 | North Dakota | 2,462,238,000 | 0.2% |
| 39 | West Virginia | 5,843,825,000 | 0.6% | 48 | Wyoming | 2,307,145,000 | 0.2% |
| 17 | Wisconsin | 21,207,549,000 | 2.0% | 49 | Vermont | 2,243,086,000 | 0.2% |
| 48 | Wyoming | 2,307,145,000 | 0.2% | 50 | South Dakota | 2,215,325,000 | 0.2% |
| | | | | | District of Columbia | 3,284,555,000 | 0.3% |

Source: U.S. Bureau of the Census, Governments Division
   "Compendium of Government Finances: 1997" (2000) (http://www.census.gov/govs/www/cog.html)
*Own source revenue includes taxes, current charges and miscellaneous general revenue. Excluded are intergovernmental transfers, insurance trust revenue and revenue from government owned utilities and other commercial or auxiliary enterprise.

# Per Capita State and Local Government Own Source Revenue in 1997

## National Per Capita = $3,901*

ALPHA ORDER

| RANK | STATE | PER CAPITA |
|------|-------|-----------|
| 46 | Alabama | $3,040 |
| 1 | Alaska | 12,865 |
| 45 | Arizona | 3,136 |
| 49 | Arkansas | 2,966 |
| 13 | California | 4,044 |
| 16 | Colorado | 3,952 |
| 3 | Connecticut | 5,080 |
| 5 | Delaware | 4,802 |
| 26 | Florida | 3,712 |
| 33 | Georgia | 3,526 |
| 8 | Hawaii | 4,520 |
| 38 | Idaho | 3,337 |
| 24 | Illinois | 3,779 |
| 30 | Indiana | 3,655 |
| 23 | Iowa | 3,786 |
| 27 | Kansas | 3,704 |
| 41 | Kentucky | 3,290 |
| 32 | Louisiana | 3,578 |
| 25 | Maine | 3,756 |
| 19 | Maryland | 3,898 |
| 9 | Massachusetts | 4,374 |
| 18 | Michigan | 3,918 |
| 6 | Minnesota | 4,754 |
| 48 | Mississippi | 3,022 |
| 42 | Missouri | 3,226 |
| 35 | Montana | 3,434 |
| 15 | Nebraska | 3,992 |
| 14 | Nevada | 3,994 |
| 37 | New Hampshire | 3,378 |
| 7 | New Jersey | 4,644 |
| 20 | New Mexico | 3,894 |
| 2 | New York | 5,643 |
| 34 | North Carolina | 3,506 |
| 21 | North Dakota | 3,842 |
| 31 | Ohio | 3,588 |
| 44 | Oklahoma | 3,192 |
| 11 | Oregon | 4,135 |
| 28 | Pennsylvania | 3,683 |
| 17 | Rhode Island | 3,926 |
| 39 | South Carolina | 3,315 |
| 47 | South Dakota | 3,031 |
| 50 | Tennessee | 2,948 |
| 40 | Texas | 3,297 |
| 35 | Utah | 3,434 |
| 22 | Vermont | 3,810 |
| 29 | Virginia | 3,668 |
| 10 | Washington | 4,214 |
| 43 | West Virginia | 3,219 |
| 12 | Wisconsin | 4,078 |
| 4 | Wyoming | 4,806 |

RANK ORDER

| RANK | STATE | PER CAPITA |
|------|-------|-----------|
| 1 | Alaska | $12,865 |
| 2 | New York | 5,643 |
| 3 | Connecticut | 5,080 |
| 4 | Wyoming | 4,806 |
| 5 | Delaware | 4,802 |
| 6 | Minnesota | 4,754 |
| 7 | New Jersey | 4,644 |
| 8 | Hawaii | 4,520 |
| 9 | Massachusetts | 4,374 |
| 10 | Washington | 4,214 |
| 11 | Oregon | 4,135 |
| 12 | Wisconsin | 4,078 |
| 13 | California | 4,044 |
| 14 | Nevada | 3,994 |
| 15 | Nebraska | 3,992 |
| 16 | Colorado | 3,952 |
| 17 | Rhode Island | 3,926 |
| 18 | Michigan | 3,918 |
| 19 | Maryland | 3,898 |
| 20 | New Mexico | 3,894 |
| 21 | North Dakota | 3,842 |
| 22 | Vermont | 3,810 |
| 23 | Iowa | 3,786 |
| 24 | Illinois | 3,779 |
| 25 | Maine | 3,756 |
| 26 | Florida | 3,712 |
| 27 | Kansas | 3,704 |
| 28 | Pennsylvania | 3,683 |
| 29 | Virginia | 3,668 |
| 30 | Indiana | 3,655 |
| 31 | Ohio | 3,588 |
| 32 | Louisiana | 3,578 |
| 33 | Georgia | 3,526 |
| 34 | North Carolina | 3,506 |
| 35 | Montana | 3,434 |
| 35 | Utah | 3,434 |
| 37 | New Hampshire | 3,378 |
| 38 | Idaho | 3,337 |
| 39 | South Carolina | 3,315 |
| 40 | Texas | 3,297 |
| 41 | Kentucky | 3,290 |
| 42 | Missouri | 3,226 |
| 43 | West Virginia | 3,219 |
| 44 | Oklahoma | 3,192 |
| 45 | Arizona | 3,136 |
| 46 | Alabama | 3,040 |
| 47 | South Dakota | 3,031 |
| 48 | Mississippi | 3,022 |
| 49 | Arkansas | 2,966 |
| 50 | Tennessee | 2,948 |

| | District of Columbia | 6,212 |

Source: Morgan Quitno Press using data from U.S. Bureau of the Census, Governments Division
"Compendium of Government Finances: 1997" (2000) (http://www.census.gov/govs/www/cog.html)
*Own source revenue includes taxes, current charges and miscellaneous general revenue. Excluded are
intergovernmental transfers, insurance trust revenue and revenue from government owned utilities and other
commercial or auxiliary enterprise.

# State and Local Government Tax Revenue in 1997

## National Total = $728,594,313,000

ALPHA ORDER

RANK ORDER

| RANK | STATE | TAX REVENUE | % of USA |
|------|-------|-------------|----------|
| 27 | Alabama | $7,958,162,000 | 1.1% |
| 44 | Alaska | 2,411,597,000 | 0.3% |
| 22 | Arizona | 10,424,677,000 | 1.4% |
| 33 | Arkansas | 5,120,299,000 | 0.7% |
| 1 | California | 90,516,873,000 | 12.4% |
| 23 | Colorado | 10,099,939,000 | 1.4% |
| 19 | Connecticut | 13,738,730,000 | 1.9% |
| 45 | Delaware | 2,155,704,000 | 0.3% |
| 4 | Florida | 35,633,024,000 | 4.9% |
| 11 | Georgia | 18,170,517,000 | 2.5% |
| 39 | Hawaii | 3,848,690,000 | 0.5% |
| 43 | Idaho | 2,719,000,000 | 0.4% |
| 5 | Illinois | 34,237,390,000 | 4.7% |
| 18 | Indiana | 14,724,298,000 | 2.0% |
| 29 | Iowa | 7,195,350,000 | 1.0% |
| 31 | Kansas | 6,762,663,000 | 0.9% |
| 25 | Kentucky | 8,895,688,000 | 1.2% |
| 24 | Louisiana | 9,630,044,000 | 1.3% |
| 40 | Maine | 3,554,711,000 | 0.5% |
| 17 | Maryland | 14,837,824,000 | 2.0% |
| 10 | Massachusetts | 20,119,738,000 | 2.8% |
| 9 | Michigan | 26,616,525,000 | 3.7% |
| 15 | Minnesota | 15,730,821,000 | 2.2% |
| 32 | Mississippi | 5,361,806,000 | 0.7% |
| 20 | Missouri | 12,595,398,000 | 1.7% |
| 46 | Montana | 1,931,092,000 | 0.3% |
| 36 | Nebraska | 4,492,416,000 | 0.6% |
| 35 | Nevada | 4,567,339,000 | 0.6% |
| 42 | New Hampshire | 2,751,584,000 | 0.4% |
| 8 | New Jersey | 27,403,361,000 | 3.8% |
| 37 | New Mexico | 4,244,527,000 | 0.6% |
| 2 | New York | 75,468,453,000 | 10.4% |
| 12 | North Carolina | 17,740,952,000 | 2.4% |
| 48 | North Dakota | 1,579,118,000 | 0.2% |
| 7 | Ohio | 29,065,488,000 | 4.0% |
| 30 | Oklahoma | 7,125,909,000 | 1.0% |
| 26 | Oregon | 8,066,469,000 | 1.1% |
| 6 | Pennsylvania | 31,879,726,000 | 4.4% |
| 41 | Rhode Island | 2,915,945,000 | 0.4% |
| 28 | South Carolina | 7,802,480,000 | 1.1% |
| 49 | South Dakota | 1,463,604,000 | 0.2% |
| 21 | Tennessee | 10,626,115,000 | 1.5% |
| 3 | Texas | 43,561,750,000 | 6.0% |
| 34 | Utah | 4,677,396,000 | 0.6% |
| 47 | Vermont | 1,617,650,000 | 0.2% |
| 13 | Virginia | 16,828,227,000 | 2.3% |
| 14 | Washington | 16,369,783,000 | 2.2% |
| 38 | West Virginia | 3,852,130,000 | 0.5% |
| 16 | Wisconsin | 15,625,389,000 | 2.1% |
| 50 | Wyoming | 1,240,534,000 | 0.2% |

| RANK | STATE | TAX REVENUE | % of USA |
|------|-------|-------------|----------|
| 1 | California | $90,516,873,000 | 12.4% |
| 2 | New York | 75,468,453,000 | 10.4% |
| 3 | Texas | 43,561,750,000 | 6.0% |
| 4 | Florida | 35,633,024,000 | 4.9% |
| 5 | Illinois | 34,237,390,000 | 4.7% |
| 6 | Pennsylvania | 31,879,726,000 | 4.4% |
| 7 | Ohio | 29,065,488,000 | 4.0% |
| 8 | New Jersey | 27,403,361,000 | 3.8% |
| 9 | Michigan | 26,616,525,000 | 3.7% |
| 10 | Massachusetts | 20,119,738,000 | 2.8% |
| 11 | Georgia | 18,170,517,000 | 2.5% |
| 12 | North Carolina | 17,740,952,000 | 2.4% |
| 13 | Virginia | 16,828,227,000 | 2.3% |
| 14 | Washington | 16,369,783,000 | 2.2% |
| 15 | Minnesota | 15,730,821,000 | 2.2% |
| 16 | Wisconsin | 15,625,389,000 | 2.1% |
| 17 | Maryland | 14,837,824,000 | 2.0% |
| 18 | Indiana | 14,724,298,000 | 2.0% |
| 19 | Connecticut | 13,738,730,000 | 1.9% |
| 20 | Missouri | 12,595,398,000 | 1.7% |
| 21 | Tennessee | 10,626,115,000 | 1.5% |
| 22 | Arizona | 10,424,677,000 | 1.4% |
| 23 | Colorado | 10,099,939,000 | 1.4% |
| 24 | Louisiana | 9,630,044,000 | 1.3% |
| 25 | Kentucky | 8,895,688,000 | 1.2% |
| 26 | Oregon | 8,066,469,000 | 1.1% |
| 27 | Alabama | 7,958,162,000 | 1.1% |
| 28 | South Carolina | 7,802,480,000 | 1.1% |
| 29 | Iowa | 7,195,350,000 | 1.0% |
| 30 | Oklahoma | 7,125,909,000 | 1.0% |
| 31 | Kansas | 6,762,663,000 | 0.9% |
| 32 | Mississippi | 5,361,806,000 | 0.7% |
| 33 | Arkansas | 5,120,299,000 | 0.7% |
| 34 | Utah | 4,677,396,000 | 0.6% |
| 35 | Nevada | 4,567,339,000 | 0.6% |
| 36 | Nebraska | 4,492,416,000 | 0.6% |
| 37 | New Mexico | 4,244,527,000 | 0.6% |
| 38 | West Virginia | 3,852,130,000 | 0.5% |
| 39 | Hawaii | 3,848,690,000 | 0.5% |
| 40 | Maine | 3,554,711,000 | 0.5% |
| 41 | Rhode Island | 2,915,945,000 | 0.4% |
| 42 | New Hampshire | 2,751,584,000 | 0.4% |
| 43 | Idaho | 2,719,000,000 | 0.4% |
| 44 | Alaska | 2,411,597,000 | 0.3% |
| 45 | Delaware | 2,155,704,000 | 0.3% |
| 46 | Montana | 1,931,092,000 | 0.3% |
| 47 | Vermont | 1,617,650,000 | 0.2% |
| 48 | North Dakota | 1,579,118,000 | 0.2% |
| 49 | South Dakota | 1,463,604,000 | 0.2% |
| 50 | Wyoming | 1,240,534,000 | 0.2% |
| | District of Columbia | 2,637,408,000 | 0.4% |

*Source: U.S. Bureau of the Census, Governments Division*
*"Compendium of Government Finances: 1997" (2000) (http://www.census.gov/govs/www/cog.html)*

# Per Capita State and Local Government Tax Revenue in 1997

## National Per Capita = $2,721

ALPHA ORDER

| RANK | STATE | PER CAPITA |
|------|-------|-----------|
| 50 | Alabama | $1,842 |
| 3 | Alaska | 3,961 |
| 36 | Arizona | 2,290 |
| 46 | Arkansas | 2,029 |
| 15 | California | 2,810 |
| 21 | Colorado | 2,596 |
| 1 | Connecticut | 4,203 |
| 10 | Delaware | 2,933 |
| 31 | Florida | 2,427 |
| 31 | Georgia | 2,427 |
| 7 | Hawaii | 3,236 |
| 40 | Idaho | 2,246 |
| 14 | Illinois | 2,850 |
| 26 | Indiana | 2,507 |
| 25 | Iowa | 2,521 |
| 23 | Kansas | 2,585 |
| 37 | Kentucky | 2,276 |
| 41 | Louisiana | 2,213 |
| 13 | Maine | 2,855 |
| 12 | Maryland | 2,913 |
| 6 | Massachusetts | 3,290 |
| 18 | Michigan | 2,720 |
| 5 | Minnesota | 3,356 |
| 49 | Mississippi | 1,963 |
| 35 | Missouri | 2,329 |
| 42 | Montana | 2,198 |
| 19 | Nebraska | 2,713 |
| 17 | Nevada | 2,726 |
| 34 | New Hampshire | 2,345 |
| 4 | New Jersey | 3,402 |
| 29 | New Mexico | 2,464 |
| 2 | New York | 4,160 |
| 33 | North Carolina | 2,388 |
| 29 | North Dakota | 2,464 |
| 22 | Ohio | 2,592 |
| 43 | Oklahoma | 2,150 |
| 28 | Oregon | 2,487 |
| 20 | Pennsylvania | 2,653 |
| 9 | Rhode Island | 2,954 |
| 45 | South Carolina | 2,059 |
| 47 | South Dakota | 2,003 |
| 48 | Tennessee | 1,976 |
| 39 | Texas | 2,251 |
| 38 | Utah | 2,265 |
| 16 | Vermont | 2,748 |
| 27 | Virginia | 2,499 |
| 11 | Washington | 2,921 |
| 44 | West Virginia | 2,122 |
| 8 | Wisconsin | 3,005 |
| 24 | Wyoming | 2,584 |

RANK ORDER

| RANK | STATE | PER CAPITA |
|------|-------|-----------|
| 1 | Connecticut | $4,203 |
| 2 | New York | 4,160 |
| 3 | Alaska | 3,961 |
| 4 | New Jersey | 3,402 |
| 5 | Minnesota | 3,356 |
| 6 | Massachusetts | 3,290 |
| 7 | Hawaii | 3,236 |
| 8 | Wisconsin | 3,005 |
| 9 | Rhode Island | 2,954 |
| 10 | Delaware | 2,933 |
| 11 | Washington | 2,921 |
| 12 | Maryland | 2,913 |
| 13 | Maine | 2,855 |
| 14 | Illinois | 2,850 |
| 15 | California | 2,810 |
| 16 | Vermont | 2,748 |
| 17 | Nevada | 2,726 |
| 18 | Michigan | 2,720 |
| 19 | Nebraska | 2,713 |
| 20 | Pennsylvania | 2,653 |
| 21 | Colorado | 2,596 |
| 22 | Ohio | 2,592 |
| 23 | Kansas | 2,585 |
| 24 | Wyoming | 2,584 |
| 25 | Iowa | 2,521 |
| 26 | Indiana | 2,507 |
| 27 | Virginia | 2,499 |
| 28 | Oregon | 2,487 |
| 29 | New Mexico | 2,464 |
| 29 | North Dakota | 2,464 |
| 31 | Florida | 2,427 |
| 31 | Georgia | 2,427 |
| 33 | North Carolina | 2,388 |
| 34 | New Hampshire | 2,345 |
| 35 | Missouri | 2,329 |
| 36 | Arizona | 2,290 |
| 37 | Kentucky | 2,276 |
| 38 | Utah | 2,265 |
| 39 | Texas | 2,251 |
| 40 | Idaho | 2,246 |
| 41 | Louisiana | 2,213 |
| 42 | Montana | 2,198 |
| 43 | Oklahoma | 2,150 |
| 44 | West Virginia | 2,122 |
| 45 | South Carolina | 2,059 |
| 46 | Arkansas | 2,029 |
| 47 | South Dakota | 2,003 |
| 48 | Tennessee | 1,976 |
| 49 | Mississippi | 1,963 |
| 50 | Alabama | 1,842 |
| | District of Columbia | 4,988 |

Source: Morgan Quitno Press using data from U.S. Bureau of the Census, Governments Division
"Compendium of Government Finances: 1997" (2000) (http://www.census.gov/govs/www/cog.html)

# State and Local Government Tax Revenue
## As a Percent of Personal Income in 1997
## National Percent = 10.5% of Personal Income*

ALPHA ORDER

RANK ORDER

| RANK | STATE | PERCENT | | RANK | STATE | PERCENT |
|------|-------|---------|---|------|-------|---------|
| 48 | Alabama | 8.7 | | 1 | Alaska | 14.6 |
| 1 | Alaska | 14.6 | | 2 | New York | 13.6 |
| 33 | Arizona | 10.1 | | 3 | Maine | 12.8 |
| 35 | Arkansas | 10.0 | | 4 | Hawaii | 12.3 |
| 25 | California | 10.5 | | 5 | Minnesota | 12.2 |
| 44 | Colorado | 9.3 | | 5 | New Mexico | 12.2 |
| 8 | Connecticut | 11.8 | | 7 | Wisconsin | 12.1 |
| 18 | Delaware | 10.7 | | 8 | Connecticut | 11.8 |
| 43 | Florida | 9.4 | | 8 | North Dakota | 11.8 |
| 38 | Georgia | 9.9 | | 8 | Vermont | 11.8 |
| 4 | Hawaii | 12.3 | | 11 | Rhode Island | 11.1 |
| 16 | Idaho | 10.8 | | 12 | Nebraska | 11.0 |
| 33 | Illinois | 10.1 | | 13 | Montana | 10.9 |
| 21 | Indiana | 10.6 | | 13 | Washington | 10.9 |
| 21 | Iowa | 10.6 | | 13 | West Virginia | 10.9 |
| 21 | Kansas | 10.6 | | 16 | Idaho | 10.8 |
| 18 | Kentucky | 10.7 | | 16 | Wyoming | 10.8 |
| 28 | Louisiana | 10.4 | | 18 | Delaware | 10.7 |
| 3 | Maine | 12.8 | | 18 | Kentucky | 10.7 |
| 35 | Maryland | 10.0 | | 18 | Utah | 10.7 |
| 25 | Massachusetts | 10.5 | | 21 | Indiana | 10.6 |
| 21 | Michigan | 10.6 | | 21 | Iowa | 10.6 |
| 5 | Minnesota | 12.2 | | 21 | Kansas | 10.6 |
| 28 | Mississippi | 10.4 | | 21 | Michigan | 10.6 |
| 41 | Missouri | 9.6 | | 25 | California | 10.5 |
| 13 | Montana | 10.9 | | 25 | Massachusetts | 10.5 |
| 12 | Nebraska | 11.0 | | 25 | New Jersey | 10.5 |
| 40 | Nevada | 9.7 | | 28 | Louisiana | 10.4 |
| 49 | New Hampshire | 8.5 | | 28 | Mississippi | 10.4 |
| 25 | New Jersey | 10.5 | | 28 | Ohio | 10.4 |
| 5 | New Mexico | 12.2 | | 31 | Oklahoma | 10.2 |
| 2 | New York | 13.6 | | 31 | Pennsylvania | 10.2 |
| 38 | North Carolina | 9.9 | | 33 | Arizona | 10.1 |
| 8 | North Dakota | 11.8 | | 33 | Illinois | 10.1 |
| 28 | Ohio | 10.4 | | 35 | Arkansas | 10.0 |
| 31 | Oklahoma | 10.2 | | 35 | Maryland | 10.0 |
| 35 | Oregon | 10.0 | | 35 | Oregon | 10.0 |
| 31 | Pennsylvania | 10.2 | | 38 | Georgia | 9.9 |
| 11 | Rhode Island | 11.1 | | 38 | North Carolina | 9.9 |
| 41 | South Carolina | 9.6 | | 40 | Nevada | 9.7 |
| 47 | South Dakota | 9.0 | | 41 | Missouri | 9.6 |
| 49 | Tennessee | 8.5 | | 41 | South Carolina | 9.6 |
| 44 | Texas | 9.3 | | 43 | Florida | 9.4 |
| 18 | Utah | 10.7 | | 44 | Colorado | 9.3 |
| 8 | Vermont | 11.8 | | 44 | Texas | 9.3 |
| 44 | Virginia | 9.3 | | 44 | Virginia | 9.3 |
| 13 | Washington | 10.9 | | 47 | South Dakota | 9.0 |
| 13 | West Virginia | 10.9 | | 48 | Alabama | 8.7 |
| 7 | Wisconsin | 12.1 | | 49 | New Hampshire | 8.5 |
| 16 | Wyoming | 10.8 | | 49 | Tennessee | 8.5 |
| | | | | | District of Columbia | 13.8 |

Source: Morgan Quitno Press using data from Bureau of Economic Analysis and U.S. Census Bureau
  "State Personal Income" and "Compendium of Government Finances: 1997"
*The personal income total used for this table is the sum of state estimates. This total differs from the national income and product accounts (NIPA) estimate of personal income because it omits the earnings of federal civilian and military personnel stationed abroad and of U.S. residents employed abroad temporarily by private U.S. firms.

# State and Local Government General Sales Tax Revenue in 1997

## National Total = $178,746,275,000*

ALPHA ORDER

| RANK | STATE | REVENUE | % of USA |
|---|---|---|---|
| 24 | Alabama | $2,505,814,000 | 1.4% |
| 46 | Alaska | 98,231,000 | 0.1% |
| 15 | Arizona | 3,657,287,000 | 2.0% |
| 30 | Arkansas | 1,863,278,000 | 1.0% |
| 1 | California | 24,108,411,000 | 13.5% |
| 20 | Colorado | 2,910,937,000 | 1.6% |
| 22 | Connecticut | 2,850,124,000 | 1.6% |
| 48 | Delaware | 0 | 0.0% |
| 4 | Florida | 12,513,191,000 | 7.0% |
| 10 | Georgia | 5,476,679,000 | 3.1% |
| 36 | Hawaii | 1,457,274,000 | 0.8% |
| 40 | Idaho | 622,250,000 | 0.3% |
| 7 | Illinois | 6,500,972,000 | 3.6% |
| 18 | Indiana | 3,042,874,000 | 1.7% |
| 34 | Iowa | 1,586,978,000 | 0.9% |
| 31 | Kansas | 1,796,842,000 | 1.0% |
| 29 | Kentucky | 1,882,771,000 | 1.1% |
| 14 | Louisiana | 3,810,886,000 | 2.1% |
| 39 | Maine | 683,207,000 | 0.4% |
| 27 | Maryland | 2,095,319,000 | 1.2% |
| 21 | Massachusetts | 2,876,066,000 | 1.6% |
| 6 | Michigan | 7,132,110,000 | 4.0% |
| 17 | Minnesota | 3,141,310,000 | 1.8% |
| 28 | Mississippi | 1,916,536,000 | 1.1% |
| 16 | Missouri | 3,643,786,000 | 2.0% |
| 48 | Montana | 0 | 0.0% |
| 37 | Nebraska | 1,024,706,000 | 0.6% |
| 32 | Nevada | 1,792,065,000 | 1.0% |
| 48 | New Hampshire | 0 | 0.0% |
| 12 | New Jersey | 4,415,428,000 | 2.5% |
| 33 | New Mexico | 1,656,499,000 | 0.9% |
| 2 | New York | 14,104,298,000 | 7.9% |
| 13 | North Carolina | 3,987,280,000 | 2.2% |
| 44 | North Dakota | 348,314,000 | 0.2% |
| 8 | Ohio | 6,173,165,000 | 3.5% |
| 25 | Oklahoma | 2,124,475,000 | 1.2% |
| 47 | Oregon | 113,000 | 0.0% |
| 9 | Pennsylvania | 6,160,545,000 | 3.4% |
| 42 | Rhode Island | 489,624,000 | 0.3% |
| 26 | South Carolina | 2,110,662,000 | 1.2% |
| 41 | South Dakota | 543,221,000 | 0.3% |
| 11 | Tennessee | 5,028,398,000 | 2.8% |
| 3 | Texas | 13,890,986,000 | 7.8% |
| 35 | Utah | 1,545,108,000 | 0.9% |
| 45 | Vermont | 183,838,000 | 0.1% |
| 23 | Virginia | 2,743,769,000 | 1.5% |
| 5 | Washington | 7,539,155,000 | 4.2% |
| 38 | West Virginia | 831,239,000 | 0.5% |
| 19 | Wisconsin | 3,017,168,000 | 1.7% |
| 43 | Wyoming | 380,732,000 | 0.2% |

RANK ORDER

| RANK | STATE | REVENUE | % of USA |
|---|---|---|---|
| 1 | California | $24,108,411,000 | 13.5% |
| 2 | New York | 14,104,298,000 | 7.9% |
| 3 | Texas | 13,890,986,000 | 7.8% |
| 4 | Florida | 12,513,191,000 | 7.0% |
| 5 | Washington | 7,539,155,000 | 4.2% |
| 6 | Michigan | 7,132,110,000 | 4.0% |
| 7 | Illinois | 6,500,972,000 | 3.6% |
| 8 | Ohio | 6,173,165,000 | 3.5% |
| 9 | Pennsylvania | 6,160,545,000 | 3.4% |
| 10 | Georgia | 5,476,679,000 | 3.1% |
| 11 | Tennessee | 5,028,398,000 | 2.8% |
| 12 | New Jersey | 4,415,428,000 | 2.5% |
| 13 | North Carolina | 3,987,280,000 | 2.2% |
| 14 | Louisiana | 3,810,886,000 | 2.1% |
| 15 | Arizona | 3,657,287,000 | 2.0% |
| 16 | Missouri | 3,643,786,000 | 2.0% |
| 17 | Minnesota | 3,141,310,000 | 1.8% |
| 18 | Indiana | 3,042,874,000 | 1.7% |
| 19 | Wisconsin | 3,017,168,000 | 1.7% |
| 20 | Colorado | 2,910,937,000 | 1.6% |
| 21 | Massachusetts | 2,876,066,000 | 1.6% |
| 22 | Connecticut | 2,850,124,000 | 1.6% |
| 23 | Virginia | 2,743,769,000 | 1.5% |
| 24 | Alabama | 2,505,814,000 | 1.4% |
| 25 | Oklahoma | 2,124,475,000 | 1.2% |
| 26 | South Carolina | 2,110,662,000 | 1.2% |
| 27 | Maryland | 2,095,319,000 | 1.2% |
| 28 | Mississippi | 1,916,536,000 | 1.1% |
| 29 | Kentucky | 1,882,771,000 | 1.1% |
| 30 | Arkansas | 1,863,278,000 | 1.0% |
| 31 | Kansas | 1,796,842,000 | 1.0% |
| 32 | Nevada | 1,792,065,000 | 1.0% |
| 33 | New Mexico | 1,656,499,000 | 0.9% |
| 34 | Iowa | 1,586,978,000 | 0.9% |
| 35 | Utah | 1,545,108,000 | 0.9% |
| 36 | Hawaii | 1,457,274,000 | 0.8% |
| 37 | Nebraska | 1,024,706,000 | 0.6% |
| 38 | West Virginia | 831,239,000 | 0.5% |
| 39 | Maine | 683,207,000 | 0.4% |
| 40 | Idaho | 622,250,000 | 0.3% |
| 41 | South Dakota | 543,221,000 | 0.3% |
| 42 | Rhode Island | 489,624,000 | 0.3% |
| 43 | Wyoming | 380,732,000 | 0.2% |
| 44 | North Dakota | 348,314,000 | 0.2% |
| 45 | Vermont | 183,838,000 | 0.1% |
| 46 | Alaska | 98,231,000 | 0.1% |
| 47 | Oregon | 113,000 | 0.0% |
| 48 | Delaware | 0 | 0.0% |
| 48 | Montana | 0 | 0.0% |
| 48 | New Hampshire | 0 | 0.0% |
| | District of Columbia | 482,354,000 | 0.3% |

Source: U.S. Bureau of the Census, Governments Division
   "Compendium of Government Finances: 1997" (2000) (http://www.census.gov/govs/www/cog.html)
*Does not include special sales taxes such as those on sale of alcohol, gasoline or tobacco.

# Per Capita State and Local Government Sales Tax Revenue in 1997

## National Per Capita = $668*

ALPHA ORDER

| RANK | STATE | PER CAPITA |
|------|-------|------------|
| 26 | Alabama | $580 |
| 46 | Alaska | 161 |
| 9 | Arizona | 803 |
| 16 | Arkansas | 738 |
| 12 | California | 748 |
| 12 | Colorado | 748 |
| 7 | Connecticut | 872 |
| 47 | Delaware | 0 |
| 8 | Florida | 852 |
| 17 | Georgia | 732 |
| 2 | Hawaii | 1,225 |
| 37 | Idaho | 514 |
| 34 | Illinois | 541 |
| 36 | Indiana | 518 |
| 29 | Iowa | 556 |
| 21 | Kansas | 687 |
| 40 | Kentucky | 482 |
| 6 | Louisiana | 876 |
| 31 | Maine | 549 |
| 43 | Maryland | 411 |
| 41 | Massachusetts | 470 |
| 18 | Michigan | 729 |
| 23 | Minnesota | 670 |
| 20 | Mississippi | 702 |
| 22 | Missouri | 674 |
| 47 | Montana | 0 |
| 25 | Nebraska | 619 |
| 3 | Nevada | 1,070 |
| 47 | New Hampshire | 0 |
| 32 | New Jersey | 548 |
| 4 | New Mexico | 961 |
| 11 | New York | 777 |
| 35 | North Carolina | 537 |
| 33 | North Dakota | 543 |
| 30 | Ohio | 551 |
| 24 | Oklahoma | 641 |
| 47 | Oregon | 0 |
| 38 | Pennsylvania | 513 |
| 39 | Rhode Island | 496 |
| 28 | South Carolina | 557 |
| 15 | South Dakota | 743 |
| 5 | Tennessee | 935 |
| 19 | Texas | 718 |
| 12 | Utah | 748 |
| 45 | Vermont | 312 |
| 44 | Virginia | 408 |
| 1 | Washington | 1,345 |
| 42 | West Virginia | 458 |
| 26 | Wisconsin | 580 |
| 10 | Wyoming | 793 |

RANK ORDER

| RANK | STATE | PER CAPITA |
|------|-------|------------|
| 1 | Washington | $1,345 |
| 2 | Hawaii | 1,225 |
| 3 | Nevada | 1,070 |
| 4 | New Mexico | 961 |
| 5 | Tennessee | 935 |
| 6 | Louisiana | 876 |
| 7 | Connecticut | 872 |
| 8 | Florida | 852 |
| 9 | Arizona | 803 |
| 10 | Wyoming | 793 |
| 11 | New York | 777 |
| 12 | California | 748 |
| 12 | Colorado | 748 |
| 12 | Utah | 748 |
| 15 | South Dakota | 743 |
| 16 | Arkansas | 738 |
| 17 | Georgia | 732 |
| 18 | Michigan | 729 |
| 19 | Texas | 718 |
| 20 | Mississippi | 702 |
| 21 | Kansas | 687 |
| 22 | Missouri | 674 |
| 23 | Minnesota | 670 |
| 24 | Oklahoma | 641 |
| 25 | Nebraska | 619 |
| 26 | Alabama | 580 |
| 26 | Wisconsin | 580 |
| 28 | South Carolina | 557 |
| 29 | Iowa | 556 |
| 30 | Ohio | 551 |
| 31 | Maine | 549 |
| 32 | New Jersey | 548 |
| 33 | North Dakota | 543 |
| 34 | Illinois | 541 |
| 35 | North Carolina | 537 |
| 36 | Indiana | 518 |
| 37 | Idaho | 514 |
| 38 | Pennsylvania | 513 |
| 39 | Rhode Island | 496 |
| 40 | Kentucky | 482 |
| 41 | Massachusetts | 470 |
| 42 | West Virginia | 458 |
| 43 | Maryland | 411 |
| 44 | Virginia | 408 |
| 45 | Vermont | 312 |
| 46 | Alaska | 161 |
| 47 | Delaware | 0 |
| 47 | Montana | 0 |
| 47 | New Hampshire | 0 |
| 47 | Oregon | 0 |

| District of Columbia | 912 |
|---|---|

Source: Morgan Quitno Press using data from U.S. Bureau of the Census, Governments Division
"Compendium of Government Finances: 1997" (2000) (http://www.census.gov/govs/www/cog.html)
*Does not include special sales taxes such as those on sale of alcohol, gasoline or tobacco.

# State and Local Government Property Tax Revenue in 1997

## National Total = $218,827,320,000

| ALPHA ORDER | | | | | RANK ORDER | | | |
|---|---|---|---|---|---|---|---|---|

| RANK | STATE | REVENUE | % of USA | | RANK | STATE | REVENUE | % of USA |
|---|---|---|---|---|---|---|---|---|
| 37 | Alabama | $1,035,388,000 | 0.5% | | 1 | New York | $24,121,718,000 | 11.0% |
| 44 | Alaska | 688,280,000 | 0.3% | | 2 | California | 23,201,040,000 | 10.6% |
| 20 | Arizona | 2,984,146,000 | 1.4% | | 3 | Texas | 16,348,847,000 | 7.5% |
| 40 | Arkansas | 815,892,000 | 0.4% | | 4 | Illinois | 12,915,218,000 | 5.9% |
| 2 | California | 23,201,040,000 | 10.6% | | 5 | New Jersey | 12,778,298,000 | 5.8% |
| 21 | Colorado | 2,966,595,000 | 1.4% | | 6 | Florida | 12,330,138,000 | 5.6% |
| 16 | Connecticut | 4,902,264,000 | 2.2% | | 7 | Pennsylvania | 9,009,480,000 | 4.1% |
| 50 | Delaware | 341,740,000 | 0.2% | | 8 | Ohio | 8,357,113,000 | 3.8% |
| 6 | Florida | 12,330,138,000 | 5.6% | | 9 | Michigan | 7,714,206,000 | 3.5% |
| 15 | Georgia | 4,946,474,000 | 2.3% | | 10 | Massachusetts | 6,612,515,000 | 3.0% |
| 45 | Hawaii | 607,265,000 | 0.3% | | 11 | Virginia | 5,249,046,000 | 2.4% |
| 43 | Idaho | 711,346,000 | 0.3% | | 12 | Wisconsin | 5,220,551,000 | 2.4% |
| 4 | Illinois | 12,915,218,000 | 5.9% | | 13 | Washington | 5,209,236,000 | 2.4% |
| 14 | Indiana | 5,091,983,000 | 2.3% | | 14 | Indiana | 5,091,983,000 | 2.3% |
| 25 | Iowa | 2,319,279,000 | 1.1% | | 15 | Georgia | 4,946,474,000 | 2.3% |
| 27 | Kansas | 2,089,168,000 | 1.0% | | 16 | Connecticut | 4,902,264,000 | 2.2% |
| 30 | Kentucky | 1,527,908,000 | 0.7% | | 17 | Minnesota | 4,278,432,000 | 2.0% |
| 32 | Louisiana | 1,435,164,000 | 0.7% | | 18 | Maryland | 3,844,385,000 | 1.8% |
| 31 | Maine | 1,521,612,000 | 0.7% | | 19 | North Carolina | 3,806,521,000 | 1.7% |
| 18 | Maryland | 3,844,385,000 | 1.8% | | 20 | Arizona | 2,984,146,000 | 1.4% |
| 10 | Massachusetts | 6,612,515,000 | 3.0% | | 21 | Colorado | 2,966,595,000 | 1.4% |
| 9 | Michigan | 7,714,206,000 | 3.5% | | 22 | Missouri | 2,804,713,000 | 1.3% |
| 17 | Minnesota | 4,278,432,000 | 2.0% | | 23 | Oregon | 2,533,167,000 | 1.2% |
| 33 | Mississippi | 1,257,163,000 | 0.6% | | 24 | Tennessee | 2,333,412,000 | 1.1% |
| 22 | Missouri | 2,804,713,000 | 1.3% | | 25 | Iowa | 2,319,279,000 | 1.1% |
| 39 | Montana | 825,083,000 | 0.4% | | 26 | South Carolina | 2,095,292,000 | 1.0% |
| 29 | Nebraska | 1,594,202,000 | 0.7% | | 27 | Kansas | 2,089,168,000 | 1.0% |
| 38 | Nevada | 998,112,000 | 0.5% | | 28 | New Hampshire | 1,815,186,000 | 0.8% |
| 28 | New Hampshire | 1,815,186,000 | 0.8% | | 29 | Nebraska | 1,594,202,000 | 0.7% |
| 5 | New Jersey | 12,778,298,000 | 5.8% | | 30 | Kentucky | 1,527,908,000 | 0.7% |
| 47 | New Mexico | 524,806,000 | 0.2% | | 31 | Maine | 1,521,612,000 | 0.7% |
| 1 | New York | 24,121,718,000 | 11.0% | | 32 | Louisiana | 1,435,164,000 | 0.7% |
| 19 | North Carolina | 3,806,521,000 | 1.7% | | 33 | Mississippi | 1,257,163,000 | 0.6% |
| 48 | North Dakota | 464,918,000 | 0.2% | | 34 | Rhode Island | 1,221,214,000 | 0.6% |
| 8 | Ohio | 8,357,113,000 | 3.8% | | 35 | Utah | 1,097,907,000 | 0.5% |
| 36 | Oklahoma | 1,095,421,000 | 0.5% | | 36 | Oklahoma | 1,095,421,000 | 0.5% |
| 23 | Oregon | 2,533,167,000 | 1.2% | | 37 | Alabama | 1,035,388,000 | 0.5% |
| 7 | Pennsylvania | 9,009,480,000 | 4.1% | | 38 | Nevada | 998,112,000 | 0.5% |
| 34 | Rhode Island | 1,221,214,000 | 0.6% | | 39 | Montana | 825,083,000 | 0.4% |
| 26 | South Carolina | 2,095,292,000 | 1.0% | | 40 | Arkansas | 815,892,000 | 0.4% |
| 46 | South Dakota | 532,956,000 | 0.2% | | 41 | West Virginia | 766,893,000 | 0.4% |
| 24 | Tennessee | 2,333,412,000 | 1.1% | | 42 | Vermont | 722,179,000 | 0.3% |
| 3 | Texas | 16,348,847,000 | 7.5% | | 43 | Idaho | 711,346,000 | 0.3% |
| 35 | Utah | 1,097,907,000 | 0.5% | | 44 | Alaska | 688,280,000 | 0.3% |
| 42 | Vermont | 722,179,000 | 0.3% | | 45 | Hawaii | 607,265,000 | 0.3% |
| 11 | Virginia | 5,249,046,000 | 2.4% | | 46 | South Dakota | 532,956,000 | 0.2% |
| 13 | Washington | 5,209,236,000 | 2.4% | | 47 | New Mexico | 524,806,000 | 0.2% |
| 41 | West Virginia | 766,893,000 | 0.4% | | 48 | North Dakota | 464,918,000 | 0.2% |
| 12 | Wisconsin | 5,220,551,000 | 2.4% | | 49 | Wyoming | 463,924,000 | 0.2% |
| 49 | Wyoming | 463,924,000 | 0.2% | | 50 | Delaware | 341,740,000 | 0.2% |
| | | | | | | District of Columbia | 699,524,000 | 0.3% |

Source: U.S. Bureau of the Census, Governments Division
"Compendium of Government Finances: 1997" (2000) (http://www.census.gov/govs/www/cog.html)

# Per Capita State and Local Government Property Tax Revenue in 1997

## National Per Capita = $817

ALPHA ORDER

| RANK | STATE | PER CAPITA |
|---|---|---|
| 50 | Alabama | $240 |
| 8 | Alaska | 1,130 |
| 33 | Arizona | 656 |
| 48 | Arkansas | 323 |
| 31 | California | 720 |
| 25 | Colorado | 762 |
| 3 | Connecticut | 1,500 |
| 41 | Delaware | 465 |
| 19 | Florida | 840 |
| 32 | Georgia | 661 |
| 40 | Hawaii | 511 |
| 35 | Idaho | 588 |
| 10 | Illinois | 1,075 |
| 17 | Indiana | 867 |
| 20 | Iowa | 813 |
| 21 | Kansas | 799 |
| 45 | Kentucky | 391 |
| 47 | Louisiana | 330 |
| 7 | Maine | 1,222 |
| 26 | Maryland | 755 |
| 9 | Massachusetts | 1,081 |
| 22 | Michigan | 788 |
| 16 | Minnesota | 913 |
| 42 | Mississippi | 460 |
| 38 | Missouri | 519 |
| 14 | Montana | 939 |
| 13 | Nebraska | 963 |
| 34 | Nevada | 596 |
| 2 | New Hampshire | 1,547 |
| 1 | New Jersey | 1,587 |
| 49 | New Mexico | 305 |
| 4 | New York | 1,330 |
| 39 | North Carolina | 512 |
| 30 | North Dakota | 725 |
| 28 | Ohio | 745 |
| 46 | Oklahoma | 331 |
| 23 | Oregon | 781 |
| 27 | Pennsylvania | 750 |
| 5 | Rhode Island | 1,237 |
| 36 | South Carolina | 553 |
| 29 | South Dakota | 729 |
| 43 | Tennessee | 434 |
| 18 | Texas | 845 |
| 37 | Utah | 532 |
| 6 | Vermont | 1,227 |
| 24 | Virginia | 780 |
| 15 | Washington | 930 |
| 44 | West Virginia | 422 |
| 11 | Wisconsin | 1,004 |
| 12 | Wyoming | 966 |

RANK ORDER

| RANK | STATE | PER CAPITA |
|---|---|---|
| 1 | New Jersey | $1,587 |
| 2 | New Hampshire | 1,547 |
| 3 | Connecticut | 1,500 |
| 4 | New York | 1,330 |
| 5 | Rhode Island | 1,237 |
| 6 | Vermont | 1,227 |
| 7 | Maine | 1,222 |
| 8 | Alaska | 1,130 |
| 9 | Massachusetts | 1,081 |
| 10 | Illinois | 1,075 |
| 11 | Wisconsin | 1,004 |
| 12 | Wyoming | 966 |
| 13 | Nebraska | 963 |
| 14 | Montana | 939 |
| 15 | Washington | 930 |
| 16 | Minnesota | 913 |
| 17 | Indiana | 867 |
| 18 | Texas | 845 |
| 19 | Florida | 840 |
| 20 | Iowa | 813 |
| 21 | Kansas | 799 |
| 22 | Michigan | 788 |
| 23 | Oregon | 781 |
| 24 | Virginia | 780 |
| 25 | Colorado | 762 |
| 26 | Maryland | 755 |
| 27 | Pennsylvania | 750 |
| 28 | Ohio | 745 |
| 29 | South Dakota | 729 |
| 30 | North Dakota | 725 |
| 31 | California | 720 |
| 32 | Georgia | 661 |
| 33 | Arizona | 656 |
| 34 | Nevada | 596 |
| 35 | Idaho | 588 |
| 36 | South Carolina | 553 |
| 37 | Utah | 532 |
| 38 | Missouri | 519 |
| 39 | North Carolina | 512 |
| 40 | Hawaii | 511 |
| 41 | Delaware | 465 |
| 42 | Mississippi | 460 |
| 43 | Tennessee | 434 |
| 44 | West Virginia | 422 |
| 45 | Kentucky | 391 |
| 46 | Oklahoma | 331 |
| 47 | Louisiana | 330 |
| 48 | Arkansas | 323 |
| 49 | New Mexico | 305 |
| 50 | Alabama | 240 |
| | District of Columbia | 1,323 |

Source: Morgan Quitno Press using data from U.S. Bureau of the Census, Governments Division
"Compendium of Government Finances: 1997" (2000) (http://www.census.gov/govs/www/cog.html)

# State and Local Government Property Tax Revenue as a Percent Of State and Local Government Total Revenue in 1997
## National Percent = 13.6%

ALPHA ORDER

| RANK | STATE | PERCENT |
|------|-------|---------|
| 50 | Alabama | 4.9 |
| 47 | Alaska | 6.1 |
| 20 | Arizona | 13.4 |
| 44 | Arkansas | 6.8 |
| 33 | California | 11.1 |
| 21 | Colorado | 13.2 |
| 3 | Connecticut | 22.2 |
| 46 | Delaware | 6.7 |
| 11 | Florida | 16.2 |
| 28 | Georgia | 12.4 |
| 42 | Hawaii | 7.5 |
| 31 | Idaho | 11.9 |
| 7 | Illinois | 19.4 |
| 8 | Indiana | 18.0 |
| 13 | Iowa | 15.8 |
| 12 | Kansas | 15.9 |
| 42 | Kentucky | 7.5 |
| 47 | Louisiana | 6.1 |
| 5 | Maine | 20.8 |
| 25 | Maryland | 12.5 |
| 9 | Massachusetts | 17.3 |
| 25 | Michigan | 12.5 |
| 23 | Minnesota | 12.9 |
| 38 | Mississippi | 9.5 |
| 34 | Missouri | 10.9 |
| 9 | Montana | 17.3 |
| 18 | Nebraska | 14.9 |
| 36 | Nevada | 9.9 |
| 1 | New Hampshire | 31.9 |
| 2 | New Jersey | 23.9 |
| 49 | New Mexico | 5.1 |
| 17 | New York | 15.1 |
| 37 | North Carolina | 9.7 |
| 30 | North Dakota | 12.3 |
| 24 | Ohio | 12.7 |
| 44 | Oklahoma | 6.8 |
| 32 | Oregon | 11.5 |
| 25 | Pennsylvania | 12.5 |
| 6 | Rhode Island | 20.7 |
| 35 | South Carolina | 10.5 |
| 16 | South Dakota | 15.2 |
| 40 | Tennessee | 8.1 |
| 14 | Texas | 15.7 |
| 39 | Utah | 9.3 |
| 4 | Vermont | 21.4 |
| 19 | Virginia | 14.3 |
| 22 | Washington | 13.0 |
| 41 | West Virginia | 8.0 |
| 15 | Wisconsin | 15.5 |
| 28 | Wyoming | 12.4 |

RANK ORDER

| RANK | STATE | PERCENT |
|------|-------|---------|
| 1 | New Hampshire | 31.9 |
| 2 | New Jersey | 23.9 |
| 3 | Connecticut | 22.2 |
| 4 | Vermont | 21.4 |
| 5 | Maine | 20.8 |
| 6 | Rhode Island | 20.7 |
| 7 | Illinois | 19.4 |
| 8 | Indiana | 18.0 |
| 9 | Massachusetts | 17.3 |
| 9 | Montana | 17.3 |
| 11 | Florida | 16.2 |
| 12 | Kansas | 15.9 |
| 13 | Iowa | 15.8 |
| 14 | Texas | 15.7 |
| 15 | Wisconsin | 15.5 |
| 16 | South Dakota | 15.2 |
| 17 | New York | 15.1 |
| 18 | Nebraska | 14.9 |
| 19 | Virginia | 14.3 |
| 20 | Arizona | 13.4 |
| 21 | Colorado | 13.2 |
| 22 | Washington | 13.0 |
| 23 | Minnesota | 12.9 |
| 24 | Ohio | 12.7 |
| 25 | Maryland | 12.5 |
| 25 | Michigan | 12.5 |
| 25 | Pennsylvania | 12.5 |
| 28 | Georgia | 12.4 |
| 28 | Wyoming | 12.4 |
| 30 | North Dakota | 12.3 |
| 31 | Idaho | 11.9 |
| 32 | Oregon | 11.5 |
| 33 | California | 11.1 |
| 34 | Missouri | 10.9 |
| 35 | South Carolina | 10.5 |
| 36 | Nevada | 9.9 |
| 37 | North Carolina | 9.7 |
| 38 | Mississippi | 9.5 |
| 39 | Utah | 9.3 |
| 40 | Tennessee | 8.1 |
| 41 | West Virginia | 8.0 |
| 42 | Hawaii | 7.5 |
| 42 | Kentucky | 7.5 |
| 44 | Arkansas | 6.8 |
| 44 | Oklahoma | 6.8 |
| 46 | Delaware | 6.7 |
| 47 | Alaska | 6.1 |
| 47 | Louisiana | 6.1 |
| 49 | New Mexico | 5.1 |
| 50 | Alabama | 4.9 |

District of Columbia — 10.9

*Source: Morgan Quitno Press using data from U.S. Bureau of the Census, Governments Division*
*"Compendium of Government Finances: 1997" (2000) (http://www.census.gov/govs/www/cog.html)*

# State and Local Government Property Tax Revenue as a Percent Of State and Local Government Own Source Revenue in 1997
## National Percent = 20.9%*

ALPHA ORDER

ALPHA ORDER / RANK ORDER

| RANK | STATE | PERCENT | RANK | STATE | PERCENT |
|------|-------|---------|------|-------|---------|
| 49 | Alabama | 7.9 | 1 | New Hampshire | 45.8 |
| 48 | Alaska | 8.8 | 2 | New Jersey | 34.2 |
| 21 | Arizona | 20.9 | 3 | Maine | 32.5 |
| 44 | Arkansas | 10.9 | 4 | Vermont | 32.2 |
| 32 | California | 17.8 | 5 | Rhode Island | 31.5 |
| 27 | Colorado | 19.3 | 6 | Connecticut | 29.5 |
| 6 | Connecticut | 29.5 | 7 | Illinois | 28.5 |
| 46 | Delaware | 9.7 | 8 | Montana | 27.3 |
| 16 | Florida | 22.6 | 9 | Texas | 25.6 |
| 31 | Georgia | 18.7 | 10 | Massachusetts | 24.7 |
| 43 | Hawaii | 11.3 | 11 | Wisconsin | 24.6 |
| 33 | Idaho | 17.6 | 12 | Nebraska | 24.1 |
| 7 | Illinois | 28.5 | 12 | South Dakota | 24.1 |
| 14 | Indiana | 23.7 | 14 | Indiana | 23.7 |
| 19 | Iowa | 21.5 | 15 | New York | 23.6 |
| 18 | Kansas | 21.6 | 16 | Florida | 22.6 |
| 42 | Kentucky | 11.9 | 17 | Washington | 22.1 |
| 47 | Louisiana | 9.2 | 18 | Kansas | 21.6 |
| 3 | Maine | 32.5 | 19 | Iowa | 21.5 |
| 26 | Maryland | 19.4 | 20 | Virginia | 21.3 |
| 10 | Massachusetts | 24.7 | 21 | Arizona | 20.9 |
| 24 | Michigan | 20.1 | 22 | Ohio | 20.8 |
| 28 | Minnesota | 19.2 | 23 | Pennsylvania | 20.4 |
| 37 | Mississippi | 15.2 | 24 | Michigan | 20.1 |
| 35 | Missouri | 16.1 | 24 | Wyoming | 20.1 |
| 8 | Montana | 27.3 | 26 | Maryland | 19.4 |
| 12 | Nebraska | 24.1 | 27 | Colorado | 19.3 |
| 38 | Nevada | 14.9 | 28 | Minnesota | 19.2 |
| 1 | New Hampshire | 45.8 | 29 | North Dakota | 18.9 |
| 2 | New Jersey | 34.2 | 29 | Oregon | 18.9 |
| 50 | New Mexico | 7.8 | 31 | Georgia | 18.7 |
| 15 | New York | 23.6 | 32 | California | 17.8 |
| 40 | North Carolina | 14.6 | 33 | Idaho | 17.6 |
| 29 | North Dakota | 18.9 | 34 | South Carolina | 16.7 |
| 22 | Ohio | 20.8 | 35 | Missouri | 16.1 |
| 45 | Oklahoma | 10.4 | 36 | Utah | 15.5 |
| 29 | Oregon | 18.9 | 37 | Mississippi | 15.2 |
| 23 | Pennsylvania | 20.4 | 38 | Nevada | 14.9 |
| 5 | Rhode Island | 31.5 | 39 | Tennessee | 14.7 |
| 34 | South Carolina | 16.7 | 40 | North Carolina | 14.6 |
| 12 | South Dakota | 24.1 | 41 | West Virginia | 13.1 |
| 39 | Tennessee | 14.7 | 42 | Kentucky | 11.9 |
| 9 | Texas | 25.6 | 43 | Hawaii | 11.3 |
| 36 | Utah | 15.5 | 44 | Arkansas | 10.9 |
| 4 | Vermont | 32.2 | 45 | Oklahoma | 10.4 |
| 20 | Virginia | 21.3 | 46 | Delaware | 9.7 |
| 17 | Washington | 22.1 | 47 | Louisiana | 9.2 |
| 41 | West Virginia | 13.1 | 48 | Alaska | 8.8 |
| 11 | Wisconsin | 24.6 | 49 | Alabama | 7.9 |
| 24 | Wyoming | 20.1 | 50 | New Mexico | 7.8 |
| | | | | District of Columbia | 21.3 |

Source: Morgan Quitno Press using data from U.S. Bureau of the Census, Governments Division
"Compendium of Government Finances: 1997" (2000) (http://www.census.gov/govs/www/cog.html)
*Own source revenue includes taxes, current charges and miscellaneous general revenue. Excluded are intergovernmental transfers, insurance trust revenue and revenue from government owned utilities and other commercial or auxiliary enterprise.

# State and Local Government Expenditures in 1997

## National Total = $1,460,748,580,000*

ALPHA ORDER

| RANK | STATE | EXPENDITURES | % of USA |
|---|---|---|---|
| 25 | Alabama | $20,173,595,000 | 1.4% |
| 40 | Alaska | 7,525,993,000 | 0.5% |
| 22 | Arizona | 21,156,437,000 | 1.4% |
| 34 | Arkansas | 10,488,400,000 | 0.7% |
| 1 | California | 196,039,816,000 | 13.4% |
| 23 | Colorado | 20,618,714,000 | 1.4% |
| 24 | Connecticut | 20,267,781,000 | 1.4% |
| 45 | Delaware | 4,379,204,000 | 0.3% |
| 4 | Florida | 71,314,473,000 | 4.9% |
| 11 | Georgia | 37,342,803,000 | 2.6% |
| 39 | Hawaii | 7,646,954,000 | 0.5% |
| 44 | Idaho | 5,423,612,000 | 0.4% |
| 6 | Illinois | 61,780,695,000 | 4.2% |
| 19 | Indiana | 25,637,406,000 | 1.8% |
| 30 | Iowa | 14,129,793,000 | 1.0% |
| 32 | Kansas | 12,367,831,000 | 0.8% |
| 28 | Kentucky | 17,784,882,000 | 1.2% |
| 21 | Louisiana | 21,209,147,000 | 1.5% |
| 41 | Maine | 6,346,785,000 | 0.4% |
| 18 | Maryland | 25,880,052,000 | 1.8% |
| 10 | Massachusetts | 37,743,985,000 | 2.6% |
| 8 | Michigan | 51,867,200,000 | 3.6% |
| 16 | Minnesota | 28,214,996,000 | 1.9% |
| 31 | Mississippi | 12,599,522,000 | 0.9% |
| 20 | Missouri | 23,014,589,000 | 1.6% |
| 46 | Montana | 4,354,961,000 | 0.3% |
| 35 | Nebraska | 9,554,897,000 | 0.7% |
| 37 | Nevada | 9,235,879,000 | 0.6% |
| 43 | New Hampshire | 5,462,875,000 | 0.4% |
| 9 | New Jersey | 47,868,258,000 | 3.3% |
| 36 | New Mexico | 9,313,310,000 | 0.6% |
| 2 | New York | 150,313,373,000 | 10.3% |
| 12 | North Carolina | 36,258,374,000 | 2.5% |
| 47 | North Dakota | 3,295,621,000 | 0.2% |
| 7 | Ohio | 56,864,760,000 | 3.9% |
| 29 | Oklahoma | 14,159,189,000 | 1.0% |
| 26 | Oregon | 19,898,069,000 | 1.4% |
| 5 | Pennsylvania | 62,205,587,000 | 4.3% |
| 42 | Rhode Island | 5,677,315,000 | 0.4% |
| 27 | South Carolina | 18,694,456,000 | 1.3% |
| 48 | South Dakota | 3,183,990,000 | 0.2% |
| 17 | Tennessee | 27,153,993,000 | 1.9% |
| 3 | Texas | 88,181,030,000 | 6.0% |
| 33 | Utah | 10,796,500,000 | 0.7% |
| 50 | Vermont | 3,069,830,000 | 0.2% |
| 14 | Virginia | 31,562,449,000 | 2.2% |
| 13 | Washington | 36,118,090,000 | 2.5% |
| 38 | West Virginia | 8,971,467,000 | 0.6% |
| 15 | Wisconsin | 28,448,813,000 | 1.9% |
| 49 | Wyoming | 3,151,478,000 | 0.2% |

RANK ORDER

| RANK | STATE | EXPENDITURES | % of USA |
|---|---|---|---|
| 1 | California | $196,039,816,000 | 13.4% |
| 2 | New York | 150,313,373,000 | 10.3% |
| 3 | Texas | 88,181,030,000 | 6.0% |
| 4 | Florida | 71,314,473,000 | 4.9% |
| 5 | Pennsylvania | 62,205,587,000 | 4.3% |
| 6 | Illinois | 61,780,695,000 | 4.2% |
| 7 | Ohio | 56,864,760,000 | 3.9% |
| 8 | Michigan | 51,867,200,000 | 3.6% |
| 9 | New Jersey | 47,868,258,000 | 3.3% |
| 10 | Massachusetts | 37,743,985,000 | 2.6% |
| 11 | Georgia | 37,342,803,000 | 2.6% |
| 12 | North Carolina | 36,258,374,000 | 2.5% |
| 13 | Washington | 36,118,090,000 | 2.5% |
| 14 | Virginia | 31,562,449,000 | 2.2% |
| 15 | Wisconsin | 28,448,813,000 | 1.9% |
| 16 | Minnesota | 28,214,996,000 | 1.9% |
| 17 | Tennessee | 27,153,993,000 | 1.9% |
| 18 | Maryland | 25,880,052,000 | 1.8% |
| 19 | Indiana | 25,637,406,000 | 1.8% |
| 20 | Missouri | 23,014,589,000 | 1.6% |
| 21 | Louisiana | 21,209,147,000 | 1.5% |
| 22 | Arizona | 21,156,437,000 | 1.4% |
| 23 | Colorado | 20,618,714,000 | 1.4% |
| 24 | Connecticut | 20,267,781,000 | 1.4% |
| 25 | Alabama | 20,173,595,000 | 1.4% |
| 26 | Oregon | 19,898,069,000 | 1.4% |
| 27 | South Carolina | 18,694,456,000 | 1.3% |
| 28 | Kentucky | 17,784,882,000 | 1.2% |
| 29 | Oklahoma | 14,159,189,000 | 1.0% |
| 30 | Iowa | 14,129,793,000 | 1.0% |
| 31 | Mississippi | 12,599,522,000 | 0.9% |
| 32 | Kansas | 12,367,831,000 | 0.8% |
| 33 | Utah | 10,796,500,000 | 0.7% |
| 34 | Arkansas | 10,488,400,000 | 0.7% |
| 35 | Nebraska | 9,554,897,000 | 0.7% |
| 36 | New Mexico | 9,313,310,000 | 0.6% |
| 37 | Nevada | 9,235,879,000 | 0.6% |
| 38 | West Virginia | 8,971,467,000 | 0.6% |
| 39 | Hawaii | 7,646,954,000 | 0.5% |
| 40 | Alaska | 7,525,993,000 | 0.5% |
| 41 | Maine | 6,346,785,000 | 0.4% |
| 42 | Rhode Island | 5,677,315,000 | 0.4% |
| 43 | New Hampshire | 5,462,875,000 | 0.4% |
| 44 | Idaho | 5,423,612,000 | 0.4% |
| 45 | Delaware | 4,379,204,000 | 0.3% |
| 46 | Montana | 4,354,961,000 | 0.3% |
| 47 | North Dakota | 3,295,621,000 | 0.2% |
| 48 | South Dakota | 3,183,990,000 | 0.2% |
| 49 | Wyoming | 3,151,478,000 | 0.2% |
| 50 | Vermont | 3,069,830,000 | 0.2% |
| | District of Columbia | 5,999,351,000 | 0.4% |

Source: U.S. Bureau of the Census, Governments Division
"Compendium of Government Finances: 1997" (2000) (http://www.census.gov/govs/www/cog.html)
*Total expenditures includes all money paid other than for retirement of debt and extension of loans. Includes payments from all sources of funds including current revenues and proceeds from borrowing and prior year fund balances. Includes intergovernmental transfers and expenditures for government owned utilities and other commercial or auxiliary enterprise and insurance trust expenditures.

# Per Capita State and Local Government Total Expenditures in 1997

## National Per Capita = $5,455*

ALPHA ORDER

| RANK | STATE | PER CAPITA |
|------|-------|------------|
| 39 | Alabama | $4,670 |
| 1 | Alaska | 12,361 |
| 41 | Arizona | 4,648 |
| 50 | Arkansas | 4,155 |
| 9 | California | 6,085 |
| 19 | Colorado | 5,299 |
| 6 | Connecticut | 6,201 |
| 11 | Delaware | 5,958 |
| 36 | Florida | 4,857 |
| 29 | Georgia | 4,988 |
| 5 | Hawaii | 6,430 |
| 45 | Idaho | 4,480 |
| 23 | Illinois | 5,143 |
| 46 | Indiana | 4,366 |
| 31 | Iowa | 4,950 |
| 37 | Kansas | 4,727 |
| 44 | Kentucky | 4,551 |
| 35 | Louisiana | 4,874 |
| 25 | Maine | 5,097 |
| 26 | Maryland | 5,082 |
| 7 | Massachusetts | 6,172 |
| 18 | Michigan | 5,300 |
| 10 | Minnesota | 6,019 |
| 42 | Mississippi | 4,612 |
| 49 | Missouri | 4,256 |
| 30 | Montana | 4,956 |
| 13 | Nebraska | 5,770 |
| 15 | Nevada | 5,512 |
| 40 | New Hampshire | 4,656 |
| 12 | New Jersey | 5,943 |
| 17 | New Mexico | 5,405 |
| 2 | New York | 8,285 |
| 34 | North Carolina | 4,881 |
| 24 | North Dakota | 5,142 |
| 27 | Ohio | 5,072 |
| 48 | Oklahoma | 4,272 |
| 8 | Oregon | 6,135 |
| 22 | Pennsylvania | 5,177 |
| 14 | Rhode Island | 5,752 |
| 33 | South Carolina | 4,932 |
| 47 | South Dakota | 4,357 |
| 28 | Tennessee | 5,049 |
| 43 | Texas | 4,556 |
| 20 | Utah | 5,227 |
| 21 | Vermont | 5,215 |
| 38 | Virginia | 4,688 |
| 4 | Washington | 6,445 |
| 32 | West Virginia | 4,941 |
| 16 | Wisconsin | 5,471 |
| 3 | Wyoming | 6,565 |

RANK ORDER

| RANK | STATE | PER CAPITA |
|------|-------|------------|
| 1 | Alaska | $12,361 |
| 2 | New York | 8,285 |
| 3 | Wyoming | 6,565 |
| 4 | Washington | 6,445 |
| 5 | Hawaii | 6,430 |
| 6 | Connecticut | 6,201 |
| 7 | Massachusetts | 6,172 |
| 8 | Oregon | 6,135 |
| 9 | California | 6,085 |
| 10 | Minnesota | 6,019 |
| 11 | Delaware | 5,958 |
| 12 | New Jersey | 5,943 |
| 13 | Nebraska | 5,770 |
| 14 | Rhode Island | 5,752 |
| 15 | Nevada | 5,512 |
| 16 | Wisconsin | 5,471 |
| 17 | New Mexico | 5,405 |
| 18 | Michigan | 5,300 |
| 19 | Colorado | 5,299 |
| 20 | Utah | 5,227 |
| 21 | Vermont | 5,215 |
| 22 | Pennsylvania | 5,177 |
| 23 | Illinois | 5,143 |
| 24 | North Dakota | 5,142 |
| 25 | Maine | 5,097 |
| 26 | Maryland | 5,082 |
| 27 | Ohio | 5,072 |
| 28 | Tennessee | 5,049 |
| 29 | Georgia | 4,988 |
| 30 | Montana | 4,956 |
| 31 | Iowa | 4,950 |
| 32 | West Virginia | 4,941 |
| 33 | South Carolina | 4,932 |
| 34 | North Carolina | 4,881 |
| 35 | Louisiana | 4,874 |
| 36 | Florida | 4,857 |
| 37 | Kansas | 4,727 |
| 38 | Virginia | 4,688 |
| 39 | Alabama | 4,670 |
| 40 | New Hampshire | 4,656 |
| 41 | Arizona | 4,648 |
| 42 | Mississippi | 4,612 |
| 43 | Texas | 4,556 |
| 44 | Kentucky | 4,551 |
| 45 | Idaho | 4,480 |
| 46 | Indiana | 4,366 |
| 47 | South Dakota | 4,357 |
| 48 | Oklahoma | 4,272 |
| 49 | Missouri | 4,256 |
| 50 | Arkansas | 4,155 |

District of Columbia     11,346

Source: Morgan Quitno Press using data from U.S. Bureau of the Census, Governments Division
    "Compendium of Government Finances: 1997" (2000) (http://www.census.gov/govs/www/cog.html)
*Total expenditures includes all money paid other than for retirement of debt and extension of loans. Includes payments from all sources of funds including current revenues and proceeds from borrowing and prior year fund balances. Includes intergovernmental transfers and expenditures for government owned utilities and other commercial or auxiliary enterprise and insurance trust expenditures.

# State and Local Government Direct General Expenditures in 1997

## National Total = $1,251,299,238,000*

ALPHA ORDER

| RANK | STATE | EXPENDITURES | % of USA |
|---|---|---|---|
| 25 | Alabama | $17,229,332,000 | 1.4% |
| 40 | Alaska | 6,705,238,000 | 0.5% |
| 23 | Arizona | 17,769,150,000 | 1.4% |
| 33 | Arkansas | 9,414,597,000 | 0.8% |
| 1 | California | 160,856,567,000 | 12.9% |
| 24 | Colorado | 17,472,887,000 | 1.4% |
| 22 | Connecticut | 17,780,083,000 | 1.4% |
| 45 | Delaware | 3,943,047,000 | 0.3% |
| 4 | Florida | 63,423,647,000 | 5.1% |
| 10 | Georgia | 32,660,513,000 | 2.6% |
| 39 | Hawaii | 6,717,896,000 | 0.5% |
| 44 | Idaho | 4,872,759,000 | 0.4% |
| 5 | Illinois | 53,121,753,000 | 4.2% |
| 17 | Indiana | 23,372,414,000 | 1.9% |
| 29 | Iowa | 12,857,886,000 | 1.0% |
| 32 | Kansas | 11,038,097,000 | 0.9% |
| 28 | Kentucky | 15,587,421,000 | 1.2% |
| 21 | Louisiana | 18,816,477,000 | 1.5% |
| 41 | Maine | 5,782,060,000 | 0.5% |
| 18 | Maryland | 22,826,931,000 | 1.8% |
| 11 | Massachusetts | 31,783,557,000 | 2.5% |
| 8 | Michigan | 45,887,584,000 | 3.7% |
| 16 | Minnesota | 25,115,859,000 | 2.0% |
| 31 | Mississippi | 11,109,261,000 | 0.9% |
| 20 | Missouri | 20,452,394,000 | 1.6% |
| 46 | Montana | 3,910,230,000 | 0.3% |
| 38 | Nebraska | 7,435,404,000 | 0.6% |
| 36 | Nevada | 7,918,011,000 | 0.6% |
| 42 | New Hampshire | 4,932,454,000 | 0.4% |
| 9 | New Jersey | 40,931,889,000 | 3.3% |
| 35 | New Mexico | 8,377,324,000 | 0.7% |
| 2 | New York | 126,294,886,000 | 10.1% |
| 12 | North Carolina | 31,222,171,000 | 2.5% |
| 47 | North Dakota | 3,001,545,000 | 0.2% |
| 7 | Ohio | 48,108,182,000 | 3.8% |
| 30 | Oklahoma | 12,218,901,000 | 1.0% |
| 26 | Oregon | 16,537,033,000 | 1.3% |
| 6 | Pennsylvania | 53,058,776,000 | 4.2% |
| 43 | Rhode Island | 4,884,329,000 | 0.4% |
| 27 | South Carolina | 15,939,282,000 | 1.3% |
| 48 | South Dakota | 2,912,034,000 | 0.2% |
| 19 | Tennessee | 21,234,091,000 | 1.7% |
| 3 | Texas | 76,431,437,000 | 6.1% |
| 34 | Utah | 8,998,342,000 | 0.7% |
| 50 | Vermont | 2,780,905,000 | 0.2% |
| 14 | Virginia | 28,524,027,000 | 2.3% |
| 13 | Washington | 28,882,454,000 | 2.3% |
| 37 | West Virginia | 7,743,592,000 | 0.6% |
| 15 | Wisconsin | 25,290,370,000 | 2.0% |
| 49 | Wyoming | 2,798,393,000 | 0.2% |

RANK ORDER

| RANK | STATE | EXPENDITURES | % of USA |
|---|---|---|---|
| 1 | California | $160,856,567,000 | 12.9% |
| 2 | New York | 126,294,886,000 | 10.1% |
| 3 | Texas | 76,431,437,000 | 6.1% |
| 4 | Florida | 63,423,647,000 | 5.1% |
| 5 | Illinois | 53,121,753,000 | 4.2% |
| 6 | Pennsylvania | 53,058,776,000 | 4.2% |
| 7 | Ohio | 48,108,182,000 | 3.8% |
| 8 | Michigan | 45,887,584,000 | 3.7% |
| 9 | New Jersey | 40,931,889,000 | 3.3% |
| 10 | Georgia | 32,660,513,000 | 2.6% |
| 11 | Massachusetts | 31,783,557,000 | 2.5% |
| 12 | North Carolina | 31,222,171,000 | 2.5% |
| 13 | Washington | 28,882,454,000 | 2.3% |
| 14 | Virginia | 28,524,027,000 | 2.3% |
| 15 | Wisconsin | 25,290,370,000 | 2.0% |
| 16 | Minnesota | 25,115,859,000 | 2.0% |
| 17 | Indiana | 23,372,414,000 | 1.9% |
| 18 | Maryland | 22,826,931,000 | 1.8% |
| 19 | Tennessee | 21,234,091,000 | 1.7% |
| 20 | Missouri | 20,452,394,000 | 1.6% |
| 21 | Louisiana | 18,816,477,000 | 1.5% |
| 22 | Connecticut | 17,780,083,000 | 1.4% |
| 23 | Arizona | 17,769,150,000 | 1.4% |
| 24 | Colorado | 17,472,887,000 | 1.4% |
| 25 | Alabama | 17,229,332,000 | 1.4% |
| 26 | Oregon | 16,537,033,000 | 1.3% |
| 27 | South Carolina | 15,939,282,000 | 1.3% |
| 28 | Kentucky | 15,587,421,000 | 1.2% |
| 29 | Iowa | 12,857,886,000 | 1.0% |
| 30 | Oklahoma | 12,218,901,000 | 1.0% |
| 31 | Mississippi | 11,109,261,000 | 0.9% |
| 32 | Kansas | 11,038,097,000 | 0.9% |
| 33 | Arkansas | 9,414,597,000 | 0.8% |
| 34 | Utah | 8,998,342,000 | 0.7% |
| 35 | New Mexico | 8,377,324,000 | 0.7% |
| 36 | Nevada | 7,918,011,000 | 0.6% |
| 37 | West Virginia | 7,743,592,000 | 0.6% |
| 38 | Nebraska | 7,435,404,000 | 0.6% |
| 39 | Hawaii | 6,717,896,000 | 0.5% |
| 40 | Alaska | 6,705,238,000 | 0.5% |
| 41 | Maine | 5,782,060,000 | 0.5% |
| 42 | New Hampshire | 4,932,454,000 | 0.4% |
| 43 | Rhode Island | 4,884,329,000 | 0.4% |
| 44 | Idaho | 4,872,759,000 | 0.4% |
| 45 | Delaware | 3,943,047,000 | 0.3% |
| 46 | Montana | 3,910,230,000 | 0.3% |
| 47 | North Dakota | 3,001,545,000 | 0.2% |
| 48 | South Dakota | 2,912,034,000 | 0.2% |
| 49 | Wyoming | 2,798,393,000 | 0.2% |
| 50 | Vermont | 2,780,905,000 | 0.2% |
| | District of Columbia | 4,335,766,000 | 0.3% |

Source: U.S. Bureau of the Census, Governments Division
"Compendium of Government Finances: 1997" (2000) (http://www.census.gov/govs/www/cog.html)
*Direct general expenditures include expenditures for current operations, assistance and subsidies, interest on debt and capital outlay. Excludes intergovernmental transfers, expenditures for government owned utilities and other commercial or auxiliary enterprise and insurance trust expenditures.

# Per Capita State and Local Government Direct General Expenditures in 1997

## National Per Capita = $4,673*

| RANK | STATE | PER CAPITA |
|------|-------|------------|
| 42 | Alabama | $3,988 |
| 1 | Alaska | 11,013 |
| 47 | Arizona | 3,903 |
| 49 | Arkansas | 3,730 |
| 12 | California | 4,993 |
| 22 | Colorado | 4,490 |
| 5 | Connecticut | 5,440 |
| 6 | Delaware | 5,365 |
| 31 | Florida | 4,319 |
| 28 | Georgia | 4,363 |
| 4 | Hawaii | 5,649 |
| 40 | Idaho | 4,025 |
| 26 | Illinois | 4,423 |
| 44 | Indiana | 3,980 |
| 21 | Iowa | 4,505 |
| 35 | Kansas | 4,219 |
| 41 | Kentucky | 3,989 |
| 30 | Louisiana | 4,324 |
| 20 | Maine | 4,643 |
| 24 | Maryland | 4,482 |
| 8 | Massachusetts | 5,197 |
| 18 | Michigan | 4,689 |
| 7 | Minnesota | 5,358 |
| 39 | Mississippi | 4,067 |
| 48 | Missouri | 3,782 |
| 25 | Montana | 4,450 |
| 22 | Nebraska | 4,490 |
| 16 | Nevada | 4,726 |
| 37 | New Hampshire | 4,204 |
| 11 | New Jersey | 5,082 |
| 15 | New Mexico | 4,862 |
| 2 | New York | 6,961 |
| 38 | North Carolina | 4,203 |
| 19 | North Dakota | 4,683 |
| 32 | Ohio | 4,291 |
| 50 | Oklahoma | 3,687 |
| 10 | Oregon | 5,099 |
| 27 | Pennsylvania | 4,416 |
| 13 | Rhode Island | 4,949 |
| 36 | South Carolina | 4,206 |
| 43 | South Dakota | 3,984 |
| 46 | Tennessee | 3,948 |
| 45 | Texas | 3,949 |
| 29 | Utah | 4,357 |
| 17 | Vermont | 4,724 |
| 34 | Virginia | 4,237 |
| 9 | Washington | 5,154 |
| 33 | West Virginia | 4,265 |
| 14 | Wisconsin | 4,863 |
| 3 | Wyoming | 5,830 |

| RANK | STATE | PER CAPITA |
|------|-------|------------|
| 1 | Alaska | $11,013 |
| 2 | New York | 6,961 |
| 3 | Wyoming | 5,830 |
| 4 | Hawaii | 5,649 |
| 5 | Connecticut | 5,440 |
| 6 | Delaware | 5,365 |
| 7 | Minnesota | 5,358 |
| 8 | Massachusetts | 5,197 |
| 9 | Washington | 5,154 |
| 10 | Oregon | 5,099 |
| 11 | New Jersey | 5,082 |
| 12 | California | 4,993 |
| 13 | Rhode Island | 4,949 |
| 14 | Wisconsin | 4,863 |
| 15 | New Mexico | 4,862 |
| 16 | Nevada | 4,726 |
| 17 | Vermont | 4,724 |
| 18 | Michigan | 4,689 |
| 19 | North Dakota | 4,683 |
| 20 | Maine | 4,643 |
| 21 | Iowa | 4,505 |
| 22 | Colorado | 4,490 |
| 22 | Nebraska | 4,490 |
| 24 | Maryland | 4,482 |
| 25 | Montana | 4,450 |
| 26 | Illinois | 4,423 |
| 27 | Pennsylvania | 4,416 |
| 28 | Georgia | 4,363 |
| 29 | Utah | 4,357 |
| 30 | Louisiana | 4,324 |
| 31 | Florida | 4,319 |
| 32 | Ohio | 4,291 |
| 33 | West Virginia | 4,265 |
| 34 | Virginia | 4,237 |
| 35 | Kansas | 4,219 |
| 36 | South Carolina | 4,206 |
| 37 | New Hampshire | 4,204 |
| 38 | North Carolina | 4,203 |
| 39 | Mississippi | 4,067 |
| 40 | Idaho | 4,025 |
| 41 | Kentucky | 3,989 |
| 42 | Alabama | 3,988 |
| 43 | South Dakota | 3,984 |
| 44 | Indiana | 3,980 |
| 45 | Texas | 3,949 |
| 46 | Tennessee | 3,948 |
| 47 | Arizona | 3,903 |
| 48 | Missouri | 3,782 |
| 49 | Arkansas | 3,730 |
| 50 | Oklahoma | 3,687 |
| | District of Columbia | 8,200 |

Source: Morgan Quitno Press using data from U.S. Bureau of the Census, Governments Division
"Compendium of Government Finances: 1997" (2000) (http://www.census.gov/govs/www/cog.html)
*Direct general expenditures include expenditures for current operations, assistance and subsidies, interest on debt and capital outlay. Excludes intergovernmental transfers, expenditures for government owned utilities and other commercial or auxiliary enterprise and insurance trust expenditures.

# State and Local Government Debt Outstanding in 1997

## National Total = $1,221,501,000,000*

ALPHA ORDER

| RANK | STATE | DEBT | % of USA |
|------|-------|------|----------|
| 28 | Alabama | $12,495,000,000 | 1.0% |
| 35 | Alaska | 7,052,000,000 | 0.6% |
| 19 | Arizona | 21,252,000,000 | 1.7% |
| 42 | Arkansas | 6,004,000,000 | 0.5% |
| 1 | California | 156,130,000,000 | 12.8% |
| 21 | Colorado | 19,440,000,000 | 1.6% |
| 18 | Connecticut | 21,637,000,000 | 1.8% |
| 44 | Delaware | 4,745,000,000 | 0.4% |
| 4 | Florida | 70,449,000,000 | 5.8% |
| 13 | Georgia | 25,884,000,000 | 2.1% |
| 33 | Hawaii | 7,379,000,000 | 0.6% |
| 48 | Idaho | 2,639,000,000 | 0.2% |
| 6 | Illinois | 52,159,000,000 | 4.3% |
| 22 | Indiana | 16,778,000,000 | 1.4% |
| 40 | Iowa | 6,258,000,000 | 0.5% |
| 32 | Kansas | 8,826,000,000 | 0.7% |
| 20 | Kentucky | 21,027,000,000 | 1.7% |
| 23 | Louisiana | 16,207,000,000 | 1.3% |
| 43 | Maine | 4,803,000,000 | 0.4% |
| 16 | Maryland | 22,515,000,000 | 1.8% |
| 8 | Massachusetts | 41,523,000,000 | 3.4% |
| 9 | Michigan | 35,559,000,000 | 2.9% |
| 15 | Minnesota | 23,477,000,000 | 1.9% |
| 36 | Mississippi | 6,994,000,000 | 0.6% |
| 25 | Missouri | 15,128,000,000 | 1.2% |
| 45 | Montana | 3,270,000,000 | 0.3% |
| 41 | Nebraska | 6,228,000,000 | 0.5% |
| 30 | Nevada | 10,251,000,000 | 0.8% |
| 34 | New Hampshire | 7,073,000,000 | 0.6% |
| 7 | New Jersey | 43,334,000,000 | 3.5% |
| 39 | New Mexico | 6,334,000,000 | 0.5% |
| 2 | New York | 151,539,000,000 | 12.4% |
| 14 | North Carolina | 23,906,000,000 | 2.0% |
| 50 | North Dakota | 1,927,000,000 | 0.2% |
| 11 | Ohio | 31,101,000,000 | 2.5% |
| 31 | Oklahoma | 9,589,000,000 | 0.8% |
| 27 | Oregon | 13,092,000,000 | 1.1% |
| 5 | Pennsylvania | 59,874,000,000 | 4.9% |
| 38 | Rhode Island | 6,414,000,000 | 0.5% |
| 26 | South Carolina | 14,103,000,000 | 1.2% |
| 46 | South Dakota | 2,675,000,000 | 0.2% |
| 24 | Tennessee | 15,500,000,000 | 1.3% |
| 3 | Texas | 78,349,000,000 | 6.4% |
| 29 | Utah | 11,991,000,000 | 1.0% |
| 47 | Vermont | 2,658,000,000 | 0.2% |
| 12 | Virginia | 27,461,000,000 | 2.2% |
| 10 | Washington | 33,564,000,000 | 2.7% |
| 37 | West Virginia | 6,704,000,000 | 0.5% |
| 17 | Wisconsin | 21,829,000,000 | 1.8% |
| 49 | Wyoming | 2,101,000,000 | 0.2% |

RANK ORDER

| RANK | STATE | DEBT | % of USA |
|------|-------|------|----------|
| 1 | California | $156,130,000,000 | 12.8% |
| 2 | New York | 151,539,000,000 | 12.4% |
| 3 | Texas | 78,349,000,000 | 6.4% |
| 4 | Florida | 70,449,000,000 | 5.8% |
| 5 | Pennsylvania | 59,874,000,000 | 4.9% |
| 6 | Illinois | 52,159,000,000 | 4.3% |
| 7 | New Jersey | 43,334,000,000 | 3.5% |
| 8 | Massachusetts | 41,523,000,000 | 3.4% |
| 9 | Michigan | 35,559,000,000 | 2.9% |
| 10 | Washington | 33,564,000,000 | 2.7% |
| 11 | Ohio | 31,101,000,000 | 2.5% |
| 12 | Virginia | 27,461,000,000 | 2.2% |
| 13 | Georgia | 25,884,000,000 | 2.1% |
| 14 | North Carolina | 23,906,000,000 | 2.0% |
| 15 | Minnesota | 23,477,000,000 | 1.9% |
| 16 | Maryland | 22,515,000,000 | 1.8% |
| 17 | Wisconsin | 21,829,000,000 | 1.8% |
| 18 | Connecticut | 21,637,000,000 | 1.8% |
| 19 | Arizona | 21,252,000,000 | 1.7% |
| 20 | Kentucky | 21,027,000,000 | 1.7% |
| 21 | Colorado | 19,440,000,000 | 1.6% |
| 22 | Indiana | 16,778,000,000 | 1.4% |
| 23 | Louisiana | 16,207,000,000 | 1.3% |
| 24 | Tennessee | 15,500,000,000 | 1.3% |
| 25 | Missouri | 15,128,000,000 | 1.2% |
| 26 | South Carolina | 14,103,000,000 | 1.2% |
| 27 | Oregon | 13,092,000,000 | 1.1% |
| 28 | Alabama | 12,495,000,000 | 1.0% |
| 29 | Utah | 11,991,000,000 | 1.0% |
| 30 | Nevada | 10,251,000,000 | 0.8% |
| 31 | Oklahoma | 9,589,000,000 | 0.8% |
| 32 | Kansas | 8,826,000,000 | 0.7% |
| 33 | Hawaii | 7,379,000,000 | 0.6% |
| 34 | New Hampshire | 7,073,000,000 | 0.6% |
| 35 | Alaska | 7,052,000,000 | 0.6% |
| 36 | Mississippi | 6,994,000,000 | 0.6% |
| 37 | West Virginia | 6,704,000,000 | 0.5% |
| 38 | Rhode Island | 6,414,000,000 | 0.5% |
| 39 | New Mexico | 6,334,000,000 | 0.5% |
| 40 | Iowa | 6,258,000,000 | 0.5% |
| 41 | Nebraska | 6,228,000,000 | 0.5% |
| 42 | Arkansas | 6,004,000,000 | 0.5% |
| 43 | Maine | 4,803,000,000 | 0.4% |
| 44 | Delaware | 4,745,000,000 | 0.4% |
| 45 | Montana | 3,270,000,000 | 0.3% |
| 46 | South Dakota | 2,675,000,000 | 0.2% |
| 47 | Vermont | 2,658,000,000 | 0.2% |
| 48 | Idaho | 2,639,000,000 | 0.2% |
| 49 | Wyoming | 2,101,000,000 | 0.2% |
| 50 | North Dakota | 1,927,000,000 | 0.2% |
|  | District of Columbia | 4,275,000,000 | 0.3% |

Source: U.S. Bureau of the Census, Governments Division
"Compendium of Government Finances: 1997" (2000) (http://www.census.gov/govs/www/cog.html)
*Includes short-term, long-term, full fail and credit, nonguaranteed and public debt for private purposes.

# Per Capita State and Local Government Debt Outstanding in 1997

## National Per Capita = $4,562*

ALPHA ORDER

ALPHA ORDER

RANK ORDER

| RANK | STATE | PER CAPITA | | RANK | STATE | PER CAPITA |
|------|-------|------------|---|------|-------|------------|
| 42 | Alabama | $2,892 | | 1 | Alaska | $11,583 |
| 1 | Alaska | 11,583 | | 2 | New York | 8,352 |
| 19 | Arizona | 4,669 | | 3 | Massachusetts | 6,790 |
| 48 | Arkansas | 2,379 | | 4 | Connecticut | 6,620 |
| 17 | California | 4,846 | | 5 | Rhode Island | 6,499 |
| 15 | Colorado | 4,996 | | 6 | Delaware | 6,456 |
| 4 | Connecticut | 6,620 | | 7 | Hawaii | 6,204 |
| 6 | Delaware | 6,456 | | 8 | Nevada | 6,118 |
| 18 | Florida | 4,798 | | 9 | New Hampshire | 6,029 |
| 37 | Georgia | 3,458 | | 10 | Washington | 5,989 |
| 7 | Hawaii | 6,204 | | 11 | Utah | 5,806 |
| 50 | Idaho | 2,180 | | 12 | Kentucky | 5,381 |
| 23 | Illinois | 4,342 | | 13 | New Jersey | 5,380 |
| 44 | Indiana | 2,857 | | 14 | Minnesota | 5,008 |
| 49 | Iowa | 2,192 | | 15 | Colorado | 4,996 |
| 38 | Kansas | 3,373 | | 16 | Pennsylvania | 4,983 |
| 12 | Kentucky | 5,381 | | 17 | California | 4,846 |
| 30 | Louisiana | 3,725 | | 18 | Florida | 4,798 |
| 28 | Maine | 3,857 | | 19 | Arizona | 4,669 |
| 21 | Maryland | 4,421 | | 20 | Vermont | 4,515 |
| 3 | Massachusetts | 6,790 | | 21 | Maryland | 4,421 |
| 36 | Michigan | 3,634 | | 22 | Wyoming | 4,377 |
| 14 | Minnesota | 5,008 | | 23 | Illinois | 4,342 |
| 47 | Mississippi | 2,560 | | 24 | Wisconsin | 4,198 |
| 45 | Missouri | 2,798 | | 25 | Virginia | 4,079 |
| 31 | Montana | 3,721 | | 26 | Texas | 4,048 |
| 29 | Nebraska | 3,761 | | 27 | Oregon | 4,037 |
| 8 | Nevada | 6,118 | | 28 | Maine | 3,857 |
| 9 | New Hampshire | 6,029 | | 29 | Nebraska | 3,761 |
| 13 | New Jersey | 5,380 | | 30 | Louisiana | 3,725 |
| 34 | New Mexico | 3,676 | | 31 | Montana | 3,721 |
| 2 | New York | 8,352 | | 31 | South Carolina | 3,721 |
| 39 | North Carolina | 3,218 | | 33 | West Virginia | 3,692 |
| 40 | North Dakota | 3,006 | | 34 | New Mexico | 3,676 |
| 46 | Ohio | 2,774 | | 35 | South Dakota | 3,660 |
| 41 | Oklahoma | 2,893 | | 36 | Michigan | 3,634 |
| 27 | Oregon | 4,037 | | 37 | Georgia | 3,458 |
| 16 | Pennsylvania | 4,983 | | 38 | Kansas | 3,373 |
| 5 | Rhode Island | 6,499 | | 39 | North Carolina | 3,218 |
| 31 | South Carolina | 3,721 | | 40 | North Dakota | 3,006 |
| 35 | South Dakota | 3,660 | | 41 | Oklahoma | 2,893 |
| 43 | Tennessee | 2,882 | | 42 | Alabama | 2,892 |
| 26 | Texas | 4,048 | | 43 | Tennessee | 2,882 |
| 11 | Utah | 5,806 | | 44 | Indiana | 2,857 |
| 20 | Vermont | 4,515 | | 45 | Missouri | 2,798 |
| 25 | Virginia | 4,079 | | 46 | Ohio | 2,774 |
| 10 | Washington | 5,989 | | 47 | Mississippi | 2,560 |
| 33 | West Virginia | 3,692 | | 48 | Arkansas | 2,379 |
| 24 | Wisconsin | 4,198 | | 49 | Iowa | 2,192 |
| 22 | Wyoming | 4,377 | | 50 | Idaho | 2,180 |

District of Columbia     8,085

*Source: Morgan Quitno Press using data from U.S. Bureau of the Census, Governments Division*
*"Compendium of Government Finances: 1997" (2000) (http://www.census.gov/govs/www/cog.html)*
*\*Includes short-term, long-term, full fail and credit, nonguaranteed and public debt for private purposes.*

# State and Local Government Full-Time Equivalent Employees in 1999

## National Total = 14,708,602 FTE Employees*

ALPHA ORDER

| RANK | STATE | EMPLOYEES | % of USA |
|---|---|---|---|
| 22 | Alabama | 261,540 | 1.8% |
| 45 | Alaska | 48,572 | 0.3% |
| 23 | Arizona | 236,752 | 1.6% |
| 33 | Arkansas | 146,546 | 1.0% |
| 1 | California | 1,589,727 | 10.8% |
| 25 | Colorado | 223,600 | 1.5% |
| 32 | Connecticut | 168,935 | 1.1% |
| 46 | Delaware | 42,853 | 0.3% |
| 4 | Florida | 733,590 | 5.0% |
| 9 | Georgia | 451,485 | 3.1% |
| 41 | Hawaii | 67,484 | 0.5% |
| 39 | Idaho | 73,521 | 0.5% |
| 5 | Illinois | 610,840 | 4.2% |
| 14 | Indiana | 309,376 | 2.1% |
| 30 | Iowa | 169,744 | 1.2% |
| 31 | Kansas | 169,190 | 1.2% |
| 26 | Kentucky | 213,434 | 1.5% |
| 18 | Louisiana | 279,023 | 1.9% |
| 40 | Maine | 69,512 | 0.5% |
| 20 | Maryland | 271,217 | 1.8% |
| 13 | Massachusetts | 314,377 | 2.1% |
| 8 | Michigan | 476,619 | 3.2% |
| 19 | Minnesota | 273,403 | 1.9% |
| 28 | Mississippi | 189,891 | 1.3% |
| 15 | Missouri | 301,912 | 2.1% |
| 44 | Montana | 50,397 | 0.3% |
| 36 | Nebraska | 104,249 | 0.7% |
| 38 | Nevada | 84,835 | 0.6% |
| 42 | New Hampshire | 61,511 | 0.4% |
| 10 | New Jersey | 443,676 | 3.0% |
| 35 | New Mexico | 115,265 | 0.8% |
| 2 | New York | 1,146,186 | 7.8% |
| 11 | North Carolina | 437,214 | 3.0% |
| 49 | North Dakota | 37,545 | 0.3% |
| 6 | Ohio | 589,010 | 4.0% |
| 27 | Oklahoma | 204,085 | 1.4% |
| 29 | Oregon | 176,708 | 1.2% |
| 7 | Pennsylvania | 527,174 | 3.6% |
| 43 | Rhode Island | 54,424 | 0.4% |
| 24 | South Carolina | 232,679 | 1.6% |
| 47 | South Dakota | 40,507 | 0.3% |
| 16 | Tennessee | 297,811 | 2.0% |
| 3 | Texas | 1,142,090 | 7.8% |
| 34 | Utah | 121,296 | 0.8% |
| 50 | Vermont | 33,588 | 0.2% |
| 12 | Virginia | 372,845 | 2.5% |
| 17 | Washington | 295,465 | 2.0% |
| 37 | West Virginia | 94,255 | 0.6% |
| 21 | Wisconsin | 270,772 | 1.8% |
| 48 | Wyoming | 38,664 | 0.3% |

RANK ORDER

| RANK | STATE | EMPLOYEES | % of USA |
|---|---|---|---|
| 1 | California | 1,589,727 | 10.8% |
| 2 | New York | 1,146,186 | 7.8% |
| 3 | Texas | 1,142,090 | 7.8% |
| 4 | Florida | 733,590 | 5.0% |
| 5 | Illinois | 610,840 | 4.2% |
| 6 | Ohio | 589,010 | 4.0% |
| 7 | Pennsylvania | 527,174 | 3.6% |
| 8 | Michigan | 476,619 | 3.2% |
| 9 | Georgia | 451,485 | 3.1% |
| 10 | New Jersey | 443,676 | 3.0% |
| 11 | North Carolina | 437,214 | 3.0% |
| 12 | Virginia | 372,845 | 2.5% |
| 13 | Massachusetts | 314,377 | 2.1% |
| 14 | Indiana | 309,376 | 2.1% |
| 15 | Missouri | 301,912 | 2.1% |
| 16 | Tennessee | 297,811 | 2.0% |
| 17 | Washington | 295,465 | 2.0% |
| 18 | Louisiana | 279,023 | 1.9% |
| 19 | Minnesota | 273,403 | 1.9% |
| 20 | Maryland | 271,217 | 1.8% |
| 21 | Wisconsin | 270,772 | 1.8% |
| 22 | Alabama | 261,540 | 1.8% |
| 23 | Arizona | 236,752 | 1.6% |
| 24 | South Carolina | 232,679 | 1.6% |
| 25 | Colorado | 223,600 | 1.5% |
| 26 | Kentucky | 213,434 | 1.5% |
| 27 | Oklahoma | 204,085 | 1.4% |
| 28 | Mississippi | 189,891 | 1.3% |
| 29 | Oregon | 176,708 | 1.2% |
| 30 | Iowa | 169,744 | 1.2% |
| 31 | Kansas | 169,190 | 1.2% |
| 32 | Connecticut | 168,935 | 1.1% |
| 33 | Arkansas | 146,546 | 1.0% |
| 34 | Utah | 121,296 | 0.8% |
| 35 | New Mexico | 115,265 | 0.8% |
| 36 | Nebraska | 104,249 | 0.7% |
| 37 | West Virginia | 94,255 | 0.6% |
| 38 | Nevada | 84,835 | 0.6% |
| 39 | Idaho | 73,521 | 0.5% |
| 40 | Maine | 69,512 | 0.5% |
| 41 | Hawaii | 67,484 | 0.5% |
| 42 | New Hampshire | 61,511 | 0.4% |
| 43 | Rhode Island | 54,424 | 0.4% |
| 44 | Montana | 50,397 | 0.3% |
| 45 | Alaska | 48,572 | 0.3% |
| 46 | Delaware | 42,853 | 0.3% |
| 47 | South Dakota | 40,507 | 0.3% |
| 48 | Wyoming | 38,664 | 0.3% |
| 49 | North Dakota | 37,545 | 0.3% |
| 50 | Vermont | 33,588 | 0.2% |
|  | District of Columbia | 43,208 | 0.3% |

Source: U.S. Bureau of the Census, Governments Division
    "State and Local Employment and Payroll - March 1999" (http://www.census.gov/govs/www/apesstl99.html)
*As of March 1999.

# Rate of State and Local Government FTE Employees in 1999

## National Rate = 539 State/Local Government Employees per 10,000 Population*

ALPHA ORDER

| RANK | STATE | RATE |
|------|-------|------|
| 10 | Alabama | 599 |
| 2 | Alaska | 784 |
| 45 | Arizona | 495 |
| 16 | Arkansas | 574 |
| 48 | California | 480 |
| 28 | Colorado | 551 |
| 40 | Connecticut | 515 |
| 22 | Delaware | 569 |
| 46 | Florida | 485 |
| 15 | Georgia | 580 |
| 22 | Hawaii | 569 |
| 14 | Idaho | 587 |
| 44 | Illinois | 504 |
| 38 | Indiana | 521 |
| 13 | Iowa | 592 |
| 6 | Kansas | 637 |
| 33 | Kentucky | 539 |
| 5 | Louisiana | 638 |
| 25 | Maine | 555 |
| 35 | Maryland | 524 |
| 43 | Massachusetts | 509 |
| 47 | Michigan | 483 |
| 17 | Minnesota | 573 |
| 3 | Mississippi | 686 |
| 27 | Missouri | 552 |
| 18 | Montana | 571 |
| 8 | Nebraska | 626 |
| 49 | Nevada | 469 |
| 42 | New Hampshire | 512 |
| 30 | New Jersey | 545 |
| 4 | New Mexico | 663 |
| 7 | New York | 630 |
| 18 | North Carolina | 571 |
| 12 | North Dakota | 593 |
| 36 | Ohio | 523 |
| 9 | Oklahoma | 608 |
| 34 | Oregon | 533 |
| 50 | Pennsylvania | 440 |
| 29 | Rhode Island | 549 |
| 10 | South Carolina | 599 |
| 26 | South Dakota | 553 |
| 31 | Tennessee | 543 |
| 20 | Texas | 570 |
| 20 | Utah | 570 |
| 24 | Vermont | 566 |
| 32 | Virginia | 542 |
| 41 | Washington | 513 |
| 37 | West Virginia | 522 |
| 39 | Wisconsin | 516 |
| 1 | Wyoming | 806 |

RANK ORDER

| RANK | STATE | RATE |
|------|-------|------|
| 1 | Wyoming | 806 |
| 2 | Alaska | 784 |
| 3 | Mississippi | 686 |
| 4 | New Mexico | 663 |
| 5 | Louisiana | 638 |
| 6 | Kansas | 637 |
| 7 | New York | 630 |
| 8 | Nebraska | 626 |
| 9 | Oklahoma | 608 |
| 10 | Alabama | 599 |
| 10 | South Carolina | 599 |
| 12 | North Dakota | 593 |
| 13 | Iowa | 592 |
| 14 | Idaho | 587 |
| 15 | Georgia | 580 |
| 16 | Arkansas | 574 |
| 17 | Minnesota | 573 |
| 18 | Montana | 571 |
| 18 | North Carolina | 571 |
| 20 | Texas | 570 |
| 20 | Utah | 570 |
| 22 | Delaware | 569 |
| 22 | Hawaii | 569 |
| 24 | Vermont | 566 |
| 25 | Maine | 555 |
| 26 | South Dakota | 553 |
| 27 | Missouri | 552 |
| 28 | Colorado | 551 |
| 29 | Rhode Island | 549 |
| 30 | New Jersey | 545 |
| 31 | Tennessee | 543 |
| 32 | Virginia | 542 |
| 33 | Kentucky | 539 |
| 34 | Oregon | 533 |
| 35 | Maryland | 524 |
| 36 | Ohio | 523 |
| 37 | West Virginia | 522 |
| 38 | Indiana | 521 |
| 39 | Wisconsin | 516 |
| 40 | Connecticut | 515 |
| 41 | Washington | 513 |
| 42 | New Hampshire | 512 |
| 43 | Massachusetts | 509 |
| 44 | Illinois | 504 |
| 45 | Arizona | 495 |
| 46 | Florida | 485 |
| 47 | Michigan | 483 |
| 48 | California | 480 |
| 49 | Nevada | 469 |
| 50 | Pennsylvania | 440 |
| | District of Columbia | 833 |

Source: Morgan Quitno Press using data from U.S. Bureau of the Census, Governments Division
   "State and Local Employment and Payroll - March 1999" (http://www.census.gov/govs/www/apesstl99.html)
*Full-time equivalent as of March 1999.

# Average Annual Earnings of Full-Time State and Local Government Employees in 1999
## National Average = $35,704*

ALPHA ORDER

| RANK | STATE | EARNINGS |
|------|-------|----------|
| 44 | Alabama | $28,737 |
| 5 | Alaska | 42,988 |
| 21 | Arizona | 33,492 |
| 49 | Arkansas | 26,670 |
| 2 | California | 44,951 |
| 17 | Colorado | 36,325 |
| 3 | Connecticut | 43,228 |
| 18 | Delaware | 35,925 |
| 23 | Florida | 32,981 |
| 31 | Georgia | 30,331 |
| 20 | Hawaii | 34,627 |
| 39 | Idaho | 29,276 |
| 11 | Illinois | 38,252 |
| 27 | Indiana | 31,397 |
| 25 | Iowa | 32,567 |
| 37 | Kansas | 29,539 |
| 43 | Kentucky | 28,877 |
| 46 | Louisiana | 27,646 |
| 34 | Maine | 29,828 |
| 12 | Maryland | 38,142 |
| 9 | Massachusetts | 39,307 |
| 10 | Michigan | 39,101 |
| 15 | Minnesota | 36,593 |
| 50 | Mississippi | 25,318 |
| 33 | Missouri | 29,932 |
| 40 | Montana | 29,009 |
| 35 | Nebraska | 29,711 |
| 7 | Nevada | 39,764 |
| 24 | New Hampshire | 32,656 |
| 1 | New Jersey | 45,326 |
| 42 | New Mexico | 28,894 |
| 4 | New York | 43,146 |
| 28 | North Carolina | 31,307 |
| 30 | North Dakota | 30,357 |
| 19 | Ohio | 35,037 |
| 47 | Oklahoma | 27,160 |
| 16 | Oregon | 36,508 |
| 13 | Pennsylvania | 37,445 |
| 6 | Rhode Island | 41,440 |
| 45 | South Carolina | 28,583 |
| 48 | South Dakota | 26,887 |
| 36 | Tennessee | 29,615 |
| 32 | Texas | 30,125 |
| 29 | Utah | 31,197 |
| 26 | Vermont | 32,388 |
| 22 | Virginia | 33,088 |
| 8 | Washington | 39,749 |
| 41 | West Virginia | 28,900 |
| 14 | Wisconsin | 37,348 |
| 38 | Wyoming | 29,454 |

RANK ORDER

| RANK | STATE | EARNINGS |
|------|-------|----------|
| 1 | New Jersey | $45,326 |
| 2 | California | 44,951 |
| 3 | Connecticut | 43,228 |
| 4 | New York | 43,146 |
| 5 | Alaska | 42,988 |
| 6 | Rhode Island | 41,440 |
| 7 | Nevada | 39,764 |
| 8 | Washington | 39,749 |
| 9 | Massachusetts | 39,307 |
| 10 | Michigan | 39,101 |
| 11 | Illinois | 38,252 |
| 12 | Maryland | 38,142 |
| 13 | Pennsylvania | 37,445 |
| 14 | Wisconsin | 37,348 |
| 15 | Minnesota | 36,593 |
| 16 | Oregon | 36,508 |
| 17 | Colorado | 36,325 |
| 18 | Delaware | 35,925 |
| 19 | Ohio | 35,037 |
| 20 | Hawaii | 34,627 |
| 21 | Arizona | 33,492 |
| 22 | Virginia | 33,088 |
| 23 | Florida | 32,981 |
| 24 | New Hampshire | 32,656 |
| 25 | Iowa | 32,567 |
| 26 | Vermont | 32,388 |
| 27 | Indiana | 31,397 |
| 28 | North Carolina | 31,307 |
| 29 | Utah | 31,197 |
| 30 | North Dakota | 30,357 |
| 31 | Georgia | 30,331 |
| 32 | Texas | 30,125 |
| 33 | Missouri | 29,932 |
| 34 | Maine | 29,828 |
| 35 | Nebraska | 29,711 |
| 36 | Tennessee | 29,615 |
| 37 | Kansas | 29,539 |
| 38 | Wyoming | 29,454 |
| 39 | Idaho | 29,276 |
| 40 | Montana | 29,009 |
| 41 | West Virginia | 28,900 |
| 42 | New Mexico | 28,894 |
| 43 | Kentucky | 28,877 |
| 44 | Alabama | 28,737 |
| 45 | South Carolina | 28,583 |
| 46 | Louisiana | 27,646 |
| 47 | Oklahoma | 27,160 |
| 48 | South Dakota | 26,887 |
| 49 | Arkansas | 26,670 |
| 50 | Mississippi | 25,318 |
| | District of Columbia | 45,880 |

Source: Morgan Quitno Press using data from U.S. Bureau of the Census, Governments Division
"State and Local Employment and Payroll - March 1999" (http://www.census.gov/govs/www/apesstl99.html)
*March 1999 payroll (multiplied by 12) for full-time equivalent employees divided by full-time equivalent employees.

# State Government Total Revenue in 1998

## National Total = 1,095,861,887,000*

ALPHA ORDER

| RANK | STATE | REVENUE | % of USA |
|---|---|---|---|
| 27 | Alabama | $14,843,951,000 | 1.4% |
| 34 | Alaska | 9,039,235,000 | 0.8% |
| 22 | Arizona | 16,582,495,000 | 1.5% |
| 32 | Arkansas | 9,487,169,000 | 0.9% |
| 1 | California | 144,984,973,000 | 13.2% |
| 28 | Colorado | 13,514,305,000 | 1.2% |
| 23 | Connecticut | 16,520,398,000 | 1.5% |
| 43 | Delaware | 4,593,997,000 | 0.4% |
| 4 | Florida | 51,751,884,000 | 4.7% |
| 14 | Georgia | 25,707,202,000 | 2.3% |
| 39 | Hawaii | 6,760,740,000 | 0.6% |
| 42 | Idaho | 4,705,173,000 | 0.4% |
| 7 | Illinois | 40,460,377,000 | 3.7% |
| 19 | Indiana | 18,507,747,000 | 1.7% |
| 31 | Iowa | 10,029,402,000 | 0.9% |
| 36 | Kansas | 8,443,997,000 | 0.8% |
| 24 | Kentucky | 15,989,084,000 | 1.5% |
| 20 | Louisiana | 17,605,336,000 | 1.6% |
| 40 | Maine | 5,689,618,000 | 0.5% |
| 17 | Maryland | 20,559,098,000 | 1.9% |
| 11 | Massachusetts | 28,234,686,000 | 2.6% |
| 8 | Michigan | 40,069,007,000 | 3.7% |
| 15 | Minnesota | 24,508,758,000 | 2.2% |
| 30 | Mississippi | 10,611,243,000 | 1.0% |
| 18 | Missouri | 19,020,637,000 | 1.7% |
| 46 | Montana | 3,625,865,000 | 0.3% |
| 41 | Nebraska | 5,635,696,000 | 0.5% |
| 38 | Nevada | 7,319,969,000 | 0.7% |
| 45 | New Hampshire | 4,010,298,000 | 0.4% |
| 9 | New Jersey | 37,007,323,000 | 3.4% |
| 33 | New Mexico | 9,058,548,000 | 0.8% |
| 2 | New York | 96,131,441,000 | 8.8% |
| 10 | North Carolina | 33,326,975,000 | 3.0% |
| 47 | North Dakota | 3,128,460,000 | 0.3% |
| 6 | Ohio | 48,133,067,000 | 4.4% |
| 29 | Oklahoma | 12,185,893,000 | 1.1% |
| 25 | Oregon | 15,688,295,000 | 1.4% |
| 5 | Pennsylvania | 48,503,491,000 | 4.4% |
| 44 | Rhode Island | 4,437,538,000 | 0.4% |
| 26 | South Carolina | 15,202,985,000 | 1.4% |
| 48 | South Dakota | 2,874,277,000 | 0.3% |
| 21 | Tennessee | 16,675,209,000 | 1.5% |
| 3 | Texas | 57,807,137,000 | 5.3% |
| 35 | Utah | 8,762,037,000 | 0.8% |
| 50 | Vermont | 2,372,580,000 | 0.2% |
| 13 | Virginia | 25,918,315,000 | 2.4% |
| 12 | Washington | 27,980,014,000 | 2.6% |
| 37 | West Virginia | 7,808,416,000 | 0.7% |
| 16 | Wisconsin | 21,394,590,000 | 2.0% |
| 49 | Wyoming | 2,652,956,000 | 0.2% |

RANK ORDER

| RANK | STATE | REVENUE | % of USA |
|---|---|---|---|
| 1 | California | $144,984,973,000 | 13.2% |
| 2 | New York | 96,131,441,000 | 8.8% |
| 3 | Texas | 57,807,137,000 | 5.3% |
| 4 | Florida | 51,751,884,000 | 4.7% |
| 5 | Pennsylvania | 48,503,491,000 | 4.4% |
| 6 | Ohio | 48,133,067,000 | 4.4% |
| 7 | Illinois | 40,460,377,000 | 3.7% |
| 8 | Michigan | 40,069,007,000 | 3.7% |
| 9 | New Jersey | 37,007,323,000 | 3.4% |
| 10 | North Carolina | 33,326,975,000 | 3.0% |
| 11 | Massachusetts | 28,234,686,000 | 2.6% |
| 12 | Washington | 27,980,014,000 | 2.6% |
| 13 | Virginia | 25,918,315,000 | 2.4% |
| 14 | Georgia | 25,707,202,000 | 2.3% |
| 15 | Minnesota | 24,508,758,000 | 2.2% |
| 16 | Wisconsin | 21,394,590,000 | 2.0% |
| 17 | Maryland | 20,559,098,000 | 1.9% |
| 18 | Missouri | 19,020,637,000 | 1.7% |
| 19 | Indiana | 18,507,747,000 | 1.7% |
| 20 | Louisiana | 17,605,336,000 | 1.6% |
| 21 | Tennessee | 16,675,209,000 | 1.5% |
| 22 | Arizona | 16,582,495,000 | 1.5% |
| 23 | Connecticut | 16,520,398,000 | 1.5% |
| 24 | Kentucky | 15,989,084,000 | 1.5% |
| 25 | Oregon | 15,688,295,000 | 1.4% |
| 26 | South Carolina | 15,202,985,000 | 1.4% |
| 27 | Alabama | 14,843,951,000 | 1.4% |
| 28 | Colorado | 13,514,305,000 | 1.2% |
| 29 | Oklahoma | 12,185,893,000 | 1.1% |
| 30 | Mississippi | 10,611,243,000 | 1.0% |
| 31 | Iowa | 10,029,402,000 | 0.9% |
| 32 | Arkansas | 9,487,169,000 | 0.9% |
| 33 | New Mexico | 9,058,548,000 | 0.8% |
| 34 | Alaska | 9,039,235,000 | 0.8% |
| 35 | Utah | 8,762,037,000 | 0.8% |
| 36 | Kansas | 8,443,997,000 | 0.8% |
| 37 | West Virginia | 7,808,416,000 | 0.7% |
| 38 | Nevada | 7,319,969,000 | 0.7% |
| 39 | Hawaii | 6,760,740,000 | 0.6% |
| 40 | Maine | 5,689,618,000 | 0.5% |
| 41 | Nebraska | 5,635,696,000 | 0.5% |
| 42 | Idaho | 4,705,173,000 | 0.4% |
| 43 | Delaware | 4,593,997,000 | 0.4% |
| 44 | Rhode Island | 4,437,538,000 | 0.4% |
| 45 | New Hampshire | 4,010,298,000 | 0.4% |
| 46 | Montana | 3,625,865,000 | 0.3% |
| 47 | North Dakota | 3,128,460,000 | 0.3% |
| 48 | South Dakota | 2,874,277,000 | 0.3% |
| 49 | Wyoming | 2,652,956,000 | 0.2% |
| 50 | Vermont | 2,372,580,000 | 0.2% |
| | District of Columbia** | NA | NA |

Source: U.S. Bureau of the Census, Governments Division
"1998 State Government Finance Data" (http://www.census.gov/govs/www/state98.html)
*Total revenue includes all money received from external sources. This includes taxes, intergovernmental transfers and insurance trust revenue and revenue from government owned utilities and other commercial or auxiliary enterprise.
**Not applicable.

# Per Capita State Government Total Revenue in 1998

## National Per Capita = $4,063*

ALPHA ORDER

| RANK | STATE | PER CAPITA |
|------|-------|------------|
| 41 | Alabama | $3,412 |
| 1 | Alaska | 14,693 |
| 37 | Arizona | 3,553 |
| 35 | Arkansas | 3,738 |
| 16 | California | 4,436 |
| 42 | Colorado | 3,405 |
| 8 | Connecticut | 5,048 |
| 2 | Delaware | 6,174 |
| 40 | Florida | 3,471 |
| 45 | Georgia | 3,366 |
| 3 | Hawaii | 5,679 |
| 33 | Idaho | 3,822 |
| 46 | Illinois | 3,352 |
| 48 | Indiana | 3,133 |
| 38 | Iowa | 3,506 |
| 47 | Kansas | 3,200 |
| 25 | Kentucky | 4,064 |
| 27 | Louisiana | 4,035 |
| 14 | Maine | 4,561 |
| 29 | Maryland | 4,008 |
| 12 | Massachusetts | 4,595 |
| 24 | Michigan | 4,080 |
| 7 | Minnesota | 5,185 |
| 32 | Mississippi | 3,857 |
| 39 | Missouri | 3,498 |
| 22 | Montana | 4,122 |
| 43 | Nebraska | 3,393 |
| 20 | Nevada | 4,198 |
| 44 | New Hampshire | 3,382 |
| 13 | New Jersey | 4,571 |
| 6 | New Mexico | 5,225 |
| 5 | New York | 5,294 |
| 17 | North Carolina | 4,417 |
| 10 | North Dakota | 4,905 |
| 19 | Ohio | 4,283 |
| 36 | Oklahoma | 3,649 |
| 11 | Oregon | 4,780 |
| 26 | Pennsylvania | 4,041 |
| 15 | Rhode Island | 4,493 |
| 30 | South Carolina | 3,960 |
| 31 | South Dakota | 3,933 |
| 49 | Tennessee | 3,069 |
| 50 | Texas | 2,933 |
| 21 | Utah | 4,171 |
| 28 | Vermont | 4,017 |
| 34 | Virginia | 3,818 |
| 9 | Washington | 4,919 |
| 18 | West Virginia | 4,310 |
| 23 | Wisconsin | 4,097 |
| 4 | Wyoming | 5,526 |

RANK ORDER

| RANK | STATE | PER CAPITA |
|------|-------|------------|
| 1 | Alaska | $14,693 |
| 2 | Delaware | 6,174 |
| 3 | Hawaii | 5,679 |
| 4 | Wyoming | 5,526 |
| 5 | New York | 5,294 |
| 6 | New Mexico | 5,225 |
| 7 | Minnesota | 5,185 |
| 8 | Connecticut | 5,048 |
| 9 | Washington | 4,919 |
| 10 | North Dakota | 4,905 |
| 11 | Oregon | 4,780 |
| 12 | Massachusetts | 4,595 |
| 13 | New Jersey | 4,571 |
| 14 | Maine | 4,561 |
| 15 | Rhode Island | 4,493 |
| 16 | California | 4,436 |
| 17 | North Carolina | 4,417 |
| 18 | West Virginia | 4,310 |
| 19 | Ohio | 4,283 |
| 20 | Nevada | 4,198 |
| 21 | Utah | 4,171 |
| 22 | Montana | 4,122 |
| 23 | Wisconsin | 4,097 |
| 24 | Michigan | 4,080 |
| 25 | Kentucky | 4,064 |
| 26 | Pennsylvania | 4,041 |
| 27 | Louisiana | 4,035 |
| 28 | Vermont | 4,017 |
| 29 | Maryland | 4,008 |
| 30 | South Carolina | 3,960 |
| 31 | South Dakota | 3,933 |
| 32 | Mississippi | 3,857 |
| 33 | Idaho | 3,822 |
| 34 | Virginia | 3,818 |
| 35 | Arkansas | 3,738 |
| 36 | Oklahoma | 3,649 |
| 37 | Arizona | 3,553 |
| 38 | Iowa | 3,506 |
| 39 | Missouri | 3,498 |
| 40 | Florida | 3,471 |
| 41 | Alabama | 3,412 |
| 42 | Colorado | 3,405 |
| 43 | Nebraska | 3,393 |
| 44 | New Hampshire | 3,382 |
| 45 | Georgia | 3,366 |
| 46 | Illinois | 3,352 |
| 47 | Kansas | 3,200 |
| 48 | Indiana | 3,133 |
| 49 | Tennessee | 3,069 |
| 50 | Texas | 2,933 |

District of Columbia**     NA

Source: Morgan Quitno Press using data from U.S. Bureau of the Census, Governments Division
 "1998 State Government Finance Data" (http://www.census.gov/govs/www/state98.html)
*Total revenue includes all money received from external sources. This includes taxes, intergovernmental transfers and insurance trust revenue and revenue from government owned utilities and other commercial or auxiliary enterprise.
**Not applicable.

# State Government Intergovernmental Revenue in 1998

## National Total = $240,788,817,000*

ALPHA ORDER

| RANK | STATE | REVENUE | % of USA |
|------|-------|---------|----------|
| 17 | Alabama | $4,021,037,000 | 1.7% |
| 41 | Alaska | 1,079,799,000 | 0.4% |
| 26 | Arizona | 3,329,995,000 | 1.4% |
| 31 | Arkansas | 2,368,339,000 | 1.0% |
| 2 | California | 30,893,821,000 | 12.8% |
| 29 | Colorado | 2,788,627,000 | 1.2% |
| 27 | Connecticut | 3,016,337,000 | 1.3% |
| 50 | Delaware | 724,706,000 | 0.3% |
| 8 | Florida | 8,301,851,000 | 3.4% |
| 12 | Georgia | 5,676,362,000 | 2.4% |
| 39 | Hawaii | 1,175,599,000 | 0.5% |
| 46 | Idaho | 862,978,000 | 0.4% |
| 5 | Illinois | 8,958,993,000 | 3.7% |
| 18 | Indiana | 3,943,070,000 | 1.6% |
| 32 | Iowa | 2,215,812,000 | 0.9% |
| 34 | Kansas | 1,862,929,000 | 0.8% |
| 22 | Kentucky | 3,602,966,000 | 1.5% |
| 16 | Louisiana | 4,026,348,000 | 1.7% |
| 37 | Maine | 1,411,320,000 | 0.6% |
| 23 | Maryland | 3,533,711,000 | 1.5% |
| 10 | Massachusetts | 6,458,265,000 | 2.7% |
| 7 | Michigan | 8,557,047,000 | 3.6% |
| 19 | Minnesota | 3,938,396,000 | 1.6% |
| 28 | Mississippi | 2,947,073,000 | 1.2% |
| 15 | Missouri | 4,246,338,000 | 1.8% |
| 42 | Montana | 1,047,919,000 | 0.4% |
| 38 | Nebraska | 1,282,063,000 | 0.5% |
| 44 | Nevada | 911,731,000 | 0.4% |
| 43 | New Hampshire | 1,023,619,000 | 0.4% |
| 11 | New Jersey | 6,391,527,000 | 2.7% |
| 35 | New Mexico | 1,846,136,000 | 0.8% |
| 1 | New York | 33,790,935,000 | 14.0% |
| 9 | North Carolina | 6,817,303,000 | 2.8% |
| 45 | North Dakota | 892,685,000 | 0.4% |
| 6 | Ohio | 8,953,346,000 | 3.7% |
| 30 | Oklahoma | 2,516,285,000 | 1.0% |
| 25 | Oregon | 3,364,556,000 | 1.4% |
| 4 | Pennsylvania | 9,608,658,000 | 4.0% |
| 40 | Rhode Island | 1,146,311,000 | 0.5% |
| 24 | South Carolina | 3,442,418,000 | 1.4% |
| 48 | South Dakota | 764,232,000 | 0.3% |
| 13 | Tennessee | 5,264,984,000 | 2.2% |
| 3 | Texas | 14,605,424,000 | 6.1% |
| 36 | Utah | 1,689,850,000 | 0.7% |
| 49 | Vermont | 729,547,000 | 0.3% |
| 21 | Virginia | 3,780,977,000 | 1.6% |
| 14 | Washington | 4,247,049,000 | 1.8% |
| 33 | West Virginia | 2,096,294,000 | 0.9% |
| 20 | Wisconsin | 3,794,650,000 | 1.6% |
| 47 | Wyoming | 838,599,000 | 0.3% |

RANK ORDER

| RANK | STATE | REVENUE | % of USA |
|------|-------|---------|----------|
| 1 | New York | $33,790,935,000 | 14.0% |
| 2 | California | 30,893,821,000 | 12.8% |
| 3 | Texas | 14,605,424,000 | 6.1% |
| 4 | Pennsylvania | 9,608,658,000 | 4.0% |
| 5 | Illinois | 8,958,993,000 | 3.7% |
| 6 | Ohio | 8,953,346,000 | 3.7% |
| 7 | Michigan | 8,557,047,000 | 3.6% |
| 8 | Florida | 8,301,851,000 | 3.4% |
| 9 | North Carolina | 6,817,303,000 | 2.8% |
| 10 | Massachusetts | 6,458,265,000 | 2.7% |
| 11 | New Jersey | 6,391,527,000 | 2.7% |
| 12 | Georgia | 5,676,362,000 | 2.4% |
| 13 | Tennessee | 5,264,984,000 | 2.2% |
| 14 | Washington | 4,247,049,000 | 1.8% |
| 15 | Missouri | 4,246,338,000 | 1.8% |
| 16 | Louisiana | 4,026,348,000 | 1.7% |
| 17 | Alabama | 4,021,037,000 | 1.7% |
| 18 | Indiana | 3,943,070,000 | 1.6% |
| 19 | Minnesota | 3,938,396,000 | 1.6% |
| 20 | Wisconsin | 3,794,650,000 | 1.6% |
| 21 | Virginia | 3,780,977,000 | 1.6% |
| 22 | Kentucky | 3,602,966,000 | 1.5% |
| 23 | Maryland | 3,533,711,000 | 1.5% |
| 24 | South Carolina | 3,442,418,000 | 1.4% |
| 25 | Oregon | 3,364,556,000 | 1.4% |
| 26 | Arizona | 3,329,995,000 | 1.4% |
| 27 | Connecticut | 3,016,337,000 | 1.3% |
| 28 | Mississippi | 2,947,073,000 | 1.2% |
| 29 | Colorado | 2,788,627,000 | 1.2% |
| 30 | Oklahoma | 2,516,285,000 | 1.0% |
| 31 | Arkansas | 2,368,339,000 | 1.0% |
| 32 | Iowa | 2,215,812,000 | 0.9% |
| 33 | West Virginia | 2,096,294,000 | 0.9% |
| 34 | Kansas | 1,862,929,000 | 0.8% |
| 35 | New Mexico | 1,846,136,000 | 0.8% |
| 36 | Utah | 1,689,850,000 | 0.7% |
| 37 | Maine | 1,411,320,000 | 0.6% |
| 38 | Nebraska | 1,282,063,000 | 0.5% |
| 39 | Hawaii | 1,175,599,000 | 0.5% |
| 40 | Rhode Island | 1,146,311,000 | 0.5% |
| 41 | Alaska | 1,079,799,000 | 0.4% |
| 42 | Montana | 1,047,919,000 | 0.4% |
| 43 | New Hampshire | 1,023,619,000 | 0.4% |
| 44 | Nevada | 911,731,000 | 0.4% |
| 45 | North Dakota | 892,685,000 | 0.4% |
| 46 | Idaho | 862,978,000 | 0.4% |
| 47 | Wyoming | 838,599,000 | 0.3% |
| 48 | South Dakota | 764,232,000 | 0.3% |
| 49 | Vermont | 729,547,000 | 0.3% |
| 50 | Delaware | 724,706,000 | 0.3% |
| | District of Columbia** | NA | NA |

Source: U.S. Bureau of the Census, Governments Division
    "1998 State Government Finance Data" (http://www.census.gov/govs/www/state98.html)
*Includes revenue from federal and local government sources.
**Not applicable.

# Per Capita State Intergovernmental Revenue in 1998

## National Per Capita = $893*

ALPHA ORDER

| RANK | STATE | PER CAPITA |
|------|-------|------------|
| 20 | Alabama | $924 |
| 2 | Alaska | 1,755 |
| 42 | Arizona | 713 |
| 19 | Arkansas | 933 |
| 18 | California | 945 |
| 44 | Colorado | 703 |
| 22 | Connecticut | 922 |
| 16 | Delaware | 974 |
| 48 | Florida | 557 |
| 38 | Georgia | 743 |
| 15 | Hawaii | 988 |
| 45 | Idaho | 701 |
| 39 | Illinois | 742 |
| 47 | Indiana | 667 |
| 34 | Iowa | 774 |
| 43 | Kansas | 706 |
| 23 | Kentucky | 916 |
| 21 | Louisiana | 923 |
| 9 | Maine | 1,131 |
| 46 | Maryland | 689 |
| 12 | Massachusetts | 1,051 |
| 26 | Michigan | 871 |
| 28 | Minnesota | 833 |
| 10 | Mississippi | 1,071 |
| 33 | Missouri | 781 |
| 6 | Montana | 1,191 |
| 35 | Nebraska | 772 |
| 50 | Nevada | 523 |
| 27 | New Hampshire | 863 |
| 32 | New Jersey | 790 |
| 11 | New Mexico | 1,065 |
| 1 | New York | 1,861 |
| 24 | North Carolina | 903 |
| 4 | North Dakota | 1,400 |
| 31 | Ohio | 797 |
| 36 | Oklahoma | 753 |
| 14 | Oregon | 1,025 |
| 30 | Pennsylvania | 801 |
| 7 | Rhode Island | 1,161 |
| 25 | South Carolina | 897 |
| 13 | South Dakota | 1,046 |
| 17 | Tennessee | 969 |
| 40 | Texas | 741 |
| 29 | Utah | 804 |
| 5 | Vermont | 1,235 |
| 48 | Virginia | 557 |
| 37 | Washington | 747 |
| 8 | West Virginia | 1,157 |
| 41 | Wisconsin | 727 |
| 3 | Wyoming | 1,747 |

RANK ORDER

| RANK | STATE | PER CAPITA |
|------|-------|------------|
| 1 | New York | $1,861 |
| 2 | Alaska | 1,755 |
| 3 | Wyoming | 1,747 |
| 4 | North Dakota | 1,400 |
| 5 | Vermont | 1,235 |
| 6 | Montana | 1,191 |
| 7 | Rhode Island | 1,161 |
| 8 | West Virginia | 1,157 |
| 9 | Maine | 1,131 |
| 10 | Mississippi | 1,071 |
| 11 | New Mexico | 1,065 |
| 12 | Massachusetts | 1,051 |
| 13 | South Dakota | 1,046 |
| 14 | Oregon | 1,025 |
| 15 | Hawaii | 988 |
| 16 | Delaware | 974 |
| 17 | Tennessee | 969 |
| 18 | California | 945 |
| 19 | Arkansas | 933 |
| 20 | Alabama | 924 |
| 21 | Louisiana | 923 |
| 22 | Connecticut | 922 |
| 23 | Kentucky | 916 |
| 24 | North Carolina | 903 |
| 25 | South Carolina | 897 |
| 26 | Michigan | 871 |
| 27 | New Hampshire | 863 |
| 28 | Minnesota | 833 |
| 29 | Utah | 804 |
| 30 | Pennsylvania | 801 |
| 31 | Ohio | 797 |
| 32 | New Jersey | 790 |
| 33 | Missouri | 781 |
| 34 | Iowa | 774 |
| 35 | Nebraska | 772 |
| 36 | Oklahoma | 753 |
| 37 | Washington | 747 |
| 38 | Georgia | 743 |
| 39 | Illinois | 742 |
| 40 | Texas | 741 |
| 41 | Wisconsin | 727 |
| 42 | Arizona | 713 |
| 43 | Kansas | 706 |
| 44 | Colorado | 703 |
| 45 | Idaho | 701 |
| 46 | Maryland | 689 |
| 47 | Indiana | 667 |
| 48 | Florida | 557 |
| 48 | Virginia | 557 |
| 50 | Nevada | 523 |

District of Columbia**    NA

Source: Morgan Quitno Press using data from U.S. Bureau of the Census, Governments Division
"1998 State Government Finance Data" (http://www.census.gov/govs/www/state98.html)
*Includes revenue from federal and local government sources.
**Not applicable.

# State Government Own Source Revenue in 1998

## National Total = $624,074,621,000*

ALPHA ORDER

| RANK | STATE | REVENUE | % of USA |
|---|---|---|---|
| 25 | Alabama | $8,412,373,000 | 1.3% |
| 30 | Alaska | 6,893,516,000 | 1.1% |
| 24 | Arizona | 8,483,767,000 | 1.4% |
| 34 | Arkansas | 5,356,120,000 | 0.9% |
| 1 | California | 80,193,916,000 | 12.9% |
| 26 | Colorado | 8,164,849,000 | 1.3% |
| 19 | Connecticut | 11,435,853,000 | 1.8% |
| 41 | Delaware | 3,158,381,000 | 0.5% |
| 4 | Florida | 28,478,482,000 | 4.6% |
| 14 | Georgia | 14,488,424,000 | 2.3% |
| 37 | Hawaii | 4,298,143,000 | 0.7% |
| 43 | Idaho | 2,728,741,000 | 0.4% |
| 7 | Illinois | 24,827,770,000 | 4.0% |
| 17 | Indiana | 13,169,641,000 | 2.1% |
| 31 | Iowa | 6,605,235,000 | 1.1% |
| 32 | Kansas | 5,922,038,000 | 0.9% |
| 22 | Kentucky | 9,365,995,000 | 1.5% |
| 21 | Louisiana | 9,622,534,000 | 1.5% |
| 42 | Maine | 3,155,557,000 | 0.5% |
| 18 | Maryland | 12,055,367,000 | 1.9% |
| 10 | Massachusetts | 19,342,877,000 | 3.1% |
| 5 | Michigan | 27,527,513,000 | 4.4% |
| 16 | Minnesota | 13,917,774,000 | 2.2% |
| 33 | Mississippi | 5,452,856,000 | 0.9% |
| 20 | Missouri | 10,637,714,000 | 1.7% |
| 46 | Montana | 1,932,500,000 | 0.3% |
| 40 | Nebraska | 3,547,243,000 | 0.6% |
| 39 | Nevada | 3,703,129,000 | 0.6% |
| 45 | New Hampshire | 1,944,504,000 | 0.3% |
| 9 | New Jersey | 21,965,799,000 | 3.5% |
| 35 | New Mexico | 5,280,896,000 | 0.8% |
| 2 | New York | 46,929,237,000 | 7.5% |
| 11 | North Carolina | 17,132,535,000 | 2.7% |
| 47 | North Dakota | 1,640,680,000 | 0.3% |
| 8 | Ohio | 23,346,538,000 | 3.7% |
| 29 | Oklahoma | 6,894,810,000 | 1.1% |
| 28 | Oregon | 7,908,603,000 | 1.3% |
| 6 | Pennsylvania | 27,224,578,000 | 4.4% |
| 44 | Rhode Island | 2,634,889,000 | 0.4% |
| 27 | South Carolina | 7,972,748,000 | 1.3% |
| 50 | South Dakota | 1,334,128,000 | 0.2% |
| 23 | Tennessee | 8,821,356,000 | 1.4% |
| 3 | Texas | 33,460,333,000 | 5.4% |
| 36 | Utah | 4,937,540,000 | 0.8% |
| 49 | Vermont | 1,466,876,000 | 0.2% |
| 12 | Virginia | 15,486,890,000 | 2.5% |
| 13 | Washington | 14,832,036,000 | 2.4% |
| 38 | West Virginia | 4,109,430,000 | 0.7% |
| 15 | Wisconsin | 14,373,982,000 | 2.3% |
| 48 | Wyoming | 1,497,925,000 | 0.2% |

RANK ORDER

| RANK | STATE | REVENUE | % of USA |
|---|---|---|---|
| 1 | California | $80,193,916,000 | 12.9% |
| 2 | New York | 46,929,237,000 | 7.5% |
| 3 | Texas | 33,460,333,000 | 5.4% |
| 4 | Florida | 28,478,482,000 | 4.6% |
| 5 | Michigan | 27,527,513,000 | 4.4% |
| 6 | Pennsylvania | 27,224,578,000 | 4.4% |
| 7 | Illinois | 24,827,770,000 | 4.0% |
| 8 | Ohio | 23,346,538,000 | 3.7% |
| 9 | New Jersey | 21,965,799,000 | 3.5% |
| 10 | Massachusetts | 19,342,877,000 | 3.1% |
| 11 | North Carolina | 17,132,535,000 | 2.7% |
| 12 | Virginia | 15,486,890,000 | 2.5% |
| 13 | Washington | 14,832,036,000 | 2.4% |
| 14 | Georgia | 14,488,424,000 | 2.3% |
| 15 | Wisconsin | 14,373,982,000 | 2.3% |
| 16 | Minnesota | 13,917,774,000 | 2.2% |
| 17 | Indiana | 13,169,641,000 | 2.1% |
| 18 | Maryland | 12,055,367,000 | 1.9% |
| 19 | Connecticut | 11,435,853,000 | 1.8% |
| 20 | Missouri | 10,637,714,000 | 1.7% |
| 21 | Louisiana | 9,622,534,000 | 1.5% |
| 22 | Kentucky | 9,365,995,000 | 1.5% |
| 23 | Tennessee | 8,821,356,000 | 1.4% |
| 24 | Arizona | 8,483,767,000 | 1.4% |
| 25 | Alabama | 8,412,373,000 | 1.3% |
| 26 | Colorado | 8,164,849,000 | 1.3% |
| 27 | South Carolina | 7,972,748,000 | 1.3% |
| 28 | Oregon | 7,908,603,000 | 1.3% |
| 29 | Oklahoma | 6,894,810,000 | 1.1% |
| 30 | Alaska | 6,893,516,000 | 1.1% |
| 31 | Iowa | 6,605,235,000 | 1.1% |
| 32 | Kansas | 5,922,038,000 | 0.9% |
| 33 | Mississippi | 5,452,856,000 | 0.9% |
| 34 | Arkansas | 5,356,120,000 | 0.9% |
| 35 | New Mexico | 5,280,896,000 | 0.8% |
| 36 | Utah | 4,937,540,000 | 0.8% |
| 37 | Hawaii | 4,298,143,000 | 0.7% |
| 38 | West Virginia | 4,109,430,000 | 0.7% |
| 39 | Nevada | 3,703,129,000 | 0.6% |
| 40 | Nebraska | 3,547,243,000 | 0.6% |
| 41 | Delaware | 3,158,381,000 | 0.5% |
| 42 | Maine | 3,155,557,000 | 0.5% |
| 43 | Idaho | 2,728,741,000 | 0.4% |
| 44 | Rhode Island | 2,634,889,000 | 0.4% |
| 45 | New Hampshire | 1,944,504,000 | 0.3% |
| 46 | Montana | 1,932,500,000 | 0.3% |
| 47 | North Dakota | 1,640,680,000 | 0.3% |
| 48 | Wyoming | 1,497,925,000 | 0.2% |
| 49 | Vermont | 1,466,876,000 | 0.2% |
| 50 | South Dakota | 1,334,128,000 | 0.2% |
| | District of Columbia** | NA | NA |

*Source: Morgan Quitno Press using data from U.S. Bureau of the Census, Governments Division "1998 State Government Finance Data" (http://www.census.gov/govs/www/state98.html)*
*Own source revenue includes taxes, current charges and miscellaneous general revenue. Excluded are intergovernmental transfers, insurance trust revenue and revenue from government owned utilities and other commercial or auxiliary enterprise.*
**Not applicable.*

# Per Capita State Government Own Source Revenue in 1998

## National Per Capita = $2,314*

| RANK | STATE | PER CAPITA | | RANK | STATE | PER CAPITA |
|---|---|---|---|---|---|---|
| 43 | Alabama | $1,933 | | 1 | Alaska | $11,205 |
| 1 | Alaska | 11,205 | | 2 | Delaware | 4,245 |
| 47 | Arizona | 1,818 | | 3 | Hawaii | 3,610 |
| 35 | Arkansas | 2,110 | | 4 | Connecticut | 3,494 |
| 18 | California | 2,454 | | 5 | Massachusetts | 3,148 |
| 39 | Colorado | 2,057 | | 6 | Wyoming | 3,120 |
| 4 | Connecticut | 3,494 | | 7 | New Mexico | 3,046 |
| 2 | Delaware | 4,245 | | 8 | Minnesota | 2,945 |
| 44 | Florida | 1,910 | | 9 | Michigan | 2,803 |
| 45 | Georgia | 1,897 | | 10 | Wisconsin | 2,753 |
| 3 | Hawaii | 3,610 | | 11 | New Jersey | 2,713 |
| 30 | Idaho | 2,217 | | 12 | Rhode Island | 2,668 |
| 39 | Illinois | 2,057 | | 13 | Washington | 2,608 |
| 29 | Indiana | 2,229 | | 14 | New York | 2,584 |
| 23 | Iowa | 2,309 | | 15 | North Dakota | 2,572 |
| 28 | Kansas | 2,244 | | 16 | Maine | 2,529 |
| 20 | Kentucky | 2,381 | | 17 | Vermont | 2,484 |
| 31 | Louisiana | 2,206 | | 18 | California | 2,454 |
| 16 | Maine | 2,529 | | 19 | Oregon | 2,410 |
| 22 | Maryland | 2,350 | | 20 | Kentucky | 2,381 |
| 5 | Massachusetts | 3,148 | | 21 | Utah | 2,351 |
| 9 | Michigan | 2,803 | | 22 | Maryland | 2,350 |
| 8 | Minnesota | 2,945 | | 23 | Iowa | 2,309 |
| 41 | Mississippi | 1,982 | | 24 | Virginia | 2,281 |
| 42 | Missouri | 1,956 | | 25 | North Carolina | 2,270 |
| 32 | Montana | 2,197 | | 26 | Pennsylvania | 2,268 |
| 33 | Nebraska | 2,136 | | 26 | West Virginia | 2,268 |
| 34 | Nevada | 2,124 | | 28 | Kansas | 2,244 |
| 49 | New Hampshire | 1,640 | | 29 | Indiana | 2,229 |
| 11 | New Jersey | 2,713 | | 30 | Idaho | 2,217 |
| 7 | New Mexico | 3,046 | | 31 | Louisiana | 2,206 |
| 14 | New York | 2,584 | | 32 | Montana | 2,197 |
| 25 | North Carolina | 2,270 | | 33 | Nebraska | 2,136 |
| 15 | North Dakota | 2,572 | | 34 | Nevada | 2,124 |
| 36 | Ohio | 2,078 | | 35 | Arkansas | 2,110 |
| 38 | Oklahoma | 2,065 | | 36 | Ohio | 2,078 |
| 19 | Oregon | 2,410 | | 37 | South Carolina | 2,076 |
| 26 | Pennsylvania | 2,268 | | 38 | Oklahoma | 2,065 |
| 12 | Rhode Island | 2,668 | | 39 | Colorado | 2,057 |
| 37 | South Carolina | 2,076 | | 39 | Illinois | 2,057 |
| 46 | South Dakota | 1,826 | | 41 | Mississippi | 1,982 |
| 50 | Tennessee | 1,624 | | 42 | Missouri | 1,956 |
| 48 | Texas | 1,697 | | 43 | Alabama | 1,933 |
| 21 | Utah | 2,351 | | 44 | Florida | 1,910 |
| 17 | Vermont | 2,484 | | 45 | Georgia | 1,897 |
| 24 | Virginia | 2,281 | | 46 | South Dakota | 1,826 |
| 13 | Washington | 2,608 | | 47 | Arizona | 1,818 |
| 26 | West Virginia | 2,268 | | 48 | Texas | 1,697 |
| 10 | Wisconsin | 2,753 | | 49 | New Hampshire | 1,640 |
| 6 | Wyoming | 3,120 | | 50 | Tennessee | 1,624 |
| | | | | | District of Columbia** | NA |

Source: Morgan Quitno Press using data from U.S. Bureau of the Census, Governments Division
    "1998 State Government Finance Data" (http://www.census.gov/govs/www/state98.html)
*Own source revenue includes taxes, current charges and miscellaneous general revenue. Excluded are
intergovernmental transfers, insurance trust revenue and revenue from government owned utilities and other
commercial or auxiliary enterprise.
**Not applicable.

# State Government Tax Revenue in 1999

## National Total = 499,510,046,000

| RANK | STATE | STATE TAXES | % of USA |
|---|---|---|---|
| 24 | Alabama | $6,032,234,000 | 1.2% |
| 48 | Alaska | 905,135,000 | 0.2% |
| 21 | Arizona | 7,542,735,000 | 1.5% |
| 31 | Arkansas | 4,608,936,000 | 0.9% |
| 1 | California | 72,387,698,000 | 14.5% |
| 26 | Colorado | 5,987,125,000 | 1.2% |
| 18 | Connecticut | 9,623,591,000 | 1.9% |
| 42 | Delaware | 2,030,789,000 | 0.4% |
| 4 | Florida | 23,791,570,000 | 4.8% |
| 13 | Georgia | 12,461,790,000 | 2.5% |
| 37 | Hawaii | 3,166,663,000 | 0.6% |
| 41 | Idaho | 2,171,127,000 | 0.4% |
| 7 | Illinois | 21,211,263,000 | 4.2% |
| 17 | Indiana | 9,736,077,000 | 1.9% |
| 30 | Iowa | 4,868,494,000 | 1.0% |
| 32 | Kansas | 4,589,475,000 | 0.9% |
| 22 | Kentucky | 7,355,861,000 | 1.5% |
| 25 | Louisiana | 6,029,883,000 | 1.2% |
| 40 | Maine | 2,540,581,000 | 0.5% |
| 19 | Maryland | 9,479,949,000 | 1.9% |
| 10 | Massachusetts | 14,731,769,000 | 2.9% |
| 5 | Michigan | 23,334,348,000 | 4.7% |
| 12 | Minnesota | 12,481,688,000 | 2.5% |
| 33 | Mississippi | 4,573,825,000 | 0.9% |
| 20 | Missouri | 8,563,594,000 | 1.7% |
| 44 | Montana | 1,365,304,000 | 0.3% |
| 39 | Nebraska | 2,662,103,000 | 0.5% |
| 36 | Nevada | 3,430,007,000 | 0.7% |
| 46 | New Hampshire | 1,070,803,000 | 0.2% |
| 9 | New Jersey | 16,926,421,000 | 3.4% |
| 35 | New Mexico | 3,484,206,000 | 0.7% |
| 2 | New York | 38,700,773,000 | 7.7% |
| 11 | North Carolina | 14,436,294,000 | 2.9% |
| 45 | North Dakota | 1,106,499,000 | 0.2% |
| 8 | Ohio | 18,175,451,000 | 3.6% |
| 28 | Oklahoma | 5,417,232,000 | 1.1% |
| 29 | Oregon | 5,341,403,000 | 1.1% |
| 6 | Pennsylvania | 21,588,754,000 | 4.3% |
| 43 | Rhode Island | 1,895,196,000 | 0.4% |
| 27 | South Carolina | 5,823,476,000 | 1.2% |
| 49 | South Dakota | 868,211,000 | 0.2% |
| 23 | Tennessee | 7,191,307,000 | 1.4% |
| 3 | Texas | 25,675,587,000 | 5.1% |
| 34 | Utah | 3,644,467,000 | 0.7% |
| 47 | Vermont | 1,011,616,000 | 0.2% |
| 16 | Virginia | 11,562,735,000 | 2.3% |
| 14 | Washington | 12,337,555,000 | 2.5% |
| 38 | West Virginia | 3,148,108,000 | 0.6% |
| 15 | Wisconsin | 11,627,782,000 | 2.3% |
| 50 | Wyoming | 812,556,000 | 0.2% |

| RANK | STATE | STATE TAXES | % of USA |
|---|---|---|---|
| 1 | California | $72,387,698,000 | 14.5% |
| 2 | New York | 38,700,773,000 | 7.7% |
| 3 | Texas | 25,675,587,000 | 5.1% |
| 4 | Florida | 23,791,570,000 | 4.8% |
| 5 | Michigan | 23,334,348,000 | 4.7% |
| 6 | Pennsylvania | 21,588,754,000 | 4.3% |
| 7 | Illinois | 21,211,263,000 | 4.2% |
| 8 | Ohio | 18,175,451,000 | 3.6% |
| 9 | New Jersey | 16,926,421,000 | 3.4% |
| 10 | Massachusetts | 14,731,769,000 | 2.9% |
| 11 | North Carolina | 14,436,294,000 | 2.9% |
| 12 | Minnesota | 12,481,688,000 | 2.5% |
| 13 | Georgia | 12,461,790,000 | 2.5% |
| 14 | Washington | 12,337,555,000 | 2.5% |
| 15 | Wisconsin | 11,627,782,000 | 2.3% |
| 16 | Virginia | 11,562,735,000 | 2.3% |
| 17 | Indiana | 9,736,077,000 | 1.9% |
| 18 | Connecticut | 9,623,591,000 | 1.9% |
| 19 | Maryland | 9,479,949,000 | 1.9% |
| 20 | Missouri | 8,563,594,000 | 1.7% |
| 21 | Arizona | 7,542,735,000 | 1.5% |
| 22 | Kentucky | 7,355,861,000 | 1.5% |
| 23 | Tennessee | 7,191,307,000 | 1.4% |
| 24 | Alabama | 6,032,234,000 | 1.2% |
| 25 | Louisiana | 6,029,883,000 | 1.2% |
| 26 | Colorado | 5,987,125,000 | 1.2% |
| 27 | South Carolina | 5,823,476,000 | 1.2% |
| 28 | Oklahoma | 5,417,232,000 | 1.1% |
| 29 | Oregon | 5,341,403,000 | 1.1% |
| 30 | Iowa | 4,868,494,000 | 1.0% |
| 31 | Arkansas | 4,608,936,000 | 0.9% |
| 32 | Kansas | 4,589,475,000 | 0.9% |
| 33 | Mississippi | 4,573,825,000 | 0.9% |
| 34 | Utah | 3,644,467,000 | 0.7% |
| 35 | New Mexico | 3,484,206,000 | 0.7% |
| 36 | Nevada | 3,430,007,000 | 0.7% |
| 37 | Hawaii | 3,166,663,000 | 0.6% |
| 38 | West Virginia | 3,148,108,000 | 0.6% |
| 39 | Nebraska | 2,662,103,000 | 0.5% |
| 40 | Maine | 2,540,581,000 | 0.5% |
| 41 | Idaho | 2,171,127,000 | 0.4% |
| 42 | Delaware | 2,030,789,000 | 0.4% |
| 43 | Rhode Island | 1,895,196,000 | 0.4% |
| 44 | Montana | 1,365,304,000 | 0.3% |
| 45 | North Dakota | 1,106,499,000 | 0.2% |
| 46 | New Hampshire | 1,070,803,000 | 0.2% |
| 47 | Vermont | 1,011,616,000 | 0.2% |
| 48 | Alaska | 905,135,000 | 0.2% |
| 49 | South Dakota | 868,211,000 | 0.2% |
| 50 | Wyoming | 812,556,000 | 0.2% |
| | District of Columbia* | NA | NA |

Source: U.S. Bureau of the Census, Governments Division
   "1999 State Government Tax Collections" (http://www.census.gov/govs/www/statetax99.html)
*Not applicable.

# Per Capita State Government Tax Revenue in 1999

## National Per Capita = $1,835

ALPHA ORDER

| RANK | STATE | PER CAPITA |
|---|---|---|
| 45 | Alabama | $1,380 |
| 44 | Alaska | 1,461 |
| 38 | Arizona | 1,579 |
| 19 | Arkansas | 1,806 |
| 8 | California | 2,184 |
| 43 | Colorado | 1,476 |
| 1 | Connecticut | 2,932 |
| 2 | Delaware | 2,695 |
| 39 | Florida | 1,574 |
| 36 | Georgia | 1,600 |
| 3 | Hawaii | 2,671 |
| 24 | Idaho | 1,735 |
| 21 | Illinois | 1,749 |
| 32 | Indiana | 1,638 |
| 28 | Iowa | 1,697 |
| 25 | Kansas | 1,729 |
| 17 | Kentucky | 1,857 |
| 46 | Louisiana | 1,379 |
| 12 | Maine | 2,028 |
| 18 | Maryland | 1,833 |
| 5 | Massachusetts | 2,386 |
| 6 | Michigan | 2,366 |
| 4 | Minnesota | 2,614 |
| 31 | Mississippi | 1,652 |
| 40 | Missouri | 1,566 |
| 41 | Montana | 1,547 |
| 37 | Nebraska | 1,598 |
| 15 | Nevada | 1,896 |
| 50 | New Hampshire | 891 |
| 11 | New Jersey | 2,079 |
| 13 | New Mexico | 2,003 |
| 10 | New York | 2,127 |
| 16 | North Carolina | 1,887 |
| 22 | North Dakota | 1,746 |
| 33 | Ohio | 1,615 |
| 34 | Oklahoma | 1,613 |
| 35 | Oregon | 1,611 |
| 20 | Pennsylvania | 1,800 |
| 14 | Rhode Island | 1,913 |
| 42 | South Carolina | 1,499 |
| 49 | South Dakota | 1,184 |
| 47 | Tennessee | 1,311 |
| 48 | Texas | 1,281 |
| 26 | Utah | 1,711 |
| 27 | Vermont | 1,704 |
| 30 | Virginia | 1,682 |
| 9 | Washington | 2,143 |
| 23 | West Virginia | 1,742 |
| 7 | Wisconsin | 2,215 |
| 29 | Wyoming | 1,694 |

RANK ORDER

| RANK | STATE | PER CAPITA |
|---|---|---|
| 1 | Connecticut | $2,932 |
| 2 | Delaware | 2,695 |
| 3 | Hawaii | 2,671 |
| 4 | Minnesota | 2,614 |
| 5 | Massachusetts | 2,386 |
| 6 | Michigan | 2,366 |
| 7 | Wisconsin | 2,215 |
| 8 | California | 2,184 |
| 9 | Washington | 2,143 |
| 10 | New York | 2,127 |
| 11 | New Jersey | 2,079 |
| 12 | Maine | 2,028 |
| 13 | New Mexico | 2,003 |
| 14 | Rhode Island | 1,913 |
| 15 | Nevada | 1,896 |
| 16 | North Carolina | 1,887 |
| 17 | Kentucky | 1,857 |
| 18 | Maryland | 1,833 |
| 19 | Arkansas | 1,806 |
| 20 | Pennsylvania | 1,800 |
| 21 | Illinois | 1,749 |
| 22 | North Dakota | 1,746 |
| 23 | West Virginia | 1,742 |
| 24 | Idaho | 1,735 |
| 25 | Kansas | 1,729 |
| 26 | Utah | 1,711 |
| 27 | Vermont | 1,704 |
| 28 | Iowa | 1,697 |
| 29 | Wyoming | 1,694 |
| 30 | Virginia | 1,682 |
| 31 | Mississippi | 1,652 |
| 32 | Indiana | 1,638 |
| 33 | Ohio | 1,615 |
| 34 | Oklahoma | 1,613 |
| 35 | Oregon | 1,611 |
| 36 | Georgia | 1,600 |
| 37 | Nebraska | 1,598 |
| 38 | Arizona | 1,579 |
| 39 | Florida | 1,574 |
| 40 | Missouri | 1,566 |
| 41 | Montana | 1,547 |
| 42 | South Carolina | 1,499 |
| 43 | Colorado | 1,476 |
| 44 | Alaska | 1,461 |
| 45 | Alabama | 1,380 |
| 46 | Louisiana | 1,379 |
| 47 | Tennessee | 1,311 |
| 48 | Texas | 1,281 |
| 49 | South Dakota | 1,184 |
| 50 | New Hampshire | 891 |

District of Columbia*    NA

Source: Morgan Quitno Press using data from U.S. Bureau of the Census, Governments Division
"1999 State Government Tax Collections" (http://www.census.gov/govs/www/statetax99.html)
*Not applicable.

# State Government Tax Revenue as a Percent of Personal Income in 1999

## National Percent = 6.4% of Personal Income*

ALPHA ORDER

| RANK | STATE | PERCENT |
|------|-------|---------|
| 33 | Alabama | 6.0 |
| 45 | Alaska | 5.1 |
| 28 | Arizona | 6.3 |
| 8 | Arkansas | 8.1 |
| 15 | California | 7.3 |
| 48 | Colorado | 4.7 |
| 13 | Connecticut | 7.5 |
| 3 | Delaware | 8.8 |
| 41 | Florida | 5.7 |
| 36 | Georgia | 5.9 |
| 1 | Hawaii | 9.7 |
| 12 | Idaho | 7.6 |
| 42 | Illinois | 5.6 |
| 28 | Indiana | 6.3 |
| 22 | Iowa | 6.6 |
| 25 | Kansas | 6.4 |
| 10 | Kentucky | 8.0 |
| 33 | Louisiana | 6.0 |
| 7 | Maine | 8.2 |
| 42 | Maryland | 5.6 |
| 21 | Massachusetts | 6.7 |
| 5 | Michigan | 8.4 |
| 4 | Minnesota | 8.5 |
| 10 | Mississippi | 8.0 |
| 36 | Missouri | 5.9 |
| 19 | Montana | 7.0 |
| 36 | Nebraska | 5.9 |
| 32 | Nevada | 6.1 |
| 50 | New Hampshire | 2.9 |
| 40 | New Jersey | 5.8 |
| 2 | New Mexico | 9.2 |
| 28 | New York | 6.3 |
| 15 | North Carolina | 7.3 |
| 13 | North Dakota | 7.5 |
| 36 | Ohio | 5.9 |
| 19 | Oklahoma | 7.0 |
| 33 | Oregon | 6.0 |
| 28 | Pennsylvania | 6.3 |
| 24 | Rhode Island | 6.5 |
| 25 | South Carolina | 6.4 |
| 48 | South Dakota | 4.7 |
| 45 | Tennessee | 5.1 |
| 47 | Texas | 4.8 |
| 15 | Utah | 7.3 |
| 22 | Vermont | 6.6 |
| 42 | Virginia | 5.6 |
| 18 | Washington | 7.1 |
| 6 | West Virginia | 8.3 |
| 8 | Wisconsin | 8.1 |
| 25 | Wyoming | 6.4 |

RANK ORDER

| RANK | STATE | PERCENT |
|------|-------|---------|
| 1 | Hawaii | 9.7 |
| 2 | New Mexico | 9.2 |
| 3 | Delaware | 8.8 |
| 4 | Minnesota | 8.5 |
| 5 | Michigan | 8.4 |
| 6 | West Virginia | 8.3 |
| 7 | Maine | 8.2 |
| 8 | Arkansas | 8.1 |
| 8 | Wisconsin | 8.1 |
| 10 | Kentucky | 8.0 |
| 10 | Mississippi | 8.0 |
| 12 | Idaho | 7.6 |
| 13 | Connecticut | 7.5 |
| 13 | North Dakota | 7.5 |
| 15 | California | 7.3 |
| 15 | North Carolina | 7.3 |
| 15 | Utah | 7.3 |
| 18 | Washington | 7.1 |
| 19 | Montana | 7.0 |
| 19 | Oklahoma | 7.0 |
| 21 | Massachusetts | 6.7 |
| 22 | Iowa | 6.6 |
| 22 | Vermont | 6.6 |
| 24 | Rhode Island | 6.5 |
| 25 | Kansas | 6.4 |
| 25 | South Carolina | 6.4 |
| 25 | Wyoming | 6.4 |
| 28 | Arizona | 6.3 |
| 28 | Indiana | 6.3 |
| 28 | New York | 6.3 |
| 28 | Pennsylvania | 6.3 |
| 32 | Nevada | 6.1 |
| 33 | Alabama | 6.0 |
| 33 | Louisiana | 6.0 |
| 33 | Oregon | 6.0 |
| 36 | Georgia | 5.9 |
| 36 | Missouri | 5.9 |
| 36 | Nebraska | 5.9 |
| 36 | Ohio | 5.9 |
| 40 | New Jersey | 5.8 |
| 41 | Florida | 5.7 |
| 42 | Illinois | 5.6 |
| 42 | Maryland | 5.6 |
| 42 | Virginia | 5.6 |
| 45 | Alaska | 5.1 |
| 45 | Tennessee | 5.1 |
| 47 | Texas | 4.8 |
| 48 | Colorado | 4.7 |
| 48 | South Dakota | 4.7 |
| 50 | New Hampshire | 2.9 |

District of Columbia**     NA

Source: Morgan Quitno Press using data from U.S. Bureau of the Census, Governments Division
"1999 State Government Tax Collections" (http://www.census.gov/govs/www/statetax99.html)
U.S. Department of Commerce, Bureau of Economic Analysis
"1999 State Per Capita Personal Income" (http://www.bea.doc.gov/bea/newsrel/spi0900.htm)
*Not applicable.  National figure does not include personal income or taxes from the District of Columbia.

# State Government Individual Income Tax Revenue in 1999

## National Total = $172,341,998,000

ALPHA ORDER

| RANK | STATE | INCOME TAX | % of USA |
|------|-------|-----------|----------|
| 24 | Alabama | $1,907,459,000 | 1.1% |
| 44 | Alaska | 0 | 0.0% |
| 21 | Arizona | 2,098,350,000 | 1.2% |
| 29 | Arkansas | 1,433,852,000 | 0.8% |
| 1 | California | 30,732,356,000 | 17.8% |
| 19 | Colorado | 2,807,793,000 | 1.6% |
| 18 | Connecticut | 3,609,595,000 | 2.1% |
| 37 | Delaware | 770,903,000 | 0.4% |
| 44 | Florida | 0 | 0.0% |
| 11 | Georgia | 5,696,757,000 | 3.3% |
| 31 | Hawaii | 1,068,974,000 | 0.6% |
| 35 | Idaho | 847,021,000 | 0.5% |
| 5 | Illinois | 7,247,472,000 | 4.2% |
| 16 | Indiana | 3,699,316,000 | 2.1% |
| 25 | Iowa | 1,715,117,000 | 1.0% |
| 26 | Kansas | 1,696,275,000 | 1.0% |
| 20 | Kentucky | 2,532,005,000 | 1.5% |
| 27 | Louisiana | 1,535,646,000 | 0.9% |
| 32 | Maine | 1,020,009,000 | 0.6% |
| 14 | Maryland | 4,178,461,000 | 2.4% |
| 3 | Massachusetts | 8,036,585,000 | 4.7% |
| 4 | Michigan | 7,394,033,000 | 4.3% |
| 12 | Minnesota | 5,306,235,000 | 3.1% |
| 33 | Mississippi | 983,045,000 | 0.6% |
| 17 | Missouri | 3,627,422,000 | 2.1% |
| 39 | Montana | 483,032,000 | 0.3% |
| 30 | Nebraska | 1,071,876,000 | 0.6% |
| 44 | Nevada | 0 | 0.0% |
| 43 | New Hampshire | 63,134,000 | 0.0% |
| 9 | New Jersey | 6,323,893,000 | 3.7% |
| 36 | New Mexico | 809,569,000 | 0.5% |
| 2 | New York | 20,576,068,000 | 11.9% |
| 7 | North Carolina | 6,586,153,000 | 3.8% |
| 41 | North Dakota | 181,973,000 | 0.1% |
| 6 | Ohio | 7,191,864,000 | 4.2% |
| 22 | Oklahoma | 2,070,452,000 | 1.2% |
| 15 | Oregon | 3,709,592,000 | 2.2% |
| 8 | Pennsylvania | 6,410,363,000 | 3.7% |
| 38 | Rhode Island | 762,784,000 | 0.4% |
| 23 | South Carolina | 1,986,164,000 | 1.2% |
| 44 | South Dakota | 0 | 0.0% |
| 42 | Tennessee | 155,670,000 | 0.1% |
| 44 | Texas | 0 | 0.0% |
| 28 | Utah | 1,461,299,000 | 0.8% |
| 40 | Vermont | 383,451,000 | 0.2% |
| 10 | Virginia | 6,087,862,000 | 3.5% |
| 44 | Washington | 0 | 0.0% |
| 34 | West Virginia | 919,879,000 | 0.5% |
| 13 | Wisconsin | 5,162,239,000 | 3.0% |
| 44 | Wyoming | 0 | 0.0% |

RANK ORDER

| RANK | STATE | INCOME TAX | % of USA |
|------|-------|-----------|----------|
| 1 | California | $30,732,356,000 | 17.8% |
| 2 | New York | 20,576,068,000 | 11.9% |
| 3 | Massachusetts | 8,036,585,000 | 4.7% |
| 4 | Michigan | 7,394,033,000 | 4.3% |
| 5 | Illinois | 7,247,472,000 | 4.2% |
| 6 | Ohio | 7,191,864,000 | 4.2% |
| 7 | North Carolina | 6,586,153,000 | 3.8% |
| 8 | Pennsylvania | 6,410,363,000 | 3.7% |
| 9 | New Jersey | 6,323,893,000 | 3.7% |
| 10 | Virginia | 6,087,862,000 | 3.5% |
| 11 | Georgia | 5,696,757,000 | 3.3% |
| 12 | Minnesota | 5,306,235,000 | 3.1% |
| 13 | Wisconsin | 5,162,239,000 | 3.0% |
| 14 | Maryland | 4,178,461,000 | 2.4% |
| 15 | Oregon | 3,709,592,000 | 2.2% |
| 16 | Indiana | 3,699,316,000 | 2.1% |
| 17 | Missouri | 3,627,422,000 | 2.1% |
| 18 | Connecticut | 3,609,595,000 | 2.1% |
| 19 | Colorado | 2,807,793,000 | 1.6% |
| 20 | Kentucky | 2,532,005,000 | 1.5% |
| 21 | Arizona | 2,098,350,000 | 1.2% |
| 22 | Oklahoma | 2,070,452,000 | 1.2% |
| 23 | South Carolina | 1,986,164,000 | 1.2% |
| 24 | Alabama | 1,907,459,000 | 1.1% |
| 25 | Iowa | 1,715,117,000 | 1.0% |
| 26 | Kansas | 1,696,275,000 | 1.0% |
| 27 | Louisiana | 1,535,646,000 | 0.9% |
| 28 | Utah | 1,461,299,000 | 0.8% |
| 29 | Arkansas | 1,433,852,000 | 0.8% |
| 30 | Nebraska | 1,071,876,000 | 0.6% |
| 31 | Hawaii | 1,068,974,000 | 0.6% |
| 32 | Maine | 1,020,009,000 | 0.6% |
| 33 | Mississippi | 983,045,000 | 0.6% |
| 34 | West Virginia | 919,879,000 | 0.5% |
| 35 | Idaho | 847,021,000 | 0.5% |
| 36 | New Mexico | 809,569,000 | 0.5% |
| 37 | Delaware | 770,903,000 | 0.4% |
| 38 | Rhode Island | 762,784,000 | 0.4% |
| 39 | Montana | 483,032,000 | 0.3% |
| 40 | Vermont | 383,451,000 | 0.2% |
| 41 | North Dakota | 181,973,000 | 0.1% |
| 42 | Tennessee | 155,670,000 | 0.1% |
| 43 | New Hampshire | 63,134,000 | 0.0% |
| 44 | Alaska | 0 | 0.0% |
| 44 | Florida | 0 | 0.0% |
| 44 | Nevada | 0 | 0.0% |
| 44 | South Dakota | 0 | 0.0% |
| 44 | Texas | 0 | 0.0% |
| 44 | Washington | 0 | 0.0% |
| 44 | Wyoming | 0 | 0.0% |
| | District of Columbia* | NA | NA |

Source: U.S. Bureau of the Census, Governments Division
    "1999 State Government Tax Collections" (http://www.census.gov/govs/www/statetax99.html)
*Not applicable.

# Per Capita State Government Individual Income Tax Revenue in 1999

## National Per Capita = $633

ALPHA ORDER

| RANK | STATE | PER CAPITA |
|---|---|---|
| 38 | Alabama | $437 |
| 44 | Alaska | 0 |
| 37 | Arizona | 439 |
| 31 | Arkansas | 562 |
| 8 | California | 927 |
| 18 | Colorado | 692 |
| 5 | Connecticut | 1,100 |
| 6 | Delaware | 1,023 |
| 44 | Florida | 0 |
| 17 | Georgia | 731 |
| 9 | Hawaii | 902 |
| 20 | Idaho | 677 |
| 29 | Illinois | 598 |
| 27 | Indiana | 622 |
| 29 | Iowa | 598 |
| 24 | Kansas | 639 |
| 24 | Kentucky | 639 |
| 40 | Louisiana | 351 |
| 12 | Maine | 814 |
| 13 | Maryland | 808 |
| 1 | Massachusetts | 1,301 |
| 16 | Michigan | 750 |
| 4 | Minnesota | 1,111 |
| 39 | Mississippi | 355 |
| 21 | Missouri | 663 |
| 32 | Montana | 547 |
| 23 | Nebraska | 643 |
| 44 | Nevada | 0 |
| 42 | New Hampshire | 53 |
| 14 | New Jersey | 777 |
| 36 | New Mexico | 465 |
| 2 | New York | 1,131 |
| 11 | North Carolina | 861 |
| 41 | North Dakota | 287 |
| 24 | Ohio | 639 |
| 28 | Oklahoma | 617 |
| 3 | Oregon | 1,119 |
| 33 | Pennsylvania | 534 |
| 15 | Rhode Island | 770 |
| 34 | South Carolina | 511 |
| 44 | South Dakota | 0 |
| 43 | Tennessee | 28 |
| 44 | Texas | 0 |
| 19 | Utah | 686 |
| 22 | Vermont | 646 |
| 10 | Virginia | 886 |
| 44 | Washington | 0 |
| 35 | West Virginia | 509 |
| 7 | Wisconsin | 983 |
| 44 | Wyoming | 0 |

RANK ORDER

| RANK | STATE | PER CAPITA |
|---|---|---|
| 1 | Massachusetts | $1,301 |
| 2 | New York | 1,131 |
| 3 | Oregon | 1,119 |
| 4 | Minnesota | 1,111 |
| 5 | Connecticut | 1,100 |
| 6 | Delaware | 1,023 |
| 7 | Wisconsin | 983 |
| 8 | California | 927 |
| 9 | Hawaii | 902 |
| 10 | Virginia | 886 |
| 11 | North Carolina | 861 |
| 12 | Maine | 814 |
| 13 | Maryland | 808 |
| 14 | New Jersey | 777 |
| 15 | Rhode Island | 770 |
| 16 | Michigan | 750 |
| 17 | Georgia | 731 |
| 18 | Colorado | 692 |
| 19 | Utah | 686 |
| 20 | Idaho | 677 |
| 21 | Missouri | 663 |
| 22 | Vermont | 646 |
| 23 | Nebraska | 643 |
| 24 | Kansas | 639 |
| 24 | Kentucky | 639 |
| 24 | Ohio | 639 |
| 27 | Indiana | 622 |
| 28 | Oklahoma | 617 |
| 29 | Illinois | 598 |
| 29 | Iowa | 598 |
| 31 | Arkansas | 562 |
| 32 | Montana | 547 |
| 33 | Pennsylvania | 534 |
| 34 | South Carolina | 511 |
| 35 | West Virginia | 509 |
| 36 | New Mexico | 465 |
| 37 | Arizona | 439 |
| 38 | Alabama | 437 |
| 39 | Mississippi | 355 |
| 40 | Louisiana | 351 |
| 41 | North Dakota | 287 |
| 42 | New Hampshire | 53 |
| 43 | Tennessee | 28 |
| 44 | Alaska | 0 |
| 44 | Florida | 0 |
| 44 | Nevada | 0 |
| 44 | South Dakota | 0 |
| 44 | Texas | 0 |
| 44 | Washington | 0 |
| 44 | Wyoming | 0 |
| | District of Columbia* | NA |

*Source: Morgan Quitno Press using data from U.S. Bureau of the Census, Governments Division*
*"1999 State Government Tax Collections" (http://www.census.gov/govs/www/statetax99.html)*
*Not applicable.*

# State Government Corporation Net Income Tax Revenue in 1999

## National Total = $30,692,483,000

ALPHA ORDER

| RANK | STATE | REVENUE | % of USA |
|------|-------|---------|----------|
| 29 | Alabama | $233,024,000 | 0.8% |
| 34 | Alaska | 211,811,000 | 0.7% |
| 16 | Arizona | 545,388,000 | 1.8% |
| 33 | Arkansas | 212,206,000 | 0.7% |
| 1 | California | 5,459,199,000 | 17.8% |
| 22 | Colorado | 301,043,000 | 1.0% |
| 17 | Connecticut | 474,512,000 | 1.5% |
| 30 | Delaware | 232,528,000 | 0.8% |
| 7 | Florida | 1,266,959,000 | 4.1% |
| 11 | Georgia | 793,173,000 | 2.6% |
| 44 | Hawaii | 52,414,000 | 0.2% |
| 40 | Idaho | 96,146,000 | 0.3% |
| 4 | Illinois | 2,103,927,000 | 6.9% |
| 9 | Indiana | 989,627,000 | 3.2% |
| 28 | Iowa | 234,540,000 | 0.8% |
| 27 | Kansas | 253,840,000 | 0.8% |
| 21 | Kentucky | 312,067,000 | 1.0% |
| 23 | Louisiana | 286,323,000 | 0.9% |
| 38 | Maine | 147,489,000 | 0.5% |
| 19 | Maryland | 404,967,000 | 1.3% |
| 8 | Massachusetts | 1,249,673,000 | 4.1% |
| 3 | Michigan | 2,366,137,000 | 7.7% |
| 12 | Minnesota | 779,176,000 | 2.5% |
| 32 | Mississippi | 229,501,000 | 0.7% |
| 24 | Missouri | 276,523,000 | 0.9% |
| 42 | Montana | 89,624,000 | 0.3% |
| 39 | Nebraska | 135,034,000 | 0.4% |
| 47 | Nevada | 0 | 0.0% |
| 26 | New Hampshire | 255,818,000 | 0.8% |
| 6 | New Jersey | 1,333,958,000 | 4.3% |
| 37 | New Mexico | 163,964,000 | 0.5% |
| 2 | New York | 2,888,041,000 | 9.4% |
| 10 | North Carolina | 920,583,000 | 3.0% |
| 41 | North Dakota | 93,595,000 | 0.3% |
| 13 | Ohio | 751,567,000 | 2.4% |
| 35 | Oklahoma | 187,308,000 | 0.6% |
| 20 | Oregon | 324,386,000 | 1.1% |
| 5 | Pennsylvania | 1,537,722,000 | 5.0% |
| 43 | Rhode Island | 66,318,000 | 0.2% |
| 31 | South Carolina | 231,821,000 | 0.8% |
| 45 | South Dakota | 50,819,000 | 0.2% |
| 15 | Tennessee | 571,428,000 | 1.9% |
| 47 | Texas | 0 | 0.0% |
| 36 | Utah | 180,141,000 | 0.6% |
| 46 | Vermont | 49,696,000 | 0.2% |
| 18 | Virginia | 414,388,000 | 1.4% |
| 47 | Washington | 0 | 0.0% |
| 25 | West Virginia | 263,121,000 | 0.9% |
| 14 | Wisconsin | 670,958,000 | 2.2% |
| 47 | Wyoming | 0 | 0.0% |

RANK ORDER

| RANK | STATE | REVENUE | % of USA |
|------|-------|---------|----------|
| 1 | California | $5,459,199,000 | 17.8% |
| 2 | New York | 2,888,041,000 | 9.4% |
| 3 | Michigan | 2,366,137,000 | 7.7% |
| 4 | Illinois | 2,103,927,000 | 6.9% |
| 5 | Pennsylvania | 1,537,722,000 | 5.0% |
| 6 | New Jersey | 1,333,958,000 | 4.3% |
| 7 | Florida | 1,266,959,000 | 4.1% |
| 8 | Massachusetts | 1,249,673,000 | 4.1% |
| 9 | Indiana | 989,627,000 | 3.2% |
| 10 | North Carolina | 920,583,000 | 3.0% |
| 11 | Georgia | 793,173,000 | 2.6% |
| 12 | Minnesota | 779,176,000 | 2.5% |
| 13 | Ohio | 751,567,000 | 2.4% |
| 14 | Wisconsin | 670,958,000 | 2.2% |
| 15 | Tennessee | 571,428,000 | 1.9% |
| 16 | Arizona | 545,388,000 | 1.8% |
| 17 | Connecticut | 474,512,000 | 1.5% |
| 18 | Virginia | 414,388,000 | 1.4% |
| 19 | Maryland | 404,967,000 | 1.3% |
| 20 | Oregon | 324,386,000 | 1.1% |
| 21 | Kentucky | 312,067,000 | 1.0% |
| 22 | Colorado | 301,043,000 | 1.0% |
| 23 | Louisiana | 286,323,000 | 0.9% |
| 24 | Missouri | 276,523,000 | 0.9% |
| 25 | West Virginia | 263,121,000 | 0.9% |
| 26 | New Hampshire | 255,818,000 | 0.8% |
| 27 | Kansas | 253,840,000 | 0.8% |
| 28 | Iowa | 234,540,000 | 0.8% |
| 29 | Alabama | 233,024,000 | 0.8% |
| 30 | Delaware | 232,528,000 | 0.8% |
| 31 | South Carolina | 231,821,000 | 0.8% |
| 32 | Mississippi | 229,501,000 | 0.7% |
| 33 | Arkansas | 212,206,000 | 0.7% |
| 34 | Alaska | 211,811,000 | 0.7% |
| 35 | Oklahoma | 187,308,000 | 0.6% |
| 36 | Utah | 180,141,000 | 0.6% |
| 37 | New Mexico | 163,964,000 | 0.5% |
| 38 | Maine | 147,489,000 | 0.5% |
| 39 | Nebraska | 135,034,000 | 0.4% |
| 40 | Idaho | 96,146,000 | 0.3% |
| 41 | North Dakota | 93,595,000 | 0.3% |
| 42 | Montana | 89,624,000 | 0.3% |
| 43 | Rhode Island | 66,318,000 | 0.2% |
| 44 | Hawaii | 52,414,000 | 0.2% |
| 45 | South Dakota | 50,819,000 | 0.2% |
| 46 | Vermont | 49,696,000 | 0.2% |
| 47 | Nevada | 0 | 0.0% |
| 47 | Texas | 0 | 0.0% |
| 47 | Washington | 0 | 0.0% |
| 47 | Wyoming | 0 | 0.0% |
| | District of Columbia* | NA | NA |

Source: U.S. Bureau of the Census, Governments Division
   "1999 State Government Tax Collections" (http://www.census.gov/govs/www/statetax99.html)
*Not applicable.

# Per Capita State Government Corporation Net Income Tax Revenue in 1999

## National Per Capita = $113

ALPHA ORDER

| RANK | STATE | PER CAPITA |
|------|-------|-----------|
| 44 | Alabama | 53 |
| 1 | Alaska | 342 |
| 19 | Arizona | 114 |
| 29 | Arkansas | 83 |
| 8 | California | 165 |
| 36 | Colorado | 74 |
| 14 | Connecticut | 145 |
| 2 | Delaware | 309 |
| 27 | Florida | 84 |
| 21 | Georgia | 102 |
| 46 | Hawaii | 44 |
| 35 | Idaho | 77 |
| 6 | Illinois | 173 |
| 7 | Indiana | 167 |
| 31 | Iowa | 82 |
| 24 | Kansas | 96 |
| 33 | Kentucky | 79 |
| 40 | Louisiana | 65 |
| 18 | Maine | 118 |
| 34 | Maryland | 78 |
| 5 | Massachusetts | 202 |
| 3 | Michigan | 240 |
| 10 | Minnesota | 163 |
| 29 | Mississippi | 83 |
| 45 | Missouri | 51 |
| 21 | Montana | 102 |
| 32 | Nebraska | 81 |
| 47 | Nevada | 0 |
| 4 | New Hampshire | 213 |
| 9 | New Jersey | 164 |
| 25 | New Mexico | 94 |
| 11 | New York | 159 |
| 17 | North Carolina | 120 |
| 12 | North Dakota | 148 |
| 38 | Ohio | 67 |
| 43 | Oklahoma | 56 |
| 23 | Oregon | 98 |
| 15 | Pennsylvania | 128 |
| 38 | Rhode Island | 67 |
| 41 | South Carolina | 60 |
| 37 | South Dakota | 69 |
| 20 | Tennessee | 104 |
| 47 | Texas | 0 |
| 26 | Utah | 85 |
| 27 | Vermont | 84 |
| 41 | Virginia | 60 |
| 47 | Washington | 0 |
| 13 | West Virginia | 146 |
| 15 | Wisconsin | 128 |
| 47 | Wyoming | 0 |

RANK ORDER

| RANK | STATE | PER CAPITA |
|------|-------|-----------|
| 1 | Alaska | 342 |
| 2 | Delaware | 309 |
| 3 | Michigan | 240 |
| 4 | New Hampshire | 213 |
| 5 | Massachusetts | 202 |
| 6 | Illinois | 173 |
| 7 | Indiana | 167 |
| 8 | California | 165 |
| 9 | New Jersey | 164 |
| 10 | Minnesota | 163 |
| 11 | New York | 159 |
| 12 | North Dakota | 148 |
| 13 | West Virginia | 146 |
| 14 | Connecticut | 145 |
| 15 | Pennsylvania | 128 |
| 15 | Wisconsin | 128 |
| 17 | North Carolina | 120 |
| 18 | Maine | 118 |
| 19 | Arizona | 114 |
| 20 | Tennessee | 104 |
| 21 | Georgia | 102 |
| 21 | Montana | 102 |
| 23 | Oregon | 98 |
| 24 | Kansas | 96 |
| 25 | New Mexico | 94 |
| 26 | Utah | 85 |
| 27 | Florida | 84 |
| 27 | Vermont | 84 |
| 29 | Arkansas | 83 |
| 29 | Mississippi | 83 |
| 31 | Iowa | 82 |
| 32 | Nebraska | 81 |
| 33 | Kentucky | 79 |
| 34 | Maryland | 78 |
| 35 | Idaho | 77 |
| 36 | Colorado | 74 |
| 37 | South Dakota | 69 |
| 38 | Ohio | 67 |
| 38 | Rhode Island | 67 |
| 40 | Louisiana | 65 |
| 41 | South Carolina | 60 |
| 41 | Virginia | 60 |
| 43 | Oklahoma | 56 |
| 44 | Alabama | 53 |
| 45 | Missouri | 51 |
| 46 | Hawaii | 44 |
| 47 | Nevada | 0 |
| 47 | Texas | 0 |
| 47 | Washington | 0 |
| 47 | Wyoming | 0 |
| | District of Columbia* | NA |

*Source: Morgan Quitno Press using data from U.S. Bureau of the Census, Governments Division*
   *"1999 State Government Tax Collections" (http://www.census.gov/govs/www/statetax99.html)*
*Not applicable.*

# State Government General Sales Tax Revenue in 1999

## National Total = $165,717,430,000*

ALPHA ORDER

| RANK | STATE | SALES TAX | % of USA |
|------|-------|-----------|----------|
| 30 | Alabama | $1,649,120,000 | 1.0% |
| 46 | Alaska | 0 | 0.0% |
| 15 | Arizona | 3,309,921,000 | 2.0% |
| 32 | Arkansas | 1,602,491,000 | 1.0% |
| 1 | California | 22,684,257,000 | 13.7% |
| 28 | Colorado | 1,703,608,000 | 1.0% |
| 19 | Connecticut | 3,218,062,000 | 1.9% |
| 46 | Delaware | 0 | 0.0% |
| 2 | Florida | 13,881,122,000 | 8.4% |
| 11 | Georgia | 4,348,817,000 | 2.6% |
| 34 | Hawaii | 1,447,278,000 | 0.9% |
| 40 | Idaho | 701,657,000 | 0.4% |
| 8 | Illinois | 5,948,973,000 | 3.6% |
| 16 | Indiana | 3,308,186,000 | 2.0% |
| 31 | Iowa | 1,646,052,000 | 1.0% |
| 29 | Kansas | 1,686,570,000 | 1.0% |
| 26 | Kentucky | 2,085,900,000 | 1.3% |
| 24 | Louisiana | 2,266,867,000 | 1.4% |
| 39 | Maine | 828,635,000 | 0.5% |
| 23 | Maryland | 2,299,610,000 | 1.4% |
| 17 | Massachusetts | 3,269,827,000 | 2.0% |
| 4 | Michigan | 8,304,882,000 | 5.0% |
| 13 | Minnesota | 3,404,441,000 | 2.1% |
| 25 | Mississippi | 2,230,309,000 | 1.3% |
| 20 | Missouri | 2,716,070,000 | 1.6% |
| 46 | Montana | 0 | 0.0% |
| 38 | Nebraska | 855,409,000 | 0.5% |
| 27 | Nevada | 1,829,874,000 | 1.1% |
| 46 | New Hampshire | 0 | 0.0% |
| 10 | New Jersey | 5,054,438,000 | 3.1% |
| 33 | New Mexico | 1,452,283,000 | 0.9% |
| 5 | New York | 7,970,189,000 | 4.8% |
| 14 | North Carolina | 3,342,157,000 | 2.0% |
| 44 | North Dakota | 332,814,000 | 0.2% |
| 9 | Ohio | 5,872,943,000 | 3.5% |
| 36 | Oklahoma | 1,375,881,000 | 0.8% |
| 46 | Oregon | 0 | 0.0% |
| 7 | Pennsylvania | 6,659,123,000 | 4.0% |
| 41 | Rhode Island | 561,193,000 | 0.3% |
| 22 | South Carolina | 2,347,155,000 | 1.4% |
| 42 | South Dakota | 461,660,000 | 0.3% |
| 12 | Tennessee | 4,216,278,000 | 2.5% |
| 3 | Texas | 13,104,114,000 | 7.9% |
| 35 | Utah | 1,376,209,000 | 0.8% |
| 45 | Vermont | 205,634,000 | 0.1% |
| 21 | Virginia | 2,394,516,000 | 1.4% |
| 6 | Washington | 7,253,611,000 | 4.4% |
| 37 | West Virginia | 897,189,000 | 0.5% |
| 18 | Wisconsin | 3,264,695,000 | 2.0% |
| 43 | Wyoming | 347,410,000 | 0.2% |

RANK ORDER

| RANK | STATE | SALES TAX | % of USA |
|------|-------|-----------|----------|
| 1 | California | $22,684,257,000 | 13.7% |
| 2 | Florida | 13,881,122,000 | 8.4% |
| 3 | Texas | 13,104,114,000 | 7.9% |
| 4 | Michigan | 8,304,882,000 | 5.0% |
| 5 | New York | 7,970,189,000 | 4.8% |
| 6 | Washington | 7,253,611,000 | 4.4% |
| 7 | Pennsylvania | 6,659,123,000 | 4.0% |
| 8 | Illinois | 5,948,973,000 | 3.6% |
| 9 | Ohio | 5,872,943,000 | 3.5% |
| 10 | New Jersey | 5,054,438,000 | 3.1% |
| 11 | Georgia | 4,348,817,000 | 2.6% |
| 12 | Tennessee | 4,216,278,000 | 2.5% |
| 13 | Minnesota | 3,404,441,000 | 2.1% |
| 14 | North Carolina | 3,342,157,000 | 2.0% |
| 15 | Arizona | 3,309,921,000 | 2.0% |
| 16 | Indiana | 3,308,186,000 | 2.0% |
| 17 | Massachusetts | 3,269,827,000 | 2.0% |
| 18 | Wisconsin | 3,264,695,000 | 2.0% |
| 19 | Connecticut | 3,218,062,000 | 1.9% |
| 20 | Missouri | 2,716,070,000 | 1.6% |
| 21 | Virginia | 2,394,516,000 | 1.4% |
| 22 | South Carolina | 2,347,155,000 | 1.4% |
| 23 | Maryland | 2,299,610,000 | 1.4% |
| 24 | Louisiana | 2,266,867,000 | 1.4% |
| 25 | Mississippi | 2,230,309,000 | 1.3% |
| 26 | Kentucky | 2,085,900,000 | 1.3% |
| 27 | Nevada | 1,829,874,000 | 1.1% |
| 28 | Colorado | 1,703,608,000 | 1.0% |
| 29 | Kansas | 1,686,570,000 | 1.0% |
| 30 | Alabama | 1,649,120,000 | 1.0% |
| 31 | Iowa | 1,646,052,000 | 1.0% |
| 32 | Arkansas | 1,602,491,000 | 1.0% |
| 33 | New Mexico | 1,452,283,000 | 0.9% |
| 34 | Hawaii | 1,447,278,000 | 0.9% |
| 35 | Utah | 1,376,209,000 | 0.8% |
| 36 | Oklahoma | 1,375,881,000 | 0.8% |
| 37 | West Virginia | 897,189,000 | 0.5% |
| 38 | Nebraska | 855,409,000 | 0.5% |
| 39 | Maine | 828,635,000 | 0.5% |
| 40 | Idaho | 701,657,000 | 0.4% |
| 41 | Rhode Island | 561,193,000 | 0.3% |
| 42 | South Dakota | 461,660,000 | 0.3% |
| 43 | Wyoming | 347,410,000 | 0.2% |
| 44 | North Dakota | 332,814,000 | 0.2% |
| 45 | Vermont | 205,634,000 | 0.1% |
| 46 | Alaska | 0 | 0.0% |
| 46 | Delaware | 0 | 0.0% |
| 46 | Montana | 0 | 0.0% |
| 46 | New Hampshire | 0 | 0.0% |
| 46 | Oregon | 0 | 0.0% |
| | District of Columbia** | NA | NA |

Source: U.S. Bureau of the Census, Governments Division
   "1999 State Government Tax Collections" (http://www.census.gov/govs/www/statetax99.html)
*Does not include special sales taxes such as those on sale of alcohol, gasoline or tobacco.
**Not applicable.

# Per Capita State Government General Sales Tax Revenue in 1999

## National Per Capita = $609*

ALPHA ORDER

| RANK | STATE | PER CAPITA |
|------|-------|-----------|
| 43 | Alabama | $377 |
| 46 | Alaska | 0 |
| 12 | Arizona | 693 |
| 19 | Arkansas | 628 |
| 13 | California | 684 |
| 41 | Colorado | 420 |
| 4 | Connecticut | 981 |
| 46 | Delaware | 0 |
| 5 | Florida | 919 |
| 26 | Georgia | 558 |
| 2 | Hawaii | 1,221 |
| 25 | Idaho | 561 |
| 37 | Illinois | 491 |
| 27 | Indiana | 557 |
| 23 | Iowa | 574 |
| 17 | Kansas | 635 |
| 30 | Kentucky | 527 |
| 33 | Louisiana | 518 |
| 14 | Maine | 661 |
| 38 | Maryland | 445 |
| 29 | Massachusetts | 530 |
| 6 | Michigan | 842 |
| 11 | Minnesota | 713 |
| 8 | Mississippi | 806 |
| 35 | Missouri | 497 |
| 46 | Montana | 0 |
| 34 | Nebraska | 513 |
| 3 | Nevada | 1,011 |
| 46 | New Hampshire | 0 |
| 21 | New Jersey | 621 |
| 7 | New Mexico | 835 |
| 39 | New York | 438 |
| 40 | North Carolina | 437 |
| 31 | North Dakota | 525 |
| 32 | Ohio | 522 |
| 42 | Oklahoma | 410 |
| 46 | Oregon | 0 |
| 28 | Pennsylvania | 555 |
| 24 | Rhode Island | 566 |
| 22 | South Carolina | 604 |
| 18 | South Dakota | 630 |
| 9 | Tennessee | 769 |
| 15 | Texas | 654 |
| 16 | Utah | 646 |
| 45 | Vermont | 346 |
| 44 | Virginia | 348 |
| 1 | Washington | 1,260 |
| 35 | West Virginia | 497 |
| 20 | Wisconsin | 622 |
| 10 | Wyoming | 724 |

RANK ORDER

| RANK | STATE | PER CAPITA |
|------|-------|-----------|
| 1 | Washington | $1,260 |
| 2 | Hawaii | 1,221 |
| 3 | Nevada | 1,011 |
| 4 | Connecticut | 981 |
| 5 | Florida | 919 |
| 6 | Michigan | 842 |
| 7 | New Mexico | 835 |
| 8 | Mississippi | 806 |
| 9 | Tennessee | 769 |
| 10 | Wyoming | 724 |
| 11 | Minnesota | 713 |
| 12 | Arizona | 693 |
| 13 | California | 684 |
| 14 | Maine | 661 |
| 15 | Texas | 654 |
| 16 | Utah | 646 |
| 17 | Kansas | 635 |
| 18 | South Dakota | 630 |
| 19 | Arkansas | 628 |
| 20 | Wisconsin | 622 |
| 21 | New Jersey | 621 |
| 22 | South Carolina | 604 |
| 23 | Iowa | 574 |
| 24 | Rhode Island | 566 |
| 25 | Idaho | 561 |
| 26 | Georgia | 558 |
| 27 | Indiana | 557 |
| 28 | Pennsylvania | 555 |
| 29 | Massachusetts | 530 |
| 30 | Kentucky | 527 |
| 31 | North Dakota | 525 |
| 32 | Ohio | 522 |
| 33 | Louisiana | 518 |
| 34 | Nebraska | 513 |
| 35 | Missouri | 497 |
| 35 | West Virginia | 497 |
| 37 | Illinois | 491 |
| 38 | Maryland | 445 |
| 39 | New York | 438 |
| 40 | North Carolina | 437 |
| 41 | Colorado | 420 |
| 42 | Oklahoma | 410 |
| 43 | Alabama | 377 |
| 44 | Virginia | 348 |
| 45 | Vermont | 346 |
| 46 | Alaska | 0 |
| 46 | Delaware | 0 |
| 46 | Montana | 0 |
| 46 | New Hampshire | 0 |
| 46 | Oregon | 0 |
| | District of Columbia** | NA |

Source: Morgan Quitno Press using data from U.S. Bureau of the Census, Governments Division
"1999 State Government Tax Collections" (http://www.census.gov/govs/www/statetax99.html)
*Does not include special sales taxes such as those on sale of alcohol, gasoline or tobacco.
**Not applicable.

# State Government Motor Fuels Sales Tax Revenue in 1999

## National Total = $29,200,869,000

| RANK | STATE | FUEL TAX | % of USA |
|------|-------|----------|----------|
| 24 | Alabama | $497,582,000 | 1.7% |
| 50 | Alaska | 38,011,000 | 0.1% |
| 17 | Arizona | 584,747,000 | 2.0% |
| 30 | Arkansas | 379,832,000 | 1.3% |
| 1 | California | 3,034,046,000 | 10.4% |
| 22 | Colorado | 515,768,000 | 1.8% |
| 20 | Connecticut | 544,667,000 | 1.9% |
| 46 | Delaware | 103,122,000 | 0.4% |
| 3 | Florida | 1,576,778,000 | 5.4% |
| 19 | Georgia | 566,402,000 | 1.9% |
| 47 | Hawaii | 73,866,000 | 0.3% |
| 39 | Idaho | 212,489,000 | 0.7% |
| 5 | Illinois | 1,328,723,000 | 4.6% |
| 14 | Indiana | 663,942,000 | 2.3% |
| 32 | Iowa | 340,767,000 | 1.2% |
| 33 | Kansas | 325,898,000 | 1.1% |
| 26 | Kentucky | 444,701,000 | 1.5% |
| 21 | Louisiana | 536,584,000 | 1.8% |
| 41 | Maine | 172,975,000 | 0.6% |
| 13 | Maryland | 680,055,000 | 2.3% |
| 16 | Massachusetts | 636,551,000 | 2.2% |
| 7 | Michigan | 1,088,370,000 | 3.7% |
| 18 | Minnesota | 580,831,000 | 2.0% |
| 28 | Mississippi | 395,007,000 | 1.4% |
| 15 | Missouri | 663,397,000 | 2.3% |
| 40 | Montana | 179,790,000 | 0.6% |
| 35 | Nebraska | 263,648,000 | 0.9% |
| 37 | Nevada | 237,491,000 | 0.8% |
| 42 | New Hampshire | 119,653,000 | 0.4% |
| 25 | New Jersey | 483,234,000 | 1.7% |
| 36 | New Mexico | 247,188,000 | 0.8% |
| 23 | New York | 505,232,000 | 1.7% |
| 6 | North Carolina | 1,145,969,000 | 3.9% |
| 45 | North Dakota | 104,893,000 | 0.4% |
| 4 | Ohio | 1,370,698,000 | 4.7% |
| 29 | Oklahoma | 383,588,000 | 1.3% |
| 27 | Oregon | 396,960,000 | 1.4% |
| 11 | Pennsylvania | 746,779,000 | 2.6% |
| 43 | Rhode Island | 119,404,000 | 0.4% |
| 31 | South Carolina | 350,998,000 | 1.2% |
| 44 | South Dakota | 107,323,000 | 0.4% |
| 10 | Tennessee | 769,912,000 | 2.6% |
| 2 | Texas | 2,592,251,000 | 8.9% |
| 34 | Utah | 312,711,000 | 1.1% |
| 49 | Vermont | 56,622,000 | 0.2% |
| 9 | Virginia | 794,798,000 | 2.7% |
| 12 | Washington | 717,813,000 | 2.5% |
| 38 | West Virginia | 237,110,000 | 0.8% |
| 8 | Wisconsin | 909,076,000 | 3.1% |
| 48 | Wyoming | 62,617,000 | 0.2% |

| RANK | STATE | FUEL TAX | % of USA |
|------|-------|----------|----------|
| 1 | California | $3,034,046,000 | 10.4% |
| 2 | Texas | 2,592,251,000 | 8.9% |
| 3 | Florida | 1,576,778,000 | 5.4% |
| 4 | Ohio | 1,370,698,000 | 4.7% |
| 5 | Illinois | 1,328,723,000 | 4.6% |
| 6 | North Carolina | 1,145,969,000 | 3.9% |
| 7 | Michigan | 1,088,370,000 | 3.7% |
| 8 | Wisconsin | 909,076,000 | 3.1% |
| 9 | Virginia | 794,798,000 | 2.7% |
| 10 | Tennessee | 769,912,000 | 2.6% |
| 11 | Pennsylvania | 746,779,000 | 2.6% |
| 12 | Washington | 717,813,000 | 2.5% |
| 13 | Maryland | 680,055,000 | 2.3% |
| 14 | Indiana | 663,942,000 | 2.3% |
| 15 | Missouri | 663,397,000 | 2.3% |
| 16 | Massachusetts | 636,551,000 | 2.2% |
| 17 | Arizona | 584,747,000 | 2.0% |
| 18 | Minnesota | 580,831,000 | 2.0% |
| 19 | Georgia | 566,402,000 | 1.9% |
| 20 | Connecticut | 544,667,000 | 1.9% |
| 21 | Louisiana | 536,584,000 | 1.8% |
| 22 | Colorado | 515,768,000 | 1.8% |
| 23 | New York | 505,232,000 | 1.7% |
| 24 | Alabama | 497,582,000 | 1.7% |
| 25 | New Jersey | 483,234,000 | 1.7% |
| 26 | Kentucky | 444,701,000 | 1.5% |
| 27 | Oregon | 396,960,000 | 1.4% |
| 28 | Mississippi | 395,007,000 | 1.4% |
| 29 | Oklahoma | 383,588,000 | 1.3% |
| 30 | Arkansas | 379,832,000 | 1.3% |
| 31 | South Carolina | 350,998,000 | 1.2% |
| 32 | Iowa | 340,767,000 | 1.2% |
| 33 | Kansas | 325,898,000 | 1.1% |
| 34 | Utah | 312,711,000 | 1.1% |
| 35 | Nebraska | 263,648,000 | 0.9% |
| 36 | New Mexico | 247,188,000 | 0.8% |
| 37 | Nevada | 237,491,000 | 0.8% |
| 38 | West Virginia | 237,110,000 | 0.8% |
| 39 | Idaho | 212,489,000 | 0.7% |
| 40 | Montana | 179,790,000 | 0.6% |
| 41 | Maine | 172,975,000 | 0.6% |
| 42 | New Hampshire | 119,653,000 | 0.4% |
| 43 | Rhode Island | 119,404,000 | 0.4% |
| 44 | South Dakota | 107,323,000 | 0.4% |
| 45 | North Dakota | 104,893,000 | 0.4% |
| 46 | Delaware | 103,122,000 | 0.4% |
| 47 | Hawaii | 73,866,000 | 0.3% |
| 48 | Wyoming | 62,617,000 | 0.2% |
| 49 | Vermont | 56,622,000 | 0.2% |
| 50 | Alaska | 38,011,000 | 0.1% |
| | District of Columbia* | NA | NA |

*Source: U.S. Bureau of the Census, Governments Division*
   *"1999 State Government Tax Collections" (http://www.census.gov/govs/www/statetax99.html)*
*Not applicable.

# Per Capita State Government Motor Fuel Sales Tax Revenue in 1999

## National Per Capita = $107

<u>ALPHA ORDER</u>

| RANK | STATE | PER CAPITA |
|------|-------|------------|
| 33 | Alabama | $114 |
| 48 | Alaska | 61 |
| 25 | Arizona | 122 |
| 8 | Arkansas | 149 |
| 43 | California | 92 |
| 21 | Colorado | 127 |
| 4 | Connecticut | 166 |
| 15 | Delaware | 137 |
| 39 | Florida | 104 |
| 45 | Georgia | 73 |
| 46 | Hawaii | 62 |
| 3 | Idaho | 170 |
| 37 | Illinois | 110 |
| 35 | Indiana | 112 |
| 31 | Iowa | 119 |
| 23 | Kansas | 123 |
| 35 | Kentucky | 112 |
| 23 | Louisiana | 123 |
| 14 | Maine | 138 |
| 16 | Maryland | 131 |
| 40 | Massachusetts | 103 |
| 37 | Michigan | 110 |
| 25 | Minnesota | 122 |
| 11 | Mississippi | 143 |
| 28 | Missouri | 121 |
| 1 | Montana | 204 |
| 6 | Nebraska | 158 |
| 16 | Nevada | 131 |
| 41 | New Hampshire | 100 |
| 49 | New Jersey | 59 |
| 12 | New Mexico | 142 |
| 50 | New York | 28 |
| 7 | North Carolina | 150 |
| 4 | North Dakota | 166 |
| 25 | Ohio | 122 |
| 33 | Oklahoma | 114 |
| 30 | Oregon | 120 |
| 46 | Pennsylvania | 62 |
| 28 | Rhode Island | 121 |
| 44 | South Carolina | 90 |
| 10 | South Dakota | 146 |
| 13 | Tennessee | 140 |
| 20 | Texas | 129 |
| 9 | Utah | 147 |
| 42 | Vermont | 95 |
| 32 | Virginia | 116 |
| 22 | Washington | 125 |
| 16 | West Virginia | 131 |
| 2 | Wisconsin | 173 |
| 16 | Wyoming | 131 |

<u>RANK ORDER</u>

| RANK | STATE | PER CAPITA |
|------|-------|------------|
| 1 | Montana | $204 |
| 2 | Wisconsin | 173 |
| 3 | Idaho | 170 |
| 4 | Connecticut | 166 |
| 4 | North Dakota | 166 |
| 6 | Nebraska | 158 |
| 7 | North Carolina | 150 |
| 8 | Arkansas | 149 |
| 9 | Utah | 147 |
| 10 | South Dakota | 146 |
| 11 | Mississippi | 143 |
| 12 | New Mexico | 142 |
| 13 | Tennessee | 140 |
| 14 | Maine | 138 |
| 15 | Delaware | 137 |
| 16 | Maryland | 131 |
| 16 | Nevada | 131 |
| 16 | West Virginia | 131 |
| 16 | Wyoming | 131 |
| 20 | Texas | 129 |
| 21 | Colorado | 127 |
| 22 | Washington | 125 |
| 23 | Kansas | 123 |
| 23 | Louisiana | 123 |
| 25 | Arizona | 122 |
| 25 | Minnesota | 122 |
| 25 | Ohio | 122 |
| 28 | Missouri | 121 |
| 28 | Rhode Island | 121 |
| 30 | Oregon | 120 |
| 31 | Iowa | 119 |
| 32 | Virginia | 116 |
| 33 | Alabama | 114 |
| 33 | Oklahoma | 114 |
| 35 | Indiana | 112 |
| 35 | Kentucky | 112 |
| 37 | Illinois | 110 |
| 37 | Michigan | 110 |
| 39 | Florida | 104 |
| 40 | Massachusetts | 103 |
| 41 | New Hampshire | 100 |
| 42 | Vermont | 95 |
| 43 | California | 92 |
| 44 | South Carolina | 90 |
| 45 | Georgia | 73 |
| 46 | Hawaii | 62 |
| 46 | Pennsylvania | 62 |
| 48 | Alaska | 61 |
| 49 | New Jersey | 59 |
| 50 | New York | 28 |
| | District of Columbia* | NA |

Source: Morgan Quitno Press using data from U.S. Bureau of the Census, Governments Division
"1999 State Government Tax Collections" (http://www.census.gov/govs/www/statetax99.html)
*Not applicable.

# State Tax Rates on Gasoline in 2001

## National Average = 19.85 Cents per Gallon*

ALPHA ORDER

| RANK | STATE | CENTS PER GALLON |
|------|-------|------------------|
| 34 | Alabama | 18.00 |
| 48 | Alaska | 8.00 |
| 34 | Arizona | 18.00 |
| 23 | Arkansas | 20.70 |
| 34 | California | 18.00 |
| 16 | Colorado | 22.00 |
| 7 | Connecticut | 25.00 |
| 14 | Delaware | 23.00 |
| 46 | Florida | 13.30 |
| 50 | Georgia | 7.50 |
| 42 | Hawaii | 16.00 |
| 4 | Idaho | 26.00 |
| 30 | Illinois | 19.30 |
| 44 | Indiana | 15.00 |
| 24 | Iowa | 20.00 |
| 24 | Kansas | 20.00 |
| 41 | Kentucky | 16.40 |
| 24 | Louisiana | 20.00 |
| 16 | Maine | 22.00 |
| 13 | Maryland | 23.50 |
| 21 | Massachusetts | 21.00 |
| 31 | Michigan | 19.00 |
| 24 | Minnesota | 20.00 |
| 33 | Mississippi | 18.40 |
| 39 | Missouri | 17.05 |
| 2 | Montana | 27.00 |
| 8 | Nebraska | 24.80 |
| 11 | Nevada | 24.00 |
| 31 | New Hampshire | 19.00 |
| 47 | New Jersey | 10.50 |
| 34 | New Mexico | 18.00 |
| 48 | New York | 8.00 |
| 9 | North Carolina | 24.55 |
| 21 | North Dakota | 21.00 |
| 16 | Ohio | 22.00 |
| 40 | Oklahoma | 17.00 |
| 11 | Oregon | 24.00 |
| 5 | Pennsylvania | 25.90 |
| 1 | Rhode Island | 29.00 |
| 42 | South Carolina | 16.00 |
| 16 | South Dakota | 22.00 |
| 20 | Tennessee | 21.40 |
| 24 | Texas | 20.00 |
| 10 | Utah | 24.50 |
| 24 | Vermont | 20.00 |
| 38 | Virginia | 17.50 |
| 14 | Washington | 23.00 |
| 6 | West Virginia | 25.65 |
| 3 | Wisconsin | 26.40 |
| 45 | Wyoming | 14.00 |

RANK ORDER

| RANK | STATE | CENTS PER GALLON |
|------|-------|------------------|
| 1 | Rhode Island | 29.00 |
| 2 | Montana | 27.00 |
| 3 | Wisconsin | 26.40 |
| 4 | Idaho | 26.00 |
| 5 | Pennsylvania | 25.90 |
| 6 | West Virginia | 25.65 |
| 7 | Connecticut | 25.00 |
| 8 | Nebraska | 24.80 |
| 9 | North Carolina | 24.55 |
| 10 | Utah | 24.50 |
| 11 | Nevada | 24.00 |
| 11 | Oregon | 24.00 |
| 13 | Maryland | 23.50 |
| 14 | Delaware | 23.00 |
| 14 | Washington | 23.00 |
| 16 | Colorado | 22.00 |
| 16 | Maine | 22.00 |
| 16 | Ohio | 22.00 |
| 16 | South Dakota | 22.00 |
| 20 | Tennessee | 21.40 |
| 21 | Massachusetts | 21.00 |
| 21 | North Dakota | 21.00 |
| 23 | Arkansas | 20.70 |
| 24 | Iowa | 20.00 |
| 24 | Kansas | 20.00 |
| 24 | Louisiana | 20.00 |
| 24 | Minnesota | 20.00 |
| 24 | Texas | 20.00 |
| 24 | Vermont | 20.00 |
| 30 | Illinois | 19.30 |
| 31 | Michigan | 19.00 |
| 31 | New Hampshire | 19.00 |
| 33 | Mississippi | 18.40 |
| 34 | Alabama | 18.00 |
| 34 | Arizona | 18.00 |
| 34 | California | 18.00 |
| 34 | New Mexico | 18.00 |
| 38 | Virginia | 17.50 |
| 39 | Missouri | 17.05 |
| 40 | Oklahoma | 17.00 |
| 41 | Kentucky | 16.40 |
| 42 | Hawaii | 16.00 |
| 42 | South Carolina | 16.00 |
| 44 | Indiana | 15.00 |
| 45 | Wyoming | 14.00 |
| 46 | Florida | 13.30 |
| 47 | New Jersey | 10.50 |
| 48 | Alaska | 8.00 |
| 48 | New York | 8.00 |
| 50 | Georgia | 7.50 |
| | District of Columbia | 20.00 |

Source: Federation of Tax Administrators
"Motor Fuel Excise Tax Rates" (http://www.taxadmin.org/fta/rate/motor_fl.html)
*As of January 1, 2001. Federal gasoline tax rate is an additional 18.4 cents per gallon. Many states also allow additional local option taxes on gasoline.

313

# State Government Motor Vehicle and Operators' License Tax Revenue in 1999

## National Total = $15,340,227,000

ALPHA ORDER

| RANK | STATE | REVENUE | % of USA |
|------|-------|---------|----------|
| 23 | Alabama | $201,005,000 | 1.3% |
| 48 | Alaska | 33,914,000 | 0.2% |
| 27 | Arizona | 156,678,000 | 1.0% |
| 34 | Arkansas | 114,181,000 | 0.7% |
| 1 | California | 1,803,858,000 | 11.8% |
| 26 | Colorado | 177,307,000 | 1.2% |
| 21 | Connecticut | 254,515,000 | 1.7% |
| 50 | Delaware | 30,428,000 | 0.2% |
| 2 | Florida | 986,060,000 | 6.4% |
| 20 | Georgia | 257,911,000 | 1.7% |
| 42 | Hawaii | 64,493,000 | 0.4% |
| 36 | Idaho | 108,775,000 | 0.7% |
| 4 | Illinois | 839,812,000 | 5.5% |
| 30 | Indiana | 139,874,000 | 0.9% |
| 14 | Iowa | 325,157,000 | 2.1% |
| 28 | Kansas | 155,467,000 | 1.0% |
| 24 | Kentucky | 189,859,000 | 1.2% |
| 35 | Louisiana | 112,353,000 | 0.7% |
| 41 | Maine | 68,460,000 | 0.4% |
| 25 | Maryland | 177,557,000 | 1.2% |
| 18 | Massachusetts | 293,427,000 | 1.9% |
| 5 | Michigan | 814,571,000 | 5.3% |
| 9 | Minnesota | 619,400,000 | 4.0% |
| 31 | Mississippi | 130,868,000 | 0.9% |
| 19 | Missouri | 272,863,000 | 1.8% |
| 43 | Montana | 56,311,000 | 0.4% |
| 37 | Nebraska | 87,528,000 | 0.6% |
| 32 | Nevada | 122,958,000 | 0.8% |
| 40 | New Hampshire | 69,647,000 | 0.5% |
| 12 | New Jersey | 394,720,000 | 2.6% |
| 29 | New Mexico | 140,003,000 | 0.9% |
| 7 | New York | 661,400,000 | 4.3% |
| 11 | North Carolina | 482,217,000 | 3.1% |
| 46 | North Dakota | 43,141,000 | 0.3% |
| 8 | Ohio | 625,716,000 | 4.1% |
| 10 | Oklahoma | 584,260,000 | 3.8% |
| 13 | Oregon | 352,747,000 | 2.3% |
| 6 | Pennsylvania | 787,699,000 | 5.1% |
| 44 | Rhode Island | 52,990,000 | 0.3% |
| 33 | South Carolina | 114,561,000 | 0.7% |
| 49 | South Dakota | 32,486,000 | 0.2% |
| 22 | Tennessee | 252,042,000 | 1.6% |
| 3 | Texas | 980,740,000 | 6.4% |
| 39 | Utah | 79,039,000 | 0.5% |
| 47 | Vermont | 37,394,000 | 0.2% |
| 15 | Virginia | 314,281,000 | 2.0% |
| 17 | Washington | 300,943,000 | 2.0% |
| 38 | West Virginia | 85,660,000 | 0.6% |
| 16 | Wisconsin | 303,433,000 | 2.0% |
| 45 | Wyoming | 49,518,000 | 0.3% |

RANK ORDER

| RANK | STATE | REVENUE | % of USA |
|------|-------|---------|----------|
| 1 | California | $1,803,858,000 | 11.8% |
| 2 | Florida | 986,060,000 | 6.4% |
| 3 | Texas | 980,740,000 | 6.4% |
| 4 | Illinois | 839,812,000 | 5.5% |
| 5 | Michigan | 814,571,000 | 5.3% |
| 6 | Pennsylvania | 787,699,000 | 5.1% |
| 7 | New York | 661,400,000 | 4.3% |
| 8 | Ohio | 625,716,000 | 4.1% |
| 9 | Minnesota | 619,400,000 | 4.0% |
| 10 | Oklahoma | 584,260,000 | 3.8% |
| 11 | North Carolina | 482,217,000 | 3.1% |
| 12 | New Jersey | 394,720,000 | 2.6% |
| 13 | Oregon | 352,747,000 | 2.3% |
| 14 | Iowa | 325,157,000 | 2.1% |
| 15 | Virginia | 314,281,000 | 2.0% |
| 16 | Wisconsin | 303,433,000 | 2.0% |
| 17 | Washington | 300,943,000 | 2.0% |
| 18 | Massachusetts | 293,427,000 | 1.9% |
| 19 | Missouri | 272,863,000 | 1.8% |
| 20 | Georgia | 257,911,000 | 1.7% |
| 21 | Connecticut | 254,515,000 | 1.7% |
| 22 | Tennessee | 252,042,000 | 1.6% |
| 23 | Alabama | 201,005,000 | 1.3% |
| 24 | Kentucky | 189,859,000 | 1.2% |
| 25 | Maryland | 177,557,000 | 1.2% |
| 26 | Colorado | 177,307,000 | 1.2% |
| 27 | Arizona | 156,678,000 | 1.0% |
| 28 | Kansas | 155,467,000 | 1.0% |
| 29 | New Mexico | 140,003,000 | 0.9% |
| 30 | Indiana | 139,874,000 | 0.9% |
| 31 | Mississippi | 130,868,000 | 0.9% |
| 32 | Nevada | 122,958,000 | 0.8% |
| 33 | South Carolina | 114,561,000 | 0.7% |
| 34 | Arkansas | 114,181,000 | 0.7% |
| 35 | Louisiana | 112,353,000 | 0.7% |
| 36 | Idaho | 108,775,000 | 0.7% |
| 37 | Nebraska | 87,528,000 | 0.6% |
| 38 | West Virginia | 85,660,000 | 0.6% |
| 39 | Utah | 79,039,000 | 0.5% |
| 40 | New Hampshire | 69,647,000 | 0.5% |
| 41 | Maine | 68,460,000 | 0.4% |
| 42 | Hawaii | 64,493,000 | 0.4% |
| 43 | Montana | 56,311,000 | 0.4% |
| 44 | Rhode Island | 52,990,000 | 0.3% |
| 45 | Wyoming | 49,518,000 | 0.3% |
| 46 | North Dakota | 43,141,000 | 0.3% |
| 47 | Vermont | 37,394,000 | 0.2% |
| 48 | Alaska | 33,914,000 | 0.2% |
| 49 | South Dakota | 32,486,000 | 0.2% |
| 50 | Delaware | 30,428,000 | 0.2% |
| | District of Columbia* | NA | NA |

*Source: U.S. Bureau of the Census, Governments Division*
*"1999 State Government Tax Collections" (http://www.census.gov/govs/www/statetax99.html)*
*Not applicable.

# Per Capita State Government Motor Vehicle and Operators' License Tax Revenue in 1999
## National Per Capita = $56.36

ALPHA ORDER

| RANK | STATE | PER CAPITA |
|------|-------|------------|
| 36 | Alabama | $46.00 |
| 22 | Alaska | 54.74 |
| 47 | Arizona | 32.79 |
| 39 | Arkansas | 44.75 |
| 24 | California | 54.42 |
| 41 | Colorado | 43.71 |
| 9 | Connecticut | 77.55 |
| 42 | Delaware | 40.38 |
| 14 | Florida | 65.25 |
| 46 | Georgia | 33.12 |
| 25 | Hawaii | 54.40 |
| 6 | Idaho | 86.90 |
| 10 | Illinois | 69.24 |
| 50 | Indiana | 23.54 |
| 3 | Iowa | 113.32 |
| 18 | Kansas | 58.58 |
| 32 | Kentucky | 47.93 |
| 49 | Louisiana | 25.70 |
| 23 | Maine | 54.64 |
| 45 | Maryland | 34.33 |
| 33 | Massachusetts | 47.52 |
| 7 | Michigan | 82.58 |
| 2 | Minnesota | 129.70 |
| 35 | Mississippi | 47.27 |
| 29 | Missouri | 49.90 |
| 15 | Montana | 63.79 |
| 27 | Nebraska | 52.54 |
| 12 | Nevada | 67.96 |
| 19 | New Hampshire | 57.98 |
| 31 | New Jersey | 48.47 |
| 8 | New Mexico | 80.47 |
| 44 | New York | 36.35 |
| 16 | North Carolina | 63.03 |
| 11 | North Dakota | 68.08 |
| 21 | Ohio | 55.59 |
| 1 | Oklahoma | 173.99 |
| 4 | Oregon | 106.37 |
| 13 | Pennsylvania | 65.67 |
| 26 | Rhode Island | 53.48 |
| 48 | South Carolina | 29.48 |
| 40 | South Dakota | 44.31 |
| 37 | Tennessee | 45.96 |
| 30 | Texas | 48.93 |
| 43 | Utah | 37.11 |
| 17 | Vermont | 62.98 |
| 38 | Virginia | 45.73 |
| 28 | Washington | 52.28 |
| 34 | West Virginia | 47.41 |
| 20 | Wisconsin | 57.79 |
| 5 | Wyoming | 103.25 |

RANK ORDER

| RANK | STATE | PER CAPITA |
|------|-------|------------|
| 1 | Oklahoma | $173.99 |
| 2 | Minnesota | 129.70 |
| 3 | Iowa | 113.32 |
| 4 | Oregon | 106.37 |
| 5 | Wyoming | 103.25 |
| 6 | Idaho | 86.90 |
| 7 | Michigan | 82.58 |
| 8 | New Mexico | 80.47 |
| 9 | Connecticut | 77.55 |
| 10 | Illinois | 69.24 |
| 11 | North Dakota | 68.08 |
| 12 | Nevada | 67.96 |
| 13 | Pennsylvania | 65.67 |
| 14 | Florida | 65.25 |
| 15 | Montana | 63.79 |
| 16 | North Carolina | 63.03 |
| 17 | Vermont | 62.98 |
| 18 | Kansas | 58.58 |
| 19 | New Hampshire | 57.98 |
| 20 | Wisconsin | 57.79 |
| 21 | Ohio | 55.59 |
| 22 | Alaska | 54.74 |
| 23 | Maine | 54.64 |
| 24 | California | 54.42 |
| 25 | Hawaii | 54.40 |
| 26 | Rhode Island | 53.48 |
| 27 | Nebraska | 52.54 |
| 28 | Washington | 52.28 |
| 29 | Missouri | 49.90 |
| 30 | Texas | 48.93 |
| 31 | New Jersey | 48.47 |
| 32 | Kentucky | 47.93 |
| 33 | Massachusetts | 47.52 |
| 34 | West Virginia | 47.41 |
| 35 | Mississippi | 47.27 |
| 36 | Alabama | 46.00 |
| 37 | Tennessee | 45.96 |
| 38 | Virginia | 45.73 |
| 39 | Arkansas | 44.75 |
| 40 | South Dakota | 44.31 |
| 41 | Colorado | 43.71 |
| 42 | Delaware | 40.38 |
| 43 | Utah | 37.11 |
| 44 | New York | 36.35 |
| 45 | Maryland | 34.33 |
| 46 | Georgia | 33.12 |
| 47 | Arizona | 32.79 |
| 48 | South Carolina | 29.48 |
| 49 | Louisiana | 25.70 |
| 50 | Indiana | 23.54 |

District of Columbia*  NA

Source: Morgan Quitno Press using data from U.S. Bureau of the Census, Governments Division
"1999 State Government Tax Collections" (http://www.census.gov/govs/www/statetax99.html)
*Not applicable.

# State Government Tobacco Product Sales Tax Revenue in 1999

## National Total = $8,190,095,000

ALPHA ORDER

| RANK | STATE | TOBACCO TAX | % of USA |
|---|---|---|---|
| 29 | Alabama | $67,802,000 | 0.8% |
| 35 | Alaska | 47,584,000 | 0.6% |
| 15 | Arizona | 162,836,000 | 2.0% |
| 21 | Arkansas | 94,594,000 | 1.2% |
| 1 | California | 899,531,000 | 11.0% |
| 28 | Colorado | 68,013,000 | 0.8% |
| 16 | Connecticut | 130,537,000 | 1.6% |
| 43 | Delaware | 24,455,000 | 0.3% |
| 6 | Florida | 451,787,000 | 5.5% |
| 22 | Georgia | 92,500,000 | 1.1% |
| 38 | Hawaii | 42,281,000 | 0.5% |
| 41 | Idaho | 28,491,000 | 0.3% |
| 5 | Illinois | 501,650,000 | 6.1% |
| 23 | Indiana | 89,894,000 | 1.1% |
| 19 | Iowa | 98,305,000 | 1.2% |
| 33 | Kansas | 54,550,000 | 0.7% |
| 46 | Kentucky | 17,670,000 | 0.2% |
| 24 | Louisiana | 85,441,000 | 1.0% |
| 25 | Maine | 78,359,000 | 1.0% |
| 17 | Maryland | 128,785,000 | 1.6% |
| 10 | Massachusetts | 284,439,000 | 3.5% |
| 3 | Michigan | 625,350,000 | 7.6% |
| 14 | Minnesota | 184,885,000 | 2.3% |
| 32 | Mississippi | 56,981,000 | 0.7% |
| 18 | Missouri | 112,861,000 | 1.4% |
| 48 | Montana | 14,083,000 | 0.2% |
| 36 | Nebraska | 46,922,000 | 0.6% |
| 30 | Nevada | 63,998,000 | 0.8% |
| 27 | New Hampshire | 73,765,000 | 0.9% |
| 7 | New Jersey | 417,548,000 | 5.1% |
| 42 | New Mexico | 24,749,000 | 0.3% |
| 2 | New York | 663,286,000 | 8.1% |
| 37 | North Carolina | 44,694,000 | 0.5% |
| 44 | North Dakota | 23,026,000 | 0.3% |
| 9 | Ohio | 292,728,000 | 3.6% |
| 26 | Oklahoma | 77,761,000 | 0.9% |
| 13 | Oregon | 193,261,000 | 2.4% |
| 8 | Pennsylvania | 330,419,000 | 4.0% |
| 31 | Rhode Island | 61,467,000 | 0.8% |
| 40 | South Carolina | 30,152,000 | 0.4% |
| 45 | South Dakota | 20,423,000 | 0.2% |
| 20 | Tennessee | 94,941,000 | 1.2% |
| 4 | Texas | 623,569,000 | 7.6% |
| 34 | Utah | 50,459,000 | 0.6% |
| 49 | Vermont | 13,570,000 | 0.2% |
| 47 | Virginia | 15,525,000 | 0.2% |
| 11 | Washington | 278,488,000 | 3.4% |
| 39 | West Virginia | 33,077,000 | 0.4% |
| 12 | Wisconsin | 266,817,000 | 3.3% |
| 50 | Wyoming | 5,786,000 | 0.1% |

RANK ORDER

| RANK | STATE | TOBACCO TAX | % of USA |
|---|---|---|---|
| 1 | California | $899,531,000 | 11.0% |
| 2 | New York | 663,286,000 | 8.1% |
| 3 | Michigan | 625,350,000 | 7.6% |
| 4 | Texas | 623,569,000 | 7.6% |
| 5 | Illinois | 501,650,000 | 6.1% |
| 6 | Florida | 451,787,000 | 5.5% |
| 7 | New Jersey | 417,548,000 | 5.1% |
| 8 | Pennsylvania | 330,419,000 | 4.0% |
| 9 | Ohio | 292,728,000 | 3.6% |
| 10 | Massachusetts | 284,439,000 | 3.5% |
| 11 | Washington | 278,488,000 | 3.4% |
| 12 | Wisconsin | 266,817,000 | 3.3% |
| 13 | Oregon | 193,261,000 | 2.4% |
| 14 | Minnesota | 184,885,000 | 2.3% |
| 15 | Arizona | 162,836,000 | 2.0% |
| 16 | Connecticut | 130,537,000 | 1.6% |
| 17 | Maryland | 128,785,000 | 1.6% |
| 18 | Missouri | 112,861,000 | 1.4% |
| 19 | Iowa | 98,305,000 | 1.2% |
| 20 | Tennessee | 94,941,000 | 1.2% |
| 21 | Arkansas | 94,594,000 | 1.2% |
| 22 | Georgia | 92,500,000 | 1.1% |
| 23 | Indiana | 89,894,000 | 1.1% |
| 24 | Louisiana | 85,441,000 | 1.0% |
| 25 | Maine | 78,359,000 | 1.0% |
| 26 | Oklahoma | 77,761,000 | 0.9% |
| 27 | New Hampshire | 73,765,000 | 0.9% |
| 28 | Colorado | 68,013,000 | 0.8% |
| 29 | Alabama | 67,802,000 | 0.8% |
| 30 | Nevada | 63,998,000 | 0.8% |
| 31 | Rhode Island | 61,467,000 | 0.8% |
| 32 | Mississippi | 56,981,000 | 0.7% |
| 33 | Kansas | 54,550,000 | 0.7% |
| 34 | Utah | 50,459,000 | 0.6% |
| 35 | Alaska | 47,584,000 | 0.6% |
| 36 | Nebraska | 46,922,000 | 0.6% |
| 37 | North Carolina | 44,694,000 | 0.5% |
| 38 | Hawaii | 42,281,000 | 0.5% |
| 39 | West Virginia | 33,077,000 | 0.4% |
| 40 | South Carolina | 30,152,000 | 0.4% |
| 41 | Idaho | 28,491,000 | 0.3% |
| 42 | New Mexico | 24,749,000 | 0.3% |
| 43 | Delaware | 24,455,000 | 0.3% |
| 44 | North Dakota | 23,026,000 | 0.3% |
| 45 | South Dakota | 20,423,000 | 0.2% |
| 46 | Kentucky | 17,670,000 | 0.2% |
| 47 | Virginia | 15,525,000 | 0.2% |
| 48 | Montana | 14,083,000 | 0.2% |
| 49 | Vermont | 13,570,000 | 0.2% |
| 50 | Wyoming | 5,786,000 | 0.1% |
| | District of Columbia* | NA | NA |

Source: U.S. Bureau of the Census, Governments Division
    "1999 State Government Tax Collections" (http://www.census.gov/govs/www/statetax99.html)
*Not applicable.

# Per Capita State Government Tobacco Sales Tax Revenue in 1999

## National Per Capita = $30.09

ALPHA ORDER

| RANK | STATE | PER CAPITA |
|------|-------|------------|
| 42 | Alabama | $15.52 |
| 1 | Alaska | 76.81 |
| 20 | Arizona | 34.08 |
| 14 | Arkansas | 37.08 |
| 27 | California | 27.14 |
| 40 | Colorado | 16.77 |
| 12 | Connecticut | 39.77 |
| 21 | Delaware | 32.45 |
| 23 | Florida | 29.90 |
| 46 | Georgia | 11.88 |
| 17 | Hawaii | 35.67 |
| 33 | Idaho | 22.76 |
| 11 | Illinois | 41.36 |
| 43 | Indiana | 15.13 |
| 19 | Iowa | 34.26 |
| 36 | Kansas | 20.55 |
| 49 | Kentucky | 4.46 |
| 37 | Louisiana | 19.54 |
| 3 | Maine | 62.54 |
| 29 | Maryland | 24.90 |
| 10 | Massachusetts | 46.06 |
| 2 | Michigan | 63.40 |
| 13 | Minnesota | 38.72 |
| 35 | Mississippi | 20.58 |
| 34 | Missouri | 20.64 |
| 41 | Montana | 15.95 |
| 24 | Nebraska | 28.16 |
| 18 | Nevada | 35.37 |
| 5 | New Hampshire | 61.41 |
| 7 | New Jersey | 51.27 |
| 44 | New Mexico | 14.22 |
| 15 | New York | 36.45 |
| 48 | North Carolina | 5.84 |
| 16 | North Dakota | 36.34 |
| 28 | Ohio | 26.00 |
| 31 | Oklahoma | 23.16 |
| 6 | Oregon | 58.28 |
| 26 | Pennsylvania | 27.55 |
| 4 | Rhode Island | 62.04 |
| 47 | South Carolina | 7.76 |
| 25 | South Dakota | 27.86 |
| 39 | Tennessee | 17.31 |
| 22 | Texas | 31.11 |
| 30 | Utah | 23.69 |
| 32 | Vermont | 22.86 |
| 50 | Virginia | 2.26 |
| 9 | Washington | 48.38 |
| 38 | West Virginia | 18.31 |
| 8 | Wisconsin | 50.82 |
| 45 | Wyoming | 12.06 |

RANK ORDER

| RANK | STATE | PER CAPITA |
|------|-------|------------|
| 1 | Alaska | $76.81 |
| 2 | Michigan | 63.40 |
| 3 | Maine | 62.54 |
| 4 | Rhode Island | 62.04 |
| 5 | New Hampshire | 61.41 |
| 6 | Oregon | 58.28 |
| 7 | New Jersey | 51.27 |
| 8 | Wisconsin | 50.82 |
| 9 | Washington | 48.38 |
| 10 | Massachusetts | 46.06 |
| 11 | Illinois | 41.36 |
| 12 | Connecticut | 39.77 |
| 13 | Minnesota | 38.72 |
| 14 | Arkansas | 37.08 |
| 15 | New York | 36.45 |
| 16 | North Dakota | 36.34 |
| 17 | Hawaii | 35.67 |
| 18 | Nevada | 35.37 |
| 19 | Iowa | 34.26 |
| 20 | Arizona | 34.08 |
| 21 | Delaware | 32.45 |
| 22 | Texas | 31.11 |
| 23 | Florida | 29.90 |
| 24 | Nebraska | 28.16 |
| 25 | South Dakota | 27.86 |
| 26 | Pennsylvania | 27.55 |
| 27 | California | 27.14 |
| 28 | Ohio | 26.00 |
| 29 | Maryland | 24.90 |
| 30 | Utah | 23.69 |
| 31 | Oklahoma | 23.16 |
| 32 | Vermont | 22.86 |
| 33 | Idaho | 22.76 |
| 34 | Missouri | 20.64 |
| 35 | Mississippi | 20.58 |
| 36 | Kansas | 20.55 |
| 37 | Louisiana | 19.54 |
| 38 | West Virginia | 18.31 |
| 39 | Tennessee | 17.31 |
| 40 | Colorado | 16.77 |
| 41 | Montana | 15.95 |
| 42 | Alabama | 15.52 |
| 43 | Indiana | 15.13 |
| 44 | New Mexico | 14.22 |
| 45 | Wyoming | 12.06 |
| 46 | Georgia | 11.88 |
| 47 | South Carolina | 7.76 |
| 48 | North Carolina | 5.84 |
| 49 | Kentucky | 4.46 |
| 50 | Virginia | 2.26 |

District of Columbia*    NA

*Source: Morgan Quitno Press using data from U.S. Bureau of the Census, Governments Division*
    *"1999 State Government Tax Collections" (http://www.census.gov/govs/www/statetax99.html)*
*Not applicable.*

# State Tax on a Pack of Cigarettes in 2001

## National Median = 34.0 Cents per Pack*

ALPHA ORDER

| RANK | STATE | CENTS PER PACK |
|------|-------|----------------|
| 42 | Alabama | 16.5 |
| 2 | Alaska | 100.0 |
| 13 | Arizona | 58.0 |
| 28 | Arkansas | 31.5 |
| 4 | California | 87.0 |
| 37 | Colorado | 20.0 |
| 18 | Connecticut | 50.0 |
| 31 | Delaware | 24.0 |
| 26 | Florida | 33.9 |
| 45 | Georgia | 12.0 |
| 2 | Hawaii | 100.0 |
| 30 | Idaho | 28.0 |
| 13 | Illinois | 58.0 |
| 43 | Indiana | 15.5 |
| 23 | Iowa | 36.0 |
| 31 | Kansas | 24.0 |
| 49 | Kentucky | 3.0 |
| 31 | Louisiana | 24.0 |
| 9 | Maine | 74.0 |
| 11 | Maryland | 66.0 |
| 7 | Massachusetts | 76.0 |
| 8 | Michigan | 75.0 |
| 19 | Minnesota | 48.0 |
| 38 | Mississippi | 18.0 |
| 40 | Missouri | 17.0 |
| 38 | Montana | 18.0 |
| 25 | Nebraska | 34.0 |
| 24 | Nevada | 35.0 |
| 16 | New Hampshire | 52.0 |
| 6 | New Jersey | 80.0 |
| 36 | New Mexico | 21.0 |
| 1 | New York | 111.0 |
| 48 | North Carolina | 5.0 |
| 20 | North Dakota | 44.0 |
| 31 | Ohio | 24.0 |
| 35 | Oklahoma | 23.0 |
| 13 | Oregon | 58.0 |
| 29 | Pennsylvania | 31.0 |
| 10 | Rhode Island | 71.0 |
| 47 | South Carolina | 7.0 |
| 27 | South Dakota | 33.0 |
| 44 | Tennessee | 13.0 |
| 22 | Texas | 41.0 |
| 17 | Utah | 51.5 |
| 20 | Vermont | 44.0 |
| 50 | Virginia | 2.5 |
| 5 | Washington | 82.5 |
| 40 | West Virginia | 17.0 |
| 12 | Wisconsin | 59.0 |
| 45 | Wyoming | 12.0 |

RANK ORDER

| RANK | STATE | CENTS PER PACK |
|------|-------|----------------|
| 1 | New York | 111.0 |
| 2 | Alaska | 100.0 |
| 2 | Hawaii | 100.0 |
| 4 | California | 87.0 |
| 5 | Washington | 82.5 |
| 6 | New Jersey | 80.0 |
| 7 | Massachusetts | 76.0 |
| 8 | Michigan | 75.0 |
| 9 | Maine | 74.0 |
| 10 | Rhode Island | 71.0 |
| 11 | Maryland | 66.0 |
| 12 | Wisconsin | 59.0 |
| 13 | Arizona | 58.0 |
| 13 | Illinois | 58.0 |
| 13 | Oregon | 58.0 |
| 16 | New Hampshire | 52.0 |
| 17 | Utah | 51.5 |
| 18 | Connecticut | 50.0 |
| 19 | Minnesota | 48.0 |
| 20 | North Dakota | 44.0 |
| 20 | Vermont | 44.0 |
| 22 | Texas | 41.0 |
| 23 | Iowa | 36.0 |
| 24 | Nevada | 35.0 |
| 25 | Nebraska | 34.0 |
| 26 | Florida | 33.9 |
| 27 | South Dakota | 33.0 |
| 28 | Arkansas | 31.5 |
| 29 | Pennsylvania | 31.0 |
| 30 | Idaho | 28.0 |
| 31 | Delaware | 24.0 |
| 31 | Kansas | 24.0 |
| 31 | Louisiana | 24.0 |
| 31 | Ohio | 24.0 |
| 35 | Oklahoma | 23.0 |
| 36 | New Mexico | 21.0 |
| 37 | Colorado | 20.0 |
| 38 | Mississippi | 18.0 |
| 38 | Montana | 18.0 |
| 40 | Missouri | 17.0 |
| 40 | West Virginia | 17.0 |
| 42 | Alabama | 16.5 |
| 43 | Indiana | 15.5 |
| 44 | Tennessee | 13.0 |
| 45 | Georgia | 12.0 |
| 45 | Wyoming | 12.0 |
| 47 | South Carolina | 7.0 |
| 48 | North Carolina | 5.0 |
| 49 | Kentucky | 3.0 |
| 50 | Virginia | 2.5 |

| | | |
|---|---|---|
| District of Columbia | | 65.0 |

*Source: Federation of Tax Administrators*
*"State Cigarette Tax Rates" (http://www.taxadmin.org/fta/rate/cigarett.html)*
*As of January 1, 2001. Many states also allow additional local option taxes on cigarettes.*

# State Government Alcoholic Beverage Sales Tax Revenue in 1999

## National Total = $3,901,092,000

ALPHA ORDER

| RANK | STATE | LIQUOR TAX | % of USA |
|---|---|---|---|
| 11 | Alabama | $120,650,000 | 3.1% |
| 40 | Alaska | 12,159,000 | 0.3% |
| 23 | Arizona | 48,152,000 | 1.2% |
| 31 | Arkansas | 27,658,000 | 0.7% |
| 3 | California | 273,398,000 | 7.0% |
| 32 | Colorado | 26,193,000 | 0.7% |
| 24 | Connecticut | 44,143,000 | 1.1% |
| 44 | Delaware | 11,155,000 | 0.3% |
| 1 | Florida | 576,762,000 | 14.8% |
| 8 | Georgia | 133,219,000 | 3.4% |
| 27 | Hawaii | 38,508,000 | 1.0% |
| 49 | Idaho | 5,762,000 | 0.1% |
| 21 | Illinois | 57,235,000 | 1.5% |
| 30 | Indiana | 30,558,000 | 0.8% |
| 42 | Iowa | 11,916,000 | 0.3% |
| 16 | Kansas | 69,580,000 | 1.8% |
| 17 | Kentucky | 65,351,000 | 1.7% |
| 22 | Louisiana | 50,144,000 | 1.3% |
| 29 | Maine | 32,658,000 | 0.8% |
| 34 | Maryland | 23,908,000 | 0.6% |
| 18 | Massachusetts | 61,520,000 | 1.6% |
| 9 | Michigan | 126,906,000 | 3.3% |
| 20 | Minnesota | 58,401,000 | 1.5% |
| 26 | Mississippi | 39,778,000 | 1.0% |
| 33 | Missouri | 24,797,000 | 0.6% |
| 37 | Montana | 16,127,000 | 0.4% |
| 36 | Nebraska | 16,792,000 | 0.4% |
| 38 | Nevada | 15,342,000 | 0.4% |
| 43 | New Hampshire | 11,564,000 | 0.3% |
| 14 | New Jersey | 75,975,000 | 1.9% |
| 28 | New Mexico | 35,562,000 | 0.9% |
| 5 | New York | 181,998,000 | 4.7% |
| 4 | North Carolina | 182,970,000 | 4.7% |
| 48 | North Dakota | 5,857,000 | 0.2% |
| 13 | Ohio | 82,197,000 | 2.1% |
| 19 | Oklahoma | 58,904,000 | 1.5% |
| 41 | Oregon | 12,087,000 | 0.3% |
| 6 | Pennsylvania | 170,511,000 | 4.4% |
| 46 | Rhode Island | 9,314,000 | 0.2% |
| 10 | South Carolina | 124,925,000 | 3.2% |
| 45 | South Dakota | 10,802,000 | 0.3% |
| 15 | Tennessee | 72,442,000 | 1.9% |
| 2 | Texas | 483,172,000 | 12.4% |
| 35 | Utah | 22,610,000 | 0.6% |
| 39 | Vermont | 14,023,000 | 0.4% |
| 12 | Virginia | 116,216,000 | 3.0% |
| 7 | Washington | 159,739,000 | 4.1% |
| 47 | West Virginia | 8,080,000 | 0.2% |
| 25 | Wisconsin | 42,104,000 | 1.1% |
| 50 | Wyoming | 1,268,000 | 0.0% |

RANK ORDER

| RANK | STATE | LIQUOR TAX | % of USA |
|---|---|---|---|
| 1 | Florida | $576,762,000 | 14.8% |
| 2 | Texas | 483,172,000 | 12.4% |
| 3 | California | 273,398,000 | 7.0% |
| 4 | North Carolina | 182,970,000 | 4.7% |
| 5 | New York | 181,998,000 | 4.7% |
| 6 | Pennsylvania | 170,511,000 | 4.4% |
| 7 | Washington | 159,739,000 | 4.1% |
| 8 | Georgia | 133,219,000 | 3.4% |
| 9 | Michigan | 126,906,000 | 3.3% |
| 10 | South Carolina | 124,925,000 | 3.2% |
| 11 | Alabama | 120,650,000 | 3.1% |
| 12 | Virginia | 116,216,000 | 3.0% |
| 13 | Ohio | 82,197,000 | 2.1% |
| 14 | New Jersey | 75,975,000 | 1.9% |
| 15 | Tennessee | 72,442,000 | 1.9% |
| 16 | Kansas | 69,580,000 | 1.8% |
| 17 | Kentucky | 65,351,000 | 1.7% |
| 18 | Massachusetts | 61,520,000 | 1.6% |
| 19 | Oklahoma | 58,904,000 | 1.5% |
| 20 | Minnesota | 58,401,000 | 1.5% |
| 21 | Illinois | 57,235,000 | 1.5% |
| 22 | Louisiana | 50,144,000 | 1.3% |
| 23 | Arizona | 48,152,000 | 1.2% |
| 24 | Connecticut | 44,143,000 | 1.1% |
| 25 | Wisconsin | 42,104,000 | 1.1% |
| 26 | Mississippi | 39,778,000 | 1.0% |
| 27 | Hawaii | 38,508,000 | 1.0% |
| 28 | New Mexico | 35,562,000 | 0.9% |
| 29 | Maine | 32,658,000 | 0.8% |
| 30 | Indiana | 30,558,000 | 0.8% |
| 31 | Arkansas | 27,658,000 | 0.7% |
| 32 | Colorado | 26,193,000 | 0.7% |
| 33 | Missouri | 24,797,000 | 0.6% |
| 34 | Maryland | 23,908,000 | 0.6% |
| 35 | Utah | 22,610,000 | 0.6% |
| 36 | Nebraska | 16,792,000 | 0.4% |
| 37 | Montana | 16,127,000 | 0.4% |
| 38 | Nevada | 15,342,000 | 0.4% |
| 39 | Vermont | 14,023,000 | 0.4% |
| 40 | Alaska | 12,159,000 | 0.3% |
| 41 | Oregon | 12,087,000 | 0.3% |
| 42 | Iowa | 11,916,000 | 0.3% |
| 43 | New Hampshire | 11,564,000 | 0.3% |
| 44 | Delaware | 11,155,000 | 0.3% |
| 45 | South Dakota | 10,802,000 | 0.3% |
| 46 | Rhode Island | 9,314,000 | 0.2% |
| 47 | West Virginia | 8,080,000 | 0.2% |
| 48 | North Dakota | 5,857,000 | 0.2% |
| 49 | Idaho | 5,762,000 | 0.1% |
| 50 | Wyoming | 1,268,000 | 0.0% |
| | District of Columbia* | NA | NA |

*Source: U.S. Bureau of the Census, Governments Division*
*"1999 State Government Tax Collections" (http://www.census.gov/govs/www/statetax99.html)*
*Not applicable.*

# Per Capita State Government Alcoholic Beverage Sales Tax Revenue in 1999

## National Per Capita = $14.33

ALPHA ORDER

| RANK | STATE | PER CAPITA |
|---|---|---|
| 5 | Alabama | $27.61 |
| 12 | Alaska | 19.63 |
| 29 | Arizona | 10.08 |
| 27 | Arkansas | 10.84 |
| 38 | California | 8.25 |
| 41 | Colorado | 6.46 |
| 22 | Connecticut | 13.45 |
| 18 | Delaware | 14.80 |
| 1 | Florida | 38.17 |
| 15 | Georgia | 17.11 |
| 2 | Hawaii | 32.48 |
| 45 | Idaho | 4.60 |
| 43 | Illinois | 4.72 |
| 42 | Indiana | 5.14 |
| 48 | Iowa | 4.15 |
| 6 | Kansas | 26.22 |
| 17 | Kentucky | 16.50 |
| 26 | Louisiana | 11.47 |
| 7 | Maine | 26.06 |
| 44 | Maryland | 4.62 |
| 32 | Massachusetts | 9.96 |
| 24 | Michigan | 12.87 |
| 25 | Minnesota | 12.23 |
| 20 | Mississippi | 14.37 |
| 46 | Missouri | 4.53 |
| 13 | Montana | 18.27 |
| 29 | Nebraska | 10.08 |
| 37 | Nevada | 8.48 |
| 33 | New Hampshire | 9.63 |
| 35 | New Jersey | 9.33 |
| 11 | New Mexico | 20.44 |
| 31 | New York | 10.00 |
| 9 | North Carolina | 23.92 |
| 36 | North Dakota | 9.24 |
| 40 | Ohio | 7.30 |
| 14 | Oklahoma | 17.54 |
| 49 | Oregon | 3.64 |
| 21 | Pennsylvania | 14.22 |
| 34 | Rhode Island | 9.40 |
| 3 | South Carolina | 32.15 |
| 19 | South Dakota | 14.73 |
| 23 | Tennessee | 13.21 |
| 8 | Texas | 24.11 |
| 28 | Utah | 10.62 |
| 10 | Vermont | 23.62 |
| 16 | Virginia | 16.91 |
| 4 | Washington | 27.75 |
| 47 | West Virginia | 4.47 |
| 39 | Wisconsin | 8.02 |
| 50 | Wyoming | 2.64 |

RANK ORDER

| RANK | STATE | PER CAPITA |
|---|---|---|
| 1 | Florida | $38.17 |
| 2 | Hawaii | 32.48 |
| 3 | South Carolina | 32.15 |
| 4 | Washington | 27.75 |
| 5 | Alabama | 27.61 |
| 6 | Kansas | 26.22 |
| 7 | Maine | 26.06 |
| 8 | Texas | 24.11 |
| 9 | North Carolina | 23.92 |
| 10 | Vermont | 23.62 |
| 11 | New Mexico | 20.44 |
| 12 | Alaska | 19.63 |
| 13 | Montana | 18.27 |
| 14 | Oklahoma | 17.54 |
| 15 | Georgia | 17.11 |
| 16 | Virginia | 16.91 |
| 17 | Kentucky | 16.50 |
| 18 | Delaware | 14.80 |
| 19 | South Dakota | 14.73 |
| 20 | Mississippi | 14.37 |
| 21 | Pennsylvania | 14.22 |
| 22 | Connecticut | 13.45 |
| 23 | Tennessee | 13.21 |
| 24 | Michigan | 12.87 |
| 25 | Minnesota | 12.23 |
| 26 | Louisiana | 11.47 |
| 27 | Arkansas | 10.84 |
| 28 | Utah | 10.62 |
| 29 | Arizona | 10.08 |
| 29 | Nebraska | 10.08 |
| 31 | New York | 10.00 |
| 32 | Massachusetts | 9.96 |
| 33 | New Hampshire | 9.63 |
| 34 | Rhode Island | 9.40 |
| 35 | New Jersey | 9.33 |
| 36 | North Dakota | 9.24 |
| 37 | Nevada | 8.48 |
| 38 | California | 8.25 |
| 39 | Wisconsin | 8.02 |
| 40 | Ohio | 7.30 |
| 41 | Colorado | 6.46 |
| 42 | Indiana | 5.14 |
| 43 | Illinois | 4.72 |
| 44 | Maryland | 4.62 |
| 45 | Idaho | 4.60 |
| 46 | Missouri | 4.53 |
| 47 | West Virginia | 4.47 |
| 48 | Iowa | 4.15 |
| 49 | Oregon | 3.64 |
| 50 | Wyoming | 2.64 |
| | District of Columbia* | NA |

*Source: Morgan Quitno Press using data from U.S. Bureau of the Census, Governments Division
"1999 State Government Tax Collections" (http://www.census.gov/govs/www/statetax99.html)
*Not applicable.*

# State Government Total Expenditures in 1998

## National Total = $930,036,567,000*

ALPHA ORDER

| RANK | STATE | EXPENDITURES | % of USA |
|------|-------|--------------|----------|
| 23 | Alabama | $13,728,431,000 | 1.5% |
| 38 | Alaska | 5,803,173,000 | 0.6% |
| 27 | Arizona | 13,327,967,000 | 1.4% |
| 32 | Arkansas | 8,103,515,000 | 0.9% |
| 1 | California | 120,329,505,000 | 12.9% |
| 28 | Colorado | 11,277,701,000 | 1.2% |
| 22 | Connecticut | 14,516,273,000 | 1.6% |
| 45 | Delaware | 3,465,428,000 | 0.4% |
| 5 | Florida | 39,214,010,000 | 4.2% |
| 13 | Georgia | 21,735,461,000 | 2.3% |
| 37 | Hawaii | 5,860,425,000 | 0.6% |
| 43 | Idaho | 3,785,613,000 | 0.4% |
| 8 | Illinois | 35,685,258,000 | 3.8% |
| 17 | Indiana | 17,223,182,000 | 1.9% |
| 30 | Iowa | 9,729,171,000 | 1.0% |
| 33 | Kansas | 7,681,014,000 | 0.8% |
| 25 | Kentucky | 13,541,073,000 | 1.5% |
| 20 | Louisiana | 14,918,718,000 | 1.6% |
| 41 | Maine | 4,606,471,000 | 0.5% |
| 18 | Maryland | 16,578,483,000 | 1.8% |
| 10 | Massachusetts | 27,194,316,000 | 2.9% |
| 7 | Michigan | 37,409,791,000 | 4.0% |
| 16 | Minnesota | 18,418,302,000 | 2.0% |
| 31 | Mississippi | 9,335,836,000 | 1.0% |
| 19 | Missouri | 15,313,244,000 | 1.6% |
| 46 | Montana | 3,262,167,000 | 0.4% |
| 40 | Nebraska | 4,753,513,000 | 0.5% |
| 39 | Nevada | 5,397,584,000 | 0.6% |
| 44 | New Hampshire | 3,477,180,000 | 0.4% |
| 9 | New Jersey | 31,701,874,000 | 3.4% |
| 34 | New Mexico | 7,539,619,000 | 0.8% |
| 2 | New York | 87,338,292,000 | 9.4% |
| 11 | North Carolina | 24,604,942,000 | 2.6% |
| 47 | North Dakota | 2,526,823,000 | 0.3% |
| 6 | Ohio | 39,209,266,000 | 4.2% |
| 29 | Oklahoma | 9,952,733,000 | 1.1% |
| 26 | Oregon | 13,465,691,000 | 1.4% |
| 4 | Pennsylvania | 40,803,540,000 | 4.4% |
| 42 | Rhode Island | 3,964,337,000 | 0.4% |
| 24 | South Carolina | 13,574,926,000 | 1.5% |
| 49 | South Dakota | 2,244,814,000 | 0.2% |
| 21 | Tennessee | 14,775,178,000 | 1.6% |
| 3 | Texas | 51,064,773,000 | 5.5% |
| 35 | Utah | 7,470,282,000 | 0.8% |
| 48 | Vermont | 2,295,310,000 | 0.2% |
| 14 | Virginia | 20,529,276,000 | 2.2% |
| 12 | Washington | 22,879,901,000 | 2.5% |
| 36 | West Virginia | 7,148,810,000 | 0.8% |
| 15 | Wisconsin | 19,101,351,000 | 2.1% |
| 50 | Wyoming | 2,172,024,000 | 0.2% |

RANK ORDER

| RANK | STATE | EXPENDITURES | % of USA |
|------|-------|--------------|----------|
| 1 | California | $120,329,505,000 | 12.9% |
| 2 | New York | 87,338,292,000 | 9.4% |
| 3 | Texas | 51,064,773,000 | 5.5% |
| 4 | Pennsylvania | 40,803,540,000 | 4.4% |
| 5 | Florida | 39,214,010,000 | 4.2% |
| 6 | Ohio | 39,209,266,000 | 4.2% |
| 7 | Michigan | 37,409,791,000 | 4.0% |
| 8 | Illinois | 35,685,258,000 | 3.8% |
| 9 | New Jersey | 31,701,874,000 | 3.4% |
| 10 | Massachusetts | 27,194,316,000 | 2.9% |
| 11 | North Carolina | 24,604,942,000 | 2.6% |
| 12 | Washington | 22,879,901,000 | 2.5% |
| 13 | Georgia | 21,735,461,000 | 2.3% |
| 14 | Virginia | 20,529,276,000 | 2.2% |
| 15 | Wisconsin | 19,101,351,000 | 2.1% |
| 16 | Minnesota | 18,418,302,000 | 2.0% |
| 17 | Indiana | 17,223,182,000 | 1.9% |
| 18 | Maryland | 16,578,483,000 | 1.8% |
| 19 | Missouri | 15,313,244,000 | 1.6% |
| 20 | Louisiana | 14,918,718,000 | 1.6% |
| 21 | Tennessee | 14,775,178,000 | 1.6% |
| 22 | Connecticut | 14,516,273,000 | 1.6% |
| 23 | Alabama | 13,728,431,000 | 1.5% |
| 24 | South Carolina | 13,574,926,000 | 1.5% |
| 25 | Kentucky | 13,541,073,000 | 1.5% |
| 26 | Oregon | 13,465,691,000 | 1.4% |
| 27 | Arizona | 13,327,967,000 | 1.4% |
| 28 | Colorado | 11,277,701,000 | 1.2% |
| 29 | Oklahoma | 9,952,733,000 | 1.1% |
| 30 | Iowa | 9,729,171,000 | 1.0% |
| 31 | Mississippi | 9,335,836,000 | 1.0% |
| 32 | Arkansas | 8,103,515,000 | 0.9% |
| 33 | Kansas | 7,681,014,000 | 0.8% |
| 34 | New Mexico | 7,539,619,000 | 0.8% |
| 35 | Utah | 7,470,282,000 | 0.8% |
| 36 | West Virginia | 7,148,810,000 | 0.8% |
| 37 | Hawaii | 5,860,425,000 | 0.6% |
| 38 | Alaska | 5,803,173,000 | 0.6% |
| 39 | Nevada | 5,397,584,000 | 0.6% |
| 40 | Nebraska | 4,753,513,000 | 0.5% |
| 41 | Maine | 4,606,471,000 | 0.5% |
| 42 | Rhode Island | 3,964,337,000 | 0.4% |
| 43 | Idaho | 3,785,613,000 | 0.4% |
| 44 | New Hampshire | 3,477,180,000 | 0.4% |
| 45 | Delaware | 3,465,428,000 | 0.4% |
| 46 | Montana | 3,262,167,000 | 0.4% |
| 47 | North Dakota | 2,526,823,000 | 0.3% |
| 48 | Vermont | 2,295,310,000 | 0.2% |
| 49 | South Dakota | 2,244,814,000 | 0.2% |
| 50 | Wyoming | 2,172,024,000 | 0.2% |
| | District of Columbia** | NA | NA |

Source: U.S. Bureau of the Census, Governments Division
"1998 State Government Finance Data" (http://www.census.gov/govs/www/state98.html)
*Total expenditures includes all money paid other than for retirement of debt and extension of loans. Includes payments from all sources of funds including current revenues and proceeds from borrowing and prior year fund balances. Includes intergovernmental transfers and expenditures for government owned utilities and other commercial or auxiliary enterprise and insurance trust expenditures. **Not applicable.

# Per Capita State Government Total Expenditures in 1998

## National Per Capita = $3,448*

ALPHA ORDER

RANK ORDER

| RANK | STATE | PER CAPITA | | RANK | STATE | PER CAPITA |
|---|---|---|---|---|---|---|
| 33 | Alabama | $3,155 | | 1 | Alaska | $9,433 |
| 1 | Alaska | 9,433 | | 2 | Hawaii | 4,923 |
| 44 | Arizona | 2,856 | | 3 | New York | 4,810 |
| 32 | Arkansas | 3,193 | | 4 | Delaware | 4,657 |
| 20 | California | 3,682 | | 5 | Wyoming | 4,525 |
| 46 | Colorado | 2,841 | | 6 | Connecticut | 4,436 |
| 6 | Connecticut | 4,436 | | 7 | Massachusetts | 4,426 |
| 4 | Delaware | 4,657 | | 8 | New Mexico | 4,349 |
| 49 | Florida | 2,630 | | 9 | Oregon | 4,103 |
| 45 | Georgia | 2,846 | | 10 | Washington | 4,023 |
| 2 | Hawaii | 4,923 | | 11 | Rhode Island | 4,014 |
| 35 | Idaho | 3,075 | | 12 | North Dakota | 3,962 |
| 39 | Illinois | 2,957 | | 13 | West Virginia | 3,946 |
| 41 | Indiana | 2,915 | | 14 | New Jersey | 3,916 |
| 27 | Iowa | 3,401 | | 15 | Minnesota | 3,897 |
| 42 | Kansas | 2,911 | | 16 | Vermont | 3,887 |
| 25 | Kentucky | 3,442 | | 17 | Michigan | 3,809 |
| 26 | Louisiana | 3,420 | | 18 | Montana | 3,709 |
| 19 | Maine | 3,692 | | 19 | Maine | 3,692 |
| 31 | Maryland | 3,232 | | 20 | California | 3,682 |
| 7 | Massachusetts | 4,426 | | 21 | Wisconsin | 3,658 |
| 17 | Michigan | 3,809 | | 22 | Utah | 3,556 |
| 15 | Minnesota | 3,897 | | 23 | South Carolina | 3,536 |
| 29 | Mississippi | 3,393 | | 24 | Ohio | 3,489 |
| 47 | Missouri | 2,816 | | 25 | Kentucky | 3,442 |
| 18 | Montana | 3,709 | | 26 | Louisiana | 3,420 |
| 43 | Nebraska | 2,862 | | 27 | Iowa | 3,401 |
| 34 | Nevada | 3,095 | | 28 | Pennsylvania | 3,400 |
| 40 | New Hampshire | 2,932 | | 29 | Mississippi | 3,393 |
| 14 | New Jersey | 3,916 | | 30 | North Carolina | 3,261 |
| 8 | New Mexico | 4,349 | | 31 | Maryland | 3,232 |
| 3 | New York | 4,810 | | 32 | Arkansas | 3,193 |
| 30 | North Carolina | 3,261 | | 33 | Alabama | 3,155 |
| 12 | North Dakota | 3,962 | | 34 | Nevada | 3,095 |
| 24 | Ohio | 3,489 | | 35 | Idaho | 3,075 |
| 38 | Oklahoma | 2,980 | | 36 | South Dakota | 3,072 |
| 9 | Oregon | 4,103 | | 37 | Virginia | 3,024 |
| 28 | Pennsylvania | 3,400 | | 38 | Oklahoma | 2,980 |
| 11 | Rhode Island | 4,014 | | 39 | Illinois | 2,957 |
| 23 | South Carolina | 3,536 | | 40 | New Hampshire | 2,932 |
| 36 | South Dakota | 3,072 | | 41 | Indiana | 2,915 |
| 48 | Tennessee | 2,720 | | 42 | Kansas | 2,911 |
| 50 | Texas | 2,590 | | 43 | Nebraska | 2,862 |
| 22 | Utah | 3,556 | | 44 | Arizona | 2,856 |
| 16 | Vermont | 3,887 | | 45 | Georgia | 2,846 |
| 37 | Virginia | 3,024 | | 46 | Colorado | 2,841 |
| 10 | Washington | 4,023 | | 47 | Missouri | 2,816 |
| 13 | West Virginia | 3,946 | | 48 | Tennessee | 2,720 |
| 21 | Wisconsin | 3,658 | | 49 | Florida | 2,630 |
| 5 | Wyoming | 4,525 | | 50 | Texas | 2,590 |

District of Columbia**    NA

Source: Morgan Quitno Press using data from U.S. Bureau of the Census, Governments Division
"1998 State Government Finance Data" (http://www.census.gov/govs/www/state98.html)
*Total expenditures includes all money paid other than for retirement of debt and extension of loans. Includes payments from all sources of funds including current revenues and proceeds from borrowing and prior year fund balances. Includes intergovernmental transfers and expenditures for government owned utilities and other commercial or auxiliary enterprise and insurance trust expenditures. **Not applicable.

# State Government Direct General Expenditures in 1998

## National Total = $548,800,136,000*

ALPHA ORDER

RANK ORDER

| RANK | STATE | EXPENDITURES | % of USA | | RANK | STATE | EXPENDITURES | % of USA |
|---|---|---|---|---|---|---|---|---|
| 24 | Alabama | $9,055,769,000 | 1.7% | | 1 | California | $55,627,745,000 | 10.1% |
| 38 | Alaska | 4,247,041,000 | 0.8% | | 2 | New York | 46,597,854,000 | 8.5% |
| 27 | Arizona | 7,046,591,000 | 1.3% | | 3 | Texas | 32,378,166,000 | 5.9% |
| 32 | Arkansas | 5,462,072,000 | 1.0% | | 4 | Pennsylvania | 25,445,361,000 | 4.6% |
| 1 | California | 55,627,745,000 | 10.1% | | 5 | Florida | 24,124,998,000 | 4.4% |
| 28 | Colorado | 6,945,189,000 | 1.3% | | 6 | Illinois | 22,143,271,000 | 4.0% |
| 18 | Connecticut | 10,053,048,000 | 1.8% | | 7 | Ohio | 20,728,906,000 | 3.8% |
| 43 | Delaware | 2,612,144,000 | 0.5% | | 8 | Massachusetts | 18,937,546,000 | 3.5% |
| 5 | Florida | 24,124,998,000 | 4.4% | | 9 | New Jersey | 18,797,715,000 | 3.4% |
| 12 | Georgia | 13,970,490,000 | 2.5% | | 10 | Michigan | 18,635,615,000 | 3.4% |
| 34 | Hawaii | 5,114,420,000 | 0.9% | | 11 | North Carolina | 14,742,145,000 | 2.7% |
| 45 | Idaho | 2,272,491,000 | 0.4% | | 12 | Georgia | 13,970,490,000 | 2.5% |
| 6 | Illinois | 22,143,271,000 | 4.0% | | 13 | Washington | 13,622,783,000 | 2.5% |
| 17 | Indiana | 10,395,011,000 | 1.9% | | 14 | Virginia | 13,376,522,000 | 2.4% |
| 29 | Iowa | 6,235,861,000 | 1.1% | | 15 | Maryland | 10,770,621,000 | 2.0% |
| 37 | Kansas | 4,531,293,000 | 0.8% | | 16 | Minnesota | 10,640,213,000 | 1.9% |
| 23 | Kentucky | 9,276,651,000 | 1.7% | | 17 | Indiana | 10,395,011,000 | 1.9% |
| 20 | Louisiana | 9,972,274,000 | 1.8% | | 18 | Connecticut | 10,053,048,000 | 1.8% |
| 39 | Maine | 3,321,285,000 | 0.6% | | 19 | Missouri | 10,014,765,000 | 1.8% |
| 15 | Maryland | 10,770,621,000 | 2.0% | | 20 | Louisiana | 9,972,274,000 | 1.8% |
| 8 | Massachusetts | 18,937,546,000 | 3.5% | | 21 | Tennessee | 9,951,290,000 | 1.8% |
| 10 | Michigan | 18,635,615,000 | 3.4% | | 22 | Wisconsin | 9,498,902,000 | 1.7% |
| 16 | Minnesota | 10,640,213,000 | 1.9% | | 23 | Kentucky | 9,276,651,000 | 1.7% |
| 31 | Mississippi | 5,650,011,000 | 1.0% | | 24 | Alabama | 9,055,769,000 | 1.7% |
| 19 | Missouri | 10,014,765,000 | 1.8% | | 25 | South Carolina | 8,703,773,000 | 1.6% |
| 46 | Montana | 2,177,220,000 | 0.4% | | 26 | Oregon | 7,260,348,000 | 1.3% |
| 40 | Nebraska | 3,273,447,000 | 0.6% | | 27 | Arizona | 7,046,591,000 | 1.3% |
| 42 | Nevada | 2,781,142,000 | 0.5% | | 28 | Colorado | 6,945,189,000 | 1.3% |
| 44 | New Hampshire | 2,584,797,000 | 0.5% | | 29 | Iowa | 6,235,861,000 | 1.1% |
| 9 | New Jersey | 18,797,715,000 | 3.4% | | 30 | Oklahoma | 5,890,237,000 | 1.1% |
| 35 | New Mexico | 4,756,882,000 | 0.9% | | 31 | Mississippi | 5,650,011,000 | 1.0% |
| 2 | New York | 46,597,854,000 | 8.5% | | 32 | Arkansas | 5,462,072,000 | 1.0% |
| 11 | North Carolina | 14,742,145,000 | 2.7% | | 33 | Utah | 5,209,914,000 | 0.9% |
| 48 | North Dakota | 1,785,766,000 | 0.3% | | 34 | Hawaii | 5,114,420,000 | 0.9% |
| 7 | Ohio | 20,728,906,000 | 3.8% | | 35 | New Mexico | 4,756,882,000 | 0.9% |
| 30 | Oklahoma | 5,890,237,000 | 1.1% | | 36 | West Virginia | 4,680,644,000 | 0.9% |
| 26 | Oregon | 7,260,348,000 | 1.3% | | 37 | Kansas | 4,531,293,000 | 0.8% |
| 4 | Pennsylvania | 25,445,361,000 | 4.6% | | 38 | Alaska | 4,247,041,000 | 0.8% |
| 41 | Rhode Island | 2,865,413,000 | 0.5% | | 39 | Maine | 3,321,285,000 | 0.6% |
| 25 | South Carolina | 8,703,773,000 | 1.6% | | 40 | Nebraska | 3,273,447,000 | 0.6% |
| 49 | South Dakota | 1,626,889,000 | 0.3% | | 41 | Rhode Island | 2,865,413,000 | 0.5% |
| 21 | Tennessee | 9,951,290,000 | 1.8% | | 42 | Nevada | 2,781,142,000 | 0.5% |
| 3 | Texas | 32,378,166,000 | 5.9% | | 43 | Delaware | 2,612,144,000 | 0.5% |
| 33 | Utah | 5,209,914,000 | 0.9% | | 44 | New Hampshire | 2,584,797,000 | 0.5% |
| 47 | Vermont | 1,798,454,000 | 0.3% | | 45 | Idaho | 2,272,491,000 | 0.4% |
| 14 | Virginia | 13,376,522,000 | 2.4% | | 46 | Montana | 2,177,220,000 | 0.4% |
| 13 | Washington | 13,622,783,000 | 2.5% | | 47 | Vermont | 1,798,454,000 | 0.3% |
| 36 | West Virginia | 4,680,644,000 | 0.9% | | 48 | North Dakota | 1,785,766,000 | 0.3% |
| 22 | Wisconsin | 9,498,902,000 | 1.7% | | 49 | South Dakota | 1,626,889,000 | 0.3% |
| 50 | Wyoming | 1,209,151,000 | 0.2% | | 50 | Wyoming | 1,209,151,000 | 0.2% |
| | | | | | | District of Columbia** | NA | NA |

*Source: U.S. Bureau of the Census, Governments Division*
 *"1998 State Government Finance Data" (http://www.census.gov/govs/www/state98.html)*
*Direct general expenditures include expenditures for current operations, assistance and subsidies, interest on debt and capital outlay. Excludes intergovernmental transfers, expenditures for government owned utilities and other commercial or auxiliary enterprise and insurance trust expenditures.*
**Not applicable.*

# Per Capita State Government Direct General Expenditures in 1998

## National Per Capita = $2,035*

ALPHA ORDER

| RANK | STATE | PER CAPITA |
|---|---|---|
| 29 | Alabama | $2,081 |
| 1 | Alaska | 6,903 |
| 50 | Arizona | 1,510 |
| 26 | Arkansas | 2,152 |
| 46 | California | 1,702 |
| 44 | Colorado | 1,750 |
| 5 | Connecticut | 3,072 |
| 3 | Delaware | 3,511 |
| 48 | Florida | 1,618 |
| 40 | Georgia | 1,829 |
| 2 | Hawaii | 4,296 |
| 35 | Idaho | 1,846 |
| 38 | Illinois | 1,835 |
| 43 | Indiana | 1,760 |
| 24 | Iowa | 2,180 |
| 45 | Kansas | 1,717 |
| 17 | Kentucky | 2,358 |
| 19 | Louisiana | 2,286 |
| 10 | Maine | 2,662 |
| 28 | Maryland | 2,100 |
| 4 | Massachusetts | 3,082 |
| 34 | Michigan | 1,898 |
| 21 | Minnesota | 2,251 |
| 30 | Mississippi | 2,054 |
| 37 | Missouri | 1,842 |
| 15 | Montana | 2,475 |
| 31 | Nebraska | 1,971 |
| 49 | Nevada | 1,595 |
| 24 | New Hampshire | 2,180 |
| 18 | New Jersey | 2,322 |
| 9 | New Mexico | 2,744 |
| 12 | New York | 2,566 |
| 33 | North Carolina | 1,954 |
| 8 | North Dakota | 2,800 |
| 36 | Ohio | 1,845 |
| 42 | Oklahoma | 1,764 |
| 23 | Oregon | 2,212 |
| 27 | Pennsylvania | 2,120 |
| 7 | Rhode Island | 2,901 |
| 20 | South Carolina | 2,267 |
| 22 | South Dakota | 2,226 |
| 39 | Tennessee | 1,832 |
| 47 | Texas | 1,643 |
| 14 | Utah | 2,480 |
| 6 | Vermont | 3,045 |
| 32 | Virginia | 1,970 |
| 16 | Washington | 2,395 |
| 11 | West Virginia | 2,584 |
| 41 | Wisconsin | 1,819 |
| 13 | Wyoming | 2,519 |

RANK ORDER

| RANK | STATE | PER CAPITA |
|---|---|---|
| 1 | Alaska | $6,903 |
| 2 | Hawaii | 4,296 |
| 3 | Delaware | 3,511 |
| 4 | Massachusetts | 3,082 |
| 5 | Connecticut | 3,072 |
| 6 | Vermont | 3,045 |
| 7 | Rhode Island | 2,901 |
| 8 | North Dakota | 2,800 |
| 9 | New Mexico | 2,744 |
| 10 | Maine | 2,662 |
| 11 | West Virginia | 2,584 |
| 12 | New York | 2,566 |
| 13 | Wyoming | 2,519 |
| 14 | Utah | 2,480 |
| 15 | Montana | 2,475 |
| 16 | Washington | 2,395 |
| 17 | Kentucky | 2,358 |
| 18 | New Jersey | 2,322 |
| 19 | Louisiana | 2,286 |
| 20 | South Carolina | 2,267 |
| 21 | Minnesota | 2,251 |
| 22 | South Dakota | 2,226 |
| 23 | Oregon | 2,212 |
| 24 | Iowa | 2,180 |
| 24 | New Hampshire | 2,180 |
| 26 | Arkansas | 2,152 |
| 27 | Pennsylvania | 2,120 |
| 28 | Maryland | 2,100 |
| 29 | Alabama | 2,081 |
| 30 | Mississippi | 2,054 |
| 31 | Nebraska | 1,971 |
| 32 | Virginia | 1,970 |
| 33 | North Carolina | 1,954 |
| 34 | Michigan | 1,898 |
| 35 | Idaho | 1,846 |
| 36 | Ohio | 1,845 |
| 37 | Missouri | 1,842 |
| 38 | Illinois | 1,835 |
| 39 | Tennessee | 1,832 |
| 40 | Georgia | 1,829 |
| 41 | Wisconsin | 1,819 |
| 42 | Oklahoma | 1,764 |
| 43 | Indiana | 1,760 |
| 44 | Colorado | 1,750 |
| 45 | Kansas | 1,717 |
| 46 | California | 1,702 |
| 47 | Texas | 1,643 |
| 48 | Florida | 1,618 |
| 49 | Nevada | 1,595 |
| 50 | Arizona | 1,510 |

District of Columbia**          NA

Source: Morgan Quitno Press using data from U.S. Bureau of the Census, Governments Division
"1998 State Government Finance Data" (http://www.census.gov/govs/www/state98.html)
*Direct general expenditures include expenditures for current operations, assistance and subsidies, interest on debt and capital outlay. Excludes intergovernmental transfers, expenditures for government owned utilities and other commercial or auxiliary enterprise and insurance trust expenditures.
**Not applicable.

# State Government Debt Outstanding in 1998

## National Total = $483,117,137,000*

ALPHA ORDER

| RANK | STATE | DEBT | % of USA |
|---|---|---|---|
| 28 | Alabama | $4,166,572,000 | 0.9% |
| 30 | Alaska | 3,799,708,000 | 0.8% |
| 38 | Arizona | 2,806,922,000 | 0.6% |
| 41 | Arkansas | 2,384,116,000 | 0.5% |
| 2 | California | 50,250,539,000 | 10.4% |
| 32 | Colorado | 3,637,200,000 | 0.8% |
| 6 | Connecticut | 17,727,048,000 | 3.7% |
| 31 | Delaware | 3,770,259,000 | 0.8% |
| 7 | Florida | 16,969,289,000 | 3.5% |
| 21 | Georgia | 6,039,633,000 | 1.3% |
| 23 | Hawaii | 5,709,739,000 | 1.2% |
| 47 | Idaho | 1,883,221,000 | 0.4% |
| 5 | Illinois | 25,314,532,000 | 5.2% |
| 20 | Indiana | 6,704,287,000 | 1.4% |
| 45 | Iowa | 2,029,300,000 | 0.4% |
| 48 | Kansas | 1,411,135,000 | 0.3% |
| 19 | Kentucky | 6,813,880,000 | 1.4% |
| 17 | Louisiana | 7,093,467,000 | 1.5% |
| 33 | Maine | 3,474,244,000 | 0.7% |
| 14 | Maryland | 10,536,254,000 | 2.2% |
| 3 | Massachusetts | 32,833,163,000 | 6.8% |
| 9 | Michigan | 16,147,205,000 | 3.3% |
| 26 | Minnesota | 5,332,686,000 | 1.1% |
| 39 | Mississippi | 2,673,577,000 | 0.6% |
| 16 | Missouri | 8,091,313,000 | 1.7% |
| 42 | Montana | 2,258,784,000 | 0.5% |
| 46 | Nebraska | 1,908,357,000 | 0.4% |
| 37 | Nevada | 2,880,506,000 | 0.6% |
| 24 | New Hampshire | 5,367,479,000 | 1.1% |
| 4 | New Jersey | 27,213,664,000 | 5.6% |
| 40 | New Mexico | 2,571,766,000 | 0.5% |
| 1 | New York | 73,254,370,000 | 15.2% |
| 18 | North Carolina | 6,877,271,000 | 1.4% |
| 50 | North Dakota | 857,474,000 | 0.2% |
| 11 | Ohio | 14,182,878,000 | 2.9% |
| 29 | Oklahoma | 3,951,153,000 | 0.8% |
| 22 | Oregon | 5,729,123,000 | 1.2% |
| 8 | Pennsylvania | 16,393,928,000 | 3.4% |
| 25 | Rhode Island | 5,351,703,000 | 1.1% |
| 27 | South Carolina | 5,191,423,000 | 1.1% |
| 44 | South Dakota | 2,067,990,000 | 0.4% |
| 36 | Tennessee | 3,191,892,000 | 0.7% |
| 10 | Texas | 14,408,011,000 | 3.0% |
| 34 | Utah | 3,435,168,000 | 0.7% |
| 43 | Vermont | 2,109,788,000 | 0.4% |
| 12 | Virginia | 10,828,138,000 | 2.2% |
| 15 | Washington | 10,289,381,000 | 2.1% |
| 35 | West Virginia | 3,433,365,000 | 0.7% |
| 13 | Wisconsin | 10,720,738,000 | 2.2% |
| 49 | Wyoming | 1,043,498,000 | 0.2% |

RANK ORDER

| RANK | STATE | DEBT | % of USA |
|---|---|---|---|
| 1 | New York | $73,254,370,000 | 15.2% |
| 2 | California | 50,250,539,000 | 10.4% |
| 3 | Massachusetts | 32,833,163,000 | 6.8% |
| 4 | New Jersey | 27,213,664,000 | 5.6% |
| 5 | Illinois | 25,314,532,000 | 5.2% |
| 6 | Connecticut | 17,727,048,000 | 3.7% |
| 7 | Florida | 16,969,289,000 | 3.5% |
| 8 | Pennsylvania | 16,393,928,000 | 3.4% |
| 9 | Michigan | 16,147,205,000 | 3.3% |
| 10 | Texas | 14,408,011,000 | 3.0% |
| 11 | Ohio | 14,182,878,000 | 2.9% |
| 12 | Virginia | 10,828,138,000 | 2.2% |
| 13 | Wisconsin | 10,720,738,000 | 2.2% |
| 14 | Maryland | 10,536,254,000 | 2.2% |
| 15 | Washington | 10,289,381,000 | 2.1% |
| 16 | Missouri | 8,091,313,000 | 1.7% |
| 17 | Louisiana | 7,093,467,000 | 1.5% |
| 18 | North Carolina | 6,877,271,000 | 1.4% |
| 19 | Kentucky | 6,813,880,000 | 1.4% |
| 20 | Indiana | 6,704,287,000 | 1.4% |
| 21 | Georgia | 6,039,633,000 | 1.3% |
| 22 | Oregon | 5,729,123,000 | 1.2% |
| 23 | Hawaii | 5,709,739,000 | 1.2% |
| 24 | New Hampshire | 5,367,479,000 | 1.1% |
| 25 | Rhode Island | 5,351,703,000 | 1.1% |
| 26 | Minnesota | 5,332,686,000 | 1.1% |
| 27 | South Carolina | 5,191,423,000 | 1.1% |
| 28 | Alabama | 4,166,572,000 | 0.9% |
| 29 | Oklahoma | 3,951,153,000 | 0.8% |
| 30 | Alaska | 3,799,708,000 | 0.8% |
| 31 | Delaware | 3,770,259,000 | 0.8% |
| 32 | Colorado | 3,637,200,000 | 0.8% |
| 33 | Maine | 3,474,244,000 | 0.7% |
| 34 | Utah | 3,435,168,000 | 0.7% |
| 35 | West Virginia | 3,433,365,000 | 0.7% |
| 36 | Tennessee | 3,191,892,000 | 0.7% |
| 37 | Nevada | 2,880,506,000 | 0.6% |
| 38 | Arizona | 2,806,922,000 | 0.6% |
| 39 | Mississippi | 2,673,577,000 | 0.6% |
| 40 | New Mexico | 2,571,766,000 | 0.5% |
| 41 | Arkansas | 2,384,116,000 | 0.5% |
| 42 | Montana | 2,258,784,000 | 0.5% |
| 43 | Vermont | 2,109,788,000 | 0.4% |
| 44 | South Dakota | 2,067,990,000 | 0.4% |
| 45 | Iowa | 2,029,300,000 | 0.4% |
| 46 | Nebraska | 1,908,357,000 | 0.4% |
| 47 | Idaho | 1,883,221,000 | 0.4% |
| 48 | Kansas | 1,411,135,000 | 0.3% |
| 49 | Wyoming | 1,043,498,000 | 0.2% |
| 50 | North Dakota | 857,474,000 | 0.2% |
| | District of Columbia** | NA | NA |

Source: U.S. Bureau of the Census, Governments Division
"1998 State Government Finance Data" (http://www.census.gov/govs/www/state98.html)
*Includes short-term, long-term, full fail and credit, nonguaranteed and public debt for private purposes.
**Not applicable.

# Per Capita State Government Debt Outstanding in 1998

## National Per Capita = $1,791*

ALPHA ORDER

RANK ORDER

| RANK | STATE | PER CAPITA | | RANK | STATE | PER CAPITA |
|---|---|---|---|---|---|---|
| 41 | Alabama | $958 | | 1 | Alaska | $6,176 |
| 1 | Alaska | 6,176 | | 2 | Rhode Island | 5,418 |
| 48 | Arizona | 601 | | 3 | Connecticut | 5,417 |
| 42 | Arkansas | 939 | | 4 | Massachusetts | 5,344 |
| 27 | California | 1,538 | | 5 | Delaware | 5,067 |
| 43 | Colorado | 916 | | 6 | Hawaii | 4,796 |
| 3 | Connecticut | 5,417 | | 7 | New Hampshire | 4,526 |
| 5 | Delaware | 5,067 | | 8 | New York | 4,034 |
| 37 | Florida | 1,138 | | 9 | Vermont | 3,572 |
| 45 | Georgia | 791 | | 10 | New Jersey | 3,362 |
| 6 | Hawaii | 4,796 | | 11 | South Dakota | 2,830 |
| 28 | Idaho | 1,530 | | 12 | Maine | 2,785 |
| 15 | Illinois | 2,097 | | 13 | Montana | 2,568 |
| 38 | Indiana | 1,135 | | 14 | Wyoming | 2,174 |
| 47 | Iowa | 709 | | 15 | Illinois | 2,097 |
| 50 | Kansas | 535 | | 16 | Maryland | 2,054 |
| 21 | Kentucky | 1,732 | | 17 | Wisconsin | 2,053 |
| 25 | Louisiana | 1,626 | | 18 | West Virginia | 1,895 |
| 12 | Maine | 2,785 | | 19 | Washington | 1,809 |
| 16 | Maryland | 2,054 | | 20 | Oregon | 1,746 |
| 4 | Massachusetts | 5,344 | | 21 | Kentucky | 1,732 |
| 23 | Michigan | 1,644 | | 22 | Nevada | 1,652 |
| 39 | Minnesota | 1,128 | | 23 | Michigan | 1,644 |
| 40 | Mississippi | 972 | | 24 | Utah | 1,635 |
| 29 | Missouri | 1,488 | | 25 | Louisiana | 1,626 |
| 13 | Montana | 2,568 | | 26 | Virginia | 1,595 |
| 36 | Nebraska | 1,149 | | 27 | California | 1,538 |
| 22 | Nevada | 1,652 | | 28 | Idaho | 1,530 |
| 7 | New Hampshire | 4,526 | | 29 | Missouri | 1,488 |
| 10 | New Jersey | 3,362 | | 30 | New Mexico | 1,484 |
| 30 | New Mexico | 1,484 | | 31 | Pennsylvania | 1,366 |
| 8 | New York | 4,034 | | 32 | South Carolina | 1,352 |
| 44 | North Carolina | 911 | | 33 | North Dakota | 1,344 |
| 33 | North Dakota | 1,344 | | 34 | Ohio | 1,262 |
| 34 | Ohio | 1,262 | | 35 | Oklahoma | 1,183 |
| 35 | Oklahoma | 1,183 | | 36 | Nebraska | 1,149 |
| 20 | Oregon | 1,746 | | 37 | Florida | 1,138 |
| 31 | Pennsylvania | 1,366 | | 38 | Indiana | 1,135 |
| 2 | Rhode Island | 5,418 | | 39 | Minnesota | 1,128 |
| 32 | South Carolina | 1,352 | | 40 | Mississippi | 972 |
| 11 | South Dakota | 2,830 | | 41 | Alabama | 958 |
| 49 | Tennessee | 588 | | 42 | Arkansas | 939 |
| 46 | Texas | 731 | | 43 | Colorado | 916 |
| 24 | Utah | 1,635 | | 44 | North Carolina | 911 |
| 9 | Vermont | 3,572 | | 45 | Georgia | 791 |
| 26 | Virginia | 1,595 | | 46 | Texas | 731 |
| 19 | Washington | 1,809 | | 47 | Iowa | 709 |
| 18 | West Virginia | 1,895 | | 48 | Arizona | 601 |
| 17 | Wisconsin | 2,053 | | 49 | Tennessee | 588 |
| 14 | Wyoming | 2,174 | | 50 | Kansas | 535 |

District of Columbia**  NA

Source: Morgan Quitno Press using data from U.S. Bureau of the Census, Governments Division
"1998 State Government Finance Data" (http://www.census.gov/govs/www/state98.html)
*Includes short-term, long-term, full fail and credit, nonguaranteed and public debt for private purposes.
**Not applicable.

# State Government Full-Time Equivalent Employees in 1999

## National Total = 4,043,265 FTE Employees*

ALPHA ORDER

| RANK | STATE | EMPLOYEES | % of USA |
|---|---|---|---|
| 20 | Alabama | 81,001 | 2.0% |
| 41 | Alaska | 22,647 | 0.6% |
| 27 | Arizona | 62,823 | 1.6% |
| 33 | Arkansas | 51,477 | 1.3% |
| 1 | California | 350,161 | 8.7% |
| 28 | Colorado | 62,112 | 1.5% |
| 25 | Connecticut | 63,486 | 1.6% |
| 42 | Delaware | 22,519 | 0.6% |
| 4 | Florida | 179,654 | 4.4% |
| 11 | Georgia | 115,608 | 2.9% |
| 31 | Hawaii | 53,363 | 1.3% |
| 39 | Idaho | 23,933 | 0.6% |
| 6 | Illinois | 140,207 | 3.5% |
| 18 | Indiana | 81,570 | 2.0% |
| 32 | Iowa | 53,059 | 1.3% |
| 36 | Kansas | 43,207 | 1.1% |
| 24 | Kentucky | 69,908 | 1.7% |
| 14 | Louisiana | 95,588 | 2.4% |
| 43 | Maine | 20,093 | 0.5% |
| 16 | Maryland | 88,903 | 2.2% |
| 17 | Massachusetts | 87,393 | 2.2% |
| 7 | Michigan | 137,275 | 3.4% |
| 23 | Minnesota | 70,710 | 1.7% |
| 30 | Mississippi | 54,222 | 1.3% |
| 15 | Missouri | 92,543 | 2.3% |
| 45 | Montana | 18,715 | 0.5% |
| 38 | Nebraska | 29,575 | 0.7% |
| 40 | Nevada | 23,315 | 0.6% |
| 46 | New Hampshire | 18,580 | 0.5% |
| 9 | New Jersey | 130,131 | 3.2% |
| 35 | New Mexico | 44,075 | 1.1% |
| 3 | New York | 249,596 | 6.2% |
| 10 | North Carolina | 124,601 | 3.1% |
| 47 | North Dakota | 15,697 | 0.4% |
| 8 | Ohio | 137,103 | 3.4% |
| 22 | Oklahoma | 73,007 | 1.8% |
| 29 | Oregon | 55,119 | 1.4% |
| 5 | Pennsylvania | 146,798 | 3.6% |
| 44 | Rhode Island | 19,801 | 0.5% |
| 21 | South Carolina | 78,975 | 2.0% |
| 48 | South Dakota | 13,030 | 0.3% |
| 19 | Tennessee | 81,407 | 2.0% |
| 2 | Texas | 269,450 | 6.7% |
| 34 | Utah | 48,679 | 1.2% |
| 49 | Vermont | 12,714 | 0.3% |
| 12 | Virginia | 113,823 | 2.8% |
| 13 | Washington | 108,514 | 2.7% |
| 37 | West Virginia | 32,857 | 0.8% |
| 26 | Wisconsin | 63,185 | 1.6% |
| 50 | Wyoming | 11,056 | 0.3% |

RANK ORDER

| RANK | STATE | EMPLOYEES | % of USA |
|---|---|---|---|
| 1 | California | 350,161 | 8.7% |
| 2 | Texas | 269,450 | 6.7% |
| 3 | New York | 249,596 | 6.2% |
| 4 | Florida | 179,654 | 4.4% |
| 5 | Pennsylvania | 146,798 | 3.6% |
| 6 | Illinois | 140,207 | 3.5% |
| 7 | Michigan | 137,275 | 3.4% |
| 8 | Ohio | 137,103 | 3.4% |
| 9 | New Jersey | 130,131 | 3.2% |
| 10 | North Carolina | 124,601 | 3.1% |
| 11 | Georgia | 115,608 | 2.9% |
| 12 | Virginia | 113,823 | 2.8% |
| 13 | Washington | 108,514 | 2.7% |
| 14 | Louisiana | 95,588 | 2.4% |
| 15 | Missouri | 92,543 | 2.3% |
| 16 | Maryland | 88,903 | 2.2% |
| 17 | Massachusetts | 87,393 | 2.2% |
| 18 | Indiana | 81,570 | 2.0% |
| 19 | Tennessee | 81,407 | 2.0% |
| 20 | Alabama | 81,001 | 2.0% |
| 21 | South Carolina | 78,975 | 2.0% |
| 22 | Oklahoma | 73,007 | 1.8% |
| 23 | Minnesota | 70,710 | 1.7% |
| 24 | Kentucky | 69,908 | 1.7% |
| 25 | Connecticut | 63,486 | 1.6% |
| 26 | Wisconsin | 63,185 | 1.6% |
| 27 | Arizona | 62,823 | 1.6% |
| 28 | Colorado | 62,112 | 1.5% |
| 29 | Oregon | 55,119 | 1.4% |
| 30 | Mississippi | 54,222 | 1.3% |
| 31 | Hawaii | 53,363 | 1.3% |
| 32 | Iowa | 53,059 | 1.3% |
| 33 | Arkansas | 51,477 | 1.3% |
| 34 | Utah | 48,679 | 1.2% |
| 35 | New Mexico | 44,075 | 1.1% |
| 36 | Kansas | 43,207 | 1.1% |
| 37 | West Virginia | 32,857 | 0.8% |
| 38 | Nebraska | 29,575 | 0.7% |
| 39 | Idaho | 23,933 | 0.6% |
| 40 | Nevada | 23,315 | 0.6% |
| 41 | Alaska | 22,647 | 0.6% |
| 42 | Delaware | 22,519 | 0.6% |
| 43 | Maine | 20,093 | 0.5% |
| 44 | Rhode Island | 19,801 | 0.5% |
| 45 | Montana | 18,715 | 0.5% |
| 46 | New Hampshire | 18,580 | 0.5% |
| 47 | North Dakota | 15,697 | 0.4% |
| 48 | South Dakota | 13,030 | 0.3% |
| 49 | Vermont | 12,714 | 0.3% |
| 50 | Wyoming | 11,056 | 0.3% |
| | District of Columbia** | NA | NA |

*Source: U.S. Bureau of the Census, Governments Division*
    *"1999 State Government Employment and Payroll" (http://www.census.gov/govs/www/apesst99.html)*
*As of March 1999.
**Not applicable.

# Rate of State Government FTE Employment in 1999

## National Rate = 148 State Government Employees per 10,000 Population*

| ALPHA ORDER | | | | RANK ORDER | | |
|---|---|---|---|---|---|---|
| RANK | STATE | RATE | | RANK | STATE | RATE |
| 19 | Alabama | 185 | | 1 | Hawaii | 450 |
| 2 | Alaska | 366 | | 2 | Alaska | 366 |
| 43 | Arizona | 131 | | 3 | Delaware | 299 |
| 13 | Arkansas | 202 | | 4 | New Mexico | 253 |
| 50 | California | 106 | | 5 | North Dakota | 248 |
| 34 | Colorado | 153 | | 6 | Wyoming | 231 |
| 16 | Connecticut | 193 | | 7 | Utah | 229 |
| 3 | Delaware | 299 | | 8 | Louisiana | 219 |
| 48 | Florida | 119 | | 9 | Oklahoma | 217 |
| 35 | Georgia | 148 | | 10 | Vermont | 214 |
| 1 | Hawaii | 450 | | 11 | Montana | 212 |
| 17 | Idaho | 191 | | 12 | South Carolina | 203 |
| 49 | Illinois | 116 | | 13 | Arkansas | 202 |
| 40 | Indiana | 137 | | 14 | Rhode Island | 200 |
| 19 | Iowa | 185 | | 15 | Mississippi | 196 |
| 29 | Kansas | 163 | | 16 | Connecticut | 193 |
| 24 | Kentucky | 176 | | 17 | Idaho | 191 |
| 8 | Louisiana | 219 | | 18 | Washington | 189 |
| 31 | Maine | 160 | | 19 | Alabama | 185 |
| 25 | Maryland | 172 | | 19 | Iowa | 185 |
| 38 | Massachusetts | 142 | | 21 | West Virginia | 182 |
| 39 | Michigan | 139 | | 22 | Nebraska | 178 |
| 35 | Minnesota | 148 | | 22 | South Dakota | 178 |
| 15 | Mississippi | 196 | | 24 | Kentucky | 176 |
| 26 | Missouri | 169 | | 25 | Maryland | 172 |
| 11 | Montana | 212 | | 26 | Missouri | 169 |
| 22 | Nebraska | 178 | | 27 | Oregon | 166 |
| 44 | Nevada | 129 | | 27 | Virginia | 166 |
| 33 | New Hampshire | 155 | | 29 | Kansas | 163 |
| 31 | New Jersey | 160 | | 29 | North Carolina | 163 |
| 4 | New Mexico | 253 | | 31 | Maine | 160 |
| 40 | New York | 137 | | 31 | New Jersey | 160 |
| 29 | North Carolina | 163 | | 33 | New Hampshire | 155 |
| 5 | North Dakota | 248 | | 34 | Colorado | 153 |
| 45 | Ohio | 122 | | 35 | Georgia | 148 |
| 9 | Oklahoma | 217 | | 35 | Minnesota | 148 |
| 27 | Oregon | 166 | | 35 | Tennessee | 148 |
| 45 | Pennsylvania | 122 | | 38 | Massachusetts | 142 |
| 14 | Rhode Island | 200 | | 39 | Michigan | 139 |
| 12 | South Carolina | 203 | | 40 | Indiana | 137 |
| 22 | South Dakota | 178 | | 40 | New York | 137 |
| 35 | Tennessee | 148 | | 42 | Texas | 134 |
| 42 | Texas | 134 | | 43 | Arizona | 131 |
| 7 | Utah | 229 | | 44 | Nevada | 129 |
| 10 | Vermont | 214 | | 45 | Ohio | 122 |
| 27 | Virginia | 166 | | 45 | Pennsylvania | 122 |
| 18 | Washington | 189 | | 47 | Wisconsin | 120 |
| 21 | West Virginia | 182 | | 48 | Florida | 119 |
| 47 | Wisconsin | 120 | | 49 | Illinois | 116 |
| 6 | Wyoming | 231 | | 50 | California | 106 |
| | | | | | District of Columbia** | NA |

Source: Morgan Quitno Press using data from U.S. Bureau of the Census, Governments Division
    "1999 State Government Employment and Payroll" (http://www.census.gov/govs/www/apesst99.html)
*Full-time equivalent as of March 1999.
**Not applicable.

# Local Government Total Revenue in 1997

## National Total = $847,769,879,000*

ALPHA ORDER

| RANK | STATE | REVENUE | % of USA |
|---|---|---|---|
| 23 | Alabama | $10,603,550,000 | 1.3% |
| 41 | Alaska | 2,712,835,000 | 0.3% |
| 20 | Arizona | 13,645,670,000 | 1.6% |
| 36 | Arkansas | 4,914,056,000 | 0.6% |
| 1 | California | 130,510,365,000 | 15.4% |
| 22 | Colorado | 12,827,527,000 | 1.5% |
| 26 | Connecticut | 9,231,394,000 | 1.1% |
| 47 | Delaware | 1,596,882,000 | 0.2% |
| 4 | Florida | 46,461,900,000 | 5.5% |
| 10 | Georgia | 22,073,881,000 | 2.6% |
| 46 | Hawaii | 1,620,451,000 | 0.2% |
| 40 | Idaho | 2,761,767,000 | 0.3% |
| 5 | Illinois | 37,782,363,000 | 4.5% |
| 18 | Indiana | 15,548,558,000 | 1.8% |
| 29 | Iowa | 7,785,806,000 | 0.9% |
| 30 | Kansas | 7,372,394,000 | 0.9% |
| 28 | Kentucky | 7,917,853,000 | 0.9% |
| 24 | Louisiana | 10,485,269,000 | 1.2% |
| 39 | Maine | 2,839,790,000 | 0.3% |
| 19 | Maryland | 14,303,664,000 | 1.7% |
| 13 | Massachusetts | 18,007,356,000 | 2.1% |
| 8 | Michigan | 29,942,304,000 | 3.5% |
| 16 | Minnesota | 16,502,760,000 | 1.9% |
| 33 | Mississippi | 6,236,043,000 | 0.7% |
| 21 | Missouri | 12,836,512,000 | 1.5% |
| 44 | Montana | 1,895,830,000 | 0.2% |
| 32 | Nebraska | 6,243,699,000 | 0.7% |
| 35 | Nevada | 5,508,102,000 | 0.6% |
| 42 | New Hampshire | 2,605,214,000 | 0.3% |
| 9 | New Jersey | 25,346,587,000 | 3.0% |
| 37 | New Mexico | 4,116,814,000 | 0.5% |
| 2 | New York | 96,811,209,000 | 11.4% |
| 11 | North Carolina | 20,947,344,000 | 2.5% |
| 49 | North Dakota | 1,448,209,000 | 0.2% |
| 7 | Ohio | 30,712,896,000 | 3.6% |
| 31 | Oklahoma | 7,267,858,000 | 0.9% |
| 25 | Oregon | 10,345,636,000 | 1.2% |
| 6 | Pennsylvania | 33,228,951,000 | 3.9% |
| 43 | Rhode Island | 2,285,741,000 | 0.3% |
| 27 | South Carolina | 8,860,540,000 | 1.0% |
| 48 | South Dakota | 1,569,601,000 | 0.2% |
| 17 | Tennessee | 16,482,826,000 | 1.9% |
| 3 | Texas | 53,534,527,000 | 6.3% |
| 34 | Utah | 5,682,467,000 | 0.7% |
| 50 | Vermont | 1,295,106,000 | 0.2% |
| 14 | Virginia | 17,270,319,000 | 2.0% |
| 12 | Washington | 19,363,535,000 | 2.3% |
| 38 | West Virginia | 3,525,381,000 | 0.4% |
| 15 | Wisconsin | 16,802,293,000 | 2.0% |
| 45 | Wyoming | 1,709,386,000 | 0.2% |

RANK ORDER

| RANK | STATE | REVENUE | % of USA |
|---|---|---|---|
| 1 | California | $130,510,365,000 | 15.4% |
| 2 | New York | 96,811,209,000 | 11.4% |
| 3 | Texas | 53,534,527,000 | 6.3% |
| 4 | Florida | 46,461,900,000 | 5.5% |
| 5 | Illinois | 37,782,363,000 | 4.5% |
| 6 | Pennsylvania | 33,228,951,000 | 3.9% |
| 7 | Ohio | 30,712,896,000 | 3.6% |
| 8 | Michigan | 29,942,304,000 | 3.5% |
| 9 | New Jersey | 25,346,587,000 | 3.0% |
| 10 | Georgia | 22,073,881,000 | 2.6% |
| 11 | North Carolina | 20,947,344,000 | 2.5% |
| 12 | Washington | 19,363,535,000 | 2.3% |
| 13 | Massachusetts | 18,007,356,000 | 2.1% |
| 14 | Virginia | 17,270,319,000 | 2.0% |
| 15 | Wisconsin | 16,802,293,000 | 2.0% |
| 16 | Minnesota | 16,502,760,000 | 1.9% |
| 17 | Tennessee | 16,482,826,000 | 1.9% |
| 18 | Indiana | 15,548,558,000 | 1.8% |
| 19 | Maryland | 14,303,664,000 | 1.7% |
| 20 | Arizona | 13,645,670,000 | 1.6% |
| 21 | Missouri | 12,836,512,000 | 1.5% |
| 22 | Colorado | 12,827,527,000 | 1.5% |
| 23 | Alabama | 10,603,550,000 | 1.3% |
| 24 | Louisiana | 10,485,269,000 | 1.2% |
| 25 | Oregon | 10,345,636,000 | 1.2% |
| 26 | Connecticut | 9,231,394,000 | 1.1% |
| 27 | South Carolina | 8,860,540,000 | 1.0% |
| 28 | Kentucky | 7,917,853,000 | 0.9% |
| 29 | Iowa | 7,785,806,000 | 0.9% |
| 30 | Kansas | 7,372,394,000 | 0.9% |
| 31 | Oklahoma | 7,267,858,000 | 0.9% |
| 32 | Nebraska | 6,243,699,000 | 0.7% |
| 33 | Mississippi | 6,236,043,000 | 0.7% |
| 34 | Utah | 5,682,467,000 | 0.7% |
| 35 | Nevada | 5,508,102,000 | 0.6% |
| 36 | Arkansas | 4,914,056,000 | 0.6% |
| 37 | New Mexico | 4,116,814,000 | 0.5% |
| 38 | West Virginia | 3,525,381,000 | 0.4% |
| 39 | Maine | 2,839,790,000 | 0.3% |
| 40 | Idaho | 2,761,767,000 | 0.3% |
| 41 | Alaska | 2,712,835,000 | 0.3% |
| 42 | New Hampshire | 2,605,214,000 | 0.3% |
| 43 | Rhode Island | 2,285,741,000 | 0.3% |
| 44 | Montana | 1,895,830,000 | 0.2% |
| 45 | Wyoming | 1,709,386,000 | 0.2% |
| 46 | Hawaii | 1,620,451,000 | 0.2% |
| 47 | Delaware | 1,596,882,000 | 0.2% |
| 48 | South Dakota | 1,569,601,000 | 0.2% |
| 49 | North Dakota | 1,448,209,000 | 0.2% |
| 50 | Vermont | 1,295,106,000 | 0.2% |
| | District of Columbia | 6,388,858,000 | 0.8% |

Source: U.S. Bureau of the Census, Governments Division
   "Compendium of Government Finances: 1997" (2000) (http://www.census.gov/govs/www/cog.html)
*Total revenue includes all money received from external sources.  This includes taxes, intergovernmental transfers and insurance trust revenue and revenue from government owned utilities and other commercial or auxiliary enterprise.

# Per Capita Local Government Total Revenue in 1997

## National Per Capita = $3,166*

ALPHA ORDER

RANK ORDER

| RANK | STATE | PER CAPITA | | RANK | STATE | PER CAPITA |
|------|-------|------------|---|------|-------|------------|
| 31 | Alabama | $2,454 | | 1 | New York | $5,336 |
| 2 | Alaska | 4,456 | | 2 | Alaska | 4,456 |
| 17 | Arizona | 2,998 | | 3 | California | 4,051 |
| 48 | Arkansas | 1,947 | | 4 | Nebraska | 3,770 |
| 3 | California | 4,051 | | 5 | Wyoming | 3,561 |
| 8 | Colorado | 3,296 | | 6 | Minnesota | 3,520 |
| 20 | Connecticut | 2,824 | | 7 | Washington | 3,455 |
| 44 | Delaware | 2,173 | | 8 | Colorado | 3,296 |
| 12 | Florida | 3,164 | | 9 | Nevada | 3,287 |
| 18 | Georgia | 2,949 | | 10 | Wisconsin | 3,231 |
| 50 | Hawaii | 1,362 | | 11 | Oregon | 3,190 |
| 38 | Idaho | 2,281 | | 12 | Florida | 3,164 |
| 14 | Illinois | 3,146 | | 13 | New Jersey | 3,147 |
| 29 | Indiana | 2,648 | | 14 | Illinois | 3,146 |
| 28 | Iowa | 2,728 | | 15 | Tennessee | 3,065 |
| 22 | Kansas | 2,818 | | 16 | Michigan | 3,060 |
| 47 | Kentucky | 2,026 | | 17 | Arizona | 2,998 |
| 32 | Louisiana | 2,410 | | 18 | Georgia | 2,949 |
| 38 | Maine | 2,281 | | 19 | Massachusetts | 2,945 |
| 23 | Maryland | 2,809 | | 20 | Connecticut | 2,824 |
| 19 | Massachusetts | 2,945 | | 21 | North Carolina | 2,820 |
| 16 | Michigan | 3,060 | | 22 | Kansas | 2,818 |
| 6 | Minnesota | 3,520 | | 23 | Maryland | 2,809 |
| 37 | Mississippi | 2,283 | | 24 | Texas | 2,766 |
| 34 | Missouri | 2,374 | | 25 | Pennsylvania | 2,765 |
| 45 | Montana | 2,158 | | 26 | Utah | 2,751 |
| 4 | Nebraska | 3,770 | | 27 | Ohio | 2,739 |
| 9 | Nevada | 3,287 | | 28 | Iowa | 2,728 |
| 41 | New Hampshire | 2,221 | | 29 | Indiana | 2,648 |
| 13 | New Jersey | 3,147 | | 30 | Virginia | 2,565 |
| 33 | New Mexico | 2,389 | | 31 | Alabama | 2,454 |
| 1 | New York | 5,336 | | 32 | Louisiana | 2,410 |
| 21 | North Carolina | 2,820 | | 33 | New Mexico | 2,389 |
| 40 | North Dakota | 2,259 | | 34 | Missouri | 2,374 |
| 27 | Ohio | 2,739 | | 35 | South Carolina | 2,338 |
| 43 | Oklahoma | 2,193 | | 36 | Rhode Island | 2,316 |
| 11 | Oregon | 3,190 | | 37 | Mississippi | 2,283 |
| 25 | Pennsylvania | 2,765 | | 38 | Idaho | 2,281 |
| 36 | Rhode Island | 2,316 | | 38 | Maine | 2,281 |
| 35 | South Carolina | 2,338 | | 40 | North Dakota | 2,259 |
| 46 | South Dakota | 2,148 | | 41 | New Hampshire | 2,221 |
| 15 | Tennessee | 3,065 | | 42 | Vermont | 2,200 |
| 24 | Texas | 2,766 | | 43 | Oklahoma | 2,193 |
| 26 | Utah | 2,751 | | 44 | Delaware | 2,173 |
| 42 | Vermont | 2,200 | | 45 | Montana | 2,158 |
| 30 | Virginia | 2,565 | | 46 | South Dakota | 2,148 |
| 7 | Washington | 3,455 | | 47 | Kentucky | 2,026 |
| 49 | West Virginia | 1,942 | | 48 | Arkansas | 1,947 |
| 10 | Wisconsin | 3,231 | | 49 | West Virginia | 1,942 |
| 5 | Wyoming | 3,561 | | 50 | Hawaii | 1,362 |

District of Columbia 12,083

*Source: Morgan Quitno Press using data from U.S. Bureau of the Census, Governments Division*
*"Compendium of Government Finances: 1997" (2000) (http://www.census.gov/govs/www/cog.html)*
*\*Total revenue includes all money received from external sources. This includes taxes, intergovernmental transfers and insurance trust revenue and revenue from government owned utilities and other commercial or auxiliary enterprise.*

# Local Government Revenue from the Federal Government in 1997

## National Total = $28,767,625,000

ALPHA ORDER

RANK ORDER

| RANK | STATE | REVENUE | % of USA |
|---|---|---|---|
| 22 | Alabama | $327,286,000 | 1.1% |
| 34 | Alaska | 172,595,000 | 0.6% |
| 16 | Arizona | 479,290,000 | 1.7% |
| 38 | Arkansas | 132,587,000 | 0.5% |
| 1 | California | 3,680,003,000 | 12.8% |
| 21 | Colorado | 355,145,000 | 1.2% |
| 25 | Connecticut | 293,535,000 | 1.0% |
| 48 | Delaware | 48,245,000 | 0.2% |
| 6 | Florida | 1,300,985,000 | 4.5% |
| 13 | Georgia | 616,139,000 | 2.1% |
| 39 | Hawaii | 123,823,000 | 0.4% |
| 46 | Idaho | 67,791,000 | 0.2% |
| 3 | Illinois | 1,762,286,000 | 6.1% |
| 26 | Indiana | 274,934,000 | 1.0% |
| 27 | Iowa | 272,978,000 | 0.9% |
| 37 | Kansas | 138,963,000 | 0.5% |
| 30 | Kentucky | 225,246,000 | 0.8% |
| 23 | Louisiana | 302,220,000 | 1.1% |
| 43 | Maine | 80,130,000 | 0.3% |
| 11 | Maryland | 721,433,000 | 2.5% |
| 9 | Massachusetts | 780,925,000 | 2.7% |
| 8 | Michigan | 880,105,000 | 3.1% |
| 20 | Minnesota | 371,695,000 | 1.3% |
| 32 | Mississippi | 190,452,000 | 0.7% |
| 17 | Missouri | 409,686,000 | 1.4% |
| 42 | Montana | 91,641,000 | 0.3% |
| 36 | Nebraska | 165,479,000 | 0.6% |
| 33 | Nevada | 186,221,000 | 0.6% |
| 47 | New Hampshire | 51,815,000 | 0.2% |
| 18 | New Jersey | 409,410,000 | 1.4% |
| 31 | New Mexico | 212,813,000 | 0.7% |
| 2 | New York | 3,266,349,000 | 11.4% |
| 12 | North Carolina | 651,996,000 | 2.3% |
| 44 | North Dakota | 75,892,000 | 0.3% |
| 7 | Ohio | 929,131,000 | 3.2% |
| 35 | Oklahoma | 168,023,000 | 0.6% |
| 10 | Oregon | 745,105,000 | 2.6% |
| 4 | Pennsylvania | 1,721,564,000 | 6.0% |
| 41 | Rhode Island | 102,786,000 | 0.4% |
| 28 | South Carolina | 267,440,000 | 0.9% |
| 45 | South Dakota | 68,904,000 | 0.2% |
| 24 | Tennessee | 300,397,000 | 1.0% |
| 5 | Texas | 1,560,004,000 | 5.4% |
| 29 | Utah | 241,769,000 | 0.8% |
| 50 | Vermont | 18,385,000 | 0.1% |
| 15 | Virginia | 479,895,000 | 1.7% |
| 14 | Washington | 513,365,000 | 1.8% |
| 40 | West Virginia | 112,585,000 | 0.4% |
| 19 | Wisconsin | 387,766,000 | 1.3% |
| 49 | Wyoming | 35,954,000 | 0.1% |

| RANK | STATE | REVENUE | % of USA |
|---|---|---|---|
| 1 | California | $3,680,003,000 | 12.8% |
| 2 | New York | 3,266,349,000 | 11.4% |
| 3 | Illinois | 1,762,286,000 | 6.1% |
| 4 | Pennsylvania | 1,721,564,000 | 6.0% |
| 5 | Texas | 1,560,004,000 | 5.4% |
| 6 | Florida | 1,300,985,000 | 4.5% |
| 7 | Ohio | 929,131,000 | 3.2% |
| 8 | Michigan | 880,105,000 | 3.1% |
| 9 | Massachusetts | 780,925,000 | 2.7% |
| 10 | Oregon | 745,105,000 | 2.6% |
| 11 | Maryland | 721,433,000 | 2.5% |
| 12 | North Carolina | 651,996,000 | 2.3% |
| 13 | Georgia | 616,139,000 | 2.1% |
| 14 | Washington | 513,365,000 | 1.8% |
| 15 | Virginia | 479,895,000 | 1.7% |
| 16 | Arizona | 479,290,000 | 1.7% |
| 17 | Missouri | 409,686,000 | 1.4% |
| 18 | New Jersey | 409,410,000 | 1.4% |
| 19 | Wisconsin | 387,766,000 | 1.3% |
| 20 | Minnesota | 371,695,000 | 1.3% |
| 21 | Colorado | 355,145,000 | 1.2% |
| 22 | Alabama | 327,286,000 | 1.1% |
| 23 | Louisiana | 302,220,000 | 1.1% |
| 24 | Tennessee | 300,397,000 | 1.0% |
| 25 | Connecticut | 293,535,000 | 1.0% |
| 26 | Indiana | 274,934,000 | 1.0% |
| 27 | Iowa | 272,978,000 | 0.9% |
| 28 | South Carolina | 267,440,000 | 0.9% |
| 29 | Utah | 241,769,000 | 0.8% |
| 30 | Kentucky | 225,246,000 | 0.8% |
| 31 | New Mexico | 212,813,000 | 0.7% |
| 32 | Mississippi | 190,452,000 | 0.7% |
| 33 | Nevada | 186,221,000 | 0.6% |
| 34 | Alaska | 172,595,000 | 0.6% |
| 35 | Oklahoma | 168,023,000 | 0.6% |
| 36 | Nebraska | 165,479,000 | 0.6% |
| 37 | Kansas | 138,963,000 | 0.5% |
| 38 | Arkansas | 132,587,000 | 0.5% |
| 39 | Hawaii | 123,823,000 | 0.4% |
| 40 | West Virginia | 112,585,000 | 0.4% |
| 41 | Rhode Island | 102,786,000 | 0.4% |
| 42 | Montana | 91,641,000 | 0.3% |
| 43 | Maine | 80,130,000 | 0.3% |
| 44 | North Dakota | 75,892,000 | 0.3% |
| 45 | South Dakota | 68,904,000 | 0.2% |
| 46 | Idaho | 67,791,000 | 0.2% |
| 47 | New Hampshire | 51,815,000 | 0.2% |
| 48 | Delaware | 48,245,000 | 0.2% |
| 49 | Wyoming | 35,954,000 | 0.1% |
| 50 | Vermont | 18,385,000 | 0.1% |
| | District of Columbia | 1,994,459,000 | 6.9% |

*Source: U.S. Bureau of the Census, Governments Division*
*"Compendium of Government Finances: 1997" (2000) (http://www.census.gov/govs/www/cog.html)*

# Per Capita Local Government Revenue from the Federal Government in 1997

## National Per Capita = $107

ALPHA ORDER

| RANK | STATE | PER CAPITA |
|------|-------|-----------|
| 30 | Alabama | $76 |
| 1 | Alaska | 283 |
| 13 | Arizona | 105 |
| 44 | Arkansas | 53 |
| 11 | California | 114 |
| 21 | Colorado | 91 |
| 22 | Connecticut | 90 |
| 38 | Delaware | 66 |
| 24 | Florida | 89 |
| 27 | Georgia | 82 |
| 14 | Hawaii | 104 |
| 42 | Idaho | 56 |
| 4 | Illinois | 147 |
| 48 | Indiana | 47 |
| 18 | Iowa | 96 |
| 44 | Kansas | 53 |
| 41 | Kentucky | 58 |
| 37 | Louisiana | 69 |
| 39 | Maine | 64 |
| 6 | Maryland | 142 |
| 7 | Massachusetts | 128 |
| 22 | Michigan | 90 |
| 29 | Minnesota | 79 |
| 36 | Mississippi | 70 |
| 30 | Missouri | 76 |
| 14 | Montana | 104 |
| 17 | Nebraska | 100 |
| 12 | Nevada | 111 |
| 49 | New Hampshire | 44 |
| 46 | New Jersey | 51 |
| 8 | New Mexico | 124 |
| 3 | New York | 180 |
| 25 | North Carolina | 88 |
| 9 | North Dakota | 118 |
| 26 | Ohio | 83 |
| 46 | Oklahoma | 51 |
| 2 | Oregon | 230 |
| 5 | Pennsylvania | 143 |
| 14 | Rhode Island | 104 |
| 34 | South Carolina | 71 |
| 19 | South Dakota | 94 |
| 42 | Tennessee | 56 |
| 28 | Texas | 81 |
| 10 | Utah | 117 |
| 50 | Vermont | 31 |
| 34 | Virginia | 71 |
| 20 | Washington | 92 |
| 40 | West Virginia | 62 |
| 32 | Wisconsin | 75 |
| 32 | Wyoming | 75 |

RANK ORDER

| RANK | STATE | PER CAPITA |
|------|-------|-----------|
| 1 | Alaska | $283 |
| 2 | Oregon | 230 |
| 3 | New York | 180 |
| 4 | Illinois | 147 |
| 5 | Pennsylvania | 143 |
| 6 | Maryland | 142 |
| 7 | Massachusetts | 128 |
| 8 | New Mexico | 124 |
| 9 | North Dakota | 118 |
| 10 | Utah | 117 |
| 11 | California | 114 |
| 12 | Nevada | 111 |
| 13 | Arizona | 105 |
| 14 | Hawaii | 104 |
| 14 | Montana | 104 |
| 14 | Rhode Island | 104 |
| 17 | Nebraska | 100 |
| 18 | Iowa | 96 |
| 19 | South Dakota | 94 |
| 20 | Washington | 92 |
| 21 | Colorado | 91 |
| 22 | Connecticut | 90 |
| 22 | Michigan | 90 |
| 24 | Florida | 89 |
| 25 | North Carolina | 88 |
| 26 | Ohio | 83 |
| 27 | Georgia | 82 |
| 28 | Texas | 81 |
| 29 | Minnesota | 79 |
| 30 | Alabama | 76 |
| 30 | Missouri | 76 |
| 32 | Wisconsin | 75 |
| 32 | Wyoming | 75 |
| 34 | South Carolina | 71 |
| 34 | Virginia | 71 |
| 36 | Mississippi | 70 |
| 37 | Louisiana | 69 |
| 38 | Delaware | 66 |
| 39 | Maine | 64 |
| 40 | West Virginia | 62 |
| 41 | Kentucky | 58 |
| 42 | Idaho | 56 |
| 42 | Tennessee | 56 |
| 44 | Arkansas | 53 |
| 44 | Kansas | 53 |
| 46 | New Jersey | 51 |
| 46 | Oklahoma | 51 |
| 48 | Indiana | 47 |
| 49 | New Hampshire | 44 |
| 50 | Vermont | 31 |
| | District of Columbia | 3,772 |

Source: Morgan Quitno Press using data from U.S. Bureau of the Census, Governments Division
"Compendium of Government Finances: 1997" (2000) (http://www.census.gov/govs/www/cog.html)

# Local Government Own Source Revenue in 1997

## National Total = $460,027,471,000*

ALPHA ORDER

| RANK | STATE | REVENUE | % of USA |
|------|-------|---------|----------|
| 26 | Alabama | $5,201,293,000 | 1.1% |
| 42 | Alaska | 1,450,128,000 | 0.3% |
| 23 | Arizona | 6,250,027,000 | 1.4% |
| 36 | Arkansas | 2,461,317,000 | 0.5% |
| 2 | California | 56,696,839,000 | 12.3% |
| 19 | Colorado | 8,030,442,000 | 1.7% |
| 24 | Connecticut | 5,904,510,000 | 1.3% |
| 50 | Delaware | 732,378,000 | 0.2% |
| 4 | Florida | 28,619,946,000 | 6.2% |
| 10 | Georgia | 12,686,078,000 | 2.8% |
| 44 | Hawaii | 1,151,610,000 | 0.3% |
| 41 | Idaho | 1,487,891,000 | 0.3% |
| 5 | Illinois | 22,065,684,000 | 4.8% |
| 14 | Indiana | 9,234,747,000 | 2.0% |
| 28 | Iowa | 4,455,623,000 | 1.0% |
| 29 | Kansas | 4,265,450,000 | 0.9% |
| 31 | Kentucky | 3,888,488,000 | 0.8% |
| 22 | Louisiana | 6,291,843,000 | 1.4% |
| 38 | Maine | 1,917,280,000 | 0.4% |
| 17 | Maryland | 8,436,433,000 | 1.8% |
| 15 | Massachusetts | 8,749,614,000 | 1.9% |
| 9 | Michigan | 12,749,009,000 | 2.8% |
| 16 | Minnesota | 8,703,163,000 | 1.9% |
| 32 | Mississippi | 3,265,441,000 | 0.7% |
| 21 | Missouri | 7,391,302,000 | 1.6% |
| 45 | Montana | 1,097,635,000 | 0.2% |
| 34 | Nebraska | 3,034,383,000 | 0.7% |
| 33 | Nevada | 3,125,343,000 | 0.7% |
| 37 | New Hampshire | 2,156,302,000 | 0.5% |
| 8 | New Jersey | 16,820,982,000 | 3.7% |
| 40 | New Mexico | 1,677,070,000 | 0.4% |
| 1 | New York | 57,475,409,000 | 12.5% |
| 11 | North Carolina | 10,670,812,000 | 2.3% |
| 49 | North Dakota | 847,254,000 | 0.2% |
| 7 | Ohio | 18,433,559,000 | 4.0% |
| 30 | Oklahoma | 4,043,354,000 | 0.9% |
| 25 | Oregon | 5,643,619,000 | 1.2% |
| 6 | Pennsylvania | 18,456,838,000 | 4.0% |
| 43 | Rhode Island | 1,445,229,000 | 0.3% |
| 27 | South Carolina | 4,975,322,000 | 1.1% |
| 47 | South Dakota | 968,126,000 | 0.2% |
| 20 | Tennessee | 7,552,712,000 | 1.6% |
| 3 | Texas | 32,068,316,000 | 7.0% |
| 35 | Utah | 2,647,645,000 | 0.6% |
| 48 | Vermont | 859,736,000 | 0.2% |
| 12 | Virginia | 10,152,934,000 | 2.2% |
| 13 | Washington | 9,513,258,000 | 2.1% |
| 39 | West Virginia | 1,825,406,000 | 0.4% |
| 18 | Wisconsin | 8,195,174,000 | 1.8% |
| 46 | Wyoming | 969,962,000 | 0.2% |

RANK ORDER

| RANK | STATE | REVENUE | % of USA |
|------|-------|---------|----------|
| 1 | New York | $57,475,409,000 | 12.5% |
| 2 | California | 56,696,839,000 | 12.3% |
| 3 | Texas | 32,068,316,000 | 7.0% |
| 4 | Florida | 28,619,946,000 | 6.2% |
| 5 | Illinois | 22,065,684,000 | 4.8% |
| 6 | Pennsylvania | 18,456,838,000 | 4.0% |
| 7 | Ohio | 18,433,559,000 | 4.0% |
| 8 | New Jersey | 16,820,982,000 | 3.7% |
| 9 | Michigan | 12,749,009,000 | 2.8% |
| 10 | Georgia | 12,686,078,000 | 2.8% |
| 11 | North Carolina | 10,670,812,000 | 2.3% |
| 12 | Virginia | 10,152,934,000 | 2.2% |
| 13 | Washington | 9,513,258,000 | 2.1% |
| 14 | Indiana | 9,234,747,000 | 2.0% |
| 15 | Massachusetts | 8,749,614,000 | 1.9% |
| 16 | Minnesota | 8,703,163,000 | 1.9% |
| 17 | Maryland | 8,436,433,000 | 1.8% |
| 18 | Wisconsin | 8,195,174,000 | 1.8% |
| 19 | Colorado | 8,030,442,000 | 1.7% |
| 20 | Tennessee | 7,552,712,000 | 1.6% |
| 21 | Missouri | 7,391,302,000 | 1.6% |
| 22 | Louisiana | 6,291,843,000 | 1.4% |
| 23 | Arizona | 6,250,027,000 | 1.4% |
| 24 | Connecticut | 5,904,510,000 | 1.3% |
| 25 | Oregon | 5,643,619,000 | 1.2% |
| 26 | Alabama | 5,201,293,000 | 1.1% |
| 27 | South Carolina | 4,975,322,000 | 1.1% |
| 28 | Iowa | 4,455,623,000 | 1.0% |
| 29 | Kansas | 4,265,450,000 | 0.9% |
| 30 | Oklahoma | 4,043,354,000 | 0.9% |
| 31 | Kentucky | 3,888,488,000 | 0.8% |
| 32 | Mississippi | 3,265,441,000 | 0.7% |
| 33 | Nevada | 3,125,343,000 | 0.7% |
| 34 | Nebraska | 3,034,383,000 | 0.7% |
| 35 | Utah | 2,647,645,000 | 0.6% |
| 36 | Arkansas | 2,461,317,000 | 0.5% |
| 37 | New Hampshire | 2,156,302,000 | 0.5% |
| 38 | Maine | 1,917,280,000 | 0.4% |
| 39 | West Virginia | 1,825,406,000 | 0.4% |
| 40 | New Mexico | 1,677,070,000 | 0.4% |
| 41 | Idaho | 1,487,891,000 | 0.3% |
| 42 | Alaska | 1,450,128,000 | 0.3% |
| 43 | Rhode Island | 1,445,229,000 | 0.3% |
| 44 | Hawaii | 1,151,610,000 | 0.3% |
| 45 | Montana | 1,097,635,000 | 0.2% |
| 46 | Wyoming | 969,962,000 | 0.2% |
| 47 | South Dakota | 968,126,000 | 0.2% |
| 48 | Vermont | 859,736,000 | 0.2% |
| 49 | North Dakota | 847,254,000 | 0.2% |
| 50 | Delaware | 732,378,000 | 0.2% |
| | District of Columbia | 3,284,555,000 | 0.7% |

Source: U.S. Bureau of the Census, Governments Division
"Compendium of Government Finances: 1997" (2000) (http://www.census.gov/govs/www/cog.html)
*Own source revenue includes taxes, current charges and miscellaneous general revenue. Excluded are intergovernmental transfers, insurance trust revenue and revenue from government owned utilities and other commercial or auxiliary enterprise.

# Per Capita Local Government Own Source Revenue in 1997

## National Per Capita = $1,718*

<table>
<tr><td colspan="3">ALPHA ORDER</td><td colspan="3">RANK ORDER</td></tr>
<tr><td>RANK</td><td>STATE</td><td>PER CAPITA</td><td>RANK</td><td>STATE</td><td>PER CAPITA</td></tr>
<tr><td>43</td><td>Alabama</td><td>$1,204</td><td>1</td><td>New York</td><td>$3,168</td></tr>
<tr><td>2</td><td>Alaska</td><td>2,382</td><td>2</td><td>Alaska</td><td>2,382</td></tr>
<tr><td>33</td><td>Arizona</td><td>1,373</td><td>3</td><td>New Jersey</td><td>2,088</td></tr>
<tr><td>48</td><td>Arkansas</td><td>975</td><td>4</td><td>Colorado</td><td>2,064</td></tr>
<tr><td>13</td><td>California</td><td>1,760</td><td>5</td><td>Wyoming</td><td>2,021</td></tr>
<tr><td>4</td><td>Colorado</td><td>2,064</td><td>6</td><td>Florida</td><td>1,949</td></tr>
<tr><td>12</td><td>Connecticut</td><td>1,806</td><td>7</td><td>Nevada</td><td>1,865</td></tr>
<tr><td>46</td><td>Delaware</td><td>996</td><td>8</td><td>Minnesota</td><td>1,857</td></tr>
<tr><td>6</td><td>Florida</td><td>1,949</td><td>9</td><td>New Hampshire</td><td>1,838</td></tr>
<tr><td>16</td><td>Georgia</td><td>1,695</td><td>10</td><td>Illinois</td><td>1,837</td></tr>
<tr><td>50</td><td>Hawaii</td><td>968</td><td>11</td><td>Nebraska</td><td>1,832</td></tr>
<tr><td>41</td><td>Idaho</td><td>1,229</td><td>12</td><td>Connecticut</td><td>1,806</td></tr>
<tr><td>10</td><td>Illinois</td><td>1,837</td><td>13</td><td>California</td><td>1,760</td></tr>
<tr><td>22</td><td>Indiana</td><td>1,573</td><td>14</td><td>Oregon</td><td>1,740</td></tr>
<tr><td>23</td><td>Iowa</td><td>1,561</td><td>15</td><td>Washington</td><td>1,698</td></tr>
<tr><td>20</td><td>Kansas</td><td>1,630</td><td>16</td><td>Georgia</td><td>1,695</td></tr>
<tr><td>47</td><td>Kentucky</td><td>995</td><td>17</td><td>Maryland</td><td>1,657</td></tr>
<tr><td>29</td><td>Louisiana</td><td>1,446</td><td>17</td><td>Texas</td><td>1,657</td></tr>
<tr><td>24</td><td>Maine</td><td>1,540</td><td>19</td><td>Ohio</td><td>1,644</td></tr>
<tr><td>17</td><td>Maryland</td><td>1,657</td><td>20</td><td>Kansas</td><td>1,630</td></tr>
<tr><td>31</td><td>Massachusetts</td><td>1,431</td><td>21</td><td>Wisconsin</td><td>1,576</td></tr>
<tr><td>38</td><td>Michigan</td><td>1,303</td><td>22</td><td>Indiana</td><td>1,573</td></tr>
<tr><td>8</td><td>Minnesota</td><td>1,857</td><td>23</td><td>Iowa</td><td>1,561</td></tr>
<tr><td>44</td><td>Mississippi</td><td>1,195</td><td>24</td><td>Maine</td><td>1,540</td></tr>
<tr><td>34</td><td>Missouri</td><td>1,367</td><td>25</td><td>Pennsylvania</td><td>1,536</td></tr>
<tr><td>40</td><td>Montana</td><td>1,249</td><td>26</td><td>Virginia</td><td>1,508</td></tr>
<tr><td>11</td><td>Nebraska</td><td>1,832</td><td>27</td><td>Rhode Island</td><td>1,464</td></tr>
<tr><td>7</td><td>Nevada</td><td>1,865</td><td>28</td><td>Vermont</td><td>1,460</td></tr>
<tr><td>9</td><td>New Hampshire</td><td>1,838</td><td>29</td><td>Louisiana</td><td>1,446</td></tr>
<tr><td>3</td><td>New Jersey</td><td>2,088</td><td>30</td><td>North Carolina</td><td>1,436</td></tr>
<tr><td>49</td><td>New Mexico</td><td>973</td><td>31</td><td>Massachusetts</td><td>1,431</td></tr>
<tr><td>1</td><td>New York</td><td>3,168</td><td>32</td><td>Tennessee</td><td>1,404</td></tr>
<tr><td>30</td><td>North Carolina</td><td>1,436</td><td>33</td><td>Arizona</td><td>1,373</td></tr>
<tr><td>36</td><td>North Dakota</td><td>1,322</td><td>34</td><td>Missouri</td><td>1,367</td></tr>
<tr><td>19</td><td>Ohio</td><td>1,644</td><td>35</td><td>South Dakota</td><td>1,325</td></tr>
<tr><td>42</td><td>Oklahoma</td><td>1,220</td><td>36</td><td>North Dakota</td><td>1,322</td></tr>
<tr><td>14</td><td>Oregon</td><td>1,740</td><td>37</td><td>South Carolina</td><td>1,313</td></tr>
<tr><td>25</td><td>Pennsylvania</td><td>1,536</td><td>38</td><td>Michigan</td><td>1,303</td></tr>
<tr><td>27</td><td>Rhode Island</td><td>1,464</td><td>39</td><td>Utah</td><td>1,282</td></tr>
<tr><td>37</td><td>South Carolina</td><td>1,313</td><td>40</td><td>Montana</td><td>1,249</td></tr>
<tr><td>35</td><td>South Dakota</td><td>1,325</td><td>41</td><td>Idaho</td><td>1,229</td></tr>
<tr><td>32</td><td>Tennessee</td><td>1,404</td><td>42</td><td>Oklahoma</td><td>1,220</td></tr>
<tr><td>17</td><td>Texas</td><td>1,657</td><td>43</td><td>Alabama</td><td>1,204</td></tr>
<tr><td>39</td><td>Utah</td><td>1,282</td><td>44</td><td>Mississippi</td><td>1,195</td></tr>
<tr><td>28</td><td>Vermont</td><td>1,460</td><td>45</td><td>West Virginia</td><td>1,005</td></tr>
<tr><td>26</td><td>Virginia</td><td>1,508</td><td>46</td><td>Delaware</td><td>996</td></tr>
<tr><td>15</td><td>Washington</td><td>1,698</td><td>47</td><td>Kentucky</td><td>995</td></tr>
<tr><td>45</td><td>West Virginia</td><td>1,005</td><td>48</td><td>Arkansas</td><td>975</td></tr>
<tr><td>21</td><td>Wisconsin</td><td>1,576</td><td>49</td><td>New Mexico</td><td>973</td></tr>
<tr><td>5</td><td>Wyoming</td><td>2,021</td><td>50</td><td>Hawaii</td><td>968</td></tr>
<tr><td></td><td></td><td></td><td></td><td>District of Columbia</td><td>6,212</td></tr>
</table>

Source: Morgan Quitno Press using data from U.S. Bureau of the Census, Governments Division
    "Compendium of Government Finances: 1997" (2000) (http://www.census.gov/govs/www/cog.html)
*Own source revenue includes taxes, current charges and miscellaneous general revenue. Excluded are
intergovernmental transfers, insurance trust revenue and revenue from government owned utilities and other
commercial or auxiliary enterprise.

# Local Government Tax Revenue in 1997

## National Total = $284,397,653,000

ALPHA ORDER

| RANK | STATE | TAX REVENUE | % of USA |
|------|-------|-------------|----------|
| 28 | Alabama | $2,474,001,000 | 0.9% |
| 42 | Alaska | 792,487,000 | 0.3% |
| 23 | Arizona | 3,824,965,000 | 1.3% |
| 38 | Arkansas | 1,343,699,000 | 0.5% |
| 2 | California | 28,849,987,000 | 10.1% |
| 19 | Colorado | 4,809,808,000 | 1.7% |
| 18 | Connecticut | 4,965,472,000 | 1.7% |
| 50 | Delaware | 412,470,000 | 0.1% |
| 5 | Florida | 14,647,445,000 | 5.2% |
| 9 | Georgia | 7,272,979,000 | 2.6% |
| 43 | Hawaii | 760,744,000 | 0.3% |
| 44 | Idaho | 758,485,000 | 0.3% |
| 4 | Illinois | 15,718,213,000 | 5.5% |
| 14 | Indiana | 5,623,456,000 | 2.0% |
| 27 | Iowa | 2,509,106,000 | 0.9% |
| 26 | Kansas | 2,529,799,000 | 0.9% |
| 30 | Kentucky | 2,076,696,000 | 0.7% |
| 24 | Louisiana | 3,760,408,000 | 1.3% |
| 34 | Maine | 1,535,220,000 | 0.5% |
| 13 | Maryland | 6,206,546,000 | 2.2% |
| 11 | Massachusetts | 6,814,267,000 | 2.4% |
| 12 | Michigan | 6,760,584,000 | 2.4% |
| 21 | Minnesota | 4,507,552,000 | 1.6% |
| 37 | Mississippi | 1,345,257,000 | 0.5% |
| 20 | Missouri | 4,779,432,000 | 1.7% |
| 47 | Montana | 622,237,000 | 0.2% |
| 32 | Nebraska | 1,944,242,000 | 0.7% |
| 36 | Nevada | 1,522,791,000 | 0.5% |
| 33 | New Hampshire | 1,836,737,000 | 0.6% |
| 6 | New Jersey | 12,988,583,000 | 4.6% |
| 41 | New Mexico | 880,956,000 | 0.3% |
| 1 | New York | 40,603,830,000 | 14.3% |
| 17 | North Carolina | 5,062,753,000 | 1.8% |
| 48 | North Dakota | 515,108,000 | 0.2% |
| 7 | Ohio | 12,647,727,000 | 4.4% |
| 31 | Oklahoma | 2,065,308,000 | 0.7% |
| 25 | Oregon | 3,120,165,000 | 1.1% |
| 8 | Pennsylvania | 12,502,270,000 | 4.4% |
| 39 | Rhode Island | 1,234,506,000 | 0.4% |
| 29 | South Carolina | 2,421,068,000 | 0.9% |
| 46 | South Dakota | 695,113,000 | 0.2% |
| 22 | Tennessee | 4,009,754,000 | 1.4% |
| 3 | Texas | 20,537,122,000 | 7.2% |
| 35 | Utah | 1,532,392,000 | 0.5% |
| 45 | Vermont | 720,738,000 | 0.3% |
| 10 | Virginia | 7,200,636,000 | 2.5% |
| 16 | Washington | 5,167,487,000 | 1.8% |
| 40 | West Virginia | 925,931,000 | 0.3% |
| 15 | Wisconsin | 5,438,621,000 | 1.9% |
| 49 | Wyoming | 485,092,000 | 0.2% |

RANK ORDER

| RANK | STATE | TAX REVENUE | % of USA |
|------|-------|-------------|----------|
| 1 | New York | $40,603,830,000 | 14.3% |
| 2 | California | 28,849,987,000 | 10.1% |
| 3 | Texas | 20,537,122,000 | 7.2% |
| 4 | Illinois | 15,718,213,000 | 5.5% |
| 5 | Florida | 14,647,445,000 | 5.2% |
| 6 | New Jersey | 12,988,583,000 | 4.6% |
| 7 | Ohio | 12,647,727,000 | 4.4% |
| 8 | Pennsylvania | 12,502,270,000 | 4.4% |
| 9 | Georgia | 7,272,979,000 | 2.6% |
| 10 | Virginia | 7,200,636,000 | 2.5% |
| 11 | Massachusetts | 6,814,267,000 | 2.4% |
| 12 | Michigan | 6,760,584,000 | 2.4% |
| 13 | Maryland | 6,206,546,000 | 2.2% |
| 14 | Indiana | 5,623,456,000 | 2.0% |
| 15 | Wisconsin | 5,438,621,000 | 1.9% |
| 16 | Washington | 5,167,487,000 | 1.8% |
| 17 | North Carolina | 5,062,753,000 | 1.8% |
| 18 | Connecticut | 4,965,472,000 | 1.7% |
| 19 | Colorado | 4,809,808,000 | 1.7% |
| 20 | Missouri | 4,779,432,000 | 1.7% |
| 21 | Minnesota | 4,507,552,000 | 1.6% |
| 22 | Tennessee | 4,009,754,000 | 1.4% |
| 23 | Arizona | 3,824,965,000 | 1.3% |
| 24 | Louisiana | 3,760,408,000 | 1.3% |
| 25 | Oregon | 3,120,165,000 | 1.1% |
| 26 | Kansas | 2,529,799,000 | 0.9% |
| 27 | Iowa | 2,509,106,000 | 0.9% |
| 28 | Alabama | 2,474,001,000 | 0.9% |
| 29 | South Carolina | 2,421,068,000 | 0.9% |
| 30 | Kentucky | 2,076,696,000 | 0.7% |
| 31 | Oklahoma | 2,065,308,000 | 0.7% |
| 32 | Nebraska | 1,944,242,000 | 0.7% |
| 33 | New Hampshire | 1,836,737,000 | 0.6% |
| 34 | Maine | 1,535,220,000 | 0.5% |
| 35 | Utah | 1,532,392,000 | 0.5% |
| 36 | Nevada | 1,522,791,000 | 0.5% |
| 37 | Mississippi | 1,345,257,000 | 0.5% |
| 38 | Arkansas | 1,343,699,000 | 0.5% |
| 39 | Rhode Island | 1,234,506,000 | 0.4% |
| 40 | West Virginia | 925,931,000 | 0.3% |
| 41 | New Mexico | 880,956,000 | 0.3% |
| 42 | Alaska | 792,487,000 | 0.3% |
| 43 | Hawaii | 760,744,000 | 0.3% |
| 44 | Idaho | 758,485,000 | 0.3% |
| 45 | Vermont | 720,738,000 | 0.3% |
| 46 | South Dakota | 695,113,000 | 0.2% |
| 47 | Montana | 622,237,000 | 0.2% |
| 48 | North Dakota | 515,108,000 | 0.2% |
| 49 | Wyoming | 485,092,000 | 0.2% |
| 50 | Delaware | 412,470,000 | 0.1% |
| | District of Columbia | 2,637,408,000 | 0.9% |

Source: U.S. Bureau of the Census, Governments Division
"Compendium of Government Finances: 1997" (2000) (http://www.census.gov/govs/www/cog.html)

# Per Capita Local Government Revenue in 1997

## National Per Capita = $1,062

ALPHA ORDER

| RANK | STATE | PER CAPITA |
|------|-------|-----------|
| 44 | Alabama | $573 |
| 6 | Alaska | 1,302 |
| 33 | Arizona | 840 |
| 46 | Arkansas | 532 |
| 29 | California | 895 |
| 8 | Colorado | 1,236 |
| 4 | Connecticut | 1,519 |
| 45 | Delaware | 561 |
| 20 | Florida | 998 |
| 21 | Georgia | 972 |
| 40 | Hawaii | 640 |
| 42 | Idaho | 627 |
| 5 | Illinois | 1,309 |
| 25 | Indiana | 958 |
| 31 | Iowa | 879 |
| 22 | Kansas | 967 |
| 47 | Kentucky | 531 |
| 32 | Louisiana | 864 |
| 9 | Maine | 1,233 |
| 11 | Maryland | 1,219 |
| 14 | Massachusetts | 1,114 |
| 38 | Michigan | 691 |
| 23 | Minnesota | 962 |
| 50 | Mississippi | 492 |
| 30 | Missouri | 884 |
| 37 | Montana | 708 |
| 12 | Nebraska | 1,174 |
| 28 | Nevada | 909 |
| 3 | New Hampshire | 1,566 |
| 2 | New Jersey | 1,613 |
| 48 | New Mexico | 511 |
| 1 | New York | 2,238 |
| 39 | North Carolina | 682 |
| 34 | North Dakota | 804 |
| 13 | Ohio | 1,128 |
| 43 | Oklahoma | 623 |
| 23 | Oregon | 962 |
| 18 | Pennsylvania | 1,040 |
| 7 | Rhode Island | 1,251 |
| 41 | South Carolina | 639 |
| 26 | South Dakota | 951 |
| 35 | Tennessee | 746 |
| 16 | Texas | 1,061 |
| 36 | Utah | 742 |
| 10 | Vermont | 1,224 |
| 15 | Virginia | 1,069 |
| 27 | Washington | 922 |
| 49 | West Virginia | 510 |
| 17 | Wisconsin | 1,046 |
| 19 | Wyoming | 1,011 |

RANK ORDER

| RANK | STATE | PER CAPITA |
|------|-------|-----------|
| 1 | New York | $2,238 |
| 2 | New Jersey | 1,613 |
| 3 | New Hampshire | 1,566 |
| 4 | Connecticut | 1,519 |
| 5 | Illinois | 1,309 |
| 6 | Alaska | 1,302 |
| 7 | Rhode Island | 1,251 |
| 8 | Colorado | 1,236 |
| 9 | Maine | 1,233 |
| 10 | Vermont | 1,224 |
| 11 | Maryland | 1,219 |
| 12 | Nebraska | 1,174 |
| 13 | Ohio | 1,128 |
| 14 | Massachusetts | 1,114 |
| 15 | Virginia | 1,069 |
| 16 | Texas | 1,061 |
| 17 | Wisconsin | 1,046 |
| 18 | Pennsylvania | 1,040 |
| 19 | Wyoming | 1,011 |
| 20 | Florida | 998 |
| 21 | Georgia | 972 |
| 22 | Kansas | 967 |
| 23 | Minnesota | 962 |
| 23 | Oregon | 962 |
| 25 | Indiana | 958 |
| 26 | South Dakota | 951 |
| 27 | Washington | 922 |
| 28 | Nevada | 909 |
| 29 | California | 895 |
| 30 | Missouri | 884 |
| 31 | Iowa | 879 |
| 32 | Louisiana | 864 |
| 33 | Arizona | 840 |
| 34 | North Dakota | 804 |
| 35 | Tennessee | 746 |
| 36 | Utah | 742 |
| 37 | Montana | 708 |
| 38 | Michigan | 691 |
| 39 | North Carolina | 682 |
| 40 | Hawaii | 640 |
| 41 | South Carolina | 639 |
| 42 | Idaho | 627 |
| 43 | Oklahoma | 623 |
| 44 | Alabama | 573 |
| 45 | Delaware | 561 |
| 46 | Arkansas | 532 |
| 47 | Kentucky | 531 |
| 48 | New Mexico | 511 |
| 49 | West Virginia | 510 |
| 50 | Mississippi | 492 |

District of Columbia — 4,988

Source: Morgan Quitno Press using data from U.S. Bureau of the Census, Governments Division
"Compendium of Government Finances: 1997" (2000) (http://www.census.gov/govs/www/cog.html)

# Local Government Total Expenditures in 1997

## National Total = $836,577,403,000*

ALPHA ORDER

RANK ORDER

| RANK | STATE | EXPENDITURES | % of USA | | RANK | STATE | EXPENDITURES | % of USA |
|---|---|---|---|---|---|---|---|---|
| 24 | Alabama | $10,527,785,000 | 1.3% | | 1 | California | $127,496,784,000 | 15.2% |
| 40 | Alaska | 2,711,483,000 | 0.3% | | 2 | New York | 96,369,034,000 | 11.5% |
| 19 | Arizona | 13,562,122,000 | 1.6% | | 3 | Texas | 52,447,777,000 | 6.3% |
| 36 | Arkansas | 4,769,718,000 | 0.6% | | 4 | Florida | 45,883,018,000 | 5.5% |
| 1 | California | 127,496,784,000 | 15.2% | | 5 | Illinois | 35,658,447,000 | 4.3% |
| 21 | Colorado | 12,812,055,000 | 1.5% | | 6 | Pennsylvania | 32,657,124,000 | 3.9% |
| 26 | Connecticut | 8,923,954,000 | 1.1% | | 7 | Ohio | 30,023,654,000 | 3.6% |
| 47 | Delaware | 1,553,846,000 | 0.2% | | 8 | Michigan | 30,012,615,000 | 3.6% |
| 4 | Florida | 45,883,018,000 | 5.5% | | 9 | New Jersey | 25,085,555,000 | 3.0% |
| 10 | Georgia | 21,547,773,000 | 2.6% | | 10 | Georgia | 21,547,773,000 | 2.6% |
| 46 | Hawaii | 1,697,123,000 | 0.2% | | 11 | North Carolina | 21,017,855,000 | 2.5% |
| 39 | Idaho | 2,821,824,000 | 0.3% | | 12 | Washington | 19,596,162,000 | 2.3% |
| 5 | Illinois | 35,658,447,000 | 4.3% | | 13 | Massachusetts | 17,960,218,000 | 2.1% |
| 18 | Indiana | 14,865,488,000 | 1.8% | | 14 | Virginia | 17,633,824,000 | 2.1% |
| 29 | Iowa | 7,698,693,000 | 0.9% | | 15 | Wisconsin | 17,139,825,000 | 2.0% |
| 30 | Kansas | 7,282,076,000 | 0.9% | | 16 | Minnesota | 16,798,423,000 | 2.0% |
| 28 | Kentucky | 7,756,176,000 | 0.9% | | 17 | Tennessee | 16,551,239,000 | 2.0% |
| 25 | Louisiana | 10,102,801,000 | 1.2% | | 18 | Indiana | 14,865,488,000 | 1.8% |
| 41 | Maine | 2,671,640,000 | 0.3% | | 19 | Arizona | 13,562,122,000 | 1.6% |
| 20 | Maryland | 13,308,559,000 | 1.6% | | 20 | Maryland | 13,308,559,000 | 1.6% |
| 13 | Massachusetts | 17,960,218,000 | 2.1% | | 21 | Colorado | 12,812,055,000 | 1.5% |
| 8 | Michigan | 30,012,615,000 | 3.6% | | 22 | Missouri | 12,731,089,000 | 1.5% |
| 16 | Minnesota | 16,798,423,000 | 2.0% | | 23 | Oregon | 10,730,357,000 | 1.3% |
| 32 | Mississippi | 6,281,388,000 | 0.8% | | 24 | Alabama | 10,527,785,000 | 1.3% |
| 22 | Missouri | 12,731,089,000 | 1.5% | | 25 | Louisiana | 10,102,801,000 | 1.2% |
| 44 | Montana | 1,869,516,000 | 0.2% | | 26 | Connecticut | 8,923,954,000 | 1.1% |
| 33 | Nebraska | 5,962,598,000 | 0.7% | | 27 | South Carolina | 8,828,242,000 | 1.1% |
| 34 | Nevada | 5,874,720,000 | 0.7% | | 28 | Kentucky | 7,756,176,000 | 0.9% |
| 42 | New Hampshire | 2,621,271,000 | 0.3% | | 29 | Iowa | 7,698,693,000 | 0.9% |
| 9 | New Jersey | 25,085,555,000 | 3.0% | | 30 | Kansas | 7,282,076,000 | 0.9% |
| 37 | New Mexico | 4,352,846,000 | 0.5% | | 31 | Oklahoma | 7,153,311,000 | 0.9% |
| 2 | New York | 96,369,034,000 | 11.5% | | 32 | Mississippi | 6,281,388,000 | 0.8% |
| 11 | North Carolina | 21,017,855,000 | 2.5% | | 33 | Nebraska | 5,962,598,000 | 0.7% |
| 49 | North Dakota | 1,423,709,000 | 0.2% | | 34 | Nevada | 5,874,720,000 | 0.7% |
| 7 | Ohio | 30,023,654,000 | 3.6% | | 35 | Utah | 5,659,141,000 | 0.7% |
| 31 | Oklahoma | 7,153,311,000 | 0.9% | | 36 | Arkansas | 4,769,718,000 | 0.6% |
| 23 | Oregon | 10,730,357,000 | 1.3% | | 37 | New Mexico | 4,352,846,000 | 0.5% |
| 6 | Pennsylvania | 32,657,124,000 | 3.9% | | 38 | West Virginia | 3,455,439,000 | 0.4% |
| 43 | Rhode Island | 2,162,077,000 | 0.3% | | 39 | Idaho | 2,821,824,000 | 0.3% |
| 27 | South Carolina | 8,828,242,000 | 1.1% | | 40 | Alaska | 2,711,483,000 | 0.3% |
| 48 | South Dakota | 1,550,372,000 | 0.2% | | 41 | Maine | 2,671,640,000 | 0.3% |
| 17 | Tennessee | 16,551,239,000 | 2.0% | | 42 | New Hampshire | 2,621,271,000 | 0.3% |
| 3 | Texas | 52,447,777,000 | 6.3% | | 43 | Rhode Island | 2,162,077,000 | 0.3% |
| 35 | Utah | 5,659,141,000 | 0.7% | | 44 | Montana | 1,869,516,000 | 0.2% |
| 50 | Vermont | 1,249,718,000 | 0.1% | | 45 | Wyoming | 1,727,588,000 | 0.2% |
| 14 | Virginia | 17,633,824,000 | 2.1% | | 46 | Hawaii | 1,697,123,000 | 0.2% |
| 12 | Washington | 19,596,162,000 | 2.3% | | 47 | Delaware | 1,553,846,000 | 0.2% |
| 38 | West Virginia | 3,455,439,000 | 0.4% | | 48 | South Dakota | 1,550,372,000 | 0.2% |
| 15 | Wisconsin | 17,139,825,000 | 2.0% | | 49 | North Dakota | 1,423,709,000 | 0.2% |
| 45 | Wyoming | 1,727,588,000 | 0.2% | | 50 | Vermont | 1,249,718,000 | 0.1% |
| | | | | | | District of Columbia | 5,999,351,000 | 0.7% |

Source: U.S. Bureau of the Census, Governments Division
   "Compendium of Government Finances: 1997" (2000) (http://www.census.gov/govs/www/cog.html)
*Total expenditures includes all money paid other than for retirement of debt and extension of loans.  Includes
payments from all sources of funds including current revenues and proceeds from borrowing and prior year fund
balances.  Includes intergovernmental transfers and expenditures for government owned utilities and other
commercial or auxiliary enterprise and insurance trust expenditures.

# Per Capita Local Government Total Expenditures in 1997

## National Per Capita = $3,124*

<table>
<tr><td colspan="3">ALPHA ORDER</td><td colspan="3">RANK ORDER</td></tr>
<tr><td>RANK</td><td>STATE</td><td>PER CAPITA</td><td>RANK</td><td>STATE</td><td>PER CAPITA</td></tr>
<tr><td>32</td><td>Alabama</td><td>$2,437</td><td>1</td><td>New York</td><td>$5,312</td></tr>
<tr><td>2</td><td>Alaska</td><td>4,453</td><td>2</td><td>Alaska</td><td>4,453</td></tr>
<tr><td>16</td><td>Arizona</td><td>2,979</td><td>3</td><td>California</td><td>3,957</td></tr>
<tr><td>49</td><td>Arkansas</td><td>1,890</td><td>4</td><td>Nebraska</td><td>3,601</td></tr>
<tr><td>3</td><td>California</td><td>3,957</td><td>5</td><td>Wyoming</td><td>3,599</td></tr>
<tr><td>11</td><td>Colorado</td><td>3,292</td><td>6</td><td>Minnesota</td><td>3,583</td></tr>
<tr><td>23</td><td>Connecticut</td><td>2,730</td><td>7</td><td>Nevada</td><td>3,506</td></tr>
<tr><td>46</td><td>Delaware</td><td>2,114</td><td>8</td><td>Washington</td><td>3,497</td></tr>
<tr><td>12</td><td>Florida</td><td>3,125</td><td>9</td><td>Oregon</td><td>3,309</td></tr>
<tr><td>19</td><td>Georgia</td><td>2,878</td><td>10</td><td>Wisconsin</td><td>3,296</td></tr>
<tr><td>50</td><td>Hawaii</td><td>1,427</td><td>11</td><td>Colorado</td><td>3,292</td></tr>
<tr><td>34</td><td>Idaho</td><td>2,331</td><td>12</td><td>Florida</td><td>3,125</td></tr>
<tr><td>17</td><td>Illinois</td><td>2,969</td><td>13</td><td>New Jersey</td><td>3,115</td></tr>
<tr><td>30</td><td>Indiana</td><td>2,531</td><td>14</td><td>Tennessee</td><td>3,077</td></tr>
<tr><td>26</td><td>Iowa</td><td>2,697</td><td>15</td><td>Michigan</td><td>3,067</td></tr>
<tr><td>21</td><td>Kansas</td><td>2,783</td><td>16</td><td>Arizona</td><td>2,979</td></tr>
<tr><td>47</td><td>Kentucky</td><td>1,985</td><td>17</td><td>Illinois</td><td>2,969</td></tr>
<tr><td>36</td><td>Louisiana</td><td>2,322</td><td>18</td><td>Massachusetts</td><td>2,937</td></tr>
<tr><td>42</td><td>Maine</td><td>2,146</td><td>19</td><td>Georgia</td><td>2,878</td></tr>
<tr><td>29</td><td>Maryland</td><td>2,613</td><td>20</td><td>North Carolina</td><td>2,829</td></tr>
<tr><td>18</td><td>Massachusetts</td><td>2,937</td><td>21</td><td>Kansas</td><td>2,783</td></tr>
<tr><td>15</td><td>Michigan</td><td>3,067</td><td>22</td><td>Utah</td><td>2,740</td></tr>
<tr><td>6</td><td>Minnesota</td><td>3,583</td><td>23</td><td>Connecticut</td><td>2,730</td></tr>
<tr><td>37</td><td>Mississippi</td><td>2,299</td><td>24</td><td>Pennsylvania</td><td>2,718</td></tr>
<tr><td>33</td><td>Missouri</td><td>2,355</td><td>25</td><td>Texas</td><td>2,710</td></tr>
<tr><td>43</td><td>Montana</td><td>2,128</td><td>26</td><td>Iowa</td><td>2,697</td></tr>
<tr><td>4</td><td>Nebraska</td><td>3,601</td><td>27</td><td>Ohio</td><td>2,678</td></tr>
<tr><td>7</td><td>Nevada</td><td>3,506</td><td>28</td><td>Virginia</td><td>2,619</td></tr>
<tr><td>38</td><td>New Hampshire</td><td>2,234</td><td>29</td><td>Maryland</td><td>2,613</td></tr>
<tr><td>13</td><td>New Jersey</td><td>3,115</td><td>30</td><td>Indiana</td><td>2,531</td></tr>
<tr><td>31</td><td>New Mexico</td><td>2,526</td><td>31</td><td>New Mexico</td><td>2,526</td></tr>
<tr><td>1</td><td>New York</td><td>5,312</td><td>32</td><td>Alabama</td><td>2,437</td></tr>
<tr><td>20</td><td>North Carolina</td><td>2,829</td><td>33</td><td>Missouri</td><td>2,355</td></tr>
<tr><td>39</td><td>North Dakota</td><td>2,221</td><td>34</td><td>Idaho</td><td>2,331</td></tr>
<tr><td>27</td><td>Ohio</td><td>2,678</td><td>35</td><td>South Carolina</td><td>2,329</td></tr>
<tr><td>41</td><td>Oklahoma</td><td>2,158</td><td>36</td><td>Louisiana</td><td>2,322</td></tr>
<tr><td>9</td><td>Oregon</td><td>3,309</td><td>37</td><td>Mississippi</td><td>2,299</td></tr>
<tr><td>24</td><td>Pennsylvania</td><td>2,718</td><td>38</td><td>New Hampshire</td><td>2,234</td></tr>
<tr><td>40</td><td>Rhode Island</td><td>2,191</td><td>39</td><td>North Dakota</td><td>2,221</td></tr>
<tr><td>35</td><td>South Carolina</td><td>2,329</td><td>40</td><td>Rhode Island</td><td>2,191</td></tr>
<tr><td>45</td><td>South Dakota</td><td>2,121</td><td>41</td><td>Oklahoma</td><td>2,158</td></tr>
<tr><td>14</td><td>Tennessee</td><td>3,077</td><td>42</td><td>Maine</td><td>2,146</td></tr>
<tr><td>25</td><td>Texas</td><td>2,710</td><td>43</td><td>Montana</td><td>2,128</td></tr>
<tr><td>22</td><td>Utah</td><td>2,740</td><td>44</td><td>Vermont</td><td>2,123</td></tr>
<tr><td>44</td><td>Vermont</td><td>2,123</td><td>45</td><td>South Dakota</td><td>2,121</td></tr>
<tr><td>28</td><td>Virginia</td><td>2,619</td><td>46</td><td>Delaware</td><td>2,114</td></tr>
<tr><td>8</td><td>Washington</td><td>3,497</td><td>47</td><td>Kentucky</td><td>1,985</td></tr>
<tr><td>48</td><td>West Virginia</td><td>1,903</td><td>48</td><td>West Virginia</td><td>1,903</td></tr>
<tr><td>10</td><td>Wisconsin</td><td>3,296</td><td>49</td><td>Arkansas</td><td>1,890</td></tr>
<tr><td>5</td><td>Wyoming</td><td>3,599</td><td>50</td><td>Hawaii</td><td>1,427</td></tr>
<tr><td></td><td></td><td></td><td></td><td>District of Columbia</td><td>11,346</td></tr>
</table>

Source: Morgan Quitno Press using data from U.S. Bureau of the Census, Governments Division
    "Compendium of Government Finances: 1997" (2000) (http://www.census.gov/govs/www/cog.html)
*Total expenditures includes all money paid other than for retirement of debt and extension of loans. Includes
payments from all sources of funds including current revenues and proceeds from borrowing and prior year fund
balances. Includes intergovernmental transfers and expenditures for government owned utilities and other
commercial or auxiliary enterprise and insurance trust expenditures.

# Federal Medicaid Matching Fund Rate for 2001

## National Average = 72.55% of States' Funds Matched by Federal Government*

ALPHA ORDER

| RANK | STATE | RATE |
|------|-------|------|
| 12 | Alabama | 78.99 |
| 33 | Alaska | 69.23 |
| 16 | Arizona | 76.04 |
| 5 | Arkansas | 81.11 |
| 38 | California | 65.88 |
| 42 | Colorado | 65.00 |
| 42 | Connecticut | 65.00 |
| 42 | Delaware | 65.00 |
| 31 | Florida | 69.63 |
| 28 | Georgia | 71.77 |
| 34 | Hawaii | 67.70 |
| 8 | Idaho | 79.53 |
| 42 | Illinois | 65.00 |
| 22 | Indiana | 73.43 |
| 19 | Iowa | 73.87 |
| 27 | Kansas | 71.90 |
| 11 | Kentucky | 79.27 |
| 9 | Louisiana | 79.37 |
| 15 | Maine | 76.28 |
| 42 | Maryland | 65.00 |
| 42 | Massachusetts | 65.00 |
| 32 | Michigan | 69.33 |
| 39 | Minnesota | 65.78 |
| 1 | Mississippi | 83.77 |
| 23 | Missouri | 72.72 |
| 4 | Montana | 81.13 |
| 25 | Nebraska | 72.27 |
| 41 | Nevada | 65.25 |
| 42 | New Hampshire | 65.00 |
| 42 | New Jersey | 65.00 |
| 3 | New Mexico | 81.66 |
| 42 | New York | 65.00 |
| 20 | North Carolina | 73.73 |
| 12 | North Dakota | 78.99 |
| 30 | Ohio | 71.32 |
| 7 | Oklahoma | 79.87 |
| 26 | Oregon | 72.00 |
| 36 | Pennsylvania | 67.53 |
| 35 | Rhode Island | 67.65 |
| 10 | South Carolina | 79.31 |
| 14 | South Dakota | 77.82 |
| 18 | Tennessee | 74.65 |
| 24 | Texas | 72.40 |
| 6 | Utah | 80.01 |
| 21 | Vermont | 73.68 |
| 37 | Virginia | 66.30 |
| 40 | Washington | 65.49 |
| 2 | West Virginia | 82.74 |
| 29 | Wisconsin | 71.50 |
| 17 | Wyoming | 75.22 |

RANK ORDER

| RANK | STATE | RATE |
|------|-------|------|
| 1 | Mississippi | 83.77 |
| 2 | West Virginia | 82.74 |
| 3 | New Mexico | 81.66 |
| 4 | Montana | 81.13 |
| 5 | Arkansas | 81.11 |
| 6 | Utah | 80.01 |
| 7 | Oklahoma | 79.87 |
| 8 | Idaho | 79.53 |
| 9 | Louisiana | 79.37 |
| 10 | South Carolina | 79.31 |
| 11 | Kentucky | 79.27 |
| 12 | Alabama | 78.99 |
| 12 | North Dakota | 78.99 |
| 14 | South Dakota | 77.82 |
| 15 | Maine | 76.28 |
| 16 | Arizona | 76.04 |
| 17 | Wyoming | 75.22 |
| 18 | Tennessee | 74.65 |
| 19 | Iowa | 73.87 |
| 20 | North Carolina | 73.73 |
| 21 | Vermont | 73.68 |
| 22 | Indiana | 73.43 |
| 23 | Missouri | 72.72 |
| 24 | Texas | 72.40 |
| 25 | Nebraska | 72.27 |
| 26 | Oregon | 72.00 |
| 27 | Kansas | 71.90 |
| 28 | Georgia | 71.77 |
| 29 | Wisconsin | 71.50 |
| 30 | Ohio | 71.32 |
| 31 | Florida | 69.63 |
| 32 | Michigan | 69.33 |
| 33 | Alaska | 69.23 |
| 34 | Hawaii | 67.70 |
| 35 | Rhode Island | 67.65 |
| 36 | Pennsylvania | 67.53 |
| 37 | Virginia | 66.30 |
| 38 | California | 65.88 |
| 39 | Minnesota | 65.78 |
| 40 | Washington | 65.49 |
| 41 | Nevada | 65.25 |
| 42 | Colorado | 65.00 |
| 42 | Connecticut | 65.00 |
| 42 | Delaware | 65.00 |
| 42 | Illinois | 65.00 |
| 42 | Maryland | 65.00 |
| 42 | Massachusetts | 65.00 |
| 42 | New Hampshire | 65.00 |
| 42 | New Jersey | 65.00 |
| 42 | New York | 65.00 |
| | District of Columbia | 79.00 |

Source: U.S. Department of Health and Human Services, Health Care Financing Administration
    "Enhanced Federal Medical Assistance Percentages" (Federal Register, 2/23/00)
*For fiscal year 2001. These are "enhanced" matching rates established by the Children's Health Insurance
Program, signed into law in August 1997. Sixty-five percent is the minimum. National average is a simple average of
the 51 individual rates and is not weighted for population or funds.

# Per Capita Local Government Direct General Expenditures in 1997

## National Per Capita = $2,702*

ALPHA ORDER

| RANK | STATE | PER CAPITA |
|------|-------|-----------|
| 40 | Alabama | $2,049 |
| 2 | Alaska | 4,029 |
| 22 | Arizona | 2,423 |
| 49 | Arkansas | 1,695 |
| 4 | California | 3,278 |
| 10 | Colorado | 2,853 |
| 15 | Connecticut | 2,542 |
| 44 | Delaware | 1,932 |
| 13 | Florida | 2,769 |
| 20 | Georgia | 2,452 |
| 50 | Hawaii | 1,211 |
| 30 | Idaho | 2,221 |
| 14 | Illinois | 2,581 |
| 28 | Indiana | 2,301 |
| 18 | Iowa | 2,477 |
| 16 | Kansas | 2,500 |
| 48 | Kentucky | 1,758 |
| 34 | Louisiana | 2,114 |
| 37 | Maine | 2,076 |
| 21 | Maryland | 2,427 |
| 29 | Massachusetts | 2,232 |
| 12 | Michigan | 2,803 |
| 5 | Minnesota | 3,256 |
| 33 | Mississippi | 2,116 |
| 35 | Missouri | 2,093 |
| 41 | Montana | 2,048 |
| 19 | Nebraska | 2,469 |
| 6 | Nevada | 3,197 |
| 36 | New Hampshire | 2,092 |
| 8 | New Jersey | 3,005 |
| 27 | New Mexico | 2,302 |
| 1 | New York | 4,462 |
| 25 | North Carolina | 2,367 |
| 38 | North Dakota | 2,059 |
| 17 | Ohio | 2,483 |
| 43 | Oklahoma | 1,966 |
| 9 | Oregon | 2,891 |
| 23 | Pennsylvania | 2,421 |
| 42 | Rhode Island | 2,023 |
| 39 | South Carolina | 2,052 |
| 45 | South Dakota | 1,916 |
| 31 | Tennessee | 2,152 |
| 26 | Texas | 2,331 |
| 32 | Utah | 2,124 |
| 46 | Vermont | 1,889 |
| 24 | Virginia | 2,384 |
| 11 | Washington | 2,807 |
| 47 | West Virginia | 1,801 |
| 7 | Wisconsin | 3,062 |
| 3 | Wyoming | 3,380 |

RANK ORDER

| RANK | STATE | PER CAPITA |
|------|-------|-----------|
| 1 | New York | $4,462 |
| 2 | Alaska | 4,029 |
| 3 | Wyoming | 3,380 |
| 4 | California | 3,278 |
| 5 | Minnesota | 3,256 |
| 6 | Nevada | 3,197 |
| 7 | Wisconsin | 3,062 |
| 8 | New Jersey | 3,005 |
| 9 | Oregon | 2,891 |
| 10 | Colorado | 2,853 |
| 11 | Washington | 2,807 |
| 12 | Michigan | 2,803 |
| 13 | Florida | 2,769 |
| 14 | Illinois | 2,581 |
| 15 | Connecticut | 2,542 |
| 16 | Kansas | 2,500 |
| 17 | Ohio | 2,483 |
| 18 | Iowa | 2,477 |
| 19 | Nebraska | 2,469 |
| 20 | Georgia | 2,452 |
| 21 | Maryland | 2,427 |
| 22 | Arizona | 2,423 |
| 23 | Pennsylvania | 2,421 |
| 24 | Virginia | 2,384 |
| 25 | North Carolina | 2,367 |
| 26 | Texas | 2,331 |
| 27 | New Mexico | 2,302 |
| 28 | Indiana | 2,301 |
| 29 | Massachusetts | 2,232 |
| 30 | Idaho | 2,221 |
| 31 | Tennessee | 2,152 |
| 32 | Utah | 2,124 |
| 33 | Mississippi | 2,116 |
| 34 | Louisiana | 2,114 |
| 35 | Missouri | 2,093 |
| 36 | New Hampshire | 2,092 |
| 37 | Maine | 2,076 |
| 38 | North Dakota | 2,059 |
| 39 | South Carolina | 2,052 |
| 40 | Alabama | 2,049 |
| 41 | Montana | 2,048 |
| 42 | Rhode Island | 2,023 |
| 43 | Oklahoma | 1,966 |
| 44 | Delaware | 1,932 |
| 45 | South Dakota | 1,916 |
| 46 | Vermont | 1,889 |
| 47 | West Virginia | 1,801 |
| 48 | Kentucky | 1,758 |
| 49 | Arkansas | 1,695 |
| 50 | Hawaii | 1,211 |

District of Columbia    8,200

Source: Morgan Quitno Press using data from U.S. Bureau of the Census, Governments Division
"Compendium of Government Finances: 1997" (2000) (http://www.census.gov/govs/www/cog.html)
*Direct general expenditures include expenditures for current operations, assistance and subsidies, interest on debt and capital outlay. Excludes intergovernmental transfers, expenditures for government owned utilities and other commercial or auxiliary enterprise and insurance trust expenditures.

# Local Government Debt Outstanding in 1997

## National Total = $764,844,001,000*

ALPHA ORDER

| RANK | STATE | DEBT | % of USA |
|------|-------|------|----------|
| 26 | Alabama | $8,398,136,000 | 1.1% |
| 37 | Alaska | 3,761,411,000 | 0.5% |
| 11 | Arizona | 18,510,302,000 | 2.4% |
| 38 | Arkansas | 3,756,483,000 | 0.5% |
| 1 | California | 110,792,754,000 | 14.5% |
| 16 | Colorado | 16,037,735,000 | 2.1% |
| 33 | Connecticut | 4,586,663,000 | 0.6% |
| 42 | Delaware | 1,311,108,000 | 0.2% |
| 4 | Florida | 54,427,039,000 | 7.1% |
| 9 | Georgia | 19,697,930,000 | 2.6% |
| 40 | Hawaii | 2,126,510,000 | 0.3% |
| 47 | Idaho | 1,041,078,000 | 0.1% |
| 6 | Illinois | 28,358,521,000 | 3.7% |
| 22 | Indiana | 9,994,303,000 | 1.3% |
| 35 | Iowa | 4,243,617,000 | 0.6% |
| 27 | Kansas | 7,614,941,000 | 1.0% |
| 17 | Kentucky | 13,906,953,000 | 1.8% |
| 24 | Louisiana | 9,176,604,000 | 1.2% |
| 41 | Maine | 1,600,449,000 | 0.2% |
| 18 | Maryland | 12,641,489,000 | 1.7% |
| 20 | Massachusetts | 12,137,089,000 | 1.6% |
| 8 | Michigan | 21,128,085,000 | 2.8% |
| 10 | Minnesota | 18,615,093,000 | 2.4% |
| 34 | Mississippi | 4,539,487,000 | 0.6% |
| 28 | Missouri | 7,548,587,000 | 1.0% |
| 45 | Montana | 1,214,519,000 | 0.2% |
| 32 | Nebraska | 4,733,392,000 | 0.6% |
| 29 | Nevada | 7,481,784,000 | 1.0% |
| 44 | New Hampshire | 1,224,180,000 | 0.2% |
| 15 | New Jersey | 16,743,259,000 | 2.2% |
| 36 | New Mexico | 3,875,957,000 | 0.5% |
| 2 | New York | 77,460,094,000 | 10.1% |
| 12 | North Carolina | 18,228,376,000 | 2.4% |
| 48 | North Dakota | 1,026,626,000 | 0.1% |
| 13 | Ohio | 17,663,479,000 | 2.3% |
| 31 | Oklahoma | 5,794,055,000 | 0.8% |
| 30 | Oregon | 7,251,164,000 | 0.9% |
| 5 | Pennsylvania | 44,506,008,000 | 5.8% |
| 46 | Rhode Island | 1,112,626,000 | 0.1% |
| 25 | South Carolina | 8,752,803,000 | 1.1% |
| 49 | South Dakota | 834,220,000 | 0.1% |
| 19 | Tennessee | 12,185,202,000 | 1.6% |
| 3 | Texas | 65,886,732,000 | 8.6% |
| 23 | Utah | 9,539,802,000 | 1.2% |
| 50 | Vermont | 620,605,000 | 0.1% |
| 14 | Virginia | 17,520,494,000 | 2.3% |
| 7 | Washington | 24,070,355,000 | 3.1% |
| 39 | West Virginia | 3,664,973,000 | 0.5% |
| 21 | Wisconsin | 11,997,603,000 | 1.6% |
| 43 | Wyoming | 1,228,730,000 | 0.2% |

RANK ORDER

| RANK | STATE | DEBT | % of USA |
|------|-------|------|----------|
| 1 | California | $110,792,754,000 | 14.5% |
| 2 | New York | 77,460,094,000 | 10.1% |
| 3 | Texas | 65,886,732,000 | 8.6% |
| 4 | Florida | 54,427,039,000 | 7.1% |
| 5 | Pennsylvania | 44,506,008,000 | 5.8% |
| 6 | Illinois | 28,358,521,000 | 3.7% |
| 7 | Washington | 24,070,355,000 | 3.1% |
| 8 | Michigan | 21,128,085,000 | 2.8% |
| 9 | Georgia | 19,697,930,000 | 2.6% |
| 10 | Minnesota | 18,615,093,000 | 2.4% |
| 11 | Arizona | 18,510,302,000 | 2.4% |
| 12 | North Carolina | 18,228,376,000 | 2.4% |
| 13 | Ohio | 17,663,479,000 | 2.3% |
| 14 | Virginia | 17,520,494,000 | 2.3% |
| 15 | New Jersey | 16,743,259,000 | 2.2% |
| 16 | Colorado | 16,037,735,000 | 2.1% |
| 17 | Kentucky | 13,906,953,000 | 1.8% |
| 18 | Maryland | 12,641,489,000 | 1.7% |
| 19 | Tennessee | 12,185,202,000 | 1.6% |
| 20 | Massachusetts | 12,137,089,000 | 1.6% |
| 21 | Wisconsin | 11,997,603,000 | 1.6% |
| 22 | Indiana | 9,994,303,000 | 1.3% |
| 23 | Utah | 9,539,802,000 | 1.2% |
| 24 | Louisiana | 9,176,604,000 | 1.2% |
| 25 | South Carolina | 8,752,803,000 | 1.1% |
| 26 | Alabama | 8,398,136,000 | 1.1% |
| 27 | Kansas | 7,614,941,000 | 1.0% |
| 28 | Missouri | 7,548,587,000 | 1.0% |
| 29 | Nevada | 7,481,784,000 | 1.0% |
| 30 | Oregon | 7,251,164,000 | 0.9% |
| 31 | Oklahoma | 5,794,055,000 | 0.8% |
| 32 | Nebraska | 4,733,392,000 | 0.6% |
| 33 | Connecticut | 4,586,663,000 | 0.6% |
| 34 | Mississippi | 4,539,487,000 | 0.6% |
| 35 | Iowa | 4,243,617,000 | 0.6% |
| 36 | New Mexico | 3,875,957,000 | 0.5% |
| 37 | Alaska | 3,761,411,000 | 0.5% |
| 38 | Arkansas | 3,756,483,000 | 0.5% |
| 39 | West Virginia | 3,664,973,000 | 0.5% |
| 40 | Hawaii | 2,126,510,000 | 0.3% |
| 41 | Maine | 1,600,449,000 | 0.2% |
| 42 | Delaware | 1,311,108,000 | 0.2% |
| 43 | Wyoming | 1,228,730,000 | 0.2% |
| 44 | New Hampshire | 1,224,180,000 | 0.2% |
| 45 | Montana | 1,214,519,000 | 0.2% |
| 46 | Rhode Island | 1,112,626,000 | 0.1% |
| 47 | Idaho | 1,041,078,000 | 0.1% |
| 48 | North Dakota | 1,026,626,000 | 0.1% |
| 49 | South Dakota | 834,220,000 | 0.1% |
| 50 | Vermont | 620,605,000 | 0.1% |
| | District of Columbia | 4,274,596,000 | 0.6% |

*Source: U.S. Bureau of the Census, Governments Division*
*"Compendium of Government Finances: 1997" (2000) (http://www.census.gov/govs/www/cog.html)*
*\*Includes short-term, long-term, full fail and credit, nonguaranteed and public debt for private purposes.*

# Per Capita Local Government Debt Outstanding in 1997

## National Per Capita = $2,856*

ALPHA ORDER

| RANK | STATE | PER CAPITA |
|---|---|---|
| 32 | Alabama | $1,944 |
| 1 | Alaska | 6,178 |
| 7 | Arizona | 4,066 |
| 40 | Arkansas | 1,488 |
| 12 | California | 3,439 |
| 6 | Colorado | 4,121 |
| 42 | Connecticut | 1,403 |
| 34 | Delaware | 1,784 |
| 9 | Florida | 3,707 |
| 16 | Georgia | 2,631 |
| 33 | Hawaii | 1,788 |
| 50 | Idaho | 860 |
| 21 | Illinois | 2,361 |
| 36 | Indiana | 1,702 |
| 41 | Iowa | 1,487 |
| 14 | Kansas | 2,911 |
| 11 | Kentucky | 3,559 |
| 28 | Louisiana | 2,109 |
| 45 | Maine | 1,285 |
| 19 | Maryland | 2,482 |
| 31 | Massachusetts | 1,985 |
| 27 | Michigan | 2,159 |
| 8 | Minnesota | 3,971 |
| 37 | Mississippi | 1,662 |
| 43 | Missouri | 1,396 |
| 44 | Montana | 1,382 |
| 15 | Nebraska | 2,858 |
| 3 | Nevada | 4,465 |
| 49 | New Hampshire | 1,043 |
| 29 | New Jersey | 2,079 |
| 25 | New Mexico | 2,250 |
| 5 | New York | 4,269 |
| 20 | North Carolina | 2,454 |
| 38 | North Dakota | 1,602 |
| 39 | Ohio | 1,575 |
| 35 | Oklahoma | 1,748 |
| 26 | Oregon | 2,236 |
| 10 | Pennsylvania | 3,704 |
| 47 | Rhode Island | 1,127 |
| 22 | South Carolina | 2,309 |
| 46 | South Dakota | 1,141 |
| 24 | Tennessee | 2,266 |
| 13 | Texas | 3,404 |
| 2 | Utah | 4,619 |
| 48 | Vermont | 1,054 |
| 17 | Virginia | 2,602 |
| 4 | Washington | 4,295 |
| 30 | West Virginia | 2,019 |
| 23 | Wisconsin | 2,307 |
| 18 | Wyoming | 2,560 |

RANK ORDER

| RANK | STATE | PER CAPITA |
|---|---|---|
| 1 | Alaska | $6,178 |
| 2 | Utah | 4,619 |
| 3 | Nevada | 4,465 |
| 4 | Washington | 4,295 |
| 5 | New York | 4,269 |
| 6 | Colorado | 4,121 |
| 7 | Arizona | 4,066 |
| 8 | Minnesota | 3,971 |
| 9 | Florida | 3,707 |
| 10 | Pennsylvania | 3,704 |
| 11 | Kentucky | 3,559 |
| 12 | California | 3,439 |
| 13 | Texas | 3,404 |
| 14 | Kansas | 2,911 |
| 15 | Nebraska | 2,858 |
| 16 | Georgia | 2,631 |
| 17 | Virginia | 2,602 |
| 18 | Wyoming | 2,560 |
| 19 | Maryland | 2,482 |
| 20 | North Carolina | 2,454 |
| 21 | Illinois | 2,361 |
| 22 | South Carolina | 2,309 |
| 23 | Wisconsin | 2,307 |
| 24 | Tennessee | 2,266 |
| 25 | New Mexico | 2,250 |
| 26 | Oregon | 2,236 |
| 27 | Michigan | 2,159 |
| 28 | Louisiana | 2,109 |
| 29 | New Jersey | 2,079 |
| 30 | West Virginia | 2,019 |
| 31 | Massachusetts | 1,985 |
| 32 | Alabama | 1,944 |
| 33 | Hawaii | 1,788 |
| 34 | Delaware | 1,784 |
| 35 | Oklahoma | 1,748 |
| 36 | Indiana | 1,702 |
| 37 | Mississippi | 1,662 |
| 38 | North Dakota | 1,602 |
| 39 | Ohio | 1,575 |
| 40 | Arkansas | 1,488 |
| 41 | Iowa | 1,487 |
| 42 | Connecticut | 1,403 |
| 43 | Missouri | 1,396 |
| 44 | Montana | 1,382 |
| 45 | Maine | 1,285 |
| 46 | South Dakota | 1,141 |
| 47 | Rhode Island | 1,127 |
| 48 | Vermont | 1,054 |
| 49 | New Hampshire | 1,043 |
| 50 | Idaho | 860 |

District of Columbia 8,084

Source: Morgan Quitno Press using data from U.S. Bureau of the Census, Governments Division
"Compendium of Government Finances: 1997" (2000) (http://www.census.gov/govs/www/cog.html)
*Includes short-term, long-term, full fail and credit, nonguaranteed and public debt for private purposes.

# Local Government Full-Time Equivalent Employees in 1999

## National Total = 10,665,337 FTE Employees*

ALPHA ORDER

| RANK | STATE | EMPLOYEES | % of USA |
|---|---|---|---|
| 22 | Alabama | 180,539 | 1.7% |
| 46 | Alaska | 25,925 | 0.2% |
| 23 | Arizona | 173,929 | 1.6% |
| 33 | Arkansas | 95,069 | 0.9% |
| 1 | California | 1,239,566 | 11.6% |
| 24 | Colorado | 161,488 | 1.5% |
| 32 | Connecticut | 105,449 | 1.0% |
| 49 | Delaware | 20,334 | 0.2% |
| 4 | Florida | 553,936 | 5.2% |
| 9 | Georgia | 335,877 | 3.1% |
| 50 | Hawaii | 14,121 | 0.1% |
| 39 | Idaho | 49,588 | 0.5% |
| 5 | Illinois | 470,633 | 4.4% |
| 13 | Indiana | 227,806 | 2.1% |
| 31 | Iowa | 116,685 | 1.1% |
| 29 | Kansas | 125,983 | 1.2% |
| 26 | Kentucky | 143,526 | 1.3% |
| 20 | Louisiana | 183,435 | 1.7% |
| 40 | Maine | 49,419 | 0.5% |
| 21 | Maryland | 182,314 | 1.7% |
| 14 | Massachusetts | 226,984 | 2.1% |
| 8 | Michigan | 339,344 | 3.2% |
| 18 | Minnesota | 202,693 | 1.9% |
| 27 | Mississippi | 135,669 | 1.3% |
| 16 | Missouri | 209,369 | 2.0% |
| 43 | Montana | 31,682 | 0.3% |
| 34 | Nebraska | 74,674 | 0.7% |
| 37 | Nevada | 61,520 | 0.6% |
| 41 | New Hampshire | 42,931 | 0.4% |
| 10 | New Jersey | 313,545 | 2.9% |
| 36 | New Mexico | 71,190 | 0.7% |
| 2 | New York | 896,590 | 8.4% |
| 11 | North Carolina | 312,613 | 2.9% |
| 47 | North Dakota | 21,848 | 0.2% |
| 6 | Ohio | 451,907 | 4.2% |
| 28 | Oklahoma | 131,078 | 1.2% |
| 30 | Oregon | 121,589 | 1.1% |
| 7 | Pennsylvania | 380,376 | 3.6% |
| 42 | Rhode Island | 34,623 | 0.3% |
| 25 | South Carolina | 153,704 | 1.4% |
| 45 | South Dakota | 27,477 | 0.3% |
| 15 | Tennessee | 216,404 | 2.0% |
| 3 | Texas | 872,640 | 8.2% |
| 35 | Utah | 72,617 | 0.7% |
| 48 | Vermont | 20,874 | 0.2% |
| 12 | Virginia | 259,022 | 2.4% |
| 19 | Washington | 186,951 | 1.8% |
| 38 | West Virginia | 61,398 | 0.6% |
| 17 | Wisconsin | 207,587 | 1.9% |
| 44 | Wyoming | 27,608 | 0.3% |

RANK ORDER

| RANK | STATE | EMPLOYEES | % of USA |
|---|---|---|---|
| 1 | California | 1,239,566 | 11.6% |
| 2 | New York | 896,590 | 8.4% |
| 3 | Texas | 872,640 | 8.2% |
| 4 | Florida | 553,936 | 5.2% |
| 5 | Illinois | 470,633 | 4.4% |
| 6 | Ohio | 451,907 | 4.2% |
| 7 | Pennsylvania | 380,376 | 3.6% |
| 8 | Michigan | 339,344 | 3.2% |
| 9 | Georgia | 335,877 | 3.1% |
| 10 | New Jersey | 313,545 | 2.9% |
| 11 | North Carolina | 312,613 | 2.9% |
| 12 | Virginia | 259,022 | 2.4% |
| 13 | Indiana | 227,806 | 2.1% |
| 14 | Massachusetts | 226,984 | 2.1% |
| 15 | Tennessee | 216,404 | 2.0% |
| 16 | Missouri | 209,369 | 2.0% |
| 17 | Wisconsin | 207,587 | 1.9% |
| 18 | Minnesota | 202,693 | 1.9% |
| 19 | Washington | 186,951 | 1.8% |
| 20 | Louisiana | 183,435 | 1.7% |
| 21 | Maryland | 182,314 | 1.7% |
| 22 | Alabama | 180,539 | 1.7% |
| 23 | Arizona | 173,929 | 1.6% |
| 24 | Colorado | 161,488 | 1.5% |
| 25 | South Carolina | 153,704 | 1.4% |
| 26 | Kentucky | 143,526 | 1.3% |
| 27 | Mississippi | 135,669 | 1.3% |
| 28 | Oklahoma | 131,078 | 1.2% |
| 29 | Kansas | 125,983 | 1.2% |
| 30 | Oregon | 121,589 | 1.1% |
| 31 | Iowa | 116,685 | 1.1% |
| 32 | Connecticut | 105,449 | 1.0% |
| 33 | Arkansas | 95,069 | 0.9% |
| 34 | Nebraska | 74,674 | 0.7% |
| 35 | Utah | 72,617 | 0.7% |
| 36 | New Mexico | 71,190 | 0.7% |
| 37 | Nevada | 61,520 | 0.6% |
| 38 | West Virginia | 61,398 | 0.6% |
| 39 | Idaho | 49,588 | 0.5% |
| 40 | Maine | 49,419 | 0.5% |
| 41 | New Hampshire | 42,931 | 0.4% |
| 42 | Rhode Island | 34,623 | 0.3% |
| 43 | Montana | 31,682 | 0.3% |
| 44 | Wyoming | 27,608 | 0.3% |
| 45 | South Dakota | 27,477 | 0.3% |
| 46 | Alaska | 25,925 | 0.2% |
| 47 | North Dakota | 21,848 | 0.2% |
| 48 | Vermont | 20,874 | 0.2% |
| 49 | Delaware | 20,334 | 0.2% |
| 50 | Hawaii | 14,121 | 0.1% |
| | District of Columbia | 43,208 | 0.4% |

Source: U.S. Bureau of the Census, Governments Division
   "Local Employment and Payroll Estimates - March 1999" (http://www.census.gov/govs/www/apesloc99.html)
*As of March 1999.

# Rate of Local Government FTE Employees in 1999

## National Rate = 391 Local Government Employees per 10,000 Population*

ALPHA ORDER

| RANK | STATE | RATE |
|------|-------|------|
| 11 | Alabama | 413 |
| 10 | Alaska | 418 |
| 34 | Arizona | 364 |
| 30 | Arkansas | 373 |
| 29 | California | 374 |
| 16 | Colorado | 398 |
| 47 | Connecticut | 321 |
| 49 | Delaware | 270 |
| 32 | Florida | 367 |
| 7 | Georgia | 431 |
| 50 | Hawaii | 119 |
| 17 | Idaho | 396 |
| 23 | Illinois | 388 |
| 25 | Indiana | 383 |
| 14 | Iowa | 407 |
| 4 | Kansas | 475 |
| 35 | Kentucky | 362 |
| 9 | Louisiana | 420 |
| 21 | Maine | 394 |
| 38 | Maryland | 353 |
| 31 | Massachusetts | 368 |
| 42 | Michigan | 344 |
| 8 | Minnesota | 424 |
| 3 | Mississippi | 490 |
| 25 | Missouri | 383 |
| 36 | Montana | 359 |
| 5 | Nebraska | 448 |
| 44 | Nevada | 340 |
| 37 | New Hampshire | 357 |
| 24 | New Jersey | 385 |
| 12 | New Mexico | 409 |
| 2 | New York | 493 |
| 12 | North Carolina | 409 |
| 41 | North Dakota | 345 |
| 15 | Ohio | 401 |
| 22 | Oklahoma | 390 |
| 32 | Oregon | 367 |
| 48 | Pennsylvania | 317 |
| 40 | Rhode Island | 349 |
| 17 | South Carolina | 396 |
| 28 | South Dakota | 375 |
| 19 | Tennessee | 395 |
| 6 | Texas | 435 |
| 43 | Utah | 341 |
| 39 | Vermont | 352 |
| 27 | Virginia | 377 |
| 46 | Washington | 325 |
| 44 | West Virginia | 340 |
| 19 | Wisconsin | 395 |
| 1 | Wyoming | 576 |

RANK ORDER

| RANK | STATE | RATE |
|------|-------|------|
| 1 | Wyoming | 576 |
| 2 | New York | 493 |
| 3 | Mississippi | 490 |
| 4 | Kansas | 475 |
| 5 | Nebraska | 448 |
| 6 | Texas | 435 |
| 7 | Georgia | 431 |
| 8 | Minnesota | 424 |
| 9 | Louisiana | 420 |
| 10 | Alaska | 418 |
| 11 | Alabama | 413 |
| 12 | New Mexico | 409 |
| 12 | North Carolina | 409 |
| 14 | Iowa | 407 |
| 15 | Ohio | 401 |
| 16 | Colorado | 398 |
| 17 | Idaho | 396 |
| 17 | South Carolina | 396 |
| 19 | Tennessee | 395 |
| 19 | Wisconsin | 395 |
| 21 | Maine | 394 |
| 22 | Oklahoma | 390 |
| 23 | Illinois | 388 |
| 24 | New Jersey | 385 |
| 25 | Indiana | 383 |
| 25 | Missouri | 383 |
| 27 | Virginia | 377 |
| 28 | South Dakota | 375 |
| 29 | California | 374 |
| 30 | Arkansas | 373 |
| 31 | Massachusetts | 368 |
| 32 | Florida | 367 |
| 32 | Oregon | 367 |
| 34 | Arizona | 364 |
| 35 | Kentucky | 362 |
| 36 | Montana | 359 |
| 37 | New Hampshire | 357 |
| 38 | Maryland | 353 |
| 39 | Vermont | 352 |
| 40 | Rhode Island | 349 |
| 41 | North Dakota | 345 |
| 42 | Michigan | 344 |
| 43 | Utah | 341 |
| 44 | Nevada | 340 |
| 44 | West Virginia | 340 |
| 46 | Washington | 325 |
| 47 | Connecticut | 321 |
| 48 | Pennsylvania | 317 |
| 49 | Delaware | 270 |
| 50 | Hawaii | 119 |
| | District of Columbia | 833 |

Source: Morgan Quitno Press using data from U.S. Bureau of the Census, Governments Division
"Local Employment and Payroll Estimates - March 1999" (http://www.census.gov/govs/www/apesloc99.html)
*Full-time equivalent as of March 1999.

# XI. HEALTH

# Persons Not Covered by Health Insurance in 1999

## National Total = 42,267,000 Uninsured

ALPHA ORDER

| RANK | STATE | UNINSURED | % of USA |
|------|-------|-----------|----------|
| 21 | Alabama | 625,000 | 1.5% |
| 44 | Alaska | 118,000 | 0.3% |
| 12 | Arizona | 1,013,000 | 2.4% |
| 31 | Arkansas | 375,000 | 0.9% |
| 1 | California | 6,728,000 | 15.9% |
| 17 | Colorado | 681,000 | 1.6% |
| 33 | Connecticut | 322,000 | 0.8% |
| 46 | Delaware | 86,000 | 0.2% |
| 4 | Florida | 2,901,000 | 6.9% |
| 6 | Georgia | 1,254,000 | 3.0% |
| 42 | Hawaii | 132,000 | 0.3% |
| 37 | Idaho | 239,000 | 0.6% |
| 5 | Illinois | 1,710,000 | 4.0% |
| 19 | Indiana | 642,000 | 1.5% |
| 38 | Iowa | 238,000 | 0.6% |
| 34 | Kansas | 321,000 | 0.8% |
| 25 | Kentucky | 574,000 | 1.4% |
| 13 | Louisiana | 984,000 | 2.3% |
| 41 | Maine | 149,000 | 0.4% |
| 22 | Maryland | 610,000 | 1.4% |
| 18 | Massachusetts | 648,000 | 1.5% |
| 10 | Michigan | 1,105,000 | 2.6% |
| 30 | Minnesota | 382,000 | 0.9% |
| 28 | Mississippi | 460,000 | 1.1% |
| 27 | Missouri | 470,000 | 1.1% |
| 40 | Montana | 164,000 | 0.4% |
| 39 | Nebraska | 180,000 | 0.4% |
| 31 | Nevada | 375,000 | 0.9% |
| 43 | New Hampshire | 123,000 | 0.3% |
| 11 | New Jersey | 1,091,000 | 2.6% |
| 29 | New Mexico | 449,000 | 1.1% |
| 3 | New York | 2,984,000 | 7.1% |
| 8 | North Carolina | 1,178,000 | 2.8% |
| 48 | North Dakota | 75,000 | 0.2% |
| 7 | Ohio | 1,238,000 | 2.9% |
| 23 | Oklahoma | 588,000 | 1.4% |
| 26 | Oregon | 484,000 | 1.1% |
| 9 | Pennsylvania | 1,127,000 | 2.7% |
| 50 | Rhode Island | 68,000 | 0.2% |
| 16 | South Carolina | 684,000 | 1.6% |
| 45 | South Dakota | 87,000 | 0.2% |
| 20 | Tennessee | 631,000 | 1.5% |
| 2 | Texas | 4,670,000 | 11.0% |
| 36 | Utah | 302,000 | 0.7% |
| 49 | Vermont | 73,000 | 0.2% |
| 14 | Virginia | 969,000 | 2.3% |
| 15 | Washington | 910,000 | 2.2% |
| 35 | West Virginia | 309,000 | 0.7% |
| 24 | Wisconsin | 578,000 | 1.4% |
| 47 | Wyoming | 77,000 | 0.2% |

RANK ORDER

| RANK | STATE | UNINSURED | % of USA |
|------|-------|-----------|----------|
| 1 | California | 6,728,000 | 15.9% |
| 2 | Texas | 4,670,000 | 11.0% |
| 3 | New York | 2,984,000 | 7.1% |
| 4 | Florida | 2,901,000 | 6.9% |
| 5 | Illinois | 1,710,000 | 4.0% |
| 6 | Georgia | 1,254,000 | 3.0% |
| 7 | Ohio | 1,238,000 | 2.9% |
| 8 | North Carolina | 1,178,000 | 2.8% |
| 9 | Pennsylvania | 1,127,000 | 2.7% |
| 10 | Michigan | 1,105,000 | 2.6% |
| 11 | New Jersey | 1,091,000 | 2.6% |
| 12 | Arizona | 1,013,000 | 2.4% |
| 13 | Louisiana | 984,000 | 2.3% |
| 14 | Virginia | 969,000 | 2.3% |
| 15 | Washington | 910,000 | 2.2% |
| 16 | South Carolina | 684,000 | 1.6% |
| 17 | Colorado | 681,000 | 1.6% |
| 18 | Massachusetts | 648,000 | 1.5% |
| 19 | Indiana | 642,000 | 1.5% |
| 20 | Tennessee | 631,000 | 1.5% |
| 21 | Alabama | 625,000 | 1.5% |
| 22 | Maryland | 610,000 | 1.4% |
| 23 | Oklahoma | 588,000 | 1.4% |
| 24 | Wisconsin | 578,000 | 1.4% |
| 25 | Kentucky | 574,000 | 1.4% |
| 26 | Oregon | 484,000 | 1.1% |
| 27 | Missouri | 470,000 | 1.1% |
| 28 | Mississippi | 460,000 | 1.1% |
| 29 | New Mexico | 449,000 | 1.1% |
| 30 | Minnesota | 382,000 | 0.9% |
| 31 | Arkansas | 375,000 | 0.9% |
| 31 | Nevada | 375,000 | 0.9% |
| 33 | Connecticut | 322,000 | 0.8% |
| 34 | Kansas | 321,000 | 0.8% |
| 35 | West Virginia | 309,000 | 0.7% |
| 36 | Utah | 302,000 | 0.7% |
| 37 | Idaho | 239,000 | 0.6% |
| 38 | Iowa | 238,000 | 0.6% |
| 39 | Nebraska | 180,000 | 0.4% |
| 40 | Montana | 164,000 | 0.4% |
| 41 | Maine | 149,000 | 0.4% |
| 42 | Hawaii | 132,000 | 0.3% |
| 43 | New Hampshire | 123,000 | 0.3% |
| 44 | Alaska | 118,000 | 0.3% |
| 45 | South Dakota | 87,000 | 0.2% |
| 46 | Delaware | 86,000 | 0.2% |
| 47 | Wyoming | 77,000 | 0.2% |
| 48 | North Dakota | 75,000 | 0.2% |
| 49 | Vermont | 73,000 | 0.2% |
| 50 | Rhode Island | 68,000 | 0.2% |
| | District of Columbia | 80,000 | 0.2% |

Source: Morgan Quitno Press using data from U.S. Bureau of the Census
"Health Insurance Historical Table 4" (http://www.census.gov/hhes/hlthins/historic/hihistt4.html)

# Percent of Population Not Covered by Health Insurance in 1999

## National Percent = 15.5% of Population*

ALPHA ORDER

| RANK | STATE | PERCENT |
|------|-------|---------|
| 24 | Alabama | 14.3 |
| 8 | Alaska | 19.1 |
| 4 | Arizona | 21.2 |
| 21 | Arkansas | 14.7 |
| 6 | California | 20.3 |
| 14 | Colorado | 16.8 |
| 45 | Connecticut | 9.8 |
| 36 | Delaware | 11.4 |
| 7 | Florida | 19.2 |
| 17 | Georgia | 16.1 |
| 38 | Hawaii | 11.1 |
| 8 | Idaho | 19.1 |
| 26 | Illinois | 14.1 |
| 41 | Indiana | 10.8 |
| 48 | Iowa | 8.3 |
| 30 | Kansas | 12.1 |
| 23 | Kentucky | 14.5 |
| 3 | Louisiana | 22.5 |
| 31 | Maine | 11.9 |
| 32 | Maryland | 11.8 |
| 43 | Massachusetts | 10.5 |
| 37 | Michigan | 11.2 |
| 49 | Minnesota | 8.0 |
| 15 | Mississippi | 16.6 |
| 47 | Missouri | 8.6 |
| 10 | Montana | 18.6 |
| 41 | Nebraska | 10.8 |
| 5 | Nevada | 20.7 |
| 44 | New Hampshire | 10.2 |
| 28 | New Jersey | 13.4 |
| 1 | New Mexico | 25.8 |
| 16 | New York | 16.4 |
| 20 | North Carolina | 15.4 |
| 32 | North Dakota | 11.8 |
| 39 | Ohio | 11.0 |
| 12 | Oklahoma | 17.5 |
| 22 | Oregon | 14.6 |
| 46 | Pennsylvania | 9.4 |
| 50 | Rhode Island | 6.9 |
| 11 | South Carolina | 17.6 |
| 32 | South Dakota | 11.8 |
| 35 | Tennessee | 11.5 |
| 2 | Texas | 23.3 |
| 25 | Utah | 14.2 |
| 29 | Vermont | 12.3 |
| 26 | Virginia | 14.1 |
| 19 | Washington | 15.8 |
| 13 | West Virginia | 17.1 |
| 39 | Wisconsin | 11.0 |
| 17 | Wyoming | 16.1 |

RANK ORDER

| RANK | STATE | PERCENT |
|------|-------|---------|
| 1 | New Mexico | 25.8 |
| 2 | Texas | 23.3 |
| 3 | Louisiana | 22.5 |
| 4 | Arizona | 21.2 |
| 5 | Nevada | 20.7 |
| 6 | California | 20.3 |
| 7 | Florida | 19.2 |
| 8 | Alaska | 19.1 |
| 8 | Idaho | 19.1 |
| 10 | Montana | 18.6 |
| 11 | South Carolina | 17.6 |
| 12 | Oklahoma | 17.5 |
| 13 | West Virginia | 17.1 |
| 14 | Colorado | 16.8 |
| 15 | Mississippi | 16.6 |
| 16 | New York | 16.4 |
| 17 | Georgia | 16.1 |
| 17 | Wyoming | 16.1 |
| 19 | Washington | 15.8 |
| 20 | North Carolina | 15.4 |
| 21 | Arkansas | 14.7 |
| 22 | Oregon | 14.6 |
| 23 | Kentucky | 14.5 |
| 24 | Alabama | 14.3 |
| 25 | Utah | 14.2 |
| 26 | Illinois | 14.1 |
| 26 | Virginia | 14.1 |
| 28 | New Jersey | 13.4 |
| 29 | Vermont | 12.3 |
| 30 | Kansas | 12.1 |
| 31 | Maine | 11.9 |
| 32 | Maryland | 11.8 |
| 32 | North Dakota | 11.8 |
| 32 | South Dakota | 11.8 |
| 35 | Tennessee | 11.5 |
| 36 | Delaware | 11.4 |
| 37 | Michigan | 11.2 |
| 38 | Hawaii | 11.1 |
| 39 | Ohio | 11.0 |
| 39 | Wisconsin | 11.0 |
| 41 | Indiana | 10.8 |
| 41 | Nebraska | 10.8 |
| 43 | Massachusetts | 10.5 |
| 44 | New Hampshire | 10.2 |
| 45 | Connecticut | 9.8 |
| 46 | Pennsylvania | 9.4 |
| 47 | Missouri | 8.6 |
| 48 | Iowa | 8.3 |
| 49 | Minnesota | 8.0 |
| 50 | Rhode Island | 6.9 |
| | District of Columbia | 15.4 |

*Source: U.S. Bureau of the Census*
*"Health Insurance Coverage: 1999" (http://www.census.gov/hhes/hlthins/hlthin99/hi99te.html)*

# Percent of Population Enrolled in Health Maintenance Organizations (HMOs) in 2000
## National Percent = 28.3% Enrolled in HMOs*

ALPHA ORDER

| RANK | STATE | PERCENT |
|------|-------|---------|
| 43 | Alabama | 7.2 |
| 50 | Alaska | 0.0 |
| 17 | Arizona | 30.9 |
| 38 | Arkansas | 10.4 |
| 1 | California | 53.5 |
| 6 | Colorado | 39.5 |
| 3 | Connecticut | 44.6 |
| 26 | Delaware | 22.0 |
| 16 | Florida | 31.4 |
| 32 | Georgia | 17.4 |
| 20 | Hawaii | 30.0 |
| 41 | Idaho | 7.9 |
| 27 | Illinois | 21.0 |
| 36 | Indiana | 12.4 |
| 42 | Iowa | 7.4 |
| 30 | Kansas | 17.9 |
| 15 | Kentucky | 31.5 |
| 33 | Louisiana | 17.0 |
| 25 | Maine | 22.3 |
| 4 | Maryland | 43.9 |
| 2 | Massachusetts | 53.0 |
| 22 | Michigan | 27.1 |
| 21 | Minnesota | 29.9 |
| 49 | Mississippi | 1.1 |
| 11 | Missouri | 35.2 |
| 44 | Montana | 7.0 |
| 37 | Nebraska | 11.2 |
| 24 | Nevada | 23.5 |
| 13 | New Hampshire | 33.7 |
| 17 | New Jersey | 30.9 |
| 8 | New Mexico | 37.7 |
| 9 | New York | 35.8 |
| 31 | North Carolina | 17.8 |
| 47 | North Dakota | 2.5 |
| 23 | Ohio | 25.1 |
| 35 | Oklahoma | 14.7 |
| 5 | Oregon | 41.1 |
| 12 | Pennsylvania | 33.9 |
| 7 | Rhode Island | 38.1 |
| 40 | South Carolina | 9.9 |
| 45 | South Dakota | 6.7 |
| 14 | Tennessee | 33.0 |
| 28 | Texas | 18.5 |
| 10 | Utah | 35.3 |
| 46 | Vermont | 4.6 |
| 28 | Virginia | 18.5 |
| 34 | Washington | 15.2 |
| 39 | West Virginia | 10.3 |
| 19 | Wisconsin | 30.2 |
| 48 | Wyoming | 1.4 |

RANK ORDER

| RANK | STATE | PERCENT |
|------|-------|---------|
| 1 | California | 53.5 |
| 2 | Massachusetts | 53.0 |
| 3 | Connecticut | 44.6 |
| 4 | Maryland | 43.9 |
| 5 | Oregon | 41.1 |
| 6 | Colorado | 39.5 |
| 7 | Rhode Island | 38.1 |
| 8 | New Mexico | 37.7 |
| 9 | New York | 35.8 |
| 10 | Utah | 35.3 |
| 11 | Missouri | 35.2 |
| 12 | Pennsylvania | 33.9 |
| 13 | New Hampshire | 33.7 |
| 14 | Tennessee | 33.0 |
| 15 | Kentucky | 31.5 |
| 16 | Florida | 31.4 |
| 17 | Arizona | 30.9 |
| 17 | New Jersey | 30.9 |
| 19 | Wisconsin | 30.2 |
| 20 | Hawaii | 30.0 |
| 21 | Minnesota | 29.9 |
| 22 | Michigan | 27.1 |
| 23 | Ohio | 25.1 |
| 24 | Nevada | 23.5 |
| 25 | Maine | 22.3 |
| 26 | Delaware | 22.0 |
| 27 | Illinois | 21.0 |
| 28 | Texas | 18.5 |
| 28 | Virginia | 18.5 |
| 30 | Kansas | 17.9 |
| 31 | North Carolina | 17.8 |
| 32 | Georgia | 17.4 |
| 33 | Louisiana | 17.0 |
| 34 | Washington | 15.2 |
| 35 | Oklahoma | 14.7 |
| 36 | Indiana | 12.4 |
| 37 | Nebraska | 11.2 |
| 38 | Arkansas | 10.4 |
| 39 | West Virginia | 10.3 |
| 40 | South Carolina | 9.9 |
| 41 | Idaho | 7.9 |
| 42 | Iowa | 7.4 |
| 43 | Alabama | 7.2 |
| 44 | Montana | 7.0 |
| 45 | South Dakota | 6.7 |
| 46 | Vermont | 4.6 |
| 47 | North Dakota | 2.5 |
| 48 | Wyoming | 1.4 |
| 49 | Mississippi | 1.1 |
| 50 | Alaska | 0.0 |
|  | District of Columbia | 35.2 |

Source: InterStudy Publications (Minneapolis, MN)
   "HMO Industry Report 10.2" (Press Release, October 30, 2000)
*As of January 1, 2000.  National percent does not include enrollees or population in U.S. territories.

# Percent of Population Lacking Access to Primary Care in 2000

## National Percent = 9.3% of Population*

| ALPHA ORDER | | | | RANK ORDER | | |
|---|---|---|---|---|---|---|
| RANK | STATE | PERCENT | | RANK | STATE | PERCENT |
| 2 | Alabama | 22.7 | | 1 | Mississippi | 26.9 |
| 13 | Alaska | 14.2 | | 2 | Alabama | 22.7 |
| 33 | Arizona | 7.7 | | 3 | Utah | 21.0 |
| 18 | Arkansas | 11.2 | | 4 | Idaho | 20.3 |
| 44 | California | 4.9 | | 5 | South Dakota | 19.2 |
| 34 | Colorado | 7.4 | | 6 | Louisiana | 18.3 |
| 42 | Connecticut | 5.7 | | 7 | Wyoming | 17.9 |
| 45 | Delaware | 4.5 | | 8 | Missouri | 17.8 |
| 27 | Florida | 8.8 | | 9 | Georgia | 16.3 |
| 9 | Georgia | 16.3 | | 10 | South Carolina | 16.0 |
| 50 | Hawaii | 2.9 | | 11 | New Mexico | 15.9 |
| 4 | Idaho | 20.3 | | 12 | North Dakota | 15.5 |
| 38 | Illinois | 6.7 | | 13 | Alaska | 14.2 |
| 27 | Indiana | 8.8 | | 13 | Kentucky | 14.2 |
| 30 | Iowa | 8.4 | | 15 | Montana | 13.5 |
| 41 | Kansas | 6.0 | | 16 | West Virginia | 12.7 |
| 13 | Kentucky | 14.2 | | 17 | Texas | 11.6 |
| 6 | Louisiana | 18.3 | | 18 | Arkansas | 11.2 |
| 35 | Maine | 7.2 | | 19 | Minnesota | 10.8 |
| 40 | Maryland | 6.2 | | 20 | Michigan | 10.5 |
| 47 | Massachusetts | 4.0 | | 21 | Tennessee | 10.1 |
| 20 | Michigan | 10.5 | | 22 | Nevada | 9.8 |
| 19 | Minnesota | 10.8 | | 23 | North Carolina | 9.5 |
| 1 | Mississippi | 26.9 | | 24 | Wisconsin | 9.3 |
| 8 | Missouri | 17.8 | | 25 | New York | 9.2 |
| 15 | Montana | 13.5 | | 26 | Washington | 9.0 |
| 39 | Nebraska | 6.6 | | 27 | Florida | 8.8 |
| 22 | Nevada | 9.8 | | 27 | Indiana | 8.8 |
| 46 | New Hampshire | 4.3 | | 29 | Oregon | 8.7 |
| 49 | New Jersey | 3.5 | | 30 | Iowa | 8.4 |
| 11 | New Mexico | 15.9 | | 31 | Rhode Island | 8.1 |
| 25 | New York | 9.2 | | 32 | Oklahoma | 7.9 |
| 23 | North Carolina | 9.5 | | 33 | Arizona | 7.7 |
| 12 | North Dakota | 15.5 | | 34 | Colorado | 7.4 |
| 37 | Ohio | 7.0 | | 35 | Maine | 7.2 |
| 32 | Oklahoma | 7.9 | | 35 | Virginia | 7.2 |
| 29 | Oregon | 8.7 | | 37 | Ohio | 7.0 |
| 43 | Pennsylvania | 5.5 | | 38 | Illinois | 6.7 |
| 31 | Rhode Island | 8.1 | | 39 | Nebraska | 6.6 |
| 10 | South Carolina | 16.0 | | 40 | Maryland | 6.2 |
| 5 | South Dakota | 19.2 | | 41 | Kansas | 6.0 |
| 21 | Tennessee | 10.1 | | 42 | Connecticut | 5.7 |
| 17 | Texas | 11.6 | | 43 | Pennsylvania | 5.5 |
| 3 | Utah | 21.0 | | 44 | California | 4.9 |
| 48 | Vermont | 3.7 | | 45 | Delaware | 4.5 |
| 35 | Virginia | 7.2 | | 46 | New Hampshire | 4.3 |
| 26 | Washington | 9.0 | | 47 | Massachusetts | 4.0 |
| 16 | West Virginia | 12.7 | | 48 | Vermont | 3.7 |
| 24 | Wisconsin | 9.3 | | 49 | New Jersey | 3.5 |
| 7 | Wyoming | 17.9 | | 50 | Hawaii | 2.9 |

District of Columbia 19.5

Source: Morgan Quitno Press using data from U.S. Dept. of Health and Human Services, Div. of Shortage Designation
"Selected Statistics on Health Manpower Shortage Areas, As of December 31, 2000"
*Percent of population considered under-served by primary medical practitioners (Family & General Practice doctors, Internists, Ob/Gyns and Pediatricians). An under-served population does not have primary medical care within reasonable economic and geographic bounds.

# Personal Health Care Expenditures in 1998

## National Total = $1,016,383,000,000*

ALPHA ORDER

| RANK | STATE | EXPENDITURES | % of USA |
|---|---|---|---|
| 22 | Alabama | $16,056,000,000 | 1.6% |
| 48 | Alaska | 2,299,000,000 | 0.2% |
| 24 | Arizona | 14,782,000,000 | 1.5% |
| 33 | Arkansas | 8,463,000,000 | 0.8% |
| 1 | California | 110,057,000,000 | 10.8% |
| 26 | Colorado | 13,669,000,000 | 1.3% |
| 23 | Connecticut | 15,221,000,000 | 1.5% |
| 44 | Delaware | 3,106,000,000 | 0.3% |
| 4 | Florida | 59,724,000,000 | 5.9% |
| 12 | Georgia | 27,219,000,000 | 2.7% |
| 40 | Hawaii | 4,658,000,000 | 0.5% |
| 43 | Idaho | 3,397,000,000 | 0.3% |
| 6 | Illinois | 44,305,000,000 | 4.4% |
| 15 | Indiana | 21,259,000,000 | 2.1% |
| 30 | Iowa | 10,198,000,000 | 1.0% |
| 31 | Kansas | 9,394,000,000 | 0.9% |
| 25 | Kentucky | 14,414,000,000 | 1.4% |
| 21 | Louisiana | 16,500,000,000 | 1.6% |
| 39 | Maine | 4,925,000,000 | 0.5% |
| 19 | Maryland | 19,646,000,000 | 1.9% |
| 10 | Massachusetts | 30,039,000,000 | 3.0% |
| 8 | Michigan | 35,647,000,000 | 3.5% |
| 17 | Minnesota | 20,313,000,000 | 2.0% |
| 32 | Mississippi | 8,882,000,000 | 0.9% |
| 16 | Missouri | 20,911,000,000 | 2.1% |
| 46 | Montana | 2,838,000,000 | 0.3% |
| 35 | Nebraska | 6,095,000,000 | 0.6% |
| 37 | Nevada | 5,606,000,000 | 0.6% |
| 40 | New Hampshire | 4,658,000,000 | 0.5% |
| 9 | New Jersey | 32,695,000,000 | 3.2% |
| 38 | New Mexico | 5,344,000,000 | 0.5% |
| 2 | New York | 85,785,000,000 | 8.4% |
| 11 | North Carolina | 27,327,000,000 | 2.7% |
| 47 | North Dakota | 2,680,000,000 | 0.3% |
| 7 | Ohio | 42,581,000,000 | 4.2% |
| 28 | Oklahoma | 10,988,000,000 | 1.1% |
| 29 | Oregon | 10,840,000,000 | 1.1% |
| 5 | Pennsylvania | 51,322,000,000 | 5.0% |
| 42 | Rhode Island | 4,515,000,000 | 0.4% |
| 27 | South Carolina | 13,204,000,000 | 1.3% |
| 45 | South Dakota | 2,842,000,000 | 0.3% |
| 14 | Tennessee | 22,021,000,000 | 2.2% |
| 3 | Texas | 67,750,000,000 | 6.7% |
| 36 | Utah | 5,944,000,000 | 0.6% |
| 49 | Vermont | 2,066,000,000 | 0.2% |
| 13 | Virginia | 22,261,000,000 | 2.2% |
| 20 | Washington | 19,292,000,000 | 1.9% |
| 34 | West Virginia | 7,037,000,000 | 0.7% |
| 18 | Wisconsin | 19,945,000,000 | 2.0% |
| 50 | Wyoming | 1,407,000,000 | 0.1% |

RANK ORDER

| RANK | STATE | EXPENDITURES | % of USA |
|---|---|---|---|
| 1 | California | $110,057,000,000 | 10.8% |
| 2 | New York | 85,785,000,000 | 8.4% |
| 3 | Texas | 67,750,000,000 | 6.7% |
| 4 | Florida | 59,724,000,000 | 5.9% |
| 5 | Pennsylvania | 51,322,000,000 | 5.0% |
| 6 | Illinois | 44,305,000,000 | 4.4% |
| 7 | Ohio | 42,581,000,000 | 4.2% |
| 8 | Michigan | 35,647,000,000 | 3.5% |
| 9 | New Jersey | 32,695,000,000 | 3.2% |
| 10 | Massachusetts | 30,039,000,000 | 3.0% |
| 11 | North Carolina | 27,327,000,000 | 2.7% |
| 12 | Georgia | 27,219,000,000 | 2.7% |
| 13 | Virginia | 22,261,000,000 | 2.2% |
| 14 | Tennessee | 22,021,000,000 | 2.2% |
| 15 | Indiana | 21,259,000,000 | 2.1% |
| 16 | Missouri | 20,911,000,000 | 2.1% |
| 17 | Minnesota | 20,313,000,000 | 2.0% |
| 18 | Wisconsin | 19,945,000,000 | 2.0% |
| 19 | Maryland | 19,646,000,000 | 1.9% |
| 20 | Washington | 19,292,000,000 | 1.9% |
| 21 | Louisiana | 16,500,000,000 | 1.6% |
| 22 | Alabama | 16,056,000,000 | 1.6% |
| 23 | Connecticut | 15,221,000,000 | 1.5% |
| 24 | Arizona | 14,782,000,000 | 1.5% |
| 25 | Kentucky | 14,414,000,000 | 1.4% |
| 26 | Colorado | 13,669,000,000 | 1.3% |
| 27 | South Carolina | 13,204,000,000 | 1.3% |
| 28 | Oklahoma | 10,988,000,000 | 1.1% |
| 29 | Oregon | 10,840,000,000 | 1.1% |
| 30 | Iowa | 10,198,000,000 | 1.0% |
| 31 | Kansas | 9,394,000,000 | 0.9% |
| 32 | Mississippi | 8,882,000,000 | 0.9% |
| 33 | Arkansas | 8,463,000,000 | 0.8% |
| 34 | West Virginia | 7,037,000,000 | 0.7% |
| 35 | Nebraska | 6,095,000,000 | 0.6% |
| 36 | Utah | 5,944,000,000 | 0.6% |
| 37 | Nevada | 5,606,000,000 | 0.6% |
| 38 | New Mexico | 5,344,000,000 | 0.5% |
| 39 | Maine | 4,925,000,000 | 0.5% |
| 40 | Hawaii | 4,658,000,000 | 0.5% |
| 40 | New Hampshire | 4,658,000,000 | 0.5% |
| 42 | Rhode Island | 4,515,000,000 | 0.4% |
| 43 | Idaho | 3,397,000,000 | 0.3% |
| 44 | Delaware | 3,106,000,000 | 0.3% |
| 45 | South Dakota | 2,842,000,000 | 0.3% |
| 46 | Montana | 2,838,000,000 | 0.3% |
| 47 | North Dakota | 2,680,000,000 | 0.3% |
| 48 | Alaska | 2,299,000,000 | 0.2% |
| 49 | Vermont | 2,066,000,000 | 0.2% |
| 50 | Wyoming | 1,407,000,000 | 0.1% |
|  | District of Columbia | 4,258,000,000 | 0.4% |

*Source: U.S. Department of Health and Human Services, Health Care Financing Administration*
*"State Health Care Expenditures" (http://www.hcfa.gov/stats/nhe-oact/stateestimates/)*
*\*By state of provider. Includes hospital care, physician services, dental services, home health care, drugs, vision products, nursing home care and other personal health care services and products.*

# Per Capita Personal Health Care Expenditures in 1998

## National Per Capita = $3,761*

ALPHA ORDER

| RANK | STATE | PER CAPITA |
|---|---|---|
| 23 | Alabama | $3,690 |
| 22 | Alaska | 3,737 |
| 46 | Arizona | 3,167 |
| 39 | Arkansas | 3,334 |
| 38 | California | 3,367 |
| 34 | Colorado | 3,444 |
| 3 | Connecticut | 4,651 |
| 8 | Delaware | 4,174 |
| 11 | Florida | 4,006 |
| 30 | Georgia | 3,564 |
| 14 | Hawaii | 3,913 |
| 50 | Idaho | 2,760 |
| 24 | Illinois | 3,671 |
| 29 | Indiana | 3,599 |
| 30 | Iowa | 3,564 |
| 32 | Kansas | 3,560 |
| 26 | Kentucky | 3,664 |
| 21 | Louisiana | 3,782 |
| 12 | Maine | 3,948 |
| 18 | Maryland | 3,830 |
| 1 | Massachusetts | 4,889 |
| 27 | Michigan | 3,630 |
| 5 | Minnesota | 4,298 |
| 43 | Mississippi | 3,228 |
| 17 | Missouri | 3,846 |
| 44 | Montana | 3,227 |
| 25 | Nebraska | 3,670 |
| 45 | Nevada | 3,215 |
| 13 | New Hampshire | 3,928 |
| 10 | New Jersey | 4,039 |
| 47 | New Mexico | 3,083 |
| 2 | New York | 4,724 |
| 28 | North Carolina | 3,621 |
| 7 | North Dakota | 4,202 |
| 20 | Ohio | 3,789 |
| 41 | Oklahoma | 3,290 |
| 40 | Oregon | 3,303 |
| 6 | Pennsylvania | 4,276 |
| 4 | Rhode Island | 4,571 |
| 35 | South Carolina | 3,439 |
| 15 | South Dakota | 3,889 |
| 9 | Tennessee | 4,053 |
| 36 | Texas | 3,437 |
| 49 | Utah | 2,830 |
| 33 | Vermont | 3,498 |
| 42 | Virginia | 3,279 |
| 37 | Washington | 3,392 |
| 16 | West Virginia | 3,884 |
| 19 | Wisconsin | 3,819 |
| 48 | Wyoming | 2,931 |

RANK ORDER

| RANK | STATE | PER CAPITA |
|---|---|---|
| 1 | Massachusetts | $4,889 |
| 2 | New York | 4,724 |
| 3 | Connecticut | 4,651 |
| 4 | Rhode Island | 4,571 |
| 5 | Minnesota | 4,298 |
| 6 | Pennsylvania | 4,276 |
| 7 | North Dakota | 4,202 |
| 8 | Delaware | 4,174 |
| 9 | Tennessee | 4,053 |
| 10 | New Jersey | 4,039 |
| 11 | Florida | 4,006 |
| 12 | Maine | 3,948 |
| 13 | New Hampshire | 3,928 |
| 14 | Hawaii | 3,913 |
| 15 | South Dakota | 3,889 |
| 16 | West Virginia | 3,884 |
| 17 | Missouri | 3,846 |
| 18 | Maryland | 3,830 |
| 19 | Wisconsin | 3,819 |
| 20 | Ohio | 3,789 |
| 21 | Louisiana | 3,782 |
| 22 | Alaska | 3,737 |
| 23 | Alabama | 3,690 |
| 24 | Illinois | 3,671 |
| 25 | Nebraska | 3,670 |
| 26 | Kentucky | 3,664 |
| 27 | Michigan | 3,630 |
| 28 | North Carolina | 3,621 |
| 29 | Indiana | 3,599 |
| 30 | Georgia | 3,564 |
| 30 | Iowa | 3,564 |
| 32 | Kansas | 3,560 |
| 33 | Vermont | 3,498 |
| 34 | Colorado | 3,444 |
| 35 | South Carolina | 3,439 |
| 36 | Texas | 3,437 |
| 37 | Washington | 3,392 |
| 38 | California | 3,367 |
| 39 | Arkansas | 3,334 |
| 40 | Oregon | 3,303 |
| 41 | Oklahoma | 3,290 |
| 42 | Virginia | 3,279 |
| 43 | Mississippi | 3,228 |
| 44 | Montana | 3,227 |
| 45 | Nevada | 3,215 |
| 46 | Arizona | 3,167 |
| 47 | New Mexico | 3,083 |
| 48 | Wyoming | 2,931 |
| 49 | Utah | 2,830 |
| 50 | Idaho | 2,760 |

District of Columbia    8,166

*Source: Morgan Quitno Press using data from U.S. Dept of Health & Human Services, Health Care Financing Admin.*
*"State Health Care Expenditures" (http://www.hcfa.gov/stats/nhe-oact/stateestimates/)*
*\*By state of provider. Per capita calculated using resident population. These figures may be skewed due to residents crossing state borders for care. Includes hospital care, physician services, dental services, home health care, drugs, vision products, nursing home care and other personal health care services and products.*

# Nonfederal Physicians in 1999

## National Total = 767,592 Physicians*

ALPHA ORDER

| RANK | STATE | PHYSICIANS | % of USA |
|------|-------|-----------|----------|
| 25 | Alabama | 9,487 | 1.2% |
| 49 | Alaska | 1,150 | 0.1% |
| 23 | Arizona | 11,487 | 1.5% |
| 32 | Arkansas | 5,458 | 0.7% |
| 1 | California | 92,985 | 12.1% |
| 24 | Colorado | 11,115 | 1.4% |
| 20 | Connecticut | 13,020 | 1.7% |
| 46 | Delaware | 1,985 | 0.3% |
| 4 | Florida | 43,835 | 5.7% |
| 14 | Georgia | 17,945 | 2.3% |
| 39 | Hawaii | 3,632 | 0.5% |
| 43 | Idaho | 2,240 | 0.3% |
| 6 | Illinois | 34,840 | 4.5% |
| 21 | Indiana | 13,000 | 1.7% |
| 31 | Iowa | 5,734 | 0.7% |
| 30 | Kansas | 6,171 | 0.8% |
| 26 | Kentucky | 9,187 | 1.2% |
| 22 | Louisiana | 11,806 | 1.5% |
| 41 | Maine | 3,356 | 0.4% |
| 11 | Maryland | 21,360 | 2.8% |
| 8 | Massachusetts | 28,062 | 3.7% |
| 10 | Michigan | 24,551 | 3.2% |
| 18 | Minnesota | 13,485 | 1.8% |
| 33 | Mississippi | 4,982 | 0.6% |
| 17 | Missouri | 13,674 | 1.8% |
| 45 | Montana | 2,010 | 0.3% |
| 37 | Nebraska | 4,111 | 0.5% |
| 40 | Nevada | 3,611 | 0.5% |
| 42 | New Hampshire | 3,274 | 0.4% |
| 9 | New Jersey | 26,606 | 3.5% |
| 36 | New Mexico | 4,231 | 0.6% |
| 2 | New York | 77,003 | 10.0% |
| 12 | North Carolina | 20,036 | 2.6% |
| 47 | North Dakota | 1,560 | 0.2% |
| 7 | Ohio | 29,358 | 3.8% |
| 29 | Oklahoma | 6,285 | 0.8% |
| 28 | Oregon | 8,825 | 1.1% |
| 5 | Pennsylvania | 38,524 | 5.0% |
| 38 | Rhode Island | 3,676 | 0.5% |
| 27 | South Carolina | 9,114 | 1.2% |
| 48 | South Dakota | 1,551 | 0.2% |
| 16 | Tennessee | 14,774 | 1.9% |
| 3 | Texas | 44,433 | 5.8% |
| 34 | Utah | 4,787 | 0.6% |
| 44 | Vermont | 2,148 | 0.3% |
| 13 | Virginia | 18,504 | 2.4% |
| 15 | Washington | 15,688 | 2.0% |
| 35 | West Virginia | 4,323 | 0.6% |
| 19 | Wisconsin | 13,452 | 1.8% |
| 50 | Wyoming | 950 | 0.1% |

RANK ORDER

| RANK | STATE | PHYSICIANS | % of USA |
|------|-------|-----------|----------|
| 1 | California | 92,985 | 12.1% |
| 2 | New York | 77,003 | 10.0% |
| 3 | Texas | 44,433 | 5.8% |
| 4 | Florida | 43,835 | 5.7% |
| 5 | Pennsylvania | 38,524 | 5.0% |
| 6 | Illinois | 34,840 | 4.5% |
| 7 | Ohio | 29,358 | 3.8% |
| 8 | Massachusetts | 28,062 | 3.7% |
| 9 | New Jersey | 26,606 | 3.5% |
| 10 | Michigan | 24,551 | 3.2% |
| 11 | Maryland | 21,360 | 2.8% |
| 12 | North Carolina | 20,036 | 2.6% |
| 13 | Virginia | 18,504 | 2.4% |
| 14 | Georgia | 17,945 | 2.3% |
| 15 | Washington | 15,688 | 2.0% |
| 16 | Tennessee | 14,774 | 1.9% |
| 17 | Missouri | 13,674 | 1.8% |
| 18 | Minnesota | 13,485 | 1.8% |
| 19 | Wisconsin | 13,452 | 1.8% |
| 20 | Connecticut | 13,020 | 1.7% |
| 21 | Indiana | 13,000 | 1.7% |
| 22 | Louisiana | 11,806 | 1.5% |
| 23 | Arizona | 11,487 | 1.5% |
| 24 | Colorado | 11,115 | 1.4% |
| 25 | Alabama | 9,487 | 1.2% |
| 26 | Kentucky | 9,187 | 1.2% |
| 27 | South Carolina | 9,114 | 1.2% |
| 28 | Oregon | 8,825 | 1.1% |
| 29 | Oklahoma | 6,285 | 0.8% |
| 30 | Kansas | 6,171 | 0.8% |
| 31 | Iowa | 5,734 | 0.7% |
| 32 | Arkansas | 5,458 | 0.7% |
| 33 | Mississippi | 4,982 | 0.6% |
| 34 | Utah | 4,787 | 0.6% |
| 35 | West Virginia | 4,323 | 0.6% |
| 36 | New Mexico | 4,231 | 0.6% |
| 37 | Nebraska | 4,111 | 0.5% |
| 38 | Rhode Island | 3,676 | 0.5% |
| 39 | Hawaii | 3,632 | 0.5% |
| 40 | Nevada | 3,611 | 0.5% |
| 41 | Maine | 3,356 | 0.4% |
| 42 | New Hampshire | 3,274 | 0.4% |
| 43 | Idaho | 2,240 | 0.3% |
| 44 | Vermont | 2,148 | 0.3% |
| 45 | Montana | 2,010 | 0.3% |
| 46 | Delaware | 1,985 | 0.3% |
| 47 | North Dakota | 1,560 | 0.2% |
| 48 | South Dakota | 1,551 | 0.2% |
| 49 | Alaska | 1,150 | 0.1% |
| 50 | Wyoming | 950 | 0.1% |
| | District of Columbia | 4,211 | 0.5% |

Source: American Medical Association (Chicago, Illinois)
"Physician Characteristics and Distribution in the U.S." (2001-2002 Edition)
*As of December 31, 1999. Total does not include 10,899 nonfederal physicians in U.S. territories and possessions.

# Rate of Nonfederal Physicians in 1999

## National Rate = 281 Physicians per 100,000 Population*

ALPHA ORDER

| RANK | STATE | RATE |
|------|-------|------|
| 41 | Alabama | 217 |
| 48 | Alaska | 186 |
| 31 | Arizona | 240 |
| 42 | Arkansas | 214 |
| 13 | California | 281 |
| 14 | Colorado | 274 |
| 4 | Connecticut | 397 |
| 22 | Delaware | 263 |
| 10 | Florida | 290 |
| 36 | Georgia | 230 |
| 9 | Hawaii | 306 |
| 50 | Idaho | 179 |
| 11 | Illinois | 287 |
| 40 | Indiana | 219 |
| 44 | Iowa | 200 |
| 34 | Kansas | 233 |
| 35 | Kentucky | 232 |
| 17 | Louisiana | 270 |
| 20 | Maine | 268 |
| 3 | Maryland | 413 |
| 1 | Massachusetts | 454 |
| 27 | Michigan | 249 |
| 12 | Minnesota | 282 |
| 49 | Mississippi | 180 |
| 26 | Missouri | 250 |
| 37 | Montana | 228 |
| 28 | Nebraska | 247 |
| 44 | Nevada | 200 |
| 15 | New Hampshire | 273 |
| 7 | New Jersey | 327 |
| 30 | New Mexico | 243 |
| 2 | New York | 423 |
| 23 | North Carolina | 262 |
| 29 | North Dakota | 246 |
| 24 | Ohio | 261 |
| 47 | Oklahoma | 187 |
| 21 | Oregon | 266 |
| 8 | Pennsylvania | 321 |
| 5 | Rhode Island | 371 |
| 33 | South Carolina | 235 |
| 43 | South Dakota | 212 |
| 18 | Tennessee | 269 |
| 39 | Texas | 222 |
| 38 | Utah | 225 |
| 6 | Vermont | 362 |
| 18 | Virginia | 269 |
| 15 | Washington | 273 |
| 32 | West Virginia | 239 |
| 25 | Wisconsin | 256 |
| 46 | Wyoming | 198 |

RANK ORDER

| RANK | STATE | RATE |
|------|-------|------|
| 1 | Massachusetts | 454 |
| 2 | New York | 423 |
| 3 | Maryland | 413 |
| 4 | Connecticut | 397 |
| 5 | Rhode Island | 371 |
| 6 | Vermont | 362 |
| 7 | New Jersey | 327 |
| 8 | Pennsylvania | 321 |
| 9 | Hawaii | 306 |
| 10 | Florida | 290 |
| 11 | Illinois | 287 |
| 12 | Minnesota | 282 |
| 13 | California | 281 |
| 14 | Colorado | 274 |
| 15 | New Hampshire | 273 |
| 15 | Washington | 273 |
| 17 | Louisiana | 270 |
| 18 | Tennessee | 269 |
| 18 | Virginia | 269 |
| 20 | Maine | 268 |
| 21 | Oregon | 266 |
| 22 | Delaware | 263 |
| 23 | North Carolina | 262 |
| 24 | Ohio | 261 |
| 25 | Wisconsin | 256 |
| 26 | Missouri | 250 |
| 27 | Michigan | 249 |
| 28 | Nebraska | 247 |
| 29 | North Dakota | 246 |
| 30 | New Mexico | 243 |
| 31 | Arizona | 240 |
| 32 | West Virginia | 239 |
| 33 | South Carolina | 235 |
| 34 | Kansas | 233 |
| 35 | Kentucky | 232 |
| 36 | Georgia | 230 |
| 37 | Montana | 228 |
| 38 | Utah | 225 |
| 39 | Texas | 222 |
| 40 | Indiana | 219 |
| 41 | Alabama | 217 |
| 42 | Arkansas | 214 |
| 43 | South Dakota | 212 |
| 44 | Iowa | 200 |
| 44 | Nevada | 200 |
| 46 | Wyoming | 198 |
| 47 | Oklahoma | 187 |
| 48 | Alaska | 186 |
| 49 | Mississippi | 180 |
| 50 | Idaho | 179 |
| | District of Columbia | 811 |

*Source: Morgan Quitno Press using data from American Medical Association (Chicago, Illinois) "Physician Characteristics and Distribution in the U.S." (2001-2002 Edition)*
*As of December 31, 1999.*

# Rate of Dentists in 1998

## National Rate = 55 Dentists per 100,000 Population*

ALPHA ORDER

| RANK | STATE | RATE |
|------|-------|------|
| 43 | Alabama | 41 |
| 6 | Alaska | 69 |
| 39 | Arizona | 44 |
| 46 | Arkansas | 40 |
| 10 | California | 62 |
| 8 | Colorado | 63 |
| 2 | Connecticut | 73 |
| 39 | Delaware | 44 |
| 29 | Florida | 48 |
| 43 | Georgia | 41 |
| 1 | Hawaii | 79 |
| 23 | Idaho | 52 |
| 10 | Illinois | 62 |
| 35 | Indiana | 46 |
| 23 | Iowa | 52 |
| 29 | Kansas | 48 |
| 23 | Kentucky | 52 |
| 38 | Louisiana | 45 |
| 33 | Maine | 47 |
| 7 | Maryland | 68 |
| 5 | Massachusetts | 71 |
| 18 | Michigan | 56 |
| 15 | Minnesota | 59 |
| 49 | Mississippi | 37 |
| 33 | Missouri | 47 |
| 23 | Montana | 52 |
| 10 | Nebraska | 62 |
| 50 | Nevada | 36 |
| 19 | New Hampshire | 55 |
| 4 | New Jersey | 72 |
| 46 | New Mexico | 40 |
| 2 | New York | 73 |
| 46 | North Carolina | 40 |
| 29 | North Dakota | 48 |
| 27 | Ohio | 51 |
| 35 | Oklahoma | 46 |
| 8 | Oregon | 63 |
| 13 | Pennsylvania | 61 |
| 19 | Rhode Island | 55 |
| 43 | South Carolina | 41 |
| 35 | South Dakota | 46 |
| 29 | Tennessee | 48 |
| 39 | Texas | 44 |
| 15 | Utah | 59 |
| 17 | Vermont | 57 |
| 22 | Virginia | 54 |
| 14 | Washington | 60 |
| 42 | West Virginia | 43 |
| 19 | Wisconsin | 55 |
| 28 | Wyoming | 50 |

RANK ORDER

| RANK | STATE | RATE |
|------|-------|------|
| 1 | Hawaii | 79 |
| 2 | Connecticut | 73 |
| 2 | New York | 73 |
| 4 | New Jersey | 72 |
| 5 | Massachusetts | 71 |
| 6 | Alaska | 69 |
| 7 | Maryland | 68 |
| 8 | Colorado | 63 |
| 8 | Oregon | 63 |
| 10 | California | 62 |
| 10 | Illinois | 62 |
| 10 | Nebraska | 62 |
| 13 | Pennsylvania | 61 |
| 14 | Washington | 60 |
| 15 | Minnesota | 59 |
| 15 | Utah | 59 |
| 17 | Vermont | 57 |
| 18 | Michigan | 56 |
| 19 | New Hampshire | 55 |
| 19 | Rhode Island | 55 |
| 19 | Wisconsin | 55 |
| 22 | Virginia | 54 |
| 23 | Idaho | 52 |
| 23 | Iowa | 52 |
| 23 | Kentucky | 52 |
| 23 | Montana | 52 |
| 27 | Ohio | 51 |
| 28 | Wyoming | 50 |
| 29 | Florida | 48 |
| 29 | Kansas | 48 |
| 29 | North Dakota | 48 |
| 29 | Tennessee | 48 |
| 33 | Maine | 47 |
| 33 | Missouri | 47 |
| 35 | Indiana | 46 |
| 35 | Oklahoma | 46 |
| 35 | South Dakota | 46 |
| 38 | Louisiana | 45 |
| 39 | Arizona | 44 |
| 39 | Delaware | 44 |
| 39 | Texas | 44 |
| 42 | West Virginia | 43 |
| 43 | Alabama | 41 |
| 43 | Georgia | 41 |
| 43 | South Carolina | 41 |
| 46 | Arkansas | 40 |
| 46 | New Mexico | 40 |
| 46 | North Carolina | 40 |
| 49 | Mississippi | 37 |
| 50 | Nevada | 36 |
| | District of Columbia | 114 |

*Source: Morgan Quitno Press using data from American Dental Association
"Distribution of Dentists, by Region and State, 1998"*
*Professionally active dentists.  Total does not include 1,714 dentists in territories nor dentists in the Armed Forces stationed overseas.*

# Community Hospitals in 1999

## National Total = 4,956 Hospitals*

### ALPHA ORDER

| RANK | STATE | HOSPITALS | % of USA |
|---|---|---|---|
| 19 | Alabama | 109 | 2.2% |
| 47 | Alaska | 17 | 0.3% |
| 31 | Arizona | 61 | 1.2% |
| 26 | Arkansas | 83 | 1.7% |
| 2 | California | 395 | 8.0% |
| 29 | Colorado | 67 | 1.4% |
| 42 | Connecticut | 35 | 0.7% |
| 50 | Delaware | 6 | 0.1% |
| 5 | Florida | 203 | 4.1% |
| 8 | Georgia | 154 | 3.1% |
| 45 | Hawaii | 22 | 0.4% |
| 37 | Idaho | 42 | 0.8% |
| 6 | Illinois | 198 | 4.0% |
| 18 | Indiana | 111 | 2.2% |
| 16 | Iowa | 115 | 2.3% |
| 11 | Kansas | 131 | 2.6% |
| 21 | Kentucky | 105 | 2.1% |
| 13 | Louisiana | 122 | 2.5% |
| 40 | Maine | 37 | 0.7% |
| 35 | Maryland | 49 | 1.0% |
| 28 | Massachusetts | 79 | 1.6% |
| 9 | Michigan | 145 | 2.9% |
| 10 | Minnesota | 134 | 2.7% |
| 22 | Mississippi | 96 | 1.9% |
| 15 | Missouri | 118 | 2.4% |
| 34 | Montana | 53 | 1.1% |
| 25 | Nebraska | 85 | 1.7% |
| 45 | Nevada | 22 | 0.4% |
| 43 | New Hampshire | 28 | 0.6% |
| 27 | New Jersey | 81 | 1.6% |
| 41 | New Mexico | 36 | 0.7% |
| 3 | New York | 218 | 4.4% |
| 17 | North Carolina | 114 | 2.3% |
| 39 | North Dakota | 41 | 0.8% |
| 7 | Ohio | 167 | 3.4% |
| 19 | Oklahoma | 109 | 2.2% |
| 32 | Oregon | 59 | 1.2% |
| 4 | Pennsylvania | 210 | 4.2% |
| 49 | Rhode Island | 11 | 0.2% |
| 30 | South Carolina | 64 | 1.3% |
| 36 | South Dakota | 48 | 1.0% |
| 14 | Tennessee | 121 | 2.4% |
| 1 | Texas | 408 | 8.2% |
| 37 | Utah | 42 | 0.8% |
| 48 | Vermont | 14 | 0.3% |
| 23 | Virginia | 89 | 1.8% |
| 24 | Washington | 86 | 1.7% |
| 33 | West Virginia | 58 | 1.2% |
| 12 | Wisconsin | 123 | 2.5% |
| 44 | Wyoming | 23 | 0.5% |

### RANK ORDER

| RANK | STATE | HOSPITALS | % of USA |
|---|---|---|---|
| 1 | Texas | 408 | 8.2% |
| 2 | California | 395 | 8.0% |
| 3 | New York | 218 | 4.4% |
| 4 | Pennsylvania | 210 | 4.2% |
| 5 | Florida | 203 | 4.1% |
| 6 | Illinois | 198 | 4.0% |
| 7 | Ohio | 167 | 3.4% |
| 8 | Georgia | 154 | 3.1% |
| 9 | Michigan | 145 | 2.9% |
| 10 | Minnesota | 134 | 2.7% |
| 11 | Kansas | 131 | 2.6% |
| 12 | Wisconsin | 123 | 2.5% |
| 13 | Louisiana | 122 | 2.5% |
| 14 | Tennessee | 121 | 2.4% |
| 15 | Missouri | 118 | 2.4% |
| 16 | Iowa | 115 | 2.3% |
| 17 | North Carolina | 114 | 2.3% |
| 18 | Indiana | 111 | 2.2% |
| 19 | Alabama | 109 | 2.2% |
| 19 | Oklahoma | 109 | 2.2% |
| 21 | Kentucky | 105 | 2.1% |
| 22 | Mississippi | 96 | 1.9% |
| 23 | Virginia | 89 | 1.8% |
| 24 | Washington | 86 | 1.7% |
| 25 | Nebraska | 85 | 1.7% |
| 26 | Arkansas | 83 | 1.7% |
| 27 | New Jersey | 81 | 1.6% |
| 28 | Massachusetts | 79 | 1.6% |
| 29 | Colorado | 67 | 1.4% |
| 30 | South Carolina | 64 | 1.3% |
| 31 | Arizona | 61 | 1.2% |
| 32 | Oregon | 59 | 1.2% |
| 33 | West Virginia | 58 | 1.2% |
| 34 | Montana | 53 | 1.1% |
| 35 | Maryland | 49 | 1.0% |
| 36 | South Dakota | 48 | 1.0% |
| 37 | Idaho | 42 | 0.8% |
| 37 | Utah | 42 | 0.8% |
| 39 | North Dakota | 41 | 0.8% |
| 40 | Maine | 37 | 0.7% |
| 41 | New Mexico | 36 | 0.7% |
| 42 | Connecticut | 35 | 0.7% |
| 43 | New Hampshire | 28 | 0.6% |
| 44 | Wyoming | 23 | 0.5% |
| 45 | Hawaii | 22 | 0.4% |
| 45 | Nevada | 22 | 0.4% |
| 47 | Alaska | 17 | 0.3% |
| 48 | Vermont | 14 | 0.3% |
| 49 | Rhode Island | 11 | 0.2% |
| 50 | Delaware | 6 | 0.1% |
|  | District of Columbia | 12 | 0.2% |

Source: American Hospital Association (Chicago, IL)
     "Hospital Statistics" (2001 edition)
*Community hospitals are all nonfederal, short-term, general and special hospitals whose facilities and services are available to the public.

# Rate of Community Hospitals in 1999

## National Rate = 1.8 Community Hospitals per 100,000 Population*

ALPHA ORDER

| RANK | STATE | RATE |
|------|-------|------|
| 18 | Alabama | 2.5 |
| 16 | Alaska | 2.7 |
| 39 | Arizona | 1.3 |
| 10 | Arkansas | 3.3 |
| 43 | California | 1.2 |
| 32 | Colorado | 1.7 |
| 46 | Connecticut | 1.1 |
| 50 | Delaware | 0.8 |
| 39 | Florida | 1.3 |
| 25 | Georgia | 2.0 |
| 28 | Hawaii | 1.9 |
| 9 | Idaho | 3.4 |
| 33 | Illinois | 1.6 |
| 28 | Indiana | 1.9 |
| 7 | Iowa | 4.0 |
| 5 | Kansas | 4.9 |
| 16 | Kentucky | 2.7 |
| 14 | Louisiana | 2.8 |
| 13 | Maine | 3.0 |
| 49 | Maryland | 0.9 |
| 39 | Massachusetts | 1.3 |
| 35 | Michigan | 1.5 |
| 14 | Minnesota | 2.8 |
| 8 | Mississippi | 3.5 |
| 22 | Missouri | 2.2 |
| 3 | Montana | 6.0 |
| 4 | Nebraska | 5.1 |
| 43 | Nevada | 1.2 |
| 20 | New Hampshire | 2.3 |
| 48 | New Jersey | 1.0 |
| 24 | New Mexico | 2.1 |
| 43 | New York | 1.2 |
| 35 | North Carolina | 1.5 |
| 1 | North Dakota | 6.5 |
| 35 | Ohio | 1.5 |
| 11 | Oklahoma | 3.2 |
| 30 | Oregon | 1.8 |
| 30 | Pennsylvania | 1.8 |
| 46 | Rhode Island | 1.1 |
| 33 | South Carolina | 1.6 |
| 1 | South Dakota | 6.5 |
| 22 | Tennessee | 2.2 |
| 25 | Texas | 2.0 |
| 25 | Utah | 2.0 |
| 19 | Vermont | 2.4 |
| 39 | Virginia | 1.3 |
| 35 | Washington | 1.5 |
| 11 | West Virginia | 3.2 |
| 20 | Wisconsin | 2.3 |
| 6 | Wyoming | 4.8 |

RANK ORDER

| RANK | STATE | RATE |
|------|-------|------|
| 1 | North Dakota | 6.5 |
| 1 | South Dakota | 6.5 |
| 3 | Montana | 6.0 |
| 4 | Nebraska | 5.1 |
| 5 | Kansas | 4.9 |
| 6 | Wyoming | 4.8 |
| 7 | Iowa | 4.0 |
| 8 | Mississippi | 3.5 |
| 9 | Idaho | 3.4 |
| 10 | Arkansas | 3.3 |
| 11 | Oklahoma | 3.2 |
| 11 | West Virginia | 3.2 |
| 13 | Maine | 3.0 |
| 14 | Louisiana | 2.8 |
| 14 | Minnesota | 2.8 |
| 16 | Alaska | 2.7 |
| 16 | Kentucky | 2.7 |
| 18 | Alabama | 2.5 |
| 19 | Vermont | 2.4 |
| 20 | New Hampshire | 2.3 |
| 20 | Wisconsin | 2.3 |
| 22 | Missouri | 2.2 |
| 22 | Tennessee | 2.2 |
| 24 | New Mexico | 2.1 |
| 25 | Georgia | 2.0 |
| 25 | Texas | 2.0 |
| 25 | Utah | 2.0 |
| 28 | Hawaii | 1.9 |
| 28 | Indiana | 1.9 |
| 30 | Oregon | 1.8 |
| 30 | Pennsylvania | 1.8 |
| 32 | Colorado | 1.7 |
| 33 | Illinois | 1.6 |
| 33 | South Carolina | 1.6 |
| 35 | Michigan | 1.5 |
| 35 | North Carolina | 1.5 |
| 35 | Ohio | 1.5 |
| 35 | Washington | 1.5 |
| 39 | Arizona | 1.3 |
| 39 | Florida | 1.3 |
| 39 | Massachusetts | 1.3 |
| 39 | Virginia | 1.3 |
| 43 | California | 1.2 |
| 43 | Nevada | 1.2 |
| 43 | New York | 1.2 |
| 46 | Connecticut | 1.1 |
| 46 | Rhode Island | 1.1 |
| 48 | New Jersey | 1.0 |
| 49 | Maryland | 0.9 |
| 50 | Delaware | 0.8 |
| | District of Columbia | 2.3 |

Source: Morgan Quitno Press using data from American Hospital Association (Chicago, IL)
    "Hospital Statistics" (2001 edition)
*Community hospitals are all nonfederal, short-term, general and special hospitals whose facilities and services are available to the public.

# Births in 1999

## National Total = 3,957,829 Live Births*

ALPHA ORDER

| RANK | STATE | BIRTHS | % of USA |
|---|---|---|---|
| 24 | Alabama | 62,123 | 1.6% |
| 47 | Alaska | 9,953 | 0.3% |
| 14 | Arizona | 81,225 | 2.1% |
| 34 | Arkansas | 36,832 | 0.9% |
| 1 | California | 518,229 | 13.1% |
| 23 | Colorado | 62,161 | 1.6% |
| 30 | Connecticut | 43,471 | 1.1% |
| 45 | Delaware | 10,675 | 0.3% |
| 4 | Florida | 197,014 | 5.0% |
| 9 | Georgia | 126,744 | 3.2% |
| 40 | Hawaii | 17,047 | 0.4% |
| 39 | Idaho | 19,871 | 0.5% |
| 5 | Illinois | 182,174 | 4.6% |
| 13 | Indiana | 86,040 | 2.2% |
| 33 | Iowa | 37,541 | 0.9% |
| 32 | Kansas | 38,788 | 1.0% |
| 26 | Kentucky | 54,344 | 1.4% |
| 21 | Louisiana | 66,913 | 1.7% |
| 42 | Maine | 13,615 | 0.3% |
| 19 | Maryland | 72,207 | 1.8% |
| 15 | Massachusetts | 80,998 | 2.0% |
| 8 | Michigan | 133,562 | 3.4% |
| 22 | Minnesota | 65,966 | 1.7% |
| 31 | Mississippi | 42,694 | 1.1% |
| 18 | Missouri | 75,352 | 1.9% |
| 44 | Montana | 10,789 | 0.3% |
| 37 | Nebraska | 23,907 | 0.6% |
| 35 | Nevada | 29,357 | 0.7% |
| 41 | New Hampshire | 14,071 | 0.4% |
| 10 | New Jersey | 114,097 | 2.9% |
| 36 | New Mexico | 27,065 | 0.7% |
| 3 | New York | 258,412 | 6.5% |
| 11 | North Carolina | 113,800 | 2.9% |
| 48 | North Dakota | 7,637 | 0.2% |
| 6 | Ohio | 150,292 | 3.8% |
| 27 | Oklahoma | 49,054 | 1.2% |
| 29 | Oregon | 45,205 | 1.1% |
| 7 | Pennsylvania | 145,497 | 3.7% |
| 43 | Rhode Island | 12,356 | 0.3% |
| 25 | South Carolina | 54,984 | 1.4% |
| 46 | South Dakota | 10,523 | 0.3% |
| 17 | Tennessee | 77,839 | 2.0% |
| 2 | Texas | 346,774 | 8.8% |
| 28 | Utah | 46,289 | 1.2% |
| 49 | Vermont | 6,565 | 0.2% |
| 12 | Virginia | 95,538 | 2.4% |
| 16 | Washington | 79,603 | 2.0% |
| 38 | West Virginia | 20,764 | 0.5% |
| 20 | Wisconsin | 68,216 | 1.7% |
| 50 | Wyoming | 6,135 | 0.2% |

RANK ORDER

| RANK | STATE | BIRTHS | % of USA |
|---|---|---|---|
| 1 | California | 518,229 | 13.1% |
| 2 | Texas | 346,774 | 8.8% |
| 3 | New York | 258,412 | 6.5% |
| 4 | Florida | 197,014 | 5.0% |
| 5 | Illinois | 182,174 | 4.6% |
| 6 | Ohio | 150,292 | 3.8% |
| 7 | Pennsylvania | 145,497 | 3.7% |
| 8 | Michigan | 133,562 | 3.4% |
| 9 | Georgia | 126,744 | 3.2% |
| 10 | New Jersey | 114,097 | 2.9% |
| 11 | North Carolina | 113,800 | 2.9% |
| 12 | Virginia | 95,538 | 2.4% |
| 13 | Indiana | 86,040 | 2.2% |
| 14 | Arizona | 81,225 | 2.1% |
| 15 | Massachusetts | 80,998 | 2.0% |
| 16 | Washington | 79,603 | 2.0% |
| 17 | Tennessee | 77,839 | 2.0% |
| 18 | Missouri | 75,352 | 1.9% |
| 19 | Maryland | 72,207 | 1.8% |
| 20 | Wisconsin | 68,216 | 1.7% |
| 21 | Louisiana | 66,913 | 1.7% |
| 22 | Minnesota | 65,966 | 1.7% |
| 23 | Colorado | 62,161 | 1.6% |
| 24 | Alabama | 62,123 | 1.6% |
| 25 | South Carolina | 54,984 | 1.4% |
| 26 | Kentucky | 54,344 | 1.4% |
| 27 | Oklahoma | 49,054 | 1.2% |
| 28 | Utah | 46,289 | 1.2% |
| 29 | Oregon | 45,205 | 1.1% |
| 30 | Connecticut | 43,471 | 1.1% |
| 31 | Mississippi | 42,694 | 1.1% |
| 32 | Kansas | 38,788 | 1.0% |
| 33 | Iowa | 37,541 | 0.9% |
| 34 | Arkansas | 36,832 | 0.9% |
| 35 | Nevada | 29,357 | 0.7% |
| 36 | New Mexico | 27,065 | 0.7% |
| 37 | Nebraska | 23,907 | 0.6% |
| 38 | West Virginia | 20,764 | 0.5% |
| 39 | Idaho | 19,871 | 0.5% |
| 40 | Hawaii | 17,047 | 0.4% |
| 41 | New Hampshire | 14,071 | 0.4% |
| 42 | Maine | 13,615 | 0.3% |
| 43 | Rhode Island | 12,356 | 0.3% |
| 44 | Montana | 10,789 | 0.3% |
| 45 | Delaware | 10,675 | 0.3% |
| 46 | South Dakota | 10,523 | 0.3% |
| 47 | Alaska | 9,953 | 0.3% |
| 48 | North Dakota | 7,637 | 0.2% |
| 49 | Vermont | 6,565 | 0.2% |
| 50 | Wyoming | 6,135 | 0.2% |
| | District of Columbia | 7,523 | 0.2% |

Source: U.S. Department of Health and Human Services, National Center for Health Statistics
     "National Vital Statistics Reports" (Vol. 48, No. 14, August 8, 2000)
*Data are preliminary estimates by state of residence.

# Birth Rate in 1999

## National Rate = 14.5 Live Births per 1,000 Population*

ALPHA ORDER

RANK ORDER

| RANK | STATE | RATE | | RANK | STATE | RATE |
|---|---|---|---|---|---|---|
| 22 | Alabama | 14.2 | | 1 | Utah | 21.7 |
| 6 | Alaska | 16.1 | | 2 | Texas | 17.3 |
| 3 | Arizona | 17.0 | | 3 | Arizona | 17.0 |
| 18 | Arkansas | 14.4 | | 4 | Georgia | 16.3 |
| 8 | California | 15.6 | | 5 | Nevada | 16.2 |
| 11 | Colorado | 15.3 | | 6 | Alaska | 16.1 |
| 37 | Connecticut | 13.2 | | 7 | Idaho | 15.9 |
| 22 | Delaware | 14.2 | | 8 | California | 15.6 |
| 40 | Florida | 13.0 | | 8 | New Mexico | 15.6 |
| 4 | Georgia | 16.3 | | 10 | Mississippi | 15.4 |
| 18 | Hawaii | 14.4 | | 11 | Colorado | 15.3 |
| 7 | Idaho | 15.9 | | 11 | Louisiana | 15.3 |
| 13 | Illinois | 15.0 | | 13 | Illinois | 15.0 |
| 17 | Indiana | 14.5 | | 14 | North Carolina | 14.9 |
| 38 | Iowa | 13.1 | | 15 | Kansas | 14.6 |
| 15 | Kansas | 14.6 | | 15 | Oklahoma | 14.6 |
| 33 | Kentucky | 13.7 | | 17 | Indiana | 14.5 |
| 11 | Louisiana | 15.3 | | 18 | Arkansas | 14.4 |
| 50 | Maine | 10.9 | | 18 | Hawaii | 14.4 |
| 27 | Maryland | 14.0 | | 18 | South Dakota | 14.4 |
| 38 | Massachusetts | 13.1 | | 21 | Nebraska | 14.3 |
| 35 | Michigan | 13.5 | | 22 | Alabama | 14.2 |
| 30 | Minnesota | 13.8 | | 22 | Delaware | 14.2 |
| 10 | Mississippi | 15.4 | | 22 | New York | 14.2 |
| 30 | Missouri | 13.8 | | 22 | South Carolina | 14.2 |
| 44 | Montana | 12.2 | | 22 | Tennessee | 14.2 |
| 21 | Nebraska | 14.3 | | 27 | Maryland | 14.0 |
| 5 | Nevada | 16.2 | | 27 | New Jersey | 14.0 |
| 47 | New Hampshire | 11.7 | | 29 | Virginia | 13.9 |
| 27 | New Jersey | 14.0 | | 30 | Minnesota | 13.8 |
| 8 | New Mexico | 15.6 | | 30 | Missouri | 13.8 |
| 22 | New York | 14.2 | | 30 | Washington | 13.8 |
| 14 | North Carolina | 14.9 | | 33 | Kentucky | 13.7 |
| 45 | North Dakota | 12.1 | | 34 | Oregon | 13.6 |
| 36 | Ohio | 13.4 | | 35 | Michigan | 13.5 |
| 15 | Oklahoma | 14.6 | | 36 | Ohio | 13.4 |
| 34 | Oregon | 13.6 | | 37 | Connecticut | 13.2 |
| 45 | Pennsylvania | 12.1 | | 38 | Iowa | 13.1 |
| 43 | Rhode Island | 12.5 | | 38 | Massachusetts | 13.1 |
| 22 | South Carolina | 14.2 | | 40 | Florida | 13.0 |
| 18 | South Dakota | 14.4 | | 40 | Wisconsin | 13.0 |
| 22 | Tennessee | 14.2 | | 42 | Wyoming | 12.8 |
| 2 | Texas | 17.3 | | 43 | Rhode Island | 12.5 |
| 1 | Utah | 21.7 | | 44 | Montana | 12.2 |
| 49 | Vermont | 11.1 | | 45 | North Dakota | 12.1 |
| 29 | Virginia | 13.9 | | 45 | Pennsylvania | 12.1 |
| 30 | Washington | 13.8 | | 47 | New Hampshire | 11.7 |
| 48 | West Virginia | 11.5 | | 48 | West Virginia | 11.5 |
| 40 | Wisconsin | 13.0 | | 49 | Vermont | 11.1 |
| 42 | Wyoming | 12.8 | | 50 | Maine | 10.9 |
| | | | | | District of Columbia | 14.5 |

Source: U.S. Department of Health and Human Services, National Center for Health Statistics
   "National Vital Statistics Reports" (Vol. 48, No. 14, August 8, 2000)
*Data are preliminary estimates by state of residence.

# Births to White Women in 1999

## National Total = 3,130,100 Live Births to White Women*

ALPHA ORDER

| RANK | STATE | BIRTHS | % of USA |
|---|---|---|---|
| 25 | Alabama | 41,729 | 1.3% |
| 47 | Alaska | 6,529 | 0.2% |
| 13 | Arizona | 71,125 | 2.3% |
| 33 | Arkansas | 28,476 | 0.9% |
| 1 | California | 420,188 | 13.4% |
| 21 | Colorado | 56,706 | 1.8% |
| 29 | Connecticut | 36,502 | 1.2% |
| 45 | Delaware | 7,678 | 0.2% |
| 4 | Florida | 146,663 | 4.7% |
| 11 | Georgia | 81,140 | 2.6% |
| 50 | Hawaii | 4,001 | 0.1% |
| 39 | Idaho | 19,211 | 0.6% |
| 5 | Illinois | 140,805 | 4.5% |
| 12 | Indiana | 75,448 | 2.4% |
| 30 | Iowa | 35,348 | 1.1% |
| 32 | Kansas | 34,611 | 1.1% |
| 22 | Kentucky | 48,747 | 1.6% |
| 28 | Louisiana | 38,408 | 1.2% |
| 41 | Maine | 13,241 | 0.4% |
| 23 | Maryland | 44,296 | 1.4% |
| 15 | Massachusetts | 68,218 | 2.2% |
| 8 | Michigan | 105,293 | 3.4% |
| 20 | Minnesota | 57,491 | 1.8% |
| 36 | Mississippi | 22,668 | 0.7% |
| 17 | Missouri | 62,531 | 2.0% |
| 43 | Montana | 9,387 | 0.3% |
| 37 | Nebraska | 21,727 | 0.7% |
| 34 | Nevada | 24,975 | 0.8% |
| 40 | New Hampshire | 13,657 | 0.4% |
| 9 | New Jersey | 84,103 | 2.7% |
| 35 | New Mexico | 22,791 | 0.7% |
| 3 | New York | 186,128 | 5.9% |
| 10 | North Carolina | 81,232 | 2.6% |
| 46 | North Dakota | 6,742 | 0.2% |
| 6 | Ohio | 126,636 | 4.0% |
| 27 | Oklahoma | 38,628 | 1.2% |
| 26 | Oregon | 41,410 | 1.3% |
| 7 | Pennsylvania | 121,063 | 3.9% |
| 42 | Rhode Island | 10,796 | 0.3% |
| 31 | South Carolina | 34,987 | 1.1% |
| 44 | South Dakota | 8,669 | 0.3% |
| 18 | Tennessee | 59,998 | 1.9% |
| 2 | Texas | 297,150 | 9.5% |
| 24 | Utah | 44,033 | 1.4% |
| 48 | Vermont | 6,469 | 0.2% |
| 16 | Virginia | 68,199 | 2.2% |
| 14 | Washington | 68,227 | 2.2% |
| 38 | West Virginia | 19,828 | 0.6% |
| 19 | Wisconsin | 58,777 | 1.9% |
| 49 | Wyoming | 5,745 | 0.2% |

RANK ORDER

| RANK | STATE | BIRTHS | % of USA |
|---|---|---|---|
| 1 | California | 420,188 | 13.4% |
| 2 | Texas | 297,150 | 9.5% |
| 3 | New York | 186,128 | 5.9% |
| 4 | Florida | 146,663 | 4.7% |
| 5 | Illinois | 140,805 | 4.5% |
| 6 | Ohio | 126,636 | 4.0% |
| 7 | Pennsylvania | 121,063 | 3.9% |
| 8 | Michigan | 105,293 | 3.4% |
| 9 | New Jersey | 84,103 | 2.7% |
| 10 | North Carolina | 81,232 | 2.6% |
| 11 | Georgia | 81,140 | 2.6% |
| 12 | Indiana | 75,448 | 2.4% |
| 13 | Arizona | 71,125 | 2.3% |
| 14 | Washington | 68,227 | 2.2% |
| 15 | Massachusetts | 68,218 | 2.2% |
| 16 | Virginia | 68,199 | 2.2% |
| 17 | Missouri | 62,531 | 2.0% |
| 18 | Tennessee | 59,998 | 1.9% |
| 19 | Wisconsin | 58,777 | 1.9% |
| 20 | Minnesota | 57,491 | 1.8% |
| 21 | Colorado | 56,706 | 1.8% |
| 22 | Kentucky | 48,747 | 1.6% |
| 23 | Maryland | 44,296 | 1.4% |
| 24 | Utah | 44,033 | 1.4% |
| 25 | Alabama | 41,729 | 1.3% |
| 26 | Oregon | 41,410 | 1.3% |
| 27 | Oklahoma | 38,628 | 1.2% |
| 28 | Louisiana | 38,408 | 1.2% |
| 29 | Connecticut | 36,502 | 1.2% |
| 30 | Iowa | 35,348 | 1.1% |
| 31 | South Carolina | 34,987 | 1.1% |
| 32 | Kansas | 34,611 | 1.1% |
| 33 | Arkansas | 28,476 | 0.9% |
| 34 | Nevada | 24,975 | 0.8% |
| 35 | New Mexico | 22,791 | 0.7% |
| 36 | Mississippi | 22,668 | 0.7% |
| 37 | Nebraska | 21,727 | 0.7% |
| 38 | West Virginia | 19,828 | 0.6% |
| 39 | Idaho | 19,211 | 0.6% |
| 40 | New Hampshire | 13,657 | 0.4% |
| 41 | Maine | 13,241 | 0.4% |
| 42 | Rhode Island | 10,796 | 0.3% |
| 43 | Montana | 9,387 | 0.3% |
| 44 | South Dakota | 8,669 | 0.3% |
| 45 | Delaware | 7,678 | 0.2% |
| 46 | North Dakota | 6,742 | 0.2% |
| 47 | Alaska | 6,529 | 0.2% |
| 48 | Vermont | 6,469 | 0.2% |
| 49 | Wyoming | 5,745 | 0.2% |
| 50 | Hawaii | 4,001 | 0.1% |
| | District of Columbia | 1,687 | 0.1% |

*Source: U.S. Department of Health and Human Services, National Center for Health Statistics*
*"National Vital Statistics Reports" (Vol. 48, No. 14, August 8, 2000)*
*Preliminary data by state of residence. By race of mother.

# Births to Black Women in 1999

## National Total = 606,720 Live Births to Black Women*

ALPHA ORDER

| RANK | STATE | BIRTHS | % of USA |
|------|-------|--------|----------|
| 15 | Alabama | 19,771 | 3.3% |
| 40 | Alaska | 460 | 0.1% |
| 31 | Arizona | 2,803 | 0.5% |
| 22 | Arkansas | 7,717 | 1.3% |
| 5 | California | 35,991 | 5.9% |
| 29 | Colorado | 2,900 | 0.5% |
| 24 | Connecticut | 5,314 | 0.9% |
| 32 | Delaware | 2,688 | 0.4% |
| 2 | Florida | 45,095 | 7.4% |
| 3 | Georgia | 42,113 | 6.9% |
| 40 | Hawaii | 460 | 0.1% |
| 47 | Idaho | 77 | 0.0% |
| 6 | Illinois | 34,254 | 5.6% |
| 20 | Indiana | 9,323 | 1.5% |
| 35 | Iowa | 1,165 | 0.2% |
| 30 | Kansas | 2,858 | 0.5% |
| 25 | Kentucky | 4,959 | 0.8% |
| 8 | Louisiana | 27,225 | 4.5% |
| 44 | Maine | 106 | 0.0% |
| 9 | Maryland | 24,568 | 4.0% |
| 21 | Massachusetts | 8,292 | 1.4% |
| 10 | Michigan | 24,057 | 4.0% |
| 27 | Minnesota | 4,034 | 0.7% |
| 16 | Mississippi | 19,417 | 3.2% |
| 19 | Missouri | 11,253 | 1.9% |
| 50 | Montana | 35 | 0.0% |
| 34 | Nebraska | 1,281 | 0.2% |
| 33 | Nevada | 2,223 | 0.4% |
| 43 | New Hampshire | 139 | 0.0% |
| 12 | New Jersey | 21,385 | 3.5% |
| 39 | New Mexico | 497 | 0.1% |
| 1 | New York | 53,798 | 8.9% |
| 7 | North Carolina | 28,446 | 4.7% |
| 46 | North Dakota | 86 | 0.0% |
| 13 | Ohio | 21,020 | 3.5% |
| 26 | Oklahoma | 4,649 | 0.8% |
| 37 | Oregon | 905 | 0.1% |
| 14 | Pennsylvania | 20,608 | 3.4% |
| 36 | Rhode Island | 967 | 0.2% |
| 17 | South Carolina | 19,103 | 3.1% |
| 45 | South Dakota | 89 | 0.0% |
| 18 | Tennessee | 16,537 | 2.7% |
| 4 | Texas | 38,883 | 6.4% |
| 42 | Utah | 270 | 0.0% |
| 49 | Vermont | 40 | 0.0% |
| 11 | Virginia | 22,498 | 3.7% |
| 28 | Washington | 3,363 | 0.6% |
| 38 | West Virginia | 752 | 0.1% |
| 23 | Wisconsin | 6,509 | 1.1% |
| 48 | Wyoming | 73 | 0.0% |

RANK ORDER

| RANK | STATE | BIRTHS | % of USA |
|------|-------|--------|----------|
| 1 | New York | 53,798 | 8.9% |
| 2 | Florida | 45,095 | 7.4% |
| 3 | Georgia | 42,113 | 6.9% |
| 4 | Texas | 38,883 | 6.4% |
| 5 | California | 35,991 | 5.9% |
| 6 | Illinois | 34,254 | 5.6% |
| 7 | North Carolina | 28,446 | 4.7% |
| 8 | Louisiana | 27,225 | 4.5% |
| 9 | Maryland | 24,568 | 4.0% |
| 10 | Michigan | 24,057 | 4.0% |
| 11 | Virginia | 22,498 | 3.7% |
| 12 | New Jersey | 21,385 | 3.5% |
| 13 | Ohio | 21,020 | 3.5% |
| 14 | Pennsylvania | 20,608 | 3.4% |
| 15 | Alabama | 19,771 | 3.3% |
| 16 | Mississippi | 19,417 | 3.2% |
| 17 | South Carolina | 19,103 | 3.1% |
| 18 | Tennessee | 16,537 | 2.7% |
| 19 | Missouri | 11,253 | 1.9% |
| 20 | Indiana | 9,323 | 1.5% |
| 21 | Massachusetts | 8,292 | 1.4% |
| 22 | Arkansas | 7,717 | 1.3% |
| 23 | Wisconsin | 6,509 | 1.1% |
| 24 | Connecticut | 5,314 | 0.9% |
| 25 | Kentucky | 4,959 | 0.8% |
| 26 | Oklahoma | 4,649 | 0.8% |
| 27 | Minnesota | 4,034 | 0.7% |
| 28 | Washington | 3,363 | 0.6% |
| 29 | Colorado | 2,900 | 0.5% |
| 30 | Kansas | 2,858 | 0.5% |
| 31 | Arizona | 2,803 | 0.5% |
| 32 | Delaware | 2,688 | 0.4% |
| 33 | Nevada | 2,223 | 0.4% |
| 34 | Nebraska | 1,281 | 0.2% |
| 35 | Iowa | 1,165 | 0.2% |
| 36 | Rhode Island | 967 | 0.2% |
| 37 | Oregon | 905 | 0.1% |
| 38 | West Virginia | 752 | 0.1% |
| 39 | New Mexico | 497 | 0.1% |
| 40 | Alaska | 460 | 0.1% |
| 40 | Hawaii | 460 | 0.1% |
| 42 | Utah | 270 | 0.0% |
| 43 | New Hampshire | 139 | 0.0% |
| 44 | Maine | 106 | 0.0% |
| 45 | South Dakota | 89 | 0.0% |
| 46 | North Dakota | 86 | 0.0% |
| 47 | Idaho | 77 | 0.0% |
| 48 | Wyoming | 73 | 0.0% |
| 49 | Vermont | 40 | 0.0% |
| 50 | Montana | 35 | 0.0% |
| | District of Columbia | 5,662 | 0.9% |

*Source: U.S. Department of Health and Human Services, National Center for Health Statistics*
  *"National Vital Statistics Reports" (Vol. 48, No. 14, August 8, 2000)*
*\*Preliminary data by state of residence. By race of mother.*

# Births of Low Birthweight in 1999

## National Total = 300,795 Live Births*

ALPHA ORDER

| RANK | STATE | BIRTHS | % of USA |
|---|---|---|---|
| 18 | Alabama | 5,777 | 1.9% |
| 47 | Alaska | 577 | 0.2% |
| 20 | Arizona | 5,686 | 1.9% |
| 30 | Arkansas | 3,168 | 1.1% |
| 1 | California | 31,612 | 10.5% |
| 22 | Colorado | 5,159 | 1.7% |
| 29 | Connecticut | 3,304 | 1.1% |
| 41 | Delaware | 918 | 0.3% |
| 4 | Florida | 16,155 | 5.4% |
| 8 | Georgia | 11,027 | 3.7% |
| 39 | Hawaii | 1,279 | 0.4% |
| 40 | Idaho | 1,232 | 0.4% |
| 5 | Illinois | 14,574 | 4.8% |
| 14 | Indiana | 6,797 | 2.3% |
| 34 | Iowa | 2,328 | 0.8% |
| 32 | Kansas | 2,754 | 0.9% |
| 25 | Kentucky | 4,456 | 1.5% |
| 15 | Louisiana | 6,691 | 2.2% |
| 44 | Maine | 817 | 0.3% |
| 16 | Maryland | 6,499 | 2.2% |
| 19 | Massachusetts | 5,751 | 1.9% |
| 9 | Michigan | 10,819 | 3.6% |
| 27 | Minnesota | 4,024 | 1.3% |
| 26 | Mississippi | 4,397 | 1.5% |
| 17 | Missouri | 5,802 | 1.9% |
| 45 | Montana | 734 | 0.2% |
| 38 | Nebraska | 1,602 | 0.5% |
| 35 | Nevada | 2,231 | 0.7% |
| 43 | New Hampshire | 872 | 0.3% |
| 11 | New Jersey | 9,242 | 3.1% |
| 36 | New Mexico | 2,084 | 0.7% |
| 3 | New York | 20,156 | 6.7% |
| 10 | North Carolina | 10,128 | 3.4% |
| 49 | North Dakota | 473 | 0.2% |
| 6 | Ohio | 11,572 | 3.8% |
| 28 | Oklahoma | 3,630 | 1.2% |
| 33 | Oregon | 2,441 | 0.8% |
| 7 | Pennsylvania | 11,349 | 3.8% |
| 42 | Rhode Island | 902 | 0.3% |
| 21 | South Carolina | 5,388 | 1.8% |
| 46 | South Dakota | 621 | 0.2% |
| 13 | Tennessee | 7,161 | 2.4% |
| 2 | Texas | 25,315 | 8.4% |
| 31 | Utah | 3,148 | 1.0% |
| 50 | Vermont | 374 | 0.1% |
| 12 | Virginia | 7,452 | 2.5% |
| 23 | Washington | 4,617 | 1.5% |
| 37 | West Virginia | 1,661 | 0.6% |
| 24 | Wisconsin | 4,570 | 1.5% |
| 48 | Wyoming | 515 | 0.2% |

RANK ORDER

| RANK | STATE | BIRTHS | % of USA |
|---|---|---|---|
| 1 | California | 31,612 | 10.5% |
| 2 | Texas | 25,315 | 8.4% |
| 3 | New York | 20,156 | 6.7% |
| 4 | Florida | 16,155 | 5.4% |
| 5 | Illinois | 14,574 | 4.8% |
| 6 | Ohio | 11,572 | 3.8% |
| 7 | Pennsylvania | 11,349 | 3.8% |
| 8 | Georgia | 11,027 | 3.7% |
| 9 | Michigan | 10,819 | 3.6% |
| 10 | North Carolina | 10,128 | 3.4% |
| 11 | New Jersey | 9,242 | 3.1% |
| 12 | Virginia | 7,452 | 2.5% |
| 13 | Tennessee | 7,161 | 2.4% |
| 14 | Indiana | 6,797 | 2.3% |
| 15 | Louisiana | 6,691 | 2.2% |
| 16 | Maryland | 6,499 | 2.2% |
| 17 | Missouri | 5,802 | 1.9% |
| 18 | Alabama | 5,777 | 1.9% |
| 19 | Massachusetts | 5,751 | 1.9% |
| 20 | Arizona | 5,686 | 1.9% |
| 21 | South Carolina | 5,388 | 1.8% |
| 22 | Colorado | 5,159 | 1.7% |
| 23 | Washington | 4,617 | 1.5% |
| 24 | Wisconsin | 4,570 | 1.5% |
| 25 | Kentucky | 4,456 | 1.5% |
| 26 | Mississippi | 4,397 | 1.5% |
| 27 | Minnesota | 4,024 | 1.3% |
| 28 | Oklahoma | 3,630 | 1.2% |
| 29 | Connecticut | 3,304 | 1.1% |
| 30 | Arkansas | 3,168 | 1.1% |
| 31 | Utah | 3,148 | 1.0% |
| 32 | Kansas | 2,754 | 0.9% |
| 33 | Oregon | 2,441 | 0.8% |
| 34 | Iowa | 2,328 | 0.8% |
| 35 | Nevada | 2,231 | 0.7% |
| 36 | New Mexico | 2,084 | 0.7% |
| 37 | West Virginia | 1,661 | 0.6% |
| 38 | Nebraska | 1,602 | 0.5% |
| 39 | Hawaii | 1,279 | 0.4% |
| 40 | Idaho | 1,232 | 0.4% |
| 41 | Delaware | 918 | 0.3% |
| 42 | Rhode Island | 902 | 0.3% |
| 43 | New Hampshire | 872 | 0.3% |
| 44 | Maine | 817 | 0.3% |
| 45 | Montana | 734 | 0.2% |
| 46 | South Dakota | 621 | 0.2% |
| 47 | Alaska | 577 | 0.2% |
| 48 | Wyoming | 515 | 0.2% |
| 49 | North Dakota | 473 | 0.2% |
| 50 | Vermont | 374 | 0.1% |
| | District of Columbia | 986 | 0.3% |

Source: Morgan Quitno Press using data from U.S. Dept. of Health and Human Services, Nat'l Center for Health Statistics "National Vital Statistics Reports" (Vol. 48, No. 14, August 8, 2000)
*Births of less than 2,500 grams (5 pounds 8 ounces). Preliminary data by state of residence. Calculated by the editors by multiplying total number of births by percent of such births reported as being low birthweight.

# Births of Low Birthweight as a Percent of All Births in 1999

## National Percent = 7.6% of Live Births*

ALPHA ORDER

RANK ORDER

| RANK | STATE | PERCENT | | RANK | STATE | PERCENT |
|------|-------|---------|---|------|-------|---------|
| 4 | Alabama | 9.3 | | 1 | Mississippi | 10.3 |
| 47 | Alaska | 5.8 | | 2 | Louisiana | 10.0 |
| 34 | Arizona | 7.0 | | 3 | South Carolina | 9.8 |
| 9 | Arkansas | 8.6 | | 4 | Alabama | 9.3 |
| 43 | California | 6.1 | | 5 | Tennessee | 9.2 |
| 12 | Colorado | 8.3 | | 6 | Maryland | 9.0 |
| 26 | Connecticut | 7.6 | | 7 | North Carolina | 8.9 |
| 9 | Delaware | 8.6 | | 8 | Georgia | 8.7 |
| 13 | Florida | 8.2 | | 9 | Arkansas | 8.6 |
| 8 | Georgia | 8.7 | | 9 | Delaware | 8.6 |
| 28 | Hawaii | 7.5 | | 11 | Wyoming | 8.4 |
| 39 | Idaho | 6.2 | | 12 | Colorado | 8.3 |
| 17 | Illinois | 8.0 | | 13 | Florida | 8.2 |
| 19 | Indiana | 7.9 | | 13 | Kentucky | 8.2 |
| 39 | Iowa | 6.2 | | 15 | Michigan | 8.1 |
| 32 | Kansas | 7.1 | | 15 | New Jersey | 8.1 |
| 13 | Kentucky | 8.2 | | 17 | Illinois | 8.0 |
| 2 | Louisiana | 10.0 | | 17 | West Virginia | 8.0 |
| 45 | Maine | 6.0 | | 19 | Indiana | 7.9 |
| 6 | Maryland | 9.0 | | 20 | New York | 7.8 |
| 32 | Massachusetts | 7.1 | | 20 | Pennsylvania | 7.8 |
| 15 | Michigan | 8.1 | | 20 | Virginia | 7.8 |
| 43 | Minnesota | 6.1 | | 23 | Missouri | 7.7 |
| 1 | Mississippi | 10.3 | | 23 | New Mexico | 7.7 |
| 23 | Missouri | 7.7 | | 23 | Ohio | 7.7 |
| 35 | Montana | 6.8 | | 26 | Connecticut | 7.6 |
| 37 | Nebraska | 6.7 | | 26 | Nevada | 7.6 |
| 26 | Nevada | 7.6 | | 28 | Hawaii | 7.5 |
| 39 | New Hampshire | 6.2 | | 29 | Oklahoma | 7.4 |
| 15 | New Jersey | 8.1 | | 30 | Rhode Island | 7.3 |
| 23 | New Mexico | 7.7 | | 30 | Texas | 7.3 |
| 20 | New York | 7.8 | | 32 | Kansas | 7.1 |
| 7 | North Carolina | 8.9 | | 32 | Massachusetts | 7.1 |
| 39 | North Dakota | 6.2 | | 34 | Arizona | 7.0 |
| 23 | Ohio | 7.7 | | 35 | Montana | 6.8 |
| 29 | Oklahoma | 7.4 | | 35 | Utah | 6.8 |
| 50 | Oregon | 5.4 | | 37 | Nebraska | 6.7 |
| 20 | Pennsylvania | 7.8 | | 37 | Wisconsin | 6.7 |
| 30 | Rhode Island | 7.3 | | 39 | Idaho | 6.2 |
| 3 | South Carolina | 9.8 | | 39 | Iowa | 6.2 |
| 46 | South Dakota | 5.9 | | 39 | New Hampshire | 6.2 |
| 5 | Tennessee | 9.2 | | 39 | North Dakota | 6.2 |
| 30 | Texas | 7.3 | | 43 | California | 6.1 |
| 35 | Utah | 6.8 | | 43 | Minnesota | 6.1 |
| 49 | Vermont | 5.7 | | 45 | Maine | 6.0 |
| 20 | Virginia | 7.8 | | 46 | South Dakota | 5.9 |
| 47 | Washington | 5.8 | | 47 | Alaska | 5.8 |
| 17 | West Virginia | 8.0 | | 47 | Washington | 5.8 |
| 37 | Wisconsin | 6.7 | | 49 | Vermont | 5.7 |
| 11 | Wyoming | 8.4 | | 50 | Oregon | 5.4 |

| | | |
|---|---|---|
| | District of Columbia | 13.1 |

Source: U.S. Department of Health and Human Services, National Center for Health Statistics
   "National Vital Statistics Reports" (Vol. 48, No. 14, August 8, 2000)
*Estimates based on preliminary data by state of residence.  Births of less than 2,500 grams (5 pounds 8 ounces).

# Teenage Birth Rate in 1998

## National Rate = 51.1 Births per 1,000 Teenage Women*

ALPHA ORDER

| RANK | STATE | RATE |
|---|---|---|
| 7 | Alabama | 65.5 |
| 32 | Alaska | 42.4 |
| 4 | Arizona | 70.5 |
| 3 | Arkansas | 70.8 |
| 17 | California | 53.5 |
| 22 | Colorado | 48.7 |
| 41 | Connecticut | 35.8 |
| 16 | Delaware | 53.9 |
| 15 | Florida | 55.5 |
| 8 | Georgia | 65.4 |
| 27 | Hawaii | 45.7 |
| 28 | Idaho | 44.8 |
| 19 | Illinois | 53.2 |
| 18 | Indiana | 53.3 |
| 42 | Iowa | 35.2 |
| 26 | Kansas | 47.0 |
| 14 | Kentucky | 57.0 |
| 8 | Louisiana | 65.4 |
| 47 | Maine | 30.4 |
| 30 | Maryland | 43.1 |
| 45 | Massachusetts | 30.8 |
| 31 | Michigan | 42.6 |
| 46 | Minnesota | 30.6 |
| 1 | Mississippi | 73.0 |
| 20 | Missouri | 51.2 |
| 38 | Montana | 37.1 |
| 39 | Nebraska | 37.0 |
| 6 | Nevada | 65.7 |
| 49 | New Hampshire | 27.1 |
| 44 | New Jersey | 34.6 |
| 5 | New Mexico | 69.0 |
| 36 | New York | 38.5 |
| 12 | North Carolina | 61.0 |
| 47 | North Dakota | 30.4 |
| 23 | Ohio | 48.1 |
| 11 | Oklahoma | 61.6 |
| 25 | Oregon | 47.4 |
| 40 | Pennsylvania | 36.9 |
| 34 | Rhode Island | 41.0 |
| 13 | South Carolina | 60.4 |
| 36 | South Dakota | 38.5 |
| 10 | Tennessee | 64.3 |
| 2 | Texas | 70.9 |
| 35 | Utah | 40.9 |
| 50 | Vermont | 24.4 |
| 29 | Virginia | 43.5 |
| 33 | Washington | 41.7 |
| 21 | West Virginia | 49.2 |
| 43 | Wisconsin | 34.8 |
| 24 | Wyoming | 47.8 |

RANK ORDER

| RANK | STATE | RATE |
|---|---|---|
| 1 | Mississippi | 73.0 |
| 2 | Texas | 70.9 |
| 3 | Arkansas | 70.8 |
| 4 | Arizona | 70.5 |
| 5 | New Mexico | 69.0 |
| 6 | Nevada | 65.7 |
| 7 | Alabama | 65.5 |
| 8 | Georgia | 65.4 |
| 8 | Louisiana | 65.4 |
| 10 | Tennessee | 64.3 |
| 11 | Oklahoma | 61.6 |
| 12 | North Carolina | 61.0 |
| 13 | South Carolina | 60.4 |
| 14 | Kentucky | 57.0 |
| 15 | Florida | 55.5 |
| 16 | Delaware | 53.9 |
| 17 | California | 53.5 |
| 18 | Indiana | 53.3 |
| 19 | Illinois | 53.2 |
| 20 | Missouri | 51.2 |
| 21 | West Virginia | 49.2 |
| 22 | Colorado | 48.7 |
| 23 | Ohio | 48.1 |
| 24 | Wyoming | 47.8 |
| 25 | Oregon | 47.4 |
| 26 | Kansas | 47.0 |
| 27 | Hawaii | 45.7 |
| 28 | Idaho | 44.8 |
| 29 | Virginia | 43.5 |
| 30 | Maryland | 43.1 |
| 31 | Michigan | 42.6 |
| 32 | Alaska | 42.4 |
| 33 | Washington | 41.7 |
| 34 | Rhode Island | 41.0 |
| 35 | Utah | 40.9 |
| 36 | New York | 38.5 |
| 36 | South Dakota | 38.5 |
| 38 | Montana | 37.1 |
| 39 | Nebraska | 37.0 |
| 40 | Pennsylvania | 36.9 |
| 41 | Connecticut | 35.8 |
| 42 | Iowa | 35.2 |
| 43 | Wisconsin | 34.8 |
| 44 | New Jersey | 34.6 |
| 45 | Massachusetts | 30.8 |
| 46 | Minnesota | 30.6 |
| 47 | Maine | 30.4 |
| 47 | North Dakota | 30.4 |
| 49 | New Hampshire | 27.1 |
| 50 | Vermont | 24.4 |
| | District of Columbia | 86.7 |

Source: U.S. Department of Health and Human Services, National Center for Health Statistics
      "National Vital Statistics Reports" (Vol. 48, No. 3, March 28, 2000)
*Women aged 15 to 19 years old.

# Births to Unmarried Women as a Percent of All Births in 1999

## National Percent = 33.0% of Live Births*

| ALPHA ORDER | | | | RANK ORDER | | |
|---|---|---|---|---|---|---|
| RANK | STATE | PERCENT | | RANK | STATE | PERCENT |
| 18 | Alabama | 33.3 | | 1 | Mississippi | 46.0 |
| 21 | Alaska | 33.1 | | 2 | New Mexico | 45.0 |
| 6 | Arizona | 38.7 | | 3 | Louisiana | 44.8 |
| 11 | Arkansas | 35.2 | | 4 | South Carolina | 39.0 |
| 23 | California | 32.9 | | 5 | Delaware | 38.9 |
| 47 | Colorado | 25.4 | | 6 | Arizona | 38.7 |
| 38 | Connecticut | 28.9 | | 7 | Florida | 37.5 |
| 5 | Delaware | 38.9 | | 8 | Georgia | 36.6 |
| 7 | Florida | 37.5 | | 9 | New York | 36.5 |
| 8 | Georgia | 36.6 | | 10 | Nevada | 35.7 |
| 26 | Hawaii | 32.7 | | 11 | Arkansas | 35.2 |
| 49 | Idaho | 21.6 | | 12 | Maryland | 34.9 |
| 15 | Illinois | 34.1 | | 13 | Tennessee | 34.6 |
| 14 | Indiana | 34.5 | | 14 | Indiana | 34.5 |
| 41 | Iowa | 27.5 | | 15 | Illinois | 34.1 |
| 39 | Kansas | 28.6 | | 15 | Missouri | 34.1 |
| 32 | Kentucky | 30.3 | | 17 | Ohio | 34.0 |
| 3 | Louisiana | 44.8 | | 18 | Alabama | 33.3 |
| 29 | Maine | 31.3 | | 18 | Rhode Island | 33.3 |
| 12 | Maryland | 34.9 | | 20 | North Carolina | 33.2 |
| 43 | Massachusetts | 26.5 | | 21 | Alaska | 33.1 |
| 21 | Michigan | 33.1 | | 21 | Michigan | 33.1 |
| 46 | Minnesota | 25.8 | | 23 | California | 32.9 |
| 1 | Mississippi | 46.0 | | 23 | Oklahoma | 32.9 |
| 15 | Missouri | 34.1 | | 23 | Pennsylvania | 32.9 |
| 34 | Montana | 29.7 | | 26 | Hawaii | 32.7 |
| 45 | Nebraska | 25.9 | | 27 | South Dakota | 31.8 |
| 10 | Nevada | 35.7 | | 28 | West Virginia | 31.7 |
| 48 | New Hampshire | 24.2 | | 29 | Maine | 31.3 |
| 40 | New Jersey | 28.2 | | 30 | Texas | 31.0 |
| 2 | New Mexico | 45.0 | | 31 | Oregon | 30.4 |
| 9 | New York | 36.5 | | 32 | Kentucky | 30.3 |
| 20 | North Carolina | 33.2 | | 33 | Virginia | 29.8 |
| 41 | North Dakota | 27.5 | | 34 | Montana | 29.7 |
| 17 | Ohio | 34.0 | | 35 | Wisconsin | 29.2 |
| 23 | Oklahoma | 32.9 | | 36 | Wyoming | 29.1 |
| 31 | Oregon | 30.4 | | 37 | Vermont | 29.0 |
| 23 | Pennsylvania | 32.9 | | 38 | Connecticut | 28.9 |
| 18 | Rhode Island | 33.3 | | 39 | Kansas | 28.6 |
| 4 | South Carolina | 39.0 | | 40 | New Jersey | 28.2 |
| 27 | South Dakota | 31.8 | | 41 | Iowa | 27.5 |
| 13 | Tennessee | 34.6 | | 41 | North Dakota | 27.5 |
| 30 | Texas | 31.0 | | 43 | Massachusetts | 26.5 |
| 50 | Utah | 16.7 | | 43 | Washington | 26.5 |
| 37 | Vermont | 29.0 | | 45 | Nebraska | 25.9 |
| 33 | Virginia | 29.8 | | 46 | Minnesota | 25.8 |
| 43 | Washington | 26.5 | | 47 | Colorado | 25.4 |
| 28 | West Virginia | 31.7 | | 48 | New Hampshire | 24.2 |
| 35 | Wisconsin | 29.2 | | 49 | Idaho | 21.6 |
| 36 | Wyoming | 29.1 | | 50 | Utah | 16.7 |
| | | | | | District of Columbia | 61.7 |

Source: U.S. Department of Health and Human Services, National Center for Health Statistics
"National Vital Statistics Reports" (Vol. 48, No. 14, August 8, 2000)
*Preliminary data by state of residence.

# Percent of Mothers Receiving Late or No Prenatal Care in 1998

## National Percent = 3.9% of Mothers*

ALPHA ORDER

| RANK | STATE | PERCENT |
|---|---|---|
| 18 | Alabama | 3.9 |
| 9 | Alaska | 4.5 |
| 2 | Arizona | 7.2 |
| 5 | Arkansas | 5.1 |
| 22 | California | 3.6 |
| 11 | Colorado | 4.3 |
| 35 | Connecticut | 3.0 |
| 22 | Delaware | 3.6 |
| 25 | Florida | 3.5 |
| 40 | Georgia | 2.8 |
| 34 | Hawaii | 3.1 |
| 10 | Idaho | 4.4 |
| 18 | Illinois | 3.9 |
| 16 | Indiana | 4.0 |
| 45 | Iowa | 2.4 |
| 40 | Kansas | 2.8 |
| 43 | Kentucky | 2.5 |
| 18 | Louisiana | 3.9 |
| 49 | Maine | 1.7 |
| 35 | Maryland | 3.0 |
| 45 | Massachusetts | 2.4 |
| 27 | Michigan | 3.4 |
| 37 | Minnesota | 2.9 |
| 16 | Mississippi | 4.0 |
| 37 | Missouri | 2.9 |
| 30 | Montana | 3.2 |
| 30 | Nebraska | 3.2 |
| 3 | Nevada | 7.0 |
| 48 | New Hampshire | 1.9 |
| 8 | New Jersey | 4.6 |
| 1 | New Mexico | 8.5 |
| 7 | New York | 4.8 |
| 37 | North Carolina | 2.9 |
| 43 | North Dakota | 2.5 |
| 12 | Ohio | 4.2 |
| 5 | Oklahoma | 5.1 |
| 21 | Oregon | 3.8 |
| 25 | Pennsylvania | 3.5 |
| 50 | Rhode Island | 1.5 |
| 12 | South Carolina | 4.2 |
| 30 | South Dakota | 3.2 |
| 22 | Tennessee | 3.6 |
| 4 | Texas | 5.3 |
| 14 | Utah | 4.1 |
| 47 | Vermont | 2.0 |
| 29 | Virginia | 3.3 |
| 30 | Washington | 3.2 |
| 42 | West Virginia | 2.6 |
| 27 | Wisconsin | 3.4 |
| 14 | Wyoming | 4.1 |

RANK ORDER

| RANK | STATE | PERCENT |
|---|---|---|
| 1 | New Mexico | 8.5 |
| 2 | Arizona | 7.2 |
| 3 | Nevada | 7.0 |
| 4 | Texas | 5.3 |
| 5 | Arkansas | 5.1 |
| 5 | Oklahoma | 5.1 |
| 7 | New York | 4.8 |
| 8 | New Jersey | 4.6 |
| 9 | Alaska | 4.5 |
| 10 | Idaho | 4.4 |
| 11 | Colorado | 4.3 |
| 12 | Ohio | 4.2 |
| 12 | South Carolina | 4.2 |
| 14 | Utah | 4.1 |
| 14 | Wyoming | 4.1 |
| 16 | Indiana | 4.0 |
| 16 | Mississippi | 4.0 |
| 18 | Alabama | 3.9 |
| 18 | Illinois | 3.9 |
| 18 | Louisiana | 3.9 |
| 21 | Oregon | 3.8 |
| 22 | California | 3.6 |
| 22 | Delaware | 3.6 |
| 22 | Tennessee | 3.6 |
| 25 | Florida | 3.5 |
| 25 | Pennsylvania | 3.5 |
| 27 | Michigan | 3.4 |
| 27 | Wisconsin | 3.4 |
| 29 | Virginia | 3.3 |
| 30 | Montana | 3.2 |
| 30 | Nebraska | 3.2 |
| 30 | South Dakota | 3.2 |
| 30 | Washington | 3.2 |
| 34 | Hawaii | 3.1 |
| 35 | Connecticut | 3.0 |
| 35 | Maryland | 3.0 |
| 37 | Minnesota | 2.9 |
| 37 | Missouri | 2.9 |
| 37 | North Carolina | 2.9 |
| 40 | Georgia | 2.8 |
| 40 | Kansas | 2.8 |
| 42 | West Virginia | 2.6 |
| 43 | Kentucky | 2.5 |
| 43 | North Dakota | 2.5 |
| 45 | Iowa | 2.4 |
| 45 | Massachusetts | 2.4 |
| 47 | Vermont | 2.0 |
| 48 | New Hampshire | 1.9 |
| 49 | Maine | 1.7 |
| 50 | Rhode Island | 1.5 |
| | District of Columbia | 10.2 |

Source: U.S. Department of Health and Human Services, National Center for Health Statistics
      "National Vital Statistics Reports" (Vol. 48, No. 3, March 28, 2000)
*Final data by state of residence.  "Late" means care begun in third trimester.

# Reported Legal Abortions in 1997

## National Total = 1,186,039 Abortions*

ALPHA ORDER

| RANK | STATE | ABORTIONS | % of USA |
|---|---|---|---|
| 21 | Alabama | 13,063 | 1.1% |
| 46 | Alaska | 1,632 | 0.1% |
| 23 | Arizona | 11,266 | 0.9% |
| 33 | Arkansas | 5,782 | 0.5% |
| 1 | California | 275,739 | 23.2% |
| 29 | Colorado | 9,183 | 0.8% |
| 18 | Connecticut | 13,802 | 1.2% |
| 36 | Delaware | 5,138 | 0.4% |
| 4 | Florida | 81,692 | 6.9% |
| 8 | Georgia | 35,702 | 3.0% |
| 38 | Hawaii | 4,520 | 0.4% |
| 49 | Idaho | 878 | 0.1% |
| 5 | Illinois | 50,147 | 4.2% |
| 20 | Indiana | 13,208 | 1.1% |
| 26 | Iowa | 10,022 | 0.8% |
| 24 | Kansas | 11,249 | 0.9% |
| 30 | Kentucky | 7,033 | 0.6% |
| 22 | Louisiana | 11,739 | 1.0% |
| 43 | Maine | 2,545 | 0.2% |
| 27 | Maryland | 9,869 | 0.8% |
| 12 | Massachusetts | 28,477 | 2.4% |
| 11 | Michigan | 29,528 | 2.5% |
| 17 | Minnesota | 14,229 | 1.2% |
| 39 | Mississippi | 4,325 | 0.4% |
| 25 | Missouri | 10,202 | 0.9% |
| 41 | Montana | 2,809 | 0.2% |
| 37 | Nebraska | 5,129 | 0.4% |
| 31 | Nevada | 6,887 | 0.6% |
| 44 | New Hampshire | 2,069 | 0.2% |
| 10 | New Jersey | 30,654 | 2.6% |
| 35 | New Mexico | 5,382 | 0.5% |
| 2 | New York | 140,834 | 11.9% |
| 9 | North Carolina | 31,495 | 2.7% |
| 47 | North Dakota | 1,226 | 0.1% |
| 6 | Ohio | 38,242 | 3.2% |
| 32 | Oklahoma | 6,428 | 0.5% |
| 16 | Oregon | 14,834 | 1.3% |
| 7 | Pennsylvania | 37,135 | 3.1% |
| 34 | Rhode Island | 5,478 | 0.5% |
| 28 | South Carolina | 9,212 | 0.8% |
| 48 | South Dakota | 919 | 0.1% |
| 15 | Tennessee | 18,283 | 1.5% |
| 3 | Texas | 84,680 | 7.1% |
| 40 | Utah | 3,408 | 0.3% |
| 45 | Vermont | 1,955 | 0.2% |
| 14 | Virginia | 26,089 | 2.2% |
| 13 | Washington | 26,932 | 2.3% |
| 42 | West Virginia | 2,808 | 0.2% |
| 19 | Wisconsin | 13,218 | 1.1% |
| 50 | Wyoming | 192 | 0.0% |

RANK ORDER

| RANK | STATE | ABORTIONS | % of USA |
|---|---|---|---|
| 1 | California | 275,739 | 23.2% |
| 2 | New York | 140,834 | 11.9% |
| 3 | Texas | 84,680 | 7.1% |
| 4 | Florida | 81,692 | 6.9% |
| 5 | Illinois | 50,147 | 4.2% |
| 6 | Ohio | 38,242 | 3.2% |
| 7 | Pennsylvania | 37,135 | 3.1% |
| 8 | Georgia | 35,702 | 3.0% |
| 9 | North Carolina | 31,495 | 2.7% |
| 10 | New Jersey | 30,654 | 2.6% |
| 11 | Michigan | 29,528 | 2.5% |
| 12 | Massachusetts | 28,477 | 2.4% |
| 13 | Washington | 26,932 | 2.3% |
| 14 | Virginia | 26,089 | 2.2% |
| 15 | Tennessee | 18,283 | 1.5% |
| 16 | Oregon | 14,834 | 1.3% |
| 17 | Minnesota | 14,229 | 1.2% |
| 18 | Connecticut | 13,802 | 1.2% |
| 19 | Wisconsin | 13,218 | 1.1% |
| 20 | Indiana | 13,208 | 1.1% |
| 21 | Alabama | 13,063 | 1.1% |
| 22 | Louisiana | 11,739 | 1.0% |
| 23 | Arizona | 11,266 | 0.9% |
| 24 | Kansas | 11,249 | 0.9% |
| 25 | Missouri | 10,202 | 0.9% |
| 26 | Iowa | 10,022 | 0.8% |
| 27 | Maryland | 9,869 | 0.8% |
| 28 | South Carolina | 9,212 | 0.8% |
| 29 | Colorado | 9,183 | 0.8% |
| 30 | Kentucky | 7,033 | 0.6% |
| 31 | Nevada | 6,887 | 0.6% |
| 32 | Oklahoma | 6,428 | 0.5% |
| 33 | Arkansas | 5,782 | 0.5% |
| 34 | Rhode Island | 5,478 | 0.5% |
| 35 | New Mexico | 5,382 | 0.5% |
| 36 | Delaware | 5,138 | 0.4% |
| 37 | Nebraska | 5,129 | 0.4% |
| 38 | Hawaii | 4,520 | 0.4% |
| 39 | Mississippi | 4,325 | 0.4% |
| 40 | Utah | 3,408 | 0.3% |
| 41 | Montana | 2,809 | 0.2% |
| 42 | West Virginia | 2,808 | 0.2% |
| 43 | Maine | 2,545 | 0.2% |
| 44 | New Hampshire | 2,069 | 0.2% |
| 45 | Vermont | 1,955 | 0.2% |
| 46 | Alaska | 1,632 | 0.1% |
| 47 | North Dakota | 1,226 | 0.1% |
| 48 | South Dakota | 919 | 0.1% |
| 49 | Idaho | 878 | 0.1% |
| 50 | Wyoming | 192 | 0.0% |
| | District of Columbia | 8,771 | 0.7% |

Source: U.S. Department of Health and Human Services, Centers for Disease Control and Prevention
"Abortion Surveillance-United States, 1997" (Morbidity Mortality Weekly Report, Vol. 49, No. SS-11, 12/08/00)
*By state of occurrence.

# Reported Legal Abortions per 1,000 Live Births in 1997

## National Rate = 306 Abortions per 1,000 Live Births*

ALPHA ORDER

| RANK | STATE | RATE |
|---|---|---|
| 28 | Alabama | 214 |
| 34 | Alaska | 164 |
| 38 | Arizona | 149 |
| 36 | Arkansas | 159 |
| 2 | California | 525 |
| 35 | Colorado | 162 |
| 9 | Connecticut | 320 |
| 3 | Delaware | 501 |
| 5 | Florida | 425 |
| 10 | Georgia | 302 |
| 18 | Hawaii | 260 |
| 49 | Idaho | 47 |
| 15 | Illinois | 277 |
| 37 | Indiana | 158 |
| 16 | Iowa | 273 |
| 10 | Kansas | 302 |
| 45 | Kentucky | 132 |
| 32 | Louisiana | 178 |
| 31 | Maine | 186 |
| 41 | Maryland | 141 |
| 6 | Massachusetts | 354 |
| 25 | Michigan | 221 |
| 25 | Minnesota | 221 |
| 46 | Mississippi | 104 |
| 42 | Missouri | 138 |
| 19 | Montana | 259 |
| 27 | Nebraska | 220 |
| 21 | Nevada | 256 |
| 40 | New Hampshire | 145 |
| 17 | New Jersey | 271 |
| 29 | New Mexico | 200 |
| 1 | New York | 547 |
| 13 | North Carolina | 294 |
| 39 | North Dakota | 147 |
| 23 | Ohio | 252 |
| 44 | Oklahoma | 133 |
| 8 | Oregon | 339 |
| 20 | Pennsylvania | 257 |
| 4 | Rhode Island | 440 |
| 33 | South Carolina | 176 |
| 47 | South Dakota | 90 |
| 24 | Tennessee | 245 |
| 22 | Texas | 254 |
| 48 | Utah | 79 |
| 12 | Vermont | 296 |
| 14 | Virginia | 284 |
| 7 | Washington | 344 |
| 43 | West Virginia | 135 |
| 30 | Wisconsin | 199 |
| 50 | Wyoming | 30 |

RANK ORDER

| RANK | STATE | RATE |
|---|---|---|
| 1 | New York | 547 |
| 2 | California | 525 |
| 3 | Delaware | 501 |
| 4 | Rhode Island | 440 |
| 5 | Florida | 425 |
| 6 | Massachusetts | 354 |
| 7 | Washington | 344 |
| 8 | Oregon | 339 |
| 9 | Connecticut | 320 |
| 10 | Georgia | 302 |
| 10 | Kansas | 302 |
| 12 | Vermont | 296 |
| 13 | North Carolina | 294 |
| 14 | Virginia | 284 |
| 15 | Illinois | 277 |
| 16 | Iowa | 273 |
| 17 | New Jersey | 271 |
| 18 | Hawaii | 260 |
| 19 | Montana | 259 |
| 20 | Pennsylvania | 257 |
| 21 | Nevada | 256 |
| 22 | Texas | 254 |
| 23 | Ohio | 252 |
| 24 | Tennessee | 245 |
| 25 | Michigan | 221 |
| 25 | Minnesota | 221 |
| 27 | Nebraska | 220 |
| 28 | Alabama | 214 |
| 29 | New Mexico | 200 |
| 30 | Wisconsin | 199 |
| 31 | Maine | 186 |
| 32 | Louisiana | 178 |
| 33 | South Carolina | 176 |
| 34 | Alaska | 164 |
| 35 | Colorado | 162 |
| 36 | Arkansas | 159 |
| 37 | Indiana | 158 |
| 38 | Arizona | 149 |
| 39 | North Dakota | 147 |
| 40 | New Hampshire | 145 |
| 41 | Maryland | 141 |
| 42 | Missouri | 138 |
| 43 | West Virginia | 135 |
| 44 | Oklahoma | 133 |
| 45 | Kentucky | 132 |
| 46 | Mississippi | 104 |
| 47 | South Dakota | 90 |
| 48 | Utah | 79 |
| 49 | Idaho | 47 |
| 50 | Wyoming | 30 |
| | District of Columbia** | NA |

*Source: U.S. Department of Health and Human Services, Centers for Disease Control and Prevention*
*"Abortion Surveillance-United States, 1997" (Morbidity Mortality Weekly Report, Vol. 49, No. SS-11, 12/08/00)*
*\*By state of occurrence.*
*\*\*The District of Columbia's ratio was not listed but was noted as being greater than 1,000 abortions per 1,000 live births.*

# Infant Deaths in 1998

## National Total = 28,371 Infant Deaths*

ALPHA ORDER

| RANK | STATE | DEATHS | % of USA |
|------|-------|--------|----------|
| 15 | Alabama | 633 | 2.2% |
| 48 | Alaska | 59 | 0.2% |
| 18 | Arizona | 590 | 2.1% |
| 29 | Arkansas | 329 | 1.2% |
| 1 | California | 3,007 | 10.6% |
| 27 | Colorado | 399 | 1.4% |
| 30 | Connecticut | 307 | 1.1% |
| 41 | Delaware | 102 | 0.4% |
| 5 | Florida | 1,417 | 5.0% |
| 10 | Georgia | 1,035 | 3.6% |
| 40 | Hawaii | 121 | 0.4% |
| 39 | Idaho | 140 | 0.5% |
| 4 | Illinois | 1,539 | 5.4% |
| 13 | Indiana | 649 | 2.3% |
| 33 | Iowa | 246 | 0.9% |
| 31 | Kansas | 270 | 1.0% |
| 26 | Kentucky | 409 | 1.4% |
| 17 | Louisiana | 609 | 2.1% |
| 44 | Maine | 87 | 0.3% |
| 16 | Maryland | 616 | 2.2% |
| 25 | Massachusetts | 416 | 1.5% |
| 7 | Michigan | 1,098 | 3.9% |
| 28 | Minnesota | 386 | 1.4% |
| 23 | Mississippi | 435 | 1.5% |
| 19 | Missouri | 577 | 2.0% |
| 45 | Montana | 80 | 0.3% |
| 37 | Nebraska | 172 | 0.6% |
| 35 | Nevada | 200 | 0.7% |
| 47 | New Hampshire | 63 | 0.2% |
| 11 | New Jersey | 734 | 2.6% |
| 36 | New Mexico | 197 | 0.7% |
| 3 | New York | 1,623 | 5.7% |
| 9 | North Carolina | 1,038 | 3.7% |
| 46 | North Dakota | 68 | 0.2% |
| 6 | Ohio | 1,221 | 4.3% |
| 24 | Oklahoma | 420 | 1.5% |
| 34 | Oregon | 245 | 0.9% |
| 8 | Pennsylvania | 1,043 | 3.7% |
| 43 | Rhode Island | 88 | 0.3% |
| 20 | South Carolina | 515 | 1.8% |
| 42 | South Dakota | 94 | 0.3% |
| 14 | Tennessee | 635 | 2.2% |
| 2 | Texas | 2,185 | 7.7% |
| 32 | Utah | 255 | 0.9% |
| 49 | Vermont | 46 | 0.2% |
| 12 | Virginia | 722 | 2.5% |
| 22 | Washington | 455 | 1.6% |
| 38 | West Virginia | 166 | 0.6% |
| 21 | Wisconsin | 489 | 1.7% |
| 50 | Wyoming | 45 | 0.2% |

RANK ORDER

| RANK | STATE | DEATHS | % of USA |
|------|-------|--------|----------|
| 1 | California | 3,007 | 10.6% |
| 2 | Texas | 2,185 | 7.7% |
| 3 | New York | 1,623 | 5.7% |
| 4 | Illinois | 1,539 | 5.4% |
| 5 | Florida | 1,417 | 5.0% |
| 6 | Ohio | 1,221 | 4.3% |
| 7 | Michigan | 1,098 | 3.9% |
| 8 | Pennsylvania | 1,043 | 3.7% |
| 9 | North Carolina | 1,038 | 3.7% |
| 10 | Georgia | 1,035 | 3.6% |
| 11 | New Jersey | 734 | 2.6% |
| 12 | Virginia | 722 | 2.5% |
| 13 | Indiana | 649 | 2.3% |
| 14 | Tennessee | 635 | 2.2% |
| 15 | Alabama | 633 | 2.2% |
| 16 | Maryland | 616 | 2.2% |
| 17 | Louisiana | 609 | 2.1% |
| 18 | Arizona | 590 | 2.1% |
| 19 | Missouri | 577 | 2.0% |
| 20 | South Carolina | 515 | 1.8% |
| 21 | Wisconsin | 489 | 1.7% |
| 22 | Washington | 455 | 1.6% |
| 23 | Mississippi | 435 | 1.5% |
| 24 | Oklahoma | 420 | 1.5% |
| 25 | Massachusetts | 416 | 1.5% |
| 26 | Kentucky | 409 | 1.4% |
| 27 | Colorado | 399 | 1.4% |
| 28 | Minnesota | 386 | 1.4% |
| 29 | Arkansas | 329 | 1.2% |
| 30 | Connecticut | 307 | 1.1% |
| 31 | Kansas | 270 | 1.0% |
| 32 | Utah | 255 | 0.9% |
| 33 | Iowa | 246 | 0.9% |
| 34 | Oregon | 245 | 0.9% |
| 35 | Nevada | 200 | 0.7% |
| 36 | New Mexico | 197 | 0.7% |
| 37 | Nebraska | 172 | 0.6% |
| 38 | West Virginia | 166 | 0.6% |
| 39 | Idaho | 140 | 0.5% |
| 40 | Hawaii | 121 | 0.4% |
| 41 | Delaware | 102 | 0.4% |
| 42 | South Dakota | 94 | 0.3% |
| 43 | Rhode Island | 88 | 0.3% |
| 44 | Maine | 87 | 0.3% |
| 45 | Montana | 80 | 0.3% |
| 46 | North Dakota | 68 | 0.2% |
| 47 | New Hampshire | 63 | 0.2% |
| 48 | Alaska | 59 | 0.2% |
| 49 | Vermont | 46 | 0.2% |
| 50 | Wyoming | 45 | 0.2% |
| | District of Columbia | 96 | 0.3% |

Source: U.S. Department of Health and Human Services, National Center for Health Statistics
"National Vital Statistics Reports" (Vol. 48, No. 11, July 24, 2000)
*Final data. Deaths under 1 year old by state of residence.

# Infant Mortality Rate in 1998

## National Rate = 7.2 Infant Deaths per 1,000 Live Births*

ALPHA ORDER

| RANK | STATE | RATE |
|---|---|---|
| 1 | Alabama | 10.2 |
| 43 | Alaska | 5.9 |
| 21 | Arizona | 7.5 |
| 8 | Arkansas | 8.9 |
| 45 | California | 5.8 |
| 37 | Colorado | 6.7 |
| 31 | Connecticut | 7.0 |
| 3 | Delaware | 9.6 |
| 25 | Florida | 7.2 |
| 11 | Georgia | 8.5 |
| 36 | Hawaii | 6.9 |
| 25 | Idaho | 7.2 |
| 13 | Illinois | 8.4 |
| 20 | Indiana | 7.6 |
| 38 | Iowa | 6.6 |
| 31 | Kansas | 7.0 |
| 21 | Kentucky | 7.5 |
| 6 | Louisiana | 9.1 |
| 41 | Maine | 6.3 |
| 9 | Maryland | 8.6 |
| 49 | Massachusetts | 5.1 |
| 14 | Michigan | 8.2 |
| 43 | Minnesota | 5.9 |
| 2 | Mississippi | 10.1 |
| 18 | Missouri | 7.7 |
| 23 | Montana | 7.4 |
| 24 | Nebraska | 7.3 |
| 31 | Nevada | 7.0 |
| 50 | New Hampshire | 4.4 |
| 39 | New Jersey | 6.4 |
| 25 | New Mexico | 7.2 |
| 41 | New York | 6.3 |
| 5 | North Carolina | 9.3 |
| 9 | North Dakota | 8.6 |
| 16 | Ohio | 8.0 |
| 11 | Oklahoma | 8.5 |
| 48 | Oregon | 5.4 |
| 30 | Pennsylvania | 7.1 |
| 31 | Rhode Island | 7.0 |
| 3 | South Carolina | 9.6 |
| 6 | South Dakota | 9.1 |
| 14 | Tennessee | 8.2 |
| 39 | Texas | 6.4 |
| 47 | Utah | 5.6 |
| 31 | Vermont | 7.0 |
| 18 | Virginia | 7.7 |
| 46 | Washington | 5.7 |
| 16 | West Virginia | 8.0 |
| 25 | Wisconsin | 7.2 |
| 25 | Wyoming | 7.2 |

RANK ORDER

| RANK | STATE | RATE |
|---|---|---|
| 1 | Alabama | 10.2 |
| 2 | Mississippi | 10.1 |
| 3 | Delaware | 9.6 |
| 3 | South Carolina | 9.6 |
| 5 | North Carolina | 9.3 |
| 6 | Louisiana | 9.1 |
| 6 | South Dakota | 9.1 |
| 8 | Arkansas | 8.9 |
| 9 | Maryland | 8.6 |
| 9 | North Dakota | 8.6 |
| 11 | Georgia | 8.5 |
| 11 | Oklahoma | 8.5 |
| 13 | Illinois | 8.4 |
| 14 | Michigan | 8.2 |
| 14 | Tennessee | 8.2 |
| 16 | Ohio | 8.0 |
| 16 | West Virginia | 8.0 |
| 18 | Missouri | 7.7 |
| 18 | Virginia | 7.7 |
| 20 | Indiana | 7.6 |
| 21 | Arizona | 7.5 |
| 21 | Kentucky | 7.5 |
| 23 | Montana | 7.4 |
| 24 | Nebraska | 7.3 |
| 25 | Florida | 7.2 |
| 25 | Idaho | 7.2 |
| 25 | New Mexico | 7.2 |
| 25 | Wisconsin | 7.2 |
| 25 | Wyoming | 7.2 |
| 30 | Pennsylvania | 7.1 |
| 31 | Connecticut | 7.0 |
| 31 | Kansas | 7.0 |
| 31 | Nevada | 7.0 |
| 31 | Rhode Island | 7.0 |
| 31 | Vermont | 7.0 |
| 36 | Hawaii | 6.9 |
| 37 | Colorado | 6.7 |
| 38 | Iowa | 6.6 |
| 39 | New Jersey | 6.4 |
| 39 | Texas | 6.4 |
| 41 | Maine | 6.3 |
| 41 | New York | 6.3 |
| 43 | Alaska | 5.9 |
| 43 | Minnesota | 5.9 |
| 45 | California | 5.8 |
| 46 | Washington | 5.7 |
| 47 | Utah | 5.6 |
| 48 | Oregon | 5.4 |
| 49 | Massachusetts | 5.1 |
| 50 | New Hampshire | 4.4 |

| District of Columbia | 12.5 |
|---|---|

Source: U.S. Department of Health and Human Services, National Center for Health Statistics
"National Vital Statistics Reports" (Vol. 48, No. 11, July 24, 2000)
*Final data.  Deaths under 1 year old by state of residence.

# White Infant Mortality Rate in 1998

## National Rate = 6.0 White Infant Deaths per 1,000 White Live Births*

ALPHA ORDER

| RANK | STATE | RATE |
|---|---|---|
| 4 | Alabama | 7.7 |
| 49 | Alaska | 4.7 |
| 11 | Arizona | 6.9 |
| 5 | Arkansas | 7.6 |
| 40 | California | 5.3 |
| 19 | Colorado | 6.4 |
| 39 | Connecticut | 5.6 |
| 11 | Delaware | 6.9 |
| 32 | Florida | 5.9 |
| 28 | Georgia | 6.0 |
| 40 | Hawaii | 5.3 |
| 8 | Idaho | 7.1 |
| 19 | Illinois | 6.4 |
| 17 | Indiana | 6.5 |
| 25 | Iowa | 6.2 |
| 9 | Kansas | 7.0 |
| 14 | Kentucky | 6.8 |
| 36 | Louisiana | 5.7 |
| 19 | Maine | 6.4 |
| 44 | Maryland | 5.2 |
| 48 | Massachusetts | 4.9 |
| 22 | Michigan | 6.3 |
| 46 | Minnesota | 5.1 |
| 22 | Mississippi | 6.3 |
| 27 | Missouri | 6.1 |
| 7 | Montana | 7.2 |
| 16 | Nebraska | 6.7 |
| 28 | Nevada | 6.0 |
| 50 | New Hampshire | 4.3 |
| 47 | New Jersey | 5.0 |
| 11 | New Mexico | 6.9 |
| 40 | New York | 5.3 |
| 17 | North Carolina | 6.5 |
| 1 | North Dakota | 8.2 |
| 9 | Ohio | 7.0 |
| 2 | Oklahoma | 8.1 |
| 40 | Oregon | 5.3 |
| 33 | Pennsylvania | 5.8 |
| 25 | Rhode Island | 6.2 |
| 28 | South Carolina | 6.0 |
| 6 | South Dakota | 7.5 |
| 22 | Tennessee | 6.3 |
| 33 | Texas | 5.8 |
| 36 | Utah | 5.7 |
| 14 | Vermont | 6.8 |
| 36 | Virginia | 5.7 |
| 44 | Washington | 5.2 |
| 3 | West Virginia | 8.0 |
| 28 | Wisconsin | 6.0 |
| 33 | Wyoming | 5.8 |

RANK ORDER

| RANK | STATE | RATE |
|---|---|---|
| 1 | North Dakota | 8.2 |
| 2 | Oklahoma | 8.1 |
| 3 | West Virginia | 8.0 |
| 4 | Alabama | 7.7 |
| 5 | Arkansas | 7.6 |
| 6 | South Dakota | 7.5 |
| 7 | Montana | 7.2 |
| 8 | Idaho | 7.1 |
| 9 | Kansas | 7.0 |
| 9 | Ohio | 7.0 |
| 11 | Arizona | 6.9 |
| 11 | Delaware | 6.9 |
| 11 | New Mexico | 6.9 |
| 14 | Kentucky | 6.8 |
| 14 | Vermont | 6.8 |
| 16 | Nebraska | 6.7 |
| 17 | Indiana | 6.5 |
| 17 | North Carolina | 6.5 |
| 19 | Colorado | 6.4 |
| 19 | Illinois | 6.4 |
| 19 | Maine | 6.4 |
| 22 | Michigan | 6.3 |
| 22 | Mississippi | 6.3 |
| 22 | Tennessee | 6.3 |
| 25 | Iowa | 6.2 |
| 25 | Rhode Island | 6.2 |
| 27 | Missouri | 6.1 |
| 28 | Georgia | 6.0 |
| 28 | Nevada | 6.0 |
| 28 | South Carolina | 6.0 |
| 28 | Wisconsin | 6.0 |
| 32 | Florida | 5.9 |
| 33 | Pennsylvania | 5.8 |
| 33 | Texas | 5.8 |
| 33 | Wyoming | 5.8 |
| 36 | Louisiana | 5.7 |
| 36 | Utah | 5.7 |
| 36 | Virginia | 5.7 |
| 39 | Connecticut | 5.6 |
| 40 | California | 5.3 |
| 40 | Hawaii | 5.3 |
| 40 | New York | 5.3 |
| 40 | Oregon | 5.3 |
| 44 | Maryland | 5.2 |
| 44 | Washington | 5.2 |
| 46 | Minnesota | 5.1 |
| 47 | New Jersey | 5.0 |
| 48 | Massachusetts | 4.9 |
| 49 | Alaska | 4.7 |
| 50 | New Hampshire | 4.3 |
| | District of Columbia** | NA |

*Source: U.S. Department of Health and Human Services, National Center for Health Statistics*
*"National Vital Statistics Reports" (Vol. 48, No. 11, July 24, 2000)*
*Final data. Deaths of infants under 1 year old, exclusive of fetal deaths. Based on race of the mother.*
**Not available, fewer than 20 white infant deaths.*

# Black Infant Mortality Rate in 1998

## National Rate = 14.3 Black Infant Deaths per 1,000 Black Live Births*

<table>
<tr><td colspan="3">ALPHA ORDER</td><td colspan="3">RANK ORDER</td></tr>
<tr><th>RANK</th><th>STATE</th><th>RATE</th><th>RANK</th><th>STATE</th><th>RATE</th></tr>
<tr><td>15</td><td>Alabama</td><td>15.5</td><td>1</td><td>Arizona</td><td>20.0</td></tr>
<tr><td>NA</td><td>Alaska**</td><td>NA</td><td>2</td><td>Nebraska</td><td>19.4</td></tr>
<tr><td>1</td><td>Arizona</td><td>20.0</td><td>3</td><td>Delaware</td><td>18.7</td></tr>
<tr><td>23</td><td>Arkansas</td><td>14.0</td><td>3</td><td>Wisconsin</td><td>18.7</td></tr>
<tr><td>25</td><td>California</td><td>13.7</td><td>5</td><td>Iowa</td><td>18.3</td></tr>
<tr><td>14</td><td>Colorado</td><td>16.0</td><td>6</td><td>North Carolina</td><td>17.6</td></tr>
<tr><td>7</td><td>Connecticut</td><td>17.4</td><td>7</td><td>Connecticut</td><td>17.4</td></tr>
<tr><td>3</td><td>Delaware</td><td>18.7</td><td>8</td><td>Indiana</td><td>17.3</td></tr>
<tr><td>31</td><td>Florida</td><td>12.3</td><td>8</td><td>Nevada</td><td>17.3</td></tr>
<tr><td>28</td><td>Georgia</td><td>13.4</td><td>10</td><td>Illinois</td><td>17.2</td></tr>
<tr><td>NA</td><td>Hawaii**</td><td>NA</td><td>11</td><td>Michigan</td><td>16.8</td></tr>
<tr><td>NA</td><td>Idaho**</td><td>NA</td><td>11</td><td>Missouri</td><td>16.8</td></tr>
<tr><td>10</td><td>Illinois</td><td>17.2</td><td>13</td><td>South Carolina</td><td>16.2</td></tr>
<tr><td>8</td><td>Indiana</td><td>17.3</td><td>14</td><td>Colorado</td><td>16.0</td></tr>
<tr><td>5</td><td>Iowa</td><td>18.3</td><td>15</td><td>Alabama</td><td>15.5</td></tr>
<tr><td>34</td><td>Kansas</td><td>10.0</td><td>16</td><td>Kentucky</td><td>15.4</td></tr>
<tr><td>16</td><td>Kentucky</td><td>15.4</td><td>16</td><td>Pennsylvania</td><td>15.4</td></tr>
<tr><td>23</td><td>Louisiana</td><td>14.0</td><td>18</td><td>Maryland</td><td>15.3</td></tr>
<tr><td>NA</td><td>Maine**</td><td>NA</td><td>19</td><td>Tennessee</td><td>15.0</td></tr>
<tr><td>18</td><td>Maryland</td><td>15.3</td><td>20</td><td>Virginia</td><td>14.9</td></tr>
<tr><td>35</td><td>Massachusetts</td><td>8.3</td><td>21</td><td>Mississippi</td><td>14.8</td></tr>
<tr><td>11</td><td>Michigan</td><td>16.8</td><td>22</td><td>Ohio</td><td>14.2</td></tr>
<tr><td>28</td><td>Minnesota</td><td>13.4</td><td>23</td><td>Arkansas</td><td>14.0</td></tr>
<tr><td>21</td><td>Mississippi</td><td>14.8</td><td>23</td><td>Louisiana</td><td>14.0</td></tr>
<tr><td>11</td><td>Missouri</td><td>16.8</td><td>25</td><td>California</td><td>13.7</td></tr>
<tr><td>NA</td><td>Montana**</td><td>NA</td><td>26</td><td>Oklahoma</td><td>13.5</td></tr>
<tr><td>2</td><td>Nebraska</td><td>19.4</td><td>26</td><td>Washington</td><td>13.5</td></tr>
<tr><td>8</td><td>Nevada</td><td>17.3</td><td>28</td><td>Georgia</td><td>13.4</td></tr>
<tr><td>NA</td><td>New Hampshire**</td><td>NA</td><td>28</td><td>Minnesota</td><td>13.4</td></tr>
<tr><td>30</td><td>New Jersey</td><td>12.8</td><td>30</td><td>New Jersey</td><td>12.8</td></tr>
<tr><td>NA</td><td>New Mexico**</td><td>NA</td><td>31</td><td>Florida</td><td>12.3</td></tr>
<tr><td>33</td><td>New York</td><td>10.9</td><td>32</td><td>Texas</td><td>11.6</td></tr>
<tr><td>6</td><td>North Carolina</td><td>17.6</td><td>33</td><td>New York</td><td>10.9</td></tr>
<tr><td>NA</td><td>North Dakota**</td><td>NA</td><td>34</td><td>Kansas</td><td>10.0</td></tr>
<tr><td>22</td><td>Ohio</td><td>14.2</td><td>35</td><td>Massachusetts</td><td>8.3</td></tr>
<tr><td>26</td><td>Oklahoma</td><td>13.5</td><td>NA</td><td>Alaska**</td><td>NA</td></tr>
<tr><td>NA</td><td>Oregon**</td><td>NA</td><td>NA</td><td>Hawaii**</td><td>NA</td></tr>
<tr><td>16</td><td>Pennsylvania</td><td>15.4</td><td>NA</td><td>Idaho**</td><td>NA</td></tr>
<tr><td>NA</td><td>Rhode Island**</td><td>NA</td><td>NA</td><td>Maine**</td><td>NA</td></tr>
<tr><td>13</td><td>South Carolina</td><td>16.2</td><td>NA</td><td>Montana**</td><td>NA</td></tr>
<tr><td>NA</td><td>South Dakota**</td><td>NA</td><td>NA</td><td>New Hampshire**</td><td>NA</td></tr>
<tr><td>19</td><td>Tennessee</td><td>15.0</td><td>NA</td><td>New Mexico**</td><td>NA</td></tr>
<tr><td>32</td><td>Texas</td><td>11.6</td><td>NA</td><td>North Dakota**</td><td>NA</td></tr>
<tr><td>NA</td><td>Utah**</td><td>NA</td><td>NA</td><td>Oregon**</td><td>NA</td></tr>
<tr><td>NA</td><td>Vermont**</td><td>NA</td><td>NA</td><td>Rhode Island**</td><td>NA</td></tr>
<tr><td>20</td><td>Virginia</td><td>14.9</td><td>NA</td><td>South Dakota**</td><td>NA</td></tr>
<tr><td>26</td><td>Washington</td><td>13.5</td><td>NA</td><td>Utah**</td><td>NA</td></tr>
<tr><td>NA</td><td>West Virginia**</td><td>NA</td><td>NA</td><td>Vermont**</td><td>NA</td></tr>
<tr><td>3</td><td>Wisconsin</td><td>18.7</td><td>NA</td><td>West Virginia**</td><td>NA</td></tr>
<tr><td>NA</td><td>Wyoming**</td><td>NA</td><td>NA</td><td>Wyoming**</td><td>NA</td></tr>
<tr><td></td><td></td><td></td><td></td><td>District of Columbia</td><td>15.5</td></tr>
</table>

Source: U.S. Department of Health and Human Services, National Center for Health Statistics
    "National Vital Statistics Reports" (Vol. 48, No. 11, July 24, 2000)
*Final data. Deaths of infants under 1 year old, exclusive of fetal deaths. Based on race of the mother.
**Not available, fewer than 20 black infant deaths.

# Deaths in 1998

## National Total = 2,337,256 Deaths*

ALPHA ORDER

RANK ORDER

| RANK | STATE | DEATHS | % of USA |
|------|-------|--------|----------|
| 18 | Alabama | 43,950 | 1.9% |
| 50 | Alaska | 2,571 | 0.1% |
| 22 | Arizona | 38,300 | 1.6% |
| 31 | Arkansas | 27,510 | 1.2% |
| 1 | California | 226,954 | 9.7% |
| 32 | Colorado | 26,640 | 1.1% |
| 27 | Connecticut | 29,710 | 1.3% |
| 46 | Delaware | 6,578 | 0.3% |
| 2 | Florida | 158,167 | 6.8% |
| 11 | Georgia | 60,428 | 2.6% |
| 43 | Hawaii | 8,091 | 0.3% |
| 42 | Idaho | 9,155 | 0.4% |
| 7 | Illinois | 104,480 | 4.5% |
| 15 | Indiana | 53,477 | 2.3% |
| 29 | Iowa | 28,362 | 1.2% |
| 33 | Kansas | 24,057 | 1.0% |
| 23 | Kentucky | 37,832 | 1.6% |
| 21 | Louisiana | 40,337 | 1.7% |
| 38 | Maine | 12,135 | 0.5% |
| 20 | Maryland | 42,059 | 1.8% |
| 12 | Massachusetts | 55,237 | 2.4% |
| 8 | Michigan | 85,160 | 3.6% |
| 24 | Minnesota | 37,195 | 1.6% |
| 30 | Mississippi | 27,847 | 1.2% |
| 13 | Missouri | 55,070 | 2.4% |
| 44 | Montana | 7,981 | 0.3% |
| 35 | Nebraska | 15,198 | 0.7% |
| 36 | Nevada | 14,464 | 0.6% |
| 41 | New Hampshire | 9,495 | 0.4% |
| 9 | New Jersey | 71,611 | 3.1% |
| 37 | New Mexico | 12,907 | 0.6% |
| 3 | New York | 156,619 | 6.7% |
| 10 | North Carolina | 67,993 | 2.9% |
| 47 | North Dakota | 5,920 | 0.3% |
| 6 | Ohio | 105,891 | 4.5% |
| 26 | Oklahoma | 33,929 | 1.5% |
| 28 | Oregon | 29,383 | 1.3% |
| 5 | Pennsylvania | 126,700 | 5.4% |
| 40 | Rhode Island | 9,604 | 0.4% |
| 25 | South Carolina | 34,827 | 1.5% |
| 45 | South Dakota | 6,867 | 0.3% |
| 16 | Tennessee | 53,415 | 2.3% |
| 4 | Texas | 142,605 | 6.1% |
| 39 | Utah | 11,824 | 0.5% |
| 48 | Vermont | 4,948 | 0.2% |
| 14 | Virginia | 54,446 | 2.3% |
| 19 | Washington | 42,706 | 1.8% |
| 34 | West Virginia | 20,767 | 0.9% |
| 17 | Wisconsin | 45,947 | 2.0% |
| 49 | Wyoming | 3,853 | 0.2% |

| RANK | STATE | DEATHS | % of USA |
|------|-------|--------|----------|
| 1 | California | 226,954 | 9.7% |
| 2 | Florida | 158,167 | 6.8% |
| 3 | New York | 156,619 | 6.7% |
| 4 | Texas | 142,605 | 6.1% |
| 5 | Pennsylvania | 126,700 | 5.4% |
| 6 | Ohio | 105,891 | 4.5% |
| 7 | Illinois | 104,480 | 4.5% |
| 8 | Michigan | 85,160 | 3.6% |
| 9 | New Jersey | 71,611 | 3.1% |
| 10 | North Carolina | 67,993 | 2.9% |
| 11 | Georgia | 60,428 | 2.6% |
| 12 | Massachusetts | 55,237 | 2.4% |
| 13 | Missouri | 55,070 | 2.4% |
| 14 | Virginia | 54,446 | 2.3% |
| 15 | Indiana | 53,477 | 2.3% |
| 16 | Tennessee | 53,415 | 2.3% |
| 17 | Wisconsin | 45,947 | 2.0% |
| 18 | Alabama | 43,950 | 1.9% |
| 19 | Washington | 42,706 | 1.8% |
| 20 | Maryland | 42,059 | 1.8% |
| 21 | Louisiana | 40,337 | 1.7% |
| 22 | Arizona | 38,300 | 1.6% |
| 23 | Kentucky | 37,832 | 1.6% |
| 24 | Minnesota | 37,195 | 1.6% |
| 25 | South Carolina | 34,827 | 1.5% |
| 26 | Oklahoma | 33,929 | 1.5% |
| 27 | Connecticut | 29,710 | 1.3% |
| 28 | Oregon | 29,383 | 1.3% |
| 29 | Iowa | 28,362 | 1.2% |
| 30 | Mississippi | 27,847 | 1.2% |
| 31 | Arkansas | 27,510 | 1.2% |
| 32 | Colorado | 26,640 | 1.1% |
| 33 | Kansas | 24,057 | 1.0% |
| 34 | West Virginia | 20,767 | 0.9% |
| 35 | Nebraska | 15,198 | 0.7% |
| 36 | Nevada | 14,464 | 0.6% |
| 37 | New Mexico | 12,907 | 0.6% |
| 38 | Maine | 12,135 | 0.5% |
| 39 | Utah | 11,824 | 0.5% |
| 40 | Rhode Island | 9,604 | 0.4% |
| 41 | New Hampshire | 9,495 | 0.4% |
| 42 | Idaho | 9,155 | 0.4% |
| 43 | Hawaii | 8,091 | 0.3% |
| 44 | Montana | 7,981 | 0.3% |
| 45 | South Dakota | 6,867 | 0.3% |
| 46 | Delaware | 6,578 | 0.3% |
| 47 | North Dakota | 5,920 | 0.3% |
| 48 | Vermont | 4,948 | 0.2% |
| 49 | Wyoming | 3,853 | 0.2% |
| 50 | Alaska | 2,571 | 0.1% |
| | District of Columbia | 6,054 | 0.3% |

Source: U.S. Department of Health and Human Services, National Center for Health Statistics
   "National Vital Statistics Reports" (Vol. 48, No. 11, July 24, 2000)
*Final data by state of residence.

# Death Rate in 1998

## National Rate = 864.7 Deaths per 100,000 Population*

ALPHA ORDER

| RANK | STATE | RATE |
|---|---|---|
| 8 | Alabama | 1,009.9 |
| 50 | Alaska | 418.7 |
| 35 | Arizona | 820.4 |
| 2 | Arkansas | 1,083.8 |
| 46 | California | 694.8 |
| 48 | Colorado | 670.9 |
| 21 | Connecticut | 907.4 |
| 27 | Delaware | 884.6 |
| 3 | Florida | 1,060.4 |
| 40 | Georgia | 790.7 |
| 47 | Hawaii | 678.2 |
| 43 | Idaho | 745.1 |
| 31 | Illinois | 867.4 |
| 22 | Indiana | 906.5 |
| 9 | Iowa | 990.8 |
| 18 | Kansas | 915.0 |
| 13 | Kentucky | 961.1 |
| 17 | Louisiana | 923.3 |
| 11 | Maine | 975.3 |
| 36 | Maryland | 819.1 |
| 25 | Massachusetts | 898.6 |
| 30 | Michigan | 867.5 |
| 41 | Minnesota | 787.1 |
| 7 | Mississippi | 1,011.8 |
| 6 | Missouri | 1,012.6 |
| 22 | Montana | 906.5 |
| 19 | Nebraska | 914.0 |
| 34 | Nevada | 828.0 |
| 38 | New Hampshire | 801.2 |
| 28 | New Jersey | 882.5 |
| 44 | New Mexico | 743.1 |
| 32 | New York | 861.7 |
| 24 | North Carolina | 901.0 |
| 16 | North Dakota | 927.5 |
| 14 | Ohio | 944.7 |
| 5 | Oklahoma | 1,013.8 |
| 26 | Oregon | 895.3 |
| 4 | Pennsylvania | 1,055.7 |
| 12 | Rhode Island | 971.6 |
| 20 | South Carolina | 907.9 |
| 15 | South Dakota | 930.3 |
| 10 | Tennessee | 983.6 |
| 45 | Texas | 721.7 |
| 49 | Utah | 563.1 |
| 33 | Vermont | 837.4 |
| 37 | Virginia | 801.7 |
| 42 | Washington | 750.6 |
| 1 | West Virginia | 1,146.6 |
| 29 | Wisconsin | 879.6 |
| 38 | Wyoming | 801.2 |

RANK ORDER

| RANK | STATE | RATE |
|---|---|---|
| 1 | West Virginia | 1,146.6 |
| 2 | Arkansas | 1,083.8 |
| 3 | Florida | 1,060.4 |
| 4 | Pennsylvania | 1,055.7 |
| 5 | Oklahoma | 1,013.8 |
| 6 | Missouri | 1,012.6 |
| 7 | Mississippi | 1,011.8 |
| 8 | Alabama | 1,009.9 |
| 9 | Iowa | 990.8 |
| 10 | Tennessee | 983.6 |
| 11 | Maine | 975.3 |
| 12 | Rhode Island | 971.6 |
| 13 | Kentucky | 961.1 |
| 14 | Ohio | 944.7 |
| 15 | South Dakota | 930.3 |
| 16 | North Dakota | 927.5 |
| 17 | Louisiana | 923.3 |
| 18 | Kansas | 915.0 |
| 19 | Nebraska | 914.0 |
| 20 | South Carolina | 907.9 |
| 21 | Connecticut | 907.4 |
| 22 | Indiana | 906.5 |
| 22 | Montana | 906.5 |
| 24 | North Carolina | 901.0 |
| 25 | Massachusetts | 898.6 |
| 26 | Oregon | 895.3 |
| 27 | Delaware | 884.6 |
| 28 | New Jersey | 882.5 |
| 29 | Wisconsin | 879.6 |
| 30 | Michigan | 867.5 |
| 31 | Illinois | 867.4 |
| 32 | New York | 861.7 |
| 33 | Vermont | 837.4 |
| 34 | Nevada | 828.0 |
| 35 | Arizona | 820.4 |
| 36 | Maryland | 819.1 |
| 37 | Virginia | 801.7 |
| 38 | New Hampshire | 801.2 |
| 38 | Wyoming | 801.2 |
| 40 | Georgia | 790.7 |
| 41 | Minnesota | 787.1 |
| 42 | Washington | 750.6 |
| 43 | Idaho | 745.1 |
| 44 | New Mexico | 743.1 |
| 45 | Texas | 721.7 |
| 46 | California | 694.8 |
| 47 | Hawaii | 678.2 |
| 48 | Colorado | 670.9 |
| 49 | Utah | 563.1 |
| 50 | Alaska | 418.7 |
| | District of Columbia | 1,157.3 |

Source: U.S. Department of Health and Human Services, National Center for Health Statistics
    "National Vital Statistics Reports" (Vol. 48, No. 11, July 24, 2000)
*Final data by state of residence.  Not age-adjusted.

# Age-Adjusted Death Rate in 1998

## National Rate = 471.7 Deaths per 100,000 Population*

ALPHA ORDER

| RANK | STATE | RATE |
|---|---|---|
| 3 | Alabama | 565.9 |
| 34 | Alaska | 441.9 |
| 25 | Arizona | 461.7 |
| 5 | Arkansas | 551.0 |
| 41 | California | 425.4 |
| 46 | Colorado | 419.0 |
| 40 | Connecticut | 425.6 |
| 14 | Delaware | 496.9 |
| 26 | Florida | 458.4 |
| 8 | Georgia | 539.8 |
| 50 | Hawaii | 370.1 |
| 42 | Idaho | 424.4 |
| 19 | Illinois | 480.5 |
| 15 | Indiana | 496.5 |
| 45 | Iowa | 421.6 |
| 30 | Kansas | 447.8 |
| 10 | Kentucky | 533.6 |
| 2 | Louisiana | 575.2 |
| 24 | Maine | 462.4 |
| 16 | Maryland | 494.8 |
| 44 | Massachusetts | 421.9 |
| 18 | Michigan | 484.6 |
| 49 | Minnesota | 394.5 |
| 1 | Mississippi | 606.6 |
| 13 | Missouri | 511.1 |
| 29 | Montana | 449.9 |
| 39 | Nebraska | 431.9 |
| 9 | Nevada | 539.1 |
| 35 | New Hampshire | 440.0 |
| 31 | New Jersey | 445.3 |
| 27 | New Mexico | 457.5 |
| 32 | New York | 443.5 |
| 12 | North Carolina | 518.6 |
| 47 | North Dakota | 414.8 |
| 17 | Ohio | 489.8 |
| 11 | Oklahoma | 529.5 |
| 28 | Oregon | 451.4 |
| 21 | Pennsylvania | 475.4 |
| 38 | Rhode Island | 433.5 |
| 6 | South Carolina | 550.8 |
| 33 | South Dakota | 442.6 |
| 4 | Tennessee | 557.0 |
| 22 | Texas | 475.3 |
| 48 | Utah | 404.5 |
| 36 | Vermont | 434.4 |
| 20 | Virginia | 480.0 |
| 43 | Washington | 423.2 |
| 7 | West Virginia | 547.9 |
| 37 | Wisconsin | 433.9 |
| 23 | Wyoming | 464.8 |

RANK ORDER

| RANK | STATE | RATE |
|---|---|---|
| 1 | Mississippi | 606.6 |
| 2 | Louisiana | 575.2 |
| 3 | Alabama | 565.9 |
| 4 | Tennessee | 557.0 |
| 5 | Arkansas | 551.0 |
| 6 | South Carolina | 550.8 |
| 7 | West Virginia | 547.9 |
| 8 | Georgia | 539.8 |
| 9 | Nevada | 539.1 |
| 10 | Kentucky | 533.6 |
| 11 | Oklahoma | 529.5 |
| 12 | North Carolina | 518.6 |
| 13 | Missouri | 511.1 |
| 14 | Delaware | 496.9 |
| 15 | Indiana | 496.5 |
| 16 | Maryland | 494.8 |
| 17 | Ohio | 489.8 |
| 18 | Michigan | 484.6 |
| 19 | Illinois | 480.5 |
| 20 | Virginia | 480.0 |
| 21 | Pennsylvania | 475.4 |
| 22 | Texas | 475.3 |
| 23 | Wyoming | 464.8 |
| 24 | Maine | 462.4 |
| 25 | Arizona | 461.7 |
| 26 | Florida | 458.4 |
| 27 | New Mexico | 457.5 |
| 28 | Oregon | 451.4 |
| 29 | Montana | 449.9 |
| 30 | Kansas | 447.8 |
| 31 | New Jersey | 445.3 |
| 32 | New York | 443.5 |
| 33 | South Dakota | 442.6 |
| 34 | Alaska | 441.9 |
| 35 | New Hampshire | 440.0 |
| 36 | Vermont | 434.4 |
| 37 | Wisconsin | 433.9 |
| 38 | Rhode Island | 433.5 |
| 39 | Nebraska | 431.9 |
| 40 | Connecticut | 425.6 |
| 41 | California | 425.4 |
| 42 | Idaho | 424.4 |
| 43 | Washington | 423.2 |
| 44 | Massachusetts | 421.9 |
| 45 | Iowa | 421.6 |
| 46 | Colorado | 419.0 |
| 47 | North Dakota | 414.8 |
| 48 | Utah | 404.5 |
| 49 | Minnesota | 394.5 |
| 50 | Hawaii | 370.1 |
| | District of Columbia | 684.8 |

Source: U.S. Department of Health and Human Services, National Center for Health Statistics
    "National Vital Statistics Reports" (Vol. 48, No. 11, July 24, 2000)
*Final data by state of residence.  Age-adjusted rates eliminate the distorting effects of the aging of the population.

# Deaths by Accidents in 1998

## National Total = 97,835 Deaths*

| RANK | STATE | DEATHS | % of USA |
|------|-------|--------|----------|
| 16 | Alabama | 2,204 | 2.3% |
| 47 | Alaska | 251 | 0.3% |
| 14 | Arizona | 2,228 | 2.3% |
| 30 | Arkansas | 1,287 | 1.3% |
| 1 | California | 9,264 | 9.5% |
| 26 | Colorado | 1,530 | 1.6% |
| 33 | Connecticut | 1,067 | 1.1% |
| 46 | Delaware | 289 | 0.3% |
| 3 | Florida | 5,877 | 6.0% |
| 9 | Georgia | 3,156 | 3.2% |
| 44 | Hawaii | 299 | 0.3% |
| 39 | Idaho | 571 | 0.6% |
| 6 | Illinois | 3,891 | 4.0% |
| 17 | Indiana | 2,199 | 2.2% |
| 32 | Iowa | 1,094 | 1.1% |
| 31 | Kansas | 1,152 | 1.2% |
| 24 | Kentucky | 1,715 | 1.8% |
| 19 | Louisiana | 1,939 | 2.0% |
| 41 | Maine | 448 | 0.5% |
| 28 | Maryland | 1,398 | 1.4% |
| 29 | Massachusetts | 1,336 | 1.4% |
| 10 | Michigan | 3,133 | 3.2% |
| 22 | Minnesota | 1,728 | 1.8% |
| 23 | Mississippi | 1,716 | 1.8% |
| 12 | Missouri | 2,455 | 2.5% |
| 40 | Montana | 461 | 0.5% |
| 37 | Nebraska | 676 | 0.7% |
| 38 | Nevada | 665 | 0.7% |
| 43 | New Hampshire | 343 | 0.4% |
| 15 | New Jersey | 2,215 | 2.3% |
| 34 | New Mexico | 996 | 1.0% |
| 4 | New York | 4,676 | 4.8% |
| 8 | North Carolina | 3,278 | 3.4% |
| 45 | North Dakota | 296 | 0.3% |
| 7 | Ohio | 3,546 | 3.6% |
| 25 | Oklahoma | 1,610 | 1.6% |
| 27 | Oregon | 1,405 | 1.4% |
| 5 | Pennsylvania | 4,573 | 4.7% |
| 48 | Rhode Island | 242 | 0.2% |
| 21 | South Carolina | 1,803 | 1.8% |
| 42 | South Dakota | 360 | 0.4% |
| 11 | Tennessee | 2,627 | 2.7% |
| 2 | Texas | 7,421 | 7.6% |
| 36 | Utah | 713 | 0.7% |
| 50 | Vermont | 216 | 0.2% |
| 13 | Virginia | 2,334 | 2.4% |
| 18 | Washington | 1,950 | 2.0% |
| 35 | West Virginia | 840 | 0.9% |
| 20 | Wisconsin | 1,924 | 2.0% |
| 49 | Wyoming | 231 | 0.2% |

| RANK | STATE | DEATHS | % of USA |
|------|-------|--------|----------|
| 1 | California | 9,264 | 9.5% |
| 2 | Texas | 7,421 | 7.6% |
| 3 | Florida | 5,877 | 6.0% |
| 4 | New York | 4,676 | 4.8% |
| 5 | Pennsylvania | 4,573 | 4.7% |
| 6 | Illinois | 3,891 | 4.0% |
| 7 | Ohio | 3,546 | 3.6% |
| 8 | North Carolina | 3,278 | 3.4% |
| 9 | Georgia | 3,156 | 3.2% |
| 10 | Michigan | 3,133 | 3.2% |
| 11 | Tennessee | 2,627 | 2.7% |
| 12 | Missouri | 2,455 | 2.5% |
| 13 | Virginia | 2,334 | 2.4% |
| 14 | Arizona | 2,228 | 2.3% |
| 15 | New Jersey | 2,215 | 2.3% |
| 16 | Alabama | 2,204 | 2.3% |
| 17 | Indiana | 2,199 | 2.2% |
| 18 | Washington | 1,950 | 2.0% |
| 19 | Louisiana | 1,939 | 2.0% |
| 20 | Wisconsin | 1,924 | 2.0% |
| 21 | South Carolina | 1,803 | 1.8% |
| 22 | Minnesota | 1,728 | 1.8% |
| 23 | Mississippi | 1,716 | 1.8% |
| 24 | Kentucky | 1,715 | 1.8% |
| 25 | Oklahoma | 1,610 | 1.6% |
| 26 | Colorado | 1,530 | 1.6% |
| 27 | Oregon | 1,405 | 1.4% |
| 28 | Maryland | 1,398 | 1.4% |
| 29 | Massachusetts | 1,336 | 1.4% |
| 30 | Arkansas | 1,287 | 1.3% |
| 31 | Kansas | 1,152 | 1.2% |
| 32 | Iowa | 1,094 | 1.1% |
| 33 | Connecticut | 1,067 | 1.1% |
| 34 | New Mexico | 996 | 1.0% |
| 35 | West Virginia | 840 | 0.9% |
| 36 | Utah | 713 | 0.7% |
| 37 | Nebraska | 676 | 0.7% |
| 38 | Nevada | 665 | 0.7% |
| 39 | Idaho | 571 | 0.6% |
| 40 | Montana | 461 | 0.5% |
| 41 | Maine | 448 | 0.5% |
| 42 | South Dakota | 360 | 0.4% |
| 43 | New Hampshire | 343 | 0.4% |
| 44 | Hawaii | 299 | 0.3% |
| 45 | North Dakota | 296 | 0.3% |
| 46 | Delaware | 289 | 0.3% |
| 47 | Alaska | 251 | 0.3% |
| 48 | Rhode Island | 242 | 0.2% |
| 49 | Wyoming | 231 | 0.2% |
| 50 | Vermont | 216 | 0.2% |
| | District of Columbia | 207 | 0.2% |

*Source: U.S. Department of Health and Human Services, National Center for Health Statistics*
*"National Vital Statistics Reports" (Vol. 48, No. 11, July 24, 2000)*
*Final data by state of residence. Includes motor vehicle deaths, poisoning, falls, drowning and other accidents.

# Death Rate by Accidents in 1998

## National Rate = 36.2 Deaths per 100,000 Population*

| ALPHA ORDER | | | | RANK ORDER | | |
|:---:|:---|:---:|:---|:---:|:---|:---:|
| RANK | STATE | RATE | | RANK | STATE | RATE |
| 5 | Alabama | 50.6 | | 1 | Mississippi | 62.4 |
| 22 | Alaska | 40.9 | | 2 | New Mexico | 57.3 |
| 10 | Arizona | 47.7 | | 3 | Montana | 52.4 |
| 4 | Arkansas | 50.7 | | 4 | Arkansas | 50.7 |
| 44 | California | 28.4 | | 5 | Alabama | 50.6 |
| 26 | Colorado | 38.5 | | 6 | South Dakota | 48.8 |
| 39 | Connecticut | 32.6 | | 7 | Tennessee | 48.4 |
| 25 | Delaware | 38.9 | | 8 | Oklahoma | 48.1 |
| 24 | Florida | 39.4 | | 9 | Wyoming | 48.0 |
| 21 | Georgia | 41.3 | | 10 | Arizona | 47.7 |
| 48 | Hawaii | 25.1 | | 11 | South Carolina | 47.0 |
| 12 | Idaho | 46.5 | | 12 | Idaho | 46.5 |
| 40 | Illinois | 32.3 | | 13 | North Dakota | 46.4 |
| 31 | Indiana | 37.3 | | 13 | West Virginia | 46.4 |
| 27 | Iowa | 38.2 | | 15 | Missouri | 45.1 |
| 17 | Kansas | 43.8 | | 16 | Louisiana | 44.4 |
| 18 | Kentucky | 43.6 | | 17 | Kansas | 43.8 |
| 16 | Louisiana | 44.4 | | 18 | Kentucky | 43.6 |
| 35 | Maine | 36.0 | | 19 | North Carolina | 43.4 |
| 46 | Maryland | 27.2 | | 20 | Oregon | 42.8 |
| 50 | Massachusetts | 21.7 | | 21 | Georgia | 41.3 |
| 41 | Michigan | 31.9 | | 22 | Alaska | 40.9 |
| 33 | Minnesota | 36.6 | | 23 | Nebraska | 40.7 |
| 1 | Mississippi | 62.4 | | 24 | Florida | 39.4 |
| 15 | Missouri | 45.1 | | 25 | Delaware | 38.9 |
| 3 | Montana | 52.4 | | 26 | Colorado | 38.5 |
| 23 | Nebraska | 40.7 | | 27 | Iowa | 38.2 |
| 28 | Nevada | 38.1 | | 28 | Nevada | 38.1 |
| 43 | New Hampshire | 28.9 | | 28 | Pennsylvania | 38.1 |
| 45 | New Jersey | 27.3 | | 30 | Texas | 37.6 |
| 2 | New Mexico | 57.3 | | 31 | Indiana | 37.3 |
| 47 | New York | 25.7 | | 32 | Wisconsin | 36.8 |
| 19 | North Carolina | 43.4 | | 33 | Minnesota | 36.6 |
| 13 | North Dakota | 46.4 | | 33 | Vermont | 36.6 |
| 42 | Ohio | 31.6 | | 35 | Maine | 36.0 |
| 8 | Oklahoma | 48.1 | | 36 | Virginia | 34.4 |
| 20 | Oregon | 42.8 | | 37 | Washington | 34.3 |
| 28 | Pennsylvania | 38.1 | | 38 | Utah | 34.0 |
| 49 | Rhode Island | 24.5 | | 39 | Connecticut | 32.6 |
| 11 | South Carolina | 47.0 | | 40 | Illinois | 32.3 |
| 6 | South Dakota | 48.8 | | 41 | Michigan | 31.9 |
| 7 | Tennessee | 48.4 | | 42 | Ohio | 31.6 |
| 30 | Texas | 37.6 | | 43 | New Hampshire | 28.9 |
| 38 | Utah | 34.0 | | 44 | California | 28.4 |
| 33 | Vermont | 36.6 | | 45 | New Jersey | 27.3 |
| 36 | Virginia | 34.4 | | 46 | Maryland | 27.2 |
| 37 | Washington | 34.3 | | 47 | New York | 25.7 |
| 13 | West Virginia | 46.4 | | 48 | Hawaii | 25.1 |
| 32 | Wisconsin | 36.8 | | 49 | Rhode Island | 24.5 |
| 9 | Wyoming | 48.0 | | 50 | Massachusetts | 21.7 |
| | | | | | District of Columbia | 39.6 |

Source: U.S. Department of Health and Human Services, National Center for Health Statistics
    "National Vital Statistics Reports" (Vol. 48, No. 11, July 24, 2000)
*Final data by state of residence. Includes motor vehicle deaths, poisoning, falls, drowning and other accidents.
Not age-adjusted.

# Estimated Deaths by Cancer in 2001

## National Estimated Total = 553,400 Deaths

ALPHA ORDER

RANK ORDER

| RANK | STATE | DEATHS | % of USA |
|---|---|---|---|
| 20 | Alabama | 9,900 | 1.8% |
| 50 | Alaska | 700 | 0.1% |
| 22 | Arizona | 9,300 | 1.7% |
| 31 | Arkansas | 6,100 | 1.1% |
| 1 | California | 51,200 | 9.3% |
| 30 | Colorado | 6,200 | 1.1% |
| 28 | Connecticut | 7,000 | 1.3% |
| 45 | Delaware | 1,800 | 0.3% |
| 2 | Florida | 40,000 | 7.2% |
| 12 | Georgia | 13,600 | 2.5% |
| 43 | Hawaii | 2,000 | 0.4% |
| 42 | Idaho | 2,200 | 0.4% |
| 7 | Illinois | 24,800 | 4.5% |
| 14 | Indiana | 12,800 | 2.3% |
| 29 | Iowa | 6,500 | 1.2% |
| 33 | Kansas | 5,300 | 1.0% |
| 23 | Kentucky | 9,200 | 1.7% |
| 21 | Louisiana | 9,500 | 1.7% |
| 37 | Maine | 3,000 | 0.5% |
| 19 | Maryland | 10,300 | 1.9% |
| 11 | Massachusetts | 13,700 | 2.5% |
| 8 | Michigan | 19,800 | 3.6% |
| 24 | Minnesota | 9,000 | 1.6% |
| 31 | Mississippi | 6,100 | 1.1% |
| 16 | Missouri | 12,400 | 2.2% |
| 44 | Montana | 1,900 | 0.3% |
| 36 | Nebraska | 3,300 | 0.6% |
| 35 | Nevada | 4,000 | 0.7% |
| 39 | New Hampshire | 2,500 | 0.5% |
| 9 | New Jersey | 18,000 | 3.3% |
| 37 | New Mexico | 3,000 | 0.5% |
| 3 | New York | 36,300 | 6.6% |
| 10 | North Carolina | 16,300 | 2.9% |
| 47 | North Dakota | 1,300 | 0.2% |
| 6 | Ohio | 25,400 | 4.6% |
| 26 | Oklahoma | 7,300 | 1.3% |
| 26 | Oregon | 7,300 | 1.3% |
| 5 | Pennsylvania | 29,800 | 5.4% |
| 41 | Rhode Island | 2,400 | 0.4% |
| 25 | South Carolina | 8,200 | 1.5% |
| 46 | South Dakota | 1,600 | 0.3% |
| 15 | Tennessee | 12,600 | 2.3% |
| 4 | Texas | 34,400 | 6.2% |
| 39 | Utah | 2,500 | 0.5% |
| 48 | Vermont | 1,200 | 0.2% |
| 13 | Virginia | 13,300 | 2.4% |
| 18 | Washington | 10,800 | 2.0% |
| 34 | West Virginia | 4,800 | 0.9% |
| 17 | Wisconsin | 10,900 | 2.0% |
| 49 | Wyoming | 1,000 | 0.2% |

| RANK | STATE | DEATHS | % of USA |
|---|---|---|---|
| 1 | California | 51,200 | 9.3% |
| 2 | Florida | 40,000 | 7.2% |
| 3 | New York | 36,300 | 6.6% |
| 4 | Texas | 34,400 | 6.2% |
| 5 | Pennsylvania | 29,800 | 5.4% |
| 6 | Ohio | 25,400 | 4.6% |
| 7 | Illinois | 24,800 | 4.5% |
| 8 | Michigan | 19,800 | 3.6% |
| 9 | New Jersey | 18,000 | 3.3% |
| 10 | North Carolina | 16,300 | 2.9% |
| 11 | Massachusetts | 13,700 | 2.5% |
| 12 | Georgia | 13,600 | 2.5% |
| 13 | Virginia | 13,300 | 2.4% |
| 14 | Indiana | 12,800 | 2.3% |
| 15 | Tennessee | 12,600 | 2.3% |
| 16 | Missouri | 12,400 | 2.2% |
| 17 | Wisconsin | 10,900 | 2.0% |
| 18 | Washington | 10,800 | 2.0% |
| 19 | Maryland | 10,300 | 1.9% |
| 20 | Alabama | 9,900 | 1.8% |
| 21 | Louisiana | 9,500 | 1.7% |
| 22 | Arizona | 9,300 | 1.7% |
| 23 | Kentucky | 9,200 | 1.7% |
| 24 | Minnesota | 9,000 | 1.6% |
| 25 | South Carolina | 8,200 | 1.5% |
| 26 | Oklahoma | 7,300 | 1.3% |
| 26 | Oregon | 7,300 | 1.3% |
| 28 | Connecticut | 7,000 | 1.3% |
| 29 | Iowa | 6,500 | 1.2% |
| 30 | Colorado | 6,200 | 1.1% |
| 31 | Arkansas | 6,100 | 1.1% |
| 31 | Mississippi | 6,100 | 1.1% |
| 33 | Kansas | 5,300 | 1.0% |
| 34 | West Virginia | 4,800 | 0.9% |
| 35 | Nevada | 4,000 | 0.7% |
| 36 | Nebraska | 3,300 | 0.6% |
| 37 | Maine | 3,000 | 0.5% |
| 37 | New Mexico | 3,000 | 0.5% |
| 39 | New Hampshire | 2,500 | 0.5% |
| 39 | Utah | 2,500 | 0.5% |
| 41 | Rhode Island | 2,400 | 0.4% |
| 42 | Idaho | 2,200 | 0.4% |
| 43 | Hawaii | 2,000 | 0.4% |
| 44 | Montana | 1,900 | 0.3% |
| 45 | Delaware | 1,800 | 0.3% |
| 46 | South Dakota | 1,600 | 0.3% |
| 47 | North Dakota | 1,300 | 0.2% |
| 48 | Vermont | 1,200 | 0.2% |
| 49 | Wyoming | 1,000 | 0.2% |
| 50 | Alaska | 700 | 0.1% |
| | District of Columbia | 1,200 | 0.2% |

*Source: American Cancer Society*
*"Cancer Facts & Figures 2001" (Copyright 2001, Reprinted with permission from the American Cancer Society)*

# Estimated Death Rate by Cancer in 2001

## National Estimated Rate = 196.6 Deaths per 100,000 Population*

ALPHA ORDER

| RANK | STATE | RATE |
|------|-------|------|
| 10 | Alabama | 222.6 |
| 50 | Alaska | 111.7 |
| 41 | Arizona | 181.3 |
| 7 | Arkansas | 228.2 |
| 47 | California | 151.2 |
| 48 | Colorado | 144.1 |
| 23 | Connecticut | 205.5 |
| 5 | Delaware | 229.7 |
| 2 | Florida | 250.3 |
| 43 | Georgia | 166.1 |
| 44 | Hawaii | 165.1 |
| 42 | Idaho | 170.0 |
| 31 | Illinois | 199.7 |
| 22 | Indiana | 210.5 |
| 11 | Iowa | 222.1 |
| 33 | Kansas | 197.1 |
| 8 | Kentucky | 227.6 |
| 18 | Louisiana | 212.6 |
| 4 | Maine | 235.3 |
| 35 | Maryland | 194.5 |
| 14 | Massachusetts | 215.8 |
| 32 | Michigan | 199.2 |
| 40 | Minnesota | 182.9 |
| 15 | Mississippi | 214.4 |
| 12 | Missouri | 221.6 |
| 21 | Montana | 210.6 |
| 36 | Nebraska | 192.8 |
| 30 | Nevada | 200.2 |
| 29 | New Hampshire | 202.3 |
| 16 | New Jersey | 213.9 |
| 46 | New Mexico | 164.9 |
| 37 | New York | 191.3 |
| 26 | North Carolina | 202.5 |
| 28 | North Dakota | 202.4 |
| 9 | Ohio | 223.7 |
| 20 | Oklahoma | 211.6 |
| 17 | Oregon | 213.4 |
| 3 | Pennsylvania | 242.7 |
| 6 | Rhode Island | 228.9 |
| 24 | South Carolina | 204.4 |
| 19 | South Dakota | 212.0 |
| 13 | Tennessee | 221.5 |
| 45 | Texas | 165.0 |
| 49 | Utah | 111.9 |
| 33 | Vermont | 197.1 |
| 38 | Virginia | 187.9 |
| 39 | Washington | 183.2 |
| 1 | West Virginia | 265.4 |
| 25 | Wisconsin | 203.2 |
| 26 | Wyoming | 202.5 |

RANK ORDER

| RANK | STATE | RATE |
|------|-------|------|
| 1 | West Virginia | 265.4 |
| 2 | Florida | 250.3 |
| 3 | Pennsylvania | 242.7 |
| 4 | Maine | 235.3 |
| 5 | Delaware | 229.7 |
| 6 | Rhode Island | 228.9 |
| 7 | Arkansas | 228.2 |
| 8 | Kentucky | 227.6 |
| 9 | Ohio | 223.7 |
| 10 | Alabama | 222.6 |
| 11 | Iowa | 222.1 |
| 12 | Missouri | 221.6 |
| 13 | Tennessee | 221.5 |
| 14 | Massachusetts | 215.8 |
| 15 | Mississippi | 214.4 |
| 16 | New Jersey | 213.9 |
| 17 | Oregon | 213.4 |
| 18 | Louisiana | 212.6 |
| 19 | South Dakota | 212.0 |
| 20 | Oklahoma | 211.6 |
| 21 | Montana | 210.6 |
| 22 | Indiana | 210.5 |
| 23 | Connecticut | 205.5 |
| 24 | South Carolina | 204.4 |
| 25 | Wisconsin | 203.2 |
| 26 | North Carolina | 202.5 |
| 26 | Wyoming | 202.5 |
| 28 | North Dakota | 202.4 |
| 29 | New Hampshire | 202.3 |
| 30 | Nevada | 200.2 |
| 31 | Illinois | 199.7 |
| 32 | Michigan | 199.2 |
| 33 | Kansas | 197.1 |
| 33 | Vermont | 197.1 |
| 35 | Maryland | 194.5 |
| 36 | Nebraska | 192.8 |
| 37 | New York | 191.3 |
| 38 | Virginia | 187.9 |
| 39 | Washington | 183.2 |
| 40 | Minnesota | 182.9 |
| 41 | Arizona | 181.3 |
| 42 | Idaho | 170.0 |
| 43 | Georgia | 166.1 |
| 44 | Hawaii | 165.1 |
| 45 | Texas | 165.0 |
| 46 | New Mexico | 164.9 |
| 47 | California | 151.2 |
| 48 | Colorado | 144.1 |
| 49 | Utah | 111.9 |
| 50 | Alaska | 111.7 |
| | District of Columbia | 209.8 |

Source: Morgan Quitno Press using data from American Cancer Society
*"Cancer Facts & Figures 2001" (Copyright 2001, Reprinted with permission from the American Cancer Society)
*Rates calculated using 2000 Census resident population figures. Not age-adjusted.

# Estimated New Cancer Cases in 2001

## National Estimated Total = 1,268,000 New Cases*

ALPHA ORDER

| RANK | STATE | CASES | % of USA |
|------|-------|-------|----------|
| 20 | Alabama | 22,600 | 1.8% |
| 50 | Alaska | 1,600 | 0.1% |
| 22 | Arizona | 21,300 | 1.7% |
| 31 | Arkansas | 14,100 | 1.1% |
| 1 | California | 117,400 | 9.3% |
| 30 | Colorado | 14,300 | 1.1% |
| 28 | Connecticut | 16,000 | 1.3% |
| 45 | Delaware | 4,000 | 0.3% |
| 2 | Florida | 91,600 | 7.2% |
| 12 | Georgia | 31,100 | 2.5% |
| 43 | Hawaii | 4,700 | 0.4% |
| 42 | Idaho | 5,000 | 0.4% |
| 7 | Illinois | 56,800 | 4.5% |
| 14 | Indiana | 29,300 | 2.3% |
| 29 | Iowa | 14,800 | 1.2% |
| 33 | Kansas | 12,100 | 1.0% |
| 23 | Kentucky | 21,100 | 1.7% |
| 21 | Louisiana | 21,700 | 1.7% |
| 37 | Maine | 6,900 | 0.5% |
| 19 | Maryland | 23,500 | 1.9% |
| 11 | Massachusetts | 31,300 | 2.5% |
| 8 | Michigan | 45,300 | 3.6% |
| 24 | Minnesota | 20,600 | 1.6% |
| 32 | Mississippi | 13,900 | 1.1% |
| 16 | Missouri | 28,400 | 2.2% |
| 44 | Montana | 4,300 | 0.3% |
| 36 | Nebraska | 7,500 | 0.6% |
| 35 | Nevada | 9,200 | 0.7% |
| 39 | New Hampshire | 5,800 | 0.5% |
| 9 | New Jersey | 41,200 | 3.2% |
| 37 | New Mexico | 6,900 | 0.5% |
| 3 | New York | 83,200 | 6.6% |
| 10 | North Carolina | 37,300 | 2.9% |
| 47 | North Dakota | 3,100 | 0.2% |
| 6 | Ohio | 58,200 | 4.6% |
| 27 | Oklahoma | 16,600 | 1.3% |
| 26 | Oregon | 16,700 | 1.3% |
| 5 | Pennsylvania | 68,400 | 5.4% |
| 40 | Rhode Island | 5,600 | 0.4% |
| 25 | South Carolina | 18,800 | 1.5% |
| 46 | South Dakota | 3,600 | 0.3% |
| 15 | Tennessee | 28,800 | 2.3% |
| 4 | Texas | 78,900 | 6.2% |
| 40 | Utah | 5,600 | 0.4% |
| 48 | Vermont | 2,900 | 0.2% |
| 13 | Virginia | 30,500 | 2.4% |
| 18 | Washington | 24,800 | 2.0% |
| 34 | West Virginia | 10,900 | 0.9% |
| 17 | Wisconsin | 25,000 | 2.0% |
| 49 | Wyoming | 2,200 | 0.2% |

RANK ORDER

| RANK | STATE | CASES | % of USA |
|------|-------|-------|----------|
| 1 | California | 117,400 | 9.3% |
| 2 | Florida | 91,600 | 7.2% |
| 3 | New York | 83,200 | 6.6% |
| 4 | Texas | 78,900 | 6.2% |
| 5 | Pennsylvania | 68,400 | 5.4% |
| 6 | Ohio | 58,200 | 4.6% |
| 7 | Illinois | 56,800 | 4.5% |
| 8 | Michigan | 45,300 | 3.6% |
| 9 | New Jersey | 41,200 | 3.2% |
| 10 | North Carolina | 37,300 | 2.9% |
| 11 | Massachusetts | 31,300 | 2.5% |
| 12 | Georgia | 31,100 | 2.5% |
| 13 | Virginia | 30,500 | 2.4% |
| 14 | Indiana | 29,300 | 2.3% |
| 15 | Tennessee | 28,800 | 2.3% |
| 16 | Missouri | 28,400 | 2.2% |
| 17 | Wisconsin | 25,000 | 2.0% |
| 18 | Washington | 24,800 | 2.0% |
| 19 | Maryland | 23,500 | 1.9% |
| 20 | Alabama | 22,600 | 1.8% |
| 21 | Louisiana | 21,700 | 1.7% |
| 22 | Arizona | 21,300 | 1.7% |
| 23 | Kentucky | 21,100 | 1.7% |
| 24 | Minnesota | 20,600 | 1.6% |
| 25 | South Carolina | 18,800 | 1.5% |
| 26 | Oregon | 16,700 | 1.3% |
| 27 | Oklahoma | 16,600 | 1.3% |
| 28 | Connecticut | 16,000 | 1.3% |
| 29 | Iowa | 14,800 | 1.2% |
| 30 | Colorado | 14,300 | 1.1% |
| 31 | Arkansas | 14,100 | 1.1% |
| 32 | Mississippi | 13,900 | 1.1% |
| 33 | Kansas | 12,100 | 1.0% |
| 34 | West Virginia | 10,900 | 0.9% |
| 35 | Nevada | 9,200 | 0.7% |
| 36 | Nebraska | 7,500 | 0.6% |
| 37 | Maine | 6,900 | 0.5% |
| 37 | New Mexico | 6,900 | 0.5% |
| 39 | New Hampshire | 5,800 | 0.5% |
| 40 | Rhode Island | 5,600 | 0.4% |
| 40 | Utah | 5,600 | 0.4% |
| 42 | Idaho | 5,000 | 0.4% |
| 43 | Hawaii | 4,700 | 0.4% |
| 44 | Montana | 4,300 | 0.3% |
| 45 | Delaware | 4,000 | 0.3% |
| 46 | South Dakota | 3,600 | 0.3% |
| 47 | North Dakota | 3,100 | 0.2% |
| 48 | Vermont | 2,900 | 0.2% |
| 49 | Wyoming | 2,200 | 0.2% |
| 50 | Alaska | 1,600 | 0.1% |
| | District of Columbia | 2,800 | 0.2% |

Source: American Cancer Society
   "Cancer Facts & Figures 2001" (Copyright 2001, Reprinted with permission from the American Cancer Society)
*These estimates are offered as a rough guide and should not be regarded as definitive. They are calculated according to the distribution of estimated 2001 cancer deaths by state. Totals do not include basal and squamous cell skin cancers or in situ carcinomas except urinary bladder.

# Estimated Rate of New Cancer Cases in 2001

## National Estimated Rate = 450.6 New Cases per 100,000 Population*

ALPHA ORDER

| RANK | STATE | RATE |
|------|-------|------|
| 10 | Alabama | 508.2 |
| 49 | Alaska | 255.2 |
| 41 | Arizona | 415.2 |
| 6 | Arkansas | 527.4 |
| 47 | California | 346.6 |
| 48 | Colorado | 332.5 |
| 25 | Connecticut | 469.8 |
| 9 | Delaware | 510.5 |
| 2 | Florida | 573.1 |
| 44 | Georgia | 379.9 |
| 42 | Hawaii | 387.9 |
| 43 | Idaho | 386.4 |
| 31 | Illinois | 457.4 |
| 20 | Indiana | 481.9 |
| 13 | Iowa | 505.8 |
| 33 | Kansas | 450.1 |
| 7 | Kentucky | 522.0 |
| 18 | Louisiana | 485.6 |
| 4 | Maine | 541.2 |
| 35 | Maryland | 443.7 |
| 14 | Massachusetts | 493.0 |
| 32 | Michigan | 455.8 |
| 40 | Minnesota | 418.7 |
| 16 | Mississippi | 488.6 |
| 11 | Missouri | 507.6 |
| 23 | Montana | 476.6 |
| 37 | Nebraska | 438.3 |
| 30 | Nevada | 460.4 |
| 26 | New Hampshire | 469.3 |
| 15 | New Jersey | 489.6 |
| 45 | New Mexico | 379.3 |
| 36 | New York | 438.4 |
| 29 | North Carolina | 463.4 |
| 19 | North Dakota | 482.7 |
| 8 | Ohio | 512.6 |
| 21 | Oklahoma | 481.1 |
| 17 | Oregon | 488.1 |
| 3 | Pennsylvania | 557.0 |
| 5 | Rhode Island | 534.2 |
| 27 | South Carolina | 468.6 |
| 22 | South Dakota | 476.9 |
| 12 | Tennessee | 506.2 |
| 46 | Texas | 378.4 |
| 50 | Utah | 250.8 |
| 24 | Vermont | 476.3 |
| 38 | Virginia | 430.9 |
| 39 | Washington | 420.8 |
| 1 | West Virginia | 602.8 |
| 28 | Wisconsin | 466.1 |
| 34 | Wyoming | 445.5 |

RANK ORDER

| RANK | STATE | RATE |
|------|-------|------|
| 1 | West Virginia | 602.8 |
| 2 | Florida | 573.1 |
| 3 | Pennsylvania | 557.0 |
| 4 | Maine | 541.2 |
| 5 | Rhode Island | 534.2 |
| 6 | Arkansas | 527.4 |
| 7 | Kentucky | 522.0 |
| 8 | Ohio | 512.6 |
| 9 | Delaware | 510.5 |
| 10 | Alabama | 508.2 |
| 11 | Missouri | 507.6 |
| 12 | Tennessee | 506.2 |
| 13 | Iowa | 505.8 |
| 14 | Massachusetts | 493.0 |
| 15 | New Jersey | 489.6 |
| 16 | Mississippi | 488.6 |
| 17 | Oregon | 488.1 |
| 18 | Louisiana | 485.6 |
| 19 | North Dakota | 482.7 |
| 20 | Indiana | 481.9 |
| 21 | Oklahoma | 481.1 |
| 22 | South Dakota | 476.9 |
| 23 | Montana | 476.6 |
| 24 | Vermont | 476.3 |
| 25 | Connecticut | 469.8 |
| 26 | New Hampshire | 469.3 |
| 27 | South Carolina | 468.6 |
| 28 | Wisconsin | 466.1 |
| 29 | North Carolina | 463.4 |
| 30 | Nevada | 460.4 |
| 31 | Illinois | 457.4 |
| 32 | Michigan | 455.8 |
| 33 | Kansas | 450.1 |
| 34 | Wyoming | 445.5 |
| 35 | Maryland | 443.7 |
| 36 | New York | 438.4 |
| 37 | Nebraska | 438.3 |
| 38 | Virginia | 430.9 |
| 39 | Washington | 420.8 |
| 40 | Minnesota | 418.7 |
| 41 | Arizona | 415.2 |
| 42 | Hawaii | 387.9 |
| 43 | Idaho | 386.4 |
| 44 | Georgia | 379.9 |
| 45 | New Mexico | 379.3 |
| 46 | Texas | 378.4 |
| 47 | California | 346.6 |
| 48 | Colorado | 332.5 |
| 49 | Alaska | 255.2 |
| 50 | Utah | 250.8 |
| | District of Columbia | 489.5 |

Source: Morgan Quitno Press using data from American Cancer Society
    "Cancer Facts & Figures 2001" (Copyright 2001, Reprinted with permission from the American Cancer Society)
*These estimates are offered as a rough guide and should not be regarded as definitive. They are calculated according to the distribution of estimated 2001 cancer deaths by state. Totals do not include basal and squamous cell skin cancers or in situ carcinomas except urinary bladder. Rates calculated using 2000 Census resident population figures

# Deaths by Cerebrovascular Diseases in 1998

## National Total = 158,448 Deaths*

ALPHA ORDER

| RANK | STATE | DEATHS | % of USA |
|---|---|---|---|
| 19 | Alabama | 2,929 | 1.8% |
| 50 | Alaska | 153 | 0.1% |
| 26 | Arizona | 2,472 | 1.6% |
| 27 | Arkansas | 2,355 | 1.5% |
| 1 | California | 16,512 | 10.4% |
| 33 | Colorado | 1,740 | 1.1% |
| 30 | Connecticut | 1,947 | 1.2% |
| 47 | Delaware | 367 | 0.2% |
| 2 | Florida | 10,085 | 6.4% |
| 10 | Georgia | 4,158 | 2.6% |
| 41 | Hawaii | 658 | 0.4% |
| 40 | Idaho | 704 | 0.4% |
| 6 | Illinois | 7,172 | 4.5% |
| 14 | Indiana | 3,892 | 2.5% |
| 29 | Iowa | 2,208 | 1.4% |
| 31 | Kansas | 1,831 | 1.2% |
| 25 | Kentucky | 2,488 | 1.6% |
| 24 | Louisiana | 2,526 | 1.6% |
| 38 | Maine | 788 | 0.5% |
| 22 | Maryland | 2,636 | 1.7% |
| 18 | Massachusetts | 3,322 | 2.1% |
| 8 | Michigan | 5,768 | 3.6% |
| 21 | Minnesota | 2,858 | 1.8% |
| 32 | Mississippi | 1,816 | 1.1% |
| 13 | Missouri | 3,898 | 2.5% |
| 44 | Montana | 579 | 0.4% |
| 35 | Nebraska | 1,158 | 0.7% |
| 36 | Nevada | 812 | 0.5% |
| 42 | New Hampshire | 618 | 0.4% |
| 11 | New Jersey | 4,094 | 2.6% |
| 39 | New Mexico | 719 | 0.5% |
| 5 | New York | 7,776 | 4.9% |
| 9 | North Carolina | 5,439 | 3.4% |
| 46 | North Dakota | 461 | 0.3% |
| 7 | Ohio | 6,719 | 4.2% |
| 28 | Oklahoma | 2,290 | 1.4% |
| 23 | Oregon | 2,621 | 1.7% |
| 4 | Pennsylvania | 8,224 | 5.2% |
| 43 | Rhode Island | 591 | 0.4% |
| 20 | South Carolina | 2,900 | 1.8% |
| 45 | South Dakota | 538 | 0.3% |
| 12 | Tennessee | 3,958 | 2.5% |
| 3 | Texas | 9,827 | 6.2% |
| 37 | Utah | 796 | 0.5% |
| 48 | Vermont | 330 | 0.2% |
| 15 | Virginia | 3,820 | 2.4% |
| 17 | Washington | 3,428 | 2.2% |
| 34 | West Virginia | 1,215 | 0.8% |
| 16 | Wisconsin | 3,648 | 2.3% |
| 49 | Wyoming | 289 | 0.2% |

RANK ORDER

| RANK | STATE | DEATHS | % of USA |
|---|---|---|---|
| 1 | California | 16,512 | 10.4% |
| 2 | Florida | 10,085 | 6.4% |
| 3 | Texas | 9,827 | 6.2% |
| 4 | Pennsylvania | 8,224 | 5.2% |
| 5 | New York | 7,776 | 4.9% |
| 6 | Illinois | 7,172 | 4.5% |
| 7 | Ohio | 6,719 | 4.2% |
| 8 | Michigan | 5,768 | 3.6% |
| 9 | North Carolina | 5,439 | 3.4% |
| 10 | Georgia | 4,158 | 2.6% |
| 11 | New Jersey | 4,094 | 2.6% |
| 12 | Tennessee | 3,958 | 2.5% |
| 13 | Missouri | 3,898 | 2.5% |
| 14 | Indiana | 3,892 | 2.5% |
| 15 | Virginia | 3,820 | 2.4% |
| 16 | Wisconsin | 3,648 | 2.3% |
| 17 | Washington | 3,428 | 2.2% |
| 18 | Massachusetts | 3,322 | 2.1% |
| 19 | Alabama | 2,929 | 1.8% |
| 20 | South Carolina | 2,900 | 1.8% |
| 21 | Minnesota | 2,858 | 1.8% |
| 22 | Maryland | 2,636 | 1.7% |
| 23 | Oregon | 2,621 | 1.7% |
| 24 | Louisiana | 2,526 | 1.6% |
| 25 | Kentucky | 2,488 | 1.6% |
| 26 | Arizona | 2,472 | 1.6% |
| 27 | Arkansas | 2,355 | 1.5% |
| 28 | Oklahoma | 2,290 | 1.4% |
| 29 | Iowa | 2,208 | 1.4% |
| 30 | Connecticut | 1,947 | 1.2% |
| 31 | Kansas | 1,831 | 1.2% |
| 32 | Mississippi | 1,816 | 1.1% |
| 33 | Colorado | 1,740 | 1.1% |
| 34 | West Virginia | 1,215 | 0.8% |
| 35 | Nebraska | 1,158 | 0.7% |
| 36 | Nevada | 812 | 0.5% |
| 37 | Utah | 796 | 0.5% |
| 38 | Maine | 788 | 0.5% |
| 39 | New Mexico | 719 | 0.5% |
| 40 | Idaho | 704 | 0.4% |
| 41 | Hawaii | 658 | 0.4% |
| 42 | New Hampshire | 618 | 0.4% |
| 43 | Rhode Island | 591 | 0.4% |
| 44 | Montana | 579 | 0.4% |
| 45 | South Dakota | 538 | 0.3% |
| 46 | North Dakota | 461 | 0.3% |
| 47 | Delaware | 367 | 0.2% |
| 48 | Vermont | 330 | 0.2% |
| 49 | Wyoming | 289 | 0.2% |
| 50 | Alaska | 153 | 0.1% |
| | District of Columbia | 315 | 0.2% |

Source: U.S. Department of Health and Human Services, National Center for Health Statistics
        "National Vital Statistics Reports" (Vol. 48, No. 11, July 24, 2000)
*Final data by state of residence.  Cerebrovascular diseases include stroke and other disorders of the blood vessels of the brain.

# Age-Adjusted Death Rate by Cerebrovascular Diseases in 1998

## National Rate = 25.1 Deaths per 100,000 Population*

ALPHA ORDER

RANK ORDER

| RANK | STATE | RATE | RANK | STATE | RATE |
|---|---|---|---|---|---|
| 7 | Alabama | 30.6 | 1 | South Carolina | 37.0 |
| 22 | Alaska | 25.2 | 2 | Arkansas | 35.3 |
| 38 | Arizona | 22.5 | 3 | Mississippi | 33.4 |
| 2 | Arkansas | 35.3 | 4 | North Carolina | 33.1 |
| 25 | California | 25.0 | 5 | Tennessee | 32.6 |
| 43 | Colorado | 21.8 | 6 | Georgia | 31.6 |
| 45 | Connecticut | 20.9 | 7 | Alabama | 30.6 |
| 33 | Delaware | 23.2 | 8 | Louisiana | 30.0 |
| 40 | Florida | 22.0 | 9 | Oregon | 29.0 |
| 6 | Georgia | 31.6 | 10 | Indiana | 28.1 |
| 31 | Hawaii | 24.1 | 11 | Oklahoma | 27.7 |
| 26 | Idaho | 24.7 | 12 | Kentucky | 27.6 |
| 20 | Illinois | 25.4 | 13 | Missouri | 27.3 |
| 10 | Indiana | 28.1 | 14 | Virginia | 27.2 |
| 36 | Iowa | 23.1 | 15 | Texas | 26.4 |
| 26 | Kansas | 24.7 | 16 | Wyoming | 26.2 |
| 12 | Kentucky | 27.6 | 17 | Wisconsin | 26.0 |
| 8 | Louisiana | 30.0 | 18 | Michigan | 25.9 |
| 37 | Maine | 22.6 | 19 | Washington | 25.6 |
| 24 | Maryland | 25.1 | 20 | Illinois | 25.4 |
| 49 | Massachusetts | 18.6 | 21 | Nevada | 25.3 |
| 18 | Michigan | 25.9 | 22 | Alaska | 25.2 |
| 42 | Minnesota | 21.9 | 22 | Nebraska | 25.2 |
| 3 | Mississippi | 33.4 | 24 | Maryland | 25.1 |
| 13 | Missouri | 27.3 | 25 | California | 25.0 |
| 33 | Montana | 23.2 | 26 | Idaho | 24.7 |
| 22 | Nebraska | 25.2 | 26 | Kansas | 24.7 |
| 21 | Nevada | 25.3 | 26 | West Virginia | 24.7 |
| 46 | New Hampshire | 20.5 | 29 | Ohio | 24.3 |
| 44 | New Jersey | 21.1 | 29 | South Dakota | 24.3 |
| 48 | New Mexico | 19.6 | 31 | Hawaii | 24.1 |
| 50 | New York | 18.3 | 32 | Pennsylvania | 23.5 |
| 4 | North Carolina | 33.1 | 33 | Delaware | 23.2 |
| 38 | North Dakota | 22.5 | 33 | Montana | 23.2 |
| 29 | Ohio | 24.3 | 33 | Vermont | 23.2 |
| 11 | Oklahoma | 27.7 | 36 | Iowa | 23.1 |
| 9 | Oregon | 29.0 | 37 | Maine | 22.6 |
| 32 | Pennsylvania | 23.5 | 38 | Arizona | 22.5 |
| 47 | Rhode Island | 20.0 | 38 | North Dakota | 22.5 |
| 1 | South Carolina | 37.0 | 40 | Florida | 22.0 |
| 29 | South Dakota | 24.3 | 40 | Utah | 22.0 |
| 5 | Tennessee | 32.6 | 42 | Minnesota | 21.9 |
| 15 | Texas | 26.4 | 43 | Colorado | 21.8 |
| 40 | Utah | 22.0 | 44 | New Jersey | 21.1 |
| 33 | Vermont | 23.2 | 45 | Connecticut | 20.9 |
| 14 | Virginia | 27.2 | 46 | New Hampshire | 20.5 |
| 19 | Washington | 25.6 | 47 | Rhode Island | 20.0 |
| 26 | West Virginia | 24.7 | 48 | New Mexico | 19.6 |
| 17 | Wisconsin | 26.0 | 49 | Massachusetts | 18.6 |
| 16 | Wyoming | 26.2 | 50 | New York | 18.3 |
| | | | | District of Columbia | 28.4 |

Source: U.S. Department of Health and Human Services, National Center for Health Statistics
    "National Vital Statistics Reports" (Vol. 48, No. 11, July 24, 2000)
*Final data by state of residence.  Cerebrovascular diseases include stroke and other disorders of the blood
vessels of the brain.

# Deaths by Chronic Obstructive Pulmonary Diseases in 1998

## National Total = 112,584 Deaths*

ALPHA ORDER

| RANK | STATE | DEATHS | % of USA |
|------|-------|--------|----------|
| 20 | Alabama | 1,985 | 1.8% |
| 50 | Alaska | 112 | 0.1% |
| 18 | Arizona | 2,401 | 2.1% |
| 30 | Arkansas | 1,244 | 1.1% |
| 1 | California | 12,341 | 11.0% |
| 22 | Colorado | 1,836 | 1.6% |
| 31 | Connecticut | 1,243 | 1.1% |
| 44 | Delaware | 327 | 0.3% |
| 2 | Florida | 8,188 | 7.3% |
| 12 | Georgia | 2,744 | 2.4% |
| 47 | Hawaii | 266 | 0.2% |
| 40 | Idaho | 540 | 0.5% |
| 7 | Illinois | 4,542 | 4.0% |
| 11 | Indiana | 2,762 | 2.5% |
| 29 | Iowa | 1,439 | 1.3% |
| 32 | Kansas | 1,198 | 1.1% |
| 21 | Kentucky | 1,963 | 1.7% |
| 28 | Louisiana | 1,566 | 1.4% |
| 37 | Maine | 769 | 0.7% |
| 25 | Maryland | 1,708 | 1.5% |
| 15 | Massachusetts | 2,546 | 2.3% |
| 8 | Michigan | 3,813 | 3.4% |
| 24 | Minnesota | 1,745 | 1.5% |
| 34 | Mississippi | 1,141 | 1.0% |
| 13 | Missouri | 2,725 | 2.4% |
| 41 | Montana | 505 | 0.4% |
| 36 | Nebraska | 784 | 0.7% |
| 35 | Nevada | 947 | 0.8% |
| 39 | New Hampshire | 572 | 0.5% |
| 10 | New Jersey | 2,794 | 2.5% |
| 38 | New Mexico | 764 | 0.7% |
| 4 | New York | 6,430 | 5.7% |
| 9 | North Carolina | 3,204 | 2.8% |
| 46 | North Dakota | 272 | 0.2% |
| 6 | Ohio | 5,404 | 4.8% |
| 23 | Oklahoma | 1,750 | 1.6% |
| 26 | Oregon | 1,612 | 1.4% |
| 5 | Pennsylvania | 5,596 | 5.0% |
| 43 | Rhode Island | 454 | 0.4% |
| 27 | South Carolina | 1,568 | 1.4% |
| 45 | South Dakota | 317 | 0.3% |
| 14 | Tennessee | 2,641 | 2.3% |
| 3 | Texas | 6,603 | 5.9% |
| 42 | Utah | 483 | 0.4% |
| 48 | Vermont | 250 | 0.2% |
| 16 | Virginia | 2,481 | 2.2% |
| 17 | Washington | 2,403 | 2.1% |
| 33 | West Virginia | 1,146 | 1.0% |
| 19 | Wisconsin | 2,062 | 1.8% |
| 49 | Wyoming | 240 | 0.2% |

RANK ORDER

| RANK | STATE | DEATHS | % of USA |
|------|-------|--------|----------|
| 1 | California | 12,341 | 11.0% |
| 2 | Florida | 8,188 | 7.3% |
| 3 | Texas | 6,603 | 5.9% |
| 4 | New York | 6,430 | 5.7% |
| 5 | Pennsylvania | 5,596 | 5.0% |
| 6 | Ohio | 5,404 | 4.8% |
| 7 | Illinois | 4,542 | 4.0% |
| 8 | Michigan | 3,813 | 3.4% |
| 9 | North Carolina | 3,204 | 2.8% |
| 10 | New Jersey | 2,794 | 2.5% |
| 11 | Indiana | 2,762 | 2.5% |
| 12 | Georgia | 2,744 | 2.4% |
| 13 | Missouri | 2,725 | 2.4% |
| 14 | Tennessee | 2,641 | 2.3% |
| 15 | Massachusetts | 2,546 | 2.3% |
| 16 | Virginia | 2,481 | 2.2% |
| 17 | Washington | 2,403 | 2.1% |
| 18 | Arizona | 2,401 | 2.1% |
| 19 | Wisconsin | 2,062 | 1.8% |
| 20 | Alabama | 1,985 | 1.8% |
| 21 | Kentucky | 1,963 | 1.7% |
| 22 | Colorado | 1,836 | 1.6% |
| 23 | Oklahoma | 1,750 | 1.6% |
| 24 | Minnesota | 1,745 | 1.5% |
| 25 | Maryland | 1,708 | 1.5% |
| 26 | Oregon | 1,612 | 1.4% |
| 27 | South Carolina | 1,568 | 1.4% |
| 28 | Louisiana | 1,566 | 1.4% |
| 29 | Iowa | 1,439 | 1.3% |
| 30 | Arkansas | 1,244 | 1.1% |
| 31 | Connecticut | 1,243 | 1.1% |
| 32 | Kansas | 1,198 | 1.1% |
| 33 | West Virginia | 1,146 | 1.0% |
| 34 | Mississippi | 1,141 | 1.0% |
| 35 | Nevada | 947 | 0.8% |
| 36 | Nebraska | 784 | 0.7% |
| 37 | Maine | 769 | 0.7% |
| 38 | New Mexico | 764 | 0.7% |
| 39 | New Hampshire | 572 | 0.5% |
| 40 | Idaho | 540 | 0.5% |
| 41 | Montana | 505 | 0.4% |
| 42 | Utah | 483 | 0.4% |
| 43 | Rhode Island | 454 | 0.4% |
| 44 | Delaware | 327 | 0.3% |
| 45 | South Dakota | 317 | 0.3% |
| 46 | North Dakota | 272 | 0.2% |
| 47 | Hawaii | 266 | 0.2% |
| 48 | Vermont | 250 | 0.2% |
| 49 | Wyoming | 240 | 0.2% |
| 50 | Alaska | 112 | 0.1% |
| | District of Columbia | 158 | 0.1% |

Source: U.S. Department of Health and Human Services, National Center for Health Statistics
    "National Vital Statistics Reports" (Vol. 48, No. 11, July 24, 2000)
*Final data by state of residence. Chronic obstructive pulmonary diseases are diseases of the lungs including bronchitis, emphysema and asthma. Includes allied conditions.

# Age-Adjusted Death Rate by Chronic Obstructive Pulmonary Diseases in 1998

## National Rate = 21.3 Deaths per 100,000 Population*

ALPHA ORDER

RANK ORDER

| RANK | STATE | RATE | | RANK | STATE | RATE |
|------|-------|------|---|------|-------|------|
| 20 | Alabama | 23.6 | | 1 | Nevada | 32.1 |
| 33 | Alaska | 20.8 | | 2 | Colorado | 28.5 |
| 11 | Arizona | 25.4 | | 3 | Wyoming | 28.4 |
| 20 | Arkansas | 23.6 | | 4 | West Virginia | 27.6 |
| 28 | California | 21.5 | | 5 | Maine | 26.9 |
| 2 | Colorado | 28.5 | | 6 | Kentucky | 26.7 |
| 48 | Connecticut | 16.0 | | 6 | Montana | 26.7 |
| 29 | Delaware | 21.2 | | 8 | Oklahoma | 26.4 |
| 36 | Florida | 20.2 | | 9 | Tennessee | 26.3 |
| 15 | Georgia | 23.8 | | 10 | New Hampshire | 26.1 |
| 50 | Hawaii | 10.8 | | 11 | Arizona | 25.4 |
| 12 | Idaho | 25.1 | | 12 | Idaho | 25.1 |
| 37 | Illinois | 19.9 | | 13 | Indiana | 24.6 |
| 13 | Indiana | 24.6 | | 14 | Missouri | 24.4 |
| 31 | Iowa | 21.0 | | 15 | Georgia | 23.8 |
| 25 | Kansas | 22.3 | | 15 | Mississippi | 23.8 |
| 6 | Kentucky | 26.7 | | 15 | Oregon | 23.8 |
| 32 | Louisiana | 20.9 | | 15 | South Carolina | 23.8 |
| 5 | Maine | 26.9 | | 19 | New Mexico | 23.7 |
| 44 | Maryland | 18.1 | | 20 | Alabama | 23.6 |
| 42 | Massachusetts | 18.4 | | 20 | Arkansas | 23.6 |
| 35 | Michigan | 20.7 | | 20 | Ohio | 23.6 |
| 45 | Minnesota | 17.9 | | 23 | North Carolina | 23.3 |
| 15 | Mississippi | 23.8 | | 24 | Washington | 22.9 |
| 14 | Missouri | 24.4 | | 25 | Kansas | 22.3 |
| 6 | Montana | 26.7 | | 26 | Nebraska | 21.8 |
| 26 | Nebraska | 21.8 | | 26 | Vermont | 21.8 |
| 1 | Nevada | 32.1 | | 28 | California | 21.5 |
| 10 | New Hampshire | 26.1 | | 29 | Delaware | 21.2 |
| 49 | New Jersey | 15.6 | | 30 | Texas | 21.1 |
| 19 | New Mexico | 23.7 | | 31 | Iowa | 21.0 |
| 47 | New York | 17.1 | | 32 | Louisiana | 20.9 |
| 23 | North Carolina | 23.3 | | 33 | Alaska | 20.8 |
| 43 | North Dakota | 18.3 | | 33 | Virginia | 20.8 |
| 20 | Ohio | 23.6 | | 35 | Michigan | 20.7 |
| 8 | Oklahoma | 26.4 | | 36 | Florida | 20.2 |
| 15 | Oregon | 23.8 | | 37 | Illinois | 19.9 |
| 38 | Pennsylvania | 19.1 | | 38 | Pennsylvania | 19.1 |
| 38 | Rhode Island | 19.1 | | 38 | Rhode Island | 19.1 |
| 15 | South Carolina | 23.8 | | 40 | South Dakota | 18.7 |
| 40 | South Dakota | 18.7 | | 41 | Wisconsin | 18.5 |
| 9 | Tennessee | 26.3 | | 42 | Massachusetts | 18.4 |
| 30 | Texas | 21.1 | | 43 | North Dakota | 18.3 |
| 46 | Utah | 17.3 | | 44 | Maryland | 18.1 |
| 26 | Vermont | 21.8 | | 45 | Minnesota | 17.9 |
| 33 | Virginia | 20.8 | | 46 | Utah | 17.3 |
| 24 | Washington | 22.9 | | 47 | New York | 17.1 |
| 4 | West Virginia | 27.6 | | 48 | Connecticut | 16.0 |
| 41 | Wisconsin | 18.5 | | 49 | New Jersey | 15.6 |
| 3 | Wyoming | 28.4 | | 50 | Hawaii | 10.8 |
| | | | | | District of Columbia | 15.7 |

Source: U.S. Department of Health and Human Services, National Center for Health Statistics
"National Vital Statistics Reports" (Vol. 48, No. 11, July 24, 2000)
*Final data by state of residence. Chronic obstructive pulmonary diseases are diseases of the lungs including
bronchitis, emphysema and asthma. Includes allied conditions.

# Deaths by Diseases of the Heart in 1998

## National Total = 724,859 Deaths*

ALPHA ORDER

ALPHA ORDER

| RANK | STATE | DEATHS | % of USA |
|------|-------|--------|----------|
| 18 | Alabama | 13,480 | 1.9% |
| 50 | Alaska | 564 | 0.1% |
| 24 | Arizona | 10,543 | 1.5% |
| 30 | Arkansas | 8,461 | 1.2% |
| 1 | California | 69,747 | 9.6% |
| 34 | Colorado | 6,644 | 0.9% |
| 26 | Connecticut | 9,639 | 1.3% |
| 46 | Delaware | 1,917 | 0.3% |
| 3 | Florida | 51,131 | 7.1% |
| 12 | Georgia | 17,964 | 2.5% |
| 42 | Hawaii | 2,458 | 0.3% |
| 43 | Idaho | 2,422 | 0.3% |
| 7 | Illinois | 32,816 | 4.5% |
| 14 | Indiana | 16,483 | 2.3% |
| 29 | Iowa | 9,148 | 1.3% |
| 32 | Kansas | 7,207 | 1.0% |
| 20 | Kentucky | 11,924 | 1.6% |
| 21 | Louisiana | 11,866 | 1.6% |
| 37 | Maine | 3,562 | 0.5% |
| 19 | Maryland | 11,939 | 1.6% |
| 16 | Massachusetts | 16,007 | 2.2% |
| 8 | Michigan | 28,005 | 3.9% |
| 28 | Minnesota | 9,372 | 1.3% |
| 27 | Mississippi | 9,539 | 1.3% |
| 11 | Missouri | 17,968 | 2.5% |
| 45 | Montana | 2,006 | 0.3% |
| 35 | Nebraska | 4,733 | 0.7% |
| 36 | Nevada | 4,120 | 0.6% |
| 41 | New Hampshire | 2,833 | 0.4% |
| 9 | New Jersey | 23,384 | 3.2% |
| 38 | New Mexico | 3,221 | 0.4% |
| 2 | New York | 59,531 | 8.2% |
| 10 | North Carolina | 19,489 | 2.7% |
| 47 | North Dakota | 1,738 | 0.2% |
| 6 | Ohio | 33,355 | 4.6% |
| 23 | Oklahoma | 11,297 | 1.6% |
| 31 | Oregon | 7,290 | 1.0% |
| 5 | Pennsylvania | 41,413 | 5.7% |
| 39 | Rhode Island | 3,070 | 0.4% |
| 25 | South Carolina | 10,026 | 1.4% |
| 44 | South Dakota | 2,108 | 0.3% |
| 13 | Tennessee | 16,516 | 2.3% |
| 4 | Texas | 42,788 | 5.9% |
| 40 | Utah | 2,881 | 0.4% |
| 48 | Vermont | 1,434 | 0.2% |
| 15 | Virginia | 16,022 | 2.2% |
| 22 | Washington | 11,517 | 1.6% |
| 33 | West Virginia | 6,883 | 0.9% |
| 17 | Wisconsin | 13,685 | 1.9% |
| 49 | Wyoming | 1,051 | 0.1% |

RANK ORDER

| RANK | STATE | DEATHS | % of USA |
|------|-------|--------|----------|
| 1 | California | 69,747 | 9.6% |
| 2 | New York | 59,531 | 8.2% |
| 3 | Florida | 51,131 | 7.1% |
| 4 | Texas | 42,788 | 5.9% |
| 5 | Pennsylvania | 41,413 | 5.7% |
| 6 | Ohio | 33,355 | 4.6% |
| 7 | Illinois | 32,816 | 4.5% |
| 8 | Michigan | 28,005 | 3.9% |
| 9 | New Jersey | 23,384 | 3.2% |
| 10 | North Carolina | 19,489 | 2.7% |
| 11 | Missouri | 17,968 | 2.5% |
| 12 | Georgia | 17,964 | 2.5% |
| 13 | Tennessee | 16,516 | 2.3% |
| 14 | Indiana | 16,483 | 2.3% |
| 15 | Virginia | 16,022 | 2.2% |
| 16 | Massachusetts | 16,007 | 2.2% |
| 17 | Wisconsin | 13,685 | 1.9% |
| 18 | Alabama | 13,480 | 1.9% |
| 19 | Maryland | 11,939 | 1.6% |
| 20 | Kentucky | 11,924 | 1.6% |
| 21 | Louisiana | 11,866 | 1.6% |
| 22 | Washington | 11,517 | 1.6% |
| 23 | Oklahoma | 11,297 | 1.6% |
| 24 | Arizona | 10,543 | 1.5% |
| 25 | South Carolina | 10,026 | 1.4% |
| 26 | Connecticut | 9,639 | 1.3% |
| 27 | Mississippi | 9,539 | 1.3% |
| 28 | Minnesota | 9,372 | 1.3% |
| 29 | Iowa | 9,148 | 1.3% |
| 30 | Arkansas | 8,461 | 1.2% |
| 31 | Oregon | 7,290 | 1.0% |
| 32 | Kansas | 7,207 | 1.0% |
| 33 | West Virginia | 6,883 | 0.9% |
| 34 | Colorado | 6,644 | 0.9% |
| 35 | Nebraska | 4,733 | 0.7% |
| 36 | Nevada | 4,120 | 0.6% |
| 37 | Maine | 3,562 | 0.5% |
| 38 | New Mexico | 3,221 | 0.4% |
| 39 | Rhode Island | 3,070 | 0.4% |
| 40 | Utah | 2,881 | 0.4% |
| 41 | New Hampshire | 2,833 | 0.4% |
| 42 | Hawaii | 2,458 | 0.3% |
| 43 | Idaho | 2,422 | 0.3% |
| 44 | South Dakota | 2,108 | 0.3% |
| 45 | Montana | 2,006 | 0.3% |
| 46 | Delaware | 1,917 | 0.3% |
| 47 | North Dakota | 1,738 | 0.2% |
| 48 | Vermont | 1,434 | 0.2% |
| 49 | Wyoming | 1,051 | 0.1% |
| 50 | Alaska | 564 | 0.1% |
| | District of Columbia | 1,662 | 0.2% |

*Source: U.S. Department of Health and Human Services, National Center for Health Statistics
"National Vital Statistics Reports" (Vol. 48, No. 11, July 24, 2000)*
*Final data by state of residence.*

# Age-Adjusted Death Rate by Diseases of the Heart in 1998

## National Rate = 126.6 Deaths per 100,000 Population*

ALPHA ORDER

| RANK | STATE | RATE |
|------|-------|------|
| 4 | Alabama | 152.3 |
| 46 | Alaska | 96.5 |
| 37 | Arizona | 109.2 |
| 8 | Arkansas | 147.6 |
| 33 | California | 113.1 |
| 48 | Colorado | 92.9 |
| 29 | Connecticut | 115.9 |
| 22 | Delaware | 127.4 |
| 26 | Florida | 118.0 |
| 9 | Georgia | 147.2 |
| 42 | Hawaii | 100.4 |
| 44 | Idaho | 96.8 |
| 19 | Illinois | 131.5 |
| 16 | Indiana | 134.5 |
| 28 | Iowa | 117.4 |
| 30 | Kansas | 114.8 |
| 7 | Kentucky | 148.7 |
| 6 | Louisiana | 150.0 |
| 25 | Maine | 118.1 |
| 23 | Maryland | 124.2 |
| 39 | Massachusetts | 106.6 |
| 13 | Michigan | 138.8 |
| 49 | Minnesota | 88.4 |
| 1 | Mississippi | 181.4 |
| 11 | Missouri | 142.7 |
| 43 | Montana | 100.2 |
| 36 | Nebraska | 111.5 |
| 12 | Nevada | 139.7 |
| 30 | New Hampshire | 114.8 |
| 24 | New Jersey | 121.4 |
| 45 | New Mexico | 96.6 |
| 13 | New York | 138.8 |
| 17 | North Carolina | 132.9 |
| 38 | North Dakota | 107.5 |
| 15 | Ohio | 136.5 |
| 5 | Oklahoma | 150.8 |
| 46 | Oregon | 96.5 |
| 18 | Pennsylvania | 132.3 |
| 27 | Rhode Island | 117.7 |
| 10 | South Carolina | 143.0 |
| 32 | South Dakota | 114.3 |
| 3 | Tennessee | 153.5 |
| 21 | Texas | 127.9 |
| 50 | Utah | 87.4 |
| 40 | Vermont | 105.2 |
| 20 | Virginia | 128.0 |
| 41 | Washington | 100.7 |
| 2 | West Virginia | 160.9 |
| 34 | Wisconsin | 112.9 |
| 35 | Wyoming | 111.6 |

RANK ORDER

| RANK | STATE | RATE |
|------|-------|------|
| 1 | Mississippi | 181.4 |
| 2 | West Virginia | 160.9 |
| 3 | Tennessee | 153.5 |
| 4 | Alabama | 152.3 |
| 5 | Oklahoma | 150.8 |
| 6 | Louisiana | 150.0 |
| 7 | Kentucky | 148.7 |
| 8 | Arkansas | 147.6 |
| 9 | Georgia | 147.2 |
| 10 | South Carolina | 143.0 |
| 11 | Missouri | 142.7 |
| 12 | Nevada | 139.7 |
| 13 | Michigan | 138.8 |
| 13 | New York | 138.8 |
| 15 | Ohio | 136.5 |
| 16 | Indiana | 134.5 |
| 17 | North Carolina | 132.9 |
| 18 | Pennsylvania | 132.3 |
| 19 | Illinois | 131.5 |
| 20 | Virginia | 128.0 |
| 21 | Texas | 127.9 |
| 22 | Delaware | 127.4 |
| 23 | Maryland | 124.2 |
| 24 | New Jersey | 121.4 |
| 25 | Maine | 118.1 |
| 26 | Florida | 118.0 |
| 27 | Rhode Island | 117.7 |
| 28 | Iowa | 117.4 |
| 29 | Connecticut | 115.9 |
| 30 | Kansas | 114.8 |
| 30 | New Hampshire | 114.8 |
| 32 | South Dakota | 114.3 |
| 33 | California | 113.1 |
| 34 | Wisconsin | 112.9 |
| 35 | Wyoming | 111.6 |
| 36 | Nebraska | 111.5 |
| 37 | Arizona | 109.2 |
| 38 | North Dakota | 107.5 |
| 39 | Massachusetts | 106.6 |
| 40 | Vermont | 105.2 |
| 41 | Washington | 100.7 |
| 42 | Hawaii | 100.4 |
| 43 | Montana | 100.2 |
| 44 | Idaho | 96.8 |
| 45 | New Mexico | 96.6 |
| 46 | Alaska | 96.5 |
| 46 | Oregon | 96.5 |
| 48 | Colorado | 92.9 |
| 49 | Minnesota | 88.4 |
| 50 | Utah | 87.4 |
| | District of Columbia | 161.5 |

Source: U.S. Department of Health and Human Services, National Center for Health Statistics
"National Vital Statistics Reports" (Vol. 48, No. 11, July 24, 2000)
*Final data by state of residence.

# Deaths by Suicide in 1998

## National Total = 30,575 Suicides*

ALPHA ORDER

| RANK | STATE | SUICIDES | % of USA |
|---|---|---|---|
| 20 | Alabama | 569 | 1.9% |
| 43 | Alaska | 129 | 0.4% |
| 12 | Arizona | 804 | 2.6% |
| 30 | Arkansas | 344 | 1.1% |
| 1 | California | 3,415 | 11.2% |
| 17 | Colorado | 611 | 2.0% |
| 36 | Connecticut | 257 | 0.8% |
| 50 | Delaware | 68 | 0.2% |
| 2 | Florida | 2,172 | 7.1% |
| 11 | Georgia | 822 | 2.7% |
| 44 | Hawaii | 116 | 0.4% |
| 39 | Idaho | 201 | 0.7% |
| 7 | Illinois | 1,036 | 3.4% |
| 15 | Indiana | 699 | 2.3% |
| 32 | Iowa | 329 | 1.1% |
| 34 | Kansas | 325 | 1.1% |
| 22 | Kentucky | 526 | 1.7% |
| 25 | Louisiana | 480 | 1.6% |
| 40 | Maine | 196 | 0.6% |
| 24 | Maryland | 497 | 1.6% |
| 23 | Massachusetts | 506 | 1.7% |
| 8 | Michigan | 969 | 3.2% |
| 27 | Minnesota | 459 | 1.5% |
| 32 | Mississippi | 329 | 1.1% |
| 16 | Missouri | 698 | 2.3% |
| 41 | Montana | 158 | 0.5% |
| 38 | Nebraska | 204 | 0.7% |
| 29 | Nevada | 397 | 1.3% |
| 42 | New Hampshire | 154 | 0.5% |
| 19 | New Jersey | 581 | 1.9% |
| 35 | New Mexico | 297 | 1.0% |
| 5 | New York | 1,364 | 4.5% |
| 9 | North Carolina | 857 | 2.8% |
| 49 | North Dakota | 72 | 0.2% |
| 6 | Ohio | 1,108 | 3.6% |
| 26 | Oklahoma | 471 | 1.5% |
| 21 | Oregon | 545 | 1.8% |
| 4 | Pennsylvania | 1,370 | 4.5% |
| 47 | Rhode Island | 86 | 0.3% |
| 28 | South Carolina | 449 | 1.5% |
| 45 | South Dakota | 115 | 0.4% |
| 13 | Tennessee | 744 | 2.4% |
| 3 | Texas | 2,133 | 7.0% |
| 31 | Utah | 336 | 1.1% |
| 47 | Vermont | 86 | 0.3% |
| 10 | Virginia | 827 | 2.7% |
| 14 | Washington | 708 | 2.3% |
| 37 | West Virginia | 232 | 0.8% |
| 18 | Wisconsin | 594 | 1.9% |
| 46 | Wyoming | 87 | 0.3% |

RANK ORDER

| RANK | STATE | SUICIDES | % of USA |
|---|---|---|---|
| 1 | California | 3,415 | 11.2% |
| 2 | Florida | 2,172 | 7.1% |
| 3 | Texas | 2,133 | 7.0% |
| 4 | Pennsylvania | 1,370 | 4.5% |
| 5 | New York | 1,364 | 4.5% |
| 6 | Ohio | 1,108 | 3.6% |
| 7 | Illinois | 1,036 | 3.4% |
| 8 | Michigan | 969 | 3.2% |
| 9 | North Carolina | 857 | 2.8% |
| 10 | Virginia | 827 | 2.7% |
| 11 | Georgia | 822 | 2.7% |
| 12 | Arizona | 804 | 2.6% |
| 13 | Tennessee | 744 | 2.4% |
| 14 | Washington | 708 | 2.3% |
| 15 | Indiana | 699 | 2.3% |
| 16 | Missouri | 698 | 2.3% |
| 17 | Colorado | 611 | 2.0% |
| 18 | Wisconsin | 594 | 1.9% |
| 19 | New Jersey | 581 | 1.9% |
| 20 | Alabama | 569 | 1.9% |
| 21 | Oregon | 545 | 1.8% |
| 22 | Kentucky | 526 | 1.7% |
| 23 | Massachusetts | 506 | 1.7% |
| 24 | Maryland | 497 | 1.6% |
| 25 | Louisiana | 480 | 1.6% |
| 26 | Oklahoma | 471 | 1.5% |
| 27 | Minnesota | 459 | 1.5% |
| 28 | South Carolina | 449 | 1.5% |
| 29 | Nevada | 397 | 1.3% |
| 30 | Arkansas | 344 | 1.1% |
| 31 | Utah | 336 | 1.1% |
| 32 | Iowa | 329 | 1.1% |
| 32 | Mississippi | 329 | 1.1% |
| 34 | Kansas | 325 | 1.1% |
| 35 | New Mexico | 297 | 1.0% |
| 36 | Connecticut | 257 | 0.8% |
| 37 | West Virginia | 232 | 0.8% |
| 38 | Nebraska | 204 | 0.7% |
| 39 | Idaho | 201 | 0.7% |
| 40 | Maine | 196 | 0.6% |
| 41 | Montana | 158 | 0.5% |
| 42 | New Hampshire | 154 | 0.5% |
| 43 | Alaska | 129 | 0.4% |
| 44 | Hawaii | 116 | 0.4% |
| 45 | South Dakota | 115 | 0.4% |
| 46 | Wyoming | 87 | 0.3% |
| 47 | Rhode Island | 86 | 0.3% |
| 47 | Vermont | 86 | 0.3% |
| 49 | North Dakota | 72 | 0.2% |
| 50 | Delaware | 68 | 0.2% |
| | District of Columbia | 43 | 0.1% |

Source: U.S. Department of Health and Human Services, National Center for Health Statistics
"National Vital Statistics Reports" (Vol. 48, No. 11, July 24, 2000)
*Final data by state of residence.

# Age-Adjusted Death Rate by Suicide in 1998

## National Rate = 10.4 Suicides per 100,000 Population*

ALPHA ORDER

| RANK | STATE | RATE |
|------|-------|------|
| 20 | Alabama | 12.0 |
| 1 | Alaska | 22.1 |
| 7 | Arizona | 16.0 |
| 13 | Arkansas | 13.1 |
| 38 | California | 9.6 |
| 12 | Colorado | 14.2 |
| 48 | Connecticut | 7.2 |
| 46 | Delaware | 8.0 |
| 17 | Florida | 12.6 |
| 37 | Georgia | 10.0 |
| 40 | Hawaii | 9.2 |
| 9 | Idaho | 15.2 |
| 44 | Illinois | 8.1 |
| 27 | Indiana | 11.1 |
| 29 | Iowa | 10.7 |
| 21 | Kansas | 11.9 |
| 22 | Kentucky | 11.8 |
| 33 | Louisiana | 10.4 |
| 11 | Maine | 14.5 |
| 43 | Maryland | 8.9 |
| 47 | Massachusetts | 7.5 |
| 41 | Michigan | 9.1 |
| 39 | Minnesota | 9.4 |
| 24 | Mississippi | 11.5 |
| 19 | Missouri | 12.1 |
| 6 | Montana | 16.3 |
| 23 | Nebraska | 11.6 |
| 2 | Nevada | 21.2 |
| 16 | New Hampshire | 12.7 |
| 50 | New Jersey | 6.4 |
| 5 | New Mexico | 16.4 |
| 49 | New York | 6.9 |
| 33 | North Carolina | 10.4 |
| 32 | North Dakota | 10.6 |
| 42 | Ohio | 9.0 |
| 13 | Oklahoma | 13.1 |
| 10 | Oregon | 14.8 |
| 33 | Pennsylvania | 10.4 |
| 44 | Rhode Island | 8.1 |
| 29 | South Carolina | 10.7 |
| 8 | South Dakota | 15.4 |
| 17 | Tennessee | 12.6 |
| 36 | Texas | 10.3 |
| 4 | Utah | 16.6 |
| 15 | Vermont | 12.9 |
| 28 | Virginia | 11.0 |
| 26 | Washington | 11.4 |
| 24 | West Virginia | 11.5 |
| 29 | Wisconsin | 10.7 |
| 3 | Wyoming | 16.8 |

RANK ORDER

| RANK | STATE | RATE |
|------|-------|------|
| 1 | Alaska | 22.1 |
| 2 | Nevada | 21.2 |
| 3 | Wyoming | 16.8 |
| 4 | Utah | 16.6 |
| 5 | New Mexico | 16.4 |
| 6 | Montana | 16.3 |
| 7 | Arizona | 16.0 |
| 8 | South Dakota | 15.4 |
| 9 | Idaho | 15.2 |
| 10 | Oregon | 14.8 |
| 11 | Maine | 14.5 |
| 12 | Colorado | 14.2 |
| 13 | Arkansas | 13.1 |
| 13 | Oklahoma | 13.1 |
| 15 | Vermont | 12.9 |
| 16 | New Hampshire | 12.7 |
| 17 | Florida | 12.6 |
| 17 | Tennessee | 12.6 |
| 19 | Missouri | 12.1 |
| 20 | Alabama | 12.0 |
| 21 | Kansas | 11.9 |
| 22 | Kentucky | 11.8 |
| 23 | Nebraska | 11.6 |
| 24 | Mississippi | 11.5 |
| 24 | West Virginia | 11.5 |
| 26 | Washington | 11.4 |
| 27 | Indiana | 11.1 |
| 28 | Virginia | 11.0 |
| 29 | Iowa | 10.7 |
| 29 | South Carolina | 10.7 |
| 29 | Wisconsin | 10.7 |
| 32 | North Dakota | 10.6 |
| 33 | Louisiana | 10.4 |
| 33 | North Carolina | 10.4 |
| 33 | Pennsylvania | 10.4 |
| 36 | Texas | 10.3 |
| 37 | Georgia | 10.0 |
| 38 | California | 9.6 |
| 39 | Minnesota | 9.4 |
| 40 | Hawaii | 9.2 |
| 41 | Michigan | 9.1 |
| 42 | Ohio | 9.0 |
| 43 | Maryland | 8.9 |
| 44 | Illinois | 8.1 |
| 44 | Rhode Island | 8.1 |
| 46 | Delaware | 8.0 |
| 47 | Massachusetts | 7.5 |
| 48 | Connecticut | 7.2 |
| 49 | New York | 6.9 |
| 50 | New Jersey | 6.4 |
| | District of Columbia | 7.3 |

Source: U.S. Department of Health and Human Services, National Center for Health Statistics
   "National Vital Statistics Reports" (Vol. 48, No. 11, July 24, 2000)
*Final data by state of residence.

# Deaths by AIDS in 1998

## National Total = 13,426 Deaths*

ALPHA ORDER

| RANK | STATE | DEATHS | % of USA |
|---|---|---|---|
| 18 | Alabama | 175 | 1.3% |
| 46 | Alaska | 6 | 0.0% |
| 22 | Arizona | 138 | 1.0% |
| 29 | Arkansas | 66 | 0.5% |
| 3 | California | 1,444 | 10.8% |
| 26 | Colorado | 84 | 0.6% |
| 19 | Connecticut | 168 | 1.3% |
| 32 | Delaware | 55 | 0.4% |
| 2 | Florida | 1,546 | 11.5% |
| 6 | Georgia | 692 | 5.2% |
| 38 | Hawaii | 22 | 0.2% |
| 42 | Idaho | 13 | 0.1% |
| 8 | Illinois | 488 | 3.6% |
| 24 | Indiana | 98 | 0.7% |
| 44 | Iowa | 9 | 0.1% |
| 35 | Kansas | 26 | 0.2% |
| 27 | Kentucky | 78 | 0.6% |
| 11 | Louisiana | 361 | 2.7% |
| 41 | Maine | 15 | 0.1% |
| 7 | Maryland | 502 | 3.7% |
| 17 | Massachusetts | 213 | 1.6% |
| 13 | Michigan | 271 | 2.0% |
| 32 | Minnesota | 55 | 0.4% |
| 21 | Mississippi | 140 | 1.0% |
| 20 | Missouri | 146 | 1.1% |
| 45 | Montana | 7 | 0.1% |
| 37 | Nebraska | 24 | 0.2% |
| 28 | Nevada | 73 | 0.5% |
| 42 | New Hampshire | 13 | 0.1% |
| 5 | New Jersey | 730 | 5.4% |
| 34 | New Mexico | 41 | 0.3% |
| 1 | New York | 2,195 | 16.3% |
| 10 | North Carolina | 436 | 3.2% |
| 49 | North Dakota | 2 | 0.0% |
| 16 | Ohio | 220 | 1.6% |
| 25 | Oklahoma | 85 | 0.6% |
| 31 | Oregon | 57 | 0.4% |
| 9 | Pennsylvania | 483 | 3.6% |
| 35 | Rhode Island | 26 | 0.2% |
| 14 | South Carolina | 270 | 2.0% |
| 46 | South Dakota | 6 | 0.0% |
| 15 | Tennessee | 231 | 1.7% |
| 4 | Texas | 938 | 7.0% |
| 40 | Utah | 17 | 0.1% |
| 46 | Vermont | 6 | 0.0% |
| 12 | Virginia | 307 | 2.3% |
| 23 | Washington | 116 | 0.9% |
| 39 | West Virginia | 20 | 0.1% |
| 30 | Wisconsin | 60 | 0.4% |
| 49 | Wyoming | 2 | 0.0% |

RANK ORDER

| RANK | STATE | DEATHS | % of USA |
|---|---|---|---|
| 1 | New York | 2,195 | 16.3% |
| 2 | Florida | 1,546 | 11.5% |
| 3 | California | 1,444 | 10.8% |
| 4 | Texas | 938 | 7.0% |
| 5 | New Jersey | 730 | 5.4% |
| 6 | Georgia | 692 | 5.2% |
| 7 | Maryland | 502 | 3.7% |
| 8 | Illinois | 488 | 3.6% |
| 9 | Pennsylvania | 483 | 3.6% |
| 10 | North Carolina | 436 | 3.2% |
| 11 | Louisiana | 361 | 2.7% |
| 12 | Virginia | 307 | 2.3% |
| 13 | Michigan | 271 | 2.0% |
| 14 | South Carolina | 270 | 2.0% |
| 15 | Tennessee | 231 | 1.7% |
| 16 | Ohio | 220 | 1.6% |
| 17 | Massachusetts | 213 | 1.6% |
| 18 | Alabama | 175 | 1.3% |
| 19 | Connecticut | 168 | 1.3% |
| 20 | Missouri | 146 | 1.1% |
| 21 | Mississippi | 140 | 1.0% |
| 22 | Arizona | 138 | 1.0% |
| 23 | Washington | 116 | 0.9% |
| 24 | Indiana | 98 | 0.7% |
| 25 | Oklahoma | 85 | 0.6% |
| 26 | Colorado | 84 | 0.6% |
| 27 | Kentucky | 78 | 0.6% |
| 28 | Nevada | 73 | 0.5% |
| 29 | Arkansas | 66 | 0.5% |
| 30 | Wisconsin | 60 | 0.4% |
| 31 | Oregon | 57 | 0.4% |
| 32 | Delaware | 55 | 0.4% |
| 32 | Minnesota | 55 | 0.4% |
| 34 | New Mexico | 41 | 0.3% |
| 35 | Kansas | 26 | 0.2% |
| 35 | Rhode Island | 26 | 0.2% |
| 37 | Nebraska | 24 | 0.2% |
| 38 | Hawaii | 22 | 0.2% |
| 39 | West Virginia | 20 | 0.1% |
| 40 | Utah | 17 | 0.1% |
| 41 | Maine | 15 | 0.1% |
| 42 | Idaho | 13 | 0.1% |
| 42 | New Hampshire | 13 | 0.1% |
| 44 | Iowa | 9 | 0.1% |
| 45 | Montana | 7 | 0.1% |
| 46 | Alaska | 6 | 0.0% |
| 46 | South Dakota | 6 | 0.0% |
| 46 | Vermont | 6 | 0.0% |
| 49 | North Dakota | 2 | 0.0% |
| 49 | Wyoming | 2 | 0.0% |
| | District of Columbia | 250 | 1.9% |

*Source: U.S. Department of Health and Human Services, National Center for Health Statistics
"National Vital Statistics Reports" (Vol. 48, No. 11, July 24, 2000)*
*\*AIDS is Acquired Immunodeficiency Syndrome. It is a specific group of diseases or conditions which are indicative of severe immunosuppression related to infection with the Human Immunodeficiency Virus (HIV).*

# Age-Adjusted Death Rate by AIDS in 1998

## National Rate = 4.6 Deaths per 100,000 Population*

ALPHA ORDER

| RANK | STATE | RATE |
|------|-------|------|
| 17 | Alabama | 3.8 |
| NA | Alaska** | NA |
| 21 | Arizona | 2.9 |
| 22 | Arkansas | 2.6 |
| 13 | California | 4.1 |
| 28 | Colorado | 1.9 |
| 11 | Connecticut | 4.7 |
| 7 | Delaware | 6.6 |
| 2 | Florida | 10.2 |
| 4 | Georgia | 8.2 |
| 32 | Hawaii | 1.8 |
| NA | Idaho** | NA |
| 17 | Illinois | 3.8 |
| 33 | Indiana | 1.6 |
| NA | Iowa** | NA |
| 38 | Kansas | 1.0 |
| 28 | Kentucky | 1.9 |
| 4 | Louisiana | 8.2 |
| NA | Maine** | NA |
| 3 | Maryland | 8.7 |
| 20 | Massachusetts | 3.1 |
| 25 | Michigan | 2.5 |
| 36 | Minnesota | 1.1 |
| 10 | Mississippi | 5.0 |
| 22 | Missouri | 2.6 |
| NA | Montana** | NA |
| 35 | Nebraska | 1.4 |
| 15 | Nevada | 3.9 |
| NA | New Hampshire** | NA |
| 6 | New Jersey | 8.0 |
| 26 | New Mexico | 2.4 |
| 1 | New York | 11.0 |
| 9 | North Carolina | 5.4 |
| NA | North Dakota** | NA |
| 28 | Ohio | 1.9 |
| 22 | Oklahoma | 2.6 |
| 33 | Oregon | 1.6 |
| 17 | Pennsylvania | 3.8 |
| 27 | Rhode Island | 2.3 |
| 8 | South Carolina | 6.5 |
| NA | South Dakota** | NA |
| 15 | Tennessee | 3.9 |
| 12 | Texas | 4.6 |
| NA | Utah** | NA |
| NA | Vermont** | NA |
| 14 | Virginia | 4.0 |
| 28 | Washington | 1.9 |
| 38 | West Virginia | 1.0 |
| 36 | Wisconsin | 1.1 |
| NA | Wyoming** | NA |

RANK ORDER

| RANK | STATE | RATE |
|------|-------|------|
| 1 | New York | 11.0 |
| 2 | Florida | 10.2 |
| 3 | Maryland | 8.7 |
| 4 | Georgia | 8.2 |
| 4 | Louisiana | 8.2 |
| 6 | New Jersey | 8.0 |
| 7 | Delaware | 6.6 |
| 8 | South Carolina | 6.5 |
| 9 | North Carolina | 5.4 |
| 10 | Mississippi | 5.0 |
| 11 | Connecticut | 4.7 |
| 12 | Texas | 4.6 |
| 13 | California | 4.1 |
| 14 | Virginia | 4.0 |
| 15 | Nevada | 3.9 |
| 15 | Tennessee | 3.9 |
| 17 | Alabama | 3.8 |
| 17 | Illinois | 3.8 |
| 17 | Pennsylvania | 3.8 |
| 20 | Massachusetts | 3.1 |
| 21 | Arizona | 2.9 |
| 22 | Arkansas | 2.6 |
| 22 | Missouri | 2.6 |
| 22 | Oklahoma | 2.6 |
| 25 | Michigan | 2.5 |
| 26 | New Mexico | 2.4 |
| 27 | Rhode Island | 2.3 |
| 28 | Colorado | 1.9 |
| 28 | Kentucky | 1.9 |
| 28 | Ohio | 1.9 |
| 28 | Washington | 1.9 |
| 32 | Hawaii | 1.8 |
| 33 | Indiana | 1.6 |
| 33 | Oregon | 1.6 |
| 35 | Nebraska | 1.4 |
| 36 | Minnesota | 1.1 |
| 36 | Wisconsin | 1.1 |
| 38 | Kansas | 1.0 |
| 38 | West Virginia | 1.0 |
| NA | Alaska** | NA |
| NA | Idaho** | NA |
| NA | Iowa** | NA |
| NA | Maine** | NA |
| NA | Montana** | NA |
| NA | New Hampshire** | NA |
| NA | North Dakota** | NA |
| NA | South Dakota** | NA |
| NA | Utah** | NA |
| NA | Vermont** | NA |
| NA | Wyoming** | NA |
| | District of Columbia | 41.3 |

Source: U.S. Department of Health and Human Services, National Center for Health Statistics
   "National Vital Statistics Reports" (Vol. 48, No. 11, July 24, 2000)
*AIDS is Acquired Immunodeficiency Syndrome. It is a specific group of diseases or conditions which are indicative
of severe immunosuppression related to infection with the Human Immunodeficiency Virus (HIV).
**Insufficient data to determine a reliable rate.

# AIDS Cases Reported in 2000

## National Total = 36,091 New AIDS Cases*

ALPHA ORDER

| RANK | STATE | CASES | % of USA |
|------|-------|------:|---------:|
| 20 | Alabama | 457 | 1.3% |
| 45 | Alaska | 22 | 0.1% |
| 21 | Arizona | 427 | 1.2% |
| 31 | Arkansas | 172 | 0.5% |
| 3 | California | 4,479 | 12.4% |
| 26 | Colorado | 300 | 0.8% |
| 17 | Connecticut | 546 | 1.5% |
| 28 | Delaware | 199 | 0.6% |
| 2 | Florida | 4,613 | 12.8% |
| 10 | Georgia | 1,117 | 3.1% |
| 37 | Hawaii | 99 | 0.3% |
| 46 | Idaho | 20 | 0.1% |
| 5 | Illinois | 1,693 | 4.7% |
| 24 | Indiana | 352 | 1.0% |
| 39 | Iowa | 86 | 0.2% |
| 36 | Kansas | 121 | 0.3% |
| 30 | Kentucky | 186 | 0.5% |
| 16 | Louisiana | 649 | 1.8% |
| 42 | Maine | 38 | 0.1% |
| 8 | Maryland | 1,197 | 3.3% |
| 9 | Massachusetts | 1,137 | 3.2% |
| 15 | Michigan | 652 | 1.8% |
| 33 | Minnesota | 160 | 0.4% |
| 22 | Mississippi | 395 | 1.1% |
| 23 | Missouri | 368 | 1.0% |
| 47 | Montana | 14 | 0.0% |
| 40 | Nebraska | 68 | 0.2% |
| 27 | Nevada | 275 | 0.8% |
| 44 | New Hampshire | 31 | 0.1% |
| 6 | New Jersey | 1,592 | 4.4% |
| 34 | New Mexico | 140 | 0.4% |
| 1 | New York | 4,634 | 12.8% |
| 14 | North Carolina | 667 | 1.8% |
| 50 | North Dakota | 3 | 0.0% |
| 17 | Ohio | 546 | 1.5% |
| 25 | Oklahoma | 320 | 0.9% |
| 32 | Oregon | 171 | 0.5% |
| 7 | Pennsylvania | 1,479 | 4.1% |
| 38 | Rhode Island | 95 | 0.3% |
| 13 | South Carolina | 755 | 2.1% |
| 49 | South Dakota | 7 | 0.0% |
| 11 | Tennessee | 771 | 2.1% |
| 4 | Texas | 2,567 | 7.1% |
| 35 | Utah | 137 | 0.4% |
| 43 | Vermont | 37 | 0.1% |
| 12 | Virginia | 764 | 2.1% |
| 19 | Washington | 480 | 1.3% |
| 41 | West Virginia | 60 | 0.2% |
| 28 | Wisconsin | 199 | 0.6% |
| 48 | Wyoming | 9 | 0.0% |

RANK ORDER

| RANK | STATE | CASES | % of USA |
|------|-------|------:|---------:|
| 1 | New York | 4,634 | 12.8% |
| 2 | Florida | 4,613 | 12.8% |
| 3 | California | 4,479 | 12.4% |
| 4 | Texas | 2,567 | 7.1% |
| 5 | Illinois | 1,693 | 4.7% |
| 6 | New Jersey | 1,592 | 4.4% |
| 7 | Pennsylvania | 1,479 | 4.1% |
| 8 | Maryland | 1,197 | 3.3% |
| 9 | Massachusetts | 1,137 | 3.2% |
| 10 | Georgia | 1,117 | 3.1% |
| 11 | Tennessee | 771 | 2.1% |
| 12 | Virginia | 764 | 2.1% |
| 13 | South Carolina | 755 | 2.1% |
| 14 | North Carolina | 667 | 1.8% |
| 15 | Michigan | 652 | 1.8% |
| 16 | Louisiana | 649 | 1.8% |
| 17 | Connecticut | 546 | 1.5% |
| 17 | Ohio | 546 | 1.5% |
| 19 | Washington | 480 | 1.3% |
| 20 | Alabama | 457 | 1.3% |
| 21 | Arizona | 427 | 1.2% |
| 22 | Mississippi | 395 | 1.1% |
| 23 | Missouri | 368 | 1.0% |
| 24 | Indiana | 352 | 1.0% |
| 25 | Oklahoma | 320 | 0.9% |
| 26 | Colorado | 300 | 0.8% |
| 27 | Nevada | 275 | 0.8% |
| 28 | Delaware | 199 | 0.6% |
| 28 | Wisconsin | 199 | 0.6% |
| 30 | Kentucky | 186 | 0.5% |
| 31 | Arkansas | 172 | 0.5% |
| 32 | Oregon | 171 | 0.5% |
| 33 | Minnesota | 160 | 0.4% |
| 34 | New Mexico | 140 | 0.4% |
| 35 | Utah | 137 | 0.4% |
| 36 | Kansas | 121 | 0.3% |
| 37 | Hawaii | 99 | 0.3% |
| 38 | Rhode Island | 95 | 0.3% |
| 39 | Iowa | 86 | 0.2% |
| 40 | Nebraska | 68 | 0.2% |
| 41 | West Virginia | 60 | 0.2% |
| 42 | Maine | 38 | 0.1% |
| 43 | Vermont | 37 | 0.1% |
| 44 | New Hampshire | 31 | 0.1% |
| 45 | Alaska | 22 | 0.1% |
| 46 | Idaho | 20 | 0.1% |
| 47 | Montana | 14 | 0.0% |
| 48 | Wyoming | 9 | 0.0% |
| 49 | South Dakota | 7 | 0.0% |
| 50 | North Dakota | 3 | 0.0% |
| | District of Columbia | 785 | 2.2% |

*Source: U.S. Department of Health and Human Services, National Center for Health Statistics*
*"Morbidity and Mortality Weekly Report" (January 5, 2001, Vol. 49, No. 51)*
*Provisional data. AIDS is Acquired Immunodeficiency Syndrome. It is a specific group of diseases or conditions which are indicative of severe immunosuppression related to infection with the Human Immunodeficiency Virus (HIV). National total does not include 589 cases in Puerto Rico.*

# AIDS Rate in 2000

## National Rate = 12.8 New AIDS Cases Reported per 100,000 Population*

ALPHA ORDER

| RANK | STATE | RATE |
|------|-------|------|
| 19 | Alabama | 10.3 |
| 40 | Alaska | 3.5 |
| 22 | Arizona | 8.3 |
| 30 | Arkansas | 6.4 |
| 15 | California | 13.2 |
| 27 | Colorado | 7.0 |
| 8 | Connecticut | 16.0 |
| 2 | Delaware | 25.4 |
| 1 | Florida | 28.9 |
| 12 | Georgia | 13.6 |
| 24 | Hawaii | 8.2 |
| 48 | Idaho | 1.5 |
| 12 | Illinois | 13.6 |
| 33 | Indiana | 5.8 |
| 44 | Iowa | 2.9 |
| 37 | Kansas | 4.5 |
| 36 | Kentucky | 4.6 |
| 9 | Louisiana | 14.5 |
| 43 | Maine | 3.0 |
| 4 | Maryland | 22.6 |
| 7 | Massachusetts | 17.9 |
| 28 | Michigan | 6.6 |
| 41 | Minnesota | 3.3 |
| 10 | Mississippi | 13.9 |
| 28 | Missouri | 6.6 |
| 47 | Montana | 1.6 |
| 38 | Nebraska | 4.0 |
| 11 | Nevada | 13.8 |
| 45 | New Hampshire | 2.5 |
| 5 | New Jersey | 18.9 |
| 26 | New Mexico | 7.7 |
| 3 | New York | 24.4 |
| 22 | North Carolina | 8.3 |
| 50 | North Dakota | 0.5 |
| 35 | Ohio | 4.8 |
| 20 | Oklahoma | 9.3 |
| 34 | Oregon | 5.0 |
| 17 | Pennsylvania | 12.0 |
| 21 | Rhode Island | 9.1 |
| 6 | South Carolina | 18.8 |
| 49 | South Dakota | 0.9 |
| 12 | Tennessee | 13.6 |
| 16 | Texas | 12.3 |
| 31 | Utah | 6.1 |
| 31 | Vermont | 6.1 |
| 18 | Virginia | 10.8 |
| 25 | Washington | 8.1 |
| 41 | West Virginia | 3.3 |
| 39 | Wisconsin | 3.7 |
| 46 | Wyoming | 1.8 |

RANK ORDER

| RANK | STATE | RATE |
|------|-------|------|
| 1 | Florida | 28.9 |
| 2 | Delaware | 25.4 |
| 3 | New York | 24.4 |
| 4 | Maryland | 22.6 |
| 5 | New Jersey | 18.9 |
| 6 | South Carolina | 18.8 |
| 7 | Massachusetts | 17.9 |
| 8 | Connecticut | 16.0 |
| 9 | Louisiana | 14.5 |
| 10 | Mississippi | 13.9 |
| 11 | Nevada | 13.8 |
| 12 | Georgia | 13.6 |
| 12 | Illinois | 13.6 |
| 12 | Tennessee | 13.6 |
| 15 | California | 13.2 |
| 16 | Texas | 12.3 |
| 17 | Pennsylvania | 12.0 |
| 18 | Virginia | 10.8 |
| 19 | Alabama | 10.3 |
| 20 | Oklahoma | 9.3 |
| 21 | Rhode Island | 9.1 |
| 22 | Arizona | 8.3 |
| 22 | North Carolina | 8.3 |
| 24 | Hawaii | 8.2 |
| 25 | Washington | 8.1 |
| 26 | New Mexico | 7.7 |
| 27 | Colorado | 7.0 |
| 28 | Michigan | 6.6 |
| 28 | Missouri | 6.6 |
| 30 | Arkansas | 6.4 |
| 31 | Utah | 6.1 |
| 31 | Vermont | 6.1 |
| 33 | Indiana | 5.8 |
| 34 | Oregon | 5.0 |
| 35 | Ohio | 4.8 |
| 36 | Kentucky | 4.6 |
| 37 | Kansas | 4.5 |
| 38 | Nebraska | 4.0 |
| 39 | Wisconsin | 3.7 |
| 40 | Alaska | 3.5 |
| 41 | Minnesota | 3.3 |
| 41 | West Virginia | 3.3 |
| 43 | Maine | 3.0 |
| 44 | Iowa | 2.9 |
| 45 | New Hampshire | 2.5 |
| 46 | Wyoming | 1.8 |
| 47 | Montana | 1.6 |
| 48 | Idaho | 1.5 |
| 49 | South Dakota | 0.9 |
| 50 | North Dakota | 0.5 |

District of Columbia    137.2

Source: Morgan Quitno Press using data from U.S. Dept. of Health & Human Serv's, National Center for Health Statistics
"Morbidity and Mortality Weekly Report" (January 5, 2001, Vol. 49, No. 51)
*Provisional data. AIDS is Acquired Immunodeficiency Syndrome. It is a specific group of diseases or conditions
which are indicative of severe immunosuppression related to infection with the Human Immunodeficiency Virus
(HIV). National rate does not include cases or population.

# AIDS Cases Reported Through June 2000

## National Total = 720,299 Reported AIDS Cases*

ALPHA ORDER

| RANK | STATE | CASES | % of USA |
|---|---|---|---|
| 23 | Alabama | 5,979 | 0.8% |
| 45 | Alaska | 459 | 0.1% |
| 21 | Arizona | 7,196 | 1.0% |
| 32 | Arkansas | 2,848 | 0.4% |
| 2 | California | 116,925 | 16.2% |
| 22 | Colorado | 6,888 | 1.0% |
| 13 | Connecticut | 11,139 | 1.5% |
| 33 | Delaware | 2,436 | 0.3% |
| 3 | Florida | 76,656 | 10.6% |
| 8 | Georgia | 21,995 | 3.1% |
| 34 | Hawaii | 2,410 | 0.3% |
| 44 | Idaho | 486 | 0.1% |
| 6 | Illinois | 24,158 | 3.4% |
| 24 | Indiana | 5,910 | 0.8% |
| 39 | Iowa | 1,267 | 0.2% |
| 35 | Kansas | 2,322 | 0.3% |
| 31 | Kentucky | 3,221 | 0.4% |
| 12 | Louisiana | 12,185 | 1.7% |
| 42 | Maine | 923 | 0.1% |
| 9 | Maryland | 20,534 | 2.9% |
| 10 | Massachusetts | 15,701 | 2.2% |
| 15 | Michigan | 10,714 | 1.5% |
| 28 | Minnesota | 3,643 | 0.5% |
| 27 | Mississippi | 4,201 | 0.6% |
| 19 | Missouri | 8,863 | 1.2% |
| 47 | Montana | 316 | 0.0% |
| 40 | Nebraska | 1,038 | 0.1% |
| 26 | Nevada | 4,265 | 0.6% |
| 43 | New Hampshire | 860 | 0.1% |
| 5 | New Jersey | 40,501 | 5.6% |
| 36 | New Mexico | 1,987 | 0.3% |
| 1 | New York | 137,015 | 19.0% |
| 16 | North Carolina | 9,962 | 1.4% |
| 50 | North Dakota | 104 | 0.0% |
| 14 | Ohio | 10,980 | 1.5% |
| 29 | Oklahoma | 3,567 | 0.5% |
| 25 | Oregon | 4,662 | 0.6% |
| 7 | Pennsylvania | 23,365 | 3.2% |
| 37 | Rhode Island | 1,981 | 0.3% |
| 18 | South Carolina | 9,075 | 1.3% |
| 49 | South Dakota | 158 | 0.0% |
| 20 | Tennessee | 8,082 | 1.1% |
| 4 | Texas | 52,292 | 7.3% |
| 38 | Utah | 1,872 | 0.3% |
| 46 | Vermont | 374 | 0.1% |
| 11 | Virginia | 12,422 | 1.7% |
| 17 | Washington | 9,246 | 1.3% |
| 40 | West Virginia | 1,038 | 0.1% |
| 30 | Wisconsin | 3,453 | 0.5% |
| 48 | Wyoming | 178 | 0.0% |

RANK ORDER

| RANK | STATE | CASES | % of USA |
|---|---|---|---|
| 1 | New York | 137,015 | 19.0% |
| 2 | California | 116,925 | 16.2% |
| 3 | Florida | 76,656 | 10.6% |
| 4 | Texas | 52,292 | 7.3% |
| 5 | New Jersey | 40,501 | 5.6% |
| 6 | Illinois | 24,158 | 3.4% |
| 7 | Pennsylvania | 23,365 | 3.2% |
| 8 | Georgia | 21,995 | 3.1% |
| 9 | Maryland | 20,534 | 2.9% |
| 10 | Massachusetts | 15,701 | 2.2% |
| 11 | Virginia | 12,422 | 1.7% |
| 12 | Louisiana | 12,185 | 1.7% |
| 13 | Connecticut | 11,139 | 1.5% |
| 14 | Ohio | 10,980 | 1.5% |
| 15 | Michigan | 10,714 | 1.5% |
| 16 | North Carolina | 9,962 | 1.4% |
| 17 | Washington | 9,246 | 1.3% |
| 18 | South Carolina | 9,075 | 1.3% |
| 19 | Missouri | 8,863 | 1.2% |
| 20 | Tennessee | 8,082 | 1.1% |
| 21 | Arizona | 7,196 | 1.0% |
| 22 | Colorado | 6,888 | 1.0% |
| 23 | Alabama | 5,979 | 0.8% |
| 24 | Indiana | 5,910 | 0.8% |
| 25 | Oregon | 4,662 | 0.6% |
| 26 | Nevada | 4,265 | 0.6% |
| 27 | Mississippi | 4,201 | 0.6% |
| 28 | Minnesota | 3,643 | 0.5% |
| 29 | Oklahoma | 3,567 | 0.5% |
| 30 | Wisconsin | 3,453 | 0.5% |
| 31 | Kentucky | 3,221 | 0.4% |
| 32 | Arkansas | 2,848 | 0.4% |
| 33 | Delaware | 2,436 | 0.3% |
| 34 | Hawaii | 2,410 | 0.3% |
| 35 | Kansas | 2,322 | 0.3% |
| 36 | New Mexico | 1,987 | 0.3% |
| 37 | Rhode Island | 1,981 | 0.3% |
| 38 | Utah | 1,872 | 0.3% |
| 39 | Iowa | 1,267 | 0.2% |
| 40 | Nebraska | 1,038 | 0.1% |
| 40 | West Virginia | 1,038 | 0.1% |
| 42 | Maine | 923 | 0.1% |
| 43 | New Hampshire | 860 | 0.1% |
| 44 | Idaho | 486 | 0.1% |
| 45 | Alaska | 459 | 0.1% |
| 46 | Vermont | 374 | 0.1% |
| 47 | Montana | 316 | 0.0% |
| 48 | Wyoming | 178 | 0.0% |
| 49 | South Dakota | 158 | 0.0% |
| 50 | North Dakota | 104 | 0.0% |
| | District of Columbia | 12,447 | 1.7% |

Source: U.S. Department of Health and Human Services, Centers for Disease Control and Prevention
"HIV/AIDS Surveillance Report, 2000" (Mid-year Edition, Vol. 12, No. 1)
*Cumulative through June 2000. AIDS is Acquired Immunodeficiency Syndrome. It is a specific group of diseases or conditions which are indicative of severe immunosuppression related to infection with the Human Immunodeficiency Virus (HIV). National total does not include 23,675 cases in Puerto Rico, 453 cases in the Virgin Islands and 50 cases in other U.S. territories.

# Adult Per Capita Alcohol Consumption in 1997

## National Per Capita = 2.5 Gallons Consumed per Adult Age 21 & Older*

ALPHA ORDER

| RANK | STATE | PER CAPITA |
|---|---|---|
| 42 | Alabama | 2.1 |
| 5 | Alaska | 3.1 |
| 7 | Arizona | 2.9 |
| 45 | Arkansas | 2.0 |
| 20 | California | 2.6 |
| 6 | Colorado | 3.0 |
| 25 | Connecticut | 2.5 |
| 3 | Delaware | 3.2 |
| 7 | Florida | 2.9 |
| 25 | Georgia | 2.5 |
| 13 | Hawaii | 2.7 |
| 33 | Idaho | 2.4 |
| 20 | Illinois | 2.6 |
| 36 | Indiana | 2.2 |
| 36 | Iowa | 2.2 |
| 45 | Kansas | 2.0 |
| 45 | Kentucky | 2.0 |
| 7 | Louisiana | 2.9 |
| 25 | Maine | 2.5 |
| 35 | Maryland | 2.3 |
| 13 | Massachusetts | 2.7 |
| 33 | Michigan | 2.4 |
| 13 | Minnesota | 2.7 |
| 25 | Mississippi | 2.5 |
| 25 | Missouri | 2.5 |
| 10 | Montana | 2.8 |
| 25 | Nebraska | 2.5 |
| 2 | Nevada | 4.5 |
| 1 | New Hampshire | 4.6 |
| 25 | New Jersey | 2.5 |
| 10 | New Mexico | 2.8 |
| 36 | New York | 2.2 |
| 36 | North Carolina | 2.2 |
| 13 | North Dakota | 2.7 |
| 36 | Ohio | 2.2 |
| 48 | Oklahoma | 1.9 |
| 20 | Oregon | 2.6 |
| 42 | Pennsylvania | 2.1 |
| 13 | Rhode Island | 2.7 |
| 13 | South Carolina | 2.7 |
| 20 | South Dakota | 2.6 |
| 42 | Tennessee | 2.1 |
| 20 | Texas | 2.6 |
| 50 | Utah | 1.6 |
| 13 | Vermont | 2.7 |
| 36 | Virginia | 2.2 |
| 25 | Washington | 2.5 |
| 49 | West Virginia | 1.8 |
| 3 | Wisconsin | 3.2 |
| 10 | Wyoming | 2.8 |

RANK ORDER

| RANK | STATE | PER CAPITA |
|---|---|---|
| 1 | New Hampshire | 4.6 |
| 2 | Nevada | 4.5 |
| 3 | Delaware | 3.2 |
| 3 | Wisconsin | 3.2 |
| 5 | Alaska | 3.1 |
| 6 | Colorado | 3.0 |
| 7 | Arizona | 2.9 |
| 7 | Florida | 2.9 |
| 7 | Louisiana | 2.9 |
| 10 | Montana | 2.8 |
| 10 | New Mexico | 2.8 |
| 10 | Wyoming | 2.8 |
| 13 | Hawaii | 2.7 |
| 13 | Massachusetts | 2.7 |
| 13 | Minnesota | 2.7 |
| 13 | North Dakota | 2.7 |
| 13 | Rhode Island | 2.7 |
| 13 | South Carolina | 2.7 |
| 13 | Vermont | 2.7 |
| 20 | California | 2.6 |
| 20 | Illinois | 2.6 |
| 20 | Oregon | 2.6 |
| 20 | South Dakota | 2.6 |
| 20 | Texas | 2.6 |
| 25 | Connecticut | 2.5 |
| 25 | Georgia | 2.5 |
| 25 | Maine | 2.5 |
| 25 | Mississippi | 2.5 |
| 25 | Missouri | 2.5 |
| 25 | Nebraska | 2.5 |
| 25 | New Jersey | 2.5 |
| 25 | Washington | 2.5 |
| 33 | Idaho | 2.4 |
| 33 | Michigan | 2.4 |
| 35 | Maryland | 2.3 |
| 36 | Indiana | 2.2 |
| 36 | Iowa | 2.2 |
| 36 | New York | 2.2 |
| 36 | North Carolina | 2.2 |
| 36 | Ohio | 2.2 |
| 36 | Virginia | 2.2 |
| 42 | Alabama | 2.1 |
| 42 | Pennsylvania | 2.1 |
| 42 | Tennessee | 2.1 |
| 45 | Arkansas | 2.0 |
| 45 | Kansas | 2.0 |
| 45 | Kentucky | 2.0 |
| 48 | Oklahoma | 1.9 |
| 49 | West Virginia | 1.8 |
| 50 | Utah | 1.6 |
| | District of Columbia | 4.3 |

*Source: Morgan Quitno Press using data from U.S. Department of Health and Human Services, National Institute on Alcohol Abuse and Alcoholism "Volume Beverage and Ethanol Consumption for States"*
*\*This is apparent consumption of actual alcohol, not entire volume of an alcoholic beverage (e.g. wine is roughly 11% absolute alcohol content). Apparent consumption is based on several sources which together approximate sales but do not actually measure consumption. Accordingly, figures for some states may be skewed by purchases by nonresidents.*

# Percent of Adults Who Smoke: 1999

## National Median = 22.7% of Adults*

ALPHA ORDER

RANK STATE | PERCENT | RANK STATE | PERCENT

| RANK | STATE | PERCENT |
|------|-------|---------|
| 19 | Alabama | 23.5 |
| 4 | Alaska | 27.3 |
| 45 | Arizona | 20.1 |
| 5 | Arkansas | 27.2 |
| 48 | California | 18.7 |
| 27 | Colorado | 22.5 |
| 26 | Connecticut | 22.8 |
| 9 | Delaware | 25.5 |
| 41 | Florida | 20.6 |
| 16 | Georgia | 23.8 |
| 49 | Hawaii | 18.5 |
| 37 | Idaho | 21.5 |
| 14 | Illinois | 24.2 |
| 8 | Indiana | 27.0 |
| 19 | Iowa | 23.5 |
| 40 | Kansas | 21.0 |
| 2 | Kentucky | 29.7 |
| 19 | Louisiana | 23.5 |
| 22 | Maine | 23.3 |
| 43 | Maryland | 20.3 |
| 47 | Massachusetts | 19.3 |
| 11 | Michigan | 25.1 |
| 46 | Minnesota | 19.5 |
| 25 | Mississippi | 22.9 |
| 6 | Missouri | 27.1 |
| 44 | Montana | 20.2 |
| 23 | Nebraska | 23.2 |
| 1 | Nevada | 31.5 |
| 32 | New Hampshire | 22.3 |
| 41 | New Jersey | 20.6 |
| 27 | New Mexico | 22.5 |
| 35 | New York | 21.8 |
| 11 | North Carolina | 25.1 |
| 34 | North Dakota | 22.1 |
| 3 | Ohio | 27.6 |
| 10 | Oklahoma | 25.2 |
| 38 | Oregon | 21.4 |
| 24 | Pennsylvania | 23.1 |
| 32 | Rhode Island | 22.3 |
| 18 | South Carolina | 23.6 |
| 27 | South Dakota | 22.5 |
| 13 | Tennessee | 24.8 |
| 30 | Texas | 22.4 |
| 50 | Utah | 14.0 |
| 36 | Vermont | 21.7 |
| 38 | Virginia | 21.4 |
| 30 | Washington | 22.4 |
| 6 | West Virginia | 27.1 |
| 17 | Wisconsin | 23.7 |
| 15 | Wyoming | 23.9 |

RANK ORDER

| RANK | STATE | PERCENT |
|------|-------|---------|
| 1 | Nevada | 31.5 |
| 2 | Kentucky | 29.7 |
| 3 | Ohio | 27.6 |
| 4 | Alaska | 27.3 |
| 5 | Arkansas | 27.2 |
| 6 | Missouri | 27.1 |
| 6 | West Virginia | 27.1 |
| 8 | Indiana | 27.0 |
| 9 | Delaware | 25.5 |
| 10 | Oklahoma | 25.2 |
| 11 | Michigan | 25.1 |
| 11 | North Carolina | 25.1 |
| 13 | Tennessee | 24.8 |
| 14 | Illinois | 24.2 |
| 15 | Wyoming | 23.9 |
| 16 | Georgia | 23.8 |
| 17 | Wisconsin | 23.7 |
| 18 | South Carolina | 23.6 |
| 19 | Alabama | 23.5 |
| 19 | Iowa | 23.5 |
| 19 | Louisiana | 23.5 |
| 22 | Maine | 23.3 |
| 23 | Nebraska | 23.2 |
| 24 | Pennsylvania | 23.1 |
| 25 | Mississippi | 22.9 |
| 26 | Connecticut | 22.8 |
| 27 | Colorado | 22.5 |
| 27 | New Mexico | 22.5 |
| 27 | South Dakota | 22.5 |
| 30 | Texas | 22.4 |
| 30 | Washington | 22.4 |
| 32 | New Hampshire | 22.3 |
| 32 | Rhode Island | 22.3 |
| 34 | North Dakota | 22.1 |
| 35 | New York | 21.8 |
| 36 | Vermont | 21.7 |
| 37 | Idaho | 21.5 |
| 38 | Oregon | 21.4 |
| 38 | Virginia | 21.4 |
| 40 | Kansas | 21.0 |
| 41 | Florida | 20.6 |
| 41 | New Jersey | 20.6 |
| 43 | Maryland | 20.3 |
| 44 | Montana | 20.2 |
| 45 | Arizona | 20.1 |
| 46 | Minnesota | 19.5 |
| 47 | Massachusetts | 19.3 |
| 48 | California | 18.7 |
| 49 | Hawaii | 18.5 |
| 50 | Utah | 14.0 |

District of Columbia | 20.6

*Source: U.S. Department of Health and Human Services, Centers for Disease Control and Prevention*
*"1999 Behavioral Risk Factor Surveillance Summary Prevalence Report" (June 23, 2000)*
*Persons 18 and older who have ever smoked 100 cigarettes and currently smoke.

# Percent of Adults Overweight or Obese: 1999

## National Median = 56.2% of Adults*

| RANK | STATE | PERCENT |
|------|-------|---------|
| 4 | Alabama | 60.9 |
| 3 | Alaska | 61.1 |
| 45 | Arizona | 51.6 |
| 8 | Arkansas | 58.8 |
| 34 | California | 54.8 |
| 50 | Colorado | 47.9 |
| 43 | Connecticut | 52.6 |
| 29 | Delaware | 55.5 |
| 20 | Florida | 56.9 |
| 19 | Georgia | 57.6 |
| 48 | Hawaii | 50.2 |
| 33 | Idaho | 55.2 |
| 20 | Illinois | 56.9 |
| 23 | Indiana | 56.7 |
| 11 | Iowa | 58.4 |
| 26 | Kansas | 56.1 |
| 10 | Kentucky | 58.5 |
| 12 | Louisiana | 58.3 |
| 34 | Maine | 54.8 |
| 30 | Maryland | 55.4 |
| 47 | Massachusetts | 50.3 |
| 6 | Michigan | 59.6 |
| 27 | Minnesota | 55.9 |
| 1 | Mississippi | 62.3 |
| 18 | Missouri | 57.7 |
| 42 | Montana | 52.7 |
| 16 | Nebraska | 57.8 |
| 41 | Nevada | 53.7 |
| 49 | New Hampshire | 50.1 |
| 36 | New Jersey | 54.5 |
| 32 | New Mexico | 55.3 |
| 40 | New York | 54.0 |
| 15 | North Carolina | 57.9 |
| 5 | North Dakota | 60.1 |
| 20 | Ohio | 56.9 |
| 16 | Oklahoma | 57.8 |
| 36 | Oregon | 54.5 |
| 25 | Pennsylvania | 56.2 |
| 39 | Rhode Island | 54.2 |
| 12 | South Carolina | 58.3 |
| 7 | South Dakota | 59.3 |
| 24 | Tennessee | 56.6 |
| 12 | Texas | 58.3 |
| 46 | Utah | 50.9 |
| 44 | Vermont | 52.3 |
| 9 | Virginia | 58.7 |
| 38 | Washington | 54.4 |
| 2 | West Virginia | 62.0 |
| 28 | Wisconsin | 55.7 |
| 30 | Wyoming | 55.4 |

RANK ORDER

| RANK | STATE | PERCENT |
|------|-------|---------|
| 1 | Mississippi | 62.3 |
| 2 | West Virginia | 62.0 |
| 3 | Alaska | 61.1 |
| 4 | Alabama | 60.9 |
| 5 | North Dakota | 60.1 |
| 6 | Michigan | 59.6 |
| 7 | South Dakota | 59.3 |
| 8 | Arkansas | 58.8 |
| 9 | Virginia | 58.7 |
| 10 | Kentucky | 58.5 |
| 11 | Iowa | 58.4 |
| 12 | Louisiana | 58.3 |
| 12 | South Carolina | 58.3 |
| 12 | Texas | 58.3 |
| 15 | North Carolina | 57.9 |
| 16 | Nebraska | 57.8 |
| 16 | Oklahoma | 57.8 |
| 18 | Missouri | 57.7 |
| 19 | Georgia | 57.6 |
| 20 | Florida | 56.9 |
| 20 | Illinois | 56.9 |
| 20 | Ohio | 56.9 |
| 23 | Indiana | 56.7 |
| 24 | Tennessee | 56.6 |
| 25 | Pennsylvania | 56.2 |
| 26 | Kansas | 56.1 |
| 27 | Minnesota | 55.9 |
| 28 | Wisconsin | 55.7 |
| 29 | Delaware | 55.5 |
| 30 | Maryland | 55.4 |
| 30 | Wyoming | 55.4 |
| 32 | New Mexico | 55.3 |
| 33 | Idaho | 55.2 |
| 34 | California | 54.8 |
| 34 | Maine | 54.8 |
| 36 | New Jersey | 54.5 |
| 36 | Oregon | 54.5 |
| 38 | Washington | 54.4 |
| 39 | Rhode Island | 54.2 |
| 40 | New York | 54.0 |
| 41 | Nevada | 53.7 |
| 42 | Montana | 52.7 |
| 43 | Connecticut | 52.6 |
| 44 | Vermont | 52.3 |
| 45 | Arizona | 51.6 |
| 46 | Utah | 50.9 |
| 47 | Massachusetts | 50.3 |
| 48 | Hawaii | 50.2 |
| 49 | New Hampshire | 50.1 |
| 50 | Colorado | 47.9 |
| | District of Columbia | 50.9 |

*Source: U.S. Department of Health and Human Services, Centers for Disease Control and Prevention*
*"1999 Prevalence Report for New Body Weight Measures" (2000)*
*Persons 18 and older. This table reflects a revised definition of overweight and differs from previous years. It is now defined as a Body Mass Index (BMI) of 25.0 to 29.9 and obese is defined as a BMI of 30.0 or more regardless of sex. BMI is a ratio of height to weight. As an example, a person 5' 8" and weighing 185 pounds has a BMI of 28. See http://www.cdc.gov/nccdphp/dnpa/bmi/bmi-adult.htm.*

# Percent of Children Aged 19 to 35 Months Fully Immunized in 1999

## National Percent = 78.4%*

| ALPHA ORDER | | | RANK ORDER | | |
|---|---|---|---|---|---|
| RANK | STATE | PERCENT | RANK | STATE | PERCENT |
| 31 | Alabama | 78.4 | 1 | Vermont | 90.5 |
| 28 | Alaska | 80.1 | 2 | Kentucky | 87.6 |
| 47 | Arizona | 72.4 | 3 | Rhode Island | 87.4 |
| 36 | Arkansas | 77.1 | 4 | Pennsylvania | 86.0 |
| 39 | California | 75.3 | 5 | Connecticut | 85.9 |
| 38 | Colorado | 75.8 | 6 | Massachusetts | 85.2 |
| 5 | Connecticut | 85.9 | 6 | Minnesota | 85.2 |
| 32 | Delaware | 78.2 | 8 | New Hampshire | 84.5 |
| 25 | Florida | 80.3 | 8 | Wisconsin | 84.5 |
| 14 | Georgia | 81.9 | 10 | Iowa | 83.4 |
| 19 | Hawaii | 81.6 | 11 | Maine | 82.9 |
| 50 | Idaho | 69.4 | 12 | Wyoming | 82.8 |
| 35 | Illinois | 77.4 | 13 | Montana | 82.5 |
| 43 | Indiana | 74.3 | 14 | Georgia | 81.9 |
| 10 | Iowa | 83.4 | 15 | Nebraska | 81.8 |
| 30 | Kansas | 78.9 | 15 | North Carolina | 81.8 |
| 2 | Kentucky | 87.6 | 17 | Mississippi | 81.7 |
| 37 | Louisiana | 76.8 | 17 | South Dakota | 81.7 |
| 11 | Maine | 82.9 | 19 | Hawaii | 81.6 |
| 29 | Maryland | 79.4 | 20 | New York | 81.0 |
| 6 | Massachusetts | 85.2 | 20 | West Virginia | 81.0 |
| 42 | Michigan | 74.4 | 22 | New Jersey | 80.8 |
| 6 | Minnesota | 85.2 | 23 | South Carolina | 80.6 |
| 17 | Mississippi | 81.7 | 24 | North Dakota | 80.4 |
| 40 | Missouri | 75.0 | 25 | Florida | 80.3 |
| 13 | Montana | 82.5 | 25 | Virginia | 80.3 |
| 15 | Nebraska | 81.8 | 27 | Utah | 80.2 |
| 44 | Nevada | 73.1 | 28 | Alaska | 80.1 |
| 8 | New Hampshire | 84.5 | 29 | Maryland | 79.4 |
| 22 | New Jersey | 80.8 | 30 | Kansas | 78.9 |
| 45 | New Mexico | 73.0 | 31 | Alabama | 78.4 |
| 20 | New York | 81.0 | 32 | Delaware | 78.2 |
| 15 | North Carolina | 81.8 | 33 | Ohio | 78.1 |
| 24 | North Dakota | 80.4 | 34 | Tennessee | 77.7 |
| 33 | Ohio | 78.1 | 35 | Illinois | 77.4 |
| 46 | Oklahoma | 72.9 | 36 | Arkansas | 77.1 |
| 49 | Oregon | 72.3 | 37 | Louisiana | 76.8 |
| 4 | Pennsylvania | 86.0 | 38 | Colorado | 75.8 |
| 3 | Rhode Island | 87.4 | 39 | California | 75.3 |
| 23 | South Carolina | 80.6 | 40 | Missouri | 75.0 |
| 17 | South Dakota | 81.7 | 41 | Washington | 74.9 |
| 34 | Tennessee | 77.7 | 42 | Michigan | 74.4 |
| 47 | Texas | 72.4 | 43 | Indiana | 74.3 |
| 27 | Utah | 80.2 | 44 | Nevada | 73.1 |
| 1 | Vermont | 90.5 | 45 | New Mexico | 73.0 |
| 25 | Virginia | 80.3 | 46 | Oklahoma | 72.9 |
| 41 | Washington | 74.9 | 47 | Arizona | 72.4 |
| 20 | West Virginia | 81.0 | 47 | Texas | 72.4 |
| 8 | Wisconsin | 84.5 | 49 | Oregon | 72.3 |
| 12 | Wyoming | 82.8 | 50 | Idaho | 69.4 |
| | | | | District of Columbia | 77.5 |

*Source: U.S. Department of Health and Human Services, Centers for Disease Control and Prevention*
  *"State Vaccination Coverage Levels" (Morbidity and Mortality Weekly Report, Vol. 49, No. 26, July 7, 2000)*
*\*Fully immunized children received four doses of DTP/DT (Diphtheria, Tetanus, Pertussis (Whooping Cough)), three doses of OPV (Poliovirus), one dose of MCV (Measles Containing Vaccine) and three doses of Hib (Haemophilus influenzae type b).*

# Rate of Registered Nurses in 2000

## National Rate = 782 Nurses per 100,000 Population*

ALPHA ORDER

| RANK | STATE | RATE |
|---|---|---|
| 33 | Alabama | 766 |
| 31 | Alaska | 784 |
| 46 | Arizona | 628 |
| 41 | Arkansas | 701 |
| 49 | California | 544 |
| 37 | Colorado | 737 |
| 12 | Connecticut | 942 |
| 13 | Delaware | 936 |
| 30 | Florida | 785 |
| 42 | Georgia | 683 |
| 40 | Hawaii | 703 |
| 44 | Idaho | 636 |
| 25 | Illinois | 819 |
| 34 | Indiana | 761 |
| 5 | Iowa | 1,060 |
| 16 | Kansas | 885 |
| 24 | Kentucky | 833 |
| 23 | Louisiana | 834 |
| 6 | Maine | 1,025 |
| 21 | Maryland | 856 |
| 1 | Massachusetts | 1,194 |
| 28 | Michigan | 798 |
| 10 | Minnesota | 957 |
| 35 | Mississippi | 750 |
| 8 | Missouri | 960 |
| 26 | Montana | 812 |
| 9 | Nebraska | 958 |
| 50 | Nevada | 520 |
| 14 | New Hampshire | 916 |
| 27 | New Jersey | 800 |
| 43 | New Mexico | 656 |
| 22 | New York | 843 |
| 19 | North Carolina | 858 |
| 4 | North Dakota | 1,096 |
| 17 | Ohio | 882 |
| 45 | Oklahoma | 635 |
| 29 | Oregon | 793 |
| 7 | Pennsylvania | 1,010 |
| 3 | Rhode Island | 1,101 |
| 38 | South Carolina | 728 |
| 2 | South Dakota | 1,128 |
| 18 | Tennessee | 872 |
| 47 | Texas | 606 |
| 48 | Utah | 592 |
| 10 | Vermont | 957 |
| 39 | Virginia | 711 |
| 36 | Washington | 738 |
| 19 | West Virginia | 858 |
| 15 | Wisconsin | 893 |
| 32 | Wyoming | 780 |

RANK ORDER

| RANK | STATE | RATE |
|---|---|---|
| 1 | Massachusetts | 1,194 |
| 2 | South Dakota | 1,128 |
| 3 | Rhode Island | 1,101 |
| 4 | North Dakota | 1,096 |
| 5 | Iowa | 1,060 |
| 6 | Maine | 1,025 |
| 7 | Pennsylvania | 1,010 |
| 8 | Missouri | 960 |
| 9 | Nebraska | 958 |
| 10 | Minnesota | 957 |
| 10 | Vermont | 957 |
| 12 | Connecticut | 942 |
| 13 | Delaware | 936 |
| 14 | New Hampshire | 916 |
| 15 | Wisconsin | 893 |
| 16 | Kansas | 885 |
| 17 | Ohio | 882 |
| 18 | Tennessee | 872 |
| 19 | North Carolina | 858 |
| 19 | West Virginia | 858 |
| 21 | Maryland | 856 |
| 22 | New York | 843 |
| 23 | Louisiana | 834 |
| 24 | Kentucky | 833 |
| 25 | Illinois | 819 |
| 26 | Montana | 812 |
| 27 | New Jersey | 800 |
| 28 | Michigan | 798 |
| 29 | Oregon | 793 |
| 30 | Florida | 785 |
| 31 | Alaska | 784 |
| 32 | Wyoming | 780 |
| 33 | Alabama | 766 |
| 34 | Indiana | 761 |
| 35 | Mississippi | 750 |
| 36 | Washington | 738 |
| 37 | Colorado | 737 |
| 38 | South Carolina | 728 |
| 39 | Virginia | 711 |
| 40 | Hawaii | 703 |
| 41 | Arkansas | 701 |
| 42 | Georgia | 683 |
| 43 | New Mexico | 656 |
| 44 | Idaho | 636 |
| 45 | Oklahoma | 635 |
| 46 | Arizona | 628 |
| 47 | Texas | 606 |
| 48 | Utah | 592 |
| 49 | California | 544 |
| 50 | Nevada | 520 |
| | District of Columbia | 1,675 |

Source: U.S. Department of Health and Human Services, Health Resources and Services Administration
"The Registered Nurse Population" (February 2001)
*Preliminary as of March 2000. Rates do not include registered nurses not employed in nursing.

# XII. HOUSING

# Households in 1998

## National Total = 101,041,000 Households*

ALPHA ORDER

| RANK | STATE | HOUSEHOLDS | % of USA |
|---|---|---|---|
| 22 | Alabama | 1,663,000 | 1.6% |
| 49 | Alaska | 215,000 | 0.2% |
| 21 | Arizona | 1,762,000 | 1.7% |
| 33 | Arkansas | 970,000 | 1.0% |
| 1 | California | 11,446,000 | 11.3% |
| 24 | Colorado | 1,561,000 | 1.5% |
| 29 | Connecticut | 1,238,000 | 1.2% |
| 45 | Delaware | 284,000 | 0.3% |
| 4 | Florida | 5,881,000 | 5.8% |
| 11 | Georgia | 2,843,000 | 2.8% |
| 42 | Hawaii | 401,000 | 0.4% |
| 41 | Idaho | 448,000 | 0.4% |
| 6 | Illinois | 4,438,000 | 4.4% |
| 14 | Indiana | 2,231,000 | 2.2% |
| 30 | Iowa | 1,103,000 | 1.1% |
| 31 | Kansas | 999,000 | 1.0% |
| 25 | Kentucky | 1,497,000 | 1.5% |
| 23 | Louisiana | 1,599,000 | 1.6% |
| 39 | Maine | 490,000 | 0.5% |
| 19 | Maryland | 1,906,000 | 1.9% |
| 13 | Massachusetts | 2,349,000 | 2.3% |
| 8 | Michigan | 3,693,000 | 3.7% |
| 20 | Minnesota | 1,791,000 | 1.8% |
| 32 | Mississippi | 997,000 | 1.0% |
| 17 | Missouri | 2,089,000 | 2.1% |
| 44 | Montana | 346,000 | 0.3% |
| 37 | Nebraska | 636,000 | 0.6% |
| 36 | Nevada | 676,000 | 0.7% |
| 40 | New Hampshire | 450,000 | 0.4% |
| 9 | New Jersey | 2,957,000 | 2.9% |
| 38 | New Mexico | 632,000 | 0.6% |
| 3 | New York | 6,766,000 | 6.7% |
| 10 | North Carolina | 2,883,000 | 2.9% |
| 47 | North Dakota | 247,000 | 0.2% |
| 7 | Ohio | 4,285,000 | 4.2% |
| 27 | Oklahoma | 1,288,000 | 1.3% |
| 28 | Oregon | 1,286,000 | 1.3% |
| 5 | Pennsylvania | 4,593,000 | 4.5% |
| 43 | Rhode Island | 376,000 | 0.4% |
| 26 | South Carolina | 1,441,000 | 1.4% |
| 46 | South Dakota | 277,000 | 0.3% |
| 16 | Tennessee | 2,100,000 | 2.1% |
| 2 | Texas | 7,113,000 | 7.0% |
| 35 | Utah | 677,000 | 0.7% |
| 48 | Vermont | 231,000 | 0.2% |
| 12 | Virginia | 2,579,000 | 2.6% |
| 15 | Washington | 2,211,000 | 2.2% |
| 34 | West Virginia | 716,000 | 0.7% |
| 18 | Wisconsin | 1,973,000 | 2.0% |
| 50 | Wyoming | 185,000 | 0.2% |

RANK ORDER

| RANK | STATE | HOUSEHOLDS | % of USA |
|---|---|---|---|
| 1 | California | 11,446,000 | 11.3% |
| 2 | Texas | 7,113,000 | 7.0% |
| 3 | New York | 6,766,000 | 6.7% |
| 4 | Florida | 5,881,000 | 5.8% |
| 5 | Pennsylvania | 4,593,000 | 4.5% |
| 6 | Illinois | 4,438,000 | 4.4% |
| 7 | Ohio | 4,285,000 | 4.2% |
| 8 | Michigan | 3,693,000 | 3.7% |
| 9 | New Jersey | 2,957,000 | 2.9% |
| 10 | North Carolina | 2,883,000 | 2.9% |
| 11 | Georgia | 2,843,000 | 2.8% |
| 12 | Virginia | 2,579,000 | 2.6% |
| 13 | Massachusetts | 2,349,000 | 2.3% |
| 14 | Indiana | 2,231,000 | 2.2% |
| 15 | Washington | 2,211,000 | 2.2% |
| 16 | Tennessee | 2,100,000 | 2.1% |
| 17 | Missouri | 2,089,000 | 2.1% |
| 18 | Wisconsin | 1,973,000 | 2.0% |
| 19 | Maryland | 1,906,000 | 1.9% |
| 20 | Minnesota | 1,791,000 | 1.8% |
| 21 | Arizona | 1,762,000 | 1.7% |
| 22 | Alabama | 1,663,000 | 1.6% |
| 23 | Louisiana | 1,599,000 | 1.6% |
| 24 | Colorado | 1,561,000 | 1.5% |
| 25 | Kentucky | 1,497,000 | 1.5% |
| 26 | South Carolina | 1,441,000 | 1.4% |
| 27 | Oklahoma | 1,288,000 | 1.3% |
| 28 | Oregon | 1,286,000 | 1.3% |
| 29 | Connecticut | 1,238,000 | 1.2% |
| 30 | Iowa | 1,103,000 | 1.1% |
| 31 | Kansas | 999,000 | 1.0% |
| 32 | Mississippi | 997,000 | 1.0% |
| 33 | Arkansas | 970,000 | 1.0% |
| 34 | West Virginia | 716,000 | 0.7% |
| 35 | Utah | 677,000 | 0.7% |
| 36 | Nevada | 676,000 | 0.7% |
| 37 | Nebraska | 636,000 | 0.6% |
| 38 | New Mexico | 632,000 | 0.6% |
| 39 | Maine | 490,000 | 0.5% |
| 40 | New Hampshire | 450,000 | 0.4% |
| 41 | Idaho | 448,000 | 0.4% |
| 42 | Hawaii | 401,000 | 0.4% |
| 43 | Rhode Island | 376,000 | 0.4% |
| 44 | Montana | 346,000 | 0.3% |
| 45 | Delaware | 284,000 | 0.3% |
| 46 | South Dakota | 277,000 | 0.3% |
| 47 | North Dakota | 247,000 | 0.2% |
| 48 | Vermont | 231,000 | 0.2% |
| 49 | Alaska | 215,000 | 0.2% |
| 50 | Wyoming | 185,000 | 0.2% |
| | District of Columbia | 225,000 | 0.2% |

Source: U.S. Bureau of the Census
"Estimates of Housing Units, Households, and Persons per Household" (ST-98-46)
(http://www.census.gov/population/estimates/housing/sthuhh1.txt)
*As of July 1, 1998.  A household includes all persons who occupy a housing unit.  A household consists of a single family, one person living alone, two or more families living together, or any other group of related or unrelated persons who share living arrangements.

# Percent Change in Households: 1994 to 1998

## National Percent Change = 5.3% Increase*

ALPHA ORDER

| RANK | STATE | PERCENT CHANGE |
|------|-------|----------------|
| 26 | Alabama | 4.3 |
| 33 | Alaska | 3.9 |
| 2 | Arizona | 13.9 |
| 23 | Arkansas | 5.0 |
| 18 | California | 6.0 |
| 6 | Colorado | 9.9 |
| 47 | Connecticut | 1.6 |
| 13 | Delaware | 7.3 |
| 9 | Florida | 8.0 |
| 4 | Georgia | 10.2 |
| 22 | Hawaii | 5.2 |
| 3 | Idaho | 10.8 |
| 42 | Illinois | 2.6 |
| 37 | Indiana | 3.7 |
| 44 | Iowa | 1.9 |
| 40 | Kansas | 3.1 |
| 28 | Kentucky | 4.2 |
| 36 | Louisiana | 3.8 |
| 33 | Maine | 3.9 |
| 25 | Maryland | 4.5 |
| 33 | Massachusetts | 3.9 |
| 29 | Michigan | 4.1 |
| 24 | Minnesota | 4.6 |
| 21 | Mississippi | 5.3 |
| 38 | Missouri | 3.5 |
| 17 | Montana | 6.3 |
| 38 | Nebraska | 3.5 |
| 1 | Nevada | 20.9 |
| 16 | New Hampshire | 6.6 |
| 31 | New Jersey | 4.0 |
| 15 | New Mexico | 7.2 |
| 47 | New York | 1.6 |
| 10 | North Carolina | 7.9 |
| 44 | North Dakota | 1.9 |
| 43 | Ohio | 2.3 |
| 26 | Oklahoma | 4.3 |
| 11 | Oregon | 7.8 |
| 49 | Pennsylvania | 1.1 |
| 50 | Rhode Island | 0.6 |
| 12 | South Carolina | 7.4 |
| 41 | South Dakota | 2.9 |
| 13 | Tennessee | 7.3 |
| 7 | Texas | 8.9 |
| 5 | Utah | 10.1 |
| 20 | Vermont | 5.6 |
| 18 | Virginia | 6.0 |
| 8 | Washington | 8.3 |
| 44 | West Virginia | 1.9 |
| 31 | Wisconsin | 4.0 |
| 29 | Wyoming | 4.1 |

RANK ORDER

| RANK | STATE | PERCENT CHANGE |
|------|-------|----------------|
| 1 | Nevada | 20.9 |
| 2 | Arizona | 13.9 |
| 3 | Idaho | 10.8 |
| 4 | Georgia | 10.2 |
| 5 | Utah | 10.1 |
| 6 | Colorado | 9.9 |
| 7 | Texas | 8.9 |
| 8 | Washington | 8.3 |
| 9 | Florida | 8.0 |
| 10 | North Carolina | 7.9 |
| 11 | Oregon | 7.8 |
| 12 | South Carolina | 7.4 |
| 13 | Delaware | 7.3 |
| 13 | Tennessee | 7.3 |
| 15 | New Mexico | 7.2 |
| 16 | New Hampshire | 6.6 |
| 17 | Montana | 6.3 |
| 18 | California | 6.0 |
| 18 | Virginia | 6.0 |
| 20 | Vermont | 5.6 |
| 21 | Mississippi | 5.3 |
| 22 | Hawaii | 5.2 |
| 23 | Arkansas | 5.0 |
| 24 | Minnesota | 4.6 |
| 25 | Maryland | 4.5 |
| 26 | Alabama | 4.3 |
| 26 | Oklahoma | 4.3 |
| 28 | Kentucky | 4.2 |
| 29 | Michigan | 4.1 |
| 29 | Wyoming | 4.1 |
| 31 | New Jersey | 4.0 |
| 31 | Wisconsin | 4.0 |
| 33 | Alaska | 3.9 |
| 33 | Maine | 3.9 |
| 33 | Massachusetts | 3.9 |
| 36 | Louisiana | 3.8 |
| 37 | Indiana | 3.7 |
| 38 | Missouri | 3.5 |
| 38 | Nebraska | 3.5 |
| 40 | Kansas | 3.1 |
| 41 | South Dakota | 2.9 |
| 42 | Illinois | 2.6 |
| 43 | Ohio | 2.3 |
| 44 | Iowa | 1.9 |
| 44 | North Dakota | 1.9 |
| 44 | West Virginia | 1.9 |
| 47 | Connecticut | 1.6 |
| 47 | New York | 1.6 |
| 49 | Pennsylvania | 1.1 |
| 50 | Rhode Island | 0.6 |
| | District of Columbia | (4.8) |

Source: Morgan Quitno Press using data from U.S. Bureau of the Census
  "Estimates of Housing Units, Households, Households by Age of Householder and Persons per Household"
*As of July 1. A household includes all persons who occupy a housing unit. A household consists of a single
family, one person living alone, two or more families living together, or any other group of related or unrelated
persons who share living arrangements.

# Persons per Household in 1998

## National Rate = 2.61 Persons per Household*

| RANK | STATE | PERSONS |
|------|-------|---------|
| 22 | Alabama | 2.56 |
| 4 | Alaska | 2.78 |
| 15 | Arizona | 2.60 |
| 22 | Arkansas | 2.56 |
| 3 | California | 2.79 |
| 44 | Colorado | 2.49 |
| 20 | Connecticut | 2.57 |
| 30 | Delaware | 2.54 |
| 45 | Florida | 2.48 |
| 12 | Georgia | 2.63 |
| 2 | Hawaii | 2.87 |
| 7 | Idaho | 2.69 |
| 11 | Illinois | 2.65 |
| 20 | Indiana | 2.57 |
| 42 | Iowa | 2.50 |
| 26 | Kansas | 2.55 |
| 22 | Kentucky | 2.56 |
| 10 | Louisiana | 2.66 |
| 45 | Maine | 2.48 |
| 12 | Maryland | 2.63 |
| 38 | Massachusetts | 2.52 |
| 15 | Michigan | 2.60 |
| 17 | Minnesota | 2.58 |
| 9 | Mississippi | 2.68 |
| 36 | Missouri | 2.53 |
| 49 | Montana | 2.47 |
| 30 | Nebraska | 2.54 |
| 30 | Nevada | 2.54 |
| 22 | New Hampshire | 2.56 |
| 7 | New Jersey | 2.69 |
| 6 | New Mexico | 2.70 |
| 14 | New York | 2.61 |
| 30 | North Carolina | 2.54 |
| 45 | North Dakota | 2.48 |
| 26 | Ohio | 2.55 |
| 38 | Oklahoma | 2.52 |
| 42 | Oregon | 2.50 |
| 30 | Pennsylvania | 2.54 |
| 36 | Rhode Island | 2.53 |
| 17 | South Carolina | 2.58 |
| 26 | South Dakota | 2.55 |
| 38 | Tennessee | 2.52 |
| 5 | Texas | 2.71 |
| 1 | Utah | 3.06 |
| 50 | Vermont | 2.46 |
| 26 | Virginia | 2.55 |
| 38 | Washington | 2.52 |
| 45 | West Virginia | 2.48 |
| 17 | Wisconsin | 2.58 |
| 30 | Wyoming | 2.54 |

| RANK | STATE | PERSONS |
|------|-------|---------|
| 1 | Utah | 3.06 |
| 2 | Hawaii | 2.87 |
| 3 | California | 2.79 |
| 4 | Alaska | 2.78 |
| 5 | Texas | 2.71 |
| 6 | New Mexico | 2.70 |
| 7 | Idaho | 2.69 |
| 7 | New Jersey | 2.69 |
| 9 | Mississippi | 2.68 |
| 10 | Louisiana | 2.66 |
| 11 | Illinois | 2.65 |
| 12 | Georgia | 2.63 |
| 12 | Maryland | 2.63 |
| 14 | New York | 2.61 |
| 15 | Arizona | 2.60 |
| 15 | Michigan | 2.60 |
| 17 | Minnesota | 2.58 |
| 17 | South Carolina | 2.58 |
| 17 | Wisconsin | 2.58 |
| 20 | Connecticut | 2.57 |
| 20 | Indiana | 2.57 |
| 22 | Alabama | 2.56 |
| 22 | Arkansas | 2.56 |
| 22 | Kentucky | 2.56 |
| 22 | New Hampshire | 2.56 |
| 26 | Kansas | 2.55 |
| 26 | Ohio | 2.55 |
| 26 | South Dakota | 2.55 |
| 26 | Virginia | 2.55 |
| 30 | Delaware | 2.54 |
| 30 | Nebraska | 2.54 |
| 30 | Nevada | 2.54 |
| 30 | North Carolina | 2.54 |
| 30 | Pennsylvania | 2.54 |
| 30 | Wyoming | 2.54 |
| 36 | Missouri | 2.53 |
| 36 | Rhode Island | 2.53 |
| 38 | Massachusetts | 2.52 |
| 38 | Oklahoma | 2.52 |
| 38 | Tennessee | 2.52 |
| 38 | Washington | 2.52 |
| 42 | Iowa | 2.50 |
| 42 | Oregon | 2.50 |
| 44 | Colorado | 2.49 |
| 45 | Florida | 2.48 |
| 45 | Maine | 2.48 |
| 45 | North Dakota | 2.48 |
| 45 | West Virginia | 2.48 |
| 49 | Montana | 2.47 |
| 50 | Vermont | 2.46 |
| | District of Columbia | 2.15 |

Source: U.S. Bureau of the Census
"Estimates of Housing Units, Households, and Persons per Household" (ST-98-46)
(http://www.census.gov/population/estimates/housing/sthuhh1.txt)
*As of July 1, 1998. A household includes all persons who occupy a housing unit. A household consists of a single family, one person living alone, two or more families living together, or any other group of related or unrelated persons who share living arrangements.

# Housing Units in 1998

## National Total = 112,499,000 Housing Units*

ALPHA ORDER

| RANK | STATE | HOUSING UNITS | % of USA |
|------|-------|---------------|----------|
| 22 | Alabama | 1,866,000 | 1.7% |
| 49 | Alaska | 248,000 | 0.2% |
| 21 | Arizona | 2,006,000 | 1.8% |
| 33 | Arkansas | 1,092,000 | 1.0% |
| 1 | California | 12,037,000 | 10.7% |
| 24 | Colorado | 1,722,000 | 1.5% |
| 29 | Connecticut | 1,379,000 | 1.2% |
| 45 | Delaware | 326,000 | 0.3% |
| 4 | Florida | 7,007,000 | 6.2% |
| 11 | Georgia | 3,184,000 | 2.8% |
| 42 | Hawaii | 440,000 | 0.4% |
| 41 | Idaho | 503,000 | 0.4% |
| 6 | Illinois | 4,777,000 | 4.2% |
| 14 | Indiana | 2,503,000 | 2.2% |
| 30 | Iowa | 1,208,000 | 1.1% |
| 31 | Kansas | 1,130,000 | 1.0% |
| 26 | Kentucky | 1,664,000 | 1.5% |
| 23 | Louisiana | 1,806,000 | 1.6% |
| 39 | Maine | 626,000 | 0.6% |
| 19 | Maryland | 2,091,000 | 1.9% |
| 13 | Massachusetts | 2,568,000 | 2.3% |
| 8 | Michigan | 4,168,000 | 3.7% |
| 20 | Minnesota | 2,021,000 | 1.8% |
| 32 | Mississippi | 1,106,000 | 1.0% |
| 15 | Missouri | 2,394,000 | 2.1% |
| 44 | Montana | 383,000 | 0.3% |
| 38 | Nebraska | 711,000 | 0.6% |
| 35 | Nevada | 767,000 | 0.7% |
| 40 | New Hampshire | 539,000 | 0.5% |
| 10 | New Jersey | 3,237,000 | 2.9% |
| 36 | New Mexico | 747,000 | 0.7% |
| 3 | New York | 7,455,000 | 6.6% |
| 9 | North Carolina | 3,367,000 | 3.0% |
| 47 | North Dakota | 293,000 | 0.3% |
| 7 | Ohio | 4,682,000 | 4.2% |
| 27 | Oklahoma | 1,459,000 | 1.3% |
| 28 | Oregon | 1,401,000 | 1.2% |
| 5 | Pennsylvania | 5,229,000 | 4.6% |
| 43 | Rhode Island | 431,000 | 0.4% |
| 25 | South Carolina | 1,683,000 | 1.5% |
| 46 | South Dakota | 322,000 | 0.3% |
| 17 | Tennessee | 2,318,000 | 2.1% |
| 2 | Texas | 7,808,000 | 6.9% |
| 37 | Utah | 731,000 | 0.6% |
| 48 | Vermont | 289,000 | 0.3% |
| 12 | Virginia | 2,837,000 | 2.5% |
| 16 | Washington | 2,386,000 | 2.1% |
| 34 | West Virginia | 794,000 | 0.7% |
| 18 | Wisconsin | 2,279,000 | 2.0% |
| 50 | Wyoming | 213,000 | 0.2% |

RANK ORDER

| RANK | STATE | HOUSING UNITS | % of USA |
|------|-------|---------------|----------|
| 1 | California | 12,037,000 | 10.7% |
| 2 | Texas | 7,808,000 | 6.9% |
| 3 | New York | 7,455,000 | 6.6% |
| 4 | Florida | 7,007,000 | 6.2% |
| 5 | Pennsylvania | 5,229,000 | 4.6% |
| 6 | Illinois | 4,777,000 | 4.2% |
| 7 | Ohio | 4,682,000 | 4.2% |
| 8 | Michigan | 4,168,000 | 3.7% |
| 9 | North Carolina | 3,367,000 | 3.0% |
| 10 | New Jersey | 3,237,000 | 2.9% |
| 11 | Georgia | 3,184,000 | 2.8% |
| 12 | Virginia | 2,837,000 | 2.5% |
| 13 | Massachusetts | 2,568,000 | 2.3% |
| 14 | Indiana | 2,503,000 | 2.2% |
| 15 | Missouri | 2,394,000 | 2.1% |
| 16 | Washington | 2,386,000 | 2.1% |
| 17 | Tennessee | 2,318,000 | 2.1% |
| 18 | Wisconsin | 2,279,000 | 2.0% |
| 19 | Maryland | 2,091,000 | 1.9% |
| 20 | Minnesota | 2,021,000 | 1.8% |
| 21 | Arizona | 2,006,000 | 1.8% |
| 22 | Alabama | 1,866,000 | 1.7% |
| 23 | Louisiana | 1,806,000 | 1.6% |
| 24 | Colorado | 1,722,000 | 1.5% |
| 25 | South Carolina | 1,683,000 | 1.5% |
| 26 | Kentucky | 1,664,000 | 1.5% |
| 27 | Oklahoma | 1,459,000 | 1.3% |
| 28 | Oregon | 1,401,000 | 1.2% |
| 29 | Connecticut | 1,379,000 | 1.2% |
| 30 | Iowa | 1,208,000 | 1.1% |
| 31 | Kansas | 1,130,000 | 1.0% |
| 32 | Mississippi | 1,106,000 | 1.0% |
| 33 | Arkansas | 1,092,000 | 1.0% |
| 34 | West Virginia | 794,000 | 0.7% |
| 35 | Nevada | 767,000 | 0.7% |
| 36 | New Mexico | 747,000 | 0.7% |
| 37 | Utah | 731,000 | 0.6% |
| 38 | Nebraska | 711,000 | 0.6% |
| 39 | Maine | 626,000 | 0.6% |
| 40 | New Hampshire | 539,000 | 0.5% |
| 41 | Idaho | 503,000 | 0.4% |
| 42 | Hawaii | 440,000 | 0.4% |
| 43 | Rhode Island | 431,000 | 0.4% |
| 44 | Montana | 383,000 | 0.3% |
| 45 | Delaware | 326,000 | 0.3% |
| 46 | South Dakota | 322,000 | 0.3% |
| 47 | North Dakota | 293,000 | 0.3% |
| 48 | Vermont | 289,000 | 0.3% |
| 49 | Alaska | 248,000 | 0.2% |
| 50 | Wyoming | 213,000 | 0.2% |
| | District of Columbia | 265,000 | 0.2% |

Source: U.S. Bureau of the Census
    "Estimates of Housing Units, Households and Persons per Household" (ST-98-46)
*A housing unit is a house, an apartment, a mobile home, a group of rooms, or a single room that is occupied (or if vacant, is intended for occupancy) as separate living quarters. Separate living quarters are those in which the occupants live and eat separately from any other persons in the building and which have direct access from the outside of the building or through a common hall.

# Percent Change in Housing Units: 1994 to 1998

## National Percent Change = 5.3% Increase*

| ALPHA ORDER | | | | RANK ORDER | | |
|---|---|---|---|---|---|---|
| RANK | STATE | PERCENT CHANGE | | RANK | STATE | PERCENT CHANGE |
| 15 | Alabama | 6.8 | | 1 | Nevada | 23.4 |
| 27 | Alaska | 4.7 | | 2 | Arizona | 12.8 |
| 2 | Arizona | 12.8 | | 3 | Utah | 11.7 |
| 20 | Arkansas | 5.7 | | 4 | Georgia | 11.6 |
| 40 | California | 3.0 | | 5 | Idaho | 11.4 |
| 7 | Colorado | 10.9 | | 6 | New Mexico | 11.3 |
| 46 | Connecticut | 2.2 | | 7 | Colorado | 10.9 |
| 22 | Delaware | 5.4 | | 8 | North Carolina | 10.6 |
| 13 | Florida | 7.2 | | 9 | South Carolina | 10.0 |
| 4 | Georgia | 11.6 | | 10 | Oregon | 9.1 |
| 25 | Hawaii | 4.9 | | 11 | Tennessee | 8.1 |
| 5 | Idaho | 11.4 | | 12 | Washington | 7.5 |
| 39 | Illinois | 3.1 | | 13 | Florida | 7.2 |
| 17 | Indiana | 6.2 | | 13 | Texas | 7.2 |
| 38 | Iowa | 3.2 | | 15 | Alabama | 6.8 |
| 25 | Kansas | 4.9 | | 16 | Virginia | 6.5 |
| 20 | Kentucky | 5.7 | | 17 | Indiana | 6.2 |
| 32 | Louisiana | 3.9 | | 18 | Mississippi | 6.0 |
| 40 | Maine | 3.0 | | 19 | South Dakota | 5.8 |
| 30 | Maryland | 4.4 | | 20 | Arkansas | 5.7 |
| 47 | Massachusetts | 2.0 | | 20 | Kentucky | 5.7 |
| 28 | Michigan | 4.6 | | 22 | Delaware | 5.4 |
| 29 | Minnesota | 4.5 | | 23 | Missouri | 5.3 |
| 18 | Mississippi | 6.0 | | 23 | Wisconsin | 5.3 |
| 23 | Missouri | 5.3 | | 25 | Hawaii | 4.9 |
| 33 | Montana | 3.8 | | 25 | Kansas | 4.9 |
| 30 | Nebraska | 4.4 | | 27 | Alaska | 4.7 |
| 1 | Nevada | 23.4 | | 28 | Michigan | 4.6 |
| 37 | New Hampshire | 3.5 | | 29 | Minnesota | 4.5 |
| 44 | New Jersey | 2.8 | | 30 | Maryland | 4.4 |
| 6 | New Mexico | 11.3 | | 30 | Nebraska | 4.4 |
| 49 | New York | 1.5 | | 32 | Louisiana | 3.9 |
| 8 | North Carolina | 10.6 | | 33 | Montana | 3.8 |
| 36 | North Dakota | 3.6 | | 33 | Wyoming | 3.8 |
| 35 | Ohio | 3.7 | | 35 | Ohio | 3.7 |
| 43 | Oklahoma | 2.9 | | 36 | North Dakota | 3.6 |
| 10 | Oregon | 9.1 | | 37 | New Hampshire | 3.5 |
| 44 | Pennsylvania | 2.8 | | 38 | Iowa | 3.2 |
| 48 | Rhode Island | 1.8 | | 39 | Illinois | 3.1 |
| 9 | South Carolina | 10.0 | | 40 | California | 3.0 |
| 19 | South Dakota | 5.8 | | 40 | Maine | 3.0 |
| 11 | Tennessee | 8.1 | | 40 | Vermont | 3.0 |
| 13 | Texas | 7.2 | | 43 | Oklahoma | 2.9 |
| 3 | Utah | 11.7 | | 44 | New Jersey | 2.8 |
| 40 | Vermont | 3.0 | | 44 | Pennsylvania | 2.8 |
| 16 | Virginia | 6.5 | | 46 | Connecticut | 2.2 |
| 12 | Washington | 7.5 | | 47 | Massachusetts | 2.0 |
| 50 | West Virginia | 1.4 | | 48 | Rhode Island | 1.8 |
| 23 | Wisconsin | 5.3 | | 49 | New York | 1.5 |
| 33 | Wyoming | 3.8 | | 50 | West Virginia | 1.4 |
| | | | | | District of Columbia | (2.5) |

*Source: Morgan Quitno Press using data from U.S. Bureau of the Census*
*"Estimates of Housing Units, Households and Persons per Household"*
*"*A housing unit is a house, an apartment, a mobile home, a group of rooms, or a single room that is occupied (or if vacant, is intended for occupancy) as separate living quarters. Separate living quarters are those in which the occupants live and eat separately from any other persons in the building and which have direct access from the outside of the building or through a common hall.*

# New Housing Units Authorized in 2000

## National Total = 1,574,361 Units*

ALPHA ORDER

RANK ORDER

| RANK | STATE | UNITS | % of USA | RANK | STATE | UNITS | % of USA |
|------|-------|-------|----------|------|-------|-------|----------|
| 25 | Alabama | 19,433 | 1.2% | 1 | Florida | 152,738 | 9.7% |
| 48 | Alaska | 2,117 | 0.1% | 2 | California | 143,913 | 9.1% |
| 6 | Arizona | 60,111 | 3.8% | 3 | Texas | 136,541 | 8.7% |
| 35 | Arkansas | 9,546 | 0.6% | 4 | Georgia | 93,328 | 5.9% |
| 2 | California | 143,913 | 9.1% | 5 | North Carolina | 77,884 | 4.9% |
| 7 | Colorado | 53,749 | 3.4% | 6 | Arizona | 60,111 | 3.8% |
| 36 | Connecticut | 9,354 | 0.6% | 7 | Colorado | 53,749 | 3.4% |
| 42 | Delaware | 4,662 | 0.3% | 8 | Illinois | 52,011 | 3.3% |
| 1 | Florida | 152,738 | 9.7% | 9 | Michigan | 50,940 | 3.2% |
| 4 | Georgia | 93,328 | 5.9% | 10 | Ohio | 49,325 | 3.1% |
| 41 | Hawaii | 4,783 | 0.3% | 11 | Virginia | 48,479 | 3.1% |
| 34 | Idaho | 10,192 | 0.6% | 12 | New York | 45,365 | 2.9% |
| 8 | Illinois | 52,011 | 3.3% | 13 | Washington | 41,369 | 2.6% |
| 15 | Indiana | 37,466 | 2.4% | 14 | Pennsylvania | 39,550 | 2.5% |
| 30 | Iowa | 12,559 | 0.8% | 15 | Indiana | 37,466 | 2.4% |
| 31 | Kansas | 12,170 | 0.8% | 16 | Tennessee | 34,128 | 2.2% |
| 26 | Kentucky | 18,258 | 1.2% | 17 | Wisconsin | 32,789 | 2.1% |
| 29 | Louisiana | 13,606 | 0.9% | 18 | Minnesota | 32,697 | 2.1% |
| 40 | Maine | 5,818 | 0.4% | 19 | Nevada | 32,550 | 2.1% |
| 22 | Maryland | 29,417 | 1.9% | 20 | South Carolina | 32,396 | 2.1% |
| 27 | Massachusetts | 17,385 | 1.1% | 21 | New Jersey | 32,311 | 2.1% |
| 9 | Michigan | 50,940 | 3.2% | 22 | Maryland | 29,417 | 1.9% |
| 18 | Minnesota | 32,697 | 2.1% | 23 | Missouri | 23,212 | 1.5% |
| 32 | Mississippi | 11,424 | 0.7% | 24 | Oregon | 19,785 | 1.3% |
| 23 | Missouri | 23,212 | 1.5% | 25 | Alabama | 19,433 | 1.2% |
| 46 | Montana | 2,426 | 0.2% | 26 | Kentucky | 18,258 | 1.2% |
| 38 | Nebraska | 8,684 | 0.6% | 27 | Massachusetts | 17,385 | 1.1% |
| 19 | Nevada | 32,550 | 2.1% | 28 | Utah | 16,512 | 1.0% |
| 39 | New Hampshire | 6,445 | 0.4% | 29 | Louisiana | 13,606 | 0.9% |
| 21 | New Jersey | 32,311 | 2.1% | 30 | Iowa | 12,559 | 0.8% |
| 37 | New Mexico | 8,740 | 0.6% | 31 | Kansas | 12,170 | 0.8% |
| 12 | New York | 45,365 | 2.9% | 32 | Mississippi | 11,424 | 0.7% |
| 5 | North Carolina | 77,884 | 4.9% | 33 | Oklahoma | 11,251 | 0.7% |
| 49 | North Dakota | 1,983 | 0.1% | 34 | Idaho | 10,192 | 0.6% |
| 10 | Ohio | 49,325 | 3.1% | 35 | Arkansas | 9,546 | 0.6% |
| 33 | Oklahoma | 11,251 | 0.7% | 36 | Connecticut | 9,354 | 0.6% |
| 24 | Oregon | 19,785 | 1.3% | 37 | New Mexico | 8,740 | 0.6% |
| 14 | Pennsylvania | 39,550 | 2.5% | 38 | Nebraska | 8,684 | 0.6% |
| 45 | Rhode Island | 2,576 | 0.2% | 39 | New Hampshire | 6,445 | 0.4% |
| 20 | South Carolina | 32,396 | 2.1% | 40 | Maine | 5,818 | 0.4% |
| 43 | South Dakota | 4,268 | 0.3% | 41 | Hawaii | 4,783 | 0.3% |
| 16 | Tennessee | 34,128 | 2.2% | 42 | Delaware | 4,662 | 0.3% |
| 3 | Texas | 136,541 | 8.7% | 43 | South Dakota | 4,268 | 0.3% |
| 28 | Utah | 16,512 | 1.0% | 44 | West Virginia | 3,504 | 0.2% |
| 47 | Vermont | 2,278 | 0.1% | 45 | Rhode Island | 2,576 | 0.2% |
| 11 | Virginia | 48,479 | 3.1% | 46 | Montana | 2,426 | 0.2% |
| 13 | Washington | 41,369 | 2.6% | 47 | Vermont | 2,278 | 0.1% |
| 44 | West Virginia | 3,504 | 0.2% | 48 | Alaska | 2,117 | 0.1% |
| 17 | Wisconsin | 32,789 | 2.1% | 49 | North Dakota | 1,983 | 0.1% |
| 50 | Wyoming | 1,527 | 0.1% | 50 | Wyoming | 1,527 | 0.1% |
| | | | | | District of Columbia | 806 | 0.1% |

Source: U.S. Bureau of the Census
   "New Privately Owned Housing Units Authorized" (http://www.census.gov/const/C40/Table2/t2yu0012.txt)
*Preliminary and unadjusted. Includes single and multifamily privately owned units. Based on approximately 19,000 places in the U.S. having building permit systems.

# Value of New Housing Units Authorized in 2000

## National Total = $182,590,023,000*

ALPHA ORDER

| RANK | STATE | VALUE | % of USA |
|------|-------|-------|----------|
| 27 | Alabama | $1,933,594,000 | 1.1% |
| 45 | Alaska | 319,823,000 | 0.2% |
| 6 | Arizona | 7,058,774,000 | 3.9% |
| 38 | Arkansas | 881,861,000 | 0.5% |
| 1 | California | 23,051,969,000 | 12.6% |
| 7 | Colorado | 6,704,084,000 | 3.7% |
| 30 | Connecticut | 1,412,331,000 | 0.8% |
| 42 | Delaware | 427,195,000 | 0.2% |
| 2 | Florida | 16,937,457,000 | 9.3% |
| 4 | Georgia | 8,749,459,000 | 4.8% |
| 40 | Hawaii | 798,610,000 | 0.4% |
| 33 | Idaho | 1,298,441,000 | 0.7% |
| 8 | Illinois | 6,542,127,000 | 3.6% |
| 15 | Indiana | 4,390,215,000 | 2.4% |
| 31 | Iowa | 1,360,189,000 | 0.7% |
| 32 | Kansas | 1,341,918,000 | 0.7% |
| 28 | Kentucky | 1,670,691,000 | 0.9% |
| 29 | Louisiana | 1,430,675,000 | 0.8% |
| 41 | Maine | 700,370,000 | 0.4% |
| 22 | Maryland | 3,178,084,000 | 1.7% |
| 23 | Massachusetts | 2,620,425,000 | 1.4% |
| 10 | Michigan | 6,045,938,000 | 3.3% |
| 16 | Minnesota | 4,111,150,000 | 2.3% |
| 36 | Mississippi | 925,688,000 | 0.5% |
| 25 | Missouri | 2,450,158,000 | 1.3% |
| 49 | Montana | 210,964,000 | 0.1% |
| 39 | Nebraska | 809,725,000 | 0.4% |
| 20 | Nevada | 3,322,965,000 | 1.8% |
| 37 | New Hampshire | 894,686,000 | 0.5% |
| 21 | New Jersey | 3,243,821,000 | 1.8% |
| 35 | New Mexico | 1,058,956,000 | 0.6% |
| 12 | New York | 4,824,285,000 | 2.6% |
| 5 | North Carolina | 8,565,100,000 | 4.7% |
| 50 | North Dakota | 180,383,000 | 0.1% |
| 9 | Ohio | 6,046,425,000 | 3.3% |
| 34 | Oklahoma | 1,161,252,000 | 0.6% |
| 24 | Oregon | 2,546,290,000 | 1.4% |
| 14 | Pennsylvania | 4,478,684,000 | 2.5% |
| 47 | Rhode Island | 293,690,000 | 0.2% |
| 19 | South Carolina | 3,455,028,000 | 1.9% |
| 43 | South Dakota | 367,360,000 | 0.2% |
| 18 | Tennessee | 3,519,505,000 | 1.9% |
| 3 | Texas | 14,989,905,000 | 8.2% |
| 26 | Utah | 1,956,975,000 | 1.1% |
| 48 | Vermont | 268,236,000 | 0.1% |
| 11 | Virginia | 5,009,493,000 | 2.7% |
| 13 | Washington | 4,605,017,000 | 2.5% |
| 44 | West Virginia | 338,380,000 | 0.2% |
| 17 | Wisconsin | 3,743,224,000 | 2.1% |
| 46 | Wyoming | 304,461,000 | 0.2% |

RANK ORDER

| RANK | STATE | VALUE | % of USA |
|------|-------|-------|----------|
| 1 | California | $23,051,969,000 | 12.6% |
| 2 | Florida | 16,937,457,000 | 9.3% |
| 3 | Texas | 14,989,905,000 | 8.2% |
| 4 | Georgia | 8,749,459,000 | 4.8% |
| 5 | North Carolina | 8,565,100,000 | 4.7% |
| 6 | Arizona | 7,058,774,000 | 3.9% |
| 7 | Colorado | 6,704,084,000 | 3.7% |
| 8 | Illinois | 6,542,127,000 | 3.6% |
| 9 | Ohio | 6,046,425,000 | 3.3% |
| 10 | Michigan | 6,045,938,000 | 3.3% |
| 11 | Virginia | 5,009,493,000 | 2.7% |
| 12 | New York | 4,824,285,000 | 2.6% |
| 13 | Washington | 4,605,017,000 | 2.5% |
| 14 | Pennsylvania | 4,478,684,000 | 2.5% |
| 15 | Indiana | 4,390,215,000 | 2.4% |
| 16 | Minnesota | 4,111,150,000 | 2.3% |
| 17 | Wisconsin | 3,743,224,000 | 2.1% |
| 18 | Tennessee | 3,519,505,000 | 1.9% |
| 19 | South Carolina | 3,455,028,000 | 1.9% |
| 20 | Nevada | 3,322,965,000 | 1.8% |
| 21 | New Jersey | 3,243,821,000 | 1.8% |
| 22 | Maryland | 3,178,084,000 | 1.7% |
| 23 | Massachusetts | 2,620,425,000 | 1.4% |
| 24 | Oregon | 2,546,290,000 | 1.4% |
| 25 | Missouri | 2,450,158,000 | 1.3% |
| 26 | Utah | 1,956,975,000 | 1.1% |
| 27 | Alabama | 1,933,594,000 | 1.1% |
| 28 | Kentucky | 1,670,691,000 | 0.9% |
| 29 | Louisiana | 1,430,675,000 | 0.8% |
| 30 | Connecticut | 1,412,331,000 | 0.8% |
| 31 | Iowa | 1,360,189,000 | 0.7% |
| 32 | Kansas | 1,341,918,000 | 0.7% |
| 33 | Idaho | 1,298,441,000 | 0.7% |
| 34 | Oklahoma | 1,161,252,000 | 0.6% |
| 35 | New Mexico | 1,058,956,000 | 0.6% |
| 36 | Mississippi | 925,688,000 | 0.5% |
| 37 | New Hampshire | 894,686,000 | 0.5% |
| 38 | Arkansas | 881,861,000 | 0.5% |
| 39 | Nebraska | 809,725,000 | 0.4% |
| 40 | Hawaii | 798,610,000 | 0.4% |
| 41 | Maine | 700,370,000 | 0.4% |
| 42 | Delaware | 427,195,000 | 0.2% |
| 43 | South Dakota | 367,360,000 | 0.2% |
| 44 | West Virginia | 338,380,000 | 0.2% |
| 45 | Alaska | 319,823,000 | 0.2% |
| 46 | Wyoming | 304,461,000 | 0.2% |
| 47 | Rhode Island | 293,690,000 | 0.2% |
| 48 | Vermont | 268,236,000 | 0.1% |
| 49 | Montana | 210,964,000 | 0.1% |
| 50 | North Dakota | 180,383,000 | 0.1% |
| | District of Columbia | 53,992,000 | 0.0% |

Source: U.S. Bureau of the Census
    "New Privately Owned Housing Units Authorized" (http://www.census.gov/const/C40/Table2/t2yv0012.txt)
*Preliminary and unadjusted. Includes single and multifamily privately owned units. Based on approximately 19,000 places in the U.S. having building permit systems.

# Average Value of New Housing Units in 2000

## National Average = $115,977 per Unit*

| ALPHA ORDER | | | | RANK ORDER | | |
|---|---|---|---|---|---|---|
| RANK | STATE | VALUE | | RANK | STATE | VALUE |
| 40 | Alabama | $99,501 | | 1 | Wyoming | $199,385 |
| 4 | Alaska | 151,074 | | 2 | Hawaii | 166,968 |
| 19 | Arizona | 117,429 | | 3 | California | 160,180 |
| 44 | Arkansas | 92,380 | | 4 | Alaska | 151,074 |
| 3 | California | 160,180 | | 5 | Connecticut | 150,987 |
| 12 | Colorado | 124,729 | | 6 | Massachusetts | 150,729 |
| 5 | Connecticut | 150,987 | | 7 | New Hampshire | 138,819 |
| 45 | Delaware | 91,633 | | 8 | Oregon | 128,698 |
| 25 | Florida | 110,892 | | 9 | Idaho | 127,398 |
| 42 | Georgia | 93,750 | | 10 | Illinois | 125,784 |
| 2 | Hawaii | 166,968 | | 11 | Minnesota | 125,735 |
| 9 | Idaho | 127,398 | | 12 | Colorado | 124,729 |
| 10 | Illinois | 125,784 | | 13 | Ohio | 122,583 |
| 20 | Indiana | 117,179 | | 14 | New Mexico | 121,162 |
| 29 | Iowa | 108,304 | | 15 | Maine | 120,380 |
| 26 | Kansas | 110,264 | | 16 | Michigan | 118,687 |
| 46 | Kentucky | 91,505 | | 17 | Utah | 118,518 |
| 34 | Louisiana | 105,150 | | 18 | Vermont | 117,751 |
| 15 | Maine | 120,380 | | 19 | Arizona | 117,429 |
| 30 | Maryland | 108,036 | | 20 | Indiana | 117,179 |
| 6 | Massachusetts | 150,729 | | 21 | Wisconsin | 114,161 |
| 16 | Michigan | 118,687 | | 22 | Rhode Island | 114,010 |
| 11 | Minnesota | 125,735 | | 23 | Pennsylvania | 113,241 |
| 50 | Mississippi | 81,030 | | 24 | Washington | 111,316 |
| 33 | Missouri | 105,556 | | 25 | Florida | 110,892 |
| 48 | Montana | 86,960 | | 26 | Kansas | 110,264 |
| 43 | Nebraska | 93,243 | | 27 | North Carolina | 109,973 |
| 38 | Nevada | 102,088 | | 28 | Texas | 109,783 |
| 7 | New Hampshire | 138,819 | | 29 | Iowa | 108,304 |
| 39 | New Jersey | 100,394 | | 30 | Maryland | 108,036 |
| 14 | New Mexico | 121,162 | | 31 | South Carolina | 106,650 |
| 32 | New York | 106,344 | | 32 | New York | 106,344 |
| 27 | North Carolina | 109,973 | | 33 | Missouri | 105,556 |
| 47 | North Dakota | 90,965 | | 34 | Louisiana | 105,150 |
| 13 | Ohio | 122,583 | | 35 | Virginia | 103,333 |
| 36 | Oklahoma | 103,213 | | 36 | Oklahoma | 103,213 |
| 8 | Oregon | 128,698 | | 37 | Tennessee | 103,127 |
| 23 | Pennsylvania | 113,241 | | 38 | Nevada | 102,088 |
| 22 | Rhode Island | 114,010 | | 39 | New Jersey | 100,394 |
| 31 | South Carolina | 106,650 | | 40 | Alabama | 99,501 |
| 49 | South Dakota | 86,073 | | 41 | West Virginia | 96,570 |
| 37 | Tennessee | 103,127 | | 42 | Georgia | 93,750 |
| 28 | Texas | 109,783 | | 43 | Nebraska | 93,243 |
| 17 | Utah | 118,518 | | 44 | Arkansas | 92,380 |
| 18 | Vermont | 117,751 | | 45 | Delaware | 91,633 |
| 35 | Virginia | 103,333 | | 46 | Kentucky | 91,505 |
| 24 | Washington | 111,316 | | 47 | North Dakota | 90,965 |
| 41 | West Virginia | 96,570 | | 48 | Montana | 86,960 |
| 21 | Wisconsin | 114,161 | | 49 | South Dakota | 86,073 |
| 1 | Wyoming | 199,385 | | 50 | Mississippi | 81,030 |
| | | | | | District of Columbia | 66,988 |

Source: Morgan Quitno Press using data from U.S. Bureau of the Census
"New Privately Owned Housing Units Authorized"
*Preliminary and unadjusted. Includes single and multifamily privately owned units. Based on approximately 19,000 places in the U.S. having building permit systems.

# Percent Change in Number of New Housing Units Authorized: 1999 to 2000

## National Percent Change = 5.4% Decrease*

ALPHA ORDER

| RANK | STATE | PERCENT CHANGE |
|------|-------|----------------|
| 8 | Alabama | 2.1 |
| 17 | Alaska | (4.3) |
| 24 | Arizona | (7.7) |
| 42 | Arkansas | (17.0) |
| 5 | California | 4.3 |
| 3 | Colorado | 9.0 |
| 36 | Connecticut | (12.1) |
| 35 | Delaware | (11.8) |
| 22 | Florida | (7.3) |
| 6 | Georgia | 4.2 |
| 2 | Hawaii | 13.6 |
| 41 | Idaho | (16.3) |
| 16 | Illinois | (3.6) |
| 30 | Indiana | (9.7) |
| 20 | Iowa | (6.6) |
| 47 | Kansas | (22.4) |
| 40 | Kentucky | (15.4) |
| 49 | Louisiana | (23.7) |
| 7 | Maine | 2.3 |
| 13 | Maryland | (1.1) |
| 28 | Massachusetts | (8.3) |
| 19 | Michigan | (6.1) |
| 14 | Minnesota | (1.9) |
| 33 | Mississippi | (11.2) |
| 38 | Missouri | (13.5) |
| 18 | Montana | (5.5) |
| 11 | Nebraska | (0.1) |
| 12 | Nevada | (0.3) |
| 9 | New Hampshire | 1.9 |
| 10 | New Jersey | 1.0 |
| 31 | New Mexico | (10.0) |
| 4 | New York | 6.5 |
| 27 | North Carolina | (8.1) |
| 48 | North Dakota | (23.1) |
| 34 | Ohio | (11.7) |
| 46 | Oklahoma | (20.7) |
| 39 | Oregon | (14.9) |
| 22 | Pennsylvania | (7.3) |
| 50 | Rhode Island | (24.5) |
| 32 | South Carolina | (10.4) |
| 1 | South Dakota | 16.2 |
| 25 | Tennessee | (7.8) |
| 21 | Texas | (6.8) |
| 44 | Utah | (19.3) |
| 37 | Vermont | (12.4) |
| 29 | Virginia | (8.8) |
| 15 | Washington | (3.2) |
| 43 | West Virginia | (17.2) |
| 25 | Wisconsin | (7.8) |
| 45 | Wyoming | (19.6) |

RANK ORDER

| RANK | STATE | PERCENT CHANGE |
|------|-------|----------------|
| 1 | South Dakota | 16.2 |
| 2 | Hawaii | 13.6 |
| 3 | Colorado | 9.0 |
| 4 | New York | 6.5 |
| 5 | California | 4.3 |
| 6 | Georgia | 4.2 |
| 7 | Maine | 2.3 |
| 8 | Alabama | 2.1 |
| 9 | New Hampshire | 1.9 |
| 10 | New Jersey | 1.0 |
| 11 | Nebraska | (0.1) |
| 12 | Nevada | (0.3) |
| 13 | Maryland | (1.1) |
| 14 | Minnesota | (1.9) |
| 15 | Washington | (3.2) |
| 16 | Illinois | (3.6) |
| 17 | Alaska | (4.3) |
| 18 | Montana | (5.5) |
| 19 | Michigan | (6.1) |
| 20 | Iowa | (6.6) |
| 21 | Texas | (6.8) |
| 22 | Florida | (7.3) |
| 22 | Pennsylvania | (7.3) |
| 24 | Arizona | (7.7) |
| 25 | Tennessee | (7.8) |
| 25 | Wisconsin | (7.8) |
| 27 | North Carolina | (8.1) |
| 28 | Massachusetts | (8.3) |
| 29 | Virginia | (8.8) |
| 30 | Indiana | (9.7) |
| 31 | New Mexico | (10.0) |
| 32 | South Carolina | (10.4) |
| 33 | Mississippi | (11.2) |
| 34 | Ohio | (11.7) |
| 35 | Delaware | (11.8) |
| 36 | Connecticut | (12.1) |
| 37 | Vermont | (12.4) |
| 38 | Missouri | (13.5) |
| 39 | Oregon | (14.9) |
| 40 | Kentucky | (15.4) |
| 41 | Idaho | (16.3) |
| 42 | Arkansas | (17.0) |
| 43 | West Virginia | (17.2) |
| 44 | Utah | (19.3) |
| 45 | Wyoming | (19.6) |
| 46 | Oklahoma | (20.7) |
| 47 | Kansas | (22.4) |
| 48 | North Dakota | (23.1) |
| 49 | Louisiana | (23.7) |
| 50 | Rhode Island | (24.5) |

District of Columbia     18.0

*Source: Morgan Quitno Press using data from U.S. Bureau of the Census*
    *"New Privately Owned Housing Units Authorized" (http://www.census.gov/const/C40/Table2/t2yu0012.txt)*
*2000 figures are preliminary and unadjusted. 1999 figures are revised and final. Includes single and multifamily privately owned units. Based on approximately 19,000 places in the U.S. having building permit systems.*

# Percent Change in Value of New Housing Units Authorized: 1999 to 2000

## National Percent Change = 0.7% Increase*

*Source: Morgan Quitno Press using data from U.S. Bureau of the Census*
   *"New Privately Owned Housing Units Authorized" (http://www.census.gov/const/C40/Table2/t2yu0012.txt)*
*\*2000 figures are preliminary and unadjusted.  1999 figures are revised and final.  Includes single and multifamily privately owned units.  Based on approximately 19,000 places in the U.S. having building permit systems.*

# Percent Change in House Prices: 1996 to 2000

## National Average = 28.5% Increase*

<table>
<tr><td colspan="3">ALPHA ORDER</td><td colspan="3">RANK ORDER</td></tr>
<tr><td>RANK</td><td>STATE</td><td>PERCENT CHANGE</td><td>RANK</td><td>STATE</td><td>PERCENT CHANGE</td></tr>
<tr><td>34</td><td>Alabama</td><td>22.4</td><td>1</td><td>Massachusetts</td><td>49.3</td></tr>
<tr><td>47</td><td>Alaska</td><td>14.0</td><td>2</td><td>Colorado</td><td>46.2</td></tr>
<tr><td>13</td><td>Arizona</td><td>28.4</td><td>3</td><td>Michigan</td><td>43.6</td></tr>
<tr><td>44</td><td>Arkansas</td><td>16.4</td><td>4</td><td>Minnesota</td><td>43.1</td></tr>
<tr><td>6</td><td>California</td><td>36.3</td><td>5</td><td>New Hampshire</td><td>42.5</td></tr>
<tr><td>2</td><td>Colorado</td><td>46.2</td><td>6</td><td>California</td><td>36.3</td></tr>
<tr><td>32</td><td>Connecticut</td><td>23.4</td><td>7</td><td>Georgia</td><td>33.4</td></tr>
<tr><td>42</td><td>Delaware</td><td>17.6</td><td>8</td><td>Kansas</td><td>30.6</td></tr>
<tr><td>29</td><td>Florida</td><td>23.7</td><td>9</td><td>Washington</td><td>29.8</td></tr>
<tr><td>7</td><td>Georgia</td><td>33.4</td><td>10</td><td>Maine</td><td>29.3</td></tr>
<tr><td>50</td><td>Hawaii</td><td>(8.6)</td><td>11</td><td>New York</td><td>28.7</td></tr>
<tr><td>45</td><td>Idaho</td><td>16.0</td><td>11</td><td>South Carolina</td><td>28.7</td></tr>
<tr><td>34</td><td>Illinois</td><td>22.4</td><td>13</td><td>Arizona</td><td>28.4</td></tr>
<tr><td>30</td><td>Indiana</td><td>23.5</td><td>14</td><td>Oregon</td><td>28.1</td></tr>
<tr><td>21</td><td>Iowa</td><td>25.7</td><td>15</td><td>Nebraska</td><td>27.9</td></tr>
<tr><td>8</td><td>Kansas</td><td>30.6</td><td>16</td><td>Missouri</td><td>26.9</td></tr>
<tr><td>23</td><td>Kentucky</td><td>25.5</td><td>17</td><td>North Carolina</td><td>26.7</td></tr>
<tr><td>19</td><td>Louisiana</td><td>26.3</td><td>17</td><td>Wisconsin</td><td>26.7</td></tr>
<tr><td>10</td><td>Maine</td><td>29.3</td><td>19</td><td>Louisiana</td><td>26.3</td></tr>
<tr><td>43</td><td>Maryland</td><td>16.8</td><td>20</td><td>Ohio</td><td>26.1</td></tr>
<tr><td>1</td><td>Massachusetts</td><td>49.3</td><td>21</td><td>Iowa</td><td>25.7</td></tr>
<tr><td>3</td><td>Michigan</td><td>43.6</td><td>22</td><td>New Jersey</td><td>25.6</td></tr>
<tr><td>4</td><td>Minnesota</td><td>43.1</td><td>23</td><td>Kentucky</td><td>25.5</td></tr>
<tr><td>26</td><td>Mississippi</td><td>24.4</td><td>23</td><td>Texas</td><td>25.5</td></tr>
<tr><td>16</td><td>Missouri</td><td>26.9</td><td>25</td><td>Tennessee</td><td>25.2</td></tr>
<tr><td>38</td><td>Montana</td><td>20.1</td><td>26</td><td>Mississippi</td><td>24.4</td></tr>
<tr><td>15</td><td>Nebraska</td><td>27.9</td><td>26</td><td>South Dakota</td><td>24.4</td></tr>
<tr><td>48</td><td>Nevada</td><td>13.2</td><td>28</td><td>Oklahoma</td><td>24.2</td></tr>
<tr><td>5</td><td>New Hampshire</td><td>42.5</td><td>29</td><td>Florida</td><td>23.7</td></tr>
<tr><td>22</td><td>New Jersey</td><td>25.6</td><td>30</td><td>Indiana</td><td>23.5</td></tr>
<tr><td>49</td><td>New Mexico</td><td>12.3</td><td>30</td><td>Utah</td><td>23.5</td></tr>
<tr><td>11</td><td>New York</td><td>28.7</td><td>32</td><td>Connecticut</td><td>23.4</td></tr>
<tr><td>17</td><td>North Carolina</td><td>26.7</td><td>33</td><td>Rhode Island</td><td>23.1</td></tr>
<tr><td>41</td><td>North Dakota</td><td>17.9</td><td>34</td><td>Alabama</td><td>22.4</td></tr>
<tr><td>20</td><td>Ohio</td><td>26.1</td><td>34</td><td>Illinois</td><td>22.4</td></tr>
<tr><td>28</td><td>Oklahoma</td><td>24.2</td><td>36</td><td>Virginia</td><td>21.3</td></tr>
<tr><td>14</td><td>Oregon</td><td>28.1</td><td>37</td><td>Vermont</td><td>20.9</td></tr>
<tr><td>46</td><td>Pennsylvania</td><td>15.2</td><td>38</td><td>Montana</td><td>20.1</td></tr>
<tr><td>33</td><td>Rhode Island</td><td>23.1</td><td>39</td><td>West Virginia</td><td>19.1</td></tr>
<tr><td>11</td><td>South Carolina</td><td>28.7</td><td>40</td><td>Wyoming</td><td>19.0</td></tr>
<tr><td>26</td><td>South Dakota</td><td>24.4</td><td>41</td><td>North Dakota</td><td>17.9</td></tr>
<tr><td>25</td><td>Tennessee</td><td>25.2</td><td>42</td><td>Delaware</td><td>17.6</td></tr>
<tr><td>23</td><td>Texas</td><td>25.5</td><td>43</td><td>Maryland</td><td>16.8</td></tr>
<tr><td>30</td><td>Utah</td><td>23.5</td><td>44</td><td>Arkansas</td><td>16.4</td></tr>
<tr><td>37</td><td>Vermont</td><td>20.9</td><td>45</td><td>Idaho</td><td>16.0</td></tr>
<tr><td>36</td><td>Virginia</td><td>21.3</td><td>46</td><td>Pennsylvania</td><td>15.2</td></tr>
<tr><td>9</td><td>Washington</td><td>29.8</td><td>47</td><td>Alaska</td><td>14.0</td></tr>
<tr><td>39</td><td>West Virginia</td><td>19.1</td><td>48</td><td>Nevada</td><td>13.2</td></tr>
<tr><td>17</td><td>Wisconsin</td><td>26.7</td><td>49</td><td>New Mexico</td><td>12.3</td></tr>
<tr><td>40</td><td>Wyoming</td><td>19.0</td><td>50</td><td>Hawaii</td><td>(8.6)</td></tr>
<tr><td></td><td></td><td></td><td colspan="2">District of Columbia</td><td>30.4</td></tr>
</table>

*Source: Office of Federal Housing Enterprise Oversight
"House Price Index" (http://www.ofheo.gov/house/)
*Single-family house prices.  As of September 30, 2000.*

# Existing Home Sales in 2000

## National Total = 5,853,000 Homes*

ALPHA ORDER

| RANK | STATE | HOMES | % of USA |
|---|---|---|---|
| 26 | Alabama | 77,800 | 1.3% |
| 45 | Alaska | 18,300 | 0.3% |
| 9 | Arizona | 169,800 | 2.9% |
| 30 | Arkansas | 58,400 | 1.0% |
| 1 | California | 690,200 | 11.8% |
| 13 | Colorado | 149,200 | 2.5% |
| 33 | Connecticut | 49,000 | 0.8% |
| 49 | Delaware | 7,900 | 0.1% |
| 3 | Florida | 519,800 | 8.9% |
| 12 | Georgia | 149,600 | 2.6% |
| 42 | Hawaii | 21,700 | 0.4% |
| 39 | Idaho | 28,900 | 0.5% |
| 4 | Illinois | 242,300 | 4.1% |
| 17 | Indiana | 130,100 | 2.2% |
| 31 | Iowa | 54,900 | 0.9% |
| 28 | Kansas | 66,200 | 1.1% |
| 27 | Kentucky | 73,300 | 1.3% |
| 25 | Louisiana | 87,000 | 1.5% |
| 37 | Maine | 37,100 | 0.6% |
| 20 | Maryland | 104,900 | 1.8% |
| 24 | Massachusetts | 93,000 | 1.6% |
| 11 | Michigan | 156,900 | 2.7% |
| 19 | Minnesota | 108,500 | 1.9% |
| 35 | Mississippi | 46,600 | 0.8% |
| 18 | Missouri | 120,500 | 2.1% |
| 44 | Montana | 18,700 | 0.3% |
| 38 | Nebraska | 31,300 | 0.5% |
| 32 | Nevada | 53,200 | 0.9% |
| 36 | New Hampshire | 40,900 | 0.7% |
| 15 | New Jersey | 139,000 | 2.4% |
| 40 | New Mexico | 28,600 | 0.5% |
| 7 | New York | 179,300 | 3.1% |
| 5 | North Carolina | 239,300 | 4.1% |
| 48 | North Dakota | 10,400 | 0.2% |
| 6 | Ohio | 189,200 | 3.2% |
| 22 | Oklahoma | 96,900 | 1.7% |
| 29 | Oregon | 61,800 | 1.1% |
| 10 | Pennsylvania | 168,500 | 2.9% |
| 43 | Rhode Island | 19,300 | 0.3% |
| 21 | South Carolina | 100,200 | 1.7% |
| 46 | South Dakota | 15,500 | 0.3% |
| 14 | Tennessee | 148,600 | 2.5% |
| 2 | Texas | 545,300 | 9.3% |
| 34 | Utah | 47,800 | 0.8% |
| 50 | Vermont | 6,700 | 0.1% |
| 16 | Virginia | 135,200 | 2.3% |
| 8 | Washington | 171,600 | 2.9% |
| 41 | West Virginia | 23,600 | 0.4% |
| 23 | Wisconsin | 94,600 | 1.6% |
| 47 | Wyoming | 12,600 | 0.2% |

RANK ORDER

| RANK | STATE | HOMES | % of USA |
|---|---|---|---|
| 1 | California | 690,200 | 11.8% |
| 2 | Texas | 545,300 | 9.3% |
| 3 | Florida | 519,800 | 8.9% |
| 4 | Illinois | 242,300 | 4.1% |
| 5 | North Carolina | 239,300 | 4.1% |
| 6 | Ohio | 189,200 | 3.2% |
| 7 | New York | 179,300 | 3.1% |
| 8 | Washington | 171,600 | 2.9% |
| 9 | Arizona | 169,800 | 2.9% |
| 10 | Pennsylvania | 168,500 | 2.9% |
| 11 | Michigan | 156,900 | 2.7% |
| 12 | Georgia | 149,600 | 2.6% |
| 13 | Colorado | 149,200 | 2.5% |
| 14 | Tennessee | 148,600 | 2.5% |
| 15 | New Jersey | 139,000 | 2.4% |
| 16 | Virginia | 135,200 | 2.3% |
| 17 | Indiana | 130,100 | 2.2% |
| 18 | Missouri | 120,500 | 2.1% |
| 19 | Minnesota | 108,500 | 1.9% |
| 20 | Maryland | 104,900 | 1.8% |
| 21 | South Carolina | 100,200 | 1.7% |
| 22 | Oklahoma | 96,900 | 1.7% |
| 23 | Wisconsin | 94,600 | 1.6% |
| 24 | Massachusetts | 93,000 | 1.6% |
| 25 | Louisiana | 87,000 | 1.5% |
| 26 | Alabama | 77,800 | 1.3% |
| 27 | Kentucky | 73,300 | 1.3% |
| 28 | Kansas | 66,200 | 1.1% |
| 29 | Oregon | 61,800 | 1.1% |
| 30 | Arkansas | 58,400 | 1.0% |
| 31 | Iowa | 54,900 | 0.9% |
| 32 | Nevada | 53,200 | 0.9% |
| 33 | Connecticut | 49,000 | 0.8% |
| 34 | Utah | 47,800 | 0.8% |
| 35 | Mississippi | 46,600 | 0.8% |
| 36 | New Hampshire | 40,900 | 0.7% |
| 37 | Maine | 37,100 | 0.6% |
| 38 | Nebraska | 31,300 | 0.5% |
| 39 | Idaho | 28,900 | 0.5% |
| 40 | New Mexico | 28,600 | 0.5% |
| 41 | West Virginia | 23,600 | 0.4% |
| 42 | Hawaii | 21,700 | 0.4% |
| 43 | Rhode Island | 19,300 | 0.3% |
| 44 | Montana | 18,700 | 0.3% |
| 45 | Alaska | 18,300 | 0.3% |
| 46 | South Dakota | 15,500 | 0.3% |
| 47 | Wyoming | 12,600 | 0.2% |
| 48 | North Dakota | 10,400 | 0.2% |
| 49 | Delaware | 7,900 | 0.1% |
| 50 | Vermont | 6,700 | 0.1% |
|  | District of Columbia | 13,100 | 0.2% |

Source: National Association of Realtors®, Economics and Research Division
"Existing Home Sales" (http://nar.realtor.com/databank/ehs.htm)
*Preliminary data. Includes existing houses, apartment condos and co-ops. Excludes new construction.

# Percent Change in Existing Home Sales: 1999 to 2000

## National Percent Change = 1.3% Decrease*

ALPHA ORDER

| RANK | STATE | PERCENT CHANGE |
|---|---|---|
| 49 | Alabama | (10.6) |
| 2 | Alaska | 14.4 |
| 16 | Arizona | (0.1) |
| 44 | Arkansas | (8.0) |
| 30 | California | (2.6) |
| 4 | Colorado | 9.5 |
| 35 | Connecticut | (3.9) |
| 46 | Delaware | (8.1) |
| 8 | Florida | 2.0 |
| 15 | Georgia | 0.3 |
| 1 | Hawaii | 21.9 |
| 11 | Idaho | 1.0 |
| 19 | Illinois | (0.7) |
| 22 | Indiana | (1.4) |
| 39 | Iowa | (5.0) |
| 29 | Kansas | (2.5) |
| 41 | Kentucky | (5.8) |
| 23 | Louisiana | (2.0) |
| 5 | Maine | 6.9 |
| 10 | Maryland | 1.7 |
| 38 | Massachusetts | (4.8) |
| 27 | Michigan | (2.2) |
| 9 | Minnesota | 1.9 |
| 48 | Mississippi | (8.8) |
| 23 | Missouri | (2.0) |
| 26 | Montana | (2.1) |
| 47 | Nebraska | (8.7) |
| 3 | Nevada | 12.5 |
| 13 | New Hampshire | 0.7 |
| 23 | New Jersey | (2.0) |
| 37 | New Mexico | (4.0) |
| 16 | New York | (0.1) |
| 6 | North Carolina | 4.7 |
| 11 | North Dakota | 1.0 |
| 31 | Ohio | (2.9) |
| 33 | Oklahoma | (3.2) |
| 20 | Oregon | (1.0) |
| 40 | Pennsylvania | (5.3) |
| 43 | Rhode Island | (6.8) |
| 35 | South Carolina | (3.9) |
| 14 | South Dakota | 0.6 |
| 18 | Tennessee | (0.3) |
| 21 | Texas | (1.2) |
| 7 | Utah | 2.8 |
| 31 | Vermont | (2.9) |
| 44 | Virginia | (8.0) |
| 28 | Washington | (2.3) |
| 50 | West Virginia | (11.6) |
| 42 | Wisconsin | (6.2) |
| 34 | Wyoming | (3.8) |

RANK ORDER

| RANK | STATE | PERCENT CHANGE |
|---|---|---|
| 1 | Hawaii | 21.9 |
| 2 | Alaska | 14.4 |
| 3 | Nevada | 12.5 |
| 4 | Colorado | 9.5 |
| 5 | Maine | 6.9 |
| 6 | North Carolina | 4.7 |
| 7 | Utah | 2.8 |
| 8 | Florida | 2.0 |
| 9 | Minnesota | 1.9 |
| 10 | Maryland | 1.7 |
| 11 | Idaho | 1.0 |
| 11 | North Dakota | 1.0 |
| 13 | New Hampshire | 0.7 |
| 14 | South Dakota | 0.6 |
| 15 | Georgia | 0.3 |
| 16 | Arizona | (0.1) |
| 16 | New York | (0.1) |
| 18 | Tennessee | (0.3) |
| 19 | Illinois | (0.7) |
| 20 | Oregon | (1.0) |
| 21 | Texas | (1.2) |
| 22 | Indiana | (1.4) |
| 23 | Louisiana | (2.0) |
| 23 | Missouri | (2.0) |
| 23 | New Jersey | (2.0) |
| 26 | Montana | (2.1) |
| 27 | Michigan | (2.2) |
| 28 | Washington | (2.3) |
| 29 | Kansas | (2.5) |
| 30 | California | (2.6) |
| 31 | Ohio | (2.9) |
| 31 | Vermont | (2.9) |
| 33 | Oklahoma | (3.2) |
| 34 | Wyoming | (3.8) |
| 35 | Connecticut | (3.9) |
| 35 | South Carolina | (3.9) |
| 37 | New Mexico | (4.0) |
| 38 | Massachusetts | (4.8) |
| 39 | Iowa | (5.0) |
| 40 | Pennsylvania | (5.3) |
| 41 | Kentucky | (5.8) |
| 42 | Wisconsin | (6.2) |
| 43 | Rhode Island | (6.8) |
| 44 | Arkansas | (8.0) |
| 44 | Virginia | (8.0) |
| 46 | Delaware | (8.1) |
| 47 | Nebraska | (8.7) |
| 48 | Mississippi | (8.8) |
| 49 | Alabama | (10.6) |
| 50 | West Virginia | (11.6) |
| | District of Columbia | (5.1) |

Source: Morgan Quitno Press using data from National Association of Realtors®, Economics and Research Division
        "Existing Home Sales" (http://nar.realtor.com/databank/ehs.htm)
*2000 data are preliminary, 1999 data are revised. Includes existing houses, apartment condos and co-ops.
Excludes new construction.
**Not available.

# Homeownership Rate in 2000

## National Rate = 67.4%*

ALPHA ORDER

| RANK | STATE | PERCENT |
|------|-------|---------|
| 14 | Alabama | 73.2 |
| 40 | Alaska | 66.4 |
| 38 | Arizona | 68.0 |
| 33 | Arkansas | 68.9 |
| 48 | California | 57.1 |
| 36 | Colorado | 68.3 |
| 28 | Connecticut | 70.0 |
| 17 | Delaware | 72.0 |
| 35 | Florida | 68.4 |
| 30 | Georgia | 69.8 |
| 49 | Hawaii | 55.2 |
| 25 | Idaho | 70.5 |
| 39 | Illinois | 67.9 |
| 8 | Indiana | 74.9 |
| 6 | Iowa | 75.2 |
| 31 | Kansas | 69.3 |
| 13 | Kentucky | 73.4 |
| 37 | Louisiana | 68.1 |
| 2 | Maine | 76.5 |
| 29 | Maryland | 69.9 |
| 47 | Massachusetts | 59.9 |
| 1 | Michigan | 77.2 |
| 4 | Minnesota | 76.1 |
| 6 | Mississippi | 75.2 |
| 10 | Missouri | 74.2 |
| 26 | Montana | 70.2 |
| 26 | Nebraska | 70.2 |
| 43 | Nevada | 64.0 |
| 32 | New Hampshire | 69.2 |
| 41 | New Jersey | 66.2 |
| 12 | New Mexico | 73.7 |
| 50 | New York | 53.4 |
| 21 | North Carolina | 71.1 |
| 24 | North Dakota | 70.7 |
| 19 | Ohio | 71.3 |
| 15 | Oklahoma | 72.7 |
| 42 | Oregon | 65.3 |
| 9 | Pennsylvania | 74.7 |
| 46 | Rhode Island | 61.5 |
| 2 | South Carolina | 76.5 |
| 20 | South Dakota | 71.2 |
| 23 | Tennessee | 70.9 |
| 44 | Texas | 63.8 |
| 15 | Utah | 72.7 |
| 34 | Vermont | 68.7 |
| 11 | Virginia | 73.9 |
| 45 | Washington | 63.6 |
| 5 | West Virginia | 75.9 |
| 18 | Wisconsin | 71.8 |
| 22 | Wyoming | 71.0 |

RANK ORDER

| RANK | STATE | PERCENT |
|------|-------|---------|
| 1 | Michigan | 77.2 |
| 2 | Maine | 76.5 |
| 2 | South Carolina | 76.5 |
| 4 | Minnesota | 76.1 |
| 5 | West Virginia | 75.9 |
| 6 | Iowa | 75.2 |
| 6 | Mississippi | 75.2 |
| 8 | Indiana | 74.9 |
| 9 | Pennsylvania | 74.7 |
| 10 | Missouri | 74.2 |
| 11 | Virginia | 73.9 |
| 12 | New Mexico | 73.7 |
| 13 | Kentucky | 73.4 |
| 14 | Alabama | 73.2 |
| 15 | Oklahoma | 72.7 |
| 15 | Utah | 72.7 |
| 17 | Delaware | 72.0 |
| 18 | Wisconsin | 71.8 |
| 19 | Ohio | 71.3 |
| 20 | South Dakota | 71.2 |
| 21 | North Carolina | 71.1 |
| 22 | Wyoming | 71.0 |
| 23 | Tennessee | 70.9 |
| 24 | North Dakota | 70.7 |
| 25 | Idaho | 70.5 |
| 26 | Montana | 70.2 |
| 26 | Nebraska | 70.2 |
| 28 | Connecticut | 70.0 |
| 29 | Maryland | 69.9 |
| 30 | Georgia | 69.8 |
| 31 | Kansas | 69.3 |
| 32 | New Hampshire | 69.2 |
| 33 | Arkansas | 68.9 |
| 34 | Vermont | 68.7 |
| 35 | Florida | 68.4 |
| 36 | Colorado | 68.3 |
| 37 | Louisiana | 68.1 |
| 38 | Arizona | 68.0 |
| 39 | Illinois | 67.9 |
| 40 | Alaska | 66.4 |
| 41 | New Jersey | 66.2 |
| 42 | Oregon | 65.3 |
| 43 | Nevada | 64.0 |
| 44 | Texas | 63.8 |
| 45 | Washington | 63.6 |
| 46 | Rhode Island | 61.5 |
| 47 | Massachusetts | 59.9 |
| 48 | California | 57.1 |
| 49 | Hawaii | 55.2 |
| 50 | New York | 53.4 |
| | District of Columbia | 41.9 |

Source: U.S. Bureau of the Census
   "Housing Vacancies and Homeownership, Annual Statistics: 2000"
      (http://www.census.gov/hhes/www/housing/hvs/annual00/ann00t13.html)
*Percent of households occupied by the owner.

# Percent Change in Homeownership Rate: 1990 to 2000

## National Percent Change = 5.5% Increase*

ALPHA ORDER

| RANK | STATE | PERCENT CHANGE |
|------|-------|----------------|
| 15 | Alabama | 7.0 |
| 4 | Alaska | 13.7 |
| 23 | Arizona | 5.4 |
| 41 | Arkansas | 1.6 |
| 21 | California | 6.1 |
| 2 | Colorado | 15.8 |
| 34 | Connecticut | 3.1 |
| 19 | Delaware | 6.4 |
| 26 | Florida | 5.1 |
| 8 | Georgia | 8.6 |
| 49 | Hawaii | (0.5) |
| 41 | Idaho | 1.6 |
| 10 | Illinois | 7.8 |
| 6 | Indiana | 11.8 |
| 19 | Iowa | 6.4 |
| 46 | Kansas | 0.4 |
| 7 | Kentucky | 11.6 |
| 46 | Louisiana | 0.4 |
| 34 | Maine | 3.1 |
| 11 | Maryland | 7.7 |
| 39 | Massachusetts | 2.2 |
| 17 | Michigan | 6.8 |
| 5 | Minnesota | 11.9 |
| 9 | Mississippi | 8.4 |
| 1 | Missouri | 15.9 |
| 41 | Montana | 1.6 |
| 29 | Nebraska | 4.3 |
| 3 | Nevada | 14.7 |
| 18 | New Hampshire | 6.5 |
| 40 | New Jersey | 1.8 |
| 13 | New Mexico | 7.4 |
| 48 | New York | 0.2 |
| 36 | North Carolina | 3.0 |
| 25 | North Dakota | 5.2 |
| 30 | Ohio | 3.8 |
| 33 | Oklahoma | 3.4 |
| 44 | Oregon | 1.4 |
| 45 | Pennsylvania | 1.2 |
| 26 | Rhode Island | 5.1 |
| 14 | South Carolina | 7.1 |
| 12 | South Dakota | 7.6 |
| 30 | Tennessee | 3.8 |
| 16 | Texas | 6.9 |
| 32 | Utah | 3.7 |
| 50 | Vermont | (5.4) |
| 22 | Virginia | 5.9 |
| 38 | Washington | 2.9 |
| 23 | West Virginia | 5.4 |
| 26 | Wisconsin | 5.1 |
| 36 | Wyoming | 3.0 |

RANK ORDER

| RANK | STATE | PERCENT CHANGE |
|------|-------|----------------|
| 1 | Missouri | 15.9 |
| 2 | Colorado | 15.8 |
| 3 | Nevada | 14.7 |
| 4 | Alaska | 13.7 |
| 5 | Minnesota | 11.9 |
| 6 | Indiana | 11.8 |
| 7 | Kentucky | 11.6 |
| 8 | Georgia | 8.6 |
| 9 | Mississippi | 8.4 |
| 10 | Illinois | 7.8 |
| 11 | Maryland | 7.7 |
| 12 | South Dakota | 7.6 |
| 13 | New Mexico | 7.4 |
| 14 | South Carolina | 7.1 |
| 15 | Alabama | 7.0 |
| 16 | Texas | 6.9 |
| 17 | Michigan | 6.8 |
| 18 | New Hampshire | 6.5 |
| 19 | Delaware | 6.4 |
| 19 | Iowa | 6.4 |
| 21 | California | 6.1 |
| 22 | Virginia | 5.9 |
| 23 | Arizona | 5.4 |
| 23 | West Virginia | 5.4 |
| 25 | North Dakota | 5.2 |
| 26 | Florida | 5.1 |
| 26 | Rhode Island | 5.1 |
| 26 | Wisconsin | 5.1 |
| 29 | Nebraska | 4.3 |
| 30 | Ohio | 3.8 |
| 30 | Tennessee | 3.8 |
| 32 | Utah | 3.7 |
| 33 | Oklahoma | 3.4 |
| 34 | Connecticut | 3.1 |
| 34 | Maine | 3.1 |
| 36 | North Carolina | 3.0 |
| 36 | Wyoming | 3.0 |
| 38 | Washington | 2.9 |
| 39 | Massachusetts | 2.2 |
| 40 | New Jersey | 1.8 |
| 41 | Arkansas | 1.6 |
| 41 | Idaho | 1.6 |
| 41 | Montana | 1.6 |
| 44 | Oregon | 1.4 |
| 45 | Pennsylvania | 1.2 |
| 46 | Kansas | 0.4 |
| 46 | Louisiana | 0.4 |
| 48 | New York | 0.2 |
| 49 | Hawaii | (0.5) |
| 50 | Vermont | (5.4) |
| | District of Columbia | 15.1 |

*Source: Morgan Quitno Press using data from U.S. Bureau of the Census*
*"Housing Vacancies and Homeownership, Annual Statistics: 2000"*
*(http://www.census.gov/hhes/www/housing/hvs/annual00/ann00t13.html)*
*Percent of households occupied by the owner.*

# Homeowner Vacancy Rate in 2000

## National Rate = 1.6% Vacant*

| ALPHA ORDER | | | RANK ORDER | | |
|---|---|---|---|---|---|
| RANK | STATE | PERCENT | RANK | STATE | PERCENT |
| 6 | Alabama | 2.3 | 1 | Florida | 2.6 |
| 30 | Alaska | 1.5 | 2 | Arkansas | 2.4 |
| 24 | Arizona | 1.6 | 2 | New Mexico | 2.4 |
| 2 | Arkansas | 2.4 | 2 | Oregon | 2.4 |
| 39 | California | 1.2 | 2 | West Virginia | 2.4 |
| 24 | Colorado | 1.6 | 6 | Alabama | 2.3 |
| 48 | Connecticut | 0.7 | 6 | Nevada | 2.3 |
| 24 | Delaware | 1.6 | 6 | Wyoming | 2.3 |
| 1 | Florida | 2.6 | 9 | Oklahoma | 2.2 |
| 13 | Georgia | 1.9 | 9 | Virginia | 2.2 |
| 45 | Hawaii | 0.9 | 11 | Mississippi | 2.0 |
| 18 | Idaho | 1.8 | 11 | Nebraska | 2.0 |
| 41 | Illinois | 1.1 | 13 | Georgia | 1.9 |
| 41 | Indiana | 1.1 | 13 | Montana | 1.9 |
| 24 | Iowa | 1.6 | 13 | North Carolina | 1.9 |
| 22 | Kansas | 1.7 | 13 | Tennessee | 1.9 |
| 30 | Kentucky | 1.5 | 13 | Washington | 1.9 |
| 22 | Louisiana | 1.7 | 18 | Idaho | 1.8 |
| 36 | Maine | 1.3 | 18 | Missouri | 1.8 |
| 30 | Maryland | 1.5 | 18 | North Dakota | 1.8 |
| 50 | Massachusetts | 0.6 | 18 | Utah | 1.8 |
| 36 | Michigan | 1.3 | 22 | Kansas | 1.7 |
| 45 | Minnesota | 0.9 | 22 | Louisiana | 1.7 |
| 11 | Mississippi | 2.0 | 24 | Arizona | 1.6 |
| 18 | Missouri | 1.8 | 24 | Colorado | 1.6 |
| 13 | Montana | 1.9 | 24 | Delaware | 1.6 |
| 11 | Nebraska | 2.0 | 24 | Iowa | 1.6 |
| 6 | Nevada | 2.3 | 24 | South Dakota | 1.6 |
| 48 | New Hampshire | 0.7 | 24 | Texas | 1.6 |
| 44 | New Jersey | 1.0 | 30 | Alaska | 1.5 |
| 2 | New Mexico | 2.4 | 30 | Kentucky | 1.5 |
| 30 | New York | 1.5 | 30 | Maryland | 1.5 |
| 13 | North Carolina | 1.9 | 30 | New York | 1.5 |
| 18 | North Dakota | 1.8 | 34 | Pennsylvania | 1.4 |
| 36 | Ohio | 1.3 | 34 | South Carolina | 1.4 |
| 9 | Oklahoma | 2.2 | 36 | Maine | 1.3 |
| 2 | Oregon | 2.4 | 36 | Michigan | 1.3 |
| 34 | Pennsylvania | 1.4 | 36 | Ohio | 1.3 |
| 41 | Rhode Island | 1.1 | 39 | California | 1.2 |
| 34 | South Carolina | 1.4 | 39 | Wisconsin | 1.2 |
| 24 | South Dakota | 1.6 | 41 | Illinois | 1.1 |
| 13 | Tennessee | 1.9 | 41 | Indiana | 1.1 |
| 24 | Texas | 1.6 | 41 | Rhode Island | 1.1 |
| 18 | Utah | 1.8 | 44 | New Jersey | 1.0 |
| 45 | Vermont | 0.9 | 45 | Hawaii | 0.9 |
| 9 | Virginia | 2.2 | 45 | Minnesota | 0.9 |
| 13 | Washington | 1.9 | 45 | Vermont | 0.9 |
| 2 | West Virginia | 2.4 | 48 | Connecticut | 0.7 |
| 39 | Wisconsin | 1.2 | 48 | New Hampshire | 0.7 |
| 6 | Wyoming | 2.3 | 50 | Massachusetts | 0.6 |
| | | | | District of Columbia | 1.9 |

Source: U.S. Bureau of the Census
"Housing Vacancies and Homeownership, Annual Statistics: 2000"
(http://www.census.gov/hhes/www/housing/hvs/annual00/ann00t4.html)
*Represents homes previously occupied by owners that are vacant and for sale.

# Rental Vacancy Rate in 2000

## National Rate = 8.0% Vacant

ALPHA ORDER

| RANK | STATE | PERCENT |
|------|-------|---------|
| 4 | Alabama | 14.4 |
| 33 | Alaska | 6.9 |
| 14 | Arizona | 10.7 |
| 9 | Arkansas | 11.4 |
| 46 | California | 4.5 |
| 39 | Colorado | 5.4 |
| 23 | Connecticut | 8.6 |
| 15 | Delaware | 10.6 |
| 12 | Florida | 10.8 |
| 18 | Georgia | 9.7 |
| 40 | Hawaii | 5.3 |
| 36 | Idaho | 6.7 |
| 26 | Illinois | 7.8 |
| 15 | Indiana | 10.6 |
| 33 | Iowa | 6.9 |
| 21 | Kansas | 9.2 |
| 20 | Kentucky | 9.5 |
| 10 | Louisiana | 11.2 |
| 37 | Maine | 6.0 |
| 45 | Maryland | 4.6 |
| 49 | Massachusetts | 3.5 |
| 19 | Michigan | 9.6 |
| 42 | Minnesota | 5.2 |
| 7 | Mississippi | 11.6 |
| 3 | Missouri | 15.0 |
| 30 | Montana | 7.5 |
| 31 | Nebraska | 7.4 |
| 7 | Nevada | 11.6 |
| 50 | New Hampshire | 3.2 |
| 47 | New Jersey | 4.3 |
| 5 | New Mexico | 13.2 |
| 38 | New York | 5.5 |
| 10 | North Carolina | 11.2 |
| 6 | North Dakota | 11.7 |
| 22 | Ohio | 9.0 |
| 2 | Oklahoma | 15.2 |
| 35 | Oregon | 6.8 |
| 24 | Pennsylvania | 8.3 |
| 40 | Rhode Island | 5.3 |
| 1 | South Carolina | 15.5 |
| 27 | South Dakota | 7.7 |
| 32 | Tennessee | 7.1 |
| 12 | Texas | 10.8 |
| 29 | Utah | 7.6 |
| 48 | Vermont | 3.8 |
| 27 | Virginia | 7.7 |
| 43 | Washington | 4.9 |
| 17 | West Virginia | 10.0 |
| 44 | Wisconsin | 4.7 |
| 25 | Wyoming | 8.1 |

RANK ORDER

| RANK | STATE | PERCENT |
|------|-------|---------|
| 1 | South Carolina | 15.5 |
| 2 | Oklahoma | 15.2 |
| 3 | Missouri | 15.0 |
| 4 | Alabama | 14.4 |
| 5 | New Mexico | 13.2 |
| 6 | North Dakota | 11.7 |
| 7 | Mississippi | 11.6 |
| 7 | Nevada | 11.6 |
| 9 | Arkansas | 11.4 |
| 10 | Louisiana | 11.2 |
| 10 | North Carolina | 11.2 |
| 12 | Florida | 10.8 |
| 12 | Texas | 10.8 |
| 14 | Arizona | 10.7 |
| 15 | Delaware | 10.6 |
| 15 | Indiana | 10.6 |
| 17 | West Virginia | 10.0 |
| 18 | Georgia | 9.7 |
| 19 | Michigan | 9.6 |
| 20 | Kentucky | 9.5 |
| 21 | Kansas | 9.2 |
| 22 | Ohio | 9.0 |
| 23 | Connecticut | 8.6 |
| 24 | Pennsylvania | 8.3 |
| 25 | Wyoming | 8.1 |
| 26 | Illinois | 7.8 |
| 27 | South Dakota | 7.7 |
| 27 | Virginia | 7.7 |
| 29 | Utah | 7.6 |
| 30 | Montana | 7.5 |
| 31 | Nebraska | 7.4 |
| 32 | Tennessee | 7.1 |
| 33 | Alaska | 6.9 |
| 33 | Iowa | 6.9 |
| 35 | Oregon | 6.8 |
| 36 | Idaho | 6.7 |
| 37 | Maine | 6.0 |
| 38 | New York | 5.5 |
| 39 | Colorado | 5.4 |
| 40 | Hawaii | 5.3 |
| 40 | Rhode Island | 5.3 |
| 42 | Minnesota | 5.2 |
| 43 | Washington | 4.9 |
| 44 | Wisconsin | 4.7 |
| 45 | Maryland | 4.6 |
| 46 | California | 4.5 |
| 47 | New Jersey | 4.3 |
| 48 | Vermont | 3.8 |
| 49 | Massachusetts | 3.5 |
| 50 | New Hampshire | 3.2 |
| | District of Columbia | 11.7 |

*Source: U.S. Bureau of the Census*
*"Housing Vacancies and Homeownership, Annual Statistics: 2000"*
*(http://www.census.gov/hhes/www/housing/hvs/annual00/ann00t3.html)*

# State and Local Government Expenditures
# For Housing and Community Development in 1997
# National Total = $23,229,554,000*

| RANK | STATE | EXPENDITURES | % of USA |
|---|---|---|---|
| 20 | Alabama | $309,565,000 | 1.3% |
| 29 | Alaska | 144,823,000 | 0.6% |
| 26 | Arizona | 222,183,000 | 1.0% |
| 38 | Arkansas | 100,730,000 | 0.4% |
| 1 | California | 4,583,639,000 | 19.7% |
| 23 | Colorado | 289,040,000 | 1.2% |
| 18 | Connecticut | 365,190,000 | 1.6% |
| 42 | Delaware | 78,526,000 | 0.3% |
| 5 | Florida | 878,062,000 | 3.8% |
| 12 | Georgia | 530,433,000 | 2.3% |
| 24 | Hawaii | 243,972,000 | 1.1% |
| 49 | Idaho | 23,293,000 | 0.1% |
| 3 | Illinois | 1,332,554,000 | 5.7% |
| 22 | Indiana | 302,012,000 | 1.3% |
| 30 | Iowa | 137,817,000 | 0.6% |
| 36 | Kansas | 108,896,000 | 0.5% |
| 32 | Kentucky | 122,347,000 | 0.5% |
| 25 | Louisiana | 229,743,000 | 1.0% |
| 40 | Maine | 93,581,000 | 0.4% |
| 9 | Maryland | 604,216,000 | 2.6% |
| 6 | Massachusetts | 870,163,000 | 3.7% |
| 27 | Michigan | 221,727,000 | 1.0% |
| 15 | Minnesota | 407,215,000 | 1.8% |
| 31 | Mississippi | 134,439,000 | 0.6% |
| 21 | Missouri | 307,551,000 | 1.3% |
| 44 | Montana | 69,369,000 | 0.3% |
| 39 | Nebraska | 99,637,000 | 0.4% |
| 34 | Nevada | 112,754,000 | 0.5% |
| 43 | New Hampshire | 76,896,000 | 0.3% |
| 10 | New Jersey | 590,275,000 | 2.5% |
| 45 | New Mexico | 68,647,000 | 0.3% |
| 2 | New York | 3,389,266,000 | 14.6% |
| 16 | North Carolina | 395,166,000 | 1.7% |
| 47 | North Dakota | 43,109,000 | 0.2% |
| 8 | Ohio | 799,052,000 | 3.4% |
| 35 | Oklahoma | 109,957,000 | 0.5% |
| 17 | Oregon | 365,339,000 | 1.6% |
| 4 | Pennsylvania | 1,132,483,000 | 4.9% |
| 33 | Rhode Island | 121,854,000 | 0.5% |
| 28 | South Carolina | 148,177,000 | 0.6% |
| 48 | South Dakota | 23,797,000 | 0.1% |
| 14 | Tennessee | 428,475,000 | 1.8% |
| 7 | Texas | 824,791,000 | 3.6% |
| 37 | Utah | 108,087,000 | 0.5% |
| 46 | Vermont | 59,989,000 | 0.3% |
| 13 | Virginia | 528,154,000 | 2.3% |
| 11 | Washington | 560,686,000 | 2.4% |
| 41 | West Virginia | 89,901,000 | 0.4% |
| 19 | Wisconsin | 316,675,000 | 1.4% |
| 50 | Wyoming | 9,233,000 | 0.0% |

| RANK | STATE | EXPENDITURES | % of USA |
|---|---|---|---|
| 1 | California | $4,583,639,000 | 19.7% |
| 2 | New York | 3,389,266,000 | 14.6% |
| 3 | Illinois | 1,332,554,000 | 5.7% |
| 4 | Pennsylvania | 1,132,483,000 | 4.9% |
| 5 | Florida | 878,062,000 | 3.8% |
| 6 | Massachusetts | 870,163,000 | 3.7% |
| 7 | Texas | 824,791,000 | 3.6% |
| 8 | Ohio | 799,052,000 | 3.4% |
| 9 | Maryland | 604,216,000 | 2.6% |
| 10 | New Jersey | 590,275,000 | 2.5% |
| 11 | Washington | 560,686,000 | 2.4% |
| 12 | Georgia | 530,433,000 | 2.3% |
| 13 | Virginia | 528,154,000 | 2.3% |
| 14 | Tennessee | 428,475,000 | 1.8% |
| 15 | Minnesota | 407,215,000 | 1.8% |
| 16 | North Carolina | 395,166,000 | 1.7% |
| 17 | Oregon | 365,339,000 | 1.6% |
| 18 | Connecticut | 365,190,000 | 1.6% |
| 19 | Wisconsin | 316,675,000 | 1.4% |
| 20 | Alabama | 309,565,000 | 1.3% |
| 21 | Missouri | 307,551,000 | 1.3% |
| 22 | Indiana | 302,012,000 | 1.3% |
| 23 | Colorado | 289,040,000 | 1.2% |
| 24 | Hawaii | 243,972,000 | 1.1% |
| 25 | Louisiana | 229,743,000 | 1.0% |
| 26 | Arizona | 222,183,000 | 1.0% |
| 27 | Michigan | 221,727,000 | 1.0% |
| 28 | South Carolina | 148,177,000 | 0.6% |
| 29 | Alaska | 144,823,000 | 0.6% |
| 30 | Iowa | 137,817,000 | 0.6% |
| 31 | Mississippi | 134,439,000 | 0.6% |
| 32 | Kentucky | 122,347,000 | 0.5% |
| 33 | Rhode Island | 121,854,000 | 0.5% |
| 34 | Nevada | 112,754,000 | 0.5% |
| 35 | Oklahoma | 109,957,000 | 0.5% |
| 36 | Kansas | 108,896,000 | 0.5% |
| 37 | Utah | 108,087,000 | 0.5% |
| 38 | Arkansas | 100,730,000 | 0.4% |
| 39 | Nebraska | 99,637,000 | 0.4% |
| 40 | Maine | 93,581,000 | 0.4% |
| 41 | West Virginia | 89,901,000 | 0.4% |
| 42 | Delaware | 78,526,000 | 0.3% |
| 43 | New Hampshire | 76,896,000 | 0.3% |
| 44 | Montana | 69,369,000 | 0.3% |
| 45 | New Mexico | 68,647,000 | 0.3% |
| 46 | Vermont | 59,989,000 | 0.3% |
| 47 | North Dakota | 43,109,000 | 0.2% |
| 48 | South Dakota | 23,797,000 | 0.1% |
| 49 | Idaho | 23,293,000 | 0.1% |
| 50 | Wyoming | 9,233,000 | 0.0% |
| | District of Columbia | 116,068,000 | 0.5% |

Source: U.S. Bureau of the Census, Governments Division
"Compendium of Government Finances: 1997" (2000) (http://www.census.gov/govs/www/cog.html)
*Direct general expenditures.

# Per Capita State and Local Government Expenditures
## For Housing and Community Development in 1997
## National Per Capita = $86.75*

ALPHA ORDER

RANK ORDER

| RANK | STATE | PER CAPITA |
|------|-------|------------|
| 22 | Alabama | $71.65 |
| 1 | Alaska | 237.86 |
| 38 | Arizona | 48.81 |
| 42 | Arkansas | 39.91 |
| 5 | California | 142.27 |
| 20 | Colorado | 74.28 |
| 9 | Connecticut | 111.73 |
| 11 | Delaware | 106.83 |
| 30 | Florida | 59.80 |
| 24 | Georgia | 70.86 |
| 2 | Hawaii | 205.14 |
| 49 | Idaho | 19.24 |
| 10 | Illinois | 110.94 |
| 35 | Indiana | 51.43 |
| 39 | Iowa | 48.28 |
| 41 | Kansas | 41.62 |
| 47 | Kentucky | 31.31 |
| 33 | Louisiana | 52.80 |
| 19 | Maine | 75.15 |
| 7 | Maryland | 118.64 |
| 4 | Massachusetts | 142.29 |
| 48 | Michigan | 22.66 |
| 15 | Minnesota | 86.87 |
| 37 | Mississippi | 49.21 |
| 31 | Missouri | 56.88 |
| 17 | Montana | 78.94 |
| 29 | Nebraska | 60.17 |
| 25 | Nevada | 67.29 |
| 27 | New Hampshire | 65.54 |
| 21 | New Jersey | 73.29 |
| 43 | New Mexico | 39.84 |
| 3 | New York | 186.81 |
| 32 | North Carolina | 53.19 |
| 26 | North Dakota | 67.26 |
| 23 | Ohio | 71.26 |
| 45 | Oklahoma | 33.18 |
| 8 | Oregon | 112.65 |
| 14 | Pennsylvania | 94.25 |
| 6 | Rhode Island | 123.46 |
| 44 | South Carolina | 39.10 |
| 46 | South Dakota | 32.56 |
| 16 | Tennessee | 79.67 |
| 40 | Texas | 42.61 |
| 34 | Utah | 52.33 |
| 12 | Vermont | 101.91 |
| 18 | Virginia | 78.44 |
| 13 | Washington | 100.05 |
| 36 | West Virginia | 49.52 |
| 28 | Wisconsin | 60.90 |
| 50 | Wyoming | 19.23 |

| RANK | STATE | PER CAPITA |
|------|-------|------------|
| 1 | Alaska | $237.86 |
| 2 | Hawaii | 205.14 |
| 3 | New York | 186.81 |
| 4 | Massachusetts | 142.29 |
| 5 | California | 142.27 |
| 6 | Rhode Island | 123.46 |
| 7 | Maryland | 118.64 |
| 8 | Oregon | 112.65 |
| 9 | Connecticut | 111.73 |
| 10 | Illinois | 110.94 |
| 11 | Delaware | 106.83 |
| 12 | Vermont | 101.91 |
| 13 | Washington | 100.05 |
| 14 | Pennsylvania | 94.25 |
| 15 | Minnesota | 86.87 |
| 16 | Tennessee | 79.67 |
| 17 | Montana | 78.94 |
| 18 | Virginia | 78.44 |
| 19 | Maine | 75.15 |
| 20 | Colorado | 74.28 |
| 21 | New Jersey | 73.29 |
| 22 | Alabama | 71.65 |
| 23 | Ohio | 71.26 |
| 24 | Georgia | 70.86 |
| 25 | Nevada | 67.29 |
| 26 | North Dakota | 67.26 |
| 27 | New Hampshire | 65.54 |
| 28 | Wisconsin | 60.90 |
| 29 | Nebraska | 60.17 |
| 30 | Florida | 59.80 |
| 31 | Missouri | 56.88 |
| 32 | North Carolina | 53.19 |
| 33 | Louisiana | 52.80 |
| 34 | Utah | 52.33 |
| 35 | Indiana | 51.43 |
| 36 | West Virginia | 49.52 |
| 37 | Mississippi | 49.21 |
| 38 | Arizona | 48.81 |
| 39 | Iowa | 48.28 |
| 40 | Texas | 42.61 |
| 41 | Kansas | 41.62 |
| 42 | Arkansas | 39.91 |
| 43 | New Mexico | 39.84 |
| 44 | South Carolina | 39.10 |
| 45 | Oklahoma | 33.18 |
| 46 | South Dakota | 32.56 |
| 47 | Kentucky | 31.31 |
| 48 | Michigan | 22.66 |
| 49 | Idaho | 19.24 |
| 50 | Wyoming | 19.23 |

District of Columbia     219.51

*Source: Morgan Quitno Press using data from U.S. Bureau of the Census, Governments Division "Compendium of Government Finances: 1997" (2000) (http://www.census.gov/govs/www/cog.html)*
*Direct general expenditures.*

# XIII. POPULATION

# XIII. POPULATION (continued)

# Population in 2000

## National Total = 281,421,906*

ALPHA ORDER

| RANK | STATE | POPULATION | % of USA |
|------|-------|-----------:|----------|
| 23 | Alabama | 4,447,100 | 1.6% |
| 48 | Alaska | 626,932 | 0.2% |
| 20 | Arizona | 5,130,632 | 1.8% |
| 33 | Arkansas | 2,673,400 | 0.9% |
| 1 | California | 33,871,648 | 12.0% |
| 24 | Colorado | 4,301,261 | 1.5% |
| 29 | Connecticut | 3,405,565 | 1.2% |
| 45 | Delaware | 783,600 | 0.3% |
| 4 | Florida | 15,982,378 | 5.7% |
| 10 | Georgia | 8,186,453 | 2.9% |
| 42 | Hawaii | 1,211,537 | 0.4% |
| 39 | Idaho | 1,293,953 | 0.5% |
| 5 | Illinois | 12,419,293 | 4.4% |
| 14 | Indiana | 6,080,485 | 2.2% |
| 30 | Iowa | 2,926,324 | 1.0% |
| 32 | Kansas | 2,688,418 | 1.0% |
| 25 | Kentucky | 4,041,769 | 1.4% |
| 22 | Louisiana | 4,468,976 | 1.6% |
| 40 | Maine | 1,274,923 | 0.5% |
| 19 | Maryland | 5,296,486 | 1.9% |
| 13 | Massachusetts | 6,349,097 | 2.3% |
| 8 | Michigan | 9,938,444 | 3.5% |
| 21 | Minnesota | 4,919,479 | 1.7% |
| 31 | Mississippi | 2,844,658 | 1.0% |
| 17 | Missouri | 5,595,211 | 2.0% |
| 44 | Montana | 902,195 | 0.3% |
| 38 | Nebraska | 1,711,263 | 0.6% |
| 35 | Nevada | 1,998,257 | 0.7% |
| 41 | New Hampshire | 1,235,786 | 0.4% |
| 9 | New Jersey | 8,414,350 | 3.0% |
| 36 | New Mexico | 1,819,046 | 0.6% |
| 3 | New York | 18,976,457 | 6.7% |
| 11 | North Carolina | 8,049,313 | 2.9% |
| 47 | North Dakota | 642,200 | 0.2% |
| 7 | Ohio | 11,353,140 | 4.0% |
| 27 | Oklahoma | 3,450,654 | 1.2% |
| 28 | Oregon | 3,421,399 | 1.2% |
| 6 | Pennsylvania | 12,281,054 | 4.4% |
| 43 | Rhode Island | 1,048,319 | 0.4% |
| 26 | South Carolina | 4,012,012 | 1.4% |
| 46 | South Dakota | 754,844 | 0.3% |
| 16 | Tennessee | 5,689,283 | 2.0% |
| 2 | Texas | 20,851,820 | 7.4% |
| 34 | Utah | 2,233,169 | 0.8% |
| 49 | Vermont | 608,827 | 0.2% |
| 12 | Virginia | 7,078,515 | 2.5% |
| 15 | Washington | 5,894,121 | 2.1% |
| 37 | West Virginia | 1,808,344 | 0.6% |
| 18 | Wisconsin | 5,363,675 | 1.9% |
| 50 | Wyoming | 493,782 | 0.2% |

RANK ORDER

| RANK | STATE | POPULATION | % of USA |
|------|-------|-----------:|----------|
| 1 | California | 33,871,648 | 12.0% |
| 2 | Texas | 20,851,820 | 7.4% |
| 3 | New York | 18,976,457 | 6.7% |
| 4 | Florida | 15,982,378 | 5.7% |
| 5 | Illinois | 12,419,293 | 4.4% |
| 6 | Pennsylvania | 12,281,054 | 4.4% |
| 7 | Ohio | 11,353,140 | 4.0% |
| 8 | Michigan | 9,938,444 | 3.5% |
| 9 | New Jersey | 8,414,350 | 3.0% |
| 10 | Georgia | 8,186,453 | 2.9% |
| 11 | North Carolina | 8,049,313 | 2.9% |
| 12 | Virginia | 7,078,515 | 2.5% |
| 13 | Massachusetts | 6,349,097 | 2.3% |
| 14 | Indiana | 6,080,485 | 2.2% |
| 15 | Washington | 5,894,121 | 2.1% |
| 16 | Tennessee | 5,689,283 | 2.0% |
| 17 | Missouri | 5,595,211 | 2.0% |
| 18 | Wisconsin | 5,363,675 | 1.9% |
| 19 | Maryland | 5,296,486 | 1.9% |
| 20 | Arizona | 5,130,632 | 1.8% |
| 21 | Minnesota | 4,919,479 | 1.7% |
| 22 | Louisiana | 4,468,976 | 1.6% |
| 23 | Alabama | 4,447,100 | 1.6% |
| 24 | Colorado | 4,301,261 | 1.5% |
| 25 | Kentucky | 4,041,769 | 1.4% |
| 26 | South Carolina | 4,012,012 | 1.4% |
| 27 | Oklahoma | 3,450,654 | 1.2% |
| 28 | Oregon | 3,421,399 | 1.2% |
| 29 | Connecticut | 3,405,565 | 1.2% |
| 30 | Iowa | 2,926,324 | 1.0% |
| 31 | Mississippi | 2,844,658 | 1.0% |
| 32 | Kansas | 2,688,418 | 1.0% |
| 33 | Arkansas | 2,673,400 | 0.9% |
| 34 | Utah | 2,233,169 | 0.8% |
| 35 | Nevada | 1,998,257 | 0.7% |
| 36 | New Mexico | 1,819,046 | 0.6% |
| 37 | West Virginia | 1,808,344 | 0.6% |
| 38 | Nebraska | 1,711,263 | 0.6% |
| 39 | Idaho | 1,293,953 | 0.5% |
| 40 | Maine | 1,274,923 | 0.5% |
| 41 | New Hampshire | 1,235,786 | 0.4% |
| 42 | Hawaii | 1,211,537 | 0.4% |
| 43 | Rhode Island | 1,048,319 | 0.4% |
| 44 | Montana | 902,195 | 0.3% |
| 45 | Delaware | 783,600 | 0.3% |
| 46 | South Dakota | 754,844 | 0.3% |
| 47 | North Dakota | 642,200 | 0.2% |
| 48 | Alaska | 626,932 | 0.2% |
| 49 | Vermont | 608,827 | 0.2% |
| 50 | Wyoming | 493,782 | 0.2% |
| | District of Columbia | 572,059 | 0.2% |

Source: U.S. Bureau of the Census
   "First Census 2000 Results" (December 28, 2000, http://www.census.gov/main/www/cen2000.html)
*Resident population.

# Population (Resident and Overseas) in 2000

## National Total = 281,998,273*

ALPHA ORDER

| RANK | STATE | POPULATION | % of USA |
|---|---|---|---|
| 23 | Alabama | 4,461,130 | 1.6% |
| 48 | Alaska | 628,933 | 0.2% |
| 20 | Arizona | 5,140,683 | 1.8% |
| 33 | Arkansas | 2,679,733 | 1.0% |
| 1 | California | 33,930,798 | 12.0% |
| 24 | Colorado | 4,311,882 | 1.5% |
| 29 | Connecticut | 3,409,535 | 1.2% |
| 45 | Delaware | 785,068 | 0.3% |
| 4 | Florida | 16,028,890 | 5.7% |
| 10 | Georgia | 8,206,975 | 2.9% |
| 42 | Hawaii | 1,216,642 | 0.4% |
| 39 | Idaho | 1,297,274 | 0.5% |
| 5 | Illinois | 12,439,042 | 4.4% |
| 14 | Indiana | 6,090,782 | 2.2% |
| 30 | Iowa | 2,931,923 | 1.0% |
| 32 | Kansas | 2,693,824 | 1.0% |
| 25 | Kentucky | 4,049,431 | 1.4% |
| 22 | Louisiana | 4,480,271 | 1.6% |
| 40 | Maine | 1,277,731 | 0.5% |
| 19 | Maryland | 5,307,886 | 1.9% |
| 13 | Massachusetts | 6,355,568 | 2.3% |
| 8 | Michigan | 9,955,829 | 3.5% |
| 21 | Minnesota | 4,925,670 | 1.7% |
| 31 | Mississippi | 2,852,927 | 1.0% |
| 17 | Missouri | 5,606,260 | 2.0% |
| 44 | Montana | 905,316 | 0.3% |
| 38 | Nebraska | 1,715,369 | 0.6% |
| 35 | Nevada | 2,002,032 | 0.7% |
| 41 | New Hampshire | 1,238,415 | 0.4% |
| 9 | New Jersey | 8,424,354 | 3.0% |
| 36 | New Mexico | 1,823,821 | 0.6% |
| 3 | New York | 19,004,973 | 6.7% |
| 11 | North Carolina | 8,067,673 | 2.9% |
| 47 | North Dakota | 643,756 | 0.2% |
| 7 | Ohio | 11,374,540 | 4.0% |
| 27 | Oklahoma | 3,458,819 | 1.2% |
| 28 | Oregon | 3,428,543 | 1.2% |
| 6 | Pennsylvania | 12,300,670 | 4.4% |
| 43 | Rhode Island | 1,049,662 | 0.4% |
| 26 | South Carolina | 4,025,061 | 1.4% |
| 46 | South Dakota | 756,874 | 0.3% |
| 16 | Tennessee | 5,700,037 | 2.0% |
| 2 | Texas | 20,903,994 | 7.4% |
| 34 | Utah | 2,236,714 | 0.8% |
| 49 | Vermont | 609,890 | 0.2% |
| 12 | Virginia | 7,100,702 | 2.5% |
| 15 | Washington | 5,908,684 | 2.1% |
| 37 | West Virginia | 1,813,077 | 0.6% |
| 18 | Wisconsin | 5,371,210 | 1.9% |
| 50 | Wyoming | 495,304 | 0.2% |

RANK ORDER

| RANK | STATE | POPULATION | % of USA |
|---|---|---|---|
| 1 | California | 33,930,798 | 12.0% |
| 2 | Texas | 20,903,994 | 7.4% |
| 3 | New York | 19,004,973 | 6.7% |
| 4 | Florida | 16,028,890 | 5.7% |
| 5 | Illinois | 12,439,042 | 4.4% |
| 6 | Pennsylvania | 12,300,670 | 4.4% |
| 7 | Ohio | 11,374,540 | 4.0% |
| 8 | Michigan | 9,955,829 | 3.5% |
| 9 | New Jersey | 8,424,354 | 3.0% |
| 10 | Georgia | 8,206,975 | 2.9% |
| 11 | North Carolina | 8,067,673 | 2.9% |
| 12 | Virginia | 7,100,702 | 2.5% |
| 13 | Massachusetts | 6,355,568 | 2.3% |
| 14 | Indiana | 6,090,782 | 2.2% |
| 15 | Washington | 5,908,684 | 2.1% |
| 16 | Tennessee | 5,700,037 | 2.0% |
| 17 | Missouri | 5,606,260 | 2.0% |
| 18 | Wisconsin | 5,371,210 | 1.9% |
| 19 | Maryland | 5,307,886 | 1.9% |
| 20 | Arizona | 5,140,683 | 1.8% |
| 21 | Minnesota | 4,925,670 | 1.7% |
| 22 | Louisiana | 4,480,271 | 1.6% |
| 23 | Alabama | 4,461,130 | 1.6% |
| 24 | Colorado | 4,311,882 | 1.5% |
| 25 | Kentucky | 4,049,431 | 1.4% |
| 26 | South Carolina | 4,025,061 | 1.4% |
| 27 | Oklahoma | 3,458,819 | 1.2% |
| 28 | Oregon | 3,428,543 | 1.2% |
| 29 | Connecticut | 3,409,535 | 1.2% |
| 30 | Iowa | 2,931,923 | 1.0% |
| 31 | Mississippi | 2,852,927 | 1.0% |
| 32 | Kansas | 2,693,824 | 1.0% |
| 33 | Arkansas | 2,679,733 | 1.0% |
| 34 | Utah | 2,236,714 | 0.8% |
| 35 | Nevada | 2,002,032 | 0.7% |
| 36 | New Mexico | 1,823,821 | 0.6% |
| 37 | West Virginia | 1,813,077 | 0.6% |
| 38 | Nebraska | 1,715,369 | 0.6% |
| 39 | Idaho | 1,297,274 | 0.5% |
| 40 | Maine | 1,277,731 | 0.5% |
| 41 | New Hampshire | 1,238,415 | 0.4% |
| 42 | Hawaii | 1,216,642 | 0.4% |
| 43 | Rhode Island | 1,049,662 | 0.4% |
| 44 | Montana | 905,316 | 0.3% |
| 45 | Delaware | 785,068 | 0.3% |
| 46 | South Dakota | 756,874 | 0.3% |
| 47 | North Dakota | 643,756 | 0.2% |
| 48 | Alaska | 628,933 | 0.2% |
| 49 | Vermont | 609,890 | 0.2% |
| 50 | Wyoming | 495,304 | 0.2% |
|  | District of Columbia | 574,096 | 0.2% |

Source: Morgan Quitno Press using data from U.S. Bureau of the Census
   "First Census 2000 Results" (December 28, 2000, http://www.census.gov/main/www/cen2000.html)
*This is the total of resident and overseas population. Overseas population includes U.S. military and federal civilian employees (and their dependents living with them) allocated to their home state or the District of Columbia, as reported by the employing federal agencies. This is the same population as that used for congressional apportionment except that the population for the District of Columbia is removed for that purpose.

# U.S. Population Living Overseas in 2000

## National Total = 576,367*

ALPHA ORDER

| RANK | STATE | OVERSEAS | % of USA |
|---|---|---|---|
| 13 | Alabama | 14,030 | 2.4% |
| 45 | Alaska | 2,001 | 0.3% |
| 21 | Arizona | 10,051 | 1.7% |
| 29 | Arkansas | 6,333 | 1.1% |
| 1 | California | 59,150 | 10.3% |
| 19 | Colorado | 10,621 | 1.8% |
| 37 | Connecticut | 3,970 | 0.7% |
| 48 | Delaware | 1,468 | 0.3% |
| 3 | Florida | 46,512 | 8.1% |
| 7 | Georgia | 20,522 | 3.6% |
| 33 | Hawaii | 5,105 | 0.9% |
| 40 | Idaho | 3,321 | 0.6% |
| 8 | Illinois | 19,749 | 3.4% |
| 20 | Indiana | 10,297 | 1.8% |
| 31 | Iowa | 5,599 | 1.0% |
| 32 | Kansas | 5,406 | 0.9% |
| 25 | Kentucky | 7,662 | 1.3% |
| 16 | Louisiana | 11,295 | 2.0% |
| 42 | Maine | 2,808 | 0.5% |
| 15 | Maryland | 11,400 | 2.0% |
| 28 | Massachusetts | 6,471 | 1.1% |
| 11 | Michigan | 17,385 | 3.0% |
| 30 | Minnesota | 6,191 | 1.1% |
| 23 | Mississippi | 8,269 | 1.4% |
| 17 | Missouri | 11,049 | 1.9% |
| 41 | Montana | 3,121 | 0.5% |
| 36 | Nebraska | 4,106 | 0.7% |
| 38 | Nevada | 3,775 | 0.7% |
| 43 | New Hampshire | 2,629 | 0.5% |
| 22 | New Jersey | 10,004 | 1.7% |
| 34 | New Mexico | 4,775 | 0.8% |
| 4 | New York | 28,516 | 4.9% |
| 10 | North Carolina | 18,360 | 3.2% |
| 46 | North Dakota | 1,556 | 0.3% |
| 6 | Ohio | 21,400 | 3.7% |
| 24 | Oklahoma | 8,165 | 1.4% |
| 27 | Oregon | 7,144 | 1.2% |
| 9 | Pennsylvania | 19,616 | 3.4% |
| 49 | Rhode Island | 1,343 | 0.2% |
| 14 | South Carolina | 13,049 | 2.3% |
| 44 | South Dakota | 2,030 | 0.4% |
| 18 | Tennessee | 10,754 | 1.9% |
| 2 | Texas | 52,174 | 9.1% |
| 39 | Utah | 3,545 | 0.6% |
| 50 | Vermont | 1,063 | 0.2% |
| 5 | Virginia | 22,187 | 3.8% |
| 12 | Washington | 14,563 | 2.5% |
| 35 | West Virginia | 4,733 | 0.8% |
| 26 | Wisconsin | 7,535 | 1.3% |
| 47 | Wyoming | 1,522 | 0.3% |

RANK ORDER

| RANK | STATE | OVERSEAS | % of USA |
|---|---|---|---|
| 1 | California | 59,150 | 10.3% |
| 2 | Texas | 52,174 | 9.1% |
| 3 | Florida | 46,512 | 8.1% |
| 4 | New York | 28,516 | 4.9% |
| 5 | Virginia | 22,187 | 3.8% |
| 6 | Ohio | 21,400 | 3.7% |
| 7 | Georgia | 20,522 | 3.6% |
| 8 | Illinois | 19,749 | 3.4% |
| 9 | Pennsylvania | 19,616 | 3.4% |
| 10 | North Carolina | 18,360 | 3.2% |
| 11 | Michigan | 17,385 | 3.0% |
| 12 | Washington | 14,563 | 2.5% |
| 13 | Alabama | 14,030 | 2.4% |
| 14 | South Carolina | 13,049 | 2.3% |
| 15 | Maryland | 11,400 | 2.0% |
| 16 | Louisiana | 11,295 | 2.0% |
| 17 | Missouri | 11,049 | 1.9% |
| 18 | Tennessee | 10,754 | 1.9% |
| 19 | Colorado | 10,621 | 1.8% |
| 20 | Indiana | 10,297 | 1.8% |
| 21 | Arizona | 10,051 | 1.7% |
| 22 | New Jersey | 10,004 | 1.7% |
| 23 | Mississippi | 8,269 | 1.4% |
| 24 | Oklahoma | 8,165 | 1.4% |
| 25 | Kentucky | 7,662 | 1.3% |
| 26 | Wisconsin | 7,535 | 1.3% |
| 27 | Oregon | 7,144 | 1.2% |
| 28 | Massachusetts | 6,471 | 1.1% |
| 29 | Arkansas | 6,333 | 1.1% |
| 30 | Minnesota | 6,191 | 1.1% |
| 31 | Iowa | 5,599 | 1.0% |
| 32 | Kansas | 5,406 | 0.9% |
| 33 | Hawaii | 5,105 | 0.9% |
| 34 | New Mexico | 4,775 | 0.8% |
| 35 | West Virginia | 4,733 | 0.8% |
| 36 | Nebraska | 4,106 | 0.7% |
| 37 | Connecticut | 3,970 | 0.7% |
| 38 | Nevada | 3,775 | 0.7% |
| 39 | Utah | 3,545 | 0.6% |
| 40 | Idaho | 3,321 | 0.6% |
| 41 | Montana | 3,121 | 0.5% |
| 42 | Maine | 2,808 | 0.5% |
| 43 | New Hampshire | 2,629 | 0.5% |
| 44 | South Dakota | 2,030 | 0.4% |
| 45 | Alaska | 2,001 | 0.3% |
| 46 | North Dakota | 1,556 | 0.3% |
| 47 | Wyoming | 1,522 | 0.3% |
| 48 | Delaware | 1,468 | 0.3% |
| 49 | Rhode Island | 1,343 | 0.2% |
| 50 | Vermont | 1,063 | 0.2% |
| | District of Columbia | 2,037 | 0.4% |

Source: U.S. Bureau of the Census
    "First Census 2000 Results" (December 28, 2000, http://www.census.gov/main/www/cen2000.html)
*Includes overseas U.S. military and federal civilian employees (and their dependents living with them) allocated to their home state or the District of Columbia, as reported by the employing federal agencies.

# Population in 1999

## National Total = 272,690,813*

ALPHA ORDER

| RANK | STATE | POPULATION | % of USA |
|------|-------|-----------:|----------|
| 23 | Alabama | 4,369,862 | 1.6% |
| 48 | Alaska | 619,500 | 0.2% |
| 20 | Arizona | 4,778,332 | 1.8% |
| 33 | Arkansas | 2,551,373 | 0.9% |
| 1 | California | 33,145,121 | 12.2% |
| 24 | Colorado | 4,056,133 | 1.5% |
| 29 | Connecticut | 3,282,031 | 1.2% |
| 45 | Delaware | 753,538 | 0.3% |
| 4 | Florida | 15,111,244 | 5.5% |
| 10 | Georgia | 7,788,240 | 2.9% |
| 42 | Hawaii | 1,185,497 | 0.4% |
| 40 | Idaho | 1,251,700 | 0.5% |
| 5 | Illinois | 12,128,370 | 4.4% |
| 14 | Indiana | 5,942,901 | 2.2% |
| 30 | Iowa | 2,869,413 | 1.1% |
| 32 | Kansas | 2,654,052 | 1.0% |
| 25 | Kentucky | 3,960,825 | 1.5% |
| 22 | Louisiana | 4,372,035 | 1.6% |
| 39 | Maine | 1,253,040 | 0.5% |
| 19 | Maryland | 5,171,634 | 1.9% |
| 13 | Massachusetts | 6,175,169 | 2.3% |
| 8 | Michigan | 9,863,775 | 3.6% |
| 21 | Minnesota | 4,775,508 | 1.8% |
| 31 | Mississippi | 2,768,619 | 1.0% |
| 17 | Missouri | 5,468,338 | 2.0% |
| 44 | Montana | 882,779 | 0.3% |
| 38 | Nebraska | 1,666,028 | 0.6% |
| 35 | Nevada | 1,809,253 | 0.7% |
| 41 | New Hampshire | 1,201,134 | 0.4% |
| 9 | New Jersey | 8,143,412 | 3.0% |
| 37 | New Mexico | 1,739,844 | 0.6% |
| 3 | New York | 18,196,601 | 6.7% |
| 11 | North Carolina | 7,650,789 | 2.8% |
| 47 | North Dakota | 633,666 | 0.2% |
| 7 | Ohio | 11,256,654 | 4.1% |
| 27 | Oklahoma | 3,358,044 | 1.2% |
| 28 | Oregon | 3,316,154 | 1.2% |
| 6 | Pennsylvania | 11,994,016 | 4.4% |
| 43 | Rhode Island | 990,819 | 0.4% |
| 26 | South Carolina | 3,885,736 | 1.4% |
| 46 | South Dakota | 733,133 | 0.3% |
| 16 | Tennessee | 5,483,535 | 2.0% |
| 2 | Texas | 20,044,141 | 7.4% |
| 34 | Utah | 2,129,836 | 0.8% |
| 49 | Vermont | 593,740 | 0.2% |
| 12 | Virginia | 6,872,912 | 2.5% |
| 15 | Washington | 5,756,361 | 2.1% |
| 36 | West Virginia | 1,806,928 | 0.7% |
| 18 | Wisconsin | 5,250,446 | 1.9% |
| 50 | Wyoming | 479,602 | 0.2% |

RANK ORDER

| RANK | STATE | POPULATION | % of USA |
|------|-------|-----------:|----------|
| 1 | California | 33,145,121 | 12.2% |
| 2 | Texas | 20,044,141 | 7.4% |
| 3 | New York | 18,196,601 | 6.7% |
| 4 | Florida | 15,111,244 | 5.5% |
| 5 | Illinois | 12,128,370 | 4.4% |
| 6 | Pennsylvania | 11,994,016 | 4.4% |
| 7 | Ohio | 11,256,654 | 4.1% |
| 8 | Michigan | 9,863,775 | 3.6% |
| 9 | New Jersey | 8,143,412 | 3.0% |
| 10 | Georgia | 7,788,240 | 2.9% |
| 11 | North Carolina | 7,650,789 | 2.8% |
| 12 | Virginia | 6,872,912 | 2.5% |
| 13 | Massachusetts | 6,175,169 | 2.3% |
| 14 | Indiana | 5,942,901 | 2.2% |
| 15 | Washington | 5,756,361 | 2.1% |
| 16 | Tennessee | 5,483,535 | 2.0% |
| 17 | Missouri | 5,468,338 | 2.0% |
| 18 | Wisconsin | 5,250,446 | 1.9% |
| 19 | Maryland | 5,171,634 | 1.9% |
| 20 | Arizona | 4,778,332 | 1.8% |
| 21 | Minnesota | 4,775,508 | 1.8% |
| 22 | Louisiana | 4,372,035 | 1.6% |
| 23 | Alabama | 4,369,862 | 1.6% |
| 24 | Colorado | 4,056,133 | 1.5% |
| 25 | Kentucky | 3,960,825 | 1.5% |
| 26 | South Carolina | 3,885,736 | 1.4% |
| 27 | Oklahoma | 3,358,044 | 1.2% |
| 28 | Oregon | 3,316,154 | 1.2% |
| 29 | Connecticut | 3,282,031 | 1.2% |
| 30 | Iowa | 2,869,413 | 1.1% |
| 31 | Mississippi | 2,768,619 | 1.0% |
| 32 | Kansas | 2,654,052 | 1.0% |
| 33 | Arkansas | 2,551,373 | 0.9% |
| 34 | Utah | 2,129,836 | 0.8% |
| 35 | Nevada | 1,809,253 | 0.7% |
| 36 | West Virginia | 1,806,928 | 0.7% |
| 37 | New Mexico | 1,739,844 | 0.6% |
| 38 | Nebraska | 1,666,028 | 0.6% |
| 39 | Maine | 1,253,040 | 0.5% |
| 40 | Idaho | 1,251,700 | 0.5% |
| 41 | New Hampshire | 1,201,134 | 0.4% |
| 42 | Hawaii | 1,185,497 | 0.4% |
| 43 | Rhode Island | 990,819 | 0.4% |
| 44 | Montana | 882,779 | 0.3% |
| 45 | Delaware | 753,538 | 0.3% |
| 46 | South Dakota | 733,133 | 0.3% |
| 47 | North Dakota | 633,666 | 0.2% |
| 48 | Alaska | 619,500 | 0.2% |
| 49 | Vermont | 593,740 | 0.2% |
| 50 | Wyoming | 479,602 | 0.2% |
|  | District of Columbia | 519,000 | 0.2% |

Source: U.S. Bureau of the Census
*"State Population Estimates"* (December 29, 1999, http://www.census.gov/population/estimates/state/st-99-3.txt)
*Includes armed forces residing in each state.

# Population Change: 1999 to 2000

## National Total = 8,731,093 Increase*

| RANK | STATE | GAIN | % of USA |
|---|---|---|---|
| 32 | Alabama | 77,238 | 0.9% |
| 49 | Alaska | 7,432 | 0.1% |
| 7 | Arizona | 352,300 | 4.0% |
| 23 | Arkansas | 122,027 | 1.4% |
| 4 | California | 726,527 | 8.3% |
| 11 | Colorado | 245,128 | 2.8% |
| 22 | Connecticut | 123,534 | 1.4% |
| 41 | Delaware | 30,062 | 0.3% |
| 1 | Florida | 871,134 | 10.0% |
| 6 | Georgia | 398,213 | 4.6% |
| 42 | Hawaii | 26,040 | 0.3% |
| 38 | Idaho | 42,253 | 0.5% |
| 8 | Illinois | 290,923 | 3.3% |
| 18 | Indiana | 137,584 | 1.6% |
| 36 | Iowa | 56,911 | 0.7% |
| 40 | Kansas | 34,366 | 0.4% |
| 30 | Kentucky | 80,944 | 0.9% |
| 27 | Louisiana | 96,941 | 1.1% |
| 43 | Maine | 21,883 | 0.3% |
| 21 | Maryland | 124,852 | 1.4% |
| 15 | Massachusetts | 173,928 | 2.0% |
| 34 | Michigan | 74,669 | 0.9% |
| 16 | Minnesota | 143,971 | 1.6% |
| 33 | Mississippi | 76,039 | 0.9% |
| 19 | Missouri | 126,873 | 1.5% |
| 45 | Montana | 19,416 | 0.2% |
| 37 | Nebraska | 45,235 | 0.5% |
| 14 | Nevada | 189,004 | 2.2% |
| 39 | New Hampshire | 34,652 | 0.4% |
| 10 | New Jersey | 270,938 | 3.1% |
| 31 | New Mexico | 79,202 | 0.9% |
| 3 | New York | 779,856 | 8.9% |
| 5 | North Carolina | 398,524 | 4.6% |
| 48 | North Dakota | 8,534 | 0.1% |
| 28 | Ohio | 96,486 | 1.1% |
| 29 | Oklahoma | 92,610 | 1.1% |
| 25 | Oregon | 105,245 | 1.2% |
| 9 | Pennsylvania | 287,038 | 3.3% |
| 35 | Rhode Island | 57,500 | 0.7% |
| 20 | South Carolina | 126,276 | 1.4% |
| 44 | South Dakota | 21,711 | 0.2% |
| 12 | Tennessee | 205,748 | 2.4% |
| 2 | Texas | 807,679 | 9.3% |
| 26 | Utah | 103,333 | 1.2% |
| 46 | Vermont | 15,087 | 0.2% |
| 13 | Virginia | 205,603 | 2.4% |
| 17 | Washington | 137,760 | 1.6% |
| 50 | West Virginia | 1,416 | 0.0% |
| 24 | Wisconsin | 113,229 | 1.3% |
| 47 | Wyoming | 14,180 | 0.2% |

| RANK | STATE | GAIN | % of USA |
|---|---|---|---|
| 1 | Florida | 871,134 | 10.0% |
| 2 | Texas | 807,679 | 9.3% |
| 3 | New York | 779,856 | 8.9% |
| 4 | California | 726,527 | 8.3% |
| 5 | North Carolina | 398,524 | 4.6% |
| 6 | Georgia | 398,213 | 4.6% |
| 7 | Arizona | 352,300 | 4.0% |
| 8 | Illinois | 290,923 | 3.3% |
| 9 | Pennsylvania | 287,038 | 3.3% |
| 10 | New Jersey | 270,938 | 3.1% |
| 11 | Colorado | 245,128 | 2.8% |
| 12 | Tennessee | 205,748 | 2.4% |
| 13 | Virginia | 205,603 | 2.4% |
| 14 | Nevada | 189,004 | 2.2% |
| 15 | Massachusetts | 173,928 | 2.0% |
| 16 | Minnesota | 143,971 | 1.6% |
| 17 | Washington | 137,760 | 1.6% |
| 18 | Indiana | 137,584 | 1.6% |
| 19 | Missouri | 126,873 | 1.5% |
| 20 | South Carolina | 126,276 | 1.4% |
| 21 | Maryland | 124,852 | 1.4% |
| 22 | Connecticut | 123,534 | 1.4% |
| 23 | Arkansas | 122,027 | 1.4% |
| 24 | Wisconsin | 113,229 | 1.3% |
| 25 | Oregon | 105,245 | 1.2% |
| 26 | Utah | 103,333 | 1.2% |
| 27 | Louisiana | 96,941 | 1.1% |
| 28 | Ohio | 96,486 | 1.1% |
| 29 | Oklahoma | 92,610 | 1.1% |
| 30 | Kentucky | 80,944 | 0.9% |
| 31 | New Mexico | 79,202 | 0.9% |
| 32 | Alabama | 77,238 | 0.9% |
| 33 | Mississippi | 76,039 | 0.9% |
| 34 | Michigan | 74,669 | 0.9% |
| 35 | Rhode Island | 57,500 | 0.7% |
| 36 | Iowa | 56,911 | 0.7% |
| 37 | Nebraska | 45,235 | 0.5% |
| 38 | Idaho | 42,253 | 0.5% |
| 39 | New Hampshire | 34,652 | 0.4% |
| 40 | Kansas | 34,366 | 0.4% |
| 41 | Delaware | 30,062 | 0.3% |
| 42 | Hawaii | 26,040 | 0.3% |
| 43 | Maine | 21,883 | 0.3% |
| 44 | South Dakota | 21,711 | 0.2% |
| 45 | Montana | 19,416 | 0.2% |
| 46 | Vermont | 15,087 | 0.2% |
| 47 | Wyoming | 14,180 | 0.2% |
| 48 | North Dakota | 8,534 | 0.1% |
| 49 | Alaska | 7,432 | 0.1% |
| 50 | West Virginia | 1,416 | 0.0% |
| | District of Columbia | 53,059 | 0.6% |

Source: Morgan Quitno Press using data from U.S. Bureau of the Census
"First Census 2000 Results" (December 28, 2000, http://www.census.gov/main/www/cen2000.html) and
"State Population Estimates" (December 29, 1999, http://www.census.gov/population/estimates/state/st-99-3.txt)
*Resident population. This table is simply the numeric difference between the last population estimate of July 1999 and the actual Census 2000 count of April 2000. This table reflects more of a correction in estimates than actual change over one year.

# Percent Change in Population: 1999 to 2000

## National Percent Change = 3.2% Increase*

*Source: Morgan Quitno Press using data from U.S. Bureau of the Census*
*"First Census 2000 Results" (December 28, 2000, http://www.census.gov/main/www/cen2000.html) and*
*"State Population Estimates" (December 29, 1999, http://www.census.gov/population/estimates/state/st-99-3.txt)*
*\*Resident population. This table is simply the percent difference between the last population estimate of July 1999 and the actual Census 2000 count of April 2000. This table reflects more of a correction in estimates than actual change over one year.*

# Population in 1998

## National Total = 270,248,003*

| RANK | STATE | POPULATION | % of USA | RANK | STATE | POPULATION | % of USA |
|---|---|---|---|---|---|---|---|
| 23 | Alabama | 4,351,037 | 1.6% | 1 | California | 32,682,794 | 12.1% |
| 48 | Alaska | 615,205 | 0.2% | 2 | Texas | 19,712,389 | 7.3% |
| 21 | Arizona | 4,667,277 | 1.7% | 3 | New York | 18,159,175 | 6.7% |
| 33 | Arkansas | 2,538,202 | 0.9% | 4 | Florida | 14,908,230 | 5.5% |
| 1 | California | 32,682,794 | 12.1% | 5 | Illinois | 12,069,774 | 4.5% |
| 24 | Colorado | 3,968,967 | 1.5% | 6 | Pennsylvania | 12,002,329 | 4.4% |
| 29 | Connecticut | 3,272,563 | 1.2% | 7 | Ohio | 11,237,752 | 4.2% |
| 45 | Delaware | 744,066 | 0.3% | 8 | Michigan | 9,820,231 | 3.6% |
| 4 | Florida | 14,908,230 | 5.5% | 9 | New Jersey | 8,095,542 | 3.0% |
| 10 | Georgia | 7,636,522 | 2.8% | 10 | Georgia | 7,636,522 | 2.8% |
| 41 | Hawaii | 1,190,472 | 0.4% | 11 | North Carolina | 7,545,828 | 2.8% |
| 40 | Idaho | 1,230,923 | 0.5% | 12 | Virginia | 6,789,225 | 2.5% |
| 5 | Illinois | 12,069,774 | 4.5% | 13 | Massachusetts | 6,144,407 | 2.3% |
| 14 | Indiana | 5,907,617 | 2.2% | 14 | Indiana | 5,907,617 | 2.2% |
| 30 | Iowa | 2,861,025 | 1.1% | 15 | Washington | 5,687,832 | 2.1% |
| 32 | Kansas | 2,638,667 | 1.0% | 16 | Missouri | 5,437,562 | 2.0% |
| 25 | Kentucky | 3,934,310 | 1.5% | 17 | Tennessee | 5,432,679 | 2.0% |
| 22 | Louisiana | 4,362,758 | 1.6% | 18 | Wisconsin | 5,222,124 | 1.9% |
| 39 | Maine | 1,247,554 | 0.5% | 19 | Maryland | 5,130,072 | 1.9% |
| 19 | Maryland | 5,130,072 | 1.9% | 20 | Minnesota | 4,726,411 | 1.7% |
| 13 | Massachusetts | 6,144,407 | 2.3% | 21 | Arizona | 4,667,277 | 1.7% |
| 8 | Michigan | 9,820,231 | 3.6% | 22 | Louisiana | 4,362,758 | 1.6% |
| 20 | Minnesota | 4,726,411 | 1.7% | 23 | Alabama | 4,351,037 | 1.6% |
| 31 | Mississippi | 2,751,335 | 1.0% | 24 | Colorado | 3,968,967 | 1.5% |
| 16 | Missouri | 5,437,562 | 2.0% | 25 | Kentucky | 3,934,310 | 1.5% |
| 44 | Montana | 879,533 | 0.3% | 26 | South Carolina | 3,839,578 | 1.4% |
| 38 | Nebraska | 1,660,772 | 0.6% | 27 | Oklahoma | 3,339,478 | 1.2% |
| 36 | Nevada | 1,743,772 | 0.6% | 28 | Oregon | 3,282,055 | 1.2% |
| 42 | New Hampshire | 1,185,823 | 0.4% | 29 | Connecticut | 3,272,563 | 1.2% |
| 9 | New Jersey | 8,095,542 | 3.0% | 30 | Iowa | 2,861,025 | 1.1% |
| 37 | New Mexico | 1,733,535 | 0.6% | 31 | Mississippi | 2,751,335 | 1.0% |
| 3 | New York | 18,159,175 | 6.7% | 32 | Kansas | 2,638,667 | 1.0% |
| 11 | North Carolina | 7,545,828 | 2.8% | 33 | Arkansas | 2,538,202 | 0.9% |
| 47 | North Dakota | 637,808 | 0.2% | 34 | Utah | 2,100,562 | 0.8% |
| 7 | Ohio | 11,237,752 | 4.2% | 35 | West Virginia | 1,811,688 | 0.7% |
| 27 | Oklahoma | 3,339,478 | 1.2% | 36 | Nevada | 1,743,772 | 0.6% |
| 28 | Oregon | 3,282,055 | 1.2% | 37 | New Mexico | 1,733,535 | 0.6% |
| 6 | Pennsylvania | 12,002,329 | 4.4% | 38 | Nebraska | 1,660,772 | 0.6% |
| 43 | Rhode Island | 987,704 | 0.4% | 39 | Maine | 1,247,554 | 0.5% |
| 26 | South Carolina | 3,839,578 | 1.4% | 40 | Idaho | 1,230,923 | 0.5% |
| 46 | South Dakota | 730,789 | 0.3% | 41 | Hawaii | 1,190,472 | 0.4% |
| 17 | Tennessee | 5,432,679 | 2.0% | 42 | New Hampshire | 1,185,823 | 0.4% |
| 2 | Texas | 19,712,389 | 7.3% | 43 | Rhode Island | 987,704 | 0.4% |
| 34 | Utah | 2,100,562 | 0.8% | 44 | Montana | 879,533 | 0.3% |
| 49 | Vermont | 590,579 | 0.2% | 45 | Delaware | 744,066 | 0.3% |
| 12 | Virginia | 6,789,225 | 2.5% | 46 | South Dakota | 730,789 | 0.3% |
| 15 | Washington | 5,687,832 | 2.1% | 47 | North Dakota | 637,808 | 0.2% |
| 35 | West Virginia | 1,811,688 | 0.7% | 48 | Alaska | 615,205 | 0.2% |
| 18 | Wisconsin | 5,222,124 | 1.9% | 49 | Vermont | 590,579 | 0.2% |
| 50 | Wyoming | 480,045 | 0.2% | 50 | Wyoming | 480,045 | 0.2% |
| | | | | | District of Columbia | 521,426 | 0.2% |

Source: U.S. Bureau of the Census
"State Population Estimates" (December 29, 1999, http://www.census.gov/population/estimates/state/st-99-3.txt)
*Includes armed forces residing in each state. This updates earlier 1998 population estimates.

# Resident State Population in 1990

## National Total = 248,790,925*

ALPHA ORDER

| RANK | STATE | POPULATION | % of USA |
|---|---|---|---|
| 22 | Alabama | 4,040,389 | 1.6% |
| 49 | Alaska | 550,043 | 0.2% |
| 24 | Arizona | 3,665,339 | 1.5% |
| 33 | Arkansas | 2,350,624 | 0.9% |
| 1 | California | 29,811,427 | 12.0% |
| 26 | Colorado | 3,294,473 | 1.3% |
| 27 | Connecticut | 3,287,116 | 1.3% |
| 46 | Delaware | 666,168 | 0.3% |
| 4 | Florida | 12,938,071 | 5.2% |
| 11 | Georgia | 6,478,149 | 2.6% |
| 41 | Hawaii | 1,108,229 | 0.4% |
| 42 | Idaho | 1,006,734 | 0.4% |
| 6 | Illinois | 11,430,602 | 4.6% |
| 14 | Indiana | 5,544,156 | 2.2% |
| 30 | Iowa | 2,776,831 | 1.1% |
| 32 | Kansas | 2,477,588 | 1.0% |
| 23 | Kentucky | 3,686,892 | 1.5% |
| 21 | Louisiana | 4,221,826 | 1.7% |
| 38 | Maine | 1,227,928 | 0.5% |
| 19 | Maryland | 4,780,753 | 1.9% |
| 13 | Massachusetts | 6,016,425 | 2.4% |
| 8 | Michigan | 9,295,287 | 3.7% |
| 20 | Minnesota | 4,375,665 | 1.8% |
| 31 | Mississippi | 2,575,475 | 1.0% |
| 15 | Missouri | 5,116,901 | 2.1% |
| 44 | Montana | 799,065 | 0.3% |
| 36 | Nebraska | 1,578,417 | 0.6% |
| 39 | Nevada | 1,201,675 | 0.5% |
| 40 | New Hampshire | 1,109,252 | 0.4% |
| 9 | New Jersey | 7,747,750 | 3.1% |
| 37 | New Mexico | 1,515,069 | 0.6% |
| 2 | New York | 17,990,778 | 7.2% |
| 10 | North Carolina | 6,632,448 | 2.7% |
| 47 | North Dakota | 638,800 | 0.3% |
| 7 | Ohio | 10,847,115 | 4.4% |
| 28 | Oklahoma | 3,145,576 | 1.3% |
| 29 | Oregon | 2,842,337 | 1.1% |
| 5 | Pennsylvania | 11,882,842 | 4.8% |
| 43 | Rhode Island | 1,003,464 | 0.4% |
| 25 | South Carolina | 3,486,310 | 1.4% |
| 45 | South Dakota | 696,004 | 0.3% |
| 17 | Tennessee | 4,877,203 | 2.0% |
| 3 | Texas | 16,986,335 | 6.8% |
| 35 | Utah | 1,722,850 | 0.7% |
| 48 | Vermont | 562,758 | 0.2% |
| 12 | Virginia | 6,189,197 | 2.5% |
| 18 | Washington | 4,866,669 | 2.0% |
| 34 | West Virginia | 1,793,477 | 0.7% |
| 16 | Wisconsin | 4,891,954 | 2.0% |
| 50 | Wyoming | 453,589 | 0.2% |

RANK ORDER

| RANK | STATE | POPULATION | % of USA |
|---|---|---|---|
| 1 | California | 29,811,427 | 12.0% |
| 2 | New York | 17,990,778 | 7.2% |
| 3 | Texas | 16,986,335 | 6.8% |
| 4 | Florida | 12,938,071 | 5.2% |
| 5 | Pennsylvania | 11,882,842 | 4.8% |
| 6 | Illinois | 11,430,602 | 4.6% |
| 7 | Ohio | 10,847,115 | 4.4% |
| 8 | Michigan | 9,295,287 | 3.7% |
| 9 | New Jersey | 7,747,750 | 3.1% |
| 10 | North Carolina | 6,632,448 | 2.7% |
| 11 | Georgia | 6,478,149 | 2.6% |
| 12 | Virginia | 6,189,197 | 2.5% |
| 13 | Massachusetts | 6,016,425 | 2.4% |
| 14 | Indiana | 5,544,156 | 2.2% |
| 15 | Missouri | 5,116,901 | 2.1% |
| 16 | Wisconsin | 4,891,954 | 2.0% |
| 17 | Tennessee | 4,877,203 | 2.0% |
| 18 | Washington | 4,866,669 | 2.0% |
| 19 | Maryland | 4,780,753 | 1.9% |
| 20 | Minnesota | 4,375,665 | 1.8% |
| 21 | Louisiana | 4,221,826 | 1.7% |
| 22 | Alabama | 4,040,389 | 1.6% |
| 23 | Kentucky | 3,686,892 | 1.5% |
| 24 | Arizona | 3,665,339 | 1.5% |
| 25 | South Carolina | 3,486,310 | 1.4% |
| 26 | Colorado | 3,294,473 | 1.3% |
| 27 | Connecticut | 3,287,116 | 1.3% |
| 28 | Oklahoma | 3,145,576 | 1.3% |
| 29 | Oregon | 2,842,337 | 1.1% |
| 30 | Iowa | 2,776,831 | 1.1% |
| 31 | Mississippi | 2,575,475 | 1.0% |
| 32 | Kansas | 2,477,588 | 1.0% |
| 33 | Arkansas | 2,350,624 | 0.9% |
| 34 | West Virginia | 1,793,477 | 0.7% |
| 35 | Utah | 1,722,850 | 0.7% |
| 36 | Nebraska | 1,578,417 | 0.6% |
| 37 | New Mexico | 1,515,069 | 0.6% |
| 38 | Maine | 1,227,928 | 0.5% |
| 39 | Nevada | 1,201,675 | 0.5% |
| 40 | New Hampshire | 1,109,252 | 0.4% |
| 41 | Hawaii | 1,108,229 | 0.4% |
| 42 | Idaho | 1,006,734 | 0.4% |
| 43 | Rhode Island | 1,003,464 | 0.4% |
| 44 | Montana | 799,065 | 0.3% |
| 45 | South Dakota | 696,004 | 0.3% |
| 46 | Delaware | 666,168 | 0.3% |
| 47 | North Dakota | 638,800 | 0.3% |
| 48 | Vermont | 562,758 | 0.2% |
| 49 | Alaska | 550,043 | 0.2% |
| 50 | Wyoming | 453,589 | 0.2% |
| | District of Columbia | 606,900 | 0.2% |

*Source: U.S. Bureau of the Census*
    *"State Population Estimates" (December 29, 1999, http://www.census.gov/population/estimates/state/st-99-3.txt)*
*The is the decennial census dated April 1, 1990. The counts shown here include corrections processed through December 1998.*

# Population Change: 1990 to 2000

## National Total = 32,712,033 Increase*

ALPHA ORDER

| RANK | STATE | GAIN/LOSS | % of USA |
|------|-------|-----------|----------|
| 25 | Alabama | 406,513 | 1.2% |
| 43 | Alaska | 76,889 | 0.2% |
| 5 | Arizona | 1,465,404 | 4.5% |
| 29 | Arkansas | 322,675 | 1.0% |
| 1 | California | 4,111,627 | 12.6% |
| 8 | Colorado | 1,006,867 | 3.1% |
| 39 | Connecticut | 118,449 | 0.4% |
| 40 | Delaware | 117,432 | 0.4% |
| 3 | Florida | 3,044,452 | 9.3% |
| 4 | Georgia | 1,708,237 | 5.2% |
| 41 | Hawaii | 103,308 | 0.3% |
| 32 | Idaho | 287,204 | 0.9% |
| 9 | Illinois | 988,691 | 3.0% |
| 18 | Indiana | 536,326 | 1.6% |
| 36 | Iowa | 149,569 | 0.5% |
| 35 | Kansas | 210,844 | 0.6% |
| 27 | Kentucky | 356,473 | 1.1% |
| 34 | Louisiana | 249,003 | 0.8% |
| 45 | Maine | 46,995 | 0.1% |
| 20 | Maryland | 515,018 | 1.6% |
| 28 | Massachusetts | 332,672 | 1.0% |
| 15 | Michigan | 643,147 | 2.0% |
| 17 | Minnesota | 544,380 | 1.7% |
| 33 | Mississippi | 271,442 | 0.8% |
| 23 | Missouri | 478,138 | 1.5% |
| 42 | Montana | 103,130 | 0.3% |
| 37 | Nebraska | 132,878 | 0.4% |
| 13 | Nevada | 796,424 | 2.4% |
| 38 | New Hampshire | 126,534 | 0.4% |
| 14 | New Jersey | 684,162 | 2.1% |
| 31 | New Mexico | 303,977 | 0.9% |
| 10 | New York | 986,002 | 3.0% |
| 6 | North Carolina | 1,420,676 | 4.3% |
| 50 | North Dakota | 3,400 | 0.0% |
| 22 | Ohio | 506,025 | 1.5% |
| 30 | Oklahoma | 305,069 | 0.9% |
| 16 | Oregon | 579,078 | 1.8% |
| 26 | Pennsylvania | 399,411 | 1.2% |
| 47 | Rhode Island | 44,855 | 0.1% |
| 19 | South Carolina | 525,309 | 1.6% |
| 44 | South Dakota | 58,840 | 0.2% |
| 12 | Tennessee | 812,098 | 2.5% |
| 2 | Texas | 3,865,310 | 11.8% |
| 21 | Utah | 510,319 | 1.6% |
| 46 | Vermont | 46,069 | 0.1% |
| 11 | Virginia | 891,157 | 2.7% |
| 7 | Washington | 1,027,429 | 3.1% |
| 49 | West Virginia | 14,867 | 0.0% |
| 24 | Wisconsin | 471,906 | 1.4% |
| 48 | Wyoming | 40,194 | 0.1% |

RANK ORDER

| RANK | STATE | GAIN/LOSS | % of USA |
|------|-------|-----------|----------|
| 1 | California | 4,111,627 | 12.6% |
| 2 | Texas | 3,865,310 | 11.8% |
| 3 | Florida | 3,044,452 | 9.3% |
| 4 | Georgia | 1,708,237 | 5.2% |
| 5 | Arizona | 1,465,404 | 4.5% |
| 6 | North Carolina | 1,420,676 | 4.3% |
| 7 | Washington | 1,027,429 | 3.1% |
| 8 | Colorado | 1,006,867 | 3.1% |
| 9 | Illinois | 988,691 | 3.0% |
| 10 | New York | 986,002 | 3.0% |
| 11 | Virginia | 891,157 | 2.7% |
| 12 | Tennessee | 812,098 | 2.5% |
| 13 | Nevada | 796,424 | 2.4% |
| 14 | New Jersey | 684,162 | 2.1% |
| 15 | Michigan | 643,147 | 2.0% |
| 16 | Oregon | 579,078 | 1.8% |
| 17 | Minnesota | 544,380 | 1.7% |
| 18 | Indiana | 536,326 | 1.6% |
| 19 | South Carolina | 525,309 | 1.6% |
| 20 | Maryland | 515,018 | 1.6% |
| 21 | Utah | 510,319 | 1.6% |
| 22 | Ohio | 506,025 | 1.5% |
| 23 | Missouri | 478,138 | 1.5% |
| 24 | Wisconsin | 471,906 | 1.4% |
| 25 | Alabama | 406,513 | 1.2% |
| 26 | Pennsylvania | 399,411 | 1.2% |
| 27 | Kentucky | 356,473 | 1.1% |
| 28 | Massachusetts | 332,672 | 1.0% |
| 29 | Arkansas | 322,675 | 1.0% |
| 30 | Oklahoma | 305,069 | 0.9% |
| 31 | New Mexico | 303,977 | 0.9% |
| 32 | Idaho | 287,204 | 0.9% |
| 33 | Mississippi | 271,442 | 0.8% |
| 34 | Louisiana | 249,003 | 0.8% |
| 35 | Kansas | 210,844 | 0.6% |
| 36 | Iowa | 149,569 | 0.5% |
| 37 | Nebraska | 132,878 | 0.4% |
| 38 | New Hampshire | 126,534 | 0.4% |
| 39 | Connecticut | 118,449 | 0.4% |
| 40 | Delaware | 117,432 | 0.4% |
| 41 | Hawaii | 103,308 | 0.3% |
| 42 | Montana | 103,130 | 0.3% |
| 43 | Alaska | 76,889 | 0.2% |
| 44 | South Dakota | 58,840 | 0.2% |
| 45 | Maine | 46,995 | 0.1% |
| 46 | Vermont | 46,069 | 0.1% |
| 47 | Rhode Island | 44,855 | 0.1% |
| 48 | Wyoming | 40,194 | 0.1% |
| 49 | West Virginia | 14,867 | 0.0% |
| 50 | North Dakota | 3,400 | 0.0% |
| | District of Columbia | (34,841) | |

Source: U.S. Bureau of the Census
"First Census 2000 Results" (December 28, 2000, http://www.census.gov/main/www/cen2000.html)
*From April 1, 1990 to April 1, 2000.

# Percent Change in Population: 1990 to 2000

## National Percent Change = 13.2% Increase*

| RANK | STATE | PERCENT CHANGE |
|------|-------|----------------|
| 25 | Alabama | 10.1 |
| 17 | Alaska | 14.0 |
| 2 | Arizona | 40.0 |
| 19 | Arkansas | 13.7 |
| 18 | California | 13.8 |
| 3 | Colorado | 30.6 |
| 47 | Connecticut | 3.6 |
| 13 | Delaware | 17.6 |
| 7 | Florida | 23.5 |
| 6 | Georgia | 26.4 |
| 30 | Hawaii | 9.3 |
| 5 | Idaho | 28.5 |
| 34 | Illinois | 8.6 |
| 26 | Indiana | 9.7 |
| 43 | Iowa | 5.4 |
| 35 | Kansas | 8.5 |
| 26 | Kentucky | 9.7 |
| 40 | Louisiana | 5.9 |
| 46 | Maine | 3.8 |
| 23 | Maryland | 10.8 |
| 41 | Massachusetts | 5.5 |
| 39 | Michigan | 6.9 |
| 21 | Minnesota | 12.4 |
| 24 | Mississippi | 10.5 |
| 30 | Missouri | 9.3 |
| 20 | Montana | 12.9 |
| 37 | Nebraska | 8.4 |
| 1 | Nevada | 66.3 |
| 22 | New Hampshire | 11.4 |
| 32 | New Jersey | 8.9 |
| 12 | New Mexico | 20.1 |
| 41 | New York | 5.5 |
| 9 | North Carolina | 21.4 |
| 50 | North Dakota | 0.5 |
| 44 | Ohio | 4.7 |
| 26 | Oklahoma | 9.7 |
| 11 | Oregon | 20.4 |
| 48 | Pennsylvania | 3.4 |
| 45 | Rhode Island | 4.5 |
| 15 | South Carolina | 15.1 |
| 35 | South Dakota | 8.5 |
| 14 | Tennessee | 16.7 |
| 8 | Texas | 22.8 |
| 4 | Utah | 29.6 |
| 38 | Vermont | 8.2 |
| 16 | Virginia | 14.4 |
| 10 | Washington | 21.1 |
| 49 | West Virginia | 0.8 |
| 29 | Wisconsin | 9.6 |
| 32 | Wyoming | 8.9 |

| RANK | STATE | PERCENT CHANGE |
|------|-------|----------------|
| 1 | Nevada | 66.3 |
| 2 | Arizona | 40.0 |
| 3 | Colorado | 30.6 |
| 4 | Utah | 29.6 |
| 5 | Idaho | 28.5 |
| 6 | Georgia | 26.4 |
| 7 | Florida | 23.5 |
| 8 | Texas | 22.8 |
| 9 | North Carolina | 21.4 |
| 10 | Washington | 21.1 |
| 11 | Oregon | 20.4 |
| 12 | New Mexico | 20.1 |
| 13 | Delaware | 17.6 |
| 14 | Tennessee | 16.7 |
| 15 | South Carolina | 15.1 |
| 16 | Virginia | 14.4 |
| 17 | Alaska | 14.0 |
| 18 | California | 13.8 |
| 19 | Arkansas | 13.7 |
| 20 | Montana | 12.9 |
| 21 | Minnesota | 12.4 |
| 22 | New Hampshire | 11.4 |
| 23 | Maryland | 10.8 |
| 24 | Mississippi | 10.5 |
| 25 | Alabama | 10.1 |
| 26 | Indiana | 9.7 |
| 26 | Kentucky | 9.7 |
| 26 | Oklahoma | 9.7 |
| 29 | Wisconsin | 9.6 |
| 30 | Hawaii | 9.3 |
| 30 | Missouri | 9.3 |
| 32 | New Jersey | 8.9 |
| 32 | Wyoming | 8.9 |
| 34 | Illinois | 8.6 |
| 35 | Kansas | 8.5 |
| 35 | South Dakota | 8.5 |
| 37 | Nebraska | 8.4 |
| 38 | Vermont | 8.2 |
| 39 | Michigan | 6.9 |
| 40 | Louisiana | 5.9 |
| 41 | Massachusetts | 5.5 |
| 41 | New York | 5.5 |
| 43 | Iowa | 5.4 |
| 44 | Ohio | 4.7 |
| 45 | Rhode Island | 4.5 |
| 46 | Maine | 3.8 |
| 47 | Connecticut | 3.6 |
| 48 | Pennsylvania | 3.4 |
| 49 | West Virginia | 0.8 |
| 50 | North Dakota | 0.5 |
| | District of Columbia | (5.7) |

*Source: U.S. Bureau of the Census*
*"First Census 2000 Results" (December 28, 2000, http://www.census.gov/main/www/cen2000.html)*
*\*From April 1, 1990 to April 1, 2000.*

# Resident State Population in 1980

## National Total = 226,504,825

ALPHA ORDER

| RANK | STATE | POPULATION | % of USA |
|---|---|---|---|
| 22 | Alabama | 3,893,888 | 1.7% |
| 50 | Alaska | 401,851 | 0.2% |
| 29 | Arizona | 2,718,215 | 1.2% |
| 33 | Arkansas | 2,286,435 | 1.0% |
| 1 | California | 23,667,902 | 10.4% |
| 28 | Colorado | 2,889,964 | 1.3% |
| 25 | Connecticut | 3,107,576 | 1.4% |
| 47 | Delaware | 594,338 | 0.3% |
| 7 | Florida | 9,746,324 | 4.3% |
| 13 | Georgia | 5,463,105 | 2.4% |
| 39 | Hawaii | 964,691 | 0.4% |
| 41 | Idaho | 943,935 | 0.4% |
| 5 | Illinois | 11,426,518 | 5.0% |
| 12 | Indiana | 5,490,224 | 2.4% |
| 27 | Iowa | 2,913,808 | 1.3% |
| 32 | Kansas | 2,363,679 | 1.0% |
| 23 | Kentucky | 3,660,777 | 1.6% |
| 19 | Louisiana | 4,205,900 | 1.9% |
| 38 | Maine | 1,124,660 | 0.5% |
| 18 | Maryland | 4,216,975 | 1.9% |
| 11 | Massachusetts | 5,737,037 | 2.5% |
| 8 | Michigan | 9,262,078 | 4.1% |
| 21 | Minnesota | 4,075,970 | 1.8% |
| 31 | Mississippi | 2,520,638 | 1.1% |
| 15 | Missouri | 4,916,686 | 2.2% |
| 44 | Montana | 786,690 | 0.3% |
| 35 | Nebraska | 1,569,825 | 0.7% |
| 43 | Nevada | 800,493 | 0.4% |
| 42 | New Hampshire | 920,610 | 0.4% |
| 9 | New Jersey | 7,364,823 | 3.3% |
| 37 | New Mexico | 1,302,894 | 0.6% |
| 2 | New York | 17,558,072 | 7.8% |
| 10 | North Carolina | 5,881,766 | 2.6% |
| 46 | North Dakota | 652,717 | 0.3% |
| 6 | Ohio | 10,797,630 | 4.8% |
| 26 | Oklahoma | 3,025,290 | 1.3% |
| 30 | Oregon | 2,633,105 | 1.2% |
| 4 | Pennsylvania | 11,863,895 | 5.2% |
| 40 | Rhode Island | 947,154 | 0.4% |
| 24 | South Carolina | 3,121,820 | 1.4% |
| 45 | South Dakota | 690,768 | 0.3% |
| 17 | Tennessee | 4,591,120 | 2.0% |
| 3 | Texas | 14,229,191 | 6.3% |
| 36 | Utah | 1,461,037 | 0.6% |
| 48 | Vermont | 511,456 | 0.2% |
| 14 | Virginia | 5,346,818 | 2.4% |
| 20 | Washington | 4,132,156 | 1.8% |
| 34 | West Virginia | 1,949,644 | 0.9% |
| 16 | Wisconsin | 4,705,767 | 2.1% |
| 49 | Wyoming | 469,557 | 0.2% |

RANK ORDER

| RANK | STATE | POPULATION | % of USA |
|---|---|---|---|
| 1 | California | 23,667,902 | 10.4% |
| 2 | New York | 17,558,072 | 7.8% |
| 3 | Texas | 14,229,191 | 6.3% |
| 4 | Pennsylvania | 11,863,895 | 5.2% |
| 5 | Illinois | 11,426,518 | 5.0% |
| 6 | Ohio | 10,797,630 | 4.8% |
| 7 | Florida | 9,746,324 | 4.3% |
| 8 | Michigan | 9,262,078 | 4.1% |
| 9 | New Jersey | 7,364,823 | 3.3% |
| 10 | North Carolina | 5,881,766 | 2.6% |
| 11 | Massachusetts | 5,737,037 | 2.5% |
| 12 | Indiana | 5,490,224 | 2.4% |
| 13 | Georgia | 5,463,105 | 2.4% |
| 14 | Virginia | 5,346,818 | 2.4% |
| 15 | Missouri | 4,916,686 | 2.2% |
| 16 | Wisconsin | 4,705,767 | 2.1% |
| 17 | Tennessee | 4,591,120 | 2.0% |
| 18 | Maryland | 4,216,975 | 1.9% |
| 19 | Louisiana | 4,205,900 | 1.9% |
| 20 | Washington | 4,132,156 | 1.8% |
| 21 | Minnesota | 4,075,970 | 1.8% |
| 22 | Alabama | 3,893,888 | 1.7% |
| 23 | Kentucky | 3,660,777 | 1.6% |
| 24 | South Carolina | 3,121,820 | 1.4% |
| 25 | Connecticut | 3,107,576 | 1.4% |
| 26 | Oklahoma | 3,025,290 | 1.3% |
| 27 | Iowa | 2,913,808 | 1.3% |
| 28 | Colorado | 2,889,964 | 1.3% |
| 29 | Arizona | 2,718,215 | 1.2% |
| 30 | Oregon | 2,633,105 | 1.2% |
| 31 | Mississippi | 2,520,638 | 1.1% |
| 32 | Kansas | 2,363,679 | 1.0% |
| 33 | Arkansas | 2,286,435 | 1.0% |
| 34 | West Virginia | 1,949,644 | 0.9% |
| 35 | Nebraska | 1,569,825 | 0.7% |
| 36 | Utah | 1,461,037 | 0.6% |
| 37 | New Mexico | 1,302,894 | 0.6% |
| 38 | Maine | 1,124,660 | 0.5% |
| 39 | Hawaii | 964,691 | 0.4% |
| 40 | Rhode Island | 947,154 | 0.4% |
| 41 | Idaho | 943,935 | 0.4% |
| 42 | New Hampshire | 920,610 | 0.4% |
| 43 | Nevada | 800,493 | 0.4% |
| 44 | Montana | 786,690 | 0.3% |
| 45 | South Dakota | 690,768 | 0.3% |
| 46 | North Dakota | 652,717 | 0.3% |
| 47 | Delaware | 594,338 | 0.3% |
| 48 | Vermont | 511,456 | 0.2% |
| 49 | Wyoming | 469,557 | 0.2% |
| 50 | Alaska | 401,851 | 0.2% |
|  | District of Columbia | 638,333 | 0.3% |

Source: U.S. Bureau of the Census
Press Release CB 91-07 (January 7, 1991)

# Resident State Population in 1970

## National Total = 203,302,000

ALPHA ORDER

| RANK | STATE | POPULATION | % of USA |
|------|-------|-----------|----------|
| 21 | Alabama | 3,444,000 | 1.7% |
| 50 | Alaska | 303,000 | 0.1% |
| 33 | Arizona | 1,775,000 | 0.9% |
| 32 | Arkansas | 1,923,000 | 0.9% |
| 1 | California | 19,971,000 | 9.8% |
| 30 | Colorado | 2,210,000 | 1.1% |
| 24 | Connecticut | 3,032,000 | 1.5% |
| 46 | Delaware | 548,000 | 0.3% |
| 9 | Florida | 6,791,000 | 3.3% |
| 15 | Georgia | 4,588,000 | 2.3% |
| 40 | Hawaii | 770,000 | 0.4% |
| 42 | Idaho | 713,000 | 0.4% |
| 5 | Illinois | 11,110,000 | 5.5% |
| 11 | Indiana | 5,195,000 | 2.6% |
| 25 | Iowa | 2,825,000 | 1.4% |
| 28 | Kansas | 2,249,000 | 1.1% |
| 23 | Kentucky | 3,221,000 | 1.6% |
| 20 | Louisiana | 3,645,000 | 1.8% |
| 38 | Maine | 994,000 | 0.5% |
| 18 | Maryland | 3,924,000 | 1.9% |
| 10 | Massachusetts | 5,689,000 | 2.8% |
| 7 | Michigan | 8,882,000 | 4.4% |
| 19 | Minnesota | 3,806,000 | 1.9% |
| 29 | Mississippi | 2,217,000 | 1.1% |
| 13 | Missouri | 4,678,000 | 2.3% |
| 43 | Montana | 694,000 | 0.3% |
| 35 | Nebraska | 1,485,000 | 0.7% |
| 47 | Nevada | 489,000 | 0.2% |
| 41 | New Hampshire | 738,000 | 0.4% |
| 8 | New Jersey | 7,171,000 | 3.5% |
| 37 | New Mexico | 1,017,000 | 0.5% |
| 2 | New York | 18,241,000 | 9.0% |
| 12 | North Carolina | 5,084,000 | 2.5% |
| 45 | North Dakota | 618,000 | 0.3% |
| 6 | Ohio | 10,657,000 | 5.2% |
| 27 | Oklahoma | 2,559,000 | 1.3% |
| 31 | Oregon | 2,092,000 | 1.0% |
| 3 | Pennsylvania | 11,801,000 | 5.8% |
| 39 | Rhode Island | 950,000 | 0.5% |
| 26 | South Carolina | 2,591,000 | 1.3% |
| 44 | South Dakota | 666,000 | 0.3% |
| 17 | Tennessee | 3,926,000 | 1.9% |
| 4 | Texas | 11,199,000 | 5.5% |
| 36 | Utah | 1,059,000 | 0.5% |
| 48 | Vermont | 445,000 | 0.2% |
| 14 | Virginia | 4,651,000 | 2.3% |
| 22 | Washington | 3,413,000 | 1.7% |
| 34 | West Virginia | 1,744,000 | 0.9% |
| 16 | Wisconsin | 4,418,000 | 2.2% |
| 49 | Wyoming | 332,000 | 0.2% |

RANK ORDER

| RANK | STATE | POPULATION | % of USA |
|------|-------|-----------|----------|
| 1 | California | 19,971,000 | 9.8% |
| 2 | New York | 18,241,000 | 9.0% |
| 3 | Pennsylvania | 11,801,000 | 5.8% |
| 4 | Texas | 11,199,000 | 5.5% |
| 5 | Illinois | 11,110,000 | 5.5% |
| 6 | Ohio | 10,657,000 | 5.2% |
| 7 | Michigan | 8,882,000 | 4.4% |
| 8 | New Jersey | 7,171,000 | 3.5% |
| 9 | Florida | 6,791,000 | 3.3% |
| 10 | Massachusetts | 5,689,000 | 2.8% |
| 11 | Indiana | 5,195,000 | 2.6% |
| 12 | North Carolina | 5,084,000 | 2.5% |
| 13 | Missouri | 4,678,000 | 2.3% |
| 14 | Virginia | 4,651,000 | 2.3% |
| 15 | Georgia | 4,588,000 | 2.3% |
| 16 | Wisconsin | 4,418,000 | 2.2% |
| 17 | Tennessee | 3,926,000 | 1.9% |
| 18 | Maryland | 3,924,000 | 1.9% |
| 19 | Minnesota | 3,806,000 | 1.9% |
| 20 | Louisiana | 3,645,000 | 1.8% |
| 21 | Alabama | 3,444,000 | 1.7% |
| 22 | Washington | 3,413,000 | 1.7% |
| 23 | Kentucky | 3,221,000 | 1.6% |
| 24 | Connecticut | 3,032,000 | 1.5% |
| 25 | Iowa | 2,825,000 | 1.4% |
| 26 | South Carolina | 2,591,000 | 1.3% |
| 27 | Oklahoma | 2,559,000 | 1.3% |
| 28 | Kansas | 2,249,000 | 1.1% |
| 29 | Mississippi | 2,217,000 | 1.1% |
| 30 | Colorado | 2,210,000 | 1.1% |
| 31 | Oregon | 2,092,000 | 1.0% |
| 32 | Arkansas | 1,923,000 | 0.9% |
| 33 | Arizona | 1,775,000 | 0.9% |
| 34 | West Virginia | 1,744,000 | 0.9% |
| 35 | Nebraska | 1,485,000 | 0.7% |
| 36 | Utah | 1,059,000 | 0.5% |
| 37 | New Mexico | 1,017,000 | 0.5% |
| 38 | Maine | 994,000 | 0.5% |
| 39 | Rhode Island | 950,000 | 0.5% |
| 40 | Hawaii | 770,000 | 0.4% |
| 41 | New Hampshire | 738,000 | 0.4% |
| 42 | Idaho | 713,000 | 0.4% |
| 43 | Montana | 694,000 | 0.3% |
| 44 | South Dakota | 666,000 | 0.3% |
| 45 | North Dakota | 618,000 | 0.3% |
| 46 | Delaware | 548,000 | 0.3% |
| 47 | Nevada | 489,000 | 0.2% |
| 48 | Vermont | 445,000 | 0.2% |
| 49 | Wyoming | 332,000 | 0.2% |
| 50 | Alaska | 303,000 | 0.1% |
| | District of Columbia | 757,000 | 0.4% |

*Source: U.S. Bureau of the Census*
*"Census of Population: 1970" (vol. 1)*

# Resident State Population in 1960

## National Total = 179,323,000

ALPHA ORDER

| RANK | STATE | POPULATION | % of USA |
|---|---|---|---|
| 19 | Alabama | 3,267,000 | 1.8% |
| 50 | Alaska | 226,000 | 0.1% |
| 35 | Arizona | 1,302,000 | 0.7% |
| 31 | Arkansas | 1,786,000 | 1.0% |
| 2 | California | 15,717,000 | 8.8% |
| 33 | Colorado | 1,754,000 | 1.0% |
| 25 | Connecticut | 2,535,000 | 1.4% |
| 46 | Delaware | 446,000 | 0.2% |
| 10 | Florida | 4,952,000 | 2.8% |
| 16 | Georgia | 3,943,000 | 2.2% |
| 43 | Hawaii | 633,000 | 0.4% |
| 42 | Idaho | 667,000 | 0.4% |
| 4 | Illinois | 10,081,000 | 5.6% |
| 11 | Indiana | 4,662,000 | 2.6% |
| 24 | Iowa | 2,758,000 | 1.5% |
| 28 | Kansas | 2,179,000 | 1.2% |
| 22 | Kentucky | 3,038,000 | 1.7% |
| 20 | Louisiana | 3,257,000 | 1.8% |
| 36 | Maine | 969,000 | 0.5% |
| 21 | Maryland | 3,101,000 | 1.7% |
| 9 | Massachusetts | 5,149,000 | 2.9% |
| 7 | Michigan | 7,823,000 | 4.4% |
| 18 | Minnesota | 3,414,000 | 1.9% |
| 29 | Mississippi | 2,178,000 | 1.2% |
| 13 | Missouri | 4,320,000 | 2.4% |
| 41 | Montana | 675,000 | 0.4% |
| 34 | Nebraska | 1,411,000 | 0.8% |
| 49 | Nevada | 285,000 | 0.2% |
| 45 | New Hampshire | 607,000 | 0.3% |
| 8 | New Jersey | 6,067,000 | 3.4% |
| 37 | New Mexico | 951,000 | 0.5% |
| 1 | New York | 16,782,000 | 9.4% |
| 12 | North Carolina | 4,556,000 | 2.5% |
| 44 | North Dakota | 632,000 | 0.4% |
| 5 | Ohio | 9,706,000 | 5.4% |
| 27 | Oklahoma | 2,328,000 | 1.3% |
| 32 | Oregon | 1,769,000 | 1.0% |
| 3 | Pennsylvania | 11,319,000 | 6.3% |
| 39 | Rhode Island | 859,000 | 0.5% |
| 26 | South Carolina | 2,383,000 | 1.3% |
| 40 | South Dakota | 681,000 | 0.4% |
| 17 | Tennessee | 3,567,000 | 2.0% |
| 6 | Texas | 9,580,000 | 5.3% |
| 38 | Utah | 891,000 | 0.5% |
| 47 | Vermont | 390,000 | 0.2% |
| 14 | Virginia | 3,967,000 | 2.2% |
| 23 | Washington | 2,853,000 | 1.6% |
| 30 | West Virginia | 1,860,000 | 1.0% |
| 15 | Wisconsin | 3,952,000 | 2.2% |
| 48 | Wyoming | 330,000 | 0.2% |

RANK ORDER

| RANK | STATE | POPULATION | % of USA |
|---|---|---|---|
| 1 | New York | 16,782,000 | 9.4% |
| 2 | California | 15,717,000 | 8.8% |
| 3 | Pennsylvania | 11,319,000 | 6.3% |
| 4 | Illinois | 10,081,000 | 5.6% |
| 5 | Ohio | 9,706,000 | 5.4% |
| 6 | Texas | 9,580,000 | 5.3% |
| 7 | Michigan | 7,823,000 | 4.4% |
| 8 | New Jersey | 6,067,000 | 3.4% |
| 9 | Massachusetts | 5,149,000 | 2.9% |
| 10 | Florida | 4,952,000 | 2.8% |
| 11 | Indiana | 4,662,000 | 2.6% |
| 12 | North Carolina | 4,556,000 | 2.5% |
| 13 | Missouri | 4,320,000 | 2.4% |
| 14 | Virginia | 3,967,000 | 2.2% |
| 15 | Wisconsin | 3,952,000 | 2.2% |
| 16 | Georgia | 3,943,000 | 2.2% |
| 17 | Tennessee | 3,567,000 | 2.0% |
| 18 | Minnesota | 3,414,000 | 1.9% |
| 19 | Alabama | 3,267,000 | 1.8% |
| 20 | Louisiana | 3,257,000 | 1.8% |
| 21 | Maryland | 3,101,000 | 1.7% |
| 22 | Kentucky | 3,038,000 | 1.7% |
| 23 | Washington | 2,853,000 | 1.6% |
| 24 | Iowa | 2,758,000 | 1.5% |
| 25 | Connecticut | 2,535,000 | 1.4% |
| 26 | South Carolina | 2,383,000 | 1.3% |
| 27 | Oklahoma | 2,328,000 | 1.3% |
| 28 | Kansas | 2,179,000 | 1.2% |
| 29 | Mississippi | 2,178,000 | 1.2% |
| 30 | West Virginia | 1,860,000 | 1.0% |
| 31 | Arkansas | 1,786,000 | 1.0% |
| 32 | Oregon | 1,769,000 | 1.0% |
| 33 | Colorado | 1,754,000 | 1.0% |
| 34 | Nebraska | 1,411,000 | 0.8% |
| 35 | Arizona | 1,302,000 | 0.7% |
| 36 | Maine | 969,000 | 0.5% |
| 37 | New Mexico | 951,000 | 0.5% |
| 38 | Utah | 891,000 | 0.5% |
| 39 | Rhode Island | 859,000 | 0.5% |
| 40 | South Dakota | 681,000 | 0.4% |
| 41 | Montana | 675,000 | 0.4% |
| 42 | Idaho | 667,000 | 0.4% |
| 43 | Hawaii | 633,000 | 0.4% |
| 44 | North Dakota | 632,000 | 0.4% |
| 45 | New Hampshire | 607,000 | 0.3% |
| 46 | Delaware | 446,000 | 0.2% |
| 47 | Vermont | 390,000 | 0.2% |
| 48 | Wyoming | 330,000 | 0.2% |
| 49 | Nevada | 285,000 | 0.2% |
| 50 | Alaska | 226,000 | 0.1% |
|  | District of Columbia | 764,000 | 0.4% |

*Source: U.S. Bureau of the Census*
*"Census of Population: 1970" (vol. 1)*

# Population per Square Mile in 2000

## National Rate = 79.6 Persons per Square Mile*

<u>ALPHA ORDER</u>

| RANK | STATE | RATE |
|---|---|---|
| 26 | Alabama | 87.6 |
| 50 | Alaska | 1.1 |
| 36 | Arizona | 45.1 |
| 34 | Arkansas | 51.3 |
| 12 | California | 217.2 |
| 37 | Colorado | 41.5 |
| 4 | Connecticut | 702.9 |
| 7 | Delaware | 400.8 |
| 8 | Florida | 296.3 |
| 18 | Georgia | 141.3 |
| 13 | Hawaii | 188.6 |
| 44 | Idaho | 15.6 |
| 11 | Illinois | 223.4 |
| 16 | Indiana | 169.5 |
| 33 | Iowa | 52.4 |
| 40 | Kansas | 32.9 |
| 23 | Kentucky | 101.7 |
| 22 | Louisiana | 102.6 |
| 38 | Maine | 41.3 |
| 5 | Maryland | 541.8 |
| 3 | Massachusetts | 810.0 |
| 15 | Michigan | 174.9 |
| 31 | Minnesota | 61.8 |
| 32 | Mississippi | 60.6 |
| 27 | Missouri | 81.2 |
| 48 | Montana | 6.2 |
| 42 | Nebraska | 22.3 |
| 43 | Nevada | 18.2 |
| 20 | New Hampshire | 137.8 |
| 1 | New Jersey | 1,134.2 |
| 45 | New Mexico | 15.0 |
| 6 | New York | 401.8 |
| 17 | North Carolina | 165.2 |
| 47 | North Dakota | 9.3 |
| 9 | Ohio | 277.2 |
| 35 | Oklahoma | 50.2 |
| 39 | Oregon | 35.6 |
| 10 | Pennsylvania | 274.0 |
| 2 | Rhode Island | 1,003.2 |
| 21 | South Carolina | 133.2 |
| 46 | South Dakota | 9.9 |
| 19 | Tennessee | 138.0 |
| 28 | Texas | 79.6 |
| 41 | Utah | 27.2 |
| 30 | Vermont | 65.8 |
| 14 | Virginia | 178.8 |
| 25 | Washington | 88.5 |
| 29 | West Virginia | 75.1 |
| 24 | Wisconsin | 98.8 |
| 49 | Wyoming | 5.1 |

<u>RANK ORDER</u>

| RANK | STATE | RATE |
|---|---|---|
| 1 | New Jersey | 1,134.2 |
| 2 | Rhode Island | 1,003.2 |
| 3 | Massachusetts | 810.0 |
| 4 | Connecticut | 702.9 |
| 5 | Maryland | 541.8 |
| 6 | New York | 401.8 |
| 7 | Delaware | 400.8 |
| 8 | Florida | 296.3 |
| 9 | Ohio | 277.2 |
| 10 | Pennsylvania | 274.0 |
| 11 | Illinois | 223.4 |
| 12 | California | 217.2 |
| 13 | Hawaii | 188.6 |
| 14 | Virginia | 178.8 |
| 15 | Michigan | 174.9 |
| 16 | Indiana | 169.5 |
| 17 | North Carolina | 165.2 |
| 18 | Georgia | 141.3 |
| 19 | Tennessee | 138.0 |
| 20 | New Hampshire | 137.8 |
| 21 | South Carolina | 133.2 |
| 22 | Louisiana | 102.6 |
| 23 | Kentucky | 101.7 |
| 24 | Wisconsin | 98.8 |
| 25 | Washington | 88.5 |
| 26 | Alabama | 87.6 |
| 27 | Missouri | 81.2 |
| 28 | Texas | 79.6 |
| 29 | West Virginia | 75.1 |
| 30 | Vermont | 65.8 |
| 31 | Minnesota | 61.8 |
| 32 | Mississippi | 60.6 |
| 33 | Iowa | 52.4 |
| 34 | Arkansas | 51.3 |
| 35 | Oklahoma | 50.2 |
| 36 | Arizona | 45.1 |
| 37 | Colorado | 41.5 |
| 38 | Maine | 41.3 |
| 39 | Oregon | 35.6 |
| 40 | Kansas | 32.9 |
| 41 | Utah | 27.2 |
| 42 | Nebraska | 22.3 |
| 43 | Nevada | 18.2 |
| 44 | Idaho | 15.6 |
| 45 | New Mexico | 15.0 |
| 46 | South Dakota | 9.9 |
| 47 | North Dakota | 9.3 |
| 48 | Montana | 6.2 |
| 49 | Wyoming | 5.1 |
| 50 | Alaska | 1.1 |

| | District of Columbia | 9,378.0 |

Source: Morgan Quitno Press using data from U.S. Bureau of the Census
   "First Census 2000 Results" (December 28, 2000, http://www.census.gov/main/www/cen2000.html)
*Resident population. Based on land area of states.

# Population per Square Mile in 1990

## National Rate = 70.4 Persons per Square Mile*

| ALPHA ORDER | | | | RANK ORDER | | |
|---|---|---|---|---|---|---|
| RANK | STATE | RATE | | RANK | STATE | RATE |
| 25 | Alabama | 79.6 | | 1 | New Jersey | 1,044.3 |
| 50 | Alaska | 1.0 | | 2 | Rhode Island | 960.3 |
| 37 | Arizona | 32.3 | | 3 | Massachusetts | 767.6 |
| 35 | Arkansas | 45.1 | | 4 | Connecticut | 678.5 |
| 12 | California | 191.1 | | 5 | Maryland | 489.1 |
| 38 | Colorado | 31.8 | | 6 | New York | 381.0 |
| 4 | Connecticut | 678.5 | | 7 | Delaware | 340.8 |
| 7 | Delaware | 340.8 | | 8 | Pennsylvania | 265.1 |
| 10 | Florida | 239.9 | | 9 | Ohio | 264.9 |
| 21 | Georgia | 111.8 | | 10 | Florida | 239.9 |
| 13 | Hawaii | 172.5 | | 11 | Illinois | 205.6 |
| 44 | Idaho | 12.2 | | 12 | California | 191.1 |
| 11 | Illinois | 205.6 | | 13 | Hawaii | 172.5 |
| 16 | Indiana | 154.6 | | 14 | Michigan | 163.6 |
| 33 | Iowa | 49.7 | | 15 | Virginia | 156.3 |
| 39 | Kansas | 30.3 | | 16 | Indiana | 154.6 |
| 23 | Kentucky | 92.8 | | 17 | North Carolina | 136.1 |
| 22 | Louisiana | 96.9 | | 18 | New Hampshire | 123.7 |
| 36 | Maine | 39.8 | | 19 | Tennessee | 118.3 |
| 5 | Maryland | 489.1 | | 20 | South Carolina | 115.8 |
| 3 | Massachusetts | 767.6 | | 21 | Georgia | 111.8 |
| 14 | Michigan | 163.6 | | 22 | Louisiana | 96.9 |
| 31 | Minnesota | 55.0 | | 23 | Kentucky | 92.8 |
| 32 | Mississippi | 54.9 | | 24 | Wisconsin | 90.1 |
| 27 | Missouri | 74.3 | | 25 | Alabama | 79.6 |
| 48 | Montana | 5.5 | | 26 | West Virginia | 74.5 |
| 42 | Nebraska | 20.5 | | 27 | Missouri | 74.3 |
| 45 | Nevada | 10.9 | | 28 | Washington | 73.1 |
| 18 | New Hampshire | 123.7 | | 29 | Texas | 64.9 |
| 1 | New Jersey | 1,044.3 | | 30 | Vermont | 60.8 |
| 43 | New Mexico | 12.5 | | 31 | Minnesota | 55.0 |
| 6 | New York | 381.0 | | 32 | Mississippi | 54.9 |
| 17 | North Carolina | 136.1 | | 33 | Iowa | 49.7 |
| 46 | North Dakota | 9.3 | | 34 | Oklahoma | 45.8 |
| 9 | Ohio | 264.9 | | 35 | Arkansas | 45.1 |
| 34 | Oklahoma | 45.8 | | 36 | Maine | 39.8 |
| 40 | Oregon | 29.6 | | 37 | Arizona | 32.3 |
| 8 | Pennsylvania | 265.1 | | 38 | Colorado | 31.8 |
| 2 | Rhode Island | 960.3 | | 39 | Kansas | 30.3 |
| 20 | South Carolina | 115.8 | | 40 | Oregon | 29.6 |
| 47 | South Dakota | 9.2 | | 41 | Utah | 21.0 |
| 19 | Tennessee | 118.3 | | 42 | Nebraska | 20.5 |
| 29 | Texas | 64.9 | | 43 | New Mexico | 12.5 |
| 41 | Utah | 21.0 | | 44 | Idaho | 12.2 |
| 30 | Vermont | 60.8 | | 45 | Nevada | 10.9 |
| 15 | Virginia | 156.3 | | 46 | North Dakota | 9.3 |
| 28 | Washington | 73.1 | | 47 | South Dakota | 9.2 |
| 26 | West Virginia | 74.5 | | 48 | Montana | 5.5 |
| 24 | Wisconsin | 90.1 | | 49 | Wyoming | 4.7 |
| 49 | Wyoming | 4.7 | | 50 | Alaska | 1.0 |
| | | | | | District of Columbia | 9,949.2 |

Source: Morgan Quitno Press using data from U.S. Bureau of the Census
    "State Population Estimates" (December 29, 1999, http://www.census.gov/population/estimates/state/st-99-3.txt)
*The is the decennial census dated April 1, 1990.  The counts shown here include corrections processed through December 1998.

# Population per Square Mile in 1980

## National Rate = 64.0 Persons per Square Mile

ALPHA ORDER

| RANK | STATE | POPULATION |
|---|---|---|
| 26 | Alabama | 76.7 |
| 50 | Alaska | 0.7 |
| 40 | Arizona | 23.9 |
| 35 | Arkansas | 43.9 |
| 14 | California | 151.4 |
| 38 | Colorado | 27.9 |
| 4 | Connecticut | 637.8 |
| 7 | Delaware | 307.6 |
| 11 | Florida | 180.0 |
| 22 | Georgia | 94.1 |
| 15 | Hawaii | 150.1 |
| 43 | Idaho | 11.5 |
| 10 | Illinois | 205.3 |
| 13 | Indiana | 152.8 |
| 32 | Iowa | 52.1 |
| 37 | Kansas | 28.9 |
| 23 | Kentucky | 92.3 |
| 21 | Louisiana | 94.5 |
| 36 | Maine | 36.3 |
| 5 | Maryland | 428.7 |
| 3 | Massachusetts | 733.3 |
| 12 | Michigan | 162.6 |
| 33 | Minnesota | 51.2 |
| 31 | Mississippi | 53.4 |
| 27 | Missouri | 71.3 |
| 48 | Montana | 5.4 |
| 41 | Nebraska | 20.5 |
| 47 | Nevada | 7.3 |
| 20 | New Hampshire | 102.4 |
| 1 | New Jersey | 986.2 |
| 44 | New Mexico | 10.7 |
| 6 | New York | 370.6 |
| 17 | North Carolina | 120.4 |
| 45 | North Dakota | 9.4 |
| 9 | Ohio | 263.3 |
| 34 | Oklahoma | 44.1 |
| 39 | Oregon | 27.4 |
| 8 | Pennsylvania | 264.3 |
| 2 | Rhode Island | 897.8 |
| 19 | South Carolina | 103.4 |
| 46 | South Dakota | 9.1 |
| 18 | Tennessee | 111.6 |
| 30 | Texas | 54.3 |
| 42 | Utah | 17.8 |
| 29 | Vermont | 55.2 |
| 16 | Virginia | 134.7 |
| 28 | Washington | 62.1 |
| 25 | West Virginia | 80.8 |
| 24 | Wisconsin | 86.5 |
| 49 | Wyoming | 4.8 |

RANK ORDER

| RANK | STATE | POPULATION |
|---|---|---|
| 1 | New Jersey | 986.2 |
| 2 | Rhode Island | 897.8 |
| 3 | Massachusetts | 733.3 |
| 4 | Connecticut | 637.8 |
| 5 | Maryland | 428.7 |
| 6 | New York | 370.6 |
| 7 | Delaware | 307.6 |
| 8 | Pennsylvania | 264.3 |
| 9 | Ohio | 263.3 |
| 10 | Illinois | 205.3 |
| 11 | Florida | 180.0 |
| 12 | Michigan | 162.6 |
| 13 | Indiana | 152.8 |
| 14 | California | 151.4 |
| 15 | Hawaii | 150.1 |
| 16 | Virginia | 134.7 |
| 17 | North Carolina | 120.4 |
| 18 | Tennessee | 111.6 |
| 19 | South Carolina | 103.4 |
| 20 | New Hampshire | 102.4 |
| 21 | Louisiana | 94.5 |
| 22 | Georgia | 94.1 |
| 23 | Kentucky | 92.3 |
| 24 | Wisconsin | 86.5 |
| 25 | West Virginia | 80.8 |
| 26 | Alabama | 76.7 |
| 27 | Missouri | 71.3 |
| 28 | Washington | 62.1 |
| 29 | Vermont | 55.2 |
| 30 | Texas | 54.3 |
| 31 | Mississippi | 53.4 |
| 32 | Iowa | 52.1 |
| 33 | Minnesota | 51.2 |
| 34 | Oklahoma | 44.1 |
| 35 | Arkansas | 43.9 |
| 36 | Maine | 36.3 |
| 37 | Kansas | 28.9 |
| 38 | Colorado | 27.9 |
| 39 | Oregon | 27.4 |
| 40 | Arizona | 23.9 |
| 41 | Nebraska | 20.5 |
| 42 | Utah | 17.8 |
| 43 | Idaho | 11.5 |
| 44 | New Mexico | 10.7 |
| 45 | North Dakota | 9.4 |
| 46 | South Dakota | 9.1 |
| 47 | Nevada | 7.3 |
| 48 | Montana | 5.4 |
| 49 | Wyoming | 4.8 |
| 50 | Alaska | 0.7 |
| | District of Columbia | 10,132.0 |

Source: U.S. Bureau of the Census
"1980 Census of Population" (vol. 1, part A, PC80-1-A)

# Population per Square Mile in 1970

## National Rate = 57.4 Persons per Square Mile

<u>ALPHA ORDER</u>

| RANK | STATE | POPULATION |
|---|---|---|
| 26 | Alabama | 67.9 |
| 50 | Alaska | 0.5 |
| 41 | Arizona | 15.6 |
| 35 | Arkansas | 37.0 |
| 13 | California | 127.6 |
| 39 | Colorado | 21.3 |
| 4 | Connecticut | 623.6 |
| 7 | Delaware | 276.5 |
| 14 | Florida | 125.5 |
| 24 | Georgia | 79.0 |
| 15 | Hawaii | 119.6 |
| 45 | Idaho | 8.6 |
| 10 | Illinois | 199.4 |
| 12 | Indiana | 143.9 |
| 29 | Iowa | 50.5 |
| 37 | Kansas | 27.5 |
| 21 | Kentucky | 81.2 |
| 23 | Louisiana | 81.0 |
| 36 | Maine | 32.1 |
| 5 | Maryland | 396.6 |
| 3 | Massachusetts | 727.0 |
| 11 | Michigan | 156.2 |
| 30 | Minnesota | 48.0 |
| 32 | Mississippi | 46.9 |
| 27 | Missouri | 67.8 |
| 47 | Montana | 4.8 |
| 40 | Nebraska | 19.4 |
| 48 | Nevada | 4.4 |
| 20 | New Hampshire | 81.7 |
| 1 | New Jersey | 953.1 |
| 46 | New Mexico | 8.4 |
| 6 | New York | 381.3 |
| 17 | North Carolina | 104.1 |
| 43 | North Dakota | 8.9 |
| 9 | Ohio | 260.0 |
| 34 | Oklahoma | 37.2 |
| 38 | Oregon | 21.7 |
| 8 | Pennsylvania | 262.3 |
| 2 | Rhode Island | 902.5 |
| 19 | South Carolina | 85.7 |
| 44 | South Dakota | 8.8 |
| 18 | Tennessee | 94.9 |
| 33 | Texas | 42.7 |
| 42 | Utah | 12.9 |
| 31 | Vermont | 47.9 |
| 16 | Virginia | 116.9 |
| 28 | Washington | 51.2 |
| 25 | West Virginia | 72.5 |
| 22 | Wisconsin | 81.1 |
| 49 | Wyoming | 3.4 |

<u>RANK ORDER</u>

| RANK | STATE | POPULATION |
|---|---|---|
| 1 | New Jersey | 953.1 |
| 2 | Rhode Island | 902.5 |
| 3 | Massachusetts | 727.0 |
| 4 | Connecticut | 623.6 |
| 5 | Maryland | 396.6 |
| 6 | New York | 381.3 |
| 7 | Delaware | 276.5 |
| 8 | Pennsylvania | 262.3 |
| 9 | Ohio | 260.0 |
| 10 | Illinois | 199.4 |
| 11 | Michigan | 156.2 |
| 12 | Indiana | 143.9 |
| 13 | California | 127.6 |
| 14 | Florida | 125.5 |
| 15 | Hawaii | 119.6 |
| 16 | Virginia | 116.9 |
| 17 | North Carolina | 104.1 |
| 18 | Tennessee | 94.9 |
| 19 | South Carolina | 85.7 |
| 20 | New Hampshire | 81.7 |
| 21 | Kentucky | 81.2 |
| 22 | Wisconsin | 81.1 |
| 23 | Louisiana | 81.0 |
| 24 | Georgia | 79.0 |
| 25 | West Virginia | 72.5 |
| 26 | Alabama | 67.9 |
| 27 | Missouri | 67.8 |
| 28 | Washington | 51.2 |
| 29 | Iowa | 50.5 |
| 30 | Minnesota | 48.0 |
| 31 | Vermont | 47.9 |
| 32 | Mississippi | 46.9 |
| 33 | Texas | 42.7 |
| 34 | Oklahoma | 37.2 |
| 35 | Arkansas | 37.0 |
| 36 | Maine | 32.1 |
| 37 | Kansas | 27.5 |
| 38 | Oregon | 21.7 |
| 39 | Colorado | 21.3 |
| 40 | Nebraska | 19.4 |
| 41 | Arizona | 15.6 |
| 42 | Utah | 12.9 |
| 43 | North Dakota | 8.9 |
| 44 | South Dakota | 8.8 |
| 45 | Idaho | 8.6 |
| 46 | New Mexico | 8.4 |
| 47 | Montana | 4.8 |
| 48 | Nevada | 4.4 |
| 49 | Wyoming | 3.4 |
| 50 | Alaska | 0.5 |
| | District of Columbia | 12,402.0 |

*Source: U.S. Bureau of the Census*
   *"Census of Population: 1970" (vol. 1)*

# Population per Square Mile in 1960

## National Rate = 50.6 Persons per Square Mile

<u>ALPHA ORDER</u>

| RANK | STATE | POPULATION |
|---|---|---|
| 26 | Alabama | 64.2 |
| 50 | Alaska | 0.4 |
| 41 | Arizona | 11.5 |
| 34 | Arkansas | 34.2 |
| 13 | California | 100.4 |
| 40 | Colorado | 16.9 |
| 4 | Connecticut | 520.6 |
| 9 | Delaware | 225.2 |
| 17 | Florida | 91.5 |
| 24 | Georgia | 67.8 |
| 15 | Hawaii | 98.5 |
| 45 | Idaho | 8.1 |
| 10 | Illinois | 180.4 |
| 12 | Indiana | 128.8 |
| 28 | Iowa | 49.2 |
| 37 | Kansas | 26.6 |
| 21 | Kentucky | 76.2 |
| 23 | Louisiana | 72.2 |
| 36 | Maine | 31.3 |
| 6 | Maryland | 313.5 |
| 3 | Massachusetts | 657.3 |
| 11 | Michigan | 137.7 |
| 30 | Minnesota | 43.1 |
| 29 | Mississippi | 46.0 |
| 27 | Missouri | 62.6 |
| 47 | Montana | 4.6 |
| 38 | Nebraska | 18.4 |
| 49 | Nevada | 2.6 |
| 25 | New Hampshire | 67.2 |
| 2 | New Jersey | 805.5 |
| 46 | New Mexico | 7.8 |
| 5 | New York | 350.6 |
| 16 | North Carolina | 93.2 |
| 43 | North Dakota | 9.1 |
| 8 | Ohio | 236.6 |
| 35 | Oklahoma | 33.8 |
| 38 | Oregon | 18.4 |
| 7 | Pennsylvania | 251.4 |
| 1 | Rhode Island | 819.3 |
| 19 | South Carolina | 78.7 |
| 44 | South Dakota | 9.0 |
| 18 | Tennessee | 86.2 |
| 33 | Texas | 36.4 |
| 42 | Utah | 10.8 |
| 32 | Vermont | 42.0 |
| 14 | Virginia | 99.6 |
| 31 | Washington | 42.8 |
| 20 | West Virginia | 77.2 |
| 22 | Wisconsin | 72.6 |
| 48 | Wyoming | 3.4 |

<u>RANK ORDER</u>

| RANK | STATE | POPULATION |
|---|---|---|
| 1 | Rhode Island | 819.3 |
| 2 | New Jersey | 805.5 |
| 3 | Massachusetts | 657.3 |
| 4 | Connecticut | 520.6 |
| 5 | New York | 350.6 |
| 6 | Maryland | 313.5 |
| 7 | Pennsylvania | 251.4 |
| 8 | Ohio | 236.6 |
| 9 | Delaware | 225.2 |
| 10 | Illinois | 180.4 |
| 11 | Michigan | 137.7 |
| 12 | Indiana | 128.8 |
| 13 | California | 100.4 |
| 14 | Virginia | 99.6 |
| 15 | Hawaii | 98.5 |
| 16 | North Carolina | 93.2 |
| 17 | Florida | 91.5 |
| 18 | Tennessee | 86.2 |
| 19 | South Carolina | 78.7 |
| 20 | West Virginia | 77.2 |
| 21 | Kentucky | 76.2 |
| 22 | Wisconsin | 72.6 |
| 23 | Louisiana | 72.2 |
| 24 | Georgia | 67.8 |
| 25 | New Hampshire | 67.2 |
| 26 | Alabama | 64.2 |
| 27 | Missouri | 62.6 |
| 28 | Iowa | 49.2 |
| 29 | Mississippi | 46.0 |
| 30 | Minnesota | 43.1 |
| 31 | Washington | 42.8 |
| 32 | Vermont | 42.0 |
| 33 | Texas | 36.4 |
| 34 | Arkansas | 34.2 |
| 35 | Oklahoma | 33.8 |
| 36 | Maine | 31.3 |
| 37 | Kansas | 26.6 |
| 38 | Nebraska | 18.4 |
| 38 | Oregon | 18.4 |
| 40 | Colorado | 16.9 |
| 41 | Arizona | 11.5 |
| 42 | Utah | 10.8 |
| 43 | North Dakota | 9.1 |
| 44 | South Dakota | 9.0 |
| 45 | Idaho | 8.1 |
| 46 | New Mexico | 7.8 |
| 47 | Montana | 4.6 |
| 48 | Wyoming | 3.4 |
| 49 | Nevada | 2.6 |
| 50 | Alaska | 0.4 |

District of Columbia     12,524.0

*Source: U.S. Bureau of the Census*
*"Census of Population: 1970" (vol. 1)*

# Metropolitan Population in 1998

## National Total = 216,478,000*

ALPHA ORDER

| RANK | STATE | POPULATION | % of USA |
|------|-------|-----------|----------|
| 25 | Alabama | 3,050,000 | 1.4% |
| 47 | Alaska | 255,000 | 0.1% |
| 17 | Arizona | 4,099,000 | 1.9% |
| 34 | Arkansas | 1,234,000 | 0.6% |
| 1 | California | 31,581,000 | 14.6% |
| 21 | Colorado | 3,335,000 | 1.5% |
| 24 | Connecticut | 3,129,000 | 1.4% |
| 42 | Delaware | 607,000 | 0.3% |
| 4 | Florida | 13,866,000 | 6.4% |
| 12 | Georgia | 5,262,000 | 2.4% |
| 38 | Hawaii | 872,000 | 0.4% |
| 43 | Idaho | 471,000 | 0.2% |
| 5 | Illinois | 10,175,000 | 4.7% |
| 16 | Indiana | 4,230,000 | 2.0% |
| 33 | Iowa | 1,278,000 | 0.6% |
| 32 | Kansas | 1,483,000 | 0.7% |
| 29 | Kentucky | 1,902,000 | 0.9% |
| 23 | Louisiana | 3,287,000 | 1.5% |
| 44 | Maine | 446,000 | 0.2% |
| 14 | Maryland | 4,760,000 | 2.2% |
| 10 | Massachusetts | 5,908,000 | 2.7% |
| 9 | Michigan | 8,110,000 | 3.7% |
| 22 | Minnesota | 3,311,000 | 1.5% |
| 36 | Mississippi | 987,000 | 0.5% |
| 18 | Missouri | 3,696,000 | 1.7% |
| 45 | Montana | 294,000 | 0.1% |
| 39 | Nebraska | 862,000 | 0.4% |
| 31 | Nevada | 1,505,000 | 0.7% |
| 41 | New Hampshire | 713,000 | 0.3% |
| 8 | New Jersey | 8,115,000 | 3.7% |
| 35 | New Mexico | 990,000 | 0.5% |
| 2 | New York | 16,697,000 | 7.7% |
| 13 | North Carolina | 5,061,000 | 2.3% |
| 46 | North Dakota | 275,000 | 0.1% |
| 7 | Ohio | 9,075,000 | 4.2% |
| 28 | Oklahoma | 2,024,000 | 0.9% |
| 27 | Oregon | 2,387,000 | 1.1% |
| 6 | Pennsylvania | 10,144,000 | 4.7% |
| 37 | Rhode Island | 927,000 | 0.4% |
| 26 | South Carolina | 2,687,000 | 1.2% |
| 48 | South Dakota | 251,000 | 0.1% |
| 19 | Tennessee | 3,685,000 | 1.7% |
| 3 | Texas | 16,688,000 | 7.7% |
| 30 | Utah | 1,610,000 | 0.7% |
| 49 | Vermont | 165,000 | 0.1% |
| 11 | Virginia | 5,307,000 | 2.5% |
| 15 | Washington | 4,718,000 | 2.2% |
| 40 | West Virginia | 759,000 | 0.4% |
| 20 | Wisconsin | 3,543,000 | 1.6% |
| 50 | Wyoming | 142,000 | 0.1% |

RANK ORDER

| RANK | STATE | POPULATION | % of USA |
|------|-------|-----------|----------|
| 1 | California | 31,581,000 | 14.6% |
| 2 | New York | 16,697,000 | 7.7% |
| 3 | Texas | 16,688,000 | 7.7% |
| 4 | Florida | 13,866,000 | 6.4% |
| 5 | Illinois | 10,175,000 | 4.7% |
| 6 | Pennsylvania | 10,144,000 | 4.7% |
| 7 | Ohio | 9,075,000 | 4.2% |
| 8 | New Jersey | 8,115,000 | 3.7% |
| 9 | Michigan | 8,110,000 | 3.7% |
| 10 | Massachusetts | 5,908,000 | 2.7% |
| 11 | Virginia | 5,307,000 | 2.5% |
| 12 | Georgia | 5,262,000 | 2.4% |
| 13 | North Carolina | 5,061,000 | 2.3% |
| 14 | Maryland | 4,760,000 | 2.2% |
| 15 | Washington | 4,718,000 | 2.2% |
| 16 | Indiana | 4,230,000 | 2.0% |
| 17 | Arizona | 4,099,000 | 1.9% |
| 18 | Missouri | 3,696,000 | 1.7% |
| 19 | Tennessee | 3,685,000 | 1.7% |
| 20 | Wisconsin | 3,543,000 | 1.6% |
| 21 | Colorado | 3,335,000 | 1.5% |
| 22 | Minnesota | 3,311,000 | 1.5% |
| 23 | Louisiana | 3,287,000 | 1.5% |
| 24 | Connecticut | 3,129,000 | 1.4% |
| 25 | Alabama | 3,050,000 | 1.4% |
| 26 | South Carolina | 2,687,000 | 1.2% |
| 27 | Oregon | 2,387,000 | 1.1% |
| 28 | Oklahoma | 2,024,000 | 0.9% |
| 29 | Kentucky | 1,902,000 | 0.9% |
| 30 | Utah | 1,610,000 | 0.7% |
| 31 | Nevada | 1,505,000 | 0.7% |
| 32 | Kansas | 1,483,000 | 0.7% |
| 33 | Iowa | 1,278,000 | 0.6% |
| 34 | Arkansas | 1,234,000 | 0.6% |
| 35 | New Mexico | 990,000 | 0.5% |
| 36 | Mississippi | 987,000 | 0.5% |
| 37 | Rhode Island | 927,000 | 0.4% |
| 38 | Hawaii | 872,000 | 0.4% |
| 39 | Nebraska | 862,000 | 0.4% |
| 40 | West Virginia | 759,000 | 0.4% |
| 41 | New Hampshire | 713,000 | 0.3% |
| 42 | Delaware | 607,000 | 0.3% |
| 43 | Idaho | 471,000 | 0.2% |
| 44 | Maine | 446,000 | 0.2% |
| 45 | Montana | 294,000 | 0.1% |
| 46 | North Dakota | 275,000 | 0.1% |
| 47 | Alaska | 255,000 | 0.1% |
| 48 | South Dakota | 251,000 | 0.1% |
| 49 | Vermont | 165,000 | 0.1% |
| 50 | Wyoming | 142,000 | 0.1% |
| | District of Columbia | 523,000 | 0.2% |

Source: U.S. Bureau of the Census
   "Population Estimates for Metropolitan Areas and Components" (December 17, 1999)
*"Metropolitan" refers to metropolitan statistical areas and consolidated metropolitan statistical areas as defined by the U.S. Office of Management and Budget, June 30, 1999.

# Percent of Population Living in a Metropolitan Area in 1998

## National Percent = 80.1% of Population*

<u>ALPHA ORDER</u>

| RANK | STATE | PERCENT |
|---|---|---|
| 25 | Alabama | 70.1 |
| 43 | Alaska | 41.5 |
| 9 | Arizona | 87.8 |
| 38 | Arkansas | 48.6 |
| 2 | California | 96.7 |
| 14 | Colorado | 84.0 |
| 4 | Connecticut | 95.6 |
| 17 | Delaware | 81.6 |
| 6 | Florida | 93.0 |
| 28 | Georgia | 68.9 |
| 22 | Hawaii | 73.1 |
| 44 | Idaho | 38.3 |
| 11 | Illinois | 84.5 |
| 24 | Indiana | 71.7 |
| 40 | Iowa | 44.6 |
| 36 | Kansas | 56.4 |
| 39 | Kentucky | 48.3 |
| 21 | Louisiana | 75.2 |
| 46 | Maine | 35.8 |
| 7 | Maryland | 92.7 |
| 3 | Massachusetts | 96.1 |
| 16 | Michigan | 82.6 |
| 25 | Minnesota | 70.1 |
| 45 | Mississippi | 35.9 |
| 29 | Missouri | 68.0 |
| 48 | Montana | 33.4 |
| 37 | Nebraska | 51.8 |
| 10 | Nevada | 86.1 |
| 34 | New Hampshire | 60.2 |
| 1 | New Jersey | 100.0 |
| 35 | New Mexico | 57.0 |
| 8 | New York | 91.9 |
| 32 | North Carolina | 67.1 |
| 41 | North Dakota | 43.1 |
| 18 | Ohio | 81.0 |
| 33 | Oklahoma | 60.5 |
| 23 | Oregon | 72.7 |
| 11 | Pennsylvania | 84.5 |
| 5 | Rhode Island | 93.8 |
| 27 | South Carolina | 70.0 |
| 47 | South Dakota | 34.0 |
| 30 | Tennessee | 67.8 |
| 11 | Texas | 84.5 |
| 20 | Utah | 76.7 |
| 50 | Vermont | 27.9 |
| 19 | Virginia | 78.1 |
| 15 | Washington | 82.9 |
| 42 | West Virginia | 41.9 |
| 30 | Wisconsin | 67.8 |
| 49 | Wyoming | 29.6 |

<u>RANK ORDER</u>

| RANK | STATE | PERCENT |
|---|---|---|
| 1 | New Jersey | 100.0 |
| 2 | California | 96.7 |
| 3 | Massachusetts | 96.1 |
| 4 | Connecticut | 95.6 |
| 5 | Rhode Island | 93.8 |
| 6 | Florida | 93.0 |
| 7 | Maryland | 92.7 |
| 8 | New York | 91.9 |
| 9 | Arizona | 87.8 |
| 10 | Nevada | 86.1 |
| 11 | Illinois | 84.5 |
| 11 | Pennsylvania | 84.5 |
| 11 | Texas | 84.5 |
| 14 | Colorado | 84.0 |
| 15 | Washington | 82.9 |
| 16 | Michigan | 82.6 |
| 17 | Delaware | 81.6 |
| 18 | Ohio | 81.0 |
| 19 | Virginia | 78.1 |
| 20 | Utah | 76.7 |
| 21 | Louisiana | 75.2 |
| 22 | Hawaii | 73.1 |
| 23 | Oregon | 72.7 |
| 24 | Indiana | 71.7 |
| 25 | Alabama | 70.1 |
| 25 | Minnesota | 70.1 |
| 27 | South Carolina | 70.0 |
| 28 | Georgia | 68.9 |
| 29 | Missouri | 68.0 |
| 30 | Tennessee | 67.8 |
| 30 | Wisconsin | 67.8 |
| 32 | North Carolina | 67.1 |
| 33 | Oklahoma | 60.5 |
| 34 | New Hampshire | 60.2 |
| 35 | New Mexico | 57.0 |
| 36 | Kansas | 56.4 |
| 37 | Nebraska | 51.8 |
| 38 | Arkansas | 48.6 |
| 39 | Kentucky | 48.3 |
| 40 | Iowa | 44.6 |
| 41 | North Dakota | 43.1 |
| 42 | West Virginia | 41.9 |
| 43 | Alaska | 41.5 |
| 44 | Idaho | 38.3 |
| 45 | Mississippi | 35.9 |
| 46 | Maine | 35.8 |
| 47 | South Dakota | 34.0 |
| 48 | Montana | 33.4 |
| 49 | Wyoming | 29.6 |
| 50 | Vermont | 27.9 |
| | District of Columbia | 100.0 |

*Source: U.S. Bureau of the Census*
   *"Population Estimates for Metropolitan Areas and Components" (December 17, 1999)*
*"Metropolitan" refers to metropolitan statistical areas and consolidated metropolitan statistical areas as defined by the U.S. Office of Management and Budget, June 30, 1999.*

# Nonmetropolitan Population in 1998

## National Total = 53,820,000*

ALPHA ORDER

| RANK | STATE | POPULATION | % of USA |
|---|---|---|---|
| 20 | Alabama | 1,302,000 | 2.4% |
| 42 | Alaska | 359,000 | 0.7% |
| 35 | Arizona | 570,000 | 1.1% |
| 19 | Arkansas | 1,304,000 | 2.4% |
| 23 | California | 1,086,000 | 2.0% |
| 33 | Colorado | 636,000 | 1.2% |
| 47 | Connecticut | 145,000 | 0.3% |
| 48 | Delaware | 137,000 | 0.3% |
| 26 | Florida | 1,050,000 | 2.0% |
| 3 | Georgia | 2,380,000 | 4.4% |
| 44 | Hawaii | 321,000 | 0.6% |
| 31 | Idaho | 758,000 | 1.4% |
| 6 | Illinois | 1,870,000 | 3.5% |
| 13 | Indiana | 1,669,000 | 3.1% |
| 14 | Iowa | 1,585,000 | 2.9% |
| 22 | Kansas | 1,146,000 | 2.1% |
| 5 | Kentucky | 2,035,000 | 3.8% |
| 24 | Louisiana | 1,082,000 | 2.0% |
| 30 | Maine | 798,000 | 1.5% |
| 40 | Maryland | 374,000 | 0.7% |
| 46 | Massachusetts | 239,000 | 0.4% |
| 11 | Michigan | 1,707,000 | 3.2% |
| 17 | Minnesota | 1,415,000 | 2.6% |
| 8 | Mississippi | 1,765,000 | 3.3% |
| 10 | Missouri | 1,742,000 | 3.2% |
| 34 | Montana | 586,000 | 1.1% |
| 29 | Nebraska | 801,000 | 1.5% |
| 45 | Nevada | 242,000 | 0.4% |
| 38 | New Hampshire | 472,000 | 0.9% |
| 50 | New Jersey | 0 | 0.0% |
| 32 | New Mexico | 747,000 | 1.4% |
| 16 | New York | 1,478,000 | 2.7% |
| 2 | North Carolina | 2,486,000 | 4.6% |
| 41 | North Dakota | 363,000 | 0.7% |
| 4 | Ohio | 2,135,000 | 4.0% |
| 18 | Oklahoma | 1,323,000 | 2.5% |
| 28 | Oregon | 895,000 | 1.7% |
| 7 | Pennsylvania | 1,858,000 | 3.5% |
| 49 | Rhode Island | 61,000 | 0.1% |
| 21 | South Carolina | 1,149,000 | 2.1% |
| 37 | South Dakota | 487,000 | 0.9% |
| 9 | Tennessee | 1,746,000 | 3.2% |
| 1 | Texas | 3,072,000 | 5.7% |
| 36 | Utah | 490,000 | 0.9% |
| 39 | Vermont | 426,000 | 0.8% |
| 15 | Virginia | 1,484,000 | 2.8% |
| 27 | Washington | 972,000 | 1.8% |
| 25 | West Virginia | 1,052,000 | 2.0% |
| 12 | Wisconsin | 1,681,000 | 3.1% |
| 43 | Wyoming | 339,000 | 0.6% |

RANK ORDER

| RANK | STATE | POPULATION | % of USA |
|---|---|---|---|
| 1 | Texas | 3,072,000 | 5.7% |
| 2 | North Carolina | 2,486,000 | 4.6% |
| 3 | Georgia | 2,380,000 | 4.4% |
| 4 | Ohio | 2,135,000 | 4.0% |
| 5 | Kentucky | 2,035,000 | 3.8% |
| 6 | Illinois | 1,870,000 | 3.5% |
| 7 | Pennsylvania | 1,858,000 | 3.5% |
| 8 | Mississippi | 1,765,000 | 3.3% |
| 9 | Tennessee | 1,746,000 | 3.2% |
| 10 | Missouri | 1,742,000 | 3.2% |
| 11 | Michigan | 1,707,000 | 3.2% |
| 12 | Wisconsin | 1,681,000 | 3.1% |
| 13 | Indiana | 1,669,000 | 3.1% |
| 14 | Iowa | 1,585,000 | 2.9% |
| 15 | Virginia | 1,484,000 | 2.8% |
| 16 | New York | 1,478,000 | 2.7% |
| 17 | Minnesota | 1,415,000 | 2.6% |
| 18 | Oklahoma | 1,323,000 | 2.5% |
| 19 | Arkansas | 1,304,000 | 2.4% |
| 20 | Alabama | 1,302,000 | 2.4% |
| 21 | South Carolina | 1,149,000 | 2.1% |
| 22 | Kansas | 1,146,000 | 2.1% |
| 23 | California | 1,086,000 | 2.0% |
| 24 | Louisiana | 1,082,000 | 2.0% |
| 25 | West Virginia | 1,052,000 | 2.0% |
| 26 | Florida | 1,050,000 | 2.0% |
| 27 | Washington | 972,000 | 1.8% |
| 28 | Oregon | 895,000 | 1.7% |
| 29 | Nebraska | 801,000 | 1.5% |
| 30 | Maine | 798,000 | 1.5% |
| 31 | Idaho | 758,000 | 1.4% |
| 32 | New Mexico | 747,000 | 1.4% |
| 33 | Colorado | 636,000 | 1.2% |
| 34 | Montana | 586,000 | 1.1% |
| 35 | Arizona | 570,000 | 1.1% |
| 36 | Utah | 490,000 | 0.9% |
| 37 | South Dakota | 487,000 | 0.9% |
| 38 | New Hampshire | 472,000 | 0.9% |
| 39 | Vermont | 426,000 | 0.8% |
| 40 | Maryland | 374,000 | 0.7% |
| 41 | North Dakota | 363,000 | 0.7% |
| 42 | Alaska | 359,000 | 0.7% |
| 43 | Wyoming | 339,000 | 0.6% |
| 44 | Hawaii | 321,000 | 0.6% |
| 45 | Nevada | 242,000 | 0.4% |
| 46 | Massachusetts | 239,000 | 0.4% |
| 47 | Connecticut | 145,000 | 0.3% |
| 48 | Delaware | 137,000 | 0.3% |
| 49 | Rhode Island | 61,000 | 0.1% |
| 50 | New Jersey | 0 | 0.0% |
| | District of Columbia | 0 | 0.0% |

Source: U.S. Bureau of the Census
   "Population Estimates for Metropolitan Areas and Components" (December 17, 1999)
*"Nonmetropolitan" are the areas outside metropolitan areas as defined by the Office of Management and Budget
as of June 30, 1999.

# Percent of Population Living in a Nonmetropolitan Area in 1998

## National Percent = 19.9% of Population*

### ALPHA ORDER

| RANK | STATE | PERCENT |
|------|-------|---------|
| 25 | Alabama | 29.9 |
| 8 | Alaska | 58.5 |
| 42 | Arizona | 12.2 |
| 13 | Arkansas | 51.4 |
| 49 | California | 3.3 |
| 37 | Colorado | 16.0 |
| 47 | Connecticut | 4.4 |
| 34 | Delaware | 18.4 |
| 45 | Florida | 7.0 |
| 23 | Georgia | 31.1 |
| 29 | Hawaii | 26.9 |
| 7 | Idaho | 61.7 |
| 38 | Illinois | 15.5 |
| 27 | Indiana | 28.3 |
| 11 | Iowa | 55.4 |
| 15 | Kansas | 43.6 |
| 12 | Kentucky | 51.7 |
| 30 | Louisiana | 24.8 |
| 5 | Maine | 64.2 |
| 44 | Maryland | 7.3 |
| 48 | Massachusetts | 3.9 |
| 35 | Michigan | 17.4 |
| 25 | Minnesota | 29.9 |
| 6 | Mississippi | 64.1 |
| 22 | Missouri | 32.0 |
| 3 | Montana | 66.6 |
| 14 | Nebraska | 48.2 |
| 41 | Nevada | 13.9 |
| 17 | New Hampshire | 39.8 |
| 50 | New Jersey | 0.0 |
| 16 | New Mexico | 43.0 |
| 43 | New York | 8.1 |
| 19 | North Carolina | 32.9 |
| 10 | North Dakota | 56.9 |
| 33 | Ohio | 19.0 |
| 18 | Oklahoma | 39.5 |
| 28 | Oregon | 27.3 |
| 38 | Pennsylvania | 15.5 |
| 46 | Rhode Island | 6.2 |
| 24 | South Carolina | 30.0 |
| 4 | South Dakota | 66.0 |
| 20 | Tennessee | 32.2 |
| 38 | Texas | 15.5 |
| 31 | Utah | 23.3 |
| 1 | Vermont | 72.1 |
| 32 | Virginia | 21.9 |
| 36 | Washington | 17.1 |
| 9 | West Virginia | 58.1 |
| 20 | Wisconsin | 32.2 |
| 2 | Wyoming | 70.4 |

### RANK ORDER

| RANK | STATE | PERCENT |
|------|-------|---------|
| 1 | Vermont | 72.1 |
| 2 | Wyoming | 70.4 |
| 3 | Montana | 66.6 |
| 4 | South Dakota | 66.0 |
| 5 | Maine | 64.2 |
| 6 | Mississippi | 64.1 |
| 7 | Idaho | 61.7 |
| 8 | Alaska | 58.5 |
| 9 | West Virginia | 58.1 |
| 10 | North Dakota | 56.9 |
| 11 | Iowa | 55.4 |
| 12 | Kentucky | 51.7 |
| 13 | Arkansas | 51.4 |
| 14 | Nebraska | 48.2 |
| 15 | Kansas | 43.6 |
| 16 | New Mexico | 43.0 |
| 17 | New Hampshire | 39.8 |
| 18 | Oklahoma | 39.5 |
| 19 | North Carolina | 32.9 |
| 20 | Tennessee | 32.2 |
| 20 | Wisconsin | 32.2 |
| 22 | Missouri | 32.0 |
| 23 | Georgia | 31.1 |
| 24 | South Carolina | 30.0 |
| 25 | Alabama | 29.9 |
| 25 | Minnesota | 29.9 |
| 27 | Indiana | 28.3 |
| 28 | Oregon | 27.3 |
| 29 | Hawaii | 26.9 |
| 30 | Louisiana | 24.8 |
| 31 | Utah | 23.3 |
| 32 | Virginia | 21.9 |
| 33 | Ohio | 19.0 |
| 34 | Delaware | 18.4 |
| 35 | Michigan | 17.4 |
| 36 | Washington | 17.1 |
| 37 | Colorado | 16.0 |
| 38 | Illinois | 15.5 |
| 38 | Pennsylvania | 15.5 |
| 38 | Texas | 15.5 |
| 41 | Nevada | 13.9 |
| 42 | Arizona | 12.2 |
| 43 | New York | 8.1 |
| 44 | Maryland | 7.3 |
| 45 | Florida | 7.0 |
| 46 | Rhode Island | 6.2 |
| 47 | Connecticut | 4.4 |
| 48 | Massachusetts | 3.9 |
| 49 | California | 3.3 |
| 50 | New Jersey | 0.0 |

District of Columbia                    0.0

Source: U.S. Bureau of the Census
   "Population Estimates for Metropolitan Areas and Components" (December 17, 1999)
*"Nonmetropolitan" are the areas outside metropolitan areas as defined by the Office of Management and Budget as of June 30, 1999.

# Male Population in 1999

## National Total = 133,276,559 Males

ALPHA ORDER

| RANK | STATE | MALES | % of USA |
|---|---|---|---|
| 23 | Alabama | 2,097,319 | 1.6% |
| 47 | Alaska | 325,077 | 0.2% |
| 20 | Arizona | 2,364,468 | 1.8% |
| 33 | Arkansas | 1,232,955 | 0.9% |
| 1 | California | 16,579,707 | 12.4% |
| 24 | Colorado | 2,010,784 | 1.5% |
| 29 | Connecticut | 1,592,801 | 1.2% |
| 45 | Delaware | 366,275 | 0.3% |
| 4 | Florida | 7,330,099 | 5.5% |
| 10 | Georgia | 3,791,130 | 2.8% |
| 41 | Hawaii | 592,037 | 0.4% |
| 39 | Idaho | 624,504 | 0.5% |
| 5 | Illinois | 5,916,083 | 4.4% |
| 14 | Indiana | 2,891,620 | 2.2% |
| 30 | Iowa | 1,397,208 | 1.0% |
| 32 | Kansas | 1,305,408 | 1.0% |
| 25 | Kentucky | 1,923,606 | 1.4% |
| 22 | Louisiana | 2,103,825 | 1.6% |
| 40 | Maine | 611,437 | 0.5% |
| 19 | Maryland | 2,513,133 | 1.9% |
| 13 | Massachusetts | 2,977,965 | 2.2% |
| 8 | Michigan | 4,799,912 | 3.6% |
| 21 | Minnesota | 2,353,020 | 1.8% |
| 31 | Mississippi | 1,326,704 | 1.0% |
| 16 | Missouri | 2,649,479 | 2.0% |
| 44 | Montana | 438,758 | 0.3% |
| 38 | Nebraska | 814,663 | 0.6% |
| 35 | Nevada | 921,070 | 0.7% |
| 42 | New Hampshire | 590,941 | 0.4% |
| 9 | New Jersey | 3,946,443 | 3.0% |
| 37 | New Mexico | 856,048 | 0.6% |
| 3 | New York | 8,770,974 | 6.6% |
| 11 | North Carolina | 3,710,119 | 2.8% |
| 48 | North Dakota | 315,167 | 0.2% |
| 7 | Ohio | 5,441,233 | 4.1% |
| 27 | Oklahoma | 1,639,559 | 1.2% |
| 28 | Oregon | 1,637,721 | 1.2% |
| 6 | Pennsylvania | 5,765,533 | 4.3% |
| 43 | Rhode Island | 476,331 | 0.4% |
| 26 | South Carolina | 1,875,030 | 1.4% |
| 46 | South Dakota | 360,485 | 0.3% |
| 17 | Tennessee | 2,646,694 | 2.0% |
| 2 | Texas | 9,887,415 | 7.4% |
| 34 | Utah | 1,058,639 | 0.8% |
| 49 | Vermont | 292,120 | 0.2% |
| 12 | Virginia | 3,358,569 | 2.5% |
| 15 | Washington | 2,862,019 | 2.1% |
| 36 | West Virginia | 870,356 | 0.7% |
| 18 | Wisconsin | 2,580,153 | 1.9% |
| 50 | Wyoming | 240,943 | 0.2% |

RANK ORDER

| RANK | STATE | MALES | % of USA |
|---|---|---|---|
| 1 | California | 16,579,707 | 12.4% |
| 2 | Texas | 9,887,415 | 7.4% |
| 3 | New York | 8,770,974 | 6.6% |
| 4 | Florida | 7,330,099 | 5.5% |
| 5 | Illinois | 5,916,083 | 4.4% |
| 6 | Pennsylvania | 5,765,533 | 4.3% |
| 7 | Ohio | 5,441,233 | 4.1% |
| 8 | Michigan | 4,799,912 | 3.6% |
| 9 | New Jersey | 3,946,443 | 3.0% |
| 10 | Georgia | 3,791,130 | 2.8% |
| 11 | North Carolina | 3,710,119 | 2.8% |
| 12 | Virginia | 3,358,569 | 2.5% |
| 13 | Massachusetts | 2,977,965 | 2.2% |
| 14 | Indiana | 2,891,620 | 2.2% |
| 15 | Washington | 2,862,019 | 2.1% |
| 16 | Missouri | 2,649,479 | 2.0% |
| 17 | Tennessee | 2,646,694 | 2.0% |
| 18 | Wisconsin | 2,580,153 | 1.9% |
| 19 | Maryland | 2,513,133 | 1.9% |
| 20 | Arizona | 2,364,468 | 1.8% |
| 21 | Minnesota | 2,353,020 | 1.8% |
| 22 | Louisiana | 2,103,825 | 1.6% |
| 23 | Alabama | 2,097,319 | 1.6% |
| 24 | Colorado | 2,010,784 | 1.5% |
| 25 | Kentucky | 1,923,606 | 1.4% |
| 26 | South Carolina | 1,875,030 | 1.4% |
| 27 | Oklahoma | 1,639,559 | 1.2% |
| 28 | Oregon | 1,637,721 | 1.2% |
| 29 | Connecticut | 1,592,801 | 1.2% |
| 30 | Iowa | 1,397,208 | 1.0% |
| 31 | Mississippi | 1,326,704 | 1.0% |
| 32 | Kansas | 1,305,408 | 1.0% |
| 33 | Arkansas | 1,232,955 | 0.9% |
| 34 | Utah | 1,058,639 | 0.8% |
| 35 | Nevada | 921,070 | 0.7% |
| 36 | West Virginia | 870,356 | 0.7% |
| 37 | New Mexico | 856,048 | 0.6% |
| 38 | Nebraska | 814,663 | 0.6% |
| 39 | Idaho | 624,504 | 0.5% |
| 40 | Maine | 611,437 | 0.5% |
| 41 | Hawaii | 592,037 | 0.4% |
| 42 | New Hampshire | 590,941 | 0.4% |
| 43 | Rhode Island | 476,331 | 0.4% |
| 44 | Montana | 438,758 | 0.3% |
| 45 | Delaware | 366,275 | 0.3% |
| 46 | South Dakota | 360,485 | 0.3% |
| 47 | Alaska | 325,077 | 0.2% |
| 48 | North Dakota | 315,167 | 0.2% |
| 49 | Vermont | 292,120 | 0.2% |
| 50 | Wyoming | 240,943 | 0.2% |
| | District of Columbia | 243,020 | 0.2% |

*Source: U.S. Bureau of the Census*
*"Population Estimates for the U.S., Regions, and States by Selected Age Groups and Sex" (ST-99-9, March 9, 2000)*
*(http://www.census.gov/population/estimates/state/st-99-09.txt)*

# Female Population in 1999

## National Total = 139,414,254 Females

ALPHA ORDER

| RANK | STATE | FEMALES | % of USA |
|---|---|---|---|
| 22 | Alabama | 2,272,543 | 1.6% |
| 49 | Alaska | 294,423 | 0.2% |
| 21 | Arizona | 2,413,864 | 1.7% |
| 33 | Arkansas | 1,318,418 | 0.9% |
| 1 | California | 16,565,414 | 11.9% |
| 24 | Colorado | 2,045,349 | 1.5% |
| 28 | Connecticut | 1,689,230 | 1.2% |
| 45 | Delaware | 387,263 | 0.3% |
| 4 | Florida | 7,781,145 | 5.6% |
| 10 | Georgia | 3,997,110 | 2.9% |
| 42 | Hawaii | 593,460 | 0.4% |
| 40 | Idaho | 627,196 | 0.4% |
| 6 | Illinois | 6,212,287 | 4.5% |
| 14 | Indiana | 3,051,281 | 2.2% |
| 30 | Iowa | 1,472,205 | 1.1% |
| 32 | Kansas | 1,348,644 | 1.0% |
| 25 | Kentucky | 2,037,219 | 1.5% |
| 23 | Louisiana | 2,268,210 | 1.6% |
| 39 | Maine | 641,603 | 0.5% |
| 19 | Maryland | 2,658,501 | 1.9% |
| 13 | Massachusetts | 3,197,204 | 2.3% |
| 8 | Michigan | 5,063,863 | 3.6% |
| 20 | Minnesota | 2,422,488 | 1.7% |
| 31 | Mississippi | 1,441,915 | 1.0% |
| 17 | Missouri | 2,818,859 | 2.0% |
| 44 | Montana | 444,021 | 0.3% |
| 38 | Nebraska | 851,365 | 0.6% |
| 36 | Nevada | 888,183 | 0.6% |
| 41 | New Hampshire | 610,193 | 0.4% |
| 9 | New Jersey | 4,196,969 | 3.0% |
| 37 | New Mexico | 883,796 | 0.6% |
| 3 | New York | 9,425,627 | 6.8% |
| 11 | North Carolina | 3,940,670 | 2.8% |
| 47 | North Dakota | 318,499 | 0.2% |
| 7 | Ohio | 5,815,421 | 4.2% |
| 27 | Oklahoma | 1,718,485 | 1.2% |
| 29 | Oregon | 1,678,433 | 1.2% |
| 5 | Pennsylvania | 6,228,483 | 4.5% |
| 43 | Rhode Island | 514,488 | 0.4% |
| 26 | South Carolina | 2,010,706 | 1.4% |
| 46 | South Dakota | 372,648 | 0.3% |
| 16 | Tennessee | 2,836,841 | 2.0% |
| 2 | Texas | 10,156,726 | 7.3% |
| 34 | Utah | 1,071,197 | 0.8% |
| 48 | Vermont | 301,620 | 0.2% |
| 12 | Virginia | 3,514,343 | 2.5% |
| 15 | Washington | 2,894,342 | 2.1% |
| 35 | West Virginia | 936,572 | 0.7% |
| 18 | Wisconsin | 2,670,293 | 1.9% |
| 50 | Wyoming | 238,659 | 0.2% |

RANK ORDER

| RANK | STATE | FEMALES | % of USA |
|---|---|---|---|
| 1 | California | 16,565,414 | 11.9% |
| 2 | Texas | 10,156,726 | 7.3% |
| 3 | New York | 9,425,627 | 6.8% |
| 4 | Florida | 7,781,145 | 5.6% |
| 5 | Pennsylvania | 6,228,483 | 4.5% |
| 6 | Illinois | 6,212,287 | 4.5% |
| 7 | Ohio | 5,815,421 | 4.2% |
| 8 | Michigan | 5,063,863 | 3.6% |
| 9 | New Jersey | 4,196,969 | 3.0% |
| 10 | Georgia | 3,997,110 | 2.9% |
| 11 | North Carolina | 3,940,670 | 2.8% |
| 12 | Virginia | 3,514,343 | 2.5% |
| 13 | Massachusetts | 3,197,204 | 2.3% |
| 14 | Indiana | 3,051,281 | 2.2% |
| 15 | Washington | 2,894,342 | 2.1% |
| 16 | Tennessee | 2,836,841 | 2.0% |
| 17 | Missouri | 2,818,859 | 2.0% |
| 18 | Wisconsin | 2,670,293 | 1.9% |
| 19 | Maryland | 2,658,501 | 1.9% |
| 20 | Minnesota | 2,422,488 | 1.7% |
| 21 | Arizona | 2,413,864 | 1.7% |
| 22 | Alabama | 2,272,543 | 1.6% |
| 23 | Louisiana | 2,268,210 | 1.6% |
| 24 | Colorado | 2,045,349 | 1.5% |
| 25 | Kentucky | 2,037,219 | 1.5% |
| 26 | South Carolina | 2,010,706 | 1.4% |
| 27 | Oklahoma | 1,718,485 | 1.2% |
| 28 | Connecticut | 1,689,230 | 1.2% |
| 29 | Oregon | 1,678,433 | 1.2% |
| 30 | Iowa | 1,472,205 | 1.1% |
| 31 | Mississippi | 1,441,915 | 1.0% |
| 32 | Kansas | 1,348,644 | 1.0% |
| 33 | Arkansas | 1,318,418 | 0.9% |
| 34 | Utah | 1,071,197 | 0.8% |
| 35 | West Virginia | 936,572 | 0.7% |
| 36 | Nevada | 888,183 | 0.6% |
| 37 | New Mexico | 883,796 | 0.6% |
| 38 | Nebraska | 851,365 | 0.6% |
| 39 | Maine | 641,603 | 0.5% |
| 40 | Idaho | 627,196 | 0.4% |
| 41 | New Hampshire | 610,193 | 0.4% |
| 42 | Hawaii | 593,460 | 0.4% |
| 43 | Rhode Island | 514,488 | 0.4% |
| 44 | Montana | 444,021 | 0.3% |
| 45 | Delaware | 387,263 | 0.3% |
| 46 | South Dakota | 372,648 | 0.3% |
| 47 | North Dakota | 318,499 | 0.2% |
| 48 | Vermont | 301,620 | 0.2% |
| 49 | Alaska | 294,423 | 0.2% |
| 50 | Wyoming | 238,659 | 0.2% |
|  | District of Columbia | 275,980 | 0.2% |

*Source: U.S. Bureau of the Census*
*"Population Estimates for the U.S., Regions, and States by Selected Age Groups and Sex" (ST-99-9, March 9, 2000)*
*(http://www.census.gov/population/estimates/state/st-99-09.txt)*

# White Population in 1999

## National Total = 224,610,797 White Persons*

ALPHA ORDER

| RANK | STATE | WHITES | % of USA |
|---|---|---|---|
| 24 | Alabama | 3,188,102 | 1.4% |
| 48 | Alaska | 466,041 | 0.2% |
| 20 | Arizona | 4,239,119 | 1.9% |
| 32 | Arkansas | 2,107,797 | 0.9% |
| 1 | California | 26,306,164 | 11.7% |
| 21 | Colorado | 3,742,369 | 1.7% |
| 27 | Connecticut | 2,880,829 | 1.3% |
| 46 | Delaware | 585,805 | 0.3% |
| 4 | Florida | 12,436,096 | 5.5% |
| 12 | Georgia | 5,373,060 | 2.4% |
| 50 | Hawaii | 391,489 | 0.2% |
| 40 | Idaho | 1,213,053 | 0.5% |
| 6 | Illinois | 9,830,204 | 4.4% |
| 13 | Indiana | 5,371,185 | 2.4% |
| 29 | Iowa | 2,765,593 | 1.2% |
| 31 | Kansas | 2,425,555 | 1.1% |
| 22 | Kentucky | 3,638,891 | 1.6% |
| 26 | Louisiana | 2,882,781 | 1.3% |
| 39 | Maine | 1,231,546 | 0.5% |
| 23 | Maryland | 3,492,062 | 1.6% |
| 11 | Massachusetts | 5,521,542 | 2.5% |
| 8 | Michigan | 8,222,390 | 3.7% |
| 19 | Minnesota | 4,437,800 | 2.0% |
| 35 | Mississippi | 1,728,520 | 0.8% |
| 17 | Missouri | 4,769,006 | 2.1% |
| 43 | Montana | 816,995 | 0.4% |
| 36 | Nebraska | 1,560,171 | 0.7% |
| 37 | Nevada | 1,548,143 | 0.7% |
| 41 | New Hampshire | 1,174,519 | 0.5% |
| 9 | New Jersey | 6,453,922 | 2.9% |
| 38 | New Mexico | 1,501,681 | 0.7% |
| 3 | New York | 13,872,760 | 6.2% |
| 10 | North Carolina | 5,759,680 | 2.6% |
| 45 | North Dakota | 593,754 | 0.3% |
| 7 | Ohio | 9,796,553 | 4.4% |
| 28 | Oklahoma | 2,788,026 | 1.2% |
| 25 | Oregon | 3,098,494 | 1.4% |
| 5 | Pennsylvania | 10,602,898 | 4.7% |
| 42 | Rhode Island | 912,101 | 0.4% |
| 30 | South Carolina | 2,683,585 | 1.2% |
| 44 | South Dakota | 662,823 | 0.3% |
| 18 | Tennessee | 4,504,674 | 2.0% |
| 2 | Texas | 16,899,229 | 7.5% |
| 33 | Utah | 2,025,663 | 0.9% |
| 47 | Vermont | 584,176 | 0.3% |
| 14 | Virginia | 5,210,494 | 2.3% |
| 15 | Washington | 5,103,999 | 2.3% |
| 34 | West Virginia | 1,739,602 | 0.8% |
| 16 | Wisconsin | 4,826,984 | 2.1% |
| 49 | Wyoming | 460,434 | 0.2% |

RANK ORDER

| RANK | STATE | WHITES | % of USA |
|---|---|---|---|
| 1 | California | 26,306,164 | 11.7% |
| 2 | Texas | 16,899,229 | 7.5% |
| 3 | New York | 13,872,760 | 6.2% |
| 4 | Florida | 12,436,096 | 5.5% |
| 5 | Pennsylvania | 10,602,898 | 4.7% |
| 6 | Illinois | 9,830,204 | 4.4% |
| 7 | Ohio | 9,796,553 | 4.4% |
| 8 | Michigan | 8,222,390 | 3.7% |
| 9 | New Jersey | 6,453,922 | 2.9% |
| 10 | North Carolina | 5,759,680 | 2.6% |
| 11 | Massachusetts | 5,521,542 | 2.5% |
| 12 | Georgia | 5,373,060 | 2.4% |
| 13 | Indiana | 5,371,185 | 2.4% |
| 14 | Virginia | 5,210,494 | 2.3% |
| 15 | Washington | 5,103,999 | 2.3% |
| 16 | Wisconsin | 4,826,984 | 2.1% |
| 17 | Missouri | 4,769,006 | 2.1% |
| 18 | Tennessee | 4,504,674 | 2.0% |
| 19 | Minnesota | 4,437,800 | 2.0% |
| 20 | Arizona | 4,239,119 | 1.9% |
| 21 | Colorado | 3,742,369 | 1.7% |
| 22 | Kentucky | 3,638,891 | 1.6% |
| 23 | Maryland | 3,492,062 | 1.6% |
| 24 | Alabama | 3,188,102 | 1.4% |
| 25 | Oregon | 3,098,494 | 1.4% |
| 26 | Louisiana | 2,882,781 | 1.3% |
| 27 | Connecticut | 2,880,829 | 1.3% |
| 28 | Oklahoma | 2,788,026 | 1.2% |
| 29 | Iowa | 2,765,593 | 1.2% |
| 30 | South Carolina | 2,683,585 | 1.2% |
| 31 | Kansas | 2,425,555 | 1.1% |
| 32 | Arkansas | 2,107,797 | 0.9% |
| 33 | Utah | 2,025,663 | 0.9% |
| 34 | West Virginia | 1,739,602 | 0.8% |
| 35 | Mississippi | 1,728,520 | 0.8% |
| 36 | Nebraska | 1,560,171 | 0.7% |
| 37 | Nevada | 1,548,143 | 0.7% |
| 38 | New Mexico | 1,501,681 | 0.7% |
| 39 | Maine | 1,231,546 | 0.5% |
| 40 | Idaho | 1,213,053 | 0.5% |
| 41 | New Hampshire | 1,174,519 | 0.5% |
| 42 | Rhode Island | 912,101 | 0.4% |
| 43 | Montana | 816,995 | 0.4% |
| 44 | South Dakota | 662,823 | 0.3% |
| 45 | North Dakota | 593,754 | 0.3% |
| 46 | Delaware | 585,805 | 0.3% |
| 47 | Vermont | 584,176 | 0.3% |
| 48 | Alaska | 466,041 | 0.2% |
| 49 | Wyoming | 460,434 | 0.2% |
| 50 | Hawaii | 391,489 | 0.2% |
|  | District of Columbia | 182,438 | 0.1% |

Source: U.S. Bureau of the Census
  "Population Estimates for States by Race and Hispanic Origin: July 1, 1999 " (August 30, 2000)
    (http://www.census.gov/population/estimates/state/srh/srh99.txt)
*Estimates. "White" is defined by Census as a person having origins in any of the original peoples of Europe, North Africa, or the Middle East. There are 196,049,435 non-Hispanic whites and 28,561,362 Hispanic whites.

# Percent of Population White in 1999

## National Percent = 82.4% White*

<table>
<tr><td colspan="3">ALPHA ORDER</td><td colspan="3">RANK ORDER</td></tr>
<tr><td>RANK</td><td>STATE</td><td>PERCENT</td><td>RANK</td><td>STATE</td><td>PERCENT</td></tr>
<tr><td>44</td><td>Alabama</td><td>73.0</td><td>1</td><td>Vermont</td><td>98.4</td></tr>
<tr><td>43</td><td>Alaska</td><td>75.2</td><td>2</td><td>Maine</td><td>98.3</td></tr>
<tr><td>22</td><td>Arizona</td><td>88.7</td><td>3</td><td>New Hampshire</td><td>97.8</td></tr>
<tr><td>33</td><td>Arkansas</td><td>82.6</td><td>4</td><td>Idaho</td><td>96.9</td></tr>
<tr><td>37</td><td>California</td><td>79.4</td><td>5</td><td>Iowa</td><td>96.4</td></tr>
<tr><td>14</td><td>Colorado</td><td>92.3</td><td>6</td><td>West Virginia</td><td>96.3</td></tr>
<tr><td>25</td><td>Connecticut</td><td>87.8</td><td>7</td><td>Wyoming</td><td>96.0</td></tr>
<tr><td>39</td><td>Delaware</td><td>77.7</td><td>8</td><td>Utah</td><td>95.1</td></tr>
<tr><td>34</td><td>Florida</td><td>82.3</td><td>9</td><td>North Dakota</td><td>93.7</td></tr>
<tr><td>46</td><td>Georgia</td><td>69.0</td><td>10</td><td>Nebraska</td><td>93.6</td></tr>
<tr><td>50</td><td>Hawaii</td><td>33.0</td><td>11</td><td>Oregon</td><td>93.4</td></tr>
<tr><td>4</td><td>Idaho</td><td>96.9</td><td>12</td><td>Minnesota</td><td>92.9</td></tr>
<tr><td>36</td><td>Illinois</td><td>81.1</td><td>13</td><td>Montana</td><td>92.5</td></tr>
<tr><td>19</td><td>Indiana</td><td>90.4</td><td>14</td><td>Colorado</td><td>92.3</td></tr>
<tr><td>5</td><td>Iowa</td><td>96.4</td><td>15</td><td>Rhode Island</td><td>92.1</td></tr>
<tr><td>18</td><td>Kansas</td><td>91.4</td><td>16</td><td>Kentucky</td><td>91.9</td></tr>
<tr><td>16</td><td>Kentucky</td><td>91.9</td><td>16</td><td>Wisconsin</td><td>91.9</td></tr>
<tr><td>48</td><td>Louisiana</td><td>65.9</td><td>18</td><td>Kansas</td><td>91.4</td></tr>
<tr><td>2</td><td>Maine</td><td>98.3</td><td>19</td><td>Indiana</td><td>90.4</td></tr>
<tr><td>47</td><td>Maryland</td><td>67.5</td><td>19</td><td>South Dakota</td><td>90.4</td></tr>
<tr><td>21</td><td>Massachusetts</td><td>89.4</td><td>21</td><td>Massachusetts</td><td>89.4</td></tr>
<tr><td>31</td><td>Michigan</td><td>83.4</td><td>22</td><td>Arizona</td><td>88.7</td></tr>
<tr><td>12</td><td>Minnesota</td><td>92.9</td><td>22</td><td>Washington</td><td>88.7</td></tr>
<tr><td>49</td><td>Mississippi</td><td>62.4</td><td>24</td><td>Pennsylvania</td><td>88.4</td></tr>
<tr><td>26</td><td>Missouri</td><td>87.2</td><td>25</td><td>Connecticut</td><td>87.8</td></tr>
<tr><td>13</td><td>Montana</td><td>92.5</td><td>26</td><td>Missouri</td><td>87.2</td></tr>
<tr><td>10</td><td>Nebraska</td><td>93.6</td><td>27</td><td>Ohio</td><td>87.0</td></tr>
<tr><td>29</td><td>Nevada</td><td>85.6</td><td>28</td><td>New Mexico</td><td>86.3</td></tr>
<tr><td>3</td><td>New Hampshire</td><td>97.8</td><td>29</td><td>Nevada</td><td>85.6</td></tr>
<tr><td>38</td><td>New Jersey</td><td>79.3</td><td>30</td><td>Texas</td><td>84.3</td></tr>
<tr><td>28</td><td>New Mexico</td><td>86.3</td><td>31</td><td>Michigan</td><td>83.4</td></tr>
<tr><td>40</td><td>New York</td><td>76.2</td><td>32</td><td>Oklahoma</td><td>83.0</td></tr>
<tr><td>42</td><td>North Carolina</td><td>75.3</td><td>33</td><td>Arkansas</td><td>82.6</td></tr>
<tr><td>9</td><td>North Dakota</td><td>93.7</td><td>34</td><td>Florida</td><td>82.3</td></tr>
<tr><td>27</td><td>Ohio</td><td>87.0</td><td>35</td><td>Tennessee</td><td>82.1</td></tr>
<tr><td>32</td><td>Oklahoma</td><td>83.0</td><td>36</td><td>Illinois</td><td>81.1</td></tr>
<tr><td>11</td><td>Oregon</td><td>93.4</td><td>37</td><td>California</td><td>79.4</td></tr>
<tr><td>24</td><td>Pennsylvania</td><td>88.4</td><td>38</td><td>New Jersey</td><td>79.3</td></tr>
<tr><td>15</td><td>Rhode Island</td><td>92.1</td><td>39</td><td>Delaware</td><td>77.7</td></tr>
<tr><td>45</td><td>South Carolina</td><td>69.1</td><td>40</td><td>New York</td><td>76.2</td></tr>
<tr><td>19</td><td>South Dakota</td><td>90.4</td><td>41</td><td>Virginia</td><td>75.8</td></tr>
<tr><td>35</td><td>Tennessee</td><td>82.1</td><td>42</td><td>North Carolina</td><td>75.3</td></tr>
<tr><td>30</td><td>Texas</td><td>84.3</td><td>43</td><td>Alaska</td><td>75.2</td></tr>
<tr><td>8</td><td>Utah</td><td>95.1</td><td>44</td><td>Alabama</td><td>73.0</td></tr>
<tr><td>1</td><td>Vermont</td><td>98.4</td><td>45</td><td>South Carolina</td><td>69.1</td></tr>
<tr><td>41</td><td>Virginia</td><td>75.8</td><td>46</td><td>Georgia</td><td>69.0</td></tr>
<tr><td>22</td><td>Washington</td><td>88.7</td><td>47</td><td>Maryland</td><td>67.5</td></tr>
<tr><td>6</td><td>West Virginia</td><td>96.3</td><td>48</td><td>Louisiana</td><td>65.9</td></tr>
<tr><td>16</td><td>Wisconsin</td><td>91.9</td><td>49</td><td>Mississippi</td><td>62.4</td></tr>
<tr><td>7</td><td>Wyoming</td><td>96.0</td><td>50</td><td>Hawaii</td><td>33.0</td></tr>
<tr><td></td><td></td><td></td><td></td><td>District of Columbia</td><td>35.2</td></tr>
</table>

Source: U.S. Bureau of the Census
"Population Estimates for States by Race and Hispanic Origin: July 1, 1999 " (August 30, 2000)
(http://www.census.gov/population/estimates/state/srh/srh99.txt)
*Estimates. "White" is defined by Census as a person having origins in any of the original peoples of Europe, North Africa, or the Middle East. Non-Hispanic whites comprise 71.9% of the total population while Hispanic whites comprise 10.5%.

# Black Population in 1999

## National Total = 34,862,169 Black Persons*

ALPHA ORDER

| RANK | STATE | BLACKS | % of USA |
|------|-------|--------|----------|
| 16 | Alabama | 1,138,726 | 3.3% |
| 41 | Alaska | 24,067 | 0.1% |
| 29 | Arizona | 175,506 | 0.5% |
| 21 | Arkansas | 410,821 | 1.2% |
| 2 | California | 2,487,006 | 7.1% |
| 28 | Colorado | 176,277 | 0.5% |
| 23 | Connecticut | 308,772 | 0.9% |
| 31 | Delaware | 149,290 | 0.4% |
| 4 | Florida | 2,333,424 | 6.7% |
| 5 | Georgia | 2,235,897 | 6.4% |
| 40 | Hawaii | 33,752 | 0.1% |
| 44 | Idaho | 7,561 | 0.0% |
| 6 | Illinois | 1,854,173 | 5.3% |
| 20 | Indiana | 497,976 | 1.4% |
| 36 | Iowa | 58,013 | 0.2% |
| 30 | Kansas | 157,176 | 0.5% |
| 25 | Kentucky | 288,336 | 0.8% |
| 10 | Louisiana | 1,415,195 | 4.1% |
| 45 | Maine | 6,258 | 0.0% |
| 8 | Maryland | 1,454,381 | 4.2% |
| 22 | Massachusetts | 405,159 | 1.2% |
| 9 | Michigan | 1,415,201 | 4.1% |
| 32 | Minnesota | 148,596 | 0.4% |
| 17 | Mississippi | 1,010,216 | 2.9% |
| 19 | Missouri | 617,148 | 1.8% |
| 50 | Montana | 3,168 | 0.0% |
| 34 | Nebraska | 68,067 | 0.2% |
| 33 | Nevada | 140,031 | 0.4% |
| 43 | New Hampshire | 9,044 | 0.0% |
| 13 | New Jersey | 1,197,430 | 3.4% |
| 39 | New Mexico | 45,792 | 0.1% |
| 1 | New York | 3,222,461 | 9.2% |
| 7 | North Carolina | 1,686,143 | 4.8% |
| 48 | North Dakota | 4,118 | 0.0% |
| 12 | Ohio | 1,304,126 | 3.7% |
| 26 | Oklahoma | 262,136 | 0.8% |
| 35 | Oregon | 62,012 | 0.2% |
| 14 | Pennsylvania | 1,170,095 | 3.4% |
| 38 | Rhode Island | 50,292 | 0.1% |
| 15 | South Carolina | 1,156,946 | 3.3% |
| 46 | South Dakota | 5,099 | 0.0% |
| 18 | Tennessee | 912,577 | 2.6% |
| 3 | Texas | 2,470,194 | 7.1% |
| 42 | Utah | 19,481 | 0.1% |
| 49 | Vermont | 3,184 | 0.0% |
| 11 | Virginia | 1,384,651 | 4.0% |
| 27 | Washington | 203,853 | 0.6% |
| 37 | West Virginia | 56,108 | 0.2% |
| 24 | Wisconsin | 293,367 | 0.8% |
| 47 | Wyoming | 4,210 | 0.0% |

RANK ORDER

| RANK | STATE | BLACKS | % of USA |
|------|-------|--------|----------|
| 1 | New York | 3,222,461 | 9.2% |
| 2 | California | 2,487,006 | 7.1% |
| 3 | Texas | 2,470,194 | 7.1% |
| 4 | Florida | 2,333,424 | 6.7% |
| 5 | Georgia | 2,235,897 | 6.4% |
| 6 | Illinois | 1,854,173 | 5.3% |
| 7 | North Carolina | 1,686,143 | 4.8% |
| 8 | Maryland | 1,454,381 | 4.2% |
| 9 | Michigan | 1,415,201 | 4.1% |
| 10 | Louisiana | 1,415,195 | 4.1% |
| 11 | Virginia | 1,384,651 | 4.0% |
| 12 | Ohio | 1,304,126 | 3.7% |
| 13 | New Jersey | 1,197,430 | 3.4% |
| 14 | Pennsylvania | 1,170,095 | 3.4% |
| 15 | South Carolina | 1,156,946 | 3.3% |
| 16 | Alabama | 1,138,726 | 3.3% |
| 17 | Mississippi | 1,010,216 | 2.9% |
| 18 | Tennessee | 912,577 | 2.6% |
| 19 | Missouri | 617,148 | 1.8% |
| 20 | Indiana | 497,976 | 1.4% |
| 21 | Arkansas | 410,821 | 1.2% |
| 22 | Massachusetts | 405,159 | 1.2% |
| 23 | Connecticut | 308,772 | 0.9% |
| 24 | Wisconsin | 293,367 | 0.8% |
| 25 | Kentucky | 288,336 | 0.8% |
| 26 | Oklahoma | 262,136 | 0.8% |
| 27 | Washington | 203,853 | 0.6% |
| 28 | Colorado | 176,277 | 0.5% |
| 29 | Arizona | 175,506 | 0.5% |
| 30 | Kansas | 157,176 | 0.5% |
| 31 | Delaware | 149,290 | 0.4% |
| 32 | Minnesota | 148,596 | 0.4% |
| 33 | Nevada | 140,031 | 0.4% |
| 34 | Nebraska | 68,067 | 0.2% |
| 35 | Oregon | 62,012 | 0.2% |
| 36 | Iowa | 58,013 | 0.2% |
| 37 | West Virginia | 56,108 | 0.2% |
| 38 | Rhode Island | 50,292 | 0.1% |
| 39 | New Mexico | 45,792 | 0.1% |
| 40 | Hawaii | 33,752 | 0.1% |
| 41 | Alaska | 24,067 | 0.1% |
| 42 | Utah | 19,481 | 0.1% |
| 43 | New Hampshire | 9,044 | 0.0% |
| 44 | Idaho | 7,561 | 0.0% |
| 45 | Maine | 6,258 | 0.0% |
| 46 | South Dakota | 5,099 | 0.0% |
| 47 | Wyoming | 4,210 | 0.0% |
| 48 | North Dakota | 4,118 | 0.0% |
| 49 | Vermont | 3,184 | 0.0% |
| 50 | Montana | 3,168 | 0.0% |
| | District of Columbia | 318,657 | 0.9% |

Source: U.S. Bureau of the Census
"Population Estimates for States by Race and Hispanic Origin: July 1, 1999 " (August 30, 2000)
(http://www.census.gov/population/estimates/state/srh/srh99.txt)
*Estimates. "Black" is defined by Census as a person having origins in any of the Black racial groups of Africa.

# Percent of Population Black in 1999

## National Percent = 12.8% Black*

ALPHA ORDER

| RANK | STATE | PERCENT |
|------|-------|---------|
| 6 | Alabama | 26.1 |
| 33 | Alaska | 3.9 |
| 34 | Arizona | 3.7 |
| 12 | Arkansas | 16.1 |
| 25 | California | 7.5 |
| 31 | Colorado | 4.3 |
| 21 | Connecticut | 9.4 |
| 9 | Delaware | 19.8 |
| 13 | Florida | 15.4 |
| 4 | Georgia | 28.7 |
| 38 | Hawaii | 2.8 |
| 46 | Idaho | 0.6 |
| 14 | Illinois | 15.3 |
| 22 | Indiana | 8.4 |
| 40 | Iowa | 2.0 |
| 28 | Kansas | 5.9 |
| 26 | Kentucky | 7.3 |
| 2 | Louisiana | 32.4 |
| 48 | Maine | 0.5 |
| 5 | Maryland | 28.1 |
| 27 | Massachusetts | 6.6 |
| 16 | Michigan | 14.3 |
| 36 | Minnesota | 3.1 |
| 1 | Mississippi | 36.5 |
| 19 | Missouri | 11.3 |
| 50 | Montana | 0.4 |
| 32 | Nebraska | 4.1 |
| 24 | Nevada | 7.7 |
| 44 | New Hampshire | 0.8 |
| 15 | New Jersey | 14.7 |
| 39 | New Mexico | 2.6 |
| 10 | New York | 17.7 |
| 7 | North Carolina | 22.0 |
| 46 | North Dakota | 0.6 |
| 18 | Ohio | 11.6 |
| 23 | Oklahoma | 7.8 |
| 41 | Oregon | 1.9 |
| 20 | Pennsylvania | 9.8 |
| 30 | Rhode Island | 5.1 |
| 3 | South Carolina | 29.8 |
| 45 | South Dakota | 0.7 |
| 11 | Tennessee | 16.6 |
| 17 | Texas | 12.3 |
| 42 | Utah | 0.9 |
| 48 | Vermont | 0.5 |
| 8 | Virginia | 20.1 |
| 35 | Washington | 3.5 |
| 36 | West Virginia | 3.1 |
| 29 | Wisconsin | 5.6 |
| 42 | Wyoming | 0.9 |

RANK ORDER

| RANK | STATE | PERCENT |
|------|-------|---------|
| 1 | Mississippi | 36.5 |
| 2 | Louisiana | 32.4 |
| 3 | South Carolina | 29.8 |
| 4 | Georgia | 28.7 |
| 5 | Maryland | 28.1 |
| 6 | Alabama | 26.1 |
| 7 | North Carolina | 22.0 |
| 8 | Virginia | 20.1 |
| 9 | Delaware | 19.8 |
| 10 | New York | 17.7 |
| 11 | Tennessee | 16.6 |
| 12 | Arkansas | 16.1 |
| 13 | Florida | 15.4 |
| 14 | Illinois | 15.3 |
| 15 | New Jersey | 14.7 |
| 16 | Michigan | 14.3 |
| 17 | Texas | 12.3 |
| 18 | Ohio | 11.6 |
| 19 | Missouri | 11.3 |
| 20 | Pennsylvania | 9.8 |
| 21 | Connecticut | 9.4 |
| 22 | Indiana | 8.4 |
| 23 | Oklahoma | 7.8 |
| 24 | Nevada | 7.7 |
| 25 | California | 7.5 |
| 26 | Kentucky | 7.3 |
| 27 | Massachusetts | 6.6 |
| 28 | Kansas | 5.9 |
| 29 | Wisconsin | 5.6 |
| 30 | Rhode Island | 5.1 |
| 31 | Colorado | 4.3 |
| 32 | Nebraska | 4.1 |
| 33 | Alaska | 3.9 |
| 34 | Arizona | 3.7 |
| 35 | Washington | 3.5 |
| 36 | Minnesota | 3.1 |
| 36 | West Virginia | 3.1 |
| 38 | Hawaii | 2.8 |
| 39 | New Mexico | 2.6 |
| 40 | Iowa | 2.0 |
| 41 | Oregon | 1.9 |
| 42 | Utah | 0.9 |
| 42 | Wyoming | 0.9 |
| 44 | New Hampshire | 0.8 |
| 45 | South Dakota | 0.7 |
| 46 | Idaho | 0.6 |
| 46 | North Dakota | 0.6 |
| 48 | Maine | 0.5 |
| 48 | Vermont | 0.5 |
| 50 | Montana | 0.4 |

| District of Columbia | 61.4 |
|---|---|

Source: Morgan Quitno Press using data from U.S. Bureau of the Census
   "Population Estimates for States by Race and Hispanic Origin: July 1, 1999 " (August 30, 2000)
      (http://www.census.gov/population/estimates/state/srh/srhus98.txt)
*Estimates. "Black" is defined by Census as a person having origins in any of the Black racial groups of Africa.

# Hispanic Population in 1999

## National Total = 31,337,122 Hispanics*

ALPHA ORDER

RANK ORDER

| RANK | STATE | HISPANICS | % of USA | | RANK | STATE | HISPANICS | % of USA |
|------|-------|-----------|----------|---|------|-------|-----------|----------|
| 38 | Alabama | 45,349 | 0.1% | | 1 | California | 10,459,616 | 33.4% |
| 42 | Alaska | 24,795 | 0.1% | | 2 | Texas | 6,045,430 | 19.3% |
| 6 | Arizona | 1,084,250 | 3.5% | | 3 | New York | 2,660,685 | 8.5% |
| 37 | Arkansas | 53,729 | 0.2% | | 4 | Florida | 2,334,403 | 7.4% |
| 1 | California | 10,459,616 | 33.4% | | 5 | Illinois | 1,276,193 | 4.1% |
| 9 | Colorado | 603,582 | 1.9% | | 6 | Arizona | 1,084,250 | 3.5% |
| 14 | Connecticut | 279,164 | 0.9% | | 7 | New Jersey | 1,027,277 | 3.3% |
| 41 | Delaware | 27,769 | 0.1% | | 8 | New Mexico | 708,407 | 2.3% |
| 4 | Florida | 2,334,403 | 7.4% | | 9 | Colorado | 603,582 | 1.9% |
| 17 | Georgia | 239,566 | 0.8% | | 10 | Massachusetts | 390,947 | 1.2% |
| 28 | Hawaii | 95,456 | 0.3% | | 11 | Washington | 376,664 | 1.2% |
| 29 | Idaho | 93,028 | 0.3% | | 12 | Pennsylvania | 326,218 | 1.0% |
| 5 | Illinois | 1,276,193 | 4.1% | | 13 | Nevada | 304,364 | 1.0% |
| 22 | Indiana | 153,960 | 0.5% | | 14 | Connecticut | 279,164 | 0.9% |
| 35 | Iowa | 61,570 | 0.2% | | 15 | Michigan | 275,849 | 0.9% |
| 24 | Kansas | 148,479 | 0.5% | | 16 | Virginia | 266,228 | 0.8% |
| 39 | Kentucky | 35,322 | 0.1% | | 17 | Georgia | 239,566 | 0.8% |
| 27 | Louisiana | 119,496 | 0.4% | | 18 | Oregon | 212,870 | 0.7% |
| 47 | Maine | 9,178 | 0.0% | | 19 | Maryland | 199,156 | 0.6% |
| 19 | Maryland | 199,156 | 0.6% | | 20 | Ohio | 184,902 | 0.6% |
| 10 | Massachusetts | 390,947 | 1.2% | | 21 | North Carolina | 175,707 | 0.6% |
| 15 | Michigan | 275,849 | 0.9% | | 22 | Indiana | 153,960 | 0.5% |
| 30 | Minnesota | 92,589 | 0.3% | | 23 | Utah | 150,699 | 0.5% |
| 43 | Mississippi | 23,975 | 0.1% | | 24 | Kansas | 148,479 | 0.5% |
| 31 | Missouri | 91,476 | 0.3% | | 25 | Wisconsin | 140,235 | 0.4% |
| 45 | Montana | 16,152 | 0.1% | | 26 | Oklahoma | 136,634 | 0.4% |
| 32 | Nebraska | 76,998 | 0.2% | | 27 | Louisiana | 119,496 | 0.4% |
| 13 | Nevada | 304,364 | 1.0% | | 28 | Hawaii | 95,456 | 0.3% |
| 44 | New Hampshire | 19,552 | 0.1% | | 29 | Idaho | 93,028 | 0.3% |
| 7 | New Jersey | 1,027,277 | 3.3% | | 30 | Minnesota | 92,589 | 0.3% |
| 8 | New Mexico | 708,407 | 2.3% | | 31 | Missouri | 91,476 | 0.3% |
| 3 | New York | 2,660,685 | 8.5% | | 32 | Nebraska | 76,998 | 0.2% |
| 21 | North Carolina | 175,707 | 0.6% | | 33 | Rhode Island | 68,644 | 0.2% |
| 49 | North Dakota | 7,269 | 0.0% | | 34 | Tennessee | 67,078 | 0.2% |
| 20 | Ohio | 184,902 | 0.6% | | 35 | Iowa | 61,570 | 0.2% |
| 26 | Oklahoma | 136,634 | 0.4% | | 36 | South Carolina | 54,299 | 0.2% |
| 18 | Oregon | 212,870 | 0.7% | | 37 | Arkansas | 53,729 | 0.2% |
| 12 | Pennsylvania | 326,218 | 1.0% | | 38 | Alabama | 45,349 | 0.1% |
| 33 | Rhode Island | 68,644 | 0.2% | | 39 | Kentucky | 35,322 | 0.1% |
| 36 | South Carolina | 54,299 | 0.2% | | 40 | Wyoming | 29,022 | 0.1% |
| 48 | South Dakota | 8,980 | 0.0% | | 41 | Delaware | 27,769 | 0.1% |
| 34 | Tennessee | 67,078 | 0.2% | | 42 | Alaska | 24,795 | 0.1% |
| 2 | Texas | 6,045,430 | 19.3% | | 43 | Mississippi | 23,975 | 0.1% |
| 23 | Utah | 150,699 | 0.5% | | 44 | New Hampshire | 19,552 | 0.1% |
| 50 | Vermont | 5,128 | 0.0% | | 45 | Montana | 16,152 | 0.1% |
| 16 | Virginia | 266,228 | 0.8% | | 46 | West Virginia | 10,330 | 0.0% |
| 11 | Washington | 376,664 | 1.2% | | 47 | Maine | 9,178 | 0.0% |
| 46 | West Virginia | 10,330 | 0.0% | | 48 | South Dakota | 8,980 | 0.0% |
| 25 | Wisconsin | 140,235 | 0.4% | | 49 | North Dakota | 7,269 | 0.0% |
| 40 | Wyoming | 29,022 | 0.1% | | 50 | Vermont | 5,128 | 0.0% |
| | | | | | | District of Columbia | 38,453 | 0.1% |

Source: U.S. Bureau of the Census
  "Population Estimates for States by Race and Hispanic Origin: July 1, 1999 " (August 30, 2000)
    (http://www.census.gov/population/estimates/state/srh/srh99.txt)
*Estimates.  Persons of Hispanic origin may be of any race.

# Percent of Population Hispanic in 1999

## National Percent = 11.5% Hispanic*

<table>
<tr><td colspan="3">ALPHA ORDER</td><td colspan="3">RANK ORDER</td></tr>
<tr><td>RANK</td><td>STATE</td><td>PERCENT</td><td>RANK</td><td>STATE</td><td>PERCENT</td></tr>
<tr><td>45</td><td>Alabama</td><td>1.0</td><td>1</td><td>New Mexico</td><td>40.7</td></tr>
<tr><td>23</td><td>Alaska</td><td>4.0</td><td>2</td><td>California</td><td>31.6</td></tr>
<tr><td>4</td><td>Arizona</td><td>22.7</td><td>3</td><td>Texas</td><td>30.2</td></tr>
<tr><td>34</td><td>Arkansas</td><td>2.1</td><td>4</td><td>Arizona</td><td>22.7</td></tr>
<tr><td>2</td><td>California</td><td>31.6</td><td>5</td><td>Nevada</td><td>16.8</td></tr>
<tr><td>7</td><td>Colorado</td><td>14.9</td><td>6</td><td>Florida</td><td>15.4</td></tr>
<tr><td>11</td><td>Connecticut</td><td>8.5</td><td>7</td><td>Colorado</td><td>14.9</td></tr>
<tr><td>26</td><td>Delaware</td><td>3.7</td><td>8</td><td>New York</td><td>14.6</td></tr>
<tr><td>6</td><td>Florida</td><td>15.4</td><td>9</td><td>New Jersey</td><td>12.6</td></tr>
<tr><td>27</td><td>Georgia</td><td>3.1</td><td>10</td><td>Illinois</td><td>10.5</td></tr>
<tr><td>12</td><td>Hawaii</td><td>8.1</td><td>11</td><td>Connecticut</td><td>8.5</td></tr>
<tr><td>13</td><td>Idaho</td><td>7.4</td><td>12</td><td>Hawaii</td><td>8.1</td></tr>
<tr><td>10</td><td>Illinois</td><td>10.5</td><td>13</td><td>Idaho</td><td>7.4</td></tr>
<tr><td>32</td><td>Indiana</td><td>2.6</td><td>14</td><td>Utah</td><td>7.1</td></tr>
<tr><td>34</td><td>Iowa</td><td>2.1</td><td>15</td><td>Rhode Island</td><td>6.9</td></tr>
<tr><td>20</td><td>Kansas</td><td>5.6</td><td>16</td><td>Washington</td><td>6.5</td></tr>
<tr><td>46</td><td>Kentucky</td><td>0.9</td><td>17</td><td>Oregon</td><td>6.4</td></tr>
<tr><td>29</td><td>Louisiana</td><td>2.7</td><td>18</td><td>Massachusetts</td><td>6.3</td></tr>
<tr><td>49</td><td>Maine</td><td>0.7</td><td>19</td><td>Wyoming</td><td>6.1</td></tr>
<tr><td>24</td><td>Maryland</td><td>3.9</td><td>20</td><td>Kansas</td><td>5.6</td></tr>
<tr><td>18</td><td>Massachusetts</td><td>6.3</td><td>21</td><td>Nebraska</td><td>4.6</td></tr>
<tr><td>28</td><td>Michigan</td><td>2.8</td><td>22</td><td>Oklahoma</td><td>4.1</td></tr>
<tr><td>36</td><td>Minnesota</td><td>1.9</td><td>23</td><td>Alaska</td><td>4.0</td></tr>
<tr><td>46</td><td>Mississippi</td><td>0.9</td><td>24</td><td>Maryland</td><td>3.9</td></tr>
<tr><td>38</td><td>Missouri</td><td>1.7</td><td>24</td><td>Virginia</td><td>3.9</td></tr>
<tr><td>37</td><td>Montana</td><td>1.8</td><td>26</td><td>Delaware</td><td>3.7</td></tr>
<tr><td>21</td><td>Nebraska</td><td>4.6</td><td>27</td><td>Georgia</td><td>3.1</td></tr>
<tr><td>5</td><td>Nevada</td><td>16.8</td><td>28</td><td>Michigan</td><td>2.8</td></tr>
<tr><td>39</td><td>New Hampshire</td><td>1.6</td><td>29</td><td>Louisiana</td><td>2.7</td></tr>
<tr><td>9</td><td>New Jersey</td><td>12.6</td><td>29</td><td>Pennsylvania</td><td>2.7</td></tr>
<tr><td>1</td><td>New Mexico</td><td>40.7</td><td>29</td><td>Wisconsin</td><td>2.7</td></tr>
<tr><td>8</td><td>New York</td><td>14.6</td><td>32</td><td>Indiana</td><td>2.6</td></tr>
<tr><td>33</td><td>North Carolina</td><td>2.3</td><td>33</td><td>North Carolina</td><td>2.3</td></tr>
<tr><td>44</td><td>North Dakota</td><td>1.1</td><td>34</td><td>Arkansas</td><td>2.1</td></tr>
<tr><td>39</td><td>Ohio</td><td>1.6</td><td>34</td><td>Iowa</td><td>2.1</td></tr>
<tr><td>22</td><td>Oklahoma</td><td>4.1</td><td>36</td><td>Minnesota</td><td>1.9</td></tr>
<tr><td>17</td><td>Oregon</td><td>6.4</td><td>37</td><td>Montana</td><td>1.8</td></tr>
<tr><td>29</td><td>Pennsylvania</td><td>2.7</td><td>38</td><td>Missouri</td><td>1.7</td></tr>
<tr><td>15</td><td>Rhode Island</td><td>6.9</td><td>39</td><td>New Hampshire</td><td>1.6</td></tr>
<tr><td>41</td><td>South Carolina</td><td>1.4</td><td>39</td><td>Ohio</td><td>1.6</td></tr>
<tr><td>42</td><td>South Dakota</td><td>1.2</td><td>41</td><td>South Carolina</td><td>1.4</td></tr>
<tr><td>42</td><td>Tennessee</td><td>1.2</td><td>42</td><td>South Dakota</td><td>1.2</td></tr>
<tr><td>3</td><td>Texas</td><td>30.2</td><td>42</td><td>Tennessee</td><td>1.2</td></tr>
<tr><td>14</td><td>Utah</td><td>7.1</td><td>44</td><td>North Dakota</td><td>1.1</td></tr>
<tr><td>46</td><td>Vermont</td><td>0.9</td><td>45</td><td>Alabama</td><td>1.0</td></tr>
<tr><td>24</td><td>Virginia</td><td>3.9</td><td>46</td><td>Kentucky</td><td>0.9</td></tr>
<tr><td>16</td><td>Washington</td><td>6.5</td><td>46</td><td>Mississippi</td><td>0.9</td></tr>
<tr><td>50</td><td>West Virginia</td><td>0.6</td><td>46</td><td>Vermont</td><td>0.9</td></tr>
<tr><td>29</td><td>Wisconsin</td><td>2.7</td><td>49</td><td>Maine</td><td>0.7</td></tr>
<tr><td>19</td><td>Wyoming</td><td>6.1</td><td>50</td><td>West Virginia</td><td>0.6</td></tr>
<tr><td></td><td></td><td></td><td></td><td>District of Columbia</td><td>7.4</td></tr>
</table>

*Source: Morgan Quitno Press using data from U.S. Bureau of the Census*
    *"Population Estimates for States by Race and Hispanic Origin: July 1, 1999 " (August 30, 2000)*
    *(http://www.census.gov/population/estimates/state/srh/srh99.txt)*
*Estimates. Persons of Hispanic origin may be of any race.*

# Asian Population in 1999

## National Total = 10,820,421 Asians*

ALPHA ORDER

| RANK | STATE | ASIANS | % of USA |
|---|---|---|---|
| 33 | Alabama | 28,435 | 0.3% |
| 34 | Alaska | 28,040 | 0.3% |
| 19 | Arizona | 102,539 | 0.9% |
| 40 | Arkansas | 18,790 | 0.2% |
| 1 | California | 4,038,309 | 37.3% |
| 20 | Colorado | 99,939 | 0.9% |
| 22 | Connecticut | 84,337 | 0.8% |
| 41 | Delaware | 16,054 | 0.1% |
| 8 | Florida | 281,366 | 2.6% |
| 14 | Georgia | 160,566 | 1.5% |
| 3 | Hawaii | 753,691 | 7.0% |
| 43 | Idaho | 14,430 | 0.1% |
| 6 | Illinois | 416,006 | 3.8% |
| 25 | Indiana | 58,665 | 0.5% |
| 31 | Iowa | 37,047 | 0.3% |
| 29 | Kansas | 47,767 | 0.4% |
| 35 | Kentucky | 27,662 | 0.3% |
| 26 | Louisiana | 54,652 | 0.5% |
| 44 | Maine | 9,484 | 0.1% |
| 11 | Maryland | 209,147 | 1.9% |
| 10 | Massachusetts | 233,239 | 2.2% |
| 13 | Michigan | 166,287 | 1.5% |
| 16 | Minnesota | 130,537 | 1.2% |
| 39 | Mississippi | 19,601 | 0.2% |
| 24 | Missouri | 61,483 | 0.6% |
| 46 | Montana | 5,391 | 0.0% |
| 38 | Nebraska | 22,574 | 0.2% |
| 21 | Nevada | 88,208 | 0.8% |
| 42 | New Hampshire | 14,974 | 0.1% |
| 5 | New Jersey | 469,435 | 4.3% |
| 36 | New Mexico | 26,427 | 0.2% |
| 2 | New York | 1,024,625 | 9.5% |
| 18 | North Carolina | 105,689 | 1.0% |
| 47 | North Dakota | 5,272 | 0.0% |
| 15 | Ohio | 132,638 | 1.2% |
| 30 | Oklahoma | 45,301 | 0.4% |
| 17 | Oregon | 110,015 | 1.0% |
| 12 | Pennsylvania | 202,969 | 1.9% |
| 37 | Rhode Island | 23,140 | 0.2% |
| 32 | South Carolina | 35,604 | 0.3% |
| 49 | South Dakota | 4,876 | 0.0% |
| 28 | Tennessee | 54,053 | 0.5% |
| 4 | Texas | 577,306 | 5.3% |
| 27 | Utah | 54,647 | 0.5% |
| 48 | Vermont | 4,921 | 0.0% |
| 9 | Virginia | 258,371 | 2.4% |
| 7 | Washington | 343,690 | 3.2% |
| 45 | West Virginia | 8,746 | 0.1% |
| 23 | Wisconsin | 83,265 | 0.8% |
| 50 | Wyoming | 4,091 | 0.0% |

RANK ORDER

| RANK | STATE | ASIANS | % of USA |
|---|---|---|---|
| 1 | California | 4,038,309 | 37.3% |
| 2 | New York | 1,024,625 | 9.5% |
| 3 | Hawaii | 753,691 | 7.0% |
| 4 | Texas | 577,306 | 5.3% |
| 5 | New Jersey | 469,435 | 4.3% |
| 6 | Illinois | 416,006 | 3.8% |
| 7 | Washington | 343,690 | 3.2% |
| 8 | Florida | 281,366 | 2.6% |
| 9 | Virginia | 258,371 | 2.4% |
| 10 | Massachusetts | 233,239 | 2.2% |
| 11 | Maryland | 209,147 | 1.9% |
| 12 | Pennsylvania | 202,969 | 1.9% |
| 13 | Michigan | 166,287 | 1.5% |
| 14 | Georgia | 160,566 | 1.5% |
| 15 | Ohio | 132,638 | 1.2% |
| 16 | Minnesota | 130,537 | 1.2% |
| 17 | Oregon | 110,015 | 1.0% |
| 18 | North Carolina | 105,689 | 1.0% |
| 19 | Arizona | 102,539 | 0.9% |
| 20 | Colorado | 99,939 | 0.9% |
| 21 | Nevada | 88,208 | 0.8% |
| 22 | Connecticut | 84,337 | 0.8% |
| 23 | Wisconsin | 83,265 | 0.8% |
| 24 | Missouri | 61,483 | 0.6% |
| 25 | Indiana | 58,665 | 0.5% |
| 26 | Louisiana | 54,652 | 0.5% |
| 27 | Utah | 54,647 | 0.5% |
| 28 | Tennessee | 54,053 | 0.5% |
| 29 | Kansas | 47,767 | 0.4% |
| 30 | Oklahoma | 45,301 | 0.4% |
| 31 | Iowa | 37,047 | 0.3% |
| 32 | South Carolina | 35,604 | 0.3% |
| 33 | Alabama | 28,435 | 0.3% |
| 34 | Alaska | 28,040 | 0.3% |
| 35 | Kentucky | 27,662 | 0.3% |
| 36 | New Mexico | 26,427 | 0.2% |
| 37 | Rhode Island | 23,140 | 0.2% |
| 38 | Nebraska | 22,574 | 0.2% |
| 39 | Mississippi | 19,601 | 0.2% |
| 40 | Arkansas | 18,790 | 0.2% |
| 41 | Delaware | 16,054 | 0.1% |
| 42 | New Hampshire | 14,974 | 0.1% |
| 43 | Idaho | 14,430 | 0.1% |
| 44 | Maine | 9,484 | 0.1% |
| 45 | West Virginia | 8,746 | 0.1% |
| 46 | Montana | 5,391 | 0.0% |
| 47 | North Dakota | 5,272 | 0.0% |
| 48 | Vermont | 4,921 | 0.0% |
| 49 | South Dakota | 4,876 | 0.0% |
| 50 | Wyoming | 4,091 | 0.0% |
| | District of Columbia | 16,120 | 0.1% |

Source: U.S. Bureau of the Census
   "Population Estimates for States by Race and Hispanic Origin: July 1, 1999 " (August 30, 2000)
      (http://www.census.gov/population/estimates/state/srh/srh99.txt)
*Estimates.  Includes Pacific Islanders.

# Percent of Population Asian in 1999

## National Percent = 4.0% Asian*

<table>
<tr><td colspan="3">ALPHA ORDER</td><td colspan="3">RANK ORDER</td></tr>
<tr><td>RANK</td><td>STATE</td><td>PERCENT</td><td>RANK</td><td>STATE</td><td>PERCENT</td></tr>
<tr><td>44</td><td>Alabama</td><td>0.7</td><td>1</td><td>Hawaii</td><td>63.6</td></tr>
<tr><td>7</td><td>Alaska</td><td>4.5</td><td>2</td><td>California</td><td>12.2</td></tr>
<tr><td>19</td><td>Arizona</td><td>2.1</td><td>3</td><td>Washington</td><td>6.0</td></tr>
<tr><td>44</td><td>Arkansas</td><td>0.7</td><td>4</td><td>New Jersey</td><td>5.8</td></tr>
<tr><td>2</td><td>California</td><td>12.2</td><td>5</td><td>New York</td><td>5.6</td></tr>
<tr><td>17</td><td>Colorado</td><td>2.5</td><td>6</td><td>Nevada</td><td>4.9</td></tr>
<tr><td>15</td><td>Connecticut</td><td>2.6</td><td>7</td><td>Alaska</td><td>4.5</td></tr>
<tr><td>19</td><td>Delaware</td><td>2.1</td><td>8</td><td>Maryland</td><td>4.0</td></tr>
<tr><td>22</td><td>Florida</td><td>1.9</td><td>9</td><td>Massachusetts</td><td>3.8</td></tr>
<tr><td>19</td><td>Georgia</td><td>2.1</td><td>9</td><td>Virginia</td><td>3.8</td></tr>
<tr><td>1</td><td>Hawaii</td><td>63.6</td><td>11</td><td>Illinois</td><td>3.4</td></tr>
<tr><td>33</td><td>Idaho</td><td>1.2</td><td>12</td><td>Oregon</td><td>3.3</td></tr>
<tr><td>11</td><td>Illinois</td><td>3.4</td><td>13</td><td>Texas</td><td>2.9</td></tr>
<tr><td>37</td><td>Indiana</td><td>1.0</td><td>14</td><td>Minnesota</td><td>2.7</td></tr>
<tr><td>30</td><td>Iowa</td><td>1.3</td><td>15</td><td>Connecticut</td><td>2.6</td></tr>
<tr><td>23</td><td>Kansas</td><td>1.8</td><td>15</td><td>Utah</td><td>2.6</td></tr>
<tr><td>44</td><td>Kentucky</td><td>0.7</td><td>17</td><td>Colorado</td><td>2.5</td></tr>
<tr><td>30</td><td>Louisiana</td><td>1.3</td><td>18</td><td>Rhode Island</td><td>2.3</td></tr>
<tr><td>41</td><td>Maine</td><td>0.8</td><td>19</td><td>Arizona</td><td>2.1</td></tr>
<tr><td>8</td><td>Maryland</td><td>4.0</td><td>19</td><td>Delaware</td><td>2.1</td></tr>
<tr><td>9</td><td>Massachusetts</td><td>3.8</td><td>19</td><td>Georgia</td><td>2.1</td></tr>
<tr><td>24</td><td>Michigan</td><td>1.7</td><td>22</td><td>Florida</td><td>1.9</td></tr>
<tr><td>14</td><td>Minnesota</td><td>2.7</td><td>23</td><td>Kansas</td><td>1.8</td></tr>
<tr><td>44</td><td>Mississippi</td><td>0.7</td><td>24</td><td>Michigan</td><td>1.7</td></tr>
<tr><td>36</td><td>Missouri</td><td>1.1</td><td>24</td><td>Pennsylvania</td><td>1.7</td></tr>
<tr><td>49</td><td>Montana</td><td>0.6</td><td>26</td><td>Wisconsin</td><td>1.6</td></tr>
<tr><td>28</td><td>Nebraska</td><td>1.4</td><td>27</td><td>New Mexico</td><td>1.5</td></tr>
<tr><td>6</td><td>Nevada</td><td>4.9</td><td>28</td><td>Nebraska</td><td>1.4</td></tr>
<tr><td>33</td><td>New Hampshire</td><td>1.2</td><td>28</td><td>North Carolina</td><td>1.4</td></tr>
<tr><td>4</td><td>New Jersey</td><td>5.8</td><td>30</td><td>Iowa</td><td>1.3</td></tr>
<tr><td>27</td><td>New Mexico</td><td>1.5</td><td>30</td><td>Louisiana</td><td>1.3</td></tr>
<tr><td>5</td><td>New York</td><td>5.6</td><td>30</td><td>Oklahoma</td><td>1.3</td></tr>
<tr><td>28</td><td>North Carolina</td><td>1.4</td><td>33</td><td>Idaho</td><td>1.2</td></tr>
<tr><td>41</td><td>North Dakota</td><td>0.8</td><td>33</td><td>New Hampshire</td><td>1.2</td></tr>
<tr><td>33</td><td>Ohio</td><td>1.2</td><td>33</td><td>Ohio</td><td>1.2</td></tr>
<tr><td>30</td><td>Oklahoma</td><td>1.3</td><td>36</td><td>Missouri</td><td>1.1</td></tr>
<tr><td>12</td><td>Oregon</td><td>3.3</td><td>37</td><td>Indiana</td><td>1.0</td></tr>
<tr><td>24</td><td>Pennsylvania</td><td>1.7</td><td>37</td><td>Tennessee</td><td>1.0</td></tr>
<tr><td>18</td><td>Rhode Island</td><td>2.3</td><td>39</td><td>South Carolina</td><td>0.9</td></tr>
<tr><td>39</td><td>South Carolina</td><td>0.9</td><td>39</td><td>Wyoming</td><td>0.9</td></tr>
<tr><td>44</td><td>South Dakota</td><td>0.7</td><td>41</td><td>Maine</td><td>0.8</td></tr>
<tr><td>37</td><td>Tennessee</td><td>1.0</td><td>41</td><td>North Dakota</td><td>0.8</td></tr>
<tr><td>13</td><td>Texas</td><td>2.9</td><td>41</td><td>Vermont</td><td>0.8</td></tr>
<tr><td>15</td><td>Utah</td><td>2.6</td><td>44</td><td>Alabama</td><td>0.7</td></tr>
<tr><td>41</td><td>Vermont</td><td>0.8</td><td>44</td><td>Arkansas</td><td>0.7</td></tr>
<tr><td>9</td><td>Virginia</td><td>3.8</td><td>44</td><td>Kentucky</td><td>0.7</td></tr>
<tr><td>3</td><td>Washington</td><td>6.0</td><td>44</td><td>Mississippi</td><td>0.7</td></tr>
<tr><td>50</td><td>West Virginia</td><td>0.5</td><td>44</td><td>South Dakota</td><td>0.7</td></tr>
<tr><td>26</td><td>Wisconsin</td><td>1.6</td><td>49</td><td>Montana</td><td>0.6</td></tr>
<tr><td>39</td><td>Wyoming</td><td>0.9</td><td>50</td><td>West Virginia</td><td>0.5</td></tr>
<tr><td></td><td></td><td></td><td></td><td>District of Columbia</td><td>3.1</td></tr>
</table>

Source: Morgan Quitno Press using data from U.S. Bureau of the Census
   "Population Estimates for States by Race and Hispanic Origin: July 1, 1999 " (August 30, 2000)
      (http://www.census.gov/population/estimates/state/srh/srh99.txt)
*Estimates.  Includes Pacific Islanders.

# American Indian Population in 1999

## National Total = 2,397,426 American Indians*

ALPHA ORDER

| RANK | STATE | INDIANS | % of USA |
|------|-------|---------|----------|
| 35 | Alabama | 14,599 | 0.6% |
| 6 | Alaska | 101,352 | 4.2% |
| 3 | Arizona | 261,168 | 10.9% |
| 36 | Arkansas | 13,965 | 0.6% |
| 1 | California | 313,642 | 13.1% |
| 17 | Colorado | 37,548 | 1.6% |
| 42 | Connecticut | 8,093 | 0.3% |
| 49 | Delaware | 2,389 | 0.1% |
| 10 | Florida | 60,358 | 2.5% |
| 28 | Georgia | 18,717 | 0.8% |
| 43 | Hawaii | 6,565 | 0.3% |
| 30 | Idaho | 16,656 | 0.7% |
| 21 | Illinois | 27,987 | 1.2% |
| 34 | Indiana | 15,075 | 0.6% |
| 41 | Iowa | 8,760 | 0.4% |
| 22 | Kansas | 23,554 | 1.0% |
| 44 | Kentucky | 5,936 | 0.2% |
| 26 | Louisiana | 19,407 | 0.8% |
| 45 | Maine | 5,752 | 0.2% |
| 31 | Maryland | 16,044 | 0.7% |
| 32 | Massachusetts | 15,229 | 0.6% |
| 12 | Michigan | 59,897 | 2.5% |
| 13 | Minnesota | 58,575 | 2.4% |
| 39 | Mississippi | 10,282 | 0.4% |
| 25 | Missouri | 20,701 | 0.9% |
| 14 | Montana | 57,225 | 2.4% |
| 33 | Nebraska | 15,216 | 0.6% |
| 18 | Nevada | 32,871 | 1.4% |
| 47 | New Hampshire | 2,597 | 0.1% |
| 24 | New Jersey | 22,625 | 0.9% |
| 4 | New Mexico | 165,944 | 6.9% |
| 9 | New York | 76,755 | 3.2% |
| 7 | North Carolina | 99,277 | 4.1% |
| 19 | North Dakota | 30,522 | 1.3% |
| 23 | Ohio | 23,337 | 1.0% |
| 2 | Oklahoma | 262,581 | 11.0% |
| 16 | Oregon | 45,633 | 1.9% |
| 29 | Pennsylvania | 18,054 | 0.8% |
| 46 | Rhode Island | 5,286 | 0.2% |
| 40 | South Carolina | 9,601 | 0.4% |
| 11 | South Dakota | 60,335 | 2.5% |
| 37 | Tennessee | 12,231 | 0.5% |
| 8 | Texas | 97,412 | 4.1% |
| 20 | Utah | 30,045 | 1.3% |
| 50 | Vermont | 1,459 | 0.1% |
| 27 | Virginia | 19,396 | 0.8% |
| 5 | Washington | 104,819 | 4.4% |
| 48 | West Virginia | 2,472 | 0.1% |
| 15 | Wisconsin | 46,830 | 2.0% |
| 38 | Wyoming | 10,867 | 0.5% |

RANK ORDER

| RANK | STATE | INDIANS | % of USA |
|------|-------|---------|----------|
| 1 | California | 313,642 | 13.1% |
| 2 | Oklahoma | 262,581 | 11.0% |
| 3 | Arizona | 261,168 | 10.9% |
| 4 | New Mexico | 165,944 | 6.9% |
| 5 | Washington | 104,819 | 4.4% |
| 6 | Alaska | 101,352 | 4.2% |
| 7 | North Carolina | 99,277 | 4.1% |
| 8 | Texas | 97,412 | 4.1% |
| 9 | New York | 76,755 | 3.2% |
| 10 | Florida | 60,358 | 2.5% |
| 11 | South Dakota | 60,335 | 2.5% |
| 12 | Michigan | 59,897 | 2.5% |
| 13 | Minnesota | 58,575 | 2.4% |
| 14 | Montana | 57,225 | 2.4% |
| 15 | Wisconsin | 46,830 | 2.0% |
| 16 | Oregon | 45,633 | 1.9% |
| 17 | Colorado | 37,548 | 1.6% |
| 18 | Nevada | 32,871 | 1.4% |
| 19 | North Dakota | 30,522 | 1.3% |
| 20 | Utah | 30,045 | 1.3% |
| 21 | Illinois | 27,987 | 1.2% |
| 22 | Kansas | 23,554 | 1.0% |
| 23 | Ohio | 23,337 | 1.0% |
| 24 | New Jersey | 22,625 | 0.9% |
| 25 | Missouri | 20,701 | 0.9% |
| 26 | Louisiana | 19,407 | 0.8% |
| 27 | Virginia | 19,396 | 0.8% |
| 28 | Georgia | 18,717 | 0.8% |
| 29 | Pennsylvania | 18,054 | 0.8% |
| 30 | Idaho | 16,656 | 0.7% |
| 31 | Maryland | 16,044 | 0.7% |
| 32 | Massachusetts | 15,229 | 0.6% |
| 33 | Nebraska | 15,216 | 0.6% |
| 34 | Indiana | 15,075 | 0.6% |
| 35 | Alabama | 14,599 | 0.6% |
| 36 | Arkansas | 13,965 | 0.6% |
| 37 | Tennessee | 12,231 | 0.5% |
| 38 | Wyoming | 10,867 | 0.5% |
| 39 | Mississippi | 10,282 | 0.4% |
| 40 | South Carolina | 9,601 | 0.4% |
| 41 | Iowa | 8,760 | 0.4% |
| 42 | Connecticut | 8,093 | 0.3% |
| 43 | Hawaii | 6,565 | 0.3% |
| 44 | Kentucky | 5,936 | 0.2% |
| 45 | Maine | 5,752 | 0.2% |
| 46 | Rhode Island | 5,286 | 0.2% |
| 47 | New Hampshire | 2,597 | 0.1% |
| 48 | West Virginia | 2,472 | 0.1% |
| 49 | Delaware | 2,389 | 0.1% |
| 50 | Vermont | 1,459 | 0.1% |
|  | District of Columbia | 1,785 | 0.1% |

Source: U.S. Bureau of the Census
"Population Estimates for States by Race and Hispanic Origin: July 1, 1999 " (August 30, 2000)
(http://www.census.gov/population/estimates/state/srh/srh99.txt)
*Estimates. Includes Eskimo and Aleut populations.

# Percent of Population American Indian in 1999

## National Percent = 0.9% American Indian*

ALPHA ORDER

| RANK | STATE | PERCENT |
|------|-------|---------|
| 32 | Alabama | 0.3 |
| 1 | Alaska | 16.4 |
| 6 | Arizona | 5.5 |
| 23 | Arkansas | 0.5 |
| 16 | California | 0.9 |
| 16 | Colorado | 0.9 |
| 39 | Connecticut | 0.2 |
| 32 | Delaware | 0.3 |
| 27 | Florida | 0.4 |
| 39 | Georgia | 0.2 |
| 21 | Hawaii | 0.6 |
| 13 | Idaho | 1.3 |
| 39 | Illinois | 0.2 |
| 32 | Indiana | 0.3 |
| 32 | Iowa | 0.3 |
| 16 | Kansas | 0.9 |
| 49 | Kentucky | 0.1 |
| 27 | Louisiana | 0.4 |
| 23 | Maine | 0.5 |
| 32 | Maryland | 0.3 |
| 39 | Massachusetts | 0.2 |
| 21 | Michigan | 0.6 |
| 15 | Minnesota | 1.2 |
| 27 | Mississippi | 0.4 |
| 27 | Missouri | 0.4 |
| 5 | Montana | 6.5 |
| 16 | Nebraska | 0.9 |
| 9 | Nevada | 1.8 |
| 39 | New Hampshire | 0.2 |
| 32 | New Jersey | 0.3 |
| 2 | New Mexico | 9.5 |
| 27 | New York | 0.4 |
| 13 | North Carolina | 1.3 |
| 7 | North Dakota | 4.8 |
| 39 | Ohio | 0.2 |
| 4 | Oklahoma | 7.8 |
| 11 | Oregon | 1.4 |
| 39 | Pennsylvania | 0.2 |
| 23 | Rhode Island | 0.5 |
| 39 | South Carolina | 0.2 |
| 3 | South Dakota | 8.2 |
| 39 | Tennessee | 0.2 |
| 23 | Texas | 0.5 |
| 11 | Utah | 1.4 |
| 39 | Vermont | 0.2 |
| 32 | Virginia | 0.3 |
| 9 | Washington | 1.8 |
| 49 | West Virginia | 0.1 |
| 16 | Wisconsin | 0.9 |
| 8 | Wyoming | 2.3 |

RANK ORDER

| RANK | STATE | PERCENT |
|------|-------|---------|
| 1 | Alaska | 16.4 |
| 2 | New Mexico | 9.5 |
| 3 | South Dakota | 8.2 |
| 4 | Oklahoma | 7.8 |
| 5 | Montana | 6.5 |
| 6 | Arizona | 5.5 |
| 7 | North Dakota | 4.8 |
| 8 | Wyoming | 2.3 |
| 9 | Nevada | 1.8 |
| 9 | Washington | 1.8 |
| 11 | Oregon | 1.4 |
| 11 | Utah | 1.4 |
| 13 | Idaho | 1.3 |
| 13 | North Carolina | 1.3 |
| 15 | Minnesota | 1.2 |
| 16 | California | 0.9 |
| 16 | Colorado | 0.9 |
| 16 | Kansas | 0.9 |
| 16 | Nebraska | 0.9 |
| 16 | Wisconsin | 0.9 |
| 21 | Hawaii | 0.6 |
| 21 | Michigan | 0.6 |
| 23 | Arkansas | 0.5 |
| 23 | Maine | 0.5 |
| 23 | Rhode Island | 0.5 |
| 23 | Texas | 0.5 |
| 27 | Florida | 0.4 |
| 27 | Louisiana | 0.4 |
| 27 | Mississippi | 0.4 |
| 27 | Missouri | 0.4 |
| 27 | New York | 0.4 |
| 32 | Alabama | 0.3 |
| 32 | Delaware | 0.3 |
| 32 | Indiana | 0.3 |
| 32 | Iowa | 0.3 |
| 32 | Maryland | 0.3 |
| 32 | New Jersey | 0.3 |
| 32 | Virginia | 0.3 |
| 39 | Connecticut | 0.2 |
| 39 | Georgia | 0.2 |
| 39 | Illinois | 0.2 |
| 39 | Massachusetts | 0.2 |
| 39 | New Hampshire | 0.2 |
| 39 | Ohio | 0.2 |
| 39 | Pennsylvania | 0.2 |
| 39 | South Carolina | 0.2 |
| 39 | Tennessee | 0.2 |
| 39 | Vermont | 0.2 |
| 49 | Kentucky | 0.1 |
| 49 | West Virginia | 0.1 |
| | District of Columbia | 0.3 |

Source: Morgan Quitno Press using data from U.S. Bureau of the Census
  "Population Estimates for States by Race and Hispanic Origin: July 1, 1999 " (August 30, 2000)
    (http://www.census.gov/population/estimates/state/srh/srh99.txt)
*Estimates.  Includes Eskimo and Aleut populations.

# Projected State Population in 2025

## National Total = 335,050,000

| RANK | STATE | POPULATION | % of USA |
|---|---|---|---|
| 22 | Alabama | 5,224,000 | 1.6% |
| 45 | Alaska | 885,000 | 0.3% |
| 17 | Arizona | 6,412,000 | 1.9% |
| 32 | Arkansas | 3,055,000 | 0.9% |
| 1 | California | 49,285,000 | 14.7% |
| 23 | Colorado | 5,188,000 | 1.5% |
| 29 | Connecticut | 3,739,000 | 1.1% |
| 47 | Delaware | 861,000 | 0.3% |
| 3 | Florida | 20,710,000 | 6.2% |
| 9 | Georgia | 9,869,000 | 2.9% |
| 39 | Hawaii | 1,812,000 | 0.5% |
| 40 | Idaho | 1,739,000 | 0.5% |
| 5 | Illinois | 13,440,000 | 4.0% |
| 16 | Indiana | 6,546,000 | 2.0% |
| 33 | Iowa | 3,040,000 | 0.9% |
| 31 | Kansas | 3,108,000 | 0.9% |
| 27 | Kentucky | 4,314,000 | 1.3% |
| 24 | Louisiana | 5,133,000 | 1.5% |
| 42 | Maine | 1,423,000 | 0.4% |
| 18 | Maryland | 6,274,000 | 1.9% |
| 14 | Massachusetts | 6,902,000 | 2.1% |
| 8 | Michigan | 10,078,000 | 3.0% |
| 21 | Minnesota | 5,510,000 | 1.6% |
| 30 | Mississippi | 3,142,000 | 0.9% |
| 19 | Missouri | 6,250,000 | 1.9% |
| 44 | Montana | 1,121,000 | 0.3% |
| 37 | Nebraska | 1,930,000 | 0.6% |
| 36 | Nevada | 2,312,000 | 0.7% |
| 41 | New Hampshire | 1,439,000 | 0.4% |
| 10 | New Jersey | 9,558,000 | 2.9% |
| 35 | New Mexico | 2,612,000 | 0.8% |
| 4 | New York | 19,830,000 | 5.9% |
| 11 | North Carolina | 9,349,000 | 2.8% |
| 48 | North Dakota | 729,000 | 0.2% |
| 7 | Ohio | 11,744,000 | 3.5% |
| 28 | Oklahoma | 4,057,000 | 1.2% |
| 26 | Oregon | 4,349,000 | 1.3% |
| 6 | Pennsylvania | 12,683,000 | 3.8% |
| 43 | Rhode Island | 1,141,000 | 0.3% |
| 25 | South Carolina | 4,645,000 | 1.4% |
| 46 | South Dakota | 866,000 | 0.3% |
| 15 | Tennessee | 6,665,000 | 2.0% |
| 2 | Texas | 27,183,000 | 8.1% |
| 34 | Utah | 2,883,000 | 0.9% |
| 50 | Vermont | 678,000 | 0.2% |
| 12 | Virginia | 8,466,000 | 2.5% |
| 13 | Washington | 7,808,000 | 2.3% |
| 38 | West Virginia | 1,845,000 | 0.6% |
| 20 | Wisconsin | 5,867,000 | 1.8% |
| 49 | Wyoming | 694,000 | 0.2% |

| RANK | STATE | POPULATION | % of USA |
|---|---|---|---|
| 1 | California | 49,285,000 | 14.7% |
| 2 | Texas | 27,183,000 | 8.1% |
| 3 | Florida | 20,710,000 | 6.2% |
| 4 | New York | 19,830,000 | 5.9% |
| 5 | Illinois | 13,440,000 | 4.0% |
| 6 | Pennsylvania | 12,683,000 | 3.8% |
| 7 | Ohio | 11,744,000 | 3.5% |
| 8 | Michigan | 10,078,000 | 3.0% |
| 9 | Georgia | 9,869,000 | 2.9% |
| 10 | New Jersey | 9,558,000 | 2.9% |
| 11 | North Carolina | 9,349,000 | 2.8% |
| 12 | Virginia | 8,466,000 | 2.5% |
| 13 | Washington | 7,808,000 | 2.3% |
| 14 | Massachusetts | 6,902,000 | 2.1% |
| 15 | Tennessee | 6,665,000 | 2.0% |
| 16 | Indiana | 6,546,000 | 2.0% |
| 17 | Arizona | 6,412,000 | 1.9% |
| 18 | Maryland | 6,274,000 | 1.9% |
| 19 | Missouri | 6,250,000 | 1.9% |
| 20 | Wisconsin | 5,867,000 | 1.8% |
| 21 | Minnesota | 5,510,000 | 1.6% |
| 22 | Alabama | 5,224,000 | 1.6% |
| 23 | Colorado | 5,188,000 | 1.5% |
| 24 | Louisiana | 5,133,000 | 1.5% |
| 25 | South Carolina | 4,645,000 | 1.4% |
| 26 | Oregon | 4,349,000 | 1.3% |
| 27 | Kentucky | 4,314,000 | 1.3% |
| 28 | Oklahoma | 4,057,000 | 1.2% |
| 29 | Connecticut | 3,739,000 | 1.1% |
| 30 | Mississippi | 3,142,000 | 0.9% |
| 31 | Kansas | 3,108,000 | 0.9% |
| 32 | Arkansas | 3,055,000 | 0.9% |
| 33 | Iowa | 3,040,000 | 0.9% |
| 34 | Utah | 2,883,000 | 0.9% |
| 35 | New Mexico | 2,612,000 | 0.8% |
| 36 | Nevada | 2,312,000 | 0.7% |
| 37 | Nebraska | 1,930,000 | 0.6% |
| 38 | West Virginia | 1,845,000 | 0.6% |
| 39 | Hawaii | 1,812,000 | 0.5% |
| 40 | Idaho | 1,739,000 | 0.5% |
| 41 | New Hampshire | 1,439,000 | 0.4% |
| 42 | Maine | 1,423,000 | 0.4% |
| 43 | Rhode Island | 1,141,000 | 0.3% |
| 44 | Montana | 1,121,000 | 0.3% |
| 45 | Alaska | 885,000 | 0.3% |
| 46 | South Dakota | 866,000 | 0.3% |
| 47 | Delaware | 861,000 | 0.3% |
| 48 | North Dakota | 729,000 | 0.2% |
| 49 | Wyoming | 694,000 | 0.2% |
| 50 | Vermont | 678,000 | 0.2% |
| | District of Columbia | 655,000 | 0.2% |

*Source: U.S. Bureau of the Census*
*"Projections of Total Population of States: 1995-2025 "*
*(http://www.census.gov/population/projections/state/stpjpop.txt)*

# Projected Population Change: 2000 to 2025

## National Projected Change = 53,626,094 Increase

ALPHA ORDER

| RANK | STATE | GAIN | % of USA |
|---|---|---|---|
| 17 | Alabama | 776,900 | 1.4% |
| 37 | Alaska | 258,068 | 0.5% |
| 8 | Arizona | 1,281,368 | 2.4% |
| 32 | Arkansas | 381,600 | 0.7% |
| 1 | California | 15,413,352 | 28.7% |
| 14 | Colorado | 886,739 | 1.7% |
| 33 | Connecticut | 333,435 | 0.6% |
| 48 | Delaware | 77,400 | 0.1% |
| 3 | Florida | 4,727,622 | 8.8% |
| 5 | Georgia | 1,682,547 | 3.1% |
| 23 | Hawaii | 600,463 | 1.1% |
| 28 | Idaho | 445,047 | 0.8% |
| 10 | Illinois | 1,020,707 | 1.9% |
| 27 | Indiana | 465,515 | 0.9% |
| 44 | Iowa | 113,676 | 0.2% |
| 29 | Kansas | 419,582 | 0.8% |
| 36 | Kentucky | 272,231 | 0.5% |
| 18 | Louisiana | 664,024 | 1.2% |
| 42 | Maine | 148,077 | 0.3% |
| 11 | Maryland | 977,514 | 1.8% |
| 25 | Massachusetts | 552,903 | 1.0% |
| 43 | Michigan | 139,556 | 0.3% |
| 24 | Minnesota | 590,521 | 1.1% |
| 35 | Mississippi | 297,342 | 0.6% |
| 19 | Missouri | 654,789 | 1.2% |
| 38 | Montana | 218,805 | 0.4% |
| 39 | Nebraska | 218,737 | 0.4% |
| 34 | Nevada | 313,743 | 0.6% |
| 40 | New Hampshire | 203,214 | 0.4% |
| 9 | New Jersey | 1,143,650 | 2.1% |
| 16 | New Mexico | 792,954 | 1.5% |
| 15 | New York | 853,543 | 1.6% |
| 7 | North Carolina | 1,299,687 | 2.4% |
| 47 | North Dakota | 86,800 | 0.2% |
| 31 | Ohio | 390,860 | 0.7% |
| 22 | Oklahoma | 606,346 | 1.1% |
| 13 | Oregon | 927,601 | 1.7% |
| 30 | Pennsylvania | 401,946 | 0.7% |
| 46 | Rhode Island | 92,681 | 0.2% |
| 21 | South Carolina | 632,988 | 1.2% |
| 45 | South Dakota | 111,156 | 0.2% |
| 12 | Tennessee | 975,717 | 1.8% |
| 2 | Texas | 6,331,180 | 11.8% |
| 20 | Utah | 649,831 | 1.2% |
| 49 | Vermont | 69,173 | 0.1% |
| 6 | Virginia | 1,387,485 | 2.6% |
| 4 | Washington | 1,913,879 | 3.6% |
| 50 | West Virginia | 36,656 | 0.1% |
| 26 | Wisconsin | 503,325 | 0.9% |
| 41 | Wyoming | 200,218 | 0.4% |

RANK ORDER

| RANK | STATE | GAIN | % of USA |
|---|---|---|---|
| 1 | California | 15,413,352 | 28.7% |
| 2 | Texas | 6,331,180 | 11.8% |
| 3 | Florida | 4,727,622 | 8.8% |
| 4 | Washington | 1,913,879 | 3.6% |
| 5 | Georgia | 1,682,547 | 3.1% |
| 6 | Virginia | 1,387,485 | 2.6% |
| 7 | North Carolina | 1,299,687 | 2.4% |
| 8 | Arizona | 1,281,368 | 2.4% |
| 9 | New Jersey | 1,143,650 | 2.1% |
| 10 | Illinois | 1,020,707 | 1.9% |
| 11 | Maryland | 977,514 | 1.8% |
| 12 | Tennessee | 975,717 | 1.8% |
| 13 | Oregon | 927,601 | 1.7% |
| 14 | Colorado | 886,739 | 1.7% |
| 15 | New York | 853,543 | 1.6% |
| 16 | New Mexico | 792,954 | 1.5% |
| 17 | Alabama | 776,900 | 1.4% |
| 18 | Louisiana | 664,024 | 1.2% |
| 19 | Missouri | 654,789 | 1.2% |
| 20 | Utah | 649,831 | 1.2% |
| 21 | South Carolina | 632,988 | 1.2% |
| 22 | Oklahoma | 606,346 | 1.1% |
| 23 | Hawaii | 600,463 | 1.1% |
| 24 | Minnesota | 590,521 | 1.1% |
| 25 | Massachusetts | 552,903 | 1.0% |
| 26 | Wisconsin | 503,325 | 0.9% |
| 27 | Indiana | 465,515 | 0.9% |
| 28 | Idaho | 445,047 | 0.8% |
| 29 | Kansas | 419,582 | 0.8% |
| 30 | Pennsylvania | 401,946 | 0.7% |
| 31 | Ohio | 390,860 | 0.7% |
| 32 | Arkansas | 381,600 | 0.7% |
| 33 | Connecticut | 333,435 | 0.6% |
| 34 | Nevada | 313,743 | 0.6% |
| 35 | Mississippi | 297,342 | 0.6% |
| 36 | Kentucky | 272,231 | 0.5% |
| 37 | Alaska | 258,068 | 0.5% |
| 38 | Montana | 218,805 | 0.4% |
| 39 | Nebraska | 218,737 | 0.4% |
| 40 | New Hampshire | 203,214 | 0.4% |
| 41 | Wyoming | 200,218 | 0.4% |
| 42 | Maine | 148,077 | 0.3% |
| 43 | Michigan | 139,556 | 0.3% |
| 44 | Iowa | 113,676 | 0.2% |
| 45 | South Dakota | 111,156 | 0.2% |
| 46 | Rhode Island | 92,681 | 0.2% |
| 47 | North Dakota | 86,800 | 0.2% |
| 48 | Delaware | 77,400 | 0.1% |
| 49 | Vermont | 69,173 | 0.1% |
| 50 | West Virginia | 36,656 | 0.1% |
| | District of Columbia | 82,941 | 0.2% |

*Source: Morgan Quitno Press using data from U.S. Bureau of the Census*
*"Projections of Total Population of States: 1995-2025 " (www.census.gov/population/projections/state/stpjpop.txt)*
*and "First Census 2000 Results" (December 28, 2000, http://www.census.gov/main/www/cen2000.html)*

# Projected Percent Change in Population: 2000 to 2025

## National Projected Percent Change = 19.1% Increase*

ALPHA ORDER

RANK ORDER

| RANK | STATE | PERCENT CHANGE |
|---|---|---|
| 19 | Alabama | 17.5 |
| 4 | Alaska | 41.2 |
| 12 | Arizona | 25.0 |
| 28 | Arkansas | 14.3 |
| 2 | California | 45.5 |
| 14 | Colorado | 20.6 |
| 38 | Connecticut | 9.8 |
| 37 | Delaware | 9.9 |
| 9 | Florida | 29.6 |
| 14 | Georgia | 20.6 |
| 1 | Hawaii | 49.6 |
| 6 | Idaho | 34.4 |
| 42 | Illinois | 8.2 |
| 43 | Indiana | 7.7 |
| 46 | Iowa | 3.9 |
| 25 | Kansas | 15.6 |
| 44 | Kentucky | 6.7 |
| 26 | Louisiana | 14.9 |
| 34 | Maine | 11.6 |
| 17 | Maryland | 18.5 |
| 41 | Massachusetts | 8.7 |
| 50 | Michigan | 1.4 |
| 32 | Minnesota | 12.0 |
| 36 | Mississippi | 10.5 |
| 33 | Missouri | 11.7 |
| 13 | Montana | 24.3 |
| 31 | Nebraska | 12.8 |
| 24 | Nevada | 15.7 |
| 21 | New Hampshire | 16.4 |
| 29 | New Jersey | 13.6 |
| 3 | New Mexico | 43.6 |
| 45 | New York | 4.5 |
| 22 | North Carolina | 16.1 |
| 30 | North Dakota | 13.5 |
| 47 | Ohio | 3.4 |
| 18 | Oklahoma | 17.6 |
| 11 | Oregon | 27.1 |
| 48 | Pennsylvania | 3.3 |
| 40 | Rhode Island | 8.8 |
| 23 | South Carolina | 15.8 |
| 27 | South Dakota | 14.7 |
| 20 | Tennessee | 17.2 |
| 8 | Texas | 30.4 |
| 10 | Utah | 29.1 |
| 35 | Vermont | 11.4 |
| 16 | Virginia | 19.6 |
| 7 | Washington | 32.5 |
| 49 | West Virginia | 2.0 |
| 39 | Wisconsin | 9.4 |
| 5 | Wyoming | 40.5 |

| RANK | STATE | PERCENT CHANGE |
|---|---|---|
| 1 | Hawaii | 49.6 |
| 2 | California | 45.5 |
| 3 | New Mexico | 43.6 |
| 4 | Alaska | 41.2 |
| 5 | Wyoming | 40.5 |
| 6 | Idaho | 34.4 |
| 7 | Washington | 32.5 |
| 8 | Texas | 30.4 |
| 9 | Florida | 29.6 |
| 10 | Utah | 29.1 |
| 11 | Oregon | 27.1 |
| 12 | Arizona | 25.0 |
| 13 | Montana | 24.3 |
| 14 | Colorado | 20.6 |
| 14 | Georgia | 20.6 |
| 16 | Virginia | 19.6 |
| 17 | Maryland | 18.5 |
| 18 | Oklahoma | 17.6 |
| 19 | Alabama | 17.5 |
| 20 | Tennessee | 17.2 |
| 21 | New Hampshire | 16.4 |
| 22 | North Carolina | 16.1 |
| 23 | South Carolina | 15.8 |
| 24 | Nevada | 15.7 |
| 25 | Kansas | 15.6 |
| 26 | Louisiana | 14.9 |
| 27 | South Dakota | 14.7 |
| 28 | Arkansas | 14.3 |
| 29 | New Jersey | 13.6 |
| 30 | North Dakota | 13.5 |
| 31 | Nebraska | 12.8 |
| 32 | Minnesota | 12.0 |
| 33 | Missouri | 11.7 |
| 34 | Maine | 11.6 |
| 35 | Vermont | 11.4 |
| 36 | Mississippi | 10.5 |
| 37 | Delaware | 9.9 |
| 38 | Connecticut | 9.8 |
| 39 | Wisconsin | 9.4 |
| 40 | Rhode Island | 8.8 |
| 41 | Massachusetts | 8.7 |
| 42 | Illinois | 8.2 |
| 43 | Indiana | 7.7 |
| 44 | Kentucky | 6.7 |
| 45 | New York | 4.5 |
| 46 | Iowa | 3.9 |
| 47 | Ohio | 3.4 |
| 48 | Pennsylvania | 3.3 |
| 49 | West Virginia | 2.0 |
| 50 | Michigan | 1.4 |
| | District of Columbia | 14.5 |

Source: Morgan Quitno Press using data from U.S. Bureau of the Census
"Projections of Total Population of States: 1995-2025 " (www.census.gov/population/projections/state/stpjpop.txt)
and "First Census 2000 Results" (December 28, 2000, http://www.census.gov/main/www/cen2000.html)

# Projected White Population in 2025

## National Projected Total = 262,222,000 White Persons*

ALPHA ORDER

| RANK | STATE | WHITES | % of USA |
|---|---|---|---|
| 24 | Alabama | 3,780,000 | 1.4% |
| 50 | Alaska | 558,000 | 0.2% |
| 16 | Arizona | 5,599,000 | 2.1% |
| 33 | Arkansas | 2,536,000 | 1.0% |
| 1 | California | 36,388,000 | 13.9% |
| 21 | Colorado | 4,621,000 | 1.8% |
| 29 | Connecticut | 3,065,000 | 1.2% |
| 48 | Delaware | 633,000 | 0.2% |
| 3 | Florida | 16,541,000 | 6.3% |
| 12 | Georgia | 6,282,000 | 2.4% |
| 49 | Hawaii | 566,000 | 0.2% |
| 39 | Idaho | 1,661,000 | 0.6% |
| 6 | Illinois | 10,504,000 | 4.0% |
| 14 | Indiana | 5,811,000 | 2.2% |
| 30 | Iowa | 2,858,000 | 1.1% |
| 31 | Kansas | 2,741,000 | 1.0% |
| 23 | Kentucky | 3,916,000 | 1.5% |
| 28 | Louisiana | 3,145,000 | 1.2% |
| 41 | Maine | 1,388,000 | 0.5% |
| 25 | Maryland | 3,775,000 | 1.4% |
| 15 | Massachusetts | 5,694,000 | 2.2% |
| 8 | Michigan | 8,011,000 | 3.1% |
| 20 | Minnesota | 4,855,000 | 1.9% |
| 35 | Mississippi | 1,939,000 | 0.7% |
| 18 | Missouri | 5,317,000 | 2.0% |
| 42 | Montana | 1,007,000 | 0.4% |
| 38 | Nebraska | 1,754,000 | 0.7% |
| 36 | Nevada | 1,933,000 | 0.7% |
| 40 | New Hampshire | 1,389,000 | 0.5% |
| 10 | New Jersey | 6,815,000 | 2.6% |
| 34 | New Mexico | 2,192,000 | 0.8% |
| 4 | New York | 13,813,000 | 5.3% |
| 9 | North Carolina | 6,824,000 | 2.6% |
| 46 | North Dakota | 654,000 | 0.2% |
| 7 | Ohio | 9,805,000 | 3.7% |
| 27 | Oklahoma | 3,166,000 | 1.2% |
| 22 | Oregon | 3,960,000 | 1.5% |
| 5 | Pennsylvania | 10,716,000 | 4.1% |
| 43 | Rhode Island | 977,000 | 0.4% |
| 26 | South Carolina | 3,174,000 | 1.2% |
| 44 | South Dakota | 759,000 | 0.3% |
| 17 | Tennessee | 5,332,000 | 2.0% |
| 2 | Texas | 22,089,000 | 8.4% |
| 32 | Utah | 2,672,000 | 1.0% |
| 45 | Vermont | 659,000 | 0.3% |
| 13 | Virginia | 5,951,000 | 2.3% |
| 11 | Washington | 6,662,000 | 2.5% |
| 37 | West Virginia | 1,755,000 | 0.7% |
| 19 | Wisconsin | 5,093,000 | 1.9% |
| 47 | Wyoming | 648,000 | 0.2% |

RANK ORDER

| RANK | STATE | WHITES | % of USA |
|---|---|---|---|
| 1 | California | 36,388,000 | 13.9% |
| 2 | Texas | 22,089,000 | 8.4% |
| 3 | Florida | 16,541,000 | 6.3% |
| 4 | New York | 13,813,000 | 5.3% |
| 5 | Pennsylvania | 10,716,000 | 4.1% |
| 6 | Illinois | 10,504,000 | 4.0% |
| 7 | Ohio | 9,805,000 | 3.7% |
| 8 | Michigan | 8,011,000 | 3.1% |
| 9 | North Carolina | 6,824,000 | 2.6% |
| 10 | New Jersey | 6,815,000 | 2.6% |
| 11 | Washington | 6,662,000 | 2.5% |
| 12 | Georgia | 6,282,000 | 2.4% |
| 13 | Virginia | 5,951,000 | 2.3% |
| 14 | Indiana | 5,811,000 | 2.2% |
| 15 | Massachusetts | 5,694,000 | 2.2% |
| 16 | Arizona | 5,599,000 | 2.1% |
| 17 | Tennessee | 5,332,000 | 2.0% |
| 18 | Missouri | 5,317,000 | 2.0% |
| 19 | Wisconsin | 5,093,000 | 1.9% |
| 20 | Minnesota | 4,855,000 | 1.9% |
| 21 | Colorado | 4,621,000 | 1.8% |
| 22 | Oregon | 3,960,000 | 1.5% |
| 23 | Kentucky | 3,916,000 | 1.5% |
| 24 | Alabama | 3,780,000 | 1.4% |
| 25 | Maryland | 3,775,000 | 1.4% |
| 26 | South Carolina | 3,174,000 | 1.2% |
| 27 | Oklahoma | 3,166,000 | 1.2% |
| 28 | Louisiana | 3,145,000 | 1.2% |
| 29 | Connecticut | 3,065,000 | 1.2% |
| 30 | Iowa | 2,858,000 | 1.1% |
| 31 | Kansas | 2,741,000 | 1.0% |
| 32 | Utah | 2,672,000 | 1.0% |
| 33 | Arkansas | 2,536,000 | 1.0% |
| 34 | New Mexico | 2,192,000 | 0.8% |
| 35 | Mississippi | 1,939,000 | 0.7% |
| 36 | Nevada | 1,933,000 | 0.7% |
| 37 | West Virginia | 1,755,000 | 0.7% |
| 38 | Nebraska | 1,754,000 | 0.7% |
| 39 | Idaho | 1,661,000 | 0.6% |
| 40 | New Hampshire | 1,389,000 | 0.5% |
| 41 | Maine | 1,388,000 | 0.5% |
| 42 | Montana | 1,007,000 | 0.4% |
| 43 | Rhode Island | 977,000 | 0.4% |
| 44 | South Dakota | 759,000 | 0.3% |
| 45 | Vermont | 659,000 | 0.3% |
| 46 | North Dakota | 654,000 | 0.2% |
| 47 | Wyoming | 648,000 | 0.2% |
| 48 | Delaware | 633,000 | 0.2% |
| 49 | Hawaii | 566,000 | 0.2% |
| 50 | Alaska | 558,000 | 0.2% |
|  | District of Columbia | 239,000 | 0.1% |

*Source: U.S. Bureau of the Census*
*"Projected State Populations, by Sex, Race, and Hispanic Origin: 1995-2025 "*
*(http://www.census.gov/population/projections/state/stpjrace.txt)*
*\*"White" is defined by Census as a person having origins in any of the original peoples of Europe, North Africa, or the Middle East.*

# Projected Percent of Population White in 2025

## National Projected Percent = 78.3% White*

ALPHA ORDER

| RANK | STATE | PERCENT |
|------|-------|---------|
| 40 | Alabama | 72.4 |
| 46 | Alaska | 63.1 |
| 19 | Arizona | 87.3 |
| 28 | Arkansas | 83.0 |
| 37 | California | 73.8 |
| 14 | Colorado | 89.1 |
| 30 | Connecticut | 82.0 |
| 38 | Delaware | 73.5 |
| 33 | Florida | 79.9 |
| 45 | Georgia | 63.7 |
| 50 | Hawaii | 31.2 |
| 4 | Idaho | 95.5 |
| 35 | Illinois | 78.2 |
| 15 | Indiana | 88.8 |
| 6 | Iowa | 94.0 |
| 16 | Kansas | 88.2 |
| 11 | Kentucky | 90.8 |
| 48 | Louisiana | 61.3 |
| 1 | Maine | 97.5 |
| 49 | Maryland | 60.2 |
| 29 | Massachusetts | 82.5 |
| 34 | Michigan | 79.5 |
| 17 | Minnesota | 88.1 |
| 47 | Mississippi | 61.7 |
| 23 | Missouri | 85.1 |
| 12 | Montana | 89.8 |
| 10 | Nebraska | 90.9 |
| 26 | Nevada | 83.6 |
| 3 | New Hampshire | 96.5 |
| 41 | New Jersey | 71.3 |
| 25 | New Mexico | 83.9 |
| 43 | New York | 69.7 |
| 39 | North Carolina | 73.0 |
| 13 | North Dakota | 89.7 |
| 27 | Ohio | 83.5 |
| 36 | Oklahoma | 78.0 |
| 9 | Oregon | 91.1 |
| 24 | Pennsylvania | 84.5 |
| 21 | Rhode Island | 85.6 |
| 44 | South Carolina | 68.3 |
| 18 | South Dakota | 87.6 |
| 32 | Tennessee | 80.0 |
| 31 | Texas | 81.3 |
| 8 | Utah | 92.7 |
| 2 | Vermont | 97.2 |
| 42 | Virginia | 70.3 |
| 22 | Washington | 85.3 |
| 5 | West Virginia | 95.1 |
| 20 | Wisconsin | 86.8 |
| 7 | Wyoming | 93.4 |

RANK ORDER

| RANK | STATE | PERCENT |
|------|-------|---------|
| 1 | Maine | 97.5 |
| 2 | Vermont | 97.2 |
| 3 | New Hampshire | 96.5 |
| 4 | Idaho | 95.5 |
| 5 | West Virginia | 95.1 |
| 6 | Iowa | 94.0 |
| 7 | Wyoming | 93.4 |
| 8 | Utah | 92.7 |
| 9 | Oregon | 91.1 |
| 10 | Nebraska | 90.9 |
| 11 | Kentucky | 90.8 |
| 12 | Montana | 89.8 |
| 13 | North Dakota | 89.7 |
| 14 | Colorado | 89.1 |
| 15 | Indiana | 88.8 |
| 16 | Kansas | 88.2 |
| 17 | Minnesota | 88.1 |
| 18 | South Dakota | 87.6 |
| 19 | Arizona | 87.3 |
| 20 | Wisconsin | 86.8 |
| 21 | Rhode Island | 85.6 |
| 22 | Washington | 85.3 |
| 23 | Missouri | 85.1 |
| 24 | Pennsylvania | 84.5 |
| 25 | New Mexico | 83.9 |
| 26 | Nevada | 83.6 |
| 27 | Ohio | 83.5 |
| 28 | Arkansas | 83.0 |
| 29 | Massachusetts | 82.5 |
| 30 | Connecticut | 82.0 |
| 31 | Texas | 81.3 |
| 32 | Tennessee | 80.0 |
| 33 | Florida | 79.9 |
| 34 | Michigan | 79.5 |
| 35 | Illinois | 78.2 |
| 36 | Oklahoma | 78.0 |
| 37 | California | 73.8 |
| 38 | Delaware | 73.5 |
| 39 | North Carolina | 73.0 |
| 40 | Alabama | 72.4 |
| 41 | New Jersey | 71.3 |
| 42 | Virginia | 70.3 |
| 43 | New York | 69.7 |
| 44 | South Carolina | 68.3 |
| 45 | Georgia | 63.7 |
| 46 | Alaska | 63.1 |
| 47 | Mississippi | 61.7 |
| 48 | Louisiana | 61.3 |
| 49 | Maryland | 60.2 |
| 50 | Hawaii | 31.2 |
| | District of Columbia | 36.5 |

Source: Morgan Quitno Press using data from U.S. Bureau of the Census
"Projected State Populations, by Sex, Race, and Hispanic Origin: 1995-2025"
(http://www.census.gov/population/projections/state/stpjrace.txt)
*"White" is defined by Census as a person having origins in any of the original peoples of Europe, North Africa, or the Middle East.

# Projected Black Population 2025

## National Projected Total = 47,539,000 Black Persons*

ALPHA ORDER

RANK ORDER

| RANK | STATE | BLACKS | % of USA | RANK | STATE | BLACKS | % of USA |
|------|-------|--------|----------|------|-------|--------|----------|
| 16 | Alabama | 1,364,000 | 2.9% | 1 | New York | 4,048,000 | 8.5% |
| 41 | Alaska | 39,000 | 0.1% | 2 | Texas | 3,871,000 | 8.1% |
| 28 | Arizona | 285,000 | 0.6% | 3 | Florida | 3,556,000 | 7.5% |
| 24 | Arkansas | 468,000 | 1.0% | 4 | California | 3,426,000 | 7.2% |
| 4 | California | 3,426,000 | 7.2% | 5 | Georgia | 3,322,000 | 7.0% |
| 27 | Colorado | 309,000 | 0.6% | 6 | North Carolina | 2,244,000 | 4.7% |
| 23 | Connecticut | 490,000 | 1.0% | 7 | Illinois | 2,176,000 | 4.6% |
| 33 | Delaware | 199,000 | 0.4% | 8 | Maryland | 2,073,000 | 4.4% |
| 3 | Florida | 3,556,000 | 7.5% | 9 | Virginia | 1,973,000 | 4.2% |
| 5 | Georgia | 3,322,000 | 7.0% | 10 | Louisiana | 1,849,000 | 3.9% |
| 40 | Hawaii | 42,000 | 0.1% | 11 | New Jersey | 1,721,000 | 3.6% |
| 43 | Idaho | 17,000 | 0.0% | 12 | Michigan | 1,705,000 | 3.6% |
| 7 | Illinois | 2,176,000 | 4.6% | 13 | Ohio | 1,660,000 | 3.5% |
| 21 | Indiana | 615,000 | 1.3% | 14 | Pennsylvania | 1,530,000 | 3.2% |
| 36 | Iowa | 91,000 | 0.2% | 15 | South Carolina | 1,402,000 | 2.9% |
| 31 | Kansas | 249,000 | 0.5% | 16 | Alabama | 1,364,000 | 2.9% |
| 26 | Kentucky | 343,000 | 0.7% | 17 | Tennessee | 1,223,000 | 2.6% |
| 10 | Louisiana | 1,849,000 | 3.9% | 18 | Mississippi | 1,162,000 | 2.4% |
| 46 | Maine | 8,000 | 0.0% | 19 | Missouri | 800,000 | 1.7% |
| 8 | Maryland | 2,073,000 | 4.4% | 20 | Massachusetts | 655,000 | 1.4% |
| 20 | Massachusetts | 655,000 | 1.4% | 21 | Indiana | 615,000 | 1.3% |
| 12 | Michigan | 1,705,000 | 3.6% | 22 | Wisconsin | 501,000 | 1.1% |
| 29 | Minnesota | 279,000 | 0.6% | 23 | Connecticut | 490,000 | 1.0% |
| 18 | Mississippi | 1,162,000 | 2.4% | 24 | Arkansas | 468,000 | 1.0% |
| 19 | Missouri | 800,000 | 1.7% | 25 | Oklahoma | 433,000 | 0.9% |
| 48 | Montana | 6,000 | 0.0% | 26 | Kentucky | 343,000 | 0.7% |
| 34 | Nebraska | 109,000 | 0.2% | 27 | Colorado | 309,000 | 0.6% |
| 32 | Nevada | 202,000 | 0.4% | 28 | Arizona | 285,000 | 0.6% |
| 44 | New Hampshire | 14,000 | 0.0% | 29 | Minnesota | 279,000 | 0.6% |
| 11 | New Jersey | 1,721,000 | 3.6% | 29 | Washington | 279,000 | 0.6% |
| 38 | New Mexico | 89,000 | 0.2% | 31 | Kansas | 249,000 | 0.5% |
| 1 | New York | 4,048,000 | 8.5% | 32 | Nevada | 202,000 | 0.4% |
| 6 | North Carolina | 2,244,000 | 4.7% | 33 | Delaware | 199,000 | 0.4% |
| 50 | North Dakota | 5,000 | 0.0% | 34 | Nebraska | 109,000 | 0.2% |
| 13 | Ohio | 1,660,000 | 3.5% | 35 | Oregon | 101,000 | 0.2% |
| 25 | Oklahoma | 433,000 | 0.9% | 36 | Iowa | 91,000 | 0.2% |
| 35 | Oregon | 101,000 | 0.2% | 36 | Rhode Island | 91,000 | 0.2% |
| 14 | Pennsylvania | 1,530,000 | 3.2% | 38 | New Mexico | 89,000 | 0.2% |
| 36 | Rhode Island | 91,000 | 0.2% | 39 | West Virginia | 66,000 | 0.1% |
| 15 | South Carolina | 1,402,000 | 2.9% | 40 | Hawaii | 42,000 | 0.1% |
| 47 | South Dakota | 7,000 | 0.0% | 41 | Alaska | 39,000 | 0.1% |
| 17 | Tennessee | 1,223,000 | 2.6% | 41 | Utah | 39,000 | 0.1% |
| 2 | Texas | 3,871,000 | 8.1% | 43 | Idaho | 17,000 | 0.0% |
| 41 | Utah | 39,000 | 0.1% | 44 | New Hampshire | 14,000 | 0.0% |
| 48 | Vermont | 6,000 | 0.0% | 45 | Wyoming | 11,000 | 0.0% |
| 9 | Virginia | 1,973,000 | 4.2% | 46 | Maine | 8,000 | 0.0% |
| 29 | Washington | 279,000 | 0.6% | 47 | South Dakota | 7,000 | 0.0% |
| 39 | West Virginia | 66,000 | 0.1% | 48 | Montana | 6,000 | 0.0% |
| 22 | Wisconsin | 501,000 | 1.1% | 48 | Vermont | 6,000 | 0.0% |
| 45 | Wyoming | 11,000 | 0.0% | 50 | North Dakota | 5,000 | 0.0% |
| | | | | | District of Columbia | 386,000 | 0.8% |

*Source: U.S. Bureau of the Census*
*"Projected State Populations, by Sex, Race, and Hispanic Origin: 1995-2025 "*
*(http://www.census.gov/population/projections/state/stpjrace.txt)*
*\*"Black" is defined by Census as a person having origins in any of the Black racial groups of Africa.*

# Projected Percent of Population Black in 2025

## National Projected Percent = 14.2% Black*

| ALPHA ORDER | | | | RANK ORDER | | |
|---|---|---|---|---|---|---|
| RANK | STATE | PERCENT | | RANK | STATE | PERCENT |
| 6 | Alabama | 26.1 | | 1 | Mississippi | 37.0 |
| 34 | Alaska | 4.4 | | 2 | Louisiana | 36.0 |
| 34 | Arizona | 4.4 | | 3 | Georgia | 33.7 |
| 16 | Arkansas | 15.3 | | 4 | Maryland | 33.0 |
| 30 | California | 7.0 | | 5 | South Carolina | 30.2 |
| 31 | Colorado | 6.0 | | 6 | Alabama | 26.1 |
| 19 | Connecticut | 13.1 | | 7 | North Carolina | 24.0 |
| 9 | Delaware | 23.1 | | 8 | Virginia | 23.3 |
| 13 | Florida | 17.2 | | 9 | Delaware | 23.1 |
| 3 | Georgia | 33.7 | | 10 | New York | 20.4 |
| 40 | Hawaii | 2.3 | | 11 | Tennessee | 18.3 |
| 44 | Idaho | 1.0 | | 12 | New Jersey | 18.0 |
| 15 | Illinois | 16.2 | | 13 | Florida | 17.2 |
| 24 | Indiana | 9.4 | | 14 | Michigan | 16.9 |
| 39 | Iowa | 3.0 | | 15 | Illinois | 16.2 |
| 27 | Kansas | 8.0 | | 16 | Arkansas | 15.3 |
| 27 | Kentucky | 8.0 | | 17 | Texas | 14.2 |
| 2 | Louisiana | 36.0 | | 18 | Ohio | 14.1 |
| 49 | Maine | 0.6 | | 19 | Connecticut | 13.1 |
| 4 | Maryland | 33.0 | | 20 | Missouri | 12.8 |
| 23 | Massachusetts | 9.5 | | 21 | Pennsylvania | 12.1 |
| 14 | Michigan | 16.9 | | 22 | Oklahoma | 10.7 |
| 33 | Minnesota | 5.1 | | 23 | Massachusetts | 9.5 |
| 1 | Mississippi | 37.0 | | 24 | Indiana | 9.4 |
| 20 | Missouri | 12.8 | | 25 | Nevada | 8.7 |
| 50 | Montana | 0.5 | | 26 | Wisconsin | 8.5 |
| 32 | Nebraska | 5.6 | | 27 | Kansas | 8.0 |
| 25 | Nevada | 8.7 | | 27 | Kentucky | 8.0 |
| 44 | New Hampshire | 1.0 | | 27 | Rhode Island | 8.0 |
| 12 | New Jersey | 18.0 | | 30 | California | 7.0 |
| 38 | New Mexico | 3.4 | | 31 | Colorado | 6.0 |
| 10 | New York | 20.4 | | 32 | Nebraska | 5.6 |
| 7 | North Carolina | 24.0 | | 33 | Minnesota | 5.1 |
| 48 | North Dakota | 0.7 | | 34 | Alaska | 4.4 |
| 18 | Ohio | 14.1 | | 34 | Arizona | 4.4 |
| 22 | Oklahoma | 10.7 | | 36 | Washington | 3.6 |
| 40 | Oregon | 2.3 | | 36 | West Virginia | 3.6 |
| 21 | Pennsylvania | 12.1 | | 38 | New Mexico | 3.4 |
| 27 | Rhode Island | 8.0 | | 39 | Iowa | 3.0 |
| 5 | South Carolina | 30.2 | | 40 | Hawaii | 2.3 |
| 47 | South Dakota | 0.8 | | 40 | Oregon | 2.3 |
| 11 | Tennessee | 18.3 | | 42 | Wyoming | 1.6 |
| 17 | Texas | 14.2 | | 43 | Utah | 1.4 |
| 43 | Utah | 1.4 | | 44 | Idaho | 1.0 |
| 46 | Vermont | 0.9 | | 44 | New Hampshire | 1.0 |
| 8 | Virginia | 23.3 | | 46 | Vermont | 0.9 |
| 36 | Washington | 3.6 | | 47 | South Dakota | 0.8 |
| 36 | West Virginia | 3.6 | | 48 | North Dakota | 0.7 |
| 26 | Wisconsin | 8.5 | | 49 | Maine | 0.6 |
| 42 | Wyoming | 1.6 | | 50 | Montana | 0.5 |
| | | | | | District of Columbia | 58.9 |

*Source: Morgan Quitno Press using data from U.S. Bureau of the Census*
*"Projected State Populations, by Sex, Race, and Hispanic Origin: 1995-2025 "*
*(http://www.census.gov/population/projections/state/stpjrace.txt)*
*"Black" is defined by Census as a person having origins in any of the Black racial groups of Africa.*

# Projected Hispanic Population in 2025

## National Projected Total = 58,925,000 Hispanics*

ALPHA ORDER

| RANK | STATE | HISPANICS | % of USA |
|------|-------|-----------|----------|
| 39 | Alabama | 63,000 | 0.1% |
| 40 | Alaska | 59,000 | 0.1% |
| 6 | Arizona | 2,065,000 | 3.5% |
| 38 | Arkansas | 67,000 | 0.1% |
| 1 | California | 21,232,000 | 36.0% |
| 9 | Colorado | 1,067,000 | 1.8% |
| 14 | Connecticut | 574,000 | 1.0% |
| 42 | Delaware | 48,000 | 0.1% |
| 3 | Florida | 4,944,000 | 8.4% |
| 19 | Georgia | 346,000 | 0.6% |
| 30 | Hawaii | 186,000 | 0.3% |
| 28 | Idaho | 205,000 | 0.3% |
| 5 | Illinois | 2,275,000 | 3.9% |
| 24 | Indiana | 243,000 | 0.4% |
| 35 | Iowa | 96,000 | 0.2% |
| 21 | Kansas | 281,000 | 0.5% |
| 41 | Kentucky | 55,000 | 0.1% |
| 26 | Louisiana | 227,000 | 0.4% |
| 47 | Maine | 20,000 | 0.0% |
| 16 | Maryland | 438,000 | 0.7% |
| 10 | Massachusetts | 934,000 | 1.6% |
| 17 | Michigan | 431,000 | 0.7% |
| 29 | Minnesota | 193,000 | 0.3% |
| 43 | Mississippi | 39,000 | 0.1% |
| 32 | Missouri | 172,000 | 0.3% |
| 43 | Montana | 39,000 | 0.1% |
| 33 | Nebraska | 111,000 | 0.2% |
| 13 | Nevada | 583,000 | 1.0% |
| 45 | New Hampshire | 34,000 | 0.1% |
| 7 | New Jersey | 1,861,000 | 3.2% |
| 8 | New Mexico | 1,241,000 | 2.1% |
| 4 | New York | 4,309,000 | 7.3% |
| 27 | North Carolina | 210,000 | 0.4% |
| 48 | North Dakota | 14,000 | 0.0% |
| 20 | Ohio | 319,000 | 0.5% |
| 23 | Oklahoma | 245,000 | 0.4% |
| 18 | Oregon | 429,000 | 0.7% |
| 12 | Pennsylvania | 639,000 | 1.1% |
| 31 | Rhode Island | 176,000 | 0.3% |
| 36 | South Carolina | 81,000 | 0.1% |
| 48 | South Dakota | 14,000 | 0.0% |
| 34 | Tennessee | 104,000 | 0.2% |
| 2 | Texas | 10,230,000 | 17.4% |
| 22 | Utah | 265,000 | 0.4% |
| 50 | Vermont | 12,000 | 0.0% |
| 15 | Virginia | 538,000 | 0.9% |
| 11 | Washington | 797,000 | 1.4% |
| 46 | West Virginia | 24,000 | 0.0% |
| 25 | Wisconsin | 236,000 | 0.4% |
| 37 | Wyoming | 74,000 | 0.1% |

RANK ORDER

| RANK | STATE | HISPANICS | % of USA |
|------|-------|-----------|----------|
| 1 | California | 21,232,000 | 36.0% |
| 2 | Texas | 10,230,000 | 17.4% |
| 3 | Florida | 4,944,000 | 8.4% |
| 4 | New York | 4,309,000 | 7.3% |
| 5 | Illinois | 2,275,000 | 3.9% |
| 6 | Arizona | 2,065,000 | 3.5% |
| 7 | New Jersey | 1,861,000 | 3.2% |
| 8 | New Mexico | 1,241,000 | 2.1% |
| 9 | Colorado | 1,067,000 | 1.8% |
| 10 | Massachusetts | 934,000 | 1.6% |
| 11 | Washington | 797,000 | 1.4% |
| 12 | Pennsylvania | 639,000 | 1.1% |
| 13 | Nevada | 583,000 | 1.0% |
| 14 | Connecticut | 574,000 | 1.0% |
| 15 | Virginia | 538,000 | 0.9% |
| 16 | Maryland | 438,000 | 0.7% |
| 17 | Michigan | 431,000 | 0.7% |
| 18 | Oregon | 429,000 | 0.7% |
| 19 | Georgia | 346,000 | 0.6% |
| 20 | Ohio | 319,000 | 0.5% |
| 21 | Kansas | 281,000 | 0.5% |
| 22 | Utah | 265,000 | 0.4% |
| 23 | Oklahoma | 245,000 | 0.4% |
| 24 | Indiana | 243,000 | 0.4% |
| 25 | Wisconsin | 236,000 | 0.4% |
| 26 | Louisiana | 227,000 | 0.4% |
| 27 | North Carolina | 210,000 | 0.4% |
| 28 | Idaho | 205,000 | 0.3% |
| 29 | Minnesota | 193,000 | 0.3% |
| 30 | Hawaii | 186,000 | 0.3% |
| 31 | Rhode Island | 176,000 | 0.3% |
| 32 | Missouri | 172,000 | 0.3% |
| 33 | Nebraska | 111,000 | 0.2% |
| 34 | Tennessee | 104,000 | 0.2% |
| 35 | Iowa | 96,000 | 0.2% |
| 36 | South Carolina | 81,000 | 0.1% |
| 37 | Wyoming | 74,000 | 0.1% |
| 38 | Arkansas | 67,000 | 0.1% |
| 39 | Alabama | 63,000 | 0.1% |
| 40 | Alaska | 59,000 | 0.1% |
| 41 | Kentucky | 55,000 | 0.1% |
| 42 | Delaware | 48,000 | 0.1% |
| 43 | Mississippi | 39,000 | 0.1% |
| 43 | Montana | 39,000 | 0.1% |
| 45 | New Hampshire | 34,000 | 0.1% |
| 46 | West Virginia | 24,000 | 0.0% |
| 47 | Maine | 20,000 | 0.0% |
| 48 | North Dakota | 14,000 | 0.0% |
| 48 | South Dakota | 14,000 | 0.0% |
| 50 | Vermont | 12,000 | 0.0% |
| | District of Columbia | 80,000 | 0.1% |

*Source: U.S. Bureau of the Census*
  *"Projected State Populations, by Sex, Race, and Hispanic Origin: 1995-2025 "*
    *(http://www.census.gov/population/projections/state/stpjrace.txt)*
*Persons of Hispanic origin may be of any race.*

# Projected Percent of Population Hispanic in 2025

## National Projected Percent = 17.6% Hispanic*

<table>
<tr><td colspan="3">ALPHA ORDER</td><td colspan="3">RANK ORDER</td></tr>
<tr><th>RANK</th><th>STATE</th><th>PERCENT</th><th>RANK</th><th>STATE</th><th>PERCENT</th></tr>
<tr><td>49</td><td>Alabama</td><td>1.2</td><td>1</td><td>New Mexico</td><td>47.5</td></tr>
<tr><td>22</td><td>Alaska</td><td>6.7</td><td>2</td><td>California</td><td>43.1</td></tr>
<tr><td>4</td><td>Arizona</td><td>32.2</td><td>3</td><td>Texas</td><td>37.6</td></tr>
<tr><td>39</td><td>Arkansas</td><td>2.2</td><td>4</td><td>Arizona</td><td>32.2</td></tr>
<tr><td>2</td><td>California</td><td>43.1</td><td>5</td><td>Nevada</td><td>25.2</td></tr>
<tr><td>8</td><td>Colorado</td><td>20.6</td><td>6</td><td>Florida</td><td>23.9</td></tr>
<tr><td>11</td><td>Connecticut</td><td>15.4</td><td>7</td><td>New York</td><td>21.7</td></tr>
<tr><td>26</td><td>Delaware</td><td>5.6</td><td>8</td><td>Colorado</td><td>20.6</td></tr>
<tr><td>6</td><td>Florida</td><td>23.9</td><td>9</td><td>New Jersey</td><td>19.5</td></tr>
<tr><td>32</td><td>Georgia</td><td>3.5</td><td>10</td><td>Illinois</td><td>16.9</td></tr>
<tr><td>16</td><td>Hawaii</td><td>10.3</td><td>11</td><td>Connecticut</td><td>15.4</td></tr>
<tr><td>14</td><td>Idaho</td><td>11.8</td><td>11</td><td>Rhode Island</td><td>15.4</td></tr>
<tr><td>10</td><td>Illinois</td><td>16.9</td><td>13</td><td>Massachusetts</td><td>13.5</td></tr>
<tr><td>31</td><td>Indiana</td><td>3.7</td><td>14</td><td>Idaho</td><td>11.8</td></tr>
<tr><td>35</td><td>Iowa</td><td>3.2</td><td>15</td><td>Wyoming</td><td>10.7</td></tr>
<tr><td>20</td><td>Kansas</td><td>9.0</td><td>16</td><td>Hawaii</td><td>10.3</td></tr>
<tr><td>47</td><td>Kentucky</td><td>1.3</td><td>17</td><td>Washington</td><td>10.2</td></tr>
<tr><td>28</td><td>Louisiana</td><td>4.4</td><td>18</td><td>Oregon</td><td>9.9</td></tr>
<tr><td>46</td><td>Maine</td><td>1.4</td><td>19</td><td>Utah</td><td>9.2</td></tr>
<tr><td>21</td><td>Maryland</td><td>7.0</td><td>20</td><td>Kansas</td><td>9.0</td></tr>
<tr><td>13</td><td>Massachusetts</td><td>13.5</td><td>21</td><td>Maryland</td><td>7.0</td></tr>
<tr><td>29</td><td>Michigan</td><td>4.3</td><td>22</td><td>Alaska</td><td>6.7</td></tr>
<tr><td>32</td><td>Minnesota</td><td>3.5</td><td>23</td><td>Virginia</td><td>6.4</td></tr>
<tr><td>49</td><td>Mississippi</td><td>1.2</td><td>24</td><td>Oklahoma</td><td>6.0</td></tr>
<tr><td>36</td><td>Missouri</td><td>2.8</td><td>25</td><td>Nebraska</td><td>5.8</td></tr>
<tr><td>32</td><td>Montana</td><td>3.5</td><td>26</td><td>Delaware</td><td>5.6</td></tr>
<tr><td>25</td><td>Nebraska</td><td>5.8</td><td>27</td><td>Pennsylvania</td><td>5.0</td></tr>
<tr><td>5</td><td>Nevada</td><td>25.2</td><td>28</td><td>Louisiana</td><td>4.4</td></tr>
<tr><td>38</td><td>New Hampshire</td><td>2.4</td><td>29</td><td>Michigan</td><td>4.3</td></tr>
<tr><td>9</td><td>New Jersey</td><td>19.5</td><td>30</td><td>Wisconsin</td><td>4.0</td></tr>
<tr><td>1</td><td>New Mexico</td><td>47.5</td><td>31</td><td>Indiana</td><td>3.7</td></tr>
<tr><td>7</td><td>New York</td><td>21.7</td><td>32</td><td>Georgia</td><td>3.5</td></tr>
<tr><td>39</td><td>North Carolina</td><td>2.2</td><td>32</td><td>Minnesota</td><td>3.5</td></tr>
<tr><td>41</td><td>North Dakota</td><td>1.9</td><td>32</td><td>Montana</td><td>3.5</td></tr>
<tr><td>37</td><td>Ohio</td><td>2.7</td><td>35</td><td>Iowa</td><td>3.2</td></tr>
<tr><td>24</td><td>Oklahoma</td><td>6.0</td><td>36</td><td>Missouri</td><td>2.8</td></tr>
<tr><td>18</td><td>Oregon</td><td>9.9</td><td>37</td><td>Ohio</td><td>2.7</td></tr>
<tr><td>27</td><td>Pennsylvania</td><td>5.0</td><td>38</td><td>New Hampshire</td><td>2.4</td></tr>
<tr><td>11</td><td>Rhode Island</td><td>15.4</td><td>39</td><td>Arkansas</td><td>2.2</td></tr>
<tr><td>43</td><td>South Carolina</td><td>1.7</td><td>39</td><td>North Carolina</td><td>2.2</td></tr>
<tr><td>44</td><td>South Dakota</td><td>1.6</td><td>41</td><td>North Dakota</td><td>1.9</td></tr>
<tr><td>44</td><td>Tennessee</td><td>1.6</td><td>42</td><td>Vermont</td><td>1.8</td></tr>
<tr><td>3</td><td>Texas</td><td>37.6</td><td>43</td><td>South Carolina</td><td>1.7</td></tr>
<tr><td>19</td><td>Utah</td><td>9.2</td><td>44</td><td>South Dakota</td><td>1.6</td></tr>
<tr><td>42</td><td>Vermont</td><td>1.8</td><td>44</td><td>Tennessee</td><td>1.6</td></tr>
<tr><td>23</td><td>Virginia</td><td>6.4</td><td>46</td><td>Maine</td><td>1.4</td></tr>
<tr><td>17</td><td>Washington</td><td>10.2</td><td>47</td><td>Kentucky</td><td>1.3</td></tr>
<tr><td>47</td><td>West Virginia</td><td>1.3</td><td>47</td><td>West Virginia</td><td>1.3</td></tr>
<tr><td>30</td><td>Wisconsin</td><td>4.0</td><td>49</td><td>Alabama</td><td>1.2</td></tr>
<tr><td>15</td><td>Wyoming</td><td>10.7</td><td>49</td><td>Mississippi</td><td>1.2</td></tr>
<tr><td></td><td></td><td></td><td></td><td>District of Columbia</td><td>12.2</td></tr>
</table>

Source: Morgan Quitno Press using data from U.S. Bureau of the Census
"Projected State Populations, by Sex, Race, and Hispanic Origin: 1995-2025 "
(http://www.census.gov/population/projections/state/stpjrace.txt)
*Persons of Hispanic origin may be of any race.

# Projected Asian Population in 2025

## National Projected Total = 21,971,000 Asians*

<u>ALPHA ORDER</u>

| RANK | STATE | ASIANS | % of USA |
|---|---|---|---|
| 34 | Alabama | 57,000 | 0.3% |
| 21 | Alaska | 193,000 | 0.9% |
| 20 | Arizona | 195,000 | 0.9% |
| 39 | Arkansas | 32,000 | 0.1% |
| 1 | California | 9,078,000 | 41.3% |
| 19 | Colorado | 199,000 | 0.9% |
| 23 | Connecticut | 171,000 | 0.8% |
| 43 | Delaware | 27,000 | 0.1% |
| 9 | Florida | 526,000 | 2.4% |
| 16 | Georgia | 247,000 | 1.1% |
| 3 | Hawaii | 1,198,000 | 5.5% |
| 42 | Idaho | 29,000 | 0.1% |
| 6 | Illinois | 721,000 | 3.3% |
| 28 | Indiana | 100,000 | 0.5% |
| 32 | Iowa | 76,000 | 0.3% |
| 31 | Kansas | 84,000 | 0.4% |
| 37 | Kentucky | 46,000 | 0.2% |
| 25 | Louisiana | 115,000 | 0.5% |
| 45 | Maine | 19,000 | 0.1% |
| 12 | Maryland | 406,000 | 1.8% |
| 8 | Massachusetts | 534,000 | 2.4% |
| 13 | Michigan | 290,000 | 1.3% |
| 14 | Minnesota | 274,000 | 1.2% |
| 39 | Mississippi | 32,000 | 0.1% |
| 27 | Missouri | 102,000 | 0.5% |
| 46 | Montana | 14,000 | 0.1% |
| 38 | Nebraska | 42,000 | 0.2% |
| 24 | Nevada | 142,000 | 0.6% |
| 41 | New Hampshire | 30,000 | 0.1% |
| 5 | New Jersey | 995,000 | 4.5% |
| 34 | New Mexico | 57,000 | 0.3% |
| 2 | New York | 1,877,000 | 8.5% |
| 22 | North Carolina | 173,000 | 0.8% |
| 49 | North Dakota | 10,000 | 0.0% |
| 15 | Ohio | 250,000 | 1.1% |
| 30 | Oklahoma | 90,000 | 0.4% |
| 17 | Oregon | 215,000 | 1.0% |
| 11 | Pennsylvania | 410,000 | 1.9% |
| 33 | Rhode Island | 63,000 | 0.3% |
| 34 | South Carolina | 57,000 | 0.3% |
| 50 | South Dakota | 9,000 | 0.0% |
| 29 | Tennessee | 93,000 | 0.4% |
| 4 | Texas | 1,065,000 | 4.8% |
| 26 | Utah | 113,000 | 0.5% |
| 48 | Vermont | 11,000 | 0.1% |
| 10 | Virginia | 519,000 | 2.4% |
| 7 | Washington | 714,000 | 3.2% |
| 44 | West Virginia | 20,000 | 0.1% |
| 18 | Wisconsin | 210,000 | 1.0% |
| 47 | Wyoming | 12,000 | 0.1% |

<u>RANK ORDER</u>

| RANK | STATE | ASIANS | % of USA |
|---|---|---|---|
| 1 | California | 9,078,000 | 41.3% |
| 2 | New York | 1,877,000 | 8.5% |
| 3 | Hawaii | 1,198,000 | 5.5% |
| 4 | Texas | 1,065,000 | 4.8% |
| 5 | New Jersey | 995,000 | 4.5% |
| 6 | Illinois | 721,000 | 3.3% |
| 7 | Washington | 714,000 | 3.2% |
| 8 | Massachusetts | 534,000 | 2.4% |
| 9 | Florida | 526,000 | 2.4% |
| 10 | Virginia | 519,000 | 2.4% |
| 11 | Pennsylvania | 410,000 | 1.9% |
| 12 | Maryland | 406,000 | 1.8% |
| 13 | Michigan | 290,000 | 1.3% |
| 14 | Minnesota | 274,000 | 1.2% |
| 15 | Ohio | 250,000 | 1.1% |
| 16 | Georgia | 247,000 | 1.1% |
| 17 | Oregon | 215,000 | 1.0% |
| 18 | Wisconsin | 210,000 | 1.0% |
| 19 | Colorado | 199,000 | 0.9% |
| 20 | Arizona | 195,000 | 0.9% |
| 21 | Alaska | 193,000 | 0.9% |
| 22 | North Carolina | 173,000 | 0.8% |
| 23 | Connecticut | 171,000 | 0.8% |
| 24 | Nevada | 142,000 | 0.6% |
| 25 | Louisiana | 115,000 | 0.5% |
| 26 | Utah | 113,000 | 0.5% |
| 27 | Missouri | 102,000 | 0.5% |
| 28 | Indiana | 100,000 | 0.5% |
| 29 | Tennessee | 93,000 | 0.4% |
| 30 | Oklahoma | 90,000 | 0.4% |
| 31 | Kansas | 84,000 | 0.4% |
| 32 | Iowa | 76,000 | 0.3% |
| 33 | Rhode Island | 63,000 | 0.3% |
| 34 | Alabama | 57,000 | 0.3% |
| 34 | New Mexico | 57,000 | 0.3% |
| 34 | South Carolina | 57,000 | 0.3% |
| 37 | Kentucky | 46,000 | 0.2% |
| 38 | Nebraska | 42,000 | 0.2% |
| 39 | Arkansas | 32,000 | 0.1% |
| 39 | Mississippi | 32,000 | 0.1% |
| 41 | New Hampshire | 30,000 | 0.1% |
| 42 | Idaho | 29,000 | 0.1% |
| 43 | Delaware | 27,000 | 0.1% |
| 44 | West Virginia | 20,000 | 0.1% |
| 45 | Maine | 19,000 | 0.1% |
| 46 | Montana | 14,000 | 0.1% |
| 47 | Wyoming | 12,000 | 0.1% |
| 48 | Vermont | 11,000 | 0.1% |
| 49 | North Dakota | 10,000 | 0.0% |
| 50 | South Dakota | 9,000 | 0.0% |
| | District of Columbia | 29,000 | 0.1% |

Source: U.S. Bureau of the Census
"Projected State Populations, by Sex, Race, and Hispanic Origin: 1995-2025"
(http://www.census.gov/population/projections/state/stpjrace.txt)
*Includes Pacific Islanders.

# Projected Percent of Population Asian in 2025

## National Percent = 6.6% Asian*

ALPHA ORDER

| RANK | STATE | PERCENT |
|---|---|---|
| 45 | Alabama | 1.1 |
| 2 | Alaska | 21.8 |
| 22 | Arizona | 3.0 |
| 48 | Arkansas | 1.0 |
| 3 | California | 18.4 |
| 18 | Colorado | 3.8 |
| 15 | Connecticut | 4.6 |
| 21 | Delaware | 3.1 |
| 25 | Florida | 2.5 |
| 25 | Georgia | 2.5 |
| 1 | Hawaii | 66.1 |
| 35 | Idaho | 1.7 |
| 12 | Illinois | 5.4 |
| 39 | Indiana | 1.5 |
| 25 | Iowa | 2.5 |
| 24 | Kansas | 2.7 |
| 45 | Kentucky | 1.1 |
| 28 | Louisiana | 2.2 |
| 42 | Maine | 1.3 |
| 8 | Maryland | 6.5 |
| 7 | Massachusetts | 7.7 |
| 23 | Michigan | 2.9 |
| 13 | Minnesota | 5.0 |
| 48 | Mississippi | 1.0 |
| 37 | Missouri | 1.6 |
| 43 | Montana | 1.2 |
| 28 | Nebraska | 2.2 |
| 9 | Nevada | 6.1 |
| 32 | New Hampshire | 2.1 |
| 4 | New Jersey | 10.4 |
| 28 | New Mexico | 2.2 |
| 5 | New York | 9.5 |
| 34 | North Carolina | 1.9 |
| 40 | North Dakota | 1.4 |
| 32 | Ohio | 2.1 |
| 28 | Oklahoma | 2.2 |
| 14 | Oregon | 4.9 |
| 20 | Pennsylvania | 3.2 |
| 11 | Rhode Island | 5.5 |
| 43 | South Carolina | 1.2 |
| 48 | South Dakota | 1.0 |
| 40 | Tennessee | 1.4 |
| 16 | Texas | 3.9 |
| 16 | Utah | 3.9 |
| 37 | Vermont | 1.6 |
| 9 | Virginia | 6.1 |
| 6 | Washington | 9.1 |
| 45 | West Virginia | 1.1 |
| 19 | Wisconsin | 3.6 |
| 35 | Wyoming | 1.7 |

RANK ORDER

| RANK | STATE | PERCENT |
|---|---|---|
| 1 | Hawaii | 66.1 |
| 2 | Alaska | 21.8 |
| 3 | California | 18.4 |
| 4 | New Jersey | 10.4 |
| 5 | New York | 9.5 |
| 6 | Washington | 9.1 |
| 7 | Massachusetts | 7.7 |
| 8 | Maryland | 6.5 |
| 9 | Nevada | 6.1 |
| 9 | Virginia | 6.1 |
| 11 | Rhode Island | 5.5 |
| 12 | Illinois | 5.4 |
| 13 | Minnesota | 5.0 |
| 14 | Oregon | 4.9 |
| 15 | Connecticut | 4.6 |
| 16 | Texas | 3.9 |
| 16 | Utah | 3.9 |
| 18 | Colorado | 3.8 |
| 19 | Wisconsin | 3.6 |
| 20 | Pennsylvania | 3.2 |
| 21 | Delaware | 3.1 |
| 22 | Arizona | 3.0 |
| 23 | Michigan | 2.9 |
| 24 | Kansas | 2.7 |
| 25 | Florida | 2.5 |
| 25 | Georgia | 2.5 |
| 25 | Iowa | 2.5 |
| 28 | Louisiana | 2.2 |
| 28 | Nebraska | 2.2 |
| 28 | New Mexico | 2.2 |
| 28 | Oklahoma | 2.2 |
| 32 | New Hampshire | 2.1 |
| 32 | Ohio | 2.1 |
| 34 | North Carolina | 1.9 |
| 35 | Idaho | 1.7 |
| 35 | Wyoming | 1.7 |
| 37 | Missouri | 1.6 |
| 37 | Vermont | 1.6 |
| 39 | Indiana | 1.5 |
| 40 | North Dakota | 1.4 |
| 40 | Tennessee | 1.4 |
| 42 | Maine | 1.3 |
| 43 | Montana | 1.2 |
| 43 | South Carolina | 1.2 |
| 45 | Alabama | 1.1 |
| 45 | Kentucky | 1.1 |
| 45 | West Virginia | 1.1 |
| 48 | Arkansas | 1.0 |
| 48 | Mississippi | 1.0 |
| 48 | South Dakota | 1.0 |
|  | District of Columbia | 4.4 |

*Source: Morgan Quitno Press using data from U.S. Bureau of the Census*
*"Projected State Populations, by Sex, Race, and Hispanic Origin: 1995-2025 "*
*(http://www.census.gov/population/projections/state/stpjrace.txt)*
*\*Includes Pacific Islanders.*

# Projected American Indian Population in 2025

## National Projected Total = 3,317,000 American Indians*

ALPHA ORDER

ALPHA ORDER

| RANK | STATE | INDIANS | % of USA |
|------|-------|---------|----------|
| 32 | Alabama | 23,000 | 0.7% |
| 9 | Alaska | 95,000 | 2.9% |
| 3 | Arizona | 332,000 | 10.0% |
| 35 | Arkansas | 20,000 | 0.6% |
| 1 | California | 393,000 | 11.8% |
| 17 | Colorado | 61,000 | 1.8% |
| 40 | Connecticut | 11,000 | 0.3% |
| 48 | Delaware | 2,000 | 0.1% |
| 13 | Florida | 84,000 | 2.5% |
| 33 | Georgia | 21,000 | 0.6% |
| 43 | Hawaii | 8,000 | 0.2% |
| 23 | Idaho | 32,000 | 1.0% |
| 20 | Illinois | 39,000 | 1.2% |
| 36 | Indiana | 19,000 | 0.6% |
| 39 | Iowa | 14,000 | 0.4% |
| 21 | Kansas | 36,000 | 1.1% |
| 43 | Kentucky | 8,000 | 0.2% |
| 29 | Louisiana | 25,000 | 0.8% |
| 46 | Maine | 7,000 | 0.2% |
| 33 | Maryland | 21,000 | 0.6% |
| 36 | Massachusetts | 19,000 | 0.6% |
| 15 | Michigan | 72,000 | 2.2% |
| 8 | Minnesota | 104,000 | 3.1% |
| 43 | Mississippi | 8,000 | 0.2% |
| 23 | Missouri | 32,000 | 1.0% |
| 10 | Montana | 92,000 | 2.8% |
| 29 | Nebraska | 25,000 | 0.8% |
| 22 | Nevada | 34,000 | 1.0% |
| 47 | New Hampshire | 4,000 | 0.1% |
| 26 | New Jersey | 29,000 | 0.9% |
| 4 | New Mexico | 275,000 | 8.3% |
| 10 | New York | 92,000 | 2.8% |
| 7 | North Carolina | 110,000 | 3.3% |
| 18 | North Dakota | 59,000 | 1.8% |
| 25 | Ohio | 30,000 | 0.9% |
| 2 | Oklahoma | 367,000 | 11.1% |
| 14 | Oregon | 73,000 | 2.2% |
| 27 | Pennsylvania | 27,000 | 0.8% |
| 41 | Rhode Island | 10,000 | 0.3% |
| 41 | South Carolina | 10,000 | 0.3% |
| 12 | South Dakota | 89,000 | 2.7% |
| 38 | Tennessee | 18,000 | 0.5% |
| 5 | Texas | 159,000 | 4.8% |
| 18 | Utah | 59,000 | 1.8% |
| 48 | Vermont | 2,000 | 0.1% |
| 31 | Virginia | 24,000 | 0.7% |
| 6 | Washington | 151,000 | 4.6% |
| 48 | West Virginia | 2,000 | 0.1% |
| 16 | Wisconsin | 63,000 | 1.9% |
| 27 | Wyoming | 27,000 | 0.8% |

RANK ORDER

| RANK | STATE | INDIANS | % of USA |
|------|-------|---------|----------|
| 1 | California | 393,000 | 11.8% |
| 2 | Oklahoma | 367,000 | 11.1% |
| 3 | Arizona | 332,000 | 10.0% |
| 4 | New Mexico | 275,000 | 8.3% |
| 5 | Texas | 159,000 | 4.8% |
| 6 | Washington | 151,000 | 4.6% |
| 7 | North Carolina | 110,000 | 3.3% |
| 8 | Minnesota | 104,000 | 3.1% |
| 9 | Alaska | 95,000 | 2.9% |
| 10 | Montana | 92,000 | 2.8% |
| 10 | New York | 92,000 | 2.8% |
| 12 | South Dakota | 89,000 | 2.7% |
| 13 | Florida | 84,000 | 2.5% |
| 14 | Oregon | 73,000 | 2.2% |
| 15 | Michigan | 72,000 | 2.2% |
| 16 | Wisconsin | 63,000 | 1.9% |
| 17 | Colorado | 61,000 | 1.8% |
| 18 | North Dakota | 59,000 | 1.8% |
| 18 | Utah | 59,000 | 1.8% |
| 20 | Illinois | 39,000 | 1.2% |
| 21 | Kansas | 36,000 | 1.1% |
| 22 | Nevada | 34,000 | 1.0% |
| 23 | Idaho | 32,000 | 1.0% |
| 23 | Missouri | 32,000 | 1.0% |
| 25 | Ohio | 30,000 | 0.9% |
| 26 | New Jersey | 29,000 | 0.9% |
| 27 | Pennsylvania | 27,000 | 0.8% |
| 27 | Wyoming | 27,000 | 0.8% |
| 29 | Louisiana | 25,000 | 0.8% |
| 29 | Nebraska | 25,000 | 0.8% |
| 31 | Virginia | 24,000 | 0.7% |
| 32 | Alabama | 23,000 | 0.7% |
| 33 | Georgia | 21,000 | 0.6% |
| 33 | Maryland | 21,000 | 0.6% |
| 35 | Arkansas | 20,000 | 0.6% |
| 36 | Indiana | 19,000 | 0.6% |
| 36 | Massachusetts | 19,000 | 0.6% |
| 38 | Tennessee | 18,000 | 0.5% |
| 39 | Iowa | 14,000 | 0.4% |
| 40 | Connecticut | 11,000 | 0.3% |
| 41 | Rhode Island | 10,000 | 0.3% |
| 41 | South Carolina | 10,000 | 0.3% |
| 43 | Hawaii | 8,000 | 0.2% |
| 43 | Kentucky | 8,000 | 0.2% |
| 43 | Mississippi | 8,000 | 0.2% |
| 46 | Maine | 7,000 | 0.2% |
| 47 | New Hampshire | 4,000 | 0.1% |
| 48 | Delaware | 2,000 | 0.1% |
| 48 | Vermont | 2,000 | 0.1% |
| 48 | West Virginia | 2,000 | 0.1% |
| | District of Columbia | 0 | 0.0% |

Source: U.S. Bureau of the Census
"Projected State Populations, by Sex, Race, and Hispanic Origin: 1995-2025 "
(http://www.census.gov/population/projections/state/stpjrace.txt)
*Includes Eskimo and Aleut populations.

# Projected Percent of Population American Indian 2025

## National Projected Percent = 1.0% American Indian*

ALPHA ORDER

| RANK | STATE | PERCENT |
|---|---|---|
| 30 | Alabama | 0.4 |
| 1 | Alaska | 10.7 |
| 7 | Arizona | 5.2 |
| 22 | Arkansas | 0.7 |
| 21 | California | 0.8 |
| 16 | Colorado | 1.2 |
| 33 | Connecticut | 0.3 |
| 45 | Delaware | 0.2 |
| 30 | Florida | 0.4 |
| 45 | Georgia | 0.2 |
| 30 | Hawaii | 0.4 |
| 12 | Idaho | 1.8 |
| 33 | Illinois | 0.3 |
| 33 | Indiana | 0.3 |
| 25 | Iowa | 0.5 |
| 16 | Kansas | 1.2 |
| 45 | Kentucky | 0.2 |
| 25 | Louisiana | 0.5 |
| 25 | Maine | 0.5 |
| 33 | Maryland | 0.3 |
| 33 | Massachusetts | 0.3 |
| 22 | Michigan | 0.7 |
| 10 | Minnesota | 1.9 |
| 33 | Mississippi | 0.3 |
| 25 | Missouri | 0.5 |
| 5 | Montana | 8.2 |
| 15 | Nebraska | 1.3 |
| 14 | Nevada | 1.5 |
| 33 | New Hampshire | 0.3 |
| 33 | New Jersey | 0.3 |
| 2 | New Mexico | 10.5 |
| 25 | New York | 0.5 |
| 16 | North Carolina | 1.2 |
| 6 | North Dakota | 8.1 |
| 33 | Ohio | 0.3 |
| 4 | Oklahoma | 9.0 |
| 13 | Oregon | 1.7 |
| 45 | Pennsylvania | 0.2 |
| 20 | Rhode Island | 0.9 |
| 45 | South Carolina | 0.2 |
| 3 | South Dakota | 10.3 |
| 33 | Tennessee | 0.3 |
| 24 | Texas | 0.6 |
| 9 | Utah | 2.0 |
| 33 | Vermont | 0.3 |
| 33 | Virginia | 0.3 |
| 10 | Washington | 1.9 |
| 50 | West Virginia | 0.1 |
| 19 | Wisconsin | 1.1 |
| 8 | Wyoming | 3.9 |

RANK ORDER

| RANK | STATE | PERCENT |
|---|---|---|
| 1 | Alaska | 10.7 |
| 2 | New Mexico | 10.5 |
| 3 | South Dakota | 10.3 |
| 4 | Oklahoma | 9.0 |
| 5 | Montana | 8.2 |
| 6 | North Dakota | 8.1 |
| 7 | Arizona | 5.2 |
| 8 | Wyoming | 3.9 |
| 9 | Utah | 2.0 |
| 10 | Minnesota | 1.9 |
| 10 | Washington | 1.9 |
| 12 | Idaho | 1.8 |
| 13 | Oregon | 1.7 |
| 14 | Nevada | 1.5 |
| 15 | Nebraska | 1.3 |
| 16 | Colorado | 1.2 |
| 16 | Kansas | 1.2 |
| 16 | North Carolina | 1.2 |
| 19 | Wisconsin | 1.1 |
| 20 | Rhode Island | 0.9 |
| 21 | California | 0.8 |
| 22 | Arkansas | 0.7 |
| 22 | Michigan | 0.7 |
| 24 | Texas | 0.6 |
| 25 | Iowa | 0.5 |
| 25 | Louisiana | 0.5 |
| 25 | Maine | 0.5 |
| 25 | Missouri | 0.5 |
| 25 | New York | 0.5 |
| 30 | Alabama | 0.4 |
| 30 | Florida | 0.4 |
| 30 | Hawaii | 0.4 |
| 33 | Connecticut | 0.3 |
| 33 | Illinois | 0.3 |
| 33 | Indiana | 0.3 |
| 33 | Maryland | 0.3 |
| 33 | Massachusetts | 0.3 |
| 33 | Mississippi | 0.3 |
| 33 | New Hampshire | 0.3 |
| 33 | New Jersey | 0.3 |
| 33 | Ohio | 0.3 |
| 33 | Tennessee | 0.3 |
| 33 | Vermont | 0.3 |
| 33 | Virginia | 0.3 |
| 45 | Delaware | 0.2 |
| 45 | Georgia | 0.2 |
| 45 | Kentucky | 0.2 |
| 45 | Pennsylvania | 0.2 |
| 45 | South Carolina | 0.2 |
| 50 | West Virginia | 0.1 |
| | District of Columbia | 0.0 |

Source: Morgan Quitno Press using data from U.S. Bureau of the Census
"Projected State Populations, by Sex, Race, and Hispanic Origin: 1995-2025"
(http://www.census.gov/population/projections/state/stpjrace.txt)
*Includes Eskimo and Aleut populations.

# Median Age in 1999

## National Median = 35.5 Years Old

ALPHA ORDER

| RANK | STATE | MEDIAN AGE |
|------|-------|-----------|
| 21 | Alabama | 36.0 |
| 49 | Alaska | 30.9 |
| 41 | Arizona | 34.5 |
| 21 | Arkansas | 36.0 |
| 46 | California | 33.6 |
| 27 | Colorado | 35.7 |
| 7 | Connecticut | 37.0 |
| 24 | Delaware | 35.9 |
| 2 | Florida | 38.7 |
| 44 | Georgia | 34.0 |
| 9 | Hawaii | 36.9 |
| 47 | Idaho | 33.5 |
| 40 | Illinois | 35.2 |
| 34 | Indiana | 35.4 |
| 9 | Iowa | 36.9 |
| 34 | Kansas | 35.4 |
| 17 | Kentucky | 36.1 |
| 43 | Louisiana | 34.1 |
| 4 | Maine | 37.8 |
| 27 | Maryland | 35.7 |
| 13 | Massachusetts | 36.5 |
| 29 | Michigan | 35.5 |
| 34 | Minnesota | 35.4 |
| 45 | Mississippi | 33.7 |
| 17 | Missouri | 36.1 |
| 4 | Montana | 37.8 |
| 29 | Nebraska | 35.5 |
| 39 | Nevada | 35.3 |
| 24 | New Hampshire | 35.9 |
| 7 | New Jersey | 37.0 |
| 41 | New Mexico | 34.5 |
| 14 | New York | 36.4 |
| 29 | North Carolina | 35.5 |
| 15 | North Dakota | 36.2 |
| 17 | Ohio | 36.1 |
| 26 | Oklahoma | 35.8 |
| 9 | Oregon | 36.9 |
| 3 | Pennsylvania | 37.9 |
| 12 | Rhode Island | 36.6 |
| 29 | South Carolina | 35.5 |
| 34 | South Dakota | 35.4 |
| 15 | Tennessee | 36.2 |
| 48 | Texas | 33.0 |
| 50 | Utah | 26.7 |
| 6 | Vermont | 37.2 |
| 34 | Virginia | 35.4 |
| 29 | Washington | 35.5 |
| 1 | West Virginia | 38.9 |
| 21 | Wisconsin | 36.0 |
| 17 | Wyoming | 36.1 |

RANK ORDER

| RANK | STATE | MEDIAN AGE |
|------|-------|-----------|
| 1 | West Virginia | 38.9 |
| 2 | Florida | 38.7 |
| 3 | Pennsylvania | 37.9 |
| 4 | Maine | 37.8 |
| 4 | Montana | 37.8 |
| 6 | Vermont | 37.2 |
| 7 | Connecticut | 37.0 |
| 7 | New Jersey | 37.0 |
| 9 | Hawaii | 36.9 |
| 9 | Iowa | 36.9 |
| 9 | Oregon | 36.9 |
| 12 | Rhode Island | 36.6 |
| 13 | Massachusetts | 36.5 |
| 14 | New York | 36.4 |
| 15 | North Dakota | 36.2 |
| 15 | Tennessee | 36.2 |
| 17 | Kentucky | 36.1 |
| 17 | Missouri | 36.1 |
| 17 | Ohio | 36.1 |
| 17 | Wyoming | 36.1 |
| 21 | Alabama | 36.0 |
| 21 | Arkansas | 36.0 |
| 21 | Wisconsin | 36.0 |
| 24 | Delaware | 35.9 |
| 24 | New Hampshire | 35.9 |
| 26 | Oklahoma | 35.8 |
| 27 | Colorado | 35.7 |
| 27 | Maryland | 35.7 |
| 29 | Michigan | 35.5 |
| 29 | Nebraska | 35.5 |
| 29 | North Carolina | 35.5 |
| 29 | South Carolina | 35.5 |
| 29 | Washington | 35.5 |
| 34 | Indiana | 35.4 |
| 34 | Kansas | 35.4 |
| 34 | Minnesota | 35.4 |
| 34 | South Dakota | 35.4 |
| 34 | Virginia | 35.4 |
| 39 | Nevada | 35.3 |
| 40 | Illinois | 35.2 |
| 41 | Arizona | 34.5 |
| 41 | New Mexico | 34.5 |
| 43 | Louisiana | 34.1 |
| 44 | Georgia | 34.0 |
| 45 | Mississippi | 33.7 |
| 46 | California | 33.6 |
| 47 | Idaho | 33.5 |
| 48 | Texas | 33.0 |
| 49 | Alaska | 30.9 |
| 50 | Utah | 26.7 |
| | District of Columbia | 37.6 |

*Source: U.S. Bureau of the Census*
*"Population Estimates for the U.S., Regions, and States by Selected Age Groups and Sex" (ST-99-9, March 9, 2000)*
*(http://www.census.gov/population/estimates/state/st-99-09.txt)*

# Population Under 5 Years Old in 1999

## National Total = 18,942,142

ALPHA ORDER

ALPHA ORDER

| RANK | STATE | POPULATION | % of USA |
|---|---|---|---|
| 23 | Alabama | 290,833 | 1.5% |
| 47 | Alaska | 49,765 | 0.3% |
| 16 | Arizona | 385,988 | 2.0% |
| 34 | Arkansas | 177,649 | 0.9% |
| 1 | California | 2,499,258 | 13.2% |
| 24 | Colorado | 288,215 | 1.5% |
| 29 | Connecticut | 218,165 | 1.2% |
| 45 | Delaware | 50,165 | 0.3% |
| 4 | Florida | 952,374 | 5.0% |
| 9 | Georgia | 580,150 | 3.1% |
| 40 | Hawaii | 80,387 | 0.4% |
| 39 | Idaho | 92,835 | 0.5% |
| 5 | Illinois | 877,679 | 4.6% |
| 13 | Indiana | 413,675 | 2.2% |
| 33 | Iowa | 182,820 | 1.0% |
| 32 | Kansas | 184,013 | 1.0% |
| 25 | Kentucky | 259,093 | 1.4% |
| 22 | Louisiana | 314,150 | 1.7% |
| 42 | Maine | 67,218 | 0.4% |
| 19 | Maryland | 346,858 | 1.8% |
| 14 | Massachusetts | 392,240 | 2.1% |
| 8 | Michigan | 654,835 | 3.5% |
| 21 | Minnesota | 321,623 | 1.7% |
| 31 | Mississippi | 202,435 | 1.1% |
| 18 | Missouri | 363,041 | 1.9% |
| 44 | Montana | 53,060 | 0.3% |
| 37 | Nebraska | 114,802 | 0.6% |
| 35 | Nevada | 142,984 | 0.8% |
| 41 | New Hampshire | 73,915 | 0.4% |
| 10 | New Jersey | 543,263 | 2.9% |
| 36 | New Mexico | 131,400 | 0.7% |
| 3 | New York | 1,214,195 | 6.4% |
| 11 | North Carolina | 534,227 | 2.8% |
| 48 | North Dakota | 39,298 | 0.2% |
| 6 | Ohio | 740,212 | 3.9% |
| 27 | Oklahoma | 232,617 | 1.2% |
| 28 | Oregon | 219,601 | 1.2% |
| 7 | Pennsylvania | 712,092 | 3.8% |
| 43 | Rhode Island | 62,037 | 0.3% |
| 26 | South Carolina | 253,462 | 1.3% |
| 46 | South Dakota | 49,786 | 0.3% |
| 17 | Tennessee | 366,844 | 1.9% |
| 2 | Texas | 1,639,575 | 8.7% |
| 30 | Utah | 210,441 | 1.1% |
| 49 | Vermont | 32,036 | 0.2% |
| 12 | Virginia | 450,638 | 2.4% |
| 15 | Washington | 389,936 | 2.1% |
| 38 | West Virginia | 100,758 | 0.5% |
| 20 | Wisconsin | 331,822 | 1.8% |
| 50 | Wyoming | 30,377 | 0.2% |

RANK ORDER

| RANK | STATE | POPULATION | % of USA |
|---|---|---|---|
| 1 | California | 2,499,258 | 13.2% |
| 2 | Texas | 1,639,575 | 8.7% |
| 3 | New York | 1,214,195 | 6.4% |
| 4 | Florida | 952,374 | 5.0% |
| 5 | Illinois | 877,679 | 4.6% |
| 6 | Ohio | 740,212 | 3.9% |
| 7 | Pennsylvania | 712,092 | 3.8% |
| 8 | Michigan | 654,835 | 3.5% |
| 9 | Georgia | 580,150 | 3.1% |
| 10 | New Jersey | 543,263 | 2.9% |
| 11 | North Carolina | 534,227 | 2.8% |
| 12 | Virginia | 450,638 | 2.4% |
| 13 | Indiana | 413,675 | 2.2% |
| 14 | Massachusetts | 392,240 | 2.1% |
| 15 | Washington | 389,936 | 2.1% |
| 16 | Arizona | 385,988 | 2.0% |
| 17 | Tennessee | 366,844 | 1.9% |
| 18 | Missouri | 363,041 | 1.9% |
| 19 | Maryland | 346,858 | 1.8% |
| 20 | Wisconsin | 331,822 | 1.8% |
| 21 | Minnesota | 321,623 | 1.7% |
| 22 | Louisiana | 314,150 | 1.7% |
| 23 | Alabama | 290,833 | 1.5% |
| 24 | Colorado | 288,215 | 1.5% |
| 25 | Kentucky | 259,093 | 1.4% |
| 26 | South Carolina | 253,462 | 1.3% |
| 27 | Oklahoma | 232,617 | 1.2% |
| 28 | Oregon | 219,601 | 1.2% |
| 29 | Connecticut | 218,165 | 1.2% |
| 30 | Utah | 210,441 | 1.1% |
| 31 | Mississippi | 202,435 | 1.1% |
| 32 | Kansas | 184,013 | 1.0% |
| 33 | Iowa | 182,820 | 1.0% |
| 34 | Arkansas | 177,649 | 0.9% |
| 35 | Nevada | 142,984 | 0.8% |
| 36 | New Mexico | 131,400 | 0.7% |
| 37 | Nebraska | 114,802 | 0.6% |
| 38 | West Virginia | 100,758 | 0.5% |
| 39 | Idaho | 92,835 | 0.5% |
| 40 | Hawaii | 80,387 | 0.4% |
| 41 | New Hampshire | 73,915 | 0.4% |
| 42 | Maine | 67,218 | 0.4% |
| 43 | Rhode Island | 62,037 | 0.3% |
| 44 | Montana | 53,060 | 0.3% |
| 45 | Delaware | 50,165 | 0.3% |
| 46 | South Dakota | 49,786 | 0.3% |
| 47 | Alaska | 49,765 | 0.3% |
| 48 | North Dakota | 39,298 | 0.2% |
| 49 | Vermont | 32,036 | 0.2% |
| 50 | Wyoming | 30,377 | 0.2% |
| | District of Columbia | 27,300 | 0.1% |

*Source: U.S. Bureau of the Census*
*"Population Estimates for the U.S., Regions, and States by Selected Age Groups and Sex" (ST-99-9, March 9, 2000)*
*(http://www.census.gov/population/estimates/state/st-99-09.txt)*

# Percent Change in Population Under 5 Years Old: 1990 to 1999

## National Percent Change = 1.0% Increase*

ALPHA ORDER

| RANK | STATE | PERCENT CHANGE |
|------|-------|----------------|
| 22 | Alabama | 0.3 |
| 43 | Alaska | (11.1) |
| 2 | Arizona | 28.5 |
| 12 | Arkansas | 5.5 |
| 19 | California | 0.9 |
| 8 | Colorado | 12.2 |
| 33 | Connecticut | (6.5) |
| 21 | Delaware | 0.5 |
| 9 | Florida | 9.1 |
| 5 | Georgia | 14.6 |
| 31 | Hawaii | (5.9) |
| 7 | Idaho | 13.8 |
| 17 | Illinois | 1.3 |
| 14 | Indiana | 2.2 |
| 33 | Iowa | (6.5) |
| 27 | Kansas | (3.7) |
| 15 | Kentucky | 1.8 |
| 39 | Louisiana | (8.3) |
| 49 | Maine | (23.0) |
| 28 | Maryland | (5.0) |
| 35 | Massachusetts | (6.9) |
| 38 | Michigan | (8.2) |
| 30 | Minnesota | (5.8) |
| 18 | Mississippi | 1.1 |
| 25 | Missouri | (3.2) |
| 44 | Montana | (11.9) |
| 29 | Nebraska | (5.3) |
| 1 | Nevada | 51.4 |
| 46 | New Hampshire | (13.8) |
| 24 | New Jersey | (0.8) |
| 16 | New Mexico | 1.6 |
| 32 | New York | (6.0) |
| 6 | North Carolina | 13.9 |
| 48 | North Dakota | (19.0) |
| 36 | Ohio | (7.1) |
| 20 | Oklahoma | 0.8 |
| 11 | Oregon | 6.8 |
| 45 | Pennsylvania | (12.2) |
| 41 | Rhode Island | (9.4) |
| 26 | South Carolina | (3.6) |
| 42 | South Dakota | (10.0) |
| 10 | Tennessee | 7.9 |
| 4 | Texas | 15.4 |
| 3 | Utah | 22.2 |
| 50 | Vermont | (23.7) |
| 23 | Virginia | 0.0 |
| 13 | Washington | 4.2 |
| 36 | West Virginia | (7.1) |
| 40 | Wisconsin | (9.2) |
| 47 | Wyoming | (14.3) |

RANK ORDER

| RANK | STATE | PERCENT CHANGE |
|------|-------|----------------|
| 1 | Nevada | 51.4 |
| 2 | Arizona | 28.5 |
| 3 | Utah | 22.2 |
| 4 | Texas | 15.4 |
| 5 | Georgia | 14.6 |
| 6 | North Carolina | 13.9 |
| 7 | Idaho | 13.8 |
| 8 | Colorado | 12.2 |
| 9 | Florida | 9.1 |
| 10 | Tennessee | 7.9 |
| 11 | Oregon | 6.8 |
| 12 | Arkansas | 5.5 |
| 13 | Washington | 4.2 |
| 14 | Indiana | 2.2 |
| 15 | Kentucky | 1.8 |
| 16 | New Mexico | 1.6 |
| 17 | Illinois | 1.3 |
| 18 | Mississippi | 1.1 |
| 19 | California | 0.9 |
| 20 | Oklahoma | 0.8 |
| 21 | Delaware | 0.5 |
| 22 | Alabama | 0.3 |
| 23 | Virginia | 0.0 |
| 24 | New Jersey | (0.8) |
| 25 | Missouri | (3.2) |
| 26 | South Carolina | (3.6) |
| 27 | Kansas | (3.7) |
| 28 | Maryland | (5.0) |
| 29 | Nebraska | (5.3) |
| 30 | Minnesota | (5.8) |
| 31 | Hawaii | (5.9) |
| 32 | New York | (6.0) |
| 33 | Connecticut | (6.5) |
| 33 | Iowa | (6.5) |
| 35 | Massachusetts | (6.9) |
| 36 | Ohio | (7.1) |
| 36 | West Virginia | (7.1) |
| 38 | Michigan | (8.2) |
| 39 | Louisiana | (8.3) |
| 40 | Wisconsin | (9.2) |
| 41 | Rhode Island | (9.4) |
| 42 | South Dakota | (10.0) |
| 43 | Alaska | (11.1) |
| 44 | Montana | (11.9) |
| 45 | Pennsylvania | (12.2) |
| 46 | New Hampshire | (13.8) |
| 47 | Wyoming | (14.3) |
| 48 | North Dakota | (19.0) |
| 49 | Maine | (23.0) |
| 50 | Vermont | (23.7) |
| | District of Columbia | (29.0) |

*Source: Morgan Quitno Press using data from U.S. Bureau of the Census*
*"Estimates of the Population of the States by Selected Age Groups and Sex" (ST-99-9, March 9, 2000)*
*From April 1, 1990 to July 1, 1999.*

# Population 5 to 17 Years Old in 1999

## National Total = 51,257,293

ALPHA ORDER

| RANK | STATE | POPULATION | % of USA |
|---|---|---|---|
| 24 | Alabama | 775,344 | 1.5% |
| 46 | Alaska | 147,060 | 0.3% |
| 21 | Arizona | 948,576 | 1.9% |
| 34 | Arkansas | 482,575 | 0.9% |
| 1 | California | 6,424,165 | 12.5% |
| 23 | Colorado | 777,295 | 1.5% |
| 28 | Connecticut | 610,095 | 1.2% |
| 47 | Delaware | 132,285 | 0.3% |
| 4 | Florida | 2,617,504 | 5.1% |
| 9 | Georgia | 1,476,735 | 2.9% |
| 42 | Hawaii | 208,953 | 0.4% |
| 39 | Idaho | 257,629 | 0.5% |
| 5 | Illinois | 2,303,659 | 4.5% |
| 13 | Indiana | 1,115,316 | 2.2% |
| 31 | Iowa | 536,865 | 1.0% |
| 32 | Kansas | 514,624 | 1.0% |
| 25 | Kentucky | 706,435 | 1.4% |
| 22 | Louisiana | 875,851 | 1.7% |
| 41 | Maine | 223,221 | 0.4% |
| 19 | Maryland | 962,574 | 1.9% |
| 15 | Massachusetts | 1,076,314 | 2.1% |
| 8 | Michigan | 1,906,304 | 3.7% |
| 20 | Minnesota | 950,227 | 1.9% |
| 30 | Mississippi | 550,431 | 1.1% |
| 16 | Missouri | 1,036,451 | 2.0% |
| 44 | Montana | 170,759 | 0.3% |
| 37 | Nebraska | 328,998 | 0.6% |
| 36 | Nevada | 348,492 | 0.7% |
| 40 | New Hampshire | 230,521 | 0.4% |
| 10 | New Jersey | 1,459,941 | 2.8% |
| 35 | New Mexico | 364,212 | 0.7% |
| 3 | New York | 3,226,729 | 6.3% |
| 11 | North Carolina | 1,406,720 | 2.7% |
| 48 | North Dakota | 120,794 | 0.2% |
| 7 | Ohio | 2,103,859 | 4.1% |
| 27 | Oklahoma | 649,445 | 1.3% |
| 29 | Oregon | 607,900 | 1.2% |
| 6 | Pennsylvania | 2,140,428 | 4.2% |
| 43 | Rhode Island | 179,143 | 0.3% |
| 26 | South Carolina | 702,468 | 1.4% |
| 45 | South Dakota | 148,251 | 0.3% |
| 18 | Tennessee | 974,086 | 1.9% |
| 2 | Texas | 4,079,659 | 8.0% |
| 33 | Utah | 496,925 | 1.0% |
| 49 | Vermont | 107,310 | 0.2% |
| 12 | Virginia | 1,214,172 | 2.4% |
| 14 | Washington | 1,096,404 | 2.1% |
| 38 | West Virginia | 302,723 | 0.6% |
| 17 | Wisconsin | 1,016,446 | 2.0% |
| 50 | Wyoming | 96,430 | 0.2% |

RANK ORDER

| RANK | STATE | POPULATION | % of USA |
|---|---|---|---|
| 1 | California | 6,424,165 | 12.5% |
| 2 | Texas | 4,079,659 | 8.0% |
| 3 | New York | 3,226,729 | 6.3% |
| 4 | Florida | 2,617,504 | 5.1% |
| 5 | Illinois | 2,303,659 | 4.5% |
| 6 | Pennsylvania | 2,140,428 | 4.2% |
| 7 | Ohio | 2,103,859 | 4.1% |
| 8 | Michigan | 1,906,304 | 3.7% |
| 9 | Georgia | 1,476,735 | 2.9% |
| 10 | New Jersey | 1,459,941 | 2.8% |
| 11 | North Carolina | 1,406,720 | 2.7% |
| 12 | Virginia | 1,214,172 | 2.4% |
| 13 | Indiana | 1,115,316 | 2.2% |
| 14 | Washington | 1,096,404 | 2.1% |
| 15 | Massachusetts | 1,076,314 | 2.1% |
| 16 | Missouri | 1,036,451 | 2.0% |
| 17 | Wisconsin | 1,016,446 | 2.0% |
| 18 | Tennessee | 974,086 | 1.9% |
| 19 | Maryland | 962,574 | 1.9% |
| 20 | Minnesota | 950,227 | 1.9% |
| 21 | Arizona | 948,576 | 1.9% |
| 22 | Louisiana | 875,851 | 1.7% |
| 23 | Colorado | 777,295 | 1.5% |
| 24 | Alabama | 775,344 | 1.5% |
| 25 | Kentucky | 706,435 | 1.4% |
| 26 | South Carolina | 702,468 | 1.4% |
| 27 | Oklahoma | 649,445 | 1.3% |
| 28 | Connecticut | 610,095 | 1.2% |
| 29 | Oregon | 607,900 | 1.2% |
| 30 | Mississippi | 550,431 | 1.1% |
| 31 | Iowa | 536,865 | 1.0% |
| 32 | Kansas | 514,624 | 1.0% |
| 33 | Utah | 496,925 | 1.0% |
| 34 | Arkansas | 482,575 | 0.9% |
| 35 | New Mexico | 364,212 | 0.7% |
| 36 | Nevada | 348,492 | 0.7% |
| 37 | Nebraska | 328,998 | 0.6% |
| 38 | West Virginia | 302,723 | 0.6% |
| 39 | Idaho | 257,629 | 0.5% |
| 40 | New Hampshire | 230,521 | 0.4% |
| 41 | Maine | 223,221 | 0.4% |
| 42 | Hawaii | 208,953 | 0.4% |
| 43 | Rhode Island | 179,143 | 0.3% |
| 44 | Montana | 170,759 | 0.3% |
| 45 | South Dakota | 148,251 | 0.3% |
| 46 | Alaska | 147,060 | 0.3% |
| 47 | Delaware | 132,285 | 0.3% |
| 48 | North Dakota | 120,794 | 0.2% |
| 49 | Vermont | 107,310 | 0.2% |
| 50 | Wyoming | 96,430 | 0.2% |
|  | District of Columbia | 67,990 | 0.1% |

*Source: U.S. Bureau of the Census*
*"Population Estimates for the U.S., Regions, and States by Selected Age Groups and Sex" (ST-99-9, March 9, 2000)*
*(http://www.census.gov/population/estimates/state/st-99-09.txt)*

# Percent Change in Population 5 to 17 Years Old: 1990 to 1999

## National Percent Change = 13.5% Increase*

| ALPHA ORDER | | | RANK ORDER | | |
|---|---|---|---|---|---|
| RANK | STATE | PERCENT CHANGE | RANK | STATE | PERCENT CHANGE |
| 44 | Alabama | 0.1 | 1 | Nevada | 70.7 |
| 5 | Alaska | 25.8 | 2 | Arizona | 38.3 |
| 2 | Arizona | 38.3 | 3 | Florida | 30.2 |
| 36 | Arkansas | 6.0 | 4 | Colorado | 28.0 |
| 8 | California | 20.2 | 5 | Alaska | 25.8 |
| 4 | Colorado | 28.0 | 6 | Washington | 22.8 |
| 13 | Connecticut | 17.2 | 7 | North Carolina | 22.7 |
| 15 | Delaware | 15.7 | 8 | California | 20.2 |
| 3 | Florida | 30.2 | 9 | Georgia | 20.1 |
| 9 | Georgia | 20.1 | 10 | Maryland | 19.9 |
| 34 | Hawaii | 6.4 | 11 | New Hampshire | 18.8 |
| 21 | Idaho | 13.1 | 12 | Texas | 18.7 |
| 24 | Illinois | 9.9 | 13 | Connecticut | 17.2 |
| 37 | Indiana | 5.6 | 14 | Oregon | 16.6 |
| 42 | Iowa | 2.2 | 15 | Delaware | 15.7 |
| 27 | Kansas | 9.0 | 16 | New Jersey | 15.0 |
| 43 | Kentucky | 0.5 | 17 | Minnesota | 14.7 |
| 47 | Louisiana | (1.7) | 18 | Massachusetts | 14.5 |
| 44 | Maine | 0.1 | 18 | Virginia | 14.5 |
| 10 | Maryland | 19.9 | 20 | New Mexico | 13.9 |
| 18 | Massachusetts | 14.5 | 21 | Idaho | 13.1 |
| 29 | Michigan | 8.7 | 22 | Rhode Island | 12.9 |
| 17 | Minnesota | 14.7 | 23 | Tennessee | 10.4 |
| 44 | Mississippi | 0.1 | 24 | Illinois | 9.9 |
| 25 | Missouri | 9.8 | 25 | Missouri | 9.8 |
| 39 | Montana | 5.1 | 26 | Wisconsin | 9.7 |
| 33 | Nebraska | 6.5 | 27 | Kansas | 9.0 |
| 1 | Nevada | 70.7 | 28 | Utah | 8.8 |
| 11 | New Hampshire | 18.8 | 29 | Michigan | 8.7 |
| 16 | New Jersey | 15.0 | 30 | New York | 7.6 |
| 20 | New Mexico | 13.9 | 31 | Pennsylvania | 7.2 |
| 30 | New York | 7.6 | 32 | Oklahoma | 6.6 |
| 7 | North Carolina | 22.7 | 33 | Nebraska | 6.5 |
| 49 | North Dakota | (5.1) | 34 | Hawaii | 6.4 |
| 40 | Ohio | 4.6 | 35 | South Carolina | 6.1 |
| 32 | Oklahoma | 6.6 | 36 | Arkansas | 6.0 |
| 14 | Oregon | 16.6 | 37 | Indiana | 5.6 |
| 31 | Pennsylvania | 7.2 | 37 | Vermont | 5.6 |
| 22 | Rhode Island | 12.9 | 39 | Montana | 5.1 |
| 35 | South Carolina | 6.1 | 40 | Ohio | 4.6 |
| 41 | South Dakota | 3.2 | 41 | South Dakota | 3.2 |
| 23 | Tennessee | 10.4 | 42 | Iowa | 2.2 |
| 12 | Texas | 18.7 | 43 | Kentucky | 0.5 |
| 28 | Utah | 8.8 | 44 | Alabama | 0.1 |
| 37 | Vermont | 5.6 | 44 | Maine | 0.1 |
| 18 | Virginia | 14.5 | 44 | Mississippi | 0.1 |
| 6 | Washington | 22.8 | 47 | Louisiana | (1.7) |
| 50 | West Virginia | (10.1) | 48 | Wyoming | (4.1) |
| 26 | Wisconsin | 9.7 | 49 | North Dakota | (5.1) |
| 48 | Wyoming | (4.1) | 50 | West Virginia | (10.1) |
| | | | | District of Columbia | (15.2) |

Source: Morgan Quitno Press using data from U.S. Bureau of the Census
"Estimates of the Population of the States by Selected Age Groups and Sex" (ST-99-9, March 9, 2000)
*From April 1, 1990 to July 1, 1999.

# Population 18 Years Old and Older in 1999

## National Total = 202,491,378

ALPHA ORDER

| RANK | STATE | POPULATION | % of USA |
|---|---|---|---|
| 22 | Alabama | 3,303,685 | 1.6% |
| 49 | Alaska | 422,675 | 0.2% |
| 21 | Arizona | 3,443,768 | 1.7% |
| 33 | Arkansas | 1,891,149 | 0.9% |
| 1 | California | 24,221,698 | 12.0% |
| 25 | Colorado | 2,990,623 | 1.5% |
| 29 | Connecticut | 2,453,771 | 1.2% |
| 45 | Delaware | 571,088 | 0.3% |
| 4 | Florida | 11,541,366 | 5.7% |
| 10 | Georgia | 5,731,355 | 2.8% |
| 42 | Hawaii | 896,157 | 0.4% |
| 40 | Idaho | 901,236 | 0.4% |
| 6 | Illinois | 8,947,032 | 4.4% |
| 14 | Indiana | 4,413,910 | 2.2% |
| 30 | Iowa | 2,149,728 | 1.1% |
| 32 | Kansas | 1,955,415 | 1.0% |
| 24 | Kentucky | 2,995,297 | 1.5% |
| 23 | Louisiana | 3,182,034 | 1.6% |
| 39 | Maine | 962,601 | 0.5% |
| 19 | Maryland | 3,862,202 | 1.9% |
| 13 | Massachusetts | 4,706,615 | 2.3% |
| 8 | Michigan | 7,302,636 | 3.6% |
| 20 | Minnesota | 3,503,658 | 1.7% |
| 31 | Mississippi | 2,015,753 | 1.0% |
| 17 | Missouri | 4,068,846 | 2.0% |
| 44 | Montana | 658,960 | 0.3% |
| 38 | Nebraska | 1,222,228 | 0.6% |
| 36 | Nevada | 1,317,777 | 0.7% |
| 41 | New Hampshire | 896,698 | 0.4% |
| 9 | New Jersey | 6,140,208 | 3.0% |
| 37 | New Mexico | 1,244,232 | 0.6% |
| 3 | New York | 13,755,677 | 6.8% |
| 11 | North Carolina | 5,709,842 | 2.8% |
| 47 | North Dakota | 473,574 | 0.2% |
| 7 | Ohio | 8,412,583 | 4.2% |
| 28 | Oklahoma | 2,475,982 | 1.2% |
| 27 | Oregon | 2,488,653 | 1.2% |
| 5 | Pennsylvania | 9,141,496 | 4.5% |
| 43 | Rhode Island | 749,639 | 0.4% |
| 26 | South Carolina | 2,929,806 | 1.4% |
| 46 | South Dakota | 535,096 | 0.3% |
| 16 | Tennessee | 4,142,605 | 2.0% |
| 2 | Texas | 14,324,907 | 7.1% |
| 34 | Utah | 1,422,470 | 0.7% |
| 48 | Vermont | 454,394 | 0.2% |
| 12 | Virginia | 5,208,102 | 2.6% |
| 15 | Washington | 4,270,021 | 2.1% |
| 35 | West Virginia | 1,403,447 | 0.7% |
| 18 | Wisconsin | 3,902,178 | 1.9% |
| 50 | Wyoming | 352,795 | 0.2% |

RANK ORDER

| RANK | STATE | POPULATION | % of USA |
|---|---|---|---|
| 1 | California | 24,221,698 | 12.0% |
| 2 | Texas | 14,324,907 | 7.1% |
| 3 | New York | 13,755,677 | 6.8% |
| 4 | Florida | 11,541,366 | 5.7% |
| 5 | Pennsylvania | 9,141,496 | 4.5% |
| 6 | Illinois | 8,947,032 | 4.4% |
| 7 | Ohio | 8,412,583 | 4.2% |
| 8 | Michigan | 7,302,636 | 3.6% |
| 9 | New Jersey | 6,140,208 | 3.0% |
| 10 | Georgia | 5,731,355 | 2.8% |
| 11 | North Carolina | 5,709,842 | 2.8% |
| 12 | Virginia | 5,208,102 | 2.6% |
| 13 | Massachusetts | 4,706,615 | 2.3% |
| 14 | Indiana | 4,413,910 | 2.2% |
| 15 | Washington | 4,270,021 | 2.1% |
| 16 | Tennessee | 4,142,605 | 2.0% |
| 17 | Missouri | 4,068,846 | 2.0% |
| 18 | Wisconsin | 3,902,178 | 1.9% |
| 19 | Maryland | 3,862,202 | 1.9% |
| 20 | Minnesota | 3,503,658 | 1.7% |
| 21 | Arizona | 3,443,768 | 1.7% |
| 22 | Alabama | 3,303,685 | 1.6% |
| 23 | Louisiana | 3,182,034 | 1.6% |
| 24 | Kentucky | 2,995,297 | 1.5% |
| 25 | Colorado | 2,990,623 | 1.5% |
| 26 | South Carolina | 2,929,806 | 1.4% |
| 27 | Oregon | 2,488,653 | 1.2% |
| 28 | Oklahoma | 2,475,982 | 1.2% |
| 29 | Connecticut | 2,453,771 | 1.2% |
| 30 | Iowa | 2,149,728 | 1.1% |
| 31 | Mississippi | 2,015,753 | 1.0% |
| 32 | Kansas | 1,955,415 | 1.0% |
| 33 | Arkansas | 1,891,149 | 0.9% |
| 34 | Utah | 1,422,470 | 0.7% |
| 35 | West Virginia | 1,403,447 | 0.7% |
| 36 | Nevada | 1,317,777 | 0.7% |
| 37 | New Mexico | 1,244,232 | 0.6% |
| 38 | Nebraska | 1,222,228 | 0.6% |
| 39 | Maine | 962,601 | 0.5% |
| 40 | Idaho | 901,236 | 0.4% |
| 41 | New Hampshire | 896,698 | 0.4% |
| 42 | Hawaii | 896,157 | 0.4% |
| 43 | Rhode Island | 749,639 | 0.4% |
| 44 | Montana | 658,960 | 0.3% |
| 45 | Delaware | 571,088 | 0.3% |
| 46 | South Dakota | 535,096 | 0.3% |
| 47 | North Dakota | 473,574 | 0.2% |
| 48 | Vermont | 454,394 | 0.2% |
| 49 | Alaska | 422,675 | 0.2% |
| 50 | Wyoming | 352,795 | 0.2% |
| | District of Columbia | 423,710 | 0.2% |

Source: U.S. Bureau of the Census
"Population Estimates for the U.S., Regions, and States by Selected Age Groups and Sex" (ST-99-9, March 9, 2000)
(http://www.census.gov/population/estimates/state/st-99-09.txt)

# Percent of Population 18 Years Old and Older in 1999

## National Percent = 74.3% of Population*

ALPHA ORDER

RANK ORDER

| RANK | STATE | PERCENT | RANK | STATE | PERCENT |
|------|-------|---------|------|-------|---------|
| 10 | Alabama | 75.6 | 1 | West Virginia | 77.7 |
| 49 | Alaska | 68.2 | 2 | Maine | 76.8 |
| 45 | Arizona | 72.1 | 3 | Vermont | 76.5 |
| 30 | Arkansas | 74.1 | 4 | Florida | 76.4 |
| 40 | California | 73.1 | 5 | Massachusetts | 76.2 |
| 33 | Colorado | 73.7 | 5 | Pennsylvania | 76.2 |
| 19 | Connecticut | 74.8 | 7 | Delaware | 75.8 |
| 7 | Delaware | 75.8 | 7 | Virginia | 75.8 |
| 4 | Florida | 76.4 | 9 | Rhode Island | 75.7 |
| 36 | Georgia | 73.6 | 10 | Alabama | 75.6 |
| 10 | Hawaii | 75.6 | 10 | Hawaii | 75.6 |
| 46 | Idaho | 72.0 | 10 | Kentucky | 75.6 |
| 32 | Illinois | 73.8 | 10 | New York | 75.6 |
| 27 | Indiana | 74.3 | 14 | Tennessee | 75.5 |
| 18 | Iowa | 74.9 | 15 | New Jersey | 75.4 |
| 33 | Kansas | 73.7 | 15 | South Carolina | 75.4 |
| 10 | Kentucky | 75.6 | 17 | Oregon | 75.0 |
| 42 | Louisiana | 72.8 | 18 | Iowa | 74.9 |
| 2 | Maine | 76.8 | 19 | Connecticut | 74.8 |
| 20 | Maryland | 74.7 | 20 | Maryland | 74.7 |
| 5 | Massachusetts | 76.2 | 20 | New Hampshire | 74.7 |
| 31 | Michigan | 74.0 | 20 | North Dakota | 74.7 |
| 38 | Minnesota | 73.4 | 20 | Ohio | 74.7 |
| 42 | Mississippi | 72.8 | 24 | Montana | 74.6 |
| 26 | Missouri | 74.4 | 24 | North Carolina | 74.6 |
| 24 | Montana | 74.6 | 26 | Missouri | 74.4 |
| 38 | Nebraska | 73.4 | 27 | Indiana | 74.3 |
| 42 | Nevada | 72.8 | 27 | Wisconsin | 74.3 |
| 20 | New Hampshire | 74.7 | 29 | Washington | 74.2 |
| 15 | New Jersey | 75.4 | 30 | Arkansas | 74.1 |
| 47 | New Mexico | 71.5 | 31 | Michigan | 74.0 |
| 10 | New York | 75.6 | 32 | Illinois | 73.8 |
| 24 | North Carolina | 74.6 | 33 | Colorado | 73.7 |
| 20 | North Dakota | 74.7 | 33 | Kansas | 73.7 |
| 20 | Ohio | 74.7 | 33 | Oklahoma | 73.7 |
| 33 | Oklahoma | 73.7 | 36 | Georgia | 73.6 |
| 17 | Oregon | 75.0 | 36 | Wyoming | 73.6 |
| 5 | Pennsylvania | 76.2 | 38 | Minnesota | 73.4 |
| 9 | Rhode Island | 75.7 | 38 | Nebraska | 73.4 |
| 15 | South Carolina | 75.4 | 40 | California | 73.1 |
| 41 | South Dakota | 73.0 | 41 | South Dakota | 73.0 |
| 14 | Tennessee | 75.5 | 42 | Louisiana | 72.8 |
| 47 | Texas | 71.5 | 42 | Mississippi | 72.8 |
| 50 | Utah | 66.8 | 42 | Nevada | 72.8 |
| 3 | Vermont | 76.5 | 45 | Arizona | 72.1 |
| 7 | Virginia | 75.8 | 46 | Idaho | 72.0 |
| 29 | Washington | 74.2 | 47 | New Mexico | 71.5 |
| 1 | West Virginia | 77.7 | 47 | Texas | 71.5 |
| 27 | Wisconsin | 74.3 | 49 | Alaska | 68.2 |
| 36 | Wyoming | 73.6 | 50 | Utah | 66.8 |

District of Columbia 81.6

Source: Morgan Quitno Press using data from U.S. Bureau of the Census
"Population Estimates for the U.S., Regions, and States by Selected Age Groups and Sex" (ST-99-9, March 9, 2000)
(http://www.census.gov/population/estimates/state/st-99-09.txt)

# Population 18 to 24 Years Old in 1999

## National Total = 26,011,449

ALPHA ORDER

ALPHA ORDER

RANK ORDER

| RANK | STATE | POPULATION | % of USA |
|------|-------|-----------:|----------|
| 23 | Alabama | 439,534 | 1.7% |
| 46 | Alaska | 70,923 | 0.3% |
| 20 | Arizona | 459,678 | 1.8% |
| 34 | Arkansas | 251,473 | 1.0% |
| 1 | California | 3,318,684 | 12.8% |
| 25 | Colorado | 392,703 | 1.5% |
| 33 | Connecticut | 255,714 | 1.0% |
| 47 | Delaware | 69,255 | 0.3% |
| 4 | Florida | 1,235,957 | 4.8% |
| 9 | Georgia | 773,918 | 3.0% |
| 40 | Hawaii | 119,733 | 0.5% |
| 39 | Idaho | 143,975 | 0.6% |
| 5 | Illinois | 1,143,197 | 4.4% |
| 13 | Indiana | 576,310 | 2.2% |
| 31 | Iowa | 282,178 | 1.1% |
| 32 | Kansas | 271,382 | 1.0% |
| 24 | Kentucky | 404,621 | 1.6% |
| 19 | Louisiana | 481,018 | 1.8% |
| 41 | Maine | 110,630 | 0.4% |
| 22 | Maryland | 441,978 | 1.7% |
| 17 | Massachusetts | 512,732 | 2.0% |
| 8 | Michigan | 927,893 | 3.6% |
| 21 | Minnesota | 454,001 | 1.7% |
| 29 | Mississippi | 302,471 | 1.2% |
| 15 | Missouri | 520,487 | 2.0% |
| 43 | Montana | 89,389 | 0.3% |
| 37 | Nebraska | 170,141 | 0.7% |
| 38 | Nevada | 155,758 | 0.6% |
| 42 | New Hampshire | 98,125 | 0.4% |
| 12 | New Jersey | 672,511 | 2.6% |
| 36 | New Mexico | 176,216 | 0.7% |
| 3 | New York | 1,618,762 | 6.2% |
| 10 | North Carolina | 709,470 | 2.7% |
| 48 | North Dakota | 68,507 | 0.3% |
| 6 | Ohio | 1,065,274 | 4.1% |
| 27 | Oklahoma | 342,931 | 1.3% |
| 28 | Oregon | 311,544 | 1.2% |
| 7 | Pennsylvania | 1,025,209 | 3.9% |
| 44 | Rhode Island | 83,921 | 0.3% |
| 26 | South Carolina | 392,508 | 1.5% |
| 45 | South Dakota | 78,159 | 0.3% |
| 16 | Tennessee | 519,799 | 2.0% |
| 2 | Texas | 2,100,197 | 8.1% |
| 30 | Utah | 300,984 | 1.2% |
| 50 | Vermont | 53,195 | 0.2% |
| 11 | Virginia | 673,268 | 2.6% |
| 14 | Washington | 557,946 | 2.1% |
| 35 | West Virginia | 179,418 | 0.7% |
| 18 | Wisconsin | 508,317 | 2.0% |
| 49 | Wyoming | 53,784 | 0.2% |

| RANK | STATE | POPULATION | % of USA |
|------|-------|-----------:|----------|
| 1 | California | 3,3˙8,684 | 12.8% |
| 2 | Texas | 2,100,197 | 8.1% |
| 3 | New York | 1,618,762 | 6.2% |
| 4 | Florida | 1,235,957 | 4.8% |
| 5 | Illinois | 1,143,197 | 4.4% |
| 6 | Ohio | 1,065,274 | 4.1% |
| 7 | Pennsylvania | 1,025,209 | 3.9% |
| 8 | Michigan | 927,893 | 3.6% |
| 9 | Georgia | 773,918 | 3.0% |
| 10 | North Carolina | 709,470 | 2.7% |
| 11 | Virginia | 673,268 | 2.6% |
| 12 | New Jersey | 672,511 | 2.6% |
| 13 | Indiana | 576,310 | 2.2% |
| 14 | Washington | 557,946 | 2.1% |
| 15 | Missouri | 520,487 | 2.0% |
| 16 | Tennessee | 519,799 | 2.0% |
| 17 | Massachusetts | 512,732 | 2.0% |
| 18 | Wisconsin | 508,317 | 2.0% |
| 19 | Louisiana | 481,018 | 1.8% |
| 20 | Arizona | 459,678 | 1.8% |
| 21 | Minnesota | 454,001 | 1.7% |
| 22 | Maryland | 441,978 | 1.7% |
| 23 | Alabama | 439,534 | 1.7% |
| 24 | Kentucky | 404,621 | 1.6% |
| 25 | Colorado | 392,703 | 1.5% |
| 26 | South Carolina | 392,508 | 1.5% |
| 27 | Oklahoma | 342,931 | 1.3% |
| 28 | Oregon | 311,544 | 1.2% |
| 29 | Mississippi | 302,471 | 1.2% |
| 30 | Utah | 300,984 | 1.2% |
| 31 | Iowa | 282,178 | 1.1% |
| 32 | Kansas | 271,382 | 1.0% |
| 33 | Connecticut | 255,714 | 1.0% |
| 34 | Arkansas | 251,473 | 1.0% |
| 35 | West Virginia | 179,418 | 0.7% |
| 36 | New Mexico | 176,216 | 0.7% |
| 37 | Nebraska | 170,141 | 0.7% |
| 38 | Nevada | 155,758 | 0.6% |
| 39 | Idaho | 143,975 | 0.6% |
| 40 | Hawaii | 119,733 | 0.5% |
| 41 | Maine | 110,630 | 0.4% |
| 42 | New Hampshire | 98,125 | 0.4% |
| 43 | Montana | 89,389 | 0.3% |
| 44 | Rhode Island | 83,921 | 0.3% |
| 45 | South Dakota | 78,159 | 0.3% |
| 46 | Alaska | 70,923 | 0.3% |
| 47 | Delaware | 69,255 | 0.3% |
| 48 | North Dakota | 68,507 | 0.3% |
| 49 | Wyoming | 53,784 | 0.2% |
| 50 | Vermont | 53,195 | 0.2% |
|  | District of Columbia | 45,671 | 0.2% |

Source: U.S. Bureau of the Census
"Population Estimates for the U.S., Regions, and States by Selected Age Groups and Sex" (ST-99-9, March 9, 2000)
(http://www.census.gov/population/estimates/state/st-99-09.txt)

# Percent Change in Population 18 to 24 Years Old: 1990 to 1999

## National Percent Change = 3.5% Decrease*

| ALPHA ORDER | | | RANK ORDER | | |
|---|---|---|---|---|---|
| RANK | STATE | PERCENT CHANGE | RANK | STATE | PERCENT CHANGE |
| 29 | Alabama | (1.3) | 1 | Utah | 50.0 |
| 6 | Alaska | 25.2 | 2 | Idaho | 46.3 |
| 7 | Arizona | 16.1 | 3 | Wyoming | 29.3 |
| 17 | Arkansas | 5.7 | 4 | Nevada | 29.0 |
| 33 | California | (4.1) | 5 | Montana | 27.3 |
| 7 | Colorado | 16.1 | 6 | Alaska | 25.2 |
| 48 | Connecticut | (26.7) | 7 | Arizona | 16.1 |
| 39 | Delaware | (9.9) | 7 | Colorado | 16.1 |
| 22 | Florida | 0.7 | 9 | Oregon | 15.7 |
| 18 | Georgia | 4.0 | 10 | New Mexico | 15.4 |
| 31 | Hawaii | (2.3) | 11 | South Dakota | 14.3 |
| 2 | Idaho | 46.3 | 12 | Washington | 13.3 |
| 35 | Illinois | (6.4) | 13 | Texas | 10.4 |
| 34 | Indiana | (5.1) | 14 | Nebraska | 8.6 |
| 27 | Iowa | (0.9) | 15 | Oklahoma | 6.2 |
| 16 | Kansas | 6.0 | 16 | Kansas | 6.0 |
| 23 | Kentucky | 0.5 | 17 | Arkansas | 5.7 |
| 19 | Louisiana | 3.1 | 18 | Georgia | 4.0 |
| 41 | Maine | (11.0) | 19 | Louisiana | 3.1 |
| 42 | Maryland | (13.4) | 20 | Mississippi | 2.8 |
| 49 | Massachusetts | (28.5) | 21 | Minnesota | 2.0 |
| 38 | Michigan | (8.0) | 22 | Florida | 0.7 |
| 21 | Minnesota | 2.0 | 23 | Kentucky | 0.5 |
| 20 | Mississippi | 2.8 | 24 | North Dakota | 0.3 |
| 25 | Missouri | 0.2 | 25 | Missouri | 0.2 |
| 5 | Montana | 27.3 | 26 | West Virginia | (0.5) |
| 14 | Nebraska | 8.6 | 27 | Iowa | (0.9) |
| 4 | Nevada | 29.0 | 28 | Wisconsin | (1.2) |
| 46 | New Hampshire | (17.2) | 29 | Alabama | (1.3) |
| 43 | New Jersey | (14.9) | 30 | Tennessee | (2.0) |
| 10 | New Mexico | 15.4 | 31 | Hawaii | (2.3) |
| 47 | New York | (18.2) | 32 | South Carolina | (4.0) |
| 40 | North Carolina | (10.0) | 33 | California | (4.1) |
| 24 | North Dakota | 0.3 | 34 | Indiana | (5.1) |
| 36 | Ohio | (6.6) | 35 | Illinois | (6.4) |
| 15 | Oklahoma | 6.2 | 36 | Ohio | (6.6) |
| 9 | Oregon | 15.7 | 37 | Virginia | (7.3) |
| 45 | Pennsylvania | (17.0) | 38 | Michigan | (8.0) |
| 50 | Rhode Island | (30.8) | 39 | Delaware | (9.9) |
| 32 | South Carolina | (4.0) | 40 | North Carolina | (10.0) |
| 11 | South Dakota | 14.3 | 41 | Maine | (11.0) |
| 30 | Tennessee | (2.0) | 42 | Maryland | (13.4) |
| 13 | Texas | 10.4 | 43 | New Jersey | (14.9) |
| 1 | Utah | 50.0 | 44 | Vermont | (16.3) |
| 44 | Vermont | (16.3) | 45 | Pennsylvania | (17.0) |
| 37 | Virginia | (7.3) | 46 | New Hampshire | (17.2) |
| 12 | Washington | 13.3 | 47 | New York | (18.2) |
| 26 | West Virginia | (0.5) | 48 | Connecticut | (26.7) |
| 28 | Wisconsin | (1.2) | 49 | Massachusetts | (28.5) |
| 3 | Wyoming | 29.3 | 50 | Rhode Island | (30.8) |
| | | | | District of Columbia | (45.2) |

Source: Morgan Quitno Press using data from U.S. Bureau of the Census
    "Estimates of the Population of the States by Selected Age Groups and Sex" (ST-99-9, March 9, 2000)
*From April 1, 1990 to July 1, 1999.

# Population 25 to 44 Years Old in 1999

## National Total = 82,748,461

ALPHA ORDER

| RANK | STATE | POPULATION | % of USA |
|------|-------|-----------|----------|
| 22 | Alabama | 1,307,387 | 1.6% |
| 48 | Alaska | 178,632 | 0.2% |
| 21 | Arizona | 1,364,930 | 1.6% |
| 33 | Arkansas | 706,286 | 0.9% |
| 1 | California | 10,707,327 | 12.9% |
| 24 | Colorado | 1,222,649 | 1.5% |
| 27 | Connecticut | 1,010,142 | 1.2% |
| 44 | Delaware | 243,440 | 0.3% |
| 4 | Florida | 4,238,337 | 5.1% |
| 9 | Georgia | 2,543,095 | 3.1% |
| 41 | Hawaii | 345,029 | 0.4% |
| 42 | Idaho | 340,915 | 0.4% |
| 5 | Illinois | 3,704,773 | 4.5% |
| 14 | Indiana | 1,786,877 | 2.2% |
| 30 | Iowa | 797,177 | 1.0% |
| 32 | Kansas | 767,666 | 0.9% |
| 26 | Kentucky | 1,183,166 | 1.4% |
| 23 | Louisiana | 1,246,875 | 1.5% |
| 40 | Maine | 384,752 | 0.5% |
| 16 | Maryland | 1,697,871 | 2.1% |
| 13 | Massachusetts | 1,995,953 | 2.4% |
| 8 | Michigan | 2,994,551 | 3.6% |
| 20 | Minnesota | 1,442,600 | 1.7% |
| 31 | Mississippi | 795,404 | 1.0% |
| 18 | Missouri | 1,610,880 | 1.9% |
| 45 | Montana | 231,490 | 0.3% |
| 38 | Nebraska | 467,472 | 0.6% |
| 35 | Nevada | 545,126 | 0.7% |
| 39 | New Hampshire | 400,851 | 0.5% |
| 10 | New Jersey | 2,532,018 | 3.1% |
| 37 | New Mexico | 488,961 | 0.6% |
| 3 | New York | 5,644,373 | 6.8% |
| 11 | North Carolina | 2,351,743 | 2.8% |
| 49 | North Dakota | 175,142 | 0.2% |
| 7 | Ohio | 3,359,012 | 4.1% |
| 29 | Oklahoma | 925,817 | 1.1% |
| 28 | Oregon | 951,665 | 1.2% |
| 6 | Pennsylvania | 3,515,421 | 4.2% |
| 43 | Rhode Island | 308,082 | 0.4% |
| 25 | South Carolina | 1,189,420 | 1.4% |
| 46 | South Dakota | 198,201 | 0.2% |
| 17 | Tennessee | 1,673,697 | 2.0% |
| 2 | Texas | 6,033,741 | 7.3% |
| 34 | Utah | 572,493 | 0.7% |
| 47 | Vermont | 187,907 | 0.2% |
| 12 | Virginia | 2,241,185 | 2.7% |
| 15 | Washington | 1,774,957 | 2.1% |
| 36 | West Virginia | 496,143 | 0.6% |
| 19 | Wisconsin | 1,556,187 | 1.9% |
| 50 | Wyoming | 126,918 | 0.2% |

RANK ORDER

| RANK | STATE | POPULATION | % of USA |
|------|-------|-----------|----------|
| 1 | California | 10,707,327 | 12.9% |
| 2 | Texas | 6,033,741 | 7.3% |
| 3 | New York | 5,644,373 | 6.8% |
| 4 | Florida | 4,238,337 | 5.1% |
| 5 | Illinois | 3,704,773 | 4.5% |
| 6 | Pennsylvania | 3,515,421 | 4.2% |
| 7 | Ohio | 3,359,012 | 4.1% |
| 8 | Michigan | 2,994,551 | 3.6% |
| 9 | Georgia | 2,543,095 | 3.1% |
| 10 | New Jersey | 2,532,018 | 3.1% |
| 11 | North Carolina | 2,351,743 | 2.8% |
| 12 | Virginia | 2,241,185 | 2.7% |
| 13 | Massachusetts | 1,995,953 | 2.4% |
| 14 | Indiana | 1,786,877 | 2.2% |
| 15 | Washington | 1,774,957 | 2.1% |
| 16 | Maryland | 1,697,871 | 2.1% |
| 17 | Tennessee | 1,673,697 | 2.0% |
| 18 | Missouri | 1,610,880 | 1.9% |
| 19 | Wisconsin | 1,556,187 | 1.9% |
| 20 | Minnesota | 1,442,600 | 1.7% |
| 21 | Arizona | 1,364,930 | 1.6% |
| 22 | Alabama | 1,307,387 | 1.6% |
| 23 | Louisiana | 1,246,875 | 1.5% |
| 24 | Colorado | 1,222,649 | 1.5% |
| 25 | South Carolina | 1,189,420 | 1.4% |
| 26 | Kentucky | 1,183,166 | 1.4% |
| 27 | Connecticut | 1,010,142 | 1.2% |
| 28 | Oregon | 951,665 | 1.2% |
| 29 | Oklahoma | 925,817 | 1.1% |
| 30 | Iowa | 797,177 | 1.0% |
| 31 | Mississippi | 795,404 | 1.0% |
| 32 | Kansas | 767,666 | 0.9% |
| 33 | Arkansas | 706,286 | 0.9% |
| 34 | Utah | 572,493 | 0.7% |
| 35 | Nevada | 545,126 | 0.7% |
| 36 | West Virginia | 496,143 | 0.6% |
| 37 | New Mexico | 488,961 | 0.6% |
| 38 | Nebraska | 467,472 | 0.6% |
| 39 | New Hampshire | 400,851 | 0.5% |
| 40 | Maine | 384,752 | 0.5% |
| 41 | Hawaii | 345,029 | 0.4% |
| 42 | Idaho | 340,915 | 0.4% |
| 43 | Rhode Island | 308,082 | 0.4% |
| 44 | Delaware | 243,440 | 0.3% |
| 45 | Montana | 231,490 | 0.3% |
| 46 | South Dakota | 198,201 | 0.2% |
| 47 | Vermont | 187,907 | 0.2% |
| 48 | Alaska | 178,632 | 0.2% |
| 49 | North Dakota | 175,142 | 0.2% |
| 50 | Wyoming | 126,918 | 0.2% |
| | District of Columbia | 183,725 | 0.2% |

*Source: U.S. Bureau of the Census*
*"Population Estimates for the U.S., Regions, and States by Selected Age Groups and Sex" (ST-99-9, March 9, 2000)*
*(http://www.census.gov/population/estimates/state/st-99-09.txt)*

473

# Percent Change in Population 25 to 44 Years Old: 1990 to 1999

## National Percent Change = 2.7% Increase*

ALPHA ORDER

| RANK | STATE | PERCENT CHANGE |
|------|-------|----------------|
| 13 | Alabama | 6.3 |
| 50 | Alaska | (17.3) |
| 2 | Arizona | 17.6 |
| 19 | Arkansas | 3.1 |
| 16 | California | 4.1 |
| 17 | Colorado | 3.8 |
| 46 | Connecticut | (7.5) |
| 6 | Delaware | 12.0 |
| 8 | Florida | 8.1 |
| 3 | Georgia | 16.4 |
| 47 | Hawaii | (8.8) |
| 5 | Idaho | 12.9 |
| 28 | Illinois | 0.5 |
| 19 | Indiana | 3.1 |
| 36 | Iowa | (3.1) |
| 31 | Kansas | (0.8) |
| 22 | Kentucky | 2.2 |
| 43 | Louisiana | (4.7) |
| 37 | Maine | (3.4) |
| 24 | Maryland | 1.5 |
| 32 | Massachusetts | (0.9) |
| 27 | Michigan | 0.6 |
| 30 | Minnesota | (0.1) |
| 14 | Mississippi | 6.0 |
| 23 | Missouri | 1.7 |
| 45 | Montana | (7.4) |
| 40 | Nebraska | (3.7) |
| 1 | Nevada | 31.9 |
| 18 | New Hampshire | 3.6 |
| 33 | New Jersey | (1.0) |
| 25 | New Mexico | 1.1 |
| 38 | New York | (3.5) |
| 7 | North Carolina | 9.5 |
| 48 | North Dakota | (9.6) |
| 34 | Ohio | (1.4) |
| 39 | Oklahoma | (3.6) |
| 21 | Oregon | 2.8 |
| 40 | Pennsylvania | (3.7) |
| 42 | Rhode Island | (3.8) |
| 12 | South Carolina | 6.9 |
| 35 | South Dakota | (3.0) |
| 9 | Tennessee | 7.9 |
| 10 | Texas | 7.4 |
| 4 | Utah | 14.8 |
| 29 | Vermont | 0.2 |
| 15 | Virginia | 5.3 |
| 11 | Washington | 7.2 |
| 44 | West Virginia | (6.9) |
| 26 | Wisconsin | 0.7 |
| 49 | Wyoming | (14.5) |

RANK ORDER

| RANK | STATE | PERCENT CHANGE |
|------|-------|----------------|
| 1 | Nevada | 31.9 |
| 2 | Arizona | 17.6 |
| 3 | Georgia | 16.4 |
| 4 | Utah | 14.8 |
| 5 | Idaho | 12.9 |
| 6 | Delaware | 12.0 |
| 7 | North Carolina | 9.5 |
| 8 | Florida | 8.1 |
| 9 | Tennessee | 7.9 |
| 10 | Texas | 7.4 |
| 11 | Washington | 7.2 |
| 12 | South Carolina | 6.9 |
| 13 | Alabama | 6.3 |
| 14 | Mississippi | 6.0 |
| 15 | Virginia | 5.3 |
| 16 | California | 4.1 |
| 17 | Colorado | 3.8 |
| 18 | New Hampshire | 3.6 |
| 19 | Arkansas | 3.1 |
| 19 | Indiana | 3.1 |
| 21 | Oregon | 2.8 |
| 22 | Kentucky | 2.2 |
| 23 | Missouri | 1.7 |
| 24 | Maryland | 1.5 |
| 25 | New Mexico | 1.1 |
| 26 | Wisconsin | 0.7 |
| 27 | Michigan | 0.6 |
| 28 | Illinois | 0.5 |
| 29 | Vermont | 0.2 |
| 30 | Minnesota | (0.1) |
| 31 | Kansas | (0.8) |
| 32 | Massachusetts | (0.9) |
| 33 | New Jersey | (1.0) |
| 34 | Ohio | (1.4) |
| 35 | South Dakota | (3.0) |
| 36 | Iowa | (3.1) |
| 37 | Maine | (3.4) |
| 38 | New York | (3.5) |
| 39 | Oklahoma | (3.6) |
| 40 | Nebraska | (3.7) |
| 40 | Pennsylvania | (3.7) |
| 42 | Rhode Island | (3.8) |
| 43 | Louisiana | (4.7) |
| 44 | West Virginia | (6.9) |
| 45 | Montana | (7.4) |
| 46 | Connecticut | (7.5) |
| 47 | Hawaii | (8.8) |
| 48 | North Dakota | (9.6) |
| 49 | Wyoming | (14.5) |
| 50 | Alaska | (17.3) |
| | District of Columbia | (14.8) |

Source: Morgan Quitno Press using data from U.S. Bureau of the Census
  "Estimates of the Population of the States by Selected Age Groups and Sex" (ST-99-9, March 9, 2000)
*From April 1, 1990 to July 1, 1999.

# Population 45 to 64 Years Old in 1999

## National Total = 59,191,443

ALPHA ORDER

| RANK | STATE | POPULATION | % of USA |
|---|---|---|---|
| 22 | Alabama | 988,812 | 1.7% |
| 48 | Alaska | 138,370 | 0.2% |
| 21 | Arizona | 990,527 | 1.7% |
| 32 | Arkansas | 572,048 | 1.0% |
| 1 | California | 6,548,155 | 11.1% |
| 23 | Colorado | 967,498 | 1.6% |
| 29 | Connecticut | 719,339 | 1.2% |
| 45 | Delaware | 160,258 | 0.3% |
| 4 | Florida | 3,325,223 | 5.6% |
| 11 | Georgia | 1,653,199 | 2.8% |
| 41 | Hawaii | 269,506 | 0.5% |
| 40 | Idaho | 274,317 | 0.5% |
| 6 | Illinois | 2,602,885 | 4.4% |
| 14 | Indiana | 1,307,703 | 2.2% |
| 30 | Iowa | 641,886 | 1.1% |
| 33 | Kansas | 562,288 | 0.9% |
| 25 | Kentucky | 914,356 | 1.5% |
| 24 | Louisiana | 952,683 | 1.6% |
| 39 | Maine | 291,862 | 0.5% |
| 19 | Maryland | 1,125,392 | 1.9% |
| 13 | Massachusetts | 1,338,199 | 2.3% |
| 8 | Michigan | 2,156,632 | 3.6% |
| 20 | Minnesota | 1,021,663 | 1.7% |
| 31 | Mississippi | 582,386 | 1.0% |
| 17 | Missouri | 1,191,795 | 2.0% |
| 43 | Montana | 220,842 | 0.4% |
| 38 | Nebraska | 356,329 | 0.6% |
| 35 | Nevada | 409,481 | 0.7% |
| 42 | New Hampshire | 253,137 | 0.4% |
| 9 | New Jersey | 1,827,422 | 3.1% |
| 36 | New Mexico | 379,081 | 0.6% |
| 3 | New York | 4,062,910 | 6.9% |
| 10 | North Carolina | 1,693,763 | 2.9% |
| 49 | North Dakota | 137,542 | 0.2% |
| 7 | Ohio | 2,487,161 | 4.2% |
| 28 | Oklahoma | 758,536 | 1.3% |
| 27 | Oregon | 790,345 | 1.3% |
| 5 | Pennsylvania | 2,701,930 | 4.6% |
| 44 | Rhode Island | 203,288 | 0.3% |
| 26 | South Carolina | 874,507 | 1.5% |
| 46 | South Dakota | 153,294 | 0.3% |
| 16 | Tennessee | 1,268,155 | 2.1% |
| 2 | Texas | 4,174,472 | 7.1% |
| 37 | Utah | 363,390 | 0.6% |
| 47 | Vermont | 140,376 | 0.2% |
| 12 | Virginia | 1,518,764 | 2.6% |
| 15 | Washington | 1,279,806 | 2.2% |
| 34 | West Virginia | 454,990 | 0.8% |
| 18 | Wisconsin | 1,146,265 | 1.9% |
| 50 | Wyoming | 116,463 | 0.2% |

RANK ORDER

| RANK | STATE | POPULATION | % of USA |
|---|---|---|---|
| 1 | California | 6,548,155 | 11.1% |
| 2 | Texas | 4,174,472 | 7.1% |
| 3 | New York | 4,062,910 | 6.9% |
| 4 | Florida | 3,325,223 | 5.6% |
| 5 | Pennsylvania | 2,701,930 | 4.6% |
| 6 | Illinois | 2,602,885 | 4.4% |
| 7 | Ohio | 2,487,161 | 4.2% |
| 8 | Michigan | 2,156,632 | 3.6% |
| 9 | New Jersey | 1,827,422 | 3.1% |
| 10 | North Carolina | 1,693,763 | 2.9% |
| 11 | Georgia | 1,653,199 | 2.8% |
| 12 | Virginia | 1,518,764 | 2.6% |
| 13 | Massachusetts | 1,338,199 | 2.3% |
| 14 | Indiana | 1,307,703 | 2.2% |
| 15 | Washington | 1,279,806 | 2.2% |
| 16 | Tennessee | 1,268,155 | 2.1% |
| 17 | Missouri | 1,191,795 | 2.0% |
| 18 | Wisconsin | 1,146,265 | 1.9% |
| 19 | Maryland | 1,125,392 | 1.9% |
| 20 | Minnesota | 1,021,663 | 1.7% |
| 21 | Arizona | 990,527 | 1.7% |
| 22 | Alabama | 988,812 | 1.7% |
| 23 | Colorado | 967,498 | 1.6% |
| 24 | Louisiana | 952,683 | 1.6% |
| 25 | Kentucky | 914,356 | 1.5% |
| 26 | South Carolina | 874,507 | 1.5% |
| 27 | Oregon | 790,345 | 1.3% |
| 28 | Oklahoma | 758,536 | 1.3% |
| 29 | Connecticut | 719,339 | 1.2% |
| 30 | Iowa | 641,886 | 1.1% |
| 31 | Mississippi | 582,386 | 1.0% |
| 32 | Arkansas | 572,048 | 1.0% |
| 33 | Kansas | 562,288 | 0.9% |
| 34 | West Virginia | 454,990 | 0.8% |
| 35 | Nevada | 409,481 | 0.7% |
| 36 | New Mexico | 379,081 | 0.6% |
| 37 | Utah | 363,390 | 0.6% |
| 38 | Nebraska | 356,329 | 0.6% |
| 39 | Maine | 291,862 | 0.5% |
| 40 | Idaho | 274,317 | 0.5% |
| 41 | Hawaii | 269,506 | 0.5% |
| 42 | New Hampshire | 253,137 | 0.4% |
| 43 | Montana | 220,842 | 0.4% |
| 44 | Rhode Island | 203,288 | 0.3% |
| 45 | Delaware | 160,258 | 0.3% |
| 46 | South Dakota | 153,294 | 0.3% |
| 47 | Vermont | 140,376 | 0.2% |
| 48 | Alaska | 138,370 | 0.2% |
| 49 | North Dakota | 137,542 | 0.2% |
| 50 | Wyoming | 116,463 | 0.2% |
| | District of Columbia | 122,212 | 0.2% |

Source: U.S. Bureau of the Census
"Population Estimates for the U.S., Regions, and States by Selected Age Groups and Sex" (ST-99-9, March 9, 2000)
(http://www.census.gov/population/estimates/state/st-99-09.txt)

# Percent Change in Population 45 to 64 Years Old: 1990 to 1999

## National Percent Change = 28.2% Increase*

ALPHA ORDER

RANK ORDER

| RANK | STATE | PERCENT CHANGE | RANK | STATE | PERCENT CHANGE |
|------|-------|----------------|------|-------|----------------|
| 28 | Alabama | 26.6 | 1 | Nevada | 68.9 |
| 2 | Alaska | 67.8 | 2 | Alaska | 67.8 |
| 5 | Arizona | 53.3 | 3 | Colorado | 65.2 |
| 32 | Arkansas | 25.7 | 4 | Idaho | 55.7 |
| 24 | California | 28.4 | 5 | Arizona | 53.3 |
| 3 | Colorado | 65.2 | 6 | Oregon | 48.9 |
| 49 | Connecticut | 11.0 | 7 | Utah | 48.4 |
| 31 | Delaware | 25.8 | 8 | Montana | 47.2 |
| 21 | Florida | 30.4 | 9 | Washington | 45.8 |
| 12 | Georgia | 42.3 | 10 | Wyoming | 44.4 |
| 16 | Hawaii | 33.6 | 11 | Texas | 43.8 |
| 4 | Idaho | 55.7 | 12 | Georgia | 42.3 |
| 42 | Illinois | 22.0 | 13 | New Mexico | 41.6 |
| 37 | Indiana | 24.5 | 14 | Vermont | 37.3 |
| 41 | Iowa | 22.7 | 15 | South Carolina | 35.5 |
| 26 | Kansas | 27.0 | 16 | Hawaii | 33.6 |
| 22 | Kentucky | 30.0 | 17 | Minnesota | 32.6 |
| 25 | Louisiana | 27.6 | 18 | Tennessee | 32.5 |
| 33 | Maine | 25.6 | 19 | North Carolina | 32.3 |
| 40 | Maryland | 23.0 | 20 | Virginia | 30.8 |
| 44 | Massachusetts | 20.6 | 21 | Florida | 30.4 |
| 38 | Michigan | 24.1 | 22 | Kentucky | 30.0 |
| 17 | Minnesota | 32.6 | 23 | Wisconsin | 28.8 |
| 30 | Mississippi | 26.3 | 24 | California | 28.4 |
| 43 | Missouri | 21.8 | 25 | Louisiana | 27.6 |
| 8 | Montana | 47.2 | 26 | Kansas | 27.0 |
| 33 | Nebraska | 25.6 | 27 | New Hampshire | 26.9 |
| 1 | Nevada | 68.9 | 28 | Alabama | 26.6 |
| 27 | New Hampshire | 26.9 | 28 | Oklahoma | 26.6 |
| 46 | New Jersey | 17.4 | 30 | Mississippi | 26.3 |
| 13 | New Mexico | 41.6 | 31 | Delaware | 25.8 |
| 47 | New York | 15.1 | 32 | Arkansas | 25.7 |
| 19 | North Carolina | 32.3 | 33 | Maine | 25.6 |
| 36 | North Dakota | 24.9 | 33 | Nebraska | 25.6 |
| 45 | Ohio | 19.1 | 35 | South Dakota | 25.5 |
| 28 | Oklahoma | 26.6 | 36 | North Dakota | 24.9 |
| 6 | Oregon | 48.9 | 37 | Indiana | 24.5 |
| 48 | Pennsylvania | 14.1 | 38 | Michigan | 24.1 |
| 50 | Rhode Island | 9.9 | 39 | West Virginia | 23.9 |
| 15 | South Carolina | 35.5 | 40 | Maryland | 23.0 |
| 35 | South Dakota | 25.5 | 41 | Iowa | 22.7 |
| 18 | Tennessee | 32.5 | 42 | Illinois | 22.0 |
| 11 | Texas | 43.8 | 43 | Missouri | 21.8 |
| 7 | Utah | 48.4 | 44 | Massachusetts | 20.6 |
| 14 | Vermont | 37.3 | 45 | Ohio | 19.1 |
| 20 | Virginia | 30.8 | 46 | New Jersey | 17.4 |
| 9 | Washington | 45.8 | 47 | New York | 15.1 |
| 39 | West Virginia | 23.9 | 48 | Pennsylvania | 14.1 |
| 23 | Wisconsin | 28.8 | 49 | Connecticut | 11.0 |
| 10 | Wyoming | 44.4 | 50 | Rhode Island | 9.9 |
| | | | | District of Columbia | 8.9 |

Source: Morgan Quitno Press using data from U.S. Bureau of the Census
"Estimates of the Population of the States by Selected Age Groups and Sex" (ST-99-9, March 9, 2000)
*From April 1, 1990 to July 1, 1999.

# Population 65 Years Old and Older in 1999

## National Total = 34,540,025

ALPHA ORDER

| RANK | STATE | POPULATION | % of USA |
|---|---|---|---|
| 22 | Alabama | 567,952 | 1.6% |
| 50 | Alaska | 34,750 | 0.1% |
| 19 | Arizona | 628,633 | 1.8% |
| 31 | Arkansas | 361,342 | 1.0% |
| 1 | California | 3,647,532 | 10.6% |
| 30 | Colorado | 407,773 | 1.2% |
| 26 | Connecticut | 468,576 | 1.4% |
| 46 | Delaware | 98,135 | 0.3% |
| 2 | Florida | 2,741,849 | 7.9% |
| 13 | Georgia | 761,143 | 2.2% |
| 40 | Hawaii | 161,889 | 0.5% |
| 43 | Idaho | 142,029 | 0.4% |
| 7 | Illinois | 1,496,177 | 4.3% |
| 15 | Indiana | 743,020 | 2.2% |
| 29 | Iowa | 428,487 | 1.2% |
| 32 | Kansas | 354,079 | 1.0% |
| 24 | Kentucky | 493,154 | 1.4% |
| 23 | Louisiana | 501,458 | 1.5% |
| 39 | Maine | 175,357 | 0.5% |
| 20 | Maryland | 596,961 | 1.7% |
| 11 | Massachusetts | 859,731 | 2.5% |
| 8 | Michigan | 1,223,560 | 3.5% |
| 21 | Minnesota | 585,394 | 1.7% |
| 33 | Mississippi | 335,492 | 1.0% |
| 14 | Missouri | 745,684 | 2.2% |
| 44 | Montana | 117,239 | 0.3% |
| 35 | Nebraska | 228,286 | 0.7% |
| 36 | Nevada | 207,412 | 0.6% |
| 42 | New Hampshire | 144,585 | 0.4% |
| 9 | New Jersey | 1,108,257 | 3.2% |
| 37 | New Mexico | 199,974 | 0.6% |
| 3 | New York | 2,429,632 | 7.0% |
| 10 | North Carolina | 954,866 | 2.8% |
| 47 | North Dakota | 92,383 | 0.3% |
| 6 | Ohio | 1,501,136 | 4.3% |
| 27 | Oklahoma | 448,698 | 1.3% |
| 28 | Oregon | 435,099 | 1.3% |
| 5 | Pennsylvania | 1,898,936 | 5.5% |
| 41 | Rhode Island | 154,348 | 0.4% |
| 25 | South Carolina | 473,371 | 1.4% |
| 45 | South Dakota | 105,442 | 0.3% |
| 17 | Tennessee | 680,954 | 2.0% |
| 4 | Texas | 2,016,497 | 5.8% |
| 38 | Utah | 185,603 | 0.5% |
| 48 | Vermont | 72,916 | 0.2% |
| 12 | Virginia | 774,885 | 2.2% |
| 18 | Washington | 657,312 | 1.9% |
| 34 | West Virginia | 272,896 | 0.8% |
| 16 | Wisconsin | 691,409 | 2.0% |
| 49 | Wyoming | 55,630 | 0.2% |

RANK ORDER

| RANK | STATE | POPULATION | % of USA |
|---|---|---|---|
| 1 | California | 3,647,532 | 10.6% |
| 2 | Florida | 2,741,849 | 7.9% |
| 3 | New York | 2,429,632 | 7.0% |
| 4 | Texas | 2,016,497 | 5.8% |
| 5 | Pennsylvania | 1,898,936 | 5.5% |
| 6 | Ohio | 1,501,136 | 4.3% |
| 7 | Illinois | 1,496,177 | 4.3% |
| 8 | Michigan | 1,223,560 | 3.5% |
| 9 | New Jersey | 1,108,257 | 3.2% |
| 10 | North Carolina | 954,866 | 2.8% |
| 11 | Massachusetts | 859,731 | 2.5% |
| 12 | Virginia | 774,885 | 2.2% |
| 13 | Georgia | 761,143 | 2.2% |
| 14 | Missouri | 745,684 | 2.2% |
| 15 | Indiana | 743,020 | 2.2% |
| 16 | Wisconsin | 691,409 | 2.0% |
| 17 | Tennessee | 680,954 | 2.0% |
| 18 | Washington | 657,312 | 1.9% |
| 19 | Arizona | 628,633 | 1.8% |
| 20 | Maryland | 596,961 | 1.7% |
| 21 | Minnesota | 585,394 | 1.7% |
| 22 | Alabama | 567,952 | 1.6% |
| 23 | Louisiana | 501,458 | 1.5% |
| 24 | Kentucky | 493,154 | 1.4% |
| 25 | South Carolina | 473,371 | 1.4% |
| 26 | Connecticut | 468,576 | 1.4% |
| 27 | Oklahoma | 448,698 | 1.3% |
| 28 | Oregon | 435,099 | 1.3% |
| 29 | Iowa | 428,487 | 1.2% |
| 30 | Colorado | 407,773 | 1.2% |
| 31 | Arkansas | 361,342 | 1.0% |
| 32 | Kansas | 354,079 | 1.0% |
| 33 | Mississippi | 335,492 | 1.0% |
| 34 | West Virginia | 272,896 | 0.8% |
| 35 | Nebraska | 228,286 | 0.7% |
| 36 | Nevada | 207,412 | 0.6% |
| 37 | New Mexico | 199,974 | 0.6% |
| 38 | Utah | 185,603 | 0.5% |
| 39 | Maine | 175,357 | 0.5% |
| 40 | Hawaii | 161,889 | 0.5% |
| 41 | Rhode Island | 154,348 | 0.4% |
| 42 | New Hampshire | 144,585 | 0.4% |
| 43 | Idaho | 142,029 | 0.4% |
| 44 | Montana | 117,239 | 0.3% |
| 45 | South Dakota | 105,442 | 0.3% |
| 46 | Delaware | 98,135 | 0.3% |
| 47 | North Dakota | 92,383 | 0.3% |
| 48 | Vermont | 72,916 | 0.2% |
| 49 | Wyoming | 55,630 | 0.2% |
| 50 | Alaska | 34,750 | 0.1% |
| | District of Columbia | 72,102 | 0.2% |

Source: U.S. Bureau of the Census
"Population Estimates for the U.S., Regions, and States by Selected Age Groups and Sex" (ST-99-9, March 9, 2000)
(http://www.census.gov/population/estimates/state/st-99-09.txt)

# Percent of Population 65 Years Old and Older in 1999

## National Percent = 12.7% of Population

ALPHA ORDER

| RANK | STATE | PERCENT |
|------|-------|---------|
| 24 | Alabama | 13.0 |
| 50 | Alaska | 5.6 |
| 21 | Arizona | 13.2 |
| 9 | Arkansas | 14.2 |
| 45 | California | 11.0 |
| 46 | Colorado | 10.1 |
| 8 | Connecticut | 14.3 |
| 24 | Delaware | 13.0 |
| 1 | Florida | 18.1 |
| 48 | Georgia | 9.8 |
| 12 | Hawaii | 13.7 |
| 43 | Idaho | 11.3 |
| 31 | Illinois | 12.3 |
| 26 | Indiana | 12.5 |
| 5 | Iowa | 14.9 |
| 18 | Kansas | 13.3 |
| 26 | Kentucky | 12.5 |
| 38 | Louisiana | 11.5 |
| 10 | Maine | 14.0 |
| 38 | Maryland | 11.5 |
| 11 | Massachusetts | 13.9 |
| 29 | Michigan | 12.4 |
| 31 | Minnesota | 12.3 |
| 35 | Mississippi | 12.1 |
| 14 | Missouri | 13.6 |
| 18 | Montana | 13.3 |
| 12 | Nebraska | 13.7 |
| 38 | Nevada | 11.5 |
| 36 | New Hampshire | 12.0 |
| 14 | New Jersey | 13.6 |
| 38 | New Mexico | 11.5 |
| 16 | New York | 13.4 |
| 26 | North Carolina | 12.5 |
| 6 | North Dakota | 14.6 |
| 18 | Ohio | 13.3 |
| 16 | Oklahoma | 13.4 |
| 23 | Oregon | 13.1 |
| 2 | Pennsylvania | 15.8 |
| 3 | Rhode Island | 15.6 |
| 34 | South Carolina | 12.2 |
| 7 | South Dakota | 14.4 |
| 29 | Tennessee | 12.4 |
| 46 | Texas | 10.1 |
| 49 | Utah | 8.7 |
| 31 | Vermont | 12.3 |
| 43 | Virginia | 11.3 |
| 42 | Washington | 11.4 |
| 4 | West Virginia | 15.1 |
| 21 | Wisconsin | 13.2 |
| 37 | Wyoming | 11.6 |

RANK ORDER

| RANK | STATE | PERCENT |
|------|-------|---------|
| 1 | Florida | 18.1 |
| 2 | Pennsylvania | 15.8 |
| 3 | Rhode Island | 15.6 |
| 4 | West Virginia | 15.1 |
| 5 | Iowa | 14.9 |
| 6 | North Dakota | 14.6 |
| 7 | South Dakota | 14.4 |
| 8 | Connecticut | 14.3 |
| 9 | Arkansas | 14.2 |
| 10 | Maine | 14.0 |
| 11 | Massachusetts | 13.9 |
| 12 | Hawaii | 13.7 |
| 12 | Nebraska | 13.7 |
| 14 | Missouri | 13.6 |
| 14 | New Jersey | 13.6 |
| 16 | New York | 13.4 |
| 16 | Oklahoma | 13.4 |
| 18 | Kansas | 13.3 |
| 18 | Montana | 13.3 |
| 18 | Ohio | 13.3 |
| 21 | Arizona | 13.2 |
| 21 | Wisconsin | 13.2 |
| 23 | Oregon | 13.1 |
| 24 | Alabama | 13.0 |
| 24 | Delaware | 13.0 |
| 26 | Indiana | 12.5 |
| 26 | Kentucky | 12.5 |
| 26 | North Carolina | 12.5 |
| 29 | Michigan | 12.4 |
| 29 | Tennessee | 12.4 |
| 31 | Illinois | 12.3 |
| 31 | Minnesota | 12.3 |
| 31 | Vermont | 12.3 |
| 34 | South Carolina | 12.2 |
| 35 | Mississippi | 12.1 |
| 36 | New Hampshire | 12.0 |
| 37 | Wyoming | 11.6 |
| 38 | Louisiana | 11.5 |
| 38 | Maryland | 11.5 |
| 38 | Nevada | 11.5 |
| 38 | New Mexico | 11.5 |
| 42 | Washington | 11.4 |
| 43 | Idaho | 11.3 |
| 43 | Virginia | 11.3 |
| 45 | California | 11.0 |
| 46 | Colorado | 10.1 |
| 46 | Texas | 10.1 |
| 48 | Georgia | 9.8 |
| 49 | Utah | 8.7 |
| 50 | Alaska | 5.6 |
| | District of Columbia | 13.9 |

Source: Morgan Quitno Press using data from U.S. Bureau of the Census
  "Population Estimates for the U.S., Regions, and States by Selected Age Groups and Sex" (ST-99-9, March 9, 2000)
    (http://www.census.gov/population/estimates/state/st-99-09.txt)

# Percent Change in Population 65 Years Old and Older: 1990 to 1999

## National Percent Change = 11.1% Increase*

ALPHA ORDER

| RANK | STATE | PERCENT CHANGE |
|---|---|---|
| 26 | Alabama | 9.3 |
| 2 | Alaska | 57.3 |
| 3 | Arizona | 32.0 |
| 43 | Arkansas | 3.6 |
| 14 | California | 17.2 |
| 5 | Colorado | 24.2 |
| 36 | Connecticut | 5.6 |
| 8 | Delaware | 22.2 |
| 17 | Florida | 16.4 |
| 16 | Georgia | 17.0 |
| 4 | Hawaii | 30.8 |
| 13 | Idaho | 17.5 |
| 39 | Illinois | 4.7 |
| 31 | Indiana | 7.1 |
| 50 | Iowa | 0.6 |
| 44 | Kansas | 3.5 |
| 35 | Kentucky | 6.0 |
| 29 | Louisiana | 7.4 |
| 28 | Maine | 7.7 |
| 18 | Maryland | 16.1 |
| 37 | Massachusetts | 5.5 |
| 22 | Michigan | 10.8 |
| 30 | Minnesota | 7.2 |
| 38 | Mississippi | 5.0 |
| 41 | Missouri | 4.2 |
| 25 | Montana | 10.4 |
| 47 | Nebraska | 2.5 |
| 1 | Nevada | 63.8 |
| 18 | New Hampshire | 16.1 |
| 27 | New Jersey | 8.1 |
| 7 | New Mexico | 23.5 |
| 42 | New York | 3.8 |
| 10 | North Carolina | 19.3 |
| 49 | North Dakota | 1.6 |
| 32 | Ohio | 7.0 |
| 34 | Oklahoma | 6.1 |
| 21 | Oregon | 11.6 |
| 40 | Pennsylvania | 4.3 |
| 46 | Rhode Island | 3.1 |
| 9 | South Carolina | 20.1 |
| 45 | South Dakota | 3.3 |
| 24 | Tennessee | 10.5 |
| 12 | Texas | 18.0 |
| 5 | Utah | 24.2 |
| 23 | Vermont | 10.7 |
| 14 | Virginia | 17.2 |
| 20 | Washington | 14.7 |
| 48 | West Virginia | 1.9 |
| 33 | Wisconsin | 6.3 |
| 11 | Wyoming | 18.4 |

RANK ORDER

| RANK | STATE | PERCENT CHANGE |
|---|---|---|
| 1 | Nevada | 63.8 |
| 2 | Alaska | 57.3 |
| 3 | Arizona | 32.0 |
| 4 | Hawaii | 30.8 |
| 5 | Colorado | 24.2 |
| 5 | Utah | 24.2 |
| 7 | New Mexico | 23.5 |
| 8 | Delaware | 22.2 |
| 9 | South Carolina | 20.1 |
| 10 | North Carolina | 19.3 |
| 11 | Wyoming | 18.4 |
| 12 | Texas | 18.0 |
| 13 | Idaho | 17.5 |
| 14 | California | 17.2 |
| 14 | Virginia | 17.2 |
| 16 | Georgia | 17.0 |
| 17 | Florida | 16.4 |
| 18 | Maryland | 16.1 |
| 18 | New Hampshire | 16.1 |
| 20 | Washington | 14.7 |
| 21 | Oregon | 11.6 |
| 22 | Michigan | 10.8 |
| 23 | Vermont | 10.7 |
| 24 | Tennessee | 10.5 |
| 25 | Montana | 10.4 |
| 26 | Alabama | 9.3 |
| 27 | New Jersey | 8.1 |
| 28 | Maine | 7.7 |
| 29 | Louisiana | 7.4 |
| 30 | Minnesota | 7.2 |
| 31 | Indiana | 7.1 |
| 32 | Ohio | 7.0 |
| 33 | Wisconsin | 6.3 |
| 34 | Oklahoma | 6.1 |
| 35 | Kentucky | 6.0 |
| 36 | Connecticut | 5.6 |
| 37 | Massachusetts | 5.5 |
| 38 | Mississippi | 5.0 |
| 39 | Illinois | 4.7 |
| 40 | Pennsylvania | 4.3 |
| 41 | Missouri | 4.2 |
| 42 | New York | 3.8 |
| 43 | Arkansas | 3.6 |
| 44 | Kansas | 3.5 |
| 45 | South Dakota | 3.3 |
| 46 | Rhode Island | 3.1 |
| 47 | Nebraska | 2.5 |
| 48 | West Virginia | 1.9 |
| 49 | North Dakota | 1.6 |
| 50 | Iowa | 0.6 |

District of Columbia (6.5)

Source: Morgan Quitno Press using data from U.S. Bureau of the Census
   "Estimates of the Population of the States by Selected Age Groups and Sex" (ST-99-9, March 9, 2000)
*From April 1, 1990 to July 1, 1999.

# Population 85 Years Old and Older in 1999

## National Total = 4,175,082

ALPHA ORDER

| RANK | STATE | POPULATION | % of USA |
|------|-------|-----------:|---------:|
| 22 | Alabama | 64,972 | 1.6% |
| 50 | Alaska | 2,398 | 0.1% |
| 21 | Arizona | 65,905 | 1.6% |
| 32 | Arkansas | 44,499 | 1.1% |
| 1 | California | 424,077 | 10.2% |
| 30 | Colorado | 47,621 | 1.1% |
| 24 | Connecticut | 63,211 | 1.5% |
| 47 | Delaware | 10,141 | 0.2% |
| 2 | Florida | 320,603 | 7.7% |
| 15 | Georgia | 85,338 | 2.0% |
| 42 | Hawaii | 17,295 | 0.4% |
| 40 | Idaho | 17,927 | 0.4% |
| 6 | Illinois | 192,388 | 4.6% |
| 14 | Indiana | 90,255 | 2.2% |
| 23 | Iowa | 64,500 | 1.5% |
| 29 | Kansas | 51,642 | 1.2% |
| 25 | Kentucky | 57,442 | 1.4% |
| 28 | Louisiana | 55,908 | 1.3% |
| 36 | Maine | 22,181 | 0.5% |
| 20 | Maryland | 66,461 | 1.6% |
| 10 | Massachusetts | 115,384 | 2.8% |
| 8 | Michigan | 144,219 | 3.5% |
| 16 | Minnesota | 84,450 | 2.0% |
| 33 | Mississippi | 41,119 | 1.0% |
| 12 | Missouri | 98,055 | 2.3% |
| 45 | Montana | 15,326 | 0.4% |
| 34 | Nebraska | 34,313 | 0.8% |
| 43 | Nevada | 16,349 | 0.4% |
| 41 | New Hampshire | 17,874 | 0.4% |
| 9 | New Jersey | 133,363 | 3.2% |
| 37 | New Mexico | 21,620 | 0.5% |
| 3 | New York | 310,167 | 7.4% |
| 11 | North Carolina | 104,845 | 2.5% |
| 46 | North Dakota | 14,761 | 0.4% |
| 7 | Ohio | 176,493 | 4.2% |
| 26 | Oklahoma | 57,209 | 1.4% |
| 27 | Oregon | 56,266 | 1.3% |
| 5 | Pennsylvania | 232,295 | 5.6% |
| 39 | Rhode Island | 21,121 | 0.5% |
| 31 | South Carolina | 46,726 | 1.1% |
| 44 | South Dakota | 15,899 | 0.4% |
| 19 | Tennessee | 78,895 | 1.9% |
| 4 | Texas | 233,547 | 5.6% |
| 38 | Utah | 21,492 | 0.5% |
| 48 | Vermont | 9,688 | 0.2% |
| 17 | Virginia | 84,016 | 2.0% |
| 18 | Washington | 82,559 | 2.0% |
| 35 | West Virginia | 31,922 | 0.8% |
| 13 | Wisconsin | 94,658 | 2.3% |
| 49 | Wyoming | 6,464 | 0.2% |

RANK ORDER

| RANK | STATE | POPULATION | % of USA |
|------|-------|-----------:|---------:|
| 1 | California | 424,077 | 10.2% |
| 2 | Florida | 320,603 | 7.7% |
| 3 | New York | 310,167 | 7.4% |
| 4 | Texas | 233,547 | 5.6% |
| 5 | Pennsylvania | 232,295 | 5.6% |
| 6 | Illinois | 192,388 | 4.6% |
| 7 | Ohio | 176,493 | 4.2% |
| 8 | Michigan | 144,219 | 3.5% |
| 9 | New Jersey | 133,363 | 3.2% |
| 10 | Massachusetts | 115,384 | 2.8% |
| 11 | North Carolina | 104,845 | 2.5% |
| 12 | Missouri | 98,055 | 2.3% |
| 13 | Wisconsin | 94,658 | 2.3% |
| 14 | Indiana | 90,255 | 2.2% |
| 15 | Georgia | 85,338 | 2.0% |
| 16 | Minnesota | 84,450 | 2.0% |
| 17 | Virginia | 84,016 | 2.0% |
| 18 | Washington | 82,559 | 2.0% |
| 19 | Tennessee | 78,895 | 1.9% |
| 20 | Maryland | 66,461 | 1.6% |
| 21 | Arizona | 65,905 | 1.6% |
| 22 | Alabama | 64,972 | 1.6% |
| 23 | Iowa | 64,500 | 1.5% |
| 24 | Connecticut | 63,211 | 1.5% |
| 25 | Kentucky | 57,442 | 1.4% |
| 26 | Oklahoma | 57,209 | 1.4% |
| 27 | Oregon | 56,266 | 1.3% |
| 28 | Louisiana | 55,908 | 1.3% |
| 29 | Kansas | 51,642 | 1.2% |
| 30 | Colorado | 47,621 | 1.1% |
| 31 | South Carolina | 46,726 | 1.1% |
| 32 | Arkansas | 44,499 | 1.1% |
| 33 | Mississippi | 41,119 | 1.0% |
| 34 | Nebraska | 34,313 | 0.8% |
| 35 | West Virginia | 31,922 | 0.8% |
| 36 | Maine | 22,181 | 0.5% |
| 37 | New Mexico | 21,620 | 0.5% |
| 38 | Utah | 21,492 | 0.5% |
| 39 | Rhode Island | 21,121 | 0.5% |
| 40 | Idaho | 17,927 | 0.4% |
| 41 | New Hampshire | 17,874 | 0.4% |
| 42 | Hawaii | 17,295 | 0.4% |
| 43 | Nevada | 16,349 | 0.4% |
| 44 | South Dakota | 15,899 | 0.4% |
| 45 | Montana | 15,326 | 0.4% |
| 46 | North Dakota | 14,761 | 0.4% |
| 47 | Delaware | 10,141 | 0.2% |
| 48 | Vermont | 9,688 | 0.2% |
| 49 | Wyoming | 6,464 | 0.2% |
| 50 | Alaska | 2,398 | 0.1% |
|  | District of Columbia | 9,223 | 0.2% |

*Source: U.S. Bureau of the Census*
*"Population Estimates for the U.S., Regions, and States by Selected Age Groups and Sex" (ST-99-9, March 9, 2000)*
*(http://www.census.gov/population/estimates/state/st-99-09.txt)*

# Percent of Population 85 Years Old and Older in 1999

## National Percent = 1.5% of Population

ALPHA ORDER

| RANK | STATE | PERCENT |
|------|-------|---------|
| 25 | Alabama | 1.5 |
| 50 | Alaska | 0.4 |
| 32 | Arizona | 1.4 |
| 16 | Arkansas | 1.7 |
| 37 | California | 1.3 |
| 42 | Colorado | 1.2 |
| 7 | Connecticut | 1.9 |
| 37 | Delaware | 1.3 |
| 4 | Florida | 2.1 |
| 47 | Georgia | 1.1 |
| 25 | Hawaii | 1.5 |
| 32 | Idaho | 1.4 |
| 21 | Illinois | 1.6 |
| 25 | Indiana | 1.5 |
| 2 | Iowa | 2.2 |
| 7 | Kansas | 1.9 |
| 25 | Kentucky | 1.5 |
| 37 | Louisiana | 1.3 |
| 11 | Maine | 1.8 |
| 37 | Maryland | 1.3 |
| 7 | Massachusetts | 1.9 |
| 25 | Michigan | 1.5 |
| 11 | Minnesota | 1.8 |
| 25 | Mississippi | 1.5 |
| 11 | Missouri | 1.8 |
| 16 | Montana | 1.7 |
| 4 | Nebraska | 2.1 |
| 49 | Nevada | 0.9 |
| 25 | New Hampshire | 1.5 |
| 21 | New Jersey | 1.6 |
| 42 | New Mexico | 1.2 |
| 16 | New York | 1.7 |
| 32 | North Carolina | 1.4 |
| 1 | North Dakota | 2.3 |
| 21 | Ohio | 1.6 |
| 16 | Oklahoma | 1.7 |
| 16 | Oregon | 1.7 |
| 7 | Pennsylvania | 1.9 |
| 4 | Rhode Island | 2.1 |
| 42 | South Carolina | 1.2 |
| 2 | South Dakota | 2.2 |
| 32 | Tennessee | 1.4 |
| 42 | Texas | 1.2 |
| 48 | Utah | 1.0 |
| 21 | Vermont | 1.6 |
| 42 | Virginia | 1.2 |
| 32 | Washington | 1.4 |
| 11 | West Virginia | 1.8 |
| 11 | Wisconsin | 1.8 |
| 37 | Wyoming | 1.3 |

RANK ORDER

| RANK | STATE | PERCENT |
|------|-------|---------|
| 1 | North Dakota | 2.3 |
| 2 | Iowa | 2.2 |
| 2 | South Dakota | 2.2 |
| 4 | Florida | 2.1 |
| 4 | Nebraska | 2.1 |
| 4 | Rhode Island | 2.1 |
| 7 | Connecticut | 1.9 |
| 7 | Kansas | 1.9 |
| 7 | Massachusetts | 1.9 |
| 7 | Pennsylvania | 1.9 |
| 11 | Maine | 1.8 |
| 11 | Minnesota | 1.8 |
| 11 | Missouri | 1.8 |
| 11 | West Virginia | 1.8 |
| 11 | Wisconsin | 1.8 |
| 16 | Arkansas | 1.7 |
| 16 | Montana | 1.7 |
| 16 | New York | 1.7 |
| 16 | Oklahoma | 1.7 |
| 16 | Oregon | 1.7 |
| 21 | Illinois | 1.6 |
| 21 | New Jersey | 1.6 |
| 21 | Ohio | 1.6 |
| 21 | Vermont | 1.6 |
| 25 | Alabama | 1.5 |
| 25 | Hawaii | 1.5 |
| 25 | Indiana | 1.5 |
| 25 | Kentucky | 1.5 |
| 25 | Michigan | 1.5 |
| 25 | Mississippi | 1.5 |
| 25 | New Hampshire | 1.5 |
| 32 | Arizona | 1.4 |
| 32 | Idaho | 1.4 |
| 32 | North Carolina | 1.4 |
| 32 | Tennessee | 1.4 |
| 32 | Washington | 1.4 |
| 37 | California | 1.3 |
| 37 | Delaware | 1.3 |
| 37 | Louisiana | 1.3 |
| 37 | Maryland | 1.3 |
| 37 | Wyoming | 1.3 |
| 42 | Colorado | 1.2 |
| 42 | New Mexico | 1.2 |
| 42 | South Carolina | 1.2 |
| 42 | Texas | 1.2 |
| 42 | Virginia | 1.2 |
| 47 | Georgia | 1.1 |
| 48 | Utah | 1.0 |
| 49 | Nevada | 0.9 |
| 50 | Alaska | 0.4 |

| District of Columbia | 1.8 |

Source: Morgan Quitno Press using data from U.S. Bureau of the Census
"Population Estimates for the U.S., Regions, and States by Selected Age Groups and Sex" (ST-99-9, March 9, 2000)
(http://www.census.gov/population/estimates/state/st-99-09.txt)

# Percent Change in Population 85 Years Old and Older: 1990 to 1999

## National Percent Change = 38.2% Increase*

ALPHA ORDER

| RANK | STATE | PERCENT CHANGE |
|------|-------|----------------|
| 25 | Alabama | 37.4 |
| 2 | Alaska | 99.8 |
| 3 | Arizona | 77.7 |
| 36 | Arkansas | 28.9 |
| 18 | California | 45.1 |
| 14 | Colorado | 46.3 |
| 24 | Connecticut | 37.5 |
| 19 | Delaware | 44.8 |
| 7 | Florida | 56.0 |
| 11 | Georgia | 52.2 |
| 4 | Hawaii | 71.9 |
| 6 | Idaho | 59.2 |
| 31 | Illinois | 32.7 |
| 41 | Indiana | 27.2 |
| 50 | Iowa | 17.8 |
| 45 | Kansas | 23.5 |
| 43 | Kentucky | 25.6 |
| 32 | Louisiana | 31.6 |
| 45 | Maine | 23.5 |
| 15 | Maryland | 45.8 |
| 39 | Massachusetts | 27.7 |
| 26 | Michigan | 37.1 |
| 44 | Minnesota | 24.1 |
| 33 | Mississippi | 30.6 |
| 47 | Missouri | 22.6 |
| 16 | Montana | 45.3 |
| 49 | Nebraska | 18.7 |
| 1 | Nevada | 123.2 |
| 27 | New Hampshire | 36.7 |
| 20 | New Jersey | 43.1 |
| 9 | New Mexico | 55.7 |
| 38 | New York | 28.7 |
| 10 | North Carolina | 52.5 |
| 30 | North Dakota | 33.1 |
| 35 | Ohio | 29.6 |
| 42 | Oklahoma | 26.9 |
| 13 | Oregon | 47.0 |
| 23 | Pennsylvania | 37.8 |
| 29 | Rhode Island | 35.0 |
| 8 | South Carolina | 55.8 |
| 48 | South Dakota | 20.3 |
| 28 | Tennessee | 36.6 |
| 21 | Texas | 42.9 |
| 5 | Utah | 59.9 |
| 34 | Vermont | 30.5 |
| 22 | Virginia | 42.8 |
| 12 | Washington | 48.9 |
| 40 | West Virginia | 27.4 |
| 37 | Wisconsin | 28.8 |
| 17 | Wyoming | 45.2 |

RANK ORDER

| RANK | STATE | PERCENT CHANGE |
|------|-------|----------------|
| 1 | Nevada | 123.2 |
| 2 | Alaska | 99.8 |
| 3 | Arizona | 77.7 |
| 4 | Hawaii | 71.9 |
| 5 | Utah | 59.9 |
| 6 | Idaho | 59.2 |
| 7 | Florida | 56.0 |
| 8 | South Carolina | 55.8 |
| 9 | New Mexico | 55.7 |
| 10 | North Carolina | 52.5 |
| 11 | Georgia | 52.2 |
| 12 | Washington | 48.9 |
| 13 | Oregon | 47.0 |
| 14 | Colorado | 46.3 |
| 15 | Maryland | 45.8 |
| 16 | Montana | 45.3 |
| 17 | Wyoming | 45.2 |
| 18 | California | 45.1 |
| 19 | Delaware | 44.8 |
| 20 | New Jersey | 43.1 |
| 21 | Texas | 42.9 |
| 22 | Virginia | 42.8 |
| 23 | Pennsylvania | 37.8 |
| 24 | Connecticut | 37.5 |
| 25 | Alabama | 37.4 |
| 26 | Michigan | 37.1 |
| 27 | New Hampshire | 36.7 |
| 28 | Tennessee | 36.6 |
| 29 | Rhode Island | 35.0 |
| 30 | North Dakota | 33.1 |
| 31 | Illinois | 32.7 |
| 32 | Louisiana | 31.6 |
| 33 | Mississippi | 30.6 |
| 34 | Vermont | 30.5 |
| 35 | Ohio | 29.6 |
| 36 | Arkansas | 28.9 |
| 37 | Wisconsin | 28.8 |
| 38 | New York | 28.7 |
| 39 | Massachusetts | 27.7 |
| 40 | West Virginia | 27.4 |
| 41 | Indiana | 27.2 |
| 42 | Oklahoma | 26.9 |
| 43 | Kentucky | 25.6 |
| 44 | Minnesota | 24.1 |
| 45 | Kansas | 23.5 |
| 45 | Maine | 23.5 |
| 47 | Missouri | 22.6 |
| 48 | South Dakota | 20.3 |
| 49 | Nebraska | 18.7 |
| 50 | Iowa | 17.8 |
| | District of Columbia | 21.5 |

*Source: Morgan Quitno Press using data from U.S. Bureau of the Census*
  *"Estimates of the Population of the States by Selected Age Groups and Sex" (ST-99-9, March 9, 2000)*
*From April 1, 1990 to July 1, 1999.*

# Domestic Migration of Population: 1998 to 1999

## National Net Migration = 0 People*

| RANK | STATE | NET MIGRATION |
|---|---|---|
| 26 | Alabama | (611) |
| 33 | Alaska | (4,076) |
| 3 | Arizona | 59,196 |
| 21 | Arkansas | 2,422 |
| 49 | California | (80,952) |
| 6 | Colorado | 44,614 |
| 40 | Connecticut | (11,447) |
| 19 | Delaware | 4,512 |
| 1 | Florida | 86,511 |
| 2 | Georgia | 73,084 |
| 44 | Hawaii | (20,112) |
| 16 | Idaho | 7,457 |
| 48 | Illinois | (65,930) |
| 27 | Indiana | (659) |
| 32 | Iowa | (3,008) |
| 30 | Kansas | (2,915) |
| 15 | Kentucky | 8,090 |
| 43 | Louisiana | (19,050) |
| 20 | Maine | 3,611 |
| 34 | Maryland | (4,472) |
| 38 | Massachusetts | (8,656) |
| 42 | Michigan | (16,966) |
| 11 | Minnesota | 13,743 |
| 22 | Mississippi | 1,227 |
| 18 | Missouri | 5,414 |
| 24 | Montana | 249 |
| 35 | Nebraska | (4,627) |
| 7 | Nevada | 40,912 |
| 14 | New Hampshire | 9,185 |
| 45 | New Jersey | (31,294) |
| 41 | New Mexico | (12,554) |
| 50 | New York | (167,818) |
| 4 | North Carolina | 52,806 |
| 37 | North Dakota | (7,051) |
| 46 | Ohio | (32,671) |
| 25 | Oklahoma | 224 |
| 13 | Oregon | 10,592 |
| 47 | Pennsylvania | (37,935) |
| 28 | Rhode Island | (1,029) |
| 8 | South Carolina | 24,995 |
| 29 | South Dakota | (1,782) |
| 10 | Tennessee | 22,918 |
| 5 | Texas | 47,471 |
| 39 | Utah | (8,657) |
| 23 | Vermont | 715 |
| 9 | Virginia | 24,326 |
| 12 | Washington | 11,058 |
| 36 | West Virginia | (6,298) |
| 17 | Wisconsin | 5,472 |
| 31 | Wyoming | (3,007) |

| RANK | STATE | NET MIGRATION |
|---|---|---|
| 1 | Florida | 86,511 |
| 2 | Georgia | 73,084 |
| 3 | Arizona | 59,196 |
| 4 | North Carolina | 52,806 |
| 5 | Texas | 47,471 |
| 6 | Colorado | 44,614 |
| 7 | Nevada | 40,912 |
| 8 | South Carolina | 24,995 |
| 9 | Virginia | 24,326 |
| 10 | Tennessee | 22,918 |
| 11 | Minnesota | 13,743 |
| 12 | Washington | 11,058 |
| 13 | Oregon | 10,592 |
| 14 | New Hampshire | 9,185 |
| 15 | Kentucky | 8,090 |
| 16 | Idaho | 7,457 |
| 17 | Wisconsin | 5,472 |
| 18 | Missouri | 5,414 |
| 19 | Delaware | 4,512 |
| 20 | Maine | 3,611 |
| 21 | Arkansas | 2,422 |
| 22 | Mississippi | 1,227 |
| 23 | Vermont | 715 |
| 24 | Montana | 249 |
| 25 | Oklahoma | 224 |
| 26 | Alabama | (611) |
| 27 | Indiana | (659) |
| 28 | Rhode Island | (1,029) |
| 29 | South Dakota | (1,782) |
| 30 | Kansas | (2,915) |
| 31 | Wyoming | (3,007) |
| 32 | Iowa | (3,008) |
| 33 | Alaska | (4,076) |
| 34 | Maryland | (4,472) |
| 35 | Nebraska | (4,627) |
| 36 | West Virginia | (6,298) |
| 37 | North Dakota | (7,051) |
| 38 | Massachusetts | (8,656) |
| 39 | Utah | (8,657) |
| 40 | Connecticut | (11,447) |
| 41 | New Mexico | (12,554) |
| 42 | Michigan | (16,966) |
| 43 | Louisiana | (19,050) |
| 44 | Hawaii | (20,112) |
| 45 | New Jersey | (31,294) |
| 46 | Ohio | (32,671) |
| 47 | Pennsylvania | (37,935) |
| 48 | Illinois | (65,930) |
| 49 | California | (80,952) |
| 50 | New York | (167,818) |
| | District of Columbia | (7,227) |

Source: U.S. Bureau of the Census
"State Population Estimates and Demographic Components of Population Change" (ST-99-1, December 29, 1999)
*As of July 1, 1999. Includes armed forces residing in each state. Net Domestic Migration is the difference between domestic inmigration to an area and domestic outmigration from it during the period. Domestic inmigration and outmigration consist of moves where both the origins and destinations are within the United States (excluding Puerto Rico).

# Net International Migration: 1998 to 1999

## National Net = 851,541 Immigrants*

ALPHA ORDER

| RANK | STATE | NET MIGRATION | % of USA |
|------|-------|---------------|----------|
| 37 | Alabama | 1,590 | 0.2% |
| 42 | Alaska | 963 | 0.1% |
| 14 | Arizona | 11,634 | 1.4% |
| 39 | Arkansas | 1,330 | 0.2% |
| 1 | California | 248,490 | 29.2% |
| 16 | Colorado | 8,639 | 1.0% |
| 18 | Connecticut | 8,259 | 1.0% |
| 40 | Delaware | 1,160 | 0.1% |
| 4 | Florida | 80,463 | 9.4% |
| 11 | Georgia | 14,776 | 1.7% |
| 24 | Hawaii | 4,721 | 0.6% |
| 31 | Idaho | 2,866 | 0.3% |
| 5 | Illinois | 47,172 | 5.5% |
| 23 | Indiana | 4,801 | 0.6% |
| 30 | Iowa | 3,398 | 0.4% |
| 28 | Kansas | 4,110 | 0.5% |
| 34 | Kentucky | 2,339 | 0.3% |
| 35 | Louisiana | 2,267 | 0.3% |
| 47 | Maine | 527 | 0.1% |
| 9 | Maryland | 17,174 | 2.0% |
| 10 | Massachusetts | 14,939 | 1.8% |
| 12 | Michigan | 13,576 | 1.6% |
| 20 | Minnesota | 7,877 | 0.9% |
| 45 | Mississippi | 791 | 0.1% |
| 22 | Missouri | 5,266 | 0.6% |
| 49 | Montana | 231 | 0.0% |
| 36 | Nebraska | 2,003 | 0.2% |
| 15 | Nevada | 9,097 | 1.1% |
| 41 | New Hampshire | 1,133 | 0.1% |
| 6 | New Jersey | 39,749 | 4.7% |
| 26 | New Mexico | 4,170 | 0.5% |
| 2 | New York | 103,745 | 12.2% |
| 17 | North Carolina | 8,261 | 1.0% |
| 44 | North Dakota | 854 | 0.1% |
| 21 | Ohio | 6,476 | 0.8% |
| 29 | Oklahoma | 3,510 | 0.4% |
| 19 | Oregon | 8,126 | 1.0% |
| 13 | Pennsylvania | 13,038 | 1.5% |
| 38 | Rhode Island | 1,553 | 0.2% |
| 33 | South Carolina | 2,458 | 0.3% |
| 46 | South Dakota | 790 | 0.1% |
| 27 | Tennessee | 4,145 | 0.5% |
| 3 | Texas | 81,934 | 9.6% |
| 25 | Utah | 4,330 | 0.5% |
| 43 | Vermont | 928 | 0.1% |
| 8 | Virginia | 18,540 | 2.2% |
| 7 | Washington | 21,360 | 2.5% |
| 48 | West Virginia | 238 | 0.0% |
| 32 | Wisconsin | 2,633 | 0.3% |
| 50 | Wyoming | 170 | 0.0% |

RANK ORDER

| RANK | STATE | NET MIGRATION | % of USA |
|------|-------|---------------|----------|
| 1 | California | 248,490 | 29.2% |
| 2 | New York | 103,745 | 12.2% |
| 3 | Texas | 81,934 | 9.6% |
| 4 | Florida | 80,463 | 9.4% |
| 5 | Illinois | 47,172 | 5.5% |
| 6 | New Jersey | 39,749 | 4.7% |
| 7 | Washington | 21,360 | 2.5% |
| 8 | Virginia | 18,540 | 2.2% |
| 9 | Maryland | 17,174 | 2.0% |
| 10 | Massachusetts | 14,939 | 1.8% |
| 11 | Georgia | 14,776 | 1.7% |
| 12 | Michigan | 13,576 | 1.6% |
| 13 | Pennsylvania | 13,038 | 1.5% |
| 14 | Arizona | 11,634 | 1.4% |
| 15 | Nevada | 9,097 | 1.1% |
| 16 | Colorado | 8,639 | 1.0% |
| 17 | North Carolina | 8,261 | 1.0% |
| 18 | Connecticut | 8,259 | 1.0% |
| 19 | Oregon | 8,126 | 1.0% |
| 20 | Minnesota | 7,877 | 0.9% |
| 21 | Ohio | 6,476 | 0.8% |
| 22 | Missouri | 5,266 | 0.6% |
| 23 | Indiana | 4,801 | 0.6% |
| 24 | Hawaii | 4,721 | 0.6% |
| 25 | Utah | 4,330 | 0.5% |
| 26 | New Mexico | 4,170 | 0.5% |
| 27 | Tennessee | 4,145 | 0.5% |
| 28 | Kansas | 4,110 | 0.5% |
| 29 | Oklahoma | 3,510 | 0.4% |
| 30 | Iowa | 3,398 | 0.4% |
| 31 | Idaho | 2,866 | 0.3% |
| 32 | Wisconsin | 2,633 | 0.3% |
| 33 | South Carolina | 2,458 | 0.3% |
| 34 | Kentucky | 2,339 | 0.3% |
| 35 | Louisiana | 2,267 | 0.3% |
| 36 | Nebraska | 2,003 | 0.2% |
| 37 | Alabama | 1,590 | 0.2% |
| 38 | Rhode Island | 1,553 | 0.2% |
| 39 | Arkansas | 1,330 | 0.2% |
| 40 | Delaware | 1,160 | 0.1% |
| 41 | New Hampshire | 1,133 | 0.1% |
| 42 | Alaska | 963 | 0.1% |
| 43 | Vermont | 928 | 0.1% |
| 44 | North Dakota | 854 | 0.1% |
| 45 | Mississippi | 791 | 0.1% |
| 46 | South Dakota | 790 | 0.1% |
| 47 | Maine | 527 | 0.1% |
| 48 | West Virginia | 238 | 0.0% |
| 49 | Montana | 231 | 0.0% |
| 50 | Wyoming | 170 | 0.0% |
| | District of Columbia | 2,941 | 0.3% |

Source: U.S. Bureau of the Census
"State Population Estimates and Demographic Components of Population Change" (ST-99-1, December 29, 1999)
*As of July 1, 1999. Net International Migration the difference between migration to an area from outside the United States (immigration) and migration from the area to outside the United States (emigration) during the period. Includes legal immigration and estimates of undocumented immigration.

# Marriages in 1999

## National Total = 2,358,000 Marriages*

| ALPHA ORDER | | | | RANK ORDER | | | |
|---|---|---|---|---|---|---|---|
| RANK | STATE | MARRIAGES | % of USA | RANK | STATE | MARRIAGES | % of USA |
| 15 | Alabama | 47,700 | 2.0% | 1 | California | 215,510 | 9.1% |
| 47 | Alaska | 5,948 | 0.3% | 2 | Texas | 186,960 | 7.9% |
| 19 | Arizona | 41,174 | 1.7% | 3 | Nevada | 159,291 | 6.8% |
| 23 | Arkansas | 39,363 | 1.7% | 4 | New York | 137,153 | 5.8% |
| 1 | California | 215,510 | 9.1% | 5 | Florida | 136,889 | 5.8% |
| 26 | Colorado | 34,771 | 1.5% | 6 | Ohio | 88,638 | 3.8% |
| 35 | Connecticut | 19,748 | 0.8% | 7 | Illinois | 85,944 | 3.6% |
| 48 | Delaware | 5,180 | 0.2% | 8 | Tennessee | 83,162 | 3.5% |
| 5 | Florida | 136,889 | 5.8% | 9 | Pennsylvania | 75,169 | 3.2% |
| 14 | Georgia | 62,642 | 2.7% | 10 | North Carolina | 67,496 | 2.9% |
| 32 | Hawaii | 22,873 | 1.0% | 11 | Michigan | 67,136 | 2.8% |
| 37 | Idaho | 15,439 | 0.7% | 12 | New Jersey | 65,632 | 2.8% |
| 7 | Illinois | 85,944 | 3.6% | 13 | Virginia | 64,683 | 2.7% |
| 27 | Indiana | 33,913 | 1.4% | 14 | Georgia | 62,642 | 2.7% |
| 31 | Iowa | 22,965 | 1.0% | 15 | Alabama | 47,700 | 2.0% |
| 36 | Kansas | 19,004 | 0.8% | 16 | Missouri | 45,314 | 1.9% |
| 17 | Kentucky | 43,773 | 1.9% | 17 | Kentucky | 43,773 | 1.9% |
| 21 | Louisiana | 40,608 | 1.7% | 18 | Washington | 42,325 | 1.8% |
| 41 | Maine | 10,146 | 0.4% | 19 | Arizona | 41,174 | 1.7% |
| 24 | Maryland | 39,179 | 1.7% | 20 | South Carolina | 40,728 | 1.7% |
| 22 | Massachusetts | 39,411 | 1.7% | 21 | Louisiana | 40,608 | 1.7% |
| 11 | Michigan | 67,136 | 2.8% | 22 | Massachusetts | 39,411 | 1.7% |
| 28 | Minnesota | 33,123 | 1.4% | 23 | Arkansas | 39,363 | 1.7% |
| 33 | Mississippi | 21,944 | 0.9% | 24 | Maryland | 39,179 | 1.7% |
| 16 | Missouri | 45,314 | 1.9% | 25 | Wisconsin | 35,864 | 1.5% |
| 45 | Montana | 6,633 | 0.3% | 26 | Colorado | 34,771 | 1.5% |
| 40 | Nebraska | 12,801 | 0.5% | 27 | Indiana | 33,913 | 1.4% |
| 3 | Nevada | 159,291 | 6.8% | 28 | Minnesota | 33,123 | 1.4% |
| 42 | New Hampshire | 9,676 | 0.4% | 29 | Oregon | 25,721 | 1.1% |
| 12 | New Jersey | 65,632 | 2.8% | 30 | Oklahoma | 23,304 | 1.0% |
| 38 | New Mexico | 14,506 | 0.6% | 31 | Iowa | 22,965 | 1.0% |
| 4 | New York | 137,153 | 5.8% | 32 | Hawaii | 22,873 | 1.0% |
| 10 | North Carolina | 67,496 | 2.9% | 33 | Mississippi | 21,944 | 0.9% |
| 50 | North Dakota | 4,277 | 0.2% | 34 | Utah | 21,089 | 0.9% |
| 6 | Ohio | 88,638 | 3.8% | 35 | Connecticut | 19,748 | 0.8% |
| 30 | Oklahoma | 23,304 | 1.0% | 36 | Kansas | 19,004 | 0.8% |
| 29 | Oregon | 25,721 | 1.1% | 37 | Idaho | 15,439 | 0.7% |
| 9 | Pennsylvania | 75,169 | 3.2% | 38 | New Mexico | 14,506 | 0.6% |
| 43 | Rhode Island | 7,770 | 0.3% | 39 | West Virginia | 13,549 | 0.6% |
| 20 | South Carolina | 40,728 | 1.7% | 40 | Nebraska | 12,801 | 0.5% |
| 44 | South Dakota | 6,840 | 0.3% | 41 | Maine | 10,146 | 0.4% |
| 8 | Tennessee | 83,162 | 3.5% | 42 | New Hampshire | 9,676 | 0.4% |
| 2 | Texas | 186,960 | 7.9% | 43 | Rhode Island | 7,770 | 0.3% |
| 34 | Utah | 21,089 | 0.9% | 44 | South Dakota | 6,840 | 0.3% |
| 46 | Vermont | 6,024 | 0.3% | 45 | Montana | 6,633 | 0.3% |
| 13 | Virginia | 64,683 | 2.7% | 46 | Vermont | 6,024 | 0.3% |
| 18 | Washington | 42,325 | 1.8% | 47 | Alaska | 5,948 | 0.3% |
| 39 | West Virginia | 13,549 | 0.6% | 48 | Delaware | 5,180 | 0.2% |
| 25 | Wisconsin | 35,864 | 1.5% | 49 | Wyoming | 4,845 | 0.2% |
| 49 | Wyoming | 4,845 | 0.2% | 50 | North Dakota | 4,277 | 0.2% |
| | | | | | District of Columbia** | NA | NA |

Source: U.S. Department of Health and Human Services, National Center for Health Statistics
    "National Vital Statistics Reports" (Vol. 48, No. 19, February 22, 2001)
*Provisional data by state of occurrence.
**Not available.

# Marriage Rate in 1999

## National Rate = 8.6 Marriages per 1,000 Population*

ALPHA ORDER

| RANK | STATE | RATE |
|---|---|---|
| 7 | Alabama | 10.9 |
| 12 | Alaska | 9.6 |
| 19 | Arizona | 8.6 |
| 3 | Arkansas | 15.4 |
| 46 | California | 6.5 |
| 19 | Colorado | 8.6 |
| 49 | Connecticut | 6.0 |
| 40 | Delaware | 6.9 |
| 17 | Florida | 9.1 |
| 26 | Georgia | 8.0 |
| 2 | Hawaii | 19.3 |
| 5 | Idaho | 12.3 |
| 39 | Illinois | 7.1 |
| 50 | Indiana | 5.7 |
| 26 | Iowa | 8.0 |
| 38 | Kansas | 7.2 |
| 6 | Kentucky | 11.1 |
| 14 | Louisiana | 9.3 |
| 23 | Maine | 8.1 |
| 33 | Maryland | 7.6 |
| 47 | Massachusetts | 6.4 |
| 43 | Michigan | 6.8 |
| 40 | Minnesota | 6.9 |
| 28 | Mississippi | 7.9 |
| 21 | Missouri | 8.3 |
| 34 | Montana | 7.5 |
| 32 | Nebraska | 7.7 |
| 1 | Nevada | 88.0 |
| 23 | New Hampshire | 8.1 |
| 23 | New Jersey | 8.1 |
| 21 | New Mexico | 8.3 |
| 34 | New York | 7.5 |
| 18 | North Carolina | 8.8 |
| 45 | North Dakota | 6.7 |
| 28 | Ohio | 7.9 |
| 40 | Oklahoma | 6.9 |
| 30 | Oregon | 7.8 |
| 48 | Pennsylvania | 6.3 |
| 30 | Rhode Island | 7.8 |
| 8 | South Carolina | 10.5 |
| 14 | South Dakota | 9.3 |
| 4 | Tennessee | 15.2 |
| 14 | Texas | 9.3 |
| 11 | Utah | 9.9 |
| 9 | Vermont | 10.1 |
| 13 | Virginia | 9.4 |
| 37 | Washington | 7.4 |
| 34 | West Virginia | 7.5 |
| 43 | Wisconsin | 6.8 |
| 9 | Wyoming | 10.1 |

RANK ORDER

| RANK | STATE | RATE |
|---|---|---|
| 1 | Nevada | 88.0 |
| 2 | Hawaii | 19.3 |
| 3 | Arkansas | 15.4 |
| 4 | Tennessee | 15.2 |
| 5 | Idaho | 12.3 |
| 6 | Kentucky | 11.1 |
| 7 | Alabama | 10.9 |
| 8 | South Carolina | 10.5 |
| 9 | Vermont | 10.1 |
| 9 | Wyoming | 10.1 |
| 11 | Utah | 9.9 |
| 12 | Alaska | 9.6 |
| 13 | Virginia | 9.4 |
| 14 | Louisiana | 9.3 |
| 14 | South Dakota | 9.3 |
| 14 | Texas | 9.3 |
| 17 | Florida | 9.1 |
| 18 | North Carolina | 8.8 |
| 19 | Arizona | 8.6 |
| 19 | Colorado | 8.6 |
| 21 | Missouri | 8.3 |
| 21 | New Mexico | 8.3 |
| 23 | Maine | 8.1 |
| 23 | New Hampshire | 8.1 |
| 23 | New Jersey | 8.1 |
| 26 | Georgia | 8.0 |
| 26 | Iowa | 8.0 |
| 28 | Mississippi | 7.9 |
| 28 | Ohio | 7.9 |
| 30 | Oregon | 7.8 |
| 30 | Rhode Island | 7.8 |
| 32 | Nebraska | 7.7 |
| 33 | Maryland | 7.6 |
| 34 | Montana | 7.5 |
| 34 | New York | 7.5 |
| 34 | West Virginia | 7.5 |
| 37 | Washington | 7.4 |
| 38 | Kansas | 7.2 |
| 39 | Illinois | 7.1 |
| 40 | Delaware | 6.9 |
| 40 | Minnesota | 6.9 |
| 40 | Oklahoma | 6.9 |
| 43 | Michigan | 6.8 |
| 43 | Wisconsin | 6.8 |
| 45 | North Dakota | 6.7 |
| 46 | California | 6.5 |
| 47 | Massachusetts | 6.4 |
| 48 | Pennsylvania | 6.3 |
| 49 | Connecticut | 6.0 |
| 50 | Indiana | 5.7 |
| | District of Columbia** | NA |

Source: Morgan Quitno Press using data from U.S. Dept of Health and Human Services, Nat'l Center for Health Statistics
"National Vital Statistics Reports" (Vol. 48, No. 19, February 22, 2001)
*Provisional data by state of occurrence.
**Not available.

# Divorces in 1999

## National Reporting States' Total = 928,469 Divorces*

| ALPHA ORDER | | | | | RANK ORDER | | | |
|---|---|---|---|---|---|---|---|---|
| RANK | STATE | DIVORCES | % of USA | | RANK | STATE | DIVORCES | % of USA |
| 13 | Alabama | 25,885 | 2.8% | | 1 | Florida | 81,674 | 8.8% |
| 40 | Alaska | 3,212 | 0.3% | | 2 | Texas | 72,445 | 7.8% |
| 16 | Arizona | 22,983 | 2.5% | | 3 | New York | 61,803 | 6.7% |
| 22 | Arkansas | 15,501 | 1.7% | | 4 | Ohio | 45,695 | 4.9% |
| NA | California** | NA | NA | | 5 | Illinois | 41,025 | 4.4% |
| NA | Colorado** | NA | NA | | 6 | Michigan | 38,017 | 4.1% |
| 37 | Connecticut | 5,655 | 0.6% | | 7 | Pennsylvania | 37,829 | 4.1% |
| 39 | Delaware | 3,647 | 0.4% | | 8 | North Carolina | 36,739 | 4.0% |
| 1 | Florida | 81,674 | 8.8% | | 9 | Georgia | 34,227 | 3.7% |
| 9 | Georgia | 34,227 | 3.7% | | 10 | Tennessee | 32,737 | 3.5% |
| 38 | Hawaii | 4,377 | 0.5% | | 11 | Virginia | 31,729 | 3.4% |
| 34 | Idaho | 6,780 | 0.7% | | 12 | Washington | 28,970 | 3.1% |
| 5 | Illinois | 41,025 | 4.4% | | 13 | Alabama | 25,885 | 2.8% |
| NA | Indiana** | NA | NA | | 14 | New Jersey | 25,181 | 2.7% |
| 29 | Iowa | 9,874 | 1.1% | | 15 | Missouri | 24,656 | 2.7% |
| 28 | Kansas | 10,164 | 1.1% | | 16 | Arizona | 22,983 | 2.5% |
| 17 | Kentucky | 22,689 | 2.4% | | 17 | Kentucky | 22,689 | 2.4% |
| NA | Louisiana** | NA | NA | | 18 | Oklahoma | 19,696 | 2.1% |
| 36 | Maine | 5,731 | 0.6% | | 19 | Wisconsin | 17,758 | 1.9% |
| 20 | Maryland | 16,785 | 1.8% | | 20 | Maryland | 16,785 | 1.8% |
| 27 | Massachusetts | 13,181 | 1.4% | | 21 | Oregon | 15,867 | 1.7% |
| 6 | Michigan | 38,017 | 4.1% | | 22 | Arkansas | 15,501 | 1.7% |
| 26 | Minnesota | 13,514 | 1.5% | | 23 | Mississippi | 15,341 | 1.7% |
| 23 | Mississippi | 15,341 | 1.7% | | 24 | Nevada | 15,026 | 1.6% |
| 15 | Missouri | 24,656 | 2.7% | | 25 | South Carolina | 14,496 | 1.6% |
| 45 | Montana | 2,548 | 0.3% | | 26 | Minnesota | 13,514 | 1.5% |
| 35 | Nebraska | 6,254 | 0.7% | | 27 | Massachusetts | 13,181 | 1.4% |
| 24 | Nevada | 15,026 | 1.6% | | 28 | Kansas | 10,164 | 1.1% |
| 33 | New Hampshire | 6,966 | 0.8% | | 29 | Iowa | 9,874 | 1.1% |
| 14 | New Jersey | 25,181 | 2.7% | | 30 | Utah | 9,455 | 1.0% |
| 32 | New Mexico | 8,258 | 0.9% | | 31 | West Virginia | 8,957 | 1.0% |
| 3 | New York | 61,803 | 6.7% | | 32 | New Mexico | 8,258 | 0.9% |
| 8 | North Carolina | 36,739 | 4.0% | | 33 | New Hampshire | 6,966 | 0.8% |
| 46 | North Dakota | 2,023 | 0.2% | | 34 | Idaho | 6,780 | 0.7% |
| 4 | Ohio | 45,695 | 4.9% | | 35 | Nebraska | 6,254 | 0.7% |
| 18 | Oklahoma | 19,696 | 2.1% | | 36 | Maine | 5,731 | 0.6% |
| 21 | Oregon | 15,867 | 1.7% | | 37 | Connecticut | 5,655 | 0.6% |
| 7 | Pennsylvania | 37,829 | 4.1% | | 38 | Hawaii | 4,377 | 0.5% |
| 41 | Rhode Island | 2,857 | 0.3% | | 39 | Delaware | 3,647 | 0.4% |
| 25 | South Carolina | 14,496 | 1.6% | | 40 | Alaska | 3,212 | 0.3% |
| 43 | South Dakota | 2,768 | 0.3% | | 41 | Rhode Island | 2,857 | 0.3% |
| 10 | Tennessee | 32,737 | 3.5% | | 42 | Wyoming | 2,824 | 0.3% |
| 2 | Texas | 72,445 | 7.8% | | 43 | South Dakota | 2,768 | 0.3% |
| 30 | Utah | 9,455 | 1.0% | | 44 | Vermont | 2,603 | 0.3% |
| 44 | Vermont | 2,603 | 0.3% | | 45 | Montana | 2,548 | 0.3% |
| 11 | Virginia | 31,729 | 3.4% | | 46 | North Dakota | 2,023 | 0.2% |
| 12 | Washington | 28,970 | 3.1% | | NA | California** | NA | NA |
| 31 | West Virginia | 8,957 | 1.0% | | NA | Colorado** | NA | NA |
| 19 | Wisconsin | 17,758 | 1.9% | | NA | Indiana** | NA | NA |
| 42 | Wyoming | 2,824 | 0.3% | | NA | Louisiana** | NA | NA |
| | | | | | | District of Columbia | 2,067 | 0.2% |

*Source: U.S. Department of Health and Human Services, National Center for Health Statistics*
  *"National Vital Statistics Reports" (Vol. 48, No. 19, February 22, 2001)*
*Provisional data by state of occurrence. National total is only for reporting states.*
**Not available.*

# Divorce Rate in 1999

## National Rate = 4.1 Divorces per 1,000 Population*

ALPHA ORDER

| RANK | STATE | RATE |
|------|-------|------|
| 4 | Alabama | 5.9 |
| 12 | Alaska | 5.2 |
| 15 | Arizona | 4.8 |
| 2 | Arkansas | 6.1 |
| NA | California** | NA |
| NA | Colorado** | NA |
| 46 | Connecticut | 1.7 |
| 15 | Delaware | 4.8 |
| 10 | Florida | 5.4 |
| 23 | Georgia | 4.4 |
| 31 | Hawaii | 3.7 |
| 10 | Idaho | 5.4 |
| 34 | Illinois | 3.4 |
| NA | Indiana** | NA |
| 34 | Iowa | 3.4 |
| 28 | Kansas | 3.8 |
| 8 | Kentucky | 5.7 |
| NA | Louisiana** | NA |
| 20 | Maine | 4.6 |
| 38 | Maryland | 3.2 |
| 45 | Massachusetts | 2.1 |
| 27 | Michigan | 3.9 |
| 44 | Minnesota | 2.8 |
| 9 | Mississippi | 5.5 |
| 22 | Missouri | 4.5 |
| 42 | Montana | 2.9 |
| 28 | Nebraska | 3.8 |
| 1 | Nevada | 8.3 |
| 7 | New Hampshire | 5.8 |
| 41 | New Jersey | 3.1 |
| 19 | New Mexico | 4.7 |
| 34 | New York | 3.4 |
| 15 | North Carolina | 4.8 |
| 38 | North Dakota | 3.2 |
| 26 | Ohio | 4.1 |
| 4 | Oklahoma | 5.9 |
| 15 | Oregon | 4.8 |
| 38 | Pennsylvania | 3.2 |
| 42 | Rhode Island | 2.9 |
| 31 | South Carolina | 3.7 |
| 28 | South Dakota | 3.8 |
| 3 | Tennessee | 6.0 |
| 33 | Texas | 3.6 |
| 23 | Utah | 4.4 |
| 23 | Vermont | 4.4 |
| 20 | Virginia | 4.6 |
| 13 | Washington | 5.0 |
| 13 | West Virginia | 5.0 |
| 34 | Wisconsin | 3.4 |
| 4 | Wyoming | 5.9 |

RANK ORDER

| RANK | STATE | RATE |
|------|-------|------|
| 1 | Nevada | 8.3 |
| 2 | Arkansas | 6.1 |
| 3 | Tennessee | 6.0 |
| 4 | Alabama | 5.9 |
| 4 | Oklahoma | 5.9 |
| 4 | Wyoming | 5.9 |
| 7 | New Hampshire | 5.8 |
| 8 | Kentucky | 5.7 |
| 9 | Mississippi | 5.5 |
| 10 | Florida | 5.4 |
| 10 | Idaho | 5.4 |
| 12 | Alaska | 5.2 |
| 13 | Washington | 5.0 |
| 13 | West Virginia | 5.0 |
| 15 | Arizona | 4.8 |
| 15 | Delaware | 4.8 |
| 15 | North Carolina | 4.8 |
| 15 | Oregon | 4.8 |
| 19 | New Mexico | 4.7 |
| 20 | Maine | 4.6 |
| 20 | Virginia | 4.6 |
| 22 | Missouri | 4.5 |
| 23 | Georgia | 4.4 |
| 23 | Utah | 4.4 |
| 23 | Vermont | 4.4 |
| 26 | Ohio | 4.1 |
| 27 | Michigan | 3.9 |
| 28 | Kansas | 3.8 |
| 28 | Nebraska | 3.8 |
| 28 | South Dakota | 3.8 |
| 31 | Hawaii | 3.7 |
| 31 | South Carolina | 3.7 |
| 33 | Texas | 3.6 |
| 34 | Illinois | 3.4 |
| 34 | Iowa | 3.4 |
| 34 | New York | 3.4 |
| 34 | Wisconsin | 3.4 |
| 38 | Maryland | 3.2 |
| 38 | North Dakota | 3.2 |
| 38 | Pennsylvania | 3.2 |
| 41 | New Jersey | 3.1 |
| 42 | Montana | 2.9 |
| 42 | Rhode Island | 2.9 |
| 44 | Minnesota | 2.8 |
| 45 | Massachusetts | 2.1 |
| 46 | Connecticut | 1.7 |
| NA | California** | NA |
| NA | Colorado** | NA |
| NA | Indiana** | NA |
| NA | Louisiana** | NA |

| District of Columbia | | 4.0 |

*Source: Morgan Quitno Press using data from U.S. Dept of Health and Human Services, Nat'l Center for Health Statistics "National Vital Statistics Reports" (Vol. 48, No. 19, February 22, 2001)*
*Provisional data by state of occurrence. National rate is only for reporting states.*
**Not available.*

# Seats in the U.S. House of Representatives in 2000

## National Total = 435 Seats*

| RANK | STATE | SEATS | % of USA |
|------|-------|-------|----------|
| 21 | Alabama | 7 | 1.6% |
| 44 | Alaska | 1 | 0.2% |
| 23 | Arizona | 6 | 1.4% |
| 32 | Arkansas | 4 | 0.9% |
| 1 | California | 52 | 12.0% |
| 23 | Colorado | 6 | 1.4% |
| 23 | Connecticut | 6 | 1.4% |
| 44 | Delaware | 1 | 0.2% |
| 4 | Florida | 23 | 5.3% |
| 11 | Georgia | 11 | 2.5% |
| 38 | Hawaii | 2 | 0.5% |
| 38 | Idaho | 2 | 0.5% |
| 6 | Illinois | 20 | 4.6% |
| 13 | Indiana | 10 | 2.3% |
| 29 | Iowa | 5 | 1.1% |
| 32 | Kansas | 4 | 0.9% |
| 23 | Kentucky | 6 | 1.4% |
| 21 | Louisiana | 7 | 1.6% |
| 38 | Maine | 2 | 0.5% |
| 19 | Maryland | 8 | 1.8% |
| 13 | Massachusetts | 10 | 2.3% |
| 8 | Michigan | 16 | 3.7% |
| 19 | Minnesota | 8 | 1.8% |
| 29 | Mississippi | 5 | 1.1% |
| 15 | Missouri | 9 | 2.1% |
| 44 | Montana | 1 | 0.2% |
| 34 | Nebraska | 3 | 0.7% |
| 38 | Nevada | 2 | 0.5% |
| 38 | New Hampshire | 2 | 0.5% |
| 9 | New Jersey | 13 | 3.0% |
| 34 | New Mexico | 3 | 0.7% |
| 2 | New York | 31 | 7.1% |
| 10 | North Carolina | 12 | 2.8% |
| 44 | North Dakota | 1 | 0.2% |
| 7 | Ohio | 19 | 4.4% |
| 23 | Oklahoma | 6 | 1.4% |
| 29 | Oregon | 5 | 1.1% |
| 5 | Pennsylvania | 21 | 4.8% |
| 38 | Rhode Island | 2 | 0.5% |
| 23 | South Carolina | 6 | 1.4% |
| 44 | South Dakota | 1 | 0.2% |
| 15 | Tennessee | 9 | 2.1% |
| 3 | Texas | 30 | 6.9% |
| 34 | Utah | 3 | 0.7% |
| 44 | Vermont | 1 | 0.2% |
| 11 | Virginia | 11 | 2.5% |
| 15 | Washington | 9 | 2.1% |
| 34 | West Virginia | 3 | 0.7% |
| 15 | Wisconsin | 9 | 2.1% |
| 44 | Wyoming | 1 | 0.2% |

| RANK | STATE | SEATS | % of USA |
|------|-------|-------|----------|
| 1 | California | 52 | 12.0% |
| 2 | New York | 31 | 7.1% |
| 3 | Texas | 30 | 6.9% |
| 4 | Florida | 23 | 5.3% |
| 5 | Pennsylvania | 21 | 4.8% |
| 6 | Illinois | 20 | 4.6% |
| 7 | Ohio | 19 | 4.4% |
| 8 | Michigan | 16 | 3.7% |
| 9 | New Jersey | 13 | 3.0% |
| 10 | North Carolina | 12 | 2.8% |
| 11 | Georgia | 11 | 2.5% |
| 11 | Virginia | 11 | 2.5% |
| 13 | Indiana | 10 | 2.3% |
| 13 | Massachusetts | 10 | 2.3% |
| 15 | Missouri | 9 | 2.1% |
| 15 | Tennessee | 9 | 2.1% |
| 15 | Washington | 9 | 2.1% |
| 15 | Wisconsin | 9 | 2.1% |
| 19 | Maryland | 8 | 1.8% |
| 19 | Minnesota | 8 | 1.8% |
| 21 | Alabama | 7 | 1.6% |
| 21 | Louisiana | 7 | 1.6% |
| 23 | Arizona | 6 | 1.4% |
| 23 | Colorado | 6 | 1.4% |
| 23 | Connecticut | 6 | 1.4% |
| 23 | Kentucky | 6 | 1.4% |
| 23 | Oklahoma | 6 | 1.4% |
| 23 | South Carolina | 6 | 1.4% |
| 29 | Iowa | 5 | 1.1% |
| 29 | Mississippi | 5 | 1.1% |
| 29 | Oregon | 5 | 1.1% |
| 32 | Arkansas | 4 | 0.9% |
| 32 | Kansas | 4 | 0.9% |
| 34 | Nebraska | 3 | 0.7% |
| 34 | New Mexico | 3 | 0.7% |
| 34 | Utah | 3 | 0.7% |
| 34 | West Virginia | 3 | 0.7% |
| 38 | Hawaii | 2 | 0.5% |
| 38 | Idaho | 2 | 0.5% |
| 38 | Maine | 2 | 0.5% |
| 38 | Nevada | 2 | 0.5% |
| 38 | New Hampshire | 2 | 0.5% |
| 38 | Rhode Island | 2 | 0.5% |
| 44 | Alaska | 1 | 0.2% |
| 44 | Delaware | 1 | 0.2% |
| 44 | Montana | 1 | 0.2% |
| 44 | North Dakota | 1 | 0.2% |
| 44 | South Dakota | 1 | 0.2% |
| 44 | Vermont | 1 | 0.2% |
| 44 | Wyoming | 1 | 0.2% |
| | District of Columbia** | 0 | 0.0% |

Source: U.S. Bureau of the Census
    Press Release CB90-232
*This table does not reflect reapportionment as a result of the 2000 Census.
**The District of Columbia has one non-voting delegate. Each state has two members in the U.S. Senate.

# Population per U.S. House of Representative Seat in 2000

## National Rate = 645,632 Population per Member of Congress*

ALPHA ORDER

RANK ORDER

| RANK | STATE | RATE | RANK | STATE | RATE |
|------|-------|------|------|-------|------|
| 26 | Alabama | 635,300 | 1 | Nevada | 999,129 |
| 29 | Alaska | 626,932 | 2 | Montana | 902,195 |
| 3 | Arizona | 855,105 | 3 | Arizona | 855,105 |
| 16 | Arkansas | 668,350 | 4 | Delaware | 783,600 |
| 19 | California | 651,378 | 5 | South Dakota | 754,844 |
| 8 | Colorado | 716,877 | 6 | Utah | 744,390 |
| 48 | Connecticut | 567,594 | 7 | Georgia | 744,223 |
| 4 | Delaware | 783,600 | 8 | Colorado | 716,877 |
| 10 | Florida | 694,886 | 9 | Texas | 695,061 |
| 7 | Georgia | 744,223 | 10 | Florida | 694,886 |
| 39 | Hawaii | 605,769 | 11 | Oregon | 684,280 |
| 21 | Idaho | 646,977 | 12 | Kentucky | 673,628 |
| 32 | Illinois | 620,965 | 13 | Kansas | 672,105 |
| 37 | Indiana | 608,049 | 14 | North Carolina | 670,776 |
| 43 | Iowa | 585,265 | 15 | South Carolina | 668,669 |
| 13 | Kansas | 672,105 | 16 | Arkansas | 668,350 |
| 12 | Kentucky | 673,628 | 17 | Maryland | 662,061 |
| 24 | Louisiana | 638,425 | 18 | Washington | 654,902 |
| 25 | Maine | 637,462 | 19 | California | 651,378 |
| 17 | Maryland | 662,061 | 20 | New Jersey | 647,258 |
| 27 | Massachusetts | 634,910 | 21 | Idaho | 646,977 |
| 31 | Michigan | 621,153 | 22 | Virginia | 643,501 |
| 34 | Minnesota | 614,935 | 23 | North Dakota | 642,200 |
| 47 | Mississippi | 568,932 | 24 | Louisiana | 638,425 |
| 30 | Missouri | 621,690 | 25 | Maine | 637,462 |
| 2 | Montana | 902,195 | 26 | Alabama | 635,300 |
| 46 | Nebraska | 570,421 | 27 | Massachusetts | 634,910 |
| 1 | Nevada | 999,129 | 28 | Tennessee | 632,143 |
| 33 | New Hampshire | 617,893 | 29 | Alaska | 626,932 |
| 20 | New Jersey | 647,258 | 30 | Missouri | 621,690 |
| 38 | New Mexico | 606,349 | 31 | Michigan | 621,153 |
| 35 | New York | 612,144 | 32 | Illinois | 620,965 |
| 14 | North Carolina | 670,776 | 33 | New Hampshire | 617,893 |
| 23 | North Dakota | 642,200 | 34 | Minnesota | 614,935 |
| 41 | Ohio | 597,534 | 35 | New York | 612,144 |
| 45 | Oklahoma | 575,109 | 36 | Vermont | 608,827 |
| 11 | Oregon | 684,280 | 37 | Indiana | 608,049 |
| 44 | Pennsylvania | 584,812 | 38 | New Mexico | 606,349 |
| 49 | Rhode Island | 524,160 | 39 | Hawaii | 605,769 |
| 15 | South Carolina | 668,669 | 40 | West Virginia | 602,781 |
| 5 | South Dakota | 754,844 | 41 | Ohio | 597,534 |
| 28 | Tennessee | 632,143 | 42 | Wisconsin | 595,964 |
| 9 | Texas | 695,061 | 43 | Iowa | 585,265 |
| 6 | Utah | 744,390 | 44 | Pennsylvania | 584,812 |
| 36 | Vermont | 608,827 | 45 | Oklahoma | 575,109 |
| 22 | Virginia | 643,501 | 46 | Nebraska | 570,421 |
| 18 | Washington | 654,902 | 47 | Mississippi | 568,932 |
| 40 | West Virginia | 602,781 | 48 | Connecticut | 567,594 |
| 42 | Wisconsin | 595,964 | 49 | Rhode Island | 524,160 |
| 50 | Wyoming | 493,782 | 50 | Wyoming | 493,782 |
| | | | | District of Columbia** | NA |

Source: Morgan Quitno Press using data from U.S. Bureau of the Census
    Press Release CB90-232

*National rate does not include population of the District of Columbia. D.C. has one non-voting delegate. Each state has two members in the U.S. Senate. This table is based only on U.S. Representatives and not U.S. Senate members. It does not reflect reapportionment that will result from the 2000 census.

# Seats in the U.S. House of Representatives in 2003

## National Total = 435 Seats*

| RANK | STATE | SEATS | % of USA |
|---|---|---|---|
| 22 | Alabama | 7 | 1.6% |
| 44 | Alaska | 1 | 0.2% |
| 18 | Arizona | 8 | 1.8% |
| 31 | Arkansas | 4 | 0.9% |
| 1 | California | 53 | 12.2% |
| 22 | Colorado | 7 | 1.6% |
| 27 | Connecticut | 5 | 1.1% |
| 44 | Delaware | 1 | 0.2% |
| 4 | Florida | 25 | 5.7% |
| 9 | Georgia | 13 | 3.0% |
| 39 | Hawaii | 2 | 0.5% |
| 39 | Idaho | 2 | 0.5% |
| 5 | Illinois | 19 | 4.4% |
| 14 | Indiana | 9 | 2.1% |
| 27 | Iowa | 5 | 1.1% |
| 31 | Kansas | 4 | 0.9% |
| 25 | Kentucky | 6 | 1.4% |
| 22 | Louisiana | 7 | 1.6% |
| 39 | Maine | 2 | 0.5% |
| 18 | Maryland | 8 | 1.8% |
| 13 | Massachusetts | 10 | 2.3% |
| 8 | Michigan | 15 | 3.4% |
| 18 | Minnesota | 8 | 1.8% |
| 31 | Mississippi | 4 | 0.9% |
| 14 | Missouri | 9 | 2.1% |
| 44 | Montana | 1 | 0.2% |
| 34 | Nebraska | 3 | 0.7% |
| 34 | Nevada | 3 | 0.7% |
| 39 | New Hampshire | 2 | 0.5% |
| 9 | New Jersey | 13 | 3.0% |
| 34 | New Mexico | 3 | 0.7% |
| 3 | New York | 29 | 6.7% |
| 9 | North Carolina | 13 | 3.0% |
| 44 | North Dakota | 1 | 0.2% |
| 7 | Ohio | 18 | 4.1% |
| 27 | Oklahoma | 5 | 1.1% |
| 27 | Oregon | 5 | 1.1% |
| 5 | Pennsylvania | 19 | 4.4% |
| 39 | Rhode Island | 2 | 0.5% |
| 25 | South Carolina | 6 | 1.4% |
| 44 | South Dakota | 1 | 0.2% |
| 14 | Tennessee | 9 | 2.1% |
| 2 | Texas | 32 | 7.4% |
| 34 | Utah | 3 | 0.7% |
| 44 | Vermont | 1 | 0.2% |
| 12 | Virginia | 11 | 2.5% |
| 14 | Washington | 9 | 2.1% |
| 34 | West Virginia | 3 | 0.7% |
| 18 | Wisconsin | 8 | 1.8% |
| 44 | Wyoming | 1 | 0.2% |

| RANK | STATE | SEATS | % of USA |
|---|---|---|---|
| 1 | California | 53 | 12.2% |
| 2 | Texas | 32 | 7.4% |
| 3 | New York | 29 | 6.7% |
| 4 | Florida | 25 | 5.7% |
| 5 | Illinois | 19 | 4.4% |
| 5 | Pennsylvania | 19 | 4.4% |
| 7 | Ohio | 18 | 4.1% |
| 8 | Michigan | 15 | 3.4% |
| 9 | Georgia | 13 | 3.0% |
| 9 | New Jersey | 13 | 3.0% |
| 9 | North Carolina | 13 | 3.0% |
| 12 | Virginia | 11 | 2.5% |
| 13 | Massachusetts | 10 | 2.3% |
| 14 | Indiana | 9 | 2.1% |
| 14 | Missouri | 9 | 2.1% |
| 14 | Tennessee | 9 | 2.1% |
| 14 | Washington | 9 | 2.1% |
| 18 | Arizona | 8 | 1.8% |
| 18 | Maryland | 8 | 1.8% |
| 18 | Minnesota | 8 | 1.8% |
| 18 | Wisconsin | 8 | 1.8% |
| 22 | Alabama | 7 | 1.6% |
| 22 | Colorado | 7 | 1.6% |
| 22 | Louisiana | 7 | 1.6% |
| 25 | Kentucky | 6 | 1.4% |
| 25 | South Carolina | 6 | 1.4% |
| 27 | Connecticut | 5 | 1.1% |
| 27 | Iowa | 5 | 1.1% |
| 27 | Oklahoma | 5 | 1.1% |
| 27 | Oregon | 5 | 1.1% |
| 31 | Arkansas | 4 | 0.9% |
| 31 | Kansas | 4 | 0.9% |
| 31 | Mississippi | 4 | 0.9% |
| 34 | Nebraska | 3 | 0.7% |
| 34 | Nevada | 3 | 0.7% |
| 34 | New Mexico | 3 | 0.7% |
| 34 | Utah | 3 | 0.7% |
| 34 | West Virginia | 3 | 0.7% |
| 39 | Hawaii | 2 | 0.5% |
| 39 | Idaho | 2 | 0.5% |
| 39 | Maine | 2 | 0.5% |
| 39 | New Hampshire | 2 | 0.5% |
| 39 | Rhode Island | 2 | 0.5% |
| 44 | Alaska | 1 | 0.2% |
| 44 | Delaware | 1 | 0.2% |
| 44 | Montana | 1 | 0.2% |
| 44 | North Dakota | 1 | 0.2% |
| 44 | South Dakota | 1 | 0.2% |
| 44 | Vermont | 1 | 0.2% |
| 44 | Wyoming | 1 | 0.2% |
| | District of Columbia** | 0 | 0.0% |

Source: U.S. Bureau of the Census
    "Congressional Apportionment" (http://www.census.gov/population/www/censusdata/apportionment.html)
*This table shows the number of seats after reapportionment of the 2000 Census. This apportionment will become effective with the Congress elected in November 2002 and that will take office in January 2003.
**The District of Columbia has one non-voting delegate. Each state has two members in the U.S. Senate.

# Gain or Loss in U.S. House of Representative Seats: 1990 to 2000 Census

## National Change = 0 Seats*

ALPHA ORDER

RANK ORDER

| RANK | STATE | GAIN/LOSS |
|------|-------|-----------|
| 9 | Alabama | 0 |
| 9 | Alaska | 0 |
| 1 | Arizona | 2 |
| 9 | Arkansas | 0 |
| 5 | California | 1 |
| 5 | Colorado | 1 |
| 41 | Connecticut | (1) |
| 9 | Delaware | 0 |
| 1 | Florida | 2 |
| 1 | Georgia | 2 |
| 9 | Hawaii | 0 |
| 9 | Idaho | 0 |
| 41 | Illinois | (1) |
| 41 | Indiana | (1) |
| 9 | Iowa | 0 |
| 9 | Kansas | 0 |
| 9 | Kentucky | 0 |
| 9 | Louisiana | 0 |
| 9 | Maine | 0 |
| 9 | Maryland | 0 |
| 9 | Massachusetts | 0 |
| 41 | Michigan | (1) |
| 9 | Minnesota | 0 |
| 41 | Mississippi | (1) |
| 9 | Missouri | 0 |
| 9 | Montana | 0 |
| 9 | Nebraska | 0 |
| 5 | Nevada | 1 |
| 9 | New Hampshire | 0 |
| 9 | New Jersey | 0 |
| 9 | New Mexico | 0 |
| 49 | New York | (2) |
| 5 | North Carolina | 1 |
| 9 | North Dakota | 0 |
| 41 | Ohio | (1) |
| 41 | Oklahoma | (1) |
| 9 | Oregon | 0 |
| 49 | Pennsylvania | (2) |
| 9 | Rhode Island | 0 |
| 9 | South Carolina | 0 |
| 9 | South Dakota | 0 |
| 9 | Tennessee | 0 |
| 1 | Texas | 2 |
| 9 | Utah | 0 |
| 9 | Vermont | 0 |
| 9 | Virginia | 0 |
| 9 | Washington | 0 |
| 9 | West Virginia | 0 |
| 41 | Wisconsin | (1) |
| 9 | Wyoming | 0 |

| RANK | STATE | GAIN/LOSS |
|------|-------|-----------|
| 1 | Arizona | 2 |
| 1 | Florida | 2 |
| 1 | Georgia | 2 |
| 1 | Texas | 2 |
| 5 | California | 1 |
| 5 | Colorado | 1 |
| 5 | Nevada | 1 |
| 5 | North Carolina | 1 |
| 9 | Alabama | 0 |
| 9 | Alaska | 0 |
| 9 | Arkansas | 0 |
| 9 | Delaware | 0 |
| 9 | Hawaii | 0 |
| 9 | Idaho | 0 |
| 9 | Iowa | 0 |
| 9 | Kansas | 0 |
| 9 | Kentucky | 0 |
| 9 | Louisiana | 0 |
| 9 | Maine | 0 |
| 9 | Maryland | 0 |
| 9 | Massachusetts | 0 |
| 9 | Minnesota | 0 |
| 9 | Missouri | 0 |
| 9 | Montana | 0 |
| 9 | Nebraska | 0 |
| 9 | New Hampshire | 0 |
| 9 | New Jersey | 0 |
| 9 | New Mexico | 0 |
| 9 | North Dakota | 0 |
| 9 | Oregon | 0 |
| 9 | Rhode Island | 0 |
| 9 | South Carolina | 0 |
| 9 | South Dakota | 0 |
| 9 | Tennessee | 0 |
| 9 | Utah | 0 |
| 9 | Vermont | 0 |
| 9 | Virginia | 0 |
| 9 | Washington | 0 |
| 9 | West Virginia | 0 |
| 9 | Wyoming | 0 |
| 41 | Connecticut | (1) |
| 41 | Illinois | (1) |
| 41 | Indiana | (1) |
| 41 | Michigan | (1) |
| 41 | Mississippi | (1) |
| 41 | Ohio | (1) |
| 41 | Oklahoma | (1) |
| 41 | Wisconsin | (1) |
| 49 | New York | (2) |
| 49 | Pennsylvania | (2) |
| | District of Columbia** | 0 |

*Source: U.S. Bureau of the Census*
    *"Congressional Apportionment" (http://www.census.gov/population/www/censusdata/apportionment.html)*
*This table shows the change in number of seats after reapportionment of the 2000 Census. This apportionment will become effective with the Congress elected in November 2002 and that will take office in January 2003.*
***The District of Columbia has one non-voting delegate. Each state has two members in the U.S. Senate.*

# State Legislators in 2000

## National Total = 7,424 Legislators*

ALPHA ORDER

| RANK | STATE | LEGISLATORS | % of USA |
|------|-------|-------------|----------|
| 28 | Alabama | 140 | 1.9% |
| 49 | Alaska | 60 | 0.8% |
| 43 | Arizona | 90 | 1.2% |
| 31 | Arkansas | 135 | 1.8% |
| 36 | California | 120 | 1.6% |
| 42 | Colorado | 100 | 1.3% |
| 9 | Connecticut | 187 | 2.5% |
| 48 | Delaware | 62 | 0.8% |
| 18 | Florida | 160 | 2.2% |
| 3 | Georgia | 236 | 3.2% |
| 46 | Hawaii | 76 | 1.0% |
| 39 | Idaho | 105 | 1.4% |
| 13 | Illinois | 177 | 2.4% |
| 19 | Indiana | 150 | 2.0% |
| 19 | Iowa | 150 | 2.0% |
| 17 | Kansas | 165 | 2.2% |
| 30 | Kentucky | 138 | 1.9% |
| 27 | Louisiana | 144 | 1.9% |
| 10 | Maine | 186 | 2.5% |
| 8 | Maryland | 188 | 2.5% |
| 6 | Massachusetts | 200 | 2.7% |
| 24 | Michigan | 148 | 2.0% |
| 5 | Minnesota | 201 | 2.7% |
| 14 | Mississippi | 174 | 2.3% |
| 7 | Missouri | 197 | 2.7% |
| 19 | Montana | 150 | 2.0% |
| 50 | Nebraska | 49 | 0.7% |
| 47 | Nevada | 63 | 0.8% |
| 1 | New Hampshire | 424 | 5.7% |
| 36 | New Jersey | 120 | 1.6% |
| 38 | New Mexico | 112 | 1.5% |
| 4 | New York | 211 | 2.8% |
| 15 | North Carolina | 170 | 2.3% |
| 25 | North Dakota | 147 | 2.0% |
| 33 | Ohio | 132 | 1.8% |
| 23 | Oklahoma | 149 | 2.0% |
| 43 | Oregon | 90 | 1.2% |
| 2 | Pennsylvania | 253 | 3.4% |
| 19 | Rhode Island | 150 | 2.0% |
| 15 | South Carolina | 170 | 2.3% |
| 39 | South Dakota | 105 | 1.4% |
| 33 | Tennessee | 132 | 1.8% |
| 11 | Texas | 181 | 2.4% |
| 41 | Utah | 104 | 1.4% |
| 12 | Vermont | 180 | 2.4% |
| 28 | Virginia | 140 | 1.9% |
| 25 | Washington | 147 | 2.0% |
| 32 | West Virginia | 134 | 1.8% |
| 33 | Wisconsin | 132 | 1.8% |
| 43 | Wyoming | 90 | 1.2% |

RANK ORDER

| RANK | STATE | LEGISLATORS | % of USA |
|------|-------|-------------|----------|
| 1 | New Hampshire | 424 | 5.7% |
| 2 | Pennsylvania | 253 | 3.4% |
| 3 | Georgia | 236 | 3.2% |
| 4 | New York | 211 | 2.8% |
| 5 | Minnesota | 201 | 2.7% |
| 6 | Massachusetts | 200 | 2.7% |
| 7 | Missouri | 197 | 2.7% |
| 8 | Maryland | 188 | 2.5% |
| 9 | Connecticut | 187 | 2.5% |
| 10 | Maine | 186 | 2.5% |
| 11 | Texas | 181 | 2.4% |
| 12 | Vermont | 180 | 2.4% |
| 13 | Illinois | 177 | 2.4% |
| 14 | Mississippi | 174 | 2.3% |
| 15 | North Carolina | 170 | 2.3% |
| 15 | South Carolina | 170 | 2.3% |
| 17 | Kansas | 165 | 2.2% |
| 18 | Florida | 160 | 2.2% |
| 19 | Indiana | 150 | 2.0% |
| 19 | Iowa | 150 | 2.0% |
| 19 | Montana | 150 | 2.0% |
| 19 | Rhode Island | 150 | 2.0% |
| 23 | Oklahoma | 149 | 2.0% |
| 24 | Michigan | 148 | 2.0% |
| 25 | North Dakota | 147 | 2.0% |
| 25 | Washington | 147 | 2.0% |
| 27 | Louisiana | 144 | 1.9% |
| 28 | Alabama | 140 | 1.9% |
| 28 | Virginia | 140 | 1.9% |
| 30 | Kentucky | 138 | 1.9% |
| 31 | Arkansas | 135 | 1.8% |
| 32 | West Virginia | 134 | 1.8% |
| 33 | Ohio | 132 | 1.8% |
| 33 | Tennessee | 132 | 1.8% |
| 33 | Wisconsin | 132 | 1.8% |
| 36 | California | 120 | 1.6% |
| 36 | New Jersey | 120 | 1.6% |
| 38 | New Mexico | 112 | 1.5% |
| 39 | Idaho | 105 | 1.4% |
| 39 | South Dakota | 105 | 1.4% |
| 41 | Utah | 104 | 1.4% |
| 42 | Colorado | 100 | 1.3% |
| 43 | Arizona | 90 | 1.2% |
| 43 | Oregon | 90 | 1.2% |
| 43 | Wyoming | 90 | 1.2% |
| 46 | Hawaii | 76 | 1.0% |
| 47 | Nevada | 63 | 0.8% |
| 48 | Delaware | 62 | 0.8% |
| 49 | Alaska | 60 | 0.8% |
| 50 | Nebraska | 49 | 0.7% |
| | District of Columbia** | NA | NA |

Source: National Conference of State Legislatures (Denver, CO)
   "2000 Post-Election Partisan Composition of The State Legislatures" (1-25-01)
      (http://www.ncsl.org/programs/legman/elect/partycomp.htm)
*There are 1,984 state senators (including Nebraska's 49 unicameral seats) and 5,440 state house members.
**Not applicable.

# Population per State Legislator in 2000

## National Rate = 37,830 Population per Legislator*

### ALPHA ORDER

| RANK | STATE | RATE |
|---|---|---|
| 21 | Alabama | 31,765 |
| 42 | Alaska | 10,449 |
| 9 | Arizona | 57,007 |
| 32 | Arkansas | 19,803 |
| 1 | California | 282,264 |
| 14 | Colorado | 43,013 |
| 34 | Connecticut | 18,212 |
| 40 | Delaware | 12,639 |
| 3 | Florida | 99,890 |
| 20 | Georgia | 34,688 |
| 38 | Hawaii | 15,941 |
| 41 | Idaho | 12,323 |
| 6 | Illinois | 70,165 |
| 16 | Indiana | 40,537 |
| 33 | Iowa | 19,509 |
| 36 | Kansas | 16,293 |
| 25 | Kentucky | 29,288 |
| 24 | Louisiana | 31,035 |
| 45 | Maine | 6,854 |
| 27 | Maryland | 28,173 |
| 22 | Massachusetts | 31,745 |
| 8 | Michigan | 67,152 |
| 28 | Minnesota | 24,475 |
| 35 | Mississippi | 16,349 |
| 26 | Missouri | 28,402 |
| 46 | Montana | 6,015 |
| 19 | Nebraska | 34,924 |
| 23 | Nevada | 31,718 |
| 50 | New Hampshire | 2,915 |
| 7 | New Jersey | 70,120 |
| 37 | New Mexico | 16,241 |
| 4 | New York | 89,936 |
| 12 | North Carolina | 47,349 |
| 48 | North Dakota | 4,369 |
| 5 | Ohio | 86,009 |
| 30 | Oklahoma | 23,159 |
| 18 | Oregon | 38,016 |
| 11 | Pennsylvania | 48,542 |
| 44 | Rhode Island | 6,989 |
| 29 | South Carolina | 23,600 |
| 43 | South Dakota | 7,189 |
| 13 | Tennessee | 43,101 |
| 2 | Texas | 115,203 |
| 31 | Utah | 21,473 |
| 49 | Vermont | 3,382 |
| 10 | Virginia | 50,561 |
| 17 | Washington | 40,096 |
| 39 | West Virginia | 13,495 |
| 15 | Wisconsin | 40,634 |
| 47 | Wyoming | 5,486 |

### RANK ORDER

| RANK | STATE | RATE |
|---|---|---|
| 1 | California | 282,264 |
| 2 | Texas | 115,203 |
| 3 | Florida | 99,890 |
| 4 | New York | 89,936 |
| 5 | Ohio | 86,009 |
| 6 | Illinois | 70,165 |
| 7 | New Jersey | 70,120 |
| 8 | Michigan | 67,152 |
| 9 | Arizona | 57,007 |
| 10 | Virginia | 50,561 |
| 11 | Pennsylvania | 48,542 |
| 12 | North Carolina | 47,349 |
| 13 | Tennessee | 43,101 |
| 14 | Colorado | 43,013 |
| 15 | Wisconsin | 40,634 |
| 16 | Indiana | 40,537 |
| 17 | Washington | 40,096 |
| 18 | Oregon | 38,016 |
| 19 | Nebraska | 34,924 |
| 20 | Georgia | 34,688 |
| 21 | Alabama | 31,765 |
| 22 | Massachusetts | 31,745 |
| 23 | Nevada | 31,718 |
| 24 | Louisiana | 31,035 |
| 25 | Kentucky | 29,288 |
| 26 | Missouri | 28,402 |
| 27 | Maryland | 28,173 |
| 28 | Minnesota | 24,475 |
| 29 | South Carolina | 23,600 |
| 30 | Oklahoma | 23,159 |
| 31 | Utah | 21,473 |
| 32 | Arkansas | 19,803 |
| 33 | Iowa | 19,509 |
| 34 | Connecticut | 18,212 |
| 35 | Mississippi | 16,349 |
| 36 | Kansas | 16,293 |
| 37 | New Mexico | 16,241 |
| 38 | Hawaii | 15,941 |
| 39 | West Virginia | 13,495 |
| 40 | Delaware | 12,639 |
| 41 | Idaho | 12,323 |
| 42 | Alaska | 10,449 |
| 43 | South Dakota | 7,189 |
| 44 | Rhode Island | 6,989 |
| 45 | Maine | 6,854 |
| 46 | Montana | 6,015 |
| 47 | Wyoming | 5,486 |
| 48 | North Dakota | 4,369 |
| 49 | Vermont | 3,382 |
| 50 | New Hampshire | 2,915 |

District of Columbia**                     NA

Source: Morgan Quitno Press using data from National Conference of State Legislatures (Denver, CO)
"2000 Post-Election Partisan Composition of The State Legislatures" (1-25-01)
(http://www.ncsl.org/programs/legman/elect/partycomp.htm)
*There are 1,984 state senators (including Nebraska's 49 unicameral seats) and 5,440 state house members.
National rate does not include population for the District of Columbia.
**Not applicable.

# Registered Voters in 1998

## National Total = 141,850,558 *

ALPHA ORDER

| RANK | STATE | REGISTERED | % of USA | RANK | STATE | REGISTERED | % of USA |
|------|-------|-----------|----------|------|-------|-----------|----------|
| 22 | Alabama | 2,316,598 | 1.6% | 1 | California | 14,983,950 | 10.6% |
| 44 | Alaska | 456,914 | 0.3% | 2 | Texas | 9,582,505 | 6.8% |
| 23 | Arizona | 2,265,879 | 1.6% | 3 | New York | 9,553,665 | 6.7% |
| 31 | Arkansas | 1,412,617 | 1.0% | 4 | Florida | 7,494,005 | 5.3% |
| 1 | California | 14,983,950 | 10.6% | 5 | Pennsylvania | 6,966,461 | 4.9% |
| 24 | Colorado | 2,099,364 | 1.5% | 6 | Michigan | 6,838,858 | 4.8% |
| 27 | Connecticut | 1,806,750 | 1.3% | 7 | Illinois | 6,493,881 | 4.6% |
| 46 | Delaware | 445,067 | 0.3% | 8 | Ohio | 6,058,808 | 4.3% |
| 4 | Florida | 7,494,005 | 5.3% | 9 | North Carolina | 4,349,290 | 3.1% |
| 11 | Georgia | 3,910,740 | 2.8% | 10 | New Jersey | 4,126,782 | 2.9% |
| 42 | Hawaii | 601,404 | 0.4% | 11 | Georgia | 3,910,740 | 2.8% |
| 40 | Idaho | 661,433 | 0.5% | 12 | Virginia | 3,470,660 | 2.4% |
| 7 | Illinois | 6,493,881 | 4.6% | 13 | Massachusetts | 3,378,165 | 2.4% |
| 14 | Indiana | 3,377,956 | 2.4% | 14 | Indiana | 3,377,956 | 2.4% |
| 28 | Iowa | 1,763,827 | 1.2% | 15 | Missouri | 3,240,657 | 2.3% |
| 32 | Kansas | 1,403,682 | 1.0% | 16 | Washington | 3,119,562 | 2.2% |
| 20 | Kentucky | 2,512,318 | 1.8% | 17 | Tennessee | 3,057,008 | 2.2% |
| 21 | Louisiana | 2,511,141 | 1.8% | 18 | Minnesota | 2,667,692 | 1.9% |
| 37 | Maine | 882,329 | 0.6% | 19 | Maryland | 2,569,316 | 1.8% |
| 19 | Maryland | 2,569,316 | 1.8% | 20 | Kentucky | 2,512,318 | 1.8% |
| 13 | Massachusetts | 3,378,165 | 2.4% | 21 | Louisiana | 2,511,141 | 1.8% |
| 6 | Michigan | 6,838,858 | 4.8% | 22 | Alabama | 2,316,598 | 1.6% |
| 18 | Minnesota | 2,667,692 | 1.9% | 23 | Arizona | 2,265,879 | 1.6% |
| 30 | Mississippi | 1,729,200 | 1.2% | 24 | Colorado | 2,099,364 | 1.5% |
| 15 | Missouri | 3,240,657 | 2.3% | 25 | South Carolina | 2,021,763 | 1.4% |
| 43 | Montana | 494,763 | 0.3% | 26 | Oregon | 1,965,981 | 1.4% |
| 34 | Nebraska | 981,160 | 0.7% | 27 | Connecticut | 1,806,750 | 1.3% |
| 36 | Nevada | 904,050 | 0.6% | 28 | Iowa | 1,763,827 | 1.2% |
| 39 | New Hampshire | 763,845 | 0.5% | 29 | Oklahoma | 1,737,229 | 1.2% |
| 10 | New Jersey | 4,126,782 | 2.9% | 30 | Mississippi | 1,729,200 | 1.2% |
| 38 | New Mexico | 821,006 | 0.6% | 31 | Arkansas | 1,412,617 | 1.0% |
| 3 | New York | 9,553,665 | 6.7% | 32 | Kansas | 1,403,682 | 1.0% |
| 9 | North Carolina | 4,349,290 | 3.1% | 33 | Utah | 1,045,071 | 0.7% |
| NA | North Dakota** | NA | NA | 34 | Nebraska | 981,160 | 0.7% |
| 8 | Ohio | 6,058,808 | 4.3% | 35 | West Virginia | 951,581 | 0.7% |
| 29 | Oklahoma | 1,737,229 | 1.2% | 36 | Nevada | 904,050 | 0.6% |
| 26 | Oregon | 1,965,981 | 1.4% | 37 | Maine | 882,329 | 0.6% |
| 5 | Pennsylvania | 6,966,461 | 4.9% | 38 | New Mexico | 821,006 | 0.6% |
| 41 | Rhode Island | 629,786 | 0.4% | 39 | New Hampshire | 763,845 | 0.5% |
| 25 | South Carolina | 2,021,763 | 1.4% | 40 | Idaho | 661,433 | 0.5% |
| 45 | South Dakota | 452,785 | 0.3% | 41 | Rhode Island | 629,786 | 0.4% |
| 17 | Tennessee | 3,057,008 | 2.2% | 42 | Hawaii | 601,404 | 0.4% |
| 2 | Texas | 9,582,505 | 6.8% | 43 | Montana | 494,763 | 0.3% |
| 33 | Utah | 1,045,071 | 0.7% | 44 | Alaska | 456,914 | 0.3% |
| 47 | Vermont | 389,191 | 0.3% | 45 | South Dakota | 452,785 | 0.3% |
| 12 | Virginia | 3,470,660 | 2.4% | 46 | Delaware | 445,067 | 0.3% |
| 16 | Washington | 3,119,562 | 2.2% | 47 | Vermont | 389,191 | 0.3% |
| 35 | West Virginia | 951,581 | 0.7% | 48 | Wyoming | 230,360 | 0.2% |
| NA | Wisconsin** | NA | NA | NA | North Dakota** | NA | NA |
| 48 | Wyoming | 230,360 | 0.2% | NA | Wisconsin** | NA | NA |
| | | | | | District of Columbia | 353,503 | 0.2% |

Source: Federal Election Commission
"Voter Registration and Turnout - 1998" (http://www.fec.gov/pages/reg&to98.htm)
*As reported by states.
**North Dakota has no voter registration and Wisconsin has election day registration at the polls.

# Percent of Eligible Voters Reported Registered in 1998

## National Percent = 70.6%*

### ALPHA ORDER

| RANK | STATE | PERCENT |
|------|-------|---------|
| 33 | Alabama | 70.3 |
| 1 | Alaska | 104.5 |
| 37 | Arizona | 68.8 |
| 21 | Arkansas | 75.1 |
| 48 | California | 63.3 |
| 31 | Colorado | 70.9 |
| 25 | Connecticut | 73.3 |
| 15 | Delaware | 78.3 |
| 45 | Florida | 65.8 |
| 36 | Georgia | 68.9 |
| 39 | Hawaii | 68.5 |
| 22 | Idaho | 74.5 |
| 23 | Illinois | 74.2 |
| 16 | Indiana | 76.6 |
| 10 | Iowa | 81.8 |
| 28 | Kansas | 72.9 |
| 8 | Kentucky | 84.0 |
| 12 | Louisiana | 79.7 |
| 3 | Maine | 92.2 |
| 42 | Maryland | 67.2 |
| 30 | Massachusetts | 71.4 |
| 2 | Michigan | 94.1 |
| 16 | Minnesota | 76.6 |
| 5 | Mississippi | 85.8 |
| 11 | Missouri | 80.2 |
| 20 | Montana | 75.2 |
| 12 | Nebraska | 79.7 |
| 37 | Nevada | 68.8 |
| 5 | New Hampshire | 85.8 |
| 40 | New Jersey | 67.9 |
| 46 | New Mexico | 65.7 |
| 33 | New York | 70.3 |
| 18 | North Carolina | 76.5 |
| NA | North Dakota** | NA |
| 29 | Ohio | 72.1 |
| 32 | Oklahoma | 70.5 |
| 14 | Oregon | 79.1 |
| 19 | Pennsylvania | 76.4 |
| 8 | Rhode Island | 84.0 |
| 35 | South Carolina | 70.0 |
| 7 | South Dakota | 84.2 |
| 23 | Tennessee | 74.2 |
| 44 | Texas | 67.0 |
| 27 | Utah | 73.0 |
| 4 | Vermont | 86.9 |
| 42 | Virginia | 67.2 |
| 25 | Washington | 73.3 |
| 41 | West Virginia | 67.7 |
| NA | Wisconsin** | NA |
| 47 | Wyoming | 65.1 |

### RANK ORDER

| RANK | STATE | PERCENT |
|------|-------|---------|
| 1 | Alaska | 104.5 |
| 2 | Michigan | 94.1 |
| 3 | Maine | 92.2 |
| 4 | Vermont | 86.9 |
| 5 | Mississippi | 85.8 |
| 5 | New Hampshire | 85.8 |
| 7 | South Dakota | 84.2 |
| 8 | Kentucky | 84.0 |
| 8 | Rhode Island | 84.0 |
| 10 | Iowa | 81.8 |
| 11 | Missouri | 80.2 |
| 12 | Louisiana | 79.7 |
| 12 | Nebraska | 79.7 |
| 14 | Oregon | 79.1 |
| 15 | Delaware | 78.3 |
| 16 | Indiana | 76.6 |
| 16 | Minnesota | 76.6 |
| 18 | North Carolina | 76.5 |
| 19 | Pennsylvania | 76.4 |
| 20 | Montana | 75.2 |
| 21 | Arkansas | 75.1 |
| 22 | Idaho | 74.5 |
| 23 | Illinois | 74.2 |
| 23 | Tennessee | 74.2 |
| 25 | Connecticut | 73.3 |
| 25 | Washington | 73.3 |
| 27 | Utah | 73.0 |
| 28 | Kansas | 72.9 |
| 29 | Ohio | 72.1 |
| 30 | Massachusetts | 71.4 |
| 31 | Colorado | 70.9 |
| 32 | Oklahoma | 70.5 |
| 33 | Alabama | 70.3 |
| 33 | New York | 70.3 |
| 35 | South Carolina | 70.0 |
| 36 | Georgia | 68.9 |
| 37 | Arizona | 68.8 |
| 37 | Nevada | 68.8 |
| 39 | Hawaii | 68.5 |
| 40 | New Jersey | 67.9 |
| 41 | West Virginia | 67.7 |
| 42 | Maryland | 67.2 |
| 42 | Virginia | 67.2 |
| 44 | Texas | 67.0 |
| 45 | Florida | 65.8 |
| 46 | New Mexico | 65.7 |
| 47 | Wyoming | 65.1 |
| 48 | California | 63.3 |
| NA | North Dakota** | NA |
| NA | Wisconsin** | NA |
| | District of Columbia | 85.4 |

Source: Federal Election Commission
   "Voter Registration and Turnout - 1998" (http://www.fec.gov/pages/reg&to98.htm)
*As a percent of voting age population.
**North Dakota has no voter registration and Wisconsin has election day registration at the polls.

# Persons Voting in 1998

## National Total = 73,117,022*

| RANK | STATE | VOTERS | % of USA |
|------|-------|--------|----------|
| 21 | Alabama | 1,317,842 | 1.8% |
| 46 | Alaska | 221,807 | 0.3% |
| 25 | Arizona | 1,013,280 | 1.4% |
| 32 | Arkansas | 700,644 | 1.0% |
| 1 | California | 8,314,953 | 11.4% |
| 20 | Colorado | 1,327,235 | 1.8% |
| 28 | Connecticut | 964,457 | 1.3% |
| 49 | Delaware | 180,527 | 0.2% |
| 3 | Florida | 3,900,162 | 5.3% |
| 16 | Georgia | 1,753,911 | 2.4% |
| 39 | Hawaii | 398,124 | 0.5% |
| 40 | Idaho | 378,174 | 0.5% |
| 6 | Illinois | 3,394,521 | 4.6% |
| 17 | Indiana | 1,588,617 | 2.2% |
| 29 | Iowa | 947,907 | 1.3% |
| 31 | Kansas | 727,245 | 1.0% |
| 22 | Kentucky | 1,145,414 | 1.6% |
| 27 | Louisiana | 969,165 | 1.3% |
| 38 | Maine | 421,009 | 0.6% |
| 19 | Maryland | 1,507,447 | 2.1% |
| 11 | Massachusetts | 1,935,277 | 2.6% |
| 7 | Michigan | 3,027,104 | 4.1% |
| 9 | Minnesota | 2,091,766 | 2.9% |
| 34 | Mississippi | 517,212 | 0.7% |
| 18 | Missouri | 1,576,857 | 2.2% |
| 42 | Montana | 338,733 | 0.5% |
| 33 | Nebraska | 545,238 | 0.7% |
| 37 | Nevada | 435,790 | 0.6% |
| 43 | New Hampshire | 314,956 | 0.4% |
| 14 | New Jersey | 1,815,489 | 2.5% |
| 35 | New Mexico | 498,703 | 0.7% |
| 2 | New York | 4,989,877 | 6.8% |
| 10 | North Carolina | 2,012,143 | 2.8% |
| 48 | North Dakota | 213,358 | 0.3% |
| 5 | Ohio | 3,404,351 | 4.7% |
| 30 | Oklahoma | 859,713 | 1.2% |
| 23 | Oregon | 1,117,747 | 1.5% |
| 8 | Pennsylvania | 2,957,499 | 4.0% |
| 44 | Rhode Island | 306,383 | 0.4% |
| 24 | South Carolina | 1,068,367 | 1.5% |
| 45 | South Dakota | 262,111 | 0.4% |
| 26 | Tennessee | 976,236 | 1.3% |
| 4 | Texas | 3,738,078 | 5.1% |
| 36 | Utah | 494,909 | 0.7% |
| 47 | Vermont | 214,036 | 0.3% |
| 12 | Virginia | 1,917,261 | 2.6% |
| 13 | Washington | 1,888,561 | 2.6% |
| 41 | West Virginia | 351,277 | 0.5% |
| 15 | Wisconsin | 1,760,836 | 2.4% |
| 50 | Wyoming | 174,888 | 0.2% |

| RANK | STATE | VOTERS | % of USA |
|------|-------|--------|----------|
| 1 | California | 8,314,953 | 11.4% |
| 2 | New York | 4,989,877 | 6.8% |
| 3 | Florida | 3,900,162 | 5.3% |
| 4 | Texas | 3,738,078 | 5.1% |
| 5 | Ohio | 3,404,351 | 4.7% |
| 6 | Illinois | 3,394,521 | 4.6% |
| 7 | Michigan | 3,027,104 | 4.1% |
| 8 | Pennsylvania | 2,957,499 | 4.0% |
| 9 | Minnesota | 2,091,766 | 2.9% |
| 10 | North Carolina | 2,012,143 | 2.8% |
| 11 | Massachusetts | 1,935,277 | 2.6% |
| 12 | Virginia | 1,917,261 | 2.6% |
| 13 | Washington | 1,888,561 | 2.6% |
| 14 | New Jersey | 1,815,489 | 2.5% |
| 15 | Wisconsin | 1,760,836 | 2.4% |
| 16 | Georgia | 1,753,911 | 2.4% |
| 17 | Indiana | 1,588,617 | 2.2% |
| 18 | Missouri | 1,576,857 | 2.2% |
| 19 | Maryland | 1,507,447 | 2.1% |
| 20 | Colorado | 1,327,235 | 1.8% |
| 21 | Alabama | 1,317,842 | 1.8% |
| 22 | Kentucky | 1,145,414 | 1.6% |
| 23 | Oregon | 1,117,747 | 1.5% |
| 24 | South Carolina | 1,068,367 | 1.5% |
| 25 | Arizona | 1,013,280 | 1.4% |
| 26 | Tennessee | 976,236 | 1.3% |
| 27 | Louisiana | 969,165 | 1.3% |
| 28 | Connecticut | 964,457 | 1.3% |
| 29 | Iowa | 947,907 | 1.3% |
| 30 | Oklahoma | 859,713 | 1.2% |
| 31 | Kansas | 727,245 | 1.0% |
| 32 | Arkansas | 700,644 | 1.0% |
| 33 | Nebraska | 545,238 | 0.7% |
| 34 | Mississippi | 517,212 | 0.7% |
| 35 | New Mexico | 498,703 | 0.7% |
| 36 | Utah | 494,909 | 0.7% |
| 37 | Nevada | 435,790 | 0.6% |
| 38 | Maine | 421,009 | 0.6% |
| 39 | Hawaii | 398,124 | 0.5% |
| 40 | Idaho | 378,174 | 0.5% |
| 41 | West Virginia | 351,277 | 0.5% |
| 42 | Montana | 338,733 | 0.5% |
| 43 | New Hampshire | 314,956 | 0.4% |
| 44 | Rhode Island | 306,383 | 0.4% |
| 45 | South Dakota | 262,111 | 0.4% |
| 46 | Alaska | 221,807 | 0.3% |
| 47 | Vermont | 214,036 | 0.3% |
| 48 | North Dakota | 213,358 | 0.3% |
| 49 | Delaware | 180,527 | 0.2% |
| 50 | Wyoming | 174,888 | 0.2% |
| | District of Columbia | 139,825 | 0.2% |

Source: Federal Election Commission
   "Voter Registration and Turnout - 1998" (http://www.fec.gov/pages/reg&to98.htm)
*Refers to the total vote cast for the highest office on the ballot in 1998. These figures may be inconsistent with other reported turnout figures since research suggests that approximately 2% of voters fail to vote for the highest office on a fairly consistent basis.

# Percent of Eligible Population Reported Voting in 1998

## National Percent = 36.4%*

| RANK | STATE | PERCENT |
|---|---|---|
| 21 | Alabama | 40.0 |
| 3 | Alaska | 50.7 |
| 46 | Arizona | 28.6 |
| 29 | Arkansas | 37.2 |
| 36 | California | 35.1 |
| 10 | Colorado | 44.8 |
| 24 | Connecticut | 39.1 |
| 42 | Delaware | 31.8 |
| 39 | Florida | 34.3 |
| 43 | Georgia | 30.9 |
| 8 | Hawaii | 45.3 |
| 16 | Idaho | 42.6 |
| 26 | Illinois | 38.8 |
| 33 | Indiana | 36.0 |
| 15 | Iowa | 43.9 |
| 28 | Kansas | 37.8 |
| 27 | Kentucky | 38.3 |
| 44 | Louisiana | 30.8 |
| 14 | Maine | 44.0 |
| 23 | Maryland | 39.4 |
| 18 | Massachusetts | 40.9 |
| 17 | Michigan | 41.7 |
| 1 | Minnesota | 60.0 |
| 48 | Mississippi | 25.7 |
| 25 | Missouri | 39.0 |
| 2 | Montana | 51.5 |
| 13 | Nebraska | 44.3 |
| 40 | Nevada | 33.2 |
| 34 | New Hampshire | 35.4 |
| 45 | New Jersey | 29.9 |
| 22 | New Mexico | 39.9 |
| 32 | New York | 36.7 |
| 34 | North Carolina | 35.4 |
| 10 | North Dakota | 44.8 |
| 20 | Ohio | 40.5 |
| 37 | Oklahoma | 34.9 |
| 9 | Oregon | 45.0 |
| 41 | Pennsylvania | 32.4 |
| 19 | Rhode Island | 40.8 |
| 31 | South Carolina | 37.0 |
| 5 | South Dakota | 49.0 |
| 50 | Tennessee | 23.7 |
| 47 | Texas | 26.1 |
| 38 | Utah | 34.6 |
| 6 | Vermont | 47.8 |
| 30 | Virginia | 37.1 |
| 12 | Washington | 44.4 |
| 49 | West Virginia | 25.0 |
| 7 | Wisconsin | 45.4 |
| 4 | Wyoming | 49.4 |

| RANK | STATE | PERCENT |
|---|---|---|
| 1 | Minnesota | 60.0 |
| 2 | Montana | 51.5 |
| 3 | Alaska | 50.7 |
| 4 | Wyoming | 49.4 |
| 5 | South Dakota | 49.0 |
| 6 | Vermont | 47.8 |
| 7 | Wisconsin | 45.4 |
| 8 | Hawaii | 45.3 |
| 9 | Oregon | 45.0 |
| 10 | Colorado | 44.8 |
| 10 | North Dakota | 44.8 |
| 12 | Washington | 44.4 |
| 13 | Nebraska | 44.3 |
| 14 | Maine | 44.0 |
| 15 | Iowa | 43.9 |
| 16 | Idaho | 42.6 |
| 17 | Michigan | 41.7 |
| 18 | Massachusetts | 40.9 |
| 19 | Rhode Island | 40.8 |
| 20 | Ohio | 40.5 |
| 21 | Alabama | 40.0 |
| 22 | New Mexico | 39.9 |
| 23 | Maryland | 39.4 |
| 24 | Connecticut | 39.1 |
| 25 | Missouri | 39.0 |
| 26 | Illinois | 38.8 |
| 27 | Kentucky | 38.3 |
| 28 | Kansas | 37.8 |
| 29 | Arkansas | 37.2 |
| 30 | Virginia | 37.1 |
| 31 | South Carolina | 37.0 |
| 32 | New York | 36.7 |
| 33 | Indiana | 36.0 |
| 34 | New Hampshire | 35.4 |
| 34 | North Carolina | 35.4 |
| 36 | California | 35.1 |
| 37 | Oklahoma | 34.9 |
| 38 | Utah | 34.6 |
| 39 | Florida | 34.3 |
| 40 | Nevada | 33.2 |
| 41 | Pennsylvania | 32.4 |
| 42 | Delaware | 31.8 |
| 43 | Georgia | 30.9 |
| 44 | Louisiana | 30.8 |
| 45 | New Jersey | 29.9 |
| 46 | Arizona | 28.6 |
| 47 | Texas | 26.1 |
| 48 | Mississippi | 25.7 |
| 49 | West Virginia | 25.0 |
| 50 | Tennessee | 23.7 |
| | District of Columbia | 33.8 |

Source: Federal Election Commission
   "Voter Registration and Turnout - 1998" (http://www.fec.gov/pages/reg&to98.htm)
*Refers to the total vote cast for the highest office on the ballot in 1998. These figures may be inconsistent with other reported turnout figures since research suggests that approximately 2% of voters fail to vote for the highest office on a fairly consistent basis.

# Response Rate for Census 2000

## National Rate = 67% of Households Responded*

ALPHA ORDER

| RANK | STATE | PERCENT |
|---|---|---|
| 44 | Alabama | 61 |
| 50 | Alaska | 56 |
| 38 | Arizona | 63 |
| 33 | Arkansas | 64 |
| 11 | California | 70 |
| 11 | Colorado | 70 |
| 11 | Connecticut | 70 |
| 38 | Delaware | 63 |
| 38 | Florida | 63 |
| 31 | Georgia | 65 |
| 46 | Hawaii | 60 |
| 24 | Idaho | 67 |
| 15 | Illinois | 69 |
| 15 | Indiana | 69 |
| 1 | Iowa | 76 |
| 9 | Kansas | 71 |
| 27 | Kentucky | 66 |
| 46 | Louisiana | 60 |
| 44 | Maine | 61 |
| 15 | Maryland | 69 |
| 15 | Massachusetts | 69 |
| 9 | Michigan | 71 |
| 2 | Minnesota | 75 |
| 38 | Mississippi | 63 |
| 15 | Missouri | 69 |
| 20 | Montana | 68 |
| 2 | Nebraska | 75 |
| 27 | Nevada | 66 |
| 24 | New Hampshire | 67 |
| 20 | New Jersey | 68 |
| 43 | New Mexico | 62 |
| 38 | New York | 63 |
| 33 | North Carolina | 64 |
| 6 | North Dakota | 72 |
| 6 | Ohio | 72 |
| 33 | Oklahoma | 64 |
| 20 | Oregon | 68 |
| 11 | Pennsylvania | 70 |
| 24 | Rhode Island | 67 |
| 49 | South Carolina | 58 |
| 5 | South Dakota | 74 |
| 31 | Tennessee | 65 |
| 33 | Texas | 64 |
| 20 | Utah | 68 |
| 46 | Vermont | 60 |
| 6 | Virginia | 72 |
| 27 | Washington | 66 |
| 33 | West Virginia | 64 |
| 2 | Wisconsin | 75 |
| 27 | Wyoming | 66 |

RANK ORDER

| RANK | STATE | PERCENT |
|---|---|---|
| 1 | Iowa | 76 |
| 2 | Minnesota | 75 |
| 2 | Nebraska | 75 |
| 2 | Wisconsin | 75 |
| 5 | South Dakota | 74 |
| 6 | North Dakota | 72 |
| 6 | Ohio | 72 |
| 6 | Virginia | 72 |
| 9 | Kansas | 71 |
| 9 | Michigan | 71 |
| 11 | California | 70 |
| 11 | Colorado | 70 |
| 11 | Connecticut | 70 |
| 11 | Pennsylvania | 70 |
| 15 | Illinois | 69 |
| 15 | Indiana | 69 |
| 15 | Maryland | 69 |
| 15 | Massachusetts | 69 |
| 15 | Missouri | 69 |
| 20 | Montana | 68 |
| 20 | New Jersey | 68 |
| 20 | Oregon | 68 |
| 20 | Utah | 68 |
| 24 | Idaho | 67 |
| 24 | New Hampshire | 67 |
| 24 | Rhode Island | 67 |
| 27 | Kentucky | 66 |
| 27 | Nevada | 66 |
| 27 | Washington | 66 |
| 27 | Wyoming | 66 |
| 31 | Georgia | 65 |
| 31 | Tennessee | 65 |
| 33 | Arkansas | 64 |
| 33 | North Carolina | 64 |
| 33 | Oklahoma | 64 |
| 33 | Texas | 64 |
| 33 | West Virginia | 64 |
| 38 | Arizona | 63 |
| 38 | Delaware | 63 |
| 38 | Florida | 63 |
| 38 | Mississippi | 63 |
| 38 | New York | 63 |
| 43 | New Mexico | 62 |
| 44 | Alabama | 61 |
| 44 | Maine | 61 |
| 46 | Hawaii | 60 |
| 46 | Louisiana | 60 |
| 46 | Vermont | 60 |
| 49 | South Carolina | 58 |
| 50 | Alaska | 56 |

| | District of Columbia | 60 |
|---|---|---|

*Source: U.S. Bureau of the Census*
*"Census 2000 Final Response Rates" (September 7, 2000, http://rates.census.gov/state.html)*
*How many housing units responded by mail, telephone or over the internet.  The Final Response Rates should not be confused with mail return rates that will be calculated and released by the Census Bureau at a later date. It is at that time that vacant housing structures will be excluded from the calculation to give a true measure of census "returns."*

# XIV. SOCIAL WELFARE

# Poverty Rate in 1999

## National Rate = 12.6% of Population in Poverty*

ALPHA ORDER

| RANK | STATE | PERCENT |
|---|---|---|
| 11 | Alabama | 15.1 |
| 43 | Alaska | 8.6 |
| 10 | Arizona | 15.2 |
| 5 | Arkansas | 16.4 |
| 9 | California | 15.3 |
| 43 | Colorado | 8.6 |
| 47 | Connecticut | 8.4 |
| 36 | Delaware | 10.1 |
| 17 | Florida | 13.3 |
| 15 | Georgia | 13.7 |
| 22 | Hawaii | 11.9 |
| 12 | Idaho | 13.9 |
| 33 | Illinois | 10.4 |
| 48 | Indiana | 8.3 |
| 42 | Iowa | 8.7 |
| 32 | Kansas | 10.5 |
| 14 | Kentucky | 13.8 |
| 2 | Louisiana | 18.2 |
| 33 | Maine | 10.4 |
| 50 | Maryland | 7.6 |
| 30 | Massachusetts | 10.9 |
| 35 | Michigan | 10.3 |
| 40 | Minnesota | 9.1 |
| 3 | Mississippi | 16.8 |
| 27 | Missouri | 11.1 |
| 6 | Montana | 15.9 |
| 28 | Nebraska | 11.0 |
| 28 | Nevada | 11.0 |
| 41 | New Hampshire | 8.9 |
| 45 | New Jersey | 8.5 |
| 1 | New Mexico | 20.8 |
| 7 | New York | 15.7 |
| 20 | North Carolina | 13.0 |
| 12 | North Dakota | 13.9 |
| 25 | Ohio | 11.4 |
| 16 | Oklahoma | 13.5 |
| 19 | Oregon | 13.1 |
| 31 | Pennsylvania | 10.6 |
| 25 | Rhode Island | 11.4 |
| 21 | South Carolina | 12.8 |
| 24 | South Dakota | 11.7 |
| 18 | Tennessee | 13.2 |
| 8 | Texas | 15.6 |
| 49 | Utah | 7.9 |
| 38 | Vermont | 9.6 |
| 37 | Virginia | 9.8 |
| 39 | Washington | 9.2 |
| 4 | West Virginia | 16.7 |
| 45 | Wisconsin | 8.5 |
| 22 | Wyoming | 11.9 |

RANK ORDER

| RANK | STATE | PERCENT |
|---|---|---|
| 1 | New Mexico | 20.8 |
| 2 | Louisiana | 18.2 |
| 3 | Mississippi | 16.8 |
| 4 | West Virginia | 16.7 |
| 5 | Arkansas | 16.4 |
| 6 | Montana | 15.9 |
| 7 | New York | 15.7 |
| 8 | Texas | 15.6 |
| 9 | California | 15.3 |
| 10 | Arizona | 15.2 |
| 11 | Alabama | 15.1 |
| 12 | Idaho | 13.9 |
| 12 | North Dakota | 13.9 |
| 14 | Kentucky | 13.8 |
| 15 | Georgia | 13.7 |
| 16 | Oklahoma | 13.5 |
| 17 | Florida | 13.3 |
| 18 | Tennessee | 13.2 |
| 19 | Oregon | 13.1 |
| 20 | North Carolina | 13.0 |
| 21 | South Carolina | 12.8 |
| 22 | Hawaii | 11.9 |
| 22 | Wyoming | 11.9 |
| 24 | South Dakota | 11.7 |
| 25 | Ohio | 11.4 |
| 25 | Rhode Island | 11.4 |
| 27 | Missouri | 11.1 |
| 28 | Nebraska | 11.0 |
| 28 | Nevada | 11.0 |
| 30 | Massachusetts | 10.9 |
| 31 | Pennsylvania | 10.6 |
| 32 | Kansas | 10.5 |
| 33 | Illinois | 10.4 |
| 33 | Maine | 10.4 |
| 35 | Michigan | 10.3 |
| 36 | Delaware | 10.1 |
| 37 | Virginia | 9.8 |
| 38 | Vermont | 9.6 |
| 39 | Washington | 9.2 |
| 40 | Minnesota | 9.1 |
| 41 | New Hampshire | 8.9 |
| 42 | Iowa | 8.7 |
| 43 | Alaska | 8.6 |
| 43 | Colorado | 8.6 |
| 45 | New Jersey | 8.5 |
| 45 | Wisconsin | 8.5 |
| 47 | Connecticut | 8.4 |
| 48 | Indiana | 8.3 |
| 49 | Utah | 7.9 |
| 50 | Maryland | 7.6 |
| | District of Columbia | 19.7 |

*Source: U.S. Bureau of the Census*
*"Poverty 1999" (http://www.census.gov/hhes/poverty/poverty99/pv99state.html)*
*\*Three-year average: 1997-1999.*

# Percent of Senior Citizens Living in Poverty in 1999

## National Percent = 9.7%*

ALPHA ORDER

| RANK | STATE | PERCENT |
|------|-------|---------|
| 4 | Alabama | 14.5 |
| NA | Alaska** | NA |
| 43 | Arizona | 5.9 |
| 7 | Arkansas | 13.2 |
| 30 | California | 8.0 |
| 47 | Colorado | 4.1 |
| 14 | Connecticut | 11.4 |
| 39 | Delaware | 6.8 |
| 28 | Florida | 8.6 |
| 21 | Georgia | 10.4 |
| 35 | Hawaii | 7.4 |
| 33 | Idaho | 7.5 |
| 37 | Illinois | 7.2 |
| 45 | Indiana | 5.8 |
| 43 | Iowa | 5.9 |
| 40 | Kansas | 6.5 |
| 19 | Kentucky | 10.6 |
| 2 | Louisiana | 17.8 |
| 40 | Maine | 6.5 |
| 11 | Maryland | 12.1 |
| 22 | Massachusetts | 10.1 |
| 33 | Michigan | 7.5 |
| 16 | Minnesota | 10.8 |
| 1 | Mississippi | 18.1 |
| 16 | Missouri | 10.8 |
| 42 | Montana | 6.2 |
| 8 | Nebraska | 12.9 |
| 31 | Nevada | 7.9 |
| 20 | New Hampshire | 10.5 |
| 31 | New Jersey | 7.9 |
| 3 | New Mexico | 14.6 |
| 9 | New York | 12.4 |
| 6 | North Carolina | 13.8 |
| 15 | North Dakota | 11.1 |
| 38 | Ohio | 6.9 |
| 16 | Oklahoma | 10.8 |
| 26 | Oregon | 9.0 |
| 35 | Pennsylvania | 7.4 |
| 23 | Rhode Island | 9.9 |
| 13 | South Carolina | 11.5 |
| 29 | South Dakota | 8.4 |
| 25 | Tennessee | 9.4 |
| 10 | Texas | 12.3 |
| 46 | Utah | 5.2 |
| NA | Vermont** | NA |
| 12 | Virginia | 12.0 |
| 24 | Washington | 9.5 |
| 5 | West Virginia | 14.4 |
| 26 | Wisconsin | 9.0 |
| NA | Wyoming** | NA |

RANK ORDER

| RANK | STATE | PERCENT |
|------|-------|---------|
| 1 | Mississippi | 18.1 |
| 2 | Louisiana | 17.8 |
| 3 | New Mexico | 14.6 |
| 4 | Alabama | 14.5 |
| 5 | West Virginia | 14.4 |
| 6 | North Carolina | 13.8 |
| 7 | Arkansas | 13.2 |
| 8 | Nebraska | 12.9 |
| 9 | New York | 12.4 |
| 10 | Texas | 12.3 |
| 11 | Maryland | 12.1 |
| 12 | Virginia | 12.0 |
| 13 | South Carolina | 11.5 |
| 14 | Connecticut | 11.4 |
| 15 | North Dakota | 11.1 |
| 16 | Minnesota | 10.8 |
| 16 | Missouri | 10.8 |
| 16 | Oklahoma | 10.8 |
| 19 | Kentucky | 10.6 |
| 20 | New Hampshire | 10.5 |
| 21 | Georgia | 10.4 |
| 22 | Massachusetts | 10.1 |
| 23 | Rhode Island | 9.9 |
| 24 | Washington | 9.5 |
| 25 | Tennessee | 9.4 |
| 26 | Oregon | 9.0 |
| 26 | Wisconsin | 9.0 |
| 28 | Florida | 8.6 |
| 29 | South Dakota | 8.4 |
| 30 | California | 8.0 |
| 31 | Nevada | 7.9 |
| 31 | New Jersey | 7.9 |
| 33 | Idaho | 7.5 |
| 33 | Michigan | 7.5 |
| 35 | Hawaii | 7.4 |
| 35 | Pennsylvania | 7.4 |
| 37 | Illinois | 7.2 |
| 38 | Ohio | 6.9 |
| 39 | Delaware | 6.8 |
| 40 | Kansas | 6.5 |
| 40 | Maine | 6.5 |
| 42 | Montana | 6.2 |
| 43 | Arizona | 5.9 |
| 43 | Iowa | 5.9 |
| 45 | Indiana | 5.8 |
| 46 | Utah | 5.2 |
| 47 | Colorado | 4.1 |
| NA | Alaska** | NA |
| NA | Vermont** | NA |
| NA | Wyoming** | NA |
| | District of Columbia** | NA |

Source: U.S Bureau of the Census
    "Poverty Status by State in 1999"
*People 65 years and over living with incomes below the poverty level.  These figures are subject to a relatively large sampling error and should be interpreted accordingly.
**Not available.

# Percent of Children Living in Poverty in 1999

## National Percent = 16.3%*

ALPHA ORDER

RANK ORDER

| RANK | STATE | PERCENT | | RANK | STATE | PERCENT |
|------|-------|---------|---|------|-------|---------|
| 3 | Alabama | 23.7 | | 1 | New Mexico | 29.6 |
| 44 | Alaska | 7.7 | | 2 | Louisiana | 25.8 |
| 27 | Arizona | 14.8 | | 3 | Alabama | 23.7 |
| 15 | Arkansas | 17.8 | | 4 | Mississippi | 22.3 |
| 9 | California | 20.0 | | 5 | West Virginia | 22.2 |
| 35 | Colorado | 11.3 | | 6 | Idaho | 22.0 |
| 46 | Connecticut | 7.6 | | 7 | Texas | 21.4 |
| 16 | Delaware | 17.7 | | 8 | New York | 21.2 |
| 18 | Florida | 17.6 | | 9 | California | 20.0 |
| 11 | Georgia | 19.2 | | 10 | Montana | 19.9 |
| 33 | Hawaii | 12.6 | | 11 | Georgia | 19.2 |
| 6 | Idaho | 22.0 | | 11 | Massachusetts | 19.2 |
| 28 | Illinois | 14.7 | | 13 | North Carolina | 18.0 |
| 42 | Indiana | 8.2 | | 14 | Kansas | 17.9 |
| 41 | Iowa | 8.9 | | 15 | Arkansas | 17.8 |
| 14 | Kansas | 17.9 | | 16 | Delaware | 17.7 |
| 26 | Kentucky | 16.3 | | 16 | Tennessee | 17.7 |
| 2 | Louisiana | 25.8 | | 18 | Florida | 17.6 |
| 24 | Maine | 16.4 | | 18 | Missouri | 17.6 |
| 49 | Maryland | 6.5 | | 18 | North Dakota | 17.6 |
| 11 | Massachusetts | 19.2 | | 21 | Ohio | 17.0 |
| 32 | Michigan | 13.1 | | 21 | South Carolina | 17.0 |
| 46 | Minnesota | 7.6 | | 23 | Nevada | 16.6 |
| 4 | Mississippi | 22.3 | | 24 | Maine | 16.4 |
| 18 | Missouri | 17.6 | | 24 | Oklahoma | 16.4 |
| 10 | Montana | 19.9 | | 26 | Kentucky | 16.3 |
| 36 | Nebraska | 11.2 | | 27 | Arizona | 14.8 |
| 23 | Nevada | 16.6 | | 28 | Illinois | 14.7 |
| 44 | New Hampshire | 7.7 | | 29 | Oregon | 14.6 |
| 40 | New Jersey | 9.8 | | 30 | Rhode Island | 14.3 |
| 1 | New Mexico | 29.6 | | 31 | Wyoming | 14.1 |
| 8 | New York | 21.2 | | 32 | Michigan | 13.1 |
| 13 | North Carolina | 18.0 | | 33 | Hawaii | 12.6 |
| 18 | North Dakota | 17.6 | | 34 | Pennsylvania | 12.5 |
| 21 | Ohio | 17.0 | | 35 | Colorado | 11.3 |
| 24 | Oklahoma | 16.4 | | 36 | Nebraska | 11.2 |
| 29 | Oregon | 14.6 | | 37 | Vermont | 11.0 |
| 34 | Pennsylvania | 12.5 | | 38 | Virginia | 10.4 |
| 30 | Rhode Island | 14.3 | | 39 | Washington | 10.0 |
| 21 | South Carolina | 17.0 | | 40 | New Jersey | 9.8 |
| 48 | South Dakota | 7.4 | | 41 | Iowa | 8.9 |
| 16 | Tennessee | 17.7 | | 42 | Indiana | 8.2 |
| 7 | Texas | 21.4 | | 43 | Wisconsin | 7.9 |
| 50 | Utah | 6.2 | | 44 | Alaska | 7.7 |
| 37 | Vermont | 11.0 | | 44 | New Hampshire | 7.7 |
| 38 | Virginia | 10.4 | | 46 | Connecticut | 7.6 |
| 39 | Washington | 10.0 | | 46 | Minnesota | 7.6 |
| 5 | West Virginia | 22.2 | | 48 | South Dakota | 7.4 |
| 43 | Wisconsin | 7.9 | | 49 | Maryland | 6.5 |
| 31 | Wyoming | 14.1 | | 50 | Utah | 6.2 |
| | | | | | District of Columbia | 23.8 |

*Source: U.S Bureau of the Census*
   *"Poverty Status by State in 1999"*
*Children 17 and under living in families with incomes below the poverty level. These figures are subject to a relatively large sampling error and should be interpreted accordingly.*

# Percent of Families Living in Poverty in 1999

## National Percent = 9.3%*

| ALPHA ORDER | | | | RANK ORDER | | |
|---|---|---|---|---|---|---|
| RANK | STATE | PERCENT | | RANK | STATE | PERCENT |
| 5 | Alabama | 12.2 | | 1 | New Mexico | 15.3 |
| 48 | Alaska | 4.7 | | 2 | Louisiana | 15.2 |
| 23 | Arizona | 9.3 | | 3 | Mississippi | 13.0 |
| 8 | Arkansas | 11.7 | | 4 | Texas | 12.4 |
| 11 | California | 10.8 | | 5 | Alabama | 12.2 |
| 40 | Colorado | 5.9 | | 6 | New York | 12.1 |
| 46 | Connecticut | 5.3 | | 6 | West Virginia | 12.1 |
| 19 | Delaware | 9.9 | | 8 | Arkansas | 11.7 |
| 25 | Florida | 9.0 | | 9 | Kentucky | 11.1 |
| 16 | Georgia | 10.1 | | 9 | North Carolina | 11.1 |
| 21 | Hawaii | 9.7 | | 11 | California | 10.8 |
| 12 | Idaho | 10.6 | | 12 | Idaho | 10.6 |
| 30 | Illinois | 8.0 | | 13 | Ohio | 10.4 |
| 49 | Indiana | 4.4 | | 14 | Montana | 10.3 |
| 40 | Iowa | 5.9 | | 15 | North Dakota | 10.2 |
| 24 | Kansas | 9.1 | | 16 | Georgia | 10.1 |
| 9 | Kentucky | 11.1 | | 16 | Tennessee | 10.1 |
| 2 | Louisiana | 15.2 | | 18 | Missouri | 10.0 |
| 35 | Maine | 7.0 | | 19 | Delaware | 9.9 |
| 49 | Maryland | 4.4 | | 19 | Oklahoma | 9.9 |
| 26 | Massachusetts | 8.4 | | 21 | Hawaii | 9.7 |
| 37 | Michigan | 6.9 | | 21 | Oregon | 9.7 |
| 44 | Minnesota | 5.4 | | 23 | Arizona | 9.3 |
| 3 | Mississippi | 13.0 | | 24 | Kansas | 9.1 |
| 18 | Missouri | 10.0 | | 25 | Florida | 9.0 |
| 14 | Montana | 10.3 | | 26 | Massachusetts | 8.4 |
| 31 | Nebraska | 7.7 | | 26 | Nevada | 8.4 |
| 26 | Nevada | 8.4 | | 28 | South Carolina | 8.3 |
| 42 | New Hampshire | 5.8 | | 29 | Wyoming | 8.2 |
| 38 | New Jersey | 6.4 | | 30 | Illinois | 8.0 |
| 1 | New Mexico | 15.3 | | 31 | Nebraska | 7.7 |
| 6 | New York | 12.1 | | 31 | Rhode Island | 7.7 |
| 9 | North Carolina | 11.1 | | 33 | Pennsylvania | 7.3 |
| 15 | North Dakota | 10.2 | | 33 | Vermont | 7.3 |
| 13 | Ohio | 10.4 | | 35 | Maine | 7.0 |
| 19 | Oklahoma | 9.9 | | 35 | Washington | 7.0 |
| 21 | Oregon | 9.7 | | 37 | Michigan | 6.9 |
| 33 | Pennsylvania | 7.3 | | 38 | New Jersey | 6.4 |
| 31 | Rhode Island | 7.7 | | 39 | South Dakota | 6.1 |
| 28 | South Carolina | 8.3 | | 40 | Colorado | 5.9 |
| 39 | South Dakota | 6.1 | | 40 | Iowa | 5.9 |
| 16 | Tennessee | 10.1 | | 42 | New Hampshire | 5.8 |
| 4 | Texas | 12.4 | | 43 | Virginia | 5.6 |
| 47 | Utah | 4.9 | | 44 | Minnesota | 5.4 |
| 33 | Vermont | 7.3 | | 44 | Wisconsin | 5.4 |
| 43 | Virginia | 5.6 | | 46 | Connecticut | 5.3 |
| 35 | Washington | 7.0 | | 47 | Utah | 4.9 |
| 6 | West Virginia | 12.1 | | 48 | Alaska | 4.7 |
| 44 | Wisconsin | 5.4 | | 49 | Indiana | 4.4 |
| 29 | Wyoming | 8.2 | | 49 | Maryland | 4.4 |
| | | | | | District of Columbia | 15.1 |

Source: U.S Bureau of the Census
"Poverty Status by State in 1999"
*Families living with incomes below the poverty level. These figures are subject to a relatively large sampling error and should be interpreted accordingly.

# Percent of Female-Headed Families with Children Living in Poverty in 1999

## National Percent = 37.4%*

ALPHA ORDER

| RANK | STATE | PERCENT |
|------|-------|---------|
| 5 | Alabama | 48.5 |
| NA | Alaska** | NA |
| 33 | Arizona | 32.8 |
| 3 | Arkansas | 49.7 |
| 21 | California | 36.5 |
| 26 | Colorado | 34.6 |
| 36 | Connecticut | 29.0 |
| 31 | Delaware | 33.6 |
| 28 | Florida | 34.4 |
| 12 | Georgia | 41.6 |
| 30 | Hawaii | 33.9 |
| 16 | Idaho | 37.3 |
| 26 | Illinois | 34.6 |
| 40 | Indiana | 26.3 |
| 22 | Iowa | 36.4 |
| 7 | Kansas | 47.2 |
| 5 | Kentucky | 48.5 |
| 1 | Louisiana | 52.3 |
| 11 | Maine | 42.6 |
| 45 | Maryland | 14.5 |
| 4 | Massachusetts | 49.6 |
| 15 | Michigan | 37.7 |
| 44 | Minnesota | 21.0 |
| 8 | Mississippi | 46.7 |
| 9 | Missouri | 44.6 |
| 24 | Montana | 34.8 |
| 32 | Nebraska | 33.5 |
| 39 | Nevada | 27.1 |
| 41 | New Hampshire | 24.0 |
| 34 | New Jersey | 31.3 |
| 20 | New Mexico | 36.7 |
| 10 | New York | 44.0 |
| 14 | North Carolina | 39.6 |
| NA | North Dakota** | NA |
| 17 | Ohio | 37.1 |
| 35 | Oklahoma | 29.7 |
| 28 | Oregon | 34.4 |
| 23 | Pennsylvania | 35.2 |
| 18 | Rhode Island | 37.0 |
| 38 | South Carolina | 28.4 |
| NA | South Dakota** | NA |
| 2 | Tennessee | 51.5 |
| 13 | Texas | 39.7 |
| 37 | Utah | 28.8 |
| NA | Vermont** | NA |
| 43 | Virginia | 21.5 |
| 42 | Washington | 22.7 |
| 18 | West Virginia | 37.0 |
| 24 | Wisconsin | 34.8 |
| NA | Wyoming** | NA |

RANK ORDER

| RANK | STATE | PERCENT |
|------|-------|---------|
| 1 | Louisiana | 52.3 |
| 2 | Tennessee | 51.5 |
| 3 | Arkansas | 49.7 |
| 4 | Massachusetts | 49.6 |
| 5 | Alabama | 48.5 |
| 5 | Kentucky | 48.5 |
| 7 | Kansas | 47.2 |
| 8 | Mississippi | 46.7 |
| 9 | Missouri | 44.6 |
| 10 | New York | 44.0 |
| 11 | Maine | 42.6 |
| 12 | Georgia | 41.6 |
| 13 | Texas | 39.7 |
| 14 | North Carolina | 39.6 |
| 15 | Michigan | 37.7 |
| 16 | Idaho | 37.3 |
| 17 | Ohio | 37.1 |
| 18 | Rhode Island | 37.0 |
| 18 | West Virginia | 37.0 |
| 20 | New Mexico | 36.7 |
| 21 | California | 36.5 |
| 22 | Iowa | 36.4 |
| 23 | Pennsylvania | 35.2 |
| 24 | Montana | 34.8 |
| 24 | Wisconsin | 34.8 |
| 26 | Colorado | 34.6 |
| 26 | Illinois | 34.6 |
| 28 | Florida | 34.4 |
| 28 | Oregon | 34.4 |
| 30 | Hawaii | 33.9 |
| 31 | Delaware | 33.6 |
| 32 | Nebraska | 33.5 |
| 33 | Arizona | 32.8 |
| 34 | New Jersey | 31.3 |
| 35 | Oklahoma | 29.7 |
| 36 | Connecticut | 29.0 |
| 37 | Utah | 28.8 |
| 38 | South Carolina | 28.4 |
| 39 | Nevada | 27.1 |
| 40 | Indiana | 26.3 |
| 41 | New Hampshire | 24.0 |
| 42 | Washington | 22.7 |
| 43 | Virginia | 21.5 |
| 44 | Minnesota | 21.0 |
| 45 | Maryland | 14.5 |
| NA | Alaska** | NA |
| NA | North Dakota** | NA |
| NA | South Dakota** | NA |
| NA | Vermont** | NA |
| NA | Wyoming** | NA |

District of Columbia — 46.2

Source: U.S Bureau of the Census
    "Poverty Status by State in 1999"
*These figures are subject to a relatively large sampling error and should be interpreted accordingly.
**Not available.

# State and Local Government Expenditures for Public Welfare Programs in 1997

## National Total = $203,782,935,000*

ALPHA ORDER

| RANK | STATE | EXPENDITURES | % of USA |
|------|-------|--------------|----------|
| 26 | Alabama | $2,575,844,000 | 1.3% |
| 42 | Alaska | 760,620,000 | 0.4% |
| 25 | Arizona | 2,632,120,000 | 1.3% |
| 32 | Arkansas | 1,675,690,000 | 0.8% |
| 1 | California | 27,106,172,000 | 13.3% |
| 28 | Colorado | 2,294,525,000 | 1.1% |
| 23 | Connecticut | 2,892,553,000 | 1.4% |
| 47 | Delaware | 502,321,000 | 0.2% |
| 7 | Florida | 7,936,215,000 | 3.9% |
| 10 | Georgia | 5,423,487,000 | 2.7% |
| 38 | Hawaii | 995,813,000 | 0.5% |
| 44 | Idaho | 633,238,000 | 0.3% |
| 5 | Illinois | 8,553,340,000 | 4.2% |
| 18 | Indiana | 3,422,252,000 | 1.7% |
| 29 | Iowa | 1,838,330,000 | 0.9% |
| 36 | Kansas | 1,164,102,000 | 0.6% |
| 19 | Kentucky | 3,245,820,000 | 1.6% |
| 22 | Louisiana | 2,931,812,000 | 1.4% |
| 34 | Maine | 1,366,127,000 | 0.7% |
| 21 | Maryland | 3,081,992,000 | 1.5% |
| 9 | Massachusetts | 5,835,658,000 | 2.9% |
| 8 | Michigan | 7,172,382,000 | 3.5% |
| 13 | Minnesota | 4,709,670,000 | 2.3% |
| 30 | Mississippi | 1,778,555,000 | 0.9% |
| 20 | Missouri | 3,139,430,000 | 1.5% |
| 46 | Montana | 518,874,000 | 0.3% |
| 37 | Nebraska | 1,069,120,000 | 0.5% |
| 43 | Nevada | 712,226,000 | 0.3% |
| 40 | New Hampshire | 944,464,000 | 0.5% |
| 11 | New Jersey | 5,301,881,000 | 2.6% |
| 35 | New Mexico | 1,295,199,000 | 0.6% |
| 2 | New York | 26,872,380,000 | 13.2% |
| 12 | North Carolina | 4,956,365,000 | 2.4% |
| 48 | North Dakota | 485,325,000 | 0.2% |
| 6 | Ohio | 8,486,798,000 | 4.2% |
| 31 | Oklahoma | 1,732,900,000 | 0.9% |
| 27 | Oregon | 2,393,223,000 | 1.2% |
| 4 | Pennsylvania | 10,093,260,000 | 5.0% |
| 41 | Rhode Island | 875,695,000 | 0.4% |
| 24 | South Carolina | 2,638,242,000 | 1.3% |
| 49 | South Dakota | 403,092,000 | 0.2% |
| 16 | Tennessee | 3,781,480,000 | 1.9% |
| 3 | Texas | 11,127,889,000 | 5.5% |
| 39 | Utah | 992,504,000 | 0.5% |
| 45 | Vermont | 523,478,000 | 0.3% |
| 17 | Virginia | 3,624,293,000 | 1.8% |
| 15 | Washington | 4,080,905,000 | 2.0% |
| 33 | West Virginia | 1,604,048,000 | 0.8% |
| 14 | Wisconsin | 4,151,676,000 | 2.0% |
| 50 | Wyoming | 262,911,000 | 0.1% |

RANK ORDER

| RANK | STATE | EXPENDITURES | % of USA |
|------|-------|--------------|----------|
| 1 | California | $27,106,172,000 | 13.3% |
| 2 | New York | 26,872,380,000 | 13.2% |
| 3 | Texas | 11,127,889,000 | 5.5% |
| 4 | Pennsylvania | 10,093,260,000 | 5.0% |
| 5 | Illinois | 8,553,340,000 | 4.2% |
| 6 | Ohio | 8,486,798,000 | 4.2% |
| 7 | Florida | 7,936,215,000 | 3.9% |
| 8 | Michigan | 7,172,382,000 | 3.5% |
| 9 | Massachusetts | 5,835,658,000 | 2.9% |
| 10 | Georgia | 5,423,487,000 | 2.7% |
| 11 | New Jersey | 5,301,881,000 | 2.6% |
| 12 | North Carolina | 4,956,365,000 | 2.4% |
| 13 | Minnesota | 4,709,670,000 | 2.3% |
| 14 | Wisconsin | 4,151,676,000 | 2.0% |
| 15 | Washington | 4,080,905,000 | 2.0% |
| 16 | Tennessee | 3,781,480,000 | 1.9% |
| 17 | Virginia | 3,624,293,000 | 1.8% |
| 18 | Indiana | 3,422,252,000 | 1.7% |
| 19 | Kentucky | 3,245,820,000 | 1.6% |
| 20 | Missouri | 3,139,430,000 | 1.5% |
| 21 | Maryland | 3,081,992,000 | 1.5% |
| 22 | Louisiana | 2,931,812,000 | 1.4% |
| 23 | Connecticut | 2,892,553,000 | 1.4% |
| 24 | South Carolina | 2,638,242,000 | 1.3% |
| 25 | Arizona | 2,632,120,000 | 1.3% |
| 26 | Alabama | 2,575,844,000 | 1.3% |
| 27 | Oregon | 2,393,223,000 | 1.2% |
| 28 | Colorado | 2,294,525,000 | 1.1% |
| 29 | Iowa | 1,838,330,000 | 0.9% |
| 30 | Mississippi | 1,778,555,000 | 0.9% |
| 31 | Oklahoma | 1,732,900,000 | 0.9% |
| 32 | Arkansas | 1,675,690,000 | 0.8% |
| 33 | West Virginia | 1,604,048,000 | 0.8% |
| 34 | Maine | 1,366,127,000 | 0.7% |
| 35 | New Mexico | 1,295,199,000 | 0.6% |
| 36 | Kansas | 1,164,102,000 | 0.6% |
| 37 | Nebraska | 1,069,120,000 | 0.5% |
| 38 | Hawaii | 995,813,000 | 0.5% |
| 39 | Utah | 992,504,000 | 0.5% |
| 40 | New Hampshire | 944,464,000 | 0.5% |
| 41 | Rhode Island | 875,695,000 | 0.4% |
| 42 | Alaska | 760,620,000 | 0.4% |
| 43 | Nevada | 712,226,000 | 0.3% |
| 44 | Idaho | 633,238,000 | 0.3% |
| 45 | Vermont | 523,478,000 | 0.3% |
| 46 | Montana | 518,874,000 | 0.3% |
| 47 | Delaware | 502,321,000 | 0.2% |
| 48 | North Dakota | 485,325,000 | 0.2% |
| 49 | South Dakota | 403,092,000 | 0.2% |
| 50 | Wyoming | 262,911,000 | 0.1% |
| | District of Columbia | 1,186,639,000 | 0.6% |

Source: U.S. Bureau of the Census, Governments Division
"Compendium of Government Finances: 1997" (2000) (http://www.census.gov/govs/www/cog.html)
*Direct general expenditures. Includes funds for cash assistance programs, medical and other vendor payments, welfare institutions and other public welfare programs.

# Per Capita State and Local Government Expenditures
## For Public Welfare Programs in 1997
## National Per Capita = $761*

ALPHA ORDER

| RANK | STATE | PER CAPITA |
|---|---|---|
| 35 | Alabama | $596 |
| 2 | Alaska | 1,249 |
| 40 | Arizona | 578 |
| 29 | Arkansas | 664 |
| 10 | California | 841 |
| 36 | Colorado | 590 |
| 8 | Connecticut | 885 |
| 26 | Delaware | 683 |
| 44 | Florida | 540 |
| 22 | Georgia | 724 |
| 12 | Hawaii | 837 |
| 46 | Idaho | 523 |
| 23 | Illinois | 712 |
| 38 | Indiana | 583 |
| 33 | Iowa | 644 |
| 49 | Kansas | 445 |
| 13 | Kentucky | 831 |
| 27 | Louisiana | 674 |
| 3 | Maine | 1,097 |
| 34 | Maryland | 605 |
| 5 | Massachusetts | 954 |
| 20 | Michigan | 733 |
| 4 | Minnesota | 1,005 |
| 31 | Mississippi | 651 |
| 39 | Missouri | 581 |
| 36 | Montana | 590 |
| 32 | Nebraska | 646 |
| 50 | Nevada | 425 |
| 14 | New Hampshire | 805 |
| 30 | New Jersey | 658 |
| 18 | New Mexico | 752 |
| 1 | New York | 1,481 |
| 28 | North Carolina | 667 |
| 16 | North Dakota | 757 |
| 16 | Ohio | 757 |
| 46 | Oklahoma | 523 |
| 19 | Oregon | 738 |
| 11 | Pennsylvania | 840 |
| 7 | Rhode Island | 887 |
| 25 | South Carolina | 696 |
| 42 | South Dakota | 552 |
| 24 | Tennessee | 703 |
| 41 | Texas | 575 |
| 48 | Utah | 481 |
| 6 | Vermont | 889 |
| 45 | Virginia | 538 |
| 21 | Washington | 728 |
| 9 | West Virginia | 883 |
| 15 | Wisconsin | 798 |
| 43 | Wyoming | 548 |

RANK ORDER

| RANK | STATE | PER CAPITA |
|---|---|---|
| 1 | New York | $1,481 |
| 2 | Alaska | 1,249 |
| 3 | Maine | 1,097 |
| 4 | Minnesota | 1,005 |
| 5 | Massachusetts | 954 |
| 6 | Vermont | 889 |
| 7 | Rhode Island | 887 |
| 8 | Connecticut | 885 |
| 9 | West Virginia | 883 |
| 10 | California | 841 |
| 11 | Pennsylvania | 840 |
| 12 | Hawaii | 837 |
| 13 | Kentucky | 831 |
| 14 | New Hampshire | 805 |
| 15 | Wisconsin | 798 |
| 16 | North Dakota | 757 |
| 16 | Ohio | 757 |
| 18 | New Mexico | 752 |
| 19 | Oregon | 738 |
| 20 | Michigan | 733 |
| 21 | Washington | 728 |
| 22 | Georgia | 724 |
| 23 | Illinois | 712 |
| 24 | Tennessee | 703 |
| 25 | South Carolina | 696 |
| 26 | Delaware | 683 |
| 27 | Louisiana | 674 |
| 28 | North Carolina | 667 |
| 29 | Arkansas | 664 |
| 30 | New Jersey | 658 |
| 31 | Mississippi | 651 |
| 32 | Nebraska | 646 |
| 33 | Iowa | 644 |
| 34 | Maryland | 605 |
| 35 | Alabama | 596 |
| 36 | Colorado | 590 |
| 36 | Montana | 590 |
| 38 | Indiana | 583 |
| 39 | Missouri | 581 |
| 40 | Arizona | 578 |
| 41 | Texas | 575 |
| 42 | South Dakota | 552 |
| 43 | Wyoming | 548 |
| 44 | Florida | 540 |
| 45 | Virginia | 538 |
| 46 | Idaho | 523 |
| 46 | Oklahoma | 523 |
| 48 | Utah | 481 |
| 49 | Kansas | 445 |
| 50 | Nevada | 425 |

| District of Columbia | 2,244 |
|---|---|

Source: Morgan Quitno Press using data from U.S. Bureau of the Census, Governments Division
"Compendium of Government Finances: 1997" (2000) (http://www.census.gov/govs/www/cog.html)
*Direct general expenditures. Includes funds for cash assistance programs, medical and other vendor payments, welfare institutions and other public welfare programs.

# State and Local Government Spending for Public Welfare Programs
## As a Percent of All State and Local Government Expenditures in 1997
## National Percent = 16.3%*

ALPHA ORDER

| RANK | STATE | PERCENT |
|---|---|---|
| 27 | Alabama | 15.0 |
| 46 | Alaska | 11.3 |
| 28 | Arizona | 14.8 |
| 11 | Arkansas | 17.8 |
| 14 | California | 16.9 |
| 40 | Colorado | 13.1 |
| 18 | Connecticut | 16.3 |
| 43 | Delaware | 12.7 |
| 45 | Florida | 12.5 |
| 15 | Georgia | 16.6 |
| 28 | Hawaii | 14.8 |
| 41 | Idaho | 13.0 |
| 20 | Illinois | 16.1 |
| 30 | Indiana | 14.6 |
| 34 | Iowa | 14.3 |
| 48 | Kansas | 10.5 |
| 3 | Kentucky | 20.8 |
| 23 | Louisiana | 15.6 |
| 1 | Maine | 23.6 |
| 38 | Maryland | 13.5 |
| 9 | Massachusetts | 18.4 |
| 23 | Michigan | 15.6 |
| 7 | Minnesota | 18.8 |
| 21 | Mississippi | 16.0 |
| 26 | Missouri | 15.3 |
| 39 | Montana | 13.3 |
| 33 | Nebraska | 14.4 |
| 50 | Nevada | 9.0 |
| 5 | New Hampshire | 19.1 |
| 41 | New Jersey | 13.0 |
| 25 | New Mexico | 15.5 |
| 2 | New York | 21.3 |
| 22 | North Carolina | 15.9 |
| 19 | North Dakota | 16.2 |
| 13 | Ohio | 17.6 |
| 35 | Oklahoma | 14.2 |
| 32 | Oregon | 14.5 |
| 6 | Pennsylvania | 19.0 |
| 10 | Rhode Island | 17.9 |
| 15 | South Carolina | 16.6 |
| 37 | South Dakota | 13.8 |
| 11 | Tennessee | 17.8 |
| 30 | Texas | 14.6 |
| 47 | Utah | 11.0 |
| 7 | Vermont | 18.8 |
| 43 | Virginia | 12.7 |
| 36 | Washington | 14.1 |
| 4 | West Virginia | 20.7 |
| 17 | Wisconsin | 16.4 |
| 49 | Wyoming | 9.4 |

RANK ORDER

| RANK | STATE | PERCENT |
|---|---|---|
| 1 | Maine | 23.6 |
| 2 | New York | 21.3 |
| 3 | Kentucky | 20.8 |
| 4 | West Virginia | 20.7 |
| 5 | New Hampshire | 19.1 |
| 6 | Pennsylvania | 19.0 |
| 7 | Minnesota | 18.8 |
| 7 | Vermont | 18.8 |
| 9 | Massachusetts | 18.4 |
| 10 | Rhode Island | 17.9 |
| 11 | Arkansas | 17.8 |
| 11 | Tennessee | 17.8 |
| 13 | Ohio | 17.6 |
| 14 | California | 16.9 |
| 15 | Georgia | 16.6 |
| 15 | South Carolina | 16.6 |
| 17 | Wisconsin | 16.4 |
| 18 | Connecticut | 16.3 |
| 19 | North Dakota | 16.2 |
| 20 | Illinois | 16.1 |
| 21 | Mississippi | 16.0 |
| 22 | North Carolina | 15.9 |
| 23 | Louisiana | 15.6 |
| 23 | Michigan | 15.6 |
| 25 | New Mexico | 15.5 |
| 26 | Missouri | 15.3 |
| 27 | Alabama | 15.0 |
| 28 | Arizona | 14.8 |
| 28 | Hawaii | 14.8 |
| 30 | Indiana | 14.6 |
| 30 | Texas | 14.6 |
| 32 | Oregon | 14.5 |
| 33 | Nebraska | 14.4 |
| 34 | Iowa | 14.3 |
| 35 | Oklahoma | 14.2 |
| 36 | Washington | 14.1 |
| 37 | South Dakota | 13.8 |
| 38 | Maryland | 13.5 |
| 39 | Montana | 13.3 |
| 40 | Colorado | 13.1 |
| 41 | Idaho | 13.0 |
| 41 | New Jersey | 13.0 |
| 43 | Delaware | 12.7 |
| 43 | Virginia | 12.7 |
| 45 | Florida | 12.5 |
| 46 | Alaska | 11.3 |
| 47 | Utah | 11.0 |
| 48 | Kansas | 10.5 |
| 49 | Wyoming | 9.4 |
| 50 | Nevada | 9.0 |

| | District of Columbia | 27.4 |
|---|---|---|

*Source: Morgan Quitno Press using data from U.S. Bureau of the Census, Governments Division*
    *"Compendium of Government Finances: 1997" (2000) (http://www.census.gov/govs/www/cog.html)*
*As a percent of a direct general expenditures.*

# Social Security (OASDI) Payments in 1999

## National Total = $385,525,000,000*

ALPHA ORDER

| RANK | STATE | PAYMENTS | % of USA |
|---|---|---|---|
| 20 | Alabama | $6,546,000,000 | 1.7% |
| 50 | Alaska | 423,000,000 | 0.1% |
| 19 | Arizona | 6,702,000,000 | 1.7% |
| 31 | Arkansas | 4,046,000,000 | 1.0% |
| 1 | California | 35,933,000,000 | 9.3% |
| 30 | Colorado | 4,423,000,000 | 1.1% |
| 26 | Connecticut | 5,401,000,000 | 1.4% |
| 45 | Delaware | 1,191,000,000 | 0.3% |
| 2 | Florida | 27,253,000,000 | 7.1% |
| 13 | Georgia | 8,884,000,000 | 2.3% |
| 43 | Hawaii | 1,517,000,000 | 0.4% |
| 42 | Idaho | 1,592,000,000 | 0.4% |
| 7 | Illinois | 16,708,000,000 | 4.3% |
| 12 | Indiana | 8,917,000,000 | 2.3% |
| 29 | Iowa | 4,694,000,000 | 1.2% |
| 33 | Kansas | 3,858,000,000 | 1.0% |
| 23 | Kentucky | 5,886,000,000 | 1.5% |
| 24 | Louisiana | 5,618,000,000 | 1.5% |
| 39 | Maine | 1,964,000,000 | 0.5% |
| 22 | Maryland | 6,216,000,000 | 1.6% |
| 11 | Massachusetts | 9,220,000,000 | 2.4% |
| 8 | Michigan | 15,085,000,000 | 3.9% |
| 21 | Minnesota | 6,266,000,000 | 1.6% |
| 32 | Mississippi | 3,859,000,000 | 1.0% |
| 15 | Missouri | 8,415,000,000 | 2.2% |
| 44 | Montana | 1,309,000,000 | 0.3% |
| 35 | Nebraska | 2,422,000,000 | 0.6% |
| 36 | Nevada | 2,365,000,000 | 0.6% |
| 40 | New Hampshire | 1,728,000,000 | 0.4% |
| 9 | New Jersey | 12,748,000,000 | 3.3% |
| 37 | New Mexico | 2,163,000,000 | 0.6% |
| 3 | New York | 27,250,000,000 | 7.1% |
| 10 | North Carolina | 10,930,000,000 | 2.8% |
| 47 | North Dakota | 937,000,000 | 0.2% |
| 6 | Ohio | 16,955,000,000 | 4.4% |
| 28 | Oklahoma | 4,886,000,000 | 1.3% |
| 27 | Oregon | 4,951,000,000 | 1.3% |
| 5 | Pennsylvania | 21,130,000,000 | 5.5% |
| 41 | Rhode Island | 1,657,000,000 | 0.4% |
| 25 | South Carolina | 5,544,000,000 | 1.4% |
| 46 | South Dakota | 1,075,000,000 | 0.3% |
| 16 | Tennessee | 8,015,000,000 | 2.1% |
| 4 | Texas | 21,486,000,000 | 5.6% |
| 38 | Utah | 2,023,000,000 | 0.5% |
| 48 | Vermont | 872,000,000 | 0.2% |
| 14 | Virginia | 8,471,000,000 | 2.2% |
| 18 | Washington | 7,452,000,000 | 1.9% |
| 34 | West Virginia | 3,337,000,000 | 0.9% |
| 17 | Wisconsin | 7,955,000,000 | 2.1% |
| 49 | Wyoming | 650,000,000 | 0.2% |

RANK ORDER

| RANK | STATE | PAYMENTS | % of USA |
|---|---|---|---|
| 1 | California | $35,933,000,000 | 9.3% |
| 2 | Florida | 27,253,000,000 | 7.1% |
| 3 | New York | 27,250,000,000 | 7.1% |
| 4 | Texas | 21,486,000,000 | 5.6% |
| 5 | Pennsylvania | 21,130,000,000 | 5.5% |
| 6 | Ohio | 16,955,000,000 | 4.4% |
| 7 | Illinois | 16,708,000,000 | 4.3% |
| 8 | Michigan | 15,085,000,000 | 3.9% |
| 9 | New Jersey | 12,748,000,000 | 3.3% |
| 10 | North Carolina | 10,930,000,000 | 2.8% |
| 11 | Massachusetts | 9,220,000,000 | 2.4% |
| 12 | Indiana | 8,917,000,000 | 2.3% |
| 13 | Georgia | 8,884,000,000 | 2.3% |
| 14 | Virginia | 8,471,000,000 | 2.2% |
| 15 | Missouri | 8,415,000,000 | 2.2% |
| 16 | Tennessee | 8,015,000,000 | 2.1% |
| 17 | Wisconsin | 7,955,000,000 | 2.1% |
| 18 | Washington | 7,452,000,000 | 1.9% |
| 19 | Arizona | 6,702,000,000 | 1.7% |
| 20 | Alabama | 6,546,000,000 | 1.7% |
| 21 | Minnesota | 6,266,000,000 | 1.6% |
| 22 | Maryland | 6,216,000,000 | 1.6% |
| 23 | Kentucky | 5,886,000,000 | 1.5% |
| 24 | Louisiana | 5,618,000,000 | 1.5% |
| 25 | South Carolina | 5,544,000,000 | 1.4% |
| 26 | Connecticut | 5,401,000,000 | 1.4% |
| 27 | Oregon | 4,951,000,000 | 1.3% |
| 28 | Oklahoma | 4,886,000,000 | 1.3% |
| 29 | Iowa | 4,694,000,000 | 1.2% |
| 30 | Colorado | 4,423,000,000 | 1.1% |
| 31 | Arkansas | 4,046,000,000 | 1.0% |
| 32 | Mississippi | 3,859,000,000 | 1.0% |
| 33 | Kansas | 3,858,000,000 | 1.0% |
| 34 | West Virginia | 3,337,000,000 | 0.9% |
| 35 | Nebraska | 2,422,000,000 | 0.6% |
| 36 | Nevada | 2,365,000,000 | 0.6% |
| 37 | New Mexico | 2,163,000,000 | 0.6% |
| 38 | Utah | 2,023,000,000 | 0.5% |
| 39 | Maine | 1,964,000,000 | 0.5% |
| 40 | New Hampshire | 1,728,000,000 | 0.4% |
| 41 | Rhode Island | 1,657,000,000 | 0.4% |
| 42 | Idaho | 1,592,000,000 | 0.4% |
| 43 | Hawaii | 1,517,000,000 | 0.4% |
| 44 | Montana | 1,309,000,000 | 0.3% |
| 45 | Delaware | 1,191,000,000 | 0.3% |
| 46 | South Dakota | 1,075,000,000 | 0.3% |
| 47 | North Dakota | 937,000,000 | 0.2% |
| 48 | Vermont | 872,000,000 | 0.2% |
| 49 | Wyoming | 650,000,000 | 0.2% |
| 50 | Alaska | 423,000,000 | 0.1% |
| | District of Columbia | 555,000,000 | 0.1% |

Source: Social Security Administration
"Social Security Bulletin, Annual Statistical Supplement 2000"
*"OASDI" is Old Age, Survivors and Disability Insurance. National total includes $6,017,000,000 in payments to recipients in U.S. territories and foreign countries.

# Per Capita Social Security (OASDI) Payments in 1999

## National Per Capita = $1,392*

<table>
<tr><td colspan="3">ALPHA ORDER</td><td colspan="3">RANK ORDER</td></tr>
<tr><td>RANK</td><td>STATE</td><td>PER CAPITA</td><td>RANK</td><td>STATE</td><td>PER CAPITA</td></tr>
<tr><td>16</td><td>Alabama</td><td>$1,498</td><td>1</td><td>West Virginia</td><td>$1,847</td></tr>
<tr><td>50</td><td>Alaska</td><td>683</td><td>2</td><td>Florida</td><td>1,803</td></tr>
<tr><td>32</td><td>Arizona</td><td>1,403</td><td>3</td><td>Pennsylvania</td><td>1,762</td></tr>
<tr><td>7</td><td>Arkansas</td><td>1,586</td><td>4</td><td>Rhode Island</td><td>1,672</td></tr>
<tr><td>47</td><td>California</td><td>1,084</td><td>5</td><td>Connecticut</td><td>1,646</td></tr>
<tr><td>46</td><td>Colorado</td><td>1,090</td><td>6</td><td>Iowa</td><td>1,636</td></tr>
<tr><td>5</td><td>Connecticut</td><td>1,646</td><td>7</td><td>Arkansas</td><td>1,586</td></tr>
<tr><td>8</td><td>Delaware</td><td>1,581</td><td>8</td><td>Delaware</td><td>1,581</td></tr>
<tr><td>2</td><td>Florida</td><td>1,803</td><td>9</td><td>Maine</td><td>1,567</td></tr>
<tr><td>45</td><td>Georgia</td><td>1,141</td><td>10</td><td>New Jersey</td><td>1,565</td></tr>
<tr><td>40</td><td>Hawaii</td><td>1,280</td><td>11</td><td>Missouri</td><td>1,539</td></tr>
<tr><td>41</td><td>Idaho</td><td>1,272</td><td>12</td><td>Michigan</td><td>1,529</td></tr>
<tr><td>34</td><td>Illinois</td><td>1,378</td><td>13</td><td>Wisconsin</td><td>1,515</td></tr>
<tr><td>15</td><td>Indiana</td><td>1,500</td><td>14</td><td>Ohio</td><td>1,506</td></tr>
<tr><td>6</td><td>Iowa</td><td>1,636</td><td>15</td><td>Indiana</td><td>1,500</td></tr>
<tr><td>27</td><td>Kansas</td><td>1,454</td><td>16</td><td>Alabama</td><td>1,498</td></tr>
<tr><td>20</td><td>Kentucky</td><td>1,486</td><td>16</td><td>New York</td><td>1,498</td></tr>
<tr><td>39</td><td>Louisiana</td><td>1,285</td><td>18</td><td>Massachusetts</td><td>1,493</td></tr>
<tr><td>9</td><td>Maine</td><td>1,567</td><td>18</td><td>Oregon</td><td>1,493</td></tr>
<tr><td>44</td><td>Maryland</td><td>1,202</td><td>20</td><td>Kentucky</td><td>1,486</td></tr>
<tr><td>18</td><td>Massachusetts</td><td>1,493</td><td>21</td><td>Montana</td><td>1,483</td></tr>
<tr><td>12</td><td>Michigan</td><td>1,529</td><td>22</td><td>North Dakota</td><td>1,479</td></tr>
<tr><td>36</td><td>Minnesota</td><td>1,312</td><td>23</td><td>Vermont</td><td>1,469</td></tr>
<tr><td>33</td><td>Mississippi</td><td>1,394</td><td>24</td><td>South Dakota</td><td>1,466</td></tr>
<tr><td>11</td><td>Missouri</td><td>1,539</td><td>25</td><td>Tennessee</td><td>1,462</td></tr>
<tr><td>21</td><td>Montana</td><td>1,483</td><td>26</td><td>Oklahoma</td><td>1,455</td></tr>
<tr><td>27</td><td>Nebraska</td><td>1,454</td><td>27</td><td>Kansas</td><td>1,454</td></tr>
<tr><td>37</td><td>Nevada</td><td>1,307</td><td>27</td><td>Nebraska</td><td>1,454</td></tr>
<tr><td>29</td><td>New Hampshire</td><td>1,439</td><td>29</td><td>New Hampshire</td><td>1,439</td></tr>
<tr><td>10</td><td>New Jersey</td><td>1,565</td><td>30</td><td>North Carolina</td><td>1,429</td></tr>
<tr><td>42</td><td>New Mexico</td><td>1,243</td><td>31</td><td>South Carolina</td><td>1,427</td></tr>
<tr><td>16</td><td>New York</td><td>1,498</td><td>32</td><td>Arizona</td><td>1,403</td></tr>
<tr><td>30</td><td>North Carolina</td><td>1,429</td><td>33</td><td>Mississippi</td><td>1,394</td></tr>
<tr><td>22</td><td>North Dakota</td><td>1,479</td><td>34</td><td>Illinois</td><td>1,378</td></tr>
<tr><td>14</td><td>Ohio</td><td>1,506</td><td>35</td><td>Wyoming</td><td>1,355</td></tr>
<tr><td>26</td><td>Oklahoma</td><td>1,455</td><td>36</td><td>Minnesota</td><td>1,312</td></tr>
<tr><td>18</td><td>Oregon</td><td>1,493</td><td>37</td><td>Nevada</td><td>1,307</td></tr>
<tr><td>3</td><td>Pennsylvania</td><td>1,762</td><td>38</td><td>Washington</td><td>1,295</td></tr>
<tr><td>4</td><td>Rhode Island</td><td>1,672</td><td>39</td><td>Louisiana</td><td>1,285</td></tr>
<tr><td>31</td><td>South Carolina</td><td>1,427</td><td>40</td><td>Hawaii</td><td>1,280</td></tr>
<tr><td>24</td><td>South Dakota</td><td>1,466</td><td>41</td><td>Idaho</td><td>1,272</td></tr>
<tr><td>25</td><td>Tennessee</td><td>1,462</td><td>42</td><td>New Mexico</td><td>1,243</td></tr>
<tr><td>48</td><td>Texas</td><td>1,072</td><td>43</td><td>Virginia</td><td>1,233</td></tr>
<tr><td>49</td><td>Utah</td><td>950</td><td>44</td><td>Maryland</td><td>1,202</td></tr>
<tr><td>23</td><td>Vermont</td><td>1,469</td><td>45</td><td>Georgia</td><td>1,141</td></tr>
<tr><td>43</td><td>Virginia</td><td>1,233</td><td>46</td><td>Colorado</td><td>1,090</td></tr>
<tr><td>38</td><td>Washington</td><td>1,295</td><td>47</td><td>California</td><td>1,084</td></tr>
<tr><td>1</td><td>West Virginia</td><td>1,847</td><td>48</td><td>Texas</td><td>1,072</td></tr>
<tr><td>13</td><td>Wisconsin</td><td>1,515</td><td>49</td><td>Utah</td><td>950</td></tr>
<tr><td>35</td><td>Wyoming</td><td>1,355</td><td>50</td><td>Alaska</td><td>683</td></tr>
<tr><td></td><td></td><td></td><td></td><td>District of Columbia</td><td>1,069</td></tr>
</table>

Source: Morgan Quitno Press using data from Social Security Administration
"Social Security Bulletin, Annual Statistical Supplement 2000"
*"OASDI" is Old Age, Survivors and Disability Insurance. National per capita does not include payments or population in U.S. territories and foreign countries.

# Social Security (OASDI) Monthly Payments in 1999

## National Total = $32,577,841,000*

ALPHA ORDER

RANK ORDER

| RANK | STATE | PAYMENTS | % of USA | RANK | STATE | PAYMENTS | % of USA |
|------|-------|----------|----------|------|-------|----------|----------|
| 20 | Alabama | $545,908,000 | 1.7% | 1 | California | $3,050,268,000 | 9.4% |
| 50 | Alaska | 35,572,000 | 0.1% | 2 | Florida | 2,330,071,000 | 7.2% |
| 19 | Arizona | 573,880,000 | 1.8% | 3 | New York | 2,312,203,000 | 7.1% |
| 31 | Arkansas | 338,478,000 | 1.0% | 4 | Texas | 1,803,158,000 | 5.5% |
| 1 | California | 3,050,268,000 | 9.4% | 5 | Pennsylvania | 1,784,668,000 | 5.5% |
| 30 | Colorado | 374,454,000 | 1.1% | 6 | Ohio | 1,419,838,000 | 4.4% |
| 25 | Connecticut | 462,585,000 | 1.4% | 7 | Illinois | 1,410,159,000 | 4.3% |
| 45 | Delaware | 101,305,000 | 0.3% | 8 | Michigan | 1,270,001,000 | 3.9% |
| 2 | Florida | 2,330,071,000 | 7.2% | 9 | New Jersey | 1,086,981,000 | 3.3% |
| 13 | Georgia | 746,245,000 | 2.3% | 10 | North Carolina | 927,098,000 | 2.8% |
| 43 | Hawaii | 131,387,000 | 0.4% | 11 | Massachusetts | 781,498,000 | 2.4% |
| 42 | Idaho | 135,548,000 | 0.4% | 12 | Indiana | 752,118,000 | 2.3% |
| 7 | Illinois | 1,410,159,000 | 4.3% | 13 | Georgia | 746,245,000 | 2.3% |
| 12 | Indiana | 752,118,000 | 2.3% | 14 | Virginia | 715,013,000 | 2.2% |
| 29 | Iowa | 397,051,000 | 1.2% | 15 | Missouri | 709,848,000 | 2.2% |
| 32 | Kansas | 326,634,000 | 1.0% | 16 | Wisconsin | 675,847,000 | 2.1% |
| 23 | Kentucky | 487,177,000 | 1.5% | 17 | Tennessee | 672,973,000 | 2.1% |
| 26 | Louisiana | 461,167,000 | 1.4% | 18 | Washington | 634,518,000 | 1.9% |
| 39 | Maine | 166,105,000 | 0.5% | 19 | Arizona | 573,880,000 | 1.8% |
| 22 | Maryland | 525,407,000 | 1.6% | 20 | Alabama | 545,908,000 | 1.7% |
| 11 | Massachusetts | 781,498,000 | 2.4% | 21 | Minnesota | 531,864,000 | 1.6% |
| 8 | Michigan | 1,270,001,000 | 3.9% | 22 | Maryland | 525,407,000 | 1.6% |
| 21 | Minnesota | 531,864,000 | 1.6% | 23 | Kentucky | 487,177,000 | 1.5% |
| 33 | Mississippi | 321,245,000 | 1.0% | 24 | South Carolina | 468,048,000 | 1.4% |
| 15 | Missouri | 709,848,000 | 2.2% | 25 | Connecticut | 462,585,000 | 1.4% |
| 44 | Montana | 110,539,000 | 0.3% | 26 | Louisiana | 461,167,000 | 1.4% |
| 35 | Nebraska | 205,266,000 | 0.6% | 27 | Oregon | 421,816,000 | 1.3% |
| 36 | Nevada | 203,950,000 | 0.6% | 28 | Oklahoma | 410,026,000 | 1.3% |
| 40 | New Hampshire | 147,592,000 | 0.5% | 29 | Iowa | 397,051,000 | 1.2% |
| 9 | New Jersey | 1,086,981,000 | 3.3% | 30 | Colorado | 374,454,000 | 1.1% |
| 37 | New Mexico | 182,342,000 | 0.6% | 31 | Arkansas | 338,478,000 | 1.0% |
| 3 | New York | 2,312,203,000 | 7.1% | 32 | Kansas | 326,634,000 | 1.0% |
| 10 | North Carolina | 927,098,000 | 2.8% | 33 | Mississippi | 321,245,000 | 1.0% |
| 47 | North Dakota | 78,232,000 | 0.2% | 34 | West Virginia | 274,811,000 | 0.8% |
| 6 | Ohio | 1,419,838,000 | 4.4% | 35 | Nebraska | 205,266,000 | 0.6% |
| 28 | Oklahoma | 410,026,000 | 1.3% | 36 | Nevada | 203,950,000 | 0.6% |
| 27 | Oregon | 421,816,000 | 1.3% | 37 | New Mexico | 182,342,000 | 0.6% |
| 5 | Pennsylvania | 1,784,668,000 | 5.5% | 38 | Utah | 172,449,000 | 0.5% |
| 41 | Rhode Island | 141,748,000 | 0.4% | 39 | Maine | 166,105,000 | 0.5% |
| 24 | South Carolina | 468,048,000 | 1.4% | 40 | New Hampshire | 147,592,000 | 0.5% |
| 46 | South Dakota | 90,650,000 | 0.3% | 41 | Rhode Island | 141,748,000 | 0.4% |
| 17 | Tennessee | 672,973,000 | 2.1% | 42 | Idaho | 135,548,000 | 0.4% |
| 4 | Texas | 1,803,158,000 | 5.5% | 43 | Hawaii | 131,387,000 | 0.4% |
| 38 | Utah | 172,449,000 | 0.5% | 44 | Montana | 110,539,000 | 0.3% |
| 48 | Vermont | 74,128,000 | 0.2% | 45 | Delaware | 101,305,000 | 0.3% |
| 14 | Virginia | 715,013,000 | 2.2% | 46 | South Dakota | 90,650,000 | 0.3% |
| 18 | Washington | 634,518,000 | 1.9% | 47 | North Dakota | 78,232,000 | 0.2% |
| 34 | West Virginia | 274,811,000 | 0.8% | 48 | Vermont | 74,128,000 | 0.2% |
| 16 | Wisconsin | 675,847,000 | 2.1% | 49 | Wyoming | 55,413,000 | 0.2% |
| 49 | Wyoming | 55,413,000 | 0.2% | 50 | Alaska | 35,572,000 | 0.1% |
| | | | | | District of Columbia | 46,569,000 | 0.1% |

Source: Social Security Administration
   "Social Security Bulletin, Annual Statistical Supplement 2000"
*For December 1999.  "OASDI" is Old Age, Survivors and Disability Insurance.  National total includes
$494,060,000 in payments to recipients in U.S. territories and foreign countries.

# Social Security (OASDI) Beneficiaries in 1999

## National Total = 44,598,890 Beneficiaries*

ALPHA ORDER

| RANK | STATE | BENEFICIARIES | % of USA |
|------|-------|--------------:|---------:|
| 19 | Alabama | 811,250 | 1.8% |
| 50 | Alaska | 51,540 | 0.1% |
| 20 | Arizona | 768,920 | 1.7% |
| 31 | Arkansas | 511,080 | 1.1% |
| 1 | California | 4,110,800 | 9.2% |
| 30 | Colorado | 523,200 | 1.2% |
| 27 | Connecticut | 567,480 | 1.3% |
| 46 | Delaware | 131,620 | 0.3% |
| 2 | Florida | 3,141,370 | 7.0% |
| 11 | Georgia | 1,078,460 | 2.4% |
| 43 | Hawaii | 179,150 | 0.4% |
| 42 | Idaho | 189,670 | 0.4% |
| 7 | Illinois | 1,817,410 | 4.1% |
| 15 | Indiana | 978,750 | 2.2% |
| 29 | Iowa | 536,540 | 1.2% |
| 33 | Kansas | 433,690 | 1.0% |
| 21 | Kentucky | 729,660 | 1.6% |
| 24 | Louisiana | 702,730 | 1.6% |
| 38 | Maine | 246,610 | 0.6% |
| 23 | Maryland | 703,270 | 1.6% |
| 12 | Massachusetts | 1,048,750 | 2.4% |
| 8 | Michigan | 1,619,190 | 3.6% |
| 22 | Minnesota | 725,310 | 1.6% |
| 32 | Mississippi | 507,060 | 1.1% |
| 14 | Missouri | 987,320 | 2.2% |
| 44 | Montana | 155,360 | 0.3% |
| 35 | Nebraska | 282,510 | 0.6% |
| 37 | Nevada | 269,780 | 0.6% |
| 40 | New Hampshire | 194,930 | 0.4% |
| 9 | New Jersey | 1,325,890 | 3.0% |
| 36 | New Mexico | 273,640 | 0.6% |
| 3 | New York | 2,963,630 | 6.6% |
| 10 | North Carolina | 1,320,790 | 3.0% |
| 47 | North Dakota | 114,440 | 0.3% |
| 6 | Ohio | 1,902,090 | 4.3% |
| 26 | Oklahoma | 586,150 | 1.3% |
| 28 | Oregon | 559,980 | 1.3% |
| 5 | Pennsylvania | 2,333,490 | 5.2% |
| 41 | Rhode Island | 190,110 | 0.4% |
| 25 | South Carolina | 672,620 | 1.5% |
| 45 | South Dakota | 135,160 | 0.3% |
| 16 | Tennessee | 974,590 | 2.2% |
| 4 | Texas | 2,575,860 | 5.8% |
| 39 | Utah | 235,780 | 0.5% |
| 48 | Vermont | 103,280 | 0.2% |
| 13 | Virginia | 1,008,050 | 2.3% |
| 18 | Washington | 826,170 | 1.9% |
| 34 | West Virginia | 388,210 | 0.9% |
| 17 | Wisconsin | 887,650 | 2.0% |
| 49 | Wyoming | 75,370 | 0.2% |

RANK ORDER

| RANK | STATE | BENEFICIARIES | % of USA |
|------|-------|--------------:|---------:|
| 1 | California | 4,110,800 | 9.2% |
| 2 | Florida | 3,141,370 | 7.0% |
| 3 | New York | 2,963,630 | 6.6% |
| 4 | Texas | 2,575,860 | 5.8% |
| 5 | Pennsylvania | 2,333,490 | 5.2% |
| 6 | Ohio | 1,902,090 | 4.3% |
| 7 | Illinois | 1,817,410 | 4.1% |
| 8 | Michigan | 1,619,190 | 3.6% |
| 9 | New Jersey | 1,325,890 | 3.0% |
| 10 | North Carolina | 1,320,790 | 3.0% |
| 11 | Georgia | 1,078,460 | 2.4% |
| 12 | Massachusetts | 1,048,750 | 2.4% |
| 13 | Virginia | 1,008,050 | 2.3% |
| 14 | Missouri | 987,320 | 2.2% |
| 15 | Indiana | 978,750 | 2.2% |
| 16 | Tennessee | 974,590 | 2.2% |
| 17 | Wisconsin | 887,650 | 2.0% |
| 18 | Washington | 826,170 | 1.9% |
| 19 | Alabama | 811,250 | 1.8% |
| 20 | Arizona | 768,920 | 1.7% |
| 21 | Kentucky | 729,660 | 1.6% |
| 22 | Minnesota | 725,310 | 1.6% |
| 23 | Maryland | 703,270 | 1.6% |
| 24 | Louisiana | 702,730 | 1.6% |
| 25 | South Carolina | 672,620 | 1.5% |
| 26 | Oklahoma | 586,150 | 1.3% |
| 27 | Connecticut | 567,480 | 1.3% |
| 28 | Oregon | 559,980 | 1.3% |
| 29 | Iowa | 536,540 | 1.2% |
| 30 | Colorado | 523,200 | 1.2% |
| 31 | Arkansas | 511,080 | 1.1% |
| 32 | Mississippi | 507,060 | 1.1% |
| 33 | Kansas | 433,690 | 1.0% |
| 34 | West Virginia | 388,210 | 0.9% |
| 35 | Nebraska | 282,510 | 0.6% |
| 36 | New Mexico | 273,640 | 0.6% |
| 37 | Nevada | 269,780 | 0.6% |
| 38 | Maine | 246,610 | 0.6% |
| 39 | Utah | 235,780 | 0.5% |
| 40 | New Hampshire | 194,930 | 0.4% |
| 41 | Rhode Island | 190,110 | 0.4% |
| 42 | Idaho | 189,670 | 0.4% |
| 43 | Hawaii | 179,150 | 0.4% |
| 44 | Montana | 155,360 | 0.3% |
| 45 | South Dakota | 135,160 | 0.3% |
| 46 | Delaware | 131,620 | 0.3% |
| 47 | North Dakota | 114,440 | 0.3% |
| 48 | Vermont | 103,280 | 0.2% |
| 49 | Wyoming | 75,370 | 0.2% |
| 50 | Alaska | 51,540 | 0.1% |
| | District of Columbia | 73,730 | 0.2% |

Source: Social Security Administration
   "Social Security Bulletin, Annual Statistical Supplement 2000"
*For December 1999.  "OASDI" is Old Age, Survivors and Disability Insurance.  National total includes 1,065,750 beneficiaries in U.S. territories and foreign countries.

# Average Monthly Social Security (OASDI) Payment in 1999

## National Average = $737.00 Each Month per Beneficiary*

ALPHA ORDER

RANK ORDER

| RANK | STATE | AVERAGE BENEFIT | RANK | STATE | AVERAGE BENEFIT |
|------|-------|-----------------|------|-------|-----------------|
| 44 | Alabama | $672.92 | 1 | New Jersey | $819.81 |
| 41 | Alaska | 690.18 | 2 | Connecticut | 815.16 |
| 17 | Arizona | 746.35 | 3 | Michigan | 784.34 |
| 48 | Arkansas | 662.28 | 4 | New York | 780.19 |
| 20 | California | 742.01 | 5 | Illinois | 775.92 |
| 30 | Colorado | 715.70 | 6 | Delaware | 769.68 |
| 2 | Connecticut | 815.16 | 7 | Indiana | 768.45 |
| 6 | Delaware | 769.68 | 8 | Washington | 768.02 |
| 21 | Florida | 741.74 | 9 | Pennsylvania | 764.81 |
| 39 | Georgia | 691.95 | 10 | Wisconsin | 761.39 |
| 24 | Hawaii | 733.39 | 11 | New Hampshire | 757.15 |
| 31 | Idaho | 714.65 | 12 | Nevada | 755.99 |
| 5 | Illinois | 775.92 | 13 | Oregon | 753.27 |
| 7 | Indiana | 768.45 | 14 | Kansas | 753.15 |
| 22 | Iowa | 740.02 | 15 | Maryland | 747.09 |
| 14 | Kansas | 753.15 | 16 | Ohio | 746.46 |
| 46 | Kentucky | 667.68 | 17 | Arizona | 746.35 |
| 49 | Louisiana | 656.25 | 18 | Rhode Island | 745.61 |
| 43 | Maine | 673.55 | 19 | Massachusetts | 745.17 |
| 15 | Maryland | 747.09 | 20 | California | 742.01 |
| 19 | Massachusetts | 745.17 | 21 | Florida | 741.74 |
| 3 | Michigan | 784.34 | 22 | Iowa | 740.02 |
| 25 | Minnesota | 733.29 | 23 | Wyoming | 735.21 |
| 50 | Mississippi | 633.54 | 24 | Hawaii | 733.39 |
| 28 | Missouri | 718.96 | 25 | Minnesota | 733.29 |
| 32 | Montana | 711.50 | 26 | Utah | 731.40 |
| 27 | Nebraska | 726.58 | 27 | Nebraska | 726.58 |
| 12 | Nevada | 755.99 | 28 | Missouri | 718.96 |
| 11 | New Hampshire | 757.15 | 29 | Vermont | 717.74 |
| 1 | New Jersey | 819.81 | 30 | Colorado | 715.70 |
| 47 | New Mexico | 666.36 | 31 | Idaho | 714.65 |
| 4 | New York | 780.19 | 32 | Montana | 711.50 |
| 35 | North Carolina | 701.93 | 33 | Virginia | 709.30 |
| 42 | North Dakota | 683.61 | 34 | West Virginia | 707.89 |
| 16 | Ohio | 746.46 | 35 | North Carolina | 701.93 |
| 37 | Oklahoma | 699.52 | 36 | Texas | 700.02 |
| 13 | Oregon | 753.27 | 37 | Oklahoma | 699.52 |
| 9 | Pennsylvania | 764.81 | 38 | South Carolina | 695.86 |
| 18 | Rhode Island | 745.61 | 39 | Georgia | 691.95 |
| 38 | South Carolina | 695.86 | 40 | Tennessee | 690.52 |
| 45 | South Dakota | 670.69 | 41 | Alaska | 690.18 |
| 40 | Tennessee | 690.52 | 42 | North Dakota | 683.61 |
| 36 | Texas | 700.02 | 43 | Maine | 673.55 |
| 26 | Utah | 731.40 | 44 | Alabama | 672.92 |
| 29 | Vermont | 717.74 | 45 | South Dakota | 670.69 |
| 33 | Virginia | 709.30 | 46 | Kentucky | 667.68 |
| 8 | Washington | 768.02 | 47 | New Mexico | 666.36 |
| 34 | West Virginia | 707.89 | 48 | Arkansas | 662.28 |
| 10 | Wisconsin | 761.39 | 49 | Louisiana | 656.25 |
| 23 | Wyoming | 735.21 | 50 | Mississippi | 633.54 |
| | | | | District of Columbia | 631.62 |

Source: Morgan Quitno Press using data from Social Security Administration
"Social Security Bulletin, Annual Statistical Supplement 2000"
*As of December 1999. "OASDI" is Old Age, Survivors and Disability Insurance. National average does not include payments to beneficiaries in U.S. territories and foreign countries.

# Medicare Benefit Payments in 1999

## National Total = $208,623,563,538*

ALPHA ORDER

RANK ORDER

| RANK | STATE | BENEFITS | % of USA |
|---|---|---|---|
| 19 | Alabama | $3,817,396,530 | 1.8% |
| 50 | Alaska | 133,480,125 | 0.1% |
| 24 | Arizona | 2,827,734,758 | 1.4% |
| 30 | Arkansas | 2,044,027,481 | 1.0% |
| 1 | California | 23,305,723,494 | 11.2% |
| 27 | Colorado | 2,327,582,779 | 1.1% |
| 23 | Connecticut | 2,985,509,581 | 1.4% |
| 47 | Delaware | 386,467,560 | 0.2% |
| 2 | Florida | 18,389,206,288 | 8.8% |
| 18 | Georgia | 3,895,108,054 | 1.9% |
| 41 | Hawaii | 600,476,783 | 0.3% |
| 42 | Idaho | 580,302,396 | 0.3% |
| 7 | Illinois | 7,605,610,448 | 3.6% |
| 13 | Indiana | 4,730,109,977 | 2.3% |
| 34 | Iowa | 1,416,873,428 | 0.7% |
| 31 | Kansas | 1,739,329,004 | 0.8% |
| 21 | Kentucky | 3,120,201,506 | 1.5% |
| 14 | Louisiana | 4,257,731,541 | 2.0% |
| 40 | Maine | 659,651,613 | 0.3% |
| 15 | Maryland | 4,095,719,519 | 2.0% |
| 12 | Massachusetts | 4,832,685,785 | 2.3% |
| 9 | Michigan | 6,716,357,961 | 3.2% |
| 22 | Minnesota | 2,991,679,494 | 1.4% |
| 28 | Mississippi | 2,231,394,305 | 1.1% |
| 16 | Missouri | 4,061,920,145 | 1.9% |
| 44 | Montana | 508,924,248 | 0.2% |
| 35 | Nebraska | 1,055,877,294 | 0.5% |
| 36 | Nevada | 1,047,877,402 | 0.5% |
| 43 | New Hampshire | 557,216,453 | 0.3% |
| 8 | New Jersey | 7,474,563,686 | 3.6% |
| 39 | New Mexico | 794,664,887 | 0.4% |
| 3 | New York | 16,838,053,507 | 8.1% |
| 10 | North Carolina | 5,808,687,639 | 2.8% |
| 46 | North Dakota | 459,480,874 | 0.2% |
| 6 | Ohio | 9,304,893,988 | 4.5% |
| 29 | Oklahoma | 2,065,542,544 | 1.0% |
| 33 | Oregon | 1,648,723,895 | 0.8% |
| 5 | Pennsylvania | 12,953,469,729 | 6.2% |
| 37 | Rhode Island | 973,152,273 | 0.5% |
| 25 | South Carolina | 2,801,284,695 | 1.3% |
| 45 | South Dakota | 486,673,168 | 0.2% |
| 11 | Tennessee | 4,855,360,413 | 2.3% |
| 4 | Texas | 14,227,830,241 | 6.8% |
| 38 | Utah | 836,291,181 | 0.4% |
| 48 | Vermont | 253,949,833 | 0.1% |
| 17 | Virginia | 4,049,543,351 | 1.9% |
| 26 | Washington | 2,504,808,594 | 1.2% |
| 32 | West Virginia | 1,652,563,616 | 0.8% |
| 20 | Wisconsin | 3,355,504,649 | 1.6% |
| 49 | Wyoming | 210,883,286 | 0.1% |

| RANK | STATE | BENEFITS | % of USA |
|---|---|---|---|
| 1 | California | $23,305,723,494 | 11.2% |
| 2 | Florida | 18,389,206,288 | 8.8% |
| 3 | New York | 16,838,053,507 | 8.1% |
| 4 | Texas | 14,227,830,241 | 6.8% |
| 5 | Pennsylvania | 12,953,469,729 | 6.2% |
| 6 | Ohio | 9,304,893,988 | 4.5% |
| 7 | Illinois | 7,605,610,448 | 3.6% |
| 8 | New Jersey | 7,474,563,686 | 3.6% |
| 9 | Michigan | 6,716,357,961 | 3.2% |
| 10 | North Carolina | 5,808,687,639 | 2.8% |
| 11 | Tennessee | 4,855,360,413 | 2.3% |
| 12 | Massachusetts | 4,832,685,785 | 2.3% |
| 13 | Indiana | 4,730,109,977 | 2.3% |
| 14 | Louisiana | 4,257,731,541 | 2.0% |
| 15 | Maryland | 4,095,719,519 | 2.0% |
| 16 | Missouri | 4,061,920,145 | 1.9% |
| 17 | Virginia | 4,049,543,351 | 1.9% |
| 18 | Georgia | 3,895,108,054 | 1.9% |
| 19 | Alabama | 3,817,396,530 | 1.8% |
| 20 | Wisconsin | 3,355,504,649 | 1.6% |
| 21 | Kentucky | 3,120,201,506 | 1.5% |
| 22 | Minnesota | 2,991,679,494 | 1.4% |
| 23 | Connecticut | 2,985,509,581 | 1.4% |
| 24 | Arizona | 2,827,734,758 | 1.4% |
| 25 | South Carolina | 2,801,284,695 | 1.3% |
| 26 | Washington | 2,504,808,594 | 1.2% |
| 27 | Colorado | 2,327,582,779 | 1.1% |
| 28 | Mississippi | 2,231,394,305 | 1.1% |
| 29 | Oklahoma | 2,065,542,544 | 1.0% |
| 30 | Arkansas | 2,044,027,481 | 1.0% |
| 31 | Kansas | 1,739,329,004 | 0.8% |
| 32 | West Virginia | 1,652,563,616 | 0.8% |
| 33 | Oregon | 1,648,723,895 | 0.8% |
| 34 | Iowa | 1,416,873,428 | 0.7% |
| 35 | Nebraska | 1,055,877,294 | 0.5% |
| 36 | Nevada | 1,047,877,402 | 0.5% |
| 37 | Rhode Island | 973,152,273 | 0.5% |
| 38 | Utah | 836,291,181 | 0.4% |
| 39 | New Mexico | 794,664,887 | 0.4% |
| 40 | Maine | 659,651,613 | 0.3% |
| 41 | Hawaii | 600,476,783 | 0.3% |
| 42 | Idaho | 580,302,396 | 0.3% |
| 43 | New Hampshire | 557,216,453 | 0.3% |
| 44 | Montana | 508,924,248 | 0.2% |
| 45 | South Dakota | 486,673,168 | 0.2% |
| 46 | North Dakota | 459,480,874 | 0.2% |
| 47 | Delaware | 386,467,560 | 0.2% |
| 48 | Vermont | 253,949,833 | 0.1% |
| 49 | Wyoming | 210,883,286 | 0.1% |
| 50 | Alaska | 133,480,125 | 0.1% |
|  | District of Columbia | 825,298,033 | 0.4% |

*Source: U.S. Department of Health and Human Services, Health Care Financing Administration
"Medicare Estimated Benefit Payments by State" (http://www.hcfa.gov/stats/BENEPAY/bnpay99i.htm)
*For fiscal year 1999. Includes payments to aged and disabled enrollees. Total includes $1,264,153,750 in payments to enrollees in Puerto Rico and $56,009,752 to enrollees in "other outlying areas."*

# Medicare Enrollees in 1999

## National Total = 39,027,270 Enrollees*

ALPHA ORDER

| RANK | STATE | ENROLLEES | % of USA |
|---|---|---|---|
| 19 | Alabama | 675,013 | 1.7% |
| 50 | Alaska | 40,096 | 0.1% |
| 20 | Arizona | 658,751 | 1.7% |
| 31 | Arkansas | 434,684 | 1.1% |
| 1 | California | 3,822,301 | 9.8% |
| 30 | Colorado | 457,787 | 1.2% |
| 26 | Connecticut | 509,627 | 1.3% |
| 46 | Delaware | 109,661 | 0.3% |
| 2 | Florida | 2,763,922 | 7.1% |
| 12 | Georgia | 896,553 | 2.3% |
| 43 | Hawaii | 161,436 | 0.4% |
| 42 | Idaho | 161,575 | 0.4% |
| 7 | Illinois | 1,620,900 | 4.2% |
| 15 | Indiana | 842,865 | 2.2% |
| 29 | Iowa | 474,586 | 1.2% |
| 33 | Kansas | 387,940 | 1.0% |
| 23 | Kentucky | 614,087 | 1.6% |
| 24 | Louisiana | 595,653 | 1.5% |
| 38 | Maine | 212,942 | 0.5% |
| 22 | Maryland | 632,471 | 1.6% |
| 11 | Massachusetts | 949,735 | 2.4% |
| 8 | Michigan | 1,384,283 | 3.5% |
| 21 | Minnesota | 646,683 | 1.7% |
| 32 | Mississippi | 413,041 | 1.1% |
| 14 | Missouri | 852,418 | 2.2% |
| 44 | Montana | 135,239 | 0.3% |
| 35 | Nebraska | 251,564 | 0.6% |
| 36 | Nevada | 229,367 | 0.6% |
| 41 | New Hampshire | 166,683 | 0.4% |
| 9 | New Jersey | 1,187,988 | 3.0% |
| 37 | New Mexico | 229,029 | 0.6% |
| 3 | New York | 2,677,201 | 6.9% |
| 10 | North Carolina | 1,111,998 | 2.8% |
| 47 | North Dakota | 102,740 | 0.3% |
| 6 | Ohio | 1,686,485 | 4.3% |
| 27 | Oklahoma | 501,844 | 1.3% |
| 28 | Oregon | 482,560 | 1.2% |
| 5 | Pennsylvania | 2,080,610 | 5.3% |
| 40 | Rhode Island | 169,569 | 0.4% |
| 25 | South Carolina | 555,881 | 1.4% |
| 45 | South Dakota | 118,706 | 0.3% |
| 16 | Tennessee | 814,298 | 2.1% |
| 4 | Texas | 2,218,856 | 5.7% |
| 39 | Utah | 200,996 | 0.5% |
| 48 | Vermont | 87,573 | 0.2% |
| 13 | Virginia | 874,965 | 2.2% |
| 18 | Washington | 722,836 | 1.9% |
| 34 | West Virginia | 334,490 | 0.9% |
| 17 | Wisconsin | 775,484 | 2.0% |
| 49 | Wyoming | 64,317 | 0.2% |

RANK ORDER

| RANK | STATE | ENROLLEES | % of USA |
|---|---|---|---|
| 1 | California | 3,822,301 | 9.8% |
| 2 | Florida | 2,763,922 | 7.1% |
| 3 | New York | 2,677,201 | 6.9% |
| 4 | Texas | 2,218,856 | 5.7% |
| 5 | Pennsylvania | 2,080,610 | 5.3% |
| 6 | Ohio | 1,686,485 | 4.3% |
| 7 | Illinois | 1,620,900 | 4.2% |
| 8 | Michigan | 1,384,283 | 3.5% |
| 9 | New Jersey | 1,187,988 | 3.0% |
| 10 | North Carolina | 1,111,998 | 2.8% |
| 11 | Massachusetts | 949,735 | 2.4% |
| 12 | Georgia | 896,553 | 2.3% |
| 13 | Virginia | 874,965 | 2.2% |
| 14 | Missouri | 852,418 | 2.2% |
| 15 | Indiana | 842,865 | 2.2% |
| 16 | Tennessee | 814,298 | 2.1% |
| 17 | Wisconsin | 775,484 | 2.0% |
| 18 | Washington | 722,836 | 1.9% |
| 19 | Alabama | 675,013 | 1.7% |
| 20 | Arizona | 658,751 | 1.7% |
| 21 | Minnesota | 646,683 | 1.7% |
| 22 | Maryland | 632,471 | 1.6% |
| 23 | Kentucky | 614,087 | 1.6% |
| 24 | Louisiana | 595,653 | 1.5% |
| 25 | South Carolina | 555,881 | 1.4% |
| 26 | Connecticut | 509,627 | 1.3% |
| 27 | Oklahoma | 501,844 | 1.3% |
| 28 | Oregon | 482,560 | 1.2% |
| 29 | Iowa | 474,586 | 1.2% |
| 30 | Colorado | 457,787 | 1.2% |
| 31 | Arkansas | 434,684 | 1.1% |
| 32 | Mississippi | 413,041 | 1.1% |
| 33 | Kansas | 387,940 | 1.0% |
| 34 | West Virginia | 334,490 | 0.9% |
| 35 | Nebraska | 251,564 | 0.6% |
| 36 | Nevada | 229,367 | 0.6% |
| 37 | New Mexico | 229,029 | 0.6% |
| 38 | Maine | 212,942 | 0.5% |
| 39 | Utah | 200,996 | 0.5% |
| 40 | Rhode Island | 169,569 | 0.4% |
| 41 | New Hampshire | 166,683 | 0.4% |
| 42 | Idaho | 161,575 | 0.4% |
| 43 | Hawaii | 161,436 | 0.4% |
| 44 | Montana | 135,239 | 0.3% |
| 45 | South Dakota | 118,706 | 0.3% |
| 46 | Delaware | 109,661 | 0.3% |
| 47 | North Dakota | 102,740 | 0.3% |
| 48 | Vermont | 87,573 | 0.2% |
| 49 | Wyoming | 64,317 | 0.2% |
| 50 | Alaska | 40,096 | 0.1% |
| | District of Columbia | 75,041 | 0.2% |

*Source: U.S. Department of Health and Human Services, Health Care Financing Administration*
*"Medicare Estimated Benefit Payments by State" (http://www.hcfa.gov/stats/BENEPAY/bnpay99i.htm)*
*For fiscal year 1999. Includes aged and disabled enrollees. Total includes 523,963 enrollees in Puerto Rico and 327,977 enrollees in "other outlying areas."*

# Medicare Payments per Enrollee in 1999

## National Rate = $5,346*

| ALPHA ORDER | | | RANK ORDER | | |
|---|---|---|---|---|---|
| **RANK** | **STATE** | **PER ENROLLEE** | **RANK** | **STATE** | **PER ENROLLEE** |
| 12 | Alabama | $5,655 | 1 | Louisiana | $7,148 |
| 46 | Alaska | 3,329 | 2 | Florida | 6,653 |
| 33 | Arizona | 4,293 | 3 | Maryland | 6,476 |
| 24 | Arkansas | 4,702 | 4 | Texas | 6,412 |
| 8 | California | 6,097 | 5 | New Jersey | 6,292 |
| 18 | Colorado | 5,084 | 6 | New York | 6,289 |
| 10 | Connecticut | 5,858 | 7 | Pennsylvania | 6,226 |
| 41 | Delaware | 3,524 | 8 | California | 6,097 |
| 2 | Florida | 6,653 | 9 | Tennessee | 5,963 |
| 31 | Georgia | 4,345 | 10 | Connecticut | 5,858 |
| 39 | Hawaii | 3,720 | 11 | Rhode Island | 5,739 |
| 40 | Idaho | 3,592 | 12 | Alabama | 5,655 |
| 25 | Illinois | 4,692 | 13 | Indiana | 5,612 |
| 13 | Indiana | 5,612 | 14 | Ohio | 5,517 |
| 49 | Iowa | 2,985 | 15 | Mississippi | 5,402 |
| 29 | Kansas | 4,484 | 16 | North Carolina | 5,224 |
| 19 | Kentucky | 5,081 | 17 | Massachusetts | 5,088 |
| 1 | Louisiana | 7,148 | 18 | Colorado | 5,084 |
| 48 | Maine | 3,098 | 19 | Kentucky | 5,081 |
| 3 | Maryland | 6,476 | 20 | South Carolina | 5,039 |
| 17 | Massachusetts | 5,088 | 21 | West Virginia | 4,941 |
| 22 | Michigan | 4,852 | 22 | Michigan | 4,852 |
| 27 | Minnesota | 4,626 | 23 | Missouri | 4,765 |
| 15 | Mississippi | 5,402 | 24 | Arkansas | 4,702 |
| 23 | Missouri | 4,765 | 25 | Illinois | 4,692 |
| 38 | Montana | 3,763 | 26 | Virginia | 4,628 |
| 34 | Nebraska | 4,197 | 27 | Minnesota | 4,626 |
| 28 | Nevada | 4,569 | 28 | Nevada | 4,569 |
| 45 | New Hampshire | 3,343 | 29 | Kansas | 4,484 |
| 5 | New Jersey | 6,292 | 30 | North Dakota | 4,472 |
| 42 | New Mexico | 3,470 | 31 | Georgia | 4,345 |
| 6 | New York | 6,289 | 32 | Wisconsin | 4,327 |
| 16 | North Carolina | 5,224 | 33 | Arizona | 4,293 |
| 30 | North Dakota | 4,472 | 34 | Nebraska | 4,197 |
| 14 | Ohio | 5,517 | 35 | Utah | 4,161 |
| 36 | Oklahoma | 4,116 | 36 | Oklahoma | 4,116 |
| 44 | Oregon | 3,417 | 37 | South Dakota | 4,100 |
| 7 | Pennsylvania | 6,226 | 38 | Montana | 3,763 |
| 11 | Rhode Island | 5,739 | 39 | Hawaii | 3,720 |
| 20 | South Carolina | 5,039 | 40 | Idaho | 3,592 |
| 37 | South Dakota | 4,100 | 41 | Delaware | 3,524 |
| 9 | Tennessee | 5,963 | 42 | New Mexico | 3,470 |
| 4 | Texas | 6,412 | 43 | Washington | 3,465 |
| 35 | Utah | 4,161 | 44 | Oregon | 3,417 |
| 50 | Vermont | 2,900 | 45 | New Hampshire | 3,343 |
| 26 | Virginia | 4,628 | 46 | Alaska | 3,329 |
| 43 | Washington | 3,465 | 47 | Wyoming | 3,279 |
| 21 | West Virginia | 4,941 | 48 | Maine | 3,098 |
| 32 | Wisconsin | 4,327 | 49 | Iowa | 2,985 |
| 47 | Wyoming | 3,279 | 50 | Vermont | 2,900 |
| | | | | District of Columbia | 10,998 |

*Source: U.S. Department of Health and Human Services, Health Care Financing Administration*
    *"Medicare Estimated Benefit Payments by State" (http://www.hcfa.gov/stats/BENEPAY/bnpay99i.htm)*
*\*For fiscal year 1999. Includes aged and disabled enrollees. National rate includes payments to enrollees in Puerto Rico and in "other outlying areas."*

# Percent of Population Enrolled in Medicare in 1999

## National Percent = 14.1% of Population*

*Source: Morgan Quitno Press using data from U.S. Dept. of Health and Human Services, Health Care Financing Admn "Medicare Estimated Benefit Payments by State" (http://www.hcfa.gov/stats/BENEPAY/bnpay99i.htm)*
*\*For fiscal year 1999. Includes aged and disabled enrollees. National rate includes only residents of the 50 states and the District of Columbia.*

# Medicaid Expenditures in 1997

## National Total = $160,528,502,653*

ALPHA ORDER

RANK ORDER

| RANK | STATE | PAYMENTS | % of USA |
|------|-------|----------|----------|
| 24 | Alabama | $2,201,307,097 | 1.4% |
| 46 | Alaska | 364,110,087 | 0.2% |
| 26 | Arizona | 1,740,017,249 | 1.1% |
| 30 | Arkansas | 1,313,630,245 | 0.8% |
| 2 | California | 16,240,099,854 | 10.1% |
| 29 | Colorado | 1,523,356,381 | 0.9% |
| 17 | Connecticut | 2,932,104,706 | 1.8% |
| 44 | Delaware | 409,213,692 | 0.3% |
| 6 | Florida | 6,447,889,401 | 4.0% |
| 12 | Georgia | 3,584,015,676 | 2.2% |
| 40 | Hawaii | 628,742,323 | 0.4% |
| 43 | Idaho | 423,261,391 | 0.3% |
| 5 | Illinois | 6,503,829,004 | 4.1% |
| 22 | Indiana | 2,493,114,385 | 1.6% |
| 31 | Iowa | 1,262,327,643 | 0.8% |
| 35 | Kansas | 1,028,739,139 | 0.6% |
| 21 | Kentucky | 2,571,547,988 | 1.6% |
| 16 | Louisiana | 3,055,407,383 | 1.9% |
| 34 | Maine | 1,090,325,858 | 0.7% |
| 19 | Maryland | 2,706,411,626 | 1.7% |
| 9 | Massachusetts | 5,509,187,324 | 3.4% |
| 8 | Michigan | 5,560,326,710 | 3.5% |
| 18 | Minnesota | 2,746,987,575 | 1.7% |
| 27 | Mississippi | 1,702,265,458 | 1.1% |
| 15 | Missouri | 3,142,586,502 | 2.0% |
| 45 | Montana | 392,064,609 | 0.2% |
| 39 | Nebraska | 731,656,067 | 0.5% |
| 42 | Nevada | 489,276,626 | 0.3% |
| 38 | New Hampshire | 731,879,670 | 0.5% |
| 10 | New Jersey | 5,478,127,337 | 3.4% |
| 36 | New Mexico | 945,547,063 | 0.6% |
| 1 | New York | 24,525,116,698 | 15.3% |
| 11 | North Carolina | 4,529,992,284 | 2.8% |
| 48 | North Dakota | 331,970,747 | 0.2% |
| 7 | Ohio | 6,443,156,403 | 4.0% |
| 32 | Oklahoma | 1,195,881,195 | 0.7% |
| 28 | Oregon | 1,544,061,944 | 1.0% |
| 4 | Pennsylvania | 8,075,706,681 | 5.0% |
| 37 | Rhode Island | 917,489,179 | 0.6% |
| 25 | South Carolina | 2,152,056,132 | 1.3% |
| 49 | South Dakota | 331,629,892 | 0.2% |
| 13 | Tennessee | 3,434,971,957 | 2.1% |
| 3 | Texas | 9,600,126,934 | 6.0% |
| 41 | Utah | 626,662,383 | 0.4% |
| 47 | Vermont | 358,490,340 | 0.2% |
| 23 | Virginia | 2,274,509,097 | 1.4% |
| 14 | Washington | 3,197,051,126 | 2.0% |
| 33 | West Virginia | 1,193,977,808 | 0.7% |
| 20 | Wisconsin | 2,573,586,437 | 1.6% |
| 50 | Wyoming | 194,261,299 | 0.1% |

| RANK | STATE | PAYMENTS | % of USA |
|------|-------|----------|----------|
| 1 | New York | $24,525,116,698 | 15.3% |
| 2 | California | 16,240,099,854 | 10.1% |
| 3 | Texas | 9,600,126,934 | 6.0% |
| 4 | Pennsylvania | 8,075,706,681 | 5.0% |
| 5 | Illinois | 6,503,829,004 | 4.1% |
| 6 | Florida | 6,447,889,401 | 4.0% |
| 7 | Ohio | 6,443,156,403 | 4.0% |
| 8 | Michigan | 5,560,326,710 | 3.5% |
| 9 | Massachusetts | 5,509,187,324 | 3.4% |
| 10 | New Jersey | 5,478,127,337 | 3.4% |
| 11 | North Carolina | 4,529,992,284 | 2.8% |
| 12 | Georgia | 3,584,015,676 | 2.2% |
| 13 | Tennessee | 3,434,971,957 | 2.1% |
| 14 | Washington | 3,197,051,126 | 2.0% |
| 15 | Missouri | 3,142,586,502 | 2.0% |
| 16 | Louisiana | 3,055,407,383 | 1.9% |
| 17 | Connecticut | 2,932,104,706 | 1.8% |
| 18 | Minnesota | 2,746,987,575 | 1.7% |
| 19 | Maryland | 2,706,411,626 | 1.7% |
| 20 | Wisconsin | 2,573,586,437 | 1.6% |
| 21 | Kentucky | 2,571,547,988 | 1.6% |
| 22 | Indiana | 2,493,114,385 | 1.6% |
| 23 | Virginia | 2,274,509,097 | 1.4% |
| 24 | Alabama | 2,201,307,097 | 1.4% |
| 25 | South Carolina | 2,152,056,132 | 1.3% |
| 26 | Arizona | 1,740,017,249 | 1.1% |
| 27 | Mississippi | 1,702,265,458 | 1.1% |
| 28 | Oregon | 1,544,061,944 | 1.0% |
| 29 | Colorado | 1,523,356,381 | 0.9% |
| 30 | Arkansas | 1,313,630,245 | 0.8% |
| 31 | Iowa | 1,262,327,643 | 0.8% |
| 32 | Oklahoma | 1,195,881,195 | 0.7% |
| 33 | West Virginia | 1,193,977,808 | 0.7% |
| 34 | Maine | 1,090,325,858 | 0.7% |
| 35 | Kansas | 1,028,739,139 | 0.6% |
| 36 | New Mexico | 945,547,063 | 0.6% |
| 37 | Rhode Island | 917,489,179 | 0.6% |
| 38 | New Hampshire | 731,879,670 | 0.5% |
| 39 | Nebraska | 731,656,067 | 0.5% |
| 40 | Hawaii | 628,742,323 | 0.4% |
| 41 | Utah | 626,662,383 | 0.4% |
| 42 | Nevada | 489,276,626 | 0.3% |
| 43 | Idaho | 423,261,391 | 0.3% |
| 44 | Delaware | 409,213,692 | 0.3% |
| 45 | Montana | 392,064,609 | 0.2% |
| 46 | Alaska | 364,110,087 | 0.2% |
| 47 | Vermont | 358,490,340 | 0.2% |
| 48 | North Dakota | 331,970,747 | 0.2% |
| 49 | South Dakota | 331,629,892 | 0.2% |
| 50 | Wyoming | 194,261,299 | 0.1% |
| | District of Columbia | 796,084,288 | 0.5% |

*Source: U.S. Department of Health and Human Services, Health Care Financing Administration*
*"Medicaid Financial Statistics Tables (HCFA-64 Report)"*
*For fiscal year 1997. National total includes payments for U.S. territories. These figures differ from those previously listed in this book. In the past, we had used HCFA-2082 report. In response to reader requests, we have switched to HCFA-64 report which includes additional expenditures.*

# Percent Change in Medicaid Expenditures: 1994 to 1997

## National Percent Change = 16.7% Increase*

ALPHA ORDER

| RANK | STATE | PERCENT CHANGE |
|---|---|---|
| 21 | Alabama | 23.9 |
| 14 | Alaska | 26.9 |
| 46 | Arizona | 2.2 |
| 23 | Arkansas | 23.2 |
| 42 | California | 11.3 |
| 7 | Colorado | 37.1 |
| 13 | Connecticut | 27.3 |
| 1 | Delaware | 46.9 |
| 20 | Florida | 24.1 |
| 42 | Georgia | 11.3 |
| 6 | Hawaii | 37.4 |
| 8 | Idaho | 36.9 |
| 15 | Illinois | 26.3 |
| 47 | Indiana | 1.2 |
| 26 | Iowa | 20.9 |
| 45 | Kansas | 5.6 |
| 3 | Kentucky | 40.1 |
| 50 | Louisiana | (27.2) |
| 28 | Maine | 19.9 |
| 27 | Maryland | 20.8 |
| 15 | Massachusetts | 26.3 |
| 41 | Michigan | 11.8 |
| 42 | Minnesota | 11.3 |
| 9 | Mississippi | 29.9 |
| 17 | Missouri | 24.7 |
| 29 | Montana | 19.4 |
| 29 | Nebraska | 19.4 |
| 11 | Nevada | 28.4 |
| 49 | New Hampshire | (23.2) |
| 37 | New Jersey | 14.7 |
| 5 | New Mexico | 38.8 |
| 38 | New York | 14.2 |
| 2 | North Carolina | 45.6 |
| 25 | North Dakota | 22.1 |
| 33 | Ohio | 16.7 |
| 39 | Oklahoma | 13.6 |
| 4 | Oregon | 39.3 |
| 33 | Pennsylvania | 16.7 |
| 32 | Rhode Island | 17.0 |
| 35 | South Carolina | 16.0 |
| 36 | South Dakota | 15.1 |
| 10 | Tennessee | 28.6 |
| 31 | Texas | 17.9 |
| 22 | Utah | 23.7 |
| 18 | Vermont | 24.6 |
| 24 | Virginia | 23.0 |
| 19 | Washington | 24.3 |
| 48 | West Virginia | (3.9) |
| 40 | Wisconsin | 11.9 |
| 12 | Wyoming | 27.4 |

RANK ORDER

| RANK | STATE | PERCENT CHANGE |
|---|---|---|
| 1 | Delaware | 46.9 |
| 2 | North Carolina | 45.6 |
| 3 | Kentucky | 40.1 |
| 4 | Oregon | 39.3 |
| 5 | New Mexico | 38.8 |
| 6 | Hawaii | 37.4 |
| 7 | Colorado | 37.1 |
| 8 | Idaho | 36.9 |
| 9 | Mississippi | 29.9 |
| 10 | Tennessee | 28.6 |
| 11 | Nevada | 28.4 |
| 12 | Wyoming | 27.4 |
| 13 | Connecticut | 27.3 |
| 14 | Alaska | 26.9 |
| 15 | Illinois | 26.3 |
| 15 | Massachusetts | 26.3 |
| 17 | Missouri | 24.7 |
| 18 | Vermont | 24.6 |
| 19 | Washington | 24.3 |
| 20 | Florida | 24.1 |
| 21 | Alabama | 23.9 |
| 22 | Utah | 23.7 |
| 23 | Arkansas | 23.2 |
| 24 | Virginia | 23.0 |
| 25 | North Dakota | 22.1 |
| 26 | Iowa | 20.9 |
| 27 | Maryland | 20.8 |
| 28 | Maine | 19.9 |
| 29 | Montana | 19.4 |
| 29 | Nebraska | 19.4 |
| 31 | Texas | 17.9 |
| 32 | Rhode Island | 17.0 |
| 33 | Ohio | 16.7 |
| 33 | Pennsylvania | 16.7 |
| 35 | South Carolina | 16.0 |
| 36 | South Dakota | 15.1 |
| 37 | New Jersey | 14.7 |
| 38 | New York | 14.2 |
| 39 | Oklahoma | 13.6 |
| 40 | Wisconsin | 11.9 |
| 41 | Michigan | 11.8 |
| 42 | California | 11.3 |
| 42 | Georgia | 11.3 |
| 42 | Minnesota | 11.3 |
| 45 | Kansas | 5.6 |
| 46 | Arizona | 2.2 |
| 47 | Indiana | 1.2 |
| 48 | West Virginia | (3.9) |
| 49 | New Hampshire | (23.2) |
| 50 | Louisiana | (27.2) |

District of Columbia 1.3

Source: Morgan Quitno Press using data from U.S. Dept. of Health & Human Services, Health Care Financing Admin.
"Medicaid Financial Statistics Tables (HCFA-64 Report)"
*For fiscal years 1994 and 1997. National figure includes payments for U.S. territories. These figures differ from those previously listed in this book. In the past, we had used HCFA-2082 report. In response to reader requests, we have switched to HCFA-64 report which includes additional expenditures.

# Medicaid Recipients in 1997

## National Total = 34,872,275 Recipients*

ALPHA ORDER

RANK ORDER

| RANK | STATE | RECIPIENTS | % of USA |
|------|-------|-----------|----------|
| 17 | Alabama | 546,140 | 1.6% |
| 48 | Alaska | 73,050 | 0.2% |
| 18 | Arizona | 540,785 | 1.6% |
| 28 | Arkansas | 370,386 | 1.1% |
| 1 | California | 4,854,546 | 13.9% |
| 33 | Colorado | 251,423 | 0.7% |
| 37 | Connecticut | 201,779 | 0.6% |
| 46 | Delaware | 83,956 | 0.2% |
| 4 | Florida | 1,597,461 | 4.6% |
| 8 | Georgia | 1,208,445 | 3.5% |
| 35 | Hawaii | 206,081 | 0.6% |
| 41 | Idaho | 115,087 | 0.3% |
| 6 | Illinois | 1,399,960 | 4.0% |
| 23 | Indiana | 514,683 | 1.5% |
| 32 | Iowa | 293,596 | 0.8% |
| 34 | Kansas | 232,888 | 0.7% |
| 14 | Kentucky | 664,454 | 1.9% |
| 12 | Louisiana | 746,461 | 2.1% |
| 38 | Maine | 167,221 | 0.5% |
| 25 | Maryland | 402,002 | 1.2% |
| 13 | Massachusetts | 723,472 | 2.1% |
| 9 | Michigan | 1,132,783 | 3.2% |
| 27 | Minnesota | 371,483 | 1.1% |
| 24 | Mississippi | 504,017 | 1.4% |
| 19 | Missouri | 540,487 | 1.5% |
| 44 | Montana | 95,562 | 0.3% |
| 36 | Nebraska | 203,340 | 0.6% |
| 43 | Nevada | 105,588 | 0.3% |
| 45 | New Hampshire | 95,215 | 0.3% |
| 20 | New Jersey | 537,890 | 1.5% |
| 30 | New Mexico | 320,223 | 0.9% |
| 2 | New York | 3,151,837 | 9.0% |
| 10 | North Carolina | 1,112,931 | 3.2% |
| 49 | North Dakota | 61,117 | 0.2% |
| 7 | Ohio | 1,395,540 | 4.0% |
| 31 | Oklahoma | 315,801 | 0.9% |
| 21 | Oregon | 531,242 | 1.5% |
| 11 | Pennsylvania | 1,024,993 | 2.9% |
| 40 | Rhode Island | 116,766 | 0.3% |
| 22 | South Carolina | 519,875 | 1.5% |
| 47 | South Dakota | 75,444 | 0.2% |
| 5 | Tennessee | 1,415,612 | 4.1% |
| 3 | Texas | 2,538,655 | 7.3% |
| 39 | Utah | 144,749 | 0.4% |
| 42 | Vermont | 109,283 | 0.3% |
| 16 | Virginia | 595,234 | 1.7% |
| 15 | Washington | 630,165 | 1.8% |
| 29 | West Virginia | 359,091 | 1.0% |
| 26 | Wisconsin | 392,223 | 1.1% |
| 50 | Wyoming | 48,865 | 0.1% |

| RANK | STATE | RECIPIENTS | % of USA |
|------|-------|-----------|----------|
| 1 | California | 4,854,546 | 13.9% |
| 2 | New York | 3,151,837 | 9.0% |
| 3 | Texas | 2,538,655 | 7.3% |
| 4 | Florida | 1,597,461 | 4.6% |
| 5 | Tennessee | 1,415,612 | 4.1% |
| 6 | Illinois | 1,399,960 | 4.0% |
| 7 | Ohio | 1,395,540 | 4.0% |
| 8 | Georgia | 1,208,445 | 3.5% |
| 9 | Michigan | 1,132,783 | 3.2% |
| 10 | North Carolina | 1,112,931 | 3.2% |
| 11 | Pennsylvania | 1,024,993 | 2.9% |
| 12 | Louisiana | 746,461 | 2.1% |
| 13 | Massachusetts | 723,472 | 2.1% |
| 14 | Kentucky | 664,454 | 1.9% |
| 15 | Washington | 630,165 | 1.8% |
| 16 | Virginia | 595,234 | 1.7% |
| 17 | Alabama | 546,140 | 1.6% |
| 18 | Arizona | 540,785 | 1.6% |
| 19 | Missouri | 540,487 | 1.5% |
| 20 | New Jersey | 537,890 | 1.5% |
| 21 | Oregon | 531,242 | 1.5% |
| 22 | South Carolina | 519,875 | 1.5% |
| 23 | Indiana | 514,683 | 1.5% |
| 24 | Mississippi | 504,017 | 1.4% |
| 25 | Maryland | 402,002 | 1.2% |
| 26 | Wisconsin | 392,223 | 1.1% |
| 27 | Minnesota | 371,483 | 1.1% |
| 28 | Arkansas | 370,386 | 1.1% |
| 29 | West Virginia | 359,091 | 1.0% |
| 30 | New Mexico | 320,223 | 0.9% |
| 31 | Oklahoma | 315,801 | 0.9% |
| 32 | Iowa | 293,596 | 0.8% |
| 33 | Colorado | 251,423 | 0.7% |
| 34 | Kansas | 232,888 | 0.7% |
| 35 | Hawaii | 206,081 | 0.6% |
| 36 | Nebraska | 203,340 | 0.6% |
| 37 | Connecticut | 201,779 | 0.6% |
| 38 | Maine | 167,221 | 0.5% |
| 39 | Utah | 144,749 | 0.4% |
| 40 | Rhode Island | 116,766 | 0.3% |
| 41 | Idaho | 115,087 | 0.3% |
| 42 | Vermont | 109,283 | 0.3% |
| 43 | Nevada | 105,588 | 0.3% |
| 44 | Montana | 95,562 | 0.3% |
| 45 | New Hampshire | 95,215 | 0.3% |
| 46 | Delaware | 83,956 | 0.2% |
| 47 | South Dakota | 75,444 | 0.2% |
| 48 | Alaska | 73,050 | 0.2% |
| 49 | North Dakota | 61,117 | 0.2% |
| 50 | Wyoming | 48,865 | 0.1% |
| | District of Columbia | 128,008 | 0.4% |

Source: U.S. Department of Health and Human Services, Health Care Financing Administration
"Medicaid Recipients by Basis of Eligibility and by State: FY 1997" (HCFA-2082)
*For fiscal year 1997. National total includes recipients for U.S. territories.

# Medicaid Expenditures per Recipient in 1997

## National Rate = $4,603 per Recipient*

| ALPHA ORDER | | | | RANK ORDER | | |
|---|---|---|---|---|---|---|
| RANK | STATE | PER RECIPIENT | | RANK | STATE | PER RECIPIENT |
| 31 | Alabama | $4,031 | | 1 | New Jersey | $10,184 |
| 15 | Alaska | 4,984 | | 2 | Pennsylvania | 7,879 |
| 44 | Arizona | 3,218 | | 3 | Rhode Island | 7,858 |
| 39 | Arkansas | 3,547 | | 4 | New York | 7,781 |
| 41 | California | 3,345 | | 5 | New Hampshire | 7,687 |
| 11 | Colorado | 6,059 | | 6 | Massachusetts | 7,615 |
| NA | Connecticut** | NA | | 7 | Minnesota | 7,395 |
| 17 | Delaware | 4,874 | | 8 | Maryland | 6,732 |
| 30 | Florida | 4,036 | | 9 | Wisconsin | 6,562 |
| 46 | Georgia | 2,966 | | 10 | Maine | 6,520 |
| 45 | Hawaii | 3,051 | | 11 | Colorado | 6,059 |
| 37 | Idaho | 3,678 | | 12 | Missouri | 5,814 |
| 19 | Illinois | 4,646 | | 13 | North Dakota | 5,432 |
| 18 | Indiana | 4,844 | | 14 | Washington | 5,073 |
| 25 | Iowa | 4,300 | | 15 | Alaska | 4,984 |
| 22 | Kansas | 4,417 | | 16 | Michigan | 4,909 |
| 33 | Kentucky | 3,870 | | 17 | Delaware | 4,874 |
| 28 | Louisiana | 4,093 | | 18 | Indiana | 4,844 |
| 10 | Maine | 6,520 | | 19 | Illinois | 4,646 |
| 8 | Maryland | 6,732 | | 20 | Nevada | 4,634 |
| 6 | Massachusetts | 7,615 | | 21 | Ohio | 4,617 |
| 16 | Michigan | 4,909 | | 22 | Kansas | 4,417 |
| 7 | Minnesota | 7,395 | | 23 | South Dakota | 4,396 |
| 40 | Mississippi | 3,377 | | 24 | Utah | 4,329 |
| 12 | Missouri | 5,814 | | 25 | Iowa | 4,300 |
| 27 | Montana | 4,103 | | 26 | South Carolina | 4,140 |
| 38 | Nebraska | 3,598 | | 27 | Montana | 4,103 |
| 20 | Nevada | 4,634 | | 28 | Louisiana | 4,093 |
| 5 | New Hampshire | 7,687 | | 29 | North Carolina | 4,070 |
| 1 | New Jersey | 10,184 | | 30 | Florida | 4,036 |
| 47 | New Mexico | 2,953 | | 31 | Alabama | 4,031 |
| 4 | New York | 7,781 | | 32 | Wyoming | 3,975 |
| 29 | North Carolina | 4,070 | | 33 | Kentucky | 3,870 |
| 13 | North Dakota | 5,432 | | 34 | Virginia | 3,821 |
| 21 | Ohio | 4,617 | | 35 | Oklahoma | 3,787 |
| 35 | Oklahoma | 3,787 | | 36 | Texas | 3,782 |
| 48 | Oregon | 2,907 | | 37 | Idaho | 3,678 |
| 2 | Pennsylvania | 7,879 | | 38 | Nebraska | 3,598 |
| 3 | Rhode Island | 7,858 | | 39 | Arkansas | 3,547 |
| 26 | South Carolina | 4,140 | | 40 | Mississippi | 3,377 |
| 23 | South Dakota | 4,396 | | 41 | California | 3,345 |
| 49 | Tennessee | 2,426 | | 42 | West Virginia | 3,325 |
| 36 | Texas | 3,782 | | 43 | Vermont | 3,280 |
| 24 | Utah | 4,329 | | 44 | Arizona | 3,218 |
| 43 | Vermont | 3,280 | | 45 | Hawaii | 3,051 |
| 34 | Virginia | 3,821 | | 46 | Georgia | 2,966 |
| 14 | Washington | 5,073 | | 47 | New Mexico | 2,953 |
| 42 | West Virginia | 3,325 | | 48 | Oregon | 2,907 |
| 9 | Wisconsin | 6,562 | | 49 | Tennessee | 2,426 |
| 32 | Wyoming | 3,975 | | NA | Connecticut** | NA |
| | | | | | District of Columbia | 6,219 |

Source: Morgan Quitno Press using data from U.S. Dept. of Health & Human Services, Health Care Financing Admin.
   "Medicaid Financial Statistics Tables (HCFA-64 Report)"
*For fiscal years 1994 and 1997. National figure includes payments and recipients in U.S. territories. These figures differ from those previously listed in this book. In the past, we had used HCFA-2082 report for expenditures and recipients. In response to reader requests, we have switched to HCFA-64 report for expenditures which includes additional payments. **Not available.

# Percent of Population Receiving Public Aid in 1999

## National Percent = 4.9% of Population*

ALPHA ORDER

| RANK | STATE | PERCENT |
|---|---|---|
| 16 | Alabama | 4.7 |
| 11 | Alaska | 5.4 |
| 32 | Arizona | 3.5 |
| 18 | Arkansas | 4.6 |
| 1 | California | 8.5 |
| 46 | Colorado | 2.2 |
| 26 | Connecticut | 4.0 |
| 30 | Delaware | 3.6 |
| 30 | Florida | 3.6 |
| 23 | Georgia | 4.2 |
| 10 | Hawaii | 5.5 |
| 49 | Idaho | 1.8 |
| 14 | Illinois | 4.9 |
| 36 | Indiana | 3.3 |
| 34 | Iowa | 3.4 |
| 42 | Kansas | 2.6 |
| 5 | Kentucky | 6.7 |
| 6 | Louisiana | 6.1 |
| 12 | Maine | 5.2 |
| 34 | Maryland | 3.4 |
| 16 | Massachusetts | 4.7 |
| 18 | Michigan | 4.6 |
| 23 | Minnesota | 4.2 |
| 7 | Mississippi | 6.0 |
| 22 | Missouri | 4.3 |
| 38 | Montana | 3.1 |
| 37 | Nebraska | 3.2 |
| 44 | Nevada | 2.4 |
| 46 | New Hampshire | 2.2 |
| 28 | New Jersey | 3.7 |
| 4 | New Mexico | 7.1 |
| 3 | New York | 7.7 |
| 25 | North Carolina | 4.1 |
| 42 | North Dakota | 2.6 |
| 21 | Ohio | 4.5 |
| 28 | Oklahoma | 3.7 |
| 40 | Oregon | 2.9 |
| 14 | Pennsylvania | 4.9 |
| 2 | Rhode Island | 7.8 |
| 27 | South Carolina | 3.8 |
| 41 | South Dakota | 2.8 |
| 8 | Tennessee | 5.7 |
| 32 | Texas | 3.5 |
| 45 | Utah | 2.3 |
| 13 | Vermont | 5.1 |
| 38 | Virginia | 3.1 |
| 18 | Washington | 4.6 |
| 9 | West Virginia | 5.6 |
| 46 | Wisconsin | 2.2 |
| 50 | Wyoming | 1.5 |

RANK ORDER

| RANK | STATE | PERCENT |
|---|---|---|
| 1 | California | 8.5 |
| 2 | Rhode Island | 7.8 |
| 3 | New York | 7.7 |
| 4 | New Mexico | 7.1 |
| 5 | Kentucky | 6.7 |
| 6 | Louisiana | 6.1 |
| 7 | Mississippi | 6.0 |
| 8 | Tennessee | 5.7 |
| 9 | West Virginia | 5.6 |
| 10 | Hawaii | 5.5 |
| 11 | Alaska | 5.4 |
| 12 | Maine | 5.2 |
| 13 | Vermont | 5.1 |
| 14 | Illinois | 4.9 |
| 14 | Pennsylvania | 4.9 |
| 16 | Alabama | 4.7 |
| 16 | Massachusetts | 4.7 |
| 18 | Arkansas | 4.6 |
| 18 | Michigan | 4.6 |
| 18 | Washington | 4.6 |
| 21 | Ohio | 4.5 |
| 22 | Missouri | 4.3 |
| 23 | Georgia | 4.2 |
| 23 | Minnesota | 4.2 |
| 25 | North Carolina | 4.1 |
| 26 | Connecticut | 4.0 |
| 27 | South Carolina | 3.8 |
| 28 | New Jersey | 3.7 |
| 28 | Oklahoma | 3.7 |
| 30 | Delaware | 3.6 |
| 30 | Florida | 3.6 |
| 32 | Arizona | 3.5 |
| 32 | Texas | 3.5 |
| 34 | Iowa | 3.4 |
| 34 | Maryland | 3.4 |
| 36 | Indiana | 3.3 |
| 37 | Nebraska | 3.2 |
| 38 | Montana | 3.1 |
| 38 | Virginia | 3.1 |
| 40 | Oregon | 2.9 |
| 41 | South Dakota | 2.8 |
| 42 | Kansas | 2.6 |
| 42 | North Dakota | 2.6 |
| 44 | Nevada | 2.4 |
| 45 | Utah | 2.3 |
| 46 | Colorado | 2.2 |
| 46 | New Hampshire | 2.2 |
| 46 | Wisconsin | 2.2 |
| 49 | Idaho | 1.8 |
| 50 | Wyoming | 1.5 |

| District of Columbia | 12.9 |
|---|---|

*Source: Morgan Quitno Press using data from U.S. Social Security Administration and U.S. Department of Health and Human Services*

*As of December 1999. Includes recipients of Temporary Assistance to Needy Families (TANF) and Supplemental Security Income payments.*

# Social Security Supplemental Security Income Beneficiaries in 1999

## National Total = 6,556,634 Beneficiaries*

ALPHA ORDER

| RANK | STATE | BENEFICIARIES | % of USA |
|---|---|---|---|
| 15 | Alabama | 160,208 | 2.4% |
| 49 | Alaska | 8,156 | 0.1% |
| 26 | Arizona | 79,306 | 1.2% |
| 23 | Arkansas | 87,686 | 1.3% |
| 1 | California | 1,066,486 | 16.3% |
| 30 | Colorado | 54,588 | 0.8% |
| 32 | Connecticut | 47,609 | 0.7% |
| 46 | Delaware | 11,840 | 0.2% |
| 4 | Florida | 366,517 | 5.6% |
| 9 | Georgia | 196,784 | 3.0% |
| 40 | Hawaii | 20,404 | 0.3% |
| 42 | Idaho | 17,761 | 0.3% |
| 6 | Illinois | 251,112 | 3.8% |
| 22 | Indiana | 88,315 | 1.3% |
| 34 | Iowa | 40,450 | 0.6% |
| 35 | Kansas | 36,290 | 0.6% |
| 11 | Kentucky | 172,225 | 2.6% |
| 12 | Louisiana | 167,927 | 2.6% |
| 36 | Maine | 29,341 | 0.4% |
| 24 | Maryland | 86,684 | 1.3% |
| 13 | Massachusetts | 167,050 | 2.5% |
| 8 | Michigan | 210,022 | 3.2% |
| 29 | Minnesota | 63,626 | 1.0% |
| 18 | Mississippi | 131,247 | 2.0% |
| 19 | Missouri | 111,003 | 1.7% |
| 43 | Montana | 13,697 | 0.2% |
| 39 | Nebraska | 21,036 | 0.3% |
| 38 | Nevada | 24,303 | 0.4% |
| 47 | New Hampshire | 11,404 | 0.2% |
| 16 | New Jersey | 145,565 | 2.2% |
| 33 | New Mexico | 45,861 | 0.7% |
| 2 | New York | 609,459 | 9.3% |
| 10 | North Carolina | 191,743 | 2.9% |
| 48 | North Dakota | 8,278 | 0.1% |
| 7 | Ohio | 242,733 | 3.7% |
| 27 | Oklahoma | 72,562 | 1.1% |
| 31 | Oregon | 50,515 | 0.8% |
| 5 | Pennsylvania | 278,196 | 4.2% |
| 37 | Rhode Island | 26,897 | 0.4% |
| 20 | South Carolina | 108,093 | 1.6% |
| 44 | South Dakota | 12,735 | 0.2% |
| 14 | Tennessee | 166,327 | 2.5% |
| 3 | Texas | 407,872 | 6.2% |
| 41 | Utah | 19,968 | 0.3% |
| 45 | Vermont | 12,551 | 0.2% |
| 17 | Virginia | 131,910 | 2.0% |
| 21 | Washington | 98,314 | 1.5% |
| 28 | West Virginia | 70,993 | 1.1% |
| 25 | Wisconsin | 86,544 | 1.3% |
| 50 | Wyoming | 5,784 | 0.1% |

RANK ORDER

| RANK | STATE | BENEFICIARIES | % of USA |
|---|---|---|---|
| 1 | California | 1,066,486 | 16.3% |
| 2 | New York | 609,459 | 9.3% |
| 3 | Texas | 407,872 | 6.2% |
| 4 | Florida | 366,517 | 5.6% |
| 5 | Pennsylvania | 278,196 | 4.2% |
| 6 | Illinois | 251,112 | 3.8% |
| 7 | Ohio | 242,733 | 3.7% |
| 8 | Michigan | 210,022 | 3.2% |
| 9 | Georgia | 196,784 | 3.0% |
| 10 | North Carolina | 191,743 | 2.9% |
| 11 | Kentucky | 172,225 | 2.6% |
| 12 | Louisiana | 167,927 | 2.6% |
| 13 | Massachusetts | 167,050 | 2.5% |
| 14 | Tennessee | 166,327 | 2.5% |
| 15 | Alabama | 160,208 | 2.4% |
| 16 | New Jersey | 145,565 | 2.2% |
| 17 | Virginia | 131,910 | 2.0% |
| 18 | Mississippi | 131,247 | 2.0% |
| 19 | Missouri | 111,003 | 1.7% |
| 20 | South Carolina | 108,093 | 1.6% |
| 21 | Washington | 98,314 | 1.5% |
| 22 | Indiana | 88,315 | 1.3% |
| 23 | Arkansas | 87,686 | 1.3% |
| 24 | Maryland | 86,684 | 1.3% |
| 25 | Wisconsin | 86,544 | 1.3% |
| 26 | Arizona | 79,306 | 1.2% |
| 27 | Oklahoma | 72,562 | 1.1% |
| 28 | West Virginia | 70,993 | 1.1% |
| 29 | Minnesota | 63,626 | 1.0% |
| 30 | Colorado | 54,588 | 0.8% |
| 31 | Oregon | 50,515 | 0.8% |
| 32 | Connecticut | 47,609 | 0.7% |
| 33 | New Mexico | 45,861 | 0.7% |
| 34 | Iowa | 40,450 | 0.6% |
| 35 | Kansas | 36,290 | 0.6% |
| 36 | Maine | 29,341 | 0.4% |
| 37 | Rhode Island | 26,897 | 0.4% |
| 38 | Nevada | 24,303 | 0.4% |
| 39 | Nebraska | 21,036 | 0.3% |
| 40 | Hawaii | 20,404 | 0.3% |
| 41 | Utah | 19,968 | 0.3% |
| 42 | Idaho | 17,761 | 0.3% |
| 43 | Montana | 13,697 | 0.2% |
| 44 | South Dakota | 12,735 | 0.2% |
| 45 | Vermont | 12,551 | 0.2% |
| 46 | Delaware | 11,840 | 0.2% |
| 47 | New Hampshire | 11,404 | 0.2% |
| 48 | North Dakota | 8,278 | 0.1% |
| 49 | Alaska | 8,156 | 0.1% |
| 50 | Wyoming | 5,784 | 0.1% |
| | District of Columbia | 20,020 | 0.3% |

Source: Social Security Administration
"Social Security Bulletin, Annual Statistical Supplement 2000"
*For December 1999. National total includes 637 beneficiaries in U.S. territories or otherwise not distributed by state.

# Average Monthly Social Security Supplemental Security Income Payment: 1999

## National Average = $368.53 Each Month per Beneficiary*

ALPHA ORDER

| RANK | STATE | AVERAGE BENEFIT |
|---|---|---|
| 39 | Alabama | $316.01 |
| 21 | Alaska | 340.20 |
| 15 | Arizona | 348.98 |
| 48 | Arkansas | 302.00 |
| 1 | California | 474.03 |
| 27 | Colorado | 333.22 |
| 13 | Connecticut | 351.54 |
| 24 | Delaware | 336.80 |
| 19 | Florida | 342.25 |
| 44 | Georgia | 312.29 |
| 3 | Hawaii | 390.16 |
| 32 | Idaho | 327.95 |
| 7 | Illinois | 377.73 |
| 18 | Indiana | 343.15 |
| 41 | Iowa | 314.58 |
| 30 | Kansas | 329.09 |
| 22 | Kentucky | 339.44 |
| 26 | Louisiana | 335.57 |
| 46 | Maine | 304.88 |
| 12 | Maryland | 353.80 |
| 4 | Massachusetts | 383.93 |
| 8 | Michigan | 374.28 |
| 20 | Minnesota | 340.44 |
| 43 | Mississippi | 312.32 |
| 29 | Missouri | 331.54 |
| 31 | Montana | 328.43 |
| 40 | Nebraska | 314.81 |
| 23 | Nevada | 339.06 |
| 34 | New Hampshire | 325.83 |
| 11 | New Jersey | 364.68 |
| 33 | New Mexico | 326.22 |
| 2 | New York | 410.92 |
| 49 | North Carolina | 300.51 |
| 50 | North Dakota | 288.18 |
| 10 | Ohio | 368.40 |
| 36 | Oklahoma | 321.44 |
| 17 | Oregon | 344.64 |
| 6 | Pennsylvania | 379.59 |
| 9 | Rhode Island | 371.59 |
| 42 | South Carolina | 313.89 |
| 45 | South Dakota | 306.44 |
| 35 | Tennessee | 321.66 |
| 47 | Texas | 302.99 |
| 16 | Utah | 345.47 |
| 28 | Vermont | 332.42 |
| 37 | Virginia | 321.07 |
| 5 | Washington | 380.01 |
| 14 | West Virginia | 350.23 |
| 25 | Wisconsin | 336.54 |
| 38 | Wyoming | 320.69 |

RANK ORDER

| RANK | STATE | AVERAGE BENEFIT |
|---|---|---|
| 1 | California | $474.03 |
| 2 | New York | 410.92 |
| 3 | Hawaii | 390.16 |
| 4 | Massachusetts | 383.93 |
| 5 | Washington | 380.01 |
| 6 | Pennsylvania | 379.59 |
| 7 | Illinois | 377.73 |
| 8 | Michigan | 374.28 |
| 9 | Rhode Island | 371.59 |
| 10 | Ohio | 368.40 |
| 11 | New Jersey | 364.68 |
| 12 | Maryland | 353.80 |
| 13 | Connecticut | 351.54 |
| 14 | West Virginia | 350.23 |
| 15 | Arizona | 348.98 |
| 16 | Utah | 345.47 |
| 17 | Oregon | 344.64 |
| 18 | Indiana | 343.15 |
| 19 | Florida | 342.25 |
| 20 | Minnesota | 340.44 |
| 21 | Alaska | 340.20 |
| 22 | Kentucky | 339.44 |
| 23 | Nevada | 339.06 |
| 24 | Delaware | 336.80 |
| 25 | Wisconsin | 336.54 |
| 26 | Louisiana | 335.57 |
| 27 | Colorado | 333.22 |
| 28 | Vermont | 332.42 |
| 29 | Missouri | 331.54 |
| 30 | Kansas | 329.09 |
| 31 | Montana | 328.43 |
| 32 | Idaho | 327.95 |
| 33 | New Mexico | 326.22 |
| 34 | New Hampshire | 325.83 |
| 35 | Tennessee | 321.66 |
| 36 | Oklahoma | 321.44 |
| 37 | Virginia | 321.07 |
| 38 | Wyoming | 320.69 |
| 39 | Alabama | 316.01 |
| 40 | Nebraska | 314.81 |
| 41 | Iowa | 314.58 |
| 42 | South Carolina | 313.89 |
| 43 | Mississippi | 312.32 |
| 44 | Georgia | 312.29 |
| 45 | South Dakota | 306.44 |
| 46 | Maine | 304.88 |
| 47 | Texas | 302.99 |
| 48 | Arkansas | 302.00 |
| 49 | North Carolina | 300.51 |
| 50 | North Dakota | 288.18 |
|  | District of Columbia | 366.24 |

Source: Social Security Administration
"Social Security Bulletin, Annual Statistical Supplement 2000"
*As of December 1999. National average includes payments to beneficiaries in U.S. territories and foreign countries.

# Recipients of Temporary Assistance to Needy Families (TANF) Payments: 2000

## National Total = 5,780,543 Monthly Recipients*

ALPHA ORDER

| RANK | STATE | RECIPIENTS | % of USA |
|------|-------|-----------|----------|
| 25 | Alabama | 55,168 | 1.0% |
| 38 | Alaska | 24,389 | 0.4% |
| 19 | Arizona | 82,851 | 1.4% |
| 35 | Arkansas | 28,113 | 0.5% |
| 1 | California | 1,272,468 | 22.0% |
| 36 | Colorado | 27,699 | 0.5% |
| 24 | Connecticut | 63,589 | 1.1% |
| 40 | Delaware | 17,262 | 0.3% |
| 10 | Florida | 135,903 | 2.4% |
| 11 | Georgia | 135,381 | 2.3% |
| 28 | Hawaii | 42,824 | 0.7% |
| 49 | Idaho | 1,382 | 0.0% |
| 4 | Illinois | 259,242 | 4.5% |
| 16 | Indiana | 96,854 | 1.7% |
| 26 | Iowa | 52,293 | 0.9% |
| 31 | Kansas | 36,557 | 0.6% |
| 18 | Kentucky | 85,696 | 1.5% |
| 20 | Louisiana | 79,745 | 1.4% |
| 43 | Maine | 14,813 | 0.3% |
| 21 | Maryland | 70,910 | 1.2% |
| 17 | Massachusetts | 93,890 | 1.6% |
| 7 | Michigan | 195,101 | 3.4% |
| 14 | Minnesota | 116,589 | 2.0% |
| 33 | Mississippi | 33,781 | 0.6% |
| 13 | Missouri | 122,930 | 2.1% |
| 44 | Montana | 14,001 | 0.2% |
| 37 | Nebraska | 26,841 | 0.5% |
| 41 | Nevada | 16,478 | 0.3% |
| 45 | New Hampshire | 13,862 | 0.2% |
| 12 | New Jersey | 125,258 | 2.2% |
| 22 | New Mexico | 67,950 | 1.2% |
| 2 | New York | 693,012 | 12.0% |
| 15 | North Carolina | 97,171 | 1.7% |
| 47 | North Dakota | 7,734 | 0.1% |
| 5 | Ohio | 238,351 | 4.1% |
| 46 | Oklahoma | 13,606 | 0.2% |
| 29 | Oregon | 42,374 | 0.7% |
| 6 | Pennsylvania | 232,976 | 4.0% |
| 27 | Rhode Island | 44,826 | 0.8% |
| 32 | South Carolina | 35,721 | 0.6% |
| 48 | South Dakota | 6,702 | 0.1% |
| 9 | Tennessee | 143,823 | 2.5% |
| 3 | Texas | 343,464 | 5.9% |
| 39 | Utah | 24,101 | 0.4% |
| 42 | Vermont | 15,528 | 0.3% |
| 23 | Virginia | 67,388 | 1.2% |
| 8 | Washington | 146,375 | 2.5% |
| 34 | West Virginia | 31,500 | 0.5% |
| 30 | Wisconsin | 37,381 | 0.6% |
| 50 | Wyoming | 1,103 | 0.0% |

RANK ORDER

| RANK | STATE | RECIPIENTS | % of USA |
|------|-------|-----------|----------|
| 1 | California | 1,272,468 | 22.0% |
| 2 | New York | 693,012 | 12.0% |
| 3 | Texas | 343,464 | 5.9% |
| 4 | Illinois | 259,242 | 4.5% |
| 5 | Ohio | 238,351 | 4.1% |
| 6 | Pennsylvania | 232,976 | 4.0% |
| 7 | Michigan | 195,101 | 3.4% |
| 8 | Washington | 146,375 | 2.5% |
| 9 | Tennessee | 143,823 | 2.5% |
| 10 | Florida | 135,903 | 2.4% |
| 11 | Georgia | 135,381 | 2.3% |
| 12 | New Jersey | 125,258 | 2.2% |
| 13 | Missouri | 122,930 | 2.1% |
| 14 | Minnesota | 116,589 | 2.0% |
| 15 | North Carolina | 97,171 | 1.7% |
| 16 | Indiana | 96,854 | 1.7% |
| 17 | Massachusetts | 93,890 | 1.6% |
| 18 | Kentucky | 85,696 | 1.5% |
| 19 | Arizona | 82,851 | 1.4% |
| 20 | Louisiana | 79,745 | 1.4% |
| 21 | Maryland | 70,910 | 1.2% |
| 22 | New Mexico | 67,950 | 1.2% |
| 23 | Virginia | 67,388 | 1.2% |
| 24 | Connecticut | 63,589 | 1.1% |
| 25 | Alabama | 55,168 | 1.0% |
| 26 | Iowa | 52,293 | 0.9% |
| 27 | Rhode Island | 44,826 | 0.8% |
| 28 | Hawaii | 42,824 | 0.7% |
| 29 | Oregon | 42,374 | 0.7% |
| 30 | Wisconsin | 37,381 | 0.6% |
| 31 | Kansas | 36,557 | 0.6% |
| 32 | South Carolina | 35,721 | 0.6% |
| 33 | Mississippi | 33,781 | 0.6% |
| 34 | West Virginia | 31,500 | 0.5% |
| 35 | Arkansas | 28,113 | 0.5% |
| 36 | Colorado | 27,699 | 0.5% |
| 37 | Nebraska | 26,841 | 0.5% |
| 38 | Alaska | 24,389 | 0.4% |
| 39 | Utah | 24,101 | 0.4% |
| 40 | Delaware | 17,262 | 0.3% |
| 41 | Nevada | 16,478 | 0.3% |
| 42 | Vermont | 15,528 | 0.3% |
| 43 | Maine | 14,813 | 0.3% |
| 44 | Montana | 14,001 | 0.2% |
| 45 | New Hampshire | 13,862 | 0.2% |
| 46 | Oklahoma | 13,606 | 0.2% |
| 47 | North Dakota | 7,734 | 0.1% |
| 48 | South Dakota | 6,702 | 0.1% |
| 49 | Idaho | 1,382 | 0.0% |
| 50 | Wyoming | 1,103 | 0.0% |
| | District of Columbia | 44,487 | 0.8% |

Source: U.S. Department of Health and Human Services, Administration for Children and Families
    "Change in TANF Caseloads" (http://www.acf.dhhs.gov/news/stats/caseload.htm)
*As of June 2000. Welfare reform replaced the Aid to Families with Dependent Children program (AFDC) with Temporary Assistance to Needy Families (TANF) as of July 1, 1997. National total includes 103,100 recipients in U.S. territories (90,630 in Puerto Rico).

# Percent Change in AFDC/TANF Recipients: 1993 to 2000

## National Percent Change = 59% Decrease*

ALPHA ORDER

| RANK | STATE | PERCENT CHANGE |
|---|---|---|
| 25 | Alabama | (61) |
| 4 | Alaska | (30) |
| 20 | Arizona | (57) |
| 27 | Arkansas | (62) |
| 10 | California | (47) |
| 43 | Colorado | (78) |
| 23 | Connecticut | (60) |
| 5 | Delaware | (38) |
| 45 | Florida | (81) |
| 33 | Georgia | (66) |
| 1 | Hawaii | (21) |
| 49 | Idaho | (93) |
| 27 | Illinois | (62) |
| 16 | Indiana | (54) |
| 11 | Iowa | (48) |
| 21 | Kansas | (58) |
| 27 | Kentucky | (62) |
| 37 | Louisiana | (70) |
| 43 | Maine | (78) |
| 36 | Maryland | (68) |
| 39 | Massachusetts | (72) |
| 39 | Michigan | (72) |
| 6 | Minnesota | (39) |
| 45 | Mississippi | (81) |
| 14 | Missouri | (53) |
| 23 | Montana | (60) |
| 8 | Nebraska | (44) |
| 14 | Nevada | (53) |
| 13 | New Hampshire | (52) |
| 30 | New Jersey | (64) |
| 3 | New Mexico | (28) |
| 7 | New York | (41) |
| 38 | North Carolina | (71) |
| 22 | North Dakota | (59) |
| 34 | Ohio | (67) |
| 48 | Oklahoma | (91) |
| 30 | Oregon | (64) |
| 25 | Pennsylvania | (61) |
| 2 | Rhode Island | (27) |
| 42 | South Carolina | (76) |
| 34 | South Dakota | (67) |
| 17 | Tennessee | (55) |
| 19 | Texas | (56) |
| 17 | Utah | (55) |
| 9 | Vermont | (46) |
| 32 | Virginia | (65) |
| 12 | Washington | (49) |
| 41 | West Virginia | (74) |
| 47 | Wisconsin | (84) |
| 50 | Wyoming | (94) |

RANK ORDER

| RANK | STATE | PERCENT CHANGE |
|---|---|---|
| 1 | Hawaii | (21) |
| 2 | Rhode Island | (27) |
| 3 | New Mexico | (28) |
| 4 | Alaska | (30) |
| 5 | Delaware | (38) |
| 6 | Minnesota | (39) |
| 7 | New York | (41) |
| 8 | Nebraska | (44) |
| 9 | Vermont | (46) |
| 10 | California | (47) |
| 11 | Iowa | (48) |
| 12 | Washington | (49) |
| 13 | New Hampshire | (52) |
| 14 | Missouri | (53) |
| 14 | Nevada | (53) |
| 16 | Indiana | (54) |
| 17 | Tennessee | (55) |
| 17 | Utah | (55) |
| 19 | Texas | (56) |
| 20 | Arizona | (57) |
| 21 | Kansas | (58) |
| 22 | North Dakota | (59) |
| 23 | Connecticut | (60) |
| 23 | Montana | (60) |
| 25 | Alabama | (61) |
| 25 | Pennsylvania | (61) |
| 27 | Arkansas | (62) |
| 27 | Illinois | (62) |
| 27 | Kentucky | (62) |
| 30 | New Jersey | (64) |
| 30 | Oregon | (64) |
| 32 | Virginia | (65) |
| 33 | Georgia | (66) |
| 34 | Ohio | (67) |
| 34 | South Dakota | (67) |
| 36 | Maryland | (68) |
| 37 | Louisiana | (70) |
| 38 | North Carolina | (71) |
| 39 | Massachusetts | (72) |
| 39 | Michigan | (72) |
| 41 | West Virginia | (74) |
| 42 | South Carolina | (76) |
| 43 | Colorado | (78) |
| 43 | Maine | (78) |
| 45 | Florida | (81) |
| 45 | Mississippi | (81) |
| 47 | Wisconsin | (84) |
| 48 | Oklahoma | (91) |
| 49 | Idaho | (93) |
| 50 | Wyoming | (94) |

| | District of Columbia | (32) |

Source: U.S. Department of Health and Human Services, Administration for Children and Families
   "Change in TANF Caseloads" (http://www.acf.dhhs.gov/news/stats/caseload.htm)
*From January 1993 to June 2000. Welfare reform replaced the Aid to Families with Dependent Children
(AFDC) program as of July 1, 1997 with Temporary Assistance to Needy Families (TANF). There were 2,755,000
fewer families and 8,334,000 fewer recipients nationwide. National percent includes territories.

# Percent Change in AFDC/TANF Families: 1993 to 2000

## National Percent Change = 56% Decrease*

| RANK | STATE | PERCENT CHANGE |
|------|-------|----------------|
| 36 | Alabama | (64) |
| 4 | Alaska | (35) |
| 19 | Arizona | (54) |
| 21 | Arkansas | (55) |
| 7 | California | (42) |
| 44 | Colorado | (75) |
| 17 | Connecticut | (52) |
| 15 | Delaware | (49) |
| 44 | Florida | (75) |
| 36 | Georgia | (64) |
| 1 | Hawaii | (16) |
| 48 | Idaho | (82) |
| 33 | Illinois | (63) |
| 17 | Indiana | (52) |
| 10 | Iowa | (45) |
| 27 | Kansas | (58) |
| 21 | Kentucky | (55) |
| 41 | Louisiana | (72) |
| 21 | Maine | (55) |
| 36 | Maryland | (64) |
| 33 | Massachusetts | (63) |
| 40 | Michigan | (69) |
| 5 | Minnesota | (39) |
| 44 | Mississippi | (75) |
| 14 | Missouri | (48) |
| 31 | Montana | (62) |
| 5 | Nebraska | (39) |
| 11 | Nevada | (46) |
| 11 | New Hampshire | (46) |
| 29 | New Jersey | (60) |
| 3 | New Mexico | (27) |
| 7 | New York | (42) |
| 39 | North Carolina | (65) |
| 24 | North Dakota | (56) |
| 33 | Ohio | (63) |
| 49 | Oklahoma | (86) |
| 29 | Oregon | (60) |
| 26 | Pennsylvania | (57) |
| 2 | Rhode Island | (25) |
| 41 | South Carolina | (72) |
| 31 | South Dakota | (62) |
| 16 | Tennessee | (51) |
| 19 | Texas | (54) |
| 24 | Utah | (56) |
| 7 | Vermont | (42) |
| 28 | Virginia | (59) |
| 11 | Washington | (46) |
| 43 | West Virginia | (74) |
| 47 | Wisconsin | (80) |
| 50 | Wyoming | (91) |

| RANK | STATE | PERCENT CHANGE |
|------|-------|----------------|
| 1 | Hawaii | (16) |
| 2 | Rhode Island | (25) |
| 3 | New Mexico | (27) |
| 4 | Alaska | (35) |
| 5 | Minnesota | (39) |
| 5 | Nebraska | (39) |
| 7 | California | (42) |
| 7 | New York | (42) |
| 7 | Vermont | (42) |
| 10 | Iowa | (45) |
| 11 | Nevada | (46) |
| 11 | New Hampshire | (46) |
| 11 | Washington | (46) |
| 14 | Missouri | (48) |
| 15 | Delaware | (49) |
| 16 | Tennessee | (51) |
| 17 | Connecticut | (52) |
| 17 | Indiana | (52) |
| 19 | Arizona | (54) |
| 19 | Texas | (54) |
| 21 | Arkansas | (55) |
| 21 | Kentucky | (55) |
| 21 | Maine | (55) |
| 24 | North Dakota | (56) |
| 24 | Utah | (56) |
| 26 | Pennsylvania | (57) |
| 27 | Kansas | (58) |
| 28 | Virginia | (59) |
| 29 | New Jersey | (60) |
| 29 | Oregon | (60) |
| 31 | Montana | (62) |
| 31 | South Dakota | (62) |
| 33 | Illinois | (63) |
| 33 | Massachusetts | (63) |
| 33 | Ohio | (63) |
| 36 | Alabama | (64) |
| 36 | Georgia | (64) |
| 36 | Maryland | (64) |
| 39 | North Carolina | (65) |
| 40 | Michigan | (69) |
| 41 | Louisiana | (72) |
| 41 | South Carolina | (72) |
| 43 | West Virginia | (74) |
| 44 | Colorado | (75) |
| 44 | Florida | (75) |
| 44 | Mississippi | (75) |
| 47 | Wisconsin | (80) |
| 48 | Idaho | (82) |
| 49 | Oklahoma | (86) |
| 50 | Wyoming | (91) |
| | District of Columbia | (9) |

*Source: U.S. Department of Health and Human Services, Administration for Children and Families*
*"Change in TANF Caseloads" (http://www.acf.dhhs.gov/news/stats/case-fam.htm)*
*From January 1993 to June 2000. Welfare reform replaced the Aid to Families with Dependent Children (AFDC) program as of July 1, 1997 with Temporary Assistance to Needy Families (TANF). There were 2,755,000 fewer families and 8,334,000 fewer recipients nationwide.*

# Maximum Monthly TANF Benefit for Family of Three in 1999

## National Average = $408*

<u>ALPHA ORDER</u>

| RANK | STATE | BENEFIT |
|------|-------|---------|
| 49 | Alabama | $164 |
| 1 | Alaska | 923 |
| 33 | Arizona | 347 |
| 44 | Arkansas | 204 |
| 4 | California** | 666 |
| 30 | Colorado | 356 |
| 6 | Connecticut | 636 |
| 25 | Delaware | 388 |
| 35 | Florida | 303 |
| 39 | Georgia | 280 |
| 2 | Hawaii** | 712 |
| 41 | Idaho | 276 |
| 27 | Illinois | 377 |
| 38 | Indiana | 288 |
| 21 | Iowa | 426 |
| 20 | Kansas | 429 |
| 43 | Kentucky | 262 |
| 46 | Louisiana | 190 |
| 19 | Maine | 439 |
| 25 | Maryland | 388 |
| 7 | Massachusetts | 579 |
| 16 | Michigan | 459 |
| 13 | Minnesota | 536 |
| 50 | Mississippi | 120 |
| 36 | Missouri | 292 |
| 15 | Montana | 461 |
| 28 | Nebraska | 364 |
| 32 | Nevada | 348 |
| 10 | New Hampshire | 550 |
| 22 | New Jersey | 424 |
| 24 | New Mexico** | 389 |
| 8 | New York | 573 |
| 42 | North Carolina | 272 |
| 11 | North Dakota | 549 |
| 29 | Ohio | 362 |
| 36 | Oklahoma | 292 |
| 14 | Oregon | 503 |
| 23 | Pennsylvania | 421 |
| 9 | Rhode Island | 554 |
| 45 | South Carolina | 201 |
| 18 | South Dakota | 450 |
| 48 | Tennessee | 185 |
| 47 | Texas | 188 |
| 17 | Utah | 451 |
| 5 | Vermont | 639 |
| 31 | Virginia | 354 |
| 12 | Washington | 546 |
| 40 | West Virginia | 278 |
| 3 | Wisconsin | 681 |
| 34 | Wyoming | 340 |

<u>RANK ORDER</u>

| RANK | STATE | BENEFIT |
|------|-------|---------|
| 1 | Alaska | $923 |
| 2 | Hawaii** | 712 |
| 3 | Wisconsin | 681 |
| 4 | California** | 666 |
| 5 | Vermont | 639 |
| 6 | Connecticut | 636 |
| 7 | Massachusetts | 579 |
| 8 | New York | 573 |
| 9 | Rhode Island | 554 |
| 10 | New Hampshire | 550 |
| 11 | North Dakota | 549 |
| 12 | Washington | 546 |
| 13 | Minnesota | 536 |
| 14 | Oregon | 503 |
| 15 | Montana | 461 |
| 16 | Michigan | 459 |
| 17 | Utah | 451 |
| 18 | South Dakota | 450 |
| 19 | Maine | 439 |
| 20 | Kansas | 429 |
| 21 | Iowa | 426 |
| 22 | New Jersey | 424 |
| 23 | Pennsylvania | 421 |
| 24 | New Mexico** | 389 |
| 25 | Delaware | 388 |
| 25 | Maryland | 388 |
| 27 | Illinois | 377 |
| 28 | Nebraska | 364 |
| 29 | Ohio | 362 |
| 30 | Colorado | 356 |
| 31 | Virginia | 354 |
| 32 | Nevada | 348 |
| 33 | Arizona | 347 |
| 34 | Wyoming | 340 |
| 35 | Florida | 303 |
| 36 | Missouri | 292 |
| 36 | Oklahoma | 292 |
| 38 | Indiana | 288 |
| 39 | Georgia | 280 |
| 40 | West Virginia | 278 |
| 41 | Idaho | 276 |
| 42 | North Carolina | 272 |
| 43 | Kentucky | 262 |
| 44 | Arkansas | 204 |
| 45 | South Carolina | 201 |
| 46 | Louisiana | 190 |
| 47 | Texas | 188 |
| 48 | Tennessee | 185 |
| 49 | Alabama | 164 |
| 50 | Mississippi | 120 |
| | District of Columbia | 379 |

*Source: U.S. Department of Health and Human Services, Administration for Children and Families unpublished data (http://www.acf.dhhs.gov)*
*National is a simple average of state rates. TANF is Temporary Assistance for Needy Families. This program replaces AFDC (Aid for Families with Dependent Children) following welfare reform legislation in 1997. **California has two levels, $682 for urban areas, $649 for rural. Hawaii's $712 is for exempt families and teen parent households, others receive $570. New Mexico adds $50 for each family not living in subsidized housing.*

# Food Stamp Benefits in 2000

## National Total = $14,985,675,289*

ALPHA ORDER

| RANK | STATE | BENEFITS | % of USA |
|------|-------|----------|----------|
| 14 | Alabama | $343,835,342 | 2.3% |
| 44 | Alaska | 45,834,562 | 0.3% |
| 21 | Arizona | 240,245,624 | 1.6% |
| 24 | Arkansas | 206,236,378 | 1.4% |
| 1 | California | 1,632,774,423 | 10.9% |
| 34 | Colorado | 126,718,844 | 0.8% |
| 32 | Connecticut | 138,164,063 | 0.9% |
| 47 | Delaware | 31,126,762 | 0.2% |
| 5 | Florida | 773,654,024 | 5.2% |
| 8 | Georgia | 487,604,078 | 3.3% |
| 29 | Hawaii | 166,259,882 | 1.1% |
| 43 | Idaho | 46,163,882 | 0.3% |
| 4 | Illinois | 777,709,465 | 5.2% |
| 17 | Indiana | 270,711,740 | 1.8% |
| 35 | Iowa | 100,189,090 | 0.7% |
| 36 | Kansas | 82,700,978 | 0.6% |
| 15 | Kentucky | 336,891,842 | 2.2% |
| 10 | Louisiana | 448,096,963 | 3.0% |
| 37 | Maine | 81,408,200 | 0.5% |
| 25 | Maryland | 199,458,863 | 1.3% |
| 28 | Massachusetts | 181,640,587 | 1.2% |
| 9 | Michigan | 457,145,378 | 3.1% |
| 30 | Minnesota | 164,674,851 | 1.1% |
| 22 | Mississippi | 226,183,118 | 1.5% |
| 13 | Missouri | 358,210,309 | 2.4% |
| 42 | Montana | 51,307,579 | 0.3% |
| 39 | Nebraska | 60,888,562 | 0.4% |
| 41 | Nevada | 56,642,985 | 0.4% |
| 48 | New Hampshire | 28,129,262 | 0.2% |
| 16 | New Jersey | 303,820,096 | 2.0% |
| 31 | New Mexico | 139,569,533 | 0.9% |
| 2 | New York | 1,363,183,391 | 9.1% |
| 12 | North Carolina | 403,432,905 | 2.7% |
| 49 | North Dakota | 25,309,514 | 0.2% |
| 7 | Ohio | 519,627,537 | 3.5% |
| 23 | Oklahoma | 208,701,757 | 1.4% |
| 26 | Oregon | 198,485,589 | 1.3% |
| 6 | Pennsylvania | 655,726,257 | 4.4% |
| 40 | Rhode Island | 59,281,417 | 0.4% |
| 19 | South Carolina | 249,274,301 | 1.7% |
| 45 | South Dakota | 36,801,145 | 0.2% |
| 11 | Tennessee | 415,292,373 | 2.8% |
| 3 | Texas | 1,215,796,425 | 8.1% |
| 38 | Utah | 68,337,664 | 0.5% |
| 46 | Vermont | 31,996,215 | 0.2% |
| 18 | Virginia | 262,328,617 | 1.8% |
| 20 | Washington | 241,495,700 | 1.6% |
| 27 | West Virginia | 185,521,000 | 1.2% |
| 33 | Wisconsin | 128,898,763 | 0.9% |
| 50 | Wyoming | 18,624,607 | 0.1% |

RANK ORDER

| RANK | STATE | BENEFITS | % of USA |
|------|-------|----------|----------|
| 1 | California | $1,632,774,423 | 10.9% |
| 2 | New York | 1,363,183,391 | 9.1% |
| 3 | Texas | 1,215,796,425 | 8.1% |
| 4 | Illinois | 777,709,465 | 5.2% |
| 5 | Florida | 773,654,024 | 5.2% |
| 6 | Pennsylvania | 655,726,257 | 4.4% |
| 7 | Ohio | 519,627,537 | 3.5% |
| 8 | Georgia | 487,604,078 | 3.3% |
| 9 | Michigan | 457,145,378 | 3.1% |
| 10 | Louisiana | 448,096,963 | 3.0% |
| 11 | Tennessee | 415,292,373 | 2.8% |
| 12 | North Carolina | 403,432,905 | 2.7% |
| 13 | Missouri | 358,210,309 | 2.4% |
| 14 | Alabama | 343,835,342 | 2.3% |
| 15 | Kentucky | 336,891,842 | 2.2% |
| 16 | New Jersey | 303,820,096 | 2.0% |
| 17 | Indiana | 270,711,740 | 1.8% |
| 18 | Virginia | 262,328,617 | 1.8% |
| 19 | South Carolina | 249,274,301 | 1.7% |
| 20 | Washington | 241,495,700 | 1.6% |
| 21 | Arizona | 240,245,624 | 1.6% |
| 22 | Mississippi | 226,183,118 | 1.5% |
| 23 | Oklahoma | 208,701,757 | 1.4% |
| 24 | Arkansas | 206,236,378 | 1.4% |
| 25 | Maryland | 199,458,863 | 1.3% |
| 26 | Oregon | 198,485,589 | 1.3% |
| 27 | West Virginia | 185,521,000 | 1.2% |
| 28 | Massachusetts | 181,640,587 | 1.2% |
| 29 | Hawaii | 166,259,882 | 1.1% |
| 30 | Minnesota | 164,674,851 | 1.1% |
| 31 | New Mexico | 139,569,533 | 0.9% |
| 32 | Connecticut | 138,164,063 | 0.9% |
| 33 | Wisconsin | 128,898,763 | 0.9% |
| 34 | Colorado | 126,718,844 | 0.8% |
| 35 | Iowa | 100,189,090 | 0.7% |
| 36 | Kansas | 82,700,978 | 0.6% |
| 37 | Maine | 81,408,200 | 0.5% |
| 38 | Utah | 68,337,664 | 0.5% |
| 39 | Nebraska | 60,888,562 | 0.4% |
| 40 | Rhode Island | 59,281,417 | 0.4% |
| 41 | Nevada | 56,642,985 | 0.4% |
| 42 | Montana | 51,307,579 | 0.3% |
| 43 | Idaho | 46,163,882 | 0.3% |
| 44 | Alaska | 45,834,562 | 0.3% |
| 45 | South Dakota | 36,801,145 | 0.2% |
| 46 | Vermont | 31,996,215 | 0.2% |
| 47 | Delaware | 31,126,762 | 0.2% |
| 48 | New Hampshire | 28,129,262 | 0.2% |
| 49 | North Dakota | 25,309,514 | 0.2% |
| 50 | Wyoming | 18,624,607 | 0.1% |
| | District of Columbia | 76,672,014 | 0.5% |

*Source: U.S. Department of Agriculture, Food, Nutrition and Consumer Services*
*"Food Stamp Program: Benefits" (http://www.fns.usda.gov/pd/fsfybft.htm)*
*\*Preliminary for year ending September 30, 2000. National total includes $56,890,833 to U.S. territories. Costs are for benefits only and exclude administrative expenditures.*

# Monthly Food Stamp Recipients in 2000

## National Total = 17,163,304 Recipients*

ALPHA ORDER

| RANK | STATE | RECIPIENTS | % of USA |
|------|-------|-----------|----------|
| 15 | Alabama | 396,057 | 2.3% |
| 46 | Alaska | 37,524 | 0.2% |
| 22 | Arizona | 259,006 | 1.5% |
| 24 | Arkansas | 246,572 | 1.4% |
| 1 | California | 1,831,697 | 10.7% |
| 33 | Colorado | 155,948 | 0.9% |
| 32 | Connecticut | 165,059 | 1.0% |
| 48 | Delaware | 32,218 | 0.2% |
| 4 | Florida | 882,341 | 5.1% |
| 9 | Georgia | 559,468 | 3.3% |
| 35 | Hawaii | 118,041 | 0.7% |
| 43 | Idaho | 58,191 | 0.3% |
| 5 | Illinois | 779,420 | 4.5% |
| 18 | Indiana | 300,314 | 1.7% |
| 34 | Iowa | 123,322 | 0.7% |
| 36 | Kansas | 116,596 | 0.7% |
| 14 | Kentucky | 403,479 | 2.4% |
| 10 | Louisiana | 499,851 | 2.9% |
| 37 | Maine | 101,665 | 0.6% |
| 28 | Maryland | 219,180 | 1.3% |
| 26 | Massachusetts | 231,829 | 1.4% |
| 7 | Michigan | 610,974 | 3.6% |
| 29 | Minnesota | 196,048 | 1.1% |
| 21 | Mississippi | 275,856 | 1.6% |
| 13 | Missouri | 419,959 | 2.4% |
| 42 | Montana | 59,466 | 0.3% |
| 38 | Nebraska | 82,414 | 0.5% |
| 41 | Nevada | 60,905 | 0.4% |
| 47 | New Hampshire | 36,266 | 0.2% |
| 16 | New Jersey | 344,677 | 2.0% |
| 31 | New Mexico | 169,354 | 1.0% |
| 2 | New York | 1,438,568 | 8.4% |
| 12 | North Carolina | 488,247 | 2.8% |
| 49 | North Dakota | 31,895 | 0.2% |
| 8 | Ohio | 609,717 | 3.6% |
| 23 | Oklahoma | 253,287 | 1.5% |
| 25 | Oregon | 234,387 | 1.4% |
| 6 | Pennsylvania | 777,112 | 4.5% |
| 40 | Rhode Island | 74,256 | 0.4% |
| 19 | South Carolina | 295,335 | 1.7% |
| 44 | South Dakota | 42,962 | 0.3% |
| 11 | Tennessee | 496,031 | 2.9% |
| 3 | Texas | 1,332,785 | 7.8% |
| 39 | Utah | 81,945 | 0.5% |
| 45 | Vermont | 40,861 | 0.2% |
| 17 | Virginia | 336,080 | 2.0% |
| 20 | Washington | 295,061 | 1.7% |
| 27 | West Virginia | 226,897 | 1.3% |
| 30 | Wisconsin | 193,021 | 1.1% |
| 50 | Wyoming | 22,459 | 0.1% |

RANK ORDER

| RANK | STATE | RECIPIENTS | % of USA |
|------|-------|-----------|----------|
| 1 | California | 1,831,697 | 10.7% |
| 2 | New York | 1,438,568 | 8.4% |
| 3 | Texas | 1,332,785 | 7.8% |
| 4 | Florida | 882,341 | 5.1% |
| 5 | Illinois | 779,420 | 4.5% |
| 6 | Pennsylvania | 777,112 | 4.5% |
| 7 | Michigan | 610,974 | 3.6% |
| 8 | Ohio | 609,717 | 3.6% |
| 9 | Georgia | 559,468 | 3.3% |
| 10 | Louisiana | 499,851 | 2.9% |
| 11 | Tennessee | 496,031 | 2.9% |
| 12 | North Carolina | 488,247 | 2.8% |
| 13 | Missouri | 419,959 | 2.4% |
| 14 | Kentucky | 403,479 | 2.4% |
| 15 | Alabama | 396,057 | 2.3% |
| 16 | New Jersey | 344,677 | 2.0% |
| 17 | Virginia | 336,080 | 2.0% |
| 18 | Indiana | 300,314 | 1.7% |
| 19 | South Carolina | 295,335 | 1.7% |
| 20 | Washington | 295,061 | 1.7% |
| 21 | Mississippi | 275,856 | 1.6% |
| 22 | Arizona | 259,006 | 1.5% |
| 23 | Oklahoma | 253,287 | 1.5% |
| 24 | Arkansas | 246,572 | 1.4% |
| 25 | Oregon | 234,387 | 1.4% |
| 26 | Massachusetts | 231,829 | 1.4% |
| 27 | West Virginia | 226,897 | 1.3% |
| 28 | Maryland | 219,180 | 1.3% |
| 29 | Minnesota | 196,048 | 1.1% |
| 30 | Wisconsin | 193,021 | 1.1% |
| 31 | New Mexico | 169,354 | 1.0% |
| 32 | Connecticut | 165,059 | 1.0% |
| 33 | Colorado | 155,948 | 0.9% |
| 34 | Iowa | 123,322 | 0.7% |
| 35 | Hawaii | 118,041 | 0.7% |
| 36 | Kansas | 116,596 | 0.7% |
| 37 | Maine | 101,665 | 0.6% |
| 38 | Nebraska | 82,414 | 0.5% |
| 39 | Utah | 81,945 | 0.5% |
| 40 | Rhode Island | 74,256 | 0.4% |
| 41 | Nevada | 60,905 | 0.4% |
| 42 | Montana | 59,466 | 0.3% |
| 43 | Idaho | 58,191 | 0.3% |
| 44 | South Dakota | 42,962 | 0.3% |
| 45 | Vermont | 40,861 | 0.2% |
| 46 | Alaska | 37,524 | 0.2% |
| 47 | New Hampshire | 36,266 | 0.2% |
| 48 | Delaware | 32,218 | 0.2% |
| 49 | North Dakota | 31,895 | 0.2% |
| 50 | Wyoming | 22,459 | 0.1% |
| | District of Columbia | 80,803 | 0.5% |

*Source: U.S. Department of Agriculture, Food, Nutrition and Consumer Services*
*"Food Stamp Program: Number of Persons Participating" (http://www.fns.usda.gov/pd/fsfypart.htm)*
*Preliminary for fiscal year 2000. National total includes 37,898 recipients in U.S. territories.

# Average Monthly Food Stamp Benefit per Recipient in 2000

## National Average = $72.76 per Recipient*

ALPHA ORDER

| RANK | STATE | PER RECIPIENT |
|---|---|---|
| 16 | Alabama | $72.34 |
| 2 | Alaska | 101.78 |
| 7 | Arizona | 77.29 |
| 27 | Arkansas | 69.70 |
| 12 | California | 74.28 |
| 37 | Colorado | 67.71 |
| 26 | Connecticut | 69.75 |
| 4 | Delaware | 80.51 |
| 14 | Florida | 73.06 |
| 15 | Georgia | 72.62 |
| 1 | Hawaii | 117.37 |
| 42 | Idaho | 66.10 |
| 3 | Illinois | 83.15 |
| 10 | Indiana | 75.11 |
| 38 | Iowa | 67.70 |
| 49 | Kansas | 59.10 |
| 28 | Kentucky | 69.58 |
| 11 | Louisiana | 74.70 |
| 39 | Maine | 66.72 |
| 9 | Maryland | 75.83 |
| 43 | Massachusetts | 65.29 |
| 47 | Michigan | 62.35 |
| 24 | Minnesota | 69.99 |
| 34 | Mississippi | 68.32 |
| 19 | Missouri | 71.08 |
| 17 | Montana | 71.90 |
| 48 | Nebraska | 61.56 |
| 6 | Nevada | 77.50 |
| 46 | New Hampshire | 64.63 |
| 13 | New Jersey | 73.45 |
| 32 | New Mexico | 68.67 |
| 5 | New York | 78.96 |
| 31 | North Carolina | 68.85 |
| 41 | North Dakota | 66.12 |
| 20 | Ohio | 71.02 |
| 33 | Oklahoma | 68.66 |
| 21 | Oregon | 70.56 |
| 23 | Pennsylvania | 70.31 |
| 40 | Rhode Island | 66.52 |
| 22 | South Carolina | 70.33 |
| 18 | South Dakota | 71.38 |
| 25 | Tennessee | 69.76 |
| 8 | Texas | 76.01 |
| 29 | Utah | 69.49 |
| 44 | Vermont | 65.25 |
| 45 | Virginia | 65.04 |
| 35 | Washington | 68.20 |
| 36 | West Virginia | 68.13 |
| 50 | Wisconsin | 55.64 |
| 30 | Wyoming | 69.10 |

RANK ORDER

| RANK | STATE | PER RECIPIENT |
|---|---|---|
| 1 | Hawaii | $117.37 |
| 2 | Alaska | 101.78 |
| 3 | Illinois | 83.15 |
| 4 | Delaware | 80.51 |
| 5 | New York | 78.96 |
| 6 | Nevada | 77.50 |
| 7 | Arizona | 77.29 |
| 8 | Texas | 76.01 |
| 9 | Maryland | 75.83 |
| 10 | Indiana | 75.11 |
| 11 | Louisiana | 74.70 |
| 12 | California | 74.28 |
| 13 | New Jersey | 73.45 |
| 14 | Florida | 73.06 |
| 15 | Georgia | 72.62 |
| 16 | Alabama | 72.34 |
| 17 | Montana | 71.90 |
| 18 | South Dakota | 71.38 |
| 19 | Missouri | 71.08 |
| 20 | Ohio | 71.02 |
| 21 | Oregon | 70.56 |
| 22 | South Carolina | 70.33 |
| 23 | Pennsylvania | 70.31 |
| 24 | Minnesota | 69.99 |
| 25 | Tennessee | 69.76 |
| 26 | Connecticut | 69.75 |
| 27 | Arkansas | 69.70 |
| 28 | Kentucky | 69.58 |
| 29 | Utah | 69.49 |
| 30 | Wyoming | 69.10 |
| 31 | North Carolina | 68.85 |
| 32 | New Mexico | 68.67 |
| 33 | Oklahoma | 68.66 |
| 34 | Mississippi | 68.32 |
| 35 | Washington | 68.20 |
| 36 | West Virginia | 68.13 |
| 37 | Colorado | 67.71 |
| 38 | Iowa | 67.70 |
| 39 | Maine | 66.72 |
| 40 | Rhode Island | 66.52 |
| 41 | North Dakota | 66.12 |
| 42 | Idaho | 66.10 |
| 43 | Massachusetts | 65.29 |
| 44 | Vermont | 65.25 |
| 45 | Virginia | 65.04 |
| 46 | New Hampshire | 64.63 |
| 47 | Michigan | 62.35 |
| 48 | Nebraska | 61.56 |
| 49 | Kansas | 59.10 |
| 50 | Wisconsin | 55.64 |
| | District of Columbia | 79.07 |

Source: U.S. Department of Agriculture, Food, Nutrition and Consumer Services
"Food Stamp Program: Average Monthly Benefit per Person" (http://www.fns.usda.gov/pd/fsavgben.htm)
*Preliminary for fiscal year 2000. National average includes recipients in U.S. territories.

# Percent of Population Receiving Food Stamps in 2000

## National Percent = 6.1%*

ALPHA ORDER

| RANK | STATE | PERCENT |
|------|-------|---------|
| 8 | Alabama | 8.9 |
| 25 | Alaska | 6.0 |
| 30 | Arizona | 5.0 |
| 7 | Arkansas | 9.2 |
| 28 | California | 5.4 |
| 47 | Colorado | 3.6 |
| 34 | Connecticut | 4.8 |
| 41 | Delaware | 4.1 |
| 27 | Florida | 5.5 |
| 17 | Georgia | 6.8 |
| 4 | Hawaii | 9.7 |
| 37 | Idaho | 4.5 |
| 21 | Illinois | 6.3 |
| 33 | Indiana | 4.9 |
| 40 | Iowa | 4.2 |
| 39 | Kansas | 4.3 |
| 3 | Kentucky | 10.0 |
| 2 | Louisiana | 11.2 |
| 10 | Maine | 8.0 |
| 41 | Maryland | 4.1 |
| 45 | Massachusetts | 3.7 |
| 23 | Michigan | 6.1 |
| 44 | Minnesota | 4.0 |
| 4 | Mississippi | 9.7 |
| 12 | Missouri | 7.5 |
| 19 | Montana | 6.6 |
| 34 | Nebraska | 4.8 |
| 49 | Nevada | 3.0 |
| 50 | New Hampshire | 2.9 |
| 41 | New Jersey | 4.1 |
| 6 | New Mexico | 9.3 |
| 11 | New York | 7.6 |
| 23 | North Carolina | 6.1 |
| 30 | North Dakota | 5.0 |
| 28 | Ohio | 5.4 |
| 14 | Oklahoma | 7.3 |
| 16 | Oregon | 6.9 |
| 21 | Pennsylvania | 6.3 |
| 15 | Rhode Island | 7.1 |
| 13 | South Carolina | 7.4 |
| 26 | South Dakota | 5.7 |
| 9 | Tennessee | 8.7 |
| 20 | Texas | 6.4 |
| 45 | Utah | 3.7 |
| 18 | Vermont | 6.7 |
| 36 | Virginia | 4.7 |
| 30 | Washington | 5.0 |
| 1 | West Virginia | 12.5 |
| 47 | Wisconsin | 3.6 |
| 37 | Wyoming | 4.5 |

RANK ORDER

| RANK | STATE | PERCENT |
|------|-------|---------|
| 1 | West Virginia | 12.5 |
| 2 | Louisiana | 11.2 |
| 3 | Kentucky | 10.0 |
| 4 | Hawaii | 9.7 |
| 4 | Mississippi | 9.7 |
| 6 | New Mexico | 9.3 |
| 7 | Arkansas | 9.2 |
| 8 | Alabama | 8.9 |
| 9 | Tennessee | 8.7 |
| 10 | Maine | 8.0 |
| 11 | New York | 7.6 |
| 12 | Missouri | 7.5 |
| 13 | South Carolina | 7.4 |
| 14 | Oklahoma | 7.3 |
| 15 | Rhode Island | 7.1 |
| 16 | Oregon | 6.9 |
| 17 | Georgia | 6.8 |
| 18 | Vermont | 6.7 |
| 19 | Montana | 6.6 |
| 20 | Texas | 6.4 |
| 21 | Illinois | 6.3 |
| 21 | Pennsylvania | 6.3 |
| 23 | Michigan | 6.1 |
| 23 | North Carolina | 6.1 |
| 25 | Alaska | 6.0 |
| 26 | South Dakota | 5.7 |
| 27 | Florida | 5.5 |
| 28 | California | 5.4 |
| 28 | Ohio | 5.4 |
| 30 | Arizona | 5.0 |
| 30 | North Dakota | 5.0 |
| 30 | Washington | 5.0 |
| 33 | Indiana | 4.9 |
| 34 | Connecticut | 4.8 |
| 34 | Nebraska | 4.8 |
| 36 | Virginia | 4.7 |
| 37 | Idaho | 4.5 |
| 37 | Wyoming | 4.5 |
| 39 | Kansas | 4.3 |
| 40 | Iowa | 4.2 |
| 41 | Delaware | 4.1 |
| 41 | Maryland | 4.1 |
| 41 | New Jersey | 4.1 |
| 44 | Minnesota | 4.0 |
| 45 | Massachusetts | 3.7 |
| 45 | Utah | 3.7 |
| 47 | Colorado | 3.6 |
| 47 | Wisconsin | 3.6 |
| 49 | Nevada | 3.0 |
| 50 | New Hampshire | 2.9 |

District of Columbia 14.1

Source: Morgan Quitno Press using data from U.S. Department of Agriculture, Food, Nutrition and Consumer Services "Food Stamp Program: Number of Persons Participating" (http://www.fns.usda.gov/pd/fsfypart.htm)
*Preliminary data for fiscal year 2000. National rate does not include recipients in U.S. territories.

# Percent Change in Food Stamp Program Participation: 1996 to 2000

## National Percent Change = 32.8% Decrease*

ALPHA ORDER

| RANK | STATE | PERCENT CHANGE |
|------|-------|----------------|
| 12 | Alabama | (22.2) |
| 9 | Alaska | (18.8) |
| 44 | Arizona | (39.4) |
| 2 | Arkansas | (10.0) |
| 47 | California | (41.7) |
| 38 | Colorado | (36.0) |
| 21 | Connecticut | (25.9) |
| 50 | Delaware | (44.3) |
| 37 | Florida | (35.7) |
| 26 | Georgia | (29.4) |
| 1 | Hawaii | (9.4) |
| 22 | Idaho | (27.1) |
| 27 | Illinois | (29.5) |
| 16 | Indiana | (22.9) |
| 28 | Iowa | (30.4) |
| 34 | Kansas | (32.1) |
| 5 | Kentucky | (16.9) |
| 19 | Louisiana | (25.4) |
| 14 | Maine | (22.3) |
| 46 | Maryland | (41.5) |
| 42 | Massachusetts | (37.9) |
| 36 | Michigan | (34.7) |
| 35 | Minnesota | (33.5) |
| 45 | Mississippi | (39.7) |
| 17 | Missouri | (24.2) |
| 4 | Montana | (16.0) |
| 10 | Nebraska | (18.9) |
| 40 | Nevada | (37.0) |
| 30 | New Hampshire | (31.3) |
| 39 | New Jersey | (36.2) |
| 24 | New Mexico | (28.0) |
| 31 | New York | (31.4) |
| 15 | North Carolina | (22.6) |
| 11 | North Dakota | (19.9) |
| 47 | Ohio | (41.7) |
| 25 | Oklahoma | (28.4) |
| 8 | Oregon | (18.5) |
| 29 | Pennsylvania | (30.8) |
| 7 | Rhode Island | (18.3) |
| 6 | South Carolina | (17.6) |
| 3 | South Dakota | (12.0) |
| 12 | Tennessee | (22.2) |
| 49 | Texas | (43.8) |
| 20 | Utah | (25.5) |
| 23 | Vermont | (27.6) |
| 41 | Virginia | (37.5) |
| 43 | Washington | (38.3) |
| 18 | West Virginia | (24.3) |
| 32 | Wisconsin | (31.9) |
| 33 | Wyoming | (32.0) |

RANK ORDER

| RANK | STATE | PERCENT CHANGE |
|------|-------|----------------|
| 1 | Hawaii | (9.4) |
| 2 | Arkansas | (10.0) |
| 3 | South Dakota | (12.0) |
| 4 | Montana | (16.0) |
| 5 | Kentucky | (16.9) |
| 6 | South Carolina | (17.6) |
| 7 | Rhode Island | (18.3) |
| 8 | Oregon | (18.5) |
| 9 | Alaska | (18.8) |
| 10 | Nebraska | (18.9) |
| 11 | North Dakota | (19.9) |
| 12 | Alabama | (22.2) |
| 12 | Tennessee | (22.2) |
| 14 | Maine | (22.3) |
| 15 | North Carolina | (22.6) |
| 16 | Indiana | (22.9) |
| 17 | Missouri | (24.2) |
| 18 | West Virginia | (24.3) |
| 19 | Louisiana | (25.4) |
| 20 | Utah | (25.5) |
| 21 | Connecticut | (25.9) |
| 22 | Idaho | (27.1) |
| 23 | Vermont | (27.6) |
| 24 | New Mexico | (28.0) |
| 25 | Oklahoma | (28.4) |
| 26 | Georgia | (29.4) |
| 27 | Illinois | (29.5) |
| 28 | Iowa | (30.4) |
| 29 | Pennsylvania | (30.8) |
| 30 | New Hampshire | (31.3) |
| 31 | New York | (31.4) |
| 32 | Wisconsin | (31.9) |
| 33 | Wyoming | (32.0) |
| 34 | Kansas | (32.1) |
| 35 | Minnesota | (33.5) |
| 36 | Michigan | (34.7) |
| 37 | Florida | (35.7) |
| 38 | Colorado | (36.0) |
| 39 | New Jersey | (36.2) |
| 40 | Nevada | (37.0) |
| 41 | Virginia | (37.5) |
| 42 | Massachusetts | (37.9) |
| 43 | Washington | (38.3) |
| 44 | Arizona | (39.4) |
| 45 | Mississippi | (39.7) |
| 46 | Maryland | (41.5) |
| 47 | California | (41.7) |
| 47 | Ohio | (41.7) |
| 49 | Texas | (43.8) |
| 50 | Delaware | (44.3) |

District of Columbia (12.9)

*Source: Morgan Quitno Press using data from U.S. Department of Agriculture, Food, Nutrition and Consumer Services "Food Stamp Program: Number of Persons Participating" (http://www.fns.usda.gov/pd/fsfypart.htm)*
*\*Preliminary data for fiscal year 2000. National percent change includes recipients in U.S. territories.*

# Households Receiving Food Stamps in 2000

## National Total = 7,334,501 Households*

<u>ALPHA ORDER</u>

| RANK | STATE | HOUSEHOLDS | % of USA |
|------|-------|-----------|----------|
| 15 | Alabama | 156,105 | 2.1% |
| 49 | Alaska | 13,208 | 0.2% |
| 28 | Arizona | 95,569 | 1.3% |
| 26 | Arkansas | 98,764 | 1.3% |
| 2 | California | 672,198 | 9.2% |
| 32 | Colorado | 69,951 | 1.0% |
| 30 | Connecticut | 84,016 | 1.1% |
| 48 | Delaware | 13,463 | 0.2% |
| 4 | Florida | 415,788 | 5.7% |
| 9 | Georgia | 229,500 | 3.1% |
| 34 | Hawaii | 54,212 | 0.7% |
| 43 | Idaho | 23,174 | 0.3% |
| 6 | Illinois | 338,230 | 4.6% |
| 19 | Indiana | 127,875 | 1.7% |
| 36 | Iowa | 52,548 | 0.7% |
| 35 | Kansas | 53,383 | 0.7% |
| 14 | Kentucky | 167,971 | 2.3% |
| 12 | Louisiana | 191,891 | 2.6% |
| 37 | Maine | 51,739 | 0.7% |
| 25 | Maryland | 101,048 | 1.4% |
| 22 | Massachusetts | 110,234 | 1.5% |
| 8 | Michigan | 272,068 | 3.7% |
| 29 | Minnesota | 91,097 | 1.2% |
| 23 | Mississippi | 108,993 | 1.5% |
| 13 | Missouri | 180,401 | 2.5% |
| 42 | Montana | 25,280 | 0.3% |
| 38 | Nebraska | 35,130 | 0.5% |
| 41 | Nevada | 28,291 | 0.4% |
| 45 | New Hampshire | 18,095 | 0.2% |
| 16 | New Jersey | 152,358 | 2.1% |
| 33 | New Mexico | 63,537 | 0.9% |
| 1 | New York | 720,035 | 9.8% |
| 11 | North Carolina | 209,232 | 2.9% |
| 47 | North Dakota | 13,624 | 0.2% |
| 7 | Ohio | 279,174 | 3.8% |
| 24 | Oklahoma | 107,098 | 1.5% |
| 21 | Oregon | 114,368 | 1.6% |
| 5 | Pennsylvania | 352,491 | 4.8% |
| 39 | Rhode Island | 33,422 | 0.5% |
| 20 | South Carolina | 121,945 | 1.7% |
| 46 | South Dakota | 16,448 | 0.2% |
| 10 | Tennessee | 215,336 | 2.9% |
| 3 | Texas | 489,303 | 6.7% |
| 40 | Utah | 32,627 | 0.4% |
| 44 | Vermont | 19,663 | 0.3% |
| 17 | Virginia | 150,452 | 2.1% |
| 18 | Washington | 133,481 | 1.8% |
| 27 | West Virginia | 96,097 | 1.3% |
| 31 | Wisconsin | 76,633 | 1.0% |
| 50 | Wyoming | 8,956 | 0.1% |

<u>RANK ORDER</u>

| RANK | STATE | HOUSEHOLDS | % of USA |
|------|-------|-----------|----------|
| 1 | New York | 720,035 | 9.8% |
| 2 | California | 672,198 | 9.2% |
| 3 | Texas | 489,303 | 6.7% |
| 4 | Florida | 415,788 | 5.7% |
| 5 | Pennsylvania | 352,491 | 4.8% |
| 6 | Illinois | 338,230 | 4.6% |
| 7 | Ohio | 279,174 | 3.8% |
| 8 | Michigan | 272,068 | 3.7% |
| 9 | Georgia | 229,500 | 3.1% |
| 10 | Tennessee | 215,336 | 2.9% |
| 11 | North Carolina | 209,232 | 2.9% |
| 12 | Louisiana | 191,891 | 2.6% |
| 13 | Missouri | 180,401 | 2.5% |
| 14 | Kentucky | 167,971 | 2.3% |
| 15 | Alabama | 156,105 | 2.1% |
| 16 | New Jersey | 152,358 | 2.1% |
| 17 | Virginia | 150,452 | 2.1% |
| 18 | Washington | 133,481 | 1.8% |
| 19 | Indiana | 127,875 | 1.7% |
| 20 | South Carolina | 121,945 | 1.7% |
| 21 | Oregon | 114,368 | 1.6% |
| 22 | Massachusetts | 110,234 | 1.5% |
| 23 | Mississippi | 108,993 | 1.5% |
| 24 | Oklahoma | 107,098 | 1.5% |
| 25 | Maryland | 101,048 | 1.4% |
| 26 | Arkansas | 98,764 | 1.3% |
| 27 | West Virginia | 96,097 | 1.3% |
| 28 | Arizona | 95,569 | 1.3% |
| 29 | Minnesota | 91,097 | 1.2% |
| 30 | Connecticut | 84,016 | 1.1% |
| 31 | Wisconsin | 76,633 | 1.0% |
| 32 | Colorado | 69,951 | 1.0% |
| 33 | New Mexico | 63,537 | 0.9% |
| 34 | Hawaii | 54,212 | 0.7% |
| 35 | Kansas | 53,383 | 0.7% |
| 36 | Iowa | 52,548 | 0.7% |
| 37 | Maine | 51,739 | 0.7% |
| 38 | Nebraska | 35,130 | 0.5% |
| 39 | Rhode Island | 33,422 | 0.5% |
| 40 | Utah | 32,627 | 0.4% |
| 41 | Nevada | 28,291 | 0.4% |
| 42 | Montana | 25,280 | 0.3% |
| 43 | Idaho | 23,174 | 0.3% |
| 44 | Vermont | 19,663 | 0.3% |
| 45 | New Hampshire | 18,095 | 0.2% |
| 46 | South Dakota | 16,448 | 0.2% |
| 47 | North Dakota | 13,624 | 0.2% |
| 48 | Delaware | 13,463 | 0.2% |
| 49 | Alaska | 13,208 | 0.2% |
| 50 | Wyoming | 8,956 | 0.1% |
|  | District of Columbia | 36,194 | 0.5% |

*Source: U.S. Department of Agriculture, Food, Nutrition and Consumer Services*
*"Food Stamp Program: Number of Households Participating" (http://www.fns.usda.gov/pd/fsfyhh.htm)*
*\*Preliminary for fiscal year 2000. National total includes 11,805 households in U.S. territories.*

# Percent of Households Receiving Food Stamps in 1998

## National Percent = 8.2% of Households*

ALPHA ORDER

RANK ORDER

| RANK | STATE | PERCENT | | RANK | STATE | PERCENT |
|------|-------|---------|---|------|-------|---------|
| 11 | Alabama | 10.0 | | 1 | West Virginia | 15.4 |
| 31 | Alaska | 6.6 | | 2 | Hawaii | 13.5 |
| 34 | Arizona | 6.1 | | 3 | Mississippi | 13.0 |
| 9 | Arkansas | 10.4 | | 4 | Louisiana | 12.6 |
| 25 | California | 7.6 | | 5 | Maine | 11.3 |
| 46 | Colorado | 5.2 | | 6 | New York | 11.2 |
| 26 | Connecticut | 7.5 | | 7 | Tennessee | 11.0 |
| 37 | Delaware | 5.9 | | 8 | Kentucky | 10.9 |
| 28 | Florida | 7.3 | | 9 | Arkansas | 10.4 |
| 15 | Georgia | 9.0 | | 10 | New Mexico | 10.2 |
| 2 | Hawaii | 13.5 | | 11 | Alabama | 10.0 |
| 43 | Idaho | 5.3 | | 12 | South Carolina | 9.4 |
| 17 | Illinois | 8.8 | | 13 | Oklahoma | 9.3 |
| 38 | Indiana | 5.8 | | 13 | Vermont | 9.3 |
| 43 | Iowa | 5.3 | | 15 | Georgia | 9.0 |
| 43 | Kansas | 5.3 | | 16 | Michigan | 8.9 |
| 8 | Kentucky | 10.9 | | 17 | Illinois | 8.8 |
| 4 | Louisiana | 12.6 | | 18 | Pennsylvania | 8.7 |
| 5 | Maine | 11.3 | | 19 | Oregon | 8.6 |
| 30 | Maryland | 7.2 | | 19 | Rhode Island | 8.6 |
| 39 | Massachusetts | 5.7 | | 21 | Texas | 8.5 |
| 16 | Michigan | 8.9 | | 22 | Missouri | 8.3 |
| 41 | Minnesota | 5.4 | | 23 | North Carolina | 7.8 |
| 3 | Mississippi | 13.0 | | 24 | Ohio | 7.7 |
| 22 | Missouri | 8.3 | | 25 | California | 7.6 |
| 28 | Montana | 7.3 | | 26 | Connecticut | 7.5 |
| 34 | Nebraska | 6.1 | | 27 | Washington | 7.4 |
| 48 | Nevada | 4.8 | | 28 | Florida | 7.3 |
| 49 | New Hampshire | 4.1 | | 28 | Montana | 7.3 |
| 33 | New Jersey | 6.3 | | 30 | Maryland | 7.2 |
| 10 | New Mexico | 10.2 | | 31 | Alaska | 6.6 |
| 6 | New York | 11.2 | | 31 | Virginia | 6.6 |
| 23 | North Carolina | 7.8 | | 33 | New Jersey | 6.3 |
| 39 | North Dakota | 5.7 | | 34 | Arizona | 6.1 |
| 24 | Ohio | 7.7 | | 34 | Nebraska | 6.1 |
| 13 | Oklahoma | 9.3 | | 34 | South Dakota | 6.1 |
| 19 | Oregon | 8.6 | | 37 | Delaware | 5.9 |
| 18 | Pennsylvania | 8.7 | | 38 | Indiana | 5.8 |
| 19 | Rhode Island | 8.6 | | 39 | Massachusetts | 5.7 |
| 12 | South Carolina | 9.4 | | 39 | North Dakota | 5.7 |
| 34 | South Dakota | 6.1 | | 41 | Minnesota | 5.4 |
| 7 | Tennessee | 11.0 | | 41 | Wyoming | 5.4 |
| 21 | Texas | 8.5 | | 43 | Idaho | 5.3 |
| 46 | Utah | 5.2 | | 43 | Iowa | 5.3 |
| 13 | Vermont | 9.3 | | 43 | Kansas | 5.3 |
| 31 | Virginia | 6.6 | | 46 | Colorado | 5.2 |
| 27 | Washington | 7.4 | | 46 | Utah | 5.2 |
| 1 | West Virginia | 15.4 | | 48 | Nevada | 4.8 |
| 50 | Wisconsin | 3.8 | | 49 | New Hampshire | 4.1 |
| 41 | Wyoming | 5.4 | | 50 | Wisconsin | 3.8 |

District of Columbia     16.8

Source: Morgan Quitno Press using data from U.S. Department of Agriculture, Food, Nutrition and Consumer Services
"Food Stamp Program: Number of Households Participating" (http://www.fns.usda.gov/pd/fsfyhh.htm)
*For fiscal year 1998. National percent excludes households in U.S. territories.

# Average Monthly Participants in Women, Infants and Children (WIC) Special Nutrition Program in 2000
## National Total = 7,196,675 Participants*

ALPHA ORDER

| RANK | STATE | PARTICIPANTS | % of USA |
|---|---|---|---|
| 23 | Alabama | 103,930 | 1.4% |
| 41 | Alaska | 24,395 | 0.3% |
| 13 | Arizona | 145,391 | 2.0% |
| 29 | Arkansas | 82,131 | 1.1% |
| 1 | California | 1,219,430 | 16.9% |
| 30 | Colorado | 71,967 | 1.0% |
| 34 | Connecticut | 56,522 | 0.8% |
| 48 | Delaware | 15,816 | 0.2% |
| 4 | Florida | 296,138 | 4.1% |
| 8 | Georgia | 215,792 | 3.0% |
| 39 | Hawaii | 32,080 | 0.4% |
| 40 | Idaho | 31,286 | 0.4% |
| 5 | Illinois | 243,655 | 3.4% |
| 18 | Indiana | 120,590 | 1.7% |
| 31 | Iowa | 60,793 | 0.8% |
| 35 | Kansas | 52,948 | 0.7% |
| 20 | Kentucky | 112,150 | 1.6% |
| 14 | Louisiana | 130,042 | 1.8% |
| 42 | Maine | 21,822 | 0.3% |
| 26 | Maryland | 94,242 | 1.3% |
| 19 | Massachusetts | 114,100 | 1.6% |
| 9 | Michigan | 212,661 | 3.0% |
| 27 | Minnesota | 90,092 | 1.3% |
| 25 | Mississippi | 95,836 | 1.3% |
| 17 | Missouri | 123,738 | 1.7% |
| 44 | Montana | 21,281 | 0.3% |
| 38 | Nebraska | 32,841 | 0.5% |
| 37 | Nevada | 38,755 | 0.5% |
| 46 | New Hampshire | 17,049 | 0.2% |
| 16 | New Jersey | 127,012 | 1.8% |
| 32 | New Mexico | 57,804 | 0.8% |
| 3 | New York | 466,784 | 6.5% |
| 10 | North Carolina | 190,271 | 2.6% |
| 49 | North Dakota | 14,303 | 0.2% |
| 6 | Ohio | 242,667 | 3.4% |
| 21 | Oklahoma | 108,375 | 1.5% |
| 28 | Oregon | 86,113 | 1.2% |
| 7 | Pennsylvania | 231,642 | 3.2% |
| 43 | Rhode Island | 21,312 | 0.3% |
| 22 | South Carolina | 108,204 | 1.5% |
| 45 | South Dakota | 20,417 | 0.3% |
| 11 | Tennessee | 148,662 | 2.1% |
| 2 | Texas | 737,206 | 10.2% |
| 33 | Utah | 57,460 | 0.8% |
| 47 | Vermont | 16,401 | 0.2% |
| 15 | Virginia | 128,484 | 1.8% |
| 12 | Washington | 145,862 | 2.0% |
| 36 | West Virginia | 50,893 | 0.7% |
| 24 | Wisconsin | 100,427 | 1.4% |
| 50 | Wyoming | 10,907 | 0.2% |

RANK ORDER

| RANK | STATE | PARTICIPANTS | % of USA |
|---|---|---|---|
| 1 | California | 1,219,430 | 16.9% |
| 2 | Texas | 737,206 | 10.2% |
| 3 | New York | 466,784 | 6.5% |
| 4 | Florida | 296,138 | 4.1% |
| 5 | Illinois | 243,655 | 3.4% |
| 6 | Ohio | 242,667 | 3.4% |
| 7 | Pennsylvania | 231,642 | 3.2% |
| 8 | Georgia | 215,792 | 3.0% |
| 9 | Michigan | 212,661 | 3.0% |
| 10 | North Carolina | 190,271 | 2.6% |
| 11 | Tennessee | 148,662 | 2.1% |
| 12 | Washington | 145,862 | 2.0% |
| 13 | Arizona | 145,391 | 2.0% |
| 14 | Louisiana | 130,042 | 1.8% |
| 15 | Virginia | 128,484 | 1.8% |
| 16 | New Jersey | 127,012 | 1.8% |
| 17 | Missouri | 123,738 | 1.7% |
| 18 | Indiana | 120,590 | 1.7% |
| 19 | Massachusetts | 114,100 | 1.6% |
| 20 | Kentucky | 112,150 | 1.6% |
| 21 | Oklahoma | 108,375 | 1.5% |
| 22 | South Carolina | 108,204 | 1.5% |
| 23 | Alabama | 103,930 | 1.4% |
| 24 | Wisconsin | 100,427 | 1.4% |
| 25 | Mississippi | 95,836 | 1.3% |
| 26 | Maryland | 94,242 | 1.3% |
| 27 | Minnesota | 90,092 | 1.3% |
| 28 | Oregon | 86,113 | 1.2% |
| 29 | Arkansas | 82,131 | 1.1% |
| 30 | Colorado | 71,967 | 1.0% |
| 31 | Iowa | 60,793 | 0.8% |
| 32 | New Mexico | 57,804 | 0.8% |
| 33 | Utah | 57,460 | 0.8% |
| 34 | Connecticut | 56,522 | 0.8% |
| 35 | Kansas | 52,948 | 0.7% |
| 36 | West Virginia | 50,893 | 0.7% |
| 37 | Nevada | 38,755 | 0.5% |
| 38 | Nebraska | 32,841 | 0.5% |
| 39 | Hawaii | 32,080 | 0.4% |
| 40 | Idaho | 31,286 | 0.4% |
| 41 | Alaska | 24,395 | 0.3% |
| 42 | Maine | 21,822 | 0.3% |
| 43 | Rhode Island | 21,312 | 0.3% |
| 44 | Montana | 21,281 | 0.3% |
| 45 | South Dakota | 20,417 | 0.3% |
| 46 | New Hampshire | 17,049 | 0.2% |
| 47 | Vermont | 16,401 | 0.2% |
| 48 | Delaware | 15,816 | 0.2% |
| 49 | North Dakota | 14,303 | 0.2% |
| 50 | Wyoming | 10,907 | 0.2% |
| | District of Columbia | 15,056 | 0.2% |

Source: U.S. Department of Agriculture, Food, Nutrition and Consumer Services
    "WIC Program: Total Participation" (http://www.fns.usda.gov/pd/wifypart.htm)
*Preliminary data for fiscal year 2000. National average includes outlying areas not shown separately (Puerto Rico has 214,134 participants).

# Average Monthly Benefit per Participant for Women, Infant and Children (WIC) Special Nutrition Program in 2000
## National Monthly Average = $32.91*

ALPHA ORDER

| RANK | STATE | AVERAGE BENEFIT |
|------|-------|-----------------|
| 4 | Alabama | $37.11 |
| 2 | Alaska | 39.44 |
| 13 | Arizona | 34.52 |
| 27 | Arkansas | 31.89 |
| 14 | California | 33.87 |
| 31 | Colorado | 31.03 |
| 12 | Connecticut | 34.82 |
| 30 | Delaware | 31.12 |
| 3 | Florida | 37.44 |
| 37 | Georgia | 30.33 |
| 1 | Hawaii | 46.95 |
| 42 | Idaho | 29.60 |
| 11 | Illinois | 35.31 |
| 23 | Indiana | 32.13 |
| 47 | Iowa | 28.25 |
| 44 | Kansas | 29.46 |
| 19 | Kentucky | 33.02 |
| 7 | Louisiana | 35.72 |
| 48 | Maine | 26.87 |
| 32 | Maryland | 30.88 |
| 45 | Massachusetts | 29.38 |
| 18 | Michigan | 33.25 |
| 38 | Minnesota | 30.04 |
| 8 | Mississippi | 35.64 |
| 43 | Missouri | 29.59 |
| 20 | Montana | 32.66 |
| 21 | Nebraska | 32.36 |
| 41 | Nevada | 29.72 |
| 49 | New Hampshire | 26.18 |
| 28 | New Jersey | 31.86 |
| 24 | New Mexico | 32.09 |
| 6 | New York | 35.77 |
| 40 | North Carolina | 29.74 |
| 5 | North Dakota | 36.30 |
| 39 | Ohio | 29.77 |
| 46 | Oklahoma | 28.78 |
| 29 | Oregon | 31.19 |
| 26 | Pennsylvania | 31.97 |
| 25 | Rhode Island | 32.08 |
| 17 | South Carolina | 33.32 |
| 36 | South Dakota | 30.46 |
| 9 | Tennessee | 35.56 |
| 50 | Texas | 26.12 |
| 33 | Utah | 30.60 |
| 16 | Vermont | 33.36 |
| 15 | Virginia | 33.75 |
| 10 | Washington | 35.45 |
| 34 | West Virginia | 30.57 |
| 22 | Wisconsin | 32.26 |
| 34 | Wyoming | 30.57 |

RANK ORDER

| RANK | STATE | AVERAGE BENEFIT |
|------|-------|-----------------|
| 1 | Hawaii | $46.95 |
| 2 | Alaska | 39.44 |
| 3 | Florida | 37.44 |
| 4 | Alabama | 37.11 |
| 5 | North Dakota | 36.30 |
| 6 | New York | 35.77 |
| 7 | Louisiana | 35.72 |
| 8 | Mississippi | 35.64 |
| 9 | Tennessee | 35.56 |
| 10 | Washington | 35.45 |
| 11 | Illinois | 35.31 |
| 12 | Connecticut | 34.82 |
| 13 | Arizona | 34.52 |
| 14 | California | 33.87 |
| 15 | Virginia | 33.75 |
| 16 | Vermont | 33.36 |
| 17 | South Carolina | 33.32 |
| 18 | Michigan | 33.25 |
| 19 | Kentucky | 33.02 |
| 20 | Montana | 32.66 |
| 21 | Nebraska | 32.36 |
| 22 | Wisconsin | 32.26 |
| 23 | Indiana | 32.13 |
| 24 | New Mexico | 32.09 |
| 25 | Rhode Island | 32.08 |
| 26 | Pennsylvania | 31.97 |
| 27 | Arkansas | 31.89 |
| 28 | New Jersey | 31.86 |
| 29 | Oregon | 31.19 |
| 30 | Delaware | 31.12 |
| 31 | Colorado | 31.03 |
| 32 | Maryland | 30.88 |
| 33 | Utah | 30.60 |
| 34 | West Virginia | 30.57 |
| 34 | Wyoming | 30.57 |
| 36 | South Dakota | 30.46 |
| 37 | Georgia | 30.33 |
| 38 | Minnesota | 30.04 |
| 39 | Ohio | 29.77 |
| 40 | North Carolina | 29.74 |
| 41 | Nevada | 29.72 |
| 42 | Idaho | 29.60 |
| 43 | Missouri | 29.59 |
| 44 | Kansas | 29.46 |
| 45 | Massachusetts | 29.38 |
| 46 | Oklahoma | 28.78 |
| 47 | Iowa | 28.25 |
| 48 | Maine | 26.87 |
| 49 | New Hampshire | 26.18 |
| 50 | Texas | 26.12 |
| | District of Columbia | 34.46 |

*Source: U.S. Department of Agriculture, Food, Nutrition and Consumer Services*
   *"WIC Program: Average Benefit per Person per Month" (http://www.fns.usda.gov/pd/wifyavg.htm)*
*\*Preliminary data for fiscal year 2000. National average includes outlying areas and Indian reservations not shown separately.*

# Percent of Public Elementary and Secondary
## Students Eligible for Free Lunch in 1999
## National Average = 37.0% of Students*

| RANK | STATE | PERCENT |
|------|-------|---------|
| 9 | Alabama | 45.1 |
| 35 | Alaska | 25.6 |
| NA | Arizona** | NA |
| 9 | Arkansas | 45.1 |
| 5 | California | 47.4 |
| 40 | Colorado | 20.9 |
| 38 | Connecticut | 24.9 |
| 17 | Delaware | 33.7 |
| 12 | Florida | 43.9 |
| 13 | Georgia | 43.3 |
| 15 | Hawaii | 38.0 |
| 22 | Idaho | 31.9 |
| NA | Illinois** | NA |
| 33 | Indiana | 27.4 |
| 31 | Iowa | 27.6 |
| 21 | Kansas | 32.4 |
| 5 | Kentucky | 47.4 |
| 2 | Louisiana | 57.4 |
| 23 | Maine | 30.9 |
| 25 | Maryland | 30.5 |
| 41 | Massachusetts | 20.7 |
| 37 | Michigan | 25.0 |
| 43 | Minnesota | 18.7 |
| 1 | Mississippi | 63.4 |
| 20 | Missouri | 32.7 |
| 24 | Montana | 30.6 |
| 28 | Nebraska | 29.6 |
| 32 | Nevada | 27.5 |
| 44 | New Hampshire | 11.2 |
| 39 | New Jersey | 23.5 |
| 4 | New Mexico | 48.9 |
| 16 | New York | 37.1 |
| 14 | North Carolina | 38.4 |
| 41 | North Dakota | 20.7 |
| 34 | Ohio | 26.5 |
| 8 | Oklahoma | 45.8 |
| 18 | Oregon | 32.8 |
| NA | Pennsylvania** | NA |
| 18 | Rhode Island | 32.8 |
| 7 | South Carolina | 46.0 |
| 26 | South Dakota | 30.2 |
| NA | Tennessee** | NA |
| 11 | Texas | 45.0 |
| 30 | Utah | 28.0 |
| NA | Vermont** | NA |
| 27 | Virginia | 30.0 |
| NA | Washington** | NA |
| 3 | West Virginia | 49.4 |
| 36 | Wisconsin | 25.5 |
| 29 | Wyoming | 28.1 |

| RANK | STATE | PERCENT |
|------|-------|---------|
| 1 | Mississippi | 63.4 |
| 2 | Louisiana | 57.4 |
| 3 | West Virginia | 49.4 |
| 4 | New Mexico | 48.9 |
| 5 | California | 47.4 |
| 5 | Kentucky | 47.4 |
| 7 | South Carolina | 46.0 |
| 8 | Oklahoma | 45.8 |
| 9 | Alabama | 45.1 |
| 9 | Arkansas | 45.1 |
| 11 | Texas | 45.0 |
| 12 | Florida | 43.9 |
| 13 | Georgia | 43.3 |
| 14 | North Carolina | 38.4 |
| 15 | Hawaii | 38.0 |
| 16 | New York | 37.1 |
| 17 | Delaware | 33.7 |
| 18 | Oregon | 32.8 |
| 18 | Rhode Island | 32.8 |
| 20 | Missouri | 32.7 |
| 21 | Kansas | 32.4 |
| 22 | Idaho | 31.9 |
| 23 | Maine | 30.9 |
| 24 | Montana | 30.6 |
| 25 | Maryland | 30.5 |
| 26 | South Dakota | 30.2 |
| 27 | Virginia | 30.0 |
| 28 | Nebraska | 29.6 |
| 29 | Wyoming | 28.1 |
| 30 | Utah | 28.0 |
| 31 | Iowa | 27.6 |
| 32 | Nevada | 27.5 |
| 33 | Indiana | 27.4 |
| 34 | Ohio | 26.5 |
| 35 | Alaska | 25.6 |
| 36 | Wisconsin | 25.5 |
| 37 | Michigan | 25.0 |
| 38 | Connecticut | 24.9 |
| 39 | New Jersey | 23.5 |
| 40 | Colorado | 20.9 |
| 41 | Massachusetts | 20.7 |
| 41 | North Dakota | 20.7 |
| 43 | Minnesota | 18.7 |
| 44 | New Hampshire | 11.2 |
| NA | Arizona** | NA |
| NA | Illinois** | NA |
| NA | Pennsylvania** | NA |
| NA | Tennessee** | NA |
| NA | Vermont** | NA |
| NA | Washington** | NA |
| | District of Columbia** | NA |

Source: U.S. Department of Education, National Center for Education Statistics
    "Overview of Public Elementary and Secondary Schools and Districts" (June 2000)
*National figure is based only on reporting states. For school year 1998-99.
**Not available.

# Child Support Collections in 1999

## National Total = $15,646,954,647*

ALPHA ORDER

| RANK | STATE | COLLECTIONS | % of USA |
|---|---|---|---|
| 25 | Alabama | $185,929,914 | 1.2% |
| 39 | Alaska | 67,131,846 | 0.4% |
| 28 | Arizona | 169,232,529 | 1.1% |
| 33 | Arkansas | 108,480,840 | 0.7% |
| 1 | California | 1,604,173,701 | 10.3% |
| 29 | Colorado | 163,546,023 | 1.0% |
| 26 | Connecticut | 175,487,270 | 1.1% |
| 43 | Delaware | 44,962,003 | 0.3% |
| 8 | Florida | 579,827,499 | 3.7% |
| 14 | Georgia | 330,631,555 | 2.1% |
| 42 | Hawaii | 60,520,055 | 0.4% |
| 41 | Idaho | 64,268,499 | 0.4% |
| 15 | Illinois | 325,562,478 | 2.1% |
| 19 | Indiana | 271,110,248 | 1.7% |
| 23 | Iowa | 201,219,305 | 1.3% |
| 30 | Kansas | 137,981,151 | 0.9% |
| 22 | Kentucky | 206,241,206 | 1.3% |
| 24 | Louisiana | 188,131,410 | 1.2% |
| 38 | Maine | 80,663,945 | 0.5% |
| 12 | Maryland | 350,165,942 | 2.2% |
| 17 | Massachusetts | 291,485,832 | 1.9% |
| 3 | Michigan | 1,274,637,793 | 8.1% |
| 11 | Minnesota | 384,847,451 | 2.5% |
| 31 | Mississippi | 128,877,572 | 0.8% |
| 18 | Missouri | 285,818,836 | 1.8% |
| 48 | Montana | 38,221,855 | 0.2% |
| 32 | Nebraska | 110,565,311 | 0.7% |
| 37 | Nevada | 92,121,885 | 0.6% |
| 40 | New Hampshire | 66,166,127 | 0.4% |
| 7 | New Jersey | 635,116,977 | 4.1% |
| 49 | New Mexico | 34,894,675 | 0.2% |
| 5 | New York | 909,755,049 | 5.8% |
| 13 | North Carolina | 347,969,980 | 2.2% |
| 45 | North Dakota | 40,878,761 | 0.3% |
| 2 | Ohio | 1,301,311,021 | 8.3% |
| 35 | Oklahoma | 96,191,903 | 0.6% |
| 20 | Oregon | 231,875,332 | 1.5% |
| 4 | Pennsylvania | 1,107,687,051 | 7.1% |
| 44 | Rhode Island | 44,304,705 | 0.3% |
| 27 | South Carolina | 173,756,503 | 1.1% |
| 47 | South Dakota | 38,323,366 | 0.2% |
| 21 | Tennessee | 224,245,130 | 1.4% |
| 6 | Texas | 802,911,218 | 5.1% |
| 34 | Utah | 107,336,206 | 0.7% |
| 50 | Vermont | 34,880,355 | 0.2% |
| 16 | Virginia | 312,776,989 | 2.0% |
| 10 | Washington | 515,859,493 | 3.3% |
| 36 | West Virginia | 92,767,171 | 0.6% |
| 9 | Wisconsin | 532,502,415 | 3.4% |
| 46 | Wyoming | 38,462,270 | 0.2% |

RANK ORDER

| RANK | STATE | COLLECTIONS | % of USA |
|---|---|---|---|
| 1 | California | $1,604,173,701 | 10.3% |
| 2 | Ohio | 1,301,311,021 | 8.3% |
| 3 | Michigan | 1,274,637,793 | 8.1% |
| 4 | Pennsylvania | 1,107,687,051 | 7.1% |
| 5 | New York | 909,755,049 | 5.8% |
| 6 | Texas | 802,911,218 | 5.1% |
| 7 | New Jersey | 635,116,977 | 4.1% |
| 8 | Florida | 579,827,499 | 3.7% |
| 9 | Wisconsin | 532,502,415 | 3.4% |
| 10 | Washington | 515,859,493 | 3.3% |
| 11 | Minnesota | 384,847,451 | 2.5% |
| 12 | Maryland | 350,165,942 | 2.2% |
| 13 | North Carolina | 347,969,980 | 2.2% |
| 14 | Georgia | 330,631,555 | 2.1% |
| 15 | Illinois | 325,562,478 | 2.1% |
| 16 | Virginia | 312,776,989 | 2.0% |
| 17 | Massachusetts | 291,485,832 | 1.9% |
| 18 | Missouri | 285,818,836 | 1.8% |
| 19 | Indiana | 271,110,248 | 1.7% |
| 20 | Oregon | 231,875,332 | 1.5% |
| 21 | Tennessee | 224,245,130 | 1.4% |
| 22 | Kentucky | 206,241,206 | 1.3% |
| 23 | Iowa | 201,219,305 | 1.3% |
| 24 | Louisiana | 188,131,410 | 1.2% |
| 25 | Alabama | 185,929,914 | 1.2% |
| 26 | Connecticut | 175,487,270 | 1.1% |
| 27 | South Carolina | 173,756,503 | 1.1% |
| 28 | Arizona | 169,232,529 | 1.1% |
| 29 | Colorado | 163,546,023 | 1.0% |
| 30 | Kansas | 137,981,151 | 0.9% |
| 31 | Mississippi | 128,877,572 | 0.8% |
| 32 | Nebraska | 110,565,311 | 0.7% |
| 33 | Arkansas | 108,480,840 | 0.7% |
| 34 | Utah | 107,336,206 | 0.7% |
| 35 | Oklahoma | 96,191,903 | 0.6% |
| 36 | West Virginia | 92,767,171 | 0.6% |
| 37 | Nevada | 92,121,885 | 0.6% |
| 38 | Maine | 80,663,945 | 0.5% |
| 39 | Alaska | 67,131,846 | 0.4% |
| 40 | New Hampshire | 66,166,127 | 0.4% |
| 41 | Idaho | 64,268,499 | 0.4% |
| 42 | Hawaii | 60,520,055 | 0.4% |
| 43 | Delaware | 44,962,003 | 0.3% |
| 44 | Rhode Island | 44,304,705 | 0.3% |
| 45 | North Dakota | 40,878,761 | 0.3% |
| 46 | Wyoming | 38,462,270 | 0.2% |
| 47 | South Dakota | 38,323,366 | 0.2% |
| 48 | Montana | 38,221,855 | 0.2% |
| 49 | New Mexico | 34,894,675 | 0.2% |
| 50 | Vermont | 34,880,355 | 0.2% |
|  | District of Columbia | 35,137,996 | 0.2% |

Source: U.S. Department of Health and Human Services, Office of Child Support Enforcement
"Temporary Assistance for Needy Families (TANF) Program, 3rd Annual Report to Congress" (August 2000)
(http://www.acf.dhhs.gov/programs/opre/annual3.pdf)
*Preliminary figures for fiscal year 1999. Total does not include $179,824,004 collected in U.S. territories.

# Cost Effectiveness of Child Support Collection Efforts in 1999

## National Average = $3.92 Collected for Every Dollar of Administrative Expense

ALPHA ORDER

| RANK | STATE | RATE |
|------|-------|------|
| 31 | Alabama | $3.47 |
| 28 | Alaska | 3.74 |
| 43 | Arizona | 2.88 |
| 41 | Arkansas | 2.95 |
| 46 | California | 2.61 |
| 36 | Colorado | 3.15 |
| 12 | Connecticut | 4.55 |
| 47 | Delaware | 2.47 |
| 37 | Florida | 3.04 |
| 29 | Georgia | 3.67 |
| 39 | Hawaii | 3.01 |
| 3 | Idaho | 6.13 |
| 49 | Illinois | 2.34 |
| 2 | Indiana | 7.03 |
| 10 | Iowa | 4.72 |
| 44 | Kansas | 2.78 |
| 29 | Kentucky | 3.67 |
| 23 | Louisiana | 3.97 |
| 15 | Maine | 4.33 |
| 18 | Maryland | 4.24 |
| 26 | Massachusetts | 3.88 |
| 1 | Michigan | 7.75 |
| 33 | Minnesota | 3.40 |
| 19 | Mississippi | 4.21 |
| 38 | Missouri | 3.03 |
| 34 | Montana | 3.28 |
| 32 | Nebraska | 3.45 |
| 48 | Nevada | 2.42 |
| 25 | New Hampshire | 3.91 |
| 11 | New Jersey | 4.56 |
| 50 | New Mexico | 1.08 |
| 17 | New York | 4.27 |
| 45 | North Carolina | 2.67 |
| 21 | North Dakota | 4.11 |
| 8 | Ohio | 4.74 |
| 40 | Oklahoma | 2.98 |
| 7 | Oregon | 5.48 |
| 4 | Pennsylvania | 6.04 |
| 22 | Rhode Island | 4.06 |
| 8 | South Carolina | 4.74 |
| 5 | South Dakota | 5.85 |
| 16 | Tennessee | 4.30 |
| 24 | Texas | 3.96 |
| 41 | Utah | 2.95 |
| 27 | Vermont | 3.86 |
| 20 | Virginia | 4.13 |
| 14 | Washington | 4.37 |
| 35 | West Virginia | 3.24 |
| 6 | Wisconsin | 5.51 |
| 13 | Wyoming | 4.39 |

RANK ORDER

| RANK | STATE | RATE |
|------|-------|------|
| 1 | Michigan | $7.75 |
| 2 | Indiana | 7.03 |
| 3 | Idaho | 6.13 |
| 4 | Pennsylvania | 6.04 |
| 5 | South Dakota | 5.85 |
| 6 | Wisconsin | 5.51 |
| 7 | Oregon | 5.48 |
| 8 | Ohio | 4.74 |
| 8 | South Carolina | 4.74 |
| 10 | Iowa | 4.72 |
| 11 | New Jersey | 4.56 |
| 12 | Connecticut | 4.55 |
| 13 | Wyoming | 4.39 |
| 14 | Washington | 4.37 |
| 15 | Maine | 4.33 |
| 16 | Tennessee | 4.30 |
| 17 | New York | 4.27 |
| 18 | Maryland | 4.24 |
| 19 | Mississippi | 4.21 |
| 20 | Virginia | 4.13 |
| 21 | North Dakota | 4.11 |
| 22 | Rhode Island | 4.06 |
| 23 | Louisiana | 3.97 |
| 24 | Texas | 3.96 |
| 25 | New Hampshire | 3.91 |
| 26 | Massachusetts | 3.88 |
| 27 | Vermont | 3.86 |
| 28 | Alaska | 3.74 |
| 29 | Georgia | 3.67 |
| 29 | Kentucky | 3.67 |
| 31 | Alabama | 3.47 |
| 32 | Nebraska | 3.45 |
| 33 | Minnesota | 3.40 |
| 34 | Montana | 3.28 |
| 35 | West Virginia | 3.24 |
| 36 | Colorado | 3.15 |
| 37 | Florida | 3.04 |
| 38 | Missouri | 3.03 |
| 39 | Hawaii | 3.01 |
| 40 | Oklahoma | 2.98 |
| 41 | Arkansas | 2.95 |
| 41 | Utah | 2.95 |
| 43 | Arizona | 2.88 |
| 44 | Kansas | 2.78 |
| 45 | North Carolina | 2.67 |
| 46 | California | 2.61 |
| 47 | Delaware | 2.47 |
| 48 | Nevada | 2.42 |
| 49 | Illinois | 2.34 |
| 50 | New Mexico | 1.08 |
|  | District of Columbia | 2.65 |

*Source: U.S. Department of Health and Human Services, Office of Child Support Enforcement*
*"Preliminary FY 99 Box Scores by State" (http://www.acf.dhhs.gov/programs/cse/rpt/00report/state.html)*

# XV. TRANSPORTATION

# Federal Highway Funds in 2001

## National Total = $30,310,431,174*

ALPHA ORDER

| RANK | STATE | FUNDING | % of USA |
|------|-------|---------|----------|
| 16 | Alabama | $610,411,345 | 2.0% |
| 32 | Alaska | 352,076,763 | 1.2% |
| 21 | Arizona | 514,366,207 | 1.7% |
| 28 | Arkansas | 396,226,924 | 1.3% |
| 1 | California | 2,750,797,243 | 9.1% |
| 33 | Colorado | 351,715,554 | 1.2% |
| 26 | Connecticut | 449,902,827 | 1.5% |
| 50 | Delaware | 130,189,364 | 0.4% |
| 5 | Florida | 1,429,342,313 | 4.7% |
| 6 | Georgia | 1,057,750,028 | 3.5% |
| 48 | Hawaii | 155,218,394 | 0.5% |
| 40 | Idaho | 232,303,432 | 0.8% |
| 8 | Illinois | 1,005,508,965 | 3.3% |
| 13 | Indiana | 735,050,584 | 2.4% |
| 31 | Iowa | 360,387,309 | 1.2% |
| 34 | Kansas | 347,950,317 | 1.1% |
| 19 | Kentucky | 540,877,466 | 1.8% |
| 23 | Louisiana | 480,223,432 | 1.6% |
| 46 | Maine | 159,596,873 | 0.5% |
| 24 | Maryland | 476,906,536 | 1.6% |
| 18 | Massachusetts | 555,337,488 | 1.8% |
| 9 | Michigan | 971,423,085 | 3.2% |
| 27 | Minnesota | 445,070,351 | 1.5% |
| 29 | Mississippi | 383,894,783 | 1.3% |
| 14 | Missouri | 714,842,504 | 2.4% |
| 36 | Montana | 292,072,656 | 1.0% |
| 39 | Nebraska | 232,902,547 | 0.8% |
| 41 | Nevada | 217,311,749 | 0.7% |
| 47 | New Hampshire | 155,698,642 | 0.5% |
| 11 | New Jersey | 802,585,747 | 2.6% |
| 37 | New Mexico | 290,364,235 | 1.0% |
| 3 | New York | 1,538,938,402 | 5.1% |
| 10 | North Carolina | 848,439,274 | 2.8% |
| 44 | North Dakota | 194,375,781 | 0.6% |
| 7 | Ohio | 1,018,382,042 | 3.4% |
| 25 | Oklahoma | 463,197,165 | 1.5% |
| 30 | Oregon | 367,383,935 | 1.2% |
| 4 | Pennsylvania | 1,513,727,262 | 5.0% |
| 45 | Rhode Island | 178,271,067 | 0.6% |
| 22 | South Carolina | 504,926,420 | 1.7% |
| 42 | South Dakota | 216,529,512 | 0.7% |
| 15 | Tennessee | 680,197,484 | 2.2% |
| 2 | Texas | 2,260,214,363 | 7.5% |
| 38 | Utah | 234,791,432 | 0.8% |
| 49 | Vermont | 134,709,782 | 0.4% |
| 12 | Virginia | 771,832,403 | 2.5% |
| 20 | Washington | 535,933,706 | 1.8% |
| 35 | West Virginia | 335,505,747 | 1.1% |
| 17 | Wisconsin | 591,491,139 | 2.0% |
| 43 | Wyoming | 204,668,595 | 0.7% |

RANK ORDER

| RANK | STATE | FUNDING | % of USA |
|------|-------|---------|----------|
| 1 | California | $2,750,797,243 | 9.1% |
| 2 | Texas | 2,260,214,363 | 7.5% |
| 3 | New York | 1,538,938,402 | 5.1% |
| 4 | Pennsylvania | 1,513,727,262 | 5.0% |
| 5 | Florida | 1,429,342,313 | 4.7% |
| 6 | Georgia | 1,057,750,028 | 3.5% |
| 7 | Ohio | 1,018,382,042 | 3.4% |
| 8 | Illinois | 1,005,508,965 | 3.3% |
| 9 | Michigan | 971,423,085 | 3.2% |
| 10 | North Carolina | 848,439,274 | 2.8% |
| 11 | New Jersey | 802,585,747 | 2.6% |
| 12 | Virginia | 771,832,403 | 2.5% |
| 13 | Indiana | 735,050,584 | 2.4% |
| 14 | Missouri | 714,842,504 | 2.4% |
| 15 | Tennessee | 680,197,484 | 2.2% |
| 16 | Alabama | 610,411,345 | 2.0% |
| 17 | Wisconsin | 591,491,139 | 2.0% |
| 18 | Massachusetts | 555,337,488 | 1.8% |
| 19 | Kentucky | 540,877,466 | 1.8% |
| 20 | Washington | 535,933,706 | 1.8% |
| 21 | Arizona | 514,366,207 | 1.7% |
| 22 | South Carolina | 504,926,420 | 1.7% |
| 23 | Louisiana | 480,223,432 | 1.6% |
| 24 | Maryland | 476,906,536 | 1.6% |
| 25 | Oklahoma | 463,197,165 | 1.5% |
| 26 | Connecticut | 449,902,827 | 1.5% |
| 27 | Minnesota | 445,070,351 | 1.5% |
| 28 | Arkansas | 396,226,924 | 1.3% |
| 29 | Mississippi | 383,894,783 | 1.3% |
| 30 | Oregon | 367,383,935 | 1.2% |
| 31 | Iowa | 360,387,309 | 1.2% |
| 32 | Alaska | 352,076,763 | 1.2% |
| 33 | Colorado | 351,715,554 | 1.2% |
| 34 | Kansas | 347,950,317 | 1.1% |
| 35 | West Virginia | 335,505,747 | 1.1% |
| 36 | Montana | 292,072,656 | 1.0% |
| 37 | New Mexico | 290,364,235 | 1.0% |
| 38 | Utah | 234,791,432 | 0.8% |
| 39 | Nebraska | 232,902,547 | 0.8% |
| 40 | Idaho | 232,303,432 | 0.8% |
| 41 | Nevada | 217,311,749 | 0.7% |
| 42 | South Dakota | 216,529,512 | 0.7% |
| 43 | Wyoming | 204,668,595 | 0.7% |
| 44 | North Dakota | 194,375,781 | 0.6% |
| 45 | Rhode Island | 178,271,067 | 0.6% |
| 46 | Maine | 159,596,873 | 0.5% |
| 47 | New Hampshire | 155,698,642 | 0.5% |
| 48 | Hawaii | 155,218,394 | 0.5% |
| 49 | Vermont | 134,709,782 | 0.4% |
| 50 | Delaware | 130,189,364 | 0.4% |
| | District of Columbia | 118,610,000 | 0.4% |

Source: U.S. Department of Transportation, Federal Highway Administration
   "TEA-21 Funding Tables" (http://www.fhwa.dot.gov/tea21/funding.htm)
*Fiscal Year 2001 apportionments.

# Per Capita Federal Highway Funds in 2001

## National Per Capita = $108*

ALPHA ORDER

| RANK | STATE | PER CAPITA |
|------|-------|-----------|
| 13 | Alabama | $137 |
| 1 | Alaska | 562 |
| 38 | Arizona | 100 |
| 12 | Arkansas | 148 |
| 48 | California | 81 |
| 47 | Colorado | 82 |
| 18 | Connecticut | 132 |
| 10 | Delaware | 166 |
| 45 | Florida | 89 |
| 19 | Georgia | 129 |
| 21 | Hawaii | 128 |
| 8 | Idaho | 180 |
| 48 | Illinois | 81 |
| 28 | Indiana | 121 |
| 26 | Iowa | 123 |
| 19 | Kansas | 129 |
| 16 | Kentucky | 134 |
| 34 | Louisiana | 107 |
| 25 | Maine | 125 |
| 42 | Maryland | 90 |
| 46 | Massachusetts | 87 |
| 39 | Michigan | 98 |
| 42 | Minnesota | 90 |
| 15 | Mississippi | 135 |
| 21 | Missouri | 128 |
| 3 | Montana | 324 |
| 14 | Nebraska | 136 |
| 31 | Nevada | 109 |
| 23 | New Hampshire | 126 |
| 40 | New Jersey | 95 |
| 11 | New Mexico | 160 |
| 48 | New York | 81 |
| 36 | North Carolina | 105 |
| 4 | North Dakota | 303 |
| 42 | Ohio | 90 |
| 16 | Oklahoma | 134 |
| 34 | Oregon | 107 |
| 26 | Pennsylvania | 123 |
| 9 | Rhode Island | 170 |
| 23 | South Carolina | 126 |
| 5 | South Dakota | 287 |
| 29 | Tennessee | 120 |
| 33 | Texas | 108 |
| 36 | Utah | 105 |
| 6 | Vermont | 221 |
| 31 | Virginia | 109 |
| 41 | Washington | 91 |
| 7 | West Virginia | 186 |
| 30 | Wisconsin | 110 |
| 2 | Wyoming | 414 |

RANK ORDER

| RANK | STATE | PER CAPITA |
|------|-------|-----------|
| 1 | Alaska | $562 |
| 2 | Wyoming | 414 |
| 3 | Montana | 324 |
| 4 | North Dakota | 303 |
| 5 | South Dakota | 287 |
| 6 | Vermont | 221 |
| 7 | West Virginia | 186 |
| 8 | Idaho | 180 |
| 9 | Rhode Island | 170 |
| 10 | Delaware | 166 |
| 11 | New Mexico | 160 |
| 12 | Arkansas | 148 |
| 13 | Alabama | 137 |
| 14 | Nebraska | 136 |
| 15 | Mississippi | 135 |
| 16 | Kentucky | 134 |
| 16 | Oklahoma | 134 |
| 18 | Connecticut | 132 |
| 19 | Georgia | 129 |
| 19 | Kansas | 129 |
| 21 | Hawaii | 128 |
| 21 | Missouri | 128 |
| 23 | New Hampshire | 126 |
| 23 | South Carolina | 126 |
| 25 | Maine | 125 |
| 26 | Iowa | 123 |
| 26 | Pennsylvania | 123 |
| 28 | Indiana | 121 |
| 29 | Tennessee | 120 |
| 30 | Wisconsin | 110 |
| 31 | Nevada | 109 |
| 31 | Virginia | 109 |
| 33 | Texas | 108 |
| 34 | Louisiana | 107 |
| 34 | Oregon | 107 |
| 36 | North Carolina | 105 |
| 36 | Utah | 105 |
| 38 | Arizona | 100 |
| 39 | Michigan | 98 |
| 40 | New Jersey | 95 |
| 41 | Washington | 91 |
| 42 | Maryland | 90 |
| 42 | Minnesota | 90 |
| 42 | Ohio | 90 |
| 45 | Florida | 89 |
| 46 | Massachusetts | 87 |
| 47 | Colorado | 82 |
| 48 | California | 81 |
| 48 | Illinois | 81 |
| 48 | New York | 81 |

District of Columbia 207

Source: Morgan Quitno Press using data from U.S. Department of Transportation, Federal Highway Administration
"TEA-21 Funding Tables" (http://www.fhwa.dot.gov/tea21/funding.htm)
*Fiscal Year 2001 funds. Rates calculated with April 2000 population figures.

# Federally-Funded Road and Street Mileage in 1999

## National Total = 955,506 Miles*

ALPHA ORDER

| RANK | STATE | MILES | % of USA |
|---|---|---|---|
| 16 | Alabama | 23,621 | 2.5% |
| 45 | Alaska | 4,235 | 0.4% |
| 33 | Arizona | 12,275 | 1.3% |
| 19 | Arkansas | 21,024 | 2.2% |
| 2 | California | 53,509 | 5.6% |
| 29 | Colorado | 16,681 | 1.7% |
| 44 | Connecticut | 5,795 | 0.6% |
| 50 | Delaware | 1,456 | 0.2% |
| 15 | Florida | 24,077 | 2.5% |
| 9 | Georgia | 30,385 | 3.2% |
| 49 | Hawaii | 1,534 | 0.2% |
| 35 | Idaho | 10,306 | 1.1% |
| 4 | Illinois | 34,169 | 3.6% |
| 17 | Indiana | 22,193 | 2.3% |
| 14 | Iowa | 25,525 | 2.7% |
| 3 | Kansas | 34,230 | 3.6% |
| 32 | Kentucky | 14,486 | 1.5% |
| 30 | Louisiana | 14,618 | 1.5% |
| 43 | Maine | 6,407 | 0.7% |
| 41 | Maryland | 7,454 | 0.8% |
| 34 | Massachusetts | 10,740 | 1.1% |
| 5 | Michigan | 33,229 | 3.5% |
| 6 | Minnesota | 31,479 | 3.3% |
| 20 | Mississippi | 20,894 | 2.2% |
| 8 | Missouri | 30,411 | 3.2% |
| 31 | Montana | 14,607 | 1.5% |
| 22 | Nebraska | 20,330 | 2.1% |
| 42 | Nevada | 6,416 | 0.7% |
| 47 | New Hampshire | 3,300 | 0.3% |
| 38 | New Jersey | 9,822 | 1.0% |
| 37 | New Mexico | 9,933 | 1.0% |
| 13 | New York | 26,092 | 2.7% |
| 21 | North Carolina | 20,597 | 2.2% |
| 25 | North Dakota | 17,982 | 1.9% |
| 10 | Ohio | 27,946 | 2.9% |
| 7 | Oklahoma | 31,244 | 3.3% |
| 26 | Oregon | 17,933 | 1.9% |
| 12 | Pennsylvania | 27,217 | 2.8% |
| 48 | Rhode Island | 1,690 | 0.2% |
| 27 | South Carolina | 17,314 | 1.8% |
| 23 | South Dakota | 19,638 | 2.1% |
| 28 | Tennessee | 16,922 | 1.8% |
| 1 | Texas | 77,908 | 8.2% |
| 39 | Utah | 8,138 | 0.9% |
| 46 | Vermont | 3,856 | 0.4% |
| 18 | Virginia | 21,173 | 2.2% |
| 24 | Washington | 18,800 | 2.0% |
| 36 | West Virginia | 10,239 | 1.1% |
| 11 | Wisconsin | 27,722 | 2.9% |
| 40 | Wyoming | 7,506 | 0.8% |

RANK ORDER

| RANK | STATE | MILES | % of USA |
|---|---|---|---|
| 1 | Texas | 77,908 | 8.2% |
| 2 | California | 53,509 | 5.6% |
| 3 | Kansas | 34,230 | 3.6% |
| 4 | Illinois | 34,169 | 3.6% |
| 5 | Michigan | 33,229 | 3.5% |
| 6 | Minnesota | 31,479 | 3.3% |
| 7 | Oklahoma | 31,244 | 3.3% |
| 8 | Missouri | 30,411 | 3.2% |
| 9 | Georgia | 30,385 | 3.2% |
| 10 | Ohio | 27,946 | 2.9% |
| 11 | Wisconsin | 27,722 | 2.9% |
| 12 | Pennsylvania | 27,217 | 2.8% |
| 13 | New York | 26,092 | 2.7% |
| 14 | Iowa | 25,525 | 2.7% |
| 15 | Florida | 24,077 | 2.5% |
| 16 | Alabama | 23,621 | 2.5% |
| 17 | Indiana | 22,193 | 2.3% |
| 18 | Virginia | 21,173 | 2.2% |
| 19 | Arkansas | 21,024 | 2.2% |
| 20 | Mississippi | 20,894 | 2.2% |
| 21 | North Carolina | 20,597 | 2.2% |
| 22 | Nebraska | 20,330 | 2.1% |
| 23 | South Dakota | 19,638 | 2.1% |
| 24 | Washington | 18,800 | 2.0% |
| 25 | North Dakota | 17,982 | 1.9% |
| 26 | Oregon | 17,933 | 1.9% |
| 27 | South Carolina | 17,314 | 1.8% |
| 28 | Tennessee | 16,922 | 1.8% |
| 29 | Colorado | 16,681 | 1.7% |
| 30 | Louisiana | 14,618 | 1.5% |
| 31 | Montana | 14,607 | 1.5% |
| 32 | Kentucky | 14,486 | 1.5% |
| 33 | Arizona | 12,275 | 1.3% |
| 34 | Massachusetts | 10,740 | 1.1% |
| 35 | Idaho | 10,306 | 1.1% |
| 36 | West Virginia | 10,239 | 1.1% |
| 37 | New Mexico | 9,933 | 1.0% |
| 38 | New Jersey | 9,822 | 1.0% |
| 39 | Utah | 8,138 | 0.9% |
| 40 | Wyoming | 7,506 | 0.8% |
| 41 | Maryland | 7,454 | 0.8% |
| 42 | Nevada | 6,416 | 0.7% |
| 43 | Maine | 6,407 | 0.7% |
| 44 | Connecticut | 5,795 | 0.6% |
| 45 | Alaska | 4,235 | 0.4% |
| 46 | Vermont | 3,856 | 0.4% |
| 47 | New Hampshire | 3,300 | 0.3% |
| 48 | Rhode Island | 1,690 | 0.2% |
| 49 | Hawaii | 1,534 | 0.2% |
| 50 | Delaware | 1,456 | 0.2% |
| | District of Columbia | 448 | 0.0% |

*Source: U.S. Department of Transportation, Federal Highway Administration*
*"Highway Statistics 1999" (Table HM-15, October 2000)*
*Does not include 2,833 federally-funded miles of highway in Puerto Rico.*

# Percent of Public Road and Street Mileage Federally-Funded in 1999

## National Percent = 24.4% of Public Road and Street Mileage*

| ALPHA ORDER | | | | RANK ORDER | | |
|---|---|---|---|---|---|---|
| RANK | STATE | PERCENT | | RANK | STATE | PERCENT |
| 22 | Alabama | 25.1 | | 1 | Hawaii | 36.0 |
| 2 | Alaska | 33.4 | | 2 | Alaska | 33.4 |
| 36 | Arizona | 22.5 | | 3 | California | 32.0 |
| 40 | Arkansas | 21.6 | | 4 | Massachusetts | 30.5 |
| 3 | California | 32.0 | | 5 | Virginia | 30.1 |
| 45 | Colorado | 19.6 | | 6 | Mississippi | 28.5 |
| 10 | Connecticut | 27.9 | | 7 | Maine | 28.3 |
| 21 | Delaware | 25.3 | | 8 | West Virginia | 28.2 |
| 42 | Florida | 20.8 | | 9 | Wyoming | 28.0 |
| 17 | Georgia | 26.7 | | 10 | Connecticut | 27.9 |
| 1 | Hawaii | 36.0 | | 10 | Rhode Island | 27.9 |
| 36 | Idaho | 22.5 | | 12 | Oklahoma | 27.8 |
| 25 | Illinois | 24.7 | | 13 | Michigan | 27.3 |
| 30 | Indiana | 23.7 | | 13 | New Jersey | 27.3 |
| 35 | Iowa | 22.6 | | 15 | Vermont | 27.0 |
| 20 | Kansas | 25.6 | | 16 | Oregon | 26.8 |
| 47 | Kentucky | 19.5 | | 17 | Georgia | 26.7 |
| 27 | Louisiana | 24.0 | | 17 | South Carolina | 26.7 |
| 7 | Maine | 28.3 | | 19 | Texas | 25.9 |
| 26 | Maryland | 24.6 | | 20 | Kansas | 25.6 |
| 4 | Massachusetts | 30.5 | | 21 | Delaware | 25.3 |
| 13 | Michigan | 27.3 | | 22 | Alabama | 25.1 |
| 29 | Minnesota | 23.8 | | 23 | Missouri | 24.8 |
| 6 | Mississippi | 28.5 | | 23 | Wisconsin | 24.8 |
| 23 | Missouri | 24.8 | | 25 | Illinois | 24.7 |
| 41 | Montana | 21.0 | | 26 | Maryland | 24.6 |
| 38 | Nebraska | 21.9 | | 27 | Louisiana | 24.0 |
| 49 | Nevada | 17.9 | | 27 | Ohio | 24.0 |
| 39 | New Hampshire | 21.7 | | 29 | Minnesota | 23.8 |
| 13 | New Jersey | 27.3 | | 30 | Indiana | 23.7 |
| 50 | New Mexico | 16.6 | | 31 | South Dakota | 23.5 |
| 33 | New York | 23.2 | | 32 | Washington | 23.4 |
| 44 | North Carolina | 20.7 | | 33 | New York | 23.2 |
| 42 | North Dakota | 20.8 | | 34 | Pennsylvania | 22.8 |
| 27 | Ohio | 24.0 | | 35 | Iowa | 22.6 |
| 12 | Oklahoma | 27.8 | | 36 | Arizona | 22.5 |
| 16 | Oregon | 26.8 | | 36 | Idaho | 22.5 |
| 34 | Pennsylvania | 22.8 | | 38 | Nebraska | 21.9 |
| 10 | Rhode Island | 27.9 | | 39 | New Hampshire | 21.7 |
| 17 | South Carolina | 26.7 | | 40 | Arkansas | 21.6 |
| 31 | South Dakota | 23.5 | | 41 | Montana | 21.0 |
| 48 | Tennessee | 19.4 | | 42 | Florida | 20.8 |
| 19 | Texas | 25.9 | | 42 | North Dakota | 20.8 |
| 45 | Utah | 19.6 | | 44 | North Carolina | 20.7 |
| 15 | Vermont | 27.0 | | 45 | Colorado | 19.6 |
| 5 | Virginia | 30.1 | | 45 | Utah | 19.6 |
| 32 | Washington | 23.4 | | 47 | Kentucky | 19.5 |
| 8 | West Virginia | 28.2 | | 48 | Tennessee | 19.4 |
| 23 | Wisconsin | 24.8 | | 49 | Nevada | 17.9 |
| 9 | Wyoming | 28.0 | | 50 | New Mexico | 16.6 |
| | | | | | District of Columbia | 31.4 |

Source: Morgan Quitno Press using data from U.S. Department of Transportation, Federal Highway Administration
"Highway Statistics 1999" (Table HM-15, October 2000)
*National percent does not include federally-funded highway miles in Puerto Rico.

# Public Road and Street Mileage in 1999

## National Total = 3,917,245 Miles*

ALPHA ORDER

| RANK | STATE | MILES | % of USA |
|---|---|---|---|
| 18 | Alabama | 94,246 | 2.4% |
| 47 | Alaska | 12,666 | 0.3% |
| 34 | Arizona | 54,456 | 1.4% |
| 17 | Arkansas | 97,559 | 2.5% |
| 2 | California | 166,972 | 4.3% |
| 23 | Colorado | 85,149 | 2.2% |
| 44 | Connecticut | 20,788 | 0.5% |
| 49 | Delaware | 5,748 | 0.1% |
| 10 | Florida | 115,957 | 3.0% |
| 11 | Georgia | 113,892 | 2.9% |
| 50 | Hawaii | 4,257 | 0.1% |
| 35 | Idaho | 45,802 | 1.2% |
| 3 | Illinois | 138,245 | 3.5% |
| 19 | Indiana | 93,606 | 2.4% |
| 12 | Iowa | 112,904 | 2.9% |
| 4 | Kansas | 133,962 | 3.4% |
| 26 | Kentucky | 74,120 | 1.9% |
| 32 | Louisiana | 60,828 | 1.6% |
| 43 | Maine | 22,665 | 0.6% |
| 41 | Maryland | 30,321 | 0.8% |
| 40 | Massachusetts | 35,265 | 0.9% |
| 7 | Michigan | 121,722 | 3.1% |
| 5 | Minnesota | 131,999 | 3.4% |
| 27 | Mississippi | 73,319 | 1.9% |
| 6 | Missouri | 122,829 | 3.1% |
| 29 | Montana | 69,663 | 1.8% |
| 20 | Nebraska | 92,797 | 2.4% |
| 39 | Nevada | 35,870 | 0.9% |
| 45 | New Hampshire | 15,175 | 0.4% |
| 38 | New Jersey | 35,944 | 0.9% |
| 33 | New Mexico | 59,913 | 1.5% |
| 13 | New York | 112,661 | 2.9% |
| 16 | North Carolina | 99,301 | 2.5% |
| 22 | North Dakota | 86,616 | 2.2% |
| 9 | Ohio | 116,368 | 3.0% |
| 14 | Oklahoma | 112,510 | 2.9% |
| 30 | Oregon | 66,879 | 1.7% |
| 8 | Pennsylvania | 119,381 | 3.0% |
| 48 | Rhode Island | 6,052 | 0.2% |
| 31 | South Carolina | 64,904 | 1.7% |
| 24 | South Dakota | 83,412 | 2.1% |
| 21 | Tennessee | 87,259 | 2.2% |
| 1 | Texas | 300,507 | 7.7% |
| 36 | Utah | 41,458 | 1.1% |
| 46 | Vermont | 14,266 | 0.4% |
| 28 | Virginia | 70,325 | 1.8% |
| 25 | Washington | 80,256 | 2.0% |
| 37 | West Virginia | 36,340 | 0.9% |
| 15 | Wisconsin | 111,906 | 2.9% |
| 42 | Wyoming | 26,779 | 0.7% |

RANK ORDER

| RANK | STATE | MILES | % of USA |
|---|---|---|---|
| 1 | Texas | 300,507 | 7.7% |
| 2 | California | 166,972 | 4.3% |
| 3 | Illinois | 138,245 | 3.5% |
| 4 | Kansas | 133,962 | 3.4% |
| 5 | Minnesota | 131,999 | 3.4% |
| 6 | Missouri | 122,829 | 3.1% |
| 7 | Michigan | 121,722 | 3.1% |
| 8 | Pennsylvania | 119,381 | 3.0% |
| 9 | Ohio | 116,368 | 3.0% |
| 10 | Florida | 115,957 | 3.0% |
| 11 | Georgia | 113,892 | 2.9% |
| 12 | Iowa | 112,904 | 2.9% |
| 13 | New York | 112,661 | 2.9% |
| 14 | Oklahoma | 112,510 | 2.9% |
| 15 | Wisconsin | 111,906 | 2.9% |
| 16 | North Carolina | 99,301 | 2.5% |
| 17 | Arkansas | 97,559 | 2.5% |
| 18 | Alabama | 94,246 | 2.4% |
| 19 | Indiana | 93,606 | 2.4% |
| 20 | Nebraska | 92,797 | 2.4% |
| 21 | Tennessee | 87,259 | 2.2% |
| 22 | North Dakota | 86,616 | 2.2% |
| 23 | Colorado | 85,149 | 2.2% |
| 24 | South Dakota | 83,412 | 2.1% |
| 25 | Washington | 80,256 | 2.0% |
| 26 | Kentucky | 74,120 | 1.9% |
| 27 | Mississippi | 73,319 | 1.9% |
| 28 | Virginia | 70,325 | 1.8% |
| 29 | Montana | 69,663 | 1.8% |
| 30 | Oregon | 66,879 | 1.7% |
| 31 | South Carolina | 64,904 | 1.7% |
| 32 | Louisiana | 60,828 | 1.6% |
| 33 | New Mexico | 59,913 | 1.5% |
| 34 | Arizona | 54,456 | 1.4% |
| 35 | Idaho | 45,802 | 1.2% |
| 36 | Utah | 41,458 | 1.1% |
| 37 | West Virginia | 36,340 | 0.9% |
| 38 | New Jersey | 35,944 | 0.9% |
| 39 | Nevada | 35,870 | 0.9% |
| 40 | Massachusetts | 35,265 | 0.9% |
| 41 | Maryland | 30,321 | 0.8% |
| 42 | Wyoming | 26,779 | 0.7% |
| 43 | Maine | 22,665 | 0.6% |
| 44 | Connecticut | 20,788 | 0.5% |
| 45 | New Hampshire | 15,175 | 0.4% |
| 46 | Vermont | 14,266 | 0.4% |
| 47 | Alaska | 12,666 | 0.3% |
| 48 | Rhode Island | 6,052 | 0.2% |
| 49 | Delaware | 5,748 | 0.1% |
| 50 | Hawaii | 4,257 | 0.1% |
| | District of Columbia | 1,426 | 0.0% |

*Source: U.S. Department of Transportation, Federal Highway Administration*
*"Highway Statistics 1999" (Table HM-10, October 2000)*
*Does not include 14,772 miles of roads and streets in Puerto Rico.*

# Interstate Highway Mileage in 1999

## National Total = 46,317 Miles*

ALPHA ORDER

| RANK | STATE | MILES | % of USA |
|------|-------|-------|----------|
| 24 | Alabama | 905 | 2.0% |
| 15 | Alaska | 1,083 | 2.3% |
| 13 | Arizona | 1,168 | 2.5% |
| 40 | Arkansas | 542 | 1.2% |
| 2 | California | 2,456 | 5.3% |
| 19 | Colorado | 953 | 2.1% |
| 45 | Connecticut | 346 | 0.7% |
| 50 | Delaware | 41 | 0.1% |
| 7 | Florida | 1,472 | 3.2% |
| 8 | Georgia | 1,244 | 2.7% |
| 49 | Hawaii | 55 | 0.1% |
| 35 | Idaho | 611 | 1.3% |
| 3 | Illinois | 2,165 | 4.7% |
| 12 | Indiana | 1,169 | 2.5% |
| 28 | Iowa | 782 | 1.7% |
| 26 | Kansas | 872 | 1.9% |
| 30 | Kentucky | 762 | 1.6% |
| 25 | Louisiana | 894 | 1.9% |
| 44 | Maine | 367 | 0.8% |
| 42 | Maryland | 481 | 1.0% |
| 37 | Massachusetts | 566 | 1.2% |
| 9 | Michigan | 1,241 | 2.7% |
| 23 | Minnesota | 912 | 2.0% |
| 33 | Mississippi | 685 | 1.5% |
| 11 | Missouri | 1,178 | 2.5% |
| 10 | Montana | 1,191 | 2.6% |
| 41 | Nebraska | 482 | 1.0% |
| 38 | Nevada | 560 | 1.2% |
| 47 | New Hampshire | 225 | 0.5% |
| 43 | New Jersey | 420 | 0.9% |
| 18 | New Mexico | 1,000 | 2.2% |
| 5 | New York | 1,667 | 3.6% |
| 17 | North Carolina | 1,017 | 2.2% |
| 36 | North Dakota | 572 | 1.2% |
| 6 | Ohio | 1,573 | 3.4% |
| 21 | Oklahoma | 930 | 2.0% |
| 32 | Oregon | 727 | 1.6% |
| 4 | Pennsylvania | 1,758 | 3.8% |
| 48 | Rhode Island | 70 | 0.2% |
| 27 | South Carolina | 828 | 1.8% |
| 34 | South Dakota | 678 | 1.5% |
| 16 | Tennessee | 1,074 | 2.3% |
| 1 | Texas | 3,234 | 7.0% |
| 20 | Utah | 938 | 2.0% |
| 46 | Vermont | 320 | 0.7% |
| 14 | Virginia | 1,118 | 2.4% |
| 29 | Washington | 764 | 1.6% |
| 39 | West Virginia | 549 | 1.2% |
| 31 | Wisconsin | 745 | 1.6% |
| 22 | Wyoming | 913 | 2.0% |

RANK ORDER

| RANK | STATE | MILES | % of USA |
|------|-------|-------|----------|
| 1 | Texas | 3,234 | 7.0% |
| 2 | California | 2,456 | 5.3% |
| 3 | Illinois | 2,165 | 4.7% |
| 4 | Pennsylvania | 1,758 | 3.8% |
| 5 | New York | 1,667 | 3.6% |
| 6 | Ohio | 1,573 | 3.4% |
| 7 | Florida | 1,472 | 3.2% |
| 8 | Georgia | 1,244 | 2.7% |
| 9 | Michigan | 1,241 | 2.7% |
| 10 | Montana | 1,191 | 2.6% |
| 11 | Missouri | 1,178 | 2.5% |
| 12 | Indiana | 1,169 | 2.5% |
| 13 | Arizona | 1,168 | 2.5% |
| 14 | Virginia | 1,118 | 2.4% |
| 15 | Alaska | 1,083 | 2.3% |
| 16 | Tennessee | 1,074 | 2.3% |
| 17 | North Carolina | 1,017 | 2.2% |
| 18 | New Mexico | 1,000 | 2.2% |
| 19 | Colorado | 953 | 2.1% |
| 20 | Utah | 938 | 2.0% |
| 21 | Oklahoma | 930 | 2.0% |
| 22 | Wyoming | 913 | 2.0% |
| 23 | Minnesota | 912 | 2.0% |
| 24 | Alabama | 905 | 2.0% |
| 25 | Louisiana | 894 | 1.9% |
| 26 | Kansas | 872 | 1.9% |
| 27 | South Carolina | 828 | 1.8% |
| 28 | Iowa | 782 | 1.7% |
| 29 | Washington | 764 | 1.6% |
| 30 | Kentucky | 762 | 1.6% |
| 31 | Wisconsin | 745 | 1.6% |
| 32 | Oregon | 727 | 1.6% |
| 33 | Mississippi | 685 | 1.5% |
| 34 | South Dakota | 678 | 1.5% |
| 35 | Idaho | 611 | 1.3% |
| 36 | North Dakota | 572 | 1.2% |
| 37 | Massachusetts | 566 | 1.2% |
| 38 | Nevada | 560 | 1.2% |
| 39 | West Virginia | 549 | 1.2% |
| 40 | Arkansas | 542 | 1.2% |
| 41 | Nebraska | 482 | 1.0% |
| 42 | Maryland | 481 | 1.0% |
| 43 | New Jersey | 420 | 0.9% |
| 44 | Maine | 367 | 0.8% |
| 45 | Connecticut | 346 | 0.7% |
| 46 | Vermont | 320 | 0.7% |
| 47 | New Hampshire | 225 | 0.5% |
| 48 | Rhode Island | 70 | 0.2% |
| 49 | Hawaii | 55 | 0.1% |
| 50 | Delaware | 41 | 0.1% |
| | District of Columbia | 14 | 0.0% |

Source: U.S. Department of Transportation, Federal Highway Administration
"Highway Statistics 1999" (Table HM-15, October 2000)
*Does not include 250 miles of highway in Puerto Rico that are part of the interstate system.

# Rural Road and Street Mileage in 1999

## National Total = 3,071,181 Rural Miles*

| RANK | STATE | MILES | % of USA | RANK | STATE | MILES | % of USA |
|---|---|---|---|---|---|---|---|
| 20 | Alabama | 73,589 | 2.4% | 1 | Texas | 218,537 | 7.1% |
| 46 | Alaska | 10,858 | 0.4% | 2 | Kansas | 123,791 | 4.0% |
| 35 | Arizona | 37,178 | 1.2% | 3 | Minnesota | 116,044 | 3.8% |
| 11 | Arkansas | 86,957 | 2.8% | 4 | Missouri | 106,460 | 3.5% |
| 15 | California | 83,185 | 2.7% | 5 | Iowa | 103,385 | 3.4% |
| 22 | Colorado | 70,902 | 2.3% | 6 | Illinois | 102,053 | 3.3% |
| 47 | Connecticut | 9,014 | 0.3% | 7 | Oklahoma | 99,225 | 3.2% |
| 48 | Delaware | 3,779 | 0.1% | 8 | Wisconsin | 95,366 | 3.1% |
| 24 | Florida | 67,636 | 2.2% | 9 | Michigan | 91,791 | 3.0% |
| 12 | Georgia | 86,434 | 2.8% | 10 | Nebraska | 87,622 | 2.9% |
| 49 | Hawaii | 2,362 | 0.1% | 11 | Arkansas | 86,957 | 2.8% |
| 34 | Idaho | 41,798 | 1.4% | 12 | Georgia | 86,434 | 2.8% |
| 6 | Illinois | 102,053 | 3.3% | 13 | Pennsylvania | 85,096 | 2.8% |
| 19 | Indiana | 73,664 | 2.4% | 14 | North Dakota | 84,781 | 2.8% |
| 5 | Iowa | 103,385 | 3.4% | 15 | California | 83,185 | 2.7% |
| 2 | Kansas | 123,791 | 4.0% | 16 | Ohio | 82,874 | 2.7% |
| 27 | Kentucky | 63,041 | 2.1% | 17 | South Dakota | 81,431 | 2.7% |
| 33 | Louisiana | 46,886 | 1.5% | 18 | North Carolina | 75,906 | 2.5% |
| 40 | Maine | 20,033 | 0.7% | 19 | Indiana | 73,664 | 2.4% |
| 41 | Maryland | 16,000 | 0.5% | 20 | Alabama | 73,589 | 2.4% |
| 44 | Massachusetts | 12,202 | 0.4% | 21 | New York | 71,746 | 2.3% |
| 9 | Michigan | 91,791 | 3.0% | 22 | Colorado | 70,902 | 2.3% |
| 3 | Minnesota | 116,044 | 3.8% | 23 | Tennessee | 69,536 | 2.3% |
| 26 | Mississippi | 65,386 | 2.1% | 24 | Florida | 67,636 | 2.2% |
| 4 | Missouri | 106,460 | 3.5% | 25 | Montana | 67,078 | 2.2% |
| 25 | Montana | 67,078 | 2.2% | 26 | Mississippi | 65,386 | 2.1% |
| 10 | Nebraska | 87,622 | 2.9% | 27 | Kentucky | 63,041 | 2.1% |
| 38 | Nevada | 30,082 | 1.0% | 28 | Washington | 62,062 | 2.0% |
| 43 | New Hampshire | 12,244 | 0.4% | 29 | Oregon | 55,977 | 1.8% |
| 45 | New Jersey | 11,778 | 0.4% | 30 | South Carolina | 54,283 | 1.8% |
| 31 | New Mexico | 53,839 | 1.8% | 31 | New Mexico | 53,839 | 1.8% |
| 21 | New York | 71,746 | 2.3% | 32 | Virginia | 51,325 | 1.7% |
| 18 | North Carolina | 75,906 | 2.5% | 33 | Louisiana | 46,886 | 1.5% |
| 14 | North Dakota | 84,781 | 2.8% | 34 | Idaho | 41,798 | 1.4% |
| 16 | Ohio | 82,874 | 2.7% | 35 | Arizona | 37,178 | 1.2% |
| 7 | Oklahoma | 99,225 | 3.2% | 36 | Utah | 34,142 | 1.1% |
| 29 | Oregon | 55,977 | 1.8% | 37 | West Virginia | 33,116 | 1.1% |
| 13 | Pennsylvania | 85,096 | 2.8% | 38 | Nevada | 30,082 | 1.0% |
| 50 | Rhode Island | 1,333 | 0.0% | 39 | Wyoming | 24,484 | 0.8% |
| 30 | South Carolina | 54,283 | 1.8% | 40 | Maine | 20,033 | 0.7% |
| 17 | South Dakota | 81,431 | 2.7% | 41 | Maryland | 16,000 | 0.5% |
| 23 | Tennessee | 69,536 | 2.3% | 42 | Vermont | 12,890 | 0.4% |
| 1 | Texas | 218,537 | 7.1% | 43 | New Hampshire | 12,244 | 0.4% |
| 36 | Utah | 34,142 | 1.1% | 44 | Massachusetts | 12,202 | 0.4% |
| 42 | Vermont | 12,890 | 0.4% | 45 | New Jersey | 11,778 | 0.4% |
| 32 | Virginia | 51,325 | 1.7% | 46 | Alaska | 10,858 | 0.4% |
| 28 | Washington | 62,062 | 2.0% | 47 | Connecticut | 9,014 | 0.3% |
| 37 | West Virginia | 33,116 | 1.1% | 48 | Delaware | 3,779 | 0.1% |
| 8 | Wisconsin | 95,366 | 3.1% | 49 | Hawaii | 2,362 | 0.1% |
| 39 | Wyoming | 24,484 | 0.8% | 50 | Rhode Island | 1,333 | 0.0% |
| | | | | | District of Columbia | 0 | 0.0% |

Source: U.S. Department of Transportation, Federal Highway Administration
"Highway Statistics 1999" (Table HM-10, October 2000)
*Does not include 7,689 miles of rural roads and streets in Puerto Rico.

# Urban Road and Street Mileage in 1999

## National Total = 846,064 Urban Miles*

ALPHA ORDER

| RANK | STATE | MILES | % of USA |
|------|-------|-------|----------|
| 13 | Alabama | 20,657 | 2.4% |
| 49 | Alaska | 1,808 | 0.2% |
| 18 | Arizona | 17,278 | 2.0% |
| 30 | Arkansas | 10,602 | 1.3% |
| 1 | California | 83,787 | 9.9% |
| 23 | Colorado | 14,247 | 1.7% |
| 26 | Connecticut | 11,774 | 1.4% |
| 46 | Delaware | 1,969 | 0.2% |
| 3 | Florida | 48,321 | 5.7% |
| 9 | Georgia | 27,458 | 3.2% |
| 47 | Hawaii | 1,895 | 0.2% |
| 39 | Idaho | 4,004 | 0.5% |
| 5 | Illinois | 36,192 | 4.3% |
| 14 | Indiana | 19,942 | 2.4% |
| 32 | Iowa | 9,519 | 1.1% |
| 31 | Kansas | 10,171 | 1.2% |
| 27 | Kentucky | 11,079 | 1.3% |
| 24 | Louisiana | 13,942 | 1.6% |
| 42 | Maine | 2,632 | 0.3% |
| 22 | Maryland | 14,321 | 1.7% |
| 12 | Massachusetts | 23,063 | 2.7% |
| 8 | Michigan | 29,931 | 3.5% |
| 21 | Minnesota | 15,955 | 1.9% |
| 33 | Mississippi | 7,933 | 0.9% |
| 20 | Missouri | 16,369 | 1.9% |
| 43 | Montana | 2,585 | 0.3% |
| 37 | Nebraska | 5,175 | 0.6% |
| 36 | Nevada | 5,788 | 0.7% |
| 41 | New Hampshire | 2,931 | 0.3% |
| 10 | New Jersey | 24,166 | 2.9% |
| 35 | New Mexico | 6,074 | 0.7% |
| 4 | New York | 40,915 | 4.8% |
| 11 | North Carolina | 23,395 | 2.8% |
| 48 | North Dakota | 1,835 | 0.2% |
| 7 | Ohio | 33,494 | 4.0% |
| 25 | Oklahoma | 13,285 | 1.6% |
| 28 | Oregon | 10,902 | 1.3% |
| 6 | Pennsylvania | 34,285 | 4.1% |
| 38 | Rhode Island | 4,719 | 0.6% |
| 29 | South Carolina | 10,621 | 1.3% |
| 45 | South Dakota | 1,981 | 0.2% |
| 17 | Tennessee | 17,723 | 2.1% |
| 2 | Texas | 81,970 | 9.7% |
| 34 | Utah | 7,316 | 0.9% |
| 50 | Vermont | 1,376 | 0.2% |
| 15 | Virginia | 19,000 | 2.2% |
| 16 | Washington | 18,194 | 2.2% |
| 40 | West Virginia | 3,224 | 0.4% |
| 19 | Wisconsin | 16,540 | 2.0% |
| 44 | Wyoming | 2,295 | 0.3% |

RANK ORDER

| RANK | STATE | MILES | % of USA |
|------|-------|-------|----------|
| 1 | California | 83,787 | 9.9% |
| 2 | Texas | 81,970 | 9.7% |
| 3 | Florida | 48,321 | 5.7% |
| 4 | New York | 40,915 | 4.8% |
| 5 | Illinois | 36,192 | 4.3% |
| 6 | Pennsylvania | 34,285 | 4.1% |
| 7 | Ohio | 33,494 | 4.0% |
| 8 | Michigan | 29,931 | 3.5% |
| 9 | Georgia | 27,458 | 3.2% |
| 10 | New Jersey | 24,166 | 2.9% |
| 11 | North Carolina | 23,395 | 2.8% |
| 12 | Massachusetts | 23,063 | 2.7% |
| 13 | Alabama | 20,657 | 2.4% |
| 14 | Indiana | 19,942 | 2.4% |
| 15 | Virginia | 19,000 | 2.2% |
| 16 | Washington | 18,194 | 2.2% |
| 17 | Tennessee | 17,723 | 2.1% |
| 18 | Arizona | 17,278 | 2.0% |
| 19 | Wisconsin | 16,540 | 2.0% |
| 20 | Missouri | 16,369 | 1.9% |
| 21 | Minnesota | 15,955 | 1.9% |
| 22 | Maryland | 14,321 | 1.7% |
| 23 | Colorado | 14,247 | 1.7% |
| 24 | Louisiana | 13,942 | 1.6% |
| 25 | Oklahoma | 13,285 | 1.6% |
| 26 | Connecticut | 11,774 | 1.4% |
| 27 | Kentucky | 11,079 | 1.3% |
| 28 | Oregon | 10,902 | 1.3% |
| 29 | South Carolina | 10,621 | 1.3% |
| 30 | Arkansas | 10,602 | 1.3% |
| 31 | Kansas | 10,171 | 1.2% |
| 32 | Iowa | 9,519 | 1.1% |
| 33 | Mississippi | 7,933 | 0.9% |
| 34 | Utah | 7,316 | 0.9% |
| 35 | New Mexico | 6,074 | 0.7% |
| 36 | Nevada | 5,788 | 0.7% |
| 37 | Nebraska | 5,175 | 0.6% |
| 38 | Rhode Island | 4,719 | 0.6% |
| 39 | Idaho | 4,004 | 0.5% |
| 40 | West Virginia | 3,224 | 0.4% |
| 41 | New Hampshire | 2,931 | 0.3% |
| 42 | Maine | 2,632 | 0.3% |
| 43 | Montana | 2,585 | 0.3% |
| 44 | Wyoming | 2,295 | 0.3% |
| 45 | South Dakota | 1,981 | 0.2% |
| 46 | Delaware | 1,969 | 0.2% |
| 47 | Hawaii | 1,895 | 0.2% |
| 48 | North Dakota | 1,835 | 0.2% |
| 49 | Alaska | 1,808 | 0.2% |
| 50 | Vermont | 1,376 | 0.2% |
| | District of Columbia | 1,426 | 0.2% |

Source: U.S. Department of Transportation, Federal Highway Administration
   "Highway Statistics 1999" (Table HM-10, October 2000)
*Does not include 7,083 miles of urban roads and streets in Puerto Rico.

# Bridges in 2000

## National Total = 585,687 Bridges*

ALPHA ORDER

| RANK | STATE | BRIDGES | % of USA |
|---|---|---|---|
| 15 | Alabama | 15,635 | 2.7% |
| 47 | Alaska | 1,409 | 0.2% |
| 31 | Arizona | 6,714 | 1.1% |
| 23 | Arkansas | 12,451 | 2.1% |
| 6 | California | 23,672 | 4.0% |
| 27 | Colorado | 7,977 | 1.4% |
| 38 | Connecticut | 4,178 | 0.7% |
| 49 | Delaware | 824 | 0.1% |
| 24 | Florida | 11,187 | 1.9% |
| 17 | Georgia | 14,382 | 2.5% |
| 48 | Hawaii | 1,066 | 0.2% |
| 39 | Idaho | 4,032 | 0.7% |
| 4 | Illinois | 25,497 | 4.4% |
| 11 | Indiana | 18,002 | 3.1% |
| 5 | Iowa | 24,632 | 4.2% |
| 3 | Kansas | 25,720 | 4.4% |
| 20 | Kentucky | 13,374 | 2.3% |
| 18 | Louisiana | 13,485 | 2.3% |
| 44 | Maine | 2,360 | 0.4% |
| 35 | Maryland | 4,965 | 0.8% |
| 36 | Massachusetts | 4,953 | 0.8% |
| 25 | Michigan | 10,581 | 1.8% |
| 21 | Minnesota | 12,811 | 2.2% |
| 14 | Mississippi | 16,672 | 2.8% |
| 7 | Missouri | 23,388 | 4.0% |
| 34 | Montana | 4,981 | 0.9% |
| 16 | Nebraska | 15,507 | 2.6% |
| 46 | Nevada | 1,424 | 0.2% |
| 45 | New Hampshire | 2,348 | 0.4% |
| 32 | New Jersey | 6,350 | 1.1% |
| 40 | New Mexico | 3,694 | 0.6% |
| 12 | New York | 17,387 | 3.0% |
| 13 | North Carolina | 16,822 | 2.9% |
| 37 | North Dakota | 4,517 | 0.8% |
| 2 | Ohio | 27,902 | 4.8% |
| 8 | Oklahoma | 22,799 | 3.9% |
| 29 | Oregon | 7,257 | 1.2% |
| 9 | Pennsylvania | 22,052 | 3.8% |
| 50 | Rhode Island | 747 | 0.1% |
| 26 | South Carolina | 9,064 | 1.5% |
| 33 | South Dakota | 6,032 | 1.0% |
| 10 | Tennessee | 19,404 | 3.3% |
| 1 | Texas | 47,886 | 8.2% |
| 42 | Utah | 2,750 | 0.5% |
| 43 | Vermont | 2,703 | 0.5% |
| 22 | Virginia | 12,710 | 2.2% |
| 28 | Washington | 7,876 | 1.3% |
| 30 | West Virginia | 6,730 | 1.1% |
| 19 | Wisconsin | 13,418 | 2.3% |
| 41 | Wyoming | 3,110 | 0.5% |

RANK ORDER

| RANK | STATE | BRIDGES | % of USA |
|---|---|---|---|
| 1 | Texas | 47,886 | 8.2% |
| 2 | Ohio | 27,902 | 4.8% |
| 3 | Kansas | 25,720 | 4.4% |
| 4 | Illinois | 25,497 | 4.4% |
| 5 | Iowa | 24,632 | 4.2% |
| 6 | California | 23,672 | 4.0% |
| 7 | Missouri | 23,388 | 4.0% |
| 8 | Oklahoma | 22,799 | 3.9% |
| 9 | Pennsylvania | 22,052 | 3.8% |
| 10 | Tennessee | 19,404 | 3.3% |
| 11 | Indiana | 18,002 | 3.1% |
| 12 | New York | 17,387 | 3.0% |
| 13 | North Carolina | 16,822 | 2.9% |
| 14 | Mississippi | 16,672 | 2.8% |
| 15 | Alabama | 15,635 | 2.7% |
| 16 | Nebraska | 15,507 | 2.6% |
| 17 | Georgia | 14,382 | 2.5% |
| 18 | Louisiana | 13,485 | 2.3% |
| 19 | Wisconsin | 13,418 | 2.3% |
| 20 | Kentucky | 13,374 | 2.3% |
| 21 | Minnesota | 12,811 | 2.2% |
| 22 | Virginia | 12,710 | 2.2% |
| 23 | Arkansas | 12,451 | 2.1% |
| 24 | Florida | 11,187 | 1.9% |
| 25 | Michigan | 10,581 | 1.8% |
| 26 | South Carolina | 9,064 | 1.5% |
| 27 | Colorado | 7,977 | 1.4% |
| 28 | Washington | 7,876 | 1.3% |
| 29 | Oregon | 7,257 | 1.2% |
| 30 | West Virginia | 6,730 | 1.1% |
| 31 | Arizona | 6,714 | 1.1% |
| 32 | New Jersey | 6,350 | 1.1% |
| 33 | South Dakota | 6,032 | 1.0% |
| 34 | Montana | 4,981 | 0.9% |
| 35 | Maryland | 4,965 | 0.8% |
| 36 | Massachusetts | 4,953 | 0.8% |
| 37 | North Dakota | 4,517 | 0.8% |
| 38 | Connecticut | 4,178 | 0.7% |
| 39 | Idaho | 4,032 | 0.7% |
| 40 | New Mexico | 3,694 | 0.6% |
| 41 | Wyoming | 3,110 | 0.5% |
| 42 | Utah | 2,750 | 0.5% |
| 43 | Vermont | 2,703 | 0.5% |
| 44 | Maine | 2,360 | 0.4% |
| 45 | New Hampshire | 2,348 | 0.4% |
| 46 | Nevada | 1,424 | 0.2% |
| 47 | Alaska | 1,409 | 0.2% |
| 48 | Hawaii | 1,066 | 0.2% |
| 49 | Delaware | 824 | 0.1% |
| 50 | Rhode Island | 747 | 0.1% |
| | District of Columbia | 250 | 0.0% |

*Source: U.S. Department of Transportation, Federal Highway Administration*
*"Deficient Bridges by State and Highway System, 2000" (http://www.fhwa.dot.gov/bridge/britab.htm)*
*\*As of August 30, 2000.  Includes federal-aid and nonfederal-aid system bridges.  National total does not include 2,068 bridges in Puerto Rico.*

# Deficient Bridges in 2000

## National Total = 166,982 Deficient Bridges*

| ALPHA ORDER | | | | RANK ORDER | | | |
|---|---|---|---|---|---|---|---|
| RANK | STATE | BRIDGES | % of USA | RANK | STATE | BRIDGES | % of USA |
| 12 | Alabama | 5,053 | 3.0% | 1 | Texas | 10,378 | 6.2% |
| 47 | Alaska | 400 | 0.2% | 2 | Pennsylvania | 9,501 | 5.7% |
| 42 | Arizona | 696 | 0.4% | 3 | Oklahoma | 9,497 | 5.7% |
| 22 | Arkansas | 3,500 | 2.1% | 4 | Missouri | 9,058 | 5.4% |
| 8 | California | 6,790 | 4.1% | 5 | Ohio | 7,269 | 4.4% |
| 34 | Colorado | 1,440 | 0.9% | 6 | Iowa | 7,124 | 4.3% |
| 35 | Connecticut | 1,278 | 0.8% | 7 | New York | 7,038 | 4.2% |
| 50 | Delaware | 131 | 0.1% | 8 | California | 6,790 | 4.1% |
| 27 | Florida | 2,227 | 1.3% | 9 | Kansas | 6,651 | 4.0% |
| 19 | Georgia | 3,712 | 2.2% | 10 | North Carolina | 5,326 | 3.2% |
| 46 | Hawaii | 550 | 0.3% | 11 | Mississippi | 5,144 | 3.1% |
| 41 | Idaho | 752 | 0.5% | 12 | Alabama | 5,053 | 3.0% |
| 13 | Illinois | 4,961 | 3.0% | 13 | Illinois | 4,961 | 3.0% |
| 17 | Indiana | 4,445 | 2.7% | 14 | Tennessee | 4,954 | 3.0% |
| 6 | Iowa | 7,124 | 4.3% | 15 | Louisiana | 4,706 | 2.8% |
| 9 | Kansas | 6,651 | 4.0% | 16 | Nebraska | 4,477 | 2.7% |
| 18 | Kentucky | 4,072 | 2.4% | 17 | Indiana | 4,445 | 2.7% |
| 15 | Louisiana | 4,706 | 2.8% | 18 | Kentucky | 4,072 | 2.4% |
| 39 | Maine | 873 | 0.5% | 19 | Georgia | 3,712 | 2.2% |
| 33 | Maryland | 1,445 | 0.9% | 20 | Virginia | 3,524 | 2.1% |
| 25 | Massachusetts | 2,480 | 1.5% | 21 | Michigan | 3,517 | 2.1% |
| 21 | Michigan | 3,517 | 2.1% | 22 | Arkansas | 3,500 | 2.1% |
| 29 | Minnesota | 1,882 | 1.1% | 23 | West Virginia | 2,791 | 1.7% |
| 11 | Mississippi | 5,144 | 3.1% | 24 | Wisconsin | 2,677 | 1.6% |
| 4 | Missouri | 9,058 | 5.4% | 25 | Massachusetts | 2,480 | 1.5% |
| 36 | Montana | 1,194 | 0.7% | 26 | New Jersey | 2,367 | 1.4% |
| 16 | Nebraska | 4,477 | 2.7% | 27 | Florida | 2,227 | 1.3% |
| 49 | Nevada | 216 | 0.1% | 28 | Washington | 2,103 | 1.3% |
| 40 | New Hampshire | 799 | 0.5% | 29 | Minnesota | 1,882 | 1.1% |
| 26 | New Jersey | 2,367 | 1.4% | 30 | South Carolina | 1,878 | 1.1% |
| 43 | New Mexico | 673 | 0.4% | 31 | South Dakota | 1,802 | 1.1% |
| 7 | New York | 7,038 | 4.2% | 32 | Oregon | 1,642 | 1.0% |
| 10 | North Carolina | 5,326 | 3.2% | 33 | Maryland | 1,445 | 0.9% |
| 37 | North Dakota | 1,174 | 0.7% | 34 | Colorado | 1,440 | 0.9% |
| 5 | Ohio | 7,269 | 4.4% | 35 | Connecticut | 1,278 | 0.8% |
| 3 | Oklahoma | 9,497 | 5.7% | 36 | Montana | 1,194 | 0.7% |
| 32 | Oregon | 1,642 | 1.0% | 37 | North Dakota | 1,174 | 0.7% |
| 2 | Pennsylvania | 9,501 | 5.7% | 38 | Vermont | 1,012 | 0.6% |
| 48 | Rhode Island | 375 | 0.2% | 39 | Maine | 873 | 0.5% |
| 30 | South Carolina | 1,878 | 1.1% | 40 | New Hampshire | 799 | 0.5% |
| 31 | South Dakota | 1,802 | 1.1% | 41 | Idaho | 752 | 0.5% |
| 14 | Tennessee | 4,954 | 3.0% | 42 | Arizona | 696 | 0.4% |
| 1 | Texas | 10,378 | 6.2% | 43 | New Mexico | 673 | 0.4% |
| 45 | Utah | 604 | 0.4% | 44 | Wyoming | 662 | 0.4% |
| 38 | Vermont | 1,012 | 0.6% | 45 | Utah | 604 | 0.4% |
| 20 | Virginia | 3,524 | 2.1% | 46 | Hawaii | 550 | 0.3% |
| 28 | Washington | 2,103 | 1.3% | 47 | Alaska | 400 | 0.2% |
| 23 | West Virginia | 2,791 | 1.7% | 48 | Rhode Island | 375 | 0.2% |
| 24 | Wisconsin | 2,677 | 1.6% | 49 | Nevada | 216 | 0.1% |
| 44 | Wyoming | 662 | 0.4% | 50 | Delaware | 131 | 0.1% |
| | | | | | District of Columbia | 162 | 0.1% |

Source: U.S. Department of Transportation, Federal Highway Administration
   "Deficient Bridges by State and Highway System, 2000" (http://www.fhwa.dot.gov/bridge/britab.htm)
*As of August 30, 2000. Includes federal-aid and nonfederal-aid system bridges. National total does not include
1,011 deficient bridges in Puerto Rico. Bridges classified as deficient are either functionally obsolete or
structurally deficient and are not necessarily unsafe.

# Deficient Bridges as a Percent of Total Bridges in 2000

## National Percent = 28.5% of Bridges are Deficient*

| ALPHA ORDER | | | | RANK ORDER | | |
|---|---|---|---|---|---|---|
| RANK | STATE | PERCENT | | RANK | STATE | PERCENT |
| 15 | Alabama | 32.3 | | 1 | Hawaii | 51.6 |
| 25 | Alaska | 28.4 | | 2 | Rhode Island | 50.2 |
| 50 | Arizona | 10.4 | | 3 | Massachusetts | 50.1 |
| 26 | Arkansas | 28.1 | | 4 | Pennsylvania | 43.1 |
| 24 | California | 28.7 | | 5 | Oklahoma | 41.7 |
| 46 | Colorado | 18.1 | | 6 | West Virginia | 41.5 |
| 18 | Connecticut | 30.6 | | 7 | New York | 40.5 |
| 47 | Delaware | 15.9 | | 8 | Missouri | 38.7 |
| 42 | Florida | 19.9 | | 9 | Vermont | 37.4 |
| 32 | Georgia | 25.8 | | 10 | New Jersey | 37.3 |
| 1 | Hawaii | 51.6 | | 11 | Maine | 37.0 |
| 44 | Idaho | 18.7 | | 12 | Louisiana | 34.9 |
| 43 | Illinois | 19.5 | | 13 | New Hampshire | 34.0 |
| 34 | Indiana | 24.7 | | 14 | Michigan | 33.2 |
| 22 | Iowa | 28.9 | | 15 | Alabama | 32.3 |
| 31 | Kansas | 25.9 | | 16 | North Carolina | 31.7 |
| 19 | Kentucky | 30.4 | | 17 | Mississippi | 30.9 |
| 12 | Louisiana | 34.9 | | 18 | Connecticut | 30.6 |
| 11 | Maine | 37.0 | | 19 | Kentucky | 30.4 |
| 21 | Maryland | 29.1 | | 20 | South Dakota | 29.9 |
| 3 | Massachusetts | 50.1 | | 21 | Maryland | 29.1 |
| 14 | Michigan | 33.2 | | 22 | Iowa | 28.9 |
| 49 | Minnesota | 14.7 | | 22 | Nebraska | 28.9 |
| 17 | Mississippi | 30.9 | | 24 | California | 28.7 |
| 8 | Missouri | 38.7 | | 25 | Alaska | 28.4 |
| 35 | Montana | 24.0 | | 26 | Arkansas | 28.1 |
| 22 | Nebraska | 28.9 | | 27 | Virginia | 27.7 |
| 48 | Nevada | 15.2 | | 28 | Washington | 26.7 |
| 13 | New Hampshire | 34.0 | | 29 | Ohio | 26.1 |
| 10 | New Jersey | 37.3 | | 30 | North Dakota | 26.0 |
| 45 | New Mexico | 18.2 | | 31 | Kansas | 25.9 |
| 7 | New York | 40.5 | | 32 | Georgia | 25.8 |
| 16 | North Carolina | 31.7 | | 33 | Tennessee | 25.5 |
| 30 | North Dakota | 26.0 | | 34 | Indiana | 24.7 |
| 29 | Ohio | 26.1 | | 35 | Montana | 24.0 |
| 5 | Oklahoma | 41.7 | | 36 | Oregon | 22.6 |
| 36 | Oregon | 22.6 | | 37 | Utah | 22.0 |
| 4 | Pennsylvania | 43.1 | | 38 | Texas | 21.7 |
| 2 | Rhode Island | 50.2 | | 39 | Wyoming | 21.3 |
| 40 | South Carolina | 20.7 | | 40 | South Carolina | 20.7 |
| 20 | South Dakota | 29.9 | | 41 | Wisconsin | 20.0 |
| 33 | Tennessee | 25.5 | | 42 | Florida | 19.9 |
| 38 | Texas | 21.7 | | 43 | Illinois | 19.5 |
| 37 | Utah | 22.0 | | 44 | Idaho | 18.7 |
| 9 | Vermont | 37.4 | | 45 | New Mexico | 18.2 |
| 27 | Virginia | 27.7 | | 46 | Colorado | 18.1 |
| 28 | Washington | 26.7 | | 47 | Delaware | 15.9 |
| 6 | West Virginia | 41.5 | | 48 | Nevada | 15.2 |
| 41 | Wisconsin | 20.0 | | 49 | Minnesota | 14.7 |
| 39 | Wyoming | 21.3 | | 50 | Arizona | 10.4 |
| | | | | | District of Columbia | 64.8 |

Source: Morgan Quitno Press using data from U.S. Department of Transportation, Federal Highway Administration
"Deficient Bridges by State and Highway System, 2000" (http://www.fhwa.dot.gov/bridge/britab.htm)
*As of August 30, 2000. Includes federal-aid and nonfederal-aid system bridges. National total does not include
bridges in Puerto Rico. Bridges classified as deficient are either functionally obsolete or structurally deficient and
are not necessarily unsafe.

# Vehicle-Miles of Travel in 1999

## National Total = 2,691,335,000,000 Miles

ALPHA ORDER

RANK ORDER

| RANK | STATE | MILES | % of USA | RANK | STATE | MILES | % of USA |
|------|-------|-------|----------|------|-------|-------|----------|
| 17 | Alabama | 56,165,000,000 | 2.1% | 1 | California | 300,066,000,000 | 11.1% |
| 50 | Alaska | 4,545,000,000 | 0.2% | 2 | Texas | 210,874,000,000 | 7.8% |
| 23 | Arizona | 46,829,000,000 | 1.7% | 3 | Florida | 141,903,000,000 | 5.3% |
| 31 | Arkansas | 29,247,000,000 | 1.1% | 4 | New York | 126,491,000,000 | 4.7% |
| 1 | California | 300,066,000,000 | 11.1% | 5 | Ohio | 105,487,000,000 | 3.9% |
| 27 | Colorado | 40,732,000,000 | 1.5% | 6 | Illinois | 102,394,000,000 | 3.8% |
| 30 | Connecticut | 29,926,000,000 | 1.1% | 7 | Pennsylvania | 102,014,000,000 | 3.8% |
| 43 | Delaware | 8,542,000,000 | 0.3% | 8 | Georgia | 98,859,000,000 | 3.7% |
| 3 | Florida | 141,903,000,000 | 5.3% | 9 | Michigan | 95,644,000,000 | 3.6% |
| 8 | Georgia | 98,859,000,000 | 3.7% | 10 | North Carolina | 87,759,000,000 | 3.3% |
| 46 | Hawaii | 8,116,000,000 | 0.3% | 11 | Virginia | 73,904,000,000 | 2.7% |
| 40 | Idaho | 13,976,000,000 | 0.5% | 12 | Indiana | 70,041,000,000 | 2.6% |
| 6 | Illinois | 102,394,000,000 | 3.8% | 13 | Missouri | 66,735,000,000 | 2.5% |
| 12 | Indiana | 70,041,000,000 | 2.6% | 14 | New Jersey | 65,540,000,000 | 2.4% |
| 32 | Iowa | 29,138,000,000 | 1.1% | 15 | Tennessee | 64,755,000,000 | 2.4% |
| 33 | Kansas | 27,699,000,000 | 1.0% | 16 | Wisconsin | 56,960,000,000 | 2.1% |
| 22 | Kentucky | 47,816,000,000 | 1.8% | 17 | Alabama | 56,165,000,000 | 2.1% |
| 26 | Louisiana | 41,205,000,000 | 1.5% | 18 | Washington | 52,714,000,000 | 2.0% |
| 39 | Maine | 14,143,000,000 | 0.5% | 19 | Massachusetts | 51,820,000,000 | 1.9% |
| 21 | Maryland | 49,126,000,000 | 1.8% | 20 | Minnesota | 51,410,000,000 | 1.9% |
| 19 | Massachusetts | 51,820,000,000 | 1.9% | 21 | Maryland | 49,126,000,000 | 1.8% |
| 9 | Michigan | 95,644,000,000 | 3.6% | 22 | Kentucky | 47,816,000,000 | 1.8% |
| 20 | Minnesota | 51,410,000,000 | 1.9% | 23 | Arizona | 46,829,000,000 | 1.7% |
| 28 | Mississippi | 34,880,000,000 | 1.3% | 24 | South Carolina | 44,146,000,000 | 1.6% |
| 13 | Missouri | 66,735,000,000 | 2.5% | 25 | Oklahoma | 42,569,000,000 | 1.6% |
| 42 | Montana | 9,835,000,000 | 0.4% | 26 | Louisiana | 41,205,000,000 | 1.5% |
| 37 | Nebraska | 18,011,000,000 | 0.7% | 27 | Colorado | 40,732,000,000 | 1.5% |
| 38 | Nevada | 17,391,000,000 | 0.6% | 28 | Mississippi | 34,880,000,000 | 1.3% |
| 41 | New Hampshire | 11,894,000,000 | 0.4% | 29 | Oregon | 34,680,000,000 | 1.3% |
| 14 | New Jersey | 65,540,000,000 | 2.4% | 30 | Connecticut | 29,926,000,000 | 1.1% |
| 34 | New Mexico | 22,362,000,000 | 0.8% | 31 | Arkansas | 29,247,000,000 | 1.1% |
| 4 | New York | 126,491,000,000 | 4.7% | 32 | Iowa | 29,138,000,000 | 1.1% |
| 10 | North Carolina | 87,759,000,000 | 3.3% | 33 | Kansas | 27,699,000,000 | 1.0% |
| 48 | North Dakota | 7,262,000,000 | 0.3% | 34 | New Mexico | 22,362,000,000 | 0.8% |
| 5 | Ohio | 105,487,000,000 | 3.9% | 35 | Utah | 22,044,000,000 | 0.8% |
| 25 | Oklahoma | 42,569,000,000 | 1.6% | 36 | West Virginia | 19,033,000,000 | 0.7% |
| 29 | Oregon | 34,680,000,000 | 1.3% | 37 | Nebraska | 18,011,000,000 | 0.7% |
| 7 | Pennsylvania | 102,014,000,000 | 3.8% | 38 | Nevada | 17,391,000,000 | 0.6% |
| 44 | Rhode Island | 8,283,000,000 | 0.3% | 39 | Maine | 14,143,000,000 | 0.5% |
| 24 | South Carolina | 44,146,000,000 | 1.6% | 40 | Idaho | 13,976,000,000 | 0.5% |
| 45 | South Dakota | 8,244,000,000 | 0.3% | 41 | New Hampshire | 11,894,000,000 | 0.4% |
| 15 | Tennessee | 64,755,000,000 | 2.4% | 42 | Montana | 9,835,000,000 | 0.4% |
| 2 | Texas | 210,874,000,000 | 7.8% | 43 | Delaware | 8,542,000,000 | 0.3% |
| 35 | Utah | 22,044,000,000 | 0.8% | 44 | Rhode Island | 8,283,000,000 | 0.3% |
| 49 | Vermont | 6,867,000,000 | 0.3% | 45 | South Dakota | 8,244,000,000 | 0.3% |
| 11 | Virginia | 73,904,000,000 | 2.7% | 46 | Hawaii | 8,116,000,000 | 0.3% |
| 18 | Washington | 52,714,000,000 | 2.0% | 47 | Wyoming | 7,797,000,000 | 0.3% |
| 36 | West Virginia | 19,033,000,000 | 0.7% | 48 | North Dakota | 7,262,000,000 | 0.3% |
| 16 | Wisconsin | 56,960,000,000 | 2.1% | 49 | Vermont | 6,867,000,000 | 0.3% |
| 47 | Wyoming | 7,797,000,000 | 0.3% | 50 | Alaska | 4,545,000,000 | 0.2% |
| | | | | | District of Columbia | 3,462,000,000 | 0.1% |

Source: U.S. Department of Transportation, Federal Highway Administration
  "Highway Statistics 1999" (Table VM-2, October 2000)

# Highway Fatalities in 1999

## National Total = 41,611 Fatalities

ALPHA ORDER

| RANK | STATE | FATALITIES | % of USA |
|---|---|---|---|
| 12 | Alabama | 1,138 | 2.7% |
| 50 | Alaska | 76 | 0.2% |
| 15 | Arizona | 1,024 | 2.5% |
| 27 | Arkansas | 604 | 1.5% |
| 1 | California | 3,559 | 8.6% |
| 25 | Colorado | 626 | 1.5% |
| 37 | Connecticut | 301 | 0.7% |
| 46 | Delaware | 100 | 0.2% |
| 3 | Florida | 2,918 | 7.0% |
| 6 | Georgia | 1,508 | 3.6% |
| 47 | Hawaii | 98 | 0.2% |
| 39 | Idaho | 278 | 0.7% |
| 8 | Illinois | 1,456 | 3.5% |
| 16 | Indiana | 1,013 | 2.4% |
| 30 | Iowa | 490 | 1.2% |
| 29 | Kansas | 537 | 1.3% |
| 20 | Kentucky | 814 | 2.0% |
| 18 | Louisiana | 924 | 2.2% |
| 42 | Maine | 181 | 0.4% |
| 28 | Maryland | 590 | 1.4% |
| 32 | Massachusetts | 414 | 1.0% |
| 10 | Michigan | 1,382 | 3.3% |
| 26 | Minnesota | 625 | 1.5% |
| 17 | Mississippi | 927 | 2.2% |
| 13 | Missouri | 1,094 | 2.6% |
| 40 | Montana | 220 | 0.5% |
| 38 | Nebraska | 295 | 0.7% |
| 36 | Nevada | 350 | 0.8% |
| 44 | New Hampshire | 141 | 0.3% |
| 23 | New Jersey | 727 | 1.7% |
| 31 | New Mexico | 460 | 1.1% |
| 5 | New York | 1,548 | 3.7% |
| 7 | North Carolina | 1,505 | 3.6% |
| 45 | North Dakota | 119 | 0.3% |
| 9 | Ohio | 1,430 | 3.4% |
| 22 | Oklahoma | 739 | 1.8% |
| 32 | Oregon | 414 | 1.0% |
| 4 | Pennsylvania | 1,549 | 3.7% |
| 49 | Rhode Island | 88 | 0.2% |
| 14 | South Carolina | 1,065 | 2.6% |
| 43 | South Dakota | 150 | 0.4% |
| 11 | Tennessee | 1,285 | 3.1% |
| 2 | Texas | 3,518 | 8.5% |
| 35 | Utah | 360 | 0.9% |
| 48 | Vermont | 90 | 0.2% |
| 19 | Virginia | 877 | 2.1% |
| 24 | Washington | 634 | 1.5% |
| 34 | West Virginia | 395 | 0.9% |
| 21 | Wisconsin | 745 | 1.8% |
| 41 | Wyoming | 189 | 0.5% |

RANK ORDER

| RANK | STATE | FATALITIES | % of USA |
|---|---|---|---|
| 1 | California | 3,559 | 8.6% |
| 2 | Texas | 3,518 | 8.5% |
| 3 | Florida | 2,918 | 7.0% |
| 4 | Pennsylvania | 1,549 | 3.7% |
| 5 | New York | 1,548 | 3.7% |
| 6 | Georgia | 1,508 | 3.6% |
| 7 | North Carolina | 1,505 | 3.6% |
| 8 | Illinois | 1,456 | 3.5% |
| 9 | Ohio | 1,430 | 3.4% |
| 10 | Michigan | 1,382 | 3.3% |
| 11 | Tennessee | 1,285 | 3.1% |
| 12 | Alabama | 1,138 | 2.7% |
| 13 | Missouri | 1,094 | 2.6% |
| 14 | South Carolina | 1,065 | 2.6% |
| 15 | Arizona | 1,024 | 2.5% |
| 16 | Indiana | 1,013 | 2.4% |
| 17 | Mississippi | 927 | 2.2% |
| 18 | Louisiana | 924 | 2.2% |
| 19 | Virginia | 877 | 2.1% |
| 20 | Kentucky | 814 | 2.0% |
| 21 | Wisconsin | 745 | 1.8% |
| 22 | Oklahoma | 739 | 1.8% |
| 23 | New Jersey | 727 | 1.7% |
| 24 | Washington | 634 | 1.5% |
| 25 | Colorado | 626 | 1.5% |
| 26 | Minnesota | 625 | 1.5% |
| 27 | Arkansas | 604 | 1.5% |
| 28 | Maryland | 590 | 1.4% |
| 29 | Kansas | 537 | 1.3% |
| 30 | Iowa | 490 | 1.2% |
| 31 | New Mexico | 460 | 1.1% |
| 32 | Massachusetts | 414 | 1.0% |
| 32 | Oregon | 414 | 1.0% |
| 34 | West Virginia | 395 | 0.9% |
| 35 | Utah | 360 | 0.9% |
| 36 | Nevada | 350 | 0.8% |
| 37 | Connecticut | 301 | 0.7% |
| 38 | Nebraska | 295 | 0.7% |
| 39 | Idaho | 278 | 0.7% |
| 40 | Montana | 220 | 0.5% |
| 41 | Wyoming | 189 | 0.5% |
| 42 | Maine | 181 | 0.4% |
| 43 | South Dakota | 150 | 0.4% |
| 44 | New Hampshire | 141 | 0.3% |
| 45 | North Dakota | 119 | 0.3% |
| 46 | Delaware | 100 | 0.2% |
| 47 | Hawaii | 98 | 0.2% |
| 48 | Vermont | 90 | 0.2% |
| 49 | Rhode Island | 88 | 0.2% |
| 50 | Alaska | 76 | 0.2% |
| | District of Columbia | 41 | 0.1% |

*Source: U.S. Department of Transportation, National Highway Safety Administration*
*"Traffic Safety Facts 1999" (Table 1) (http://www.nhtsa.dot.gov/people/ncsa/pdf/STDfacts99.pdf)*

# Highway Fatality Rate in 1999

## National Rate = 1.55 Fatalities per 100 Million Vehicle-Miles of Travel

| ALPHA ORDER | | | | RANK ORDER | | |
|---|---|---|---|---|---|---|
| RANK | STATE | RATE | | RANK | STATE | RATE |
| 11 | Alabama | 2.03 | | 1 | Mississippi | 2.66 |
| 21 | Alaska | 1.67 | | 2 | Wyoming | 2.42 |
| 6 | Arizona | 2.19 | | 3 | South Carolina | 2.41 |
| 8 | Arkansas | 2.07 | | 4 | Louisiana | 2.24 |
| 42 | California | 1.19 | | 4 | Montana | 2.24 |
| 27 | Colorado | 1.54 | | 6 | Arizona | 2.19 |
| 49 | Connecticut | 1.01 | | 7 | West Virginia | 2.08 |
| 46 | Delaware | 1.17 | | 8 | Arkansas | 2.07 |
| 9 | Florida | 2.06 | | 9 | Florida | 2.06 |
| 28 | Georgia | 1.53 | | 9 | New Mexico | 2.06 |
| 39 | Hawaii | 1.21 | | 11 | Alabama | 2.03 |
| 13 | Idaho | 1.99 | | 12 | Nevada | 2.01 |
| 32 | Illinois | 1.42 | | 13 | Idaho | 1.99 |
| 30 | Indiana | 1.45 | | 14 | Tennessee | 1.98 |
| 20 | Iowa | 1.68 | | 15 | Kansas | 1.94 |
| 15 | Kansas | 1.94 | | 16 | South Dakota | 1.82 |
| 19 | Kentucky | 1.70 | | 17 | Oklahoma | 1.74 |
| 4 | Louisiana | 2.24 | | 18 | North Carolina | 1.71 |
| 36 | Maine | 1.28 | | 19 | Kentucky | 1.70 |
| 40 | Maryland | 1.20 | | 20 | Iowa | 1.68 |
| 50 | Massachusetts | 0.80 | | 21 | Alaska | 1.67 |
| 31 | Michigan | 1.44 | | 21 | Texas | 1.67 |
| 37 | Minnesota | 1.22 | | 23 | Missouri | 1.64 |
| 1 | Mississippi | 2.66 | | 23 | Nebraska | 1.64 |
| 23 | Missouri | 1.64 | | 23 | North Dakota | 1.64 |
| 4 | Montana | 2.24 | | 26 | Utah | 1.63 |
| 23 | Nebraska | 1.64 | | 27 | Colorado | 1.54 |
| 12 | Nevada | 2.01 | | 28 | Georgia | 1.53 |
| 42 | New Hampshire | 1.19 | | 29 | Pennsylvania | 1.52 |
| 47 | New Jersey | 1.11 | | 30 | Indiana | 1.45 |
| 9 | New Mexico | 2.06 | | 31 | Michigan | 1.44 |
| 37 | New York | 1.22 | | 32 | Illinois | 1.42 |
| 18 | North Carolina | 1.71 | | 33 | Ohio | 1.36 |
| 23 | North Dakota | 1.64 | | 34 | Vermont | 1.31 |
| 33 | Ohio | 1.36 | | 34 | Wisconsin | 1.31 |
| 17 | Oklahoma | 1.74 | | 36 | Maine | 1.28 |
| 42 | Oregon | 1.19 | | 37 | Minnesota | 1.22 |
| 29 | Pennsylvania | 1.52 | | 37 | New York | 1.22 |
| 48 | Rhode Island | 1.06 | | 39 | Hawaii | 1.21 |
| 3 | South Carolina | 2.41 | | 40 | Maryland | 1.20 |
| 16 | South Dakota | 1.82 | | 40 | Washington | 1.20 |
| 14 | Tennessee | 1.98 | | 42 | California | 1.19 |
| 21 | Texas | 1.67 | | 42 | New Hampshire | 1.19 |
| 26 | Utah | 1.63 | | 42 | Oregon | 1.19 |
| 34 | Vermont | 1.31 | | 42 | Virginia | 1.19 |
| 42 | Virginia | 1.19 | | 46 | Delaware | 1.17 |
| 40 | Washington | 1.20 | | 47 | New Jersey | 1.11 |
| 7 | West Virginia | 2.08 | | 48 | Rhode Island | 1.06 |
| 34 | Wisconsin | 1.31 | | 49 | Connecticut | 1.01 |
| 2 | Wyoming | 2.42 | | 50 | Massachusetts | 0.80 |
| | | | | | District of Columbia | 1.18 |

*Source: Morgan Quitno Press using data from U.S. Department of Transportation, National Highway Safety Admin.*
*"Traffic Safety Facts 1999" (Table 1) (http://www.nhtsa.dot.gov/people/ncsa/pdf/STDfacts99.pdf)*

# Percent Change in Highway Fatality Rate: 1998 to 1999

## National Percent Change = 1.9% Decrease

ALPHA ORDER

| RANK | STATE | PERCENT CHANGE |
|------|-------|----------------|
| 10 | Alabama | 4.6 |
| 9 | Alaska | 6.4 |
| 18 | Arizona | 1.9 |
| 36 | Arkansas | (5.9) |
| 26 | California | (2.5) |
| 29 | Colorado | (3.8) |
| 43 | Connecticut | (9.8) |
| 47 | Delaware | (16.4) |
| 21 | Florida | 0.5 |
| 35 | Georgia | (5.6) |
| 49 | Hawaii | (19.3) |
| 19 | Idaho | 1.0 |
| 13 | Illinois | 2.9 |
| 16 | Indiana | 2.1 |
| 5 | Iowa | 8.4 |
| 8 | Kansas | 6.6 |
| 38 | Kentucky | (7.6) |
| 25 | Louisiana | (2.2) |
| 45 | Maine | (9.9) |
| 31 | Maryland | (4.0) |
| 15 | Massachusetts | 2.6 |
| 24 | Michigan | (1.4) |
| 37 | Minnesota | (6.9) |
| 31 | Mississippi | (4.0) |
| 42 | Missouri | (9.4) |
| 41 | Montana | (9.3) |
| 39 | Nebraska | (8.4) |
| 29 | Nevada | (3.8) |
| 7 | New Hampshire | 7.2 |
| 28 | New Jersey | (3.5) |
| 6 | New Mexico | 7.9 |
| 20 | New York | 0.8 |
| 40 | North Carolina | (8.6) |
| 1 | North Dakota | 31.2 |
| 22 | Ohio | 0.0 |
| 27 | Oklahoma | (3.3) |
| 50 | Oregon | (26.1) |
| 14 | Pennsylvania | 2.7 |
| 3 | Rhode Island | 14.0 |
| 12 | South Carolina | 3.0 |
| 46 | South Dakota | (10.8) |
| 16 | Tennessee | 2.1 |
| 31 | Texas | (4.0) |
| 23 | Utah | (1.2) |
| 48 | Vermont | (17.1) |
| 43 | Virginia | (9.8) |
| 34 | Washington | (5.5) |
| 4 | West Virginia | 9.5 |
| 11 | Wisconsin | 4.0 |
| 2 | Wyoming | 26.0 |

RANK ORDER

| RANK | STATE | PERCENT CHANGE |
|------|-------|----------------|
| 1 | North Dakota | 31.2 |
| 2 | Wyoming | 26.0 |
| 3 | Rhode Island | 14.0 |
| 4 | West Virginia | 9.5 |
| 5 | Iowa | 8.4 |
| 6 | New Mexico | 7.9 |
| 7 | New Hampshire | 7.2 |
| 8 | Kansas | 6.6 |
| 9 | Alaska | 6.4 |
| 10 | Alabama | 4.6 |
| 11 | Wisconsin | 4.0 |
| 12 | South Carolina | 3.0 |
| 13 | Illinois | 2.9 |
| 14 | Pennsylvania | 2.7 |
| 15 | Massachusetts | 2.6 |
| 16 | Indiana | 2.1 |
| 16 | Tennessee | 2.1 |
| 18 | Arizona | 1.9 |
| 19 | Idaho | 1.0 |
| 20 | New York | 0.8 |
| 21 | Florida | 0.5 |
| 22 | Ohio | 0.0 |
| 23 | Utah | (1.2) |
| 24 | Michigan | (1.4) |
| 25 | Louisiana | (2.2) |
| 26 | California | (2.5) |
| 27 | Oklahoma | (3.3) |
| 28 | New Jersey | (3.5) |
| 29 | Colorado | (3.8) |
| 29 | Nevada | (3.8) |
| 31 | Maryland | (4.0) |
| 31 | Mississippi | (4.0) |
| 31 | Texas | (4.0) |
| 34 | Washington | (5.5) |
| 35 | Georgia | (5.6) |
| 36 | Arkansas | (5.9) |
| 37 | Minnesota | (6.9) |
| 38 | Kentucky | (7.6) |
| 39 | Nebraska | (8.4) |
| 40 | North Carolina | (8.6) |
| 41 | Montana | (9.3) |
| 42 | Missouri | (9.4) |
| 43 | Connecticut | (9.8) |
| 43 | Virginia | (9.8) |
| 45 | Maine | (9.9) |
| 46 | South Dakota | (10.8) |
| 47 | Delaware | (16.4) |
| 48 | Vermont | (17.1) |
| 49 | Hawaii | (19.3) |
| 50 | Oregon | (26.1) |
| | District of Columbia | (27.6) |

Source: Morgan Quitno Press using data from U.S. Department of Transportation, National Highway Safety Admin. *"Traffic Safety Facts 1999" (Table 1) (http://www.nhtsa.dot.gov/people/ncsa/pdf/STDfacts99.pdf)*

# Safety Belt Usage Rate in 1999

## National Rate = 67.0% Use Safety Belts*

ALPHA ORDER

| RANK | STATE | PERCENT |
|------|-------|---------|
| 40 | Alabama | 57.9 |
| 37 | Alaska | 60.6 |
| 16 | Arizona | 71.1 |
| 44 | Arkansas | 57.2 |
| 1 | California | 89.3 |
| 26 | Colorado | 65.2 |
| 14 | Connecticut | 72.9 |
| 30 | Delaware | 64.4 |
| 38 | Florida | 59.0 |
| 11 | Georgia | 74.2 |
| 6 | Hawaii | 80.3 |
| 40 | Idaho | 57.9 |
| 25 | Illinois | 65.9 |
| 43 | Indiana | 57.3 |
| 9 | Iowa | 78.0 |
| 33 | Kansas | 62.6 |
| 39 | Kentucky | 58.6 |
| 24 | Louisiana | 67.0 |
| 31 | Maine | 64.3 |
| 3 | Maryland | 82.7 |
| 46 | Massachusetts | 52.0 |
| 17 | Michigan | 70.1 |
| 15 | Minnesota | 71.5 |
| 45 | Mississippi | 54.5 |
| 35 | Missouri | 60.8 |
| 12 | Montana | 74.0 |
| 21 | Nebraska | 67.9 |
| 7 | Nevada | 79.8 |
| 40 | New Hampshire | 57.9 |
| 32 | New Jersey | 63.3 |
| 2 | New Mexico | 88.4 |
| 10 | New York | 76.1 |
| 8 | North Carolina | 78.1 |
| 48 | North Dakota | 46.7 |
| 29 | Ohio | 64.8 |
| 36 | Oklahoma | 60.7 |
| 3 | Oregon | 82.7 |
| 20 | Pennsylvania | 69.7 |
| 23 | Rhode Island | 67.3 |
| 26 | South Carolina | 65.2 |
| 50 | South Dakota | 38.6 |
| 34 | Tennessee | 61.0 |
| 12 | Texas | 74.0 |
| 22 | Utah | 67.4 |
| 19 | Vermont | 69.8 |
| 18 | Virginia | 69.9 |
| 5 | Washington | 81.1 |
| 47 | West Virginia | 51.9 |
| 28 | Wisconsin | 65.1 |
| 49 | Wyoming | 45.7 |

RANK ORDER

| RANK | STATE | PERCENT |
|------|-------|---------|
| 1 | California | 89.3 |
| 2 | New Mexico | 88.4 |
| 3 | Maryland | 82.7 |
| 3 | Oregon | 82.7 |
| 5 | Washington | 81.1 |
| 6 | Hawaii | 80.3 |
| 7 | Nevada | 79.8 |
| 8 | North Carolina | 78.1 |
| 9 | Iowa | 78.0 |
| 10 | New York | 76.1 |
| 11 | Georgia | 74.2 |
| 12 | Montana | 74.0 |
| 12 | Texas | 74.0 |
| 14 | Connecticut | 72.9 |
| 15 | Minnesota | 71.5 |
| 16 | Arizona | 71.1 |
| 17 | Michigan | 70.1 |
| 18 | Virginia | 69.9 |
| 19 | Vermont | 69.8 |
| 20 | Pennsylvania | 69.7 |
| 21 | Nebraska | 67.9 |
| 22 | Utah | 67.4 |
| 23 | Rhode Island | 67.3 |
| 24 | Louisiana | 67.0 |
| 25 | Illinois | 65.9 |
| 26 | Colorado | 65.2 |
| 26 | South Carolina | 65.2 |
| 28 | Wisconsin | 65.1 |
| 29 | Ohio | 64.8 |
| 30 | Delaware | 64.4 |
| 31 | Maine | 64.3 |
| 32 | New Jersey | 63.3 |
| 33 | Kansas | 62.6 |
| 34 | Tennessee | 61.0 |
| 35 | Missouri | 60.8 |
| 36 | Oklahoma | 60.7 |
| 37 | Alaska | 60.6 |
| 38 | Florida | 59.0 |
| 39 | Kentucky | 58.6 |
| 40 | Alabama | 57.9 |
| 40 | Idaho | 57.9 |
| 40 | New Hampshire | 57.9 |
| 43 | Indiana | 57.3 |
| 44 | Arkansas | 57.2 |
| 45 | Mississippi | 54.5 |
| 46 | Massachusetts | 52.0 |
| 47 | West Virginia | 51.9 |
| 48 | North Dakota | 46.7 |
| 49 | Wyoming | 45.7 |
| 50 | South Dakota | 38.6 |
| | District of Columbia | 77.9 |

*Source: U.S. Department of Transportation, National Highway Traffic Safety Administration "Traffic Safety Facts 1999" (http://www.nhtsa.dot.gov/people/ncsa/factshet.html)*
*As of December 1999.*

# Percent of Passenger Car Occupant Fatalities
## Where Victim Used a Seat Belt in 1999
## National Percent = 40.1% of Passenger Car Occupant Fatalities*

ALPHA ORDER

| RANK | STATE | PERCENT |
|------|-------|---------|
| 31 | Alabama | 36.5 |
| 24 | Alaska | 37.9 |
| 26 | Arizona | 37.3 |
| 42 | Arkansas | 27.3 |
| 4 | California | 50.9 |
| 6 | Colorado | 47.0 |
| 27 | Connecticut | 37.0 |
| 35 | Delaware | 33.3 |
| 16 | Florida | 41.3 |
| 16 | Georgia | 41.3 |
| 30 | Hawaii | 36.8 |
| 39 | Idaho | 31.5 |
| 32 | Illinois | 36.1 |
| 9 | Indiana | 43.5 |
| 14 | Iowa | 41.7 |
| 23 | Kansas | 38.0 |
| 37 | Kentucky | 32.1 |
| 36 | Louisiana | 32.5 |
| 8 | Maine | 45.9 |
| 1 | Maryland | 53.9 |
| 46 | Massachusetts | 26.6 |
| 7 | Michigan | 46.6 |
| 20 | Minnesota | 39.1 |
| 48 | Mississippi | 25.4 |
| 34 | Missouri | 34.0 |
| 50 | Montana | 21.7 |
| 45 | Nebraska | 26.8 |
| 11 | Nevada | 42.5 |
| 40 | New Hampshire | 31.4 |
| 25 | New Jersey | 37.5 |
| 13 | New Mexico | 42.1 |
| 12 | New York | 42.2 |
| 5 | North Carolina | 48.7 |
| 14 | North Dakota | 41.7 |
| 19 | Ohio | 39.3 |
| 10 | Oklahoma | 42.9 |
| 2 | Oregon | 52.8 |
| 41 | Pennsylvania | 30.3 |
| 38 | Rhode Island | 31.9 |
| 22 | South Carolina | 38.2 |
| 49 | South Dakota | 23.4 |
| 43 | Tennessee | 27.0 |
| 3 | Texas | 52.4 |
| 29 | Utah | 36.9 |
| 47 | Vermont | 26.5 |
| 27 | Virginia | 37.0 |
| 18 | Washington | 40.4 |
| 33 | West Virginia | 34.7 |
| 21 | Wisconsin | 38.4 |
| 43 | Wyoming | 27.0 |

RANK ORDER

| RANK | STATE | PERCENT |
|------|-------|---------|
| 1 | Maryland | 53.9 |
| 2 | Oregon | 52.8 |
| 3 | Texas | 52.4 |
| 4 | California | 50.9 |
| 5 | North Carolina | 48.7 |
| 6 | Colorado | 47.0 |
| 7 | Michigan | 46.6 |
| 8 | Maine | 45.9 |
| 9 | Indiana | 43.5 |
| 10 | Oklahoma | 42.9 |
| 11 | Nevada | 42.5 |
| 12 | New York | 42.2 |
| 13 | New Mexico | 42.1 |
| 14 | Iowa | 41.7 |
| 14 | North Dakota | 41.7 |
| 16 | Florida | 41.3 |
| 16 | Georgia | 41.3 |
| 18 | Washington | 40.4 |
| 19 | Ohio | 39.3 |
| 20 | Minnesota | 39.1 |
| 21 | Wisconsin | 38.4 |
| 22 | South Carolina | 38.2 |
| 23 | Kansas | 38.0 |
| 24 | Alaska | 37.9 |
| 25 | New Jersey | 37.5 |
| 26 | Arizona | 37.3 |
| 27 | Connecticut | 37.0 |
| 27 | Virginia | 37.0 |
| 29 | Utah | 36.9 |
| 30 | Hawaii | 36.8 |
| 31 | Alabama | 36.5 |
| 32 | Illinois | 36.1 |
| 33 | West Virginia | 34.7 |
| 34 | Missouri | 34.0 |
| 35 | Delaware | 33.3 |
| 36 | Louisiana | 32.5 |
| 37 | Kentucky | 32.1 |
| 38 | Rhode Island | 31.9 |
| 39 | Idaho | 31.5 |
| 40 | New Hampshire | 31.4 |
| 41 | Pennsylvania | 30.3 |
| 42 | Arkansas | 27.3 |
| 43 | Tennessee | 27.0 |
| 43 | Wyoming | 27.0 |
| 45 | Nebraska | 26.8 |
| 46 | Massachusetts | 26.6 |
| 47 | Vermont | 26.5 |
| 48 | Mississippi | 25.4 |
| 49 | South Dakota | 23.4 |
| 50 | Montana | 21.7 |
| | District of Columbia | 28.6 |

Source: U.S. Department of Transportation, National Highway Traffic Safety Administration
"Traffic Safety Facts 1999" (http://www.nhtsa.dot.gov/people/ncsa/factshet.html)
*Only those fatalities where seat belts are known to have been used are counted.

# Fatalities in Alcohol-Related Crashes in 1999

## National Total = 15,786 Fatalities*

ALPHA ORDER

| RANK | STATE | FATALITIES | % of USA |
|---|---|---|---|
| 12 | Alabama | 430 | 2.7% |
| 47 | Alaska | 40 | 0.3% |
| 14 | Arizona | 406 | 2.6% |
| 29 | Arkansas | 190 | 1.2% |
| 2 | California | 1,351 | 8.6% |
| 25 | Colorado | 220 | 1.4% |
| 36 | Connecticut | 134 | 0.8% |
| 47 | Delaware | 40 | 0.3% |
| 3 | Florida | 1,043 | 6.6% |
| 8 | Georgia | 506 | 3.2% |
| 46 | Hawaii | 43 | 0.3% |
| 39 | Idaho | 102 | 0.6% |
| 4 | Illinois | 637 | 4.0% |
| 17 | Indiana | 342 | 2.2% |
| 33 | Iowa | 160 | 1.0% |
| 30 | Kansas | 186 | 1.2% |
| 22 | Kentucky | 281 | 1.8% |
| 13 | Louisiana | 427 | 2.7% |
| 44 | Maine | 59 | 0.4% |
| 31 | Maryland | 179 | 1.1% |
| 27 | Massachusetts | 203 | 1.3% |
| 6 | Michigan | 547 | 3.5% |
| 28 | Minnesota | 201 | 1.3% |
| 15 | Mississippi | 362 | 2.3% |
| 11 | Missouri | 441 | 2.8% |
| 38 | Montana | 103 | 0.7% |
| 37 | Nebraska | 125 | 0.8% |
| 34 | Nevada | 156 | 1.0% |
| 42 | New Hampshire | 66 | 0.4% |
| 21 | New Jersey | 291 | 1.8% |
| 26 | New Mexico | 206 | 1.3% |
| 16 | New York | 344 | 2.2% |
| 7 | North Carolina | 536 | 3.4% |
| 45 | North Dakota | 56 | 0.4% |
| 10 | Ohio | 458 | 2.9% |
| 24 | Oklahoma | 245 | 1.6% |
| 32 | Oregon | 170 | 1.1% |
| 5 | Pennsylvania | 605 | 3.8% |
| 49 | Rhode Island | 36 | 0.2% |
| 18 | South Carolina | 333 | 2.1% |
| 43 | South Dakota | 65 | 0.4% |
| 9 | Tennessee | 489 | 3.1% |
| 1 | Texas | 1,734 | 11.0% |
| 40 | Utah | 74 | 0.5% |
| 50 | Vermont | 34 | 0.2% |
| 19 | Virginia | 320 | 2.0% |
| 23 | Washington | 265 | 1.7% |
| 35 | West Virginia | 145 | 0.9% |
| 20 | Wisconsin | 309 | 2.0% |
| 41 | Wyoming | 70 | 0.4% |

RANK ORDER

| RANK | STATE | FATALITIES | % of USA |
|---|---|---|---|
| 1 | Texas | 1,734 | 11.0% |
| 2 | California | 1,351 | 8.6% |
| 3 | Florida | 1,043 | 6.6% |
| 4 | Illinois | 637 | 4.0% |
| 5 | Pennsylvania | 605 | 3.8% |
| 6 | Michigan | 547 | 3.5% |
| 7 | North Carolina | 536 | 3.4% |
| 8 | Georgia | 506 | 3.2% |
| 9 | Tennessee | 489 | 3.1% |
| 10 | Ohio | 458 | 2.9% |
| 11 | Missouri | 441 | 2.8% |
| 12 | Alabama | 430 | 2.7% |
| 13 | Louisiana | 427 | 2.7% |
| 14 | Arizona | 406 | 2.6% |
| 15 | Mississippi | 362 | 2.3% |
| 16 | New York | 344 | 2.2% |
| 17 | Indiana | 342 | 2.2% |
| 18 | South Carolina | 333 | 2.1% |
| 19 | Virginia | 320 | 2.0% |
| 20 | Wisconsin | 309 | 2.0% |
| 21 | New Jersey | 291 | 1.8% |
| 22 | Kentucky | 281 | 1.8% |
| 23 | Washington | 265 | 1.7% |
| 24 | Oklahoma | 245 | 1.6% |
| 25 | Colorado | 220 | 1.4% |
| 26 | New Mexico | 206 | 1.3% |
| 27 | Massachusetts | 203 | 1.3% |
| 28 | Minnesota | 201 | 1.3% |
| 29 | Arkansas | 190 | 1.2% |
| 30 | Kansas | 186 | 1.2% |
| 31 | Maryland | 179 | 1.1% |
| 32 | Oregon | 170 | 1.1% |
| 33 | Iowa | 160 | 1.0% |
| 34 | Nevada | 156 | 1.0% |
| 35 | West Virginia | 145 | 0.9% |
| 36 | Connecticut | 134 | 0.8% |
| 37 | Nebraska | 125 | 0.8% |
| 38 | Montana | 103 | 0.7% |
| 39 | Idaho | 102 | 0.6% |
| 40 | Utah | 74 | 0.5% |
| 41 | Wyoming | 70 | 0.4% |
| 42 | New Hampshire | 66 | 0.4% |
| 43 | South Dakota | 65 | 0.4% |
| 44 | Maine | 59 | 0.4% |
| 45 | North Dakota | 56 | 0.4% |
| 46 | Hawaii | 43 | 0.3% |
| 47 | Alaska | 40 | 0.3% |
| 47 | Delaware | 40 | 0.3% |
| 49 | Rhode Island | 36 | 0.2% |
| 50 | Vermont | 34 | 0.2% |
| | District of Columbia | 22 | 0.1% |

*Source: U.S. Department of Transportation, National Highway Traffic Safety Administration*
*"Traffic Safety Facts 1999, Alcohol" (http://www.nhtsa.dot.gov/people/ncsa/pdf/Alcohol99.pdf)*
*\*Drivers with Blood Alcohol Content (BAC) of 0.01 or more. "Legally Drunk" BAC differs from state to state but is often .08 or higher.*

# Fatalities in Alcohol-Related Crashes
## As a Percent of All Highway Fatalities in 1999
## National Percent = 38% of Highway Fatalities*

ALPHA ORDER

RANK ORDER

| RANK | STATE | PERCENT | RANK | STATE | PERCENT |
|---|---|---|---|---|---|
| 26 | Alabama | 38 | 1 | Alaska | 53 |
| 1 | Alaska | 53 | 2 | Massachusetts | 49 |
| 19 | Arizona | 40 | 2 | Texas | 49 |
| 46 | Arkansas | 31 | 4 | Montana | 47 |
| 26 | California | 38 | 4 | New Hampshire | 47 |
| 36 | Colorado | 35 | 4 | North Dakota | 47 |
| 8 | Connecticut | 45 | 7 | Louisiana | 46 |
| 19 | Delaware | 40 | 8 | Connecticut | 45 |
| 33 | Florida | 36 | 8 | Nevada | 45 |
| 39 | Georgia | 34 | 8 | New Mexico | 45 |
| 11 | Hawaii | 44 | 11 | Hawaii | 44 |
| 30 | Idaho | 37 | 11 | Illinois | 44 |
| 11 | Illinois | 44 | 13 | South Dakota | 43 |
| 39 | Indiana | 34 | 14 | Nebraska | 42 |
| 41 | Iowa | 33 | 14 | Washington | 42 |
| 36 | Kansas | 35 | 16 | Oregon | 41 |
| 36 | Kentucky | 35 | 16 | Rhode Island | 41 |
| 7 | Louisiana | 46 | 16 | Wisconsin | 41 |
| 43 | Maine | 32 | 19 | Arizona | 40 |
| 48 | Maryland | 30 | 19 | Delaware | 40 |
| 2 | Massachusetts | 49 | 19 | Michigan | 40 |
| 19 | Michigan | 40 | 19 | Missouri | 40 |
| 43 | Minnesota | 32 | 19 | New Jersey | 40 |
| 24 | Mississippi | 39 | 24 | Mississippi | 39 |
| 19 | Missouri | 40 | 24 | Pennsylvania | 39 |
| 4 | Montana | 47 | 26 | Alabama | 38 |
| 14 | Nebraska | 42 | 26 | California | 38 |
| 8 | Nevada | 45 | 26 | Tennessee | 38 |
| 4 | New Hampshire | 47 | 26 | Vermont | 38 |
| 19 | New Jersey | 40 | 30 | Idaho | 37 |
| 8 | New Mexico | 45 | 30 | West Virginia | 37 |
| 49 | New York | 22 | 30 | Wyoming | 37 |
| 33 | North Carolina | 36 | 33 | Florida | 36 |
| 4 | North Dakota | 47 | 33 | North Carolina | 36 |
| 43 | Ohio | 32 | 33 | Virginia | 36 |
| 41 | Oklahoma | 33 | 36 | Colorado | 35 |
| 16 | Oregon | 41 | 36 | Kansas | 35 |
| 24 | Pennsylvania | 39 | 36 | Kentucky | 35 |
| 16 | Rhode Island | 41 | 39 | Georgia | 34 |
| 46 | South Carolina | 31 | 39 | Indiana | 34 |
| 13 | South Dakota | 43 | 41 | Iowa | 33 |
| 26 | Tennessee | 38 | 41 | Oklahoma | 33 |
| 2 | Texas | 49 | 43 | Maine | 32 |
| 50 | Utah | 21 | 43 | Minnesota | 32 |
| 26 | Vermont | 38 | 43 | Ohio | 32 |
| 33 | Virginia | 36 | 46 | Arkansas | 31 |
| 14 | Washington | 42 | 46 | South Carolina | 31 |
| 30 | West Virginia | 37 | 48 | Maryland | 30 |
| 16 | Wisconsin | 41 | 49 | New York | 22 |
| 30 | Wyoming | 37 | 50 | Utah | 21 |
| | | | | District of Columbia | 53 |

*Source: U.S. Department of Transportation, National Highway Traffic Safety Administration*
*"Traffic Safety Facts 1999, Alcohol" (http://www.nhtsa.dot.gov/people/ncsa/pdf/Alcohol99.pdf)*
*\*Drivers with Blood Alcohol Content (BAC) of 0.01 or more. "Legally Drunk" BAC differs from state to state but is often .08 or higher.*

# Licensed Drivers in 1999

## National Total = 187,170,420 Licensed Drivers

ALPHA ORDER

| RANK | STATE | DRIVERS | % of USA |
|---|---|---|---|
| 19 | Alabama | 3,445,893 | 1.8% |
| 48 | Alaska | 459,362 | 0.2% |
| 20 | Arizona | 3,297,281 | 1.8% |
| 31 | Arkansas | 1,925,733 | 1.0% |
| 1 | California | 20,830,674 | 11.1% |
| 22 | Colorado | 2,990,673 | 1.6% |
| 28 | Connecticut | 2,373,723 | 1.3% |
| 45 | Delaware | 551,787 | 0.3% |
| 3 | Florida | 12,400,841 | 6.6% |
| 11 | Georgia | 5,471,100 | 2.9% |
| 42 | Hawaii | 752,693 | 0.4% |
| 41 | Idaho | 872,825 | 0.5% |
| 7 | Illinois | 7,925,204 | 4.2% |
| 16 | Indiana | 3,856,177 | 2.1% |
| 30 | Iowa | 1,935,201 | 1.0% |
| 32 | Kansas | 1,892,478 | 1.0% |
| 26 | Kentucky | 2,660,468 | 1.4% |
| 25 | Louisiana | 2,762,571 | 1.5% |
| 40 | Maine | 911,704 | 0.5% |
| 21 | Maryland | 3,194,601 | 1.7% |
| 13 | Massachusetts | 4,421,054 | 2.4% |
| 8 | Michigan | 6,863,199 | 3.7% |
| 23 | Minnesota | 2,907,027 | 1.6% |
| 33 | Mississippi | 1,788,189 | 1.0% |
| 17 | Missouri | 3,839,764 | 2.1% |
| 44 | Montana | 660,151 | 0.4% |
| 38 | Nebraska | 1,202,517 | 0.6% |
| 35 | Nevada | 1,322,014 | 0.7% |
| 39 | New Hampshire | 918,563 | 0.5% |
| 9 | New Jersey | 5,550,772 | 3.0% |
| 37 | New Mexico | 1,221,927 | 0.7% |
| 4 | New York | 10,626,625 | 5.7% |
| 10 | North Carolina | 5,491,228 | 2.9% |
| 49 | North Dakota | 457,890 | 0.2% |
| 6 | Ohio | 8,045,787 | 4.3% |
| 29 | Oklahoma | 2,312,621 | 1.2% |
| 27 | Oregon | 2,461,639 | 1.3% |
| 5 | Pennsylvania | 8,478,276 | 4.5% |
| 43 | Rhode Island | 688,650 | 0.4% |
| 24 | South Carolina | 2,810,221 | 1.5% |
| 46 | South Dakota | 543,573 | 0.3% |
| 14 | Tennessee | 4,175,766 | 2.2% |
| 2 | Texas | 13,359,305 | 7.1% |
| 34 | Utah | 1,439,534 | 0.8% |
| 47 | Vermont | 495,824 | 0.3% |
| 12 | Virginia | 4,729,373 | 2.5% |
| 15 | Washington | 4,128,775 | 2.2% |
| 36 | West Virginia | 1,273,701 | 0.7% |
| 18 | Wisconsin | 3,733,122 | 2.0% |
| 50 | Wyoming | 363,471 | 0.2% |

RANK ORDER

| RANK | STATE | DRIVERS | % of USA |
|---|---|---|---|
| 1 | California | 20,830,674 | 11.1% |
| 2 | Texas | 13,359,305 | 7.1% |
| 3 | Florida | 12,400,841 | 6.6% |
| 4 | New York | 10,626,625 | 5.7% |
| 5 | Pennsylvania | 8,478,276 | 4.5% |
| 6 | Ohio | 8,045,787 | 4.3% |
| 7 | Illinois | 7,925,204 | 4.2% |
| 8 | Michigan | 6,863,199 | 3.7% |
| 9 | New Jersey | 5,550,772 | 3.0% |
| 10 | North Carolina | 5,491,228 | 2.9% |
| 11 | Georgia | 5,471,100 | 2.9% |
| 12 | Virginia | 4,729,373 | 2.5% |
| 13 | Massachusetts | 4,421,054 | 2.4% |
| 14 | Tennessee | 4,175,766 | 2.2% |
| 15 | Washington | 4,128,775 | 2.2% |
| 16 | Indiana | 3,856,177 | 2.1% |
| 17 | Missouri | 3,839,764 | 2.1% |
| 18 | Wisconsin | 3,733,122 | 2.0% |
| 19 | Alabama | 3,445,893 | 1.8% |
| 20 | Arizona | 3,297,281 | 1.8% |
| 21 | Maryland | 3,194,601 | 1.7% |
| 22 | Colorado | 2,990,673 | 1.6% |
| 23 | Minnesota | 2,907,027 | 1.6% |
| 24 | South Carolina | 2,810,221 | 1.5% |
| 25 | Louisiana | 2,762,571 | 1.5% |
| 26 | Kentucky | 2,660,468 | 1.4% |
| 27 | Oregon | 2,461,639 | 1.3% |
| 28 | Connecticut | 2,373,723 | 1.3% |
| 29 | Oklahoma | 2,312,621 | 1.2% |
| 30 | Iowa | 1,935,201 | 1.0% |
| 31 | Arkansas | 1,925,733 | 1.0% |
| 32 | Kansas | 1,892,478 | 1.0% |
| 33 | Mississippi | 1,788,189 | 1.0% |
| 34 | Utah | 1,439,534 | 0.8% |
| 35 | Nevada | 1,322,014 | 0.7% |
| 36 | West Virginia | 1,273,701 | 0.7% |
| 37 | New Mexico | 1,221,927 | 0.7% |
| 38 | Nebraska | 1,202,517 | 0.6% |
| 39 | New Hampshire | 918,563 | 0.5% |
| 40 | Maine | 911,704 | 0.5% |
| 41 | Idaho | 872,825 | 0.5% |
| 42 | Hawaii | 752,693 | 0.4% |
| 43 | Rhode Island | 688,650 | 0.4% |
| 44 | Montana | 660,151 | 0.4% |
| 45 | Delaware | 551,787 | 0.3% |
| 46 | South Dakota | 543,573 | 0.3% |
| 47 | Vermont | 495,824 | 0.3% |
| 48 | Alaska | 459,362 | 0.2% |
| 49 | North Dakota | 457,890 | 0.2% |
| 50 | Wyoming | 363,471 | 0.2% |
|  | District of Columbia | 348,873 | 0.2% |

*Source: U.S. Department of Transportation, Federal Highway Administration*
*"Highway Statistics 1999" (Table DL-1C, October 2000)*

# Licensed Drivers per 1,000 Driving Age Population in 1999

## National Ratio = 889 Licensed Drivers

| ALPHA ORDER | | | | RANK ORDER | | |
|---|---|---|---|---|---|---|
| RANK | STATE | RATIO | | RANK | STATE | RATIO |
| 4 | Alabama | 1,005 | | 1 | Vermont | 1,050 |
| 3 | Alaska | 1,032 | | 2 | Florida | 1,039 |
| 25 | Arizona | 920 | | 3 | Alaska | 1,032 |
| 7 | Arkansas | 978 | | 4 | Alabama | 1,005 |
| 46 | California | 828 | | 5 | New Hampshire | 986 |
| 11 | Colorado | 960 | | 6 | Wyoming | 981 |
| 17 | Connecticut | 934 | | 7 | Arkansas | 978 |
| 18 | Delaware | 933 | | 8 | Tennessee | 972 |
| 2 | Florida | 1,039 | | 9 | South Dakota | 970 |
| 27 | Georgia | 918 | | 10 | Nevada | 967 |
| 47 | Hawaii | 811 | | 11 | Colorado | 960 |
| 24 | Idaho | 923 | | 12 | Montana | 958 |
| 42 | Illinois | 852 | | 13 | Utah | 956 |
| 44 | Indiana | 840 | | 14 | Oregon | 951 |
| 40 | Iowa | 864 | | 15 | Nebraska | 941 |
| 21 | Kansas | 927 | | 16 | New Mexico | 938 |
| 41 | Kentucky | 855 | | 17 | Connecticut | 934 |
| 45 | Louisiana | 830 | | 18 | Delaware | 933 |
| 29 | Maine | 912 | | 19 | Washington | 929 |
| 48 | Maryland | 798 | | 20 | North Carolina | 928 |
| 30 | Massachusetts | 909 | | 21 | Kansas | 927 |
| 32 | Michigan | 903 | | 22 | North Dakota | 925 |
| 49 | Minnesota | 795 | | 23 | South Carolina | 924 |
| 43 | Mississippi | 848 | | 24 | Idaho | 923 |
| 31 | Missouri | 906 | | 25 | Arizona | 920 |
| 12 | Montana | 958 | | 25 | Ohio | 920 |
| 15 | Nebraska | 941 | | 27 | Georgia | 918 |
| 10 | Nevada | 967 | | 28 | Wisconsin | 917 |
| 5 | New Hampshire | 986 | | 29 | Maine | 912 |
| 39 | New Jersey | 874 | | 30 | Massachusetts | 909 |
| 16 | New Mexico | 938 | | 31 | Missouri | 906 |
| 50 | New York | 747 | | 32 | Michigan | 903 |
| 20 | North Carolina | 928 | | 33 | Oklahoma | 895 |
| 22 | North Dakota | 925 | | 34 | Pennsylvania | 894 |
| 25 | Ohio | 920 | | 35 | Texas | 893 |
| 33 | Oklahoma | 895 | | 36 | Rhode Island | 888 |
| 14 | Oregon | 951 | | 37 | Virginia | 876 |
| 34 | Pennsylvania | 894 | | 38 | West Virginia | 875 |
| 36 | Rhode Island | 888 | | 39 | New Jersey | 874 |
| 23 | South Carolina | 924 | | 40 | Iowa | 864 |
| 9 | South Dakota | 970 | | 41 | Kentucky | 855 |
| 8 | Tennessee | 972 | | 42 | Illinois | 852 |
| 35 | Texas | 893 | | 43 | Mississippi | 848 |
| 13 | Utah | 956 | | 44 | Indiana | 840 |
| 1 | Vermont | 1,050 | | 45 | Louisiana | 830 |
| 37 | Virginia | 876 | | 46 | California | 828 |
| 19 | Washington | 929 | | 47 | Hawaii | 811 |
| 38 | West Virginia | 875 | | 48 | Maryland | 798 |
| 28 | Wisconsin | 917 | | 49 | Minnesota | 795 |
| 6 | Wyoming | 981 | | 50 | New York | 747 |
| | | | | | District of Columbia | 806 |

*Source: U.S. Department of Transportation, Federal Highway Administration*
*"Highway Statistics 1999" (Table DL-1C, October 2000)*

# Motor Vehicle Registrations in 1999

## National Total = 216,308,623 Motor Vehicles*

ALPHA ORDER

RANK ORDER

| RANK | STATE | VEHICLES | % of USA | RANK | STATE | VEHICLES | % of USA |
|---|---|---|---|---|---|---|---|
| 20 | Alabama | 3,957,249 | 1.8% | 1 | California | 26,362,468 | 12.2% |
| 48 | Alaska | 571,469 | 0.3% | 2 | Texas | 14,068,720 | 6.5% |
| 23 | Arizona | 3,606,227 | 1.7% | 3 | Florida | 11,389,713 | 5.3% |
| 33 | Arkansas | 1,817,825 | 0.8% | 4 | New York | 10,756,026 | 5.0% |
| 1 | California | 26,362,468 | 12.2% | 5 | Ohio | 10,235,603 | 4.7% |
| 22 | Colorado | 3,858,148 | 1.8% | 6 | Illinois | 9,355,260 | 4.3% |
| 29 | Connecticut | 2,766,171 | 1.3% | 7 | Pennsylvania | 9,008,600 | 4.2% |
| 47 | Delaware | 615,611 | 0.3% | 8 | Michigan | 8,289,644 | 3.8% |
| 3 | Florida | 11,389,713 | 5.3% | 9 | Georgia | 6,972,710 | 3.2% |
| 9 | Georgia | 6,972,710 | 3.2% | 10 | New Jersey | 6,102,758 | 2.8% |
| 45 | Hawaii | 718,107 | 0.3% | 11 | Virginia | 5,871,157 | 2.7% |
| 39 | Idaho | 1,129,643 | 0.5% | 12 | North Carolina | 5,690,440 | 2.6% |
| 6 | Illinois | 9,355,260 | 4.3% | 13 | Indiana | 5,495,087 | 2.5% |
| 13 | Indiana | 5,495,087 | 2.5% | 14 | Massachusetts | 5,333,188 | 2.5% |
| 25 | Iowa | 3,049,967 | 1.4% | 15 | Washington | 4,862,150 | 2.2% |
| 32 | Kansas | 2,224,348 | 1.0% | 16 | Tennessee | 4,426,519 | 2.0% |
| 30 | Kentucky | 2,661,989 | 1.2% | 17 | Missouri | 4,404,244 | 2.0% |
| 24 | Louisiana | 3,504,662 | 1.6% | 18 | Wisconsin | 4,265,772 | 2.0% |
| 42 | Maine | 915,455 | 0.4% | 19 | Minnesota | 4,009,717 | 1.9% |
| 21 | Maryland | 3,896,297 | 1.8% | 20 | Alabama | 3,957,249 | 1.8% |
| 14 | Massachusetts | 5,333,188 | 2.5% | 21 | Maryland | 3,896,297 | 1.8% |
| 8 | Michigan | 8,289,644 | 3.8% | 22 | Colorado | 3,858,148 | 1.8% |
| 19 | Minnesota | 4,009,717 | 1.9% | 23 | Arizona | 3,606,227 | 1.7% |
| 31 | Mississippi | 2,316,772 | 1.1% | 24 | Louisiana | 3,504,662 | 1.6% |
| 17 | Missouri | 4,404,244 | 2.0% | 25 | Iowa | 3,049,967 | 1.4% |
| 41 | Montana | 997,905 | 0.5% | 26 | South Carolina | 3,026,247 | 1.4% |
| 36 | Nebraska | 1,569,553 | 0.7% | 27 | Oregon | 3,012,959 | 1.4% |
| 38 | Nevada | 1,162,376 | 0.5% | 28 | Oklahoma | 2,931,486 | 1.4% |
| 40 | New Hampshire | 1,050,898 | 0.5% | 29 | Connecticut | 2,766,171 | 1.3% |
| 10 | New Jersey | 6,102,758 | 2.8% | 30 | Kentucky | 2,661,989 | 1.2% |
| 35 | New Mexico | 1,576,482 | 0.7% | 31 | Mississippi | 2,316,772 | 1.1% |
| 4 | New York | 10,756,026 | 5.0% | 32 | Kansas | 2,224,348 | 1.0% |
| 12 | North Carolina | 5,690,440 | 2.6% | 33 | Arkansas | 1,817,825 | 0.8% |
| 46 | North Dakota | 704,412 | 0.3% | 34 | Utah | 1,577,180 | 0.7% |
| 5 | Ohio | 10,235,603 | 4.7% | 35 | New Mexico | 1,576,482 | 0.7% |
| 28 | Oklahoma | 2,931,486 | 1.4% | 36 | Nebraska | 1,569,553 | 0.7% |
| 27 | Oregon | 3,012,959 | 1.4% | 37 | West Virginia | 1,379,131 | 0.6% |
| 7 | Pennsylvania | 9,008,600 | 4.2% | 38 | Nevada | 1,162,376 | 0.5% |
| 44 | Rhode Island | 747,010 | 0.3% | 39 | Idaho | 1,129,643 | 0.5% |
| 26 | South Carolina | 3,026,247 | 1.4% | 40 | New Hampshire | 1,050,898 | 0.5% |
| 43 | South Dakota | 781,961 | 0.4% | 41 | Montana | 997,905 | 0.5% |
| 16 | Tennessee | 4,426,519 | 2.0% | 42 | Maine | 915,455 | 0.4% |
| 2 | Texas | 14,068,720 | 6.5% | 43 | South Dakota | 781,961 | 0.4% |
| 34 | Utah | 1,577,180 | 0.7% | 44 | Rhode Island | 747,010 | 0.3% |
| 50 | Vermont | 517,615 | 0.2% | 45 | Hawaii | 718,107 | 0.3% |
| 11 | Virginia | 5,871,157 | 2.7% | 46 | North Dakota | 704,412 | 0.3% |
| 15 | Washington | 4,862,150 | 2.2% | 47 | Delaware | 615,611 | 0.3% |
| 37 | West Virginia | 1,379,131 | 0.6% | 48 | Alaska | 571,469 | 0.3% |
| 18 | Wisconsin | 4,265,772 | 2.0% | 49 | Wyoming | 528,194 | 0.2% |
| 49 | Wyoming | 528,194 | 0.2% | 50 | Vermont | 517,615 | 0.2% |
| | | | | | District of Columbia | 235,498 | 0.1% |

Source: U.S. Department of Transportation, Federal Highway Administration
"Highway Statistics 1999" (Table MV-1, October 2000)
*Includes automobiles, trucks and buses. Does not include motorcycles.

# Motor Vehicles per Driving Age Population in 1999

## National Rate = 1.03 Motor Vehicles*

| ALPHA ORDER | | | | RANK ORDER | | |
|---|---|---|---|---|---|---|
| RANK | STATE | RATE | | RANK | STATE | RATE |
| 15 | Alabama | 1.15 | | 1 | Montana | 1.45 |
| 6 | Alaska | 1.28 | | 2 | Wyoming | 1.43 |
| 34 | Arizona | 1.01 | | 3 | North Dakota | 1.42 |
| 45 | Arkansas | 0.92 | | 4 | South Dakota | 1.39 |
| 27 | California | 1.05 | | 5 | Iowa | 1.36 |
| 7 | Colorado | 1.24 | | 6 | Alaska | 1.28 |
| 22 | Connecticut | 1.09 | | 7 | Colorado | 1.24 |
| 31 | Delaware | 1.04 | | 8 | Nebraska | 1.23 |
| 41 | Florida | 0.95 | | 9 | New Mexico | 1.21 |
| 12 | Georgia | 1.17 | | 10 | Indiana | 1.20 |
| 49 | Hawaii | 0.77 | | 11 | Idaho | 1.19 |
| 11 | Idaho | 1.19 | | 12 | Georgia | 1.17 |
| 34 | Illinois | 1.01 | | 12 | Ohio | 1.17 |
| 10 | Indiana | 1.20 | | 14 | Oregon | 1.16 |
| 5 | Iowa | 1.36 | | 15 | Alabama | 1.15 |
| 22 | Kansas | 1.09 | | 16 | New Hampshire | 1.13 |
| 47 | Kentucky | 0.86 | | 16 | Oklahoma | 1.13 |
| 27 | Louisiana | 1.05 | | 18 | Massachusetts | 1.10 |
| 45 | Maine | 0.92 | | 18 | Minnesota | 1.10 |
| 37 | Maryland | 0.97 | | 18 | Mississippi | 1.10 |
| 18 | Massachusetts | 1.10 | | 18 | Vermont | 1.10 |
| 22 | Michigan | 1.09 | | 22 | Connecticut | 1.09 |
| 18 | Minnesota | 1.10 | | 22 | Kansas | 1.09 |
| 18 | Mississippi | 1.10 | | 22 | Michigan | 1.09 |
| 31 | Missouri | 1.04 | | 22 | Virginia | 1.09 |
| 1 | Montana | 1.45 | | 22 | Washington | 1.09 |
| 8 | Nebraska | 1.23 | | 27 | California | 1.05 |
| 48 | Nevada | 0.85 | | 27 | Louisiana | 1.05 |
| 16 | New Hampshire | 1.13 | | 27 | Utah | 1.05 |
| 38 | New Jersey | 0.96 | | 27 | Wisconsin | 1.05 |
| 9 | New Mexico | 1.21 | | 31 | Delaware | 1.04 |
| 50 | New York | 0.76 | | 31 | Missouri | 1.04 |
| 38 | North Carolina | 0.96 | | 33 | Tennessee | 1.03 |
| 3 | North Dakota | 1.42 | | 34 | Arizona | 1.01 |
| 12 | Ohio | 1.17 | | 34 | Illinois | 1.01 |
| 16 | Oklahoma | 1.13 | | 36 | South Carolina | 0.99 |
| 14 | Oregon | 1.16 | | 37 | Maryland | 0.97 |
| 41 | Pennsylvania | 0.95 | | 38 | New Jersey | 0.96 |
| 38 | Rhode Island | 0.96 | | 38 | North Carolina | 0.96 |
| 36 | South Carolina | 0.99 | | 38 | Rhode Island | 0.96 |
| 4 | South Dakota | 1.39 | | 41 | Florida | 0.95 |
| 33 | Tennessee | 1.03 | | 41 | Pennsylvania | 0.95 |
| 44 | Texas | 0.94 | | 41 | West Virginia | 0.95 |
| 27 | Utah | 1.05 | | 44 | Texas | 0.94 |
| 18 | Vermont | 1.10 | | 45 | Arkansas | 0.92 |
| 22 | Virginia | 1.09 | | 45 | Maine | 0.92 |
| 22 | Washington | 1.09 | | 47 | Kentucky | 0.86 |
| 41 | West Virginia | 0.95 | | 48 | Nevada | 0.85 |
| 27 | Wisconsin | 1.05 | | 49 | Hawaii | 0.77 |
| 2 | Wyoming | 1.43 | | 50 | New York | 0.76 |
| | | | | | District of Columbia | 0.54 |

Source: Morgan Quitno Press using data from U.S. Department of Transportation, Federal Highway Administration
"Highway Statistics 1999" (Table MV-1, October 2000)
*Persons age 16 and older. Motor Vehicles include automobiles, trucks and buses. Motorcycles are not included.

# Automobile Registrations in 1999

## National Total = 132,432,044 Automobiles*

ALPHA ORDER

| RANK | STATE | AUTOMOBILES | % of USA |
|---|---|---|---|
| 25 | Alabama | 1,918,032 | 1.4% |
| 49 | Alaska | 238,202 | 0.2% |
| 22 | Arizona | 2,037,370 | 1.5% |
| 33 | Arkansas | 945,871 | 0.7% |
| 1 | California | 16,657,441 | 12.6% |
| 21 | Colorado | 2,053,579 | 1.6% |
| 23 | Connecticut | 1,994,380 | 1.5% |
| 45 | Delaware | 401,917 | 0.3% |
| 4 | Florida | 7,304,601 | 5.5% |
| 10 | Georgia | 4,011,725 | 3.0% |
| 44 | Hawaii | 454,341 | 0.3% |
| 42 | Idaho | 494,220 | 0.4% |
| 6 | Illinois | 6,307,479 | 4.8% |
| 14 | Indiana | 3,224,493 | 2.4% |
| 27 | Iowa | 1,723,848 | 1.3% |
| 32 | Kansas | 1,187,320 | 0.9% |
| 28 | Kentucky | 1,592,519 | 1.2% |
| 24 | Louisiana | 1,964,922 | 1.5% |
| 40 | Maine | 550,537 | 0.4% |
| 16 | Maryland | 2,665,572 | 2.0% |
| 11 | Massachusetts | 3,822,524 | 2.9% |
| 8 | Michigan | 5,069,808 | 3.8% |
| 20 | Minnesota | 2,265,392 | 1.7% |
| 31 | Mississippi | 1,299,441 | 1.0% |
| 18 | Missouri | 2,601,830 | 2.0% |
| 43 | Montana | 455,430 | 0.3% |
| 35 | Nebraska | 833,415 | 0.6% |
| 39 | Nevada | 620,131 | 0.5% |
| 38 | New Hampshire | 678,497 | 0.5% |
| 9 | New Jersey | 4,341,182 | 3.3% |
| 36 | New Mexico | 761,012 | 0.6% |
| 2 | New York | 7,892,118 | 6.0% |
| 13 | North Carolina | 3,423,588 | 2.6% |
| 47 | North Dakota | 342,786 | 0.3% |
| 5 | Ohio | 6,651,554 | 5.0% |
| 30 | Oklahoma | 1,524,424 | 1.2% |
| 29 | Oregon | 1,559,972 | 1.2% |
| 7 | Pennsylvania | 6,071,724 | 4.6% |
| 41 | Rhode Island | 535,034 | 0.4% |
| 26 | South Carolina | 1,872,502 | 1.4% |
| 46 | South Dakota | 379,168 | 0.3% |
| 17 | Tennessee | 2,621,508 | 2.0% |
| 3 | Texas | 7,738,292 | 5.8% |
| 34 | Utah | 856,699 | 0.6% |
| 48 | Vermont | 301,914 | 0.2% |
| 12 | Virginia | 3,769,276 | 2.8% |
| 15 | Washington | 2,741,257 | 2.1% |
| 37 | West Virginia | 759,648 | 0.6% |
| 19 | Wisconsin | 2,520,717 | 1.9% |
| 50 | Wyoming | 195,762 | 0.1% |

RANK ORDER

| RANK | STATE | AUTOMOBILES | % of USA |
|---|---|---|---|
| 1 | California | 16,657,441 | 12.6% |
| 2 | New York | 7,892,118 | 6.0% |
| 3 | Texas | 7,738,292 | 5.8% |
| 4 | Florida | 7,304,601 | 5.5% |
| 5 | Ohio | 6,651,554 | 5.0% |
| 6 | Illinois | 6,307,479 | 4.8% |
| 7 | Pennsylvania | 6,071,724 | 4.6% |
| 8 | Michigan | 5,069,808 | 3.8% |
| 9 | New Jersey | 4,341,182 | 3.3% |
| 10 | Georgia | 4,011,725 | 3.0% |
| 11 | Massachusetts | 3,822,524 | 2.9% |
| 12 | Virginia | 3,769,276 | 2.8% |
| 13 | North Carolina | 3,423,588 | 2.6% |
| 14 | Indiana | 3,224,493 | 2.4% |
| 15 | Washington | 2,741,257 | 2.1% |
| 16 | Maryland | 2,665,572 | 2.0% |
| 17 | Tennessee | 2,621,508 | 2.0% |
| 18 | Missouri | 2,601,830 | 2.0% |
| 19 | Wisconsin | 2,520,717 | 1.9% |
| 20 | Minnesota | 2,265,392 | 1.7% |
| 21 | Colorado | 2,053,579 | 1.6% |
| 22 | Arizona | 2,037,370 | 1.5% |
| 23 | Connecticut | 1,994,380 | 1.5% |
| 24 | Louisiana | 1,964,922 | 1.5% |
| 25 | Alabama | 1,918,032 | 1.4% |
| 26 | South Carolina | 1,872,502 | 1.4% |
| 27 | Iowa | 1,723,848 | 1.3% |
| 28 | Kentucky | 1,592,519 | 1.2% |
| 29 | Oregon | 1,559,972 | 1.2% |
| 30 | Oklahoma | 1,524,424 | 1.2% |
| 31 | Mississippi | 1,299,441 | 1.0% |
| 32 | Kansas | 1,187,320 | 0.9% |
| 33 | Arkansas | 945,871 | 0.7% |
| 34 | Utah | 856,699 | 0.6% |
| 35 | Nebraska | 833,415 | 0.6% |
| 36 | New Mexico | 761,012 | 0.6% |
| 37 | West Virginia | 759,648 | 0.6% |
| 38 | New Hampshire | 678,497 | 0.5% |
| 39 | Nevada | 620,131 | 0.5% |
| 40 | Maine | 550,537 | 0.4% |
| 41 | Rhode Island | 535,034 | 0.4% |
| 42 | Idaho | 494,220 | 0.4% |
| 43 | Montana | 455,430 | 0.3% |
| 44 | Hawaii | 454,341 | 0.3% |
| 45 | Delaware | 401,917 | 0.3% |
| 46 | South Dakota | 379,168 | 0.3% |
| 47 | North Dakota | 342,786 | 0.3% |
| 48 | Vermont | 301,914 | 0.2% |
| 49 | Alaska | 238,202 | 0.2% |
| 50 | Wyoming | 195,762 | 0.1% |
|  | District of Columbia | 197,070 | 0.1% |

Source: U.S. Department of Transportation, Federal Highway Administration
   "Highway Statistics 1999" (Table MV-1, October 2000)
*"Automobiles" formerly included personal passenger vans, minivans and sports-utility vehicles. These now are counted as trucks.

# Bus Registrations in 1999

## National Total = 728,777 Buses*

ALPHA ORDER

| RANK | STATE | BUSES | % of USA |
|------|-------|-------|----------|
| 28 | Alabama | 8,708 | 1.2% |
| 43 | Alaska | 2,372 | 0.3% |
| 33 | Arizona | 4,551 | 0.6% |
| 30 | Arkansas | 6,468 | 0.9% |
| 3 | California | 47,017 | 6.5% |
| 31 | Colorado | 5,803 | 0.8% |
| 26 | Connecticut | 10,011 | 1.4% |
| 45 | Delaware | 1,986 | 0.3% |
| 4 | Florida | 44,045 | 6.0% |
| 14 | Georgia | 17,520 | 2.4% |
| 34 | Hawaii | 4,184 | 0.6% |
| 36 | Idaho | 3,580 | 0.5% |
| 13 | Illinois | 17,691 | 2.4% |
| 8 | Indiana | 26,902 | 3.7% |
| 29 | Iowa | 8,115 | 1.1% |
| 35 | Kansas | 3,850 | 0.5% |
| 22 | Kentucky | 12,525 | 1.7% |
| 10 | Louisiana | 21,328 | 2.9% |
| 39 | Maine | 2,930 | 0.4% |
| 24 | Maryland | 11,476 | 1.6% |
| 23 | Massachusetts | 11,710 | 1.6% |
| 9 | Michigan | 25,536 | 3.5% |
| 18 | Minnesota | 14,664 | 2.0% |
| 25 | Mississippi | 10,544 | 1.4% |
| 19 | Missouri | 13,551 | 1.9% |
| 40 | Montana | 2,811 | 0.4% |
| 32 | Nebraska | 5,797 | 0.8% |
| 48 | Nevada | 1,771 | 0.2% |
| 49 | New Hampshire | 1,713 | 0.2% |
| 11 | New Jersey | 20,565 | 2.8% |
| 37 | New Mexico | 3,524 | 0.5% |
| 2 | New York | 50,731 | 7.0% |
| 7 | North Carolina | 29,987 | 4.1% |
| 44 | North Dakota | 2,289 | 0.3% |
| 5 | Ohio | 36,364 | 5.0% |
| 16 | Oklahoma | 16,169 | 2.2% |
| 21 | Oregon | 12,920 | 1.8% |
| 6 | Pennsylvania | 34,930 | 4.8% |
| 47 | Rhode Island | 1,900 | 0.3% |
| 17 | South Carolina | 15,816 | 2.2% |
| 41 | South Dakota | 2,721 | 0.4% |
| 15 | Tennessee | 17,380 | 2.4% |
| 1 | Texas | 82,589 | 11.3% |
| 50 | Utah | 1,242 | 0.2% |
| 46 | Vermont | 1,938 | 0.3% |
| 12 | Virginia | 17,854 | 2.4% |
| 27 | Washington | 9,137 | 1.3% |
| 38 | West Virginia | 3,211 | 0.4% |
| 20 | Wisconsin | 13,032 | 1.8% |
| 42 | Wyoming | 2,710 | 0.4% |

RANK ORDER

| RANK | STATE | BUSES | % of USA |
|------|-------|-------|----------|
| 1 | Texas | 82,589 | 11.3% |
| 2 | New York | 50,731 | 7.0% |
| 3 | California | 47,017 | 6.5% |
| 4 | Florida | 44,045 | 6.0% |
| 5 | Ohio | 36,364 | 5.0% |
| 6 | Pennsylvania | 34,930 | 4.8% |
| 7 | North Carolina | 29,987 | 4.1% |
| 8 | Indiana | 26,902 | 3.7% |
| 9 | Michigan | 25,536 | 3.5% |
| 10 | Louisiana | 21,328 | 2.9% |
| 11 | New Jersey | 20,565 | 2.8% |
| 12 | Virginia | 17,854 | 2.4% |
| 13 | Illinois | 17,691 | 2.4% |
| 14 | Georgia | 17,520 | 2.4% |
| 15 | Tennessee | 17,380 | 2.4% |
| 16 | Oklahoma | 16,169 | 2.2% |
| 17 | South Carolina | 15,816 | 2.2% |
| 18 | Minnesota | 14,664 | 2.0% |
| 19 | Missouri | 13,551 | 1.9% |
| 20 | Wisconsin | 13,032 | 1.8% |
| 21 | Oregon | 12,920 | 1.8% |
| 22 | Kentucky | 12,525 | 1.7% |
| 23 | Massachusetts | 11,710 | 1.6% |
| 24 | Maryland | 11,476 | 1.6% |
| 25 | Mississippi | 10,544 | 1.4% |
| 26 | Connecticut | 10,011 | 1.4% |
| 27 | Washington | 9,137 | 1.3% |
| 28 | Alabama | 8,708 | 1.2% |
| 29 | Iowa | 8,115 | 1.1% |
| 30 | Arkansas | 6,468 | 0.9% |
| 31 | Colorado | 5,803 | 0.8% |
| 32 | Nebraska | 5,797 | 0.8% |
| 33 | Arizona | 4,551 | 0.6% |
| 34 | Hawaii | 4,184 | 0.6% |
| 35 | Kansas | 3,850 | 0.5% |
| 36 | Idaho | 3,580 | 0.5% |
| 37 | New Mexico | 3,524 | 0.5% |
| 38 | West Virginia | 3,211 | 0.4% |
| 39 | Maine | 2,930 | 0.4% |
| 40 | Montana | 2,811 | 0.4% |
| 41 | South Dakota | 2,721 | 0.4% |
| 42 | Wyoming | 2,710 | 0.4% |
| 43 | Alaska | 2,372 | 0.3% |
| 44 | North Dakota | 2,289 | 0.3% |
| 45 | Delaware | 1,986 | 0.3% |
| 46 | Vermont | 1,938 | 0.3% |
| 47 | Rhode Island | 1,900 | 0.3% |
| 48 | Nevada | 1,771 | 0.2% |
| 49 | New Hampshire | 1,713 | 0.2% |
| 50 | Utah | 1,242 | 0.2% |
| | District of Columbia | 2,609 | 0.4% |

*Source: U.S. Department of Transportation, Federal Highway Administration*
*"Highway Statistics 1999" (Table MV-1, October 2000)*
*\*Includes private, commercial and publicly-owned buses.*

# Truck Registrations in 1999

## National Total = 83,147,802 Trucks*

ALPHA ORDER

| RANK | STATE | TRUCKS | % of USA |
|------|-------|--------|----------|
| 14 | Alabama | 2,030,509 | 2.4% |
| 45 | Alaska | 330,895 | 0.4% |
| 21 | Arizona | 1,564,306 | 1.9% |
| 32 | Arkansas | 865,486 | 1.0% |
| 1 | California | 9,658,010 | 11.6% |
| 15 | Colorado | 1,798,766 | 2.2% |
| 34 | Connecticut | 761,780 | 0.9% |
| 49 | Delaware | 211,708 | 0.3% |
| 3 | Florida | 4,041,067 | 4.9% |
| 7 | Georgia | 2,943,465 | 3.5% |
| 47 | Hawaii | 259,582 | 0.3% |
| 37 | Idaho | 631,843 | 0.8% |
| 6 | Illinois | 3,030,090 | 3.6% |
| 10 | Indiana | 2,243,692 | 2.7% |
| 26 | Iowa | 1,318,004 | 1.6% |
| 30 | Kansas | 1,033,178 | 1.2% |
| 29 | Kentucky | 1,056,945 | 1.3% |
| 22 | Louisiana | 1,518,412 | 1.8% |
| 43 | Maine | 361,988 | 0.4% |
| 27 | Maryland | 1,219,249 | 1.5% |
| 23 | Massachusetts | 1,498,954 | 1.8% |
| 5 | Michigan | 3,194,300 | 3.8% |
| 20 | Minnesota | 1,729,661 | 2.1% |
| 31 | Mississippi | 1,006,787 | 1.2% |
| 16 | Missouri | 1,788,863 | 2.2% |
| 40 | Montana | 539,664 | 0.6% |
| 35 | Nebraska | 730,341 | 0.9% |
| 39 | Nevada | 540,474 | 0.7% |
| 42 | New Hampshire | 370,688 | 0.4% |
| 18 | New Jersey | 1,741,011 | 2.1% |
| 33 | New Mexico | 811,946 | 1.0% |
| 9 | New York | 2,813,177 | 3.4% |
| 11 | North Carolina | 2,236,865 | 2.7% |
| 44 | North Dakota | 359,337 | 0.4% |
| 4 | Ohio | 3,547,685 | 4.3% |
| 25 | Oklahoma | 1,390,893 | 1.7% |
| 24 | Oregon | 1,440,067 | 1.7% |
| 8 | Pennsylvania | 2,901,946 | 3.5% |
| 50 | Rhode Island | 210,076 | 0.3% |
| 28 | South Carolina | 1,137,929 | 1.4% |
| 41 | South Dakota | 400,072 | 0.5% |
| 17 | Tennessee | 1,787,631 | 2.1% |
| 2 | Texas | 6,247,839 | 7.5% |
| 36 | Utah | 719,239 | 0.9% |
| 48 | Vermont | 213,763 | 0.3% |
| 13 | Virginia | 2,084,027 | 2.5% |
| 12 | Washington | 2,111,756 | 2.5% |
| 38 | West Virginia | 616,272 | 0.7% |
| 19 | Wisconsin | 1,732,023 | 2.1% |
| 46 | Wyoming | 329,722 | 0.4% |

RANK ORDER

| RANK | STATE | TRUCKS | % of USA |
|------|-------|--------|----------|
| 1 | California | 9,658,010 | 11.6% |
| 2 | Texas | 6,247,839 | 7.5% |
| 3 | Florida | 4,041,067 | 4.9% |
| 4 | Ohio | 3,547,685 | 4.3% |
| 5 | Michigan | 3,194,300 | 3.8% |
| 6 | Illinois | 3,030,090 | 3.6% |
| 7 | Georgia | 2,943,465 | 3.5% |
| 8 | Pennsylvania | 2,901,946 | 3.5% |
| 9 | New York | 2,813,177 | 3.4% |
| 10 | Indiana | 2,243,692 | 2.7% |
| 11 | North Carolina | 2,236,865 | 2.7% |
| 12 | Washington | 2,111,756 | 2.5% |
| 13 | Virginia | 2,084,027 | 2.5% |
| 14 | Alabama | 2,030,509 | 2.4% |
| 15 | Colorado | 1,798,766 | 2.2% |
| 16 | Missouri | 1,788,863 | 2.2% |
| 17 | Tennessee | 1,787,631 | 2.1% |
| 18 | New Jersey | 1,741,011 | 2.1% |
| 19 | Wisconsin | 1,732,023 | 2.1% |
| 20 | Minnesota | 1,729,661 | 2.1% |
| 21 | Arizona | 1,564,306 | 1.9% |
| 22 | Louisiana | 1,518,412 | 1.8% |
| 23 | Massachusetts | 1,498,954 | 1.8% |
| 24 | Oregon | 1,440,067 | 1.7% |
| 25 | Oklahoma | 1,390,893 | 1.7% |
| 26 | Iowa | 1,318,004 | 1.6% |
| 27 | Maryland | 1,219,249 | 1.5% |
| 28 | South Carolina | 1,137,929 | 1.4% |
| 29 | Kentucky | 1,056,945 | 1.3% |
| 30 | Kansas | 1,033,178 | 1.2% |
| 31 | Mississippi | 1,006,787 | 1.2% |
| 32 | Arkansas | 865,486 | 1.0% |
| 33 | New Mexico | 811,946 | 1.0% |
| 34 | Connecticut | 761,780 | 0.9% |
| 35 | Nebraska | 730,341 | 0.9% |
| 36 | Utah | 719,239 | 0.9% |
| 37 | Idaho | 631,843 | 0.8% |
| 38 | West Virginia | 616,272 | 0.7% |
| 39 | Nevada | 540,474 | 0.7% |
| 40 | Montana | 539,664 | 0.6% |
| 41 | South Dakota | 400,072 | 0.5% |
| 42 | New Hampshire | 370,688 | 0.4% |
| 43 | Maine | 361,988 | 0.4% |
| 44 | North Dakota | 359,337 | 0.4% |
| 45 | Alaska | 330,895 | 0.4% |
| 46 | Wyoming | 329,722 | 0.4% |
| 47 | Hawaii | 259,582 | 0.3% |
| 48 | Vermont | 213,763 | 0.3% |
| 49 | Delaware | 211,708 | 0.3% |
| 50 | Rhode Island | 210,076 | 0.3% |
| | District of Columbia | 35,819 | 0.0% |

*Source: U.S. Department of Transportation, Federal Highway Administration*
    *"Highway Statistics 1999" (Table MV-1, October 2000)*
*"Trucks" now include personal passenger vans, minivans and sports-utility vehicles. These were formerly classified as "automobiles."*

# Motorcycle Registrations in 1999

## National Total = 4,152,433 Motorcycles*

ALPHA ORDER

RANK ORDER

| RANK | STATE | MOTORCYCLES | % of USA | | RANK | STATE | MOTORCYCLES | % of USA |
|------|-------|-------------|----------|---|------|-------|-------------|----------|
| 27 | Alabama | 49,205 | 1.2% | | 1 | California | 419,572 | 10.1% |
| 49 | Alaska | 14,924 | 0.4% | | 2 | Ohio | 240,590 | 5.8% |
| 9 | Arizona | 145,190 | 3.5% | | 3 | Florida | 235,716 | 5.7% |
| 41 | Arkansas | 21,786 | 0.5% | | 4 | Illinois | 216,641 | 5.2% |
| 1 | California | 419,572 | 10.1% | | 5 | Pennsylvania | 200,829 | 4.8% |
| 17 | Colorado | 95,027 | 2.3% | | 6 | Wisconsin | 192,806 | 4.6% |
| 24 | Connecticut | 53,521 | 1.3% | | 7 | Texas | 168,896 | 4.1% |
| 50 | Delaware | 10,704 | 0.3% | | 8 | Michigan | 167,882 | 4.0% |
| 3 | Florida | 235,716 | 5.7% | | 9 | Arizona | 145,190 | 3.5% |
| 18 | Georgia | 87,009 | 2.1% | | 10 | New York | 143,547 | 3.5% |
| 44 | Hawaii | 19,302 | 0.5% | | 11 | Minnesota | 126,786 | 3.1% |
| 33 | Idaho | 40,779 | 1.0% | | 12 | Iowa | 125,201 | 3.0% |
| 4 | Illinois | 216,641 | 5.2% | | 13 | Indiana | 109,472 | 2.6% |
| 13 | Indiana | 109,472 | 2.6% | | 14 | Washington | 107,290 | 2.6% |
| 12 | Iowa | 125,201 | 3.0% | | 15 | New Jersey | 105,547 | 2.5% |
| 26 | Kansas | 49,682 | 1.2% | | 16 | Massachusetts | 103,110 | 2.5% |
| 32 | Kentucky | 41,905 | 1.0% | | 17 | Colorado | 95,027 | 2.3% |
| 31 | Louisiana | 42,908 | 1.0% | | 18 | Georgia | 87,009 | 2.1% |
| 35 | Maine | 30,953 | 0.7% | | 19 | North Carolina | 78,733 | 1.9% |
| 30 | Maryland | 45,973 | 1.1% | | 20 | Oregon | 66,609 | 1.6% |
| 16 | Massachusetts | 103,110 | 2.5% | | 21 | Tennessee | 62,985 | 1.5% |
| 8 | Michigan | 167,882 | 4.0% | | 22 | Virginia | 57,464 | 1.4% |
| 11 | Minnesota | 126,786 | 3.1% | | 23 | Missouri | 57,329 | 1.4% |
| 34 | Mississippi | 32,212 | 0.8% | | 24 | Connecticut | 53,521 | 1.3% |
| 23 | Missouri | 57,329 | 1.4% | | 25 | Oklahoma | 53,277 | 1.3% |
| 40 | Montana | 22,216 | 0.5% | | 26 | Kansas | 49,682 | 1.2% |
| 42 | Nebraska | 19,631 | 0.5% | | 27 | Alabama | 49,205 | 1.2% |
| 39 | Nevada | 23,499 | 0.6% | | 28 | New Hampshire | 47,656 | 1.1% |
| 28 | New Hampshire | 47,656 | 1.1% | | 29 | South Carolina | 46,844 | 1.1% |
| 15 | New Jersey | 105,547 | 2.5% | | 30 | Maryland | 45,973 | 1.1% |
| 36 | New Mexico | 30,669 | 0.7% | | 31 | Louisiana | 42,908 | 1.0% |
| 10 | New York | 143,547 | 3.5% | | 32 | Kentucky | 41,905 | 1.0% |
| 19 | North Carolina | 78,733 | 1.9% | | 33 | Idaho | 40,779 | 1.0% |
| 47 | North Dakota | 16,387 | 0.4% | | 34 | Mississippi | 32,212 | 0.8% |
| 2 | Ohio | 240,590 | 5.8% | | 35 | Maine | 30,953 | 0.7% |
| 25 | Oklahoma | 53,277 | 1.3% | | 36 | New Mexico | 30,669 | 0.7% |
| 20 | Oregon | 66,609 | 1.6% | | 37 | South Dakota | 25,761 | 0.6% |
| 5 | Pennsylvania | 200,829 | 4.8% | | 38 | Utah | 24,674 | 0.6% |
| 45 | Rhode Island | 19,210 | 0.5% | | 39 | Nevada | 23,499 | 0.6% |
| 29 | South Carolina | 46,844 | 1.1% | | 40 | Montana | 22,216 | 0.5% |
| 37 | South Dakota | 25,761 | 0.6% | | 41 | Arkansas | 21,786 | 0.5% |
| 21 | Tennessee | 62,985 | 1.5% | | 42 | Nebraska | 19,631 | 0.5% |
| 7 | Texas | 168,896 | 4.1% | | 43 | West Virginia | 19,447 | 0.5% |
| 38 | Utah | 24,674 | 0.6% | | 44 | Hawaii | 19,302 | 0.5% |
| 46 | Vermont | 17,663 | 0.4% | | 45 | Rhode Island | 19,210 | 0.5% |
| 22 | Virginia | 57,464 | 1.4% | | 46 | Vermont | 17,663 | 0.4% |
| 14 | Washington | 107,290 | 2.6% | | 47 | North Dakota | 16,387 | 0.4% |
| 43 | West Virginia | 19,447 | 0.5% | | 48 | Wyoming | 15,925 | 0.4% |
| 6 | Wisconsin | 192,806 | 4.6% | | 49 | Alaska | 14,924 | 0.4% |
| 48 | Wyoming | 15,925 | 0.4% | | 50 | Delaware | 10,704 | 0.3% |
| | | | | | | District of Columbia | 1,489 | 0.0% |

*Source: Morgan Quitno Press using data from U.S. Department of Transportation, Federal Highway Administration "Highway Statistics 1999" (Table MV-1, October 2000)*
*Includes private, commercial and publicly-owned motorcycles.*

# Annual Miles per Vehicle in 1999

## National Annual Average = 12,442 Miles*

ALPHA ORDER

| RANK | STATE | MILES |
|------|-------|-------|
| 13 | Alabama | 14,193 |
| 50 | Alaska | 7,953 |
| 21 | Arizona | 12,986 |
| 2 | Arkansas | 16,089 |
| 34 | California | 11,382 |
| 43 | Colorado | 10,557 |
| 41 | Connecticut | 10,819 |
| 17 | Delaware | 13,876 |
| 26 | Florida | 12,459 |
| 15 | Georgia | 14,178 |
| 37 | Hawaii | 11,302 |
| 28 | Idaho | 12,372 |
| 39 | Illinois | 10,945 |
| 23 | Indiana | 12,746 |
| 49 | Iowa | 9,554 |
| 27 | Kansas | 12,453 |
| 1 | Kentucky | 17,963 |
| 30 | Louisiana | 11,757 |
| 3 | Maine | 15,449 |
| 24 | Maryland | 12,608 |
| 48 | Massachusetts | 9,717 |
| 31 | Michigan | 11,538 |
| 22 | Minnesota | 12,821 |
| 6 | Mississippi | 15,055 |
| 5 | Missouri | 15,152 |
| 47 | Montana | 9,856 |
| 33 | Nebraska | 11,475 |
| 8 | Nevada | 14,962 |
| 36 | New Hampshire | 11,318 |
| 42 | New Jersey | 10,739 |
| 14 | New Mexico | 14,185 |
| 29 | New York | 11,760 |
| 4 | North Carolina | 15,422 |
| 45 | North Dakota | 10,309 |
| 46 | Ohio | 10,306 |
| 12 | Oklahoma | 14,521 |
| 32 | Oregon | 11,510 |
| 35 | Pennsylvania | 11,324 |
| 38 | Rhode Island | 11,088 |
| 11 | South Carolina | 14,588 |
| 44 | South Dakota | 10,543 |
| 10 | Tennessee | 14,629 |
| 7 | Texas | 14,989 |
| 16 | Utah | 13,977 |
| 20 | Vermont | 13,267 |
| 25 | Virginia | 12,588 |
| 40 | Washington | 10,842 |
| 18 | West Virginia | 13,801 |
| 19 | Wisconsin | 13,353 |
| 9 | Wyoming | 14,762 |

RANK ORDER

| RANK | STATE | MILES |
|------|-------|-------|
| 1 | Kentucky | 17,963 |
| 2 | Arkansas | 16,089 |
| 3 | Maine | 15,449 |
| 4 | North Carolina | 15,422 |
| 5 | Missouri | 15,152 |
| 6 | Mississippi | 15,055 |
| 7 | Texas | 14,989 |
| 8 | Nevada | 14,962 |
| 9 | Wyoming | 14,762 |
| 10 | Tennessee | 14,629 |
| 11 | South Carolina | 14,588 |
| 12 | Oklahoma | 14,521 |
| 13 | Alabama | 14,193 |
| 14 | New Mexico | 14,185 |
| 15 | Georgia | 14,178 |
| 16 | Utah | 13,977 |
| 17 | Delaware | 13,876 |
| 18 | West Virginia | 13,801 |
| 19 | Wisconsin | 13,353 |
| 20 | Vermont | 13,267 |
| 21 | Arizona | 12,986 |
| 22 | Minnesota | 12,821 |
| 23 | Indiana | 12,746 |
| 24 | Maryland | 12,608 |
| 25 | Virginia | 12,588 |
| 26 | Florida | 12,459 |
| 27 | Kansas | 12,453 |
| 28 | Idaho | 12,372 |
| 29 | New York | 11,760 |
| 30 | Louisiana | 11,757 |
| 31 | Michigan | 11,538 |
| 32 | Oregon | 11,510 |
| 33 | Nebraska | 11,475 |
| 34 | California | 11,382 |
| 35 | Pennsylvania | 11,324 |
| 36 | New Hampshire | 11,318 |
| 37 | Hawaii | 11,302 |
| 38 | Rhode Island | 11,088 |
| 39 | Illinois | 10,945 |
| 40 | Washington | 10,842 |
| 41 | Connecticut | 10,819 |
| 42 | New Jersey | 10,739 |
| 43 | Colorado | 10,557 |
| 44 | South Dakota | 10,543 |
| 45 | North Dakota | 10,309 |
| 46 | Ohio | 10,306 |
| 47 | Montana | 9,856 |
| 48 | Massachusetts | 9,717 |
| 49 | Iowa | 9,554 |
| 50 | Alaska | 7,953 |

District of Columbia     14,701

Source: Morgan Quitno Press using data from U.S. Department of Transportation, Federal Highway Administration
"Highway Statistics 1999" (Tables MV-1 and VM-2, October 2000)
*Includes automobiles, trucks, buses and motorcycles.

# Average Miles per Gallon in 1999

## National Average = 16.8 Miles per Gallon*

ALPHA ORDER

| RANK | STATE | MILES PER GALLON |
|---|---|---|
| 8 | Alabama | 17.8 |
| 49 | Alaska | 13.3 |
| 36 | Arizona | 15.7 |
| 41 | Arkansas | 15.0 |
| 7 | California | 17.9 |
| 24 | Colorado | 16.8 |
| 16 | Connecticut | 17.3 |
| 2 | Delaware | 19.4 |
| 24 | Florida | 16.8 |
| 26 | Georgia | 16.6 |
| 1 | Hawaii | 20.0 |
| 33 | Idaho | 16.1 |
| 30 | Illinois | 16.3 |
| 11 | Indiana | 17.6 |
| 47 | Iowa | 14.5 |
| 39 | Kansas | 15.6 |
| 21 | Kentucky | 16.9 |
| 40 | Louisiana | 15.5 |
| 17 | Maine | 17.1 |
| 19 | Maryland | 17.0 |
| 19 | Massachusetts | 17.0 |
| 34 | Michigan | 16.0 |
| 21 | Minnesota | 16.9 |
| 30 | Mississippi | 16.3 |
| 13 | Missouri | 17.4 |
| 43 | Montana | 14.8 |
| 41 | Nebraska | 15.0 |
| 43 | Nevada | 14.8 |
| 36 | New Hampshire | 15.7 |
| 48 | New Jersey | 14.1 |
| 21 | New Mexico | 16.9 |
| 3 | New York | 19.1 |
| 9 | North Carolina | 17.7 |
| 43 | North Dakota | 14.8 |
| 34 | Ohio | 16.0 |
| 12 | Oklahoma | 17.5 |
| 9 | Oregon | 17.7 |
| 32 | Pennsylvania | 16.2 |
| 5 | Rhode Island | 18.0 |
| 36 | South Carolina | 15.7 |
| 46 | South Dakota | 14.6 |
| 17 | Tennessee | 17.1 |
| 27 | Texas | 16.5 |
| 13 | Utah | 17.4 |
| 5 | Vermont | 18.0 |
| 28 | Virginia | 16.4 |
| 28 | Washington | 16.4 |
| 13 | West Virginia | 17.4 |
| 4 | Wisconsin | 18.2 |
| 50 | Wyoming | 11.6 |

RANK ORDER

| RANK | STATE | MILES PER GALLON |
|---|---|---|
| 1 | Hawaii | 20.0 |
| 2 | Delaware | 19.4 |
| 3 | New York | 19.1 |
| 4 | Wisconsin | 18.2 |
| 5 | Rhode Island | 18.0 |
| 5 | Vermont | 18.0 |
| 7 | California | 17.9 |
| 8 | Alabama | 17.8 |
| 9 | North Carolina | 17.7 |
| 9 | Oregon | 17.7 |
| 11 | Indiana | 17.6 |
| 12 | Oklahoma | 17.5 |
| 13 | Missouri | 17.4 |
| 13 | Utah | 17.4 |
| 13 | West Virginia | 17.4 |
| 16 | Connecticut | 17.3 |
| 17 | Maine | 17.1 |
| 17 | Tennessee | 17.1 |
| 19 | Maryland | 17.0 |
| 19 | Massachusetts | 17.0 |
| 21 | Kentucky | 16.9 |
| 21 | Minnesota | 16.9 |
| 21 | New Mexico | 16.9 |
| 24 | Colorado | 16.8 |
| 24 | Florida | 16.8 |
| 26 | Georgia | 16.6 |
| 27 | Texas | 16.5 |
| 28 | Virginia | 16.4 |
| 28 | Washington | 16.4 |
| 30 | Illinois | 16.3 |
| 30 | Mississippi | 16.3 |
| 32 | Pennsylvania | 16.2 |
| 33 | Idaho | 16.1 |
| 34 | Michigan | 16.0 |
| 34 | Ohio | 16.0 |
| 36 | Arizona | 15.7 |
| 36 | New Hampshire | 15.7 |
| 36 | South Carolina | 15.7 |
| 39 | Kansas | 15.6 |
| 40 | Louisiana | 15.5 |
| 41 | Arkansas | 15.0 |
| 41 | Nebraska | 15.0 |
| 43 | Montana | 14.8 |
| 43 | Nevada | 14.8 |
| 43 | North Dakota | 14.8 |
| 46 | South Dakota | 14.6 |
| 47 | Iowa | 14.5 |
| 48 | New Jersey | 14.1 |
| 49 | Alaska | 13.3 |
| 50 | Wyoming | 11.6 |
| | District of Columbia | 18.2 |

Source: Morgan Quitno Press using data from U.S. Department of Transportation, Federal Highway Administration
"Highway Statistics 1999" (October 2000)
*Total vehicle-miles for 1999 divided by total highway motor-fuel use. Includes gasoline, gasohol, diesel and other
"special fuels."

# Railroad Mileage Operated in 1999

## National Total = 169,954 Miles of Railroad*

ALPHA ORDER

| RANK | STATE | MILES | % of USA |
|---|---|---|---|
| 17 | Alabama | 3,689 | 2.2% |
| 46 | Alaska | 482 | 0.3% |
| 39 | Arizona | 1,909 | 1.1% |
| 19 | Arkansas | 3,619 | 2.1% |
| 3 | California | 7,424 | 4.4% |
| 22 | Colorado | 3,435 | 2.0% |
| 44 | Connecticut | 743 | 0.4% |
| 48 | Delaware | 294 | 0.2% |
| 27 | Florida | 2,961 | 1.7% |
| 9 | Georgia | 4,797 | 2.8% |
| 50 | Hawaii | 0 | 0.0% |
| 40 | Idaho | 1,850 | 1.1% |
| 2 | Illinois | 10,058 | 5.9% |
| 8 | Indiana | 5,093 | 3.0% |
| 12 | Iowa | 4,401 | 2.6% |
| 4 | Kansas | 6,794 | 4.0% |
| 26 | Kentucky | 2,962 | 1.7% |
| 25 | Louisiana | 3,195 | 1.9% |
| 42 | Maine | 1,199 | 0.7% |
| 43 | Maryland | 1,193 | 0.7% |
| 41 | Massachusetts | 1,237 | 0.7% |
| 13 | Michigan | 4,387 | 2.6% |
| 7 | Minnesota | 5,918 | 3.5% |
| 29 | Mississippi | 2,720 | 1.6% |
| 10 | Missouri | 4,558 | 2.7% |
| 24 | Montana | 3,294 | 1.9% |
| 18 | Nebraska | 3,668 | 2.2% |
| 38 | Nevada | 1,916 | 1.1% |
| 47 | New Hampshire | 453 | 0.3% |
| 34 | New Jersey | 2,276 | 1.3% |
| 33 | New Mexico | 2,404 | 1.4% |
| 15 | New York | 3,926 | 2.3% |
| 23 | North Carolina | 3,360 | 2.0% |
| 14 | North Dakota | 3,962 | 2.3% |
| 5 | Ohio | 6,503 | 3.8% |
| 16 | Oklahoma | 3,900 | 2.3% |
| 31 | Oregon | 2,635 | 1.6% |
| 6 | Pennsylvania | 6,321 | 3.7% |
| 49 | Rhode Island | 102 | 0.1% |
| 32 | South Carolina | 2,480 | 1.5% |
| 36 | South Dakota | 2,051 | 1.2% |
| 28 | Tennessee | 2,953 | 1.7% |
| 1 | Texas | 13,938 | 8.2% |
| 35 | Utah | 2,245 | 1.3% |
| 45 | Vermont | 609 | 0.4% |
| 21 | Virginia | 3,440 | 2.0% |
| 20 | Washington | 3,495 | 2.1% |
| 30 | West Virginia | 2,681 | 1.6% |
| 11 | Wisconsin | 4,427 | 2.6% |
| 37 | Wyoming | 1,958 | 1.2% |

RANK ORDER

| RANK | STATE | MILES | % of USA |
|---|---|---|---|
| 1 | Texas | 13,938 | 8.2% |
| 2 | Illinois | 10,058 | 5.9% |
| 3 | California | 7,424 | 4.4% |
| 4 | Kansas | 6,794 | 4.0% |
| 5 | Ohio | 6,503 | 3.8% |
| 6 | Pennsylvania | 6,321 | 3.7% |
| 7 | Minnesota | 5,918 | 3.5% |
| 8 | Indiana | 5,093 | 3.0% |
| 9 | Georgia | 4,797 | 2.8% |
| 10 | Missouri | 4,558 | 2.7% |
| 11 | Wisconsin | 4,427 | 2.6% |
| 12 | Iowa | 4,401 | 2.6% |
| 13 | Michigan | 4,387 | 2.6% |
| 14 | North Dakota | 3,962 | 2.3% |
| 15 | New York | 3,926 | 2.3% |
| 16 | Oklahoma | 3,900 | 2.3% |
| 17 | Alabama | 3,689 | 2.2% |
| 18 | Nebraska | 3,668 | 2.2% |
| 19 | Arkansas | 3,619 | 2.1% |
| 20 | Washington | 3,495 | 2.1% |
| 21 | Virginia | 3,440 | 2.0% |
| 22 | Colorado | 3,435 | 2.0% |
| 23 | North Carolina | 3,360 | 2.0% |
| 24 | Montana | 3,294 | 1.9% |
| 25 | Louisiana | 3,195 | 1.9% |
| 26 | Kentucky | 2,962 | 1.7% |
| 27 | Florida | 2,961 | 1.7% |
| 28 | Tennessee | 2,953 | 1.7% |
| 29 | Mississippi | 2,720 | 1.6% |
| 30 | West Virginia | 2,681 | 1.6% |
| 31 | Oregon | 2,635 | 1.6% |
| 32 | South Carolina | 2,480 | 1.5% |
| 33 | New Mexico | 2,404 | 1.4% |
| 34 | New Jersey | 2,276 | 1.3% |
| 35 | Utah | 2,245 | 1.3% |
| 36 | South Dakota | 2,051 | 1.2% |
| 37 | Wyoming | 1,958 | 1.2% |
| 38 | Nevada | 1,916 | 1.1% |
| 39 | Arizona | 1,909 | 1.1% |
| 40 | Idaho | 1,850 | 1.1% |
| 41 | Massachusetts | 1,237 | 0.7% |
| 42 | Maine | 1,199 | 0.7% |
| 43 | Maryland | 1,193 | 0.7% |
| 44 | Connecticut | 743 | 0.4% |
| 45 | Vermont | 609 | 0.4% |
| 46 | Alaska | 482 | 0.3% |
| 47 | New Hampshire | 453 | 0.3% |
| 48 | Delaware | 294 | 0.2% |
| 49 | Rhode Island | 102 | 0.1% |
| 50 | Hawaii | 0 | 0.0% |
| | District of Columbia | 39 | 0.0% |

*Source: Association of American Railroads*
   *"Railroad Ten-Year Trends"*
*Includes Class I, Regional, Linehaul and Switching & Terminal miles. In previous editions, this table reflected Class I railroad only. Does not include miles operated by non-Class 1 railroads or miles operated by Canadian railroads in the United States. Includes trackage rights.*

# XVI. SOURCES

**ACT, Inc.**
2201 N. Dodge Street, P.O. Box 168
Iowa City, IA 52243-0168
319-337-1000
Internet: www.act.org

**Administration for Children and Families**
U.S. Dept. of Health and Human Services
370 L'Enfant Promenade, SW
Washington, DC 20447
202-401-9215
Internet: www.acf.dhhs.gov

**American Cancer Society, Inc.**
1599 Clifton Road, NE
Atlanta, GA 30329-4251
800-227-2345
Internet: www.cancer.org

**American Dental Association**
211 E. Chicago Ave.
Chicago, IL 60611
312-440-2500
Internet: www.ada.org

**American Hospital Association**
One North Franklin
Chicago, IL 60606-3421
312-422-3000
Internet: www.aha.org

**American Medical Association**
515 North State Street
Chicago, IL 60610
312-464-5000
Internet: www.ama-assn.org

**Association of American Railroads**
50 F Street, NW
Washington, DC 20001-1564
202-639-2100
Internet: www.aar.org

**Bureau of the Census**
3 Silver Hill & Suitland Road
Suitland, MD 20746
301-457-2800
Internet: www.census.gov

**Bureau of Economic Analysis**
U.S. Department of Commerce
1441 L Street, NW
Washington, DC 20230
202-606-9900
Internet: www.bea.doc.gov

**Bureau of Justice Statistics**
U.S. Department of Justice
810 Seventh St., NW
Washington, DC 20531
202-307-0765
Internet: www.ojp.usdoj.gov/bjs/

**Bureau of Labor Statistics**
Department of Labor
2 Massachusetts Ave., NE.
Washington, DC 20212
202-691-5200
Internet: http://stats.bls.gov

**Centers for Disease Control**
1600 Clifton Road, NE
Atlanta, GA 30333
800-311-3435
Internet: www.cdc.gov

**College Board**
The College Board
45 Columbus Avenue
New York, NY 10023-6992
(212) 713-8000
Internet: www.collegeboard.org/

**Dun & Bradstreet Corporation**
One Diamond Hill Road
Murray Hill, NJ 07974-1218
800-234-3867
Internet: www.dnb.com

**Economic Research Service**
U.S. Department of Agriculture
1800 M Street, NW
Washington, DC 20036-5831
202-694-5050
Internet: www.econ.ag.gov

**Energy Information Administration**
1000 Independence Avenue, SW
Washington, DC 20585
202-586-8800
Internet: www.eia.doe.gov

**Environmental Protection Agency**
1200 Pennsylvania Ave
Washington, DC 20004
202-260-5922
Internet: www.epa.gov

**Federal Bureau of Investigation**
935 Pennsylvania Avenue, NW
Washington, DC 20535-0001
202-324-3000
Internet: www.fbi.gov

**Federal Deposit Insurance Corporation**
550 17th Street, NW
Washington, DC 20429
800-276-6003
Internet: www.fdic.gov

**Federal Election Commission**
999 E Street, NW
Washington, DC 20463
800-424-9530
Internet: www.fec.gov

**Federal Highway Administration**
400 7th Street, SW
Washington, DC 20590
202-366-0660
Internet: www.fhwa.dot.gov

**Federation of Tax Administrators**
444 North Capitol St., NW
Ste 348
Washington, DC 20001
(202) 624-5890
www.taxadmin.org

# XVI. SOURCES (continued)

**Food and Nutrition Service**
U.S. Department of Agriculture
3101 Park Center Drive, Room 819
Alexandria, VA 22302
703-305-2286
Internet: www.fns.usda.gov/fns/

**General Services Administration**
1800 F Street, NW
Washington, DC 20405
202-501-0705
Internet: www.gsa.gov

**Health Care Financing Administration**
7500 Security Boulevard
Baltimore, MD 21244
410-786-3000
Internet: www.hcfa.gov

**Internal Revenue Service**
U.S. Department of the Treasury
1111 Constitution Avenue, NW
Washington, DC 20224
800-829-1040
Internet: www.irs.ustreas.gov

**National Agricultural Statistics Service**
1400 Independence Ave, SW
Washington, DC 20250
800-727-9540
Internet: www.usda.gov/nass

**National Assembly of State Arts Agencies**
1029 Vermont Ave., NW 2nd Fl
Washington, DC 20005
202-347-6352
Internet: www.nasaa-arts.org

**National Association of Realtors**
700 11th Street, NW.
Washington, DC 20001
202-383-1000
Internet: http://nar.realtor.com

**National Association of State Park Directors**
9894 E. Holden Place
Tucson, AZ 85748
520-298-4924
Internet: www.indiana.edu/~naspd/

**National Association of Attorneys General**
750 First Street, NE, Ste. 1100
Washington, DC 20002
202-326-6000
Internet: www.naag.org/

**National Center for Education Statistics**
U.S. Department of Education
1900 K Street, NW
Washington, DC 20006
202-502-7300
Internet: http://nces.ed.gov

**National Center for Health Statistics**
U.S. Department of Health and Human Services
6525 Belcrest Road
Hyattsville, MD 20782-2003
301-458-4636
Internet: www.cdc.gov/nchswww/

**National Conference of State Legislatures**
1560 Broadway, Suite 700
Denver, CO 80202
303-830-2200
Internet: www.ncsl.org

**National Education Association**
1201 16th Street, NW
Washington, DC 20036
202-833-4000
Internet: www.nea.org

**National Highway Traffic Safety Admin.**
U.S. Department of Transportation
400 7th Street, SW
Washington, DC 20590
202-366-9550
Internet: www.nhtsa.dot.gov

**National Institute on Alcohol Abuse
And Alcoholism**
6000 Executive Boulevard
Bethesda, MD 20892-7003
301-443-9970
Internet: www.niaaa.nih.gov/

**National Oceanic & Atmospheric Admin.**
U.S. Department of Commerce
14th Street & Constitution Ave., NW.
Washington, DC 20230
202-482-6090
Internet: www.noaa.gov

**National Weather Service**
Storm Prediction Center
1313 Halley Circle
Norman, OK 73069
405-579-0771
Internet: www.spc.noaa.gov

**Social Security Administration**
6401 Security Boulevard
Baltimore, MD 21235
800-772-1213 (information)
Internet: www.ssa.gov

**Tax Foundation**
1250 H Street, NW
Ste 750
Washington, DC 20005
202-783-2760
Internet: www.taxfoundation.org

**U.S. Department of Defense**
The Pentagon
Washington, DC 20301
703-697-5737
Internet: www.defenselink.mil

**U.S. Department of Veterans Affairs**
810 Vermont Avenue, NW
Washington, DC 20420
202-273-5700
Internet: www.va.gov

**U.S. Geological Survey**
12201 Sunrise Valley Drive
Reston, VA 20192
1-800-ASK-USGS
Internet: www.usgs.gov

# XVII. INDEX

# XVII. INDEX (continued)

# XVII. INDEX (continued)

# XVII. INDEX (continued)

Prospect Heights Public Library
12 N. Elm St.
Prospect Heights, IL. 60070-1499

# CHAPTER INDEX

## HOW TO USE THIS INDEX

Place left thumb on the outer edge of this page. To locate the desired entry, fold back the remaining page edges and align the index edge mark with the appropriate page edge mark.

**Prospect Heights Public Library**
**12 N. Elm St.**
**Prospect Heights, IL 60070-1499**

Other books by Morgan Quitno Press:

- *State Statistical Trends (monthly journal)*
- *Crime State Rankings 2001 ($52.95)*
- *Health Care State Rankings 2001 ($52.95)*
- *City Crime Rankings, 7th Edition ($39.95)*

Call toll free: 1-800-457-0742 or
visit us at www.statestats.com